INTERTEXTUAL BIBLE COMMENTARY

THE BOOK OF REVELATION

ITS INTRODUCTION AND PROPHECY

George Wesley Buchanan

Wipf & Stock
PUBLISHERS
Eugene, Oregon

IN **MEMORY OF MY PARENTS**

GEORGE AND HELEN CECELIA KRAL BUCHANAN

Wipf and Stock Publishers
199 W 8th Ave, Suite 3
Eugene, OR 97401

The Book of Revelation
Its Introduction and Prophecy
By Buchanan, George Wesley
Copyright©2005 by Buchanan, George Wesley
ISBN: 1-59752-362-3
Publication date: 10/1/2005

TABLE OF CONTENTS

INTRODUCTION..1
  THE FUNCTION OF AN INTRODUCTION................................1
    The Place to Begin...1
    The Necessity of an Introduction..3
  INTRODUCTORY SUMMARIES...4
    Financial Metaphors..4
    Sabbatical Rules..6
    Jubilee Theology..8
    Eschatology and the Land...8
    Cycles of Time..9
    The Kingdom of God..11
    Daniel Seven..13
  TYPOLOGY...15
    Typology Defined...15
    Elijah Type..16
    Joseph Type..17
    Phineas Type..18
    Jesus Type..19
    Captivity Type..20
    Exodus Typology..20
    Erroneous Typology...22
  MIDRASHIC EXEGESIS..23
  ISAIAH'S MIDRASH...24
  PSALMS AND EXODUS FIFTEEN..27
  TEXT...28
    The Translation..30
    The Goal and Method of Presentation..31

CHAPTER ONE...33
  TEXT...33
  COMMENTARY...33
    The revelation of Jesus Christ...33
    To show to his saints..37
    The things that must happen quickly..37
    He gave a sign...39
    Having sent through his messenger..39
    To his servant, John..40
    The word of God and the testimony of Jesus..............................40
    Whatever things he saw...41
    Blessed is he who reads...41
    Those who hear . . . and keep..42
    The word of this prophecy...42
  TEXT...44

COMMENTARY.. 45
    John to the seven churches... 45
    Grace to you and peace..46
    From the One who is..46
    From the One who was...47
    From the One who is coming..47
    The seven spirits... 49
    From Jesus the Messiah.. 49
    The first born of the dead ones..50
    The One who loved us... 51
    Kingdom, priests to God... 52
    Into the age of the ages. Amen... 53
TEXT.. 53
COMMENTARY.. 54
    Look! He comes with the clouds... 54
    Even the ones who stabbed [him]... 54
    All the tribes of the land..54
    Yes. Amen... 55
TEXT.. 55
COMMENTARY.. 56
    I am the Alpha, and I am the Omega.....................................56
    The One who is coming...57
TEXT.. 57
COMMENTARY.. 57
    I, John, am your brother... 58
    Endurance in Jesus... 59
    I was on the island called Patmos...59
    Because of the word of God.. 60
TEXT.. 61
COMMENTARY..61
    I was day-dreaming... 61
    On the Lord's day.. 61
    Voice loud as a trumpet saying... 62
    On the Lord's day..63
    [That which you see] write.. 64
    To Ephesus, Pergamum, Thyatira, Smyrna, Philadelphia, and
        Laodicia.. 64
LITERARY TREATY STYLE... 65
TEXT..66
TECHNICAL DETAILS...67
COMMENTARY..68
    When I turned, I saw seven gold lamp stands........................68
    One like a Son of man..69
    The hair of his head was white... 70
    His eyes were like a flame of fire.. 71
    His feet were like burnished brass... 71

- *Like the sound of much water [running]* 72
- *From his mouth went out a sharp sword* 72
- *Like the sun [disk] in its might* 73
- **TEXT** 73
- **COMMENTARY** 74
  - *When I saw him I fell at his feet* 74
  - *I am the first and the last* 74
  - *I have the keys of death and Hades* 74
- **TEXT** 75
- **COMMENTARY** 75
  - *The things that you have seen* 75
  - *The things that are about to happen after this* 76
  - *The seven gold lampstands* 77
  - *The Mystery of the seven stars* 77
  - *The seven stars are messengers of the seven churches* 77
- **THE MESSENGER WHO CAME TO JOHN AT PATMOS** 78
  - *The angelos* 79
  - *The prophecy* 79
  - *The endorsement* 79
  - *A human messenger* 80
  - *The first and the last* 81
- **JOHN, THE ANGELOS, AND THE LITERATURE** 82
- **CONCLUSIONS** 83

CHAPTER TWO 84
- **TECHNICAL DETAILS** 84
- **TEXT** 85
- **COMMENTARY** 85
  - *To the officer* 85
  - *Of the church in Ephesus* 88
  - *The One who holds the seven stars* 89
  - *The lampstands* 89
- **TEXT** 90
- **COMMENTARY** 90
  - *Your labor and your endurance* 90
  - *Those who call themselves "apostles."* 91
  - *You have carried all afflictions* 92
  - *You have left your first love* 93
  - *The tree of life* 93
  - *Remember [the position]* 94
  - *I will come and move your lamp* 95
  - *You hate the works of the Nicolaitans* 95
  - *He who has an ear, let him hear* 97
  - *To eat of the tree of life* 98
  - *To the one who conquers* 98
  - *Paradise of God* 98
- **TEXT** 100

COMMENTARY 100
   To the officer of the church of Smyrna 100
   The first and the last 101
   I know your tribulation 101
   Those who call themselves Jews 101
   Have no fear 102
   The things you are about to suffer 102
   Throw some of you into prison 103
   [Be] faithful until death 103
   He who has an ear 104
   He who conquers 104
   Will not be judged guilty 104
TEXT 105
COMMENTARY 105
   The two edged sword 105
   I know where you live 105
   Antipas, my witness, my faithful one 106
   The teachings of Balaam 106
   A stumbling block 106
   Commit acts of sexual indecency 106
TEXT 107
COMMENTARY 108
   Even you 108
   The teachings of the Nicolaitans 108
   Repent, therefore 108
   I will battle against them 108
   He who has an ear 109
   The hidden manna . . . a white pebble 109
   I will give him . . . a new name 110
TEXT 110
TECHNICAL DETAILS 111
COMMENTARY 112
   The officer of the church in Thyatira 112
   This is what the Son of God says 112
   Whose eyes were like a flame of fire 112
   I know your works 112
   Your last works are even more than the first 112
   I hold much against you 112
   The woman, Jezebel, who says it is a prophecy 113
   But she does not want to repent 114
   I will throw her into a bed 114
   If they do not repent of her works 114
   I will kill her children with pestilence 114
   Who searches the heart and mind 115
   I will give to each according to your works 115
   The rest of you in Thyatira 115

Have not known the deep things of Satan... 115
I will not cast upon you another burden... 116
Only that which is held..116
He who keeps my works until the end... 116
I will give him authority..116
He will rule them with an iron rod..116
Early morning star.. 117
He who has an ear.. 117

CHAPTER THREE 118
TEXT 118
COMMENTARY 119
To the officer 119
The seven spirits of God 119
You have a reputation of being alive 120
Strengthen the things which remain 120
I have not found your works filled up 121
You have received and heard. So keep 121
If, therefore, you do not 122
You have a few individuals 122
I will confess his name before my Father 122
TEXT 123
COMMENTARY 124
The officer of the church 124
The church of Philadelphia 124
The holy One, the true One 124
You have a little power 125
The hour of testing which is to come 126
MIGRANTS ON THE LAND 126
Migrants on the Land 126
Hebrew hypotheses 127
MIGRANTS IN PALESTINE 128
The earth and the Land 128
First Testament usage 128
Deuteronomic ethics 129
People of the Land 129
Migrants in NT times 130
Saints and migrants 130
Palestine and the Book of Revelation 132
Cosmic influences 133
CONCLUSIONS 133
So that no one can take away your crown 134
A pillar in the temple of my God 134
Write upon him the name 135
TEXT 136
The new Jerusalem that comes down from heaven 135
The officer of the church 137

Laodicia...137
Thus says the Amen..137
You are neither hot nor cold..................................138
I am rich; I have become wealthy...........................138
You are wretched, poverty stricken, blind, and naked.................138
I advise you to buy from me...................................139
Look! I stand at the door and knock......................139

CHAPTER FOUR 141
TEXT 141
THE PROPHECY 142
COMMENTARY 142
After this, I was watching..142
I was day dreaming...143
The door opened in heaven. Now look!.................143
Like a trumpet...146
Come up here...146
Suddenly I began to day dream...............................147
A throne was set up in heaven.................................148
The one on the throne was sitting...........................149
Looked like a sapphire stone, a carnelian..............149
A rainbow on a rainy day..150
TEXT 150
COMMENTARY 152
Around the throne were twenty-four thrones........152
Twenty-four elders..153
Seven torches of fire..154
Which were the seven spirits of God......................154
A glassy sea..155
In the midst of the throne.......................................155
Around the throne were four beasts......................155
Every one of them had six wings............................156
They have no rest day or night...............................157
Holy, holy, holy, holy, holy, holy, holy, holy..........157
The One who is..157
TEXT 157
COMMENTARY 158
The One who lives into ages of ages. Amen...........158
They threw their crowns before the throne...........158
You are worthy..158
Summary..159

CHAPTER FIVE 160
INTRODUCTION 160
TEXT 160
COMMENTARY 161
I saw at the right hand...161
The One seated on the throne................................161

          [A scroll written] of the front and back..................................... 162
          Sealed with seven seals..162
          Who is worthy to open the scroll?.................................. 163
          No one was able . . . to open the scroll......................... 163
          Look! The lion of the tribe of Judah................................163
     TEXT..165
     COMMENTARY... 165
          Between the throne and the four beasts......................... 165
          A Lamb standing as slaughtered..................................... 167
          Having seven horns..169
          And seven eyes...169
          Then the Lamb came and took [the scroll].....................169
     TEXT..170
     COMMENTARY... 171
          He took the scroll...171
          The twenty-four elders... 171
          Which are the prayers of the saints................................ 171
          You are worthy... 172
          You negotiated with God...172
          They sang a new song..172
          [Some] from every tribe, language, and nation.............. 173
          You have made them . . . a kingdom and priests........... 173
          They shall rule over the Land..174
     TEXT..174
     COMMENTARY... 175
          Many angels around the throne..................................... 175
          I was watching, and I heard.. 176
          The Lamb which was slaughtered................................. 176
     TEXT..177
     COMMENTARY... 177
          Every creature...177
          To the One seated on the throne and to the Lamb........177
          Then the four beasts said, "Amen!"............................... 178
     SUMMARY..178
CHAPTER SIX.. 180
     TEXT.. 180
     TECHNICAL DETAILS 180
     COMMENTARY... 181
          The Lamb opened one of the seven seals 181
          Go.... 182
          Look! a white horse 182
          To take peace from the land 184
          Had a scale in his hand 184
     TEXT.. 185
     COMMENTARY... 186
          A koinix of wheat for a denarius 186

- *Do not damage the oil or the wine* 187
- *A sorrel horse . . . and his name was "Death"* 188
- *The sword . . . and by the wild beasts* 188

TEXT 190
COMMENTARY 191
- *The souls of those who have been slain* 191
- *On account of the testimony which they held* 192
- *How long, Master, will you not judge* 193
- *Migrants of the land* 194
- *Were about to be killed* 195

TEXT 196
COMMENTARY 197
- *A great earthquake occurred* 197
- *The sun became black* 198
- *Hid themselves in caves and rocks* 198
- *The heaven will vanish like a scroll unrolled* 199
- *From the anger of the Lamb* 200
- *The day of their great wrath has arrived* 201
- *Who can stand?* 202

CHAPTER SEVEN 203
TEXT 203
COMMENTARY 204
- *Four angels . . . holding the four winds* 204
- *The four corners* 205
- *East of the sun* 206
- *The seal of the God of life* 207
- *Upon any tree* 207
- *Do not hurt the Land, the sea, nor any tree* 207
- *Seal the servants of God on their* foreheads 208
- *From every tribe of Israel* 210
- *A hundred forty-four thousands* 212

TECHNICAL DETAILS 212
TEXT 212
COMMENTARY 213
- *A great crowd* 213
- *From every nation, tribe, people, and language* 213
- *With palm leaves in their hands* 214

TEXT 216
COMMENTARY 217
- *Salvation to our God on the throne* 217
- *All angels stood around the throne* 217

VIEWS OF OTHERS 217
TEXT 218
COMMENTARY 218
- *One of the elders answered* 218
- *Who are these who are wearing white robes* 219

      Those who have come up from great tribulation 219
      He said 220
      They have washed their garments 220
   TEXT 221
   TECHNICAL DETAILS 222
   COMMENTARY 223
      Because of this 223
      The One seated on the throne knows them 223
      The sun will not fall upon them any more 223
      The Lamb on the throne will shepherd them 224
      Springs of water of life 224

CHAPTER EIGHT 225
   FIRST TESTAMENT REACTIONS TO THE EXODUS CURSES ... 225
   TRUMPETS AND BOWLS OF REVELATION 226
   TEXT 227
   TECHNICAL DETAILS 227

COMMENTARY 228
      Silence in heaven for about half an hour 228
      Seven angels who stood before God 230
   TEXT 231
   COMMENTARY 231
      Prayers of all the saints 231
      Thunders . . . and an earthquake 233
   TEXT 234
   COMMENTARY 235
      So that they could blow the trumpets 235
      The third portion of the Land burned 236
   TEXT 237
   TECHNICAL DETAILS 238
   TEXT 238
   TECHNICAL DETAILS 239
   TEXT 240
   TECHNICAL DETAILS 240
   COMMENTARY 240
      An eagle flying in mid-heaven 240
      Woe! To the migrants on the Land 241

CHAPTER NINE 242
   TECHNICAL DETAILS 242
   TEXT 242
   COMMENTARY 243
      The fifth angel blew its trumpet 243
      I saw a star fallen from heaven 243
      Key to the pit of the abyss 244
      Smoke went up over the pit 244
      The sun and the air grew dark from the smoke 244
      From the smoke went out locusts of the Land 244
      They were given authority 244

   They were not to injure the grass..244
   The seal of god on their foreheads...246
   Five months...247
   People will look for death...248
  TEXT..248
  COMMENTARY..248
   The appearances of the locusts was like horses....................248
   They had their own king..249
   The angel of the abyss..249
   One woe is past..249
  TEXT..249
  COMMENTARY..250
   The sixth angel blew its trumpet..250
   A voice from the golden altar...250
   The four angels . . . at the Great River..................................250
   The hour, month, and year...251
   The number of the cavalry..251
   The Third..252
  TEXT..252
  COMMENTARY..253
   The rest of the people...253
   Had not repented of the works of their hands.......................253
   The gold, silver, brass, and stone idols..................................253
   Their murders, their sorceries, their sexual indecencies........253

CHAPTER TEN...255
 TECHNICAL DETAILS..255
 TEXT..255
 COMMENTARY..256
  Another strong angel..256
  Wearing a cloud..256
  The hair was upon his head..256
  Like the sun...257
  His legs were like pillars of fire..257
  A scroll...257
  His right foot on the sea, and his left [foot] was on the Land........259
  Loud as a lion roars...259
  Seal that which the seven thunders spoke..............................259
 TEXT..260
 COMMENTARY..260
  The angel which I saw standing on the sea and one the Land........260
  Swore by the One who lives into the age................................260
  Who created . . . the earth and things in it...............................261
  There will be no more time [to wait]..261
 TEXT..263
 COMMENTARY..264
  The mystery of God had been completed................................264
  He announced the good news...265
 TEXT..266

COMMENTARY	266
The voice which I heard from heaven	266
Standing on the Land	266
TEXT	266
COMMENTARY	267
I took the scroll . . . and I ate it	267
It is necessary for you to prophesy	268
CHAPTER ELEVEN	**269**
TEXT	270
COMMENTARY	270
There was given to me a reed	270
[God] said	270
Arise and measure	270
The temple and the altar	271
Count the people	271
And its worshipers	272
The Quadrangle, that is outside of the sanctuary, throw out	273
They will trample the holy city for forty–two months	276
TEXT	279
COMMENTARY	280
I will give [authority] to my two witnesses	280
They will prophesy for 1,260 days	281
These are the two olive trees	281
That are standing before the Lord of all the Land	282
Whatever woman wants to hurt them	282
Fire will go out from their mouth	283
TEXT	283
COMMENTARY	284
These have authority	284
To close up the heavens	284
They have authority over the water	285
TEXT	286
COMMENTARY	286
When they finished their testimony	286
The beast then coming up from the abyss	286
Which is spiritually Sodom and Egypt	286
Their corpses [will be] left on the street of the great city	287
Where also their Lord was crucified	288
Tribes, peoples, languages, and nations	292
The migrants of the Land	292
They celebrate and send gifts	292
TEXT	292
COMMENTARY	293
They stood upon their feet	293
A great fear fell upon those who had watched them	294

       Their enemies watched them..294
       There was a great earthquake...294
       The rest became frightened and gave glory to the God of heaven 295
       A tenth of the city fell..295
       The second woe has passed...295
   SIGNS OF THE MESSIAH..296
   TEXT...300
   COMMENTARY...301
       The seventh angel..301
       The kingdom of the world..301
       [The kingdom] of our Lord and of his Messiah....................302
       He will rule into the age of ages..302
   TEXT...303
   COMMENTARY...304
       Seated on their thrones before God....................................304
       Lord, the God of armies...305
       You have become king..305
       The gentiles became enraged...305
       The time of the dead to be judged......................................306
       Both small and great..306
       Those who plunder the Land..306
   TEXT...307
   COMMENTARY...307
       The temple of God which is in heaven................................307
       The contract of God...308
   THE SECRETS OF SHIMON BEN YOCHAI..........................308
   CONCLUSION..309
CHAPTER TWELVE...310
   TEXT...310
   COMMENTARY...313
       A great sign appeared in heaven. A woman......................313
       A woman wearing the sun [disk]..314
       Look! A huge red dragon...315
       Having seven heads and ten horns.....................................316
       His tail swept the third of the stars of heaven....................316
       The dragon stood before the woman..................................317
       She was pregnant, and she cried out in birth pangs...........318
       She bore a son, a male..319
       Who was about to rule all the gentiles with a rod of iron....320
       The woman fled to the wilderness......................................321
       They nourish her there..321
       Twelve hundred, sixty days...321
       There was a war in heaven...323
       Michael and his angels..324
       Nor then was found there..324
   TEXT...324

- COMMENTARY...325
  - *The old serpent which is called the devil and Satan* 325
  - *The large dragon . . . was thrown to the earth*.......................326
- TEXT...326
- COMMENTARY...327
  - *I heard a loud voice from heaven*..327
  - *Salvation and power*...327
  - *The Kingdom of our God*...327
  - *Their accuser before God*..328
  - *They conquered him*..328
  - *Through the blood of the Lamb*..328
  - *The word of their testimony*..328
  - *They did not love their soul until death*................................329
  - *Woe to the Land and the sea*...329
  - *Rejoice, Heavens*..329
  - *He has a little time*..329
- TEXT...330
- COMMENTARY...331
  - *It was thrown to the earth*..331
  - *It pursued the woman*...331
  - *Two wings of a great eagle*...331
  - *She might fly into the wilderness* 332
  - *From the presence of the serpent*..332
  - *The serpent poured out*...332
  - *Two times and half a time*...333
- TEXT...333
- COMMENTARY...334
  - *The dragon became angry*...334
  - *To make war on the rest of her children*...............................334
  - *Those who keep the commandment of God*............................335
  - *It stood on the sand of the sea [shore]*.................................337

CHAPTER THIRTEEN..339
FIRST DIVISION..339
TEXT...339
TECHNICAL DETAILS...340
- *The units*..340
- *Jewish use of imagery*...340
COMMENTARY...343
- *I was watching*...343
- *A beast coming out of the sea*...344
HERODIANS AND THE BEASTS..345
BEASTS AND SCHOLARS..346
THE BEASTS AND THE DRAGON...347
- *Having ten horns*..347
- *Seven heads*..348
- *As if slaughtered to death*..348
- *Blasphemous names*...350

       The Land was appalled because of the beast......................350
  TEXT..350
  COMMENTARY...351
       The dragon who gave authority to the beast..................351
       Who is like the beast?...352
       Talking excessively and [speaking] blasphemy...............352
       Authority was given him for forty-two months.................353
  TEXT..354
  COMMENTARY...355
       Blaspheming him and his tent..355
       To make war with the saints..355
       Every tribe, people, language, and nation.......................356
       The migrants of the Land worshiped him........................356
       Whose names have been written......................................356
       In the Lamb's book of life..356
       The Lamb that was slain...357
  TEXT..357
  COMMENTARY...358
       If anyone [takes others] into captivity...............................358
       Will himself go away...358
       If anyone will kill by the sword..358
  SECOND DIVISION...359
  TEXT..359
  COMMENTARY...359
       Another beast...359
       He had two horns like a Lamb...361
       He exercises all the authority of the first beast................362
       He makes the Land . . . worship the first beast................362
       Whose mortal wound was healed.....................................363
  TEXT..364
  COMMENTARY...365
       He performs great miracles..365
       Telling the migrants of the Land..368
       Who has the wound of the sword and lived....................368
       He will act so that whoever does not worship.................368
  TEXT..368
  COMMENTARY...369
       All—the small and the great..369
       To wear his mark..369
       The mark of the beast or his name...................................369
       Six hundred, sixty-six..369
       666 and the end of the Common Era...............................373
CHAPTER FOURTEEN...379
  TEXT..379
  TECHNICAL DETAILS...381
  PALESTINE AND ASIA MINOR..382

COMMENTARY	386
I was watching	386
The Lamb is standing on Mount Zion	386
His name and the name of his Father	387
Like the sound of much water [running]	388
They were singing a new song	388
The redeemed of the Land	388
For they are celibate	389
MONASTICISM IN NT TIMES	394
These are those who follow the Lamb	396
The first [with respect to] God and to the Lamb	397
They had not defiled themselves with women	398
In their mouth was not found anything false	401
TEXT	401
SCRIPTURAL CONTEXT	402
Another angel	403
Having the gospel of he age	404
To proclaim to the migrants of the Land	405
TEXT	405
COMMENTARY	406
Another, a second [angel]	406
The bracketed text	406
Fallen, fallen is great Babylon	406
Takes a mark upon his forehead or on his hand	407
TEXT	407
COMMENTARY	409
If anyone worships the beast or its image	409
He also drinks from the wine of God's anger	409
The smoke of their torture	410
They have no rest day or night	410
Here is the patience of the saints	410
The commandments of God (and the testimony of Jesus)	411
Summary	411
TEXT	412
COMMENTARY	412
Dying in the Lord until now	412
Their works will follow them	413
TEXT	413
COMMENTARY	414
I was watching	414
Another angel went out from the temple	414
Upon the white cloud was seated	415
Another angel	417
The time to harvest has come	418
The harvest of the Land is ripe	420
TEXT	420

TECHNICAL DETAILS	421
COMMENTARY	422
Another angel went out from the temple	422
The One who was seated on the cloud	422
The vine of the Land	423
Put his sickle to the Land, clusters [of grapes]	423
The great wine press of the anger	423
Outside the city	424
From sixteen hundred stadia	424
The blood poured out of the winepress	425
CHAPTER FIFTEEN	427
TEXT	427
COMMENTARY	429
I saw	429
Another sign in heaven, great and marvelous	429
Angels having the seven last plagues	429
The anger of God was completed	430
A glassy sea mixed with fire	430
Those who conquered	430
The number of its name	431
Having harps of the Lord God	431
The song of the Lamb	431
Great and marvelous are your works	433
Just and true are your ways	433
King of the ages	433
Who will nor fear you?	433
All the nations will come	434
The just deeds before you	434
TEXT	434
COMMENTARY	435
The temple of the tent of testimony in heaven	435
The seven angels who had the seven plagues	436
God who lives for ages of ages. Amen	436
The four [heavenly] beasts	436
The seven gold bowls	436
No one was able to enter the temple	438
Until the 7 plagues . . . were completed	439
CHAPTER SIXTEEN	440
INTRODUCTION	440
TEXT	440
COMMENTARY	441
A voice from the temple	441
The seven angels	441
Pour out the seven bowls of the wrath of God	442
The bracketed words	442
Evil and bad boil	442

  It became blood as dead..442
  Every soul living in the sea died..442
  Upon the rivers...443
TEXT..443
COMMENTARY..444
  "Righteous are you"...444
  Which [saints and prophets] are worthy..............................445
  Then I heard the altar saying...445
  Lord God of armies...445
TEXT..446
COMMENTARY..446
TEXT..446
COMMENTARY..446
TEN SIGNS WILL COME TO THE WORLD BEFORE THE END 447
  The first sign..447
  The second sign..448
  The third sign...448
  The fourth sign...449
  The fifth sign..449
  The sixth sign...449
  The seventh sign...450
  The eighth sign...450
  The ninth sign..450
  The tenth sign...451
  Because of their grief...451
  They did not repent..451
TEXT..451
COMMENTARY..452
  The great river Euphrates..452
  The kings of the East...453
GEOGRAPHY AND HISTORY IN REVELATION SIXTEEN........454
  Alexander's Empire...454
  The Roman heritage..455
  Rome and the Seleucids...455
  Scipio and Pompey..455
  Jews and the super powers...456
  The Parthians..456
  Rome and the Parthians..456
  Jews and the Parthians..457
  Seventh decade conflicts..457
INTERNATIONAL JEWISH PATTERNS...............................458
PARTHIA AND MEGIDDO..459
  Parthians and Megiddo...459
  Megiddo as a fortress...459
  Jewish History..460
  Megiddo and Fertile Crescent history...................................461

  Opinions of scholars... 462
  Parthian-Rome symbolism..464
 THE GREAT CITY..465
  Gentile cities.. 468
  Jerusalem..469
  Plagues...469
 TEXT..470
 COMMENTARY ON THE UNIT..470
  Variants in the Main text..471
  Variants in the separated passage...471
  The false prophet... 472
  Unclean spirits like frogs..472
  Keeps his garments[clean]..472
  The kings of the East...472
  The characters..474
 CONCLUSIONS ON THE UNIT.. 474
 TEXT REPEATED.. 474
 COMMENTARY ON TEXT..476
  The great Euphrates... 476
  Called in Hebrew "Har Megiddo"..476
  Bolts of lightning, noises, and peals of thunder............................... 476
  The cup of the wine of his wrath..478
  Every island fled, and the mountains were not found....................478
  Babylon the great was remembered before God............................478
 TEXT REPEATED.. 479
 COMMENTARY... 479
  The false prophet... 479
  Unclean spirits like frogs... 479
  He is coming like a thief.. 479
  Keeps his garments clean.. 480
CHAPTER SEVENTEEN...481
 TEXT..481
 COMMENTARY... 482
  One of the angels . . . spoke to me...482
  Come, and I will show you..483
  The judgment of the great harlot... 483
  Living on much water...486
  With whom the kings of the earth acted indecently....................... 487
 TEXT.. 488
 COMMENTARY... 489
  He took me away into the wilderness..489
  In the spirit.. 489
  Having seven heads and ten horns..490
  Having a gold cup in her hand..490
  On her forehead was written—a mystery...................................... 490

TEXT	491
COMMENTARY	491
The blood of the witnesses of Jesus	491
The mystery of the woman	492
I was tremendously appalled	492
The beast with seven heads and ten horns	492
The beast . . . is about to go away	493
TEXT	494
COMMENTARY	495
The book of life	495
Here is the mind which has wisdom	495
The seven heads are the seven mountains	495
There are seven kings	496
It will be necessary to remain	497
The beast who was	497
The five have fallen	498
TEXT	498
COMMENTARY	499
The ten horns which you saw	499
They receive authority as kings . . . together with the beast	499
The Lamb will conquer them	500
Elect and faithful	501
TEXT	501
COMMENTARY	502
The things which you saw	502
The ten horns which you saw	503
The ten horns . . . and the beast . . . hate the harlot	503
They will be devastated and naked	503
Burn her with fire	504
God has put a desire in their minds to do his will	504
To give the kingdom do the beasts	505
The woman which you saw	505
Summary	505
CHAPTER EIGHTEEN	506
INTRODUCTION	506
TEXT--POETRY	508
TEXT--MIDRASH	510
COMMENTARY	512
After this I saw another angel	512
The land shone from his glory	512
Fallen is Babylon	513
The dwelling place of demons	514
The wine of the anger of her harlotries	514
The merchants have become rich	514
TEXT	515

- COMMENTARY 516
  - *A voice from Heaven* 516
  - *Come out from her, my people* 516
  - *No sharing . . . no receiving* 517
  - *For her crimes have been glued to heaven* 517
  - *Give back to her as she has given* 517
  - *Pay her double* 518
- TEXT 518
- COMMENTARY 520
  - *She says to herself, "I sit a queen."* 520
  - *Strong is God, the Lord* 521
  - *The kings of the earth . . . will weep* 521
  - *The smoke of her fall* 521
  - *In one hour your judgment has come* 522
- TEXT 522
- COMMENTARY 523
  - *Merchants of the Land* 523
  - *Very precious wood* 524
  - *And human slaves* 524
- TEXT 524
- COMMENTARY 525
  - *The bright shining things have vanished* 525
  - *Woe! woe! the city* 525
  - *In one hour* 525
- TEXT 525
- COMMENTARY 526
  - *Everyone who sails somewhere* 526
  - *The smoke of her burning* 527
- TEXT 527
- COMMENTARY 529
  - *Rejoice over her, Heaven* 529
  - *Saints, apostles, and prophets* 529
  - *As big as a mill stone* 530
  - *Babylon the great will be thrown* 530
  - *Will no longer be heard* 531
  - *Every craftsman* 531
  - *The light of the lamp* 531
  - *The merchants were the great people* 531
  - *The blood of prophets and saints* 531
- SUMMARY 532

CHAPTER NINETEEN 533
- TEXT 533
- COMMENTARY 534
  - *After this* 534
  - *Like the loud noise* 534
  - *Hallelujah* 534

Let there be salvation 534
Just are his judgments 536
He has avenged the blood 536
TEXT... 536
COMMENTARY... 537
    The smoke goes up into the ages of ages 537
    The 24 elders… 539
    The four……… 539
    Both small and great 539
TEXT... 540
COMMENTARY... 541
    I heard……… 541
    Like the sound… 541
    The almighty One has become king 541
    Let us give them glory 541
    The wedding of the Lamb 542
    The bride has prepared herself 543
    The linen is the righteous deeds 544
TEXT... 545
COMMENTARY... 546
    He said to me… 546
    Those who are invited 546
    The wedding banquet of the Lamb 549
    The true words of God 546
    I fell on my face 547
    A fellow servant of you and your brothers 547
    The testimony of Jesus is the spirit of prophecy 547
TEXT... 547
COMMENTARY... 548
    I saw the heavens opened 548
    The one seated upon it 549
    He will judge righteously and make war 549
    He had upon his head many crowns 550
    Having a name written 550
    A garment sprinkled with blood 551
    His name was called, "The word of God" 551
TEXT... 552
COMMENTARY ….. 553
    A sharp, two-edged sword 553
    He will shatter the gentiles 554
    He will trample the wine press 554
    On his thigh the name written 555
    King of kings and Lord of Lords 555
EZEKIEL AND THE ORDER OF EVENTS 556
COMMENTARY... 557
    The great banquet of God 557

The flesh of kings 557
Might be consumed 557
TEXT 557
COMMENTARY 558
I saw the beast 558
The kings of the earth and their troops 558
The beast seized 559
The mark of the beast 559
All the birds will be filled 559
The sword of his mouth 560
Chapter Nineteen and other Chapters 560

CHAPTER TWENTY 562
TEXT 562
COMMENTARY 562
And I saw 562
An angel . . . overpowered the dragon 562
The key of the abyss and a chain 563
Who is the devil and the Satan 563
He bound him into the abyss 564
Until the thousand years are complete 565
After this it will be necessary 570
TEXT 574
COMMENTARY 575
I saw thrones, and [elders] sat on them 575
Judgment was given to them [the elders] 575
The souls of those who had been beheaded 577
On account of the testimony of Jesus 579
Which very ones did not worship 579
The saints lived and ruled with the Messiah 579
TEXT 582
COMMENTARY 582
The rest of the dead will not come to life 582
The first resurrection 583
The second death has no authority 583
Priests of God 584
Priests both of God and of his Messiah 584
TEXT 585
COMMENTARY 588
Satan will be released from prison 588
The four corners, namely Gog and Magog 589
They went up over the breadth of the land 592
They surrounded the camp 592
The saints of the beloved city 592
They surrounded the camp of the saints 593
Fire came down 594
The devil was thrown into the lake 595

TEXT	596
COMMENTARY	599
A great white throne and one seated on it	599
From whose face earth and heaven fled	600
No place for them was found	600
Standing at the throne	601
The books was opened	601
The Book of Life	601
The dead were judged	602
The sea gave up the dead who were in it	602
Death and Hades gave up the dead	602
They were judged, each according to his works	602
Death and Hades were thrown into the lake of fire	603
This was the second death	603
If anyone will be found	603
CHAPTER TWENTY-ONE	604
TEXT	604
TECHNICAL DETAILS	605
COMMENTARY	606
A new heaven and a new Land	606
The sea will be no more	611
The new Jerusalem coming down from heaven	612
HEAVENLY JERUSALEM	616
RESTORATION OF THE TEMPLE	618
COMMENTARY	619
The new Jerusalem	619
Prepared as a bride	619
TEXT	619
COMMENTARY	623
A loud voice from the throne was saying	623
The tent of God is with human beings	623
He will tentdwell with them	625
They themselves will be his people	626
There will be neither lamentation nor crying	628
The One seated on the throne said to me	628
These words are faithful and true	628
They have happened	628
TEXT	629
COMMENTARY	630
I am the Alpha and the Omega	630
The Author's Use of Second Isaiah	630
The Second Death	630
The one who conquers will inherit these things	632
The Unfaithful	632
TEXT	632
COMMENTARY	634

    One of the seven angels who had the seven bowls 634
    He brought me in the spirit 634
    I will show you the bride 634
    The holy city, Jerusalem 635
    The glory of God 636
    Twelve gates… 636
    Three gates on the north 636
    The walls of the city, having foundation stones 636
    Twelve names of the twelve apostles of the Lamb 637
TEXT 638
COMMENTARY 639
    The one who was speaking to me 639
    So that he could measure the city 639
    The city lies square 639
    Rabbinic interpretation 643
    He measured its fodder 644
    The measure of a man, that is of [the] angel 644
TEXT 645
COMMENTARY 646
    Construction [material] of its wall was jasper 646
    The city was of pure gold 646
    The foundations of the wall of the city 646
    Decorated with every kind of precious stones 646
    Each gate was [carved] from one pearl 647
    The street of the city was gold 647
TEXT 648
COMMENTARY 651
    I saw no temple in it 651
    No need of the sun or the moon 653
    Its lamp will be the Lamb 653
    The gentiles will walk through its light 654
    The gates will not be closed 656
    Nothing common will enter it 656

CHAPTER TWENTY-TWO 658
TEXT 658
COMMENTARY 659
    He showed me a river 658
    In the middle of its street 663
    Conclusions 665
    Medieval Jewish Expectations 669
    From the throne of God and the Lamb 670
    Its fruit 672
    The leaves of the trees 672
    For healing of the nations 672
TEXT 673
TECHNICAL DETAILS 674

COMMENTARY	675
There will not be any wool	667
The throne of God and the Lamb is in it	676
They will serve him	676
They will see his face	677
There will be no night	677
They shall rule as kings	678
SUMMARY...	679
JOHN'S CONCLUSION	680
TEXT………..	680
TECHNICAL DETAILS	681
THE INCLUSIO……	681
COMMENTARY	682
Sent [to] me his messenger	682
What things are necessary to happen	682
TEXT………..	682
COMMENTARY	683
These words are faithful and true	683
Look, I am coming quickly	683
TEXT………..	683
COMMENTARY	683
Who hear and see these things	683
Don't do that! I am a fellow servant of yours	683
Your brothers, the prophets	685
TEXT………..	686
COMMENTARY	687
He said to me…	687
Do not seal up the words	687
The prophecy of this scroll	687
The time is near	687
TEXT………..	688
COMMENTARY	689
Let the unjust be unjust still	689
I am coming quickly	689
I am the Alpha and the **Omega**	689
Blessed are they who wash their robes	689
Their authority will be over the tree of life	690
And they will enter the gates of the city	690
Outside are the dogs	690
Acts and loves…	691
TEXT………..	691
COMMENTARY	691
I, Jesus………..	691
The root and offspring of David	691
For the sake of the churches	691

TEXT 691
COMMENTARY 693
   The Spirit and the bride 693
   Let him who is thirsty come 693
   The water of life 693
   I, John, bear witness 693
   Who hears the prophecy of this book 693
JOHN'S COPYRIGHT 694
TEXT 694
COMMENTARY 695
   God will take away his share 695
   I am coming quickly 695
   With the saints.. 695
   The poem 695
   If anyone adds to them 695
   The plagues that are written in this scroll 695

CONCLUSIONS 697
THE BASIC MESSAGE 697
STRUCTURE AND LITERARY IDENTIFICATION 699
   The outline 699
   The Midrash 703
   Revelation and Redemption Midrash 707
   Midrash as Prophecy 709
   The Introduction and Conclusion 710
DATES AND PLACES OF COMPOSITION 711
THE AUTHORS AND THE COMMUNITIES OF THE DOCUMENT 713
   Author or Authors 713
   A Christian Leader 714
   Possible Problems 715
   The Cost of Convictions 716
   Approved Behavior 716
   Unacceptable Behavior 717
   Goats and Sheep 717
   John the Zealot 717
   John's familiarity with scripture 718
INSIGHTS FROM REVELATION 719

GENERAL INDICES 722
WORDS 722
GEOGRAPHICAL LOCATIONS 735
ANCIENT PERSONALITIES 737
MODERN SCHOLARS 742

PREFACE

My first serious interest in the Book of Revelation began in 1956 when I was pastor of Whitehall United Methodist Church in Towaco, New Jersey. There were evangelistic services being held in churches in our neighborhood at which the evangelist told the congregation that the world was coming to an end very soon. This declaration was based on the Book of Revelation. Adult members of the church asked me to teach a course on the Book of Revelation so that they could understand what this was all about. At the outset I told them that I was no expert on the Book of Revelation, but that I would read through the book with them to discover what we might learn.

The class concluded with more questions than answers. I had read enough commentaries on the book by then to realize that the problem could not be solved by reading more secondary sources. The consensus of scholars had not made any sense of that book, either. Nonetheless, I believed that it must have been written by some one to have been understood by some others, and it was preserved, so it must have been successful at that time. It was a part of the Christian canon, so I also believed that pastors should be able to learn more about this book than any pastor knew at that time. That was the beginning of my research.

Since I was completing the residence requirement for my Ph.D. at Drew University, I asked permission to write a thesis on the origin of the Book of Revelation. No one in the New Testament department at that time could be interested in the project. That was the age when the "new hermeneutic," "de-mythologization," and "existentialistic exegesis," were popular. Objective historical research was not very exciting to many scholars, but Rorschach eisegesis was in for a shock with the discovery of the Dead Sea Scrolls.

The Dead Sea Scrolls were just then coming into the forefront of New Testament studies, so I next applied for permission to write a thesis on the eschatology of the Qumran scrolls. The faculty approved, and, with the support of Horowitz and Scheuer fellowships, I spent the next three years at Hebrew Union College and the University of Cincinnati, writing my thesis, but also working intensively in Hebrew, Syriac, Aramaic, classical Greek, and the literature of these languages. From then until now I have continued to analyze the languages, literature, history, and culture necessary for understanding the thought-form of the Book of Revelation. During this time I have written several articles and books on related subjects. There was no short-cut method by which I could have learned that which was necessary to know for teaching that course for the adult members of the Whitehall United Methodist Church. The results of that study, however, is now available in this commentary for pastors and church members who face the same problems that we faced nearly fifty years ago.

During all these years of study I have learned that every language has a mythology which is taken for granted by the speakers. Expressions like "Watergate," "hippy," "Chapaquitic," and "what the meaning of is is," are well recognized expressions in USA today. Nearly all of us know the stories that go with the terms, but suppose we should read these in expressions out of context three thousand years from now in a few fragmented papers! In a Shakespearean audience a speaker can say "Sweets for the sweet," and presume the audience knows the implied context. To computer audiences a person can speak of "down loading," "up-dating," "crashes," "viruses," "default settings," etc. Take away the context and understood background, and these terms seem like garbage. Revelation was written and read by people—all of whom were trained in the same catechism. They had all read the same literature, had the same beliefs, knew the same local political and social situation, so they could express things easily in code. These contexts have to be learned to understand the message. Realizing that, I have spent these years studying to learn the literature, the geography, history, languages, thought-forms, expressions, myths, and code. Once these are understood, Revelation suddenly becomes a choice bit of intelligent literature—but I did not know all of this when I taught the class in 1956. Now, I do, however, and if you read this book, you will, too. Since I began this study, trying to help lay people in the church understand this book, I have here attempted also to explain these technical terms in ordinary American English that pastors and church school teachers can follow.

The first edition of this commentary was published by the Edwin Mellen Press, 1993. One of the reviewers, Tommy Lea (SWJT 40 [1998]:105-106), said of that edition, "Buchanan shows a significant knowledge of the Old Testament and Jewish tradition. All commentators on Revelation recognize that the author of Revelation has made significant use of the Old Testament, and Buchanan provides insight into the writer's use of his Old Testament and Jewish writings." Lea was disappointed, however, that I did not reach the same conclusions that were most widely known. If I had chosen to find agreement rather than truth, of course, I could have reached that more than 40 years ago. No one has refuted the first edition of this commentary, and there are probably many, especially the consensus scholars who concur with Lea, but had I imitated the status quo that would not have helped my church school class then, or scholars and church members today. The people I have known in the church are people of integrity. They do not want fairy tales and distortions given down condescendingly. They want the facts presented accurately in ways that make sense so that they can understand them and judge them for themselves. That is the purpose of this commentary.

Although this second edition does not deny any of the facts presented in the first edition, and it does not depart from the basic format or goals of the first commentary, it has made several important improvements. The format is still better; This edition contains pictures and a map that were not available in the first edition. I have gained new legal, rhetorical, and archaeological insights in the last twelve years; I have included reactions to later scholars; and I have been able to relate the new archaeological findings of the City of David and the true location of the temple to the Book of Revelation. This has been exciting, because there is much in the Book of Revelation related to the temple and the City of Zion. All of these become clearer when the true location of these sites are known. I have also worked harder to see that every technical term is clearly explained for non-technicians in scripture.

The goal of this research has been to bring the truth to the church. John Wesley propagated the truths his people needed to know through inexpensive pamphlets, and his movement succeeded. This commentary does not come in penny pamphlets, but it is sold as inexpensively as possible in our inflated culture.

ACKNOWLEDGEMENTS

I was twenty years of age when my parents died in 1942. I had two older sisters and six living younger brothers at the time. Our youngest was four years of age. Our parents left us more financial debits than assets, but they left us a heritage of much greater value--integrity, ability, motivation, willingness to work, sensitivity to the needs of others, and an honorable name. Wherever our parents were known their children have been respected. The deaths of our parents did not separate their children. We have continued to be very close, emotionally, even though we are often many miles apart. One of the great gifts our parents left to us is a wonderful group of brothers and sisters. Our names and birth dates are given here:

Cecelia Anne Buchanan Ahrenholtz--July 19, 1918, deceased 1972
Ruth Eleanor Buchanan Clothier--March 13, 1920
George Wesley Buchanan--December 25, 1921
Hubert William Buchanan--January 23, 1924, deceased 1927
Kenneth Stephen Buchanan--January 15, 1926
Charles Valentine Buchanan--December 3, 1927, deceased 1981
James Richard Buchanan--September 2, 1930
Leonard Francis Buchanan--December 14, 1932
Russell Howard Buchanan--February 13, 1935
Donald Edward Buchanan--May 9, 1937, deceased, 1954

It is in memory of our parents that I dedicate this book. I am also grateful to the congregation in New Jersey that first challenged me to become seriously acquainted with the Book of Revelation. It is because this is the most difficult book in the Bible to understand that I have spent a lifetime studying and clarifying that document.

After I had defined my Ph.D. thesis I spent three very helpful years at Hebrew Union College - Jewish Institute of Religion with the aid of Horowitz and Scheuer fellowships. It was at that time that I began to obtain the knowledge of literature and languages that was necessary for me to complete this project. I am very grateful to the donors of these fellowships and for the excellent scholars and research facilities from which I benefited there. I am grateful for the help received from Thomas W. Gregory, one of my former students, a genius who is skilled in many areas, one of which is computers. He has taught me nearly all I know about hardware and software necessary for producing manuscripts, such as this one. I have received invaluable library research help form Ms. Howartine L. Farrell Duncan M.Div, librarian at the Wesley Theological Seminary library.

After a book has been written there is still much work required before publication—proof reading, preparing the index, and making a table of contents. My talented wife, Harlene, has helped me so much with this part of the preparation with all of my books that I would have a difficult time preparing a book for the press without her. My books and articles are all better because her hands have touched them. More important, she always encourages my research.

Included in this manuscript are some materials that have been published previously. These have been updated and modified to suit this format, but the basic message in each case is the same.

1. "John of Patmos and the Angel of Revelation," *The Proceedings of the Sixth World Congress of Jewish Studies* (Jerusalem, 1977), I, pp.35-50.

2. The analysis of Revelation 16:12-21 is basically the same as that published in *New Testament Eschatology: Its Historical and Cultural Context* (Lewiston: The Edwin Mellen Press, 1993), pp. 172-191.

3. Several quotations have been taken from

Revelation and Redemption: Jewish Documents of Deliverance from the Fall of Jerusalem to the Death of Nahmanides (Dillsboro, North Carolina: Western North Carolina Press, c1978). This has been republished as *Jewish Messianic Movements from AD 70 to AD 1300* (Eugene, Oregon: Wipf and Stock Publishers, 2003). Individual documentation is given on the pages where each quotation is used.

4 The first edition of this book was published as *The Book of Relelation: Its Introduction and Prophecy* (Lewiston: The Edwin Mellen Press, 1993).

The editors and publishers of these documents have all kindly granted permission for these documents to be used again in the form of this commentary.

Two of the photographs used in this manuscript are views of a bowl now preserved at the University of Pennsylvania. These pictures were taken and permission for their use was granted by The University Museum, University of Pennsylvania (Negative numbers S4-140948 CBS 16096: interior view of Bowl from Nippur and S4-140949 CBS 16096: Side view of Bowl from Nippur).

The picture of the scroll with seven seals has been rephotographed with permission from Dr. Frank M. Cross, Jr. from his article, "The Discovery of the Samaria Papyri," *BA* 26 (1963):115.

The photograph of the Beth-horon area and the City of David were both taken from the air by Dr. Richard Cleave of Rohr Productions LTD. All other pictures and maps are mine or acknowledged at the illustration.

I am grateful to the editors, publishers, scholars and museums for this generosity.

THE BOOK OF REVELATION

George Wesley Buchanan

INTRODUCTION

THE FUNCTION OF AN INTRODUCTION

The Place to Begin. The Book of Revelation deserves the attention of both scholars and church men and women. Because it has been difficult to understand, it has been labeled "ridiculous," "nonsense," "irreligious," "fringe literature," and other uncomplimentary names. Because it was written for only certain people to understand, scholars and laymen and women alike have overlooked the high quality of this literature. Once understood, it will be appreciated. In this commentary the difficult parts will all be explained, so that this document will not remain a great mystery.

Nearly sixty years ago, the German scholar, Lohmeyer, thought it was strange that scholars from the United States had shown so little attention to the Book of Revelation as they had. At that time he held that there was no great work on the subject from the American scene.[1] In recent years there has been some solid research done in the United States, but that was not true in 1934. Some of the assumptions made about this literature were rather naive.

For example, in 1972, when J. R. May began his work on the Apocalypse and the American novel, he began with popular dogma about ancient notions and thought-forms. He confidently said,

> Both Judaism and Christianity developed myths of future catastrophe, of an end that would come only once in the history of the world. The apocalyptic literature that appeared late in Judaism reached its perfection in the last book of the Christian canon. The end will come only once because, in the Judaeo-Christian world view, time is linear and irreversible. Not that there are not suggestions of the cyclic in the pattern of its liturgy and in the "return to innocence" that is implicit in the *metanoia* urged upon the individual; these analogies to primitive cult are indeed there. But time is not cyclic, and this is the uniqueness of Judaeo-Christianity in the perspective of world religions. It has accepted the irreversibility of time, the terror of history. It sees the value of the historical hour for salvation. Moreover, since the Incarnation of Christ took place in history, history has shown itself capable of sustaining hierophany in a much more profound sense even than God's revelation of himself to the Hebrew people in the events of the covenant. In the Incarnation, according to Christian belief, God himself became event for man in history. So any

---

[1] E. Lohmeyer, "Die Offenbarung des Johannes 1920-1934," *TRu* 6 (1934):295.

> Judaeo-Christian expectation of an end of the world would obviously have to come in history, even if it would mean the end of time and of history.[1]

Sweet agreed that Christians and Jews were expecting the world to come to an end, and he also conceded that they expected it to happen soon, but he raised the question, If Revelation was based on the assumption--evidently wrong--that the world was about to end, of what further importance can it be? Sweet was not the first to ask this question. The early reformer, Ulrich Zwingli, refused to base Christian teaching on Revelation, holding that it was not a biblical book. Sweet's answer to his own question was that the importance of this message was "the truth of his vision of God's nature and will, and the world in that light. Lacking this, even successful predictions will soon be forgotten."[2] This is only partially correct. Caird realized that most scholars thought the Book of Revelation was written because John expected the final crisis of world history. Caird, however, did not accept that thesis. He believed

> John's coming crisis was simply the persecution of the church, and that all the varied imagery of his book has no other purpose than this, to disclose to the prospective martyrs the real nature of their suffering and its place in the eternal purposes of God.[3]

Those who wrote books like Revelation did not expect either the world or time to come to an end. They made prophecies on the bases of fulfillment of Scripture, the patterns of cycles, typology, and other standard doctrines. Typology is the study of the relationships of similar patterns. There was a type and an antitype. If the comparison was heavenly and earthly things, then the type was in heaven and the earthly object, person, or system on earth was the antitype. If both type and antitype were on earth, the earlier one was the type, and the later one was the antitype. For exampleJesus was thought to have been the new Moses—an antitype of Moses. John the was an antitype of Elijah. Ancients made prophecies on the bases of these typologies.

It was customary to think the end they expected would happen soon. Jews and Christians developed arguments to show this. When the end did not come, the argument continued and was reapplied to another anticipated future situation. This ability to reorganize conclusions has been practiced for hundreds of years. It was their conviction that caused believers to hold fast to arguments that were persuasive even after the arguments were proved false so far as that particular situation was concerned, but that was not a conviction that the world was coming to an end.

---

[1] From J. R. May, *Toward a New Earth: Apocalypse in the American Novel* (Notre Dame: University of Notre Dame Press, c1972) in H. Bloom (ed. and intro.), *The Revelation of St. John the Divine* (New York, 1988), p. 35. For similar opinions see C. Rowland, *The Open Heaven* (New York: Crossroad, c1982), pp. 37, 46-48, *et passim*.
[2] J. P. M. Sweet, *Revelation* (Philadelphia: Westminster Press, c1979), p. 2.
[3] G. B. Caird, *A Commentary on the Revelation of St. John the Divine* (London: Black, c1966), p. 12.

Their beliefs were positive and hopeful. They wanted the world to continue. They wanted only the evil sectors of the age to come to an end. This involved changing political administrations and powers. If they had believed that the world itself or its history was about to come to an end, it would not have been easy to reapply the arguments. It would also be difficult to keep on hoping that the world would come to an end. They expected an end, but not the end of the world or of its history. The notion that God wanted this world to come to an end was invented by nineteenth century Christians in Germany and accepted by other westerners for no good reason.

Caird concluded that the first readers of the Book of Revelation were no better off than we are today in discovering the meaning of the book.[1] That overlooks the fact that the original readers held the same concepts and knew the same idioms that the author did, simply because they belonged to the same period of history, spoke the same language, and believed the same doctrines. Today we have to deduce those concepts and doctrines. If we do not understand what they were, we cannot accurately understand what the author or authors meant. Anyone who reads the Book of Revelation on the assumption--

1) that Christians and Jews of New Testament (NT) times believed time was linear and irreversible,
2) that Jews and Christians of NT times believed that the world would come to an end, and
3) that time and history would run out—
   will certainly misunderstand the message of that book.

The Book of Revelation is not considered by most people to be easy bed-time reading. It is generally thought to be difficult, but it is more difficult to understand any literature if a person starts with erroneous presuppositions. In an effort to avoid that confusion and provide the reader a reasonable place to begin, this introduction will not only show that May, like many others, has accepted wrong concepts, but it will also show why they are mistaken.

The Necessity of an Introduction. Most "introductions" to commentaries are really conclusions. They ask the reader to begin reading the book with a group of presuppositions, designed to satisfy the conclusions of the author. This book will withhold the conclusions to the end, after the reader has read the entire text of the Book of Revelation, verse-by-verse, together with its interpretation. Only then will the reader be prepared to judge the conclusions fairly and to determine which of the conclusions reached seem reasonable to him or her. Readers are not expected to agree with the deductions of the author against his or her own judgment. It is more important for readers to have access to data than to be given dogmatic conclusions, and this book was written so that readers will have some basis for making their own judgments.

---

[1] Caird, *Revelation*, p. 7.

At the same time that this commentary was being prepared another book, *NT Eschatology: its Historical and Cultural Background*,[1] was also being written. That book provides the background concepts necessary for understanding the Book of Revelation, and anyone who wishes may read that before beginning to read this commentary. Here, however, there will be only a summary of *NT Eschatology*, lacking the extensive arguments, much of the data, and nearly all of the footnotes necessary to defend the position taken here.

The first five divisions of this introduction will constitute summaries of five chapters of *NT Eschatology*. They are these:

1) eschatology and financial concepts,
2) Sabbatical eschatology,
3) time and cycles,
4) the Kingdom of God, and
5) the eschatology of the Book of Daniel.

Three additional sections will include:

1) midrash,
2) typology, and
3) the basis for the translation.

This introduction will open doors for the reader to become acquainted with the kinds of thought-forms that were customary in the days when this document was written. It will also discuss some literary patterns normally used and historiography that was then accepted. These are necessary to make sense of a document that does not make much sense in modern concepts. At the time this book was written Christianity was a sect of Judaism, and there were no significant differences in Christian and Jewish methodology, so information from either tradition will be useful for understanding this document.

INTRODUCTORY SUMMARIES

Financial Metaphors. Jewish and Christian eschatology did not grow out of a cosmic myth about the end of the world. It was logically reasoned on the basis of Israel's laws about court practices of punishing and pardoning crimes. It also deals with financial justice in the market place, borrowing and lending money, foreclosing on debts, redeeming or forgiving notes, satisfying financial obligations, reconciling accounts, forgiving and releasing people from debts according to the laws of Sabbath and Jubilee years. These laws all had a theological significance that was applied to national government and Jewish and Christian eschatology.

---

[1] George Wesley Buchanan, *NewTestament Eschatology: Historical and Cultural Background* (Lewiston: Edwin Mellen Press, 1993).

Just as Israel patterned many of its theological thought-forms and metaphors from national court concepts, military organization, and political policies, so also it integrated into its theology some of its national monetary practices. This involved the national banking structure that enabled individuals to invest their money in a certain place where it could accumulate interest and be drawn later. Once money had been deposited, people could borrow against this accumulated supply when they needed it and pay it back later.

Financial metaphors were not unique to Israel's theology. A similar theological thought-form was expressed in ancient Babylon: "The man who sacrifices to his god is satisfied with the bargain. He is making loan upon loan."[1] Eliade has shown that ancients from many parts of the world think religiously in terms of borrowing and lending. This is true, for example, of the Semang pygmies and people of India.[2] The treasury of merits doctrine presumed that good deeds could be stored up for future use just as money could. It also assumed that lenders could "foreclose" whenever the account was overdrawn, and there was no immediate re-supply. Although the term "treasury of merits" does not occur in canonical Scripture, the patterns that presume its existence are evident there. Financial concepts, such as ransom, redemption, forgiveness, calculation, and reckoning were all part of Jewish and Christian theological terminology.

Offenses that can be punished in court are called "crimes," no matter how great or small. The sixteenth century English translation of "sin" is too general in use today to cover the biblical meaning. Crimes are expected to be punished, by death, prison terms, or fines. Judges can also pardon crimes, and release the criminal from punishment. When fines are not paid, they can accumulate. These are called "inequities." Because fines are financial, they can also be forgiven. That is why pardon and forgiveness have the same result for the criminal.

When money was borrowed, the borrower signed a note. When the loan was paid, the borrower redeemed his or her note, and the loan was cancelled. If the borrower could not repay the note, the note could be foreclosed or someone else could redeem the note for him or her, or the banker could forgive the note. These are all financial terms.

The day of judgment was the court day when crimes were judged, but, from a financial point of view, it was also a time when books were audited, fines had to be paid, punishments and foreclosures were assigned. A day of judgment was also a day of reckoning. Salvation meant being rescued from deserved punishment, foreclosure, bankruptcy. That is why salvation was synonymous with redemption and pardon. These metaphors have been used extensively by Hebrews, Israelites, Jews, Roman Catholics, and Protestants. Commercial concepts were basic to theology.

---

[1] W. G. Lambert, "The Dialogue of Pessimism," *Babylonian Wisdom Literature* (Oxford: Clarendon Press, 1960), p. 147.
[2] M. Eliade, *Cosmos and History: The Myth of the Eternal Return*, tr. W. R. Trask (New York: Harper, c1954), p. 99.

Believers thought God kept record of bank deposits and fines, and the fortunes of people were determined by their morality status. If they were blessed, that was the reward they received for good deeds. Any difficulties they experienced occurred because they had committed crimes, and God was punishing them. These sufferings were opportunities God had given them to pay the debts they owed him. This whole banking and marketing business concept was held to be God's way of establishing justice in the world. This was not only God's methodology for rewarding and punishing individuals, but also the way he brought about justice among nations. Israel had been driven off the Promised Land because its legal bank account had been overdrawn and bankrupt.

It was reestablished because of its increased merit. On the basis of these financial doctrines Israelites looked toward the future. How could believers cancel their debts so that God would favor them once again by giving them back the Promised Land? The end of the indebtedness and consequent "prison" sentence was the end for which they longed whenever they were not in control of that territory. These financial metaphors also became doctrines related to Israel's legal system in relationship to Sabbath justice and debtor slaves. This provided the rationale for sabbatical eschatology.

Sabbatical Rules. Thousands of years before there ever was a Jewish, Christian, Samaritan, or Hebrew people there were ancient laws and practices related to units of seven. There were seven days in a week, the seventh of which was the Sabbath. For ancients the Sabbath day was a taboo day. They believed that any work done on this day would bring them bad luck.[1] There was a week of weeks of days, or 49 days. The day after the forty-ninth day was called "the fiftieth" or "Pentecost." Early Sabbath calendars did not count the Pentecost as a day of the year. It was a day set apart for celebration. There were seven Penteacontads each year, bringing the total to 350 days (including Pentecost festivals). There were 15 or 16 days between the end of one year and the beginning of the next. Before this period began, ancients destroyed all food except unleavened bread, because they thought it was bad luck to carry over produce from the old year for use in the new year.

Believers survived during these 15 or 16 days on unleavened bread alone for food. The New Year began at the end of this fast of unleavened bread. Israelites adapted this custom to their own history in relationship to Passover. The old New Year's festival fell on the exact day that has later come to be Christian Easter. At that time people could cut the new grain and begin to eat food from the new year. This was the greatest festival day of the year. Those who observed this calendar had

---

[1] On Sabbaths and Pentacontads see J. and H. Lewy, "The Origin of the Week and the Oldest West Asiatic Calendar," *HUCA* 17 (1942/43):1-152; R. North, "The Derivation of the Sabbath," *Biblica* 36 (1955):182-201; R. North, *Sociology of the Biblical Jubilee* (Rome: Pontifical Bible Institute, 1959); J. Morgenstern, "The Calendar of the Book of Jubilees, its Origin and Character," *VT* 5 (1955):34-76; Th. Pinches, "Shapattu, the Babylonian Sabbath," *PSBA* 26 (1904):51-56; J. Meinold, "Die Entstehung des Sabbats," *ZAW* 29 (1909):81-112; Meinold, "Zur Sabbatfrage," *ZAW* 48 (1930):121-38; George Wesley Buchanan, *Jesus: The King and his Kingdom* (Macon: Mercer U. Press, 1984), pp. 316-18.

names for weeks, rather than just names for months.[1] The same reasoning was extended to years.

There were seven years in a week of years, the seventh of which was the Sabbath year. During this entire year farmers were forbidden to plant or harvest crops. They were required to live on crops that came up voluntarily. There was also a week of weeks of years, a unit of 49 years. The first year after the forty-ninth was called the Jubilee year. Just as the Pentecosts were days of celebration, so the Jubilee was a year of celebration. These sevens and multiples of seven dictated rests, celebrations, and times to abstain from producing crops. There were also civil laws that were further extensions of this system. Knowledge of these beliefs was basic for determining the ancient Jewish and Christian understanding of eschatology.

Eschatology is the study of ends. The term comes from the Greek word *éskhah-taws,* (ἔσχατος), which means "end." It can mean the end of an object, like a stick or a period of time, like a day, a week, a year, an era, or an administration.

The ancient Israelite who loaned money to another Israelite received no interest. The only protection there was for lenders was the law that gave creditors the right to force the borrower to work for the lender at half wages until the debt was paid (Deut 15:12-13, 18). Should the sabbatical year come around before the debt was paid, however, the creditor was required to release the debtor anyway, because he had worked at half wages, thus paying twice the amount of the money borrowed (Deut 15:12-13, 18).

This was part of the whole mentality of Sabbath taboo. On the seventh day everyone was required to stop working; on the seventh year everyone was obligated to release the land from production; on the seventh year creditors had to release all debts and allow their debtor slaves to go to their own homes. Because the laws that dictated these releases were in the Scripture, and therefore the word of God, Jews reasoned that it was God, like the banker, who redeemed them from their indebtedness on Sabbath years. If anyone owned property and needed money, he or she could sell the property; but on the Jubilee year, the one who bought it was required to return it to the seller or the heirs of the seller. This protected the owner and the owner's family, so that the land could not finally be taken from them.

The person who "bought" the land bought it knowing the law and the conditions of the sale, so Jubilee did not take the buyer by surprise. At the Jubilee, which happened after every 49 years, not only were the debtor slaves set free, but the land was restored to the original owners. This occasion was announced throughout the land by the blowing of trumpets (Lev 25:8-10). The restoration of the land on Jubilee years was also believed to be an act of the Lord's redemption of his people from their debts. Sabbath and Jubilee laws were rules of economic justice that enabled parties of the Mosaic contract to borrow from one another and lend to each

---

[1] 1Chron 24:7-18. This is further clear from 4Q Mishmerot HaKohanim (*4QS^e*). See B. Z. Wacholder and M. G. Abegg, *A Preliminary Edition of the Unpublished Dead Sea Scrolls* I (Washington, D.C.: Biblical Archaeological Society, c1991), pp. 104-18.

other, but the same laws also protected both borrower and lender from extensive exploitation. This concept was later transferred to national theology.

Jubilee Theology. The earliest recorded application of Jubilee justice to nationalistic theology was written during the seventh or eighth century BIA,[1] probably nearly 50 years after the North Israelites had been taken into captivity to Nineveh. The author looked forward to the New Year's Day of the next Jubilee (Isa 27:13). He thought God was obligated to observe the Sabbath rules written in the Torah. God had sent the North Israelites off the land into Assyrian captivity because of their "debts." Because of their debts, they had sold their land, but only on Jubilee terms. When the Jubilee occurred, God would let them come home and repossess their homeland. He would blow a great Jubilee trumpet that could be heard all the way from Egypt to Assyria, calling the liberated debtors home to Jerusalem.

Eschatology and the Land. In the Dead Sea Scrolls,[2] apocryphal and pseudepigraphical literature,[3] the NT,[4] and rabbinic literature,[5] terminology related to the expected end of the age and the restoration of the land in terms of Sabbath rest, Jubilee trumpets, and release of debtor captives occurs over and over again. Just as the Sabbath was a day or year of rest, so Jews and Israelites considered the secure establishment of the Promised Land to be "rest" (Deut 3:20; 12:10; 25:19; Josh 1:13, 15; 21:44; 22:4; 23:1; 2Sam 7:1, 11; 1Kings 5:4; *Sifre* Deut 1:2; #2, 65a). Those medieval rabbis and Jewish poets who calculated end times usually did so according to the Sabbath years and Jubilees. In this, Jews were consistent with biblical eschatology which is always expressed in calculations of sabbatical years and Jubilees or else in other real time-span terms related to Israel's history, such as the length of

---

[1] The abbreviation BIA (Before the International Age) is a politically correct term, preferred to the apartheid equivalents, BC (Before Christ), offensive to Jews, and BCE (Before the common era) offensive to biblically sensitive Christians (Lev 10:10; Ezek 22:26; 44:23).
  C. van Houten, *The Alien in Israelite Law* (Sheffield: JSOT, 1991), p. 128, overlooked Isaiah when she followed H. T. C. Sun in concluding, "Furthermore, there are no references to the Year of Jubilee in pre-exilic literature." For an analysis of scholarly opinion on the date for Isa 27 see S. Pagán, "Apocalyptic Poetry: Isaiah 24-27," *BT* 43 (1992):314-25. Some of those who relate Isaiah 24-27 to Isaiah of Jerusalem and the 8th century are: M. Lagrange, "L'Apocalypse d'Isaïe (24-27)," *RB* 3 (1894):200-31; C. Boutflower, *The Book of Isaiah Chapters I-XXXIX in the Light of the Assyrian Monuments* (London: S.P.C.K., 1930), pp. 328-31; and Y. Kaufmann, *Tohldóht Ha-'Emunáh Ha-Yisra'aylít (History of Israelite Faith)* [Hebrew] (Jerusalem: Mosad Bialik, 1954), VI, pp. 190-92, who denies that Isaiah 27 is apocalyptic. Pagán thought Isaiah 24-27 was a unit and was post Babylonian exilic. Like many, he ignored the Assyrian captivity.
[2] 1QS 10.3-4, 7-8; 11QMelch See also George Wesley Buchanan, *The Eschatological Expectations of the Qumran Community* (Unpublished Ph.D. Thesis for Madison: Drew University, c1959).
[3] 4Ezra 6.23; ApocAbr 31; SibOr 7:174; PssSol 11:19; *et passim*. Apocryphal literature is that which is not biblical. Pseudepigraphal literature is that which has been falsely attributed to the named author.
[4] 1Cor 15:51-52; 1Thes 4:16; Rev 11:2, 3, 5, 10, 11; Matt 13:39-40; 24:3; 28:20.
[5] See fn. 5. See also G. W. Buchanan, *Jewish Messianic Movements* (Eugene, Oregon: Wipf and Stock Publishers, 2003). Index on the various expressions.

time Israelites spent in Egypt or Babylon. Their hope was consistently related to years and ages and real restoration of the Promised Land to the chosen people.

According to biblical justice, crimes deserved punishment. Some offenses deserved corresponding injuries, but most crimes could be punished by levying a fine to be paid with money or goods. Unpaid fines constituted financial debts that might accumulate. The same was true of virtues that might be accredited, as if they were deposits in a bank account. The financial concepts that were interpreted theologically were applied to eschatological expectations in terms of Sabbath and Jubilee justice as well as Day of Atonement theology. It was by applying these laws to the situations in the diaspora where Jews could anticipate their return to the Promised Land and its restoration to Jewish government. This logic was intermingled with financial and legal terminology. The Day of Atonement was one day each year when the Lord was expected to declare his final judgments and conclude the decisions he had made as a result of his audits of the books. This could be a day of redemption or a day of punishment.

Single aspects of any of these beliefs could be used as code terms that suggested to those who had "ears to hear" the entire concept. For example, terms like "trumpets," "promised rest," or "liberation," called attention to the Jubilee, which, in turn, meant the "debtor captives" would be set free and the (promised) land restored to the original owners (the Jews). Expressions, like "a time, two times, and half a time," "42 months," "1,290 days," "1,335 days," or "the end of the days," reminded them of the end of the gentile era in the cycle of time. It was also the last half of the last week of years in a Jubilee, and the anti-type of the Maccabean revolt against the Syrian Greeks. Terms like "slavery," "captives," paying "double" for all their crimes, etc. referred to the role of debtor-slaves who were working off their debt. "The tribulation," also called "the days of the Messiah," is the antitype of the last three and a half years of the Greek era, during which Judas and his brothers fought against the Greeks for Jewish liberation. This period of tribulation would endure until "the times of the gentiles are fulfilled" (Luke 21:24) or finished.

All of these expressions were understood in a national sense. It was not just one Jew or Christian working off his own debt of crime; it was the whole people, which constituted a legal corporation, working off its accumulated national debt of crime. The Kingdom would not be restored to an individual; it was a community project that required a community endeavor.

Cycles of Time. Today most people anticipate the weather for the next day or week by watching the evening TV analysis. There meteorologists show pictures that have been taken from satellites that have been stationed in outer space. These photographs show the cloud formations, the direction of the jet streams, and the density of the clouds. With this and other data at their disposal meteorologists are often able to predict the next day's temperature within a few degrees and the rainfall within a fraction of an inch. This kind of scientific data was not available 50 years ago. In those days people guessed at the weather for the next day by reading almanacs, checking the local newspaper, and noting the way the sun set and rose.

The people who wrote almanacs based their predictions of the weather a year in advance on the basis of the moon, the average weather for that day, whether or not it was sunny on Ground Hog's Day, and whatever data they could gather from watching animals and plants. No one expected them to be very accurate, but that was the best available analysis at the time. With no better scientific bases for analysis, some financial advisors still try to predict the stock market on the basis of cycles. Before recent discoveries, most people lived on very nearly the same cyclical bases 50 years ago that were employed hundreds of years earlier. Not only were these cyclical judgments used to predict weather, but also to predict the rise, development, and fall of nations. It was on these bases that Jews and Christians developed their eschatological expectations.

Not only Greeks but many ancient peoples thought time moved in cycles. There were seven days in a week, and when the week was over it started all over again. The same was true of months, years, Sabbath years, and Jubilees. Seasons followed each other in predictable order, and feast days came each year in the same sequence. Jews also believed there were large temporal units called "ages" that followed each other in the same sequence. Each cycle had two halves, just as each day had two halves—night and day. One half of the cycle was the dark age, and the other was the age of light. Jews ruled the Promised Land during the ages of light--the Davidic-Solomonic age, the age of Ezra and Nehemiah, or the Hasmonean age. During the dark ages, Hebrews, Israelites, and Jews were in "captivity" in Egypt, Assyria, or Babylon, or they were living on the Promised Land under foreign dominance, either of the Syrian Greeks or the Romans.

After Judas the Maccabee's famous victory at Beth-horon and the rededication of the temple in 164 BIA a devoted Jewish calculator was able to trace the captivity of Babylon from 586 BIA to 164 BIA in terms of cycles, Jubilees, and Sabbath years. The important Sabbath period was the last week of years before the dedication of the temple. The Sabbath period began with a treaty made between Antiochus Epiphanes and the Jews. One half week later (168 BIA), Antiochus broke the treaty and defiled the temple. The next half week of years was devoted to a guerrilla war between Judas and his followers and the Syrian Greeks.

Typologically, each of these two 3½ year units symbolized one of the two periods before the construction of Solomon's temple. One was a wilderness period and the other was a period of conquest. This proved to those who studied cycles that there would always be a two-step development at the end of the dark age before the age of light came into existence, and this last stage was always war, called "the birth pangs of the Messiah" or the "tribulation." Those who believed in the understood system were able to match Jubilees, Sabbath years, redemption, and cycles of time together. There was no conflict among concepts of treasury of merits, debtor slavery, Sabbath justice, and cycles of time. The end for which pious Jews and Christians longed was the end of the dark age--not the end of the world, the cosmos, or of time. When the dark age came to an end, there would be a new age of light with a Jewish messiah ruling the Kingdom of God from his throne at Jerusalem.

The Kingdom of God. The term "kingdom" is a political term associated with a ruler that is a king, and all of the other political functions associated with a monarchical form of government. The first kingdom for Israel was the United Kingdom ruled at first by David and Solomon. The kingdom over which Solomon ruled was called both Solomon's kingdom and the Lord's kingdom (*mahl-koót Yeh-hoh-wáh,*[1] מלכות יהוה) (1Chron 28:5-7; 17:13; 22:10). Solomon was called God's son and he sat on the throne of Yehowah (*ahl kee-sáy Yehowáh,* על כסא יהוה) (1Chron 29:23). When Alexander Janneus was high priest and king over Israel (103-76 BIA), he was called in Hebrew "King Jonathan" (*Yóh-nah-than hah méh-lehk* יונתן המלך). A fragment from the Dead Sea Scrolls contains part of a prayer to God to bless the nation (God's kingdom, *mahl-kóo-teh-khah,* מלכותך), and all of the congregation of the people of Israel, wherever they happened to be (4Q 448.B). This prayer was for 1) the king, 2) the people, and 3) the kingdom of God, which was the kingdom over which Alexander Janneus ruled. Another fragment (4Q246) referred to a person who functioned as a king, establishing justice among his people, and leading the nation in war against the enemy. Like Solomon he was called "the Son of God" (ברה די אל). As late as the Crusades, Medieval Jews called the Promised Land the "Kingdom of God." Of course, this was exactly the term Jesus used to describe the kingdom he expected.

Windisch studied extensively the expressions in the NT that meant "entering" in relationship to the Kingdom of God or the Kingdom of Heaven. He found that the expression "enter the Kingdom of Heaven" was closely allied with "inheriting the Kingdom of Heaven" and "entering into life."[2] He found no similar equivalent in Rabbinic literature, but its counterpart occurs in the First Testament (FT) and in redemption literature. In the FT, the elect entered the Promised Land, the Land of Canaan, and the holy city. Those who entered Canaan also had life and inherited the land.[3] There were also references in relationship to the congregation of Israel or the congregation of worshipers. Those who were not properly qualified were forbidden to enter the congregation.[4] He concluded that

---

[1] The Tetragrammaton is correctly pronounced "Yehowah" or "Yehuwah." The popular pronunciation "Yahweh" was designed in the western world. It does not even sound Near Eastern. It does not rhyme when it is included in poetry, such as Exod 15. In proper names, like Jeremiah, Isaiah, Jonathan, Joshua, etc., the middle letter, which can be either a consonant or a vowel, is always treated as a vowel. See further Buchanan, "Some Unfinished Business with the Dead Sea Scrolls," *RevQ* 49-52 13 (1988) *Mémorial Jean Carmignac,* ed. F. G. Martínez et E. Peuch (Paris: Letouzey et Ané, 1988), pp. 411-20.

[2] H. Windisch, "Die Sprüche vom Eingehen in das Reich Gottes," *ZNW* 27 (1928):163-89. For an examination of the political kingdom in Israel see J. A. Soggin, *Das Königtum in Israel* (Berlin:Töpelmann, 1967).

[3] Windisch, "Reich Gottes," p. 177.

[4] Windisch, "Reich Gottes," p. 184.

> the whole complex of ideas appears much more strongly anchored in
> the Old Testament than one usually thinks.[1]

That is true, and there are also more references and ideas from FT in the Book of Revelation than one usually thinks.

The Kingdom of the Lord or the Kingdom of God in FT always referred to the Davidic or Solomonic kingdom. This is coherent with the use of the expression "Kingdom of God" or "Kingdom of Heaven" in the NT, Pseudepigraphical Literature of the FT, Rabbinic Literature, and the Dead Sea Scrolls. Josephus, a first century Jewish historian, used the Greek terms for kingdom many times--always in relationship to human kings over geographical, earthly territory. There is no biblical example of a psychological, sociological, or mystical kingdom unrelated to geographical territory.

The eschatology of Jesus, like the eschatology of other Jews of NT times was a national eschatology. In Jesus' day the Kingdom of God was hidden, so that the Romans could not realize what was going on. Underground, Jesus evidently had a government with a treasury and a cabinet. He may have had organized troops under cover. When Jesus said, "The Kingdom of Heaven is in your midst" (Luke 17:21) he meant that it already existed and was functioning, undercover within the very same borders as those held by King Solomon when he ruled the Kingdom of Yehowah (1Chron 28:5-7; 17:13; 22:10). When the Roman government came to an end this kingdom would appear in the open. The eschatology Jews and early Christians anticipated was the end of the gentile rule of the Promised Land, the completion of the times of the gentiles (Luke 21:24), a reestablishment of the Davidic or Hasmonean kingdom under the leadership of their own messiah.

Jews believed that the restoration of this kingdom was predestined, so they studied the cycles of time; they looked for antitypes to earlier events that preceded some deliverance and restoration of the land. They tried to lay up treasures in heaven to remove all obstacles to the establishment of the kingdom; zealous Jews joined celibate sects in order to provide levitically pure places for the Lord to be present; they performed works of supererogation, meaning that they did more good works than were required, to pay for the debt of crime this nation had accumulated; and Jews organized guerrilla bands in secret to be prepared to fight when the right time came to overpower the Romans.

Both in antiquity and now, events and time have been described in terms of beginnings and endings of cycles. When the end of one political administration, one stock market cycle, or one season of the year is discussed it is assumed that another similar phenomenon will follow. These are not concepts that deal with the end of time or the world. One of the reasons that the Book of Revelation is confusing to the average reader is that he or she has been misled by nineteenth century scholars who translated all of these ordinary endings into ends of the world, and modern scholars have not corrected their error.

---

[1] Windisch, "Reich Gottes," p. 187.

Many later scholars have not believed that the world was coming to an end, so they interpreted these ends in inventive and imaginary, but still incorrect, ways.[1] This commentary, however, is an attempt to find original sources that were influential in forming the Book of Revelation. These sources will not be discovered by reading authors like Bultmann and Dodd or Lindsey and White. They are found by examining biblical views about time, cycles, Sabbath and Jubilee laws, and the meaning of such basic terms as "kingdom," especially as they were understood by the author of the Book of Daniel.

Daniel Seven. The Book of Daniel is partly historical fiction and partly historical myth. Historical fiction is like "The Tale of Two Cities," "Les Miserables," or "The Scarlet Letter," in which a fictitious story is told as if it had happened in a certain historical setting. Its purpose is primarily that of convincing the reader of a point of view the author wants to propagate in relationship to that period of history. In the Book of Daniel the narrative about the Jewish scholars who achieved superior wisdom by observing Jewish dietary laws (Dan 1) or the story of Daniel in the Lion's den (Dan 6) are both historical fictions. Dan 7, on the other hand, is a historical myth. The Jewish victory over the Greeks at the Battle of Beth-horon and the rededication of the temple in 164 BIA have been dramatized as a great heavenly court scene. The judge was called the Ancient of Days, who was obviously God, because he came with the clouds of heaven, with flames of fire around his chariot. The defendants included the four beasts who were characters representing the kings of the four countries that ruled the Promised Land from 586 BIA to 164 BIA The most prominent of these was "the horn" who played the role of Antiochus Epiphanes. The plaintiff was the Son of man, who represented Judas the Maccabee.

The judge appeared at his bench with his assistant judges and the legal briefs to be considered in this trial. As in all Jewish trials where the death sentence might be given (bSan 4:1), the defendant was allowed to speak first. In Dan 7, the defendant spoke extensively, but he did not convince the judge of his case. He was given the death penalty, and his body was burned. Then the plaintiff stepped forward and received a positive verdict. He and his followers, the saints of the Most High, were given the kingdom, power, glory, and all other benefits that go with royalty.

This heavenly scene was an author's vision of events that had already happened on earth. In a conflict between Judas and his troops, on one side, and Antiochus Epiphanes and his troops on the other, Judas won, and Antiochus lost. Not only did he lose, but he died at just that time. In the Battle of Beth-horon, Judas not only won, but he succeeded so well that this was a turning point in the war, and he had enough space and time to have the temple cleansed and worship restored. At that point he not only became the military leader, but he became local ruler of the nation. This Son of man was given the kingdom, power, and glory. The kingdom he had been given was the territory which he had been able to conquer around Jerusalem.

---

[1] For a review of secondary sources, see Buchanan, Introduction to the reprinting of R. H. Charles, *Eschatology* (New York: Schocken Press, c1963), vii-xxx.

The clouds played the same role for Hebrews that the flying disk did for other Near Eastern political powers. It was the cloud that went before and behind the children of Israel when they crossed the sea. It had as its religious equivalent, the Hebrew *mahl-áhk* (מלאך), which is a messenger, angel, or agent. The cloud was moved from Sinai to the tent of meeting and finally to Solomon's temple. Maccabees expected the kind of divine help that was normally associated with the sun disk, cloud, or angels. Judas and his followers entered into battle, "with the Lord going before them" (2Macc 10:1), just as he had done when the Hebrews crossed the sea (Exod 14:19). In one of their battles the enemy of the Jews saw in the sky five majestic creatures from heaven on horses with golden bridles helping the Jews in battle (2Macc 10:29; see also 4QM 12.8).

On another occasion the heaven opened and two glorified angels confronted the enemies and frightened them into retreat (3Macc 6.18). When the Syrian governor approached Jerusalem with troops to take the temple and plunder its treasuries, mounted angels in armor appeared from heaven, filled the Syrian troops with terror, and made them withdraw (2Macc 3:22-30; 4Macc 4.10-14). These visions reflect the same kind of divine support as clouds did for early Jews and Christians. In the myth of Dan 7 the cloud accompanied Judas in his victory at Beth-horon and was reestablished at the dedication of the temple about three and a half years after the temple had been defiled.

The mythologists deliberately described the rule of the foreign power that governed the Jews during the "dark age" from 586 BIA to 164 BIA as leaders under the control of demonic powers that came up from the great deep. Correspondingly, they pictured the new kingdom Judas was establishing as having come from heaven with the power and authority coming from the Ancient of Days and accompanied with the Lord's cloud. The cloud is often accompanied by fire, lightning, and thunder. Here the cloud might be part of the atmosphere associated with the flames of fire that surrounded the seat of the Ancient of Days. When Moses went up Mount Sinai to receive the commandments, the mountain was wrapped in smoke, (or a cloud) and the Lord descended in the fire (Exod 19:18-20). The Lord was present in the pillar of cloud and fire at the tent of meeting (Exod 33:7-11).[1] On the Mount of Transfiguration, the Lord announced through the cloud that Jesus was his Son (Luke 9:34-35). In Daniel's judgment scene the fire and clouds were probably added to inform the reader that God was present in this entire judgment, and his influence

---

[1] See also J. VanderKam, "The Theophany of Enoch 1.3b-7, 9," *VT* 23 (1973):129-50; F. Schnutenhaus, "Das Kommen und Erscheinin Gottes im Alten Testament," *ZAW* 76 (1964):3; Patrick D. Miller, Jr., "Fire in the Mythology of Canaan and Israel," *CBQ* 27 (1965):256-61. Franz Cumont said that in Mazdean faith legitimate kings rule by the will of the supreme god, and they are given a special divine grace, called *Hvareno*. This did not make the king a god, but it provided him a unique destiny and supernatural power. Cf. Cumont, "Mithra," *Dict. des antiquities grecques et romaines*, ed. C. Daremberg and Saglio; *Les religions orientales dans le repandit dans paganisme romain* (Paris: Hachett, 1929), pp. 131 ff.; and *Les mysteres de Mithra* (Paris: A. Fontemoing, 1902), pp. 91-96. M. Rissi, *The Future of the World* (Naperville: A. R. Allenson, 1972), p. 19, said the white cloud was a sign of the parousia.

surrounded, not only the throne, but also the one for whom the verdict was pronounced, Judas as one like a Son of man.

It is obvious that Dan 7 and the judgment scenes in Enoch constitute a mythicization of the history of the Jews from the destruction of the Jerusalem temple in 586 BIA to its restoration in 164 BIA and the death of Antiochus Epiphanes sometime shortly before or shortly after that time. This narrative was told in terms of a judgment day scene in which the kings of the four countries that ruled Palestine after 586 BIA (Babylonia, Media, Persia, and Syria) were characterized as four "beasts." Real beasts do not often appear in court, but these kings were being insulted *posthumously* as if they were monstrous characters. In this myth the animals had the same function that animals play in Aesop's fables. They were intended to illustrate human character. They appeared in this court scene as if they all lived at the same time and appeared altogether, when, in reality, one king ruled at a time. The second king (= beast) did not begin to rule until the reign of the first one ended, but this provided no problem to the author of the myth any more than the passage of time provides an obstacle to a playwright. Scenes change, time is passed with a few stage changes, and the play goes on.[1]

TYPOLOGY

Typology Defined. Closely associated with temporal cycles was Jewish and Christian typology, and its application was prominent in the composition of the Book of Revelation. "Typology" is a belief that objects, events, persons, and institutions exist and occur in relationship to other corresponding objects, events, persons, and institutions. Typology is the term used to describe these relationships. For earthly things, when considered antitypes, there were prior and corresponding heavenly prototypes or archetypes that were patterns by which the earthly things were created. When the typology dealt with earthly things, the pattern was usually referred to as the "type," rather than the "prototype," and its corresponding antitype was also earthly and historical. When NT authors used the typological method of exegesis, the "type" was in the FT, and the "antitype" was in the NT interpretation.

The word, "type" comes from the Greek *typtein*, to strike. It has the basic meaning of a blow or a mark left by a blow or strike. It is like the impression left by a seal on wax. The impression, then, is the mold from which other seals or forms can be made. The instrument that made the impression was also called the type. The initial striker might be called the archetype, pattern, or model which could be imitated.[2] This succession of impressions could continue. For example, a heavenly prototype might make an earthly type or antitype, which, in turn, could have corresponding types or antitypes. Lampe criticized typology as an exegetical method. He held that it had some of the same problems as allegory and was sometimes little

---

[1] For arguments to support these summary conclusions see Buchanan, *The Book of Daniel* (Lewiston: The Edwin Mellen Press, c1999), pp. 179-234.
[2] G. W. Lampe and K. J. Woollcombe, *Essays on Typology* (London, SCM Press, c1957), pp. 6-61.

more than a rhetorical trick. For example, he noted that it was only by a far fetched process of reasoning that Melchizedek could be held to be superior to the Levitical priesthood. Even if that were conceded, it cannot be denied that the primary typology claimed by the author of Hebrews between the high priest's actions on the Day of Atonement and those he ascribed to Jesus were genuine type and antitype.[1]

This review will not provide an exhaustive appraisal of all examples of typology in the Bible. It will point out some of them as illustrations, examine their function in literature, and study the cultural thought-forms required to use typology in the way ancient Jews and Christians did. If this were a doctrinal study it might be proper to consider whether or not typology used by biblical authors was far-fetched and/or a legitimate discipline for theologians to practice today, but this is basically a factual analysis. The question here is, "Did the biblical authors employ typology at all?" The answer to this question is clearly, "Yes." Some of the common biblical types are Elijah, Phineas, Joseph, Jesus, the captivity, and release. These will be considered here.

Elijah Type. Elijah was a famous prophet in North Israel who is reported to have performed many miracles, stood up in resistance to an idolatrous government, and cleansed the land from pagan priests (1Kings 17:1-2; 2Kings 2:15). At a later time, when the priests of Israel were judged to be corrupt, Malachi reasoned that a new Elijah was needed in his day to cleanse the priesthood again. Malachi, therefore, promised that the Lord would cleanse the land of these wicked priests who had broken the contract Levi had once made with the Lord. The Levite, Malachi said, was the messenger for the Lord of armies (Mal 2:7), and in the day of judgment that was coming, the sons of Levi would be purified (Mal 3:2-3). When the Lord returned to his temple, there would first be a messenger, an anti-type of the old Levi, with whom the Lord had made a contract. This new messenger would be an antitype also of Elijah (Mal 4:5). From the time of Malachi on, Elijah was thought of as the Lord's messenger who would come before the Lord returned to his temple. There were several ramifications of this. The Lord would not return to the temple until the land was restored to the chosen people. At that time there would not only be a new temple, but also a high priest and a king, the Lord's anointed ones.

When Jesus referred to John as **Elijah**, he meant that John the Baptist was the antitype of the type, Elijah. He functioned in the way Elijah was supposed to function. When Herod called Jesus, **John raised from the dead**, he meant that Jesus was just another John the Baptist or an antitype of the type, John.

Woollcombe distinguished among allegory, fulfillment of Scripture, and typology. Allegory, he said, concentrates on details and is not historically controlled. He acknowledged that typology and fulfillment of Scripture sometimes overlap, but an event, such as the triumphal entry (Matt 21), was not really typology but the fulfillment of Zech 9:9. Typology relates one historical event to another, not in details, but in basics. A question such as the one that John might be Elijah (John 1:21) was typological and not the fulfillment of Scripture. John could not have

---

[1] Lampe and Woollcombe, *Essays*, pp. 34-37.

fulfilled the prophecy that Elijah must come first, because he was not really Elijah. He was an antitype of Elijah. Woollcombe thought the term "recapitulate" was the best term to describe some of the prophecy fulfillments in the NT. For example, Jesus was held to be the recapitulation of the son of David and the son of Abraham. The temple in Ezekiel's vision was a recapitulation of Solomon's temple. The deliverance from Babylon was a recapitulation of the deliverance from Egypt.[1] We will not make that distinction here. These will here be termed, "types," and the next type to be considered is Joseph.

Joseph Type. Scholars have observed that the hero of Dan 2 has been patterned after the Joseph stories in Gen 41. The following chart makes that obvious:

Daniel	Joseph
Nebuchadnezzar **had a dream** (Dan 2:1).	Pharaoh **had a dream** (Gen 41:1).
His spirit was troubled (*teet-pah-áhm róo-khoh*, תתפעם רוחו) (Dan 2:1, 3).	**His spirit was troubled** (*tee-pah-áhm róo-khoh,* תפעם רוחו) (Gen 41:8).
He called for the best wise men in Babylon (Dan 2:2).	He called for the best wise men in Egypt (Gen 41:8).
They could not interpret the dream (Dan 2:3-7).	They could not interpret the dream (Gen 41:8).
An official brought Daniel to the king (Dan 2:14-25).	An official brought Joseph to the Pharaoh (Gen 41:9-14).
Daniel **interpreted the dream** (Dan 2:27-45).	Joseph **interpreted the dream** (Gen 41:25-32).
Nebuchadnezzar praised Daniel's **God** (Dan 2:46-47).	Pharaoh acknowledged that Joseph was favored by **God** (Gen 41:37-39).
Daniel **made ruler over all** Babylon (*ahl kohl meh-dee-náht bah-váyl*, על כל מדנת בבל)(Dan 2:48).	Joseph **made ruler over all** Egypt (*ahl kohl áh-rehtz meetz-ráh-yehm*, על כל ארץ מצרים)(Gen 41:39-41).

Daniel was composed as if the hero had lived during the Babylonian diaspora, so the author easily found a type to follow from the diaspora in Egypt. Since

---

[1] Lampe and Woollcombe, *Essays*, pp. 42-44.

Joseph had once saved Israel during its Egyptian diaspora, enabling the Israelites to escape and return at a later time, Daniel was intentionally caricatured to be a new Joseph--wise, courageous, pious, prudent, and law abiding. Like Joseph, Daniel faced many dangers, but God always delivered him from them and rewarded him handsomely. This historical novel encouraged Jews to believe that Jews in the Babylonian diaspora would be rescued again and would later return to the Promised Land. Woollcombe overlooked examples such as these when he held that historical typology came into existence with Christianity.[1]

Phineas Type. At a time when Hebrews were suffering because they had mingled with the neighboring gentiles, the priest, Phineas, took the law in his own hands and killed two of the offenders (Num 25). The author of First Maccabees believed Mattathias, the patron of the Hasmoneans, was a new Phineas, and he pictured him as killing the mingling Jews together with the pagan foreigners. In the name of his forefather, Phineas, he raised his sword and began to recruit zealous patriots in an effort to throw off the yoke of the foreign rule (1Macc 2:17-28).

These details may not all have been exactly as the author of First Maccabees gave them. There was the factual basis that Mattathias rebelled against the neighboring collaborators and ruling foreigners and led the Maccabean revolt. Since this was something like that done by Phineas, the author of First Maccabees created a scene very much like the one in which Phineas was the hero, even to the extent of having Mattathias kill two people as Phineas had done--one a mingling Jew and the other, a foreigner. Because this author understood the type-antitype concept, he told the story so that Mattathias fit the antitype very well. Telling a story with Mattathias as a Phineas hero was good propaganda to support the Hasmonean government.

Many centuries later, some midrashic rabbi believed that he lived in a destructive age, like the one faced by Phineas and Mattathias. He derived comfort from Num 25, believing as he did that God would act in his day as he had in the past. There would be a new teacher of righteousness, an antitype of the priest Phineas. He would act as Phineas and Mattathias had done to purge the land from this foreign corruption. He interpreted Num 25 as follows:

> When he [Phineas] went out, he saw the angel striking the people with a plague. Thus it is written, **but one sinner** destroys **much good** (Eccles 9:18); this refers to Zimri, because of whom 24,000 Israelites perished. When Phineas executed judgment the plague was stopped, as it says, **And Phineas executed judgment** (*peen-khas vah-yeép-ah-láyl,* פינחס ויפלל) [so the plague was stopped] (Ps 106:30). *Pah-láyl* refers to judgment, for it is written, **and he shall pay as the judges determine** (*buh-péh-lee-leém,* בפללים) (Exod 21:22). So, may there come a teacher of righteousness in our lifetime and may he

---

[1] Lampe and Woollcombe, *Essays,* p. 42.

bring about judgment and justice in truth in the building up of Jerusalem, as it is written, **The Lord builds up Jerusalem**, etc. (Ps 147:2).[1]

The Hasmoneans functioned both as priests and government rulers, so the new teacher of righteousness could be both military leader and high priest. When the new Phineas came he would act just the way Mattathias and Phineas had acted in the past. In this way Phineas became a type of patriotic zealous rebel in whom Jewish zealots put their hopes. Elijah was the one anticipated in an expectation of two messiahs--one of Aaron and one of David--whereas Phineas was the priest expected to imitate the Levitical Hasmoneans. He was the type that motivated zealots to fight.

Jesus Type. Although Jesus was considered an antitype of Moses, Joshua, David, and Elisha, he himself was considered to be a type after which the apostles were patterned. It was not difficult for later authors to reason this way. An apostle was a legal agent who was legally identical to the principal for whom he or she was employed. This typological conviction was basic to the author of Acts. For example, the man who had been blind from birth was healed at once by Jesus. This caused a great furor among the religious people who tried to get the man to deny that he had been healed, but he refused (John 9:1-41). Likewise Peter healed a lame man at the temple gate. Afterward the apostles were cross-examined by the high priest and other officials who tried to suppress Peter and quiet the excitement that had aroused the people (Acts 3:1-4:22). To prove Paul's apostleship, the author also provided for him to heal a lame man (Acts 14:8-10).

Jesus raised a girl who had died by saying, **Talitha, arise**, **Little girl, arise** (Luke 8:49-56)! and Peter did the same thing, saying, "Tabitha, arise" (Acts 9:36-43)! A woman touched the hem of Jesus' garment and was healed from her hemorrhage (Mark 5:25-34). People were healed by arranging for the shadow of Peter to fall upon them (Acts 5:15). People brought scarves and other articles of clothing for Paul to touch so that the owners would be healed (Acts 19:11-12). When they brought a lame man to Jesus on a mat, Jesus ordered him to take up his bed and walk, and he did (Matt 9:1-8; Mark 2:1-12; Luke 5:17-26). Peter did the same (Acts 9:32-35).

At a certain point in Jesus' career, he set his face steadfast to go to Jerusalem, where he expected to be killed (Luke 9:51, 53). Paul, likewise, set his face steadfast to go to Jerusalem and Rome, realizing that he would not return to see the people to whom he said, "Farewell" (Acts 19:21; 20:22; 21:15, 17; 23:11). Jesus appeared before the Roman governor, Pilate, who found no guilt worthy of death (Luke 23:4, 14, 22). Paul appeared before the Roman governor, Festus, who found Paul had done nothing worthy of death (Acts 25:25). Both were under accusation of

---

[1] See Buchanan, "The Priestly Teacher of Righteousness," *RevQ* 6 (1969):553-58; "The Office of Teacher of Righteousness," *RevQ* 9 (1977):415-25; and M. Bergman, "Another Reference to 'A Teacher of Righteousness' in Midrashic Literature," *RevQ* 37 (1979):97-98.

the Jews. These statements reflect more doctrine than factual history. The narrator, whose major subject was the activities of the apostles, believed Jesus had ordained these apostles to be his legal agents. Therefore he reasoned that since the apostles were authorized to act in behalf of their principal and in his name, they must have done nearly the same things Jesus did. In this conviction, he composed examples of Jesus' actions and goals being fulfilled through the agency of the apostles.

Captivity Type. When Jews found themselves against their will in Babylon they began to interpret their lives in relationship to the captivity in Egypt. Both "captivities" were interpreted as prison terms and were consistently understood in terms of debtor slavery. The earliest analysis of a second captivity is reflected in the Isaianic redemption chapter (Isa 27). This was probably written nearly 50 years after the Assyrian captivity (722 BIA); i.e., about 685-75 BIA, because the author expected a great trumpet blast, as at Jubilee, and thought at that time all of the diaspora Israelites from Egypt and Assyria would return the way debtor slaves were to return at Jubilee.[1] This means the people taken captive into Assyria were understood by that time to have been debtor slaves, serving out a prescribed term until the first Jubilee arrived, when all debtor slaves were to be sent home, and all land taken to pay off debts would be restored (Deut 15:12-13, 18; Lev 25:8-10).

    The Deuteronomist had made that deduction sometime after the Assyrian captivity. It is unlikely that he dreamed of a future exile out of a clear blue sky. He probably interpreted an event that had already taken place. After there had been a deportation of the leaders of North Israel to Assyria, the Deuteronomist "predicted" that it would take place, and explained why the Lord let it happen (Deut 28:20-21, 41, 64). Also, like the author of the Isaianic apocalypse, the Deuteronomist promised that the Lord would restore them to the land, as he had done before when they were exiled in Egypt (Deut 29:3-10). By the time of Jeremiah, that prophet had at his disposal both the "prophecies" of Deuteronomy and the history of the North Israelite exile as bases for his prophecies that Judah also would be taken into exile. He had only to pay attention to the international events of his time to be able to predict that they would go to Babylon rather than Assyria.

    Many years later, after the Romans had taken complete control of Herod's kingdom, deposed and exiled his son, Archelaus, and organized a Roman taxation of Palestine (ca. IA 6/7), Zadok the Pharisee and Judas of Galilee led a revolt against Rome. They argued that the Romans had taken away their freedom, and they considered themselves slaves and captives again. This thought continued, and it was the basis of the great Roman-Jewish war of IA 66-72. With the typology of the Exodus captivity of Egypt and Babylon was also associated the hope of the Exodus release. This is reflected many places in the Book of Revelation.

Exodus Typology. The earliest repetition of an Exodus type in biblical account is the leadership of Joshua, the first successor to Moses. Just as Moses had sent messengers in to spy out the land, so Joshua sent messengers in to spy out the land (Josh

---

[1] On this see Buchanan *The Consequences of the Covenant* (Leiden: E. J. Brill, 1970), pp. 9-18.

2:1-24). Just as the Lord opened up the waters at the border of Egypt to allow the Israelites to cross under the leadership of Moses, so Joshua divided the waters of the Jordan so that the Israelites could cross over on dry land (Josh 3:7-17). Just as the Lord commanded Moses to take off his shoes because he was standing on holy ground, so Joshua was commanded to remove his shoes, because he was standing on holy ground (Josh 5:13-15). Just as Moses gave a farewell address before he died, so Joshua gave a farewell address before he died (Josh 23:1-16). Just as Moses called the Israelites to make a contract with the Lord, so Joshua invited the Israelites to make a contract with the Lord (Josh 24:1-28). The author of Joshua not only presented the crossing of the Jordan as an antitype of the Exodus from Egypt, but he pictured Joshua as a new Moses. The entire Exodus experience, with its theological interpretation, continued to be a type upon which later events were understood as antitypes.

Just as the Babylonian and later diaspora experiences were interpreted as captivity and as prison terms served by debtor slaves according to the Egyptian pattern, so the expectation of a new Exodus from Babylon was understood as a logical consequence. The Isaianic redemption chapter (Isaiah 27) predicted a Jubilee trumpet to announce liberty to the captives of Assyria and Egypt. Jeremiah had followed Deuteronomic logic and "prophecy" in predicting the captivity because Jews had not really let their brothers go free on years of release (Deut 15:18). He said the Lord would then fulfill the curses of the contract by giving the Jews a new type of "freedom"--freedom to the sword, pestilence, and famine (Jer 34:17). When the Lord sent the Jews into Babylon, Jeremiah argued that they would have to work off their indebtedness to the Lord at half wages, just as the law decreed. This meant paying double for all of their crimes (Jer 16:18).

When the author of Second Isaiah realized that Cyrus was willing to cooperate with Jews in overthrowing the Babylonians and allowing Jews to return to Palestine, he immediately looked for a theological justification for the return. He observed that the Jubilee was at hand, so he announced release to the Babylonian captives (Isa 61:7) in terms of Sabbath and Jubilee justice. He reasoned that if Cyrus was about to liberate them, it must be that Jews had already paid double for all their crimes (Isa 40:2), but even if they had not, they could be restored to the land according to debtor slave-release terms (Isa 40:2) because of the laws related to Jubilee. Second Isaiah expected a new Exodus, patterned after the Exodus from Egypt.

Instead of imagining that the Babylonian Jews would go back to Palestine by the same route they had taken to get there, going northwest through the Tigris-Euphrates valleys and then turning south through the Esdraelon Pass, he followed the Exodus from Egypt typology and visualized a new road being built from Babylon to Jerusalem, through the desert, because the Hebrews had traveled through a desert years before. He also expected the same kind of provisions as before--plenty of food and water, miracles of healing, and freedom from ritualistic pollution (Isa 35). Just as the Lord had brought the Hebrews out on eagles' wings to establish them in their destined portion (Deut 32:8-11), so the Jews of Babylon would mount up on wings as eagles (Isa 40:31).

As the Lord guided the Hebrews through the sea to escape from the Egyptians (Exod 14:15; Isa 63:12-14), so he would again lead the chosen people through the waters (Isa 43:2; 51:11). Just as the Lord had sent his angel before the Hebrews as a pillar of fire by night and a pillar of cloud by day and followed them across the sea in the same way (Exod 14:19-20), so Jews would return with the Lord before them and behind them (Isa 52:12; 58:8). Just as the Lord drove away all of Israel's enemies, showing himself to be the "man of war" (Exod 15:3), so Second Isaiah referred to the Lord as a "man of wars" who would prevail against the enemies of the Jews (Isa 41:12; 54:14-17).

These are only a few of the many Exodus themes echoed by the Babylon typologist.[1] Others were undertaken by the author of Revelation. A very significant typology in Revelation was related to the conclusion of the war of 66-70 IA. Jews had expected the war to result in their freedom as it had in the Hasmonean Rebellion nearly two hundred years earlier. When Vespasian left the scene at Jerusalem to settle a civil war in Rome, Jews thought victory was theirs.

Goppelt has called attention to the extensive use of typology in the NT,[2] but, following the first edition of this book, Bird mentioned the significance of typology in the FT itself.. Some of the types and antiypes he listed are:

1) Exodus of Abraham –exodus of Moses—exodus of Second Isaiah;
2) Sodom of Genesis—Sodom of Jeremiah;
3) Eden of Adam—Eden of Ezekiel;
4) Davidic shepherd, Elijah—Malachi's priestly Elijah—the baptizing Elijah;
5) Adam—Noah;
6) Moses—Joshua;
7) Moses—Elijah;
8) Jacob—the nation Israel.[3]

Bird correctly held that the NT did not manufacture typology. It already had a pattern in the FT.

Erroneous Typology. In IA 70, when Emperor Vespasian's son Titus returned to Palestine to continue the Roman war with the Jews, Titus found Jerusalem considerably weakened by famine and destruction. Just a few months earlier, when Vespasian left his military offense against Jerusalem to settle a civil war in Rome, Jews

---

[1] On this see Buchanan, *Jesus: The King and his Kingdom* (Macon: Mercer U. Press, c1984), pp. 164-68; and *Typology and the Gospel* (Lanham: University Press of America, c1987), pp. 1-27.
[2] L. Goppelt, *Typos: The Typological Interpretation of the Old Testament in the New* (Grand Rapids: Eerdmans, 1982), tr. D. H. Madvig.
[3] C. H. Bird, "Typological Interpretation within the Old Testament: Melchizedekian Typology," *Concordia Journal* 26 (2000):37-46.

were thrilled. They thought their war with Rome was nearly over, but the civil war in Jerusalem changed the perspective. The earlier Jewish exuberance had been reduced to lamentation, but religious soldiers fought until the temple burned, expecting a miracle right up to the last minute. Josephus said there had been numerous false prophets who had deluded the people during this war. One of them assured Jews, even when the temple was in flames, that God was right at the point of showing the signs of deliverance (War 6:285-8).

Parts of the Book of Revelation may have been written by some of those "false prophets" just before the temple burned. After the temple had been burned, Josephus observed that the cycle was exactly in agreement with the earlier type. The temple had been burned first in 586 BIA and again in IA 70 on exactly the same month and day, according to Josephus (War 6:268-70).[1] Whereas the "false prophets" had recognized the signs of the times to be exactly in correspondence with the period before the Maccabean victory, Josephus, following the same typological, cyclical understanding of predestined time, concluded, after the event, that the prophets had been false, and the type they had identified was the wrong one.

This was neither the beginning nor the end of Jewish reliance on signs and interpretations. During the forty or so years after the crucifixion of Jesus, Josephus reported four leaders who promised deliverance to contemporary Jews. They also offered signs to prove this would happen. Their signs were all modern equivalents of earlier prototypes that would show they were then in the very place in the cycle of time where these events occurred in the first place. Theudas promised that the river Jordan would open for him as it had for Joshua (Ant 20:97-98). Another figure led the Jews to the wilderness to see signs of liberation (Ant 20:167-68; War 2:259). A third promised that the walls of Jerusalem would fall before him as those of Jericho had before Joshua (Ant 20:168-72; War 2:261-63). A fourth led Jews into the wilderness to receive salvation and rest (Ant 20:188). These happened so often that Jews were also warned not to go out into the wilderness to meet these messiahs (Matt 24:25). The signs they promised to repeat first occurred prior to, or during, the first conquest of Canaan. Followers hoped to see proof that they were then at the same point in the cycle of time as when these first occurred.[2]

MIDRASHIC EXEGESIS

It is impossible to make sense out of the Book of Revelation without recognizing the use the author has made of the FT. FT allusions are so prevalent in the Book of Revelation that it might properly be called midrashic redemption literature. Of the 39

---

[1] Josephus probably forced the facts to fit the cycle as did also the author of Second Maccabees who said the cleansing of the temple in 164 BIA occurred on the very day and month on which the temple had been defiled (2Macc 10:5).

[2] There were non-Jews who expected the past to be reenacted just as precisely as this. Thucycides (*Hist* 1.22[4]), for instance, said, ". . . events like this will occur again." See further Buchanan, *Jesus*, pp. 264-68, and *Typology*, 1-27.

books of the FT, Revelation alludes to 24. Many have noticed the frequent use of FT in Revelation. Beale, for example, argued that Daniel was the main scriptural basis for Revelation.[1] Vogelgesang, Ruiz,[2] Vanhoye,[3] and Goulder[4] claimed that Ezekiel was the main source. Some chapters show more dependence on Daniel and others more on Ezekiel, Zechariah, Isaiah, Jeremiah, the Torah, or some of the Psalms, but the use made of the FT is significant. The authors of the various units of Revelation believed that the FT was the word of God, and they interpreted it as lawyers might exegete the United States constitution together with its later precedents. If they alluded to some of these texts, their reading publics would have recognized the entire context of the FT in which texts were contained. Rabbis called this method of composition "midrashic." It was widely employed among Jewish, Samaritan, and Christian authors of NT times. In fact it was extensively used also in the FT itself. The word "midrash" comes from the Hebrew *dah-rásh* (דרש) "search," and was used as early as the seventh or eighth century BIA.

ISAIAH'S MIDRASH

Isaiah used sources that he believed had sacred authority. In another context, while promising destruction for Edom, Isaiah exhorted readers to "search (*deer-shóo*, דרשו) the Book of Yehowah and read (*oo-keh-rah-óo*, וקראו). Not one of these will be left out" (Isa 34:16).[5] Unfortunately, we do not have this source Isaiah used,[6] but if we did, we would probably learn that the details of his prophecy against Edom were all included in that source which both he and his readers accepted as authoritative. If his readers had not accepted the Book of Yehowah as authoritative, Isaiah could not have used it to prove his prophecy. The Book of Yehowah evidently included curses like those in Isa 34, and Isaiah was confident that every curse would be carried out, since it was God's word. There were apparently other laws attributed to Moses that no longer exist.

---

[1] G. K. Beale, "The Influence of Daniel upon the Structure and Theology of John's Apocalypse," *JETS* 27 (1984):413-23.
[2] J. P. Ruiz, *Ezekiel in the Apocalypse: the Transformation of Prophetic Language in Revelation 16,17-19,10* (Frankfurt: Peter Lang, c1989).
[3] A. Vanhoye, "L'Utilisation du Livre d'Ezechiel dans l'Apocalypse," *Bib* 43 (1962):436-76.
[4] Michael D. Goulder, "The Apocalypse as an Annual Cycle of Prophecies," *NTS* 27 (1981):342-67.
[5] Looking for the Lord in this case meant reading the Scripture. Ezra set his mind to study the Torah of Yehowah (*leed-róhsh et toh-ráht Yehowáh*, לדרוש תורת יהוה, Ezra 7:10). Much of the "searching" or "looking for" on the part of Hebrews, Israelites, or Jews was looking for or asking something from the Lord. This was done by going to Moses, a judge, a priest, or a prophet to receive the Lord's judgment. The person to whom they went to ask the question or try the case was considered a valid legal agent of the Lord, one authorized to give advice or pronounce judgment. In addition to asking a legal agent, they might also check the Scripture that had been composed by a legal agent and therefore represented the Lord's opinion on a case.
[6] There are other dependencies upon materials no longer extant. For example, the Chronicler mentions that the priests sprinkled blood on the altar after they had received it from the Levites, **acting according to the Torah of Moses** (2Chron 30:16) even though this command nowhere occurs in the present Pentateuch. So M. A. Fishbane, *Biblical Interpretation in Ancient Israel* (New York: Oxford U. Press, 1985), p. 533.

The word *dah-ráhsh* (דרשׁ) was used many times in FT. It was used in close association with *shah-áhl* (שׁאל), "ask," "consult," "interrogate," "desire," *bah-káhsh* (בקשׁ), "search," "strive," "desire," "demand," "request," or *khah-káhr* (חקר), "search," "examine," "inquire." *Darásh* also holds some of these meanings. It means "looking for" something that might be found, such as a lost animal (Deut 22:2) or Yehowah (Deut 4:29; Isa 55:5-6; Jer 29:12-13). It could also mean looking for or tryng to obtain peace (Jer 29:6-7; 38:4) or "demanding," like demanding someone's blood (Ps 9:12-13) or the Lord's flock (Ezek 20:10). In certain situations it meant "investigate." When the Levites, Ithamar and Eleazar performed their assigned funcions, Moses investigated meticulously (*dah-roóhsh dah-ráhsh*, דרשׁ דרשׁ) to find out if the work had been done carefully (Lev 10:16). Isaiah anticipated a good Davidic king on the throne, judging and investigating (*dóh-resh*, דרשׁ) rules so as to establish quick justice (Isa 16:5). Even gentiles were expected to consult the Davidic king (Isa 11:10).

If anyone heard of citizens who encouraged others to serve other gods, they were commanded to investigate (*dah-ráhsh-tah*, דרשׁת), search (*khah-káhr-tah*, חקרת), and ask (*shah-áhl-tah*, שׁאלת), until they found out the facts. Then they should act accordingly (Deut 13:14-15). Whenever anyone made a vow or took an oath, he or she could expect that Yehowah would investigate the case (*dah-rawsh yeed-reh-sháy-noo*, דרשׁ ידרשׁנו) diligently so that it would not be neglected (Deut 23:22). Yehowah would also investigate (*eh-dráwsh*, אדרשׁ) anyone who would not listen to his word that was spoken in his name (Deut 18:19). The way Yehowah investigated a case and provided judgment was through a court, where a judge was Yehowah's legal agent, authorized to act and speak on the Lord's behalf.

Judges were obligated to investigate well (*dah-reh-shóo*, דרשׁו, ... *hay-táhv*, היטב), before pronouncing verdicts (Deut 19:17-18). These investigations were closely related to ethics, the fulfillment of vows or commandments, and the investigator was one whose responsibility it was to enforce justice. Looking for Yehowah meant looking for good, rather than evil (Amos 5:4-6, 14). Those who consulted Yehowah did no wrong (Ps 105:3-4), kept his testimonies, and walked in his ways (Ps 119:2-3, 10).

There were many instances in which the context was not clear how the person was to "search for," "look for," or "consult" Yehowah, although this was clearly the expectation. Some consulted Baal Zebub (2Kings 1:2, 3, 16), idols (Ezek 20:31), conjuring spirits, necromancers, or wizards (Isa 1:16, 19; 19:3). Nevertheless, there are a few clues to indicate that this "consulting" or "looking for" Yehowah was not as mysterious as it seems in the twentieth century. Moses appointed judges at the advice of his father-in-law, because Moses had told his father-in-law that the people came to Moses to consult God. This means they came to him to judge legal cases. Since he was the Lord's legal agent, consulting Moses was the legal equivalent of consulting God (Deut 1:9-17). Israelites were ordered to consult the priests, the Levites, and the judges to find the word of judgment (Deut 17:9). Some who consulted Yehowah did so by consulting a prophet (1Kings 22:4-5; 22:7-8; 2Kings 3:11; Jer 21:2; Ezek 14:7; 20:1-3).

People evidently consulted Yehowah when they needed advice, forgiveness, or vindication from some injury. If they needed atonement, they consulted the Lord through a priest; if they needed counsel, they asked a prophet; if they needed justice, they came to a judge. These were all legal agents who could speak for God. Those Israelites who came to agents of the Lord rather than pagan agents were commended. Ezekiel warned that those who went to pagan courts and temples, consulting pagan deities rather than Yehowah could not later find recourse through the agents of Yehowah (Ezek 20:1-3; 34:8). Since consulting the Lord sometimes meant utilizing the Jewish court system, those who used pagan courts were considered idolaters. They had worshiped idols. Perhaps the close relationship between consulting a deity and consulting a pagan court prompted Paul to shame the Corinthians, telling them that it would be better to suffer injury than to take cases to a gentile court (1Cor 6:1-10). In fact, those who practiced trying to achieve justice through pagan courts were worshiping the deity of whom the judge was the agent. This made the litigants in the case idolaters, and Paul reminded the Corinthians that no idolater would enter the Kingdom of Heaven (1Cor 6:9-10).[1]

Deuteronomy said the Lord would investigate the person who made an oath (Deut 23:22), but no indication was given to show how the Lord went about this. He may have done his investigation through the priest in whose presence the vow was taken, as in the case of Hanna and Eli (1Sam 1:1-18, 24-28) or a judge (CDC 9:9). In one instance whereby Yehowah did the investigating it was because someone would not listen to the Lord's word which was spoken in his name (Deut 18:19). If it was spoken in his name it was spoken by a legal agent, possibly Moses, in the Deuteronomist's judgment. Since the Lord gave so much validity to his word that was spoken in his name, he may have been satisfied with the investigation that was conducted in his name. At least the logic that gave the Lord's authority to his word through an agent might also accept his punishment administered by an agent. One of the ways by which ancient Hebrews investigated to learn what God's word was to consult the Scriptures. The community that consulted **Yehowah, God of Israel** (*leed-róhsh leh-Yehowáh eh-loh-háy yees-rah-ayl*, לדרוש ליהוה אלהי ישראל) (Ezra 6:21) was the same community that consulted **the Torah of Yehowah** (*leed-róhsh eht toh-ráht Yehowáh*, לדרש את תורת יהוה) to do and to teach in Israel the statute and the law (Ezra 7:10). Asa was reported to have destroyed the foreign religious objects, and he "told Judah to consult (*leed-róhsh*, לדרש) Yehowah the God of their fathers and observe the Torah and the commandment" (2Chron 14:3). Consulting Yehowah was closely related to the Scripture and the ethical demands recorded there. Isaiah counseled his readers to "consult" or "search" from the Book of Yehowah and read (Isa 34:15-16).

The word, *dah-ráhsh* which Isaiah used to invite his readers to check his documentation, is the very word later rabbis used in precisely the same way. It is

---

[1] For an analysis of 1Cor 6 see J. D. M. Derrett, "Judgement and 1 Corinthians 6," *NTS* 37 (1991):22-36.

from the root *dah-ráhsh* that the word "midrash" is derived.[1] Those who search or consult the text and interpret it produce a midrash or commentary on the sacred text. This is what Isaiah was doing (Isa 34:1-17). There are other prophecies in the FT against Edom (Jer 49:7-22; Ezek 25:12-14; 35; Amos 1:11-12; Obad; Mal 1:2-5; Ps 137; and Lam 4:21-22), and some of these may also have used this now unknown source, the Book of Yehowah, but none seems to have the exact detail Isa 34 produced, and none document this source.

Although this methodology was extensively utilized in medieval Judaism and Christianity, unless all of this Isaianic literature can be proved to have been composed by later authors, midrashic literature was already an accepted literary genre as early as the seventh or eighth century BIA. Isaiah employed two Psalms and Exod 15 to compose some of his literature. There is no book either in the FT or the NT that utilized the midrashic method as much as the Book of Revelation.

PSALMS AND EXODUS FIFTEEN

Exod 15 was standard liturgy by the time Ps 104-106 were written, because part of this extensive Psalm was based on that text. You can tell from the texts before you that the Psalmist not only told the story of the Exodus, but he took some of the very words from Exodus 15 and wove them into his poem, making a narrative midrash. This long historic poem shows the same kind of relationship to Genesis, Numbers, and Deuteronomy, but there is no history in the poem later than the story of Phineas and his encounter with Zimri and his new Midianite wife. Nothing is reported of the conquest of Canaan or the establishment of a kingdom. Most scholars think this is pre-exilic literature.[2]

Psalm 104	Exodus 15
[33:35]**I will sing to Yehowah** with my life; **I will sing praise** to **my God** while I exist! Let my meditation please him; I will rejoice in **Yehowah**.	[1]**I will sing to Yehowah** [2]My strength and **my praise is Yehowah.**

---

[1] Two midrashim reported in the FT are: "The rest of the acts of Abijah, his ways and his words, are written in the midrash (*buh meéd-rahsh*, במדרש) of the prophet Iddo" (2Chron 13:22). This book is no longer extant. The Prophet Iddo seems to have written a prophecy upon which someone else wrote a commentary. Concluding the account of Joash, the Chronicler said, "These are the ones who conspired against him: Zabad, the son of Shimeath, the Ammonite, Yahozabad, the son of Shimrith, the Moabite, [the account of] his sons, the many prophecies against him, [and the report that] he founded the House of God--look! they are written on the Midrash (*ahl meéd-rahsh*, על מדרש) of the Book of the Kings" (2Chron 24:26-27).

[2] Briggs, Sarna, W. R. Taylor and W. S. McCullough, Dahood, *et alia*.

Let criminals perish from the land,
> and the wicked be no more.

Bless, **Yehowah**, O my soul!
Praise Yehowah.

Psalm 105

¹⁻⁴Give thanks **to Yehowah**;
call out in his name!

Make known among **the peoples** his deeds;

Sing to him! sing for joy to him!
think of all his **miraculous deeds**.
Praise his holy name.
Let the heart rejoice, [you] who request **Yehowah**
Seek (*dahr-shóo*, דרשו) **Yehowah** and his **strength**.

Exodus 15

¹I will **sing to Yehowah.**

¹⁴**The peoples** have heard; they tremble.

¹I will **sing to Yehowah.**
¹¹**a miracle worker.**
²**I will praise him.**

²My **strength** and my song is **Yehowah.**

These Psalms were composed by authors who were already familiar with earlier texts from Exod 15. The Psalms are really midrashic Psalms. This is called "narrative midrash," because words from the text are incorporated into the Psalm itself. The text of the Book of Revelation is mostly composed in the same fashion, as the following passages will illustrate.

TEXT

Revelation 1

¹²When I **turned**,

I saw seven gold lamp stands, ¹³and in the midst of the **lamp stands** was

one like a Son of man,

First Testament

^{Zech 4:1-2}The messenger who was speaking with me **turned, and he** aroused me as a man who is awakened from his sleep. Then **he said to me, "What do you see?"** I said, "I see--now look! a **lamp stand, all of gold**, with a bowl on the top of it and **seven** lamps on it."

^{Dan 7:13}Now look! With the clouds of heaven, **one like a Son of man** was coming.

dressed in a full-length robe, **and** he **was bound** at **his waist with a gold** belt.	^{Dan 10:5}Look! A man **dressed in** linen, **and his waist was bound with gold** of Uphaz.
¹⁴**His head and** his **hair were white as wool**--**white as snow**--and	^{Dan 7:9}The Ancient of Days sat down. His garment was **white as snow,** and **the hair** of **his head was like** pure **wool.**
his eyes were like flames of fire. ¹⁵**His feet were like burnished brass**, as if smelted in a furnace.	^{Dan 10:6}**His eyes were like** torches **of fire**, and **his** arms and **legs were like** the gleam of **burnished brass**. The sound of his words **was like the sound of** a multitude.
His **voice was like the sound of much water [running]**, ¹⁶having in his right hand seven stars, and from his **mouth** went out **a sharp sword,**	^{Ezek 1:24}I heard the **sound** of their wings, **like the sound of much water [running].** ^{Isa 49:2}He set my **mouth** like **a sharp** two-edged **sword**.
his appearance **like the sun** shines **in its might**.	^{Judges 5:31}Thus let all your enemies perish, Yehowah, but his friends **like the sun** as it goes **in its might**.

According to Swete there are 404 verses in the Book of Revelation; 278 of these use the FT.[1] Most scholars working on the Book of Revelation today think there are more allusions than earlier scholars have proposed.[2] No attempt will be made in this book to give any numerical figure. Instead the most obvious allusions will be shown here by placing the relevant FT passages in parallel columns with the passages from the Book of Revelation. Readers may then judge and count for themselves which of these parallels is genuine and how many of them there are.

In this commentary, the text of Revelation will be set in one column with the texts from the FT that were used to compose the text in Revelation in a parallel column so that the reader can see the texts used to compose the Book of Revelation. A few parallels from surrounding literature are also included to show the consistency

---

[1] H. B. Swete, *The Old Testament in the Book of Revelation* (Grand Rapids: Eerdmans, 1972), p. 132.
[2] For example, C. J. Hemer, *The Letters to the Seven Churches of Asia in their Local Setting* (Sheffield: JSOT, c1986), p. 13.

with which concepts were preserved. There is less use of FT in chapters 2 and 3 than in the rest of the book.

The Translation. This translation has been made on the basis of one ancient text--Sinaiticus. This text was chosen because it is the only text that includes the entire Book of Revelation. Most modern translations are made on the basis of a composite text, such as that of Nestle and Aland. Nestle and Aland (NA) have used many good texts and have chosen in each case which variant is most likely to have been the original text. In most cases their judgment is probably correct, but there was never a church in antiquity that used the composite text they have produced. Even though Sinaiticus has many obvious scribal errors, I have chosen to use it, because it was a version of the Book of Revelation that was used, just as it is preserved today. There are problems with the Sinaiticus text that will become apparent to any reader. The scribe sometimes misheard the dictation. At other times he omitted part of a sentence, making it seem rather ludicrous, but even when that is the case, I have translated the texts just as they are, noting the problems in the commentary, and the NA choice is given for comparison.

I am responsible for every translation made in this commentary, unless I have shown otherwise. I have translated the Greek text of the Book of Revelation and all Hebrew, Aramaic, Greek, and Latin texts used that are not from the Book of Revelation. This translation of the Book of Revelation shows no absolute consistency whereby one Greek word is always rendered by the same English word. There are several reasons for this:

1) Sometimes the same Greek expression is repeated over and over in a passage. I have used synonyms in such cases to improve the English text.
2) Especially when the Greek renders an obvious FT passage I have chosen to find an English word or expression that best reflects the FT involved even though the translation is different from other English translations of the same expression or word. For example, the expression *kai áye-dawn* (καὶ εἶδον) is used over and over again in the Book of Revelation. Sometimes it introduces a vision and is a quotation from Daniel. At such times it is given an imperfect force, "I was watching." At other times it is rendered in simple aorist, "and I saw," or "and I looked."
3) Different contexts require different translations of the same Greek term. The Greek conjunction *kai* (καί) is used many times in the Book of Revelation in ways that need no English or American counterpart to convey the meaning involved. In such cases it is simply omitted in English. At other times it reflects the Hebrew *waw*, especially in a *waw* consecutive formation. In these cases it has been either omitted or sometimes rendered by some conjunction other than the usual, "and," "but," or "also."

I have used Greek, Hebrew, and Aramaic in the commentary itself to provide scholars the bases for my translations in critical places, but I have also written the commentary with the average pastor in mind. After all, it was as a pastor of a local church that I was motivated to begin this research. Therefore, I have translated and transliterated every Greek, Hebrew, and biblical Aramaic word that is printed in the commentary, with one exception. I have not transliterated the talmudic and targumic Aramaic, because the dialects of the targumists are uncertain.

The earliest western transliterations were evidently made in Eastern Europe, where they used an alphabet that has many letters not used in English, German, or American. The western scholars used letters that were familiar to westerners but then put accents over them, making them familiar to Eastern Europeans but unfamiliar to westerners. As noted traditionalists, Bible scholars, however, followed the Eastern European technique and continued to use this alphabet for transliteration purposes only, and call it "scientific transliteration." Eastern Europeans, however, did not consider it specially scientific. In their languages, it was simple transliteration according to their consonant and vowel sounds. It seems unnecessary today for people who otherwise do not use Eastern European alphabets to have to memorize them for the purposes of transliterating biblical languages only. Why not make our own transliterations, using our own alphabets? That is what will be done in this commentary, making it possible for Americans, French, German, and Spanish readers to understand it without learning the Eastern European languages. This transliteration is not scientific, and it is not intended for scholars, only. I have transliterated these words, phonetically, into American so that a person untrained in Near Eastern languages might pronounce them approximately correctly if he or she so desired.

I have tried to make the translation basically smooth, idiomatic American, avoiding the Shakespearean English expressions that are often used in biblical commentaries. To accomplish this I have sometimes ignored the historic present tense that the author of the text used. Instead I have rendered into English the tense that makes the most sense. Even though I have sometimes taken these liberties, at other times I have deliberately made the translation rather "wooden" to reflect the underlying idioms involved.

Throughout the commentary the Tetragrammaton is spelled in English "Yehowah." Although it is popular in scholarly circles to spell the name "Yahweh," and pronounce it accordingly, the omission of the central syllable is not justified. In a Greek scroll (4QLXX Lev), the name is translated into Greek ΙΑΩ, *Yah-Oh*, preserving the "oh" syllable. This is also true in proper names that continued to be pronounced: Elijah (*Eh-lee-Yah-hoo*), Jeremiah (*Yeh-reh-mee-Yáh-hoo*), Jonathan (*Yah-hóh-nah-than*), or John (*Yah-hoh-khah-nahn*), preserving either the "oh" or the "oo" syllable. Also in poetry, such as Exodus 15:1, 3, 6, 11, 17, 18, the central syllable is necessary to balance the meter.[1]

The Goal and Method of Presentation. Facts necessary to reach conclusions are given in this commentary directly. These are events, facts of history, literary data,

---
[1] For a more extensive justification, see Buchanan, "Unfinished Business," pp. 411-20.

and other unquestionable materials. In addition to facts, however, the commentary also reports opinions--opinions of other scholars and opinions that are mine. The latter are given more tenuously than facts, couched in such expressions as "it seems"--likely, reasonable, probable, possible, etc., which means this is the way it seems to me. It does not assume that the same data will seem the same way to every reader. The data that convinced me of the conclusions given are provided, and readers may pass their own judgment on every case. Final judgments are withheld until the end of the book to enable readers to reach their own conclusions first, but those who want early previews of my conclusions may read them at the end of the book before reading the commentary.

This commentary is not a rhetorical defense of nineteenth century hypotheses that were created in Western cultures and are still being held to tenaciously. The historian and the rhetoricians have different goals in mind. The historian is always looking for new data that will shed more light on the picture. As more and better information is obtained the historian will change his or her conclusions, accordingly. When new scrolls are found or new archaeological insights are discovered, the historian begins immediately to learn how they apply to literature he or she is trying to interpret. The rhetorician, on the other hand, is satisfied with the conclusion he or she already accepts, and has as the goal, only that of defending that conclusion. The rhetorician develops hypotheses to keep contradictory data away from the investigation.

There are dozens of rhetorical commentaries on the Book of Revelation that can be bought or read in a library. The defensive Christian who is satisfied with his or her current understanding of this document, who fears new insights and interpretations, is free to read these for support. The person who wants to learn as many materials as possible that effect the interpretation of the text will find this commentary interesting, refreshing, and exciting. It reflects the work of a careful historian of the Scripture.

The basic materials for this study belong to the ancient Near Eastern culture, geography, topography, languages, literature, and attitudes. The goal of the commentary is not to indoctrinate but to inspire; not to prove but to provoke imagination, thought, and discussion. Readers will learn how successful I have been after they have read the commentary.

CHAPTER ONE

TEXT

Revelation	First Testament
1:1The revelation of Jesus Christ, which God gave to him to show his saints **the things that must happen** quickly, and he gave a sign, having sent through his messenger (*'ahn-geh-laws*, ἄγγελος) to his servant, John, 2who bore witness to the word of God and the testimony of Jesus the Messiah whatever he saw. 3Blessed is he who reads and **those who hear** the word of this prophecy and **keep** the things written in it, for the time is near.	Dan 10:1On the third year of Cyrus, king of Persia, the word **was revealed** to Daniel . . . and the word was true. Dan 2:28But there is a God in heaven who reveals mysteries, and who has made known to Nebuchadnezzar **the things that must happen** in the last of days. Dan 2:45A great God has made known to the king **that which must happen** after this. Exod 24:7All that Yehowah has spoken **we will do (keep), and we will hear (obey)** (*nah-ah-seh wuh neesh-mah*, נעשה ונשמע).

COMMENTARY

The revelation of Jesus Christ. **The Revelation** is the beginning term of the entire document which is called "The Book of Revelation," or sometimes just "Revelation." The Greek for that is *ah-paw-kaw-loóp-sees* ἀποκαλύψις). This is the word from which the term "apocalyptic literature" is derived. There never was an expression "apocalyptic literature," or a type of literature now known as apocalyptic literature, however, in New Testament (NT) times. Morton Smith's extensive study shows that there were very few early uses of the term "apocalypse," either in classical or biblical sources. When it did appear, the term often meant things human, such as uncovering an ear or exposing someone's nude body for shame. Smith conjectured that during the last centuries BIA[1] the word was applied to telling

---

[1] BIA (Before the International Age) is a politically correct alternative used instead of BC (Before Christ) or BCE (Before the common era). The term "common" in biblical and Jewish usage has a

secrets. Most NT usages are related to Pauline letters or documents written by first century Paulinists in Paul's name, but there is no evidence that Paul knew of literary materials called "apocalypses."[1] Here the term is not used to describe a type of literature.

The words, **the revelation of Jesus Christ,** can mean a **revelation** which belonged to **Jesus Christ;** that is, it was Christian. It could also mean it was made by him, or it might be a **revelation** about Jesus Christ. The word translated **revelation** can mean something uncovered, such as a revealed woman is one who has no clothing, is naked. When Saul was angry with his son, Jonathan, he told Jonathan that what he was doing was being done to his own disgrace and to the disgrace of his naked mother or his **revealed** or unclothed mother (*ahr-váht eem-áy-kha*, ערות אמך = LXX ἀποκαλυψέσως μητρός σου[*ah-paw-kah-loop-séh-ohs may-tráws soo*], 1Sam 20:30). The term rendered "naked" or "unclothed" was also used to tell of a message Daniel received, informing him of the events that were to happen in the future. This was the word that was **revealed** or "uncovered" to Daniel *dah-váhr nee-gah-láy luh-Dahn-ee-áyl*, דבר נגלה לדניאל = ὁ λόγος ἀπεκαλύφθη τῷ᾽ Δανιηλ, *haw láw-gaws ahp-eh-kahl-oóf-thay toh Daniel*, Dan 10:1).[2] Later Daniel was ordered to **cover** (*káh-loop-sawn* κάλυψον) **the commandments and seal the scroll** (Old Greek [OG], Dan 12:4). *Kah-lóop-tayn* means to cover; *ah-paw-kah-lóop-tayn* means to uncover, to open, or to disclose something hidden, such as nakedness or secret information. The word that was "uncovered" for Daniel was apparently contained in a scroll that was unrolled. The way he would "cover" the commandments would have been to roll up the scroll and seal it. Jews of NT times also thought of ages rolling and unrolling like scrolls. When an age was just about over it was ready to be rolled up, closed, and sealed (4Ezra 6.20).

John of Patmos was intentionally relating his message to that of Daniel. For Daniel, the message that was sealed would not be opened and revealed for another 3½ years. In antiquity people thought time was circular. That which happened once would happen again at a later time in the circle, just as seasons recur, and days of the week happen over and over again. This was called "typological." The first occurrence was the "type," and the later occurrences were all "antitypes." John of Patmos thought he was living in an antitype period that happened earlier with Daniel. Therefore, he expected the events to conclude in the same way.

John of Patmos thought he was living in the 3½ year period that was in the same place in the circle as Daniel was when Daniel sealed the scroll, but he thought

---

pejorative meaning (Lev 10:10).

[1] M. Smith, "On the History of ΑΠΟΚΑΛΥΠΤΩ and ΑΠΟΚΑΛΥΨΙΣ," ed. D. Hellholm, *Apocalypticism in the Mediterranean World and the Near East* (Tübingen: J. C. B. Mohr, 1983), pp. 9-19.

[2] T. Zahn, *Die Offenbarung des Johannes* (Leipzig: A. Deichert, 1924) I, p. 138, noted that this translation is only in Theodotian's, which some have thought was used in the Book of Revelation. Zahn argued that Theodotian wrote many years after the Book of Revelation was composed. If there was any dependence it would have been that Theodotian used the Book of Revelation. The most likely answer is that both the authors of Revelation and Theodotian provided independent translations of Daniel, but both tried to reflect the Hebrew literally.

he was nearing the end of that period, the time when the seals should be broken, the scroll unrolled, and the message revealed. In fact he had in his hand at that moment the scroll that had already been opened. The uncovering or *ah-paw-káw-loop-sees* of the scroll that came to **John** at **Patmos** would have been the unsealing and unrolling of the scroll. The context shows what was hidden or covered and how it was shown openly, opened up, or disclosed.

Here, as in Daniel, **revelation** deals with secret information that is disclosed, but it may be intended to describe something more visual than that as well. It refers to something unrolled or opened up. This would happen, for example, when a person's will was unrolled and read. In John's judgment the scroll brought to him was a Christian prophecy, one in which Jesus Christ was the main subject and principal actor. Like Daniel's **revelation,** this **revelation** reportedly was given to **John** at this point to let him know what the future was expected to hold.[1]

One of the Dead Sea Scroll discoveries was the Habakkuk Commentary. The author of this document studied the Book of Habakkuk to learn what would happen in the future. Passage by passage, he first quoted Habakkuk and then added, "The interpretation of the word is . . ." It is apparent that this commentator thought the prophecy of Habakkuk was the word of God and that it applied to Jews of his own day. At the end of one of his interpretations (*páy-shehr hah dah-váhr*, פשר הדבר), most of which has been lost, he said, ". . . and afterward he will reveal (*tee-gah-léh*, תגלה) to them **knowledge** as **water** of the **sea** for abundance" (1QpHab 11.1-2). This was the interpretation of Hab 2:14: **For the land will be filled with the knowledge of the glory of Yehowah as water covers the sea** (1QpHab 10.14-15).

The commentator understood that the Promised Land would be filled with this special knowledge when God revealed to the Jews the knowledge involved. The author was getting his knowledge from the Scripture, and he probably thought this was the knowledge that should fill the land of Palestine, and God would reveal to the Jews this knowledge when they read the Scripture the way he did. For that author God's revelation was closely related to the Scripture. The same was true of John of Patmos, as most commentators have observed.[2]

Zahn insisted that **Jesus** could be only the subject of the **revelation**--not the object, as some have thought. The **revelation** was not about **Jesus**; it is **Jesus** who

---

[1] T. Zahn, *Die Offenbarung des Johannes* (Leipzig: A.Deichert, 1924) I, pp. 140-43, has pointed out many literary similarities between Revelation and the Apocalypse of Baruch. He held that the Apocalypse of Baruch was dependent upon the Book of Revelation, and not vice versa (p. 143).

[2] According to M. E. Boring's count (*The Continuing Voice of Jesus* [Louisville: Westminster/John Knox Press, c1991], p. 143), there are 499 passages in the Book of Revelation that are put in bold type in the Nestle-Aland Greek text of the NT. Bold type indicates passages the editors thought alluded to passages in the First Testament (FT). H. Kraft, *Die Offenbarung des Johannes* (Tübingen: J. C. B. Mohr, 1974), p.112, said that the author of Revelation applied a Scripture passage for every assertion he made. This is the same methodology employed by the authors of medieval redemption literature.

did the **revealing**.[1] Jesus was the agent through which God sent his message. God gave it to **Jesus** to show to his servants (Rev 1:1).

The entire genre, apocalypse, may be a misnomer. It gets its origin from this one word in Rev 1:1, but Mazzaferri insisted that the Book of Revelation is not an apocalypse:

> The title, apocalyptic, certainly derives from Rev, but this is irrelevant. [*Ah-paw-káw-loop-sees*], ἀποκάλυψις is not a technical term in John's day, although he employs it prophetically. In terms of actual generic definition, Rev cannot be equated with apocalyptic in form.[2]

Betz was correct in saying that apocalyptic literature has never been satisfactorily defined.[3] Rowley went too far in saying, "That apocalyptic is the child of prophecy, yet diverse from prophecy, can hardly be disputed."[4] Hill held that Revelation was more like FT prophecy than like apocalypses--assuming, of course, that some of the literature that is somewhat like the Book of Revelation consists of apocalypses, even though they never use the term **revelation** in their texts. Like earlier prophetic books, the Book of Revelation was written out of its time and for its time. Its main interest was not the sealed mystery of the distant future, but the contemporary situation. It is not a book that has been falsely ascribed to another earlier author (pseudepigrapha).[5] Mazzaferri is not quite correct in holding that in its final form, the Book of Revelation is a letter. It does not begin with a salutation. It contains letters (Rev 2-3), however, as well as a prophecy: Rev 4:1-22:5.

All of these so-called apocalyptic documents might better be called "Redemption Literature." This is similar to the designation the Israeli scholar, Ibn Shemuel gave to his collection of medieval Jewish literature of this nature. He called it *meed-reh-sháy geh-oo-láh*, מדרשי גאולה "Midrashim on the subject of Redemption" or "Redemption Midrashim."[6] A midrash is a commentary on a biblical text. It is a literature about a literature. The literature in Ibn Shemuel's volume deals with the redemption or restoration of the Promised Land. It is a collection of earlier medieval Jewish documents that were interpretations of biblical literature. The Book of Revelation, like Daniel, Zechariah, Jeremiah, Ezekiel, and many other biblical and other books written after the FT and before the NT (intertestamental), belongs to the same category.

---

[1] Zahn, *Offenbarung* I, p. 145.
[2] F. D. Mazzaferri, *The Genre of the Book of Revelation from a Source-critical Perspective* (New York: DeGruyter, 1989), p. 258.
[3] H. D. Betz, "Zum Problem des religiongeschtlichen Verständnisses der Apokalyptik," *ZTK* 63 (1966):592.
[4] H. H. Rowley, *The Relevance of Apocalyptic* (New York, Association Press, 1963), p. 15.
[5] D. Hill, "Prophecy and Prophets in the Revelation of St. John," *NTS* (1971/72):401-405.
[6] Ibn Shemuel's book, *Midreshe Ge'ulah* (Jerusalem: Bialik, 1968) exists only in Hebrew. The documents he collected plus many more have been translated into English and published with notes as Buchanan, *Jewish Messianic Movements* (Eugene, Oregon: Wipf and Stock Publishers, 2003).

Redemption literature began with the Assyrian exile of the North Israelites and was further developed with the Babylonian exile of the Jews of Judah. As soon as the members of the twelve tribes found themselves off the land that they believed God had promised them, they began to study the Scripture and try to understand where they were in the circle of time and what would have to happen before the land might be restored.

Redemption is a financial term. When a person borrows money from a bank, he or she is expected to pay it back. When it is paid, the borrower is given a note, "paid in full." This means the loan has been redeemed. If the borrower cannot meet the time and terms of payment, someone could, hypothetically, pay it for him or her. This person would be the redeemer. It is always possible for the banker to forgive the loan and become the borrower's redeemer. Israel and Judah knew that they had committed many crimes and owed many unpaid fines. Just as a wife is given a document of divorce by her husband and sent away from his house (Deut 24:1), ancient Jews and North Israelites assumed that, although they had a marriage contract with the Lord, when the temple, God's "house," was destroyed and they were sent off the land to foreign countries that they had been divorced. They wanted to become reconciled to the Lord and have the contract renewed. The terms of renewal evidently meant that they would have to pay those unpaid fines with multiple damages. This would be required for their redemption from foreign powers and restored to their home in the Promised Land. The only way they could avoid this fate was for another redeemer to pay the debt.

Exilic and post-exilic prophets were yearning for redemption, which meant a restoration of the Promised Land under rule of their own king. The literature they wrote is called "prophecy" and is strongly supported by earlier Scripture the authors considered sacred. This means post-exilic prophecy is midrashic in character;[1] it might also be called "redemption literature," as it will be in this commentary.

To show to his saints. Most texts have **to show to his servants**. The word **saints** here is a peculiarity of the Sinaiticus Greek text, translated in this commentary, that also closed John's message, with words, **with all the saints** (Rev 22:21). In Rev 1:1, however, Sinaiticus calls John **his** "servant." These terms were near synonyms. When the servants were servants of the Lord they were also **saints. The saints of the Most High** (Dan 7:27). They were Jews with the Judas 164 BIA. John and his contemporaries thought of themselves as antitypes of the Maccabean Jews.

The things which must happen quickly. This prediction was couched in the framework of Daniel's anticipation. The terms, **near** or **quickly**, probably meant that Christians were then within that last 3½ year period of the gentile age. The period of 3½ years was mentioned only once, directly, in the Book of Revelation (Rev 12:14),

---

[1] For illustrations of this claim see Buchanan, "Midrashim Pre-Tannaïtes," *RB* 72 (1965):227-39, and "Some Unfinished Business with the Dead Sea Scrolls," *RevQ* 49-52 13 (1988) *Mémorial Jean Carmignac*, ed. F. G. Martínez et E. Peuch (Paris, 1988), pp. 411-20.

but the period of the same length was referred to as 42 months (Rev 11:2; 13:5) and also as 1,260 days (Rev 11:3; 12:6). Forty-two-30-day months equals 1,260 days. This was the "end of the days" of foreign rule before Jewish or Christian rule would be established over Palestine.

This forms an antitype of the very difficult period in Daniel between the time when the Syrian king, Antiochus, defiled the temple and the time when it was cleansed by the Jewish guerrilla leader, Judas the Maccabee. Jews refer to this period as "the birth pangs of the Messiah." Christians call it "the tribulation." Both anticipate the future on the basis of the historical events just before the rededication of the temple in the time of Judas. The war between the Jews and the Greeks during this 3½ year period preceded the liberation. John thought Christians were then near the end of the tribulation, and it would be only a short time before the predestined period would be over and the nation would be free from foreign rule.

Whenever this period of time is mentioned in the Book of Revelation it is as an antitype of the same period in Daniel which is the type. It is futile to stretch the meaning of the terms **short** and **soon** to indicate something that really meant "long" or "in the far distant future." Christians who are still waiting for this end, after more than 1900 years fail to understand the meaning of John's message. Some apologists have tried to explain **near** to mean the last days of history.[1] Others say it means "suddenly"--anytime in the future, or to say that this was the "prophetic outlook" which is *always* near. Another defense is to escape in the terms of 2Peter 3:8, **With the Lord one day is as a thousand years.** But John was not expecting to wait a thousand years. Based on Daniel, he expected an end to take place within 3½ years. That did not happen, and John made a mistake, just as many other prophets have done. Both Isaiah and Jeremiah, for example, prophesied that the Medes would conquer the Babylonians and destroy the city. That never happened. Neither Media nor Babylon still exist, so those prophecies will never be fulfilled. That is all there is to it, and no one should try to claim some infallibly correct interpretation that will absolve Isaiah, Jeremiah, or John of Patmos' of their errors.[2]

Zahn correctly identified **quickly** (Rev 1:1) with **for the time is near** (Rev 1:3), but he was too confident in emphasizing the precise significance of the word, *kai-ráws* (καιρός) "time." He argued that it should not be confused with the word "*khráw-naws* (χρόνος)," which, he said, meant a duration of time.[3] That which he said is true in most classical Greek literature, but not of Jewish or Christian literature. The OG, in fact, most regularly renders the word for feast or a special time (*moh-áyd*, מועד) by χρόνος (*khráw-naws*), and it translates *ayt* (עת) extended time, by καιρός (*kai-ráws*), just the opposite of classical Greek. There are times in the NT when καιρός (*kai-ráws*) has the meaning of something appointed, but that is not consistently true. Each usage must be determined by its own context. Here John refers to the time when this "tribulation" would be over.

---

[1] Boring, *Continuing Voice*, p. 168.
[2] On this see M. P. Horgan, *Pesharim: Qumran Interpretations of Biblical Books* (Washington, D.C.: The Catholic Biblical Association of America, 1979).
[3] Zahn, *Offenbarung* I, p. 157.

He gave a sign. The **sign** that this was so was given in the **prophecy** which was commanded to be read before the congregation. The text does not say directly that the **sign** was itself a scroll containing the prophecy and that this prophecy was exactly that which John **saw** and about which he bore witness. There is a very close relationship, nonetheless, between the **prophecy** which was mentioned in the blessing which promised that the time was near and the revelation given to John, telling the things that must happen quickly.

Rhetoricians are people trained in debate and argument. Most attorneys and public speakers are rhetoricians. Ancient rhetoricians called any item used in an argument that was possible but which could not be proved **a sign**. The term seems to have been used in the rhetoric of the Book of Revelation in somewhat the same way. For Jews and Christians of NT times, a **sign** was usually something in the present that recalled something in the past. Something that happened currently reminded Jews and Christians of something that happened to Moses, Joshua, Deborah and Barak, Zerubbabel and Joshua, Judas the Maccabee, or some historical hero or heroine. Because they expected time to move around in cycles that repeated earlier cycles, religious leaders tried to match their time with an earlier period.

If someone struck a rock, for example, and water flowed, this was a **sign** that the current period corresponded to the wilderness period where Moses struck the rock and water appeared. Religious prophets studied cycles of time the way modern investors study stock market cycles, trying to deduce which phase of the bull or bear market resembled an earlier phase in the curve. Authors of weather almanacs predict the weather a year in advance in the same way. Predictions based on these cyclical studies of the stock market or weather almanacs are never perfect, and investment or weather prophets do not all agree. There are often mistaken prophecies made, but investors and weather prophets never give up studying the patterns of the stock market or the weather cycle. There is a certain amount of reliability in cyclical time. Spring always follows winter and autumn always follows summer, but when the authors of almanacs tried to predict conditions more precisely, they were often mistaken. It is much more reliable to predict weather on the basis of satellite imformation than on the basis of past history. Religious prophecy, however, has no satellite direction to follow. The religious leaders in NT times, like current "prophets," who looked for **signs** of earlier history on which to predict the future were wrong more often than not.

Having sent through his messenger. The word **messenger** here renders the Greek *áhn-geh-laws* (ἄγγελος), which is often translated "angel" and assumed to have been some heavenly being. There were heavenly angels in antiquity, to be sure, but the ancient world did not think they were the only messengers. An *áhn-geh-laws*, like the Hebrew equivalent, *mah-láhk* (מלאך), means **messenger**, and can be either a human or a heavenly **messenger.** For example, the prophet Haggai was called **a messenger of Yehowah** (Hag 1:3). A Jewish priest was called **a messenger of**

Yehowah of armies (Mal 2:7). The author of the Book of Malachi was called the Lord's **messenger** or angel (Mal 1:1). The Lord's **messenger** that was expected to prepare the way for the Messiah was called his angel (Mal 3:1-3). The reader must learn from the context whether the **messenger** of God is human or divine. King David was said to be like a Messenger of God (2Sam 19:28).

The **messenger** who came to John might have been a fellow Christian who brought this revelation, which John considered a message from God himself. It was also a Christian message, having something to do with Jesus the Messiah, and it was the word of God. Düsterdieck correctly observed that this was not an ordinary angel. It was *the* **messenger** who belonged to Jesus, and Jesus was the **messenger's** principal,[1] the one who sent him to John. In a legal relationship, the principal was the person who sent messengers. The messenger was the person sent. The messenger spoke and acted in the name of the principal, in behalf of the principal, and at the responsibility of the principal. Legally, the messenger was the principal when he had been authorized as a legal agent.

To his servant, John. There is no authoritarian title given to John. He was not designated as a prophet, an apostle, an elder, or a bishop--only a servant. Justin Martyr (110-165 IA, *Dial* 81) and Tertullian (145-220 IA) seem to have been acquainted with the Book of Revelation and believed it to have been composed by the Apostle John. Papias (IA 70-155) may have identified the author of Revelation as John in his list of disciples of Jesus, whom he called elders (*HE* 3.39). This is probably the basis for the tradition that "John the Elder" wrote the Book of Revelation. In Revelation, itself, **John** is not called "the elder." Irenaeus (IA 120-202) held that the author lived during the reign of Domitian (*HE* 5.8). Epiphanius (310-403 IA [International Age], *Haer* 51.12, 32), however, seemed to think Revelation was written about 50 years earlier, during the reign of Gaius or Claudius.[2] Normally scholars give a lot of credence to the testimony of the church fathers. After all they were closer to the events than we are, but there is no consistent agreement on the precise time when **John** lived and wrote. The church fathers may have had to deduce the dates they chose just the way we do. This means we cannot begin research on the basis that we know when **John** lived and wrote.

The word of God and the testimony of Jesus. These two objects are parallel: **The word of God** is **the testimony of Jesus**. In the judgment of the author, **Jesus** was the Messiah. As such he was, by virtue of his office, also the legal agent of God. As God's agent, his testimony had the same authority as the principal who commissioned him, Namely God. Therefore **God's word** was the same as **Jesus' testimony**. In both cases the genitive case is subjective rather than objective. It was not the word about God or the testimony about Jesus, but the word belonging to God

---

[1] F. Düsterdieck, *Critical and Exegetical Handbook to the Revelation of John*, tr. H. E. Jacobs (Winona Lake: Alpha Publications, 1884), p. 122.
[2] J. J. Gunther, "The Elder John, Author of Revelation," *JSNT* 11 (1981):3-20, holds that John was an ascetic prophet from Jerusalem and also a priest.

and the testimony belonging to Jesus. This is consistent with the use of testimony used elsewhere in the Book of Revelation. For example the souls of those who had been slain (Rev 6:9) were killed for the **testimony** which they bore, and the two witnesses were killed after they had borne their **testimony** (Rev 11:7).[1] These were John's convictions as he comprehended the **revelation**.[2]

The word **testimony** was a court term. It got its name from a liturgy used in taking oaths. In ancient Greek and Roman courts a witness was not automatically required to testify under oath. Only when **testimonies** were questioned were **witnesses** required to take oaths. If **witnesses** refused, the judge or jury assumed that the **testimony** was false. When Jews and Christians were suspected of being insurrectionists and saboteurs, they were sometimes taken to court and forced to take oaths. An oath in a Roman court required an invitation to pagan deities to enforce the oaths with punishment, if false. Christians and Jews were required by doctrine to refuse to take oaths in pagan courts, so they were often judged guilty on this basis alone. They might even have been tortured to force them to confess whether or not they were Jews or Christians. At such a point, their confession was their testimony, and it sometimes led to their deaths. That was the reason the word, "martyr" (a witness) became identical to facing death for one's beliefs.

After John read the scroll brought to him, he testified to the things he saw. When he testified to Jesus' message he was also testifying to God's word (Rev 1:9; 12:17; 14:12; 17:6; 19:10; 20:4; 22:16, 20, 21). This instruction was a message of good news to John's fellow servants, and it promised to be a blessing to those who gave this prophecy their careful attention and observed its teachings.

Whatever things he saw. Part of the **things** John **saw** were the events he reported in relationship to **the messenger** and part were things he read in the Scripture and the prophecy which the **messenger** brought to him.

Blessed is he who reads. The benedictions requested are both for the reader and the congregational hearers who kept the commandments written in the prophecy. This is the first of seven beatitudes in the book (Rev 1:3; 14:13; 16:15; 19:9; 20:6; 22:7, 14). Since the reader is singular, and the hearers are plural, John pictured a church scene where one person **read** the Scripture out loud to an audience[3]--an ordinary Jewish and Christian custom (Neh 8:2; Luke 4:16; Acts 13:15).

---

[1] So also A. A. Trites, "MARTUS and Martyrdom in the Apocalypse," *NovT* 15 (1973):72-80.
[2] So also Mazzaferri, *Genre*, p. 313: "Above all, μαρτυρία Ἰησοῦ= [*mahr-too-reé-ah yay-soó*], in apposition to (ὁ λόγος τοῦ θεοῦ [*haw láw-gaws too theh-oó*], signifies John's entire prophetic book." Mazzaferri, however, thought John wrote the entire Book of Revelation and here referred to the whole document rather than the prophecy contained in 4:1-22:5. P. Vassiliadis, "The Translation of [*Mahr-too-reé-ah Iay-soo*] μαρτυρία Ἰησοῦ in Revelation," *BT* 36 (1985):129-32, argued that in every instance in the Book of Revelation, the term *mahr-too-reé-ah* meant martyrdom and alluded to testimony at the possible cost of death.
[3] D. L. Barr, "The Apocalypse of John as Oral Enactment," *Int* 40 (1986):243-56, was correct in calling attention to the features in the Book of Revelation that would respond to oral reading. This

Those who hear . . . and keep. **Hearing** and **keeping** are terms related to the reception of the commandments given at Mount Sinai. When Moses presented these to the people, they replied, **All that the Lord has spoken we will keep (or do)** (*nah-ah-séh*, נעשה) **and we will hear (or "obey"** [*wuh neesh-máh*, ונשנע], [Exod 24:7]). This is a *hysteron-proteron* expression--one in which that which is spoken first will really happen second. The **hearing** would really be first and the **keeping** would be the second. Israelites would first **hear** and then act rather than vice versa. These terms may have been used here intentionally to put the audience in the same frame of mind as if they had been receiving the commandments from Moses at Sinai.

The Sermon on the Mount concludes with a parable based on the same passage in Exodus, picturing the reader as one standing at the foot of the new mountain, listening to the new Moses: **Everyone who *hears* these words of mine and *observes* them is like a prudent man who built his house upon a rock** (Matt 7:24). Luke has a benediction that is also based on Exod 24:7: **Blessed are those who *hear* the word of God and *keep* it** (Luke 11:28). Although Rev 1:1-2 is a beautiful liturgical paragraph which John might have appropriated from some earlier source, it is very well designed to fit exactly the use given here.

The word of this prophecy. The Greek text of Revelation called "Sinaiticus" uses the singular **word**. Nestle-Aland editors have chosen **words** as the correct text.

This prophecy which John received are not his own words, as Davis, Ruiz, and others hold.[1] He received **the prophecy** from **the messenger**, and he probably translated it before sending it to the churches, but he did not compose it. That which John had received was a revelation that was also a **prophecy**. Morris was correct in thinking that a **prophecy** was an authentic word of God, but he was mistaken in saying that the **prophecy** intended here was not a prediction. One of the important points of the message is the prediction of future events.[2] Because of the word **prophecy** many scholars classify the entire Book of Revelation as **a prophecy**. For example, Boring said,

> The Apocalypse is our most obvious, and most extensive, example of Christian prophecy . . . It is clear that the author claims to write

---

does not mean, however, that the book was *only* read or originally given in oral form. The careful exegesis of the Hebrew of Scripture is too precise to have been composed in oral form or used only orally.

[1] R. D. Davis, *The Heavenly Court Scene of Revelation 4-5* (Berrien Springs: Andrews U. PhD. Thesis, 1986), p. 9; J. P. Ruiz, *Ezekiel in the Apocalypse: The Transformation of Prophetic Language in Revelation 16,17-19,10* (Frankfurt: Peter Lang, c1989), p. 532. Ruiz noted that the references to "prophetic words" occur only in Rev 1:3; 22:7, 10, 18, and 19--all references from the introduction and conclusion made by John himself--but he thought the entire book was composed by John.

[2] L. Morris, *The Revelation of St. John* (Grand Rapids: Eerdmans, c1969), pp. 46-47.

profeteia (1:3; 19; 20; 22:7, 10, 18-10). . . It is also clear in 22:9 that the author designates himself as a prophet.[1]

Schüssler-Fiorenza said, "The author of the Apoc doubtlessly understands himself a Christian prophet and intends his work to be a 'word of prophecy.'"[2] The main point of Mazzaferri's book is the demonstration that the Book of Revelation is a **prophecy** which Mazzaferri believed John wrote. It is true that John and his colleagues were held to be **prophets**, but in this instance John was sending to the seven churches a **prophecy** that he did not write. He only received it, copied it, and sent it out to the churches. That which John wrote was a letter that included the **prophecy** which **the messenger** brought to him.

John was so favorably impressed with this message that he wanted his readers to think of this as the equivalent of the revelation of the ten commandments given at Sinai (Aboth 1:1). It was the new contract that Jeremiah promised (Jer 31:31). In John's judgment that prophecy was unquestionably God's word. It was to be received and obeyed, just as Moses and the Israelites received the Torah and agreed to obey it. Jesus probably intended a similar meaning when he said, **Blessed . . . are those who *hear* the word of God and *keep* it** (Luke 11:28). The Sermon on the Mount also compared those who *heard* Jesus' words and *did* them to a house built on rock, whereas those who *heard* his words and *did not do them* were like houses built on sand (Matt 7:24-27). Ruiz correctly observed that John would not have argued so strenuously for its authenticity if that authenticity would have been accepted without question.[3]

When Thomas listed the characteristics of the gift of **prophecy** he overlooked the one that the Scripture listed as the most important: Did that which was **prophesied** come to pass in later history?[4] John apparently accepted this document as a valid **prophecy**, probably because it was so richly laced with Scripture which had already been accepted as the word of God. The Torah warned believers against accepting prophecies until history had proved that their predictions were valid (Deut 18:21-22). Loisy thought that Rev 1:1-3 was added by a later editor to a scroll that had already been completed. The editor, he thought, found the basis for his introduction in the scroll's conclusion (Rev 22:18-19).[5] Whealon correctly observed that Rev 4:1-22:7 was a Jewish document that was later Christianized by the introduction, conclusion, and a few editorial additions (Rev 11:8; 12:17; 13:8; 14:12b-13; 16:15; 17:6; 18:13-20; 19:9b-10:13; 20:4, 6; 21:14; 22:7). Questions will be raised about some of his selections in the appropriate places of this commentary, but his main thesis is valid.[6]

---

[1] M. E. Boring, "The *Apocalypse* as Christian Prophecy: a Discussion of the Issues Raised by the Book of Revelation for the Study of Early Christian Prophecy," *SBLSP* 2 (1974):43.
[2] E. Schüssler-Fiorenza, *The Apocalypse* (Chicago: Franciscan Herald Press, 1976), p. 21.
[3] Ruiz, *Ezekiel*, p. 532.
[4] R. L. Thomas, "The Spiritual Gift of Prophecy in Rev 22:18," *JETS* 32 (1989):201-204.
[5] A. Loisy, *L'Apocalypse de Jean* (Paris: Emile Mourry, 1923), pp. 62-63.
[6] J. F. Whealon, "New Patches on an Old Garment: The Book of Revelation," *BTB* 11 (1981):54-59.

TEXT

Revelation

⁴John to the seven churches which are in Asia: Grace to you and peace from **the One who is**, the One who was,

and **the One who is coming**, and from the seven spirits which are before the throne, ⁵and from Jesus,

the Messiah, **faithful witness**

the firstborn of the dead, the ruler of the kings of the land, to one who loves us

First Testament and Other Jewish Literature

OG Exod 3:14Then God said to Moses, "I am **the One who is.**"

Ps 118:26Blessed is **the one who comes** in the name of Yehowah.

Isa 55:3-4I will make for you **faithful** ones a contract for the age, my trustworthy love for David--yes **a witness** for the gentiles I have made him.

Prov 4:25A savior of lives is a **faithful witness**.

Jer 42:5Then they said to Jeremiah, "May Yehowah be between us a **faithful** and trustworthy **witness** if we do not do according to every word which Yehowah, your God, will send to us."

Ps 89:36-38I have sworn by my holiness "May the following unmentioned curses come upon me] if I would lie to my servant, David; his dynasty will be for the age, his throne, like the sun before me, like the moon it will be firm for the age, **a trustworthy witness** in heaven."

Ps 89:28I will make him **a firstborn**, the highest **of the kings of the land**.

Ps 130:7-8For with Yehowah is loving kindness and much redemption, and

---

This thesis was proposed much earlier and is now part of this commentary.

and has released us
from our crimes, by means of his blood, ⁶and has made us

**a kingdom,
priests** to God

and his **father** to him be glory and power into the age of ages. Amen.

he will redeem Israel **from** all **its iniquities**.

^(Exod 19:6)Now if you really pay attention to my voice and listen to my contract, you will be segregated from me from all the peoples. For mine is all the land. You shall be to me **a kingdom of priests** and a holy nation.

^(Targ Onq Exod 19:6)You shall be before me **kings and priests**, and a holy people.

^(Isa 61:6)You shall be called "**priests** of Yehowah, ministers of our God."

^(Ps 89:27)He shall cry to me, "You are my **father**, my God and the rock of my salvation."

COMMENTARY

John to the seven churches. Some of the Gnostic texts discovered in Upper Egypt have a reading which identifies **John** as the brother of James, one of the sons of Zebedee.[1] Scholars have dated these texts from the first to the fifth centuries IA. This does not mean the author of this portion of the Book of Revelation was an apostle but that the church made that identification at a very early date.

  John turned at once from the benediction for the reader and hearers of this **prophecy** to his salutation to the leaders of the seven churches, who were evidently the ones who would receive the **prophecy** with the expectation that they would read it aloud to each congregation. His attribution to God and Jesus was formed by piecing together quotations from several FT passages. The seven churches were specified later (Rev 1:11), but since they received the message the members knew who they were. **The** choice of **seven churches** has two possible reasons:

1) there actually were **seven churches** for which **John** was responsible. This is the most likely reason.
2) The second reason may be based on the **seven** nations against which Ezekiel pronounced curses: 1) Ammon, 2) Moab, 3) Edom, 4) Philistia, 5) Tyre, 6) Sidon, 7) Egypt. Although John scolded some of the leaders of **the seven churches,** they did not really correspond to enemy nations. Some scholars think **seven** was only a mythical number symbolizing the church universal.

---

[1]A. Helmbold, "A Note on the Authorship of the Apocalypse," *NTS* 8 (1961/62):77-79.

That is possible but not the most likely meaning for the number and names of the churches.

Asia, in NT times, reached from the Far East to the western borders of modern Turkey. That was the extent of the Seleucid empire at the height of Antiochus III, the Great's, career. It included all of modern Turkey, most of the islands of the eastern Mediterranean, and even some part of Europe. From the view of Greeks and Romans, Asia began with the western border of what is now Turkey.

Many scholars have asked why John wrote to only **seven churches**. There were surely more than **seven churches** in Asia Minor. There may have been more than one church in each of the cities to which this letter was directed, but the churches with which John was associated would not have been the same as those to whom Paul wrote, even in the same city. We can only guess the reasons, and there is no assurance that twentieth century guesses are accurate. Some think seven was an artificial number chosen to cohere with all of the rest of the sevens in the Book of Revelation, whereas, in reality, the book was intended for the entire church. It is not likely that the entire church was involved.

If it was directed to more than **seven** churches, they would not have been churches other than those that professed **John's** doctrine. None of the Pauline **churches** would have been involved. Another possibility is that John was actually associated with only these **seven churches**. The **seven** cities involved were close enough together to form a geographical circuit at the western end of Asia Minor. **Ephesus** was a popular seaport; **Smyrna** was another well-known seaport, only 40 miles to the north. **Pergamum** was another 40 miles north of Smyrna. Thyatira was 45 miles south east of Pergamum. **Sardis** was 30 miles south of Pergamum, and **Philadelphia** was 30 miles east, southeast of **Sardis. Laodicia** was an additional 40 miles southeast of **Philadelphia.**

Grace to you and peace. John prayed for **grace and peace** that would be from God (see also Rev 22:21). Later Christians prayed, "Let grace come, and let this world pass away. Hosanna to the God of David" (Did 10:6)! John had the same hope. If **grace** came, the Davidic kingdom would be restored, and bondage to any foreign power would cease. "This world" was the current situation in which Rome ruled, and Israel was a subject nation. That is the situation or "world" which would automatically vanish as soon as grace and peace came.

From the One who is. To be correct Greek the preposition for **from** (ἀπό, *ah-póh*) should take the genitive case, but here it is the nominative. The reason Caird gives for this is, "John keeps the divine title in the nominative. God is, so to speak, always in the nominative, always the subject."[1] If that were so, however, the Greek word for God would also always be in the nominative, but that is not so. In the immediate context, the word for God occurs in the genitive in Rev 1:2, 9 and in the dative in Rev 1:6. Every time John used the expression, **the One who is**, however, he used the

---

[1] G. B. Caird, *A Commentary on the Revelation of St. John the Divine* (London: Black, c1966), p. 16.

expression exactly as it occurs in the OG. This one euphemism is one he always kept in the nominative.

This verse quotes a FT passage that alludes to the answer the Lord gave to Moses when Moses asked the Lord what name Moses should tell the people belonged to the God who sent him to release his people from bondage in Egypt. In Hebrew the answer is, **I will be that which I will be** (*eh heh-yéh ah-sháyr eh heh-yéh*, אהיה אשר אהיה). The theme continued:

> **Tell the children of Israel, "I will be" has sent me to you** (Exod 3:14); **Tell the children of Israel, "Yehowah, the God of your fathers, the God of Abraham, the God of Isaac, the God of Jacob sent me to you." This is my name for the age; this is the way I am to be remembered for generations** (Exod 3:15).

The OG translation of the relevant clause is, *eh-góh ay-mee haw ówn* (ἐγώ εἰμι ὁ ὤν), **I am the one who is**. John wanted his readers to know that the same God who called Moses and through him delivered the Israelites from Egypt also called Jesus and through him was about to redeem the Jews from Rome.

The One who was. This is very awkward Greek, because it is a finite verb rather than a participle as are the other two action words in the clause. Probably the reason is that participles in Greek have no temporal force of their own. The time in which the action takes place is controlled by whatever finite verb there is in the sentence. **John** evidently wanted to show that it was the past tense that was involved here. In Semitic languages, none of these words would have been participles. For example Targum Pseudo-Jonathan renders Exod 3:14, "I am the one who was (דהויתי), is (והוינא), and is destined to be (ועתיד למיהוי)." John was evidently one who was very familiar with Hebrew and Aramaic, so his Greek here was Semitic Greek.[1]

The one who is coming. **The one who comes in the name of Yehowah** (Ps 118:26) would be one of Yehowah's legal agents. The Messiah was expected to fill that role. He would be legally identical to the principal who sent him. He would **come** in the name of Yehowah, in the interests of Yehowah, and at the responsibility of Yehowah. When the principal's legal agent **comes,** it is legally the same as if the principal had **come** himself or herself.

Scholars, like Morris, noted the grammatical inaccuracies involved in this phrase without explaining how it came about.[2] Revelation has often been reported as having impossible Greek, but this is an unjust accusation. Mussies has shown the

---

[1] S. Thompson, *The Apocalypse in Semitic Syntax* (Cambridge: Cambridge U. Press, 1985), p. 108, said, "The Apc. can . . .with no hesitancy be categorized as 'Jewish Greek' to the fullest extent of that term . . . the Greek language was little more than a membrane, stretched tightly over a Semitic framework, showing many essential contours from beneath."

[2] Morris, *Revelation*, pp. 47-48.

care with which this book has been written. Of course there are many Semitisms in the document, and there is not a single genitive absolute in the entire document, but these Semitisms are more like FT than Mishnaic Hebrew. The word order of Revelation is not distinctively Hebraic. There seems to be a careful effort not to follow the exact order consistently. Some sentences begin with verbs and others with nouns. When the same basic meaning is repeated, the words are skillfully reorganized.[1] For example:

2:9: τῶν λεγόντων Ἰουδαίους εἶναι ἑαυτούς (*tohn leg-áwn-tohn Yoo-daí-oos áy-nai he-ow-toós*)

3:9: τῶν λεγόντων ἑαυτούς εἶναι (*tohn le-gáwn-tohn Yoo-daí-oos áy-nai*)

11:5a: καὶ εἴ τις αὐτοὺς θέλει ἀδικῆσαι (*kai ay tees ow-tóos theh-láy ah-dee-káy-sai*)
11:5b: καὶ εἴ τις θελήσῃ αὐτοὺς ἀδικῆσαι[2] (*kai ay tees theh-láy-say ow-tóos ah-dee-káy-sai*),

Mussies concluded:

> Taken all together this means that the Apocalypse of John, in spite of many grammatical restrictions and reductions, can be read as one of the most vivid and picturesque books of the NT.[3]

The authors of the Book of Revelation not only wrote picturesque literature, but they did that while working into their narratives numerous passages from FT. This requires still greater skill than Mussies observed. There were also doctrines that the authors had to observe, such as the one in this sentence. Here **John** quoted from the OG precisely, even though that meant writing in poor Greek grammar. Since the expression **the One who is** is the object of the preposition, **from** (*ah-póh*, ἀπό) which takes the genitive case, it should have been, *too áwn-too* (τοῦ ὄντου), but John was more interested in the authority of the Scripture than the accuracy of his Greek grammar.

John expanded on the Scripture by adding that God was not only the One who is, but also the one who was and the One who is to come--in other words, the God of all time. This was an important insight from which to begin this document, because the **prophecy** involved remembering that which **was**, that which was happening at the time of the writing, and that which was going to happen in the

---

[1] G. Mussies, "The Greek of the Book of Revelation," *L'Apocalypse johannique et l'Apocalyptique dans le Nouveau Testament* ed. J. Lambrecht (Gembloux: J. Duculot, 1980), pp. 167-77.
[2] Mussies, "Greek," p. 176.
[3] Mussies, "Greek," p. 177.

future. This was not a unique thought of **John**. The rabbis, commenting on the text, *I am Yehowah your God*,[1] said

> I am [the one who was] in Egypt, and I am [the one who was] at the sea; I am [the one who was] at Sinai; I am [the God of] the past; I am [the God of] the future; I am in this age; and I am in the age to come, as it is said, *Look, now, for I, I am he* (Deut 32:29; Mek *Bahodesh* 5.27-29).

Jewish and Christian belief in cyclical time and typological order prompted them to believe that the future was not obscure. Those who studied the past would be able to see their own time in relationship to it. By studying their own time in cyclical order, they thought they could predict what would happen next, just as people on Wednesday would expect that the next day would be Thursday to be followed by Friday. Jews and Christians in those days followed time cycles with just as much interest and confidence as investors watch stock market cycles today. They try to find patterns and cycles so that from that information they might be able to predict future events.

The seven spirits. The **seven spirits** probably refer to the **seven spirits** listed in Isa 11:2. They are as follows:

1) **the spirit** of Yehowah,
2) **the spirit** of wisdom,
3) [the spirit of] understanding,
4) **the spirit** of counsel,
5) [the spirit of] power,
6) **the spirit** of knowledge, and
7) [the spirit of] the fear of Yehowah.

John of Patmos, however, may have taken the expression from the **prophecy** which the angel brought him (Rev 4:5). He apparently took phrases from this document and worked them into his narrative the same way he took quotations from Scripture.

From Jesus the Messiah. In describing **Jesus** as **the faithful witness, John** may have alluded to the situation in which Jeremiah was asked to pray to the Lord and ask what the people should do. They accompanied their request with the following oath:

> **May the Lord be between us as** *a true and faithful witness.***[May the following unmentioned curses come upon us] if we do not act**

---

[1] For the pronunciation, see Buchanan, "Unfinished Business," pp. 413-20.

according to every word which the Lord your God will send to us.

This was a minced oath, omitting the understood curses.[1] A more likely possibility is the Psalm which presented the Lord taking a minced oath to affirm that the seed of David would occupy his throne, and the sun and the moon were invited as **a faithful witness in heaven. The faithful witness in heaven** was one who would appear before the throne of God and testify in behalf of the plaintiff or defendant in the heavenly court. In both cases **the faithful witness** was presented in a court context to uphold an oath.[2]

Ps 89 is a hymn in praise of David and the assurance that God made a special contract with him, guaranteeing to him that God would make him the highest of all kings and preserve his dynasty until the age [to come], but not unconditionally. If the members of David's posterity failed to keep the law they would be punished, but the contract would not be annulled. In this Psalm, David was called God's anointed (Messiah) and God's first born, the highest of kings. He was God's first born-- legally. Chronologically, he was the last born of his father, Jesse.

The first born of the dead ones. **John** of Patmos attributed the names that had been applied to David in this Psalm to Jesus. Jesus was called the Messiah (Christ), **the first born**, and the ruler of the kings of the earth. Ps 89:27 has the term **first born** in parallel relationship with "the highest of the kings of the earth." This means that one term has the same meaning as the other. According to Ps 89 God made David his **first born**. This means he had already been **born**, physically. When he was anointed king he became God's **first born**, *legally*, by virtue of his office. Being God's **first born** had nothing to do with chronological order. It applied only to his official status. At the same time the Psalmist affirmed the anointing of David, he mentioned the contract God had made with David that he would establish his dynasty for the age (Ps 89:28).

John made the same identification as the Psalmist, and he also referred to **Jesus** as an anointed one, like David, but John added a new item; Jesus was the **firstborn**, not just of God, but the **first born** of those who had died. This is the main point of Paul's sermon (Acts 13:26-38). There is not much question that **John** thought of **Jesus** as someone from the dynasty of David and also one who would fulfill the promises given to David and act like a king. God loved David, so David would never be removed from his love. In the same way, **John** of Patmos said that **Jesus** loved Christians. This was the concept that led him to Ps 130.

Minear warned his readers not to think of **Jesus** as a ruler of kings in any political sense. **John** was talking about a different kind of sovereignty, Minear claimed.[3] Jesus was associated with too many political names to be completely absolved of political interests. He was called a king, a messiah (anointed king), a

---

[1] See Buchanan, "Some Oath and Vow Formulas in the NT," *HTR* 58 (1965):319-26.
[2] See further R. H. Mounce, *The Book of Revelation* (Grand Rapids: Eerdmans, c1977), pp. 64-65.
[3] P. Minear, *I Saw a New Earth* (Washington, D.C.: Corpus Books, c1968), p. 13.

Son of God (a title given such kings as Pharaoh, Alexander the Great, and King Solomon), and a son of man (a code name for a Jewish king). He was expected to rule the Kingdom of God and to redeem Israel. In a world situation where monarchies were the most predominate governments, it is likely that Jesus did not understand kingdom, messiah, king, son of God, and son of man in a philosophical sense that modern Westerners might consider. If he had, no one of his contemporaries would have understood his message.[1] Kings were not considered as evil in antiquity as they are now. In fact, God was often referred to as a king in the FT. He was never called "president," and he did not rule over a democracy. Like other kings, God was thought to have had a cabinet of advisors, but no parliament or congress. Like other literature the Book of Revelation is understood best against its own historical context.

To One who loved us. Some texts have a definite article--*the* **One who loved us**. The Sinaiticus text is one of those that gave the best reading, which is *lóo-sahn-tee* (λύσαντι), **released**, which is a financial or legal term. It refers either to a person was being released from a prison sentence or to someone who was being **released** from a debt. A weaker reading, supported by several later texts is *loó-sahn-tee* (λούσαντι), "washed," which is a liturgical term. It recalls someone who was baptized to remove all earlier defilement. The meanings are close enough in appearance, pronunciation, and meaning that it is easy to see how one might be confused for the other.

Forgiveness, redemption, removal from crimes, and atonement are all related to the theological implications of the Day of Atonement. Forgiveness and redemption are both financial terms. A banker might forgive a loan or a debt. A person can also redeem or buy back a mortgage. The Day of Atonement functioned on the basis that crimes that had been committed demanded fines for punishment. These unpaid fines accumulated and were recorded just as debts were. Once fines for crimes were recorded and held against a person they were called "iniquities."

Ps 130 is the prayer of a defendant before a judge in court. The defendant realized that he was guilty of the accusations made against him. He pleaded only for mercy and pardon. The poem concludes with the assurance that the Lord would redeem Israel from its iniquities (Ps 130:8). It is not until that point that the reader is alerted to the fact that the defendant is the entire nation of Israel, pleading its case before the Lord on the Day of Atonement. The Day of Atonement fell just ten days after New Year's Day. New Year's Day was believed to be the day on which God would begin to judge his people. He would hold a court session for the entire ten days between New Year's Day and the Day of Atonement to hear all of the accusations and defenses. Crimes and debts were so closely related in meaning that financial terms like forgiveness, redemption, and reconciliation were also used in court to mean pardon, release from prison, and restoration to community.

---

[1] See further Buchanan, *Jesus: The King and his Kingdom* (Macon: Mercer U. Press, 1984).

If Israel were a borderline case, there was still a ten day period in which to repent and become reconciled with coreligionists against whom the believer had committed crimes before the Day of Atonement, which was treated like a Day of Reckoning, when the books would be audited. On that day the accumulated iniquities for previously committed crimes could be forgiven if the conditions were met. The believer had to bring a sacrificial offering to pay for his crimes. This would be effective only if the person had already repented and become reconciled with all of his coreligionists. If the Day of Atonement came and went but the land had not been restored to the chosen people, it was assumed that there were crimes that had not been pardoned, believers who had not been reconciled, or inadequate crime offerings made to pay up all the debt against Israel. The Psalmist tried to bargain with the Lord, appealing to him to mitigate the punishment and not to be exact and demanding about the iniquities filed against Israel. The Psalmist was counting on God's redemption and steadfast love to make atonement effective.

John was just as confident as the Psalmist that atonement would be complete, not just because he had two Psalm texts to prove it, but because the atonement offering had already been made through the blood of Jesus. Whereas the Psalmist said God would redeem Israel, **John** said **Jesus** had already released the faithful from their crimes by means of his blood. As God's legal agent he had brought about the redemption the Psalmist had promised. Since all **prophecy** was prophesied only for the days of the Messiah, and these were the days of the Messiah, **John** was certain that the Day of Atonement had been effective, and the land would soon be restored, just as it had been restored for Judas the Maccabee more than two hundred years earlier, just after the Day of Atonement, 164 BIA.

Although the Holy Scripture had promised that God would make the Israelites a kingdom of priests and a holy nation (Exod 19:6), John said God would make his people a kingdom. They did not constitute a kingdom at that point; Rome ruled them, but they would constitute a kingdom when on the Day of Atonement redemption had been demonstrated. Then they would be God's priests. They would be the ones who would minister at the altar in place of the priests who had collaborated with the Romans and were currently serving the temple in an ineffective way. This seems to mean that the communities to whom John was writing and to which he belonged were priests, like the Zadokites who wrote the Torah or Temple Scroll of the Dead Sea Scrolls. They were also probably celibate monks, but that is not clear from the text to this point.

A kingdom, priests to God. On the basis of Semitic influence, Newport translated the word rendered **made** here "appointed."[1] This is a slightly changed expression from the quotation **You shall be to me a kingdom of priests and a holy nation**. (Exod 19:6). It was probably on the basis of Exod 19:6 that Second Isaiah wrote, **You shall be called "priests of Yehowah," ministers of our God** (Isa 61:6). **Priests** were of the highest class of Jews who were ranked as **priests**, Levites, Israelites, and

---

[1] K. G. C. Newport, "Some Greek Words with Hebrew Meanings in the Book of Revelation," *AUSS* 26 (1988):27.

proselytes in descending order (CDC 14:3-6). During the Babylonian captivity, when non-**priests** functioned as **priests**, keeping their houses as undefiled as the temple, Second Isaiah concluded that they had fulfilled the requirements of the Torah and were to be called **priests**.

Not all sects of Jews and Israelites concurred, but there continued to be monastic sects that functioned as carefully as priests and treated the building in which they were housed as a temple, "a holy of holies for Aaron." Some of these refused to worship in Herod's temple at Jerusalem. They called the high priest of that temple "the wicked priest." Among those who were not celibate were members of the Damascus sect. That group continued to give priority to **priests**. If there were no **priest** in the camp to make a judgment on leprosy, some priest from outside the group should be brought in to fulfill this responsibility. If there were a **priest** who was ignorant, members of the group should instruct him, but still insist that the **priest** make the decree (CDC 13:3-7). The members of the community which **John** of Patmos was addressing were evidently priests by birth, or they considered themselves **priests** by their careful observance of purity rules.[1] Davis observed that there are two sets of trilogies in this pericope:[2]

What Christ Is	What Christ Has Done
1. Faithful Witness	1. Loves Us
2. First-born of the Dead	2. Has Freed Us from Our Crimes
3. Ruler of the Kings on Earth.	3. Made Us a Kingdom, Priests

Into the age of the ages. Amen. This is a Semitic way of making a superlative. It means "into the greatest age of all." Some texts have **ages of ages,** in the plural, meaning "the greatest ages of all." **Amen** is a legal term associated with an oath. It means here, "I swear that this is true."

TEXT

Revelation	First Testament
[7]**Look! He comes with the clouds,** and they	Dan 7:13 **Look! He comes with the clouds** of heaven up to the Ancient of Days.

---

[1] W. H. Brownlee, "The Priestly Character of the Church in the Apocalypse," *NTS* 5 (1958/59):224-25, argued that from the insights of the Dead Sea Scrolls we are justified in presuming a priestly centered community for the origin of the Book of Revelation. Furthermore, the "angels" of the first three chapters should be thought of as human messengers or bishops.

[2] Davis, *Heavenly Court Scene*, p. 97.

	^{Isa 19:1}Yehowah is riding on a swift **cloud** and **he comes** to Egypt.
	^{Ezek 30:3}A day for Yehowah is near, it will be a day of **cloud**, a time of the gentiles.
will stare at him with [their own] eye[s]--even the ones who **stabbed**	^{Zech 12:10}They **will stare at him** whom they **stabbed**, and they **will mourn** for him.
him, **and** all the tribes of **the land will mourn**. Yes. Amen!	^{Zech 12:12}**The land will mourn**.

COMMENTARY

Look! He comes with the clouds. Following the discussion based on two Psalms, John continued with a discussion based on two prophecies. Since John had already identified Jesus as the one who was **the first born from the dead**, the ruler of kings, and the one whose death had redeemed the faithful from their crimes, he followed with a further identification of Jesus with the Son of man, who was Judas the Maccabee. The Messiah, like Judas the Maccabee, would **come with the clouds,** which meant that God would go before him and make his actions successful.[1] **The clouds** symbolized the presence of the deity here, just as on Mount Sinai and the Mount of Transfiguration.

Even the ones who stabbed [him]. Some texts have "**Every eye will stare at him.**" Sinaiticus agrees with 1, *al*, and *sy*. Sinaiticus lacks the final pronoun, **him**. Since Jesus had been **stabbed** and died, he was also the one for whom the tribes of the land would mourn. These were other prophecies that had been fulfilled through Jesus, the Messiah. The OG does not include the clause, **the ones who stabbed him** (Zech 12:10).

All the tribes of the land. Other texts have **will mourn** *over him*. The author of Matthew put together two of the same texts similarly:

> Then will appear the sign of the Son of man in heaven. Then all the tribes of the land will mourn (Zech 12:10), and they will see the Son of man coming on the clouds of heaven (Dan 7:13) with power and great glory (Matt 24:30).

This probably means John and Matthew were acquainted with the tradition that used both eschatological texts.

---

[1] See further with a drawing of the god Asshur in the clouds with bow drawn, Buchanan, *The Book of Daniel* (Lewiston: Mellen Biblical Press, c1999), pp. 185-89.

Yes, Amen. **Amen** is a legal word used in oaths and vows. When the woman, suspected by her husband of having been unfaithful, was brought before the priest, the priest made her drink a solution of water used to wash ink off a parchment into which dust was mixed. The oaths she was about to take had been written on the parchment, but before she drank the solution with the vows, she was told that if she had been unfaithful she would abort, but if she had not been unfaithful her pregnancy would continue to completion. Then he asked her if she would accept these vows with these conditional curses. She responded with, **Amen**! (Num 5). It means, "I hereby solemnly swear." It was the response given in court to questions like the one asked today, "Do you hereby swear to tell the truth, the whole truth, and nothing but the truth, so help you God?" **Yes. Amen!** was a fitting conclusion to the argument given up to that point. John had argued, like a lawyer in court, using quotations from Scripture the way an attorney uses earlier laws and precedents to prove a case. This was supported by an oath.

TEXT

Revelation	First Testament
⁸**I am**	Exod 3:14 "Then God said to Moses, "**I am** what **I am**." And he said, "Thus you shall say to the children of Israel, '**I am** sent me to you.'"
	Isa 41:4 Who has acted and accomplished, calling the generations from the first? **I**, Yehowah, **am the** first, **and I am the** last.
the Alpha, **and I am the** Omega, the beginning and the end," says	
	Isa 44:6 Thus says Yehowah, king of Israel and its redeemer, Yehowah of armies. "**I am the** first; **I am the** last; and apart from me there is no God."
	Amos 3:13 "Hear and bear witness in the house of Jacob," says **the Lord** Yehowah, **the God of armies.**
the Lord God, the One who is, the One who was,	OG Exod 3:14 Then God said to Moses, "**I am the One who is.**"

and **the One who is** coming, **the almighty One**.

OG Amos 3:13"You shall hear, and you shall bear witness to the house of Jacob," says the Lord, God, **the almighty One**.

COMMENTARY

I am the Alpha, and I am the Omega. Only Sinaiticus, 1, *al*, *gig*, and *vg* add **the beginning and the end**. Nestle-Aland text also omits the second **I am**. **Alpha** (A, α) is the first letter of the Greek alphabet. The last letter is the **omega** (Ω, ω). These translate the original Hebrew *áh-lehph* (א), the first letter of the Hebrew alphabet, and the *taw* (ת), the last letter. The ancient *tau* looked like the English X. It was the mark made on Israelite houses in Egypt on the night of the Passover, and it was the sign put on the foreheads of the righteous in Jerusalem (Ezek 9:4). It became known as the "sign of the cross." The alphabet was a code formula to tell Jews that the end of the alphabet marked the end of a period of captivity. The *aleph* was the beginning of the exodus from Egypt, and the *tau* was an anticipated end of a current situation and of a future exodus, either from Babylon, or some other undesirable situation.

The expression recurs often in the Book of Revelation (Rev 1:8, 17; 2:8; 4:8; 11:7; 15:3; 16:7, 14; 19:6, 15; 21:6, 22; and 22:13). In his customary fashion, John wove together here two texts dealing with the name of God. From Exodus, he quoted from the passage where Moses asked God what his name was, and he said, **I am what I am, and thus you shall say to the sons of Israel, "I am" has sent you** (Exod 3:14). Targum Neophyte has expanded this **I am** (*eh heyéh*, אהיה) to "The One who spoke and the age came into existence from the beginning and is destined to say to it, 'Exist!' and it will come into existence [again]." The Old Greek (OG) translation Exod 3:14 is **I am the one who is** (*egó ay-mee ho ówn*, ἐγώ εἰμι ὁ ὤν) (OG Exod 3:14). From that clause, John took the words, **I am** and added some further designations, **the Alpha and the Omega**. He may have deduced these terms from Isa 41:4; 44:6; and 48:12, where God called himself, **the first and the last**. Since John treated the prophecy which the messenger brought him as if it were Scripture, he may have been motivated to compose a small midrash on this text. It was used frequently in the prophecy of Rev 4:1-22:5.

In magical spells among the magical papyri is the command, "Write the great name with seven vowels" (PGM 13.39). The list of seven vowels are ΑΕΗΙΟΥΩ, which were sometimes summarized by the first and last letters, ΑΩ (PGM 3.661). The divine name, Yehowah (ΙΑΩ) is frequently used in the papyri together with the predicate, "the one who is" (*haw óhn*) (PGM 13.1020, 045). One quotation is very similar to Rev 1:8:

The One who is, God, the ΙΑΩ, Lord, almighty One" (*haw óhn theh-áws haw Yah-oh koó-ree-aws pahn-taw-kráh-tohr*, ὁ ὤν θεὸς ὁ Ιαω, κύριος πααντοκράτωρ, PGM 71.3-4).

This does not necessarily mean that the authors of these magical prayers of the third to the sixth centuries IA had copied from Revelation. It probably means that before either wrote, these biblical terms had been formulated into liturgy that was employed both by the authors of the magical papyri and by John of Patmos. His liturgy evidently accepted the OG translation of Exod 3:14, **the One who is.**

The One who is coming. The expression **the almighty One**, was used three times in the Book of Revelation in close relationship with the title, **The One who is and the One who was** or **the One who is, the One who was, and the One who is coming**. (Rev 1:8; 4:8; 11:17). The descriptive adjective, **of armies,** is the term most frequently used to describe the Hebrew God, Yehowah. The OG translated the Hebrew word **of armies** (*tseh-váh-óht*, צבאות) as **the almighty One** (*pahn-taw-kráh-tohr*, παντοκράτωρ), which occurs in Revelation a total of nine times (Rev 1:8; 4:8; 11:17; 15:3; 16:7, 14; 19:6, 15; and 21:22). It also occurs in the magical papyri. The magical chants that included *Alpha* and *Omega* were probably accepted into Jewish and Christian traditions because they were identified with the description of God in Second Isaiah as the first and the last. Second Isaiah used the expression to describe the first (Egyptian) exodus and the last (Babylonian) exodus. There is no question that Jews and Christians at some time were influenced by Greek and Latin magic. The question is only one of when and how.[1] The fact that early Jewish and Christian translators rendered "of armies" to mean "the almighty One" says something about their concept of power. The one who controlled the armies was all powerful.

TEXT

Revelation

⁹**I**, John, am your brother and sharer in the tribulation, kingdom, and endurance in Jesus. **I** was on the Island called Patmos because of the word of God and the testimony of Jesus.

First Testament

Dan 7:15 **I**, Daniel, was confused; the visions in my head alarmed me.
Dan 8:1**I**, Daniel, after that which had appeared to me at the beginning.

Dan 9:2**I**, Daniel, was studying in the books.

---

[1] See further D. E. Aune, "The Apocalypse of John and Graeco-Roman Revelatory Magic," *NTS* 33 (1987):490-91. Texts are from H. D. Betz (ed.), *The Greek Magical Papyri in Translation. Including the Demotic Spells* (Chicago: University of Chicago Press, 1986), vol. 1.

COMMENTARY

I, John, am your brother. The author did not give any detail about his qualifications—no genealogy, no attempt to distinguish himself from all of the other **Johns** of the NT. He simply wrote affirmatively, boldly and voluntarily, **I, John,** as if he were testifying in court. He did not tell more about himself, except to identify himself with the Christian brothers, apparently a courageous thing to do during the turbulent time about which he wrote.

He identified himself with the message he sent—not as if he were the author—but as if the testimony was important and should be believed. He recommended it, and put his signature to his recommendation. As Bovon correctly said, he was not discreet about it. He made no attempt to be anonymous, but he used his own personal pronoun and his own name. This would draw him closer to his readers or listeners.[1] He used his name only twice in the entire document-- once here in the introduction, and again at the end (Rev 22:8). In both places he put his signature to his recommendation.

John followed a normal scriptural pattern of bearing witness. The same form was applied to Daniel when he reported events that he had seen or heard—**I, Daniel,** (Dan 8:1, 15, 27; 9:2; 10:2, 7; 12:50). Paul used the expression in a testimony context in parallel with another similar expression: **I, Paul, say to you . . . again, I bear witness to you** (2Cor 5:2-3). For a person to use his or her own name while making an affirmation, seems to have the force of an oath.

There were many **Johns** in NT times, because one of the Hasmonean brothers was named **John**. This does not mean he was the Apostle **John** or that he was the author of the Fourth Gospel, whose name was not given in the text. Like the Baptist and one of the apostles, his name was **John.** He called himself a **brother**. This probably does not mean that he was writing to his blood **brothers** and sisters. **Brother** was a Christian name, used mostly by monks, because they took vows to disown their blood relatives and accept the other members of the monastery as their legal **brothers**. They belonged to a religious brotherhood. He also was one who shared in the tribulation. This certainly means that both he and his readers had endured hardship because of their political and religious positions.

The term **tribulation** later came to be a technical term that meant an antitype of the suffering that was identified with the hardship the Jews endured during the 3½ years of guerrilla fighting the Hasmoneans led before they overpowered the Greeks, cleansed the temple, and celebrated the first Hanukkah. Christians call this the **tribulation**; Jews call it the "birth pangs of the Messiah." It is reasonable to think that **John** also thought of his suffering as being the antitype of the suffering of the Hasmoneans just before the end of Greek control over the temple. He thought that the remaining suffering would be short; based on Daniel, this would be at most 3½ years total. Since **John** knew the history of the **tribulation** before Hanukkah, he realized that after the war, the Hasmoneans and the contemporary Jews gained control of the Jewish kingdom.

---

[1] F. Bovon, "John's Self-presentation in Revelation 1:9-10," *CBQ* 62 (2000):693-700.

Endurance in Jesus. Because John thought he and his contemporaries were in the same place in the cycle as the Hasmoneans were, he thought of himself as **sharing in a tribulation** like theirs, but also he and his **brothers** would **share** in a **kingdom** like theirs. They would share in the kind of endurance that was typical of **Jesus**. Endurance was an important word for John and his contemporary Christians. They could bear the tortures they faced and continue to endure, because they "knew" the time table. They had compared the events of their times with those of other cycles of time. They believed that this evil age was just about over. They could hold out just a little longer. **John** said it was **in Jesus**, because he and his readers were all Christians. They were legally members of the body of Christ, the legal corporation that was identified with **Jesus**.

I was on the island called Patmos. Although there are heavenly scenes in the Book of Revelation, the opening scene takes place firmly on earth, in relationship to a certain human being in a specific geographical location. The geographical location of **John** when he wrote this was **the island called Patmos.** This is a small, crescent-shaped island, roughly eight miles long and five miles wide approximately 21 square miles in size. Some scholars say the scenery of Patmos has left a deep impression on the book,[1] but that is not very obvious. **Patmos Island** does not have caves, or mountains. It has one large hill, 800 feet tall, and for the benefit of tourists a cave has been constructed to show where **John** might have done his writing, but it is not a natural cave. The coast line of **Patmos** is about 30 miles long. **Patmos** is located west of modern Turkey, about 40 miles from the mouth of the Meander River and 65 miles from Ephesus. **John** was evidently exiled there because of his insurrectionist activities (HE 4.12, 23; Pliny, *NH*). He probably was not chained or in prison there. He may have had as much freedom as anyone might have on that island who was not free to leave. The ruling authorities did not want to kill him; they just wanted to curtail his activities. His limitations were not the kind that would have prevented him from writing or receiving messages from the outside world.

Bousset has argued that **John** was no longer on the island when he wrote.[2] He used the aorist, *eh-geh-náw-mayn* (ἐγενόμην), **I** *was*--not **I am**. He also used the term in association with other aorist verbs: **I was in the spirit** (Rev 1:9); **I heard** (Rev 1:9); **I turned** (Rev 1:12). It could, however, mean "I arrived on the Island of Patmos," as Zahn argued.[3] This would mean he reported the events in sequence: 1) he arrived; 2) he became in the spirit; and 3) he turned. Bousset's logic, however, is convincing, even though not conclusive. John may have written from some other location at a later time. This implies that his isolation on this island was not a life time sentence. Loisy argued that **John's** presence on **the Island of Patmos** for the **word of God and the testimony of Jesus** may not mean that he was exiled there.

---

[1] A. S. Peake, *The Revelation of John* (London: Holborn, 1919) p. 218.
[2] W. Bousset, *Die Offenbarung Johannis* (Göttingen: Vandenhoeck und Ruprecht, 1896), p. 79.
[3] Zahn, *Die Offenbarung des Johannes* (Leipzig: A.Deichert, 1924)I, pp. 180-81.

He may have come there as a missionary to bear **testimony to the word of God and the testimony of Jesus.**[1]

Because of the word of God. **The word of God was**, on the one hand, the FT. This was the source of all knowledge, so far as believers were concerned. This was also, on the other hand, the contract **God** had made with his people on Mount Sinai. There are echoes and allusions to this contract throughout the Book of Revelation. The communities from which this literature came evidently believed that **God** was about to establish a new contract with his people. **John** thought this contract would be inaugurated by **Jesus**.

John said he was on **the Island of Patmos because of the word of God and the testimony of Jesus.** This expression appears twice in Rev 1 (Rev 1:2, 9) and only two other times in the entire prophecy of 18 chapters (Rev 6:9; 20:4). A closely related expression occurs two more times (Rev 12:17; 14:12). These five expressions include the only times the word **Jesus** appears in the whole prophecy.

The testimony of Jesus meant either: 1) the message he was communicating about **Jesus,** 2) **the testimony** that **Jesus** had made, or 3) the new contract that **Jesus** was about to introduce. Any of these would make sense: 1) **John** acted and spoke as he did because of the way he interpreted **the word of God** and **because of the testimony Jesus** bore when he accepted death at the hands of the Romans. Romans did not usually punish people for their religious beliefs so long as they did not stir up subversive activity. Romans had already spent a tremendous amount of money and lives fighting the Jews before they captured Jerusalem and destroyed their temple. They knew about Jewish sabotage and resistance. They also knew Christians were involved in the same kind of movements.

The word of God included the Book of Daniel that led to the Hasmonean victory. Joshua told of the conquest of Canaan; the Book of Zechariah told of the reestablishment of the land under Jewish rule. It included the holy war rules of Deuteronomy and the military activities of Joshua and the Judges. Because Jews and Christians thought they could undertake wars like this again, Romans acted to keep these fifth columnist movements under control. Therefore John was exiled to **Patmos.** Jesus had been crucified because he was thought by the Romans to be a threat to their security. This may have been **because of** his **testimony,** and **John** supported **Jesus' testimony**. Therefore he was at **Patmos.** The expression, **the testimony of Jesus**, was placed in parallel relationship to **the word of God.** Both may have been considered legal expressions referring to the contract at Sinai and the new contract Jesus introduced. It was these contracts which prompted Jews and Christians to engage in political activity such as that which placed John on Rome's list of fifth columnists.

---

[1] Loisy, *L'Apocalypse*, pp. 75-76.

TEXT

¹⁰I was day dreaming on the Lord's Day when I heard behind me a loud noise, [loud] as a trumpet, ¹¹saying, "That which you see write in a scroll and send [it] to the seven churches--to Ephesus, Pergamum, Thyatira, and Smyrna, Philadelphia, and Laodicia." Then I turned to see the voice which was speaking to me.

COMMENTARY

I was day-dreaming. Literally this says in Greek, **I was in the spirit.** Aune rendered it **I fell into a prophetic trance,**[1] which may or may not be just another way of saying the same thing. Many scholars take this to mean John was under a hypnotic, ecstatic spell,[2] but that is not required of the context. Being **in the spirit** meant not being there actually and physically. The expression does not mean **John** was under the control of God's **Spirit,** as Sweet suggested.[3] This is an "as if" situation. It seemed to John as if he had heard the message given. The message came to him "loud and clear." John was obviously speaking metaphorically here. Trumpets do not speak so that they can be understood. They make loud noises. John apparently meant that while he was day dreaming this message came to him like a sudden blast that startled him with its significance. John's experience was like that of Ezekiel who was physically in Babylon when he visualized himself at the temple in Jerusalem (Ezek 1:1-28). He did not travel to Jerusalem; all of this description took place in his "mind's eye." Later rabbis had other poetic ways of expressing themselves. For example, when a person was listening to someone who had taken a journey tell of his travels, he called that "taking a journey in words" or "traveling in words."[4]

John had before him the scroll which the messenger brought to him. He thought this had the same authority as Scripture, so he used expressions from the scroll, just as he had from Scripture, to form a narrative midrash. One of the earliest expressions in the scroll (Rev 4:1-22:5) was: At once *I was day-dreaming* (*eh-geh-náw-mayn en pnoó-mah-tee*, ἐγενόμην ἐν πνεύματι) (Rev 4:2), the very same words used here in Rev 1:10.

On the Lord's Day. This has often been taken to mean that **the Lord's Day** was distinguished from the Sabbath by the time of **John of Patmos**. Indeed this seems to have been supported by Ignatius early in the second century IA. Ignatius identified Christians as those who attained the newness of hope and did not observe the

---

[1] D. E. Aune, *Revelation 1-5* (Dallas: Word Books, c1997), p. 62.
[2] Among others, this is the opinion of Zahn, *Offenbarung* I, p. 182; and Düsterdieck, *Revelation*, p. 109, who thought being "in the spirit" was the same as being "in ecstasy," but you do not have to be ecstatic to obtain an insight or imagine something.
[3] J. P. M. Sweet, *Revelation* (Philadelphia: Westminster Press, c1979), p. 64.
[4] Buchanan, *Jewish Messianic Movements*, pp. 193-94.

Sabbath, but rather fashioned their lives after **the Lord's Day** (*IgnMagn 8-9*). Guy argued for the genuineness of Ignatius's work.¹ Lewis, however, said "sabbatize" does not have to mean observing **the Lord's Day** on Sunday. It might mean following the Jewish custom of resting on the Sabbath Day. In which **case the Lord's Day** might have been Saturday.² The Day of the Lord is often used in the Scriptures to mean the day when the Lord would sit in judgment on the first day of the year. This was day of the year that was most celebrated by Jews who observed the old calendar, and it was declared to be Easter, the most celebrated day of the year by Christians. Since Easter was identified with the first day of the new year, it is likely that the first day of the week for Christians was not a sabbath day of rest but the Lord's day of celebration.

Voice, loud as a trumpet, saying. Still earlier in the scroll brought to John were the words: **the first voice which I heard [loud] as a trumpet, speaking** (Rev 4:1). The two verses are very similar in Greek:

Revelation 1:10

ἤκουσα ὀπίσω μου φωνὴν μεγάλην
áy-koo-sah oh-peé-soh moo foh-náyn meh-gáh-layn
ὡς σάλπιγγος
hohs sáhl-ping-gaws
λεγούσης
Leh-goó-says.

Revelation 4:1

ἡ φωνὴ ἡ πρώτη ἥν
hay foh-náy hay próh-tay háyn

ἤκουσα ὡς σάλπιγγος
áy-koo-sah hohs sáhl-ping-gaws
λαλούσης.
Lah-loó-says.

    John apparently took these words from the beginning of the scroll that had been brought to him and put them early into his introduction to testify to his belief that this scroll contained **the words of God**.³ This was not the only or even the first time **John** treated words of **the prophecy** as if they were Scripture. **John** also used the image of a voice speaking from heaven or from some divine being in Rev 1:15. In the prophetic section of Revelation (Rev 4:1-22:5) the word **voice** occurred as a message from heaven or through some divine messenger 33 times. John picked up the term and used it in the same way twice.
    In his very first paragraph the author referred to himself as **John, who bore witness to the word of God and the testimony of Jesus** (Rev 1:2). This was an expression that also appeared in the prophecy section of the Book of Revelation:

---

¹ F. Guy, "'The Lord's Day' in the Letter of Ignatius to the Magnesians," *AUSS* 2 (1964):1-17.
² R. B. Lewis, "Ignatius and the 'Lord's Day,'" *AUSS* 6 (1968):46-59.
³This insight was called to my attention by my former student, M. R. Mulholland, *Revelation* (Grand Rapids: Francis Asbury Press, c1990). He explained the phenomenon differently.

12:17: **Those who keep the commandments of God and have the testimony of Jesus.**
14:12: **Those who keep the commandments of God and the faith of Jesus.**
17:6: **From the blood of the saints and from the testimony of Jesus.**
20:4: **The souls of those who have been beheaded on account of the testimony of Jesus and on account of the word of God.**

When **John** read the prophecy the messenger brought him, he probably identified himself immediately as one of those who kept the commandments of God and bore the testimony of Jesus. He was so favorably impressed with the document that he treated it as the word of God and wove expressions into his introduction which he took from the prophecy, just as he wove words from the Scripture into his narrative. At the very beginning of his introduction, he reported that God had sent him this revelation through the messenger **to his servant John, who bore witness to the word of God and the testimony of Jesus the Messiah** (Rev 1:1-2). A few verses further he said, **I, John, . . . was on the island called Patmos, because of the word of God and the testimony of Jesus** (Rev 1:9).

Because there are several words in the introduction and conclusion of the Book of Revelation that are identical to those found in **the prophecy** section (Rev 4:1-22:5) many scholars have previously assumed that the same author wrote the entire document. That is not a necessary assumption. Those familiar with the methodology of forming midrash will realize that it is normal for an author to weave words from Scripture into the document in preparation.

On the Lord's Day. The expression **the day of the Lord** (*hay-méh-rah Koo-reé-oo*, ἡμέρα Κυρίου or *hay-méhrah too Koo-reé-oo*, ἡμέρα τοῦ Κυρίου) appears many times in the OG, but except for one unlikely variant text (2Macc 12:36), the term used here (*koo-ree-ah-káy*, κυριακῇ) nowhere occurs. **The day of the Lord** was the day when Israel expected the Lord to hold court and try his people for their crimes and virtues. That was not the same as a special day of the week. According to the research of Stott, the expression *koo-ree-ah-káy* does not occur among the church fathers until the time of Ignatius.[1] Stott's examination convinced him that the term could not mean Easter nor the eschatological day of the Lord. Following Charles, Stott thought it was patterned after a Roman practice in relationship to its emperors. The first day of each month was called *Sebastáy*, Σεβεστή and dedicated to the emperor. Christians refused to honor the emperor, but they called the first day of the week after their own king, Jesus. They called it, instead of *Seh-bahs-táy*

---

[1] W. Stott, "Note on the Word KURIAKH in Rev. I.10," *NTS* 12 (1965/66):70-75.

(Σεβαστή), *koo-ree-ah-káy* (κυριακή) a day to honor the Lord Jesus. John used this term to refer to Sunday, a day for Christians to worship.

[That which you see] write. The words **that which you see** do not appear in Sinaiticus. It is almost necessary for the sense of the passage. The scribe of Sinaiticus probably overlooked it as he did with other words.

This message that came to John did not tell him to write down what he had *heard*, but rather he was to write what he had *seen*. **That which he had seen** was the scroll that the messenger had brought to him--the prophecy **which he had seen** (Rev 1:1-3). Since **that which he had seen** was already written, the writing involved meant translating the prophecy from Hebrew into Greek so that the people in the seven churches could read it. He was confident that anyone who read this aloud to a congregation, and any congregation who listened to it being read, and kept that which was written in the prophecy would be blessed (Rev 1:3). When John realized that, the message came to him clearly. His task was to get this message out to the churches. These churches were all seven in the area which is now western Turkey. They were all prominent cities that were close together and had some geographical and probably some governmental connections before the time of this writing. When **John** understood what was involved in this prophecy, his imagination wandered, and he began to associate the message of the prophecy, his own local situation, and the many FT passages dealing with redemption, so he wrote down the following:

To Ephesus, Pergamum, Thyatira, Smyrna, Philadelphia, and Laodicia. **Sardis** is omitted by Sinaiticus. This is evidently an oversight, because **Sardis** is included as the recipient of one of the letters (Rev 3:1-6). Other texts have **Smyrna** and **Pergamum** reversed, with Sardis after Thyatira.

John surely intended there to be seven in this list, because seven was an important number. That does not mean that there were only seven churches in **John's** circuit, but that he intentionally listed only seven.[1] In the same way Daniel referred to four beasts (Dan 7) and four divisions of a statue (Dan 2) to represent four nations--Babylonia, Media, Persia, and Greece. He did this even though Babylonia was conquered by Persia without any rule of Media in between.

The Book of Revelation has seven churches, seven spirits of God, seven vials, seven trumpets, seven allusions to the altar, etc. This is not only true of this document. The magic number seven was used often in literature. For example Fourth Ezra has seven visions (4 Ezra 3:1; 5:21; 6:35; 9:26; 11:1; 13:1; 14:1).

---

[1] When I was in Izmir, Turkey (Smyrna) in 1973, I found a stone slab with a message engraved on it. I recognized three of the seven church cities in the text. I did not have time to decipher the entire message at the time, so I photographed it and left. The photography did not develop well, so I never learned how these cities were related, but they evidently had some administrative and political relationship apart from John's churches.

LITERARY TREATY STYLE

Following Mendenhall's work on treaties and contracts, Shea pointed out the many places where the Book of Revelation used treaty language to express thought intended. Mendenhall listed five labels used in treaties:

(1) The *preamble* to the Hittite suzerainty treaty identified the king who was the author of the covenant by giving his name, titles, attributes, and genealogy;
(2) the *historical prologue* described the past relations between the two contracting parties;
(3) the *stipulation* detailed the obligations imposed upon the vassal;
(4) the *witnesses* to the extra-biblical treaties were the gods of the participants, but monotheistic Yahwism found other elements to substitute for them; and
(5) the treaties then concluded with their religious sanctions, the *blessings and curses* that would occur in the case of loyalty to, or breach of, the covenant.[1]

Shea noted that the following passage (Rev 1:12-20) follows the description of the personal identification of the suzerain. This is also supplemented by the description of the Messiah as **King of kings and Lord of lords** (Rev 19:16). Most of the terminology Shea noted is in Rev 2 and 3.

Inspired by Shea, Strand extended the research in the Book of Revelation on the basis of its literary relationship to ancient suzerainty treaties and concluded that the entire book was structured as an ancient suzerainty with the *prologue* and *preamble* in Rev 1, especially Rev 1:5-6. The stipulations fall, of course, in the letters to the churches, but also in other parts of the document; e.g., Rev 6:9-11; 7:13-14; 12:11, 17; 14:12-13; 16:15; 18:4; 20:4. Along with these stipulations are assurances of the Lord's faithfulness and loyalty (Rev 5:9-10; 7:15-17; 11:18; 14:1-4; 16:4-7; 18:20; 19-22).

For the call upon **witnesses**, Strand offered three instances:
1) **I, Jesus, sent my messenger to testify these things to you among the churches** (Rev 22:16);
2) **the Spirit and the bride say, "come!" Let him who hears say, come!"** (Rev 22:17); and
3) **The one who witnesses to these things says, "Yes, I am coming quickly"** (Rev 22:20).

Strand found the following formulas for **blessings and/or curses**:

---

[1] W. H. Shea, "The Covenantal Form of the Letters to the Seven Churches," *AUSS* 21 (1983):71-84. This quotation is from page 72.

1) **Blessed is he who keeps the words of the prophecy of this scroll** (Rev 22:7).
2) **Blessed are those who wash their robes** (Rev 22:14);
3) **I testify to everyone who hears the words of the prophecy of this scroll. If anyone adds to them God will add to him the plagues that are written in this scroll, and if anyone takes away from the words of the book of this prophecy, God will take away his share from the tree of life and from the holy city of those things written in this scroll** (Rev 22:18-19).[1]

These insights tell more about the ability and knowledge of John of Patmos, who wrote Rev 1-3 and Rev 22:6-22. He apparently recognized the legal aspects of the prophecy that was brought to him. He considered it to be a valid prophecy and a recognized contract, like that of Exod 20 or the Book of Deuteronomy. Therefore, he structured his introduction and conclusion so as to point out the contractual character of this prophecy. The prophecy had stipulations and promises that were normal to a contract. John added the necessary preamble, historical prologue, the call for witnessses, and the blessings and curses of a contract. He further emphasized this character by writing the letters in contractual form as Shea demonstrated.

TEXT

Revelation	First Testament
[12] When I **turned**,	Zech 4:1-2 The messenger who was speaking with me **turned, and he** aroused me as a man who is awakened from his sleep. Then **he said to me, "What do you see?"** I said, "**I see**--now look! a **lamp stand, all of gold**, with a bowl on the top of it and **seven lamps** on it."
I saw **seven gold lamp stands**, [13] and [in the] midst of the **lamp stands** was	
	Exod 25:37 You shall make **seven lamps** for it [the lamp stand for the tabernacle].
one like a Son of man,	Dan 7:13 Now look! With the clouds of heaven, **one like a Son of man** was coming.

---

[1] K. A. Strand, "A Further Note on the Covenantal Form in the Book of Revelation," *AUSS* 21 (1983):251-64.

dressed in a full-length robe, and he was bound at his waist with a gold belt.	Dan 10:5 Look! A man **dressed in** linen, **and** his waist was bound with gold of Uphaz.
	Dan 7:9 The Ancient of Days sat down. His garment white as snow, and the hair of his head was like pure wool.
¹⁴His head and his hair were white as wool--as snow--and	
his eyes were like a flame of fire. ¹⁵His feet were like burnished brass, as if smelted in a furnace.	Dan 10:6 His eyes were like torches of fire, and his arms and legs were like the gleam of burnished brass. The sound of his words was like the sound of a multitude.
	Ezek 1:7 The soles of their feet were like the feet of a calf, and they shone like burnished brass.
His voice was like the sound of much water [running], ¹⁶having in his right hand seven stars,	Ezek 1:24; cf. 43:2 I heard the sound of their wings, like the sound of much water [running].
	Isa 11:4 He will strike the land with the club of his mouth, and with the breath of his lips he will kill the wicked.
and from his mouth went out a sharp two-edged sword,	Isa 49:2 He set my mouth like a sharp two-edged sword.
	Ps 149:6 Let the high praises of God be in their throats, and a two-edged sword, in their hands.
his appearance shines like the sun shines in its might.	Judges 5:31 Thus let all your enemies perish, Yehowah, but his friends like the sun [disk] as it goes in its might.

TECHNICAL DETAILS

This is the kind of passage in the Book of Revelation that makes people think it was written by someone out of his mind who spoke only in bizarre language that makes no sense. Since John put together parts of sentences from several different narratives none of the pictures to which he alluded is complete.

Without recognizing all of the allusions to scriptural passages, it is difficult indeed to understand what this passage was intended to say. John, however, and his original readers were familiar with the Scriptures. When John just alluded to these various passages in the FT, it is clear what he meant. After he had read the prophecy he knew that the prophecy dealt with the redemption of Israel. He immediately thought of all the other redemption events in Israel:

1) There was the victory of the Hasmoneans over the Greeks just before the first Hanukkah. This was reported in Daniel, so John mentioned characters in Dan 7, 10.
2) He remembered that Ezekiel pictured the restoration of the Jews to the Promised Land, so he quoted a well-known passage from Ezekiel.
3) He thought of Second Isaiah's promise of a bright return to a prosperous Promised Land, so he mentioned the sharp sword from Isa 49.
4) When he thought about the marvelous way God had gone ahead of the troops to win battles for Judas the Maccabee, he also remembered the victory of Deborah and Barak over Sisera made into a victory song in Judges 5. In ancient art are carved in stone pictures of kings returning victorious from battle with the sun disk flying in heaven just above and before the king, showing that the deity had been going before the king and his troops into battle to frighten and confuse the enemy so the king could be victorious. In the same way Israelites pictured either an angel or a pillar of fire at night and a pillar of cloud during the day time going before and behind the Israelites, protecting them from the enemies. In the "Song of Deborah" it was the sun disk that was going ahead in its power. This was one of the texts John worked into his narrative.

Like a good attorney, preparing an argument to use in a court trial, John gathered all of the precedents he could to make his case. All of these allusions were crowded into these five verses. The message is clear to those who understand all of the allusions, but it has not made sense to scholars for many years. All of these seemed to apply to John's own time, and redemption would come again within less than 3½ years. These were the last days of the Roman era. John and his readers were then living in this tribulation period. Soon they would be redeemed. John "proved" this rhetorically by quoting the appropriate texts of Scripture. This is the message John communicated through this apparently confused passage.

COMMENTARY

When I turned I saw seven gold lamp stands. A **seven** branch **lamp stand** was an object that looked like a candelabrum with seven branches, except that instead of candles on the top of each of the branches there was a **lamp stand** or place to set an oil **lamp**. The light given by each **lamp** was about the same as that given by each of the candles. The **seven gold lamp stands** were probably **seven** parts to one candelabrum that held **seven lamps**.

After reading the scroll the messenger brought him, John was convinced that he and his brothers were living in the same situation in their own day. That was the purpose of knowing typology and the cyclical order of events in time. Zechariah had written about two olive trees that symbolized two messiahs. One of these, the king, was Zerubbabel. The other, the high priest, was Joshua. The seven gold lamp stands alluded to the situation in Zerubbabel's days, but in Zerubbabel's place John introduced, as one of the olive trees, the Son of man, the main character in the vision of Dan 7. By this he understood that the Son of man was a messianic king. Dan 7 and the Son of man called the reader's attention to the Hasmonean victory.

Dan 7 surveyed Jewish history mythologically from the time when the temple was burned (586 BIA) until Judas the Maccabee had it cleansed (ca. 164 BIA). In the sixth century BIA Zechariah's vision meant that the land which had just been restored would be entrusted to the royal leadership of Zerubbabel who would be empowered by God to reestablish the government and the temple. The divine power and the anointed leaders were the necessities of the day. In the second century BIA Daniel's vision meant the Greeks were driven out and the Jews would be in charge with Judas as their leader.

Philo identified the **seven** branches of the **lamp stand** as **seven** planets that are signs of the Zodiac: the sun, the moon, Saturn, Jupiter, Mars, Mercury, and Venus (*Quest* Exod 1:75-76; *Moses* 2:102-103; *Heir* 221-25). Goodenough held that the menorah was a symbol of God.[1] Like the pillar of fire and cloud or the burning fire on the altar, it symbolized the real presence of God.

One like a Son of man. Instead of *ehn méh-soh* (ἐν μέσῳε] **midst,** Sinaiticus has *méh-sawn* (μέσον), "midst."

John intentionally brought together the promise in Daniel of the Son of man (Judas the Maccabee) who would come with the clouds (*ah-nah-neém*, ענניס) to drive out the enemies from Palestine and Zechariah's vision of the olive trees that symbolized the high priest, Joshua, and the king, Zerubbabel. These would come while the Lord was trying to overthrow all of Israel's opponents. From Daniel come the description of the Ancient of Days whose hair was white as wool, the fantastic description of the one who brought the message about the end to Daniel. It was **the one like a son of man,** whose eyes were like flames **of fire** and whose **feet** and legs **were like burnished brass**, and who was clothed in a long robe and a **gold** belt.

From Zechariah, the author took the passages about **the lamp stands**. This history was dramatized as a court scene in which the four beasts, representing the heads of four countries that had controlled Judah (Babylon, Media, Persia, and Greece) were defendants before the divine Judge, the Ancient of Days. After they had defended their actions, the Judge condemned Antiochus Epiphanes (the little

---

[1] E. R. Goodenough, *Jewish Symbols in the Greco-Roman Period* (New York: Pantheon Books, c1954) IV, pp. 71-98.

horn) to death and sentenced the other beasts to severe restrictions. He removed their governing power. After that the plaintiff, characterized as **one like a Son of man** (Judas the Maccabee), appeared before the Judge and was awarded, in conjunction with the saints of the Most High (contemporary Jews), the dominion, glory, and kingdom. This myth was a theological interpretation of the Maccabean victory. The temple that had been burned in 586 BIA was then restored, and the land that had been taken away was returned. The local leadership that had been removed was then replaced.

John of Patmos thought that he and his contemporary believers were in the same position in the predestined cycle of time in his day as Judas and the saints of the Most High had been before the first Hanukkah. He also thought that there were divinely anointed leaders ready to be introduced to the historical scene. Just as Zerubbabel appeared in the sixth century BIA and Judas in the second century BIA, in John's day another one **like a Son of man** would come and liberate the chosen people. All of this John communicated in these few words which made no sense either then or now to those who did or do not recognize all of the unwritten meanings included in the allusions to FT.

John was convinced that this new insight of his had come from God. One of his basic reasons for thinking this was from God was that he found all of these passages from the word of God in the Scripture. Like the authors of the *peh-shah-reém* (פשרים) in the Dead Sea Scrolls, John thought all of these Scripture passages applied to his own local situation, so he dramatized this conviction by identifying **the voice** that gave him the insight both with the Ancient of Days (Dan 7) who decreed the judgment against the gentiles and in favor of the Jews and also with the being that brought Daniel the assurance that the heavenly angels and clouds would fight against Persia and Greece in behalf of the Jews. John wove together parts of the terms used to describe the Ancient of Days with other parts of the descriptions of the being who gave Daniel the vision that the enemy nations were being overpowered by God to tell his readers that this insight was from God. After reading the scroll, John was convinced that this prophecy was the word of God, just like other FT. He wove many words from the FT into his narrative, and he also used words from the prophecy he had just read (Rev 4:1-22:4). The word **lamp stands**, of course, came from Zechariah, but it also appeared in the prophecy (Rev 11:4).

The hair of his head was white. The words **as snow** do not have to be a later gloss, as Loisy suggested.[1] They belong to the quotation from Daniel (Dan 7:9), which the author used. In Daniel, these attributes belonged to the Ancient of Days (God). Here they are attributed to the Lord's legal agent, the Messiah, the one like a Son of man. This is the new antitype of Judas the Maccabee. A messiah was a legal agent for God, which means that he was *legally*, though not physically, equal to God within the limits of his assignments.

---

[1] Loisy, *L'Apocalypse*, p. 80.

His eyes were like a flame of fire. This passage was taken from Daniel, but John may have been motivated to use it because it also appeared in the prophecy which he was translating (Rev 19:12). He also used this expression in Rev 2:18.

His feet were like burnished brass. Sweet said the translation **burnished bronze** was only a guess since the Greek term *khahl-kaw-lee-báhn-oh* (χαλκολιβάνῳ) is found only here and in Rev 2:18 in Greek literature.[1] He was certainly justified in avoiding absolute conclusions. Ford supported his reticence.[2] Sweet, however, was not completely right in saying that it was nowhere else found. More than 200 years ago Wetstein listed a few quotations that included either the term itself or a similar Latin term. These references suggest that *khal-kaw-lee-báh-noh* was either a precious metal or an alloy of gold and bronze,[3] but the word was not used frequently or widely known. The Latin Vulgate renders it *aurichalco* (ow-ree-kháhl-koh)— "gold bronze." On the basis of Wetstein's data, many scholars have considered this as a possibility, supposing that *khahl-kaw-lee-báh-noh* some alloy that is now unknown.[4] As early as the nineteenth century, however, scholars considered the possibility that *khahl-kaw-lee-bahn* was an etymological hybrid, composed of *khahl-koh* and *lah-bahn*, and therefore meaning "shining white bronze."[5] This possibility deserves further examination. With so little knowledge about the metal mentioned by some classical sources, it is better methodology to examine the term in relationship to the text which John of Patmos quoted when he used the term, *khahl-kaw-lee-báh-noh*, namely Dan 10:6, and presume that the translator of Rev 1:15 used a variant text but intended the same meaning.

This word is composed of two others. It is the second part of the word *khahl-kaw-lee-báh-noh* that creates the problem. Literally, the first word *khahl-káws*, (χαλκός) means "brass or bronze." *Aí-bah-naws* (αὔβανος) means "frankincense," which seems odd. The passage containing this word is a translation of Dan 10:6, whose Masoretic Hebrew is *neh-khóh-sheht kah-láhl*, (נחשת קלל). There is no problem with *neh-khó-sheht* which means brass or bronze. The problem is with *kah-láhl*, which basically means "make light," but this was used in many ways. It means to make light in weight, to disparage, belittle, curse, whet, sharpen, polish, shine, or burn to make glisten. It is difficult to see how the translator could translate this word by "frankincense." He must have rendered a different Hebrew text.

A possibility is that he read *neh-khóh-sheht leh-bóh-nah*, (נחשת לבנה). In Hebrew the word *leév-nah* (לבנה) means both make white, purify, be bright or clear and also "frankincense," a white resinous substance. It could be taken as a synonym for *kah-láhl*, and it could be translated as shining. The author may have used a

---

[1] Sweet, *Revelation*, p. 72.
[2] J. M. Ford, *Revelation* (Garden City: Doubleday & Co., 1975), p. 383.
[3] J. J. Wetstein, *Novum Testamentum Graecum* (Amsterdam: Akademische Druck, 1752) II, p. 752.
[4] R. H. Charles, *A Critical and Exegetical Commentary on the Revelation of St. John* (Edinburgh: T. & T. Clark, 1920) I, p. 29; Düsterdieck, *Revelation*, p. 113; Mounce, *Revelation*, p. 79.
[5] Düsterdieck, *Revelation*, p. 113.

variant reading for Dan 10:6, namely *neh-khoh-sheht leh-bóhn-ah*, and by his translation formed a word by making a Greek loan word of the Hebrew word *libnah* and the Greek word *chalkos*, without any acquaintance with the metal or alloy mentioned by such classical authors as Suidas and Aristophanes, or he may have known the word and assumed that this was the appropriate loan word to render the Hebrew he saw. In either case he probably understood this to mean "shining brass," but the Hebrew *leév-nah*, pointed *lee-bóhn-ah*, like the Greek *líbanos*, means "frankincense." Either the Hebrew is a Greek loan word, the Greek is a Hebrew loan word, or both are loan words from some other language.

The OG translation of the crucial term in Daniel 10:6 is *kháhl-kaws ehx-ahs-tráhp-tohn* (χαλκὸς ἐξαστράπτων), a brass that shines like the sun or lightning. Theodotian's version is *khahl-káw steel-bawn-taws* (χαλκο στίλβοντος), bright-shining bronze. The term *khahl-kaw-lee-báhn-oh* (χαλκολιβάνω), like the OG and Theodotian's rendering of the Hebrew of Daniel 10:6, should also be bright, shining, or burnished brass or bronze. This is still a conjecture, but it is not as mysterious as many scholars have thought. There is a biblical basis for this suggested hybrid.

Like the sound of much water [running]. **The voice** that had spoken to Daniel (Dan 8) was one that explained to Daniel his vision in terms that promised destruction to Israel's enemies and vindication to Israel. This voice was identified by John of Patmos with the voice in Dan 10 that also interpreted a vision for Daniel, and this voice "predicted" the kind of trouble Jews would face before they were delivered. Of this voice, Daniel said: **The sound (voice) of his words was like the sound (voice) of a multitude** (Dan 10:6), but John was not satisfied with so simple an allusion. He changed the description to read **like the sound (voice) of much water [running]** to call attention also to Ezekiel's vision. This was the same voice that spoke to John in a loud voice like a trumpet (Rev 1:10), which is not the same sound as that of a waterfall. The point John wanted to make was that it was very loud and clear. It was not a soft whisper that might be misunderstood or ignored. The vision in Ezekiel, to which John called attention, described the holy of holies in the temple at Zion, where the Spring of Siloan roared as it poured out huge amounts of water every day, and where there were cherubim over the altar. The flapping of their wings was like the sound of much water [running] (Ezek 1:24). This identified "the voice" also with the heavenly beings in the holy of holies at the City of David.

From his mouth went out a sharp sword. This probably had the same meaning as Isa 49:2 which seems to mean the same as Isa 11:4, where the Messiah was destined to judge the people, slaying the land with the rod of his mouth, killing the wicked with the breath of his lips. This means he would pass judgment, giving the wicked death sentences, and they would later be killed. His position of authority permitted him to say, **Off with his head!** and the result was the same as if he had cut off the victim's head himself with a sharp two-edged sword.

Like the sun [disk] in its might. The last situation to which John alluded in this mythological vision was the Song of Deborah (Judges 5). In that proof text Israel went out to meet the Philistine leader, Sisera, in war against overwhelming odds. Israel's soldiers had only rocks and clubs, whereas Sisera had chariots and armed soldiers. Nonetheless, the Lord sent a heavy rain to help the Israelites at Megiddo. The horses and chariots got stuck in the mud and were helpless. Then the Israelites overpowered them, and Sisera was killed. In this victory song, the poet concluded, **So perish all your enemies, Lord, but your friends be as the sun rising in its power** (Judges 5:31).

The sun that rose in its power was the **sun disk**, well known in ancient art. The **sun disk** in Near Eastern religions was the divine symbol that went ahead of divinely appointed kings to confuse the enemy and guarantee victory to the side on which the **sun disk** was fighting. In this case, the **sun disk** went ahead of the Israelites and brought down the rain to destroy the chariots of Sisera. When John quoted this passage he was adding the song of victory related to the original conquest of Canaan to the other situations during which Israel had been able to recover the land. In these few verses, John alluded to 1) the conquest of Canaan during the time of the judges, 2) Ezekiel's vision of the restored temple during the Babylonian captivity, 3) the restoration of the land during the rule of Joshua and Zerubbabel, and 4) the Hasmonean victory and restoration of the land in the second century BIA.

These were all times in past history when Israel had succeeded in acquiring the Promised Land from the control of the gentiles. John probably thought that these all occurred at the same point of time in the cycle, and he also believed that he and his contemporaries were at that very time living in the last days of the old age of gentile rule before the land was to be restored under the rule of the believers' messiah. When all of this is understood from these few verses, the passage does not seem nearly as nonsensical as it originally appears.

TEXT

Revelation	First Testament
[17]When **I saw him I fell** at his feet as though I was dead, but he laid his right hand upon me, saying,	Ezek 1:28**I saw, and I fell** on my face, and I heard a voice speaking.
	Dan 8:18When he came I was afraid, and **I fell** on my face.
"**I am the first and the last,** [18] the One who lives. I was dead, but look! I am living into the ages of ages.	Isa 44:6**I am the first**, and I am **the last**; besides me there is no god.
I have **the keys of** death and Hades."	Isa 22:22I will place on his shoulder **the key of** the house of David.

> ^{Isa 48:12-13}**I am the first; I am** also **the last**. Even my hand laid the foundation of the earth, and my right hand spread out the heavens.

COMMENTARY

When I saw him I fell at his feet.. When John **fell at** the messenger's **feet,** he reflected the kind of humility Ezekiel experienced in his call to prophecy (Ezek 1:28) and that of Daniel, when he received the message of the end time from the angel Gabriel (Dan 8:18). This narrative, however, was intentionally made to imitate the reaction of Daniel after he saw the vision of **the voice** who told him the angels of heaven were out to destroy Persia and Greece (Dan 10). After he saw the vision of **the voice,** like Daniel, John's strength left him, and he fell on his face to the ground. Then **the voice** picked up Daniel, stood him on his feet, and said, **Do not be afraid** (Dan 10:12).

John's account was very similar, but he summarized the experience of losing strength, falling to the ground, and falling asleep as falling at his feet as though dead. The **I am** here comes from Exod 3:14, as it did earlier, except here instead of concluding, **I am the one who is, who was, and the coming one,** he said, "**I am the first, the last, and the living one.**" The idiom, **the first and the last**, comes from Second Isaiah (Isa 41:4; 44:6) who used it to refer to God's creation or his delivery of the Hebrews from Egypt **at first**. The **voice**, like the heavenly angel, Gabriel (Dan 8:17), did not object to others worshiping him, but the messenger who brought the prophecy to John did (Rev 22:9). This suggests that the **voice** is a divine figure, but the messenger who brought the prophecy to John was not.

I am the first and the last. This is one of the euphemistic names for God. It is also used three other times in John's introduction and concluding recommendation (Rev 1:8; 2:23; 22:16) and once in the prophecy (Rev 21:6). The formula **I am** occurs 48 times in the NT, almost always attributed to Christ or God.[1]

Some texts begin this statement with, **Do not be afraid!** This is a text taken from Isa 44:2 and Dan 10:12. **The last** refers to the final restoration of Jews to the Promised Land. John added some expressions to that of Second Isaiah. To show that the "I am" refers to Jesus rather than to God, John added, **the One who lives. I was dead, but look! I am living into the ages of the ages. I have the keys of death and of Hades**. This refers to Jesus who was crucified but was still alive and would continue to live for ages. In John's judgment, Jesus controlled the future destiny of all people who died.

I have the keys of death and Hades. This is another expression which John picked up from the prophecy (Rev 4:1-22:5) and wove into his narrative. Originally this

---

[1] Aune, *Revelation 1-5*, p. 100.

thought form came from the Hellenistic world where the goddess Hecate was believed to hold **the keys** to the gates of **Hades**. John of Patmos read in the judgment scene of Rev. 20:1: **I saw an angel coming down from heaven having the key of the abyss and a large chain in his hand.** Further on in the same chapter he read, **Death and Hades gave up the dead people who were in them** (Rev 20:13). **Then death and Hades were thrown into the lake of fire** (Rev 20:14). A star that had fallen from heaven was given the key to the pit of the abyss (Rev 9:1). From these idioms John visualized a **voice** announcing to John that he *had the keys of death and Hades* (Rev 1:18). The expression **keys** in the NT is always used metaphorically to mean authority. Peter was given the keys to the Kingdom of Heaven (Matt 16:19). The lawyers were accused of having taken away the key to knowledge (Luke 11:52). Shea thought Rev 1:17-18, along with Rev 5:9-10; 7:14-17; 12:7-11, like Exod 20, constituted a historical prologue for a treaty.[1]

TEXT

Revelation

"¹⁹Write, therefore, the things which you have seen, both the things that are and **the things that are about to happen after this**.

²⁰**The mystery** of the seven stars **which** you saw in my right hand and the seven gold lamp stands: the seven stars are messengers of the seven

churches, and the lamp stands are the churches."

First Testament

Dan 2:45 A great good has made known to the king **that which is to happen after this**.

Dan 1:27-28 Daniel answered before the king and said, "**The mystery which** the king has asked, no wise men, enchanters, magicians, or astrologers are able to show the king, but

there is a God in the heavens who reveals **mysteries**, and he will make known to King Nebuchadnezzar that which is to happen at the end of days."

COMMENTARY

The things that you have seen. By this John meant the things he had seen and read in the scroll that was brought to him. His commandment to write meant he was commissioned to translate the prophecy in the scroll and write the messages to the churches, which he did. Hemer suggested that this verse divided the book into two units: 1) the things which are--Rev 1-3 and 2) the things that are about to happen

---

[1] Shea, "Covenantal Form," p. 73.

after this--the prophecy in Rev 4-22.[1] The things that were when John wrote were the events related in Rev 1:1-3:22 and 22:6-21. The future anticipations were contained in the prophecy (Rev 4:1-22:5).

The things that are about to happen after this. Helmbold noticed a quotation in a Coptic apocryphon which has a partial quotation that seems to be precisely this phrase in Coptic. From this fourth or fifth century document, Helmhold conjectured that it really represents the middle of the second century. Since the scribe of the document attributed it to John the brother of James, this must be a valid early witness to the early origin of the Book of Revelation.[2] There is not much basis for his conjecture.

When John read the prophecy that was brought to him, he thought that he understood how the events of his day fit into the cycles of times and the typology of events. From these he could deduce what things were to happen in the immediate future, because he believed everything was predestined to happen in a certain order, according to the cycle of time. It was like seeing a play on the stage that he had already seen before or whose script he had read before he attended the theater. The expression, **at the end of days** (Dan 2:28) is in exact parallel with the other expression, **after this** (Dan 2:29, 45), which clearly does not refer to the end of the world.[3]

In Daniel that which was expected to happen at the end of the 490-year period was that the Greek domination was to be overthrown and Jews were to be free to rule the Promised Land. John probably knew all about the Hasmonean victory that took place at the end of that era and was himself expecting this point in the cycle to appear again. This time it would be the Romans who would be driven out when the new kingdom was established. John believed time moved in cycles and that everything had to happen in a foreordained order. Since he knew what had happened just before the United Kingdom was first established, just before Joshua and Zerubbabel tried to reestablish the kingdom and rebuild the temple, and just before Judas won the battle of Beth-horon, he therefore knew that the events of his own day had the same significance as these. He also knew that after each of these past events the kingdom was established on the Promised Land; therefore he knew what things were about to happen **after this**.

John, however, was not dependent upon Daniel alone for this expression. The author of the prophecy also used the words from Daniel at the beginning of his message: **Come up here, and I will show you the things that are destined to happen after this** (Rev 4:1).[4]

Hemer suggested that John intentionally put together the expressions, **the things that are** and **the things that are destined to happen after this**, as a partial

---

[1] C. J. Hemer, *The Letters to the Seven Churches of Asia in their Local Setting* (Sheffield: JSOT, c1986), p. 31.
[2] Helmbold, "Authorship," pp. 77-79.
[3] See Buchanan, "Eschatology and the 'End of Days,'" *JNES* 20 (1961):188-93.
[4] This insight was also called to my attention by Mulholland, *Revelation*, p. 34.

outline of the book. He thought Revelation 2-3 were **the things which are** and Rev 4-22, **the things that are destined to happen after this**.[1] This is a good suggestion, but not precise. **The things that are** should also include Rev 1 and Rev 22:6-21, because the events related to John and the messenger were parts of the current historical situation.

The seven gold lamp stands. There were ten lamp stands in Solomon's temple (1Kings 7:49), but only one in the wilderness tent (Exod 26:35). In Zechariah's vision there was only one lamp stand, but it had seven lamps on it (Zech 4:2).

The mystery of the seven stars. Aune correctly renders this phrase, **the secret meaning of the seven stars.**[2] The word **mystery** was given to tell the reader who had "eyes to see and ears to hear" that the author was speaking in a secret code. The Judaic teacher of righteousness reported among the Dead Sea Scrolls was claimed to have been the "one to whom God made known all of the mysteries of the words of his servants the prophets" (1QpHab 7:4-5). This means he knew how to interpret the prophets correctly—according to the technique of the sect. **The mystery of the seven stars** was that the author was not talking about astrology. When he spoke of the **seven stars** he was referring to a specific group of **seven churches**. In a similar manner, **the myseries of the Kingdom of Heaven** referred to the secret teachings of the sect that used this formula. **The mystery** with which Nebuchadnezzar approached Daniel was, judging from Nebuchadnezzar's dream, what was to happen in the future (Dan 2:26-45). In the vision of Zechariah, **the seven** lamp stands were the **eyes of the Lord**. John reinterpreted these to mean **the seven** churches to whom he was sending the prophecy. It is not certain how **the churches** functioned as the "eyes of God" to search out the land. In a subversive atmosphere, the churches may have functioned as an underground intelligence agency, keeping tab on everything related to the land.

The seven stars are messengers of the seven churches. **The seven stars** in **the voice's** right hand was an addition of John, not taken from the FT, although he might have taken the idea of **seven messengers** (*áhn-geh-loi*, ἄγγελοι) from the prophecy he was shown. In that prophecy (Rev 4:1-22:5) there were **seven** angels (*áhn-geh-loi*) who blew the trumpets (Rev 8:2) and **seven** angels who poured out the bowls of God's anger upon the land (Rev 16:1). John said these symbolized the *áhn-geh-loi* of the churches. These might have been guardian angels of the churches,[3] officers in the churches, or messengers who carried this prophecy to the churches. John the Baptist was a human angel (Mal 3:1; Matt 11:10). A human priest was called the **messenger** of the Lord (Mal 2:7). The human prophet Haggai spoke of

---

[1] C. J. Hemer, *Letters*, p. 31.
[2] Aune, *Revelation 1-5*, p. 106.
[3] As J. Weiss, *Die Offenbarung des Johannes* (Göttingen: Vandenhoeck und Ruprecht, 1908), p. 608, believed.

himself as the Lord's **angel** (Hag 1:13). Zahn followed some church fathers in concluding that these **stars** were angels which were really bishops. He correctly held that these **angels** could not qualify as heavenly divine messengers. They had to be human beings.[1] Charles, however, argued that all angels in the Book of Revelation were superhuman beings, and these could be no exceptions.[2]

There was an office in the ancient synagogues called the *shah-leé-ahkh hah tsee-bóhr* (שליח הצבור), the agent of the congregation, who was the congregation's representative before the Lord. He was the one who prayed in behalf of the congregation. Since an angel (*ahn-geh-laws*) can also be a legal agent, this seems to have been the officer intended. It was to each of these that the message John had was being sent.

The author composed Rev 1 as a complete unit. This is evident from his *inclusio* formed by using Dan 2:28 and Dan 2:45 both at the beginning and at the end of the chapter: **The things that are necessary to happen** (Rev 1:1) and **The things that are about to happen after this** (Rev 1:20). The author of Rev 1 was apparently **John** of Patmos, but he evidently did not compose the entire scroll by himself. Instead he received a message from a certain **angel.** These relationships raise new questions that will claim our attention before continuing to Rev 2.

THE MESSENGER WHO CAME TO JOHN AT PATMOS

At the very beginning of the Book of Revelation the reader is confronted with the identity of the author and his relationship with a certain *áhn-geh-laws* which is usually taken to be a heavenly angel, but that is not required of the word or its context. Although many celestial angels in the Book of Revelation are shown engaged in heavenly activities,[3] this messenger who was closely related to John of

---

[1] Zahn, *Offenbarung* I, pp. 212-19.
[2] R. H. Charles, *A Critical and Exegetical Commentary on the Revelation of St. John* the Diviine (New York: Charles Scribner's Sons, 1920) I, p. 34.
[3] The activity of angels, mostly in heaven, is prominent in the Book of Revelation. Angels carry out assignments around the altar, the throne, or the area of the heavenly temple in general (Rev 5:11; 7:11; 8:2-5; 14:17-19; 15:6, 8, 11; 16:1). They sound trumpets or speak from heaven announcing disasters to take place on earth (Rev 5:2; 8:6, 8, 10, 12; 9:1, 14, 18; 10:7; 11:15; 14:8-9, 15). Angels fly in heaven and either come or are thrown from heaven to earth (Rev 8:13; 10:1; 12:9; 14:6; 18:1; 20:1). Some stand on the sun (Rev 19:17), ascend from the east (Rev 7:2), stand on the sea and land (Rev 10:5, 8) or at the four corners of the earth (Rev 7:1). One throws a millstone into the sea (Rev 18:21); another is in charge of the bottomless pit (Rev 9:11); Michael and his angels fight a battle in heaven (Rev 12:7); and four others are released to kill a third of mankind (Rev 9:15). Seven angels pour bowls full of plagues onto the earth (Rev 14:10; 15:7; 17:1; 21:9). Twelve angels are stationed at the gates of the new Jerusalem, and occasionally an angel communicates with a seer (Rev 10:9, 10; 17:7; 21:12). Most of this angelic activity is associated with heavenly administration. The Greek áhn-geh-laws (ἄγγελος), of course, means simply "messenger" and can refer to any person carrying a message. But since there is so much heavenly angelic activity in the Book of Revelation, scholars have commonly assumed that all angels in the book are heavenly messengers. R. C. Trench, *Commentary on the Epistles to the Seven Churches in Asia* (New York: Charles Scribner's Sons, 1867), argued strongly that the "angels of the seven churches" (Rev 1:20) were human and not celestial (pp. 52-59), but he raised no question about the *angelos* associated with John (1:1). Others,

Patmos seems to have been of a different character. He referred to himself as a fellow servant of John. Since the identity of this *áhn-geh-laws* is vital to the understanding of the apocalypse, this problem will be undertaken at once.

The áhn-geh-laws The revelation which John received was one which God sent him through God's *angelos* (Rev 1:1).[1] John, in turn, bore witness to **whatever things he saw** (*haw-sah áy-dehn*, ὅσα εἶδεν), and his testimony was **the word of God and the testimony of Jesus** Christ (Rev 1:2). The details of this communication are not clearly specified. In what way did John see these things? Did he see a vision? Or did he see something written on a scroll as Ezekiel professed to have done (Ezek 2:9)? Only an examination of the context and the conclusion of the book will clarify this question.

The Prophecy. The benediction that followed was for those who heard and the one who read **the words of the prophecy** (Rev 1:3). This means, at least, that the message was communicated from John to the next recipients by means of writing. It also makes good sense to understand the enclosed prophetic message (Rev 4:1-22:5) as the revelation which John received and the *áhn-geh-laws* as a human being who brought John a scroll which John saw with his physical eyes and read it just as others have done ever since.

The Endorsement. Except for an apparent intrusion in Rev 19:10, which is a summary of Rev 22:6-9, the dialogue between John and the *áhn-geh-laws*, which began in Rev 1, was not taken up again until the last chapter. After the basic message of the prophecy was concluded, the *áhn-geh-laws* told John, **These words are faithful and true . . . Blessed is he who keeps the words of the prophecy of this scroll** (Rev 22:6). John afterwards **fell down to worship before the feet of the *áhn-geh-laws* who showed** him these things (Rev 22:8).[2] Responding in a way similar to that

---

such as C. A. Scott, *The Book of Revelation* (London: Hodder and Stoughton, 1905), also passed over the *angelos* without comment. Düsterdieck, *Revelation*, objected to Ewald's claim that the same angel was involved in all visions, even when not named (p. 67). Düsterdieck thought it should be generically conceived, and thus applied to all the individual angels "who in the different visions have the office of significative declaration" (p. 97). He noted the close relationship between the angel of Rev 1:1 and that of Rev 22:6. H. B. Swete, *The Apocalypse of St. John* (London:MacMillan and Co., 1909), discussed the angelology of Revelation (p. clxix-c) without calling special attention either to the angel associated with John or those belonging to the seven churches. Taking celestial origin for granted, he discussed the importance of the revelation coming through the hands of an angel (p. 2). Caird, *Revelation*, p. 11, G. E. Ladd, *A Commentary on the Revelation of John* (Grand Rapids:Eerdmans, c1972), p. 23, M. Rist, "The Revelation of St. John the Divine," *The Interpreter's Bible* (New York: Abingdon Press, c1957) 12, pp. 366-67, Zahn, *Offenbarung* I, pp. 146, 318, E. Lohmeyer, *Die Offenbarung des Johannes* (Tübingen: J. C. B. Mohr, 1953), pp. 6-7, 20, et al. took the celestial quality of the *angelos* for granted.

[1] God sent (*shah-leé-ahkh*, שליח) his angel (*mah-lah-kháh*, מלכא to close the mouths of the lions (Dan 6:22) on another occasion.

[2] It was not unusual for a man to "worship" another in deference. Nebuchadnezzar worshipped

of Paul and Barnabas, who had been addressed as **Zeus** and **Hermes** (Acts 14:11-15), the *áhn-geh-laws* said, **Do not do that! I am a fellow servant of you and your brothers, the prophets and those who keep the words of this scroll. Worship God** (Rev 22:9).

A Human Messenger. This *áhn-geh-laws* did not want to be confused with God. He considered himself a **fellow servant**--one who felt some kinship with John and his fellow prophets, although he distinguished himself from them. He referred to them as **you and your brothers**, not **you and** our **brothers**. This does not necessarily mean that he was of a different ontological nature from John and his brothers. He may simply have belonged to a different sect or order. If so, the *áhn-geh-laws* is pictured as being Christian rather than Jewish, because he was sent in the name of Jesus (Rev 22:16) and the message was called a revelation of Jesus Christ (Rev 1:1). When John testified both to the word of God and the testimony of Jesus (Rev 1:2), he may have meant that he received both a prophecy which he considered the word of God, and also a Christian testimony from the Christian messenger. Both the *angelos* and John were impressed with the significance of **the words of this scroll** or **the words of the prophecy of this scroll** (Rev 22:9-10). John understood that the *áhn-geh-laws* was sent by God (Rev 1:1) and by Jesus (Rev 22:16) to show **his servants what things must happen** (Dan 2:28, 45) **quickly** (Rev 22:6). The servants were John and the **brothers** in the churches. The blessings and exhortations that accompanied the reading, hearing, and keeping of the words of the prophecy of this scroll (Rev 1:3; 22:7, 9, 10, 18, 19) suggest that to both the *áhn-geh-laws* and John the **voice** was one of event and interpretation. The *áhn-geh-laws* brought a prophecy, and God gave a revelation (Rev 1:1).

The **voice** spoke to John after John had been inspired (Rev 1:10). After John had seen the prophecy and heard the things said by the *áhn-geh-laws*, he fell down to worship him; the *áhn-geh-laws* objected (Rev 22:8-9). When he saw the **voice** he fell down **as dead** (Rev 1:17). This was a customary literary practice for those who wrote this kind of literature. It was their reaction to being **in the spirit** (Dan 8:27; 10:9-12; Enoch 13.13-14; 14:24; 60:3; 71:11; 4Ezra 5:14; 10:30). Instead of objecting, the **voice** placed his right hand on John and said, **Do not be afraid; I am the first and the last (Isa 44:2, 6) and the living one; I died, but look, I am alive for the age of ages.**[1] **I have the keys of death and Hades. Write, then, the things**

Daniel (Dan 2:46). Ezra was reported to have "fallen on his face before the angel whom he addressed as 'Lord'" (*O dominator domine, dominus meus*, or *domine*: 4 Ezra 4:3, 4, 12, 22, 38, 41; 5.33-35, 41, 56; 7.3, 10, 53, 132; 8.6, 20, 36; 10.34). The same titles are also used for God in 4 Ezra 3.4; 5.23; 6.38; 12.7; and 13.51. See also Dan 10:16-17. There was no objection to this. In the Coptic Apocalypse of Elijah, however, the same angel (E)rhmiel= U(riel) said, "Do not pray to me. I am not the Lord, the Almighty" (10.9). G. Steindorf, "Die Apokalypse des Elias Tyre de Jean a Jerusalem," *NovT* 11 (1969):225-32, held that the journey to Patmos in Rev 1:9 was also done only in the spirit. Zahn, *Offenbarung* I, pp. 147-318, noted that the nameless "voice" could not have been Jesus and therefore must have been an angel.

[1] The injunction not to fear was a typical response for an angel or other divine being who appeared in a vision (Luke 1:13, 30; 2:10; 4Ezra 5:15; 10.30; Dan 10:17).

you have seen, both of the things that are and the things that are about to happen after these things (Dan 2:29; Rev 1:17-19). The role of the **voice** was to personify John's compulsion to copy this message and publicize it.[1]

The First and the Last. Just as in **the first** chapter (Rev 1) there is a narration of a historic event followed at once by a theological interpretation couched in redemption language and scriptural allusions, so also in **the last** chapter (Rev 22) there is the reaction of John to the reception of the prophecy and the objection of the *áhn-geh-laws*, followed by an exhortation with quotations from Daniel (Rev 8:26; 12:4, 10), Isa 40:10; 44:6; 48:12, Prov 24:12, and Gen 2:9; 3:22; 49:11. The exhortation containing all these scriptural allusions was apparently attributed to the *áhn-geh-laws*.

Ancient historians, like Thucydides, Josephus, Livy, Plutarch, Tacitus, and Dio Cassius, considered it proper to create speeches for the historical personages to have given, so long as the speeches were appropriate for the speaker and the occasion.[2] This custom partially accounts for the similarity of viewpoint expressed by different personages in speeches reported by the same historian, but that did not mean that the rest of the historian's composition was also fictitious. The same canon of composition should be expected of John of Patmos. Readers were expected to understand that this speech was more than a report of historical fact. The style and viewpoint of this exhortation is similar to that of the allegory introduced by the **voice** in Rev 1. The relationship of the speech and the allegory to the historical narrative in both **the first and the last** chapters is similar, suggesting the same author and purpose.

Like other historians of antiquity, **John** of Patmos included in his historical account other literary materials, but there are introductory clues to alert the reader to the changes in type of literary material. Rev 1:1-2 seems to be a narration of event. Rev 1:3 is a benediction introduced by the normal, **Blessed** (*Mah-káh-ree-aws* μακάριος). Rev 1:4-7 is a greeting to the churches, introduced by a proper salutation. Rev 1:8 is an affirmation of faith in God, attributed to God himself. Rev 1:9 is a continuation of the historical narrative from Rev 1:2. Rev 1:10-20 is an allegory, which, like the greeting to the churches (Rev 1:4-7), is filled with theological convictions and Scripture quotations. Both were apparently composed by John. So were also the letters to the churches of Rev 2:1-3:22. In the last chapter, Rev 22:6-9 represents a historical report, but Rev 22:10-15 includes the speech attributed to the *áhn-geh-laws*, which John, like other ancient historians, probably composed himself.

---

[1] Other prophetic and apocalyptic books included historical reports as well as visions. E.g., a Jew from Jerusalem reported to Ezekiel that Jerusalem had fallen (Ezek 33:21). After that "the hand of the Lord" was upon Ezekiel and the "word of the Lord came to" him (Ezek 33:22-23). The historical events are not confused with Ezekiel's visions or message from God. The same distinction seems true of the "voice" and the *angelos*.

[2] For a carefully documented interpretation of the speeches included in the works of ancient historians, see H. J. Cadbury, *The Making of Luke-Acts* (London: S. P. C. K., 1958), pp. 184-98.

It is difficult to analyze, from a historical point of view, Rev 1-3 and Rev 22:6-21, because the historical account is proportionately very small in comparison to the speeches, allegories, and other material included. It was customary, however, to include many such materials into historical narratives. Livy's speeches were reported to have been more than 2,000, of which about 400 are still extant.[1] The numerous speeches in Acts also comprise a large percentage of that document (Acts 2:14-36; 3:12-26; 7:2-53; 10:34-43; 11:5-17; 13:16-41; 15:13-21; 17:22-31; 22:1-21; 24:10-21; 26:2-23). Although the percentage of doctrine to history is much higher in Rev 1-3 and 22:6-21 than that of other historians, the methodology seems to have been the same. The first and last chapters of Revelation contain the only biographical references, either to John or the *áhn-geh-laws* with whom he was associated. Therefore, these chapters are the ones likely to produce clues for an understanding of available knowledge about John.

JOHN, THE ANGELOS, AND THE LITERATURE

When the *áhn-geh-laws* is considered a human being and John's report considered partially historical, their combined roles in the publication of the Book of Revelation seem surprisingly clear. The *áhn-geh-laws* brought John a message which impressed John very favorably. John felt divinely inspired to send it to the churches. After he had seen the message, he copied it and introduced it with individual letters to the seven churches. The account of the way he received the message and the letters to the churches comprise the first three chapters. Rev 4 begins with an account of a heavenly vision--a typical introduction to a unit of redemption literature (see Ezek 1:1, 4).

> After these things[2] I was watching. Now look! A door was opened in heaven, and the first voice which I heard (was) like a trumpet speaking with me, saying, "Come up here, and I will show you *what things must happen* (Dan 2:28, 45) after these things" (Rev 4:1).

The prophetic document continues for 19 chapters until it concludes:

> And there shall be no longer any night there,
> and they will have no need of [the] light of a lamp
> or [the] light of the sun,

---

[1] Cadbury, *Luke-Acts*, p. 184.
[2] The connective, "after these things" (*meh-táh tów-tah,* μετὰ ταῦτα) is more of an introduction to a section of literature than to an entire document (see Rev 7:1, 9; 15:5; 18:1; 19:1).There are several imaginative ways of explaining this, none of which is completely satisfactory: The original document may have been longer, but the introduction had been omitted, either by John or someone earlier. John might have added this connecting phrase to relate the document to his introduction. The original document may have actually begun with the expression, "After these things," just as Leviticus really begins with "And."

because the Lord God will shine upon them,
and they will rule into ages of ages (Rev 22:5).

After this, John added,

> And he (the *áhn-geh-laws*) said to me, "These words are faithful and true" (Rev 22:6). Then John continued to tell his readers, "And the Lord God of the spirits of the prophets sent his *áhn-geh-laws* to show his servants **what things must happen** (Dan 2:28) quickly. **Look! I am coming soon** (Isa 13:22). Blessed is he who keeps the words of the prophecy of this scroll" (Rev 22:6-7).

John correctly defined the document he enclosed as a prophecy, composed under the inspiration of the same God who had inspired earlier prophets and also in the name of Jesus (Rev 22:16). After John had read this scroll himself, he bowed down before his fellow servant, the *áhn-geh-laws*, so grateful was he for the message (Rev 22:8). John then copied the prophecy which he published (Rev 1:19) together with his introduction and recommendation to the churches (Rev 22:16).

If this analysis is correct, John of Patmos did not compose most of the document between Rev 4:1 and 22:5, but wrote only the first three chapters and most of the last one (Rev 22:6-21). The extensive prophecy in between is the **prophecy of this scroll** (Rev 22:7) which the *áhn-geh-laws* brought to John at Patmos. This was the revelation which God showed John through the agency of John's fellow-servant, the *áhn-geh-laws*. This hypothesis is strengthened by a comparison of the contents of the prophecy with the introduction and conclusion. This hypothesis will be tested throughout the commentary.

CONCLUSIONS

John's competence in Scripture, his zeal for his country, his faithfulness to the law, his belief that he was then living in the last 3½ years of the evil era of the cycle of time, and his understanding of sabbatical eschatology were not unique features. These were concepts that were common among faithful Jews and Christians of his day, and they are reflected in the rest of the Book of Revelation. Because these concepts have been overlooked, many Christians have believed that the Book of Revelation was written by some stupid fanatic who was nearly illiterate and whose arguments make no sense. *Nothing could be farther from the truth.* As we examine the text, verse-by-verse, and relate the FT passages and concepts to the statements made, it will become apparent that neither John nor the authors of the prophecy brought to him should be considered either stupid or illiterate. They were writing in a code known by faithful Jews and early Christians in a way that Romans could not understand their beliefs or plans.

CHAPTER TWO

TECHNICAL DETAILS

Ever since the Babylonian captivity, Jews in areas away from Jerusalem (the diaspora) have continued to maintain their faith by writing letters to the great systematic theologians (*geh-oh-neém*, גאונים), either in Babylon or Jerusalem, for counsel. There were always Jewish merchants who traveled widely in the world and were able to carry these messages to the respective rabbis. The doctrinal counsel that the rabbis wrote in answer to these questions were called *responsa* (*ree-spáw-sah*). These were letters written in response to letters asking questions. Paul's letters to the churches continued this pattern, which was practiced throughout the middle ages. This practice was taken for granted in the formulation of the letters to the seven churches. The seven churches were located at the west end of modern Turkey, and the Island of Patmos was not far from the shore in the Agaean Sea. (The map of this area is between chapters twelve and thirteen).

Shea called attention to the many formulae evident in the letters to the seven churches that are similar to legal treaties and contracts found in antiquity in the Near East. Five of these formulae are the following:

Preamble:	"The word of him who . . ." (titles follow).
Prologue:	"I know your works . . ." (details follow).
Stipulations:	"Repent, [etc.] . . ." (other imperatives follow).
Witness:	"Hear what the Spirit says to the churches."
Blessing:	"To him who overcomes I will grant . . .".[1]

Shea cited many examples from Rev 2-3 where these five formulae are indigenous parts of the letters. John of Patmos evidently wrote these letters in this form, intentionally. The legal significance of the contract made at Sinai to authors of redemption literature is very important to the Book of Revelation.[2] Hemer correctly observed that the letters followed a parallel structure and appeared to be quite different from the main body of the book to which they are coherently joined.[3]

---

[1] W. H. Shea, "The Covenantal Form of the Letters to the Seven Churches," *AUSS* 21 (1983):81.
[2] Shea, "Covenantal," pp. 71-84.
[3] C. J. Hemer, *The Letters to the Seven Churches of Asia in their Local Setting* (Sheffield: JSOT, c1986), p. 14.

TEXT

Revelation

²:¹To **the officer** of the church in Ephesus write: "Thus says the One who holds the **seven** stars in his right hand, who walks in the midst of

the seven gold lamp stands.

First Testament

^(Zech 4:1)**The Messenger** who talked with me came again, and wakened me like a man awakened from his sleep, ²and he said to me, "What do you see?" I said, "I am watching. Now look! a **lamp stand** completely of **gold**; a bowl on top of it, and **seven lamps** on it."

^(Zech 4:10)**The seven?** These are the eyes of Yehowah. They wander back and forth through all the land.

COMMENTARY

To the officer. This phrase is normally rendered **to the angel.** Of course, many ancient peoples in antiquity believed in heavenly beings, called angels. These are also more evident in the Book of Revelation than in any other book in the New Testament (NT). The word, "angel," however, is only a Greek name for a **messenger.** It is deceptive to render this term "angel" today, because the word "angel" in modern Western languages has an automatic specification of a heavenly being. That was not true in ancient Greek.

The word **officer** is used here to clarify the broader meaning. The word usually rendered "angel," is a very general term in Greek. Messengers were important in antiquity when there were no telephones, cell phones, TV, e-mail, telegrams, or radios. The only way people had to communicate from one place to another was by personal travel or messenger. All of these messengers, in Greek were called "angels." There were two kinds of angels:

1) Any being, human or divine, who carried a message, such as postal mail carrier or delivering agent for Federal Express or United Parcels.
2) Other messengers traveled with authority and were authorized to act, speak, and negotiate in behalf of someone else. These were legal agents, such as ambassadors or business agents. These specially empowered angels were also called apostles (*ah-páws-taw-loi,* ἀπόστολοι) in Greek or *shah-lee-ah-keém* (שליחים) in Hebrew.

These legal agents were not always travelers. Some were officers in local areas, representing governments, businesses, or companies at some central locations different from that of the local agency. The same is true today when nearly all of the world's business is conducted by legal agents. A legal agent is a person who acts for someone else. He or she acts and speaks in the name of the other person or company (the principal), in behalf of the principal, and at the responsibility of the principal. Legally, the agent is the principal within the limits of the defined agency. Any negotiations the legal agent makes, the principal is required to uphold.

Any of these messengers or **officers** could be "angels." The type of official involved has to be learned from her or his function. As a principal in the church, John wrote to the officers of the seven local churches who held important official responsibilities. They acted in John's name, in his interest, and at his responsibility. He, in turn, acted, spoke, and wrote in the name of, in the interest of, and at the responsibility of Jesus.

This is not a deduced or imagined office. There were **officers** of this nature in synagogues in John's day, and there probably were officers like that in the early churches. They may have been called "bishops," but, because that is not certain, here they will be designated only by the general name, **officers,** without trying to determine the name that was then assigned to them. In the ancient synagogues the chief officer was called "the apostle of the congregation" (*shah-leé-ahkh hah tseeboór*, שליח הצבור). The legal agent of the congregation, was a messenger who was sent or appointed to a local congregation to perform a special function. This Jewish officer was normally rendered either *áhn-geh-laws* (ἄγγελος) or *ah-páws-taw-laws* (ἀπόστολος) in Greek. Depending on the assignment, an angel can be also an apostle, as is the case here. The general Greek word for messenger was *áhn-geh-laws;* the Hebrew word was *mah-láhk* (מלאך). The term usually used for the messenger with legal authority to act and speak in behalf of the principal who directed his function was an *ah-páws-taw-laws*, in Greek, and a *shah-leé-ahk*, in Hebrew.

Rabbis have described some of the duties of the apostle to the synagogue. He was a representative of the congregation. One of his duties was to represent the congregation to God in prayer. If, for example, while reciting the *teh-fee-láh* (a prayer), he should fall into error, this would be a bad omen not only for him, but also for the whole congregation that he represented (mBer 5:5). He was obligated by his office to say the *teh-fee-láh* every day (mRH 4:9). Some of his other duties were probably similar to those required of the apostles to the seven churches in Asia Minor. These messengers were local officials, each of whom represented one congregation. The **officers** in charge of the seven churches addressed by John of Patmos evidently functioned in a similar way to the churches as the Jewish apostles did to the Jewish synagogues. Other scholars have not quite reached this conclusion.

Peake, for example, thought all references in the Book of Revelation to **angels** must mean heavenly **angels**. Therefore **the angels** of the churches must all be heavenly **angels** as well, although Peake admitted that there was a problem with the situation in which Christ in heaven addressed **an angel** in heaven through John and the churches on earth. Peake also thought it was strange that John would scold a heavenly **angel,** as he did the messenger in Rev 2:20.[1] Peake's problem, like those of many others, was in assuming that **angel** could mean only heavenly **angel.** This was a mistake. The word **angel** was a secular term, quite apart from its theological usage. Although there are many reports of heavenly **angelic** activity in the Book of Revelation, the **angel** who brought the prophecy to John and the **angels** of the churches were evidently all human.

Schüssler-Fiorenza followed the same basic logic as Peake, concluding that the **officers** of the seven churches were patron **angels** of the church rather than bishops or other human leaders.[2] Düsterdieck argued that churches could have individual guardian **angels** just as believers could. Loisy, however, argued that the angel was the leader or chief of all the churches.[3] Hemer doubted that a human writer would write to supernatural beings, holding them guilty for the faults of the churches. His proposal, however, that the **angels** were personifications of the churches also seems unreasonable.[4] He failed to demonstrate any case in the FT or later Jewish or Christian literature where **angels** personified churches or congregations. Nor did he justify his claim that symbols were as fluid as he claimed.

Aune remained non-committal. He analyzed the views of other scholars extensively and argued that none of the solutions was without problems.[5] He acknowledged that the messages were addressed to singular people in each case, but he thought that the letters were intended to be kept as a group and all of them to be read to all of the churches, because the letters conclude, encouraging the **one who has an ear to hear** to **listen to what the spirit says to the churches** (Rev 2:7, 11, 16, 29; 3:6, 12, 21).[6] That is possible, but it is not absolutely clear. Even that message was to the **one** who had an ear to hear. The letters were not addressed, as some of Paul's letters, "To those who are in Corinth" (1Cor 1:2), "To the churches of Galatia" (Gal 1:2), "To those who are in Phillipi, together with the bishops and deacons" (Phillip 1:1), or to the Colossians with instructions that the letter be read and shared with others (Col 4:16-17). That was not the case in any of these seven letters. They were addressed to **the officers** of the churches. John of Patmos assumed that his instructions to the leaders would effect the character of the churches, but he did not address the letters to the churches, themselves. He may or may not have intended to have the letters read to the churches. Some of the things he said seemed rather personal and insulting—not for general publication. Even when he wrote in the plural, he apparently referred to all of the officers of the seven churches.

The narrative of the letter to **the officer** at **Ephesus** was patterned after the visions of Zech 4, in which a messenger (*mah-lahk,* מלאך) brought a message to

---

[1] A. S. Peake, *The Revelation of John* (London: Holborn, 1919), pp. 228-229.
[2] E. Schüssler-Fiorenza, *The Book of Revelation: Justice and Judgment* (Philadelphia: Fortress Press, c1985), pp. 52-53.
[3] A. Loisy, *L'Apocalypse de Jean* (Paris: Emile Nourry, 1923), p. 87.
[4] F. Düsterdieck, *Critical and Exegetical Handbook to the Revelation of John*, tr. H. E. Jacobs (Winona Lake: Alpha Publications, 1884), p. 53. C. J. Hemer, S*even Churches*, p. 33.
[5] D. Aune, *Revelation 1-5* (Dallas: Word Books, Publisher, c1997), p. 110.
[6] Aune, *Revelation 1-5,* p. 119.

Zechariah. He told Zechariah what political events would happen, and he said that when they began to fall into place then Zechariah would know that **Yehowah of armies has sent me** (Zech 4:9). If Zechariah had thought he had been conversing with a heavenly angel it would not have been necessary for that messenger to remind Zechariah of the approved way by which he could check the messenger's qualifications and believe that he had been given good advice.

Future events determine whether the messenger was a valid prophet of the Lord or not—not whether or not he was a heavenly being. This advice followed the directions of Deut 18:22 for determining whether or not to trust those who profess to be prophets. According to the targum, when Ruth returned to Naomi with six measures of wheat from Boaz, Naomi told her to wait to see what "the decree of heaven" was over the matter (TargRuth 3:18). The sure way to find out what God's will was in any situation was to wait and see afterward what had been predestined. Ruth found out what God had decreed when she learned how successful Boaz had been in negotiating with the nearest in kin to Naomi (Ruth 4:1-12). All of this suggests that the messenger that came to Zechariah was also a human being, and John of Patmos patterned his argument to **the officers** of the church on that of Zechariah.

Of the church in Ephesus. **Ephesus** was the largest commercial center and the most important city in Asia Minor (modern Turkey) and the third largest city in the Roman Empire. Its population is estimated to have been between 250,000 and 500,000. The city was located at the mouth of the Cayster River and on a gulf of the Aegean Sea. It was part of the kingdom which King Attalus III of Pergamum gave to Rome in 133 BIA.[1] Three great trade routes converged at this city. From the gulf to the city was a beautiful stone street, 35 feet wide, lined with marble columns on both sides. This street led directly to the large theater that would seat 25,000 people at once. Surrounding streets are still lined with statues. A photograph of that theater, together with the road from the harbor appears between chapters stwelve and thirteen.

Pliny the Elder (NH 36:95 ff.) said the Temple to Artemis was 425 feet long, 220 feet wide, and 60 feet high. It included 127 pillars of Parian marble, 36 of which were overlaid with gold and jewels. It was considered one of the seven wonders of the ancient world. Among the excavated ruins of this city exist today a large stadium, a large public rest room, buildings, streets, statues, and stone inscriptions.[2]

As in most other parts of the Roman Empire, there were Jews in **Ephesus**, with enough political power to demand special attention from the Syrian governor, Dolabella, who in 43 BIA issued a decree exempting Jews from military service, because their Sabbath laws prevented them from working on that day (Ant 14:225-28). Although the decree was sent to the Jews of **Ephesus** it applied to all Jews in Asia

---

[1] BIA (Before the International Age) is the politically correct abbreviation used instead of the exclusive abbreviations BC (Before the Christian era) and BCE (Before the common era Lev 10:10).

[2] For pictures and a map of the ruins of Ephesus see D. Cole, "Corinth & Ephesus," *BR* 6 (Dec.1988):20-30.

Minor (Ant 14:230). In another Roman decree to the Jews **of Ephesus** Jews were permitted to observe all of their Sabbath practices without interference (Ant 14:262). It is not surprising that the early Christian church had established a community there, but John's attitude toward **the officer** of that church was not all approving.

The One who holds the seven stars. This is part of a preamble, composed as if it were the introduction to a contract or treaty. **The One who holds the seven stars** in his right hand, of course, is God. His agent or apostle would have been one of his messiahs. He would have had two: One was the king, and the other, the high priest. Both were anointed. When only one messiah is mentioned it is almost always the king. Zechariah said the messiahs were King Zerubbabel and Joshua, the high priest. (Zech 3:8; 4:3-14). **The seven stars** were identified as **the officers** of the seven churches, meaning that the Lord held all of the leaders of **the seven** churches in his hand. **The lamp stands are the seven churches** (Rev 1:16, 20).

The lamp stands. Goodenough argued that the seven branched **lamp stand** represented **the tree of life** in Judaism.[1] When the prophet Ahijah met Jeroboam on the road, he prophesied the secession of North Israel from Judah and Benjamin. He promised that the ten northern tribes would be taken from Solomon, but with reference to David's son, he said, **But to his son I will give one tribe, so that there will be a lamp for David my servant all the days before me in Jerusalem** (1Kings 11:29-36). With the **lamp** was the southern kingdom, with its authority and rule of one of the sons of David in Jerusalem. If David's son ever stopped ruling from Jerusalem, then the **lamp** of David would be extinguished.

Zechariah pictured the **seven lamp stands.** These did not symbolize either the authority of the king or seven of the twelve tribes, but rather **the seven eyes of Yehowah** (Zech 4:10). The **seven eyes** were assigned the task of scouting over all the land. Since this is in preparation to the recovery of the Promised Land, these might have been spies. They were probably assigned the task of surveying the land and reporting the situation. Like Zechariah, John of Patmos spoke of **seven lamp stands**. He did not say that these were also **the eyes of Yehowah.** Rather he said they were **the seven churches** (Rev 1:20). Is it possible that he implied that the churches were supposed to act as information gathering agents?[2] A later Jewish author related the **tree of life** with several associated expressions:

---

[1] E. Goodenough, "The Menorah among Jews of the Roman World," *HUCA* 23 (1950-51): 451-52.
[2] E. Schüssler-Fiorenza, *Justice*, p. 145, said these angels could not be bishops since Revelation does not mention bishops anywhere. That is not a necessary requirement for authenticity, but these officials may or may not have been bishops. They may have qualified as the legal agents of the churches, regardless of the titles given.

It is for you that Paradise is opened, the tree of life is planted; the future time is prepared; abundance is supplied; the city is constructed; and rest is approved (4Ezra 8:52).

When any one of these conditions exist they all do. They describe the ideal conditions that will exist on the Promised Land, around the city of Zion in the age to come.

TEXT

^{2}I know your works, your labor, and your endurance. Also that you (singular) are not able to tolerate evil men. You have tested those who call themselves apostles but are not, and you have found them false. ^{3}You have patience, and you have carried all afflictions because of my name; and you have not become exhausted. ^{4}Nonetheless, I have against you [the complaint] that you have left your first love. ^{5}Remember then, [the position] from which you have fallen, repent, and do the first works. If you do not repent, I will come and move your lamp stand from its place.

Revelation

^{6}Nevertheless you also have this [merit]: you **hate** the works of the Nicolaitans, which **I** also **hate**. ^{7}He who has an ear, let him hear what the spirit says to the churches. To the one who conquers I will give him [permission] to eat

of the tree of life which is in

the paradise of God."

First Testament

$^{Ps\ 139:21\text{-}2}$Do I not **hate** them that **hate** you, Lord?. . . **I hate** them with perfect hatred; I count them as my enemies.

$^{Gen\ 3:22\text{-}24}$The Lord God said, "Look! The man has become like one of us, to know good and evil. Now [let us act] lest he put out his hand and take also **of the tree of life** and eat and live for the age. So Yehowah God sent him from **the garden (Paradise)** of Eden" (see also Gen 2:9).

COMMENTARY

Your labor, and your endurance. This is part of a legal prologue. The message is written in the singular. It is consistent with the lead sentence. The message is directed to **the officer**, the apostle of the church, and not to the church itself. The legal agent or apostle of the church, of course, was the leader in charge of the church, so the fault of the church members was the fault of its agent, and vice versa. The agent is the one being recognized, scolded and praised, but it reflects on the entire corporation, the church.

Those who call themselves apostles. **The officer** of the church was **the officer** who had the authority to determine who would and who would not qualify as guests of the community. This was an important responsibility for the chief **officer** of the church. Some leaders abused this authority with the result that Christian missionaries were refused hospitality, even though they qualified (3John 9-10). Others may have admitted false apostles without carefully testing them.

Those who called themselves apostles were supposedly important Christian leaders. They should have been trusted when they traveled to different communities, but some were frauds. **The officer** in charge at Ephesus was commended, because he did not take things like that for granted. He **tested** them.

The basis for **testing** others and judging them adversely was not for their morally or ethically bad behavior, as Hailey thought.[1] It was, rather, a matter of religious belief and doctrine. They did not observe the proper religious practices. They did not observe the same dietary laws; they did not keep their clothing undefiled. They did not observe the same purity laws. John was obviously a very exclusive, orthodox person. Those **apostles** who did not precisely fit his doctrine were considered "false" or only those who **call themselves apostles**. The **apostle** Paul would probably have fit into this category, but the reference was apparently to more than one **apostle**. **Those who called themselves apostles** but were not were not the Judaizers whom Paul opposed, but the anti-legalists who were like Paul.[2]

The **apostles** who came to the door of the Ephesian **officer** were none of the original twelve but rather later sub-**apostles**. These traveling missionaries were probably commissioned **officers** sent out from some sect as their legal agents or **apostles**. They were tested for orthodoxy before they were admitted. Sectarians had ways of interrogating people to discover whether or not they were "trustworthy" (*neh-eh-máhn,* נאמן or *áhx-ee-aws,* ἄξιος). Hosting churches had to learn whether or not the guests who appeared at their door observed all of the dietary and purity rules required of guests before admitting them into their homes. If a person entered a city where he knew no one, he might ask anyone, "Who is there here that is trustworthy? Who here pays tithes?" If that person said he was himself trustworthy, he should not be believed, but if he pointed to someone else, he might be believed (mDemai 4:6). In other ways such as this an orthodox or observant Jew or Christian might employ checks to test the care with which a stranger observed the proper dietary, tithing, and purity rules.

According to Matthew, when Jesus sent out the **apostles,** he directed them, when they came to a certain town or village, first to find out who in it was **worthy**, and there to stay (Matt 10:11). Although the exact interrogation is not recorded, it is clear that traveling Jews and Christians, as well as prospective hosts and hostesses,

---

[1] H. M. Hailey, *Revelation: Introduction and Commentary* (Grand Rapids: Baker's Book House, c1979), p. 121.
[2] So also Loisy, *L'Apocalypse*, p. 89.

had ways of **testing** one another for orthodoxy. The **officer** at **Ephesus** was careful about this, and John approved of his official leadership in this area.[1]

Those who held religious ideas different from the sect represented were said to be of a different spirit. They observed different laws. The word "spirit" in the Bible often refers to something legal. The author of First John warned Christians not to believe every spirit. Just because something was legally approved by some sect did not mean it was valid. Those who did not confess that Jesus was of God had the spirit of the antichrist and were false prophets (1John 4:1-3). Some early Christians were counseled to **test** those who said they had the spirit to see if they behaved like the Lord. If they did not, Christians were to consider them false (Didache 11:8). Without saying how it should be done Hermas warned that those who profess to have the spirit should be **tested** and the **empty** ones should not be entertained (Herm. *Mand.* 11:16-17). The **officer** at Ephesus also had methods of **testing** which John approved. This enabled Ephesians to exclude liberal Christians who were called "evil" and "false **apostles**." The exclusive hospitality practices of early Jews and Christians make hospitality a necessity. Early Jewish Christians observed dietary and cleanliness laws just as carefully as orthodox Jews did.

If people were forbidden to touch any food that was not approved by their own sect, they could not travel and buy food from ordinary market places. They had to depend on the hospitality of members of their own sect in various places. The author of Third John was very much upset by a certain Diotrephes who not only did not provide hospitality for traveling Christians, himself, but he also prohibited others from providing it (3John 10). The author reminded that community that it was good to render service to the brothers and send them on their way in God's service. Traveling church members needed Christian support because they could accept nothing from the heathen (3John 5-8). The other side of this coin is that many took advantage of free hospitality and exploited the generosity of others.

The third group consisted of genuine prophets who were not as conservative as the prospective hosts. These were the kind that called at **Ephesus** and were turned away. An **apostle** was not considered trustworthy whose authority had not been approved by the principal who sent him. Many early Christians said this could apply only to those twelve whom Jesus had appointed while he was alive. They did not accept Paul or anyone from his persuasion. John was probably of this opinion.

You have carried all afflictions. John also praised the **officer** at Ephesus for his ability to endure whatever hardship and inconvenience had been necessary because of his association with John. Being identified with John obviously had not made it easier for him in his community. Whatever it was that made the government think John should be exiled from normal civilization evidently provided a bad reputation for his friends and fellow Christians. The **officer** at Ephesus, however, had not become exhausted by this difficulty.

---

[1] See Buchanan, "Essenes," *The International Standard Bible Encyclopedia* (Grand Rapids: William B. Eerdmans Publishing Co., c1982) II, pp. 147-55.

You have left your first love. This turn in the discussion begins with *Nonetheless, I have against you [the complaint]*. The word rendered **nonetheless** is *ahl-láh* (ἀλλά). This is a strong, adversative conjunction, often rendered "but." The term occurs only 13 times in the entire Book of Revelation, eight of which occur in Rev 2-3. In the prophecy this term is seldom used. Instead the softer *kai* (καί), which means "and," "but," "both . . . and." In Jewish documents it reflects the Hebrew *waw* (ו) which has basically the same meanings. In typical Semitical form, nearly 74% of all 337 sentences in Revelation begin with *kai*. Only 20.5% of the 44 sentences in Rev 2-3 begin with *kai*. This suggests that the letters are not as Semitic as the rest of the Book of Revelation.

Along with all of his praise, the word **nonetheless** comes as a surprise to note that John accused this **official** of **leaving** his **first love.** This was serious enough that John warned him to repent and stop his back sliding or John would remove his **lamp stand** from its place. This means **the officer** would lose his official position as an authorized agent of the Lord's **eyes** (i.e., his spies). This might not mean he would be excommunicated from the order or that the church corporation would be punished. He had obviously been a faithful leader, as John had observed. This probably was not a threat to the entire church, as Aune suggested, "to obliterate the Ephesian congregation as an empirical Christian community."[1] Whatever the details of the threat involved it was directed to **the officer** himself.

The tree of life. The expression **tree of life** was not unique to Jewish or Israelite culture. Eliade said in the pagan world the **tree of life** was a symbol of **life** and also of the center of the world.[2]

In the sermon on Deut 6:4-9; 11:18-22, the author of Prov 2-7 said Wisdom was a **tree of life** (Prov 3:18). Wisdom, according to the Proverbial author, was closely associated with discipline (Prov 3:11), **paths of uprightness** (Prov 4:11), **life** (Prov 4:13, 22), **water from your own cistern** (Prov 5:15), and **the wife of your youth** (Prov 5:18). This sermon (Proverbs 2-7) was a very orthodox one, urging, in mythical language, Jews to cleave to their early Jewish teaching and not become involved with the lures of the gentiles (the wicked woman).

In Proverbs the author related the **tree of life** to the wife of youth, meaning that the one who was wise, well-disciplined, studied the Torah faithfully, and kept its admonitions would have **the tree of life**.[3] In order to understand all of these images it is necessary to know that the **tree of life** was an item in the Garden of Eden story that was basic to the meaning of the story, and the **wife of your youth** is from a marriage imagery. The reference to the marriage situation deals with the contract the Lord made with his people. It was a marriage contract in which God was the groom,

---

[1] Aune, *Revelation 1-5*, p. 147.
[2] M. Eliade, *Patterns in Comparative Religion* (New York: World Publishers, 1963), pp. 266-67, 283-90.
[3] See Buchanan, "Midrashim Pre-Tannaïtes," *RB* 72 (1965):227-39.

and the people, a legal corporation, constituted the bride. To have left the wife of his youth would have been to have broken the contract between God and his people.

New members of the church were those who recently became parties to this marriage contract. Those who had the **tree of life** would be allowed to continue in the exclusive community of orthodox Christians. The same is true also of those who keep the contract they have made with the Lord. **Life** here is a legal term that refers to existence within accepted terms of the corporation contract. The author was using these terms that have known religious meanings to those who are trained in the religious discipline of the faithful as if they were code terms. Those who understand the code know the message.

For John, the **first love** which the Ephesian **officer** had left may have had the same meaning as the Proverbial **wife of your youth**. He had fallen away from his religious teachings and had taken up some of the customs of the gentiles. This was not allowed. Even though **the officer** at Ephesus was in many ways as segregationistic as John, hated the liberal Christians as John did, refused to show tolerance toward other sects, if that **officer** started accepting practices of the gentiles, he would be terminated in his office. This kind of behavior could not be endured.

Remember, then, [the position]. This is part of a legal stipulation, similar to that normally used in a contract or treaty.

Repentance is a basic Jewish and Christian doctrine. It was a necessary part of The Day of Atonement ritual. The Day of Atonement is a festival day for Jews still today. It happens in the Autumn, usually in October. On that day those believers who fulfilled the proper requirements would obtain forgiveness from the Lord. If all believers repented and obtained forgiveness, there would no longer be any crime held against believers and they would be restored to the Promised Land. There were three necessary parts to a successful Day of Atonement:

1) The required sacrifice had to be brought to the temple; paying off all debts for earlier criminal activity.
2) all believers were required, before bringing this sacrifice, to obtain pardon from and reconciliation with all those believers whom they had injured prior to that day. This meant they must repent and make whatever amends were required.
3) God would also pardon. Rabbis said that the land would be restored to Jews if all Israel would repent for just one day. That day, of course, would be the Day of Atonement.

One rabbi taught his students to repent the day before they died. The students then asked how they could know when that day was. He answered that they could not; therefore they must repent every day. Jesus told his disciples that they must forgive offenders seven times a day if necessary. If, by oversight, they should come to the temple on the Day of Atonement and there remember some fellow believer whom they had offended, they must first go back and find that person, make the necessary amends for reconciliation, and then come with their crime offering to the temple

(Matt 5:23-24). The Day of Atonement was a special time for **remembering**. John asked the **officer** at Ephesus to **remember** what he had once been. That was necessary before he could begin to consider restoration. Then he would have to **remember** all those whom he had offended, before he could repent and be restored. Repentance and forgiveness are basic teachings and exhortations found in many places in the NT and in rabbinic literature.[1] John's exhortation to **the officer** at Ephesus is basic Christian doctrine.

The word, normally translated "sin" in popular use is such a general term that it is not very descriptive. For example a mischievous little boy might be called a "little sinner," but he would not merit any kind of legal punishment. The word in the Scripture, however, that is normally rendered "sin" in English, is not so innocent. The offense used in Scripture is always punishable by the court and should be called a "crime." The offender, then, is not a "sinner" but a criminal.

Forgiveness and redemption are financial terms. A person who borrows money and then repays it, redeems the note and has the debt cancelled. A person who cannot pay the debt, might still have the debt forgiven and the debt cancelled. A person who commits a crime can be either punished or pardoned. These are court terms. Because crimes are often punished by fines, an unpaid fine can also be a debt and need forgiveness just as the criminal needs pardoning. An unpaid debt for a crime is called iniquity. These expressions are all used in relationship to the Day of Atonement.

I will come and move your lamp. This threat is part of a curse, much like the curses used in contracts and treaties. This obviously has a symbolic meaning, but it is not clear what the meaning is. The **lamp** apparently had some legal and authoritarian significance. It may have been the symbol that accepted an **officer** into some official position. If it was removed, that may have meant that **the officer** was relieved of his **official** duties and status. The **lamp** of David still shone as long as there was someone from David's family sitting on the throne in Jerusalem. Removing the **lamp** probably did not mean his excommunication, it would not have had to be final. There was an opportunity for repentance. If **the officer** at Ephesus repented and returned to his isolationistic ghetto patterns, then he might eat of the tree of life (Rev 2:7). This meant he would be restored to intercommunion with other orthodox churches.

You hate the works of the Nicolaitans. These words constitute part of the prologue begun in Rev 2:1. John also praised **the officer** for hating the **Nicolaitans**, as John himself did. **Hating the Nicolaitans** was considered a virtue. Among sectarians love and **hatred** were prescribed attitudes with understood accompanying actions. Those who belonged to the sect by virtue of the fact that they had entered the contract were obligated to love one another (1QS 1:10. They were also under contract to **hate** all

---

[1] See further Buchanan, *The Consequences of the Covenant* (Leiden: E. J. Brill, 1970), pp. 222-37; *Jesus: the King and his Kingdom* (Macon: Mercer U. Press, c1984), pp. 223-36.

the sons of darkness or the men of the pit (1QS 9:21-22). Those who were under contract to love one another were required to provide for the needs of one another as the contract demanded. The attitude of those whom the members accepted was one of love; the attitude toward all of the rest was one of rejection, which was **hatred**. It was assumed that God loved and **hated** exactly the ones the members loved and hated. (1QS 4:1). In this context, if John **hated the works of the Nicolaitans** then God must **hate** them as well, and the addressees were also expected to **hate** them.

Jews and Christians supposedly teach only love, but literary evidence does not bear out this claim. The Lord reportedly **hated** all the things Canaanites did for their gods (Deut 12:31; 16:22), and he **hated** all evil doers (Ps 5:5). One of the Psalmists **hated** all of his enemies who he claimed also **hated** the Lord (Ps 139:21). The community that followed the Rule of the Community was told how to behave in relationship to the "men of the pit," obviously its enemies. Members were obligated to **hate** them with **the hatred** of the age (*sehn-áht oh-láhm*, שנאת עולם), but to tolerate them temporarily, keeping their hatred secret while maintaining their zeal. Members of this orthodox community should even submit to the "men of the pit," the way a slave submits to a master, but wait until the Day of Vengeance when the Lord would repay them (1QS 9:21-26). This is probably the attitude understood by those willing to turn the other cheek and walk the second mile (Matt 6:39-41). John's teaching about Christians' desirable attitude towards outsiders was not unique.

Zahn thought the name, **Nicolaitans**, may have been a loan word taken from two Hebrew words. *Nico* would come from the Hebrew *bah-láh* (בלע), to swallow, destroy, conquer and *laus* would come from the Greek *lah-áws* (λαός) which equals the Hebrew *ahm* (עם), people. Therefore Nicolaus would mean about the same as Balaam (*bah-láhm*, בלעם), a destroyer of the people.[1] In Rev 2:14-15, the teachings of Balaam seem to be the same or at least very similar to the teachings of the **Nicolaitans**. John criticized the Christians at Pergamum for holding to the teachings of both. That supports Zahn's interesting theory, but that does not mean the name, **Nicolaitans**, actually had the suggested etymological origin.

The name, **Nicolaitans**, may have come from the name Nicolaus which had a different origin. The pejorative title, "destroyer of the people," could have been applied to it by its enemies who provided this etymological insult. Jews and Christians have been resourceful in relating insults to names of their enemies. One rabbinic saying is, "As his name, so is he" (*kuh sheh-móh, kayn hoo*, כשמו כן הוא). **The Nicolaitans**, like the ones called "evil" and "false apostles," were evidently also liberal Christians, in John's judgment. Irenaeus said they were willing to eat "food offered to idols" i.e., food not sold at the *kah-sháyr* (כשר) meat market. (*AdvHaer* 1:26, 3; cf. 3:11,.1). Victorinus of Patau (*Commentary* 2:6) said the **Nicolaitans** were members of a heresy named after the elder, Nicolaus. They performed magical, exorcistic rites over food sold in ordinary meat markets. These rites were designed to cast out demons and evil spirits from food that did not meet the dietary requirements

---

[1] T. Zahn, *Die Offenbarung des Johannes* (Leipzig: A.Deichert, 1924), p. 268.

of the Torah and then declared it *kah-sháyr*, permitted for eating. They also held that anyone who committed fornication was defiled for only eight days, after which that person might receive absolution, just as those who had been defiled by leprosy or corpse uncleanness.

Nevertheless, **Nicolaitans** were not as liberal as Paulinists.[1] Orthodox Christians and Jews, like John, would not have allowed any kind of modification of orthodox practices. Therefore they would not allow their congregations to associate with people who did. Loving one's neighbor, in their judgment, did not extend to such heretics as this. Eusebius said the **Nicolaitans** did not last very long (*HE* 3:29, 1). Smith compared the church fathers with Acts 6:5 and said they clearly identified the Nicolas of Acts with the Nicolaitans of Revelation. Hyppolytus, *Deh reh-soo-rehk-tee-oh-neh* (*Merke GCS* 1:1 p. 251) said the libertinism of Nicolaitans was their belief that the resurrection occurred at baptism.[2] Since baptism was a legal liturgy by which a person was born again into a new community or existence, having a new identity, a new citizenship, or a new religion, **Nicolations** thought of resurrection of the body as the legal birth of a corporation and resurrection of the individual as being born again as new creations.

Some scholars, such as Bousset and Caird, thought the **Nicolaitans** were Paulinists, for whom "fornication" was not sexual but only metaphorical.[3] Others, like Schüssler-Fiorenza, thought they were libertine gnostics, like the enthusiasts in Corinth, and that John of Patmos, like Paul, was an anti-gnostic.[4] If **Nicolaitans** were not Paulinists, they were at least more liberal than orthodox Jews and Christians. Being "anti-gnostic" meant being a member of a different sect from yours. I.e., it had a different "gnosis" from yours. Probably all Jews and Christian sects had secret material not told to those outside the sect. It was called "gnosis," "*dah-áht*," "mysteries of the Kingdom of heaven," or "Mysteries of the Kingdom of God."

He who has an ear, let him hear. This is a call for attention to witnesses, similar to that of a treaty or contract. These exhortations are frequent in redemption literature. The ones who have ears to hear are the ones who understand the code. These are those who know FT and Jewish and Christian tradition. Therefore they understand the real meaning of the message disguised. The exhortation was to remind certain listeners that there was a hidden message here for them.

---

[1] W. Bauer, *Die Evangelien II Johannes* (Tübingen: J. C. B. Mohr, 1912), p. 368, thought the attacks against the Nicolaitans and the followers of Jezebel were really attacks against Paul.

[2] M. Smith, *Clement of Alexandria and the Secret Gospel of Mark* (Cambridge: Harvard U. Press, 1973), p.262.

[3] W. Bousset, *Die Jüdische Apokalyptik* (Berlin: Reuther & Riecharad, 1903), p. 238; G. B. Caird, *A Commentary on the Revelation of St. John the Divine* (London: Black, c1966), pp. 39-44. Others of this view were F.C. Baur, *Vorlesungen über neutestamentliche Theologie* (Leipzig: Darmstadt, 1864), pp. 207-30; A. Hilgenfeld, "Die Christus-Leute in Korinth und die Nikolaiten," *ZWT* 15 (1872):220-26.

[4] E. Schüssler-Fiorenza, "Apocalyptic and Gnosis in the Book of Revelation and in Paul," *JBL* 92 (1973):570, 574, 581.

To eat of the tree of life. The term **life** in Jewish and Christian thought means more than eating, breathing, and taking up space. Jesus said the dead should bury the dead, by which he did not mean corpses should bury corpses. Religious **life** was **life** within the community that had made a contract with the Lord. People were baptized into **life** when they joined some Jewish or Christian order. One new convert had been circumcised by the Holy Spirit and became drunk with the water of **life** that does not die (OdeSol 11:2, 7). Practically that meant that he had completed a legal ceremony which admitted him as a full member of the church. It was a different ceremony from the Jewish ceremony of circumcision, but it was just as effective, legally. It also meant that he had been baptized into the community where **life** was possible. Jews and Christians were expelled when they had committed crimes "unto death"—which means that they committed the kinds of crimes which removed them from the community where **life** was possible (1John 5:16). Some of these communities of life were monastic, and it is against that background of thought that the Garden of Eden drama was probably formed. **Eating of the tree of life** meant that they were permitted to **eat** at the same table as other "worthy," orthodox church members. They could give and receive hospitality with the orthodox.

In one of Enoch's visions he saw a flaming mountain and a fragrant **tree.** When Enoch asked the angel Michael what these were, Michael responded that the mountain was the place where the Lord's throne of glory would be; i.e., Zion. As for the **tree,** no human being could touch it until the judgment day. At that time it would be planted near the temple, and its fruit would be for the elect and the righteous (1Enoch 25:1-5). This was probably based on Ezek 47 which pictured trees in the Kidron Valley that produced fruit every month of the year in the new age. It was because of this that Jesus looked for figs in the Kidron Valley out of normal season, to learn if the new age had arrived.

To the one who conquers. The word **conquer** was an important word for John. He used it seven times (Rev 2:7, 11, 17, 26; 3:5, 12, 21) in two chapters. He may have been inspired by its use in the prophecy, where it was used twice (Rev 5:5; 21:7). In every instance a reward was promised to the one who **conquered.**

The Paradise of God. A **Paradise** is a garden or a park. **The Paradise of God** was part of one of the blessings or promises associated with a contract or treaty made between God and his people. In an early biblical drama, there were two characters. Adam and Eve, that were innocently happy in the Lord's **Paradise** or court yard (Gen 2:4-3:24). They were forbidden only to eat of **the tree** of the knowledge of good and evil. If they ate of this fruit, they were warned, they would surely die. So, they ate of it, and they did not die physically, but they were no longer celibate, so they were expelled from the garden. Adam was forced to work for a living, and Eve gave birth to children.[1]

---

[1] See Buchanan, *Consequences*, pp. 173-74.

This drama was evidently composed to illustrate a teaching about sexual behavior. **The Paradise of God** would have to be a place where only monks could live. They were the ones who did not **eat** the forbidden fruit. The term **conquer** was often used to describe the victory initiates gained when they overcame their passions and were able to endure the ascetic practices required of the monastery. John may have addressed such a group of monks at **Ephesus.** He urged them to hold fast, to **conquer,** so that they might eat of **the tree of life** in **the Paradise of God** (Gen 2:9; 3:23-24).[1] That meant that they could qualify for the monastery, eating at the holy table where only those who were ritually purified could participate. That which Jews of NT times expected to take place at the introduction of the new age was not the normal but the miraculous.

Another early seer envisioned himself being taken to the Lord's Paradise where fruit trees would be flourishing, bearing fruits, with their roots from an immortal land [probably Palestine]. These fruits were watered by the river of gladness [probably the stream that flows from the spring of Siloam in the Kidron Valley], and the area around was the land of life of the age [to come] (OdeSol 11:15-16). This is the same stream of which the psalmist said, **There is a river whose streams make glad the city of God, the holy dwelling place of the Most High** (Ps 46:5). That is the stream that flows out from the temple at Zion, through the Wady Qumran, and on into the Dead Sea, where it would sweeten the bitter waters in the age to come (Ezek 47). Among Saadia Gaon's proofs that salvation was destined to come to Israel was the promise given in Ezek 47:1-12. Whenever that prophecy would be fulfilled, then the land would be restored and salvation would take place.[2] This was also part of the Scripture expected to be fulfilled at the national redemption according to the "Book of Zerubbabel."[3] Jesus was also checking the fig tree in the Kidron Valley to learn whether or not the new age had begun. If it had there would be ripe figs every month of the year in the Kidron Valley. It would not be necessary to wait for the right season. Saadia Gaon, like Jesus, thought the clue for the new age could be found in the fulfillment of Ezekiel's prophecy.[4]

---

[1] Schüssler-Fiorenza, *Justice*, p. 116, said, "The phrase 'to eat food sacrificed to idols' refers to food which had already been consecrated to an idol as well as to participation in pagan feasts. Likewise *porneusai* (the practice of immorality) should be understood in a literal sense as well as in a metaphorical sense, namely, in reference to syncretistic tendencies and idolatry" (p. 116).
[2] Buchanan, *Jewish Messianic Movements* (Eugene, Oregon: Wipf and Stock Publishers, 2003), p. 58.
[3] Buchanan, *Jewish Messianic Movements*, p. 380.
[4] Buchanan, "Withering Fig Trees and Progression in Midrash," C. A. Evans and W. R. Stegner (eds.), *The Gospels and the Scriptures of Israel* (Sheffield: Sheffield Academic Press Ltd, c1994), pp. 249-69.

TEXT

Revelation

⁸To the officer of the church of Smyrna, write:
Thus said

**the first
and the last** who was dead and came to life. "⁹I know your tribulation and poverty, but you(s.) are rich, and [I also know] the blasphemy from those who call themselves Jews but are not, but are the synagogue of Satan.
¹⁰**Have no fear** of the things you are about to suffer. Look! The devil is about to throw some of you into prison

so that you may be **tested**. You will also have tribulation **for ten days**. [Be] faithful until death, and I shall give you the crown of life. ¹¹He who has an ear let him hear what the spirit says to the churches. He who conquers will not be judged guilty of the second death."

First Testament

Isa 44:6; see 48:12 **Thus says** Yehowah, king of Israel and its redeemer, Yehowah of armies, "I am **the first and** I am **the last**. Except for me, there is no god."

Dan 10:12 Then he said to me, "**Do not be afraid**, Daniel, for from the first day that you gave your heart to understand and to humble yourself before God, your words have been heard."

Dan 1:11-12, 14 Then Daniel said to the manager, . . . "**Test** your servants **for ten days**. Let us be given vegetables to eat and water to drink" . . . and he **tested** them for **ten days**.

COMMENTARY

To the officer of the church of Smyrna. **Smyrna** is today called Izmir, Turkey. It was a large city about 40 miles north of Ephesus on the gulf into which the Hermus river flowed. **Ephesus** and **Smyrna** were bitter rivals (Dio Chrysostom *Or* 34:48). Like **Ephesus** it was a seaport city. Its population has been estimated at 100,000. It was part of the Ionian league. It had many temples and became a center for science and medicine (Strabo 12:8, 20; Tacitus, *Annals* 3:63). **Smyrna** was a faithful ally of the Roman Empire before Rome had expanded its territory into Asia Minor, and Asia Minor was under the control of the Seleucids. Rome took control of this area more than 250 years before John wrote this message. Polycarp was bishop at Smyrna before he was burned at stake in IA 155 (*HE* 4:15, 1).

The first and the last. These words are part of a legal preamble. The message of John to the church at **Smyrna** was attributed to the Lord, whom Second Isaiah related to **the first** redemption from Egypt and **the last** redemption from Babylon.

I know your tribulation. This formula is part of the prologue to a treaty. The God who had delivered Jews from the Babylonians and Greeks would also deliver the Christians from the Romans. God's agent who gave John the message was identified with the Lord as the one who died and lived, evidently Jesus who was crucified and raised from the dead. This identity of Jesus, the Messiah, with God was probably legal identity and not physical identity. This meant Jesus acted as one who had divine authority to speak and act in God's behalf, in his name, and at his responsibility. In the name of Yehowah and his agent, the Messiah Jesus, John comforted the **officer** of the church at **Smyrna,** because he recognized his hardship and apparent economic problems, but, from another standard of values, John was convinced that **the officer** was rich! The wealth about which John spoke constituted riches in the treasury of merits. The poverty which **the officer** suffered may have been economic. He may have been a faithful monk who had given up all of his wealth to join a monastery. If that were the case the church at Smyrna might have been a monastery, but that is not a necessary conclusion. Smyrna was a prosperous city, but the church there may not have been, and it may not have provided well for its clergy leader.

Those who call themselves Jews. There are many[1] like Schüssler-Fiorenza who claim that the people insulted here were **Jews.** Although these insults were directed against **Jews,** in her opinion, they should not be considered anti-semitic![2] Caird also thought that those who attended the **synagogue of Satan** were **Jews**.[3] The insults were obviously written by one **Jew** against certain other **Jews.** There has never been perfect harmony among different sects of Jews or different sects of Christians. Insults among the elect are normal.

If this had been written *against Jews* by non-**Jews** the author would not have said they were not really **Jews**. He would have thought being **Jews** was bad and he would have accused them of being nothing but **Jews.** The author of this narrative, namely John of Patmos, thought being a **Jew** was good. He considered himself one, as did most Christians of the first and early second centuries. Instead of being members of the **synagogue** of God, as they professed, these people were really the **synagogue of Satan.** This is the kind of an attack an orthodox makes against people who are liberal. Orthodox **Jews** have traditionally thought of themselves as true

---

[1] So Hailey, *Revelation*, p. 126; M. Lohmeyer, *Die Offenbarung des Johannes* (Tübingen: J. C. B. Mohr, 1953); and E. Boring, *Revelation* (Louisville: John Knox Press, c1989), p. 13. For an additional list of these see E. *Schüssler-Fiorenza, "Apocalyptic and Gnosis," pp. 565-82. Her list is on p. 571.*
[2] *Schüssler-Fiorenza, The Book of Revelation--Justice and Judgement* (Philadelphia: Fortress, 1985),p. 55.
[3] Caird, *Revelation*, p. 131.

Jews; they think any person less observant than they are cannot be called a **Jew** at all. Liberal **Jews** do not deny that orthodox are true **Jews**, but John did accuse others of being **called Jews** and really belonging to the **synagogue of Satan.**

Schüssler-Fiorenza correctly denied that the **Nicolaitans** could be Judaizers, because they ate food offered to idols, the way the liberal Jews did. All foods sold in the open market without orthodox Jewish slaughtering and preparation were called foods offered to idols. Shüssler-Fiorenza thought, however, that they were the enthusiasts Paul confronted in Corinth. This is possible, but it is not a required conclusion. The place to begin reasoning is realizing that John was a Judaizing Christian. Those of the **synagogue of Satan** were more liberal than he. They might have been Paulinists. enthusiasts, or any other liberals, but they were not non-Christian **Jews**.

John contrasted the Christians at **Smyrna** with the liberals who hypocritically called themselves **Jews**! The **officer** at **Smyrna** who suffered was a real Jew in contrast to the liberal Christians who made peace with Rome and the gentiles and therefore did not suffer. Liberal Christians apparently went through the normal Jewish forms, celebrated feasts, had their sons trained for the *bar mitzwahs,* in preparation for undertaking personal, levitical responsibilities, attended **synagogue** on Friday nights, and considered themselves to be among the chosen people. But all of this was blasphemy, in the judgment of **John,** because they were lax about something, perhaps their dietary rules, circumcision, or something like that. Their practices were evidently to some degree like those of the gentiles that lived nearby. This made their place of study and worship a **synagogue** of Satan.

Satan was the agent of the Lord in heaven who tested Job on earth (Job 1-2), and he was the prosecuting attorney in the heavenly court trial that had to be overpowered before the Promised Land could be returned with Joshua as its high priest (Zech 3). A congregation that was on Satan's side was a primary adversary to the chosen people. From this attack it is clear that John considered himself a true **Jew** and not an anti-**Jewish** Christian. This was true of most Christians before the Bar Cochba rebellion of IA 132-35.

Have no fear. Some texts (AC, 046, *al*) have **Do not be afraid** (*may*, mh rather than *may-dehn*, μηδεν). The differences are not great. Sinaiticus concurs with K, P*pm*, latt, sy, Th.

These words constitute a stipulations formula, found frequently in legal contracts and treaties. John also called attention to the deliverance of **the Jews** from the Greeks under the leadership of the Hasmoneans by quoting from Daniel. John, like Daniel, had been faithful even in time of persecution. His being on Patmos Island was like being in the lion's den or the fiery furnace (Dan 3, 6).

The things you are about to suffer. John promised **the officer** at Smyrna that he was **about to** face **suffering** and **testing** as Daniel and his friends had done, but reminded him that God would rescue him as he had rescued Daniel and his friends. The author did not intend to communicate to **the officer** that the **testing** would last only ten days, but he put in the **ten days** to remind **the officer** that he was the new antitype of Daniel and his friends. The word **test** alone would not be enough to have that connotation, but **test** together with **ten days** would make the allusion clear. The "tribulation" or "days of the Messiah" would last, not **ten days**, but 3½ years. It would, however, come to an end as it had for the Son of man in Dan 7. John's claiming that he and the true Christians were really the true Jews was not as widely held as a compliment after the Bar Cochba revolt and Marcion's movement. This may be one of the reasons that the Book of Revelation had such a checkered career in the early church. John was one of the early leaders who represented the Judaizers with whom Paul had been in conflict.

Throw some of you(plural) *into prison.*[1] This is the first part of the message addressed in the plural, rather than to **the officer** in charge, alone. This small, one sentence, message, however, stands out from the rest of the letter, which was addressed only to the principal **officer**, himself. Of course, John may have meant by **some,** just other members of the church at Smyrna. That is not likely, however, because all of the rest of these letters are directed to various **officers** in charge of the churches, rather than any of the members of the seven churches. John began the discussion in the first person, singular, masculine, and after this sentence, continued, directing the entire message to **the officer.** In this one sentence he included the **officer** in charge of the Smyrna church, together with all of the six other churches as those leaders who were suffering the same sort of terror.

For **Jews** and early Christians **the devil** was not just some abstract figure that personified evil. **The devil** was normally identified as the force behind specific human beings who were enemies of the faithful. In this case **the devil** was the Roman authorities whose security the **Jews** and Christians threatened. John expected the conditions for Christian leaders to get worse before they got better. **The devil** would **throw some of** them into **prison** for their faith. This would give them a chance to show their faithfulness, just as Daniel and his colleagues did when they were asked to eat food that was not *kah-sháyr* in Babylon. By quoting from Daniel, John implied that this **testing** would not last forever. Daniel and his friends were **tested** for only **ten days**, after which they were allowed to follow their own diets.

[Be] faithful until death. The Greek word here rendered "Be (s.)" is *geé-noo* (γίνου). This word does not occur here in the Sinaiticus text although the sense requires it. Some scribe must have overlooked it. Evidently the problem facing **the officer** at **Smyrna** was more serious than ignoring dietary laws. He was under the kind of oppression which could have meant **death** if he maintained his **faith** steadfastly. John urged him not to be deterred by this threat. Even if he died, he would then be assured of a position in **life**, probably in the age to come. There he would receive a crown and have a royal status. Crowns were those generally

---

[1] The Greek text of Sinaiticus is ee-*doó meh-láy báh-lay báh-leen ex hoo-móhn* (ιδου μελλει βαλλει βαλιν εκ υμων). The Greek word *bálin* (balin) makes no sense in this context. The only possible explanation seems to conjecture an attempt at rendering an infinitive absolute from Hebrew into Greek. The text might have intended to say, "Look! Satan will surely throw some of you. . . ."

associated with victory in festive and athletic events. In political concepts crowns were given to governmental leaders. Such prestige as that made the suffering worth while.[1]

He who has an ear. This is a normal part of a witness formula, like those found in legal treaties and contracts. In redemption literature this formula reminds the reader that the preceding words have been written in code. The reader can understand this message only if he or she understands the Scripture quoted and the tradition implied.

He who conquers. The one **who conquer**s is the **faithful** believer. This theme is pursued throughout the Book of Revelation (Rev 2:7, 11, 17, 26; 3:5, 12, 21; 5:5; 12:11; 15:2; 17:14; 21).[2] It is also an important theme for First John (1John 2:13, 14; 4:4; 5:4, 5). For First John the ones who conquer are the celibate monks **who** have **conquered** their passions and fulfill all of the monastic rules. Mealy correctly observed that the condition and promise given to the church at **Ephesus** and the church at **Smyrna** are the same: The one **who conquers** will be permitted to **eat of the tree of life in the Paradise of God** (Rev 2:7); the one **who** is faithful until death will receive **the crown of life** (Rev 2:10); the one **who conquers** will not be judged guilty of the **second death** (Rev 2:11). In these balanced statements, the one **who** is faithful until death is also the one **who conquers** and the one **who** receives **the crown of life** is also permitted to **eat of the tree of life** and is not judged guilty of the second death.[3] These coded idioms all have basically the same meaning. They allude repetitiously to the same reward.

Will not be judged guilty. This phrase is part of a blessings formula often used in legal contracts and treaties. **Second death**, like **second** birth, was legal. All people are physically born and physically die, but when a person who is physically alive goes through some legal ceremony by which to become adopted, married, or a member of some community, such a person is born again and becomes legally "alive" by coming into existence in a new family or community. When a person becomes excommunicated, divorced, or legally removed from a family, that person faces **second death** or "legal death." The **second death** mentioned here refers to Christians who have behaved in such a way as to be excommunicated. They would not be a part of the community in the age to come. This would become evident in the **judgment** day, after the martyrs had been raised from the first **death**. In the **judgment**, martyrs would not be declared **guilty** and punished. Instead they would be introduced into the new kingdom where true life was possible. This was more important than being saved from martyrdom by the Romans.

---

[1] See further Pliny the Younger, *Letters* 10:96-97.
[2] See further K. A. Strand, "'Overcomer': A Study in the Macrodynamic of Theme Development in the Book of Revelation," *AUSS* 28 (1990):237-54.
[3] J. W. Mealy, *After the Thousand Years* (Sheffield: JSOT, c1992), p. 82.

TEXT

Revelation

¹²To the officer of the church in Pergamum, write: "Thus says the one who has the
sharp two edged **sword**, ¹³"I know where you live--where the throne of Satan is, but you hold to my name and you have not denied my faith, even in the days of Antipas, my witness, my faithful one who was killed in your midst, where Satan dwells.
¹⁴But I have a few things against you, because you have there [some] holding to the teaching of **Balaam** who taught [Balak] to place a stumbling block before **the sons of Israel** [so

that] they would eat food offered to idols and

commit acts of sexual indecency.

First Testament

$^{\text{Isa 49:2}}$He made my mouth like a **sharp sword.**

$^{\text{Num 31:16}}$They [the women] have become through the word of **Balaam**

an occasion for **the sons of Israel** to trespass against the Lord.

$^{\text{Num 25:1-2}}$When Israel dwelled at Shittim the people began **to commit acts of sexual indecency** . . . The people ate and prostrated themselves to their gods.

COMMENTARY

The two edged sword. These words constitute part of a legal preamble formula, the kind often used in contracts. John addressed the churches as from **the one who** was described in Rev 1: **the one who holds the seven stars** (Rev 1:16), **the first and the last** (Rev 1:8), and here **the one who has the sharp two edged sword** (Rev 1:16). This was part of the description of the **voice. The voice** had **the sword** in his mouth as a weapon of speech. He had the authority to kill by just giving the command: "Off with his head!"

I know where you live. This statement is part of a legal prologue. It might mean, "**I know where** you sit," because the word for **live** or **dwell** and **sit** in Hebrew are the same. The reason for considering **sit** as a possibility is that the next phrase speaks of the throne of Satan. Thrones are places where people **sit,** but the author seems to be speaking of the place where Satan's throne is. **The officer** and his fellow Christian members dwelled in this place. The place where they all lived was the city of

Pergamum. It was Satan, and not **the officer**, who was **sitting** on this throne. Satan was the prosecuting attorney in heaven who opposed the Jews and Christians (Job 1-2; Zech 3). In **Pergamum** there were pagan temples to the god Asclepius, the god of healing, who was symbolized by a serpent. This might have motivated John to refer to **Pergamum** as the place of the old serpent, Satan.[1] A more likely suggestion is that John was insulting the Romans. **Pergamum** was one of the three largest cities of the whole Roman province of Asia Minor Pliny said it was the most famous city in Asia Minor (Pliny, *Nat Hist*. 5:126). It was a large seaport city, 68 miles north of Smyrna, which Attalus III gave to Rome 133 BIA. Satan's throne was in the same city where Rome's throne was.

Antipas, my witness, my faithful one. **The officer** at **Pergamum** was both very good and very bad, in John's judgment. One from their midst, a certain **Antipas**, faced death for this faith. According to Zahn, none of the early church fathers who wrote of martyrdoms included **Antipas**.[2] He seems to have been overlooked except for John of Patmos. John thought **Antipas** was exemplary, but there were others who held to the teachings of Balaam and the **Nicolaitans.**

The teachings of Balaam. **Balaam** was one who had been hired by **Balak** to place a curse **on the sons of Israel,** but he finally blessed them, instead. This made **Balak** angry and should have made **Israelites** happy, but for some reason **Balaam** is regularly referred to as "wicked **Balaam**" in rabbinic literature. Here he is pictured as being responsible for **teaching Balak** to make trouble for **Israel**, even though that is not what he did. John here joined two stories from Numbers. The story of **Balaam** and **Balak** is in Num 22-24 and referred to again in Num 31.[3] In the words, **Which he taught [Balak],** the object of this sentence, **Balak**, is not in Sinaiticus.

A stumbling block. The Greek word is *skáhn-dah-lawn* (σκάνδαλον), which means stumbling block, trap, offense, or scandal.

Commit acts of sexual indecency. Num 25 begins with an account of the Israelites mingling with the daughters of Moab, worshiping Moabite gods, and eating food with the Moabites. This type of social mingling was called "fornication" or "adultery," implying that these social and business associations were really **sexual** brothels. While in the wilderness, **Israel** suffered a serious plague, and people thought their mingling must have been the cause. John accused **the officer** of the church at **Pergamum** of allowing teachings of these unapproved doctrines to exist

---

[1] So also Zahn, *Offenbarung* I, pp. 260-63.
[2] Zahn, *Offenbarung* I, p. 246.
[3] A. J. Beagley, *The "Sitz im Leben" of the Apocalypse with Particular Reference to the Role of the Church's Enemies* (Berlin: W. De Gruyter, 1987), p. 32, said, "We may eliminate immediately the suggestion of George Wesley Buchanan that this attack is aimed at the Paulinists who permit non-observance of the law." The claim here is not that the Nicolaitans were Paulinists but that they were liberal Christians with some characteristics like those of Paul. Beagley did not give any data to support his dismissal.

and be propagated in the church there at **Pergamum.** He had allowed Christians at **Pergamum** to become antitypes of the mingling Israelites in the wilderness. They had been mingling with the gentiles in the same way. Contrary to Hailey,[1] the members of the church at **Pergamum** probably were not engaged in **sexual** promiscuity. Their "fornication" probably involved willingness to speak to the **Nicolaitans** and deal with them in business and on social occasions. Jezebel was a queen who worshiped the Baals, but she was never accused of being promiscuous (2Kings 9:22) in her own time. Like the followers of **Balaam**, she mingled with foreign cults.

Jeremiah accused Israelites of **bowing down like a harlot on every high hill and under every green tree** (Jer 2:20). Bowing down, of course is not the normal posture for harlots. It is the posture of someone worshiping. This happened at the places of worship for the Baal worshipers. For the purpoe of insulting, Jews frequently associated sexual immorality with idolatry (Exod 32:15-16; Wis 14:12-31; T. Reuben 4:6; T. Benjamin 10:10; sDeut 171b; mSan 82a; bShab 17b).

TEXT

Revelation	First Testament
[15]Thus you, even you, have those who hold to the teaching of the Nicolaitans as well. [16]Repent therefore! If you do not, I will come to you quickly, and I will battle against them **with the sword of my mouth.** [17]He who has an ear to hear let him hear what the spirit says to the churches.	Isa 11:4 He will hit the earth **with the staff of his mouth**; with the breath of his lips he will kill the wicked.
To the one who conquers I will give him some of the hidden **manna**, and I will give	Exod 16:15 Each man said to his brother, "It is **manna**." . . . Moses said to them, "It is the bread which the Lord has given you to eat."
	Ps 78:23 He rained upon them **manna** to eat; grain from heaven he gave them.
him a white pebble, and on the pebble [will be] written **a new name** which no one knows except the one who receives [it]."	Isa 62:2 You will be called by **a new name**.

---

[1] Hailey, *Revelation*, p. 132.

COMMENTARY

Even you. After all the praise John had given to **the officer at Thytira,** it comes as a surprise that this faithful officer--**even** he--had allowed Nicolaitians to penetrate the faithful community and infect it with their heresies. This indicates how serious this heresy was in that community.

The teachings of the Nicolaitans. John thought it was terrible that **the officer of the church at Pergamum** had in his church some of those unorthodox people who observed **the teachings of the Nicolaitans. Nicolaitans** were more liberal than John. They made some of the same accommodations to pagan society as Paul did. They may have been the same people John also called followers of Balaam. This was more than John could tolerate.

Repent therefore! This is a stipulation formula--a standard part of a treaty. The verb was directed to **the officer** himself—not to the members of the church. In order for that **officer** to **repent,** he would have to put an end to all of **the teachings of Balaam** and **the Nicolaitans** that had been allowed in that church. If **the officer** failed to do that, John threatened **to come quickly.** Aune followed Beasley-Murray in thinking that this referred to the final coming of Jesus in judgment.[1] That is a reasonable conclusion, because John of Patmos claimed to be speaking in Jesus' name (**the one who has the sharp, two edged sword**, Rev 2:12). Because he was Jesus' legal agent, however, Jesus was responsible for everything he said. He also expressed his own opinion, and he may have meant only that he himself would come quickly and enforce discipline. If he did, of course, he would have done that also in Jesus' name. If that were the case, that would imply that John expected soon to be released from his confinement at Patmos and would be free to do as he threatened.

I will battle against them. This statement is part of a legal curse formula, used in contracts and treaties. The pronoun **them** evidently applies to those who follow the **teachings of Balaam** and **the Nicolaitans**. They, and not **the officer,** would be the recipients of the **battle** in which John was prepared to engage. Since Jesus was no longer alive physically, it is likely that John, himself, as Jesus' legal agent would do the battling.

Just as Phineas took the law in his own hands and killed Zimri and his new Midianite wife, so John threatened to fight with those in the church served by **the officer** to whom John addressed his letter, namely those in **the church at Pergamum,** who observed the teachings of **Balaam** and the **Nicolaitans**. His **battle** would be with **the sword of his mouth**, which probably meant he would scold, curse, or excommunicate them.[2] He expected, however, that **the officer** of that

---

[1] Aune, *Revelation 1-5*, p. 188.
[2] Schüssler-Fiorenza *Justice*, p. 195, correctly said, "It is likely that all three code names 'Nicolaitans, Balaam, and Jezebel' characterize the same group of Christian prophets who allowed eating food

church would take care of the situation before John appeared on the scene. That was the purpose of this letter. If **the officer** could solve this problem all by himself, John would not have to come.

He who has an ear. These words form part of a legal witness formula. In redemption literature this is the clue given to alert the reader that the material he or she has just read is in code.

The hidden manna . . . a white pebble. These words constitute part of a legal blessings formula. There was a Jewish legend circulating in NT times that, before the temple was destroyed in 586 BIA, the treasury of manna had been **hidden** in heaven, and after the Messiah came it would be returned to earth and Jews would eat it again at the end of the captivity when the new age would begin (2Bar 29:1-8). It was called the **bread from heaven** (Neh 9:15; Ps 105:40; John 6:31-33, 50-51). There is a tradition that Jeremiah hid the chest holding the contract to prevent it from being taken into Babylon and that the manna was hidden along with it (2Macc 2:4-6).

The pebble was a small white stone, probably of beryl, a valuable precious stone used as a ballot for voting. Only those who were privileged to be citizens were allowed to cast them.[1] Those who had the privilege of eating **the hidden manna** were those who would belong to the new age when the Messiah was ruling. Those whose names were written on ballot **pebbles** were the ones who belonged as citizens in the new kingdom of the Messiah. Victorinus (d. IA 304) said the name written on the stone was "Christian" (*Commentary* on Rev 2).

Receiving **the hidden manna** and the **white pebble** (Rev 2:17) has the same significance as receiving **the crown of life,** being permitted **to eat from the tree of life,** and being protected against a guilty verdict of **the second death** (Rev 2:7, 10,

---

sacrificed to idols and accepted compromise with the emperor cult," but she mistakenly assumed that John of Patmos wrote the entire Book of Revelation from somewhere in Asia Minor. She thought the Nicolatians were heretical Christians but the so-called Jews were not Christians (see pp. 18, 118). She said further, "Whereas the Tübingen School regarded the Nicolaitans as Pauline in tendency, scholars today consider them more as a Judaistic group" B. M. Newman, for example, characterizes them as promoting a "heretical gnostic Christianity of Jewish tint." H. Koester, "GNOMAI DIAPHOROI: The Origin and Nature of Diversification in Early Christianity," *Trajectories through Early Christianity* (Philadelphia: Fortress Press, 1971), pp. 114-57, esp. pp. 148-49, also described them with reference to Rev. 2:6, 16 as a "hostile Judaizing group" and placed them in a line with the Judaizers mentioned in Galatians, Philippians, Colossians, and the letters of Ignatius. "The Nicolaitans, therefore, should be distinguished from the opponents of Paul in 1 Corinthians" (pp. 117/118).

F. C. Baur, *Vorlesungen über neutestamentliche Theologie* (Leipzig: Darmstadt, 1864), pp. 207-30; G. Volkmar, *Kommentar zur Offenbarung Johannes* (Zurich: Drell, 1862), pp. 80, 82-85; A. Hilgenfeld, "Die Christus-Leute in Korinth an die Nikolaiten," *ZWT* 15 (1872), pp. 220-26; E. Renan, *Saint Paul* (Paris: Michel Levy Freres, 1869), pp. 303-4. Newman, *Rediscovering*, p. 30.; Koester, "GNOMAI DIAPHOROI," 114-57, esp. pp. 148-49. One of the sages said, "He overcame the anger, not by strength of body nor by force of weapons, but by means of a word he subdued the one who administers punishment" (*Sol* 18:26). John of Patmos obtained the expression not only from Isa 11:4, but also from the prophecy brought him by the messenger (Rev 19:15).

[1] G. Braumann, "ψῆφος [*psáy-phaws*]," *TDNT*, IX, pp. 606-607.

11). The conditions and promises are given to **the officers** of the churches of **Ephesus, Smyrna, and Philadelphia**. The one who receives these blessings is the one who is faithful and conquers. The one who receives one of them receives all of them, because all of these idioms are coded terms with the same meaning.

I will give him . . . a new name. John promised the faithful that God would **give** them **hidden manna**, just as he had done for Moses and the Hebrews in the wilderness (2Macc 2:4-8). The **hidden** quality of the **manna** may mean that the **manna**, like the keys and temple vessels, was **hidden** in heaven until the temple would be restored. Each of these would also have his or her **name** written on a **white pebble**. This was another way of saying that the person's **name** would be **written in the book of life** or **written in heaven**. The **new name** was to remind these Christians of Second Isaiah's promise that the Lord would distinguish the Jews and show them honor before all the kings and gentiles. At that time the Lord would **give** them **a new name**. John promised that the same would be true of faithful Christians of his day. According to the traditional Ethiopian interpretation, the **new name** given here was the baptismal **name** of believers which they are **given** after their worldly **name**.[1]

TEXT

Revelation

[18] To the **officer** of the church in Thyatira, write: "This is what the Son of God says, the One who has **eyes like a flame of fire and whose feet are like burnished brass**, [19] I know your works, love, faith, and endurance. Your last works are even more than the first, [20] but I hold much against you--you tolerate the woman, **Jezebel**, who says it (her teaching) is a prophecy. She both teaches and causes my servants to go astray--**to commit indecent acts** and to eat food offered to idols. [21] I have given her time so that she

First Testament

Dan 10:6 His **eyes like flames of fire and whose feet are like burnished brass**.

1Kings 16:31 [Ahab] took **Jezebel**, the daughter of Ethbaal . . . for a wife, and he went and served Baal and worshiped him.

Num 15:1-2 The people began **to commit indecent acts** with the daughters of Moab . . . and the people ate and prostrated themselves to their gods.

---

[1] R. W. Cowley, *The Traditional Interpretation of the Apocalypse of St. John in the Ethiopian Orthodox Church* (Cambridge: Cambridge U. Press, c1983), p. 88.

might repent of her **indecent acts**. ²²Look! I [will] throw her into a bed, and those who **commit** adultery with her, into great tribulation if they do

not repent of her **works**. ²³I will kill her children with pestilence, and all the churches will know that

I am the one who searches the heart and mind I will **give to each according to your**

works.'"
²⁴Now I say to the rest of you in Thyatira, who do not have this teaching and have not known "the deep things of Satan," as they say. I will not cast upon you another burden. ²⁵Only that which you have, [should be] held fast until I come. ²⁶He who conquers and keeps my works until the end, ²⁶ **I shall give** to him authority over **the gentiles**,

²⁷and **he will rule them with an iron rod; as pottery vessels they will be broken**. ²⁸Even as I have received from my Father, and I will give to him the early morning star. ²⁹He who has an ear, let him hear what the spirit says to the churches."

²Kings 9:22What peace can there be so long as the **indecent acts** and sorceries of your mother **Jezebel** are numerous?

OG Exod 3:14Then God said to Moses, "**I am the one who is**."

Ps 62:12You pay back to each according to his **work**.
Jer 17:10-11**I**, Yehowah, **search the mind** and test the **heart**, giving to every man according to his ways, according to the fruit of his **works**

Jer 11:20The Lord of armies judges righteousness, testing **the heart and mind**.

Ps 2:8-9; PssSol 17.23-28You are my son; today I have given you birth. Ask from me, and **I shall give** you **the gentiles** as your inheritance, the ends of the land, as your possession, and you **will rule them with an iron rod; as a potter's vessels you will break them**.

Jer 19:11Yehowah of armies said, "This is the way I **will break** this people and this city, just as one breaks a potter's vessel that cannot be repaired."

TECHNICAL DETAILS

This is the first letter to the churches addressed both to **the officer** in charge and to the church members. It was initially addressed the chief **officer**. Its main purpose was to motivate that **officer** into getting rid of the church leader called **Jezebel** who had a following of students, called "her children." First he had a message of warning for them. Then he had words of encouragement to the faithful. John apparently wrote all of this to **the officer** only, but he expected that officer to communicate his messages further to the church members, as he had directed. This is not true of the other letters.

COMMENTARY

To the officer of the church in Thyatira. **Thyatira** is an inland city located 45 miles southeast of **Pergamum**, at the most important junction of roads between Lydia and Mysia.

This is what the Son of God says. These words form part of a legal preamble formula. This is the only place in the entire Book of Revelation where the title **Son of God** appears. The title **Son of God** was often applied to a king in the ancient Near East. The description of this **Son of God** was couched in the language used in Daniel to describe the agent **God** sent to give comfort and assurance to Daniel, telling him what would happen at the end of the old age. The **Son of God,** then, was here understood to be also an agent of **God**. Since kings were understood to be both agents of the deity and sons of the deity, it is quite clear here what the author intended the readers to understand about this figure. He was the Messiah of the Lord, destined to rule over Israel.

Whose eyes were like a flame of fire. This expression came from Daniel, but it also appeared in the description of John's experience (Rev 19:14). Rev 1:13-16 consists of a fabrication of seven different passages of Scripture that were all used to describe fantastically the visionary **voice** that gave John of Patmos directions for action, following his reading of the scroll brought to him. The description of **the Son of God** here was intended to allude the reader back to the **voice** (Rev 1:12).

I know your works. This is part of a legal prologue formula. Some texts have "and ministry," which Sinaiticus omitted.

Your last works are even more than the first. Again John described the authority for his message in terms of **the voice** in Rev 1 (Rev 1:14). **The Son of God,** of course, is the Messiah or legal agent for God. This one is also identical with the **voice** (Rev 1:14) both in John's earlier dramatization and in Daniel's (Rev 10:6). **Works**, love, faith, ministry, and endurance are all merits for which the church gains credit in the heavenly treasury. **Thyatira** had not only kept up its good **works**, but it had increased them.

I hold much against you. Sinaiticus agrees here with *al*, *gig*, sy[ph], and S. Some other texts omit **much** (*paw-loó*, πολου). Without **much** it would be necessary to conjecture a **this.**

The woman, Jezebel, who says it is a prophecy. Some texts read, **Who calls herself a prophet**. These texts provide the less difficult reading. Sinaiticus does not provide an antecedent for the pronoun **it.**

Jezebel was the queen of North Israel. Her husband, King Ahab, was a worshiper of Yehowah, but **Jezebel** worshiped the Baals. She had Naboth killed and confiscated his vineyard that Ahab wanted. Elijah, the prophet of Yehowah, condemned this action. **Jezebel** had killed many of the prophets of Yehowah and tried to have Elijah killed, but he escaped. Later the prophet, Elisha, arranged to have Jehu anointed king. Jehu had to fight **Jezebel**'s husband to claim his throne. He succeeded and had Queen **Jezebel** killed **and thrown** out of a second story window on to the street where she was left unburied, for the dogs to eat her flesh. (1Kings 19, 21; 2Kings 9). She was a pagan woman who succeeded in getting into a government that had been composed of Yehowah worshipers. She tried to destroy that religion. She was later considered by Jews and Israelites as a seductress and one who sabotaged the nation she ruled, behind the scenes. She was the type for which the teacher in Thyatira was patterned. John of Patmos pictured himself as the new prophet, Elisha, who was assigned to have the new **Jezebel thrown** out of power.

Loisy held that **Jezebel** was not an individual at all, but rather, a heretical Christian sect.[1] Even if accepted as an individual, this **Jezebel** would have been a heretic. If we follow the reading given here, what is it that **is a prophecy?** With this text it is necessary to conjecture one, such as the teaching of **Jezebel,** mentioned in the same verse. This particular **Jezebel** was liberal, like those who **call themselves Jews** or those **who called themselves** apostles. The criticism John had for the church at **Thyatira** is similar to the fault he had for other churches--the members had tolerated a certain leader whom John considered a heretic. Like the false **prophet,** the so-called Jews, and the false apostle, this leader was identified with **Jezebel**, the queen who frightened Elijah and misled Ahab. Those who listened to her were like the minglers who associated with the Midianites and the Moabites in the wilderness.

Like those, these were accused of committing indecent sexual acts, when they probably only mingled in business and social events. Eating food offered to idols was food that was not purchased at a *kah-sháyr* meat market--a practice forbidden to orthodox Jews. The old **Jezebel**, the archetype of this one, was accused **of harlotries and sorceries** (1Kings 9:30-37), the Scripture narrative gives no report of promiscuous activity. Jezebel was opposed by Elijah and Elisha because she associated with the priests of Baal and had the prophets of Yehowah killed. The new **Jezebel** probably was offensive in the same way.

In NT times all food was sacrificed; there was no non-sacred food. The question was only to which deity it was sacrificed. Therefore all pagan food was idolatrous. *Did* 11-13 tells of ways and occasions for testing prophets and apostles. When one of them speaks **in the spirit** he should not be tested. After all both **prophets** and apostles were leaders of authority who spoke in the name and with the

---

[1] Loisy, *L'Apocalypse*, pp. 101-102.

authority of the one who sent them. Apparently, when they spoke **in the spirit** they spoke under the authority of the one who sent them. The **spirit** gave them the authority. It was only their behavior that prompted anyone to question their authenticity. If they taught false doctrine, asked for money, or stayed more than two days they were false. This is very similar to the testing methods prescribed in the Mishnah. Weiss thought the angel involved was a heavenly guardian angel. He opposed the idea that the word, "woman," might be taken to mean "wife." He apparently opposed some in his day who argued that since the "angel" had a wife, it must have been a bishop and not a heavenly angel.[1]

But she does not want to repent. This is a passage that is not included by Sinaiticus, probably because of a homeoteleuton error. Homeoteleuton means "the same ending." A homeoteleuton error is one made by a copyist who was copying a text that had two lines on the same page that ended with the same word. While copying, his eye unintentionally dropped from the first occurrence to the second, omitting all of the sentences in between. Here the scribe dropped from the first infinitive **to repent** to the second same word, both at the end of lines, and he left out this passage in between. The other possibility is that some later scribe added these words to expand the message homiletically.

I will throw her into a bed.[2] This is part of legal curse formula, normally used in contracts. This is a figure of speech to identify John as an antitype of Jehu who ordered Jezebel **thrown** out of the window into the street. John had given this leader time to repent, which means he or she was officially a member of the church at **Thyatira**. She, however, clearly felt no need of **repentance**. If she did not **repent** soon, John promised to punish both her and her "lovers" from the church at **Thyatira**.

If they do not repent of her works. Jezebel's lovers were her students who probably followed her teachings and actions. They probably did not commit adultery with her physically. They were warned of the necessity of **repentance. Repentance** meant that they would stop studying with her and stop following any of her teachings. John of Patmos said he would **kill Jezebel's children in death** or **with pestilence**. This was another way of saying that he would **throw her into a bed** with a disease (pestilence), as one of the promised curses guaranteed to come upon anyone who broke the contract.

I will kill her children with pestilence. RSV renders this passage, "I will strike her children dead." Literally, the Greek says, **I will kill her children with death** (*thah-náh-toh*, θανάτῳ). That expression in Hebrew simply meant, "I will really kill" or "I will slaughter." The Greek translator evidently did not know the Hebrew idiom.

---

[1] J. Weiss, *Die Offenbarung des Johannes* (Göttingen: Vandenhoeck und Ruprecht, 1908), pp. 611, 617.
[2] Sinaiticus has instead of *báh-loh* (βάλλω) *káh-loh* (κάλλω) evidently a scribal error.

The vicious killing is what Elisha ordered Jehu to have done. The new Elisha was John of Patmos. He may not have planned to kill this teacher and all of the students, physically, but if he excommunicated them, that means he had killed them legally.

Since this leader's name was not really **Jezebel,** he or she might not even have been a woman. The term **Jezebel** was used to identify this leader with Ahab's wicked foreign queen who misled the Israelites and promoted Baalism. The accusations John of Patmos directed against the new **Jezebel** were also directed against the new Balaam. The person called **Jezebel** may also have been the one called Balaam, but this is guess work. Both names were used as types of which the heretics in the Asia Minor churches were antitypes.

Jezebel did not represent any gentile. It represented parties to the contract who had broken the contract they had made with the Lord. This would include Jews, Samaritans, or Christians. Therefore its punishment would be the curses promised to those who broke the contract. (See further Rev 6:8 and OG Jer 14:12).

Who searches the heart and mind. **Mind and heart** are synonyms used here in duplicate for emphasis. To **search** another person's **mind** is to cross-examine her or him to test that person's intellect, opinions, attitudes, and ethical judgments. On the great judgment day it was assumed that God would test everyone's **mind,** motives, and actions. Semitic peoples thought of the **heart** as the human instrument, needed for thinking, just as westerners believe that is the function of the **mind.** The praiseworthy attributes that John gave the Messiah or God were increased again with the claim, **I am,** as with Moses, trying to learn God's name. This time he alluded to Psalms and Jeremiah who called God **One who searches or tests the souls and hearts of men**. He used Proverbs to prove that God would repay each according to the works done.

I will give to each according to your works. Some texts have "their" **works**; some have "her" **works.** Sinaiticus has **the works to you** *tah éhr-gah hoo-meén* (τα ἔγα ὑμῖν). *Hoo-meén* (ὑμῖν) may be a scribal error for *hoo-móhn* (ὑμῶν). The other possibility is that it is a literal rendering of the Hebrew and means **the works belonging to you.** (*luh-kháh,* לך).

To the rest of you in Thyatira. To those who are not the **children** of **Jezebel, who do not hold** to her **teachings**. This is a message that is not directed to **the officer** in charge, but to the members of the church themselves that have not been lured by the heresy.

Have not known the deep things of Satan. Some scholars have supposed that this is a satire on the doctrines which some sect called "**the deep things of** God." Jews and Christians have a wonderful way of twisting an expression by slightly mispronouncing or changing a word so as to change a compliment into an insult. For example, one of Saul's sons was given the Baalistically defensive name, "from the argument of Baal" (*muh-reév báh-ahl*). Later Jews called him "*muh-fee bóh-sheth*" ("from the mouth of shame."(2Sam 4:4). Today "genitals" are sometimes confused for "gentiles." There were those in **Thyatira** who did not subscribe to the teachings of **Jezebel**. John encouraged these to keep on being faithful as they had been so far, at least until John came. This means John was optimistic about his own future. He expected to be released from Patmos Island some day.

I will not cast upon you another burden. John had been severe with those who had been lax in their discipline. They had modified their orthodoxy and compromised their doctrine. There were **those in Thyatira,** however, who had been faithful. John was not expecting any more of them than that which they were already doing.

Only that which is held. Some other texts say, **Only that which you have, hold fast until I come**. Sinaiticus has this sentence cast in a passive mood and in third person singular rather than second person plural. This is another indication that John of Patmos planned to be released sometime in the future so that he could come and deal with the situation himself.

He who . . . keeps my works until the end. **The end** mentioned is not **the end** of the world or **the end** of time, but until **the end** of the Roman rule over the Jews and Christians.

I will give to him authority. This is part of a curse formula, common for legal treaties and contracts. This reward will come to the one who conquers (cf. also Rev 2:7, 11, 17). The one who should receive this reward and be permitted to rule **the gentiles** first had to conquer. Although the enthronement Psalms quoted were directed to kings who would rule nations, the word that means **nations** also means gentiles in Greek. Since this message is directed to church members and not to pretending messiahs, the term here is translated **gentiles**.

He will rule them with an iron rod. This is a quotation from Ps 2, but it may also have been inspired by the prophecy which John received. That prophecy used the same quotation (Rev 12:5; 19:15). With those who conquered, John shared the enthronement promises not only of Ps 2 and the prophecy he was given but also the PssSol 17:23-28:

> Look, Lord! Raise up for them their king,
>   the son of David,
> at a time which you know, God,
>   so that he may rule your servant, Israel.
> Gird him with strength, so that he may
>   bruise the wicked rulers,
> cleanse Jerusalem of those gentiles who trample [it]
>   destructively.

> Wisely, righteously, let him throw out the sinners
>> from the inheritance,
> shatter the arrogant sinner like a potter's vessel,
>> crush all their substance with an iron rod,
> destroy the lawless gentiles with the word of
>> his mouth.
> At his threat, let gentiles flee from him,
> and may he rebuke sinners by the word of
>> their hearts (PssSol 17:21-25).

This was expressed about the Messiah who promised to share these privileges with the faithful, just as the Lord had shared them with him. Ps 2 was one of the texts nationalists liked. In the main body of the Book of Revelation, the text of Ps 2 was quoted three times (Rev 11:18; 12:5; 19:15). When **the Son of man** came before the **Ancient of Days**, God gave him a positive judgment. He was given **the dominion, the glory, and the kingdom** (Dan 7:14). At the same time **the kingdom, dominion**, and **the greatness of the kingdom** was awarded to the **saints of the Most High.** The Son of man was a title for a king, so this kingdom was given both to the king and to the citizens of the country (the saints of the Most High) (Dan 7:27). John of Patmos expected that there would soon be another judgment when the faithful of Thyatira would share the victory with the Messiah.

Caird did not like the idea that the Messiah would behave like a military general or king. He said this must be a mistranslation. Instead of **smash** or **rule** with a rod of iron, the Messiah would have "pastured" or "shepherded."[1] Then he took "shepherding" to mean dying a martyr's death, but that defies the context. A messiah was a king who **ruled,** fought battles, and defended his nation. The shepherd metaphor was applied to kings, because kings, like shepherds, provided food for their flock and defended them *with their rods* against dangerous intruders. First century kings could not fit the non-violent role many Western scholars would prefer. Not only did John of Patmos use the text from Ps 2, but the authors of three portions of the prophecy used it as well. It must have been popular.

Early morning star. This expression is also mentioned in Rev 22:16, where it is applied to the Davidic Messiah.

He who has an ear. This is part of a witness formula used in ancient contracts and treaties. In redemption literature it alerts the reader to the fact that the pertinent message is in code.

---

[1] Caird, *Revelation*, pp. 45-46.

CHAPTER THREE

TEXT

¹To the officer of the church in Sardis, write:

"Thus says the one who has the seven spirits of God and the seven stars: 'I know your works, because you have a reputation for being alive, but you are dead!

Revelation

²Be watchful and **strengthen the** remaining things which are about to die, for I have not found your works filled up before my God. ³Remember, then, how

you received **and heard**. So, **keep** [the faith] and repent. If, therefore, you do not watch out, I will come like a thief, and you will not know at which hour I will come against you. ⁴But you have a few individuals in Sardis who have not defiled their garments, and they will walk with me in white, because they are worthy. ⁵He who conquers like this will be clothed in white garments, and I will **not erase** his name **from the book** of life, but I will confess his name before my Father and

before his angels. ⁶He who has an ear, **let him** hear what the Spirit says to the churches.'"

First Testament

$^{Isa\ 35:3}$**Strengthen the** weak hands and make the stumbling knees stable.

$^{Job\ 4:3}$You **strengthened the weak hands**; your words upheld the stumbling; you made stable the bent knees.

$^{Exod\ 24:7}$All that Yehowah has spoken we will **keep, and** we will **hear.**

$^{Ezek\ 34:4}$**The** weak you have not **strengthened**; the sick you have not healed.

$^{Exod\ 32:32}$Now, if you will, forgive their crime--but if **not**,
blot me out, please,
from the book which you have written.

$^{Mal\ 3:16}$Then those who fear Yehowah conversed, each man with his neighbor, and Yehowah paid attention and heard, and **a book of memory** was written before him.

> $^{Ps\ 69:29}$Let them be **blotted out from the book of life; let them** *not be* inscribed with the righteous.
>
> $^{Dan\ 12:1}$In that time your people will escape--everyone who is found written in **the book**.

COMMENTARY

To the officer. As with all of the other letters that John of Patmos addressed and sent, this letter also was directed to the leading **officer** of the church. He was the one who was responsible for the activity and character of the congregation. He was an angel, meaning that he was a legal agent of John, who was a legal agent of Jesus and therefore could speak in the name of Jesus, in his behalf, and at his responsibility. He was a human being who lived on earth, but he was legally appointed as a messenger or officer of the church.

The seven spirits of God and the seven stars. This is the same description given at the introduction of the letter to Ephesus. John of Patmos used euphemisms like this to avoid blaspheming God in some way. The conjunction, here rendered by **and** is used epexegetically. That means that the two expressions are the same in meaning and the conjunction would be translated better by "namely." That means that Jesus is the one in whose name John was speaking. He was the one who possessed the **officers** of the churches, including this one at **Sardis** who would receive this letter. It was obviously a coded expression John liked. He explained earlier,

> The seven stars are the officers of the seven churches,
> and the lamp stands are the seven churches (Rev 1:20).

The one who controlled **the seven spirits of God and the seven stars** was the one to whom all of **the officers** were responsible. John reminded **the officer** at **Sardis** that he was one of those **stars**. It is the Messiah to whom this message is attributed. He was the one who held **the seven stars**, and at this point he also held **the seven spirits of God.** This was a coded way of saying that he was the legal agent of God and had full authority to act in his name, in his behalf, and at his responsibility. The word **spirit** often is a synonym for legal authority.

There are many ruins today at **Sardis**. They have been excavated by the combined Harvard-Cornell Universities, and some buildings have been restored as the archaeologists conjectured that they were originally. Above the plain there is a tall plateau, about 1500 feet above the plain. This has been seriously eroded over the years. At one time it was probably a strong fortress. There are a few ruins of buildings still left on the plateau. On both sides of the plateau are ruins of temples and other structures. Even today this plateau can be reached from the plain only by goats and human beings, winding their way up the crooked, narrow paths. In antiquity, a small, well-armed force could easily prevent troops from climbing this precipice. A photograph of the ruins of Sardis can be seen between chapters twelve and thirteen.

Sardis was an important commercial city. For many years it was the most important city in Asia Minor. It was the capital of Lydia when Croesus was the wealthy king of that country. It was a wealthy city, because there was gold to be mined from the river Pactolus that flowed through the middle of the city. In his time King Croesus was known as the richest king in the world. The city was taken by Cyrus of Persia in 549 BIA and by Alexander the Great during his famous campaign (334 BIA). Antiochus the Great captured it in 218 BIA. Scipio, the Roman general who overpowered Hannibal, took **Sardis** from the Seleucids in 189 BIA, defeating Antiochus the Great at the Battle of Magnesia. The most popular religion of the city was the worship of Cybele or Artemis.

Among the ruins at **Sardis** was found a large synagogue with room enough to hold a thousand people. It has inscriptions of about 80 different people, mostly wealthy, who made donations. This indicates further the large number of wealthy Jewish businessmen that lived in the diaspora, away from Jerusalem.

You have a reputation for being alive. The word rendered **reputation** here is literally **name** in Greek, but the word **name** in Hebrew has the meaning of **fame** or reputation.[1] When John wrote to other **officers** he began with praise. Then he later found also criticism. With the officer at **Sardis**, John began noting that the **officer had a reputation**—but only a reputation--of **being alive.** Legal life consisted of being worthy members of the religious community. Of course, of all people, the leading **officer** had a reputation of being alive.

He had acted as if he was a Christian **officer.** He pretended to uphold the contract he and his corporation had made with God, but he did not live up to its **name.** The accusation against the **officer** of the church at **Sardis** was that he was **dead.** The words **life** and **death** refer to membership within the contract community or exclusion from it. Only those within the legal Christian corporation have **life. The officer** at **Sardis** was physically alive; he was listed not only as a member, but as a leader of the church, but John had so many misgivings about this **officer** that he claimed he was **dead**. This was evidently an exaggeration, because John urged **the officer** to hold on to the few living things that were left before they also **died.**

Strengthen the things that remain. This is a warning similar to the one Ezekiel gave to the shepherds of Israel (the kings) who had not been caring for the people of Israel faithfully. Ezekiel accused them of not feeding the sheep and not **strengthening** the weak ones of the flock (Ezek 34:1-4). He said further, **Thus says the Lord,**

---

[1] H. G. C. Newport, "Some Greek Words with Hebrew Meanings in the Book of Revelation," *AUSS* 26 (1988):28-29.

Yehowah, "Look! I am against the shepherds, and I will require the sheep at their hands" (Ezek 34:10). Aune has correctly noted that the neuter is sometimes used as masculine in Greek (1Cor 1:27-28: Heb 7:7), so he rendered this passage **strengthen** those who **remain**, meaning those people who **remain**.[1] The context, however, does not require that. Following the FT texts, **The things that remain** are weak **things,** like weak hands, stumbling knees, and sick people (Job 4:3; Isa 35:3; Ezek 34:4). The exhortation in Isa 35:5 seems to have been well enough known for Job to have composed a small midrash on it. It may also have been the basis for John's exhortation.

I have not found your works filled up. This expression pictures someone checking up on the situation. That which he discovered is that which he **found,** the nature of the situation involved. That which John **found** here was that the officer had not fulfilled his responsibility very well. He did not pass inspection.

This is a *litotes* expression. A *litotes* is an understatement or one that has been softened by using a negative with a word of opposite meaning. To say, for example, "She is not beautiful," means, "She is homely" "He is not strong," means "He is weak." John did not mean that he found them to be a little weak--just not quite completely **filled up** with works of supererogation. He meant that they not only did not have a huge balance on hand, but that they were overdrawn, completely deficient in merits. The **works** of **Sardis** were drawn against the treasury of merits to offset the merits added to it by others. Rabbis called a generation that had accumulated no merits in the heavenly treasury "a poverty stricken generation." John thought **the officer at Sardis** had not added to the merit side of the ledger, but instead to the deficit. Therefore that **officer** at **Sardis** had a lot of work to do to bring up the balance. If he did not recall the past and **repent**, then the Messiah would come to him and treat him the way the Messiah was to treat criminals--smash him like a crock or piece of china! That would happen on the day of the Lord (Mal 3:23 [4:5]) or the judgment day.

You have received and heard. So keep. When the commandments were given to the Israelites in the wilderness, they were asked if they would accept them. They responded, **We will keep and we will hear** (*nah-ah-sáy wuh neesh-mah*, נעשה ונשמע). This is called a *hysteron proteron* expression. That means that the last word expressed is really the first one to be acted upon. They meant **we will hear** (obey); **we will act** (keep the commandments). Here John of Patmos reminded **the officer** that he **had heard.** He knew the commandments and the rules required. He knew enough to be alive, religiously and legally. He really had no excuses for his behavior and failure to lead the congregation as he should have done. Therefore, he was obligated **to keep** the promises he had made, fulfill his responsibilities, act as his contract required. That would require **repentance**. That involved acknowledgement of faults and correction of damages committed.

---

[1] D. Aune, *Revelation* 1-5 (Dallas: Word Books Publisher, c1997), p. 219-222.

If, therefore, you do not. **That officer** had received just warning. If he would continue as he had, John of Patmos would be released from his confinement at some time in the future, at a time the **officer** would not be informed. Then John would arrive at **Sardis** and enforce discipline in no uncertain terms. John would not tolerate such unorthodox leadership as that **officer** had demonstrated so far.

You have a few individuals. Aune recognized that the subject here, as in other letters, is in the singular and held that this is a collective reference to the group.[1] A much more likely interpretation is that John addressed this letter, as the others, to the **officer.** He was the leading **officer** in the community. It was his group, for which he was responsible.

In Greek the word rendered **individual** here is literally **names**. In Hebrew the word for **name** (*shame*, שׁם) also means **individual**.[2] It means that they had their **names** in the membership roll. They were alive and well, religiously. Before the Day of the Lord came, the Lord would prepare a **book of remembrance** (Mal 3:16), listing the faithful in a membership book to which the Lord could refer when he held judgment.

John was disturbed because **the officer** in charge had allowed a great deal of laxity in observance, but the church was not all bad. John acknowledged that there were **a few individuals** in **Sardis** that would be included in that book. These were the "worthy" ones, who observed all of the dietary, tithing, and purity laws. They were as undefiled as the priests were supposed to be in the holy of holies. They wore **white garments** to indicate that they were not defiled with any midras uncleanness. It was safe to admit them to the pulpit (the *báy-mah,* במה) to read Scripture in the synagogue or to eat with the other careful law observers (the *khah-veh-reém,* חברים). The Messiah would confess these pious ones to his Father and his angels and bear witness on their behalf. These were the ones whose **names** were written in the **book of life**, the book containing the membership roll of those who belonged to the community where **life** was possible (see also Rev 20:12, 15; 21:27).

I will confess his name before my Father. In early Christianity Jews and Christians were both involved in subversive anti-governmental movements. When caught they could be brought before the court and tortured to obtain confessions from them. There was a normal self-protective impulse to deny any part of any association with any leader that might be considered a security threat. Jesus was obviously one of those leaders, so he taught his followers:

> Everyone then who confesses me before men I will also confess him before my Father in heaven. But whoever denies me before men I also will deny him before my Father in heaven. Do not think that I

---

[1] Aune, *Revelation 1-5*, p. 222. \
[2] Newport, "Hebrew," p. 28.

came to bring peace to the land; I did not come to bring peace but a sword (Matt 10:32-34).

Luke's variant is that instead of **my Father in heaven**, he has **the angels of God** (Luke 12:3), which has the same meaning. Since the **angels of God** were God's legal agents, who would bring the message directly to God. John of Patmos may have been acquainted with this quotation and have given it the same scriptural authority as he had just given Exod 32:32 and Ps 69:29.[1]

TEXT

⁷To the officer of the church in Philadelphia, write:

Revelation	First Testament
"Thus says the holy One,	Isa 22:20-22 On that day I will call my servant, Eliakim . . . and I will dress him with your robe . . . I will commit your authority to his hand, and he will be a father to those who live in Jerusalem . . . and I will place on his shoulder
The true One, who has **the key of David** who **opens and no one closes and** who **closes and no one opens**, ⁸'I know your works. Look! I have set before you an **open**	**the key** to the house **of David**; he will **open, and no one** will **close, and** he will **close, and no one** will **open**.
door, which **no one** can **close**, because you have a little power; you have kept my commandment; and you have not denied my name. ⁹Look! I am giving [some] of those from the synagogue of Satan, who say they are Jews, but are not. They are lying. Look! I will make them so that **they will** come and **prostrate themselves before your feet** and they will know that	Job 12:14 If he [God] destroys, no one can rebuild; if he **closes** a man out, no one can **open**. Isa 49:23 Kings will be your foster fathers, and queens, your nursing mothers (also Isa 60:14; 45:14; Ps 86:9). **They will prostrate themselves before** you, licking the dust of **your feet**, with their faces to the ground.

---

[1] So also Aune, *Revelation 1-5*, pp. 225-27.

I have loved you. ¹⁰Because you have kept my commandment to endure, I also will keep you from the hour of testing which is about to come upon the whole universe to test the migrants of the land. ¹¹I am coming quickly. Hold fast to that which you have, so that no one may take away your crown. ¹²He who conquers I will make him a pillar in the temple of my God, and I will come, and he will not go out again. I will write upon him the name of my God

and the name of the city of my God, the new Jerusalem which comes down from heaven, from my God, and [I will write upon him]

my **new name**.' ¹³He who has an ear let him hear what the Spirit says to the churches."

^(Isa 43:3)I have given Egypt as your ransom; Ethiopia and Seba instead of you. Because you are precious in my eyes and honored,

^(Isa 43:4)**I have loved you**, and I have given [other] men instead of you, gentiles in exchange for your life.

^(Ezek 48:35)The circumference of the city will be eighteen thousand cubits,

and the name of the city from that day will be "Yehowah is there."

^(Isa 62:2) Gentiles will see your vindication, and all of the kings, your glory. You will be called by a **new name** which the mouth of the Lord will call.

COMMENTARY

The officer of the church. The recipient of the letter, often translated "angel," was an **official** leader of the community, legally established as an agent of the greater Christian community of which John of Patmos was in charge. He was not any kind of a heavenly being.

The Church of Philadelphia. The community at **Philadelphia** was probably badly damaged by the earthquake of 17 IA.[1] It may have been the place where Montanism originated. There are very few remains of that city today. It was located about 28 miles southeast of Sardis and 60 miles east of Smyrna, at the foot of the Tmolus mountains (Pliny, *NatHist* 5:30).

The holy One the true One. **The holy and true One** is still the Messiah. This is clear from the allusion to Isaiah's prophecy that **Eliakim** would succeed the incumbent

---

[1] IA (Internatonal Age).A politically correct calendrical abbreviation, chosen in preference to the exclusive designations, AD (the year of our Lord) and CE (the common era, Lev 10:10).

ruler. Isaiah said the Lord would give **Eliakim** a royal robe, royal authority, and give him charge over Jerusalem. He would have exclusive responsibility for **opening and closing.** He could initiate or conclude any activity in the kingdom that he chose. No one could prevent his actions. **The key to the house of David was placed on his shoulder.** This meant that God would make Eliakim king, ruling from Jerusalem (Isa 22:20-22).

John identified the Messiah with this type. The message of the Messiah to the **officer** at **Philadelphia** was a midrash on this text from Isaiah. This Messiah who had the authority **to open and close** doors had set before the Christians at **Philadelphia** an **open door** which **no one could close.** The welcome mat was always out for them.

You have a little power. **The officer** at Philadelphia was apparently discouraged, so John's message was one of encouragement. **The officer's** situation was not as bad as it seemed, and he himself was not a failure. He **had a little power.** He was not completely helpless. He had been able **to keep** John's **word,** or commandment, and **he did not deny his name.** For this he was to be congratulated. That was not an easy assignment in this difficult situation. John admitted that he had sent **the officer** into a difficult appointment. His was not a church of the faithful observers. In fact this was **the synagogue of Satan.** There were members there **who called themselves Jews**, but they **were not** really **Jews.** Their confessions were **lies,** because they did not observe normal orthodox regulations. Members of this **synagogue** were liberal Christians who did not observe many of the forms that were considered essential by the orthodox Jewish Christians. They were not "unbelieving Jews" who were disdained because they had not accepted Christianity, as Rissi and Beagley held.[1] While making his second promise to the Christians at **Philadelphia**, John was thinking of Isa 43:3-4.

There Second Isaiah reasoned that the Lord would redeem Israel (Isa 43:1). He would pay off Israel's debt of unpaid fines (iniquities). In order to get the ransom money required, the Lord would give Egypt as a trade-in. He would give other people (probably into slavery) in order to buy Israel's freedom. Second Isaiah promised that **those who oppressed** Babylonian Jews **would bow before** them (Isa 60:14). He further held that even gentile kings and queens would become Jewish slaves and **bow down at their feet** (Isa 49:22-23). When Joshua's troops captured five local kings, Joshua forced them all to bow at his feet and had the members of his armed forces to put their feet on the necks of each of the kings. Afterwards they killed them (Josh 10:5-27).

Against that scriptural background, John told **the officer**, however, that he should not give up hope. Sooner or later, John would make these fake Jews **come and prostrate themselves before** the **officer.** Then these counterfeit Jews would know that John **loved** and supported **the officer**, and not the counterfeit Jews in this

---

[1] M. Rissi, *The Future of the World* (Naperville: A. R. Allenson, c1966), p.74; and A. J. Beagley, *The "Sitz im Leben" of the Apocalypse* (Berlin: W. De Gruyter, 1987), *passim*.

dispute. All of this would happen because **the officer** had kept John's **commandment to endure,** so John, in turn, would protect him **from the hour of testing.**

The hour of testing which is to come. The time of **testing** that was destined **to come** upon the whole Greco-Roman world would not effect the Christians at **Philadelphia**, but it was designed to test **the migrants of the land** [of Palestine], those in Palestine who were not Jews. Most of these were Romans, but there were also Greeks, and some of other nationalities. Jews hated these **migrants of the land**, and John insultingly implied that those counterfeit Jews who belonged to the **synagogue of Satan** in Philadelphia were of the same caliber as the **migrants of the land**. They also deserved the same punishment as the gentiles who were destined to **prostrate themselves before** the liberated Babylonian Jews (Isa 49:23; 60:14). The **migrants of the land** have erroneously been called "those who dwell upon the earth,"[1] but that does not describe this group at all. This is just one specific group of enemies of Israel in the land of Palestine. **The hour of testing which is to come** was an anticipated war in Palestine that would not effect **the officer** who lived in **Philadelphia**.

MIGRANTS ON THE LAND

Migrants on the land. A group of people to whom reference is made in the Book of Revelation has been called by the RSV **those who dwell on the earth** (Rev 3:10; 6:10; 11:10; 13:14; 14:6), **all who dwell on earth** (Rev 13:8), **the earth and its inhabitants** (Rev 13:12), or **the dwellers on earth** (Rev 17:2, 8).[2] There are problems with this translation, however, because the people involved do not include *all* of the people on the earth, even when the adjective "all" was used in reference to them (Rev 13:8). In that instance "all" of **the dwellers** were set in contrast to still others whose names were written in the Book of Life (Rev 13:8). Hemer said the solution was easy. They were "the enemies of the church,"[3] but that answer is too easy. They were also contrasted with those who would be kept from the hour of testing (Rev 3:10), and the seer prayed that God would punish them for the martyrdom of those who had been killed for the word of God (Rev 6:9-10). These **dwellers** rejoiced when two witnesses were killed by the "beast," because those anointed prophets had earlier tortured these dwellers (Rev 11:7-10).

---

[1] Beagley, *Sitz im Leben*, has attempted to translate this phrase differently, depending on each context throughout the Book of Revelation, as if the group would change from time to time or from context to context. Wherever possible he holds that they constitute a group of Palestinian Jews who were enemies of Christians (e.g. p., 86).

[2] Aune, *Revelation 1-5*, p. 240, rendered this expression "those who dwell on the earth." He thought, however, that they were "native Palestinians," and correctly noticed that the phrase "always occurs in a negative sense," but he could not explain why.

[3] C. J. Hemer, *The Letters to the Seven Churches of Asia in their Local Setting* (Sheffield:JSOT, c1986), p. 164.

Hebrew Hypotheses. Charles correctly noted that these could either be considered "those who dwell on the earth" or "those who dwell on the land," meaning the land of Palestine.[1] He was further accurate in observing that it would be impossible for all the inhabitants of the earth to learn of the death of the witnesses and send each other presents within 3½ days.[2] He concluded that these dwellers were Palestinian inhabitants and also Jews.[3] In other examples (Rev 3:10; 6:10), Charles thought these dwellers were non-Christians or heathen.[4] Charles held that the expressions *kaht-oi-koón-tehs epí tays gays* (κατοικοῦντες ἐπὶ τῆς γῆς) and *kaht-oi-koón-tehs tane gane* (κατοικοῦντες τὴν γῆν), rendered *yoh-sheh-veém ahl hah-áh-rehtz* (יושבים על הארץ) or *yoh-sheh-váy hah-áh-retz* (יושבי הארץ). This is a reasonable deduction, since the root *yah-sháhv* (ישב) means to sit, dwell, reside, or remain, but Charles' conjecture is not the only one possible. That root was translated by 80 different terms in the Old Greek (OG),[5] most of which were some form of *oí-kayn* (οἴκειν) or *kath-eéd-zane* (καθίζειν). Eight of these were rendered by *páh-roi-kos* (πάροικος), which translates either *gayr* (גר) or *tóh-shav* (תושב), "tenant" or "migrant."

It seems evident that the crucial Hebrew terms behind this Greek are *yah-sháv* (ישב) and *éh-retz* (ארץ), because **the dwellers** seem not to have occupied all of the earth, and because the same group in one instance is rendered *toos kath-ayménoos eh-peé tays gáys* (τοὺς καθημένους ἐπὶ τῆς γῆς)--**those seated on the land** or **earth** (Rev 14:6).[6] Since the root *yah-sháhv* can mean both "sit" and **dwell,**

---

[1] R. H. Charles, *A Critical and Exegetical Commentary on the Revelation of St. John the Divine* (New York: Charles Scribner's Sons, 1920), I, *loc. cit.*

[2] Charles, *Revelation* I, p. 289.

[3] Charles, *Revelation* I, p. 290. S. Brown, "'The Hour of Trial' (Rev 3:10)," *JBL* 85 (1966):309, held that the phrase "upon the entire earth" (3:10) precluded the possibility that the inhabitants referred to only those in Palestine. But just because the test was to come upon all the Roman world (*tays oi-koó-meh-nays háw-lehs*, (τῆς οἰκουμένες ὄλες) does not mean the dwellers who would be tested at that time were the only ones to be punished or that they inhabited the whole world, as Brown thought. He said that the expression must be translated "the inhabitants of the earth," but it could not mean all human beings without exception (p. 311-12). Therefore they must refer only to the enemies of the church. Brown clearly saw that the dwellers were enemies of the faithful and not all the inhabitants, but his deduction from this that the dwellers must not be only Palestinian does not follow. F. Düsterdieck, *Critical and Exegetical Handbook of the Revelation of John*, tr. H. E. Jacobs (Winona Lake: Alpha Publications, c1883, 1979), rendered the passages to mean inhabitants of the earth, although he once held that it meant the unbelieving inhabitants (p. 173), and at another place it meant the inhabitants of Jerusalem who represented all the inhabitants of the earth (p. 319).

[4] Charles, *ICC Revelation*, 1, pp. 90, 175.

[5] So C. Dos Santos, *An Expanded Hebrew Index for the Hatch-Redpath Concordance to the Septuagint* (Jerusalem: Dugeth Publishers, n.d.), p. 87.

[6] J. M. Ford, *Revelation* (Garden City: Doubleday & Co., c1975), p. xxxvii, rendered the passage, "those who are enthroned on the earth." She translated the other passages as those who dwelled on the earth. Brown, "Trial," thought the seer intentionally changed the verb to "seated" in the phrase "with the same conceptual content," because this context has no pejorative moral overtones (fn 7, p. 309). Brown, however, overlooked the overtones that are there. The "eternal gospel" announced to

some translator evidently mistranslated it to mean "seated," even though "seated" makes no sense in that context. Some OG translator also confused *yah-sháhv* (יֵשֵׁב) with *shoov* (שׁוּב) and rendered it by *ah-paw-stréh-phayn* (ἀποστρέφειν, Prov 20:3). With 80 different words used to translate *yah-shāhv* in the OG with *kahth-ay-méh-noi* confused for *kaht-oi-koón-tehs* in the Book of Revelation, with *éh-rehtz* meaning both "earth" and "land," there are other possibilities for the underlying Hebrew than Charles' conjecture, and English translation possibilities other than the RSV's offering. One of these will be considered here.

MIGRANTS IN PALESTINE

The Earth and the Land. The term *yoh-sheh-vay hah-ah-rehtz* was used in the FT four times when it probably meant "the inhabitants of the earth" (Isa 24:6; Jer 25:30, 31; Ps 33:14). RSV additionally renders Zeph 1:18 "inhabitants of the earth."[1] The term *yoh-sheh-váy tay-váyl* (יוֹשְׁבֵי תֵבֵל) also had this meaning (Isa 26:18; Lam 4:12; Ps 33:8). The great majority of cases, however, identify the *yoh-sheh-váy hah-áh-rehtz* as those who lived on the land of Palestine (Exod 23:31; 34:12, 15; Josh 2:9, 24; 6:12; 7:9; 9:14; 10:18; 13:21; 24:18; 25:29, 30; Judges 1:32-33; Ezek 7:7; Hos 4:1; Joel 1:2, 14; 2:1; Zech 11:6) and should be rendered "inhabitants of the land" rather than "inhabitants of the earth." From the same Hebrew root comes both the expression *yóh-shayv* (יוֹשֵׁב) one who dwells or sits, and also *tóh-shayv* (תּוֹשָׁב), meaning one who dwells, but *tóh-shahv* has the special meaning of one who dwells *temporarily*. Inhabitant is a general expression, whereas **migrant** is a more distinctive term. Those who were tenants or **migrants** in the land were those who lived in the land of Palestine but who either belonged someplace else or were believed by the citizens of Palestine to belong somewhere else. These **dwellers** seem more likely to qualify for identification with those in the Book of Revelation than do earthly inhabitants in general. The next step of this study will be to examine the migrants in the land to learn their characteristics.

First Testament Usage. **Migrants** held an important role in forming Hebrew life and religion. Abraham dwelled in Canaan as a **tenant** (*gayr* = *pár-oikos*) **and a migrant** (*tóh-shayv* = *pah-reh-peé-day-mos*) (Gen 23:4). This evidently means that he lived there but was not assimilated among the local residents. The author of Hebrews said Abraham dwelled as a **tenant** in the land of the promise, the land he was afterwards to inherit (Heb 11:9). He did not become a Canaanite citizen. Because of the strong

---

these people was not good news to them. As in Second Isaiah, the good news announced that the land was about to be restored to the Jews. That was good news to the Jews, but not to the foreigners who lived in Palestine, as well as the other gentiles of every nation, tribe, language, and people (Rev 14:6). When God acted, these would be terrified, expelled, made subject, and forced to give God (and also the Jews) glory (Rev 11:13; 14:6-7).

[1] Marvin A. Sweeney, "Zephaniah: A Prophet of His Time—Not the End Time," *Bible Review* 20.6 (2004):34-40, 43, correctly argued that Zephaniah's prophecies had nothing to do with the end of the cosmos, the world, or time. All of his predictions were expected to be fulfilled in time and known local geography.

hospitality demands a priest might be tempted to serve a tenant food limited to priests, so Israelite law prohibited him from doing that.

Israelites were reminded that even when they owned land in Palestine, which they had received as an inheritance, they were still **migrants and tenants** with the Lord (Lev 25:23). They were obligated to redeem the land. The land belonged to the Lord, so believers were only tenants, so far as the Lord was concerned. Jews could be evicted (1Chron 29:15; Ps 39:12). The fellow Israelite who had to work off his debt lived with his creditor as a **migrant and a tenant** (Lev 25:35, 40). Someone who lived in the same community but was not a member of the Israelite family was called a **migrant and a tenant,** even though he was wealthy, settled, and probably owned the property where he lived (Lev 25:47). From the point of view of the Israelite invaders, all Canaanites, Hittites, and other local residents might have been classed as temporary residents to be expelled and replaced as soon as possible, even though the land they owned had been in the family for centuries. Cities of refuge were provided for **migrants and tenants** who were fleeing from avengers (Num 35:15).

Rabbis distinguished between **the migrant**, who was a temporary resident, and **the tenant**, who was a proprietor (GenR 58:6), but that distinction was not always valid. The two terms were often applied jointly to the same person who could not have been both **a tenant** and a proprietor at the same time. These **migrants** were all short term residents or non-citizens in a certain geographical area. Abraham was a **migrant** in the midst of the Canaanites. Some were guests in a priest's house. Other **migrants** were with God on the Promised Land which they were obligated to redeem. The debtor was a **migrant** in the home of his creditor. In one way or another their **migrating** was done in relationship to **the Land** which they claimed for an inheritance.

Deuteronomic Ethics. The Deuteronomist and his followers encouraged Israelites to be hospitable and kind to the **tenant** (*gayr,* גֵר) (Deut 10:18-19; Jer 7:6; Zech 7:10; Mal 3:5) and saw to it that he received justice, remembering that Israelites themselves had once been tenants in Egypt (Deut 23:8; 24:17-18; 27:19). The tenant was classed together with widows and orphans who needed special attention, but Jews in NT times, at least, did not feel kindly to most non-Jews who were residents of Palestine. Daube argued that **migrants** were people who lived as subjects in some way.[1] They did not have full status as citizens.

People of the Land. The **migrants** or tenants were not confused with the **people of the land** (*ah-máy hah-áh-retz,* עמי הארץ) after the time of Nehemiah. When upper class Babylonian Jews (Ant 10:98) returned to reestablish the land they found in Palestine the descendants of the local Palestinian Jews who had not been taken into captivity. The reason they had been left behind was that they were not leaders, and

---

[1] D. Daube, *The Exodus Pattern in the Bible* (London: Faber and Faber, c1963), pp. 24-25.

they had no ability to organize a revolution. There was an obvious class difference between the upper class Babylonian Jews and the Palestinian Jews whom the former called **the people of the land**, probably comparing them insultingly to the pagan Canaanites that occupied the land before Joshua's conquest.

Even though the Babylonian Jews insulted the Palestinian Jews, they did not reject them from **the land**. They admitted that these Palestinian Jews had a right to be there. They were not confused with **migrants** or tenants.

Migrants in NT Times. In NT times there was a strong anti-**migrant** movement. Jews wanted Palestine for themselves alone, and there were many **migrants** there. The Jews wanted these **migrants** cleansed from the land. When Herod rebuilt Samaria and named it Sebaste after Caesar, he settled 6,000 colonists in the city. These were probably foreigners, because this was one of the few cities that did not cooperate in the anti-Roman rebellion while Archelaus was trying to obtain control of Palestine (War 1:403; 2:69). At that time Gaza, Gadara, and Hippos were known as Greek cities (War 2:97). Herod had built for the Greeks in Caesarea non-Jewish statues and temples. Greeks in that city were numerous enough to demand and obtain from Nero control of the city (War 2:266-67, 284). As the war was breaking out between Rome and the Jews, bands of Jews attacked the Syrian cities of Philadelphia, Sebonitis, Gerasa, Pella, and Scythopolis, and they burned both Sebaste and Ascalon to the ground. They also razed Gaza and Anthedon (War 2:458-60).

These settlements of foreigners in Palestine helped to keep down any type of rebellion against Rome, so they also provided a group of Roman sympathizers which Jewish nationalists resented. When it became clear that the Jews were going to fight Rome to the finish, it seemed necessary at the outset to reduce these internal saboteurs, **the migrants of the land. The migrants,** then, were unwanted non-Jewish residents in Palestine. The so-called "dwellers on the earth" in the Book of Revelation were also people whom the author disliked. This is only one of the reasons for thinking that those who have been called "dwellers on the earth" were really **migrants on the land.** The following analysis will support this possibility.

Saints and Migrants. At the hour of testing, the **migrants** of the land would be punished, but the Lord would keep those who had kept his word. On those who were not **migrants** the Lord would write his new name and the name of the new Jerusalem which comes down from heaven (Rev 3:7-12). When the fifth seal was opened, and the seer saw under the altar the souls of those who had been slaughtered because of their witness to the word of God, he cried out asking God how long before God avenged those **migrants** on the land, implying that these were the ones responsible for the deaths of the martyrs (Rev 6:9-10). Following the type of Exodus plagues, four angels blew their trumpets, after which four different plagues fell from heaven. Then the eagle flew in the sky, crying out, **Woe, woe to the migrants on the land, because of the rest of the trumpet blasts which the three angels are about to sound** (Rev 8:13).

The two witnesses, who were identified with both Elijah and Elisha and also the two olive trees in Nehemiah that symbolized the high priest and the king, were killed, and their bodies were left unburied in the streets of Jerusalem for three days. During that time, the **migrants of the land** rejoiced at their death and held celebrations, because the witnesses had previously tortured these **migrants**. From the view point of the seer, the two witnesses were God's chosen messiahs, and the migrants were some of his enemies (Rev 11:1-11).

Following the typology of Dan 7, a beast came up out of the sea who epitomized all four beasts in Daniel. This new antitype of Antiochus Epiphanes was given auhority for 42 months (or three and a half years), during which time he spoke blasphemies and made war against the saints. This beast had authority over every tribe, people, tongue, and nation. He was also worshipped by the **migrants of the land.**

These **migrants**, like all tribes, peoples, languages, and nations under the beast's authority, were the ones whose names were not written in the Book of Life. There followed another subordinate beast, who apparently acted as an agent of the first beast. It exercised the authority of the first beast and made **the Land** and its **migrants** worship the first beast. Its great signs deceived the **migrants of the Land** into making an image of the first beast. Those, then, who would not worship the image of the beast, namely the non-**migrants**, would be slain (Rev 13:1-15). The **migrant**s here were set in contrast to those who would not worship the beast. Therefore, they did not comprise all those inhabitants of the earth. In this typological narrative, the first beast was probably Rome, and the second beast, who worked under Rome's authority, probably represented some of the Herods who ruled Palestine in behalf of Rome. They instituted Roman policies, erected Roman temples and statues, and enforced Roman law on Jews in Palestine. They evidently had the cooperation of a group of non-Jews who lived in Palestine as **migrants**.

The RSV rendered Rev 14:6 as "those who dwell on earth," even though it literally means "those who are seated" either on earth or **on the land.** The translators were correct, however, in recognizing that the group involved was the same group as those others who dwelled, either on the earth or on **the Land**. In this case the **migrants** were classed again with every nation, tribe, language, and people (except the Jews) as the recipients of an eternal gospel which commanded them to fear God and give him glory. This would happen just before the new Babylon fell (Rev 14:6-8, 12). This means all gentiles in foreign countries, as well as those in Palestine, would be forced to accept the God of the Jews and submit to his decrees. Although they had trusted Rome, Rome would fall as Babylon had fallen before.

In a vision the seer was shown the great harlot (Rome), with whom the kings of the earth had committed adultery and with whose wine of adultery **the migrants of the land** became intoxicated (Rev 17:1-2). These **migrants** were cast in an unfavorable light. They were those who were aligned with all other nations, peoples, tongues, and tribes. They gave allegiance to Rome, worshipping its image and becoming intoxicated with its association. They opposed the messianic movements that originated in Jerusalem. They were responsible for the deaths of the martyrs, and when the day of God's visitation came, they would be punished along with the rest of the gentiles who lived outside **of the land**.

Palestine and the Book of Revelation. When this group of people whom the seer disliked is understood as a group of **migrants on the land** of Palestine rather than a group consisting of all the inhabitants of the earth, it becomes more obvious that the Promised Land is the central geographical unit in the Book of Revelation. The one who had authority to open the seals of the scroll was the lion from the tribe of Judah of the root of David (Rev 5:5)--obviously someone from Palestine.

After the Lamb had opened the sixth seal, there were so many plagues that leaders fled and hid in caves and rocks of the mountains (of which there are many in Palestine) from their fear of the Lamb's anger. Since the Lamb was stationed at Jerusalem, the geography seems to have been designated against a Palestinian background (Rev 6:12-17). Crowds were expected to gather before the Lamb on his throne with palm branches, Jewish nationalistic symbols (Rev 7:9-10). This is the way Jews were supposed to gather at Jerusalem from the diaspora on the Feast of Tabernacles (Zech 14:16-21).

There is no biblical command to gather in crowds at Ephesus, Antioch, Alexandria, or Rome with palm branches on the Feast of Tabernacles. That the Lamb was located at Jerusalem is evident from the claim that the 144,000 would be gathered together with him on Mount Zion (Rev 14:7). The bride of the Lamb was to be the holy city, the new Jerusalem (Rev 21:9-27). In that city, as in Ezekiel's vision of Jerusalem, was a stream of water flowing out from the spring of Siloam under the temple area, with fruit trees on either side. There also was to be the throne of God and of the Lamb (Rev 22:1-5), there in Zion in the palace near the temple. The two messianic witnesses were to have been active and to have been killed in the great city--apparently Jerusalem (Rev 11:7-8).

The northern border of the Promised Land was believed for many years to have been the river Euphrates.[1] It was probably on this basis that the seer visualized four angels released from the river Euphrates (Rev 9:13-14). The antitype of the Egyptian plagues was expected to include drying up the river Euphrates, so that the kings of the East could come to Israel's assistance. This was probably an anticipated miracle to expedite the military support of the Parthians in opposing Rome (Rev 16:1-14, esp 12), just as the Parthians had come to nationalists' rescue during the time of Herod the Great.

Following the harvest and winepress metaphors of which Joel's prophecy is the prototype, the seer visualized a great battle in the Valley of Jehoshaphat in the Kidron Valley, just opposite the temple area in Zion (Rev 14:14-20). This would also recur in the same place after the millennium was over. Then Satan would lead all nations together for battle, according to the same type. The nations would surround the beloved city (of Jerusalem) where the camp of the saints was gathered (Rev 20:7-9). Immediately following this battle, there would be a judgment, apparently right there at Jerusalem (Rev 20:11-15).

---

[1] Buchanan, *The Consequences of the Covenant* (Leiden: E. J. Brill, 1970), pp. 91-109.

When the seventh angel poured out its bowl, there would be terrible natural catastrophes, and the great city would be divided into three parts, the cities of the nations would fall, and God would remember to punish Babylon (Rev 16:17-19). This may reflect events at the beginning of 70 IA, when Jerusalem was divided into three parts, each part governed by a different, zealotish messiah--John, Simon, or Eleazar. At that time there were wars in many parts of the world, and Rome was engaged in another civil war (War 5:21). This would follow the sixth angel who poured out its bowl just before the great battle at Mount Megiddo, an important fortification at the end of the Carmel Range in Palestine (Rev 16:12-16).

Cosmic Influences. Apart from Palestinian geographical sites in the Book of Revelation were only those of typological significance, such as Sodom or Egypt, along with the enemy nation, Rome, who was represented by terms like "beast," "dragon," and "harlot." To be sure, there was a great deal of mythological activity described in relationship to heaven, but even this was patterned after Jerusalem, the temple, and the ministers who functioned there. The angels were like heavenly priests and Levites, and the heavenly temple fixtures, such as the throne and the tent, were prototypes of those in Jerusalem.[1]

Natural and supernatural heavenly activity of cosmic proportions did not preclude earthly events of local significance. When the sun stood still for Joshua, he won a battle that was important for conquering the land. The stars in their courses fought against Sisera so Deborah and Barak could win the battle along Mount Carmel on the Promised Land. When the sea at the eastern border of Egypt miraculously opened up, the Israelites escaped from Egypt. Also in the Book of Revelation, angels poured out bowls of curses, and blew trumpets. There were earthquakes, and fire fell from heaven, but the end result desired was that Rome would be defeated. Jews would be liberated to rule at least Palestine and possibly the whole Roman world under the leadership of their own messianic king from the Davidic line. When all of this happened, the Jewish merchants who dealt with Rome would weep, and God would punish those migrants of the land who had supported Rome against Jewish nationalistic efforts.

CONCLUSIONS

Although the Greek expressions, which the RSV translated to mean the inhabitants of the whole earth, can hypothetically bear that meaning from the purely linguistic point of view, there are several reasons why that meaning does not satisfy the contexts in Revelation in which the term occurs:

1) The group in question was clearly not a general group including all humankind;
2) the group was not associated with the whole world, geographically; and

---

[1] Buchanan, *To the Hebrews* (Garden City: Doubleday & Co., c1972), pp. 157-162.

3) the members were always hated by the author of Revelation, who did not hate people in general.

These same problems do not occur when the members of the group are considered **migrants in the land**, which is an equally valid translation from a purely etymological point of view. Contextually, **migrants of the land** is a much more satisfactory translation, because there were **migrants** in Palestine who were hated by nationalistic Jews of NT times. They constituted only a small portion of humankind, and they were closely related to the problems of Jews in the Promised Land in NT times. For these reasons it is more satisfactory to call this group **migrants of the land** than "inhabitants of the earth."

So that no one can take away your crown. It is not surprising that John exhorted this **officer** to be careful lest someone should deprive him of his **crown**. Since he was identified with the Messiah and was discussed in royal terms, it is normal to speak of his office in terms of a **crown**. Those who threatened the security of **the officer's** position were the members of **the synagogue of Satan**. John told **the officer** again, **Hold fast to that which you have;** don't submit or yield from your firmness.

Changing metaphors, John promised that the **one who conquered,** namely, **the officer** if he held out, would become a **pillar in the temple of God,** and the Messiah would write upon him the name of his God and the name of the city of God, the new Jerusalem.

A pillar in the temple of my God. There were, of course, **pillars in** Solomon's **temple** (1Kings 7:13-22), but the expression is here used of a person. Paul used the term **pillars** as a title for the leaders of the Jerusalem church (Gal 2:9). The blessing over the seven virgins was that they might become seven **pillars** in the city or refuge (Jos As 17:6). These **pillars** were real people and not temples or churches. The same is true of the pillar of Rev 3:12. The expression was not applied to the church at **Philadelphia** but to **the officer** in charge of that church. Newport, on the basis of Semitic influence, rendered the word **make** by **appoint**.[1] Allison noted that 4Q403.38-46 personifies the temple, assuming that **pillars** and other parts of the temple could sing praise to God. This is also true of Rev 9:13-14 where the voice from the horns of the altar speak to the angel. In the context of Rev 3:12 the promise is that a certain person, namely **the officer** of the church, might become **a pillar,** while remaining animate.[2] In antiquity memorials were sometimes placed either on mosaic floors or on **pillars**. For example, the **synagogue** at Capernaum, on the northern shore of the Sea of Galilee, has a pillar on which is engraved the name of one of the large contributors involved in building the **synagogue**.

---

[1] Newport, "Greek Words," p. 27.
[2] D. C. Allison, "4Q 403 Fragm. I, Col. I, 38-46 and the Revelation to John," *RQ* 47 (1986):409-14. Note the pillars in Solomon's temple (1Kings 7:13-22).

Write upon him the name. Ezekiel anticipated the time when Jerusalem would be restored. That event would be preceded by a destruction of all of the criminals in the city. Before the slaughter began, however, a scribe with an pen and an inkwell would be sent through the city to mark the foreheads of the faithful with the sign of the Hebrew *tau* (ת), which in antiquity looked like the Greek *khee* (X). This sign would preserve them from the slaughter, just as the marked Israelite houses protected the Israelites from the messenger of death that went through Egypt as the Israelites escaped into the wilderness (Ezek 9; Exod 11-12).

When John promised **the officer** that he would protect him from the coming **testing** and that he would **write on him the name of** his **God and the name of the city of** his **God,** he was picturing the new Jerusalem in which **the officer of Philadelphia** would not be among those slaughtered at this **testing**, but rather be among the saints who were marked on their forehead for salvation. When the **new Jerusalem** was established this **officer** would be one of **the pillars**.

The new Jerusalem that comes down from heaven. **New Jerusalem** was also called **the city of [my] God** (Rev 3:12; see also Gal 4:26; Heb 11:10; 12:22; 13:14). John of Patmos not only obtained the idea of a **new Jerusalem that came down from heaven** from Second Isaiah (Isa 62:1-2), but he also found it in that prophecy that the messenger brought him (Rev 21:1-2).

Medieval rabbis imagined that before Moses died the Lord allowed him to see the Lord building the temple in heaven. He was using as building blocks, precious stones. Instead of mortar, he sealed these stones together with the Shekinah, the legal presence of God. Upon request, the Lord gave Moses the privilege of speaking to the Messiah who explained the relationship between Jacob's vision (Gen 28:17) and the **Jerusalem** temple which was then **in heaven.** Then Moses asked the important question: "When was this temple going **to come down** to earth and function in **Jerusalem** where it belonged?" The temple not made with hands was the heavenly temple which would be constructed in the future at Jerusalem.[1] **Not made with hands** was an idiomatic way of saying that it was not idolatrous. Pagan idols were "made with hands," so this became an idiom for idolatry. The temple at **Jerusalem**, when it was cleansed and functioning with a legitimate priesthood, was held to be a temple **not made with hands**. When it was defiled, it was an idolatrous temple.

---

[1] Buchanan, *Jewish Messianic Movements from AD 70-AD 1300* (Eugene, Oregon: Wipf and Stock Publishers, 2003), pp. 526-28.

TEXT

[14]To the officer of the church at Laodicea, write:

Revelation	First Testament
	Ps 89:35-37 I have sworn by my holiness [May these unexpressed curses come upon me] if I lie to David: "His posterity will be for the age, his throne, like the sun before me; like the moon, it is established for the age."
	Prov 14:5 A **faithful witness** does not lie.
Thus says the Amen, **The faithful** and true **witness**	Ps 89:38 . . . **the faithful witness** in the sky.
the beginning of God's creation,	Prov 8:23 The Lord created me at **the beginning of** his way, the first of his acts.
[15]"**I know** your **works**, that you are neither cold nor hot. [16]Because you are luke warm, [however], and neither hot nor cold, I will vomit you from my mouth. [17]You say, 'I am rich; **I have become wealthy; I have** no need'; but you do not know that you are wretched, poverty stricken, blind, and naked. [18]I advise you to buy from me 1) gold smelted by fire so that you may be rich, 2) a white robe to wear so that the disgrace of your nakedness may not become evident, and 3) salve to anoint your eyes in order for you to see. [19]Those **whom I love** I **discipline** and instruct. Be zealous, then, and repent. [20]Look! I stand at the door	Isa 66:18 **I know** their **works** and their thoughts, and I am coming to gather all nations and languages. They will come and see my glory.
	Hos 12:9 Ephraim says, "**I have become wealthy; I have** found my strength (און); no weariness will find me." -- [Do not read, "*ohn*" (און) (strength), but read] "*ah-ohn*" (עון) (iniquity) which is crime."
	Prov 3:12 The one **whom** the Lord **loves** he **disciplines**.
and **knock**. If anyone hears my voice and **opens** the door, I will enter his home [as a guest], and I will dine with	Song of Sol 5:2 I slept but my heart was awake. [I heard] the sound of my beloved **knocking** [and saying], "**Open** for me, my sister, my

him and he with me. ²¹To the one who conquers I will give [permission] to sit with me [while I am sitting] on the throne, just as I have conquered and have taken a seat with my Father [as he is sitting] on his throne. ²²He who has an ear let him hear what the Spirit says to the churches.'"

neighbor, my dove, my perfect one."

COMMENTARY

The officer of the church. The word **officer** is a rendering of the Greek *áhn-geh-laws* (ἄγγελος) and is usually translated into English as "angel." *Áhn-geh-laws*, in Greek, however, is a general term for "messenger" and is not restricted to heavenly activity. **The officer** at **Laodicia** was not a heavenly angel but a commissioned legal agent. That is why he was called an "angel," a person who had been appointed and sent as a messenger to fulfill a certain **office** at Laodicia. In this context **the officer** involved is clearly in charge of an official responsibility on earth, rather than in heaven.

Laodicia. This is a city named after the favorite queen of King Antiochus III, the Great, of Syria. It was located 40 miles southeast of Philadelphia and 100 miles east of Ephesus. It was destroyed by an earthquake in 60 IA. It was the most important city in the Lycus Valley, near Hierapolis and Colossae (Col 4:13). There was evidently a large Jewish Population in the Lycus Valley (Ant 14:2241-43). Today **Laodicia** is a cultivated field, farmed by local citizens of Turkey. It has not been excavated. Ruins that appear above the surface of the ground include archways, a stadium, and a large theater. It was an inland city that is not a seaport and it was not near a river, so it depended on roads for communication. It was a rural city—not like the great metropolises of Ephesus, Smyrna, or Sardis. Nonetheless, it was prosperous, famous for its banking. Land there was productive and fertile.

Thus says the Amen. **The Amen** is the Messiah who functions as the Father's legal agent. He sits on his Father's throne. John of Patmos was the one who either wrote or dictated the letter, but he attributed the words of the Lord to the Messiah Jesus (Prov 3:12; Rev 3:19). Jesus was God's **faithful and true witness, the beginning of God's creation** (Rev 3:14), the **faithful witness that does not lie (Prov 14:5)**. These were only some of the terms used to praise the Messiah, who was staged as the speaker. Terms were taken from the Torah, the Psalms, and Proverbs. From Num 5:22 comes the term **Amen**, which is said to confirm a statement taken under oath. This is coherent with the next praiseworthy expression that the author took from Ps 89. Although this is a Psalm of lamentation, the first 38 verses are praise to the God of David who had established him on his throne and would not betray his contract with David in which he promised to protect David against his enemies, make him the greatest of all kings, and preserve his dynasty for the age. John quoted from the end of this eulogy, applying this text to mean that the Messiah was like the moon and the sky. He was a continuous and trustworthy witness. To this praise, he also added the adjective **true**. The next praise was taken from Proverbs, which is a poem praising wisdom. Rissi followed Wellhausen and others in calling **the faithful and true witness** a translation and explanation of the word **amen**.[1]

Wisdom is the most precious of all possessions. Kings and princes rule by wisdom; it was the beginning of all God's creation. God first created wisdom and then, in association with wisdom, created the earth, sea, and sky. John appropriated these attributes and applied them to the Messiah to whom he accredited this message. John felt free to attribute to the Messiah praise designed for God, because the Messiah was a legal agent for God and therefore legally identical to the principal, God.

You are neither hot nor cold. This was an attack on the chief **officer** of the congregation, but the metaphor was probably related to the water at **Laodicia**. It was apparently **lukewarm**, because it was brought a long distance through pipes. It also sometimes made people **vomit**, because it contained minerals that were nauseating. Nearby there were hot springs and also cold springs, but not at **Laodicia**.[2] The **heat and cold** were not descriptions of the officer's bodily temperature. They reflected his religious zeal. His enthusiasm, energy, and leadership were flat and indolent. Using a flavoring metaphor, he was tasteless. He caused no trouble, and he organized no new theological points of view. He did not stimulate the congregation to great deeds of heroism. He was just there. A congregation leading **officer** should mean more than that.

I am rich; I have become wealthy. This is apparently a quotation to John from that **officer**. He was not only lukewarm; he was also self satisfied. John compared the officer at Laodicia to Ephraim (Samaria), whom Hosea had rebuked for its pride. In one of the earliest recorded usages of the exegetical method "do not read" (*ahl teek-ráh* (אל תקרא), he altered the text a little so that it sounded almost the same to the ear, but had a different meaning. Two words, "strength" (*ohn,* און) and "iniquity" (*ah-óhn,* עון) sounded very much the same. Hosea said that, contrary to Ephraim's assumption, the pejorative attribute (iniquity) applied to Ephraim, but not the praiseworthy one (strength).[3] John applied the same logic to **Laodicia**.

You are wretched, poverty stricken, blind, and naked. This was John's response to the **officer's** claim to be wealthy. The repetition of five adjectives in rapid succession was a rhetorical device, called polysyndeton, intended to emphasize the miserableness of **the officer's** condition. **The officer** at the church of **Laodicea** obviously

---

[1] Rissi, *Future*, p. 21.
[2] So Hemer, *Seven Churches*, pp. 187-91.
[3] Oddly enough, Hosea scholars seem to have missed this rhetorical technique applied by Hosea.

did not impress John very favorably. In his judgment **the officer** was an indifferent leader. He did not become enthusiastic either about crime or righteousness. He seemed self-satisfied, but in John's opinion he had no basis for complacency. From outward appearances, he was an upper class **officer,** who belonged to the most prominent country clubs and adapted easily to upper class surroundings. Although he was financially well-to-do, from a religious point of view, John claimed that **the officer** was **wretched, poor, blind, and naked**. He had accumulated silver and gold, but he had added no merits in the heavenly treasury. Such a leader as this inspired only nausea in John. Rabbis called a generation that had added no merits to the treasury of merits a "poor generation."

I advise you to buy from me. Since **Laodicia** was a business and banking community, John spoke to the officer in terms of **buying** and selling, of being **rich** and being **poor**. The wealthy officer was able to **buy** almost anything he wanted, but John told him what he needed to **buy** that would take more than money. Although John was discouraged, he nevertheless, had not given up on this **Laodicean officer** completely. He strongly urged him to change his sense of values and face the difficulties that go with faithful witnessing. **Laodicia** was known in antiquity for its eye salve and its banks where gold was stored. This was one of the reasons for the officer's pride. John urged him to trade in his treasures on earth for treasures in heaven. To do this he was obligated to **buy** from the Messiah the gold, white garments, and healing salve necessary to avoid the embarrassment that then threatened him. The Lord's love was accompanied, not with ease and comfort, but discipline and instruction. If **the officer** were to accept this discipline, he had to become zealous and repent.

Look! I stand at the door and knock. John seems to have taken this picture of the Messiah **standing at the door and knocking** from a vision in the Song of Songs, in which the author visualized the Lord, probably understood as represented through his agent, the Messiah, **knocking** and waiting for his people (his bride) to wake up and accept him. Rabbis understood this passage as the Lord trying to wake up his people to redeem them as he had done earlier on Passover night. The **knocking** was not only to lead the people but also to motivate the faithful to passive redemption. It was intended first to stir them to repentance so that they would be prepared for redemption (*CantR* 5.2). The Messiah was pictured as **standing at the door.** He had washed his feet and removed his outer garment so that he was prepared for admission, but the hostess or host was too late. By the time he or she opened the door, the Messiah had given up and left (SongSol 5:3-4).

This picture is similar to that described in the parable of the ten virgins who waited for the bridegroom to appear at night. They had lamps to be kept burning until the bridegroom came. When he arrived, those who were ready entered with him and participated in the wedding feast. The others returned after the door had been closed. The wedding feast was at once a Passover Feast and an occasion to establish the new contract. The Messiah would be the new bridegroom and the participants would be the parties to the new contract. The contract would be a wedding contract between God and his new church (Matt 25:1-13; Luke 12:35-38).

It was on a Passover night when Jesus hosted the Last Supper with his twelve apostles, who were his legal agents. He renewed the contract in precisely the same way. Using the ordinary Passover bread as his seisin he performed the ceremony by which he created the new corporation, his legal body, the corporation of Christ, the *corpus Christi*. Then at the end of the supper, he used the fruit of the vine as another seisin for the blood of the contract which he renewed with the new church.[1]

John of Patmos had the same motivation in his message to the church at **Laodicia** as the rabbinical teaching and the parable of the ten virgins, but he spoke as if the Messiah had not yet left in disappointment. The church still had a chance.

On Passover night in many countries Jews had to celebrate the Passover in secret with doors and windows closed, but they left the door slightly ajar so the Messiah could come. They even saved food for him. To gentiles they explained that they were expecting Elijah, but the only reason Elijah was important was that he was expected to announce the Davidic Messiah.

When John of Patmos wrote to **the officer** of the church at **Philadelphia** he assured **that officer** that the welcome mat was always out. Like the Messiah, the faithful **officer** at **Philadelphia** held the key to the city. The **Laodicean** officer was not given such comfort, but he was given another chance. Although he was not provided the **open door** treatment, he was given an opportunity to **open** his door to the Messiah. If he would open his door, the Messiah would enter and become the **officer's** guest. Then he and the Messiah could dine together. In the Near East, where very much honor is given to hospitality, this was an important invitation, but **the officer** who **opened** the door to the Messiah from **Laodicea** would first have to repent and become zealous.

The one who conquered would share authority with the Messiah. He might sit alongside of him, just as the Messiah sat alongside of God. The Messiah was with God just as wisdom was. He was God's authorized agent who could act with power of attorney in God's behalf. He was the authority next in power to God. John saved **Laodicea** to the last, and he dealt with its **officer** very severely, but still with an open invitation.

This was the end of the introduction that John prepared for the churches to whom he sent the scroll that was brought to him at Patmos. The introduction told a great deal about the author. John was clearly a zealous, militaristic, orthodox Christian, and he believed that the scroll sent to him was the true word of God. This scroll seems to have been the prophecy that begins immediately at Rev 4:1.

---

[1] See further Buchanan, *The Gospel of Matthew* (Lewiston: Mellen Biblical Press, c1996) II, pp. 965-80.

CHAPTER FOUR

TEXT

Revelation	First Testament
4:1After this I was watching--Now look!	Dan 7:6**After this I was watching--now look!**
A door **opened** in **heaven**. Now look! the first	Ezek 1:1**Heaven opened**, and **I saw** a vision of God.
	Exod 19:16The morning of the third day, there were thunders, lightnings, and a heavy cloud on the mountain, and there was a loud **sound** (voice) of
voice which I heard speaking to me like **a trumpet** saying, "Come up here, and I	**a trumpet** and all the people who were in camp trembled.
	Dan 2:29Your thoughts were directed to what **would happen after this**.
will show you **the things that are destined to happen after this**." ²Suddenly I began to day-dream. Now look! [in my mind's eye] a **throne was set** up in heaven, and	Dan 2:45A great God has made known to the king **the things that are destined to happen after this**.
	Dan 7:9I was watching until **thrones were set up** and the Ancient of Days **sat down**.
on the **throne** was One **sitting**.	Isa 6:1I saw the Lord **sitting on** a **throne**.
³The one **sitting**	Ps 47:9God rules over the nations; God **sits on** his glorious **throne**.
	Ezek 1:26Above the firmament which was over their heads was something that
looked like a sapphire stone, a carnelian,	**looked like a sapphire stone**, in the form of a

and **a rainbow** on a rainy day was the apparent brightness that **encircled** the **throne**, and it **looked like** an emerald.

^{Ezek 1:28}**like a rainbow** in a cloud **encircled** it.

throne, and on that which was in the form of **a throne** was the form of something that **looked like** a man on it from above.

^{Gen 9:12-13}God said, "This is the contract which I am establishing between me and all living beings that are with you for the generations of the age: My **rainbow** I have placed in the cloud. It will be the sign of my contract between me and the earth."

THE PROPHECY

This is the beginning of **the prophecy** which the messenger brought to John at Patmos. As Caird has noticed, "Structurally the first three chapters are a covering letter."[1] Rev 1 was the really introductory chapter which tells of John's experience in receiving **the prophecy**. Rev 2 and 3 are formal epistles directed to the leading officers of the seven churches. They are not directly related to the message of **the prophecy** and may once have existed independently, although in this commentary they are treated as if John of Patmos wrote them all. The conclusion, that continues where Rev 1 (Rev 1:20) stops, begins again at Rev 22:6.

COMMENTARY

After this, I was watching. The Greek for **I was watching** is *áy-dawn*, (εἶδον). It means **I saw**, but this is a rendering of the same expression in Aramaic in Daniel (*hah-váyth khah-záh* הוית חזה) which is clearly the imperfect, made with a helping verb **to be** to show continuous action. The author was watching for a long time when suddenly he saw something. This expression appears often in the Book of Revelation (Rev 7:1, 9; 15:5; 18:1). These opening words of Rev 4 were intended to alert the reader to the very same words in the Book of Daniel. In Daniel that which was seen was a vision of a great judgment scene during which the Lord functioned as judge; Antiochus Epiphanes (the little horn) was the defendant; and Judas the Maccabee (the Son of man) was the plaintiff. The verdict was that Antiochus was given the death sentence, and Judas, together with his contemporary citizens was given back the Promised Land as the kingdom, with all of the associated benefits. The author of this unit wanted to suggest to the reader that he was visualizing a similar judgment in

---

[1] G. B. Caird, *A Commentary on the Revelation of St. John the Divine* (London: Black, c1966), p. 60.

the readers' own days during which the new saints and their new messiah would be given the heavenly verdict, and the Roman enemies would lose.

This document begins, as many units of similar literature begin, **After this** or **I was watching** (Rev 13:1; 17:3). This idiom sometimes marks an end to one unit and the beginning of another. The normal twentieth century Western question is, "**After** what?" Some scholars say it means "after the content of Rev 1-3," and in its present form that is accurate from the standpoint of sequence, but that answer is not required by the style. The Near Easterner did not seem to need something before to introduce a unit by the word, "**After**." The Oriental apparently did not bother to ask what went before. In the same way Near Easterners began discussions with the expression, "He answered and said," when no one had previously asked a question to be answered. The expression has about the same force as "He began to say." The **first voice** also seems not to refer to one of a number of voices that had been identified earlier but rather the first voice that captured the author's attention after he noticed a gate or door opening into heaven.

I was day dreaming. Düsterdieck said being **in the spirit** meant he was released from physical limitations and was able to ascend into heaven.[11] Charles and Loisy both thought "being in the spirit" meant the author fell into an ecstatic state.[2] Aune rendered this clause, "I was in a prophetic trance."[3] A **day-dream** does not have to have an ecstatic content as a necessary qualification. A **day-dream** can take place without releasing anyone from physical limitations. Being ecstatic or released from physical limitations is not the point of the expression. Not all prophecies depended on the prophet's being in an ecstatic state. Being **in the spirit** means that the author was **day-dreaming**, and in his **dreams** he imagined himself in heaven, even though he was physically right there on earth. When Ezekiel was physically in Babylon he **dreamed** he was in Jerusalem, so he said, **The Spirit lifted me . . . and brought me in visions of God to Jerusalem** (Ezek 8:3). He was not physically moved to Jerusalem, and his dreams were not altogether ecstatic.

The door opened in heaven. Now look! The words, **Now look**! do not occur in the Nestle-Aland text of the New Testament (NA).

Other visions in the Book of Revelation are also introduced by the heavens opening (Rev 11:19; 15:5). This is the beginning of the first scene of the prophecy brought to John at Patmos. It is also one of those scenes Strand labeled as "victorious."[4] It obviously took place in heaven, as indicated by **the open door to**

---

[1] F. Düsterdieck, *Critical and Exegetical Handbook to the Revelation of John*, tr. H. E. Jacobs (Winona Lake: Alpha Publications, 1884), p. 189. I, p. 111; A. Loisy, *L'Apocalypse de Jean* (Paris: Emile Nourry, 1923), p. 121.
[2] R. H. Charles, *A Critical and Exegetical Commentary on the Revelation of St. John the Divine* (New York: Charles Scribner's Sons, c1920)
[3] D. Aune, *Revelation 1-5* (Dallas: Word Books Publishers, c1997), p. 268.
[4] K. A. Strand, "The 'Victorious-Introduction' Scenes in the Visions in the Book of Revelation," *AUSS* 25 (1987):267-88.

heaven. Ancients thought of **heaven** as the region above the clouds. Above the clouds there was another whole world of existence, and Jews believed it was very much like Jerusalem, and especially the temple there.

In times of independent rule, there was both a temple and a king's palace in Jerusalem. In many Near Eastern governments the two were identical. In **heaven** it was assumed that God functioned very much the same way as earthly kings administer. His **throne** room was the place from which God made decisions, instigated action, and passed judgment on the most important legal cases. As the leader of government he had advisors, ambassadors, and messengers. Messengers were sent by ship or horseback to carry messages to distant places.

Some of these messengers had the authority of legal agents. This means they were legally identical to the king. They spoke in the name of the king, in behalf of the king, and at the responsibility of the king. Those who received the agents treated them as if they were receiving the king himself--and legally they were. The king also received messengers from other kings and important world leaders with the same understanding. **Trumpets** announced their arrival. During an age when there were no telephones, fax machines, or even telegraphs, messengers were necessary to keep in communication with the rest of the world. As the commander in chief of the nation's defense forces, the king had final authority over the nation's army and navy. This required many troops and ships.

As the highest judge in the land the king was in charge of the nation's supreme court. Unless he was a tyrant he had assistant judges gathered around his throne room, together with prosecuting and defense attorneys, witnesses, bailiffs, and clerks. In this court room legal treaties and contracts were designed, signed, interpreted, and upheld. When decisions were made, the king needed messengers to carry out the judgments and **trumpets** to announce the action. His decisions were the sword of his mouth. When he announced a death penalty, someone was ordered to fulfill the execution, and some other messenger was probably assigned the task of blowing trumpets and announcing the action to the community.

In antiquity there was no separation of religion and the state. Sometimes the king was also the high priest, and his **throne** room also functioned as both a court and a temple. Since the king was a legal agent of the deity he was both worshiped and obeyed. The principal in this case was the deity, but the king had the legal authority of God. He spoke in God's name, in behalf of God, and at the responsibility of God. Legally those who worshiped him were really worshiping God. All of this means the throne room was a very important place in any ancient government. Prosecuting and defense attorneys worshiped the king and offered prayers for relief. In the Book of Revelation, these various aspects were tied so closely together in some scenes that it is not clear whether the scene takes place in a temple, a court room, a throne room, or all three at the same time. Because the king was the agent of God, it is not always certain whether the scene takes place in a heavenly temple or the temple at Zion.

It was assumed that in heaven things were much the same as those on earth. God, as principal, functioned the same way as his earthly apostles or legal agents. He had angels to deliver messages. There were military forces,[1] temple officers, lawyers, and counselors. It is not always evident in what capacity the heavenly officers officiated in the heavenly scenes. Those around the throne could have been understood as heavenly Levites, heavenly assistant judges, court witnesses, lawyers, or prophets. While kings, like David, ruled the nation, they were believed to be legally present in the council of God (Acts 13:36). Jeremiah said true prophets were those who had stood in the council of Yehowah (Jer 23:18). He evidently meant that such prophets were legally standing in the council of God while prophesying on earth. The test of a true prophet was that his prophecies would later be fulfilled in history. If that happened, then it was understood that he had stood in the council of Yehowah.

The beasts that surround the throne, for example, may have been the heavenly counterpart of the monks in a monastery who take turns singing praises to God day and night. The elders were located in the places where assistant judges might normally sit, but they also were dressed in white like priests. When the door was opened in heaven the seer involved was permitted to see all of the personnel, furniture, and activity that went on there.

The Lord was present in heaven, to be sure, but he was also present in the holy of holies in the temple. This was the mercy seat, the earthly equivalent of his throne in heaven. He was legally present in the temple in Jerusalem, because his name dwelt there (1Kings 8:29; 2Chron 6:20; Deut 12:5, 11, 21). This may be the logic behind some of the confusion. In heaven the Lord was in his throne room. His throne on earth was in the temple. Those who worshiped him in the temple were legally performing the same duty as if they had been present, worshiping the Lord in heaven.

The **door** which **opened into heaven** was in the firmament. The firmament was the floor or ceiling that separated earth from **heaven.** This firmament was like a bedouin's tent. It sometimes was tight and at other times, it sagged. Mountains reached up through the clouds into heaven. That is why ancients built temples on mountains. The Lord could be present there in the temple itself. If the temple did not quite reach **heaven**, the smoke from the bonfire formed a pillar that would join earth to **heaven.** Sometimes the sky came down and almost touched the earth. Occasionally the Lord let down a funnel of cloud to destroy parts of the earth or sea. This was a twister that disrupted things on earth and carried them up to heaven. Most people never entered **heaven**, but a few had special contact. **Doors opened** from heaven so angels could go back and forth and specially righteous people could cross over **into heaven** (Gen 28:12; 1Enoch 14.15; TLevi 5.1).

The **door** that **opened into heaven** was like the gate of **heaven** Jacob saw in his vision at Bethel (Gen 28:17). Just as the ladder reaching **heaven** appeared to

---

[1] The military forces, the troops (*tseh-báh-oth,* צבעות), would not have been the same as the members of the divine council, as Davis (D. R. Davis, *The Heavenly Court Scene of Revelation 4-5* [Ann Arbor: PhD. Dissertation for Andrews Unversity, c1987], p. 118) suggested. The troops would have been used by the council to enforce its decisions.

Jacob in a dream, so the author of this document described himself as dreaming when he visualized an access route to heaven that would reveal to him that divine, unknown territory above the sky. Although Jacob dreamed only of the angels moving from earth to heaven, the author of this document imagined that he, himself, was allowed to enter the **open door** and see what was actually going on **in heaven.** This provided an excellent literary basis for introducing the readers to his message, which he obtained mostly from the Scripture. In his day dream he was in heaven and learned all the activities, official leaders, and furniture. From there he could also anticipate the future

Like a trumpet. In antiquity trumpets were not used primarily to make music for a symphony orchestra. They were used to call a council or a town meeting, to call together troops for war, to announce a feast, or send some other recognized notice to members of a community.

Come up here. As he was **watching** intently, a voice shouted to him. This was not just a suggestion or an invitation; it was a loud command that he enter that **door.** In his imagination, while he was day dreaming, he left the earthly sphere for the heavenly regions from which all earthly activities are administered. The **voice** promised to show the author that which was destined to happen in the future. Düsterdieck correctly observed that heaven appears as a temple to the author. It was also the palace of God, the place where he was **enthroned** (Ps 11:4; 18:7; 29:9).[1] For other references to a temple in heaven see Rev 7:9; 11:19; 15:2; TLevi 5.1; TDan 5.12; *2 Bar* 4:3; and Mid Ps 122:3

Ancients knew there were sun, moon, and stars **in heaven,** because they could be seen from the earth. They knew there was water in heaven because the rain fell. There were windows and doors in heaven because periodically the sun shone through the windows. This meant the windows could be opened or closed. Windows were like holes in a bedouin's tent where water could come through into the tent. There were also windows and doors separating the earth from **heaven**. These could be **opened** and closed at the discretion of the Lord. This continued to be the cosmology throughout the Crusades. In an eleventh century IA redemption document, called *The Book of Zerubbabel*, Zerubbabel is pictured as standing at the gate of heaven:

> 32:4) Zerubbabel said: "Hurry, go above me, where the Rock of ages is!" He answered me from the doors of heaven and said to me, "You are Zerubbabel." I answered, "I am." He answered and spoke to me **just as a man speaks to his neighbor** (Ex 33:11). He spoke to me words of very great uprightness. 32:5) He said to me, "Who are you, Sir?" Then he said to me, "I am Mettatron, general of the Lord's army," and he placed my name as his name, and he showed me a man like a pretty and handsome child. Mettatron said to me, "This is

---

[1] Düsterdieck, *Handbook*, p. 188.

the Messiah of the Lord. He was born to the house of David, but the Lord hid him to become a leader over Israel. He is Menahem Ben Amiel, who was born in the house of Nebuchadnezzar."[1]

The words, "He placed my name as his name," mean that God had made Mettatron his legal agent. He had the power of attorney to speak in the Lord's name and with his authority.

Suddenly I began to day-dream. Literally, this means **I was in the spirit** (see also Rev 1:10), but that image is not an everyday expression to most Westerners. **Being in the spirit** means that which the author saw was in his imagination and nothing that he **saw** with his naked eyes. It had mental reality. He visualized himself being taken up **into heaven. Being in the spirit** also has the force of authority. Prophets who spoke **in the spirit** spoke God's words. They were God's legal agents, and this is part of the message intended here. The author not only wanted his readers to know he had first hand visual testimony about heaven and God, but that he was **in the spirit,** so that he could speak with God's authority. The message, like Scripture, had legal validity.

Many scholars think this means simply that the author was in a state of ecstasy,[2] but that is not the main point of the idiom. Neither was Morris correct in saying that the Holy **Spirit** was meant by this expression.[3] Ancient Near Easterners thought the earth was a type of the heavenly prototype, and Jews especially thought the nearest earthly object reflecting heaven was the temple at Jerusalem. Therefore, when the author set out to attract the reader into a mood to think of heavenly things, he used scriptural allusions to the temple.

The trumpet that sounded was like the one that announced the revelation of the ten commandments at Mount Sinai, and the throne scene included quotations from Isaiah's and Ezekiel's visions of the Lord in the temple. This was all coherent. The author wanted to call attention to the contract made with the Lord at Sinai. This contract was later kept in the temple at Jerusalem. Most countries kept their treaties and national contracts in their temples, which were also national treasuries and fortresses. Since this contract had apparently been broken, Jews and Christians of NT times were eagerly anticipating the reinstitution of a new contract with the Lord which would again make the Lord responsible to them and provide the chosen people with the Promised Land. Throughout the Book of Revelation there are various kinds of allusions to the provision of the contract, because this was an important part of the deliverance believers hoped to receive from God.

---

[1] The quotation is from Buchanan, *Jewish Messianic Movements from AD 70 to AD 1300* (Eugene, Oregon: Wipf and Stock Publishers, 2003), pp. 338-39.
[2] So Düsterdieck, *Handbook*, p. 189; T. Zahn, *Die Offenbarung des Johannes* (Leipzig: A. Deichert, 1924) I, pp. 317-18.
[3] L. Morris, *The Book of Revelation* (Grand Rapids: Eerdmans Publishing Co., c1987), p. 86.

After the author had aroused the reader's interest in the possibility that the following columns of text would disclose the future that was destined to take place--even before those events happened--the prophet responsible for this text suddenly **became in the spirit**. This probably means he started to day dream, and the scenes that follow are those pictures that he visualized as existing in heaven.

These are all literary devices used by the author to stimulate the imagination of the reader to follow the message that he was trying communicate. These were ways ancient authors, without the benefit of TV or cameras, could take readers on "a journey of words," describing picturesque things through literary means, depending on vivid imaginations to fill in the pictures they described. Although the author pictured all this in an imaginary way, this does not mean he thought he was composing fairy tales. He worked under accepted doctrinal controls.

He believed that time moved in predestined cycles. This enabled a good student of history to compare contemporary events with the order of events in previous cycles in history. These points of contact between current events with earlier miracles were considered "signs" to guide the prophet in determining where his generation then was in the cycle. The author studied all of these carefully. It was like reading a play before watching the play at a theater. Then when the play was being performed, the observer knew in advance what was destined to happen next, because he or she had seen or read it before. Jews and early Christians thought, that by studying past history, they could find where in the cycle they were at that time, thinking that history would be played over very much the way it had been played before.

Jews and Christians also believed that all Scripture was destined to be fulfilled in the days of the Messiah. The days of the Messiah occurred during that 3½ year period at the end of the gentile age. The basic source of this temporal period was the Book of Daniel. The days of the Messiah were the days between the defilement of the temple and its cleansing. During these Danielic days of the Messiah, the Messiah was Judas the Maccabee, and the Maccabean Revolt was fought during these 3½ years.

If the signs indicated that believers were then in a certain critical period of the cycle, the author considered it legitimate to search the Scriptures to discover what had been prophesied. He then matched prophecies, signs, typologies, and cycles to understand what had happened in the recent past and to predict what was destined to happen before the ages changed, and Israel would again be ruled from Jerusalem with the Davidic Messiah on the throne. This was the message the author wished to communicate. He believed it was designed in heaven, so he dramatized his convictions by describing heavenly scenes. This literary form was the mythology he created to express his convictions. The reader who follows this drama is sure to be favorably impressed with the knowledge, artistry, and skill by which the author shared his beliefs.

A throne was set up in heaven. God was pictured throughout the Book of Revelation as a great king, sitting on **a throne in heaven** (Rev 1:4; 2:13; 3:21; 6:16; 7:9-11, 15, 17; 8:3; 11:16; 12:5; 13:2; 14:3; 16:10, 17; 19:4-5; 20:4, 11-12; 21:5; 22:1, 3). The word **throne** occurs 47 times in the Book of Revelation out of a total of 62 in the whole NT. In the ancient Near East there were not very many chairs. Most people either, stood, squatted, or reclined on the ground. The exception was for great leaders, like kings, who were distinguished for their ability to sit on special chairs, called **thrones**. Almost all of the king's or judge's decisions were made while sitting on his **throne**. No ordinary person ever sat on one of these thrones.

Like other kings, God had messengers (angels) to run his errands and administer his kingdom; like other kings, he also held court and made judgments. The text does not say who **set up the throne in heaven**, presumably some of the servants there. This is the same idiom as that used by the one who visualized a heavenly judgment scene in Dan 7:9; **thrones were set up**.

The One on the throne was sitting. The Nestle-Aland (NA) text omits the initial definite article. That text reads, **One upon the throne was sitting**. **The One** *seated on the throne in heaven* was obviously God. This idiom was used many times in the Book of Revelation to mean God. God was thought of as a great king (1Chron 28:5; Isa 6:1; Ezek 1:26; 10:1; Dan 7:9; Ps 11:4; 45:6; 93:2; 103:19; Rev 20:11), and he was described in the appearance of precious stones. Believers were afraid they might blaspheme God if they used his name. Therefore they employed various kinds of euphemisms, such as **the One sitting on the throne**, "The holy One blessed be He," or "the One who created all things." This was also a way of eulogizing God.

Thrones were very fancy chairs, but in an era in which chairs were reserved for people, like kings, who had a great deal of dignity, it was an honor to be able to **sit** on a throne. **Thrones** were closely associated with authority. Others who were not **enthroned** were either standing or bowing before **the one sitting on the throne**. Even the heavenly beasts were required to stand upright before **the One who was sitting on the throne** (The legs of the heavenly beasts were upright legs, *rahg-láy-hehm réh-gehl yeh-shah-ráh,* רגליהם רגל ישרה). Following Ezek 1 and Isa 6, **throne** scenes appear frequently in later literature. In the Book of Revelation alone see Rev 7:9-12; 11:19; 19:1-8; 20:11.

Looked like a sapphire stone, a carnelian. This seems to Westerners like an odd way to describe a royal deity **on** his **throne**, but apparently, this was a traditional Near Eastern way of referring to the deity. An ancient Sumerian, probably of the second millennium BIA,[1] composed a prayer,

> To my king with varicolored eyes who wears a lapis lazuli beard, speak; To the golden statue . . .[2]

---

[1] BIA (Before the International Age) is a politically correct alternative to the exclusive abbreviations BC (Before Christ) or BCE (Before the common era).
[2] S. N. Kramer (tr.), "Petition to a King," J. B. Pritchard (ed.), *Ancient Near Eastern Texts* (Princeton: Princeton U. Press, 1969), p. 381.

Apparently the **king** to whom the prayer was offered was either the deity itself, a statue of the deity, or a human king who was the legal agent of the deity. The precious stones used to describe the recipient of this prayer may not have meant that it was a graven image. It may have been a flattering, visionary way of describing either a deity or a king. The goddess Inanna, the queen of **heaven**, dressed in lapis lazuli beads when she descended to the nether world. The palace in the nether world was the lapis-lazuli mountain. When she came to the third gate, her necklace of lapis lazuli was removed.[1] The precious lapis lazuli was used for garments and scepters of kings and deities. The description in Revelation of the one sitting on the throne in terms of precious stones seems to have been customary. This text was also based on the temple vision of Ezekiel who also used precious stones to describe a **throne** scene.

A rainbow on a rainy day. This may have been simply an artistic way of describing the area around the **throne**. It may, however, have also intended to remind the readers of the contract God made with Noah after the flood. The **rainbow** was the sign that the storm was over, and a new age was about to begin. With the new age was a contract, like the contract God made with Noah (Gen 9:12-15). This was not the same contract as the one God made with Moses and the Israelites on Mount Sinai, but the situation provided the author with another opportunity to call attention to the contract.

TEXT

Revelation	First Testament and other Jewish Literature
	Isa 24:23 **Y**ehowah of armies has become king gloriously on Mount Zion and in Jerusalem. Across from his **elders** [he was seated].
⁴Around the **throne** were twenty-four **thrones**, [and upon the **thrones were** twenty-four] **elders seated**, dressed in **white**. Upon their heads were gold crowns. ⁵From the [central] **throne** went out **lightnings, sounds, and**	Dan 7:9 I was watching until **thrones were** set up, and the Ancient of Days **sat down**. His clothes were **white** as snow. Exod 19:16 There were **sounds, lightnings, and** a heavy cloud over the mountain.

---

[1] S. N. Kramer, *History Begins at Sumer* (Philadelphia: University of Pennsylvania Press, 1981), pp. 159-61.

thunder. **Seven torches**	Exod 37:23 He made the **seven lamps** . . . of pure gold.
	Zech 4:2 Look! A **lamp stand**--all gold and a bowl on its top with **seven** of its candles upon it.
	Gen 15:17 After the sun had set, and it was dark, look! a smoking fire pot and **a fiery torch** which passed between these pieces.
of fire were burning before the throne, which are the seven spirits of God.	Dan 7:9-10 His throne **was** surrounded by **fire,** wheels **of burning fire.** A river **of fire** went out **before** him.
	Ezek 1:22 Over the heads of the beasts **was** a firmament,
⁶Before the throne **was something** like a glassy **sea,**	1Kings 7:23 He made **the sea,** that was formed, fifteen feet in diameter and seven and a half feet tall. It was forty-five feet in circumference
like a crystal, and in	**like a** terrible **crystal.**
the midst of the throne and **around**	Ezek 1:4-5 A large cloud, fire was flashing, and its brightness **around** and from **the midst of** it was something like shining bronze, and from **its midst was something like four beasts**.
the throne were **four beasts**	
full of eyes, in front and back.	Ezek 1:18 The rims [of the wheels] **full of eyes** around the four of them.
	Ezek 10:20 This was **the beast** which I saw under the God of Israel at the River Cebar; I knew that they were cherubim.
⁷**The first was like a lion;**	Ezek 10:14 There were four faces for each one: **the first** face **was like** the face of

the second beast **was** like an ox; **the third** beast had a **face of a man**; **and the fourth** beast **was** like **an eagle** flying.

⁸Now the **four beasts**,

every one of them had six wings,

outside and inside, **full of eyes**. They

have no rest day or night, saying, "Holy, holy, holy, holy, holy, holy, holy, holy, Lord God of armies," the **One who** was, **who is**, and **who is** the coming **One."**

a cherub; **the second** face **was** the face of a man; the third was the face of a lion; and the fourth was the face of an eagle.

Ezek 1:5 From its midst came something like **four beasts**.

Above him stood the seraphim: **each one of them having six wings**

Isa 6:3 . . One called to the other **saying, "Holy, holy, holy Lord God of armies!**

Ezek 10:12 [The wheels] were **full of eyes**, all the way around for the four wheels.

1Enoch 39.12 Those who **do not sleep** but stand before your glory will bless you.

OGExod 3:14 I am **the One who is**.

COMMENTARY

Around the throne were twenty-four thrones. The term, **throne,** appears in the Book of Revelation 47 times. As earlier, the author composed his heavenly **throne** scene by weaving into his narrative words from other scriptural **throne** scenes in the temple. These are also supported by the revelation at Mount Sinai. The major temple scenes are from Isa 6 and Ezek 1, although the **lamp stands** come from Zech 4. **The throne** scenes picture God as a king ruling in omnipotence (Ps 29:97). On the basis of Isa 24:13, Rabbi Abin said in the future God would **sit**, as president of the court, in a circle with his elders, judging the gentiles. On the basis of Isa 24:13, rabbis said that in the messianic times Yehowah would **sit** with his elders in Jerusalem, on Mount Zion (Exod 5:12). That means that the king, as God's legal agent, would sit with his elders on Mount Zion. Legally he would be identical to God. There was, of course, a court in Jerusalem. It was called the *báyt deén* (בית דין). Jews and Christians also believed that there was a court in heaven a *báyt deén shehl shahmáh-yeem* (בית דין של שמים, Mek Nezikin 10.81-87). God was physically present in heaven, but he was also legally present in Zion.

The elders were probably stationed in a half circle with twelve on one side of **the throne** and twelve on the other. This seems to have been a standard structure for a chief judge and his assistant judges, as the elders probably were understood to be. About 15 centuries before the Book of Revelation was composed the court room of an Egyptian vizier was described. A vizier was the highest judge in Egypt.[1] His judgment seat was arranged similar to that of the elders around the king.

Twenty-four elders. The clause, **Upon the thrones** were **twenty-four,** was omitted from the Sinaiticus text. The scribe who copied the text evidently moved by mistake from the **24 thrones** to **the 24 elders** that were situated in the same place in a lower line as the **24 thrones.** In doing so, he left out the intervening words. This is a normal *homeoteleuton* copying error, which the Siniaticus copier made many times. Sinaiticus also differs from the text NA has chosen in that it says the elders were dressed in white, whereas NA text says they were dressed in white *robes*.

The theme of **24 elders** also occurs in Rev 19:4. **White** is the color of priestly robes. This indicates that the **elders** were not only assistant judges, but also priests. This is feasible; there were priestly **elders.** The Torah Scroll (11QT 15:18) refers to a group as "the elders of the priests" (*zeek-náy hah koh-heh-neém*, זקני הכוהנים). Priests were also those who were entitled to wear crowns.[2]

The **24 elders** in heaven corresponded to the **24** courses of priests who functioned in sequence at the temple in Jerusalem (1Chron 24:7-18). Düsterdieck is probably correct in holding that these elders were not cherubim, seraphim, or any heavenly angels, but human figures who wore clothes and **crowns,**[3] like the Lord's human **elders** on Mount Zion. Zahn, however, said they had to be angels.[4] Rabbis, commenting on Isa 24:23, said it was not before his troops, his angels, or his priests, but before his **elders** that there would be glory (EcclR 1.11 #1). Since the Lord's **throne** room was also a court room, with God as the supreme judge, the elders may have fulfilled the offices of assistant judges like those who occupied the additional chairs in the court session of Dan 7:9.

In Micaiah's vision, he saw Yehowah **seated** on this **throne** with all the heavenly troops around him, standing on both sides (1Kings 22:19). These troops constituted the heavenly army that was standing guard, rather than **the elders** who were seated adjacent to the heavenly judge (Rev 4:4). In Job 1:6-2:7 the Lord is pictured with his council comprised of sons of God. They seemed to function in the same capacity as the elders.

These priests (**elders**) who worshiped the Lord around his **throne in heaven** were agents, and, as such, were legally identical to the human priests who worshiped the Lord in his temple at Jerusalem, according to their respective courses. Although these priests held short term offices, during their term they were not only priests who

---

[1] J. A. Wilson (tr.), "The Vizier of Egypt," J. B. Pritchard (ed), *Ancient Near Eastern Texts* (Princeton: Princeton U. Press, 1969), pp. 212-14.
[2] G. M. Stevenson, "Conceptional Background to Golden Crown Imagery in the Apocalypse of John (4:4, 10; 14:14)," *JBL* 114 (1995): 257-72.
[3] Düsterdieck, *Handbook*, p. 193.
[4] T. Zahn, *Offenbarung des Johannes* I (Leipzig: A. Deibert, 1924), p. 323.

served in the temple at Jerusalem, but they were members of the council of God **in heaven**.

It was the doctrines and beliefs of the author of this unit that prompted him to have this kind of a vision. Before he ever began to write, the author was convinced that God was **in heaven** together with the members of his council, sitting on his great **throne**, administering the affairs of the world, with the aid of the persons on earth who were represented with God in heaven. These were doctrines that were understood by his readers, and he documented his convictions by the Scripture passages to which he alluded. All the author did was put these beliefs into literary expression.

Seven torches of fire. **Torches of fire** probably means **seven burning torches** or a lighted candelabra with seven candles. John of Patmos had earlier referred to the **seven** spirits which were before God's **throne** (Rev 1:4). John also interpreted the seven **lamp stands of** Zechariah's vision as the **seven** churches (Rev 1:11-13, 20), implying that the churches had the responsibility of being **God's eyes** that survey and keep watch over the Promised Land (Zech 4:11). The Greek word that John used (*lookh-neé-ai*, λυχνίαι) is not the same as the word for **torches** used here (*lahm-páhs*, λαμπάς). These may or may not be synonyms for the same object. John may have obtained this expression from this text, or he may have got it from the FT directly. Just because Rev 1-3 now appears earlier in the Book of Revelation than Rev 4 does not mean it was written first or by the same person, as Davis assumed.[1]

This scroll defined **the seven torches** before God's throne in the heavenly temple as the **seven** spirits of God (Rev 4:5). John interpreted the lamp stands as the **seven** churches, but he may also have understood that they belonged to the temple before God's throne. This is not certain. There were **lamp stands** inside the temple. This furniture in the heavenly throne room was intended to give it the appearance of a temple, as well as a court and a throne room. The scroll was closely identified with the contract, so the **burning torches** may also have alluded to the **fire** that was carried through between the pieces of the slaughtered animal at the time Abraham made a contract with Yehowah (Gen 15:17).

Which are the seven spirits of God. This interpretative phrase was not included in the Sinaiticus text. Either this phrase was a later addition or it was one Sinaiticus omitted but was accepted by the NA editors.

John of Patmos associated **the seven spirits** with **the seven** stars (Rev 3:1), and also said **the seven stars** were **the officers** of **seven** churches (Rev 1:20). **The seven** spirits probably came from Isa 11:2 and were:

1) The spirit of Yehowah,
2) the spirit of wisdom,
3) [the spirit of] understanding,

---

[1] Davis, *Heavenly Court*, p. 21.

4) the spirit of counsel,
5) [the spirit of] might,
6) the spirit of knowledge, and
7) [the spirit of] the fear of the Lord.

A glassy sea. A body of water as big as a **sea** is not expected inside of a building, or even part of a palatial grounds. That which is called **a sea** must be a piece of furniture that was kept in the temple. It also received attention in Rev 15:2. There was such a basin called **the sea,** described in the FT. It was 15 feet in diameter and five feet tall, and it was placed before the throne (1Kings 7:23). It was also called **the bronze sea** (*yam hah-neh-khóh-sheht,* ים הנחשת) (2Kings 25:13; 1Chron 18:8; Jer 52:17).

It may have resembled a fountain, or a basin similar to one that has been preserved in The Alhambra in Spain. In the Court of Lions there is a large cement water basin held up by several lions made of cement whose mouths function as fountains, pouring out water. The basin is carried on their backs, and the lions face outward. The **sea** in the temple was probably something like that. Instead of lions it had four different kinds of beasts holding up a bronze **sea** (Rev 4:6). One of these was like a lion; another like a cow; a third like an eagle; and the fourth, probably looked like a sphinx, having a face like a human being (Rev 4:7). The picture of the basin in the Alhumbra is placed between chapters twelve and thirteen.

In the midst of the throne. Scholars have had to conjecture many possible ways to make sense of this phrase. Hall has wisely suggested that this text be taken to mean exactly what it says. The beasts were like gargoyles carved into the wood of **the throne** itself and around **the throne** from every side. They were not all sitting on the seat of **the throne** (Rev 4:6).[1] In fact that is precisely the interpretation given by a medieval Jewish scholar, describing **the throne** of Solomon:

> The throne was of ivory with its legs different one from the other; one was like an ox; the second, like an eagle; the third was like a lion; and the fourth leg was like a man.[2]

Of course this medieval Jew based his judgment on Ezekiel. The **One sitting on the throne** was **the One who lives for ages of ages** (Rev 4:9).

Around the throne were four beasts. As in Ezekiel 1, **the four beasts** in the temple were like **four** legs of a table, but instead of a table they held up a large tank with water in it. This was probably intended for the various ablutions required of the

---

[1] R. G. Hall, "Living Creatures in the Midst of the Throne: Another Look at Revelation 4:6," *NTS* 36 (1990):609-13.
[2] Quotation from "The Story of Daniel (Upon Whom be Peace)," tr. by Buchanan, *Jewish Messianic Movements*, p. 463.

priests during the sacrifices or other necessities of feasts. The temple was stationed right behind the Spring of Siloam on top of the ridge on the western bank of the Kidron Valley where there would be lots of water available for the numerous sacrifices that were performed there. It was not located within the huge walls of Antonia, Herod's Roman fortress, where the Dome of the Rock is now located. That 35 acre fortress sometimes housed 6,000 Roman troops stationed there to keep the temple and David's Holy City under control. It was outside of the temple compound, The temple was located about 600 feet south of the Roman city. Within the temple at Zion there was a large bronze basin that that was called the 'sea."The Sphinxlike **beasts** that supported the sea seem to have been necessary parts of temples. Early mosaics, like the synagogue floors at Beth Alpha and Hamath, Tiberias, had replicas of an altar with two **lamp stands**, each holding seven candles, which may have been the same as the **torches** which were defined as the **seven spirits of God before the throne** (Rev 4:5). A photograph of the floor at Beth Alpha can be seen between chapters twelve and thirteen.

The Beth Alpha floor also shows pictorial symbols of two cherubim, grotesque **beasts** like these described by Ezekiel and copied here in Revelation. In that mosaic floor, at one end is a picture of the altar with the chest containing the contract at the center and the beasts and candelabra at both sides. At the other end of the floor is the artist's conception of Abraham, Isaac, and the lamb offered for sacrifice. In the center are the signs of the zoaiac. This floor is a replica of the temple floor, according to the description of Josephus (War 5:216-17).[1] There were also four other beasts in the temple that supported the bronze sea. Loisy held that the four **beasts** in this vision were intended to reflect four of the signs of the zodiac: 1) the lion, 2) the bull, 3) the man-scorpion, and 4) the eagle, which was Pegasus.[2] **Beasts** like these are also reported in Rev 19:4, following the NA text. Although the **beasts** must have been monstrous in appearance, they were considered good **beasts**, because they were devoted to serving God in heaven.

Every one of them had six wings. NA text is not the same as the Sinaiticus text in Greek: NA has *hehn kath' hehn éh-khohn* ἐν καθ°ἐν ἔχων-- **one by one having**. Sinaiticus, on the other hand, has *hen ehs-kháh-tohn ow-tóhn áy-chawn* (ἐν ἐσκάτων αὐτῶν εἴχον-- **every one of them had.**[3] Both texts have basically the same meaning. They are only slightly different in form.

It is the **beasts** that continue singing like a choir the very words sung by the seraphim in Isa 6:3, in the first line of their hymn. The Greek attribute to God is that he is "the almighty one," but the Hebrew text reads that he is the God **of armies**. The second line of this hymn praises God as **the one who is** (Exod 3:14), recalling

---

[1] See Düsterdieck, *Handbook*, pp. 196-97, for a survey of the many arbitrary interpretations of the symbolism of the sea and the beasts.The photograph is taken from Erwin R. Goodenough, *Jewish Symbols in the Greco-Roman Period* (New York: Pantheon Books, Inc., 1933) III, Illustration 632.
[2] Loisy, *L'Apocalypse*, p. 125.
[3] This text may reflect a hearing mistake from dictation, confusing ἐσκάτων for ἐσχάτων—"last," "every last one of them had."

God's answer to Moses' question about his name. The author, however, claimed he was not only **the one who is**, but he **was the one who was and who is to come.** This passage may have been the source of John's attribute to God at the beginning of his address to the churches (Rev 1:4). The hymn was interrupted to describe **the elders** praising God by worshiping him and throwing their crowns before God, described from Ps 47 as **the one seated upon the throne** and from Daniel as **the one who lives into the ages**. Then the hymn continued to praise God for his worthiness. The author of this chapter obviously was well acquainted with Scripture and was able to supplement his message with appropriate texts from many places.

They have no rest day or night. This is a singing quartet assigned to the task of praising God 24 hours a day. The group that followed the laws of the Rule of the Community had a regular structure to keep some of the monks reading Scripture and praying in shifts 24 hours a day. There are still monasteries today where monks sing in groups of two to four in shifts throughout the day and night.

Holy, holy, holy, holy, holy, holy, holy, holy. NA text has only three **holies.** Why the Sinaiticus text has eight is a mystery. One might have expected either three, to be consistent with Isa 6:3 or seven, to concur with the other sevens in the Book of Revelation, but why eight? NA does not even acknowledge this as a variant. Christians are so much accustomed to singing Reginald Heber's (1826 IA) hymn, **Holy, Holy, Holy**, that even if scholars should prove that Sinaiticus preserved the correct text with its eight fold repetition of **holy,** translations would probably never acknowledge it. It is called the *sanctus* or *tersanctus* in Latin and *try-sáh-gee-awn* (τρισάγιον) in Greek. These names apply only to the repetition of **holy** three times.

The One who is. This is the same being who was also called **the One who** sits on the throne and **the One who** lives into ages of ages. **The One who is** alludes to Exod 3:14, to the God whom Moses asked to tell his name. This is part of a short hymn of praise:

> **Holy, holy, holy,**
> Lord, God, the almighty One,
> The One who was, who is, and the coming One.

TEXT

Revelation	First Testament
⁹When the beasts give glory, honor, and thanksgiving to the one **seated on the throne,**	Ps 47:10 God **sits on the throne** of his glory.

who lives **into ages** of ages, Amen, ¹⁰the 24 elders fell down before the One **sitting on the throne**, and they worshiped the One who lives **into the ages of ages**, Amen. Then they threw their crowns before the throne, [say]ing:
¹¹"You are worthy, our Lord and God,
to receive glory, honor, and power,
because you created all things;
by your will they were created."

^{Isa 6:1}In the year that King Uzziah died I saw the Lord, **sitting upon a throne** high and exalted, and his train filled the temple.

^{Dan 6:27}He is the God of life, who endures **into the ages**.

COMMENTARY

The One who lives into the ages of ages. Amen. This is **the one who** survives all of the generations. Human beings seldom last more than one **age,** but God lives from one **age** to the next. This is not the same as eternity. It is a chronological concept in which one **age** follows another just as one day follows the one before it. Sinaiticus has **Amen** after the mention of **ages of ages**, both in verses 9 and 10. These are not included in the NA text.

They threw their crowns before the throne. NA adds the word **saying**. The Greek is *léh-gawn-tehs* (λέγοντες). Sinaiticus has only *ehn-tehs* (εντες), which makes no sense. Sinaiticus once probably also had **saying**, but some letters have been lost.

    Throwing crowns was an act of subjection as was their worship. If the elders were the earthly kings, then the one they worshiped was **the king of kings**, a name by which he was called in Revelation. A king of kings was the greatest of all kings. All other kings would be subject to him. For example, many kings of smaller kingdoms were subjects of the Roman emperor. **Crowns** sometimes symbolized royalty or even divinity, but they are also used to represent various other kinds of athletic or other honors. Here the **crowns** were worn by the priests, which was customary.[1] In the presence of the king, there was only one person seated on a throne. All of the other people present were required to stand or bow. In a monarchy, there could not be many people ruling or many people seated.

You are worthy. **Worthy** is a familiar Jewish and Christian word. Orthodox Jews who observed dietary and cleanliness rules precisely were called **worthy**. Bishops were called **worthy**. They were legally authorized to perform their official tasks. This line introduces another verse of praise:

---

[1] Stevenson, "Golden Crown Imagery," pp. 257-72.

> You are **worthy**, our Lord and our God,
> to receive glory, honor, and power,
> because you created all things;
> by your will they were created.

Summary. This chapter seems to constitute a complete unit. The theme is **the throne room in heaven**. Early in the narrative the reader is introduced to **the one who was sitting on a throne**. This is an echo of many FT passages which picture God **sitting on a throne**. Near the end of this chapter, the song of praise begins with praise to the one **who sits on the throne,** concluding with a creation theme which is appropriate for Sabbath worship in the temple in heaven (Gen 2:1-3). This probably was intended to form an *inclusio*, defining the limits of the unit. An *en-kloó-see-oh* is a literary form in which the author uses some of the same words at the end as at the beginning to show that the narrative ends at that point. This interesting phenomenon, however, is repeated in Rev 5, implying also that the unit ends there, except there the very first and the very last verses mention the **One sitting on a throne**. It is quite likely that they were composed independently and put together in this anthology precisely because they had some of these similarities.

Chapter 4 is related to chapter 5, but there is a development. Whereas Rev 4 describes the geography and furniture of God's throne room in heaven, Rev 5, moves from that emphasis to the activity that took place there, introducing the Messiah and the contract that God would make with his people.

CHAPTER FIVE

INTRODUCTION

Rev 4 was concentrated on the topic of the open door into heaven, into which the author entered in his vision to obtain a position from which to predict the future. Rev 5 is dedicated to the Lamb, which is the anticipated Messiah. The Lamb is a central character for the entire Book of Revelation.

TEXT

Revelation	First Testament
^{5:1}**I saw** at the right **hand** of the one **seated on the throne**	^{Isa 6:1}In the year that King Uzziah died **I saw** the Lord, high and exalted, **sitting on a throne.**
	^{Ps 47:10}God is **seated on the throne** of his holiness.
[a scroll	^{Ezek 2:9-10}Now look! **A hand** reached out to me [handing me] a scroll of **a scroll**, and it was
written] **on the front and back and sealed** with seven seals. ²Then I saw a strong angel, announcing in **a loud** voice, "Who is worthy	**written on the front and back.**.
	^{Gen 27:34}Esau cried out with **a loud** and bitter cry.
to open the scroll	^{Dan 7:10}**The scrolls were opened.**
and break its **seals**?" ³But no one was able, either in heaven or on earth to open the **scroll** or to look at it. ⁴Then I wept very much, because no one was found worthy of **opening the scroll** and looking at it. ⁵Then one of the elders said to me, "Do not weep!	^{Isa 29:11-12}It will be to you visions of everything, **sealed** in a scroll which they give to the one who can read, saying, "Read this, please." Then he said, "I cannot, because it is **sealed**." Then the **scroll** was given to one who could not read, saying, "Read this, please," but he said, "I do not know how to read."
Judah is a **lion's** cub; look! the **lion** of the tribe of Judah.	^{Gen 49:9-10}He stooped down; he crouched like a **lion.**

The root of David has conquered [and is therefore able] to open the scroll and break its seals."

⁴Ezra 12.31-32As for the **lion** that you saw--stirred up from the forest, roaring, and speaking to the eagle and scolding it for its wickedness and all its works, as you have heard--This is the Messiah.

Isa 11:1There shall grow up a **shoot** from the stump of Jesse.

Isa 11:10In that day **the root of** Jesse will stand.

COMMENTARY

I saw at the right hand. Düsterdieck has argued strongly that this does not mean that the scroll was on a table or part of the throne **at the right** of the one enthroned, but *on* the hand of the one seated.¹ It could be either. The preposition *eh-peé* (ἐπί) renders the Hebrew *ahl* (עַל) which could mean "alongside of," "over," "above," or "on." It is important that it was on **the right** side or in **the right hand** rather than the left. Near Easterners were careful not to do with their left **hands** that which might be inappropriate. There was a taboo against the left **hand** in the Near East, as in other countries, that carries over into Western cultures. For this reason children in the United States for many years have been forced to write with **the right hand**. Tools are made for **right handed** people only, and desks in school are made to suit the needs of **right handed** people, even though 27% of Americans are left handed.

The One seated on the throne. Boring thought the author of this passage was "very restrained" in dealing with **the throne** scene. His judgment was based on the fact that this scene was not introduced until Rev 5:6. This would be true if the same author who wrote the first three chapters also wrote the rest of the Book of Revelation. Once a person notices that the document involved began at Rev 4:1, this is no longer a valid conclusion. The author of the prophecy (Rev 4:1-22:5) began at once with a scene patterned after Ezek 1 which is a temple scene. This entire prophecy begins with a temple scene in heaven and the Lord **seated on his throne**. This is shown in the second chapter of this prophecy--not at all a restrained motif. As Boring noticed, there are six scenes where the Lamb is shown **seated on** God's **throne**. Since the Lamb was the Messiah, and by definition God's legal agent, he functioned in God's behalf when he **sat on** God's **throne**, ruling over the Kingdom of Yehowah (2Chron

---

[1] F. Düsterdieck, *Critical and Exegetical Handbook to the Revelation of John*, tr. H. E. Jacobs (Winona Lake: Alpha Publications, 1884), p. 205.

29:11), just as Solomon did when he sat **on the throne** of Yehowah in Jerusalem (2Chron 29:23).[1]

[A scroll written] on the front and back. The bracketed words are in NA text but not in Sinaiticus. NA also has **inside** (*éhs-oh-thehn*, ἔσωθεν) for **on the front** (*éhm-praws-then* (ἔμπροσθεν). Some texts have still further variants, but the meaning is clear in all of them. The scroll was written on both sides of the parchment.

The author pictured the way pages are located on a scroll when it is rolled up. **The front** side is rolled on the inside and **the back** is on the outside. Prior to this time, the one who was **seated on the throne** was God. The scroll may have been on a stand at his **right hand**, so that the one **seated on the throne** could easily reach it, or it could have been in his **right hand** already. The **scroll written** on both sides alludes to the **scroll** placed in Ezekiel's hand at the time of his call to prophesy. Ezekiel's **scroll** was one of lamentation, mourning, and woe (Ezek 2:10). Ezekiel's **scroll** was open, but this **scroll** was sealed with seven seals.

Sealed with seven seals. Scrolls were often **sealed with seven seals**, one beside the other, and it was necessary to break all of the **seals** before the scroll could be read. The incidents that were evoked by the breaking of the **seals** did not come as a result of the contents of the scroll, as Loisy thought. He believed the events that followed came because of the content of each part of the scroll as they were unrolled gradually.[2] That would not have been physically possible, because of the way the **seals** were placed. It was the breaking of the **seals** itself that set all of these catastrophes into action. The events that were put into motion were ones that were necessary to precede the renewal of the contract. The author of this chapter may have visualized the new contract that Jeremiah promised (Jer 31:31)as this scroll that was **sealed**.

The author is reported to have *seen* the scroll written on both sides and **sealed** with seven seals. This does not mean that he saw all that was written on both sides, Mazzaferri was correct in arguing that all **seven seals** were visible before the scroll was opened.[3] The author also said he saw the scroll written on front and back. He could have seen only a small portion of the back and none of the front if it were rolled up and sealed **with seven seals**. He did not see all of the writing. What he might have seen was a scroll, and the scroll he might have seen would have been one that was written on both sides. Actually this narrative was motivated by Scripture, namely Isa 6:1 and Ezek 2:9-10, so the vision was based more on earlier Scripture than on actual objects seen with the human eye.

The scroll theme is very important in the Book of Revelation. It appears again in Rev 10. In both instances the scroll involved was the contract necessary to renew relationships with the Lord.

---

[1] M. E. Boring, "The Theology of Revelation," *Int* 40 (1986):266.
[2] A. Loisy, *L'Apocalypse de Jean* (Paris: Emile Nourry, 1923), p. 129.
[3] F. D. Mazzaferri, *The Genre of the Book of Revelation from a Source-critical Perspective* (Berlin; New York: W. De Gruyter, 1989), p. 271.

Who is worthy to open the scroll? Seals used for **scrolls** were made of some metal, like brass, copper, or silver. **Scrolls** were rolled up tight, and sealed with metal seals that were placed proportionately across the scroll, with each ring of an equal distance from the seal next to it. The seals looked like rings with special insignia on them. There is a photograph of a **scroll with** six **seals** preserved in an article written by F. M. Cross, Jr.[1] and has been recorded with permission between chapters twelve and thirteen.

Valuable documents were sealed this way to prevent any unauthorized person from invading the privacy of the message. Being able to open these seals did not require special knowledge or physical strength. Neither was it necessary for the qualified person to possess special inner ethical qualities, as Düsterdieck thought.[2] It required legal authority, political power. The word used to describe the angel's announcement is the same word used to mean "preaching." The town crier who went through the village, announcing news the whole community should know at the top of his voice was "preaching," or "announcing."

This narrative is patterned after Isa 29 in which the community was faced with a **scroll**, and it needed to know the scroll's message. They gave it to one person, but he did not have the authority to break the seal. They found someone with authority to break the seal, but he did not know how to read (Isa 29:11-12).

No one was able in heaven or on earth to open the scroll. NA text added the following words after **on earth**: "or under **the earth**." This variant might have been original or it might have been a later addition. It is not possible to know which. Instead of **to open** (*ahn-oíx-ay*, ἀνοῖξαι) Sinaiticus has *ahn-oíx-eh* (ἀνοῖξε), **Open!** The clause requires an infinitive there, so the mistake was made by a scribe of Sinaiticus.

The scroll involved was evidently thought to be the new contract which Jeremiah promised God would make with his people. It was also a will which would contain the stipulations by which the chosen people might inherit the Promised Land. If this will could not be opened, the heirs would be left with no legal claim to the heritage they believed to be rightfully theirs. This would be a cause for weeping.

Look! The lion of the tribe of Judah. When Jacob blessed Judah at his death bed, he reportedly called Judah a "**lion's** whelp" (Gen 49:9-10). He further promised that he would become a ruler over other peoples. This name symbolized the power Jews liked to claim. Fourth Ezra 12.31-32 called **the lion** that came out of the forest "the Messiah."

The Messiah was understood to be a fierce warrior, a descendant of David, called by a midrashic fragment "the prince of the congregation" (4Q285; PssSol 18). He was expected to have such authority that he could order the wicked to be killed, and it would happen (Isa 11:1-5). Jews thought he would be victorious, rather than

---

[1] F. M. Cross, Jr., "The Discovery of the Samaritan Papyri." *BA* 26.4 (1963):112, 115, 117.
[2] Düsterdieck, *Handbook*, p. 207.

killed.[1] The text does not say what **the Lion** conquered, but whatever it was, it qualified him to break the seals and open **the scroll**. Caird could not believe the Messiah would function like **a lion**, so he said that wherever the author looked for a **lion** he saw instead a Lamb. Such a Lamb was not a warlike creature, but rather one who had been slaughtered. He continued,

> It is almost as if John were saying . . . "Wherever the Old Testament says, *'Lion'* read *'Lamb'*".[2]

Caird, however, failed to notice how often the Lamb in the Book of Revelation behaved like a **lion.**

The word used to mean **worthy** was used frequently to describe a person who was orthodox in his observation of purity, dietary, and tithing rules and therefore was **worthy** (*áhx-ee-aws*, ἄξιος = *neh-eh-máhn*, נאמן) to be admitted into another orthodox Jew's or Christian's home (mDem 2:3; tDem 2:3-24). It was also the term used to describe one qualified to be a bishop. That meant the bishop was legally qualified to fulfill the duties of his office. The angel was asking for someone who had the authority to open the scroll and read its contents.

The expression, **open the scroll and break its seals**, is a *heés-teh-rawn-praw-teh-rawn* (*hysteron proteron*) form. The order is backwards. In reality, the person involved would first break the seals and secondly open **the scroll**. The person found qualified to perform this service was from **the tribe of Judah**, the family of David. This means he is the **Lion of Judah**, the Messiah. According to TgPsJon the flag (טקסיה) of the camp of Judah had the figure of a young lion (TgOnq Num 2:3). **The lion** was a symbol for the Messiah in 4Ezra 11:36-46. There, also, **the lion** was a conqueror who accused the eagle (Rome) of being the fourth beast in Dan 7 who had conquered all of the beasts that had gone before it. When the times and age were completed, the Lord would hold a court session, and the eagle would be finished, just as Antiochus Epiphanes (the horn) was given the death sentence in Dan 7.

The **scroll** and the Messiah belonged together, just as Moses and the old contract belonged together. Without the Messiah the contract could not be opened and established. If that could not be done, the land with the contract promised to the Jews and/or Christians could not be restored to the chosen people. Therefore **the scroll** theme is basic to redemption literature. Each time the word **scroll** appears in the Book of Revelation, the reader should ask how this was intended to be understood in relationship to redemption.

---

[1] H. Shanks, "The 'Pierced Messiah' Text--An Interpretation Evaporates," *BAR* 18, 4 (1992):80-82.
[2] G. B. Caird, *A Commentary on the Revelation of St. John the Divine* (London: Black, c1966), pp. 73-75.

TEXT

Revelation	First Testament

Revelation

⁶Then I saw between the throne and the four beasts [on the one side] and [on the other] among the elders,
a Lamb standing
as slaughtered, having

seven horns and **seven eyes**, which are the **seven spirits** of God **sent** out **into all the land**.

⁷Then [the Lamb] came and took [the scroll] from the right **hand** of the one

seated on the throne.

First Testament

$^{Isa\ 53:7}$Like a sheep brought **for slaughter**, **a Lamb** before its shearers.

$^{Jer\ 11:9}$I was like a gentle **Lamb** led for **slaughter**; I did not know that they devised schemes against me.

$^{Zech\ 4:10}$These **seven** are the **eyes** of the Lord that go back and forth **in all the land**.

$^{Ezek\ 2:3}$The **spirit** entered me . . . , and he said to me, "Son of man, I am **sending** you to the children of Israel."

$^{Ezek\ 2:9}$Now look! A **hand** stretched out to me. Now look! In it was a scroll.

$^{Isa\ 6:1}$In the year that King Uzziah died I saw the Lord, **sitting on a throne**, high and exalted.

$^{Ps\ 47:9}$God is **seated on the throne** of his holiness.

$^{1Kings\ 22:19}$I saw the Lord **sitting on his throne**, and all the army of heaven over him, at his **right** and his left.

COMMENTARY

Between the throne and the four beasts. The terms, *ehn méh-soh . . . ehn méh-soh* (ἐν μέσῳ . . . ἐν μέσῳ) are the Greek for *bayn . . . oo-váyn* (וּבֵין . . . בֵּין) literally, **between . . . and between**. This is simply a Semitic way of saying **between**. The question is, "What is **between** what two or more objects?" The scene took place in **the throne** room of the temple.

1) On one side of the room there was **a throne** for the king and also a large bronze basin called the **sea** that was supported by **four** legs. These legs were sculptured **beasts.**
2) on the other side were the elders. It was the **Lamb** that was in **between** those two sides of the room.

There the **Lamb** was **standing.** He was positioned **between**

1) **the throne** and the **four beasts,** on one side, and
2) the elders, on the other.

This took place in a **throne** room, similar to the heavenly **throne** room described by Micaiah (1Kings 22:19), with the royal **throne and the four beasts** that carried the **sea** on one side, and at a respectful distance are the elders, sometimes seated on their respective **thrones** (chairs) and at other times worshiping God, who sat on **the throne.**

There is no indication in Rev 5 that the Lamb was either enthroned or invested on the occasion described here. No mention is made of either. Apparently he had already been anointed and enthroned at the time described. Here, as in Rev 14:1, the Lamb appears as one **standing.**[1] The title **Lamb** was often used to refer to kings or those pretending to become kings in Hasmonean times. Aune correctly interpreted the coded terms of 1Enoch 89:11-12 to identify Samuel, David, and Saul:

> And the Lord of the sheep sent this lamb [τὸ ἐν ἄρνα, *ahr-nah*] = Samuel] to another lamb [ἄρνα = David], to establish him as a ram [εἰς κριοῦ, *kree-oo* = David as king] in rule over the sheep [τῶν προβάτων = Israel] in place of the ram [τοῦ κριοῦ = Saul] who lost his way.[2]

From this illustration, alone, one would assume that all male Israelites were lambs, but only after ordination those who became kings were rams. The lambs that have drawn attention of the authors of the Book of Revelation, however, were either pretending kings or enthroned kings. They might have been anointed in secret, the way Saul and David were, but they were messiahs, in any event.

The one described as a **Lamb** was also the **lion**. It was not gentle at all. This **Lamb** was monstrously described as a **Lamb** who had seven horns and seven eyes and it was also the Messiah. This is not the twentieth century Western image of a messiah, but in NT times a messiah was expected to overpower all ruling forces by his military strength and take control of the Promised Land, ruling there as king. In the late Middle Ages some Jewish author described his idea of the Messiah:

---

[1] D. D. Hannah, "Of Cherubim and the Divine Throne: Rev 5:6 in Context" *NTS* 49 (2003):528-542, argued that the Lamb was standing in the midst of the throne. People usually *sit* on the midst of the throne. They do not stand on it.
[2] D. E. Aune, *Revelation 1-5* (Dallas: Word Books Publishers, c1997), p. 370.

> He is tall; his neck is thick; his face is [round] like the sun; his eyes are aflame; the hooves of his feet are thick; his back is wrinkled. He will rule over countries, and he will be given the kingdom, the glory, and the greatness (cf. Dan 7:14).[1]

This monstrous figure was called a **Lamb**, because he belonged to the Lord's chosen flock. This meant he was a Jew, but Jewish and Christian **Lambs** were not expected to be gentle at all to anyone except their own people. One of the parables of 1Enoch describes the Israelites as if they were sheep and the Land of Canaan as if it were a pasture where the sheep grazed. Their leader and judge (probably David) was a ram who drove away the dogs (gentiles) (1Enoch 89:28-47). While mythicizing the Maccabean Revolt the narrator described the Jews as sheep who grew horns, and one of them (probably Judas the Maccabee) grew a large horn (1Enoch 89:46; 90:9-16, 19; see also TJoseph 19:8; TBenj 3:8).

A Lamb standing as slaughtered. These words were taken from Second Isaiah, who applied them to the servant. They were taken here to identify the **Lamb** with the suffering servant of Isaiah. Although a **Lamb** that had been **slaughtered** would not be standing and receiving official documents, John may have added the words, **as slaughtered**, to alert the Christian reader that the Messiah involved was both the suffering servant and the crucified Christ. John of Patmos understood the Lamb to have been Jesus, but there were other messiahs before and in NT times that had been slaughtered for their country,[2] and this document may originally have been written about one of them.

One **Lamb** that was **slaughtered** was the last of the Hasmonean kings, Antigonus, whom the Parthians installed on the throne after they had overpowered the Romans and the family of Herod. Antigonus was a pre-Christian Son of man. He ruled as king from Jerusalem for more than three years, with Parathian support. When the Parthians invaded Palestine, they killed Herod the Great's brother and forced Herod to flee for his life. Herod returned with Roman authority and military supplies. He overpowered the pro-Parthian forces, and captured the Hasmonean messianic king, Antigonus, and had him crucified. The Roman general, Sossius, was prepared to take Antigonus captive back to Rome, but Herod bribed Sossius to have him killed right there in Jerusalem and hang him on a cross for display and ridicule (Ant 14:488-89). Antigonus was the last of the Hasmoneans to sit on the **throne** in Jerusalem before Herod became king. It was not likely that Jews would soon forget

---

[1] "The Signs of the Messiah," Buchanan, *Jewish Messianic Movements from AD 70 to AD 1300* (Eugene, Oregon: Wipf and Stock Publishers, 2003), p. 505.

[2] C. Rowland, *The Open Heaven: A Study of Apocalyptic in Judaism and Christianity* (New York: Crossroad, 1982), p. 516, fn. 71: "The reference to the *arnion . . . hos esphagmenon* makes it impossible to see this chapter [chapter 5] as one devoid of Christian influence."

the offensive abuse their king had suffered at the hands of the Romans—especially Herod. Jerusalem was the city where **their lord was crucified** (Rev 11:8).

Many Jews hated Herod and had strong ties to the Hasmonean family. They might have looked upon Antigonus as the true Messiah who had been killed as a **Lamb** led to the **slaughter**. As a Jew or an Israelite, the Messiah was called a ram or **a Lamb**. As a martyr who had been killed for his country he was described in sacrificial and redemptive terms related to the Day of Atonement as an animal who had been slaughtered as a crime offering for his people. The sermon in Hebrews 1:1-12:29 is devoted to interpreting Jesus' death as an Atonement Day sacrifice. The nearest type of sacrificial Atonement Day offering for Jesus was King Antigonus.

There are other bases for dating parts of the Book of Revelation. Most of which are more precise than this, but since Antigonus is the earliest king that we have on record that was slaughtered—even crucified—it is good methodology to keep this event in mind. King Antigonus was crucified about 38 BIA—much earlier than the author of Rev 5. All we can learn from this is that the author lived and wrote after 38 BIA and that this event was still alluded to in code so that those **who had ears to hear** would understand

After the death of Herod, there were three pretending messiahs, Simon, Eliezer, and Athrongeus (War 2:55-65). All of these led military forces while Herod's son, Archelaus was in Rome, having his leadership confirmed. When he returned, all Judaea had become a guerrilla battlefield. Archelaus overpowered all of these forces with Roman weapons and killed the pretending messiahs. All of these leaders had loyal followers who thought of the leaders as messiahs--**Lambs** that were slain for their nation. There were enough messiahs who had been slain before the time of Christ to have developed a strong doctrine in Judaism about the efficacy of a suffering and dying messiah in terms of servant theology. Messiahs were not called **Lambs** because they were very gentle and helpless. They were **Lambs** because they were part of the Lord's flock of chosen sheep. Ordinary **lambs** do not have horns. Horns are grown only on the rams and then only after they become mature, but this **Lamb had seven horns** (Rev 5:6).

After **lambs** have been slaughtered they are no longer able to stand. Therefore, the **Lamb** that was standing in heaven as though slaughtered was seen only in the author's imagination. Therefore it is not necessary for us to make physical sense of the situation. Whenever a legitimate king was ruling from the palace in Jerusalem, it was presumed that he was God's legal agent. As such he was automatically also a member of the council of God in heaven, by virtue of his office. For example King David was reported to have served in the council of God just before he died (Acts 13:36), so he would have been serving in that council at the same time he was ruling Palestine from Jerusalem (Acts 13:36). He was also a **Lamb** (1Enoch 89:11-12). The significance of having a messiah in heaven that had already been killed was that he might also function as an atonement sacrifice for the crimes of the nation. Since the **Lamb** was also the **lion** of Judah he was both the military leader and the redeemer for his people. This picture was intended to declare the author's conviction that the **Lamb** continued to be a representative in heaven even though he had been **slaughtered** on earth.

Having seven horns. The Lamb is a central figure in the Book of Revelation. The word **Lamb** (*ahr-neé-awn*, ἀρνίον) occurs 29 times in the book. Like the **lion from the tribe of Judah**, it is one of the symbols of the Messiah. Like the renewal of the contract, symbolized by the scroll and sound effects near Sinai, the leadership of the Messiah was necessary for the restoration of the Promised Land. **Horns** symbolized military ability. The **horns** for a goat, bull, ram, or deer were their defense weapons. The same was true of the Messiah. His **horns** were cross bows, spears, battering rams, swords, and other military weapons. Since most sheep or goats have only two **horns**, a **Lamb** with **seven horns** would have been well armed, more like a buck deer with a large rack.

Caird did not like this symbolism, so he said we should not think of this omnipotence as military power but as the power of "infinite persuasion, the invincible power of self-negating, self-sacrificing love."[1] Dr. Rorschach was the one who invented the "ink blot," test in psychology. Those who took this test could look at any blot of spilled ink to learn—not the picture drawn by this ink--but rather their own feelings and thoughts which they infused into the picture as they looked at the ink blot. Some scholars read the Bible as if it were an ink blot, finding their own notions rather than the meaning of the text. Their methodology is called "Rorschach eisegesis." If the author of Rev 5 had wanted to indicate the power of the mouth to persuade rather than the power of weapons to overpower, he might have chosen Caird's symbols rather than his own. Historians have to know something about psychology, but their purpose in research is learning the true meaning of texts rather than expressing their own feelings about the texts involved, psychologically.

And seven eyes. The Lamb's **seven eyes** were the **lamp stands** in Zechariah's vision that represented God's **eyes,** searching all over the land (Zech 4:10), perhaps to gather intelligence material. John of Patmos assigned this task to the churches. They were all authorized to observe everything that happened and report back. The author was commenting on the **seven eyes** of Zechariah. Just as Zechariah reported God as having **seven eyes** that were sent out into all the land, so the commentator deduced that the Messiah, as God's legal agent, would have **seven eyes** which would be sent out into all the land. These he believed would be the **seven** spirits of God. The author was probably relating a passage from Zechariah to another from Ezekiel. The **seven eyes** were identified with **seven** spirits that were sent. Just as these spirits were sent, so God sent the spirit into Ezekiel and sent him out with authority as a legal agent to the children of Israel. The **seven eyes** might also have had the symbolic significance of omniscience, as Weiss suggested.[2] See further Rev 4:5.

Then [the Lamb] came and took [the scroll]. God would not have given this **scroll** to anyone who was not authorized. Both John and the author of the scroll wanted the

---

[1] Caird, *Revelation*, p. 75.
[2] J. Weiss, *Die Offenbarung des Johannes* (Göttingen: Vandenhoeck and Ruprecht, 1908), p. 625.

reader to know both that this **scroll** came from God and that God had recognized the credentials of the Messiah. **The Lamb,** as one authorized, came and took **the scroll** from the hand of God, just as the Lord reached out (literally "sent" [*shah-loó-ah-kah,* שלוח]) his hand to Ezekiel with a **scroll** in it.

TEXT

Revelation

⁸When he took the scroll, the four beasts and the twenty-four elders fell down [prostrate, in a worshipful position] before the Lamb, each one having a harp and gold vials full of **incense** which are the **prayers** of the saints,

⁹and they **sang a new song**, saying,

"You are worthy to receive **the scroll and to open** its seals, because you were slaughtered, and you negotiated with God by means of your blood [for some] from **every** tribe, **language, and nation,**

First Testament

Ps 141:2 Let my **prayer** be counted as **incense** before you.

Isa 42:10 **Sing** to Yehowah **a new song**, his praise from the ends of the earth, those who go down to the sea and fill it, the islands, and their inhabitants.

Ps 89:1 Sing to the Lord **a new song**.

Ps 33:3 **Sing** to him **a new song**.

Ps 40:4 He put in my mouth **a new song**, praise to our God.

Ps 96:1 **Sing** to Yehowah **a new song**; sing to Yehowah, all the land.

Ps 98:1 **Sing** to Yehowah **a new song**, for he has performed miraculous deeds.

Ps 144:9 God, I will **sing** to you **a new song**.

Dan 7:10 **The scrolls were opened.**

Dan 7:14 To him was given the governing authority, the glory, and the kingdom. **All peoples, nations, and languages** would

serve him (cf. Dan 3:4; 5:19; 6:25; 7:14, 29).

¹⁰and you have made them **to** our God **a kingdom** and **priests** and they will rule over the land."

Exod 19:6 If you hear my voice and keep my contract, you will be segregated for me from all the peoples, for all the land is mine. You will be **to** me **a kingdom** of **priests** and a holy nation.

Dan 7:27 The **kingdom**, the governing authority, and the greatness of the **kingdoms** under all heaven will be given to the saints of the Most High.

COMMENTARY

He took the scroll. As soon as the Lamb received **the scroll,** it was evident to those around him that he was commissioned as the new Messiah. **The scroll** gave him the authority to rule.

The twenty-four elders. These were evidently human beings in the council of God. They may actually have been human officers in the temple at Jerusalem or in the royal palace who understood that God was in their midst whenever they met. While David was alive and ruling he was said to have been serving in the council (*boo-láy*, βουλῇ) of God (Acts 13:36). There was a very close proximity between heaven and the temple at Jerusalem--enough so that Hebrews called Mount **Zion, city of the living God**, also **heavenly Jerusalem** (Heb 12:22).[1]

The elders were probably the heavenly counterparts of the **24** priests who took turns assisting in the service at the temple, each with a two-week tenure (1Chron 24:7-18). They represented the priesthood from all over the nation. These elders worshiped the Messiah as if he were God, because as God's legal agent, he was thought to be God, legally. As an outsider, Pliny said Christians sang hymns to Christ as if to a god (Pliny, *Letters* 10.96,7). Many Christians, like Pliny, have confused legal with physical identity and have thought of Jesus as God also physically.

Which are the prayers of the saints. This is an obvious homiletical interpretation. Ps 141:2 asks that God give credit to those who offer their **prayers** as if they, instead, had offered incense upon the altar of the temple. The author assumed that the **prayer** had been granted, so the author pictured a scene in heaven in which these prayers became efficacious. The priestly elders who took their turns at offering sacrifices in the temple collected all of the prayers of the saints and delivered them personally to the Lord in heaven, just as a mail carrier delivers letters. There they were duly credited. The prayers became transformed into incense when the priestly elders brought

---

[1] See further, Buchanan, *To the Hebrews* (Garden City: Doubleday & Co., 1972), *loc. cit*.

them to heaven. The author of this heavenly scene visualized all of this taking place. The new song which the elders sang was probably a continuation of the hymn quoted in Rev 4:11. Both stanzas begin with the word "worthy."

You are worthy. The Lamb was the Lord's Messiah, his legal agent, the lion from the tribe of Judah (Rev 5:5), who was here authorized to open the scroll, which was the new contract that Jeremiah had promised God would make with his people (Jer 31:31). This took place in a judgment situation, just as in Dan 7:13, the Son of man (Judas the Maccabee) appeared before the Ancient of Days in a judgment scene and was given the authority to rule over the Promised Land. This means he was authorized to be the Messiah.

You negotiated with God. The **negotiator** was **the Lamb** who was slain. This implies that he was taken up to heaven after his death where he might **negotiate with God**, using the merits gained by his death as barter. The author reasoned that when **the Lamb** reached heaven he must have been ready to strike a good deal for his nation with the Lord God Almighty.[1] After all, this was no ordinary sacrifice. **This Lamb** was the lion of Judah, the Messiah of the Lord, God's legal agent on earth. How much more could the Lord require? In addition to this he was supported also by the priestly elders in heaven who supported his petition with the prayers of all the saints on earth. The prayers should have set the mood for the Lord to be receptive when **the Lamb** arrived with his sacrifice.

Schüssler-Fiorenza overlooked the role of the treasury of merits, Sabbath justice, and redemption in relationship to Sabbaths and Jubilees when she argued that the redemption took place in God's behalf and that the purchase was made from the world with Jesus as the purchasing agent. She thought it was the world that was paid rather than God.[2] She was right in thinking of the Lamb as the **negotiating** agent, but the author of this document did not think God owed the world anything. Schüssler-Fiorenza's interpretation does not follow. It was God who was the creditor; the Messiah made a terrific payment. The negotiation was to determine how much of the debt would be cancelled because of that payment. It was not the world's debt Jews and early Christians were concerned about. It was Israel's.

They sang a new song. This sentence appears in the Psalms over and over (Ps 33:3; 40:3; 96:1; 144:9; 149:1; Isa 53:10) with standard or different lines in parallel construction. This may have been a standard introduction to any new psalm that was used in worship for the first time. The Book of Revelation used the word **new** many times--**a new song,** a **new** name (Rev 2:17), the **new** Jerusalem (Rev 3:12; 21:2);

---

[1] E. Schüssler-Fiorenza, "Redemption as Liberation: Apoc 1:5f. and 5:9f.," *CBQ* 36 (1974):230-31, was correct in holding that the Kingdom of God is to be understood in "political terms as the alternative to the Roman Empire." This is not a realized or gnostic but an eschatological understanding of redemption and salvation.

[2] Schüssler-Fiorenza, "Redemption," pp. 220-32.

and all things were to be made **new** (Rev 21:5). All of this was possible, because he was thinking of a **new** age.

[For some] from every tribe, language, and nation. This is a polysyndetic list, which means several synonyms were used, one right after the other for emphasis. There is some uncertainty about the words **because you negotiated with God by means of your blood**. Some texts omit **with God** and some texts add **for us**. This poem may once have read, "because you redeemed us." Then the whole poem would make sense. Another possibility is that the ones redeemed were those **from every tribe, language, and nation**. This expression was used many times in the Book of Revelation. It refers either to the migrants of the land--i.e., the foreigners in Palestine--or the Jews from the diaspora. Since the expression comes from Isa 42, the meaning probably is intended to be the same. The servant in Isaiah was to bring forth justice.

This would be good news to all the Jews of the diaspora who would **sing a new song** from their current geographical location--anywhere in the world. They would all be redeemed! Jews in the diaspora believed that when the Messiah came, they would be redeemed, returned to the Promised Land, where they would constitute one kingdom over the Lord's land, because all the land is his, and his own chosen people would rule it. Like the servant who made his death with the wicked and received stripes for the healing of other Jews, so **the Lamb** was one who was slaughtered to **negotiate with the Lord** for the redemption of believers of every language, tribe, and nation.

Jews who lived away from the Promised Land (diaspora Jews) have always been a strategic force on which Palestinian Jews counted in their international conflicts. Just before the war of 66-70 IA broke out, Josephus pictured King Agrippa II delivering a speech to the Jews of Jerusalem. His arguments were intended to answer the plans and arguments that were circulating in Palestine. Agrippa assured them, for example, that they could expect no support from Jews in Adiabene (War 2:388), which was obviously an expectation by some Jews.

You have made them . . . a kingdom and priests. Newport, on the basis of Semitic influence, rendered the word **made** here by "appointed."[1] The poem may have been garbled by John or an earlier Christian who wanted to give credit for this redemption to Jesus who had been crucified and paid the redemption price with his blood. In order for the promise in Exodus to be fulfilled, the Israelites would have to be **made** to rule over the Promised Land. Only then could they be **a kingdom of priests and a holy nation**. The author here, however, followed by John (Rev 1:6), punctuated the promise to mean that they would become **to God a kingdom**, which involved being **priests**. "To God a kingdom" is a Semitism which means "a kingdom belonging to God." Although this seems awkward, Revelation appears to be a

---

[1] K. G. C. Newport, "Some Greek Words with Hebrew Meanings in the Book of Revelation," *AUSS* 26 (1988):27.

priestly document, something like the 11Q Torah of the Dead Sea Scrolls, which structured the entire Torah in terms of priestly leadership and concepts. The 24 elders in the council of heaven were the heavenly equivalent of the 24 priests who took turns serving in the temple. Jews were classified in ranks from the most important to the least important as follows: priests, Levites, Israelites, and proselytes. Part of the significance of being a **kingdom of priests** means it would be a **kingdom** where everyone would be first class. It also suggests that the author himself was a priest.

They shall rule over the land. Some texts (A, for example) put this verb in the present tense **They are ruling over the land**. Ulfgard correctly observed that the priests involved were not **ruling the land** at the time of the writing. At that time the beast and the harlot were really in charge. Ulgard preferred the present tense, however, because he did not like the thought that Revelation was thinking of ruling in a materialistic way.[1]

The ones who were destined to **rule over the land** would be the typological equivalents of **the saints of the Most High** (Dan 7:27). At the same time the kingdom, glory, and governing authority was given to the Son of man (Judas the Maccabee) it was given to his contemporary Jewish colleagues, the saints of the Most High. They ruled in the sense that they were citizens of the ruling power. They were not subjects of any outside force, such as Babylon, Greece, or Rome. The author of this passage in Revelation expected **the Lamb** to become the new Messiah, the new Judas the Maccabee, who, together with his Jewish colleagues, would constitute a **kingdom**. Like the Hasmoneans, they would be priests and, like the Hasmoneans, they would **rule the land.** They would be the parties to the new contract, and citizens of the new **kingdom** on the Promised Land. This is part of a verse of praise, directed to the Lamb:

> [9]You are worthy to receive the scroll
> and to open its seals, because you were slaughtered,
> and you negotiated with God by means of your blood
> [for some] from every tribe, language, and nation,
> [10]and you have made them **to** our God **a kingdom** and **priests**
> and they will rule over the land.

TEXT

Revelation

[11]**I was watching** and I heard the sound of many angels around the **throne**, together with the beasts and

First Testament

Dan 7:9-10 **I was watching** until **thrones** were set up and the Ancient of Days sat down . . . A stream of fire advanced and

---

[1] H. Ulfgard, *Feasts and Future: Revelation 7:9-17 and the Feast of Tabernacles* (Stockholm: Almquist and Wiksell, 1989), p. 49.

elders. Their number was **hundreds of millions** and **millions**, ¹²saying in a loud voice, "Worthy is the **Lamb** which was **slaughtered** to receive **power**, wealth, wisdom, **strength, honor, glory**, and praise."

went out before him. **Millions served him**, and **hundreds of millions** stood up before him [in deference].

^{1Kings 22:19}I saw Yehowah sitting on his **throne**, and all the armies of heaven were standing alongside him, on his right and on his left.

^{Isa 53:7}Like a sheep brought for **slaughter** and a **Lamb** before its shearers.

^{1Chron 29:10-11}David blessed Yehowah before the eyes of all the congregation and David said, "Blessed are you, Yehowah, the God of Israel, our Father from the age and until the age. Yours is the greatness, the **power**, the **glory**, the **strength**, and the **honor**, because all that is in heaven and on earth is yours. Yours is the kingdom, and you are exalted as head with respect to all."

^{Ps 62:12-13}Because **strength** belongs to God; yours, Lord, is steadfast love.

^{Dan 7:14}To him [the Son of man] was given the governing authority, **glory**, and a kingdom.

COMMENTARY

Many angels around the throne. When the throne room in heaven was crowded with **angels** as well as beasts and elders it resembled the court room described in Daniel, where there were thousands of assistants to the Ancient of Days, and all of the myriads of people present in the court room rose up in deference to the Ancient of Days as he approached the bench for judgment (Dan 7:9-10). On that occasion the judgment was made in favor of the Son of man, who was Judas the Maccabee. In this similar court scene the verdict was given in favor of the Son of man, **the Lamb,** who was judged **worthy.** Both leaders were given great power and authority along with other special honors.

I was watching, and I heard. The Greek here says, literally, **I saw, and I heard,** but this expression is from Dan 7:13: **I was watching** (*khah-zay hah váyth*, חזה הוית). Charles recognized years ago that parts of Revelation could not be correctly understood until it was retranslated into a Semitic language. This **watching** took place in the Scriptures where the author was looking over (reading) the works of Daniel and Second Isaiah. While he was visualizing the throne room scene, where the Lord sat in judgment and millions of people were witnesses in court, he heard beasts and elders singing.

The Lamb which was slaughtered. The three line verse seems to be part of the hymn that was quoted in Rev 4:11 and Rev 5:9-10. The first line may have been expanded by the addition of the phrase, **which was slaughtered,** but even with this phrase, these lines would pass for a verse of poetry. It is also coherent with Rev 5:9, which was also directed to one who had been slain. The virtues of the Lamb were listed in an asyndeton list to emphasize them accumulatively.

> Worthy is the Lamb that has been slaughtered
> to receive power, wealth, wisdom,
> strength, honor, glory, and praise.

נאמן הרחל הטבוח	neh-eh-máhn hah rah-kháyl hah tah-vóh-akh
לקבל כוח והון וחכמה	luh qee-báyl kóh-akh wuh-hohn wuh khakh-máh
ועז וכבוד וחדר ושבח	wah-óhz wuh kah-vóhd wuh kháy-dehr wuh sheh-bákh

This is the same **Lamb** as the one **standing as slaughtered** (Rev 5:6). It has normally been assumed by such scholars as Rowland[1] that it is impossible to see Rev 5 as devoid of Christian influence. This is an overstatement. It is certainly possible to see this verse as a Christian addition, but it is also possible to understand it as normal Jewish interpretation. Jesus was not the only Jewish Messiah to be killed for his nation. Judas the Maccabee was killed in battle for his country. Antigonus was the last of the Hasmonean kings to rule over Judah. He ruled for three years before Herod regained control of the country, after which Herod had Antigonus crucified. Immediately after the death of Herod the Great, Simon, Eliezer, and Athrongeus were all pretending messiahs or **Lambs** who led military movements against Rome and were killed by Herod the Great's son, Archelaus.

The verse was probably intentionally planned to have seven nouns in the list of praiseworthy items **the Lamb** deserved to receive. They are all qualities that would be fitting for a king, reminiscent of the tributes given to the Son of man as he appeared before the Ancient of Days. They also reflect David's praise of God before the congregation (1Chron 29:10-11). O'Rourke[2] thought Rev 5:12 was a piece of Johannine liturgy, just as it is, possibly used in a Paschal liturgy. He also thought the

---

[1] Rowland, *The Open Heaven,* p. 516, fn. 71.
[2] J. J. O'Rourke, "The Hymns of the Apocalypse," *CBQ* 30 (1968):402.

final author replaced the words, "the Lord," with **and the Lamb**, and thereby disrupted the poetry.[1]

Before **the beasts** gave the final **amen**, while the elders worshiped, the angels sang a hymn of praise. The hymn which the author employed would have continued unbroken from the line, **honor, glory, and praise** (Rev 5:12), to the line, **to the one seated upon the throne** (Rev 5:13). A later editor interrupted the poem to expand the chorus from the angels only to include every creature in the universe. This affirmation was composed in poetic form.

TEXT

[13]and every creature which is in heaven, upon earth, and in the sea, and all the things in them, I heard saying,

Revelation	First Testament
"To the one **seated on the throne**	Isa 6:1 In the year that King Uzziah died, I saw the Lord, **sitting on the throne**.
and to the Lamb be praise, honor, and glory to the ages of ages."	Ps 47:9 God is **seated on the throne** of his holiness.
[14]Then the four beasts said, "Amen!" and the elders fell down and worshiped.	1Kings 22:19 I saw the Lord **sitting on his throne**.

COMMENTARY

Every creature. Some scholars have tried to identify the kind of **creatures** that are in heaven and under the earth,[2] but that is not the point here. This is simply a periphrastic way of saying **every** single **creature** in existence anywhere. That means all that are **in heaven, on earth, and in the sea**. NA edition added after **the earth, and under the earth,** referring to worms and beasts that live in holes. NA also had **on the sea** rather than **in the sea**.

To the one seated on the throne and to the Lamb. **The one seated on the throne** was God, **and the Lamb** was his legal agent, the Messiah. The understanding is the same as the picture of Solomon **seated on the throne** of the Kingdom of Yehowah (2Chron 28:5; also 29:11, 23) while he ruled from Jerusalem. Solomon acted as Yehowah's legal agent when he **sat on the** royal **throne** at Jerusalem. At the same time God was **sitting on** a corresponding **throne** in heaven. Since the agent acted in behalf of the principal, whenever Solomon or the Messiah **sat on the throne,** God

---

[1] O'Rourke, "Hymns," p. 404.
[2] Düsterdieck, *Handbook*, p. 215.

also **sat on the throne.** To have both God **and the Lamb sitting on the throne**, it was not necessary to picture the Messiah sitting on God's lap!¹

Instead of **and power**, after **glory**, as NA text has, Sinaiticus has **[the] almighty One**. This confusion is probably the result of a dictation error. *Kai taw kráh-taws* (καὶ τὸ κράτος) sounds something like *pahn-taw-kráh-taws* (παντοκράτος). This little couplet is a verse of praise to God and to the Messiah:

> To the one *seated on the throne* and to the Lamb
> be praise, honor, and glory to the ages of ages.

Then the four beasts said, "Amen!" **The four beasts** were not **the four** monsters whom Daniel caricatured as representatives of enemy kings. These **beasts** were also monstrous, but they were heavenly cherubim and seraphim. Like **the beasts** that came **out of the sea**, they were composite sphinx-like **beasts** with wings like birds, heads like lions, feet like goats. They were able to do all of the things birds, **beasts,** and human beings could do. This is the conclusion of the scene of praise and worship of God and the Lamb in the heavenly throne room. After **the beasts**, elders, and angels had joined in worship and praise of the **Lamb** and of God, the author set the stage. Others say this was a preexisting Jewish hymn to which the words **to the Lamb** have been added. The word **amen** was used with oaths for the oath-taker to acknowledge that he or she understood the content of the oath and agreed to it. In liturgy it was added at certain points for the congregation to acknowledge its approval and willingness to accept the requirements made of the confession, prayer, or oath expressed by the leader. It was introduced by the notation, "Say, '**Amen**.'"² In this structure it was the heavenly **beasts** who responded with the **amen.**

Vogelgesang argued that Rev 5:13-14 is such a logical conclusion to a book that it is surprising to find any other text following it.³ He is correct, of course, and at one time these verses may have concluded a unit of redemption midrash. Some editor, however, used this unit as only part of a larger anthology (Rev 4:1-22:5). Rev 5 fit very nicely after Rev 4, which is an obvious introductory unit.

SUMMARY

Rev 5 is a coherent portion of the prophecy that was presented to John of Patmos (Rev 1:1-3). The entire Jewish prophecy (Rev 4:1-22:5) contained the term, **Lamb**, 28 times The term, however, does not appear at all in the portion that can justly be attributed to John of Patmos (Rev 1:1-3:22, and 22:6-21). The word, "Jesus," occurs eight times in these few verses written by John. It occurs an additional six times in the 19 chapters of the prophecy. All of these usages are interpretative, obvious

---

[1] A picture visualized, and rejected, by Loisy, *L'Apocalypse*, pp. 133-34.
[2] E.g. "The Kaddish," S. Singer, *The Authorized Daily Prayer Book* (London: Eyre and Spotteswoode, 1960), pp.86-87.
[3] J. M. Vogelgesang, *The Interpretation of Ezekiel in the Book of Revelation* (Ann Arbor: University Microfilms, 1986), p. 343-44.

additions made to give the prophecy a Christian meaning. Prior to these additions, these 19 chapters constituted a Jewish prophecy, in which the main character was the **Lamb**. This means that the **Lamb** involved was a Jewish messiah, but it was not Jesus. John of Patmos received this Jewish prophecy, and he may instantly have identified the **Lamb** that was slaughtered with Jesus, but he did not "improve" the text by calling that **Lamb** "Jesus." The particular Lamb in Rev 5 was some Jewish messiah who had been killed. The one that fits the type best is King Antigonus, the last of the Hasmonean kings, who was killed and crucified by the order of Herod about 38 BIA.

CHAPTER SIX

TEXT

$^{6:1}$I was watching when the Lamb opened one of the seven seals, and I heard one of the four beasts saying [in a voice] like the sound of thunder,

Revelation

"Go!" ^{2}I was watching--Now look! A **white horse**, and the one sitting on it had a bow, and a crown was given to him, and he went out conquering and to conquer. ^{3}When he opened the second seal, I heard **the second** beast saying, "Go!" ^{4}and another **red horse** went out.

To the one seated on it was given [authority] to take peace from the land, so that they will slaughter one another, and a great sword was given to him. ^{5}When he opened the third seal, I heard **the third** beast saying, "Go!" I was watching. Now look! A **black horse**, and the one seated upon it had a scale in his hand. ^{6}I heard something like a voice in the midst of **the four** beasts,

First Testament

$^{\text{Zech 1:8}}$Behind him were **red**, sorrel, and **white horses**.

$^{\text{Zech 1:8}}$Look! A man riding on a **red horse**.

$^{\text{Zech 6:1, 2-3, 5}}$Now look! **four** chariots came out from between the mountains . . . The first chariot had **red horses**;

the second chariot had **black horses**; **the third** chariot had **white horses**,

and **the fourth** chariot had dappled gray horses . . . The angel answered me, "These are going out to **the four** winds of heaven, stationing themselves alongside the Lord of all the land."

TECHNICAL DETAILS

Rev 4-7 fit together coherently, and many scholars assume that they were written by the same author as an intended **unit**. This unity, however, could also have been made by a good editor who was competent in organizing his materials. Rev 4 meshes nicely with Rev 5, but it also stands as a unit forming an inclusion from the verse, **The one seated upon the throne** (Isa 6:1) at the beginning and end of Rev 4. The same verse, however, also concludes Rev 5 to form another inclusion. Someone may have composed Rev 5 with Rev 4 before him, but these are only conjectures. We now have the text as it has been composed, organized, and edited. We cannot be sure where all of the borders of the various units begin and end. That which is most likely is that the prophecy began with Rev 4:1.

COMMENTARY

The Lamb opened one of the seven seals.[1] When believers saw the scroll, they were happy, because that was the new contract they wanted, but **the seals** were the obstacles that prevented it from being consummated. Breaking one of the seals was like lighting the fuse for a bomb. They had to break the seals to get to the contract, but breaking them was asking for punishment. The events that followed each seal that was broken were destined to be damaging to the Israelites. These evils were all punishments necessary to correct all offenses before God would renew his contract with his people. The contract contained the terms required by contract for the people to observe if God was to fulfill the blessings and promises contained in the contract. This contract was in one sense a will that showed what the chosen people would inherit, but it was more than that. It provided the terms and conditions according to which the Lord would continue to provide for Israel. The promises were well known, because they were part of the First Testament (FT) in which the former contract was given. The new contract was the one Jeremiah promised that God would make with his people (Jer 31:31-34).

The seven seals kept the contract from being fulfilled. Following Hosea, Jeremiah looked to Deut 24:1 to learn what the Assyrian and Babylon exiles meant. When a husband divorced his wife, all he had to do was to put the legal document in her hand that told her that she was divorced. Then he had to send her out of his house just as Abraham sent Hagar out of his house. Jeremiah thought God had also divorced his people with whom he was married by contract. The author of Rev 6 evidently also thought that the document which God put into Israel's and Judah's hands was the contract, sealed with seven seals, so that it would not be effective until all of the terms of the contract had been fulfilled. At that time Israel and Judah would both be given the same new contract. The seals kept the people from receiving the contract. The seven curses that were represented by seven seals were required of the people before the contract could be renewed.

The Lamb had his authority confirmed before the throne of God, so he was now prepared to break the **seals** and **open the** scroll. Some scrolls in antiquity, after the desired text had been written on them, were **sealed** with **seven seals** made as part

---

[1] F. Düsterdieck, *Critical and Exegetical Handbook to the Revelation of John*, tr. H. E. Jacobs (Winona Lake: Alpha Publications, 1884), p. 220, disagreed with this translation. He held that the opening of the seal was not the object of the verb, *áy-dawn* (εἶδον), *I saw*. He thought the "seeing" referred to the prophetic condition, and the object of the vision was really the hearing that followed in the same sentence. This complicates a very simple sentence: the author was watching when suddenly the Lamb began to open one of the seven seals.

of metal rings, one beside the other.[1] The scroll was fitted inside the rings. The scroll could not be read until all **seven seals** had been broken.[2] In the following narrative, the curses were instigated by breaking the seals--not from reading the scroll. This was the type of magic, which Elisha applied to Joash when Elisha told him to take some arrows and strike the ground with them to begin the destruction of Syria (2Kings 13:15-19).

The new contract would not be instituted, nor could it be read, until all of the **seals** were broken and all of the associated punishments had been made. The narrative that follows the breaking of each **seal** would not have been the content of the scroll. When **the Lamb** broke each **seal**, one of the beasts issued a command, and one of the four horsemen of Zechariah's vision appeared to carry out the orders. These horsemen, however, had a different mission from those of Zechariah. Zechariah's horsemen went out to patrol the land, and they returned to report that the land was at peace. Theirs was a mission similar to **the seven eyes of the lord** which scouted the land. This was bad news to Zechariah, because he knew the land could not be restored during a time of peace.

The horsemen of Revelation, however, had a different mission--one that would please the holy war theologian. Each horse reported something that indicated a time of war: The first seal was broken: "Snap!" and one horseman went out with a bow and arrows to fight. The second seal was broken: "Ping!" and the next horseman took peace from the land and destined people to slaughter one another in war. The third seal was broken: "Zingo!" and the third horseman indicated a shortage of grain which made prices soar. There would be famine, because the fields were left unplanted or were destroyed in war. The fourth seal was broken and: "Presto!" the fourth horseman would bring pestilence, plaguing the nation with disease.

Go! The Greek could be translated either "Come!" or **Go!** The context demands that the word be translated **Go!** because the horsemen were commanded to **go** away from the commander and perform a commission.[3] They were not being called to come to the commander from somewhere else. This was not just a quiet suggestion. Like a military command, it was an order given to be obeyed. It was said to be loud as thunder.

Look! a white horse. This text was written when the cavalry was the strongest section of a battlefield. Horses were the fastest means of transportation available.

---

[1] F. M. Cross, Jr., "The Discovery of the Samaria Papyri," *BA* 26 (1963):110-39, for pictures of ancient scrolls that had been sealed with seven seals. One of those has been rephotographed with permission and appears on p. 116 of this book.
[2] So also G. Bornkamm, "Die Komposition der apokalyptischen Visionen in der Offenbarung Johannis," *Studien zu Antike und Urchristentum* (Munich: Kaiser, 1963), pp. 205, 218-19.
[3] D. E. Aune, *Revelation 6-16* (Nashville: Thomas Nelson Publishers, c1998), p. 395, rendered this "Come," but he also noted, "The author . . . used . . . the verb [*ehx-ayl-thehn*], ἐξῆλθεν, 'he rode out,' though it is not clear whence the cavalier comes." The problem is that he did not "come" he went.

Kings rode either horseback or in chariots. There were no limousines or military tanks available.

Although there is no direct word usage, Hodges may be correct in holding that the author consciously imitated Ps 45 where a king is pictured as riding in his majesty prosperously (Ps 45:4) with peoples falling before his sharp arrows (Ps 45:6). Hodges argued that the rider on this **white horse** was the Messiah,[1] who was also armed with a bow and arrow. Weiss held that the use of the bow would have suggested the Parthians,[2] but they were not the only ones who used bows and arrows in warfare. Bows and arrows were standard military weapons in NT times. In Bachmann's extensive study he observed that for centuries scholars have interpreted this verse in different ways. Some have taken the role of this rider to be the Messiah and be positive; others have classed the rider of the **white horse**, like the riders of the other three, to be assigned a negative role.

Bachmann concluded that the rider of the **white horse** was the Messiah and was to be seen as over against the other riders. Whereas this one was a **white horse**, the others were colored. **White** was the color given to holy things, whereas colors like crimson were applied to the harlot, an enemy.[3] Bachmann argued that the rider on the **white horse** played a positive role, but the other riders had negative roles.

Hailey argued that the rider who wore the crown was the Messiah, but he went forth to conquer the world, not through military power, but in the gospel by which he would conquer human souls.[4] Feuillet argued against this view. He said this horse must be interpreted in relationship to the other two **horses** with which it was combined. Its mission was not to proclaim good news but to conquer with weapons. His assignment was not beneficial but punitive.[5]

There were negative roles for all of the riders, but their overall purpose was positive. The anticipated war was to be like the ones the Jews fought under the leadership of Judas the Maccabee against Antiochus Epiphanes. This was sometimes called "the birth pangs of the Messiah" or "the tribulation." The war was inflicted on the believers to provide enough damage to the believers to pay for their crimes before the contract could be renewed. They provided the necessary torture to develop martyrs who could testify in behalf of the chosen people at the court trial when the judgment would be made over the people. Every time a seal was broken and a horseman was sent out on a mission, there was more suffering for the saints but also a payment of their crimes that kept them divorced from God without a contract.

The more tortures that happened the sooner the contract would be renewed. This is the reason Paul rejoiced in his sufferings (Col 1:24). He reasoned **that the**

---

[1] Z. C. Hodges, "The First Horseman of the Apocalypse," *BibSac* 119 (1962):324-33.
[2] J. Weiss, *Die Offenbarung des Johannes* (Göttingen: Vandenhoeck and Ruprecht, 1908), p. 629.
[3] M. Bachmann, "Der Erste Apokalyptische Reiter und die Anlage des Letzten Buches der Bibel," *Bib* 67 (1986):240-75.
[4] H. M. Hailey, *Revelation: Introduction and Commentary* (Grand Rapids: Baker's Book House, c1979), p. 189.
[5] A. Feuillet, "Le Premier Cavalier de L'Apocalypse," *ZNW* 57 (1966):258-59.

sufferings of the current time were not worthy of being compared to the glory that was **about to be revealed** (Rom 8:18). The author of Hebrews said Jesus **through the suffering of his death was crowned with glory and honor** (Heb 2:9-10). Rabbi Nathan said that punishments caused Jews to be beloved by their father in heaven (Mek. *Bahodesh* 6:143-44); Rabbi Ishmael said,

> Blessed are those who are persecuted because of me, because they will have a place where they will not be persecuted (Strom 4:6, 41).

To take peace from the land. The typological background for this statement is the commission of the horsemen in Zechariah's vision. The horsemen in Zechariah were sent to walk around the Promised Land and come back to report the conditions. They returned and said that **the** entire **land** was peace and quiet. Then the messenger of the Lord complained to the Lord: **How long will you not have mercy on Jerusalem and on the cities of Judah with whom you have been angry these seventy years** (Zech 1:12)? Jeremiah had promised that Jews would be returned from Babylon and **the land** restored in 70 years. At the time of this vision, the 70 years had passed, and the land was not restored. It could not be restored, in the judgment of the prophet, so long as there was **peace** in **the land**. It would require war to overpower the foreign rulers.

This was the experience also of the Hasmonean rebellion. There was a 3½ year period when **peace** was taken **from the land** before the temple could be restored. The horsemen in the Book of Revelation had a more satisfying assignment than the one in Zechariah's vision. Instead of reporting **peace,** the second horseman was given authority **to take peace from the land.** This would instigate the war necessary to regain possession of **the land. Peace** under foreign rule was not good news, either to Zechariah or to the author of the prophecy in Revelation.

Düsterdieck called the group that was the subject of all of this slaying "the dwellers upon earth," not noticing that *all* people are "dwellers upon earth" (Rev 6:10). He did not think *tays gays* (τῆς γῆς) could mean **the land** of Judah, but he did not say why not, just as he did not say why this report surely could not refer to the war of IA 66-70.[1]

Had a scale in his hand. The word for **scale** is literally "yoke." A yoke was used for carrying two objects at once. It would fit over a person's shoulders, so that she or he could have a bucket of water on each side, or it could be used to bind two oxen together to pull one vehicle. This was also used to balance two weights, a known weight on one side and an unknown on the other, to learn how much it weighed. This became a symbol of judgment. After a battle, the victorious general in charge would pass judgment on the result. For example, after the destruction of Jerusalem Titus gathered his troops and held a judgment. There he awarded honors for those who had shown special leadership and bravery. He slaughtered the oxen and held a great victory banquet, and sent the prisoners to Caesarea on the Sea for temporary

---
[1] Düsterdieck, *Handbook*, p. 223.

custody (War 7:1-24). A following judgment would determine the disposition of the prisoners. This was standard practice, and that is what the **scale** symbolized after peace had been taken from the land. Those who were to be weighed in the **scale** were the participants in the war.

TEXT

Revelation

saying, "**A** koinix **of wheat for a** denarius, and three **koinixes of barley for a** denarius, but do not damage the oil or the wine."
⁷When he opened the fourth seal, I heard the voice of the fourth beast, saying, "Go!" ⁸I was watching--
Now look! **A sorrel horse**, and one was seated upon it. His name was

Death and Hades followed after him. Then there was given to them authority over **the fourth** of the

land, to kill by means of **the sword, famine, pestilence**,

First Testament

²ᴷⁱⁿᵍˢ ⁷:¹Elisha said, "Hear the word of the Lord! Thus **says** the Lord, '**A** measure **of fine** [wheat] **meal** shall be sold **for a** shekel, and two measures **of barley for a** shekel, at the gate of Samaria.'"

ᶻᵉᶜʰ ¹:⁸Now look! A man riding on a bay **horse** . . . and behind him bay, **sorrel**, and white **horses**.

ᴸᵉᵛ ²⁶:⁶I will provide peace on the land. You will lie down and there will be no fear. I will turn away the evil **beasts** from the land, and **the sword** will not pass through in your land.

²ᴷⁱⁿᵍˢ ⁶:²⁵There was a great **famine** in Samaria. Now look! They [Ben Hadad's troops] besieged it until a donkey's head [was sold for] eight [shekels] of silver, and a **fourth** of a kab of dove's dung [was sold for] five [shekels of] silver.

ᴶᵉʳ ¹⁴:¹¹⁻¹²; ᶜᶠ. ²⁴:¹⁰Do not pray for this people . . . because with **sword**, with **famine**, and with **pestilence** I will finish them off.

ᴱᶻᵉᵏ ⁵:¹²A third of you will die with **pestilence** and with **famine** be consumed in your midst, and the third will fall **with the sword** round about you.

^{Ezek 14:21}Thus says the Lord Yehowah, "Even I will send against Jerusalem four evil verdicts to cut off man and **beast: sword, famine**, evil **beasts, and pestilence.**"

^{Jer 15:3-4}"I will visit upon them **four** kinds [of curses]," said the Lord: "**the sword**, to kill, the dogs to tear, the birds of the sky and **the wild beasts** to eat and destroy, and I will make them a horror to all the kingdoms of the earth.

and by **the wild beasts**.

^{Ezek 29:5}I will give you as food for **the wild beasts** and the birds of the heaven.

COMMENTARY

A koinix of wheat for a denarius. **A koinix** is about a pint and a half. This is only enough **wheat** to last one person one day. In normal times a **denarius** would have bought twelve times as much. A **denarius** is a full day's wages for a laborer. This means a laborer could not earn enough to feed his family with **wheat**. These are conditions of famine like those that existed in Samaria after a battle (2Kings 2:16). One battle during which many people starved to death was fought in 66-70 IA. It ended with the destruction of Jerusalem.

Elisha was prophesying famine when he said that a measure of fine meal would be sold for a shekel and two measures of barley for a shekel (2Kings 7:1). Düsterdieck correctly noted that there was no special kind of symbolism of the bow. It just symbolized war, as a sword might have done. When he referred to Ps 45:6, he volunteered that this was an image "in a description which may have floated before John." Obviously, Düsterdieck thought the author was having a vision played before his eyes like a play on a stage.[1] Morris observed that this "vision" came after the scroll was opened. He even said one should have expected him to read the book after he had opened it, but instead he had a vision.[2] This "vision," however, came directly from Zechariah, the book he was reading when he was inspired.

---

[1] Düsterdieck, *Handbook*, p. 221.
[2] L. Morris, *The Book of Revelation* (Grand Rapids: Wm. B. Eerdmans, c1987), p. 103.

Do not damage the oil or the wine. The voice in the midst of the four beasts warned **not to damage the oil or wine**, regardless of the prices. Charles[1] followed others in explaining the famine as that occurring in Domitian's time when there was a surplus of **wine** and a shortage of grain. Domitian ordered that no more vineyards be planted and half the vineyards in the provinces be cut down. Before this was completely implemented, some cities complained so bitterly that Domitian withdrew the edict and, in fact, prohibited any further destruction of vineyards (Seutonius, *Dom* 7:2; 14:2). There are still scholars like Hemer who subscribe to this interpretation, even though it has many flaws.[2] The situation in Rome during the time of Domitian, scholars have held, explains the command, **Do not damage the wine**. Morris, following Charles, said the situation was one in which there was a surplus of **oil and wine** but a scarcity of grain.[3] If this were the case, we might have expected the author to say not to hurt the wheat and the barley rather than the **oil and wine.**

The argument supported by Charles and his followers offers no explanation for **the oil** or the **wheat**. Düsterdieck thought this warning referred to a famine in Rome in the time of Claudius.[4] It says nothing about a shortage of **oil and wine** in Jerusalem.

Thompson was not satisfied with Charles's explanation. He thought it meant, "Do not (fraudulently) withhold **the oil and wine**," when they are scarce so as to charge exorbitant prices for them.[5] Giblin rendered the passage, "and (yet) do not harm [cheat on, by overcharging for] the oil and wine."[6] He further explained that **oil and wine** were singled out for special treatment, because they were "associated with the life of luxury" and therefore "would not be touched."[7] Boring was of the same opinion. He said the food rationing effected only the poor who would need the **wheat** and barley, whereas the rich would continue to live with their normal luxuries--**oil and wine**.[8]

If **oil and wine** were too expensive to be touched, how would anyone hurt them? Overcharging would hurt the buyers--not **the oil or wine.** Charles looked for a solution in the Roman Empire, almost anywhere in the Mediterranean area, since he believed John wrote the entire Book of Revelation and that he wrote it from Patmos Island. This blinded him and his later followers from looking for an easy solution in the land of Palestine. A more reasonable explanation comes from the famine that occurred in Jerusalem at the end of the IA 66-70 war.

---

[1] R. H. Charles, *Critical and Exegetical Commentary on the Revelation of St. John the Divine* (New York: Charles Scribner's Sons, c1920) I, p. 67.
[2] C. J. Hemer, *The Letters to the Seven Churches of Asia in their Local Setting* (Sheffield: JSOT, c1986), p. 4.
[3] Morris, *Revelation*, p. 106.
[4] Düsterdieck, *Handbook*, p. 225.
[5] S. Thompson, *The Apocalypse in Semitic Syntax* (New York: Cambridge U. Press, 1985), p. 16.
[6] C. H. Giblin, *The Book of Revelation* (Collegeville: Liturgical Press, c1991), p. 81.
[7] Giblin, *Revelation*, p. 84.
[8] M. E. Boring, *Revelation* (Louisville: John Knox Press, c1989), p. 122.

Josephus described that condition as being one in which people would bargain all of their possessions for a single measure of **wheat**, if they were rich, of barley, if they were poor. These purchases, however, had to be made secretly. If the soldiers knew anyone possessed food they would confiscate it (War 5:424-28). No matter how great the shortage of food, it was necessary to preserve, undefiled, enough **oil** to anoint the Messiah and enough **wine** for the messianic banquet. This is consistent with the offense Josephus expressed when he learned that John, after he gained control of the temple area, not only used the vessels designed for the pure **wine**, but he and his supporters used every drop of sacred **wine and oil** (War 5:562-65; see also mMid 2.6). That which offended Josephus probably seemed proper to John and his soldiers. They probably used **the oil** to anoint John king of the Jews and **the wine** for a messianic banquet. That was the reason it had been saved in the first place. The only disagreement concerned the identity of the Messiah.

A sorrel horse . . . and his name was "Death." This was the last of the four beasts to utter a command to a horse and rider whose name was *Thah-nah-taws* (θάνατος) which can mean either **death** or "pestilence." Here it probably means **Death**, because authority was given it to kill, not only by means of disease, but also through famine, sword, and wild beasts. These were three of the Lord's four acts of adverse judgment, which are the curses of the contract. **Hades** was the place of the dead, so it would normally follow **death** more certainly than pestilence.

The sword, famine, pestilence, and by the wild beasts of the land. Each of **the horsemen** brought one of the curses, and the four riders were reported here as having authority to provide all four curses. Specifically, however, **the horsemen** delivered only three. These four curses were the ones associated with the contract Israel had made with the Lord. If Israel kept the commandments given, God would bless the Israelites with all kinds of success and prosperity (Lev 26:1-13; also see Ezek 14:21). If they did not keep the contract, God would make them fail in all their efforts, punishing them **seven** times for all their crimes. These punishments would come in the form of four plagues:

1) **Wild beasts**,
2) **the sword;**
3) **pestilence,** and
4) **famine** (Lev 26:21-26; see also Jer 14:12; 15:2; 24:10; 29:17-18; 42:17; 43:11).

Of these four the last three are associated with the first four seals. Sirach said, **Fire, hail, famine, and pestilence--these all were created for vengeance** (Sir 39:29). By this he meant they were designed to punish believers after they had broken the contract with the Lord. Other instruments of vengeance were **wild beasts**, scorpions, vipers, and **the sword** (Sir 39:30).

Instead of **wild beasts** in Rev 16, there is a **crowned** rider on a **white horse** having **a bow,** and probably some arrows. This seems to have the same intent as the second seal which released a rider on a **red horse** who had authority to **take peace from the land.** The fourth rider brought disease (**pestilence**) and **death** (Hades) and then was given a summary authority that applied all four curses. The editor of this passage apparently had before him a manuscript which included the **four horsemen,** so he included it. Since he noticed it was closely related to the curses of the **contract**, he summarized the curses in association with **the fourth horseman.** Other scholars have noticed that **the seven seals** were separated into two groups: the first four and the last three.[1] The reason for the division is clearly the relationship of the first four to the curses of the **contract.** The last three brought the total up to **the seven** promised in Lev 26.

Both Jeremiah and Ezekiel commented in detail on the curses listed in Lev 26. In Ezek 5 attention was given to the four curses of the contract. All of these curses were destined to come upon Jerusalem, because of the criminal activity of the people of Israel. The Israelites were guilty of having broken **the contract** they had made with the Lord. Therefore, they were destined to receive the promised curses of **the contract.** All of these curses express God's anger, and they were all part of the terms of the **contract**. In response to this the author of Revelation followed the curses with the terrible day during which God expressed his anger. Daniel probably interpreted mythically the kings of the four gentile nations that ruled over Palestine from 586 BIA to 164 BIA. as monstrous beasts so that they would fulfill against these generations the curses of **the contract,** one of which was that they would be cursed by evil beasts.

All four of these curses are associated with war. **The sword** was the weapon used in war; **famine** came during warfare when cities were besieged and not given access to food supplies for many months; starvation, decaying corpses, and other unhealthful conditions associated with confinement within city walls promoted disease; and wild beasts and scavengers were lured by the corpses left unburied. Since the second horseman took peace from the land, conditions were right for these four curses to be enforced. They were all designed at the time the contract was made with the Lord at Sinai. Since Israel's God was called the God "of Armies" (*tseh-váh-ohht*, צבעות), he punished his people with failure in war just as he rewarded them with victory in war if they obeyed his **contract.**

From the fact that these **horsemen** were assigned to enforce the curses of the contract which was promised Israelites if they broke the contract, it is evident that the document which **the seals** secured was **the contract**, and **the seals** were instruments which could apply the curses of the contract. When each **seal** was broken Israelites were to receive more of the curses. **The seals** had to be broken before **the contract** could be read, and the curses had to be received before **the contract** could be renewed. All of this symbolism indicates that the curses were directed at the parties to the contract and not against the enemies of Israel. It was good news for Israel

---

[1] A. S. Peake, *The Revelation of John* (London: Holborn, n.d.), p. 269.

to receive the curses and the war that accompanied them. These were the "birth pangs of the Messiah" or the "tribulation" that marked the last three and a half years of the old age. It was the antitype of the war between Judas and the Syrian Greeks before the Battle of Beth-horon and the rededication of the temple in 164 BIA.

Like many others, Caird was horrified by these verses. He offered the following apology to soften the offense:

> He is not asking us to believe that war, rebellion, famine, and disease are the deliberate creation of Christ, or that, except in an indirect way, they are what God wills for men and women he has made.[1]

The author understood precisely that these punishments were designed by God to apply to the parties to the contract if they happened to break it. Since they broke it, it was God's will that they receive the prescribed curses.

TEXT

Revelation	First Testament and Fourth Ezra
⁹When he opened the fifth seal, I saw under the altar **the souls of** those who had been slain on account of the word of God and on account of the testimony which they held. ¹⁰Then they cried in a loud voice, **saying, "How long**	4Ezra 4.35-37 Did not **the souls of** the just in their store houses ask about these things, **saying, "How long will** we wait in this way? When will the harvest of our reward come?" Jeremiel the archangel answered and said to them, "When the number of those like you is filled up, for he has weighed the age in a scales; he has measured the times by measure; by number he has numbered the times; he will not move nor arouse them until the prescribed measure is filled up."
O Master, will you not	Zech 1:12 **Yehowah of armies, how long will you not** have mercy on Jerusalem and on the cities of Judah with whom you have been angry these seventy years?

---

[1] G. B. Caird, *A Commentary on the Revelation of St. John the Divine* (London: Black, c1966), pp. 82-83.

avenge our **blood** from the migrants of the land?" ¹¹Then to each of them was given a white robe, and they were told they must continue to rest a little while, until also their

fellow **servants** and their brothers who were about to be killed as even they had been [were killed].

^(Deut 32:43)He **avenges the blood** of his servants; he takes vengeance on his opponents.

^(Ps 13:1)**How long, Yehowah? Will you** forget me forever? **How long will you** turn your face from me?

^(Ps 74:10)**How long, God, will** the enemy scoff? Will the enemy revile your name forever?

^(Ps 79:5)**How long, Yehowah?** Will you be angry for ever? Your zeal burns like fire.

^(Deut 32:43)I said, **"How long, Lord?"** Praise his people, nations, for he **avenges the blood** of his **servants** and returns **vengeance** to his enemies.

COMMENTARY

The souls of those who have been slain. The heavenly altar under which **the souls** were stored was expected to be like the altars in earthly temples. **Souls** were legal identities. In the judgment of Jews and Christians, pagans did not have **souls.** People obtained their **souls** with baptism and lost them with excommunication. Losing a soul was like losing a passport, permanently. Souls were not limited to physical life. They were stored up and filed like legal records for future identity, recorded on the nation's rolls. Physical lives could not be stored and preserved, but **souls** could.

The idea of **souls** being stored in heaven was widely held. Fourth Ezra described impatient **souls** in store houses, stored like money or grain (4Ezra 4:35-37). Second Baruch expected that **the souls of** the righteous that were stored in heavenly treasuries would all be released at the end of the evil times (2Bar 30:1-3). During those evil times the building of Zion would be shaken, but that would happen only so that the temple could later be rebuilt (2Bar 32:2-4). In the meantime those **souls** that were stored in heaven would have to wait. Like those in Revelation, the just **souls** reported by Fourth Ezra had to wait until the required number of innocent believers had been killed and their **souls** stored in the heavenly warehouses.

Rabbis said that in the Araboth (heaven) are stored treasures of peace, blessing, **souls of the** righteous, the spirits and **souls of those** not yet born, and the dew which the holy One blessed be He would use in the future to revive the dead (bHag 12b). When the fifth **seal** was opened, the author saw under the heavenly altar **the souls** that had been treasured up as sacrificial martyrs. These cried for revenge against **the migrants of the land. The migrants** were the foreigners on the Promised Land whom Palestinian Jews hated.[1] In response to their demand, the Lord gave to each martyr a white robe, symbolizing purity, and explained that there must still be more believers' blood shed before the deficit was filled up, and the account could be settled. That would take **a little while**, which probably meant 3½ years.

This is similar to the vision of Fourth Ezra, when **the souls of** the righteous were asking the same question, How long would they have to remain in their chambers? The archangel said to them,

> When the number of those like yourselves is completed, for he has weighed the age in the balance, measured the times by measure, and he will not move or disturb them until the measure is filled up (4Ezra 4:36-37).

Second Baruch was of the same basic opinion. He said the Messiah would appear at the destined time. After that the treasuries would be opened in which the souls of the righteous were stored. This would happen at the end of times, which means the last 3½ year period of the evil gentile age, just before the Jewish age came into force.

The author assumed that the tribulations he and his contemporary Jews were suffering were deserved punishments for having broken their **contract** with the Lord. Therefore it was only just that they should receive the curses associated with **the contract**. These they would receive until they had suffered enough to pay for their crimes. This meant filling up the measure of righteousness to balance out the crimes. Protestants who are convinced that salvation is by faith alone and refuse to believe in a treasury of merits have difficulty with these texts. Even Paul's doctrine of redemption depends on the same treasury of merits concept that was basic to the Day of Atonement. Salvation by faith alone was the invention of in Luther.[2] It is not a biblical doctrine. A. Y. Collins correctly observed that passive suffering was a part of the holy war theology thought-form,[3] but martyrdom is not the only ethics advocated either by holy war theology or the Book of Revelation.

On account of the testimony which they held. In ancient courts witnesses were not required to take oaths that they were telling the truth unless their veracity was

---

[1] A. J. Beagley, *The "Sitz im Leben" of the Apocalypse* (Berlin: W. De Gruyter, 1987), p. 43, expressed the confusion of most scholars when he said, "The only clue to the identity of the oppressors against whom the martyrs cry for vengeance is the description of them as 'earth-dwellers.'" Düsterdieck, *Handbook* p. 230, also called them "the dwellers on the earth" and said they were "all the nations" as over against the servants of God. For a fuller justification of the judgment given here, see Rev 3.
[2] For a defense of this claim see Buchanan, "The Day of Atonement and Paul's Doctrine of Redemption," *NovT* 32 (1990):236-49.
[3] A. Y. Collins, "The Political Perspective of the Revelation to John," *JBL* 96 (1977):241-56.

suspected. If that were the case, the judge or opposing attorney might put the witness under oath. If he or she refused to take an oath he or she was judged guilty and punished accordingly. Christians and Jews, however, refused to take oaths to a foreign deity, so they were systematically punished by courts for refusing to take oaths. Even if they were believed to be telling the truth, their truthfulness would admit that they belonged to subversive organizations that were threats to the Roman government. This also would motivate a death penalty.

Giblin said, "The language is surprisingly free of distinctively Christian phraseology."[1] It is surprising to Giblin, because he thought John of Patmos wrote the entire Book of Revelation. Except for intrusions in four places (Rev 12:17; 14:12; 17:6; 19:9), the word "Jesus" does not occur anywhere between Rev 4:1 and Rev 22:5. This should surprise Giblin still more.

How long, Master, will you not judge and avenge. This was the question Zechariah raised after the horsemen reported **peace** and quiet in the land (Zech 1:12). It was also asked by other prophets and psalmists. After all, Deuteronomy had promised that God would **avenge** his servants (Deut 32:43). Why was he not doing it? Each of these complained when they needed God to **avenge** their enemies. They thought they had already received their share of punishment for their crimes. The author of Rev 6 agreed with the prophets and psalmists who had complained before him. As with others, this author thought God's servants had already received the designated punishment, and he hoped that soon their punishment would be complete. Jews knew they were receiving these afflictions because they had broken their **contract** with the Lord. The rule was that they would have to pay **seven** times for all of their crimes, but when would that period be over? Once their punishment had been complete the Scripture promised that the Lord would again avenge Israel's enemies, but Jews and Israelites were not always satisfied with the speed of his action. The cry, "**How long?**" was repeated often (Ps 74:10; 79:5; 4Ezra 4.35). The vengeance they desired, however, was destined to come. Later in the book the Lord was pictured as judging the great harlot and **avenging** the blood of his servants (Rev 19:2).

Christians are embarrassed by the cries for **vengeance** that are prominent in the Book of Revelation, but across the centuries **vengeance** has always been considered an essential part of justice. Years ago Judge Oliver Wendell Holmes argued extensively and convincingly that courts and law were established as alternatives to private **vengeance**. There is a strong desire on the part of an injured party to gain **vengeance** for damages received. If the desire for **vengeance** is not satisfied under the orderly and controlled terms of the court it will be settled by feuds among families, war among nations, or private retaliation among individuals.[2] Not all cultures and societies demanded the same kind of **vengeance**.

---

[1] Giblin, *Revelation*, p. 86.
[2] O. W. Holmes, *The Common Law* (Boston: Little, Brown, & Co., 1881), pp. 3-6, 9-10, 40-42.

Through courts, individuals, nations, and families can prevent lengthy and destructive conflicts by reaching some satisfactory solution that involves enough injury or cost to the offending party to satisfy the person or group that has been injured. Modern American courts have tried to avoid vengeance and punishment to the criminal without considering the injury of the victim and his or her family. Hypothetically we have become too sophisticated and civilized to need vengeance. The result has been a significant increase in crime. Holmes is correct; vengeance is a necessary function of the court system. If the court does not satisfy the victim, the victim is likely to take the law into his or her own hands.

The author of Rev 6 was impatient because God had not avenged the **migrants of the land. Migrants of the land** were not "those who dwell upon the earth" as Sweet rendered the phrase, much less "all the inhabitants of the earth without distinction," as Zahn interpreted the expression.[1] Neither was this a "stock expression for the 'worldly.'"[2] **Migrants of the land** were the foreigners in the Promised Land. They were the pro-Roman forces that opposed all nationalistic movements. Naturally they were considered enemies by all zealous Jews.

The author of Fourth Ezra may have been acquainted with Rev 6, because he asked rhetorically if the souls in their chambers had not asked **how long** they would have to remain there. He knew the answer was that they would have to stay there until the required number of martyrs was completed (4Ezra 4:35-36).[3] In a medieval Jewish document Rabbi Ishmael reportedly said in his prayer,

> Lord God of armies, God of Israel, how long will we be abandoned to the gentiles? All who see us mock us and say, "These are the people of the Lord! Why has he smitten them? Why has he cast them away from him?" Because of the magnitude of their iniquity and the number of their crimes.[4]

The migrants of the land. Aune noted that this expression was used "*always* [emphasis his] of the enemies of Christianity." Nonetheless, he still rendered the expression "the inhabitants of the earth."[5] Friends of Christianity and Judaism are also "inhabitants of the earth." These people constitute a particular group of people—those who lived in the Promised Land who were not Jews or Christians. They were

---

[1] T. Zahn, *Die Offenbarung des Johannes* (Leipzig: A. Deichert, 1924), vol. 2, p. 65.
[2] J. M. P. Sweet, *Revelation* (Philadelphia: Westminster Press, c1979), p. 142; C. H. Giblin, "Revelation 1:1-13: its Form, Function and Contextual Integration," *NTS* 30 (1984):444; Caird, *Revelation*, pp. 87-88, said these were at home in the present world order.
[3] P. -M. Bogaert, "Les Apocalypses Contemporaines de Baruch, d'Esdras et de Jean," *L'Apocalypse johannique et l'Apocalyptique dans la Nouveau Testament* ed. J. Lambrecht (Gembloux: Duculot, c1980), pp. 47-67, concluded that the author of Revelation knew Second Baruch, and Fourth Ezra was familiar with the Book of Revelation.
[4] From "A Legend of Rabbi Ishmael," tr. Buchanan, *Jewish Messianic Movements from AD 70 to AD 1300*), p. 441.
[5] Aune, *Revelation 6-16*, p. 410.

Romans, Greeks, Canaanites, Egyptians, and others whom the chosen people believed had no right to live in the Promised Land (commentary on Rev 3:10).

Were about to be killed. Believers were living in such dangerous situations that they might expect death at any time. They were not expecting to wait until the last days of history, as Boring thought.[1] There is no place in the Bible where anyone expected the end of history. Boring thought the passage, **Until heaven and earth pass away, not one iota, not one horn, will pass away from the law** (Matt 5:18), meant that history would come to an end.[2] This was a hyperbolic way of saying that the law would remain forever. Not a single portion of one single letter would ever pass away from the law. This did not mean that **heaven and earth** would ever **pass away** and history come to an end. Even the story of Noah's flood did not describe the end of history. It just told of a flood that supposedly covered the entire earth. It was not the end of the earth. After the rain, the land dried up again. The expectation that the entire cosmos was destined to come to an end and there would be no more time is called "Cosmic eschatology." It is an invention of Western scholars. It has no biblical basis.

TEXT

Revelation	First Testament
¹²I watched while he opened the sixth seal, and a great **earthquake** occurred. **The sun became**	Joel 2:10 Before him **the earthquakes**; the heavens tremble; and **the sun** and **moon grow dark**. The stars stop shining.
	Amos 8:9 In that day, says Yehowah, I will bring in **the sun** at noon, and I will **darken** the land during daylight.
black as **sack cloth**;	Isa 50:3 I clothe the heavens with **black**ness and make **sack cloth** their covering.
the moon became completely like **blood**.	Joel 3:3-4 I will provide signs in heaven and on earth--blood, fire, and vaporous smoke. The sun will be changed to **become** dark, and **the moon** to **blood** before the great and terrible day of Yehowah comes.

---

[1] M. E. Boring, *The Continuing Voice of Jesus* (Louisville: John Knox Press, c1991), p. 168.
[2] Boring, *Continuing Voice*, p. 227.

	Ezek 32:8 All the shining lights in heaven I will make dark over you, and I will make all of your land dark, said the Lord Yehowah.
	Isa 13:9-10 Look! The day of Yehowah is coming--cruel with wrath and fierce anger to place upon the land . . . for **the stars of the heaven** and their planets will not give their light. The sun will be dark when it rises, and the moon will not shed its light.
13The stars of heaven fell to the earth **like a fig tree** shedding its **leaves**, being swept by a strong wind. 14The	
heaven vanished **like a scroll unrolled**.	Isa 34:4 All the armies of **heaven** will rot; **the heaven will unroll like a scroll**. All their troops will **fall like** a **leaf** from a vine, and the **falling** [of **a leaf** from] **a fig tree**.
Every **mountain** and island **was moved** from its place.	Jer 4:24 I looked at **the heaven**, and there was no light. I looked at **the mountains**. Now look! They were quaking, and all the hills **were moving**.
15The kings of the earth and the great ones--the chiliarchs, wealthy, and powerful, all free	Ps 2:2 **The kings of the earth** congregate, **and the rulers** hold counsel together.
citizens and slaves **hid** themselves **in**	Isa 2:10 Enter **into the rock, and hide in** the dust **from the face of** the terror of **Yehowah**.
the caves and rocks of the mountains.	Isa 2:19 They will go into holes of **the rocks and into caves of the** dust because of the dread of the Lord.
16**They said to the mountains** and rocks, "**Fall on us** and hide us	Hos 10:8 **They** will **say to the mountains**, "Cover us," **and** to the hills, "**Fall on us**."

from the face of the one	Jer 4:26 All its cities were destroyed **from the face of Yehowah**, from the face of the wrath of his anger.
	Ps 47:9-10 God rules over the nations; God **is seated on his** holy **throne**.
seated on the throne and from the	Isa 6:1 I saw the Lord, **seated on his throne**, high and exalted.
wrath of the Lamb, ¹⁷because the day of their great wrath has arrived.	Zeph 1:14-15 **A day of wrath** is that day.
	Nahum 1:6 Before his **anger who can stand**? Who will survive **the wrath** of his **anger**.
Who can stand?"	Joel 2:11 The day of Yehowah is great and very fearful. **Who can** endure it?
	Mal 3:2 **Who can** endure **the day** of his coming? **Who can stand** when he appears?
	Jer 30:7 **The day** is so great there is none like it. It is a time of distress for Jacob, but he will be saved from it.

COMMENTARY

A great earthquake occurred. There were many **earthquakes** in antiquity. The anticipated events listed here were those that had already been reported earlier. The author simply quoted Scripture when he listed them. At the time the author lived, as also today, the universe still existed. The idea that

> The portents in the heavens are so terrible that they can only be understood in apocalyptic terms to mean the final dissolution of the whole world,[1]

is far fetched. The notion that biblical authors expected the end of the cosmos and time was invented in the nineteenth century in Europe. Near Easterners who lived 2,000 years ago should not be blamed for this misconception. The text itself does not

---

[1] E. Schüssler-Fiorenza, *Revelation: Vision of a Just World* (Minneapolis: Fortress Press, c1991), p. 64.

justify such a conclusion as this. The author expected events to occur such as those that happened at the Exodus from Egypt, the provision of the ten commandments, or were prophesied by Isaiah, Jeremiah, Ezekiel, Joel, or Hosea. Some of these prophets anticipated **portents in heaven** but not "the final dissolution of the world," as Schüssler-Fiorenza holds.[1] When these portents occurred, the prophets expected Jews to hide in their shelters--the caves in the mountains--right there in Palestine, to protect themselves from the danger. Earthquakes were not just "symbols," as Caird thought.[2] There have been earthquakes in the Near East as well as terrible thunder and lightning storms. They have been frightening. Without seismographs and satellites to explain when and where these would happen, ancients thought they reflected God's attitude at the time so people took normal precautions, but they did not think the world was coming to an end. Western theologians and philosophers imagined that.

The sun became black. The sixth **seal** seemed to have the same magical force as the wand Aaron used or the magic of Moses' hand as he stretched it out to bring about the plagues of the Exodus. The Lord commanded Moses to extend his hand up to the sky. He did, and darkness covered the entire land of Egypt (Exod 10:21-22). When Aaron fulfilled the command Moses gave him in behalf of the Lord, Aaron raised his wand over the water, and the water of every stream and spring in Egypt became blood (Exod 7:19-20). When the Lamb opened the sixth **seal**, however, it was not the water that became blood; it was the moon, because the author of Rev 6 had also Joel to give him directions. Joel promised that when the Day of the Lord arrived the sun would become dark and the moon would become blood (Joel 3:4). The author of Rev 6 thought that prophecy would also be fulfilled. When Moses or Aaron raised their hand or wand, something magical happened. The same was true when the sixth **seal** was opened. New plagues took place against new enemies of the chosen people.

Hid themselves in caves and rocks of the mountains. Palestine is honeycombed with caves in the mountains. These have been used for hiding places for centuries. They are excellent places for guerrilla hideouts. There are no such mountains on Patmos Island, which is another reason for thinking that John did not write this entire document on that island. In the large cave in this picture, there is room for an entire town to live inside. It has many side rooms. In 1927 Bedouin told me that people had gone inside that cave and died because they were unable to find their way out. It would be easy for an entire troop to hide in this cave and be able to defend themselves from any other troop, because only one person could enter at a time, and only one guard could stand at a side tunnel near the entrance and kill each one who entered. A picture of that cave is shown between chapters twelve and thirteen.

Those who hid themselves--the kings, political officers of smaller governing bodies, great ones, wealthy people, powerful ones, free citizens, and slaves--were not identical to **the migrants of the land**, mentioned in Rev 6:10, as Minear

---

[1] Schüssler-Fiorenza, *Revelation: Vision of a Just World* (Minneapolis: Fortress Press, c1991), p. 65.
[2] Caird, *Revelation*, p. 88.

thought.¹ The **migrants** were the objects of the first **seal**; these others were objects of the sixth **seal**. Minear was correct, however, in observing that **the migrants** were enemies of the elect.

These verses of Revelation are commentaries on various FT texts that described the day of the Lord. This was a day when the Lord would hold court and pass judgment on people. The authors of the FT warned Jews that God was angry with their behavior, and this day would not be for them a day of vindication. Instead it would be a day of punishment (Amos 5:18). This day would carry out the four curses of the contract. Isaiah, Jeremiah, and Hosea pictured the parties to the contract hiding from God's anger (Isa 2:19; Jer 4:26; Hos 10:8), which they understood to have been expressed in war and natural calamities, such as earthquakes, storms, tornados, etc. Although parties to the contract could not escape the curses that were destined to come upon them because they had broken the contract, they might try to hide in fear of the impending punishment that might come in terms of natural disasters or warfare. They expected the punishment to take place in this age and in this world. Otherwise they would not have tried to hide.

The heaven will vanish like a scroll unrolled. **A scroll** is **unrolled** from one end, like a roll of wall paper. As the person reads the content on the surface that portion is rolled up again, so the person who reads has two rolls, one that is becoming smaller as it is unrolled and the other that is getting larger as it rolls up that which has been read (Isa 34:4; SibOr 3:82). Of course, the scroll just vanishes from one roller. Following Isaiah, the author of Rev 6 thought the heaven was a roof above the earth. It was like a goat skin bedouin's tent. It was rolled and unrolled regularly to change its character.

Many scholars have conjectured the contents and nature of the **scroll** whose seals were being opened, and no one has reached a very satisfactory answer,² because the contents and nature of this **scroll** have to be deduced. The **scroll** was almost like a Pandora's box. Every time a seal was opened, some new event was released. The horse appeared because the command had been given, and the events described happened because **the seal** had been broken. This is not necessarily related to the contents of the scroll. They did not break a seal and then read a portion of the **scroll** which contained the script of a play that was then enacted act by act as the **scroll was unrolled**. None of the **scroll** could be read until all seven of the seals were broken and the **scroll** could be unrolled. By that time all of the events described would have happened. It was the breaking of the seals, just as it was the

---

¹ P. S. Minear, *I Saw a New Earth* (Washington, D.C.: Corpus Books, c1968), p. 79.
² See G. E. Ladd, *A Commentary on the Revelation of John* (Grand Rapids: Eerdmans, 1972), pp. 80-81; R. H. Mounce, *The Book of Revelation* (Grand Rapids: Eerdmans, c1977), p. 142; Sweet, *Revelation*, p. 123; J. M. Ford, *Revelation* (Garden City: Doubleday and Co., 1975), pp. 93, 165. Beagley, *Sitz*, pp. 36-37.

waving of the wand for Moses and Aaron, that magically started all of these natural phenomena to move into action.

None of these predestined events could take place until the seals were broken, one by one. The events that took place, incidentally, were plagues that had happened or been prophesied in the First Testament (FT) in association with the Exodus from Egypt, the conquest of Canaan, and the provision of the contract with the Lord in the wilderness. The scroll was probably the new contract that Jeremiah had promised (Jer 31:31). It was expected to be provided together with the restoration of the Promised Land, the anointing of the new Messiah, and the natural phenomena that appeared when Moses came down from the mountain with the contract in the wilderness. The vision of the Lamb, the contract, and the plagues of Egypt were all expected repetitions of earlier history. Although there is not much verbal relationship between this passage and Ezek 7, Goulder is correct in seeing a similarity of pattern. Both deal with the Day of the Lord which is coming against the people of the land of Palestine. It is punishment that is required before the contract could be renewed. Israel was being judged according to the contract she had made with the Lord years before.

From the anger of the Lamb. Torrance said, "Who ever heard of a Lamb being angry? What a terrible thought--the gentlest of God's creature's angry? It is the wrath of love."[1] Rissi said,

> In other words, the judgments are to be understood as an expression of the 'wrath of the *Lamb,*' that is to say, of the divine love.[2]

Wrath and love are not usually thought of as synonyms. The Lamb in the Book of Revelation, was God's legal agent and, like God, according to this document (Rev 6:16), was frequently angry (Rev 11:18; 14:10; 16:19; 19:15). Since the Lamb was the Messiah, he was not expected to exhibit lamb-like qualities. He was called a Lamb only to indicate that he was a member of the Lord's flock, a true Jew or Christian--not a Roman outsider, like the procurators or **the migrants of the land.** As the Lord's legal agent he was obligated to carry out the Lord's anger, both against the chosen people (Ezek 7:8, 12) and against their enemies. Enoch pictured the Lamb as the Son of man, sitting on the throne of his glory.

> The whole judgment was given to the Son of man.
> He will make the criminals pass away
> and be destroyed from the face of the earth (1Enoch 2:164).

Would Rissi understand these death penalties to be an expression of divine love?

---

[1] T. F. Torrance, *The Apocalypse Today* (London: James Clarke & Co., 1960), p. 58.
[2] M. Rissi, *The Future of the World* (Naperville: A. R. Allenson, 1972), p. 13.

The day of their great wrath has arrived. The author wanted his readers to realize that with the breaking of the sixth **seal, the day of** the Lord began. Isa 2 described the terror that would happen because **the Lord of armies has a day**. Isa 34 called these frightening natural catastrophes the events of the Lord's **day of vengeance**. The frightening occurrences Joel described were to take place on the **day of the Lord** which was to be so terrible no one could endure it. Zephaniah called this **day of Yehowah, a day of wrath**. For the author, these things all happened because the sixth seal had been broken before the Messiah and the Lord in the throne room in heaven.

The act of breaking the sixth **seal** was the prompt necessary to notify the actors that the stage was set and the play was to begin at once. The anger of the Lord and of his Messiah would be expressed by cosmic catastrophes on earth, when the predestined time arrived. The Messiah was the legal agent of the Lord. He acted in behalf of the principal, in the interests of the principal, and at the responsibility of the principal. Therefore, if the Lord **was angry, the Messiah would be angry**. Since **the Messiah** was legally identical to the principal, the Lord's **wrath** was the **Messiah's wrath** and vice versa.

The anger that was instigated by Israel's failure to fulfill the demands of the contract was expressed both in the Lord's wrath and in the Messiah's wrath. Düsterdieck thought the entire unit, Rev 12-17, referred to the Jewish-Roman war, and the **great day of wrath** was the destruction of Jerusalem.[1] **The day of wrath** was expected to take place on New Year's Day when the Lord held court and passed judgment both on his own people and on the enemies of Israel. Weiss correctly observed that all of these hardships were parts of the birth pangs of the Messiah which Jews thought were necessary before the kingdom of God would come.[2]

Jews of NT times expected the Hasmonean type to be repeated. In 164 BIA there was a great judgment day on New Year's Day. Ten days later there was a Day of Atonement, as there is every year. This year, Jews believed, all of Israel's crimes had been forgiven, and the judgment was made in Israel's favor. The basis for this judgment was the famous Beth-horon Battle which was the turning point of the Hasmonean war. It was a judgment against the Romans. This was followed by the celebration at Hanukkah when the temple was restored. The judgment day could be a terrible day that put an end to Israel's liberty, as it had in 586 BIA and again in 6/7 IA, when the Romans installed their own government leaders and collected their own taxes, and again in 70 IA when the temple was destroyed. But the judgment could bring an end to the punishment, renew the contract, and restore the Promised Land. Sweeney correctly observed that Zephaniah's prophecy did not at all apply to the end of the cosmos, the world, or of time. He prophesied for events that he expected to take place in local geography in ordinary time.[3]

---

[1] Düsterdieck, *Revelation*, p. 232.
[2] Weiss, *Offenbarung*, p. 629.
[3] Marvin A. Sweeney, "Zephaniah: Prophet of His Time—not the End Time," *Bible Review* 20.6 (2004):34-40, 43.

Who can stand? This is a rhetorical question taken from Malachi. It means **no one can stand**. To **stand** means to stand before the judge after the trial. If the judge asks the defendant to arise and **stand** before him, that means the Judge is about to pronounce him innocent or pardoned.[1] In a medieval Jewish document, the author pictured a judgment scene in the Valley of Jehoshaphat, just outside the temple area in Jerusalem. At that time the gates of the Garden of Eden would be opened, and meritorious Jews would **stand** before the Lord in fulfillment of the Scripture, **On the third day he will raise us [and we shall live before him]** (Hos 6:2). The author said further, **This is the day of judgment**.[2] Malachi was addressing Jews, people who had made a contract with the Lord, but had broken it. Therefore they had no right to assume they would be declared innocent when an angry judge examined their case. The assumption is that the gentiles were God's enemies, and therefore they could not **stand** innocent in judgment; also the contract-breaking Jews and Christians could not stand. That meant no one could, but the author of this portion of Revelation placed this question strategically in a *position* where some might answer it positively. The answer to this question is found in the next chapter. In Rev 7 there are 144,000 servants of God who are sealed upon their foreheads who are standing before the throne and before the Lamb. See also Rev 14. Later rabbis commented on the text, **Fallen, no more to rise is the virgin daughter** (Amos 5:2), Zion, saying, "Who is destined to exalt her? The Messiah."[3]

---

[1] The custom of the judge to invite the defendant to stand and face him when he intended to give a favorable verdict is shown in Buchanan, *Biblical and Theological Insights from Ancient and Modern Civil Law* (Lewiston: Edwin Mellen Press, c1992), pp. 57-61.

[2] From "The Prayer, Secrets, and Mysteries of Rabbi Shimon Ben Yohai," tr. by Buchanan, *Jewish Messianic Movements*, pp. 405-406.

[3] Buchanan, *Jewish Messianic Movements*, p. 346.

CHAPTER SEVEN

TEXT

Revelation

$^{7:1}$After this I saw **four** angels standing

at **the four corners of the land**,

holding [back] **the four winds**

of the land so that no wind might blow upon the **land**, the sea, nor upon any tree. ^{2}Then I saw another angel arising from east of the sun, having the seal of the God of life, and

he cried out with a loud voice to the four angels to whom were given [authority] to damage the land and the sea, ^{3}saying,

First Testament

$^{Jer\ 49:36}$I will bring against Elam **the four winds** from the four borders of heaven.

$^{Ezek\ 7:2}$An end has come upon **the four corners of the land**.

$^{Zech\ 6:5}$These are **the four winds** of heaven, going out to station themselves beside the Lord **of** all **the land**.

$^{Dan\ 7:2}$I was watching in the night when, look! **the four winds of** heaven were stirring up the Great Sea.

$^{Ezek\ 37:9}$Come from **the four winds**, spirit, and breathe upon the ones that have been killed and they will live.

$^{Ezek\ 9:1}$**He cried out** in my hearing **in a loud voice**, "Let the inspectors of the city draw near."

$^{Exod\ 12:13}$The blood will be to you a sign. On the houses where you are, I will see the blood, and I will **pass over** you, and no plague will afflict you when I strike the land of Egypt.

$^{Ezek\ 9:6}$**Pass over** into the city after him, and strike! Your eye shall not spare, and you shall show no pity. The old men, teen age boys and girls, children, and women you shall kill,

"**Do not** damage the land, sea, nor any **tree,** until we seal the servants of God **on their foreheads**."

but everyone on whom there is the *tau*, **do not** touch.

Ezek 9:4 Then he said to me, "**Pass over** into the midst of the city, in the midst of Jerusalem, mark a *tau* **on the foreheads** of the men who sigh and lament over all the abominations that have occurred in its midst."

Deut 20:19 When you besiege a city for a long time, making war against it in order to take it, you shall not destroy the **trees** by wielding an ax against them.

⁴Then I heard the number of those sealed: 144,000 from every tribe of the sons of Israel: 1) ⁵from the tribe of Judah, 12,000 sealed, 2) from the tribe of Reuben, 12,000, 3) ⁶from the tribe of Asher, 12,000, 4) from the tribe of Naphthali, 12,000, 5) from the tribe of Manasseh, 12,000, 6) ⁷from the tribe of Levi, 12,000, 7) from the tribe of Issachar, 12,000, 8) ⁸from the tribe of Zebulun, 12,000, 9) from the tribe of Benjamin, 12,000, 10) from the tribe of Joseph, 12,000.

COMMENTARY

Four angels . . . holding the four winds. According to Zechariah, the **four** chariots were **the four winds** of heaven and they were sent to take their stations in the **four** respective corners of **the land.** Here in Revelation seven angels are sent to **the four** corners to hold back these **winds** so that they could not act without direction. This was done to prevent any precocious action. In the same way Baruch is reported as having seen **four angels** stationed at the **four** corners of the city of Jerusalem with torches unlighted. They **held** these and waited until one angel descended to the holy of holies from which he removed the veil and the sacred furniture. Then he issued the command, and the other **angels** lighted the torches and destroyed the city before the enemy arrived (2Bar 6:1-7:1).

This was Baruch's way of describing theologically that which happened when the temple was destroyed in 70 IA. Just before the Romans crossed over from the fortress Antonia to take the temple, Jews inside the temple lighted it afire with pitch and kindling.

This entire passage, of course, is an antitype of Ezek 9, where the terrorists were restrained until one man with a pen and an ink horn at his belt marked the righteous with the sign of the *tau* (ת) on their foreheads. The *tau* is the last letter of the Hebrew alphabet. In antiquity it looked like the Greek X and became known as the sign of the cross. Once the messengers had marked the faithful, the slaughterers destroyed all the rest in Jerusalem (Ezek 9:1-8). Daniel reported **the four winds of heaven** organized to stir up the **Great Sea** (The Mediterranean). These were all localized to form a hurricane in one spot (Dan 7:2). The expression was not used to imply that the focus was on the entire earth. Whenever the **wind** blew it came from one of these **four** directions, and it was assumed that the Lord had heavenly messengers that controlled the winds and directed their action.

The four corners. At one time the narrative might have continued from Rev 6:8. If that were the case the **four** seals would be followed immediately by **the four angels** at **the four corners** of **the land.** If that was, in fact, the case, someone later added Rev 6:9-17 to bring the number from **four** up to seven.

At first glance it would appear that the **angels** were stationed at **the four corners** of the earth rather than **the land,** since the same Hebrew word can mean either earth or **land**. Most scholars render this "earth," rather than **land**,[1] because it is related to **the four winds,** but the **land** had four corners just as the earth had, and **the winds** blew from the same directions over the **land** that blew over the earth, and the background type is taken from Ezekiel, where the prophet predicted an end that would come upon **the four corners of the land.** Fourth Ezra anticipated salvation to take place "in my land within my borders" (4Ezra 9:7-8), "throughout my borders" (4Ezra 12:34), "within my holy borders" (4Ezra 13:48). That author expected the Lamb to stand on Mount Zion (4Ezra 13:15). The blasting of the winds was part of the continued devastation of the day of the Lord about which the author had already dealt at length. The day of the Lord was believed to be the judgment day, and expected to take place on New Year's Day. On that day the Lord would take the people of Israel and its enemies to court, open the books that had been prepared by the attorneys for the plaintiff and the defense, and judge the people.

Ezekiel's narrative, upon which this passage in Revelation was based, was obviously an antitype of the **Passover** story in Exodus. Ezekiel even used the term **Pass over** in his narrative (Ezek 9:6). According to the old Pentacontad calendar New Year's Day occurred on the first day of the week after **Passover**. Following the modern Jewish calendar, New Year's Day happened in the Autumn. This is not enough to prove anything, but it stirs the imagination to ask whether or not the author who based his text on Ezekiel's **Passover** passage was himself an observer of the old Pentacontad calendar when New Year's Day was very close to **Passover.**

The Pentacontad calendar was organized according to Sabbaths. There were seven days in a week, the seventh of which was a day of rest. Seven weeks made up a Pentacontad or Pentecost; 49 working days plus a fiftieth was a day of celebration. Seven Pentacontads or Pentecosts comprised a year—350 days. The fiftieth "week" was a week of celebration which included however many days were necessary to total 365 or 366 days. This was followed by New Year's Day, which fell on exactly the same day as Christian Easter. There were still Jews in NT times observing this old calendar. This question should be kept in mind while reading the rest of the

---

[1] D. E. Aune, *Revelation 6-16* (Dallas: Word Books, c1997), pp. 450-51.

Book of Revelation. The Pentacontad calendar was still in use in NT times. It is reflected in 1Enoch and some of the Dead Sea Scrolls. It may be a way of explaining why Jesus and his disciples celebrated the Passover the day before the feast season began in popular Judaism. The more times the Pentacontad calendar fits into the narrative, the more likely it is that the author or final editor followed this calendar.

Judgment was usually accompanied by a fierce war outside Jerusalem. If Jews were meritorious, the verdict would be in their favor, and the gentiles would be destroyed. If that were the case, then the land would be restored. One judgment day, reported in Dan 7, occurred after a 3½ year war with the Seleucids, after which Judas the Maccabee (as **one like a Son of man**) was judged meritorious, and the temple was rededicated. That court trial became the basic type for all later heavenly court sessions for redemption literature. Jews and Christians continued to anticipate a court trial when they would be vindicated. The author of this narrative had something like that in mind as the practical consequences that would follow when the Messiah broke the sixth **seal**.

East of the sun. This messenger was the seventh **angel** with a **seal**. This one differed from the others, because he did not have a **seal** *to open*. His seal seemed to be an X marked on him, like a tattoo. This **angel** was one coming up from **east of the sun** (Rev 7:2), and he was a messenger, authorized by **the God of life**. **East of the sun** would have been somewhere in the far **East**—farther away than eye could see and farther **east** than the topic under discussion. That **angel** may have been an antitype of Cyrus of Persia, the Lord's anointed who came **from the east** to rescue Jews from Babylon (Isa 41:2). The word *ah-nah-taw-láys* (ἀνατολῆς) means both **east** and **rising**. It was used to allude to the verse, **a scepter** *shall arise* **out of Israel** (Num 24:17). Therefore the **rising one** was a term given to the Messiah. This may have been included in the design to have the other **angel** as one who **came up** from the **east of the sun**. Second Isaiah called Cyrus of Persia, **One from the East** (Isa 41:2). There are also **four angels** bound at the Euphrates River whom the sixth **angel** who blew the trumpet was commanded to release (Rev 9:13-14).

The sixth **angel** who poured out his bowl, poured it upon the Euphrates River so that its water would dry up and prepare the way for the kings of the **East** to cross (Rev 16:12). The Euphrates seems to have been the boundary that separated the **East** from the West for the author. There is also a coincidental relationship among Rev 7, 9, and 16. There are six **angels** in Rev 9 and 16 and **four angels** in Rev 7. In Rev 7 **an angel** came from the **East;** in Rev 9 **angels** were released from the Euphrates; and in Rev 16 the kings of the **East** were expected to cross the Euphrates River on dry land.[1] Parthia was the country **east** of the Euphrates, in which there were many Jews, and from which Jews received the military support necessary to evict Herod at one time. The Parthians were enemies of Rome. That is

---

[1] See further P. -M. Bogaert, "Les Apocalypses contemporaines de Baruch, d'Esdras et de Jean," J. Lambrecht (ed.), *L'Apocalypse johannique et l'Apocalyptique dans le Nouveau Testament* (Gembloux: J. Duculot, c1980), p. 52.

why Jews could benefit from their support. The Sibyl said, "The dread Parthians have made you [Rome] rattle through and through" (SibOr 5:38-39).

Fourth Ezra visualized the return of the ten northern tribes who had been taken **east** of the Euphrates River into captivity. When Jeremiah's prophecy that the Lord would restore the tribes of Israel to the Promised land would be fulfilled, it was understood that those tribes would be involved. When they returned, the Lord would hold back the channels feeding the Euphrates River so that it would dry up and allow the ten northern tribes to cross over on dry land (4Ezra 13:39-47) and return to the Promised Land (bBer 7a; bSan 65b; bRoshH 17a; GenR 11:73; LamR 3). This was the same technique Cyrus of Persia used when he captured Babylon. He stopped up the Euphrates River, diverting the water into an upper lake, and then entered Babylon without interference from the Euphrates River, whose defense was necessary to the security of the city (Herodotus, *History* 1:191; Xenophon, *Cyropaedia* 7:5, 1-57).[1]

The seal of the God of life. Only someone with authority would be allowed to have and use **the seal** of another person. For example Joseph was given **the seal** of the Pharaoh of Egypt (Gen 41:42). **The seal** had the same force as a signature. The mouth of the lion's den was **sealed** with the king's signet ring (Dan 6:17). **The angel** with **the seal** had the authority to speak for God and give directions to the other subordinate **angels.**

Upon any tree. Most texts have **any tree** in the accusative case, whereas **land** and **sea** are in the genitive. Hypothetically, this might mean that the preposition had a different force, such as "toward" or "against." This seems, however, to be translated Hebrew, and the Greek preposition renders the Hebrew *ahl* (על), which means "upon," "over," "above." The Greek *eh-peé* (ἐπί) with the accusative can also hold these meanings. Therefore, all three usages of the same preposition are rendered the same here.

Do not hurt the land, the sea, nor any tree. This is a repetition of Rev 6:6, which further suggests that Rev 7:1 may once have followed Rev 6:8. The order given here was said in the context of Ezek 9, where the slaughterers were told not to come near [**to hurt**] anyone on whom was the sign of the *tau*. Here before the sealing of the servants of God the order was given not to **hurt.** In Ezekiel those not to be **hurt** were the servants of God, those who had the sign of the *tau* on their foreheads. Here those things not to be **hurt** were:

---

[1] A. L. Oppenheim (tr.), "Babylonian and Assyrian Historical Texts," J. B. Pritchard (ed.) *Ancient Near Eastern Texts* (Princeton: Princeton U. Press, 1969), pp. 315-16; Buchanan, *New Testament Eschatology: Historical and Cultural Background* (Lewiston: Mellen Biblical Press, c1993), pp. 161-79

1) the [promised] **land,**
2) **the sea**--possibly **the Sea** of Galilee or the Dead **Sea,** and
3) any **tree**.

Plundering was certain to take place but it was to be done in such a way that the servants of God would be saved and **the land** with its water sources and **trees** would survive.

The context was holy war (Deut 20:19-20). When Israel tried to conquer any city in the Promised Land, the temptation would be to cut down the **trees** and use them to build towers against the walls. Deuteronomy prohibits cutting down the **trees,** because when Israel moved into the town, they would need the fruit which the trees would provide.

Seal the servants of God on their foreheads. Caird remythologized this passage in the following way: He first concluded that whenever John used the term **servant** he meant "prophet," and that prophet was synonymous with martyr. Therefore the author really intended the reader to understand these servants as martyrs.[1] His next step was to distinguish between that which the author of this passage, which Caird thought was John, *heard* and what he *saw*. "So in the present passage," said Caird,

> what John *hears* is the scriptural image of the army of Israel, but
> what he *sees* is the Christian fact of the noble army of martyrs.[2]

Since the author made no distinction between what he saw and heard, this conclusion was developed only in the mind of Caird, and there is no data in the text to justify its creation.

It is true that *some* servants were prophets (Amos 3:7; Dan 9:6, 10). But there is no indication that all servants were prophets or that prophets were identical to martyrs. When the author wanted readers to understand that the servants were martyrs he might have said so. In the absence of any such data, the servants here will be identified on the basis of the narrative. The servants of God in Revelation are the same as those in Ezekiel who have the sign of the *tau* **on their forehead.** These are the few who would *survive* the destruction of criminals in Jerusalem, and therefore *not* be martyrs.[3] Ezekiel had indicated further the punishment that would come against Jerusalem. The Lord had ordered executioners to destroy all of the living creatures in the city because of their criminal activity, but before they did that, he ordered them to wait until another man went through and marked the sign of the *tau* (a cross or X mark) **on the foreheads** of the righteous in the city.

---

[1] G. B. Caird, *A Commentary on the Revelation of St. John the Divine* (London: Black, c1966), p. 95.
[2] Caird, *Revelation*, p. 96. An army that consisted only of those who had already been killed as martyrs would not be very formidable. It is difficult to follow Caird's logic or exegesis.
[3] *Contra* Aune, *Revelation 6-16*, p. 447. Aune said, "It is possible that John understands Dan 12:1 as the time when the people of God triumph, not through waging war but through martyrdom" (p. 446), as if martyrs were developed only in time of peace.

These were the righteous whom the executioners should spare. As an antitype of this event, the author of this portion of Revelation pictured a man with the **seal of the God of life** ordering the angels to hold back the winds of destruction until the servants of God were marked with the sign **on their foreheads**. The author had artfully put together two passages from Ezekiel--one about holding back the winds (Ezek 7) and the other about the **sealing of the foreheads** of the saints (Ezek 9:4)--to visualize a new judgment day. Charles overlooked the significance of the Ezekiel passages when he said,

> Protection not from physical death, but from the demonic and Satanic enemies of the spirit, [emphasis his] became the supreme aim of the faithful. So far is it from being true that the faithful were secured by the sealing from physical death, that it is distinctly stated that they should all suffer martyrdom [emphasis his] (xiii.15).[1]

Instead of being martyrs, the servants of God in Ezekiel were the only ones in Jerusalem who were destined to be *preserved* alive. Those singled out and marked **on the forehead** were people who lived on earth, in the city of Jerusalem, and they were saved from physical death. There is no mention made of demons in the immediate context of Revelation, and **the migrants of the land** who were promised death were not the same people as the 144,000 who were sealed. Charles conjectured the demons, and he misunderstood **the migrants of the land** to be the inhabitants of all the earth.

An early Christian psalmist said God's seal was known; his troops possessed it, and his elect archangels were clothed with it (OdeSol 4:7-8). Christ was portrayed as recognizing his elect and putting his **seal** on their faces (foreheads) (OdeSol 8:13-18). A Jewish Psalmist said God had put his mark on the righteous for salvation; therefore they would not receive the curses of the contract--famine, sword, and pestilence (PssSol 15:6-7). Rabbi Aha ben R. Hanina said the holy One blessed be He said to Gabriel,

> Go, place a *tau* of ink upon the foreheads of the righteous ones, so that the destroying angels can have no power over them, and a *tau* of blood upon the foreheads of the wicked ones, so that the destroying angels may have power over them (bSab 55a).

Among the Dead Sea Scrolls is the following passage:

> These [the poor of the flock] will escape at the time of visitation, but those who hesitate will be given over to the sword at the arrival of the Messiahs of Aaron and Israel, just as it was in the time of

---

[1] R. H. Charles, *A Critical and Exegetical Commentary on the Revelation of St. John the Divine* (New York: Charles Scribner's Sons, c1920) I, p. 196.

visitation of the first ones, as he said through the hand of Ezekiel, **To mark a tau on the foreheads of those who sigh and groan** (CDC 19:12, ms. B).

The idea of marking a few to save them from the destruction destined for the rest originated from the **Passover** in Egypt when the Israelites had their houses marked before the **messenger of death** killed people in the other homes. Ezekiel took this Exodus event as a type to be repeated in an antitype in his day, but instead of Egypt and the Egyptians who would be destroyed, it would be Jerusalem and the evil people in it. The author of Rev 7 understood Ezek 9 as the primary type, and he also applied the type to Jerusalem and its inhabitants.

From every tribe of Israel. The ones marked, according to the author of Rev 7, numbered 144,000; that is, 12,000 elect **from every tribe of Israel**--well, not quite. The designation of the twelve tribes given here does not coincide with the blessing of Jacob (Gen 49:3-28), nor the list given in Num 13:4-15, nor the Exodus from Egypt, nor the blessing of Moses (Deut 33:6-25). Dan is omitted, and Manassah has been added, for no known reason.[1] All the wicked ones in Palestine, including **the migrants of the land**, were to be completely destroyed on the day of the Lord when these executioners, who were the antitypes of the **messengers of death** in Egypt, would be released against them.

Hailey and Sweet both argued that the marking was to remind all Christians (the ones marked) that they constituted the true **Israel.** The number, Sweet held, was symbolic of the entire Christian body--not just a portion.[2] There is nothing in the text that says this is spiritual **Israel.** The fact that the tribes were mentioned indicates a geographically identifiable **Israel.** It further overlooks the antitype in Ezekiel where the ones marked were distinguished from the rest of the Jews who were to be destroyed. They symbolized the remnant of **Israel,** and here were intended to mean the remnant only of the Christians or Jews. Zahn said the 144,000 probably did not constitute an actual count, resulting from a national census. It probably had more of a symbolic than actual meaning.[3] On the other hand, he thought the number was reasonable. There would not have been that many Christians in Palestine in the first century, but as Christianity spread from Antioch to Rome there would have been more conversions and more Christian children born. The total may have reached 144,000.

---

[1] T. Zahn, *Die Offenbarung des Johannes* (Leipzig: A. Deichert, 1924), p.374, thought maybe Dan was omitted, because the Antichrist was expected to come from the tribe of Dan. Jeremiah foresaw rebellion and destruction coming from Dan and said the Lord would send serpents among them (Jer 8:16-17). R. E. Winkle, "Another Look at the List of Tribes in Revelation 7," *AUSS* 27 (1989):53-67, also considered the possibility that Dan was rejected because Judas came from his tribe or because that tribe was known for its idolatry.

[2] J. P. M. Sweet, *Revelation* (Philadelphia: Westminster, c1979), p. 147; H. M. Hailey, *Revelation: An Introduction and Commentary* (Grand Rapids: Baker's Book House, c1979), pp. 147, 204.

[3] Zahn, *Offenbarung*, p. 371.

Zahn presumed that John of Patmos wrote the entire Book of Revelation and that it was composed only for and about Christians.[1] Weiss said this text allows "not the slightest doubt that born Jews are intended." Nevertheless, he held that the 144,000 constituted an elite group that consisted--not of Jews--but of Christians. Like those in Rev 14, these were ascetic Christian monks. Giblin was of the same basic opinion as Zahn. He called this group the representation of "the complete and multitudinous Israel of God."[2] Schüssler-Fiorenza thought

> the twelve tribes of Israel were no longer a historical but only a theological entity, since in John's time only two tribes were still in existence.[3]

This does not follow. There were still Samaritans who considered themselves members of the ten northern tribes of Israel in Samaria itself as well as in places of the diaspora, such as Egypt (Ant 12:10).[4]

The time reflected in Jerusalem when the author of this portion of Revelation was composed may have been early in the year 70 IA. That was a time of intense civil strife inside Jerusalem, when many Jews were starving to death; others were killed by disease, and still others were being slaughtered by troops from another fragment of the Jerusalem inhabitants. The Jews inside Jerusalem seemed to be receiving all of the curses of the contract. Vespasian had first surrounded the city and then pulled back his troops, because there was a civil war going on in Rome, and he became head of one revolutionary movement.

When in July 69 IA, Vespasian had left the Jews without an opposition, they organized three factions among themselves, trying to decide which one of the three leaders should be the new Messiah. In the process they burned the grain stores, so that when Vespasian sent his son, Titus, to complete the war, he had only to wait until the Jews in Jerusalem starved themselves to death. Some of the slaughter that went on in the city reminded someone of Ezek 9, and he thought some of the terrororists were divinely appointed to do as they were doing. These curses of the contract that were apparently being fulfilled were understood as the **signs** of the times just before deliverance. Josephus said there were prophets in Jerusalem, right up to the time when the temple was burned, who were interpreting these events as the fulfillment of Scripture. These were all **signs** that the evil era ruled by Rome was coming to an end (War 6:285-87). Rev 14 is another evaluation of the same situation

---

[1] Zahn, *Offenbarung*, p. 372.
[2] J. Weiss, *Die Offenbarung des Johannes* (Göttingen: Vandenhoeck and Ruprecht, 1908), pp. 634, 635; C. H. Giblin, *The Book of Revelation* (Collegeville: The Liturgical Press, c1991), p. 91.
[3] E. Schüssler-Fiorenza, *Revelation: Vision of a Just World* (Minneapolis: Fortress Press, c1991), p. 67.
[4] See further, Buchanan, "The Samaritan Origin of the Gospel of John," J. Neusner (ed.), *Religions in Antiquity* (Leiden: E. J. Brill, 1968), pp. 149-75.

in Jerusalem. Rev 7 and 14 were composed by commentators using the same text from Ezekiel. They may both have been written by the same author.

A hundred forty four thousand. NA edition has **a hundred forty-four thousand**, which corresponds to the claim that there are 12,000 from each of the twelve tribes. The Sinaiticus scribe probably made a mistake. The list in Sinaiticus also omits both **the tribe** of Gad and **the tribe** of Simon, which are included in the NA text. It also places the tribe of Benjamin before the tribe of Joseph.

TECHNICAL DETAILS

The editor of Rev 7 seems to have put together two literary units that were related in some way.[1] Both were associated with feast days (Rev 7:1-8; 7:9-17). The first was designed according to **the Passover** experience of Egypt and the judgment on New Year's Day, and the second narrated a festal scene which may have been patterned after the Feast of the Tabernacles. This is not certain, however, because palm branches were waved on important national celebrations, such as the first Hanukkah and the celebration of Jewish independence from the Grecian Syrians. Both told about large groups of people, one group of 144,000 and the other so large no one could count the number.

The editor put these together, because they had common themes. Both were large groups of people--the first comprised of Palestinians and the second of diaspora Jews. He may have put them together to include all the Jews of the world. Another possibility is that the editor was a conservative, orthodox Jew who observed the Pentacontad calendar. According to this calendar, the Feast of Tabernacles falls just before **Passover**. Popular Judaism celebrated New Year's Day in the Autumn. At some point in biblical history Jews accepted the lunar calendar, and probably moved both New Year's Day and Sukkoth (the Feast of Tabernacles) from Spring to Autumn. From that time on, popular Jews waved palm branches on the Feast of Tabernacles in the Fall, just after New Year's Day and the Day of Atonement. It is not likely that one of these groups consisted of Jewish Christians and the other gentile Christians, as many scholars have thought.[2]

TEXT

Revelation

⁹After this I was watching--Now look! a **great crowd which no one was able to count**, from every nation, tribe, people, and language

First Testament and Other Literature

4Ezra 13:34 An **innumerable multitude** will be gathered together, which you

---

[1] So also Zahn, *Offenbarung*, pp. 366-67, 379.
[2] Such as Zahn, *Offenbarung*, p. 379.

standing before the throne and before the Lamb, wearing white robes and	saw, wanting to come and conquer him.
	4Ezra 13:39-40When you see him [God's son] gathering to himself another peaceful **multitude**, these are the ten tribes.
[they held] **palm leaves** in their hands.	Lev 23:40On the first day you shall take the fruit of good trees, **palm leaves**, and branches of leafy trees, and willows from the creek, and you shall rejoice before Yehowah your God for seven days.
	2Macc10:6-7They held a celebration for eight days, just as in the Feast of Tabernacles, . . . They had thyrsi and beautiful **branches**, as well as **palm leaves**.

COMMENTARY

A great crowd. Jerusalem is the place to which Jews from every nation, tribe, people, and language have come every year to attend the feasts. Just because they had come from the diaspora does not mean that they were gentiles. Mounce correctly observed that the second vision stood in marked contrast to the first:

1) Instead of being preserved from injury, these come up out of great tribulation;
2) **the multitude** includes so many **no one could count them**--obviously more than 144,000.[1]

From every nation, tribe, people, and language. Charles,[2] Beagley,[3] Düsterdieck,[4] Beasley-Murray,[5] and others conclude that this group consists of both Jewish and gentile Christians and that the crowd mentioned in Rev 7:9 is comprised of the same

---

[1] R. H. Mounce, *The Book of Revelation* (Grand Rapids: Eerdmans, c1977), p. 171, also thought this gathering took place in heaven, forgetting that the throne of God and the Messiah was located in Jerusalem where people gathered for feasts.
[2] Charles, *Revelation* I, pp. 199-201.
[3] A. J. Beagley, *The "Sitz im Leben" of the Apocalypse* (Berlin: W.De Gruyter, 1987), pp. 46-47.
[4] F. Düsterdieck, *Critical and Exegetical Handbook to the Revelation of John*, tr. H. E. Jacobs (Winona Lake: Alpha Publications, 1884), p. 241.
[5] G. R. Beasley-Murray, *The Book of Revelation* (London: Oliphants, c1978), pp. 139-40.

144,000 reported in Rev 7:4-8. Although the word "Christian" or "Jesus" is nowhere mentioned in this chapter, these and other scholars have assumed that the entire book was written by John of Patmos and is Christian. Although the 144,000 were all from the twelve tribes of Israel, some scholars have concluded that the people from every nation, tribe, people, and language must all have been both Christian gentiles and at the same time Christian members of the twelve tribes of Israel. This judgment clearly has problems, and the introductions to separate visions suggests that there are two units in this chapter.

With palm leaves in their hands. **Palm leaves** were huge, sometimes six or eight feet in length. They are sometimes called **palm branches or palm fronds,** because they grow directly from the trunk of the tree; they do not cling to branches as leaves of many other trees do. Because they are soft, they would be much easier for a human being or beast of burden to walk on than would branches of wood from other trees. Because they are light, like other leaves, they could easily be waved.

The mob of people was composed of diaspora Jews, with **palm branches in their hands**, who had come from all parts of the world to one of the feasts. **Palm leaves** were normally waved on the Feast of Tabernacles, but they were also brought on other nationalistic feasts, such as Hanukkah. Jews expected mobs of Jews from the diaspora to attend the feasts at Jerusalem. Jewish revolts against Rome were planned to take place on feast days when Jews had all of this military support. Generally, **palm leaves** were waved as victory symbols. **Palm leaves** were for Jews as green clover is for the Irish or the various tartans are for the Scots. They were their national symbols and were carried in processions and waved as flags. When Jesus entered Jerusalem other Jews waved palm leaves and spread them out on the road where he would travel.

Judgment day was believed to be held on New Year's Day. Popular Judaism celebrated both of these in the Autumn.[1] The Day of Atonement followed ten days after New Year's Day, and the Feast of Tabernacles occurred ten days after the Day of Atonement. According to the old Pentacontad calendar, however, New Year's Day and the Feast of Tabernacles were both observed in the Spring. Christians still celebrate **with palm branches** the Sunday before Easter, and Easter is now celebrated on the exact date of New Year's Day, according to the old Pentacontad calendar. Although modern Judaism in NT times followed the Roman calendar, conservative Jews still used the old Pentacontad calendar. This is evident in some of the Dead Sea Scrolls, some pseudepigraphical literature, and possibly in the NT.

On the Feast of Tabernacles the Jews from the diaspora were expected to come to Jerusalem (Zech 14:16-21), so it seems likely that the author of this portion of Revelation envisioned diaspora Jews coming together to Jerusalem on that feast day, to the place where God's throne was stationed. According to Second Maccabees the first Hanukkah was celebrated shortly after the Feast of Tabernacles (2Macc 10:1-9), and **palm leaves** were waved on the first Hanukkah just as at the Feast of Tabernacles. First Maccabees reported that the celebration of complete

---

[1] See E. Nodet, "La Dedicace, Les Maccabüees et le Messie," *RB* 93 (1986):321-75.

freedom from Syria came during the leadership of Simon and was celebrated also with the waving of **palm leaves** (1Macc 13:51). This does not indicate that it was celebrated on the Feast of Tabernacles, but that it was an important national festival. The great Jewish war against Rome began in 66 IA when many Jews of the diaspora were in Jerusalem, and they remained there until the temple was burned in 70 IA.

The Feast of Tabernacles was celebrated only ten days after the Day of Atonement which followed ten days after New Year's Day, depending on the sect of Jews. Some conservative Jews still celebrated the New Year and Feast of Tabernacles according to the old Pentacontad calendar. On New Year's Day, conservative Jews celebrated the first harvesting of the New Year, after a fast of unleavened bread. At the beginning of the fast, Jews marched in procession to the temple, probably waving their **palm branches.** This seems to have been the seasonal procession with which Jesus entered Jerusalem.

Since this celebration was described in Rev 7 just after the famine described in Rev 6, the author of these passages probably interpreted the famine that occurred in Jerusalem in 69-70 IA as the fast required before the judgment on New Year's Day. He may have written sometime after January, 70 IA, and before New Year's Day (Easter), 70 IA. He may have expected the famine to have been broken on the following New Year's Day when the judgment day would be held, and Jews would be vindicated. At that time, following the directions of the feast, they would put the sickle into the grain, harvest it, give the proper tithes, then parch it and break their fast with new grain (mMen 10:2-5). There would have been no new grain to harvest in the Autumn, at the time of the New Year's Day celebrated by popular Judaism.

When Jews came to Jerusalem at the harvest time of the year, just a week before New Year's Day, they had nationalistic expectations, hoping the prophecy of Joel would be fulfilled. Joel, using New Year's Day and harvest terminology, visualized the Lord putting the sickle into the grain, by which he meant the Lord would cut down the enemy that would be gathered at Kidron Valley (Joel 4:13 [RSV 3:13]), just as the 185,000 Assyrians were killed in that valley in the time of Hezekiah and Isaiah.[1] The palm branches indicated Jewish support for such a battle. They sang praises there to God. In 70 IA the Roman troops were gathered in the Kidron Valley, waiting for the Jews to surrender because of starvation.

The author of this portion of Revelation probably expected a divine act to take place on New Year's Day whereby God would "harvest" the enemies of Israel as he had done before when he slew 186,000 Assyrians, defending the city of Jerusalem for his own sake and for the sake of his servant David (2Kings 19:32-37). At that time he left a remnant of survivors from Mount Zion (2Kings 19:31; Isa 37:32), just as Ezekiel said would happen (Ezek 9:1-11), and the survivors would have been the ones with the sign of the *tau* (ת =X) on their foreheads. Just as Isaiah had reassured Hezekiah in the midst of a threatening crisis that the Lord was just about to interfere with Sennacherib's plan and save a remnant from Zion (Isa 37:5-38), so this author who faced a crisis in Jerusalem in 70 IA assured his readers

---

[1] For details see Buchanan, "The Tower of Siloam," *ET* 115.2 (2003):41-42.

that the Lord would deliver them miraculously from this impending catastrophe. The author probably also remembered that Judas the Maccabee had been delivered during a similar crisis at Jerusalem, at a time when Jews were surrounded inside the walls of Jerusalem by the Syrians who had their siege engines set up against them. Jewish provisions of food had begun to give out, because that had been a Sabbath year (so also Isa 37:30). Then, as if by an act of God, there was a civil conflict in Syria, and the Syrian general, Lysias, was required to make peace with Judas and leave the area to assist in the conflict back in Antioch (Ant 12:375-389).

The editor of Rev 6 and 7 probably understood his contemporary situation in Jerusalem in 70 IA as an antitype of both the situation in Hezekiah's time and that of Judas. Like other ancient Jews and Israelites he thought time moved in cycles and that periods of history repeated themselves just as days of the week or seasons of the years do. Jews in 70 IA, he thought, were at that time in the very same place in the cycle of time as both of these earlier leaders had been. Josephus said that there were many prophets in Jerusalem who were promising signs of deliverance right up to the time the temple burned (War 6:285-87). All of this was based on typology, fulfillment of prophecy, and Jewish belief that time moved in predictable cycles.

TEXT

Revelation	First Testament
[10]They cried out in a loud voice, saying, **"Salvation**	Zech 9:9 Rejoice greatly, daughter of Zion! **Shout aloud** daughter of Jerusalem! Look! Your king is coming to you, righteous and **a savior.**
to our **God**	1Kings 22:19 **God** has become king over the gentiles; **God sits on his** glorious **throne**, and
who **sits on the throne**, and to the Lamb." [11]Then the angels **stood** around **the throne** together with the elders and the four beasts, and they [all] fell upon their faces before	all the army of heaven **standing** beside him, on his right and on his left.
the throne, and they worshiped God, [12]saying, "Amen!	Isa 6:1 In the year that King Uzziah died I saw Yehowah **seated on a throne**, high and exalted.
Blessing,	1Chron 29:10 David said, "**Blessed** are you, Yehowah, God of Israel, our Father **from age to age**! Yours, Yehowah, is the greatness, **the power,**
glory, and wisdom, thanksgiving,	
honor, power, and might be to our God to **ages of ages**. Amen."	**the glory, the might, and the honor.**"

Ps 47:9-10 God has become king over the gentiles; God **sits on his** glorious **throne**.

COMMENTARY

Salvation to our God on the throne. NA edition inserts **"who sits"** after God. Sinaiticus also adds after **the Lamb, "into ages of ages. Amen."**

Salvation to Jews and early Christians was never simply a mystic feeling. It always had legal and practical ramifications. For the individual salvation meant being a member of the community. For the community it meant national deliverance from foreign rule or victory in war. Since **the Lamb**, as the Messiah, was God's legal agent, whenever **salvation** came to God, it meant **the Lamb** was established **on the throne** at Jerusalem. Caird and Aune rendered this passage, "Victory to our God..."[1]

All angels stood around the throne. NA edition adds a definite article before "angels." All *the* angels.

The crowd of worshiping Jews was supported further when all the angels, elders, and beasts joined them in their hymn of praise, using seven words of ascription to God.

VIEWS OF OTHERS

O'Rourke concurred that Rev 7:12 had formerly belonged in Jewish liturgy.[2] Feuillet and Morris thought the 144,000 referred to spiritual Israel rather than Israel after the flesh.[3] Following Comblin,[4] Feuillet held that this referred to those who had been baptized who had also suffered death by persecution. The true remnant of Israel is not made of Jews according to the flesh, but (Rev 2:9; 3:9) true Jews are taken by God from all the nations.[5] In a mystical sense the Jews of the dispersion meant all of the elect Christians whose fatherland was heaven (see Epistle to Diognetus 5). This means Christ had spiritualized the restoration of the chosen nation.[6] Many scholars

---

[1] Caird, *Revelation*, p. 99; Aune, *Revelation 6-16*, p. 470.
[2] J. J. O'Rourke, "Hymns of the Apocalypse," *CBQ* 30 (1968):401.
[3] L. Morris, *The Book of Revelation* (Grand Rapids: Eerdmans, c1987), p. 116, and A. Feuillet, "Les 144,000 Israelites Marques d'un Sceau," *NovT* 9 (1967):194. Feuillet thought the 144,000 sons of Israel in Rev 7 were distinguished from the celibates of Rev 14:1-5 (p. 203). The one is the innumerable elect and the other are the elect on Mount Zion. The seal refers to Christian baptism (p. 204). Morris said the author piled one expression on top of the other to indicate the crowd's universality (p. 116).
[4] J. Comblin, *Le Christ dans l'Apocalypse* (Tournai-Paris: Desclee, 1965), p. 224.
[5] Comblin, *Le Christ*, p. 6, fn.1.
[6] Feuillet, "Les 144,000," pp. 199-200.

think the 144,000 were the Jewish Christians.[1] McKelvey argued that the feast involved here was the Feast of Tabernacles.[2] The Hosannas of Ps 118:25 were used at this feast (mSuk 4:5). The palms, trumpets, and the springs of water are all associated with the Feast of Tabernacles. Draper related Rev 7 both to the Feast of Tabernacles and to Zech 14.[3] Ulfgard suggested that the reference to the feast in Rev 7 was made with an intentional allusion to Exod 5:1; 4:23; and 7:16.[4]

TEXT

Revelation	First Testament
[13]Then one of the elders answered me saying, "Who **are these** wearing white robes, and from where have they come?" [14]I said to him, "**My Lord, you know**." Then he said to me, "These are those who have come up from great **tribulation**. They have **washed their robes** and bleached them **in the blood of the Lamb**."	[Zech 4:4, 11, 12; 5:6, 12]I said to the angel who was talking with me, "What **are these, my Lord**?" [Ezek 37:3]He said to me, "Son of man, can these bones live?" I answered, "**Lord** God, **you know**." [Dan 12:1]It will be a time of **tribulation** such as has not been during the existence of the nation until that time. [Gen 49:11]He **washes his garment** with wine, his clothing **in the blood of the** grape.

COMMENTARY

One of the elders answered. Sinaiticus added, **One of the elders, saying to me**. This is an obvious dittography, duplicated by mistake.

The elder **answered** the author, when the author had not yet asked a question, but this is a normal Semitic idiom. A person begins a conversation by "answering and saying." The "answer" the elder gave, was in fact, itself, a question, but that was the kind of question-answer dialogue typical of Zechariah and Ezekiel. The question under consideration was the identity of these diaspora Jews in Jerusalem. They had been part of the "time of tribulation" (Dan 12:1) that was destined to take place before God's people would be delivered. That which "bleached" the

---

[1] Bengel, Bleek, Holtzmann, Calmes, Bousset, Zahn, Allo, Ketter, Schrenk, Aune..
[2] R. J. McKelvey, *The New Temple: The Church of the New Testament* (London: Oxford U. Press, 1969), p. 163.
[3] J. A. Draper, "The Heavenly Feast of the Tabernacles in Revelation 7.1-17," *JSNT* 19 (1983):133-47.
[4] H. Ulfgard, *Feasts and Future: Revelation 7:9-17 and the Feast of Tabernacles* (Stockholm: Almqvist & Wilksell, 189), p. 40.

garments was the suffering of the saints in the great tribulation, which had just been described as the day of the Lord. This figure was intended metaphorically. The garments bleached were legal garments. Having garments bleached meant having their crimes forgiven. Blood does not sanitize or bleach garments, but suffering was expected to remove crimes, leaving the believer ritually clean. White was the color that symbolized ritual cleanliness or purity.

Who are these who are wearing white robes? People do not ordinarily bleach garments by washing them in blood. The words, "in the blood of the Lamb," may have been a Christian interpretive addition, but it may also have been an earlier Jewish messiah who had been killed as a martyr and held by Jews to be their redeemer. Whether Jewish or Christian, the author knew of the account where Judah had washed his garments in wine, although there is no claim that he got them **white** by so doing. The author of Rev 7, however, may have wanted his readers to know that the Lamb involved was a slain messiah, either Jesus or someone else. "Making them **white**" meant they had removed all the ritual midras defilement from their "garments" by having their crimes forgiven. Midras defilement came from having some part of clothing defiled by touching something that was ritually unclean, such as a corpse, a gentile, or otherwise defiled person.

Who have come up from great tribulation. This is an answer to the question, "**Who are these?**" **The tribulation** has come to have a technical meaning in redemption literature. It is an antitype of the **tribulation** described in Dan 12:1. That **tribulation** was the suffering Jews endured during the Maccabean rebellion against the Syrian Greeks. During this time Antiochus Epiphanes tortured and killed Jews who observed their traditional religious customs. That **tribulation came** to an end when Judas the Maccabee and his troops defeated the Syrian Greeks at Beth-horon, after which Jews had the temple cleansed and celebrated the first Hanukkah. The tribulation is sometimes called the "birth pangs of the Messiah." It was expected to last about 3½ years, as it did before the first Hanukkah. Also following Daniel 12:1, the redemption chapter in Matthew alludes to the same phenomenon:

Like most scholars, Aune held that these were Christian martyrs who were gathered in heaven,[1] but there is no word in this chapter that identifies these people who had suffered with Christians or that pictured them in heaven. **The throne of God** was right there in the temple at Zion where there **were springs of the water of life.** That is what Jews normally expected to happen whenever the land was restored to the chosen people.

> **For there will be then a great tribulation such as there has never been from the beginning of the world until now, nor will ever be** (Matt 24:21).

---

[1] Aune, *Revelation 6-16*, p.480.

He said. NA edition adds **to me.**

They have washed their garments. This was a ritual cleansing rather than a type of disinfectant. Although passages dealing with a slain Lamb may be Christian compositions, as Rowland insists, it is not the only solution.[1] Weiss thought this work was written earlier and revised by an editor who interpreted the white clothing to symbolize the victory of martyrdom.[2] The **garments** washed were probably not cotton or woolen. They were probably legal **garments.** When people were baptized they left their old **garments** on one bank of a river, entered the water, were cleansed legally, and came up on the other side to put on different clothing. The clothing they left was their gentile clothing, which contained all of their crimes and guilt. When they were cleansed, they were free from all of that guilt, legally. They had declared "bankruptcy" on all of that. They became new beings as Christians, and were then permitted to take part in the community meal or eucharist. In this way they were "washed by the blood of the Lamb," without touching any red blood, physically.

Ford correctly noted that kings could take away crime by destroying the criminals,[3] but that is not the only possibility. Kings can also get rid of crime by pardoning the criminals. Kings could also die for their countries. In fact there were other Jewish messiahs who died for their nation as well as Jesus. If this passage was of Jewish, rather than Christian, origin, then the **Lamb** whose blood cleansed people's crimes would have been some other messiah. There were several who died for their nation:

1) Judas the Maccabee was killed in battle;
2) Simon, Eliezer, and Athrongeus were all killed in war against
    Rome just after Herod's death; and
3) Antigonus, the Hasmonean Messiah who ruled Jerusalem from
    the time the Parthians captured the city until Herod the Great
    recaptured it with Roman support, was killed by Herod, crucified,
    and became a **Lamb** that was slain.

Garments in antiquity held important symbolism. Citizens and priests were forbidden by law to wear the same type of **garments** that a high priest wore (1Macc 14:44-45). There were times when some action was taking place in the Roman senate when all the senators went home, changed **garments,** and returned to conduct the business at hand (Dio, *RomHist* 46:44, 4; 51:5, and frequently). Those who

---

[1] C. Rowland, *The Open Heaven: A Study of Apocalyptic in Judaism and Christianity* (New York: Crosssroad, 1982), p. 516, fn. 71: "The reference to the *arnion . . . hos esphagmenon* makes it impossible to see this chapter [chapter 5] as one devoid of Christian influence."
[2] J. Weiss, *Offenbarung*, p. 636.
[3] J. M. Ford, *Revelation* (Garden City: Doubleday, 1975), pp. 89-90.

became Christians removed their **garments,** were baptized, and put on clean, white **garments.**[1]

An early poet told of his salvation which he described as having been "circumcised by the Holy Spirit" and having "drunk of the water of life." At that time he put away folly and turned to the Most High. Then the Lord renewed him with his **garment** (OdesSol 11:2-11). He was legally transformed. The symbolism of white **garments** as crimelessness and filthy garments as criminal guilt was earlier evident in Zechariah, where Joshua, the high priest, stood before the Lord at a court session, appearing in filthy **garments**. He was the defendant in the court case, and Satan was the prosecuting attorney. In this judgment, the Lord ruled in Joshua's favor, pardoned his crimes, and since he was the legal agent of the people, the Lord pardoned all Israel's crimes by the same act. The Judge then ordered the angel who was acting as Joshua's defense attorney to remove Joshua's filthy **garments** and clothe him with proper priestly **garments** (Zech 3:1-6).

TEXT

Revelation	First Testament
[15]Because of this they are before **the throne of God,**	[Isa 6:1]In the year that King Uzziah died I saw Yehowah, seated on **his throne**, high and exalted, and his train filled the temple.
	[Ps 47:9]God has become king over the nations; God has sat down on **his holy throne**.
and they serve him **day** and **night** in his temple. The one	[Ps 121:6]The sun will not afflict you during the day, nor the moon during **night**.
seated on the throne knows them.	[1Kings 22:19]Then [Micaiah] said, "Therefore hear the word of Yehowah! I saw Yehowah **seated on his throne** with all the troops of heaven standing alongside of him."
[16]**They will not become hungry or thirsty** any more, and **the sun** will not fall upon **them** nor any **heat,**	[Isa 49:10a]**They will not become hungry or thirsty**; the burning **heat nor sun** will strike **them**.

---

[1]Buchanan, *The Consequences of the Covenant* (Leiden: E. J. Brill, 1970), pp. 198-210.

¹⁷because

	Ps 121:6**The sun will not** afflict you during the day, nor the moon during the night.
the Lamb **on the throne will shepherd them and**	Ezek 34:23I will raise up over them one **shepherd**, my servant David. **He will shepherd them and be their shepherd**.
lead them to springs of water of life,	Isa 49:10bThe one who has mercy on **them will lead them,** and alongside **springs of water** he will guide them.
	Ps 23:1, 3Yehowah is my **shepherd . . . He leads me** in paths of righteousness
	Jer 2:13They have abandoned me, **the fountain of the water of life**.
and God will wipe away every tear from their eyes.	Isa 25:8He will swallow up death forever, and **the Lord Yehowah will wipe away** the **tear from all** faces, and the disgrace of his people he will turn away from all the land, for Yehowah has spoken.

TECHNICAL DETAILS

The author has based these promises on Isa 25 and 49, with supplemental Psalms. Both chapters in Isaiah are promises of deliverance. Isa 25 promised that the Lord's hand would rest on Mount Zion, and the Lord would hold a feast there and **wipe away tears from all faces** and remove all the disgrace of his people. The disgrace they had suffered was that of not having their own homeland, free from foreign rule. Those who waited for him would rejoice in his salvation. Isa 49 promised that the sons of Jacob would not only be raised, but they would become a light to the nations, and God's salvation would reach to the end of the earth. God would reestablish the land and bring forth the prisoners from captivity. He would pasture them on the heights of Israel, where they would neither hunger nor thirst any more, neither suffer from sun nor scorching heat. **The one who had mercy would lead them to springs of water.**

The springs of water of life are Ain Gihon and Ain Rogel at the foot of Mount Zion in the City of David. Ain Gihon (Siloam) flows out from the temple and runs down the Kidron Valley to Wadi Qumran and on into the Dead Sea (Ezek 47). Those who came to **the springs of water** would come to Zion, as Jews and Christians wanted to do when the new age came. Diaspora Jews would come to Jerusalem from distant countries--**from the east, west, and north** (Isa 49:12), because the Lord was comforting his people, which meant he was restoring them to the Promised Land by bringing them to **the springs of the water of life.**

COMMENTARY

Because of this. **They were before the throne of God**, right there at Zion, where there were the **springs of the water of life** flowed out from the temple, where **God's throne** was**, because** they had previously endured a great tribulation. Their reward was that they should appear **before the throne of God**, so that they might minister to him **day and night in his temple,** as priests do. There are other clues that this prophecy (Rev 4:1-22:5) is a priestly document. The 24 elders, for example, functioned as representatives of the 24 priestly courses (1Chron 24:7-18).

The one seated on the throne knows them. NA edition has instead of **knows** "will pitch his tent over." Both readings make sense. The claim that God knows them means he will look out for them, care for them, and protect them.

These are things the faithful could expect of God also if he pitched his tent in their midst. The One seated on the throne would pitch his tent over them to shield them from the elements of weather. He would protect them. The list of promises given here (Rev 7:15-17) are the promises the author believed would soon be fulfilled. With the sixth seal, not only was the day of the Lord coming with vengeance, but the Lord was also going to comfort his people. The dress rehearsal for all this had already happened in heaven where these diaspora parties to the contract had gathered from every nation of the earth, from all distant places, and returned to Jerusalem, where **the One who sat on the throne** would dwell with them as he had in the wilderness. Then the land would be restored, and the Lamb **in the midst of the throne** would shepherd them. The expression, which literally means **in the midst of** in Greek, is rendered here, **on.** This is probably an awkward rendering of the Hebrew *beht* (ב), which means "in," "on," "against," "through," etc. **In the midst of** a chair might mean being carved into the furniture, as was true of the ivory throne on which Solomon sat (1Kings 10:18-20). The other possibility is that he sat on the throne between the arms and on the seat.

The sun will not fall upon them any more. NA edition omits **any more** (*éh-tee.* (ἔτι). During their tribulation, these people suffered many kinds of natural afflictions. After the tribulation, however, these hardships would cease. They not only would be spared earthquakes and storms. Even the sun would not torture them.

The Lamb on the throne will shepherd them. **The Lamb on the throne** was no ordinary **Lamb**--no helpless sheep. He was called **a Lamb** to indicate that he belonged to the Lord's "flock," but he was also the **shepherd,** and he **shepherded** with an iron rod, which means he would enforce discipline firmly, and protect the nation, militarily. This was the Lord's Messiah, the king of Israel, the Lord's agent, who sat **on the** Lord's **throne**. His function **on the throne** and role as a **shepherd** identified him legally with God. He was God's legal agent. He was also called "the Son of God." His identity as a **Lamb,** meant that he was one of the chosen people of the Lord's flock. Acting as the Lord's agent, he would govern the people Israel, provide for their material needs, and remove all of their pain and discomfort. This was all the natural consequence of the day of the Lord, which would come with terror and destruction, before the Lord would comfort his faithful people who had come up through this tribulation and kept their **garments** undefiled.

Springs of water of life. Sheep are natural followers. The **shepherd** does not have to drive them. They will follow either shepherds or goats. Kings want all of their citizens to be like sheep, willing to follow the king regardless of the cost or wisdom. Citizens who are like goats usually demand a democracy, because they do not follow unquestioningly. In kingdoms goats are the rebels and therefore bad; sheep are loyal followers and therefore good. Isaiah said God would lead Israelites to **springs of water**, the way **shepherds** lead sheep to oases for drinking water. The author of this portion of Revelation, however, pictured **the Lamb,** as God's legal agent, leading the faithful--not only to **springs of water**--but to **springs of water of life**. This is a special kind of water that is used for baptism and cleansing from various kinds of defilement. It was specially identified with the water that flowed out from under the threshold of the temple, from the Spring of Siloam. It was the special water used for baptism and preparing outsiders for membership in the holy community. It would qualify people for membership in the community. It had special healing powers because it flowed out from the temple.

CHAPTER EIGHT

FIRST TESTAMENT REACTIONS TO THE EXODUS CURSES

The plagues of Egypt have influenced later biblical literature, including both the Psalms and the prophecies. Rev 8 is only one of the instances in which these plagues provide a basis for the prophecy. The plagues were delegated to punish people for their crimes. The original criminals were the Egyptians, but these afflictions were also applied to Israel or any of her enemies. Aune has prepared two tables to compare these. They are copied here.[1] The first table shows the plagues of Egypt as reflected in the First Testament (FT). The second shows the plagues in the Book of Revelation.

Seven Plagues of Ps 78:43-52	Seven Plagues of Ps 105:27-36	Seven plagues of Amos 4:6-13
1. Rivers turn to blood (v 44).	1. Darkness (v 28)	1. Famine Yet the people do not return to God (v 6).
2. Flies (v. 45a)	2. Waters become blood; fish die (v 29a)	2. Drought Yet the people do not return to God (vv. 7-8)
3. Frogs (v. 45b)	3. Frogs (v 30)	3. Blight and mildew destroy crops (v 9a)
4. Caterpillars and Locusts (v. 46)	4. Flies and gnats (v 31)	4. Locusts devour trees. Yet people do not return to God (v 9b)
5. Hail and frost destroy vegetation (v 47)	5. Hail and lightning destroy vines and trees (vv 32-33)	5. Pestilence (v 10a)
6. Hail and lightning destroy livestock (v 48)	6. Locusts destroy crops (vv 34-35)	6. Conquest in war Yet people do not return to God (v 10bc).

---

[1] D. E. Aune, *Revelation 6-16* (Dallas: Word Books, 1998), pp. 502-503 and 500-501.

7. Death of firstborn (vv 49-51).	7. Destruction of firstborn (v 36)	7. Some overthrown as were Sodom and Gomorrah (v 11) Yet people do not return to God (v 11)

TRUMPETS AND BOWLS OF REVELATION

Seven trumpets of Rev 8:1-11:19	Seven Bowls of Rev 15:1-16:21
1. Hail and fire mixed with blood. One-third of earth, trees, and grass burned up (8:7)	1. Foul and evil waters (16:2)
2. Burning mountain falls into the sea (8:8). One third of sea life dies. One third of ships destroyed (8:9)	2. Sea becomes blood. All sea animals die (16:3)
3. Blazing star falls on one-third of rivers and fountains (8:10). One-third of waters poisoned and many people die (8:11)	3. Rivers and fountains become blood (16:4)
4. One-third of sun, moon, and stars darkened. One-third of day and one-third of night kept from shining (8:12)	4. Sun allowed to scorch people. People curse God and do not repent (16:8)
5. Star falls from heaven to earth; opens bottomless pit and locusts emerge (9:1-11).	5. Kingdom of beast in darkness. People curse God and did not repent (16:10-11)
6. Four angels bound at Euphrates released; large cavalry kills one-third of humankind (9:13-21). Rest of humankind do not repent of evil (9:20-21)	6. Euphrates dries up, opening way for kings of east; kings of whole world assemble at Armageddon (16:12-16)
7. Kingdom of this world becomes the kingdom of Christ (11:15-18)	7. Earthquake splits Babylon in three parts; cities destroyed (16:17-21)

Rev 8 is devoted to the reapplication of the plagues of Egypt in NT times. The chapter begins with the trumpets sounding from heaven.

TEXT

Revelation

$^{8:1}$When [the Lamb] opened the seventh seal, there was **silence** in heaven for about half an hour. ^{2}Then I saw

the seven angels who stood before God, and they were given [authority] over **seven trumpets**.

First Testament

$^{Zeph\ 1:7}$**Hush** before the Lord Yehowah, because the day of Yehowah is near.

$^{Hab\ 2:20}$Yehowah is in his holy temple; **hush** before him all the land.

$^{Josh\ 6:4-5}$**Seven** priests will carry

seven Jubilee trumpets before the chest. On the **seventh** day you shall surround the city **seven** times, and the priests will blow **the trumpets**. It will happen while [they] continue [blowing] the rams' horns, when you hear the sound of **the trumpet**, all the people will shout loudly, and the wall of the city will fall.

TECHNICAL DETAILS

Here [the Lamb] opened **the seventh seal. The sixth seal** was opened in Rev 6. Mazzaferri asked what the subject of the sentence is in Rev 8:1. The subject here has been supplied as the Lamb. Mazzaferri thought Rev 7 had been intruded and that Rev 8 once followed immediately after Rev 6.[1] This is possible, but the unified existence may not have ever been part of the Book of Revelation, in its complete form. Revelation, like other redemption anthologies, is very composite. Some final editor put together many units to comprise one complete unit. That editor would have been the one who decided how the units should be divided and spliced together. Schüssler-Fiorenza is partially right in noting that the final editor did not separate sections or parts but rather joined parts together.[2] It is likely that he did both. He may have interrupted one of his narratives to insert Rev 7 because of the word, **stand.** Rev 6 concluded with the question, **Who can stand**? (Rev 6:17). Rev 7

---

[1] F. D. Mazzaferri, *The Genre of the Book of Revelation from a Source-critical Perspective* (Berlin; New York: W. De Gruyter, 1989), p. 336.
[2] E. Schüssler-Fiorenza, *"Composition and Structure of the Book of Revelation,"* BCQ 39 (1977):361-62.

pictures the 144,000 **standing** before the throne and before the Lamb. That answers the question and may have been inserted there because it does.

If Rev 7 were removed, the subject of Rev 8:1 would be **the Lamb** of Rev 6:16. Weiss was of the opinion that **the seventh seal** could introduce nothing other than the Day of Wrath.[1] Caird expected the end to follow immediately after **the seventh seal**, but concluded, ". . . yet the End does not come."[2] It just depends on the kind of end expected. Rev 8:1 constituted the end of the narrative of **the seven seals**, which, mythologically, included various destructive events which were completed. The world did not come to an end; neither did the Book of Revelation. The editor introduced a connecting sentence (Rev 8:2), after which another unit began.

COMMENTARY

Silence in heaven for about half an hour. This was the beginning of the second victorious scene of the prophecy brought to John. Like the first scene (Rev 4-5), this scene took place **in heaven**. Like the first scene, this scene was also situated in the temple **in heaven.** After all of the singing of praises and sound of trumpets, this unit began with a sudden **silence**. Scholars have conjectured many reasons for the **silence** and the reason why it was for just one **half hour**. Some suggested that it was really a thousand years but only appeared short, but all guesses are equally fantastic.[3] Zahn said the phenomenon was not **silence** but stillness. At this point there was no thunder, no trumpet sounds, no roaring of the sea. Only stillness.[4] So, what is the difference? Caird thought there was a period of **silence** for God to hear the prayers of the saints.[5] His basis for this is the fact that in the verses that follow the prayers were brought to God's awareness before any of the trumpets were sounded or before there were any loud meteorological noises. There really is no obvious, good reason given for this **silence in heaven.** It may have been inserted here by the author only to give dramatic effect. The idea being that everyone was still in apprehension of the **seals** that were to be opened.

Another possibility is that the **silence** reflects a court scene before the judge approached the bench. This would imply that **the sealed contract** would be opened before a judge in a court room while observers waited in **silence** to hear the contents. That would be expected after the seven seals had been broken, so that the contract might be opened and read. A scene like that would take place on the judgment day, normally on New Year's Day. This is the situation envisioned when believers, before the throne of God on judgment day, were exhorted to be still in God's presence, just as Enoch warned in a different judgment scene that there should be no frivolous talk in the presence of the divine judge (1Enoch 62:3).

---

[1] J. Weiss, *Die Offenbarung des Johannes* (Göttingen: Vandenhoeck and Ruprecht, 1908), p. 637.

[2] G. B. Caird, *A Commentary on the Revelation of St. John the Divine* (London: Black, c1966), p. 103.

[3] For a list see F. Düsterdieck, *Critical and Exegetical Handbook to the Revelation of John,* tr. H. E. Jacobs (Winona Lake: Alpha Publications, 1884), pp. 60-62.

[4] T. Zahn, *Die Offenbarung des Johannes (*Leipzig: A Deichert, 1924), p. 380.

[5] Caird, *Revelation, p. 107.*

Another possibility may be that since this was **the seventh seal,** there was stillness in honor of the Sabbath. That would be particularly true if the author wanted to direct the reader's attention to the Sabbath of Sabbaths, the year of Jubilee when Israelite captives would be liberated and their land would be restored. That Jubilee would also fall on the Day of Atonement when Israel's crimes might be pardoned.

Seven angels who stood before God. There was a tradition that there were **seven angels** who stood before the Lord, and Raphael was one of those (Tob 12:15). The **seven angels** appeared because another seal was opened. This was the last of **the seven seals** which the Lamb was authorized to open.

1) The first **seal** reversed the situation of Zech 4 and established war.
2) The second **seal** took peace from the land.
3) The third **seal** established famine.
4) The fourth **seal** brought pestilence, sufficiently dreadful to cause people to die by all four evils--**famine, pestilence, the sword, and beasts**.
5) The fifth **seal** brought about the day of the Lord with all of its natural catastrophes and fears.
6) With the sixth **seal** came utter destruction to **the migrants** and all people **on the land** except those 144,000 elect servants of God who had been **sealed on their foreheads**. This was followed by comfort and promise for those Jews from every nation who had remained faithful through the tribulation. The promise involved the restoration of the Promised Land under the leadership of the Lord's Messiah, **the Lamb**.
7) **The seventh seal**, like the Sabbath day, provided quiet. This was the lull after the storm (1Kings 19:12), but it did not last very long.

The seventh seal also introduced **seven angels** with **seven** trumpets whose activity was destined to effect the history of Palestine. Morris suggested that these **seven angels** were a special **seven** who entered and left before the glory of the Holy One (Tob 12:15): Uriel, Raphael, Raguel, Michael, Saraqael, Gabriel, and Remiel (1Enoch 20.1-8; see also Rev 8:6; 15:1, 6-9; 16:1; 17:1; 21:9).[1]

The **seven angels** with their **seven** trumpets may have been types of the **seven** priests who led the entrance into Canaan with Joshua. These were the **seven** priests who led the procession around the city of Jericho which concluded with the capture of the first city of the Promised Land. Just as the priests, with their **trumpets** and the chest containing the contract, performed the magical rites that ended with the possession of the land, so the **seven angels** with their **trumpets** were preparing for the new conquest of the Promised Land and the reestablishment of the contract. The **angels** were not only reenacting the preparation for the entrance into the land, but they also produced another eschatological sign--the Jubilee, the time when the debts were all declared "paid," and the land was restored to the "original" owners.

---

[1] L. Morris, *The Book of Revelation* (Grand Rapids: Eerdmans, c1987), pp. 119-20.

This eschatological sign signaled the end of the common era of pagan rule. **The trumpets** blown by the priests when they marched around Jericho were Jubilee **horns** (*kéh-rehn hah yóh-vayl*, בקרן היובל, Josh 6:5). These were rams **horns,** the kind of **trumpets** used to announce the Jubilee. The author of this narrative, then, created a unit where the **seventh trumpet** instituted the final stages of preparation for the restoration of the land. Just as the priests performed the proper ritual to start the conquest of Canaan, so the **seven angels** blew the trumpets to institute whatever action was necessary to restore the land. The seventh **angel** concluded with the reestablishment of the contract **in heaven** and the new Mount Sinai on earth (Rev 11:19). The new Mount Sinai was Zion.

In antiquity **trumpets** were not primarily designed to play in dance orchestras. They were used
1) as a means of warning (Num 10:1-8; Ezek 33:3-6; Hos 8:1; Joel 2:1;
2) to announce an attack by enemy forces (Num 31:6; Judges 7:8-22; 2Chron 13:12; Zeph 1:16; 2Macc 13:25);
3) to give an alarm in a city (Jer 20:16; Hos 5:8; Amos 3:6; Zeph 1:16;
4) to signal a retreat (2Sam 2:28; 18:16; 20:22; 2Kings 9:22;
5) A cry to God for help (Num 10:9; 1Macc 4:40;
6) to announce victory (Ps 47:5);
7) to announce good news (PssSol 11:1). One of the Eighteen Benedictions of the morning service is as follows;

> Sound a great shofar for our liberty!
> Raise the flag to gather our exiles.
> Gather us together from the four corners of the earth.
> Blessed are you, Lord, who gathers his rejected people, Israel.[1]

TEXT

Revelation	First Testament
[3]Another angel came and **stationed** himself **on the altar**, having a gold censor	Amos 9:1 I saw the Lord **stationed on the altar**, and he said, "Strike the capitals, and the thresholds will tremble, and cut off their heads--all of them. What are left of them--I will kill with a sword. Not one of them will get away, fleeing; not one of them will escape."
and much **incense** was given to him	Isa 6:6-7 One of the seraphim flew to me. In his hand he took a **fiery coal** with

---
[1] S. Singer, *Authorized Daily Prayer Book* (London: Eyre and Spotteswoode Limited, 1960), p. 48, translated from the Hebrew.

so that he might offer [it] by means of **the prayers** of all the saints upon **the** gold **altar** which is before the throne. ⁴Then the smoke of the **incense** by means of **the prayers** of the saints went up from the hand of the angel before God. ⁵Then the angel **took the censor**, and he **filled** it **[with coals] from the fire on the altar**,
and he threw them to the earth, and

tongs from the top **of the altar**, and he touched my mouth and said, "Look! This has touched your lips. It has turned away your iniquity and atoned for your crime."

^{Lev 16:12}He [Aaron] **will take the censor full of fiery coals from the** top **of the altar** which is before Yehowah and his two hands full of the **incense** beaten fine, from the temple to the curtain.

^{Ezek 10:2}He spoke to the man dressed in linen, and said, "Go in among the wheels to [the place] under the cherubim and **fill** your hands with **fiery coals from** between the cherubim [at the altar] and sprinkle [them] over the city."

^{Amos 7:4}Thus the Lord Yehowah showed me: Look! The Lord Yehowah is calling for a judgment by **fire**. It will consume great Tehom, and it will eat up the portion [of the land].

^{Exod 19:16}It happened on the morning of the third day that **there were noises, lightnings**, and a heavy cloud over the mountain and the very loud sound of a trumpet blast.

there were thunders, **noises, bolts of lightning**, and an earthquake.

COMMENTARY

Prayers of all the saints. **Prayer** is a legal concept that is designed to take place in court. Near the conclusion of a court trial, the plaintiff offers a **prayer** for relief to the judge or jury. He reviews the offenses committed by the defense and suggests proper punishments that the judge might enforce upon the defense. The defense would then be allowed to offer a counter **prayer,** asking for reduction of demands, mitigating the claims on the basis of circumstances, or just asking for mercy.

The setting for **the prayers of all the saints** seems to have been a **heavenly court** scene on the Day of Atonement. On the Day of Atonement, the Lord might forgive Israel's unpaid fines (her iniquities) and pardon her crimes if the conditions were right. They were these:

1) There must be an appropriate sin offering to pay for Israel's crimes.
2) All believers must be reconciled to one another, with all debts paid or forgiven.
3) God would then act to forgive Israel's iniquities and pardon her crimes committed against him.

This would be shown by his willingness to return the land to the chosen people under the leadership of their own messiah. The court session began with respectful silence in the Judge's presence. Then the atonement offering was presented to the Judge. This offering also functioned as the plaintiff's **prayer** for relief, requesting that Israel's enemies be punished and that God's promises to Israel be fulfilled. The entire process requiring **the seven seals** to be broken was scheduled to begin.

In addition to the stillness of the Sabbath, the author immediately introduced the reader to the heavenly altar in the temple, which was also the heavenly court where the Lord functioned as acting judge. The priestly angel was the attorney for the plaintiff, Israel. The priest entered the holy of holies on the Day of Atonement when **trumpets** would be sounded on Jubilee years. Just as it was **the angel** who blew the Jubilee **trumpet,** so also it was an **angel** who offered the incense necessary to cancel Israel's iniquities and crimes so that liberation would be possible. This image was designed to show the effectiveness in the heavenly court of **prayers** for relief. When the **saints prayed,** the **prayers** were changed into incense in **heaven**. **In heaven** they were duly acknowledged, accredited, and their enforcement began.

There an **angel** took a censor and filled it with the huge amount of incense which had accumulated from these **prayers.** He put these on the golden altar so that the smoke from the incense would ascend to God. As a result of these invocations, **the angel** had another assignment. He filled the same censor--not with incense--but with fire **from the altar,** and he hurled it to the earth. This caused natural catastrophes like those that occurred with the revelation of the ten commandments at Mount Sinai (Exod 19:16) or the day of the Lord (Joel 2:1-3).

These actions belong together--if **the seals** had not been **broken** there would have been no incense. Without the incense there would have been no catastrophes on the earth. This was all essential ritual. One act made the other necessary, but this was only the beginning of the plagues that would fall on the enemies of the Jews. This was all good news to the **saints**. It was done the way the seraph brought **a fiery coal** from the altar to touch Isaiah's lips. This coal cleansed his lips and atoned for his crime (Isa 6:1-7). In the same way **the angel** scattered **fiery coals** from the altar to cleanse the crime from the land of Palestine. There was a strong belief among Jews that crime must be abolished in the land before the kingdom could be restored. Jews would not sit, **everyone under his vine and fig tree**, until all the guilt was removed in one day. That day would be the Day of Atonement (Zech 3:18-19).

Before the land could be restored it was necessary to put all of the iniquity of the land into a bucket, cover it with a heavy lid and send it out of the country to Babylon (Zech 4:5-11). Jeremiah promised that the Lord would cleanse the Jews and Israelites of their crimes and restore the fortunes of Israel (Jer 33:7-8). Jesus taught that the judgment would come like the separation of fish with scales and fins from all the rest, after the nets had been drawn in (Matt 13:47-50), or like separating the wheat from the weeds at the end of the harvest (Matt 13:24-30). In the new kingdom there would be neither weeds nor sea creatures without scales and fins.

Following Rabbis Meir, Jeremiah, and Hiyya ben Abba, Rabbi Phineas said the Israelites did not all pray at once. Different synagogues **prayed** at different times. Then an angel would collect all of these **prayers**, weave them into garlands, and take them to **heaven** where he would place the crown on the head of God. Then the Lord would be crowned with the **prayers** of Israel (ExodR 21:4 [Exod 14:15]). Early Jews and Christians had various ways of picturing the **prayers of the saints** reaching **heaven**, but they believed these accumulated like money in a bank and would eventually cancel the mortgage placed against the nation. Crime had to be removed in one way or another. **Prayer** was one of the methods believed to be effective. Another method was to destroy the wicked and cleanse the righteous. This was the plan of the **seven angels** with their **seven trumpets**.

The whole theology of sacrifice is based on the ways plaintiffs treat judges on earth. When the plaintiff cannot meet the possible requirement, he or she sometimes tries to bribe or flatter the judges. Sacrifices are intended to put God into a good mood in relationship to the worshiper. In earthly courts many offenses that have been committed can be satisfied with monetary settlement. The court decides how serious the offense is and how much must be paid by the offender. Some offenders are quick to offer settlements, because they want to remove their guilt.

When the believer commits crimes against God, it is assumed that God might accept some kind of alternative compensation. The only way this can be done on earth while God is **in heaven** is to burn animals and incense and let the fragrance reach heaven. If the worshiper continues to have bad fortune he or she presumes that still more sacrifices are required. Micah complained that there would never be enough material sacrifices to satisfy God--not even **thousands of rams, ten thousand rivers of olive oil,** or his **first born son** (Micah 6:8). **Prayers** were messages that might be sent to God in an effort to negotiate a settlement. They are like the requests plaintiffs make to judges, **prayers** for relief. Defendants would offer **prayers** for mercy, pardon, and forgiveness.

Thunders, bolts of lightning, noises, and an earthquake. All of these natural phenomena were accumulated here to remind the reader of the contract given on Mount Sinai. When the seals were finished, Jews were expected to have suffered enough tribulation to gain redemption--the restoration of the contract and the land. With **the seventh seal** came all of these reminders. With them came the end of **the seven**

seals and the end of that particular unit. The next narrative begins with the **seven trumpets,** which announced a new turn of events.

TEXT

Revelation

⁶The seven angels who had the seven trumpets prepared them so that they could blow the trumpets. ⁷The first [angel] **blew the trumpet**, and there appeared

hail and **fire** mixed with **blood.**

First Testament

^(Ezek 10:2)Then he spoke to the man clothed in linen and said to him, "Go in between the wheels under the cherubim and fill your hands with coals of **fire** from among the cherubim. Scatter [them] over the city."

^(Joel 2:1)**Blow the trumpet** in Zion! Sound an alarm in my holy mountain; let all the inhabitants of the land tremble, because the Day of Yehowah is coming; it is near.

^(Ezek 38:22)I will judge him with pestilence, **blood**, torrents of rain, **hail stones**, and I will rain down upon him and upon his troops, and many people who are with him, **fire** and sulphur.

^(Isa 30:30)The blow of his arm coming down in fierce anger will be seen and a flame of devouring **fire**, a cloud-burst, a storm, and **hail**stones.

^(Josh 10:11)While they were going down the ascent of Beth-horon, Yehowah threw down huge **hail** stones from heaven upon them as far as Azekah, and they died.

^(Joel 3:3)I will produce wonders in heaven and on **earth--blood, fire**, and vaporous smoke.

^(Exod 9:23)Moses stretched out his wand up to heaven and Yehowah produced

	noises and **hail**; **fire** moved **earthward**; and Yehowah rained **hail** upon the land of Egypt.
	^{Amos 7:4}Thus the Lord Yehowah showed me: Look! The Lord Yehowah calling for a judgment by **fire**. It will consume great Tehom, and it will eat up **the portion** [of the land].
Consequently **the third portion of the land burned**;	^{Ezek 5:2}**A third portion** you shall **burn** in the fire in the midst of the city [of Jerusalem] when the days of the seige are completed; a **third portion** you shall take and strike with the sword round about the city; and a **third portion** you shall scatter to the wind and I will unsheathe the sword after them.
	^{Zech 13:8-9}In **the** whole **land**, says Yehowah, two **thirds** will be cut off and perish;
the third portion of the trees **burned**; and all green grass **burned.**	**one third** will be left alive, and I will put this **third** into the fire.

COMMENTARY

So that they could blow the trumpets. **Trumpets** were sometimes used to warn the community of dangers (Amos 3:6; Ezek 33:3), call them for battle, or to announce something, like Jubilee (Lev 25:8-9; Isa 27:13) or the New Moon (Ps 81:3). They were also used to start something, like a battle. Num 10:1-16 gives direction for the **blowing of trumpets**--what kind of blast should be **blown**, how many blasts for each need, and who the people should be who **blow the trumpets**.

This attention to earthly **trumpets** to direct community movement prompted early Jews and Christians to assume that there were divine **trumpets** in heaven that caused the natural calamities that followed. People 2,000 years ago knew a great deal about cause and effect, but they did not know as much as we know today. They knew rain, snow, and hail came when there were clouds, but they could not watch cloud formations and see the direction of jet streams on TV as people can today. That which they did not know they conjectured, just as we do today. When it rained or hailed, or when there was a drought or a plague of insects, ancients deduced that the Lord must have sent an angel to pour out a bowl full of some substance or an angel to **blow a trumpet**, or something like that to start action intended.

This was consistent with their belief that they could pour water on the altar while praying and expect the rainy season to begin. If the authorized person waved a wand in the air, the air would become filled with gnats. If someone held up his hands while a battle was in process, the side which he favored would win (Exod 17:8-13). Modern science has taught us a great deal about the causes of certain effects, but scientists can no more explain why or how God works in these natural phenomena today than religious leaders could 2,000 years ago.

The third portion of the land burned. **Trumpets** are frequently associated with Jubilee releases for Jews and/or Christians (Lev 25:9; Isa 43:6-7; 60:3-5; PssSol 11.1-9). These **trumpets** seem to deal with the negative effects of Jubilee. If Jews were to be given liberty, the enemies of Israel would have to be suppressed. Therefore, the Jubilee **trumpets** here introduce to the enemies of Israel torture and plagues. Just as at the Exodus the Israelites were liberated from Egypt as a result of the plagues afflicted on the Egyptians, here, on Jubilee, the Jews and/or Christians were to be liberated by plagues directed toward the gentiles.

The trumpets were different from the **seals**. Whenever a **seal** was broken, one of the curses of the contract was turned loose upon the Israelites. When angels **blew trumpets**, however, plagues were inflicted upon the enemies of Israel. In both instances there was magic involved. Either Moses or Aaron waved or pointed a wand or an angel appeared and blew a **trumpet.** This first **trumpet** was a repetition of the seventh plague which Moses and Aaron performed against Pharaoh in Egypt. Ezekiel promised that the Lord would similarly rain down fire and brimstone against Gog, but in both Gog and Egypt, the destruction was to be complete for the land involved. Here the amount of territory involved was either **a third** of the whole earth or **a third** of the land of Israel. Since the **migrants of the land** are mentioned in the verse just below, this entire chapter may have been written with **the land** in mind, rather than the earth.

It seems strange for the author to design for **a third** portion of the land or the sea to be destroyed or burned with fire, rather than complete destruction, but the author of this text was heavily dependent upon the First Testament (FT) for his expectations. In a situation in which the angel was hurling fire to the ground to punish and cleanse the land of Israel, it was normal to turn for direction to Amos who had previously promised to cleanse Israel with fire. He also said he would use fire to consume **the portion** (*hah kháy-lehk*, (החלק), without saying what that portion was or of what. This gave the commentator the freedom to fill in details: *the* portion would be *the* **third,** and the portion would be of the land and the sea.[1] Amos may have been supplemented by using Ezekiel's prophecy which brought punishment against Jerusalem--in **thirds.**

---

[1] S. Giet, *L'Apocalypse et L'Histoire* (Paris: Presses Universitaires de France, 1957), p. 153.

TEXT

Revelation

⁸The second angel blew his trumpet,

and [something] like a great
mountain, burning
with fire,

was **thrown** into the sea,

and **the third portion** of
the sea **became blood**. ⁹Then **the
third portion** of the creatures of the
sea--those having life--**died**,

and **the third**

First Testament

^(Jer 51:25)"Look! I am against you, destroying **mountain**," says Yehowah who destroys all the land, "and I will reach out my hand against you, and roll you from the rocks, and I will make you a **burnt mountain.**"

^(Ezek 38:20)**The mountains** will be **thrown** down, and the cliffs will fall, and every wall will fall to the ground.

^(Exod 7:20-21)Moses and Aaron did just as Yehowah had commanded them, and [Aaron] raised the wand and struck the water which was in the Nile before the eyes of Pharaoh and his servants, and all the water which was in
the Nile **became blood**. The fish

which were in the Nile **died**; the Nile became polluted, so that the Egyptians were not able to drink water from the Nile. It had
become blood in all the land of Egypt.

^(Ezek 5:11-12)I will withdraw; my eye will not spare; I will show no mercy.
The third of you will die with pestilence and be consumed with famine in your midst. **The third** of you will fall by the sword surrounding you; and **the third** of you I will scatter to every wind, and I will draw the sword after them

^(Amos 7:4)Thus the Lord Yehowah showed me: Look! The Lord Yehowah calls for a judgment by **fire**.

| portion of the ships were destroyed. | It will consume great Tehom, and it will eat up **the portion** [of the land]. |

TECHNICAL DETAILS

The type which was like a **burning mountain** was Babylon, in Jeremiah's curse against that city. This alone would account for the imagery. It is possible to guess, but never know, whether or not this was also an allusion to Mount Vesuvius, which erupted in 79 IA and sent **burning** lava into the sea on the Western shore of Italy. Zahn was convinced that this alluded only to that **mountain**, the report of which was given by Pliny (*Epistle* 6:16, 20), and not the destruction of Jerusalem by Vespasian and Titus.[1] Ancient Jews and early Christians did not think disasters in nature were "natural." If there was an earthquake, volcano, hurricane, drought, or any other event that human beings had not caused directly, it was presumed that God caused it to punish or reward people on earth.

The second type imitated here is the first plague in Egypt which made the water in the Nile to **become blood**. Rabbis said that the water **became blood** only for the Egyptians. When the Israelites drank it, it was water. The only way Egyptians could drink water was to buy it from the Israelites, and the Israelites became rich selling water to the Egyptians (GenR 7:19-21 #9.10).

The only apparent reason for limiting the destruction to *the* **third portion** seems to come from Amos 7:4 and/or Ezek 5:12. The definite article before the word **portion** in Amos and **third** in Revelation supports this possibility. Early commentators were sometimes particular about details like this.

TEXT

Revelation	First Testament
¹⁰The third angel blew his trumpet, and a great **star fell from heaven**, burning like a lamp, and it **fell** on **the** third **portion** of the rivers and upon the springs of water.	Isa 14:12-13 How you have **fallen from heaven**, Daystar! How you have been shattered to the earth! You who have slain the gentiles. You said to yourself, "I will go up to **heaven**. From above the **stars** of God I will raise my throne; I will sit on the mountain of feasts in the North."
¹¹The name of the **star** was called	Dan 8:10 It expanded up to the troops **of heaven** and it made some of the troops and some of the **stars fall** to the earth, and it trampled them.

---

[1] Zahn, *Offenbarung* I, pp. 391-94.

"Sulfur,"	Jer 9:15-16"Therefore," says Yehowah of armies, the God of Israel, "Look! I will feed this people **sulfur**, and give them poison **water** to drink."
	Amos 7:4Thus the Lord Yehowah showed me; Look! The Lord Yehowah calls for a judgment by **fire**. It will consume great Tehom, and it will eat up
and **the** third **portion**	**the portion** [of the land].
of the **water** turned into **sulfur**. Many **died** from the **water**, because they were poisoned.	Mic 1:4The mountains melt under him; the valleys break out like wax before the fire like **water** pouring down a cliff.

TECHNICAL DETAILS

The star that **fell** from heaven was an antitype of Babylon. Isaiah promised that Babylon would fall from its pristine position like a **falling star** when the Lord restored Jews to the Promised Land. Wormwood is a plant that produces a bitter oil and a putrid smell, like sulfur. Brimstone is another name for sulfur. Both terms have been used in relationship to the fiery lava that pours out from a volcanic mountain. A volcanic crater filled with boiling lava blowing off sulfurous gases is the picture of fire and brimstone the ancients had in mind. The idea, however, of anyone enduring in such boiling fluid for eternity is unrealistic. Anyone thrown into such a boiling crater would be dissolved almost instantly.

The author of this portion of Revelation was led to the curse by Jeremiah. Lamenting for the crimes of Judah, Jeremiah promised that the Lord would revenge these people. He would lay waste the **mountains** and wilderness; the cities of Judah would become a desolation. Because the people had gone after the Baals the Lord would give them wormwood to eat and poison water to drink (Jer 9:15-16). It was partly the prophecy of Jeremiah which provided the basis for the author's predictions. The desolation and destruction Jeremiah promised to the criminal chosen people of Palestine, the author of Rev 8 attributed to **the migrants** who lived in that land.

TEXT

Revelation	First Testament
¹²The fourth angel blew his **trumpet**,	

and he wounded **the** third **portion** of the sun, **the** third **portion** of the moon, and **the** third **portion** of the stars, so that the third of them would be **darkened**. The **day** would not appear during its third, and the same would be true for the night. ¹³Then I

saw and heard **an eagle** flying in the sky, saying in a loud voice, "Woe! Woe! Woe! [to] the migrants on the land, because of the rest of the sounds of the **trumpets** of the three angels who have yet to blow their **trumpets**."

^{Amos 8:9}"It will happen on that day," says the Lord Yehowah, "I will make the sun go down at noon, and I **will darken** the land in broad daylight."

^{Hab 1:8}From a distance they come; they fly like **an eagle** swift to consume.

^{Hos 8:1}[Put] the **trumpet** to your mouth. As **an eagle** [the enemy] is over the house of Yehowah, because they [the Israelites] have broken my contract; they have transgressed my law.

TECHNICAL DETAILS

At first glance, the image suggested is that of a huge catapult that shot a missile and blew off a **third** of all the disks involved--sun, moon, and each star--so that each one would look like the moon when it's a **third** past full moon. The interpretation, however, is different. The affliction is such that each heavenly body is put out of commission for **a third** of each day and each night. The sun would appear for 2/3 of the day and the moon and **stars** would appear for only 2/3 of the night. This is like the terror that Amos promised in punishment to Israel when part of the day would be dark. This seemed like a sufficiently frightening event for the citizens of Palestine, but the author promised that it would be still worse for **the migrants** (i.e., the foreigners) in the land.

COMMENTARY

An eagle flying in mid-heaven. NA edition has "one **eagle**." This is probably a translation of the Hebrew which sometimes used the number "one" where Westerners would use the indefinite article. This **eagle** pericope is forced into a unified narrative dealing with seven angels and seven **trumpets**. Only four of those angels have appeared at this point, and the fifth does not come until Rev 9:1, when the narrative of the angels and trumpets continues, but not without further interruption. Between the sixth and the seventh angels is inserted Rev 10:1-11:14. **Flying in mid-heaven** means that he was **flying** up in the sky.

Woe! Woe! Woe! to the migrants on the land. The **eagle** was thought of as a swift, mean bird which Hosea and Habakkuk compared to an invading enemy army. Here, also, the **eagle** entered the scene as an enemy to one group of people. **The eagle** was also Rome's national symbol. It came in as an intermission to warn the observers that the worst was still to come, and Israel's arch local enemies, **the migrants**, would be the victims. The three **woes** were for the following **three trumpets**. The next **three trumpets** would be directed to **the migrants**.[1] **The migrants** were the Roman collaborators and other foreigners who lived in the land of Palestine. Like many others, Weiss called these "earth dwellers." He further expatiated that they were here distinguished from the creatures who lived in the sea, the streams, or the sky.[2] Minear also called them "earth-dwellers," but correctly recognized that, according to their contexts, they could not consist of all the people of the earth. In his judgment they were the enemies of the followers of the Lamb, perhaps outsiders who persecuted the church as well as false Christians.[3]

---

[1] A. J. Beagley, *The "Sitz im Leben" of the Apocalypse* (Berlin: W. De Gruyter, 1987), p. 52, who made every effort he could to universalize the Book of Revelation, acknowledged that the term "earth-dwellers" (here called migrants) might even refer to the inhabitants of Palestine.

[2] B. Weiss, *"ΑΠΟΚΑΛΥΨΙΣ ΙΩΑΝΟΥ," Das Neue Testament* (Leipzig: J. C. Hinrichs, 1902), p. 459.

[3] P. S. Minear, *I Saw a New Earth* (Washington, D. C.: Corpus, c1968), pp. 79-82. For an extensive interpretation of the migrants, see commentary on Revelation 3.

CHAPTER NINE

TECHNICAL DETAILS

Rev 9 does not begin a new unit. This is a continuation of the trumpet series which began in Rev 8. It is the fifth angel to blow his trumpet which motivated the action which begins in Rev 9

TEXT

Revelation

^{9:1}The fifth angel blew its trumpet, and I saw a **star fallen from heaven**

to earth, and it was given the key to

the pit of the abyss. ²Then **smoke went up** over the pit **like the smoke of a** great **furnace**.

The sun and the air **grew dark** from the **smoke of** the pit.

³From the **smoke**

went out **locusts** into **the land**, and they were given authority the way scorpions have authority on **the land**.

⁴They were told not to injure

First Testament

^{Isa 14:12}How you have **fallen from heaven**, Day **Star**, son of Dawn. You have been cut down **to the earth**. Powerless over the gentiles.

^{Gen 19:28}[Abraham] looked over the surface of Sodom and Gomorrah and over the surface of all the land around, and he saw--Now look! The **smoke** of the land **went up like the smoke of** the **furnace**.

^{Joel 2:10}Before him the earth quakes, and heaven rumbles. **The sun and moon grow dark**, and the shining of the stars ceases.

^{Exod 19:18}Mount Sinai was all **smoke**, because Yehowah descended upon it in the fire, and **smoke went up like the smoke of a furnace**, and the whole mountain shook tremendously.

Locusts went up over all **the land** of Egypt . . . They ate everything **green of the land** and all the fruit of the trees which the hail left, so that there did not remain **anything green** in the

the grass of the land or any tree, but only	trees or in **the grass of the** field in all Egypt.
	^Exod 10:15^Yehowah said to him, "Go through in the midst of the city, in the midst of Jerusalem, and make a *tau*."
those who did not have the seal of God **on their foreheads**. ⁵[Authority] was given to them [the locusts] not to kill them [the unsealed], but to torture them for five months (Their torture was like the torture of a scorpion when it stings someone). ⁶In those days people will look **for death, but they will not** find it; they will long to die, **but death** will flee from them.	^Ezek 9:4^**on the foreheads** of those who mourn and lament over all the abominations that have occurred in its midst.

^Job 3:21^Those who hope **for death, but they will not** [die]. |

COMMENTARY

The fifth angel blew its trumpet. Rev 8:13 concluded with the line **Woe! Woe! Woe! To the migrants of the land, because of the rest of the sounds of the trumpets of the three angels who have yet to blow their trumpets** This was the first woe against the **migrants of the land.**

I saw a star fallen from heaven. If the verb is given the full force of the perfect (*pehp-toh-káw-tah*, (πεπτωκότα) the author did not envision a **star** in the process of **falling**. It had already **fallen,** and it was then established on earth.[1] In fact it had human characteristics. It could receive and use a key that "was given" to it, meaning God gave it the key that would open the pit of the abyss.

    As the **eagle flying** in the sky warned, the curse that followed was directed against the **migrants of the land** (Rev 8:13). At the outset, the commentator compared the **migrants of the land** to Babylon who had **fallen** like **a star from heaven** (Isa 14:12). Just as Isaiah personified Babylon as a **star**, so the author of this narrative seems to have identified the **star** with the **migrants of the land**. If that was not his intention,[2] he at least intended the **migrants of the land** to be victims of whatever action followed. The author of this portion of Revelation resented the special power the **migrants of the land** held. They supported Rome, and from Rome they received many kinds of special treatment not given nationalistic Jews.

---

[1] So also H. M. Hailey, *Revelation:Introduction and Commentary* (Grand Rapids: Baker's Book House, c1979), p. 225.
[2] For a list of the various identifications scholars have given to the star see L. Morris, *The Book of Revelation* (Grand Rapids: Eerdmans, c1987), p. 127.

The author, however, anticipated the time when **the migrants of the land**, like the Babylonians, would fall from their place and be left helpless.

Key to the pit of the abyss. The abyss was a place under the earth, sometimes called just "the pit" (1Enoch 18.10-11) or Tartarus (2Peter 2:4). It was a place of the dead where even angels and **stars** were punished (Jude 6; 2Pet 2:4; 1Enoch 18.14-16). The theme of the abyss occurs also in Rev 20:1-3.

Smoke went up over the pit. NA has before this clause, **Then it opened the pit of the abyss, and** NA also has **from** (*ehk,* ἐκ) rather than **over** or **upon** (*eh-peé,* ἐπί). These are probably errors of copying on the part of Sinaiticus, because the scribe also misspelled **smoke** in the following phrase, **as the smoke of a great furnace** (*kahp-neé-aws,* καπνίος instead of *kahp-náws,* καπνός).

The sun and the air grew dark from the smoke. This is a hendiadys. The expression means that the entire sky became **dark**. Sinaiticus omitted the following phrase which NA has, **from the pit and from the smoke**, which is probably correct. Sinaiticus apparently made a homeoteluton error. This happens when the same word occurs at the end of two nearby lines, and the scribe mistakes one word for the next, moving from the word for **smoke** in one phrase to the word for **smoke** in the next, omitting the words in between. The Sinaiticus text made several mistakes like this.

From the smoke went out locusts of the land. The destruction that would come upon them was going to be like that of Sodom and Gomorrah. These cities perished in the midst of a great cloud of **smoke**. There was also **smoke like a great furnace** when the Lord appeared at Mount Sinai, but the typology here more closely resembles the destruction of Sodom and Gomorrah than the revelation at Sinai. Like other trumpets, this one brought a curse. The curse consisted of **locusts,** just like the curse of **locusts** Moses and Aaron introduced to the land of Egypt. The difference is that the Egyptian locusts consumed everything green, including the fruit of every tree. The concept given here most nearly antitypes the **locusts** in Joel 2 which came like a mighty army.

They were given authority. The passive voice, as in Rev 9:1, was used to avoid the expression of the divine name. This means **God gave them authority**. This **authority** was limited. They could torture, but they were not allowed to kill. The locusts were compared with scorpions, Loisy held, because these events took place during the zodiacal month of the scorpion,[1] but that is not a necessary conclusion. People in the Near East all know about the sting of a scorpion, and that may have been the kind of torture the author had in mind.

They were told not to injure the grass of the land. The passive voice was used again here to indicate that God was the subject. NA has an additional phrase, **or anything**

---

[1] A. Loisy, *L'Apocalypse de Jean* (Paris: Emile Nourry, 1923), p. 183.

green. This might have been an omission on the part of Sinaiticus or an addition by other scribes.

Grass and vegetation are precisely the things **locusts** devour. These locusts, however, were located on the Promised Land where there were at the same time faithful Jews and also the **migrants of the land**. These **locusts** were commanded not to eat the green vegetation. Faithful believers would need that. This woe, like two others, was very discriminating; it was intended to **hurt** *only* a certain class of human beings. The **locusts** were created for one assignment only. They were directed to torture those human beings who did not have the sign of the *tau* (God's sign) upon their foreheads. These were the **migrants of the land** whom the Jews hated. By torturing these in **the land** the angel would succeed in punishing them without **hurting** their saintly Jewish neighbors. That is exactly the way the author of this narrative wanted events to take place.

Giet argued that all three woes reflected parts of the war between the Jews and Rome (66-70 IA). The first woe was inflicted by Florus who did not want to **injure** any of the natural part of the country, but only human beings.[1]

The plagues in Egypt afflicted only the Egyptians--not the Israelites. When swarms of flies irritated the Egyptians, Israelites had no flies (Exod 8:20-24). When the plague came upon the farm animals, it killed only Egyptian beasts; Israelite animals were not affected (Exod 9:1-4). The hail destroyed all of the Egyptians' crops, but it did not fall on Israelite fields (Exod 9:22-26). When **the** whole **land** of Egypt was covered with darkness for three days, the Israelites had light (Exod 10:21-23; Wis 18:1). When the angel of death killed the first born of all Egyptians, the Israelites alone were marked for safety (Exod 11:4-7). Jews and Christians have traditionally expected special treatment from the Lord.

Since God had not directed the **locusts** to kill the **migrants** he may have intended the **migrants** to leave **the land** or else become cleansed of their crimes, so that they would then repent and become converts, or they may have been forced to become converts against their will.[2] Following the pattern of the plagues of Egypt, however, it is more likely that the **migrants of the land** would be tortured by one plague after the other without repenting. When Alexander the Great conquered the East he left Greek settlements everywhere. Many of the people in these settlements were originally soldiers who took **land** Alexander gave them as payment for their military activity. This also protected Alexander's territories and helped spread Greek culture. Descendants of these were some of the **migrants** whom the Jews hated. Romans were added to these, and there continued to be some of the original Canaanites in the land. These were all people Jews wanted to evict. **The migrants** were not completely parallel to the Egyptians. Israelites lived in Egypt and wanted to get out.

---

[1] S. Giet, *L'Apocalypse et L'Histoire* (Paris: Presses Universitaires de France, 1957), p. 33.
[2] A. J. Beagley, *The "Sitz im Leben" of the Apocalypse* (Berlin: W. De Gruyter, 1987), p. 52, who argued as much as possible against any suggestion that the Book of Revelation was somehow related to anything so provincial as Palestine, acknowledged that the migrants in this context (which he called "earth-dwellers") might be inhabitants of Palestine.

Migrants lived in Palestine, and Jews wanted them to get out. The plagues helped the Israelites to leave Egypt. Jews hoped plagues would afflict the **migrants** so severely that they would voluntarily leave.

Those who do not have the seal of God on their foreheads. People in Palestine were from many origins, but from the standpoint of the Jews they were all divided into two classes:

1) Those with the sign of the beast or the sign of the dragon on their right hands and
2) those who had the **seal of God** on their foreheads.

1) Those who wore **the sign** of the beast were Romans, Greeks, and Jews who mingled with Romans and were dual loyalists whose primary loyalty was to the Romans. Josephus said the zealots treated Jews who had any associations with Rome as their enemies (War 2:264). These were the ones against whom the curses were directed. The locusts were ordered to torture the people zealots hated with stings like scorpions, which were not severe enough to kill people, but painful enough to make them wish they were dead. It is not clear why the author said this should go on for five months rather than four or six months, for instance. It is clear, however, that the author anticipated their torture with a sadistic glee. Giet thought that the **locusts** were really Roman soldiers who were torturing people at the direction of Florus.[1] That is not likely, since the **migrants of the land** were pro-Roman.

2) The other class consisted of those who had **the seal of God on their foreheads**. These were the faithful, the elect, those who bore up under persecution and remained undefiled. It was the former group against whom this curse was planned. Consistent with this position was Cyril of Jerusalem (MPG 133:816B) who wove together various Scripture passages in his exhortation to faithful Christians:

> Let us not be ashamed, therefore, to confess the crucified one. On the forehead (Ezekiel 9:4) with boldness before all, let there be a seal of the cross with the fingers, over the bread, while we eat, over the cup, while we drink, while coming in, while going out (Ps 121:8), while going to bed before sleeping, while arising, or while traveling (Deut 6:7-8).

When the day of judgment really came, the verdict was quite different from that expected by either the author of this redemption passage or the zealots in Palestine. At that time the temple was burned, and many thousands of Jews were taken captive, including those with **the seal of the *tau* on their foreheads**. Only those Jews were allowed to escape who also were Roman citizens. Some of these would have been **migrants of the land** against whom the curses were made.

---

[1] Giet, *L'Apocalypse*, p. 33.

Five months. The period **five months** seems odd. Some have called these months "five mystical months" which would become 150 years or possibly 79½ years.[1] It does not appear to refer to any earlier biblical period--not 70, 40, 7, 3, or 10--but **five months**.[2] Since this does not have any prophetic or typological significance, it might refer to an actual period in history.[3] When a scholar is searching for a solution the first place to look is not Patmos Island or any place in Asia Minor, but Jerusalem, because it was in Jerusalem where Ezekiel prophesied that those who had not been marked with the cross on their foreheads would be slaughtered.

A time when people in Jerusalem were being slaughtered was the period after Titus returned to Jerusalem in early 70 IA until the time the author wrote. From the time Titus returned until the temple burned was only a few months, probably seven or eight. Right up to the day the temple burned, there were prophets in Jerusalem who believed that they were just about to see God's miracle delivering them from the hand of the Romans. **Five months** was a period during which torture was intense, as described in this chapter. People may actually have been consoled by the torture, thinking that it was a sign that the end of the gentile age was about to come. These were surely the last days of the tribulation. Giet suggests that it refers to the term of office during which Gessius Florus ruled over the Jews from Jerusalem.[4] The **locusts** were Roman cavalry.

Another, less likely, possibility is that this **five month** period was just before the Spring of 37 BIA. Herod had left the area of conflict in Palestine to confer with Mark Anthony. He left the troops in the hands of his brother, Joseph. Joseph set out to take Jericho and its grain supplies. From the Jewish nationalistic point of view, he and his supporters were **the migrants of the land**. This army was defeated by the nationalistic saints, and King Antigonus cut off Joseph's head. Following this victory, Galileans rebelled against the pro-Roman forces in their country, and drowned the **migrants of the land** in the Sea of Galilee. The nationalists in Idumaea also revolted, providing the **migrants of the land** a great deal of difficulty for a few **months** until Herod returned and overpowered the rebels (Ant 14:439-50). This may have been the **five month** period when the **migrants of the land** were tortured but the movement was not destroyed. The "**locusts**" that tortured them were the nationalistic rebels who supported King Antigonus before Herod conquered Jerusalem and had Antigonus crucified.

Neither of these two guesses might be the right one, but it is likely that the **five months** was a period of history that made sense to the author in an area related to Jerusalem. They were not just "mythical months."

---

[1] For these and other guesses, see the list given by F. Düsterdieck, *Critical and Exegetical Handbook to the Revelation of John*, tr. H. E. Jacobs (Winona Lake: Alpha Publications, 1884), pp. 277-78.

[2] Some scholars have tried to relate the five to other usages of the number five in the Scripture: five sparrows, five yoke of oxen, two groups of five virgins, five days, five husbands, etc., but none of these seems relevant to this time period. See Morris, *Revelation*, p. 129.

[3] So also W. Hendrickson, *More than Conquerors* (Grand Rapids: Baker's Book House, 1944), p. 117.

[4] Giet, *L'Apocalypse*, p. 34.

People will look for death. Under Satan's torture Job longed to die but could not.

TEXT

Revelation

⁷**The appearance of the locusts**

was like horses

organized for war. On their heads [was something] like gold crowns, and their faces were like human faces, ⁸and they had hair like the hair of women. **Their teeth were like [the teeth of] lions**, ⁹and they had breast plates like iron breastplates. The noise of their wings was **like the sound of chariots**--of many **horses** running into battle. ¹⁰They had tails like scorpions, and the sting was also in their tails. Their authority to injure human beings was for five months. ¹¹They had their own king, the angel of the abyss. His name in Hebrew is **Abaddon** (destroyer), and in Greek his name is Apollyon (destroyer).
     One woe is past. ¹²Look! Two woes are still coming after this.

First Testament

Jer 51:27 Bring up **horses like** bristling **locusts**.

Joel 2:4-5 **Like the appearance of horses is** their [locusts'] **appearance**, and as **horses**, thus they run. **Like the sound of chariots** on the tops of mountains they leap. Like the flame of fire consuming chaff, like a fierce people **organized for war** [are the locusts].

Joel 1:6 **Its [the nation's] teeth are like the teeth of lions** and its fangs are [like the fangs] of a lioness.

Job 26:6; cf. also 28:22 Sheol is naked before God, and there is no covering for **Abaddon**.

Prov 15:11; cf. also Ps 88:12 Sheol and **Abaddon** are before Yehowah.

COMMENTARY

The appearances of the locusts was like horses. Joel described vividly either an army like a swarm of **locusts** or a swarm of **locusts** like an invading army. The characteristics of an army resemble a barbaric army, like the hordes from the north. The similarities between hoards of barbarians and swarms of **locusts** are so fitting that it is impossible to decide which was the fact and which was the analogy. That was no problem for the author of this narrative. He described a plague, like the **locusts** that cursed Egypt. Therefore he employed the vivid imagery of Joel to authenticate his prediction. **The locusts** were not ends in themselves. They were only a means for the author to describe the severe torture to be afflicted against his enemies--the Romans in Palestine and their sympathizers.

They had their own king. NA has **They have** over them **a king**--(*ehp ow-tóhn*, (ἐπ αὐτῶν) instead of *heh ow-tóhn* (ἑαυτῶν). This is an easy confusion, either from reading or from listening. The tense changes with Rev 9:11 from past to present. This may have come from merging two texts or from a later expansion. The English translation maintains the past tense for ease of reading.

The angel of the abyss. Consistent with the accusation that these **locusts** come from the pit and **the abyss** is the claim that they have a king who is **the angel of the abyss**. Abaddon in FT is associated with Sheol and death (Prov 15:11; Job 26:6; 28:22; 31;12). It is his Greek name that is important. It sounds like Apollo, the great god of the Romans. This contradicts Prov 30:17 that says locusts have no king. Although the eagle announced that the next three woes were directed to those who were not marked with the seal of God on their forehead, the next two woes are not specifically directed to that group. Perhaps that is understood.

One woe is past. NA has definite articles here: **the one**. This is the first woe directed at the migrants. Two more will follow.

TEXT

Revelation

¹³The sixth angel blew its trumpet, and I heard a voice from the four horns of the golden altar which was before God, ¹⁴saying to the sixth angel, who had the trumpet, "Release the four angels which are tied at **the great River Euphrates**."
¹⁵Then the four angels [who] were prepared for the hour, month, and year were released so that they could kill **the third** of the people. ¹⁶The number of the cavalry was two hundred million. I heard their number [mentioned]. ¹⁷Thus I saw the horses in the vision and the men riding on them,

First Testament

Gen 15:18; Deut 1:7; Josh 1:4 To your children I will give this land, from the river of Egypt to **the Great River, the River Euphrates**.

Zech 13:8-9 "It will happen in all the land," said Yehowah, "two thirds will be cut off and perish, **the third** will be left in it. I will bring **the third** into the fire, and I will refine them as silver is refined; I will test them as gold is tested."

having breast plates of fiery red, hyacinth, and sulfuric color. The heads of the horses were like lions' heads, and from their mouths went out fire, smoke, and sulfur. ¹⁸From these three plagues were killed **the third** of the human beings from the fire, smoke, and sulphur which went out from their mouths. ¹⁹For the authority of the horses was in their mouths and in their tails. For their tails are like serpents having heads, and they injured [people] with them.

COMMENTARY

The sixth angel blew its trumpet. **The sixth angel** announced the second woe against **the migrants**. Giet held that the second woe was the expedition of Cestius who settled his troups on the Mount of Olives to attack Jerusalem. He later retreated through the Beth-horon canyon under attack by the Jews from whom he suffered a terrible loss.[1]

A voice from the golden altar. NA has "**a voice from** one of the four horns of **the altar**." One scribe (Sinaiticus) might have omitted the detail, or another scribe might have added it.

The four angels which are tied at the great river Euphrates. The **angels tied at the Euphrates River** were left there at the beginning of Rev 7. They were standing at the four corners of the land to hold back the winds until all of the righteous ones were sealed with the mark **of God on their foreheads** (Rev 7:1-4). The fact that these **angels** are located **at the Euphrates River**, which was believed by scriptural scribes to be the **Great River,** further confirms the position that the author, when writing Rev 7 intended the four corners to be **the four corners of the land** rather than the four corners of the earth. **The Great River** has been identified as *Nahar il Kebir*, the river on the northern border of Lebanon. *Nahar il Kebir* in Arabic means **the Great River.** Some later scribe, who thought the Euphrates River was the only river big enough to deserve that name, added **the River Euphrates** to the texts of Gen 15:18; Deut 1:7; Josh 1:4--all of which were initially intended to give the boundaries of the Promised Land.[2]

---

[1] Giet, *L'Apocalypse*, p. 34.
[2] Buchanan, *The Consequences of the Covenant* (Leiden: E. J. Brill, 1970), pp. 91-109. Düsterdieck, *Handbook*, p. 287, disagreed. He said, "That the Euphrates is the boundary of the land of Abraham and David, is to be urged here as little as that it was the boundary of the Roman Empire; the only matter of consequence is, that from the Euphrates formerly 'the scourges of god' proceeded."

The scribal additions to the scriptural texts had all been made long before the Book of Revelation was written, so the author of this document assumed that **the River Euphrates** was the scriptural validation of the northern boundary of the Promised Land. This means the location of **the river Euphrates** and the northeast corner are the same. In Rev 7 the number was given of the ones sealed. That was 144,000.

Romans were apprehensive about the territory around **the Euphrates.** There had frequently been wars with the Parthians in that area. In 53 BIA the Roman general Crassus was killed and his entire army perished in a battle against the Parthians near **the Euphrates** (Ant 14:119; War 1:179). The troops of the Roman general Paetus were slaughtered near **the Euphrates** in 62 IA (Tacitus, *Annals* 15:7-12; see further commentary on Rev 16).

For the hour, month, and year. NA has, **The four angels *who* were prepared for the hour, *day*, month, and year**. The relative pronoun is necessary to make sense of the sentence, so the mistake was probably that of the Sinaiticus scribe. He may also have omitted the word **day**, but, on the other hand, some other scribe might have added that word.

The number of the cavalry was two hundred million. Literally this is two myriads of myriads. A myriad is ten thousand. $2 \times 10,000 \times 10,000 = 200,000,000$. This would have been a tremendous military force. There has never been an cavalry as large as this! The Parthian king Vologenses offered to support Vespasian's revolt against Vitellius by sending 40,000 horses and riders into battle in his behalf (Tacitus, *Hist* 4:51). This was a magnanimous offer, but it was far short of 200,000,000. Zahn thought, however, that the author knew of this offer and that it inspired the huge number in the cavalry.[1] The expectation that the Parthians would come to the aid of the Jews in Jerusalem during the civil war in Rome (Rev 16), however, indicates that the author of Rev 16 was not aware of Vespasian's treaty with the Parthians before he left Palestine.

Here the number is given of the number of the cavalry sent out to kill *the* third of the people. This probably does not mean *the* third of the whole human race, because they were only to kill the ones who worshiped demons and idols (Rev 9:20). The cavalry was stationed at the border of the Promised Land, at **the Euphrates River.** Its purpose was to remove the criminals and cleanse **the land** before the kingdom could be restored. These were the antitypes of the slaughterers in Ezek 9 who were appointed to kill all the people of the holy city who were criminals. The righteous ones were first marked on their forehead with an X so that they could be preserved. The antitype of these righteous in the Book of Revelation was made up of the 144,000 celibate followers of the Lamb (Rev 14:4). That group was localized to the city of Jerusalem. After the cavalry had killed *the* third, namely the wicked ones of Palestine, then the two thirds who would survive would all be followers of the

---

[1] T. Zahn, *Die Offenbarung des Johannes* (Leipzig: A. Deichert, 1924), p. 408.

Lamb. Only *the* third of the population in Palestine would have been idol worshipers on the Promised Land. But if the cavalry was assigned to kill all the idol worshipers of the whole world outside of Palestine, that would constitute three thirds.

The cavalry was under the control, not of Satan, as Weiss supposed,[1] but of the Lord, just as the Lord appointed the slaughterers in Ezek 9. *The* third that was scheduled for destruction was made up of the theological equivalents of **the migrants of the land** and those of every nation, tribe, language, and people who were warned by the angel to fear God and give him glory (Rev 14:6-8). Both the **horses** and riders were monstrous creatures with specially designed qualities of destruction. These had been restrained for this very predestined hour when their destructive activity would begin.

The Third. The reader would normally expect the author to have referred to the group as **a third**, as over against the remaining two-**thirds**, but the author wanted the reader to realize that he understood this predestined group was related to ***the* third** (*hah sheh-lee-sheét*, הַשְּׁלִישִׁית = *taw treé-tawn*, τὸ τρίτον) prophesied in Zechariah, so he used exactly the same expression. In Zechariah, *the* third was the surviving remnant. Here the author was more generous. The decree went out that only *the* third would be killed, whereas the two thirds of the population would survive (see 1Chron 21:7-17).

TEXT

Revelation	First Testament
	Isa 2:7-8; 17:8 [The foreigner's] land is filled with **silver and gold**, and there is no end to his treasures . . . his land is filled with **idols,**
[20] The rest of the people, those who had not been killed by these plagues, and had not repented of **the works of their hands** so that they might not **worship** the demons, and the	**the work of his hands,** **he worships** that which his fingers have made.
	Deut 31:29 I know that after my death . . . you will do evil in the eyes of Yehowah, to make him angry with **the work of your hands**.
gold silver, brass, and stone idols	Dan 5:4 [Belshazzar and his party] drank wine and praised the gods of **gold, silver, bronze,** iron, wood, **and stone**

---

[1] B. Weiss, "ΑΠΟΚΑΛΥΨΙΣ ΙΩΑΝΟΥ" *Das Neue Testament* (Leipzig: J. C. Hinrichs, 1902), p. 463.

	Ps 115:4 Their idols are **silver and gold, the work of** human **hands**.
	Dan 5:23 You have praised the gods of **silver, gold, bronze**, iron, wood, **and stone which neither see nor hear**.
which do not see, hear,	
	Ps 115:5-7 They have eyes but **do not see**; they have ears but do not **hear**; they have noses but do not smell; they have hands but do not feel; they have feet but do **not walk**.
nor walk, ²¹nor did they repent of their murders, their	
sorceries, their **sexual indecencies** nor from their thievery.	2Kings 9:22 When Joram saw Jehu, he said, "Is it peace, Jehu?" [Jehu] said, "What peace is there as long as the **sexual indecencies** and **sorceries** of your mother, Jezebel, are many?"

COMMENTARY

The rest of the people. The author did not say here what happened or would happen to these wicked people, but he alluded to those FT passages which told of other similarly wicked people who were killed or their empires destroyed for such behavior. Therefore he implied that something like that would happen to these.

Had not repented of the works of their hands. **The works of** human **hands** refer to idols which people worshipped. The references come both from Isaiah's condemnation of foreign influences and Daniel's criticism of the gods of various kinds of material which Belshazzar praised while he and his guests were drinking wine from the vessels taken by Nebuchadnezzar from the temple in Jerusalem. This was followed immediately by the handwriting on the wall which predicted the downfall of his empire.

The gold, silver, brass, and stone idols. NA has also **and wood.** Since Daniel has all of these plus "and iron," none of the scribes copied exactly from that document. One left out both iron and wood, whereas the other omitted only wood.

Their murders, their sorceries, their sexual indecencies. **The sorceries and sexual indecencies** allude to the activities of Jezebel just before Jehu came and overthrew Jezebel and Ahab. **Sorceries** described a type of magic and use of drugs. All religious liturgies that were not Jewish or Christian were held to be **sorceries**.

Schüssler-Fiorenza, like others who read the Book of Revelation sensitively, thought the cruelty of the anticipation was shocking. Therefore, she thought the text must be interpreted in such a way that it would not seem evil. She said it would be disastrous

> to understand Revelation as an accurate description of what has already happened in the time of John or as an elaborate prediction of events which will actually happen in the eschatological future.[1]

She evidently assumed that the author (she thought there was only one) of the Book of Revelation was infallible. That which he anticipated would have to happen. Therefore, in her opinion, it is necessary to interpret the text in such a way that it loses all of the obvious hatred included in the text. A better approach is to admit that our religious ancestors were imperfect and sometimes held evil thoughts which we should not emulate or confuse with God's will. For example, Jeremiah prophesied more than 20 events that never happened. Nevertheless he was called the great prophet, because the one event that was very important, namely the fall of Jerusalem, which he prophesied actually happened. Eighth century BIA Isaiah prophesied that Media would destroy Babylon. It never happened.

After the sixth **trumpet** had been sounded (Rev 9), one would normally expect Rev 10 to begin with **the seventh trumpet,** but it did not. **The seventh trumpet** was blown in Rev 11:7, but the results of the woe began with Rev 12. This suggests that Rev 10 and 11 were inserted into a complete document between Rev 9 and 12. Giet thought that the third woe was the completion of the war by Vespasian and Titus, beginning in the Spring of 67 IA and completed in August, 70 IA.[2] Giet was probably correct in relating these woes to the situation in Palestine during the seventh decade, but he ignored the fact that the woes were directed against the **migrants of the land**, rather than the saints of Jerusalem (Rev 8:13; 11:10).

---

[1] E. Schüssler-Fiorenza, *Revelation: Vision of a Just World* (Minneapolis: Fortress, c1991), p. 72.
[2] Giet, *L'Apocalypse*, pp. 36-37.

CHAPTER TEN

TECHNICAL DETAILS

The narrative containing the seven angels who blew trumpets that introduced curses continued through Rev 9, concluding with the sixth angel. Then the seventh angel did not arrive on the scene until Rev 11:15. Weiss, like many other scholars, thought some editor took an earlier source and inserted it into the narrative between the sixth and seventh angel. All of Rev 10 would have belonged to that earlier source.[1] Bergmeier attempted to conjecture that source on the basis of Rev 5 and Rev 10.[2] Many scholars have suggested parallels between these two chapters. There are enough similarities in theme and wording to evoke conjectures regarding their relationships, but it is difficult to know if any of the conjectures is correct.

TEXT

Revelation	First Testament
[10:1]I saw another strong angel coming down from heaven, wearing a **cloud**, and the hair was upon his head. His face was **like the sun**,	[Judges 5:31]So may all of your enemies perish, Yehowah, but let your friends be **like the sun** as it rises in its power.
	[Ps 18:11-12][Yehowah] rode on a cherub; he flew; he moved on the wings of the wind. He set darkness and concealed it around him. His roof is watery darkness, **clouds** of heaven.
and **his legs were like**	[Dan 10:6]**His legs were like** brass burnished in a fiery furnace.
	[Exod 13:21]Yehowah went before them during the day in a pillar of cloud and during the night in a **pillar of fire**.
pillars of fire.	
[2]He had in his **hand**	[Ezek 2:9]Now look! **A hand** reached out

---

[1] J. Weiss, *Die Offenbarung des Johannes* (Göttingen: Vandenhoeck & Ruprecht, 1908), p. 642.
[2] R. Bergmeier, "Die Buchrolle und das Lamm (Apk 5 und 10)," *ZNW* 76 (1985):225-42. This conjecture is thought-provoking, but difficult to judge.

a scroll, opened. He placed his right foot on the sea and his left foot on the land. ³He cried out in a voice as loud as a lion **roars**, ⁴and when he cried out, the seven thunders made their own noises.

When the seven **thunders** spoke I was about to write, and I heard a voice from heaven saying, "**Seal** that which the seven **thunders** spoke, and do not write them."

to me, and in it was **a** literary **scroll**.

ᴶᵉʳ ²⁵:³⁰The Lord will **roar** from on high; from his holy place he will put forth his voice.

ᴾˢ ²⁹:³The voice of Yehowah is over the water; the God of glory **thundered**, Yehowah, over much water.

ᴰᵃⁿ ¹²:⁴Close the words, and **seal** the scroll until the time of the end.

ᴰᵃⁿ ¹²:⁹For the words are closed and **sealed** until the time of the end.

COMMENTARY

Another strong angel. The only **other strong angel** mentioned earlier is that in Rev 5:2. There are other links between Rev 5 and 10.

Wearing a cloud. This is phantasmagoric speech. The same is true of the expressions **face like the sun** and **legs like pillars of fire.** Garments in Semitic thought form had important symbolic significance. A defendant in court was expected to come with his or her hair uncombed, wearing black, shabby clothing, as if he or she were in mourning. This was to earn the pity of the judge. When given a verdict of innocence, the judge ordered that the clothing be changed (Zech 3). Roman senators sometimes left the senate, went home and changed clothes before certain actions were taken in the senate. **Wearing** white clothing indicated innocence, purity, or holiness, so priests **wore** white. New converts were dressed in white after they had been baptized. The Lord was clothed in white for the same reason (Dan 7). The cloud symbolized the presence of God and was associated with the revelation at Sinai, the crossing of the sea, and the Mount of Transfiguration. In the famous judgment scene in Dan 7 the Son of man appeared in a cloud as he approached the bench as the victorious plaintiff in the court trial. The cloud was brought into the story to show that this was a divine judgment. God was present, and the conclusion of the trial was of extensive significance.

The hair was upon his head. This is not phantasmagoric, but it is probably mistaken. NA has instead the words, **a rainbow**, as that which was **upon** or over **his head**. The mistake was probably made from hearing. In Greek the words **the hair** (*hay threex*, (ἡ θρίξ) sound very much like "rainbow" (*ee-reess*, Ἶρις). In this exaggerated context, indicating the presence of God, and associate with clouds, a rainbow is much more appropriate than **the hair**, which anyone might expect on someone's head.

Like the sun. Here the angel who wore the **cloud** was like the angel who led the Israelites through the body of water at the eastern border of Egypt. It had the same significance as **the sun** disk shown in many military victory processions just ahead of the king in Near Eastern art and sculpture. **The sun** was the symbol of the deity, leading the army into battle and home from the war. The victory of Barak and Deborah over Sisera concluded with the lines: **Thus may all your enemies perish, Lord, but your friends be like the sun [disk], rising in its power** (Judges 5:31).

His legs were like pillars of fire. The Greek rendered **legs** here is *pó-dehs*, (πόδες)) which literally means feet, but the Hebrew translated was probably *ráy-gehl* (רגל) which can mean either foot or **leg**. The context requires the meaning **legs**, because feet do not look like **pillars**. This angel was described according to scriptural allusions. His **legs** were to remind the reader of the arms and **legs** of the phantasmagoric "man" described in Dan 10, whom Daniel saw in a vision.[1] This visionary man assured Daniel that he was in control of international events and was fighting against Daniel's enemies. He knew what was going to happen in the future. The **pillars of fire** were intended to remind the reader of the Exodus and the **pillar of fire** by night which led the Israelites through the sea to safety and victory.

A scroll. The **scroll** (*beeb-lah-reé-dee-awn*, (βιβλαρίδιον) is a diminutive form of the simple *beéb-laws* βίβλος, but Mazzaferri correctly observed that words that are diminutive in form are not always diminutive in force. He argued that in its four occurrences, the word used in Revelation is not really diminutive. It is simply a **scroll** that is opened.[2] The question here is, "What is the significance of the **scroll**?" Since the allusion to the **legs** referred to Dan 10, it is likely that there is a clue here to its importance. The visionary man in Dan 10 first comforted Daniel and assured him that he was in charge. Then he said,

> I will tell you what is written in the scroll of truth: there is no one who fights against these [enemy countries] except your prince, Michael (Dan 10:21).

---

[1] D. E. Aune, *Revelation 6-16* (Nashville: Thomas Nelson Publishers, 1998), p. 556, has made a thought-provoking suggestion that this image was motivated by the Colossos of Rhodes. His suggestion would have still more credence if the author of this document were not so much biblically oriented and dependent on the Book of Daniel.

[2] F. D. Mazzaferri, *The Genre of the Book of Revelation from a Source-critical Perspective* (Berlin; W. De Gruyter, 1989), pp. 267-69.

The **scroll** of truth seems to have contained the predestined order of future events and the important participants. When the strong angel of Rev 10 held in his hand an opened **scroll**, it was probably intended to be the antitype of the **scroll** of truth in Dan 7, a point overlooked by scholars in general.[1]

Many scholars have argued either for or against the theory that the call narrative in Rev 10 is a variant of the call narrative in Rev 1, since both involve eating a **scroll**. Collins argued that John was commissioned twice, once according to the report in Rev 1 and again in Rev 10.[2] She reached this conclusion because she presumed that John of Patmos wrote the entire document. Rev 1 is part of John's composition; Rev 10 is a part of the prophecy the messenger brought to him. It was composed by someone else and even edited later by someone who put together many units to make the unit, Rev 4:1-22:5. Without realizing this she examined the data with erroneous assumptions. Like most authors, Mazzaferri thought his own judgment that the two **scrolls** are identical was a "rather more cogent explanation."[3] Like Collins, Mazzaferri also assumed that John wrote the entire document. Vogelgesang thought Rev 1, 4-5, and 10 should be seen as one unit.[4] Many of the themes in one also appeared in one or more of the others. Bergmeier conjectured a source behind both narratives, organizing the two chapters in a supposed original order.[5]

The theme of the **scroll** was important to redemption hopes. So was the prophecy of Ezekiel upon which all of these depended. In Revelation the scroll usually symbolized the contract and was part of the typology necessary for the restoration of the Promised Land and the Davidic kingdom. John probably wrote Rev 1. Different other people probably wrote the other chapters. If they had all been composed into one document by one author, as Vogelgesang suggested, much of the repetition might have been omitted. Rev 10 includes a commission of the seer, an event which Vogelgesang thought should have been structured into Rev 4 and 5.[6] The probable reason is that the editor who organized these units did not compose them. He received Rev 4 and 5 either as one complete unit or two units, which he put together. Vogelgesang is correct in thinking a commissioning ceremony should appear at the beginning of a prophecy, rather than near the middle. At one time Rev 10 might have been the beginning of a prophecy. In this prophetic collection, however, the editor chose to open the collection with a different introductory

---

[1] For example, J. Moffatt, *The Revelation of St. John the Divine* (Grand Rapids:, c1979), pp. 411-14; R. H. Mounce, *The Book of Revelation* (Grand Rapids: Eerdmans, c1977), pp. 208-214; F. Düsterdieck, *Critical and Exegetical Handbook to the Revelation of John* (Winona Lake: Alpha Publications, c1883, 1979), pp. 298-306; J. M. Ford, *Revelation* (Garden City: Doubleday & Co., 1975), pp. 162-66; Mazzaferri, *Genre*, pp. 267-69; *et al.*.
[2] A. Y. Collins, *The Combat Myth in the Book of Revelation* (Missoula: Scholars Press, 1976), pp. 19-21.
[3] Mazzaferri, *Genre*, p. 355.
[4] J. M. Vogelgesang, *The Interpretation of Ezekiel in the Book of Revelation* (Ann Arbor: University Microfilms, 1986), pp. 387-88.
[5] Bergmeier, "Buchrolle," pp. 225-42.
[6] Vogelgesang, *Interpretation*, p. 325.

chapter, namely Rev 4, with the heavens opening.[1] Repetitions and imperfections like these are characteristic of anthologies. Peculiarities such as these enable us to recognize the composite character of the Book of Revelation.

His right foot on the sea and his left [foot] on the land. This may mean that he took possession of both. **The land** and **sea** visualized was probably **the land** of Palestine and the Mediterranean **Sea**--not one on the shore of Asia Minor and the other on an island, as Loisy thought.[2] This image may have been intended to allude to the two men who stood on opposite sides of a stream, and the one who was clothed in white who stood above the stream. There was no foot in the stream, but there are some associate words in the concept. The one clothed in white took an oath that the time of the wonders would continue for 3½ years (Dan 12:5-7).

As loud as a lion roars. In the First Testament (FT) God was heard speaking with the thunder (Exod 19:19; 1Sam 7:10; Job 37:2, 5; 40:9; Ps 18:13; 29:3; 68:33; 103:7; Isa 3:30; Jer 10:13; Amos 1:2). God was not expected to speak quietly.

Seal that which the seven thunders spoke. NA has, **the things which**, rather than **that which**. The angel simply cried out; the thunders spoke, but the reader never learned what they said. The fact that the messenger knows more than it was allowed or willing to tell, however, added to its credibility. Ancient peoples believed that every bolt of lightning, every rumble of thunder, was an expression of the deity. God was speaking, grumbling, complaining, or acting out his anger in violence. In Greek tradition thunder was thought to be Zeus' positive answer to prayer (Iliad 2:353; 9:236; Odyessey 20:101-104). That concept probably arose because needed rain often followed the thunder. Near Easterners more often thought of God preparing for violence.

Ps 29 visualized the Lord sitting on his bench, holding court. His bench was located over the flood (Ps 29:10) provided by the spring of Siloam that gushed water through the tunnel that connected the shaft from the spring to the temple level of the City of David, roaring under the temple threshold.[3] When he pronounced a verdict, peoples of the earth heard the thunder. In Dan 12:4, 9 the warning was given to seal the vision and not to disclose it until the end of this period took place. That would be in 3½ years. The author of this redemption narrative wanted to disclose the same message. The angel was dramatized in cosmic terms in a phantasmagoric fashion. The scroll contained the message which prompted the angel to give the author the instructions he did. The scroll in the angel's hand probably contained the contract that believers were hoping to reestablish with God.

---

[1] The commissioning of John in Rev 1 is a separate event, different from the commissioning of the prophet or seer in Rev 10. One belongs to the prophecy and the other to the letter.
[22] A. Loisy, *L'Apocalypse de Jean* (Paris: Emile Nourry, 1923), p. 196.
[3] Buchanan, "The Area of the Temple at Zion," *ET* 116.6 (2005):181-189.

TEXT

Revelation	First Testament
⁵The angel which **I saw standing on** the sea and on the land,	Dan 12:7; Deut 32:40 **Then I, Daniel, watched**. Now look! two others **stood**, one **on** one bank of the stream and one on the other. I said to the man dressed in linen who was above the water of the stream, "How long until the mysteries end?" I heard the man dressed in linen who was above the water of the stream,
raised his right hand to heaven ⁶**and swore by the** One who lives **into the ages**,	and **he raised his right hand** and his left hand **to heaven and swore by the life of the age** that [it would be] for a time, two times, and half a time.
who made heaven and the things in it, **earth and the things in** it, that there will be no more time [to wait].	Exod 20:11 **For in six days Yehowah made heaven, earth, and the sea and** all **the things that are in** them.

COMMENTARY

The angel which I saw standing on the sea and on the land. The one who brought a message to Daniel, telling him all the events that were predestined to occur between the fall of Jerusalem in 586 BIA and the Maccabean revolt, promised that his people would escape--those whose names were written in the scroll. He stood over the waters of the stream, and there were two men standing, one on one bank of the stream and the other, on the other. When asked how long it would be until these events would be finished, he took an oath by the one who lives into the age that the end would come in 3½ years (Dan 10:10-12:7).

During those 3½ years were the decisive battles of the Maccabean Revolt which concluded with the end of the gentile rule over Palestine until the time of Pompey (63 BIA). When given the same question, the author of Rev 10 provided a briefer period. He made the angel swear that this 3½ year period was over. There would be no more time to wait until the new age began.

Swore by the one who lives into the age. At his farewell speech Moses reportedly quoted God as raising his hand to heaven and **swearing** by his life that he would both punish his enemies and avenge his servants (Deut 33:40). Inspired by this event, the author of Daniel pictured the man dressed in linen raising both hands to heaven and **swearing by the life of the age** that the one who caused all of their suffering would be finished in 3½ years (Dan 12:7). Each oath was taken while the oath taker raised his right hand. The same is true of this angel in Rev 10:5. This practice is still followed in American courts before *sworn* testimony is accepted. Some oaths were taken **by the Life of Yehowah** (Judges 8:19). The author of Rev 10:5 had Daniel as his closest point of reference, and he anticipated that God would avenge the enemies of the Jews, and he would not waste any time getting it done. The 3½ years spoken by Daniel was already completed.

Who created . . . the earth and things in it. NA has additionally **the sea and the things in it.** Both readings were euphemisms for **by the life of Yehowah** (Judges 8:19). Oaths were taken in the name of something stable and unchangeable, heaven, earth, the sea. Sometimes these were called upon as witnesses in an oath swearing context. In this case the oath was taken—not by **heaven, earth, and sea,** but–by the one **who created** all of these. Sometimes only a pile of stones acted as witnesses. Usually oaths were taken in the name of something sacred, such as the altar, Jerusalem, the gift on the altar (Matt 5:35). Usually an oath ceremony went like this: 1) The name of the deity or sacred object, 2) the curses accepted and requested the deity to enforce, 3) **if** . . . the oath taker either did or did not do that which he or she claimed or **if** that which the oath-taker said were not true.

There will be no more time [to wait]. Many scholars have used this verse to justify their belief that the author was expecting the end of history, the world, or the cosmos.[1] Morris was correct in holding that this meant that there would **be no more delay**.[2] Hailey correctly reasoned that time could not be over, because the author had other things to happen after it was finished. He said,

> Therefore, what was to be without delay was something other than the end of time; thus, it must have been the completion of the mystery.[3]

Rissi said,

> It cannot therefore be a question of the suspension of time. If the beginning of a timeless eternity were really expected here, the article would certainly have been used also (*ho chronos*). The expression is best taken, with Behm, to mean "period of delay."[4]

---

[1] Such as C. H. Giblin, *The Book of Revelation* (Collegeville: The Liturgical Press, c1991), p. 105, who renders this passage, "There is no longer (ongoing) time."
[2] L. Morris, *The Book of Revelation* (Grand Rapids: Eerdmans, c1987), p. 140.
[3] H. M. Hailey, *Revelation: Introduction and Commentary* (Grand Rapids: Baker's Book House, 1979), p. 245.
[4] M. Rissi, *Time and History* (Richmond: John Knox Press, 1965), p. 24.

He rightly concluded,

> The concept of an existence outside of time is totally foreign to the Revelation [as it is in the FT, and primitive Christianity].[1]

The meaning is the same as that in Mark 1:15, **The time is fulfilled**, meaning that the predestined **time** for waiting is over. Therefore, **The Kingdom of God is near** (Mark 1:15). When the question was raised in Dan 12:6: **How long will it be before the end of these mysteries?** the answer given there was, **A time, two times, and half a time** (Dan 12:7), or **Three and a half years.** The 3½ year period "prophesied" by Daniel was finished by 164 BIA, and the mysterious events were the things that happened during the Maccabean Rebellion. In the antitype of those events in **the time** of the author of Rev 10:6 the 3½ year period was also over. The angel already had the scroll containing the new contract in his hand, and it was opened--unsealed. The seals had all been broken or they never existed. The scroll was ready to be made effective. The predestined time of tribulation (3½ years) had been fulfilled; there was **no** longer any **time** to wait.

This could not have been the same unit of literature in which the seals were broken in Rev 8-9, because the seventh seal of that contract had not yet been broken. It was to be broken in Rev 11. This incident did not mention seals Nevertheless, both units of literature were written about the expectation of the same contract.

Johnson was correct in relating the phrase, **no more time [to wait],** to sabbatical eschatology, and he was further correct in calling attention to 2Enoch 33:1-2. In that passage God told Enoch that there would be 7,000 years, then the 8,000th would be one in which **time** would not be counted.

The reference in Enoch, however, is not to unending **time,** as Johnson thought, but to the structure of the old Pentacontad calendar, which was based entirely on Sabbaths.[2] There were seven days to a week, and seven weeks to a Pentacontad. The fiftieth day, however, did not count. The fiftieth day was a Pentacontad, and there were seven of these each year. On each of those days, the community celebrated, but Pentecost was not one of the seven days of the week. The

---

[1] Rissi, *Time*, p. 33.

[2] R. Johnson, "The Eschatological Sabbath in John's Apocalypse: A Reconsideration," *AUSS* 25 (1987):44-45. Johnson "supported" his argument innocently enough by following W. G. Braude's translation of *The Midrash on Psalms 2* (New Haven: Yale U. Press, 1959), pp. 110-111. The word Braude rendered "worlds" was *oh-lah-meém*, (עולמים), which very seldom has a spacial meaning. Here the context requires that it be rendered "ages." The Lord did not create seven worlds; he created seven days of the week, seven years of a week of years, and he created seven ages. The seventh day was a day of rest for Israel, the seventh year was a year of release, and the seventh age was "the age to come," which was an age or a millennium of rest for Israel. This age of rest was called "life of the age" (*khai hah oh-láhm*, חי העולם) does not mean "life eternal" but life of the age [to come]. See further Buchanan, *The Consequences of the Covenant* (Leiden: Brill, 1970), pp. 12-18, and *Jesus: the King and his Kingdom* (Macon: Mercer U. Press, 1978), *passim* (see index). For Israel, an age of rest was an age when Jews had control of the Promised Land under the leadership of their own messiah.

day before the Pentecost was the seventh day of the week, and the day after the Pentecost was the first day of the week. There was no eighth. The same was true of a Jubilee year. The year before was the seventh year (49th); the fiftieth was a Jubilee; and the next year was the first year of the following week of years. At the end of seven Pentacontads the year reached its end, but that was only 350 days, and there were still 15 or 16 days before the new year began. These were days of unleavened bread which did not count either as part of the old year or as part of the new year.

After the 49 years were over, there would be **no more time** to wait for the Jubilee, and that is the point the author of Rev 10:6 had in mind. The context shows that the author thought it was the years of waiting that was finished.[1] That period of time would come to an end--not time in general. When the seventh angel blew the trumpet, that put an end to the **mystery** so far as the chosen people were concerned.

The **mystery** of God (Rev 10:6) was the typological equivalent of **the mysteries** of Dan 12:7. For Daniel **the mysteries** were over when Antiochus Epiphanes was dead, the Battle of Beth-horon was won, and the temple was cleansed. In Rev 10:6, the **mystery of God** was finished, and then the scroll was unrolled, and those who had the seal of the *tau* on their foreheads realized that this Roman age would be over in 3½ years. A medieval midrash, attributed to Rabbi Akiba, also pictured seven angels blowing trumpets. When the seventh angel blew its trumpet the righteous would rise up alive and stand on their feet, fully clothed, in the land of Israel (Beth Ha-midrash 3, pp. 31-32).

TEXT

Revelation

First Testament and Other Jewish Literature

⁷But in the days of the voice of the seventh angel when he was about to blow the trumpet, the **mystery of God** had been completed, as he announced the good news [to]
his own servants and **the prophets**.

Amos 3:7 For the Lord Yehowah will not do a thing without revealing **his mystery**

to **his servants, the prophets**.

Dan 2:28 There is a God in heaven who reveals **mysteries**, and he makes known to King Nebuchadnezzar what will happen in the future.

Dan 12:7; Deut 32:40 I said to the man

---

[1] For an analysis of the significance of Jubilee reckoning for Second Baruch and Fourth Ezra see E. Lupieri, "The Seventh Night-Vision of History in the Revelation of John and the Contemporary Apocalyptic," *Henoch* 14 (1992):113-32.

dressed in linen who was above the water of the stream, "How long until **the mysteries** end?" I heard the man dressed in linen who was above the water of the stream, and he raised his right hand and his left hand to heaven and swore by the life of the age that [it would be] for a time, two times, and half a time.

We have not listened to the voice of Yehowah our God, to walk in his Torah which he has given us in the hand of **his servants, the prophets** (Dan 9:10).

^{1QS1:3}[God] commanded through the hand of Moses and through the hand of all **his servants the prophets** to love all that which he has chosen and to hate all that which he has rejected.

^{1QHab2:7-10}When they hear all the things that are coming against the last generation from the mouth of the priest whom God has provided in the midst of the community to interpret all the words of **his servants the prophets** through whose hands God has told all the things that are coming against his people and his land.

COMMENTARY

The mystery of God had been completed. This was **the mystery** which God kept from the world, but which **he revealed to his servants the prophets** (Amos 3:7). The author of the Habakkuk Commentary thought it was the priest to whom God assigned the responsibility of interpreting the words of **the prophets**. He was the one who could determine from the Scripture what things were going to take place in relationship to the Israelites and the Promised Land during the last generation of the captivity before the land would be restored and Jews would be liberated from foreign rule. This was **the mystery** of which the author of this Revelation chapter was concerned.

The mystery in Daniel was also that which would happen in the future, **at the end of the days** (*buh-ah-khah-reét yoh-máh-yah*, באחרית ימיא) (Dan 2:28), at the end of the 3½ year period of conflict. Daniel was the one of God's **servants, the prophets**, who demanded the most attention of later interpreters who calculated their own times in relationship to the Scripture. Daniel reported the 3½ years that had passed from the time Antiochus IV defiled the temple until Judas had it cleansed and dedicated. As an antitype, 3½ years also transpired from the outbreak of the Jewish Roman war in 66 IA to the time when the temple burned in 70 IA.

He announced the good news. NA has **his servants, the prophets**, identifying the **servants** as **prophets**. This is the combination in Amos, Daniel, and the Dead Sea Scrolls, and the reading expected, especially since it is associated with the word **mystery**. If, however, the original reading had included the conjunction, a later scribe might easily have corrected it to conform to the FT.

Ancient Jews and Christians thought that God spoke to them through thunder and lightning and also through the Scriptures, but they were not always sure what he meant in either. They depended, therefore on **instructors** (*mahs-kee-leém*, משכלים) to interpret them (Dan 12:3). These were **the prophets** and priestly teachers of righteousness who could interpret the Scriptures and tell how they applied to their own days (1QHab 7:1-5). Caird mistakenly said, that John nowhere uses the word **prophet** except to denote the Christian martyr.[1] Caird repeatedly made this claim but never demonstrated it. It is probably a distortion of the text.

The expectation of the author was all bad news for the Romans, but it was **good news** for the believers. It is possible that the period during which the author wrote was at the end of the Jewish war of 66-70 IA with the Romans. Jews had been fighting the Romans for **a time, two times, and half a time**. That should be the extent of time necessary to pass between the time when the war broke out until the temple would be cleansed. This is the way it was with the war between the Greeks and the Hasmoneans. If this passage was written at the same time as Rev 9, they both may have been composed in 70 IA--5 months after Titus returned with Roman troops, and the Jews in Jerusalem had been tortured as the description was given here. The author of Rev 10 may have been one of **the prophets** of which Josephus spoke who assured the inhabitants of Jerusalem that the new age was just about to begin (War 6:285-87). The importance of the quotation from Amos was to justify by text the author's conviction that the message given was from heaven and directed to his chosen people. **The prophets** were the legal agents through which this message was conveyed.

---

[1] G. B. Caird, *A Commentary on the Revelation of St. John the Divine* (London: Black, c1966), p. 129.

TEXT

Revelation	First Testament
⁸The **voice** which **I heard** from heaven, again **speaking** with me **and saying**, "Go away, take the scroll which is opened in the hand of the angel which is standing on the land."	Ezek 1:28-2:1 **I heard a voice speaking, and it said** to me . . . .

COMMENTARY

The voice which I heard from heaven. This means the author received a message from God, which might have been an insight he obtained by reading the Scripture rather than looking up in the sky. The author of this redemption unit was ordered to take the unrolled scroll from the angel who was standing on the land and sea. When the author received this unrolled scroll, he too, would have access to **the mystery** of God, because the scroll had the words of God's **servants, the prophets**.

Standing on the land. NA has on the sea **and on the land**. This could be an easy homeoarchton error on the part of the Sinaiticus scribe. This kind of error occurred when a copying scribe found the same word at the beginning of two differing lines. The scribe's eye mistakenly shifted from one word to the next, omitting all of the words in between. The scribe may have moved from the definite article (*tays*, τῆς) before the word **sea** to the same one before **land**, and omitted the words in between. The other possibility is that the Sinaiticus scribe is correct. The original author may have noted that in Dan 8 the ram was **standing** near the water, but on the bank, not in the water. Also in Dan 12, there were two men **standing** on opposite banks of the river, not in the water. The man clothed in linen was above the water of the river (Dan 12:6), but not **standing**. None of these was **standing** on the stream itself, as some texts of Rev 10:8 picture as being the case of the angel. The texts approved by NA would be a conflation of the men who **stood** on the banks of the river and the man clothed in linen who was **above** the water.

TEXT

Revelation	First Testament
⁹Then I went toward the angel, telling him to give me **the scroll**, and he	Ezek 3:1 He said to me, "Son of man, that which you find, **eat--eat** this **scroll**, and go, speak to the house of Israel."
	Jer 15:16 Your words appeared, **and I ate** them, and your words became to me a joy and happiness to my heart, because your name was called over me.

said to me, "Take it and **eat** [it]. It will make **your stomach** bitter,

but **in** your **mouth it** will be **sweet as honey**," ¹⁰So I took the **scroll**

from the hand of the angel, **and I ate it, and it was in my mouth sweet as honey**, and after I had eaten

it, my **stomach** was **full**. ¹¹Then they (=God) said to me, "It is necessary for **you** to prophesy again against

peoples, nations, and languages and many kings."

^{Ezek 3:3}**Then I ate, and it was in my mouth sweet as honey**.

^{Ps 119:103}How **sweet** to my taste are your sayings, [sweeter] than **honey** to **my mouth**.

^{Ezek 3:3}He said to me, "Son of man let your **stomach** consume and your bowels be **filled** with this **scroll** which I am giving **you**."

^{Dan 7:14}To him will be given ruling authority, glory, and a kingdom, and all **peoples, nations, and languages** will worship him.

COMMENTARY

I took the scroll . . . and I ate it. Sinaiticus has a different Greek word for **scroll** from that approved by NA. Instead of *beeb-lahr-eé-dee-awn,* βιβλαρίδιον) Sinaiticus has *beeb-leé-awn* (βιβλίον). In this context, both words have the same meaning. The NA text is diminutive, but diminutive words do not always take a diminutive meaning. The emphasis here is on the fact that it is a book or **scroll**--not that **the scroll** is little.

  Like Jeremiah and Ezekiel, the author consumed a scroll, but this was probably done in all cases metaphorically. They all studied **the scroll** until they almost knew it by heart. This was what was meant by having a contract **written on their heart** (Jer 31:33). **The scroll** which they **ate** was probably the Torah, which Daniel called the **scroll of truth** (Dan 10:21) and probably also the Psalms, prophets, and wisdom literature. This picture is painted against the background of resistant prophets, such as Moses, Jeremiah, and Ezekiel. The word similarity is primarily taken from Ezekiel's description of his own call and commandment to prophesy. The problem of this assignment is that **the prophets** were required to predict **lamentation, mourning, and woe** (Ezek 1:10). Like Ezekiel, the author found his immediate task pleasant and he was filled with its content. The content became the basis for his prophesying.

  The scroll mentioned in Revelation, however, was not just the FT, which was involved with Jeremiah and Ezekiel. **This scroll** was the new contract which Jeremiah promised (Jer 31:31). The old contract had been broken when the Lord divorced his people and drove them out of his temple and off his land. The land could not be restored until there was a new contract and a new messiah. **This scroll**

came down from heaven, accompanied by the kinds of sounds that accompanied the provision of the original contract to Moses on Mount Sinai. Readers were expected to understand the significance of this **scroll** from the surroundings of the incident.

There is another variant respecting the consequences of swallowing **the scroll**. Sinaiticus reports that after he had **eaten** it his **stomach** was full. NA texts said that his **stomach** had become bitter or sour. Sinaiticus is consistent with Ezek 3:3. Ezekiel was commanded to **eat the scroll** and fill his **stomach** with it. Sinaiticus reported the recipient to have **eaten the scroll** as he was commanded by the angel, and in the process his **stomach** became full, rather than bitter.

Weiss thought the image of sweetness had to do with prophecy. When the words were in his **mouth** they **were sweet**. He was free to speak them. Later, however, he had to suppress his words. This gave him a **stomach** ache.[1]

Many scholars have noticed the similarity of the narrative in Rev 5 and Rev 10, dealing with **the scroll** which the angel ordered to be consumed.[2] Both of these narratives are based upon the mythical description that Jeremiah experienced which was used also by Ezekiel. They probably were written by different authors at different times. Some editor included both of them in his prophecy (Rev 4:1-22:5).

It is necessary for you to prophesy again against. Just as the consumption of the scroll for Jeremiah and Ezekiel was accompanied by a command **to prophesy**, so this command comes together with the consumption of a scroll. The Greek *eh-peé* (ἐπί) with the dative case can mean either **against** or "about." Here it is rendered "against," because it reflects the Hebrew *ahl* (על), **against,** "over," "concerning," "because of," *et alia*.[3] The word "again" presumes that the recipient of the scroll had **prophesied** before. The recipient, however, was probably not John of Patmos, as many scholars presume[4] (note also verse 7), but some unknown author of this unit that was composed sometime earlier and included in this manuscript that was given to John at a later time. The **prophesying** involved telling people what was involved in the new contract people were asked to accept if they wanted the land restored.

---

[1] B. Weiss, "ΑΠΟΚΑΛΥΨΙΣ ΙΩΑΝΟΥ," *Das Neue Testament* (Leipzig: J. C. Hendrichs, 1902), p. 466.
[2] A. Farrer, *The Revelation of St. John the Divine: Commentary on the English Text* (Oxford: Clarendon Press, 1964), p. 19; J. Sweet, *Revelation* (London: , 1979), p. 176.
[3] So also K. Newport, "Semitic Influences on the Use of Some Prepositions in the Book of Revelation," *The Biblical Translator* 37 (1986):330-31.
[4] Such as J. P. Ruiz, *Ezekiel in the Apocalypse: the Transformation of Prophetic Language in Revelation 16:17-19:10* (Frankfurt, 1989), p. 532.

CHAPTER ELEVEN

TEXT

Revelation	First Testament
^{11:1}There was given to me **a reed** like a rod [by someone]. [God] said, "Arise and **measure** the temple of God, the altar, and [count] those who worship in it, ²but the quadrangle which is outside **the sanctuary leave** out,	^{Ezek 40:3-4}Now look! A man whose appearance was like bronze. A **line** of flax was in his hand and a **measuring reed**.
and do not **measure**, because it has been	^{Dan 8:11}The place of **the sanctuary was thrown** down
	^{Zech 2:1-2}I raised my eyes and looked. Now look! a man with a **measuring line** in his hand. Then I said, "Where are you going?" He said to me, "To **measure** Jerusalem, to see what is its breadth and what is its length."
	^{Zech 12:3}It will be in that day I will place Jerusalem a stone being **trampled down** by all **the gentiles.**
given to **the gentiles**, and the holy city they **will trample**	^{Isa 63:3-4}I have **trampled** the wine press alone. From among **gentiles** no one was with me; I **trampled** them in my anger; I **stamped on** them in my wrath . . . for a day of vengeance was in my heart, and the year of my redemption had come.
for forty-two months."	^{Dan 12:7}He raised his right hand and his left hand to heaven, and he swore by the life of the age that [it would be] for **a time, two times, and half a time** and when the shatterer of the power of the holy people will come to an end, all these things will be accomplished.

^{Dan 7:25}He tried to change the times and the religion, and it was given into his hand **for a time, two times, and half a time**.

^{Dan 12:11}From the time the continual offering was removed and the provision of the abomination of desolations will be **twelve hundred, ninety days**.

^{Dan 12:12}Blessed is the one who waits and reaches the **thirteen hundred, thirty-five days**.

COMMENTARY

There was given to me a reed. The subject of this sentence is not given. In the passive voice it is understood that the subject was avoided to prevent blasphemy by using God's name.

[God] said. The subject was supplied. The text literally said, **saying, w**hich implied that the same subject was involved as with the previous clause. God was the one speaking. A few texts add the words, **and the angel was standing** [there], before the word **saying.** These words were supplied to provide a clear subject, which was God. The angel was God's legal agent.

Arise and measure. The expression, **arise and**, is apparently a common expression for stirring someone to action. The idiom initially developed from asking someone who was seated or lying down to get up on his or her feet and do something. It probably developed into an idiom used also to address someone already standing. When the Lord called Jonah he said, **Arise and go to Nineveh** (Jonah 1:2).

The author of Rev 11 intentionally composed a story fashioned after the vision of Ezekiel, who was given a **measuring** stick to **measure** the temple. Ezekiel was a good geographer. He not only outlined the City of David and its temple, but he has given the boundary lines of the entire Promised Land, and he gave them accurately from the southern end of the Dead Sea to the northern border of Lebanon.[1]

Zechariah was also given a **measuring** stick to **measure** Jerusalem, but he was not **measuring** the specific details of the temple (Zech 2:5-9). In all of these cases, the purpose of the **measuring** was in anticipation of the restoration of Zion and its

---
[1] Buchanan, *The Consequences of the Covenant* (Leiden: E. J. Brill, 1970), pp. 91-109.

temple. The author was sure that he could predict the future on the basis of the past. He learned from Zechariah and Joel that there would be a great war outside of Jerusalem, when foreign nations would be gathered to crush Jerusalem, but instead of their designed result, they would themselves be crushed. It would be the great day of judgment.[1]

Schüssler-Fiorenza did not like the idea offered by other commentators that this was a zealot oracle anticipating the reestablishment of Jerusalem as the center of the Promised Land in the restored kingdom, as the texts of Ezekiel and Zechariah suggest, so she said it must be understood symbolically as in 1Enoch 61:1-5.[2] This would require a distortion of both texts. First, Enoch's message was not intended symbolically.

The temple and the altar. **The altar** of incense was part of **the temple**. It was usually placed in **the holy. The altar** of sacrifice, however, was separate. It was in a separate place near **the temple**. It was large, composed of stone and mortar, and had no roof to cover it. It was 22½ feet tall and 75 feet long on each side. It was huge, like the altar recovered at Megiddo. It was not round, as the Megiddo altar was, but it was very similar. It would have had a built in stairway to reach the top as is true of the altar at Megiddo. A photograph of the Megiddo altar is found between chapters twelve and thirteen. The altar at Zion was a necessary part of the sacrificial system and was included in any reconstruction.

Count the people. The same Greek word for **measure** also means **count**. So here the temple is to be **measured** and the people are to be **counted**. The practical implications of that command meant either that he was supposed to **count the people** who were there at that particular time or to estimate how large the space for the people was, so preparation could be made for the temple's reconstruction, if the temple were ever destroyed. The author seemed to have been writing when destruction of the temple seemed possible.

The text could be interpreted to have said that the angel was going **to measure** people to learn the extent of their righteousness, so that the non-elect would not mingle with the elect (1Enoch 61:1-5). The **measuring** of character was not symbolic of something else. In Revelation, however, like Ezekiel and Zechariah, the text orders the **measurement** of the temple in the city of Jerusalem--not the measurement of human beings for their righteousness.

---

[1] Both Zechariah and Joel were probably motivated to make that prophecy, because that event had already happened before, during the time of Isaiah and Hezekiah (Isa 37). They expected a repeat performance.

[2] E. Schüssler-Fiorenza, *The Book of Revelation--Justice and Judgement* (Philadelphia: Fortress, 1985), pp. 76-77. So also J. S. Considine, "The Two Witnesses: Apocalypse 11:3-13," *CBQ* 8 (1944):377-92, who allegorized the entire event. He took "measurement" to mean divine protection; the two witnesses, he said, represented the entire church; Jerusalem represented the entire world.

Feuillet thought that, based on Rev 11:19, **the temple** here is a heavenly one; the report here is non-temporal;[1] and the heavenly **temple** has been substituted for the earthly one. Hailey said it seemed out of place to have a book of symbols and switch at once from a symbolic temple to a literal city. Either they both must be literal or both symbolical. He noted that Jerusalem was called a holy city in the New Testament (NT) (Matt 4:5; 27:53), but he thought Revelation referred to a heavenly city of the future that was going to come down from heaven.[2] The problem here is that it was not a city in heaven that was trampled for 3½ years. It was the earthly city, surrounded by Roman troops for most of 3½ years (66-70 IA).

McNicol, like Schüssler-Fiorenza, disagreed with Bousset in his theory that Rev 11:1-2 was based on a zealot pamphlet, but for different reasons. He said such a theory as that was unnecessary. The author might have used sources, but he could have found all the sources necessary for this material from the First Testament (FT) itself. The Lord gave Ezekiel a rod, just as he had given one to Moses (Ezek 29:6). A man also appeared to Ezekiel with a string and a **measuring** rod with which he **measured** the various parts of the temple of Jerusalem (Ezek 40:3-4). The author obtained the 42 months duration (Rev 11:2) from Dan 9:27. With these sources, the author of the entire unit of Rev 11 might have also composed Rev 11:1-2.[3]

McNicol, however, had a different solution for the data from the one given by Schüssler-Fiorenza. He considered these verses to be the composition of an anti-Jewish Christian. The offenders were Jews, like the ones John called members of the synagogue of Satan. The author was pro-gentile and opposed to Jerusalem. Therefore, McNicol pictured Jerusalem as Sodom and Egypt, and the gentiles as those who were the new heirs of the temple area. The two witnesses were Christians who were persecuted by Jews. The document was composed after 70 IA.[4]

And its worshipers. Strand raised a difficult question. How could anyone **measure** the people worshiping in the temple? On the one hand, since all worshipers except priests would have to worship somewhere outside the holiest areas, this **measurement** might have dealt with the area of worship allowed for non-priestly Israelite worshipers. Strand, on the other hand, thought that this was really an allusion to Lev 16, which tells the order of conducting a Day of Atonement service. The **measurement**, then, would be spiritual rather than spacial. On the Day of Atonement the Jews would have to "measure up." Although there are no passages from Lev 16 that are quoted in Rev 11, Strand noticed that the same subjects were involved--temple, altar, and worshipers.[5] There are also other items necessary for the Day of Atonement: priests, sacrifices, goats, bulls, blood, etc. There are also other

---

[1] A. Feuillet, "Essai D'Interpretation du Chapitre XI de L'Apocalypse," 4 (1954/55):183-200.
[2] H. M. Hailey, *Revelation* (Grand Rapids: Baker's Book House, 1979), p. 252.
[3] A. McNicol, "Revelation 11:1-14 and the Structure of the Apocalypse," *RQ* 22 (1979):193-98.
[4] McNicol, "Revelation 11:1-14," pp. 198-202.
[5] K. A. Strand, "An Overlooked Old-Testament Background to Revelation 11:1," *AUSS* 22 (1984):317-25. Although Prof. Strand seems to have strained his allusions a little too far this time, his methodology of using First Testament backgrounds for understanding the Book of Revelation is valid, and many of his insights are good.

FT passages where some of these words occur. This is determined by subject matter, however, rather than midrashic use by any of the authors whose works are preserved in the Book of Revelation.

There is still another item of data to consider: the Greek word for **measure** (*meh-tréh-oh*, μετρέω) also means **to count** or **estimate.** The intention may have been to **measure** the space allotted to the temple and estimate the number of worshipers that were there at the time or the number of worshipers who could worship in this space at one time. Josephus noted that just one portico of the outer courtyard held 6,000 refugees, mostly women and children, at the time Titus captured the temple area (War 6:283). Neither Ezekiel nor Revelation tells how many worshipers the entire temple could hold of all degrees--i.e., priests, Jewish men, women, children, gentiles--but that may have been the question posed by Ezekiel.

The quadrangle which is outside the sanctuary throw out. The Sinaiticus scribe pictured someone taking a court yard that is inside and throwing it outside. This could be done with an object, like a stone, but not a geographical location. Texts approved by NA read, **The court which is outside leave out,** by which he meant that it should be excluded from the architectural drawings. The author was probably influenced by the report of Antiochus Epiphanes entering the holy of holies and **throwing it down** (Dan 8:11)**,** which was a violent way of saying that he defiled the place thoroughly so as to make it unusable for holy people.[1] He did not actually destroy it. That which Antiochus Epiphanes had done with the holy of holies, the author of this text wanted done with the unholy place, **the court** of the gentiles.

The Sinaiticus scribe probably saw a problem with **throwing** that **which was** outside **out,** so he changed it to **read throwing that which was inside out**. That does not make sense either. That which is inside the temple itself was reserved only for the high priest and only on the Day of Atonement, but **inside** here referred only to the entire temple territory, that which was to be **measured**. That which was to be **left out** is that which was already **out** when the author wrote. It was **outside** the temple area and the entire city of David from the day Herod built it.

Archaeologists discovered a wall in Jerusalem that is 5,000 years old and is adjacent to a "circle" that was discovered many years ago. Its relationship to the wall enabled the archaeologists to identify this circle of rocks as the footings for the Tower of Siloam. This is part of the small, moon-shaped ridge, which is now only 10 or 12 acres in size and clearly identified as the City of David. In biblical times that sloping ridge had tall, perpendicular walls, near the bottoms of the valleys on both sidess and the ridge was masterly filled in with rocks. It made the area called Zion or the City of David about three times as large as it is now.[2]

The quadrangle is the 35 acre plot that has been walled in by huge rock walls. It is Herod's old fortress, called "Antonia." It overlooked the entire City of David, with it's temple and palace, behind the Spring of Siloam. It was a separate

---

[1] Buchanan, *The Book of Daniel* (Lewiston: Mellen Biblical Press, c1999), p 245.
[2] For more details see Buchanan, "The Area of the Temple at Zion," *ET* 116.6 (2005);181-189.

city that held as many as 6,000 soldiers part of the time, keeping Zion, its temple, and palace under subjection. It was ruled by the Romans and considered defiled by the Jews. It was enemy territory.[1]

The **quadrangle** (*ow-láyn*, αὐλήν) can be called "an open court," a "court yard" or **quadrangle**, depending upon its context. Here it is the **quadrangle** which was Herod's fortress.[2] It was not a part of the temple facilities. It lay north of the City of David with its temple and was separate from it. It was **outside**, and when it came to measuring the future temple, it should be **left out** or **omitted.** This defiled fortress, city, and tower were not to be considered a necessary part of the restored temple in the holy city. **It had been given to the gentiles** ever since the Romans first constructed it. The understood subject of that sentence is "God." God was in charge of all events. That means that God **gave it to the gentiles.** It was not really the Romans, but God who did all of this as punishment to the Jews. This **quadrangle** was not an inherent part of the temple, as scholars have normally thought. As much as the author disliked that enemy fortress, he assumed that God had allowed it, as he allowed everything else that existed. To avoid using the divine name, the author used the passive voice.

Before the time of Solomon, **the altar of God** was stationed in the City of David, very near to Ain Gihon. David may have found it already there, left by the Jebusites, when he captured the city. David's altar, however, was small, and he could easily have had it constsructed, originally, when he put up the tent. The reason we know that it was small is that when Solomon became king, both Adonijah and Joab ran to the altar and held on to its horns for protection. The horns of an altar are placed on the corners to hold the beast in place when it is being roasted. A human being could hold on to two horns at a time only if the altar was small, like the altar shown in the photograph of the altar in the court at Lachish between chapters twelve and thirteen. The altar at Arad is larger than the altar at Lachish and could probably hold two beasts at a time.

The tent was placed near the altar. It had been moved from the house of Obenedom to the City of David by King David (2Sam 6:12-17). Solomon's **altar** was much larger. According to Hecataeus, it was 30 feet by 30 feet and 15 feet tall.[3] He made a temple that corresponded to the altar. Its holy of holies was also 30 feet wide and 30 feet long. Like David's tent, Solomon's temple was separated from **the altar** so that smoke could go upward without inhibition. It was evidently a little south of the threshold of the temple, because Ezekiel described the course of the water that went out from under the threshold, running under the south edge of **the temple** toward **the altar** (Ezek 47:1).

Herod's **altar** was 75 by 75 feet and 22 ½ feet tall. Assuming that the dimensions were proportionate to those of Solomon's temple, the holy of holies for Herod's temple would also have been 75 by 75 feet. It had an open **court** in front of

---

[1] For a more detailed documentation see further Ernest Martin, *The Temples Jerusalem Forgot* (Portland: ASK Publications, c2000), pp. 1-59.
[2] This insight was called to my attention in a telephone conversation by Gary Arvidson.
[3] According to Hecataeus, quoted by Josephus, *Apion* 1:22, 198.

the building with an **altar** for sacrifice.[1] The altar was comparable to the round **altar** excavated at Megiddo. (for that altar see the photograph between chapters twelve and thirteen). Herod's temple itself was probably even taller than the temples whose ruins still survive at Baalbeck, Lebanon. The altar had horns on the corners to hold the animals in place for sacrifice (War 5:224-225). **The temple** was also a fortress and the nation's treasury (War 6:282), so Jewish soldiers were stationed there, and the Romans wanted to conquer that structure.

The word here rendered **sanctuary** is *nah-áws* (ναός). It is the same translation that scholars like Düsterdieck[2] have given for different reasons. He thought that only the holy of holies was to be **measured**, because in classical Greek literature *nah-áws* (ναός) means **the sanctuary**, distinguishing it from **the temple** (*hee ehráwn*, Ἱερόν), but that was not true of the temple in Jerusalem. In the Old Greek text (OG), and frequently in the NT, *nah-áws* was used for the entire temple. The entire temple area was one stadion wide and one stadion long. A stadion is a little less than 600 feet. Inside of this square area was the temple, the bronze sea, and the altar. Herod's temple was controlled by the Romans. The word is rendered **sanctuary** here, because of its relationship to Dan 8:11.

As the Israelites became urbanites, however, status demanded that a temple be built near the altar and that it was large enough so that it was not overshadowed by the altar. The altar may have survived the burning both of Solomon's temple and also Herod's.

The altar in the wilderness was probably more like the two found in the Negev by the archaeologist, Johanan Aharoni. The altar at Lachish is very small. It is large enough to sacrifice only one small beast at a time. It was probably used to roast only goats or sheep. It would not be big enough to hold a cow. The altar at Arad is larger. It is large enough that it could be used to roast a cow or even two beasts at at time. Both altars were adequate for local community needs, one of them was probably about the same size as the one David had in relationship to the tent near the Spring of Gihon (Siloam). After Solomon became king, and the kingdom expanded to include modern Lebanon, the altar had to be large enough to accommodate the needs of the entire nation on feast days. That was when Israelites constructed and began to use that huge altar near the Spring of Siloam.

The temple area in Lachish, shown in the photograph between chapters twelve and thirteen, consists of a court, a holy place, and a holy of holies. From the court there is a series of steps that lead up to the holy place, where only priests are allowed. There was normally a curtain covering each door, one at the top of the stairs and the other that leads from the holy place to the holy of holies where only the high priest entered and only once a year. In Arad there are no steps from the

---

[1] According to Hecataeus, quoted by Josephus, *Apion* 1:22, 198, the altar of Zerubbabel was smaller-- 30 feet X 30 feel X 15 feet tall.
[2] F. Düsterdieck, *Critical and Exegetical Handbook to the Revelation of John*, tr. H. E. Jacobs (Winona Lake: Alpha Publications, 1884), p. 313.

court into the holy place. In Arad the holy place, the holy of holy of holies, and the altar are all approximately the same size ad those in Lachish.

The holy of holies is only about 5 feet wide and 9 feet deep. There is where the altar of incense was kept. In the temple at Lachish there was also found a stone slab, known as a *bah-mah* (במה), normally expected in Baal temples. There evidently was not as much difference between Jewish and pagan worship forms as western Jews and Christians like to think. Herod's temple was not only a place for priestly sacrifice, but it was also a national fortress and the nation's treasury. Josephus' description seems to apply to a situation in Jerusalem when gentiles had control of the city, but when **the temple** was still standing. It could hypothetically apply

1) to 63 BIA when Pompey was admitted to the city;
2) to 37 BIA when Herod recaptured Jerusalem; or
3) to 70 IA after Titus captured Jerusalem but before the temple was burned.[1]

Weiss thought Rev 11 had to have been written very close to the time when **the temple** was destroyed in 70 IA. He concluded that it must have been composed while **the temple** was still standing.

Reader was of the same opinion, but only of Rev 11:1-2, which he thought was written by a different author from the one who wrote the rest of Rev 11. Since it was written earlier than the time when John wrote, in Reader's opinion, it could not have been written by John of Patmos but appropriated by him from an earlier source. This earlier source would have been Jewish, and not Christian, in his judgment. Reader was very precise in dating Rev 11:1-2. He thought this had to have been written after the Romans had taken control of the city and had already captured the court of the gentiles, but had not yet taken the holy of holies.[2] That which Reader called the "court of the gentiles" was really the fortress of Antonia which Romans captured before the temple was burned.

They will trample the holy city for forty-two months. This 3½ year period is not just a round number, as Kittel thought.[3] It is a very specific number related to the Hasmonean period, just before the successful victory over the Syrians and the institution of Hanukkah. **The holy city** was Jerusalem. The basis for this time period is an antitype of the time in Daniel--reporting the length of time between the defilement of the temple by Antiochus Epiphanes and the cleansing of the temple and its restoration by Judas the Maccabee. Antiochus was also called the abomination of desolation. In Daniel the period between the defilement and the cleansing is given inexactly by rough approximations, sometimes 3½ years, sometimes, 1,290 days, and sometimes

---

[1] A. S. Peake, *The Revelation of John* (London: Holborn, 1919), pp. 29, 80, thought this portion of Revelation was written very shortly before the temple was destroyed in 70 IA.
[2] J. Weiss, *Die Offenbarung des Johannes* (Göttingen: Vandenhoeck und Ruprecht, 1908), p. 602. W. Reader, "The Riddle of the Identification of the Polis in Rev. 11:1-3," *SE* 7: 1982):408-409.
[3] So D. E. Aune, *Revelation 6-16* (Dallas: Word Books, c1997), p. 609,

1,335 days, but the same historical period is involved. The little redemption pericope in Luke also reflects Daniel. It expected that Jerusalem in that author's day would be trampled by the gentiles, just as it had been in the period in Daniel when the Hasmoneans were fighting the war against the Syrian Greeks. Luke did not say how many days this would continue, but he called them **the times of the gentiles** (Luke 21:24), meaning the time when the gentiles were in control of Palestine. These were, in fact, expected to be the last of the **times of the gentiles** before the temple would be cleansed, and the land would be ruled by a Jewish messiah.

In Revelation the period is more exact than it is in Daniel. It is always the same length of time--**42 months** (Rev 11:2; 13:5)--which equals 3½ years (Rev 12:14), or 1,260 days (Rev 11:3; 12:6), which is **42 30-day months.** Just as the type in Daniel reports a real period of time in Jewish history, the Book of Revelation was composed by people who were analyzing their own history as an antitype of Maccabean history. Daniel, Luke, and Revelation were dealing with the same kind and basic length of time--the last of the gentile rule over Palestine, which all three believed was predestined. No one thought of some period thousands of years in the future.

Boring said there was an "already" and a "not yet" in eschatological thought. "Eschatological thought" referred to thinking about the end of things—end of a stick, end of a month, end of a king's term of ruling, end of any period of time. In biblical concepts it deals with the end of a gentile rule of the Promised Land. By "already" and "not yet" Boring meant that Jesus as the Messiah had already come, but that the end of history had not yet arrived.[1] That is not the rationale of the biblical eschatologists. They patterned their concepts typologically after the formula given in Daniel. The end of history was never a factor. Eschatologists who followed Daniel in their calculations, found something in their history that seemed to be an antitype for the defilement of the temple by Antiochus Epiphanes. In Daniel that happened about 3 or 3½ years before the death of Antiochus, the victorious battle of Beth-horon, and the cleansing of the temple. The "already" was that the temple had already been defiled, and the "not yet" was that the Battle of Beth-horon and the cleansing of the temple had not yet occurred. The 3½ year period after Jews thought the temple had been defiled was filled with anxieties.

Following that successful restoration of the Promised Land, later prophets calculated every event they could find that was similar, and zealots were daily ready to fight a war. This was the period when Jews and Christians expected to be fighting a new Hasmonean Revolt. This period was sometimes called the "birth pangs of the Messiah" or "the tribulation." It was a period spent on earth in war. Believers were not expected to be raptured into heaven to escape the pain and suffering of this **42-month** period.

One important 3½ year period of tribulation, when the author may have lived and written, was between the years 66-70 IA when the Romans surrounded the holy city. Another earlier period was the 3½ year span of time during which Herod the

---

[1] M. E. Boring, *Revelation* (Louisville: John Knox Press, c1989), pp. 78-79, 99.

Great recaptured his kingdom after he had been forced to flee from Jerusalem in about 40 BIA. Both were considered antitypes of the 3½ years the Syrians fought with the Jews in Maccabean times. The author identified the Romans as the antitypes of the Greeks who had done just as the Syrian Greeks had done, nearly two centuries earlier. From Isa 63 the author learned of the divine vengeance which would come up from Edom. Since Edom was one of the code words Jews used for Rome, the author understood this to mean the Lord would come up from Rome, covered with blood after he had trodden the "wine press" on the day of vindication.

The Lord would **trample** down the peoples in his anger (Isa 63:3, 6). This would take place the year God redeemed his people. The year of redemption had not yet happened, because the gentiles were still in control of the temple (Isa 63:18). The author of Daniel probably based his message in Rev 10 on Isa 63. Like the Lord in Isa 63 the man Daniel saw in his vision was also fighting against the Persians alone. Only Michael the prince of the Jewish people came to his help. This man came to Daniel to tell him what would happen to his people at the end of the days in which they lived (Dan 10:14, 21).

The author of Rev 11 was acquainted both with Second Isaiah and with Daniel. From Daniel the author learned that **the holy city** and the court outside the temple would be **trampled** by the gentiles before they learned that Jerusalem was a stumbling block for them. At that time the tides would turn, and it would be the gentiles who would be **trampled.** In the meantime the gentiles would have control for 42 months or 3½ years--the exact length of time Jerusalem had been held captive during a critical war with the Greeks before the famous victory of Judas the Maccabee at the Battle of Beth-horon in 164 BIA. These were the last days of the Seleucid rule over Palestine--not the last days of history, as Boring believed.[1]

In the new battle, the gentiles that confronted the author of Rev 11 were the Romans. They were expected to be driven out of Jerusalem, just as the Greeks had been driven out earlier by the Hasmoneans. The author of Rev 11 apparently wrote after the 42 months had almost expired and before the expected victory had taken place. It is not possible to know exactly when he wrote, because it is uncertain when he thought the war began. There were many military skirmishes before the all-out war was in full force. At many points a contemporary might have thought Jews were in war with Romans. At sometime, near the end of the war, the situation in Jerusalem was such that it prompted him to think of earlier Scripture that reported situations similar to his own. This was the way midrashic authors studied and composed, which is evident in the following passages.

---

[1] M. E. Boring, *The Continuing Voice of Jesus* (Louisville: John Knox Press, c1991), p. 168.

TEXT

Revelation	First Testament
³I shall give to my **two** witnesses [authority], and they will prophesy for 1,260 days, dressed in sack cloth.	^{Zech 4:1-3}Then the angel who was speaking with me returned and woke me up as a man is awakened from his sleep. He said to me, "What do you see?" I said, "I am watching--now look! **a lamp stand**, completely of gold, with a bowl on top of it and seven **lamps** on it and seven lips on each of the **lamps** which are on top of it.
⁴These are **the two olive trees** and the **two lamp stands**	There are **two olive trees**, on the right of the bowl and one on its left."
	^{Zech 4:12-14}I said to him, "What are the **two olive** branches which are beside the **two** gold pipes which pour out oil over them?" He said to me, "Do you not know what these are?" I said, "No, my Lord." He said, "These are the two sons of oil
that are standing before **the Lord of all the land**, ⁵and whatever woman might want to hurt them,	**that are standing** beside **the Lord of all the land.**"
	^{Jer 5:14}Therefore thus says the Lord God of armies, "Therefore you have spoken this word. Look! I am putting my word in **your mouth as fire**, and this people as wood, **and you will consume** them."
fire will go out **from** their **mouth and consume** their enemies. If anyone wants to hurt them thus it is necessary for him to be killed.	^{2Sam 22:7-9}I will cry to the Lord; to my God I will cry. He will hear from his temple my voice, my cry in his ears. . . . smoke **goes** up in his nostrils--**fire from** his **mouth will consume**.
	^{2Kings 1:10}Elijah answered the captain of fifty, "If I am a man of God, let **fire** descend from heaven and **consume** you

and your fifty." Then **fire** descended from heaven and **consumed** him and his fifty.

COMMENTARY

I will give [authority] to my two witnesses. Loisy may have been correct in concluding that this narrative was composed between May and August of 70 IA.[1] Because God has appointed these **witnesses** to prophesy, they were considered true prophets. If this applied to the period shortly before the destruction of Jerusalem in IA 70, as Loisy suggests, then the prophets the author thought were appointed by God were condemned by Josephus as false prophets. They were prophesying that God would save the city and drive out the Romans, but that did not happen (War 6:281-87).

If this message were applied to the time when Herod was regaining his kingdom, then the **witnesses** would have been thought to be the two leaders who were prophets at that time. Charles and Weiss both thought the **witnesses** were antitypes of Moses and Elijah.[2] This is consistent with the appearance of Moses and Elijah together with Jesus on the Mount of Transfiguration, but usually Moses was paired with Aaron, Elijah with Elisha, and Zerubbabel with Joshua. These might also have been considered the **two** messiahs, the Messiah of Aaron and the Messiah of Israel.[3] Jews expected Moses to return (Deut 18:18), and both Christians and Jews thought Elijah would return before the Messiah would come (Matt 11:14; Eduyoth 8.7).

Giet followed Munck and Boismard in thinking they were Peter and Paul and that their testimony and martyrdom took place in Rome rather than Jerusalem.[4] Hill said they did not represent any two historical human beings or ancient prophets but that they symbolized the remnant of messianism. There were two, he held, because **two** is the minimum number of **witnesses** required in court to be valid.[5] Rissi imagined that the **witnesses** were not intended as individuals, but constituted a collective idea as the Jerusalem church.[6]

Witnesses in ancient courts were not limited to answering questions asked by attorneys before a judge. **Witnesses** were allowed to argue as well as report. Judges might even be **witnesses**.[7] Christians made later identifications as well. For example, the Franciscans said these two **witnesses** were Francis and Dominic.[1]

---

[1] A. Loisy, *L'Apocalypse de Jean* (Paris: Emile Nourry, 1923), p. 207.

[2] R. H. Charles, *A Critical and Exegetical Commentary on the Revelation of St. John the Divine* (New York: Charles Scribner's Sons, c1920) I, p. 281; B. Weiss, "ΑΠΟΚΑΛΥΨΙΣ ΙΩΑΝΟΥ," *NT* (Leipzig: J.C. Hinrichs, 1902), p. 469.

[3] It may be a little imaginative to consider these witnesses merely hypothetical non-persons who represent: 1) the word of God and 2) the testimony of Jesus, as K. A. Strand, "The Two Witnesses of Rev. 11:3-12," *AUSS* 19 (1981):127-35 and "The Two Olive Trees of Zechariah 4 and Revelation 11," *AUSS* 20 (1982):257-61, suggests.

[4] S. Giet, *L'Apocalypse et L'Histoire* (Paris: Presses Universitaires de France, 1957), pp. 40-43.

[5] D. Hill, "Prophecy and Prophets in the Revelation of St John," *NTS* 18 (1971/72):408.

[6] M. Rissi, *Time and History* (Richmond: John Knox Press, 1965), p. 101.

[7] A. A. Trites, *The New Testament Concept of Witness* (Cambridge: Cambridge U. Press, 1977), p. 27. This book is an important contribution to NT studies in relationship to legal concepts. L. Köhler,

They will prophesy for 1,260 days. The 1,260 days during which the **witnesses** were wearing sack cloth (Rev 11:3) was the same period of time as the 42 months during which the enemy would **trample the holy city** (Rev 11:2). This was the antitype of the 3½ years after the temple was defiled by Antiochus Epiphanes and before the Battle of Beth-horon was fought and the temple was cleansed and rededicated by the priests under the leadership of Judas the Maccabee (164 BIA). This period is often called the tribulation or the birth pangs of the Messiah, but this period is different by one month from the type in Daniel. In Daniel the period, when reckoned according to days, is either 1,290 days or 1,335 days (Dan 12:12-13).

Why the difference? The most likely reason seems to be that the author wanted to be consistent: 3½ years is a number that was important sabbatical eschatologists. 3 ½ years = 42 months, and 42 30-day months = 1,260 days. In the Book of Revelation, all of these dates are consistently the same. They do not vary as in the Book of Daniel, so this is the simplest and probably the correct explanation of the phenomena. Another possible reason for choosing 1,260 rather than 1,290 or 1,395 may have been to make the numbers concur with some local situation. We can only speculate about the identity of such a possible local situation as this, and our guesses may be wrong. Nevertheless, here they are:

If the author was alive and writing during the last of the war of 66-70 IA, and if that war had actually been in progress for less than 1,260 days, and the situation was so critical that the author did not think the war would last 1,290 or 1,335 days, he may have eckoned accordingly. He probably did write after the war was over and count exact days, because he still expected the **witnesses** to be vindicated.

If the author was actually writing during the time when Herod recovered his kingdom, 1,260 days may have been the actual time that had expired since Herod had been driven from Jerusalem. This would have been about 37 BIA. The exact numbers of 1,290 and 1,335 were taken from Dan 12. It is possible that this narrative originated at the time of Herod and was updated later to fit the time when Jerusalem was in danger of being burned. These guesses may be inaccurate, but the prophecy was made in consideration of normal sabbatical dogma in relationship to real events within real time frames in real history. These Jewish and Christian prophets were not speaking in the same kind of symbols that many Western scholars conjecture.

These are the two olive trees. It is clear that the author was speaking symbolically here. Those who knew the Scripture understood what he meant. The two **witnesses** may epitomize **two** prophets, like Elijah and Elisha and/or the **two** anointed rulers--the high priest and the king. In Zechariah, **the two olive trees** symbolized Joshua, the anointed high priest, and Zerubbabel, the anointed king, destined to rule Palestine when the Babylonian Jews returned. Strand's argument that the oil

---

Hebrew Man, tr. P. A. Ackroyd (London: SCM Press, c1953), p. 96, fn. 1, also held that a witness might also function as a judge.

[1] B. McGinn, *Visions of the End* (New York: Columbia U. Press, 1979), p. 213.

symbolizes the Holy Spirit rather than authority as rulers is not quite accurate, but authority and the Spirit are closely related.[1] It was the descent of the spirit that provided authority, and this spirit came upon people when they were being anointed as kings or high priests. The Spirit fell upon various charismatic leaders and they became judges; the Spirit fell upon Saul, and he became king; it fell upon Jesus at his baptism; Jesus breathed upon his disciples the Holy Spirit, and they became apostles; the Spirit fell upon Paul and he was commissioned to become an apostle to the gentiles; followers of John the Baptist received the Spirit, and became Christians. In Zechariah, Zerubbabel and Joshua were anointed and then functioned by the Spirit and authority of the Lord. With the oil came the anointing and the Holy Spirit.

The author of Rev 11 intended to typologize the two messiahs of Zechariah. This is obvious from his identification of the **witnesses** with the **two olive trees** which Zechariah identified with the **two** messiahs that were destined to rule the Promised Land after their return from Babylon. The author has also identified the two lamp stands with the two messiahs or prophets. He identified the seven lamp stands of Zech 4:2 with **the seven stars** and **the seven spirits of God**--both of which seem to have been code words for **the eyes of the Lord**. John of Patmos identified them with the seven churches. King David was called **the lamp of Israel** (2Sam 21:17), so lamp stands, like oil and the Spirit may have symbolized authority, according to biblical logic and prophetic code.

That are standing before the Lord of all theLand. In one of the Dead Sea Scrolls the following assurance was given:

> Yehowah has told you that he will build a temple for you, "And I will raise up your seed after you, and I will establish the throne of his kingdom for the age [to come]. I will be to him like a father, and he will be to me like a son" (2Sam 7:13). The shoot of David will **stand** with the interpreter of the Torah who will . . . in Zion in the last days, just as it is written, "I will raise up the tent of David that has fallen" (Amos 9:11), "who will **stand** to deliver Israel" (4QFlorilegium 1:10-13).

The expectation here was not that these two parties would just **stand** up, rather than sit down. **Standing before the Lord of all the land** had certain implications. Those who were expected to **stand** up were, the Messiah of David to rule, and the interpreter of the Torah to function as high priest in the last days of the gentile era in the Messiah's kingdom for the age to come. That evil age would come to an end when the Messiah of David would deliver Israel from the Romans. Then **the Lord** would build a temple for his people. This would be a reestablishment of the tent of David. There was another Dead Sea reference to the standing of the high priest:

---

[1] K. A. Strand, "Two Olive Trees," p. 258-59.

> Its interpretation is concerning the priest, the teacher of righteousness to whom God told to **stand** and whom he established to build for him a congregation (4Q Ps37:15-16).

The two witnesses who were destined to **stand before the Lord of all the land** were the two messiahs who were expected to hold the main offices of the government in the age to come. One was to be the high priest and the other the Davidic king.

Whatever woman wants to hurt them. There is an error in the Sinaiticus text at this point. The mistake was made from listening rather than reading. In Greek the word **whatever woman** (*háy-tees*, ἥτις)) sounds almost exactly like **if anyone** (*ay-tees*, εἴτις). The correct reading should be with NA, **If anyone wants to hurt them.** Considine did not like the ethics this sentence reflects, so he changed the force to "if anyone *wills* [emphasis added] to hurt them."[1]

Fire will go out from their mouth. It was not difficult for authors of redemption literature to imagine unreal situations, such as horses with tails of snakes, breathing **fire,** a woman dressed in the sun, or an angel dressed in a cloud. Here the author had some help. He had only to allude to the poem attributed to David with promises to his seed for the age (2Sam 22:51). God was portrayed there as one with smoke going from his nostrils and fire from his mouth (2Sam 22:9; see also Ps 18:8-9). This poem reflects David's gratefulness and glory after his deliverance from the hand of his enemies (2Sam 22:1). Elisha was reported to have been able to call down **fire** from heaven to consume his enemies (2Kings 1:10-14; Sir 48:1-3). The apostles of Jesus thought that they could call down **fire** from heaven to destroy a village of Samaritans if Jesus wanted them to do so (Luke 9:54). Reflecting that the messiahs were agents of the Lord, the author attributed to them the power of God given in this psalm and held that this power would be directed against their enemies, as God had directed his power against David's enemies.

TEXT

Revelation	First Testament
⁶These have the authority to close up the heaven so that it	1Kings 17:1Elijah the Tishbite . . . said to Ahab, "By the life of the Lord God of Israel, before whom I stand [may the following unmentioned curses come upon me] if there will be during these years dew or **rain** except at my word."

---

[1] Considine, "Witnesses," p. 387.

will not **rain** during the days of their prophecies, and they have authority over the **water** to **change** it **into blood**. They may **strike** the land with any plague whenever they want.

Exod 7:17 Thus said the Lord, "In this you will know that I am the Lord. Look! I am **striking** with the wand that is in my hand the **water** that is in the Nile, and it will be **changed into blood**."

COMMENTARY

These have the authority The author showed no sympathy with the opposition. Anyone who wanted to injure these **witnesses** would have to be killed. Weiss thought the **witnesses** were antitypes of Moses and Elijah, but those are only **two** of the possibilities.[1] Many scholars hold this opinion. The reason for this judgment are obvious. The **witnesses** produced signs similar to those performed by Moses and Elijah. Like Elijah, they **had the authority** to close up the sky so that it would not rain (1Kings 17:1) **during the days of their prophecy.** Like Moses, they **had authority** over the water to turn (Exod 7:17) it **into blood** (Exod 7:17, 19-20) and to **strike the land with any plague** (1Sam 4:8), as many as they wished, but this great power did not make them invincible. Just as soon as they had finished their testimony, the beast which goes up from the abyss (Dan 7:3) would make war with them (Dan 7:21), conquer them (Dan 7:21), and kill them (Rev 11:6-7). It was Elijah who **had the authority** to close up the sky and prevent rain, and it was Moses and Aaron who had a **wand** with which they could **change water** into **blood** and perform other terrible **plagues**. The author took qualities from all of these earlier leaders and applied them to the **two witnesses**.

When the Israelites were losing in a battle with the Philistines, the sons of Eli brought the chest containing the contract into camp. Hofni and Phineas carried the chest. When the Israelites saw the chest, they cheered. When the Philistines learned the cause of this uproar, they were afraid, noting that the gods contained in that chest were the same ones who struck Egypt with **plagues** in the wilderness.

To close up the heavens. Rabbi Jonathan said there are three keys which the Lord does not give over into the hand of an agent. One of these is the key of rain. Nevertheless, God did give even this key over to Elijah at one point in history (Ps 78:5, 173b). The author took **the authority** from the Scripture that had been earlier recognized as belonging to God, Moses, Aaron, and Elijah. Therefore, these **witnesses** were held to be almost invincible, but this **authority** lasted only as long as their testimony or **prophecy** lasted. Once this was finished, the enemy moved in. Since there were **two witnesses,** and one of them was identified with Elijah, the author may have understood that the other was Elisha. Part of the freedom of typology is that a theologian could identify characters with two or more types at the

---

[1] J. Weiss, *Offenbarung*, p. 644.

same time as was done here. **The witnesses** are at once an antitype of Moses and Aaron, Elijah and Elisha, and Joshua and Zerubbabel.

They have authority over the water. Not only did these **witnesses have authority to close up the heavens**, but they **had authority over the water** generally, so that they could change it **into blood** as Moses and Aaron had done in Egypt. They were agents of the Lord and could do any of the things any prophet or king had done in the past. The enemy that moved in was a type patterned after the fourth beast which Daniel described as the most monstrous of all. The contemporary counterpart of that beast was one of its agents of Rome. This probably means the author ascribed the death of these **two witnesses** to Rome.

TEXT

Revelation	First Testament
⁷When they finish their testimony, the **beast** then **will come up from** the abyss,	^{Dan 7:3}Four large **beasts came up out of** the sea, differing one from the other.
make war with them, **and he will conquer them** and kill them.	^{Dan 7:21}I was watching, and this horn **made war with** the saints, **and he conquered them**.
₈Their corpses [will be left] on the street of the great city (which is	^{Ps 79:3-4}They poured out their blood like water around Jerusalem, and there was no one to bury them. We have become an object of ridicule to our neighbors.
	^{Isa 1:9}If the Lord of armies had not left us a small remnant, we should have been like **Sodom** and become like Gomorrah.
called spiritually **Sodom** and **Egypt** where their Lord was crucified). ⁹[Some of those] from the tribes, peoples, languages, and nations will gaze upon their corpses for three and a half days, but they did not permit [anyone] to place [them] in a tomb. ¹⁰The migrants on the land **rejoice** over them, and they celebrate and send gifts to one another, because these two prophets tortured the migrants of the land.	^{Jer 23:14}Every one of them has been to me like **Sodom** and its inhabitants, like [those of] Gomorrah.
	^{Ps 105:38} **Egypt rejoiced** when [the Israelites] departed.
	^{Est 8:17}Wherever the king's word and decree came there was **gladness and joy**

among the Jews.

^{Neh 8:19}Thus said Yehowah of armies: "The fast of the fourth, the fast of the fifth, the fast of the seventh, and the fast of the tenth [months] will be for the house of Judah for **joy, gladness,** and good feasts."

COMMENTARY

When they finished their testimony. **The witnesses** gave their testimony for 42 months after which the beast came up out of the abyss. If the beast were Herod, this would mean that **the witnesses prophesied** during the time when Herod was away from Jerusalem. This was the period from the time of his escape until his return with Roman troops. It was after **they had finished their prophecy** that the beast returned.

The beast then coming up from the abyss. Instead of **then** (*táw-teh*, τότε) NA has **that** (*taw*, τό). This was another error probably made from mistakenly hearing the text read. The correct text would render, **The beast which comes up from the abyss.**

In Medieval Jewish documents there is a mythological figure that appears in at least 13 different sources. The character is called "Armilos"--probably a Semitic adaptation of "Romulus." He is characterized in such a way as to ridicule Jesus, the Christian Church, the Roman empire, and other enemy groups or individuals. He is always associated with two messiahs, one of Samaria and one of Judah. Armilos, like the beast in Rev 11, always kills the Messiah Ephraim (of Samaria), and his corpse is allowed to lie unburied in Jerusalem until the Messiah Nehemiah (of Judah), son of David, comes and raises him from the dead. Over the centuries this myth varied to fit the needs of the time in which it was written, but it seems likely that Armilos and the two messiahs of Medieval Judaism had its origin with this story in Rev 11.[1]

Which is spiritually Sodom and Egypt. The words encompassed in parentheses of Rev 11:8 contradict the spirit of the rest of the message. They were probably added by some anti-Jerusalem Christian, who identified Jerusalem with **Sodom,** the city so wicked that the Lord destroyed it, and Egypt, the country where Israelites were captive for more than 400 years. This addition was probably made after Jerusalem had been destroyed in 70 IA. That was part of the basis for identifying it with **Sodom**. The Lord had judged both cities for destruction. Morris thought the city was symbolical and not Jerusalem.[2]

---

[1] See Buchanan, *Messianic Movements*, pp. 362-69.
[2] L. Morris, *The Book of Revelation* (Grand Rapids: Eerdmans, c1987), p. 150.

Their corpses [will be] left on the street of the great city. The expression **great city** appears in Revelation eight times:

1) Rev 16:19 (Jerusalem);
2) Rev 17:18 (Rome);
3) Rev 18:10, 16, 18, 19, 21 (Rome).

The expression in Rev 11:8 applies to Jerusalem. The identity of each **city** can only be learned by studying the context. The **corpses** of **the witnesses** were **left in the streets of the great city,** which all Jews and early Christians knew was Jerusalem--even the anti-Jerusalemite Christian who made the addition, recognized this.[1] The insulting description that would identify Jerusalem with **Sodom,** the city where not even ten innocent people could be found and **Egypt** where Israelites had been enslaved, was added to offend Jews and Palestinian Christians. Reportedly Rabbi Akiba said, "There is no city except Jerusalem, as it is said, **The city which I chose**" (1Kings 11:13).[2] Those of every people, tribe, language, and nation who saw the **corpses** were gentiles in Palestine. These were the **migrants of the land,** foreigners from Rome, Greece, and other countries who had settled in Palestine without embracing Judaism. These supported Herod after he returned with Roman troops. They joined his army and fought alongside Roman soldiers. They had been in open conflict with the **two witnesses**, who had tortured them. Therefore, they rejoiced at the death of these prophets.

Reader thought Rev 11:3-13 was composed by a different writer from Rev 11:1-2, and he declared that the **city** mentioned here could not have been Jerusalem, because Jerusalem had been destroyed, in his judgment, before this document had been written. Those called **migrants** here, Reader called "the inhabitants of the earth," and he said of them,

> This designation . . . always denotes the entire unbelieving mankind and never the inhabitants of Palestine or Jerusalem.[3]

He evidently failed to notice the geographical contexts in which this group was stationed. Whenever they were associated with a certain geographical area, that area was within the Promised Land.

---

[1] This was not a policy limited to Jews. When the Roman leader, Sejanus, earned Tiberius's disfavor, he was imprisoned, executed, and thrown down the stairway, and left there for three days. After that the corpse was thrown into the river (Dio, *RomHist* 58.11.4-5).

[2] Rabbi Akiba, "Midrash Alpha Beta," A. Jellinek (ed.) *Bet ha Midrasch* (Jerusalem: Wahrmann Books, 1967) III, p. 31 [Hebrew].

[3] Reader, "Riddle," p. 412, fn. 28. S. Giet, *L'Apocalypse,* pp. 29-30, following Boismard argued that the great city could only be Rome, because Jerusalem could not qualify as Sodom and Egypt, but, of course, neither could Rome.

A Jewish document composed during the Crusades prophesied that a foreign king named Shiroi would come to Jerusalem and kill the Messiah of Ephraim, Nehemiah ben Hoshiel. His **corpse** would lie at the gates of Jerusalem for 41 days without burial.[1] This might reflect some familiarity with Rev 11.

It was customary in Near Eastern antiquity to celebrate military victories. Jews celebrated Hanukkah after Judas had won the Battle of Beth-horon. They also celebrated as "Nicanor's Day" the second victory of Judas in the Valley of Beth-horon when the Greek army was defeated and Nicanor, the general, was killed. (Ant 12:409). Sometimes Rome voted a festivity of as much as 60 days because of some military victory. When the leaders of an enemy movement died, this was an occasion for celebration.

Where also their Lord was crucified. Chester Beatty papyrus omits the pronoun **their** (*ow-tóhn*, αὐτῶν), leaving the expression **the Lord.** This is the easier reading and was probably made by a Christian scribe. It is not likely that the pronoun **their** would have been added to confuse the text. Accepting the pronoun, the question is: Whose Lord? Did the Jews have a messiah, other than Jesus, who **also was crucified**? Indeed they did! Aune said,

> The term κύριος, "Lord," is used of Jesus here for the first time in Revelation and in a unique way.[2]

Like most other scholars, Aune thought the term "lord" could apply only to God or to his legal agent, Jesus. The term was regularly applied to any king and often to other persons of dignity. Sometimes it was used like the English word "sir."

During the time when Herod was trying to regain his throne (ca. 40-37 BIA), with the aid of the Parthians, Jews succeeded in placing on the throne their own king, Antigonus, a Jew of Hasmonean descent. After Herod had taken Jerusalem he bribed the Roman general, Sossius, to have Antigonus killed (War 1:357). The Romans obligingly hanged Antigonus on a cross and whipped him. Afterward they beheaded him. Dio called this

> a punishment which no other king had suffered at the hands of the Romans (Dio, *RomHist* 49:22, 6).

Josephus omitted these gory details and said simply that he "fell beneath the ax" (War 1:357). Jews called their Messiah "Lord." Rabbi Ishmael reportedly said,

> The Messiah is called **the Lord**, as it is said, **This is the name by which he will be called, "The Lord is our righteousness"**(Jer 23:6).[3]

---

[1] Buchanan, *Jewish Messianic Movements* (Eugene, Oregon: Wipf and Stock, 2003), p. 362.
[2] Aune, *Revelation 6-16*, p. 620.
[3] Buchanan, *Jewish Messianic Movements*, p. 518.

There seems to be a serious problem also with Josephus' account of this event. Sossius left Jerusalem, leading Antigonus captive to Anthony (*Ahn-teé-gawn-awn áh-gaw-nay Ahn-tohn-eé-oh*, Ἀντίγονουν ἄγωνη Ἀντωνίῳ (Ant 14:488). This seems to mean that the crucifixion did not take place at Jerusalem, but Josephus also said that Herod bribed Sossius to change his plans and have Antigonus killed, because Herod was afraid that if Anthony actually got control of Antigonus he might lead him on to Rome and Rome might decide not to kill him (Ant 14:488-89). This means Sossius actually did not lead Antigonus to Anthony, but instead had him killed before he went to Anthony. Once he changed his plans and decided not to lead Antigonus to Anthony, the most reasonable place to have had him killed would have been right there in Jerusalem, **the great city . . . where also their Lord was crucified** (Rev 11:8). Not only was the Christian Messiah crucified in Jerusalem, but *also their* (*kai . . . eh-stower-óh-thay*, καὶ . . . ἐσταυρώθη) i.e., the Jews' Lord was crucified.

This interpretation admits that the author of this intrusion was a Christian and not a Jew. He was also a Christian who was hostile to Jews and Jerusalem, as many Christians were after 70 IA. He labeled the city Jews called **great, spiritually Sodom and Egypt.** It also presumes that there was a tradition, that Christians knew, about the crucifixion of Antigonus at Jerusalem. They may also have realized that Jews also had a Messiah whom they identified with **the Lamb that was slain.** It also means that the "beast" involved here was Herod the Great, the agent of Rome and that Antigonus was one of the witnesses, one of the **two olive trees** mentioned by Zechariah. Antigonus would have been the antitype of Zerubbabel.

For a perfect antitype the second **witness** would have been the antitype of the high priest, Joshua. The new Joshua would have been the high priest who functioned alongside Antigonus.[1] Josephus did not report a separate high priest alongside Antigonus. John Hyrcanus I was both the highest government officer and high priest. His son Aristobulus declared himself to be king (War 1:68-71), and he was succeeded by his brother Alexander Jannaeus who was both priest and king. When Alexander Jannaeus died (78 BIA), his wife could not be high priest, so she appointed her son John Hyrcanus II as high priest (War 1:107-109), while she ruled as queen. When she became ill, her younger son seized the opportunity to overthrow the government and declare himself king (War 1:117-119). He and John Hyrcanus were fighting over the offices of king and high priest when Antipater, Herod's father, became involved and gradually prepared the government for the leadership of himself and his sons. When the Parthians made Antigonus king, he may also have claimed the role of high priest, because other Hasmoneans had done that. If that were the case, King Antigonus alone might have functioned as both high priest and king and therefore the total successor of the two offices held by the **two olive trees** in Zechariah.

---

[1] See more about this identification in the commentary on Rev 13.

Another possibility is that the other **witness** was not a high priest but instead King Antigonus' highest general, Pappus. In military conflict with Herod's troops, Pappus was killed just as Herod was beginning his attack on Jerusalem, just three years after Herod had been proclaimed king in Rome. Herod had General Pappus beheaded and sent the head to his brother, Pheroras (War 1:335-43). Antigonus was not crucified and beheaded until 3-5 months later. It would require the kind of broad interpretation that only dogmatists can accept to make both of these leaders fit the report of the **two witnesses** as antitypes of the **two olive trees** as if they had happened at once, but religious authors are often credulous dogmatists. Ancient biblical interpreters often forced their current situations to fit earlier **prophecies** or become antitypes of earlier historical situations.

The time during which the **witnesses** were given to prophesy was **42 months** (Rev 11:2); i.e., 1,260 days (Rev 11:3). Josephus reported that three years elapsed from the time Herod was declared king in Rome until he drew his army against the walls of Jerusalem. That is 1,095 days, 165 days short of the 1,260 days reported here in Rev 11, but the author of this passage probably was referring to the full length of the time from Herod's flight until his later establishment as king in Jerusalem. Several days transpired from the time Herod fled from Jerusalem and Antigonus was made king until he reached Rome. In between he fled with military guard from Jerusalem to Masada, with military conflicts all along the way. From Masada he went to Arabia where he expected to be able to receive aid from the Arabs. Those expectations failed. After he was driven from Arabian territory, he fled to Egypt, where he discussed problems with Cleopatra. From there he found one ship that took him through a severe storm to Rhodes. From Rhodes he found another ship which finally took him to Italy. There is no record of the time that elapsed while all of this was going on.

After Herod began his attack on Jerusalem he maintained the siege into the fifth month, during which he overpowered it, according to Wars (1:351), but the report is not unequivocal. In Antiquities Josephus said the victory came precisely on the 185th Olympiad, on the day of the fast. This would probably refer to the fast associated with the Day of Atonement, on Oct 3, 37 IA, but Josephus also said it was on the **third month** (Ant 14:487). The question is, "The third month of what?" The third month of the siege? The third month of the year?[1] The two periods, one before Herod reached Rome and the other after the siege of Jerusalem had begun are of uncertain length, but it is altogether possible for these two to add up to 165 days, which, together with 1,095 days between Herod's appointment as king until he attacked Jerusalem, would total 1,260, the number of days the author of Rev 11 reported as the period of the witnessing. Even if it had not, sabbatical eschatologists, like the author, would have had no difficulty in forcing the facts to fit the figures. That is the way the sabbatical eschatologist of Daniel forced the 422 years (586 BIA to 164 BIA) to conform to his sabbatical scheme of 490 years. That is close enough for a dogmatist.

---

[1] On this problem see R. Marcus, *Josephus* (New York: Putnam, 1961) VII, pp. 700-701.

This means it is reasonable to relate this passage to Herod as the beast, and the 1,260 days of prophesying or witnessing as the period from the time Herod fled from Jerusalem until he returned and conquered Jerusalem. One of the witnesses may have been King Antigonus, the last Hasmonean king, together with his general, Pappus, or without him. Antigonus and Pappus were the two leaders who fought Herod's troops for three years. They killed many people. They might have qualified as those who had such great authority that if anyone wanted to injure them that person would have to be killed (Rev 11:5). When the beast (possibly Herod) **came up from the abyss** (Rome), he made war against them, conquered them, and killed them (Rev 11:7), just as Josephus said (War 1:342-57).

The **witnesses** also functioned as prophets (Rev 11:3, 6-7), so they might have been two prophets who lived in Jerusalem at that time, of which we have no further information. The people called **migrants of the land** (Rev 11:10) might have been those who supported Herod during this conflict.

There is still another possibility. During the war of IA 66-70 the zealots invited the Idumeans into the city of Jerusalem where they added to the conflict which was already extensive. They were admitted during a rain storm at night. During that night, Josephus reported that there were 8,500 people killed. Among the dead were two chief priests, Ananus and Jesus (Joshua in Hebrew). They were singled out for special treatment. Idumaeans threw out their bodies without burial (War 4:314-17). If these chief priests had ever been high priests they would have also been messiahs. Since one of them was named Joshua he might have been thought of as the new Joshua, who was the high priest for the first restoration of Jerusalem from Babylon and referred to as one of **the olive trees** (Rev 11:4; Zech 4:1-3, 12-14), meaning one of the messiahs. These priests were also killed after the war had been going on for about three years. This would satisfy the 1,260 days during which these two witnesses might have prophesied (Rev 11:3). There are enough points here to satisfy the imagination of nationalistic Jews during the war of 66-70 IA and encourage them to identify these two priests with the two messiahs (Joshua and Zerubbabel) of the first restoration.

These conjectures are only the best guesses possible with the available data at this distance in time. They are not all mutually exclusive. This myth may once have been applied to King Antigonus and later updated to fit the chief priests Joshua and Ananus. On the other hand, they may all be inaccurate, but that which is likely is that these two **witnesses** were not just vague, hypothetical characters at the time Rev 11 was written. They probably described two individuals who fit the descriptions given. It seems unlikely that **two witnesses** would really mean a whole circle of Christian prophets, as Mazzaferri argues.[1] Mounce also held that they were not really two individuals at all, but they were only symbols for the **witnessing** church.[2]

---

[1] F. D. Mazzaferri, *The Genre of the Book of Revelation from a Source-critical Perspective* (Berlin: W. DeGruyter, 1989), p. 325.

[2] R. H. Mounce, *The Book of Revelation* (Grand Rapids: Eerdmans, c1977), p. 223, and Feuillet, "Essai," p. 95, said the resurrection of the two witnesses symbolized the resurrection of the church.

Düsterdieck thought they were particular Christian prophets who were antitypes of Joshua and Zerubbabel but were unidentified.[1] Neither Moffatt nor Ford made any attempt to identify them.[2] Whealon thought there was no question that the words, **where also their Lord was crucified** referred to Jerusalem and was a Christian addition to a Jewish document.[3] It is obvious that John of Patmos understood the Lord involved to have been Jesus, but there are other earlier possibilities.

Tribes, peoples, languages, and nations. NA has a different order: **Peoples, tribes, languages, and nations**.

The migrants of the land. It would make no sense at all to consider these people **those who dwell upon the earth**, as the RSV has done. Neither were they "worldly people," as Giblin claimed.[4] Weiss also saw a problem here. He said the expression was used hyperbolically, but that is not enough to satisfy the identfication.[5] Not only did these **migrants** dwell on the earth, but so did their enemies. The **migrants** were enemies of this author or the Lamb as also in Rev 13:8. They were not just "earth dwellers." They were the foreigners who lived in Palestine whom Jews hated. They collaborated with Rome and functioned as a fifth column for Jewish nationalists. They were the Palestinans who supported Herod in his fight to regain control of Palestine. Fourth Ezra also told of these **migrants (those who inhabit the land,** *eos qui inhabitant terram*) (4Ezra 13:30) whom the Lord would confuse and make them fight with one another. They are contrasted to those who are on the [**Promised**] **Land** (*eos qui super terram sunt*), whom the Most High would deliver (4Ezra 13:29).

They celebrate and send gifts. NA has, **They celebrate and** will **send gifts**, employing the future tense for the second verb. Sinaiticus is more consistent in its tenses.

This was a sad turn of events. Years earlier, thanks to Esther, Jews were permitted to kill all pagans that they wanted dead. Because of this privilege, they had all sorts of **celebrations.** When the second temple was built in Jerusalem, Jews were given four times a year to **celebrate** rather than fast. In this instance, however, those rejoicing were the **migrants of the land**--the pagans. They **celebrated** because of the death of two popular Jewish leaders.

TEXT

Revelation	First Testament
¹¹After 3½ days,	Ezek 37:5-6 Thus says the Lord Yehowah to

---

[1] Düsterdieck, *Revelation*, p. 315.
[2] J. M. Ford, *Revelation* (Garden City: Doubleday & Co., 1975), pp. 170-71.
[3] J. F. Whealon, "New Patches on an Old Garment: The Book of Revelation," *BTB* 11 (1981):55.
[4] C. H. Giblin, "Revelation 11:1-13: its Form, Function, and Contextual Integration," *NTS* 30 (1984):444.
[5] B. Weiss, ΑΠΟΚΑΛΥΨΙΣ, p. 470.

| | the bones, "Look! I will bring **breath** into you, and you will **live**. I will stretch over you sinews; I will put over you flesh; I will cover you with skin; I will put **breath** into you; and you will **live** and know that I am Yehowah." |

^{Ezek 37:10}I prophesied as he commanded me;

the spirit of **life** from God **entered them**
and they stood upon their feet,

breath entered them; they came to **life, and they stood upon their feet**.

^{Gen 15:12}Deep sleep **fell over** Abram. Now look! **dread** and great darkness **fell upon** him.

and a great **fear fell upon** those who watched them.

¹²Then [those observers] heard a loud voice from **heaven** saying to them, "Come up here!" and [the revived witnesses] **went up to heaven** in the cloud, and their enemies watched them. ¹³In that hour **there was a great earthquake**, and a tenth of the city fell. In **the earthquake** 7,000 names of men were killed, and the rest became frightened and gave glory to the **God** of **heaven** (Dan 2:40). ¹⁴The second woe has passed. Look! The third woe is coming at once.

^{2Kings 2:11}Look! A chariot of fire and horses of fire separated the two of them, and Elijah **went up into heaven**.

^{Ezek 38:19}**There will be a great earthquake** in the land of Israel.

COMMENTARY

They stood upon their feet. The revival of the **two witnesses** was based on Ezekiel's parable of dry bones. Although all corpses had been dead for many days, the Lord would cause **breath** to **enter them,** and they would live. Ezekiel prophesied as he had been commanded, and the bones came to life and **stood upon their feet**. These bones represented the house of Israel (Ezek 37:11) that had been in exile away from the **land** of life, without a contract with the Lord, and without a **land.** They were legally dead, even though they were doing well economically in Babylon.

The words of Rev 11:11 change the direction of the narrative. The joyful **migrants of the land** were suddenly surprised and frightened into belief, as these corpses took on new life and were taken into heaven. This may have been either a legal or a physical resurrection. Dio reported that Augustus Caesar was seen ascending to heaven (Dio 56:46, 2). Justin said a witness had sworn that he had seen Caesar ascending into the sky (Justin, *Apol* 21:3). Apollonius of Tyana vanished before jailors and was never seen again. Supposedly he ascended into heaven (Philostratus, *Vita Apoll* 8:30). If this was a legal or political resurrection, it would mean that the two witnesses that had been politically defeated and almost forgotten became active again. Herod wondered if Jesus was John the Baptist raised from the dead (Matt 14:2).

A great fear fell upon those who had watched them.[1] The importance of the quotation from Genesis is that Gen 15 tells of God's contract with Abram and his promise to him, but it also said that Abram and his descendants would be **migrants in a land** not theirs (Gen 15:13). This followed the **fear** that **fell upon** Abram. Here the **fear fell upon** the enemies of the **witnesses** who were also **migrants** in a land not theirs, in the author's judgment--a subtle way of reminding readers both of **migrants** and of the contract with Abraham and his posterity.

Their enemies watched them. Two texts (P^{47} and 1611) which read **Their** *fifteen* **enemies (ιε)** give no clue for identifying which fifteen.[2]

There was a great earthquake. This **earthquake** was an antitype of the **earthquake** God brought against Gog in the Promised Land, which would be followed by every terror against Gog (Ezek 38:21). According to Ezekiel this **earthquake** would take place in the **land** of Israel--not in Asia Minor or anywhere else. In so doing God would show his greatness and holiness to many nations (Ezek 38:23). This holiness and greatness of God, mentioned by Ezekiel, reminded the author of Nebuchadnezzar's humiliation and final subjection to **the King of heaven** whom he honored (Dan 4:37). Hai Gaon said there would have to be an **earthquake** along with the war of Gog and Magog which took place at the edge of Jerusalem, because the **earthquake** would dislodge the disintegrated parts of Jewish corpses that had become parts of bricks, buildings, and debris of various kinds. These would have to be broken up so the resurrection could take place.[3] The **earthquake** and other parts of this story remind the reader of the events after the crucifixion (Matt 27:51).

---

[1] The Chester Beatty papyrus has *ay-meh-tráy-sahn*, (ἡμετρῆσαν) (they measured, counted, estimated) for *theh-oh-roón-tahs* (θεωροῦντας) (they saw or gazed upon). As a result of a *homeoteleuton* error, the scribe of that papyrus also omitted several words. It would be difficult to make sense of this reading or to deduce how it came into being.

[2] J. R. Royce, "'Their Fifteen Enemies': The Text of Rev xi.12 in P^{47} and 1611," *JTS* 31 (1980):78-80, and H. C. Hoskier, *Concerning the Text of the Apocalypse* (London: B. Quartich, Ltd., 1929), II, p. 299, both thought this was some kind of scribal error.

[3] Buchanan, *Jewish Messianic Movements*, p. 131.

The rest became frightened and gave glory to the God of heaven. The fiendish glee with which the author predicted this antitype is obvious. Those who had embarrassed Israel would be embarrassed still more and finally be forced to worship Israel's God. This is the second woe which the angel correctly said would be directed against the **migrants of the land**.

There still exist some medieval Jewish documents that seem to echo this narrative in Rev 11. There are several versions of an eschatological myth in which the enemy character was Armilos, who was at once identified with Rome, the Christian church, and Jesus. Hero characters were Nehemiah, the Messiah of Joseph, Ephraim, or Samaria and the Messiah of David from Judah. The Messiah of Joseph was killed by Armilos, but then Elijah and the Messiah of Judah raised him from the dead in the streets of Jerusalem. The author of that narrative may have been acquainted with this earlier story in Rev 11.

A tenth of the city fell. Robinson correctly argued that this unit of Revelation was written before 70 IA. It presumes that Jerusalem was still standing. If it had been composed after 70 IA the author would have reported that more than one tenth fell, and he would not have suggested that the fall was caused by an earthquake, but a war.[1]

The second woe has passed. This is a connecting sentence. It reports that which has gone before and then introduces that which will follow **the third woe**. Weiss held that a unit was concluded here—not just one that began with Rev 11:1, but one that began with Rev 10:1. Like many other scholars, Weiss believed that a later editor used earlier sources.[2] In Rev 8 there was the introduction of the seven trumpets. After the fourth one was blown there was an eagle flying in the sky that announced three woes to the **migrants of the land**. With the introduction of the seven trumpets came natural phenomena that were similar to those that appeared at Mount Sinai when the contract was given to the chosen people. These antitypes are suggestive of the events intended to follow and the final goal designed. The symbols in the Book of Revelation are not meaningless. They are coded concepts that were intended to be understood by those who knew their Scripture and tradition. Symbols, myths, and

---

[1] J. A. T. Robinson, *Redating the New Testament* (Philadelphia: Westminster Press, 1976), pp. 238-42. A. Y. Collins, *Crisis & Catharsis: The Power of the Apocalypse* (Philadelphia: Westminster Press, 1984), p. 76, however, thought Robinson was wrong, because Rome could not have been called "Babylon" until it destroyed Jerusalem as Babylon had. Jews and early Christians did not need that much identity to apply insults. Whenever any Jews or Christians felt that they were being treated by some later country the way they were treated in Egypt or Babylon, that nation could at that time be called Egypt or Rome, typologically. A. Y. Collins, *Crisis*, also erred in assuming that John wrote the entire Book of Revelation. This prevented her from dating the earliest composition of one unit by one date and another by another date (e.g., p. 71). She also failed to consider the function of Jeremiah 51 in preparing the exegesis of Rev 17.
[2] J. Weiss, *Offenbarung*, p. 601.

codes continued to be used by Jews throughout the period of the Crusades. One of them is the updated version of the beast introduced in Revelation 11.

SIGNS OF THE MESSIAH[1]

The holy One blessed be He, the Master of wonders, will perform a miracle in the world. They say that there is in Rome a marble stone whose appearance is like a very beautiful woman. She was [a statue] not made with human hands, but the holy One blessed be He created her thus in his power. Then the wicked gentiles, sons of Beliel, will come and fall passionately in love with her and cohabit with her. The holy One blessed be He will keep their sperm inside the stone. He will then create inside her a creature; he will form a son. [The stone] will break open, and the one born from her will appear like a man. His name will be Armilos the tempter (Satan). This is the one whom the gentiles [Christians] call the anti-Christ. He will be eighteen feet long and three feet wide, and his eyes will be a span apart and be deep and bloodshot. His hair will be like gold dye. The soles of his feet will be greenish yellow, and he will have two heads.[1]

He will come to the wicked Edomites and say to them, "I am the Messiah; I am your God." Immediately they will believe in him and make him king over them. All the sons of Esau will join his followers and come to him, and he will proceed to conquer every country. He will say to the sons of Esau, "Bring me my Torah which I gave you." They will bring him their follies.[2] Then he will say to them, "This is true which I have given you." He will say to the gentiles, "Believe in me, for I am your Messiah!" At once they will believe in him. At that time he will send to Nehemiah Ben Hoshiel and to all the Israelites and say to them, "Bring me your Torah and testify that I am God!" They will immediately become frightened and bewildered.

Then Nehemiah Ben Hoshiel will rise up with thirty thousand warriors from the soldiers of Ephraim, and they will take the Book of the Torah and read it to him, **I am the Lord your God . . . You shall have no other gods before me** (Exod 20:2-3). He will say to them, "There is nothing at all in this Torah of yours, but come, bear witness to me that I am God, just as all the gentiles have done." At once Nehemiah will stand up and say to his servants, "Seize him and tie him up." Immediately Nehemiah Ben Hoshiel and the 30,000 who are with him will rise up and make war with him [Armilos] and kill 200,000 of his [soldiers]. Immediately the anger of the wicked

---

[1] Heads of the church, one at Rome and the other at Constantinople. This means this version was composed after the division of the church into two branches, the Eastern and the Western.
[2] The New Testament.

Armilos will be aroused, and he will gather all the troops of the gentiles to the Valley of Decision [outside Jerusalem]. He will join battle with the Israelites, and numerous of his soldiers will be injured. He will slay the Messiah of the Lord [Nehemiah], and the ministering angels will come and take him and hide him with the patriarchs of the age. Suddenly the hearts of the Israelites will melt, and their strength will weaken, but the wicked Armilos will not know that the Messiah is dead, because if he knew, there would not be left from the Israelites a remnant or fugitive. At that time, all the gentiles will drive the Israelites out of their countries, and they will not permit them to live with them in their countries. They will say, "Do you see this despised and defeated people who rebelled against us and set up a king?" There will be for the Israelites **harder times than there have ever been up to that time** (Dan 12:1).

At that time, Michael will stand up to purify the wicked ones in Israel, as it is said, **At that time Michael, the great prince who stands for the children of your people will arise, and there will be a time of hardship such as there never has been [from the existence of the nation until that time]** (Dan 12:1). Quickly all will resort to the gentiles and ask, "Is this the redemption for which we have been waiting, when the Messiah will be murdered?" But everyone who has not looked forward to the redemption will be embarrassed by it and will defect to the gentiles. At that time the holy One blessed be He will test the Israelites and refine them like silver and gold, as it is written in Zechariah, **I will bring the third part through the fire, and I will refine them as silver is refined** (Zech 13:9). For it is written in Ezekiel, **I will purge you out from among [the rebels and those who transgress against me]** (Ezek 20:38), and in Daniel it is written, **They will cleanse themselves and make themselves white, and many will be refined, but the wicked will act wickedly** (Dan 12:10).

Then all the remnant of the Israelites, the saints and the pure ones, will be in the Wilderness of Judah for 45 days. They will be shepherds and will eat [only] saltwort and the leaves plucked from shrubs. In them will be fulfilled that which is said in Hosea, **Therefore, look! I will allure her and lead her into the wilderness, and I will speak tenderly to her** (Hos 2:16). Where [can you find scriptural proof] that it will be 45 days? As it is said, **From the time the continual burnt-offering is taken away and the abomination of desolations is set up [there shall be]** 1,290 (Dan 12:11). It also says, Blessed is he who waits until [the time] arrives, 1,335 days (Dan 12:12). [1,335 minus 1,290 = 45].

At that time the wicked ones of Israel, who were not considered worthy to see the redemption, will die. Then Armilos will come and fight with Egypt and capture it, as it is said, **The land of Egypt shall not escape** (Dan 11:42). He will turn his face toward Jerusalem and destroy it a second time, as it is said, **He will pitch his palatial tents between the seas and the mountains of the glorious sanctuary, and he will come to his end, and no one will help him** (Dan 11:45). Michael will arise (Dan 12:1) and sound the shofar three times, as it is said, **On that day a great shofar will be blown** (Isa 27:13). For it is written, **God will blow the shofar and will come with the whirlwinds of the south** (Zech 9:14). At the first blast, the Messiah son of David and the prophet Elijah will be revealed to those refined and righteous ones of Israel and those who had fled to the Wilderness of Judah. At the end of 45 days, they will take courage, and **support their trembling hands and make steady their knocking knees** (Isa 35:3).

The rest of the Israelites in all the world will hear the sound of the shofar, and they will know that the Lord has visited them and that the complete redemption has come. Then they will gather together and come, as it is said, **Those who are lost in the land of Assyria [and those who are dispersed in the land of Egypt will worship the Lord in the holy mountain at Jerusalem]** (Isa 27:13). At that sound, fear and trembling will fall over the gentiles, and grievous illness will fall upon them. The Israelites will gird their loins and get ready to leave. Then the Messiah son of David and the prophet Elijah will come to Jerusalem with the righteous ones who have lived in the Wilderness of Judah and with all the Israelites who have congregated, and he will go up the remaining stairs of the temple and dwell there.

Then Armilos will hear that a king has arisen over Israel, and he will say, "How long will this despised and broken nation keep on doing this?" At once he will gather all the troops of the gentiles and will come and fight with the Messiah of the Lord. Then the holy One blessed be He will not require him to fight, but he will say to him, **Sit at my right hand** (Ps 110:1). He will say to the Israelites, **Stand still and see the salvation of the Lord which he will bring about for you today** (Exod 14:13). At once the holy One blessed be He will engage in conflict with them, as it is said, **The Lord will go forth and fight those nations as when he fights on the day of battle** (Zech 14:3). The holy One blessed be He will bring down fire and brimstone from heaven, as it is said, **I will plead against him with pestilence and blood, and [I will cause to rain upon him an overflowing shower, hailstones, fire, and brimstone]** (Ezek 38:22). Suddenly the wicked Armilos will die together with all his troops, and the wicked Edomites who destroyed the temple of our God and drove us into exile from our land. Then the Israelites will wreak vengeance upon them, as it is said, **Then the house of Jacob will become a fire, and the house of Joseph, a flame, and the house of Esau, stubble** (Obad 18).

Michael will sound forth a great blast, and the graves in Jerusalem will be opened, and the holy One blessed be He will revive them [the corpses]. Then the Messiah son of David and the prophet Elijah will go and revive the Messiah son of Joseph who was buried at the gates of Jerusalem. The Messiah son of David will send him out for the rest of the Israelites who are scattered in all the lands. Immediately the gentile kings will carry them on their shoulders and bring them to the Lord (see Isa 49:22-23).

Michael will sound forth a great blast,[1] and the holy One blessed be He will bring out all the tribes from the river Gozen and from Halah and from Habor, and from all the cities of Media. [All the tribes] will come together with the sons of Moses, too many to be counted or estimated. The land before them will be like the Garden of Eden, but behind them, a flaming fire [will burn] so that no living being will remain of the gentiles. When the tribes depart, clouds of glory will surround them, and the holy One blessed be He will open for them fountains of the tree of life, and he will provide them with water to drink on the way, as it is said in Isaiah, **I will open rivers on the high hills, and fountains in the midst of the valleys. I will make the wilderness a pool of water, and the dry land springs of water** (Isa 41:18). For in it is written, **They shall neither hunger nor thirst, and neither scorching wind nor sun will strike them** (Isa 49:10).[2]

There were variations of this story in different texts, but there are a number of points in which several of them reflect influences from Rev 11. For example,

1) there were two important leaders;
2) the Roman leader, Armilos, opposed them;
3) Armilos filled the same function as the beast in Rev 11;
4) Armilos killed the Messiah of Joseph, just as the beast killed the witnesses;
5) the Messiah of Joseph's corpse was thrown before the gate of Jerusalem;
6) the Messiah son of David, together with Elijah, came and raised the Messiah from the dead;
7) many believed in the resurrected Messiah.

These later narratives show also some differences from the Rev 11 narrative:

---

[1] Announcing the nationalistic Jubilee (Isa 27:13).
[2] Buchanan, *Messianic Movements*, pp. 362-69.

1) Only one of the leaders is killed; and
2) no one was taken up to heaven.

Bishop Victorinus, *Commentary on Revelation 11* (d. 304 IA), said it was Antichrist who killed the two witnesses reported in Rev 11. Armilos for Jews represented, all at once, Jesus, the Christian church, and Rome. Victorinus, *Commentary on Revelation 12*, said Antichrist symbolized Rome. This provides further reason for thinking that Jews obtained the motivation for their Armilos figure from an earlier Christian tradition of the Antichrist (see 1John 2:18, 22; 4:3; 2John 7).

TEXT

Revelation	First Testament
[15]Then the seventh angel **blew** its	Exod 19:16 The **blast** of the **trumpet** was very loud, and all the people who were in the camp trembled.
trumpet, and there were loud **noises**	Exod 19:13 When the **trumpet blast** continues, they may go up on the mountain.
in heaven, saying, "**The kingdom of the world has**	Ps 22:28 For **the kingdom** belongs to **the Lord, and he rules** over the nations.
become [the Kingdom] of our **Lord**	Obad 21 **The kingdom** will **become the Lord's**.
and of **his Messiah**	Ps 2:2 The kings of the earth take counsel together against **the Lord and** against **his Messiah**.
and he **will rule into the age of ages**. Amen."	Exod 15:18 **The Lord will rule into the age** and until [the next age].
	Ps 10:16 **The Lord will rule into the age** and until [the next age]; the gentiles will perish from his land.
	Dan 2:44 The God of heaven will raise up a **kingdom** which is for **the ages**; and his **kingdom** will not be transferred to another people.

^{Dan 7:27}**The kingdom**, the ruling authority, and the greatness of the kingdoms under all heaven will be given to the saints of the Most High.

^{Zech 14:9}**The Lord** will become king over all the land; in that day **the Lord** will be one and his name, one.

COMMENTARY

The seventh angel. Most scholars agree that Rev 11:15-19 occupies a strategic position in the structure of Revelation. Some also have noticed that there are many verses between the conclusion of the narrative associated with the sixth **angel** and the beginning of discussion surrounding **the seventh angel.** This probably means that Rev 10:1-11:14 was inserted in between these two **angels** with trumpets.[1] There may have been an intentional interruption between the sixth and the **seventh trumpet,** because the same pattern exists in the series of **seven seals**: Six seals were broken in uninterrupted sequence (Rev 6:1-17). Then there is an interruption of an entire chapter (Rev 7:1-17) before the **seventh seal** was broken (Rev 8:1-5). This was the work of the final editor who organized the various redemptive units into a composite prophecy (Rev 4:1-22:5). The insertions may have been added to enhance the effect of the **seventh seal** and the **seventh** trumpet. In the third series, however, the same pattern does not follow. The **seven** bowls are presented in unbroken sequence (Rev 16:1-21). This unit does not seem to be an original part of the earlier six **angels**, with the trumpets and bowls that introduced curses, because the **seventh angel** here introduces a throne scene rather than another curse.

The kingdom of the world. The word for **world** is *káws-maws* (κόσμος), a term used only three times in the entire Book of Revelation (Rev 11:15; 13:8; 17:8). This term was used 186 times in the NT, but the authors and editors of Revelation were much more interested in the Land than **the world. The kingdom of the world** in NT times was Rome. It belonged to "this age." At the end of this age the power would be transferred accordingly from Rome to Israel. Those who had been captives would become kings, queens, and dignified political leaders. Whenever Rome was overthrown, then Jerusalem would become the holy city and Jews would rule from there. **The kingdom** ruled by David and Solomon was called the **Kingdom of the Lord** (2Chron 13:5, 8). In those days, **the Lord's** agent was either David or Solomon, anointed kings of Israel. Whenever **the Lord** ruled over Israel, his human agent would be the king ruling from Jerusalem. **The kingdom of the Lord** was the **Kingdom of** God, the Promised Land. The claim of this hymn of praise is that the

---
[1] So Peake, *Revelation*, p. 298.

entire Roman Empire should become a part of the Promised Land—all under the rule of the Jewish or Christian king. This is an early indication of Jewish and Christian expansionistic hopes. Pressure to fulfill this hope continued until the time of Constantine and the Holy Roman Empire.

[The Kingdom] of our Lord and of his Messiah. Jews and Christians think that the Lord is always king, but he is not functioning as king in the way we want him to function until **our Messiah** has been anointed and is ruling over the Promised Land. Since **the Messiah** is the legal agent of **the Lord,** whenever **the Messiah** rules, **the Lord** rules

He will rule into the age of ages. The antecedent would seem to be **our Lord and his Messiah**, but the verb here is singular. The implication seems to be that the one who would rule would be **his Messiah.** Since whenever **the Messiah** rules, **the Lord** rules, the meaning is the same as if it read, "and they will rule." Therefore **the Kingdom of the Lord** was also the **Kingdom of the Lord's messiah**, the king of Israel. "The Messiah" was used here with the definite article as also in Rev 12:10 and Rev 20:4, 6. De Jonge correctly observed that in all instances **the Messiah** was used in close connection with God and with ruling. In the FT the term is often used as a designation for the king of Israel (Ps 2:2; 18:51; 20:7; 28:8; 83:10; 89:39, 52; 132:10, 17).[1] De Jonge also observed that the term "Messiah" was used three times in association with Jesus (*Yay-soós khrees-táws,* Ἰησοῦς χριστός) which De Jonge considered a proper name.[2] That is not certain. This might also be a title: "Jesus [the] Messiah."

When the Son of man received **the kingdom,** the saints of the Most High also received **the kingdom**--he as the ruler, and they as the citizens—and that was the part that was of strategic interest to the saints. Although the author knew of cyclical time, and he realized that the ages were predestined to rotate back into gentile control again, yet he gathered all the scriptural proof he could muster to prove his desire that Jews would never stop ruling the world.

The age of ages is a semitic way of using the superlative. **The age of ages** is the greatest of all **ages.** The anticipated **age** to come when the Messiah was destined to rule was to be such a great **age** that there would never be an **age** like it. This does not mean "forever," as many scholars assume. Ancients thought in terms of a succession of ages, just as there was a succession of days, weeks, months, and years. Ages also came to ends. There were ages when Jews ruled and other ages when gentiles ruled. This means the greatest of all ages would last until it was over. No one knew how long that would be. There was the Egyptian age, the Babylonian age, the Hasmonean age, and currently the Roman age. The traditional way of expressing this hope was **to the age and until** (Exod 15:18; Ps 10:16), meaning "until that age

---

[1] M. De Jonge, "The Use of the Expression ὁ Χριστός [*haw Christos*] in the Apocalypse of John," *L'Apocalypse johannique et l'Apocalyptique dans le Nouveau Testament*, ed., J. Lambrecht (Gembloux: Duculot, c1980), p. 267.
[2] De Jonge, "Haw Christos," p. 268.

comes to an end," but they did not like to anticipate that. Sometimes their claim was still more bold: **Your kingdom is a kingdom of all ages, your government in every generation.** (Ps 145:13).

TEXT

Revelation	First Testament and Old Greek
¹⁶Now the twenty-four elders, who were seated on **their thrones** before God, fell down on their faces and worshipped God, ¹⁷saying, "We thank you, **Lord God** of armies,	ᴰᵃⁿ ⁷:⁹I was watching until **thrones** were set up.
	ᴼᴳᴱˣᵒᵈ ³:¹⁴**God** said to Moses,
the One who is and the One who was, because you have taken your great power, and **you have become king**.	"I am **the One who is**."
	ᴾˢ ⁹⁹:¹The Lord **has become king**; the peoples **tremble**.
	ᴵˢᵃ ⁵²:⁷Tell Zion, "Your God **has become king**."
	ᴾˢ ⁴⁷:⁹⁻¹⁰God **has become king** over **the gentiles**. He sits on his holy throne.
¹⁸**The gentiles became enraged**,	ᴾˢ ²:¹Why have **the gentiles become enraged** and the nations plot vanity?
and your **anger** has come--the time for	ᴾˢ ²:⁵Then he will speak to them in his **anger**.
	ᴾˢ ²:¹²Kiss his feet lest he **become angry**, and you perish in the way, for his **wrath** kindles quickly.
the dead to be judged, [the time] to give payments	
to your servants, the prophets	ᴬᵐᵒˢ ³:⁷For **the Lord** Yehowah will not do anything unless he reveals his secret **to his servants, the prophets**.
	ᴰᵃⁿ ⁹:⁶We have not paid attention **to your servants, the prophets**.

and saints, and **those who fear your name**	^{Dan 9:10}We have not paid attention to the voice of **the Lord**, our God, to walk in his teachings which he has sent before us through the hand of **his servants, the prophets**. ^{Zech 1:6}My words and my statutes which I commanded **my servants, the prophets** have they not overtaken your fathers. ^{Neh 1:11}Please, **Lord**, let our ear be attentive to the prayer of **your servant**, and to the prayers of **your servants who** want **to fear your name.**
both small and great and to plunder those who plundered the land."	^{Ps 115:13}He will bless **those who fear the Lord, both small and great.**

COMMENTARY

Seated on their thrones before God. Aune said,

> In depictions of the heavenly court in Israelite literature, God is always *seated* (1Kgs 22:19; Isa 6:1; Dan 7:9) and is surrounded by members of the heavenly court who are always *standing* (1Kgs 22:19; Isa 6:2; Dan 7:10).[1]

Aune was basically correct, but he overlooked one point. In the court scene of Dan 7, the Ancient of Days was **seated,** but first **thrones (plural),** were set up, apparently for the great Judge, and his assistants. Those who stood before him were the observers in the court who would have been asked to stand as the judge approached his bench. There were millions of those who stood at the proper time (Dan 7:10). A court setting in Egypt during the 15th century BIA was described as follows:

> [The Vizier] shall sit upon a *judgment*-chair, with a matting on the floor, a *matting over* him, a cushion under his back and a cushion under his feet, a [*cape*] upon him, a scepter at his hand, and the forty

---

[1] Aune, *Revelation 6-16*, p. 640.

leather *straps* spread out in front of him, the Chiefs of Southern Tens on two sides in front of him, the Overseer of the Cabinet on his right hand, the Supervisor of Clients on his left hand, and the Scribe of the Vizier beside him, one *confronting* another, with every man opposite him.[1]

In this situation the judge needed the most important assistants he could find at his side as he made judgments. These would have been **seated** at his two sides, where the scribe took notes. They would not have been standing while the entire court session was going on. The same was true of the mythical judgment scene in Dan 7. The **thrones were set up** so that all of these chosen assistants could be **seated** as consultants for the Ancient of Days. Here in Rev 11:16 the same kind of situation was structured, so the 24 elders were **Seated on their thrones before God.** Solomon's elders who **stood before** him (1Kings 12:6) were not standing all of the time. Here the expression **standing before** means that they held offices in his cabinet, just as when the Messiah and the priestly teacher of righteousness were expected to **stand,** as they undertook their official responsibilities.

Lord, the God of armies. This expression appears five times in the Book of Revelation. (Rev 4:8, 11:17; 15:3; 16:21-22). Of the attributes ascribed to God in praise, the one most often used in the entire FT is, **The God of armies**. The Greek has mistranslated the term *tseh-váh-ohth* (צבעות, "armies" or "military functions") to mean "the almighty One" (*haw pahn-taw-kráh-tohr*, ὁ παντοκράτωρ). Another attribute is **the One who** which was the response Moses received when he asked God what his name was (Exod 3:14). To this the author added **and who was**.

You have become king. God was praised further as the one who had great power which he employed to **become king**. The rabbis held that God was not **king** until he had the Promised Land under control of the sons of Abraham. When he came into the world, Abraham made God **king** over heaven and the land of Canaan (Sifre Deut 32:10). Whenever there was a Jewish **king** ruling from Jerusalem, then God would become **king** again. All of that made sense legally, because the Messiah was understood to be God's legal agent and as such was legally God. The author thought this was about to happen. When God **became king** there would be a great court session, when the gentiles would become angry, because they had lost control over Palestine. By the same token, with the change of ages, the righteous Jews would be rewarded.

The gentiles became enraged. This, again, is a quotation from Ps 2, evidently a very popular Psalm in NT times (Rev 2:7; 12:5; 19:15). This was all part of the same picture. Whenever the Lord **became king**, his son and legal agent, the Messiah,

---

[1] J. A. Wilson (tr.), "Egyptian Documents," J. B. Pritchard (ed.), *Ancient Near Eastern Texts* (Princeton: Princeton University Press, 1969), pp. 213-14.

would rule from Zion, and he would govern the gentiles with an iron rod. This, of course, would make them angry.

The time of the dead to be judged. The contrast between the righteous and the wicked on the day of **judgment** (= day in court) was also reflected in the texts quoted. Ps 115, for instance, pointed out the contrasts between those who worshipped idols and those who feared the Lord. Ps 2 contrasted the gentiles who were angry with the Lord's son the **king,** who was established on his throne. On the **judgment** day, those who plundered the Promised Land would themselves be plundered, whereas the saints, prophets, and those who feared God, **both small and great**, would be rewarded.

The anger, hostility, and threats up to this point has been between the servants, the prophets, saints, and **those who fear your name** on one side and the gentiles who were enraged on the other. The king of the Promised Land would fight for control over the gentile nations. Then the nations would be punished. Still continuing this discussion, the author said it was **the time of the dead to be judged.**

Yehowah was the God of life. It was the water of life that flowed out from Zion; during the Babylonian exile, Jews were cut off from the Land of Life to make their death with the wicked in Babylon. With the return of the exiles and the restoration of the Promised Land, Ezekiel had a vision of the dead bones being revived from death into life as the chosen people returned. Existence within the contract community on the Land of Life was life. Exclusion meant death. The dead who were to be judged in this context were **the gentiles** who **became enraged** (Rev 11:18). The understanding was that the gentiles would be judged adversely and **payments** would be **given** to the Lord's **servants, the prophets.**

Both small and great. The term **small and great** is a merismus, coming from the Greek meaning "part." There are only two halves to a whole. A merismus is an expression which gives all the parts to include all that is in between. Therefore it means "everything" or "everyone."

Those who plunder the land. These were not people who **plundered** or ruined the whole earth as Weiss, Caird, Aune, and others imply by their translations. Neither is it "the people of the earth."[1] It is not the earth but **the land** which is involved. Since the same word (*hah áh-rehtz*, הארץ) is rendered either by "[promised] **land**" or "earth," this is an easy confusion. Context is the determining factor. The discussion took place, geographically, around Jerusalem. The **migrants of the land** and other enemies were **those who plundered** Palestine--not the whole earth.

---

[1] B. Weiss, ΑΠΟΚΑΛΥΨΙΣ, p. 473; G. B. Caird, *A Commentary on the Revelation of St. John the Divine* (London: Black, c1966), p. 143; Aune, *Revelation 6-16*, p 645.

TEXT

Revelation	First Testament Intertexts
	^{1Kings 8:1}Then Solomon called together the elders of Israel, all the heads of the tribes, the leaders of the fathers of the Israelites to King Solomon to
¹⁹Then the temple of God opened in heaven, and **the chest containing the contract of God** appeared in the temple, and	Jerusalem to bring up **the chest containing the contract of the Lord** from the city of David, which is Zion.
there were lightning, noises, thunders, an earthquake, and	^{Exod 19:16}**There were noises, lightning** and a heavy cloud over the mountain and the sound of a very loud trumpet, and all the people who were in camp trembled.
large **hailstones**.	^{Exod 9:24}**The Lord** sent **noises, hailstones**, and flashing fire to the earth; the Lord rained **hail** over the land of Egypt.
	^{Isa 30:30}Yehowah will make the majesty of his voice to be heard, and the descent of his arm will be seen with fierce anger, a flame of consuming fire, a cloud burst, tempest, and **hailstones**.
	^{Ps 18:12}From the brightness before him **hailstones** and coals of fire passed through his clouds.

COMMENTARY

The temple of God which is in heaven. This is the beginning of a new victorious scene. Like the opening scene of the prophecy brought to John (Rev 4-5), this scene begins at **the temple of God in heaven.** This time **the temple** had open doors so that **the chest containing the contract** was in full view, just as it had been in the tent David constructed for it behind the altar when it was first brought to the City of David from the house of Obenedom, the Gittite (2Sam 6:12-17). Not only does this scene call attention to the **contract** by mentioning it in relationship to **the temple in heaven**, but, like the second scene of the prophecy brought to John, it quoted the noises associated with the provision of **the contract** at Sinai (Rev 8:1-6; 11:19). Here is another indication of the importance of **the contract** to the Book of Revelation.

The contract of God. The contract which the Lord made with his people was the guarantee that they were still his people, and he was their God. When the temple burned, however, Jeremiah followed Hosea in decreeing that God had divorced his people. He had driven them out of his house according to the accepted rules for divorce (Deut 24:1). They would be without a contract until they had paid double for all of the fines assessed against their accumulated crimes. That would require 3½ years of tribulation. When that was completed, God would renew his contract with them. Then he would become their God, and they would be his people. When he became their husband again, he would provide for them as he had promised with prosperity, posterity, and the land. This drama pictures the temple in heaven with the contract in place. Whenever God chose to bring it down and replace it at Zion, the heavenly city of David, this would again become effective.

The temple was destined to be restored again to the City of David from heaven. This means all those who feared God would be rewarded on that day. **The temple which** opened **in heaven** was just like the one that had been established in Jerusalem. The author may have followed the author of Second Maccabees who put together the establishment of the ark of the contract in the temple in Jerusalem during the time of Solomon with the revelation of the law at Mount Sinai, when the contract first appeared. The ark was a chest or box that held the rules Israel understood to be its part of **the contract** made with the Lord. It may have held the ten commandments, the entire Book of Deuteronomy, or even the entire Torah. This was hidden in a cave by Jeremiah until the Lord again would bring his people together and again send down fire from heaven to consume the sacrifices (2Macc 2:1-15). Later Jews believed that this contract had been taken up into heaven and kept securely until it could be restored.

This data had been discerned when Judas was about to rededicate **the temple** on the first Hanukkah. The author of Rev 11 expected **the temple** to be restored again to Jerusalem from **heaven**. With this revelation would come all the natural miracles that surrounded the revelation of the law at Sinai, accompanied by the plagues that were inflicted on Israel's enemies, the Egyptians. Throughout this unit, the two-fold character of the judgment was evident blessings for the faithful and curses on the heathen. The belief that there would be a constructed **temple** brought down from **heaven** was expressed in several medieval Jewish documents, one of which is the following:

THE SECRETS OF SHIMON BEN YOCHAI

Then a fire will come down from heaven and consume Jerusalem until [only] three cubits [are left], and he [the Messiah] will clear out the strangers, the uncircumcised, and the defiled [Jews] from its midst.¹ Then the perfected, rebuilt Jerusalem will come down from heaven, in which will be seventy-two pearls which will shine from one end of the world to the other. All the gentiles will walk towards its shining, as it is said, **gentiles will walk in your light** (Isa 60:3). Then the [already] constructed temple will descend from heaven, for it is bound to the celestial abode, for this is what Moses (upon whom be peace) saw through the Holy Spirit,² as it is said, **You shall bring it, and you shall plant it [on the mountain of your inheritance; a place of your dwelling you have constructed, Lord; a temple, Lord, your hands have prepared it]** (Exod 15:17).³

CONCLUSION

Rev 11 was devoted to explaining the scriptural proofs and the accepted Jewish hopes in a time of severe national conflict. The author told of the necessity for approved national leadership with two messiahs, one a priest and the other a king. He also admitted the difficulty that would have to be overcome before that could take place.

Lambrecht, following many others, noted that the story that ends with the end of Rev 11 continues at Rev 15:5. Rev 11:19 is the end of the **seven trumpets,** and the seven bowls begins at Rev 15:5. In between are three chapters (Rev 12-14) which Lambrecht considered an intercalation.⁴ This is altogether possible. The Book of Revelation, like other redemption literature, is notoriously composite. Rev 12-14 constitutes a unit, dealing with the dragon, the beasts, and the Lamb, in that order. That unit may have existed separately at one time. The last verse of Rev 11 also helps to introduce the next chapter.

---

[1] Compare this to the cleansing of the temple in the NT. Also Buchanan, "Symbolic Money-Changers in the Temple?" *NTS* 37 (1991):280-90.
[2] The fact that it now occurs in the Torah means the Holy Spirit revealed it to Moses.
[3] Translated from the Hebrew by Buchanan, *Jewish Messianic Movements*, p. 404.
[4] J. Lambrecht, "A Structuration of Revelation 4, 1-22,5," *L'Apocalypse johannique et l'Apocalyptique dans le Nouveau Testament* ed. J. Lambrecht (Gembloux: Duculot, 1980), pp. 85-86.

CHAPTER TWELVE

TEXT

Revelation	First Testament
^{12:1}A great **sign** appeared in heaven, **a woman**	^{Isa 7:14}Therefore the Lord himself will give you **a sign**. Look! A young **woman** will **become pregnant** and **bear a son**, and you will call his name Immanuel.
wearing	^{Ps 104:1-2}Yehowah, my God, you are very great! You **wear** honor and majesty as clothing; you wear light as a robe.
the sun [disk] **and** the **moon** under her feet. Upon her head was a crown of twelve **stars**,	^{Gen 37:9}He [Joseph] dreamed another dream, and he told it to his brothers. He said, "Look! I dreamed another dream. Look! **the sun, moon, and** eleven **stars** were bowing down to me."
	^{Ps 84:12}For a **sun** and a shield is Yehowah God; grace and honor Yehowah will give.
²and she **was pregnant**.	^{1Sam 4:19}His daughter-in-law, the wife of Phineas **was pregnant**, about to bear. When she heard the report that the chest of God had been taken, and that her father-in-law and her husband were dead, she bent over and **gave birth**, because her **labor pangs** came upon her.
She **cried out** in **labor pangs**, **agonizing to give birth**. ³Then another sign appeared in heaven.	^{Jer 4:31}I heard a cry, like a woman in labor, **agonizing to give birth** to her first child, the cry of the daughter of Zion, gasping for breath, spreading

out her hands, [saying], "Woe is me! I am worn out before murderers."

Micah 4:10 Writhe and **give birth**, daughter of Zion, like a woman **bearing**, for now you will leave the city and lie down in the field.

Isa 26:16-18 Lord, in tribulation I was reminded of you; the wind whispers your instruction to us; just as **a pregnant woman** is near to **giving birth**. She is in **pain**; she cries out in her **birth pangs**. Thus we have been to you, Yehowah. We were **pregnant**; we suffered birth pangs; and we **have given birth**--to the wind.

Isa 66:7 Before she [Zion] was in labor **she gave birth** before pain came upon her she bore a son.

2Kings 19:3 This is what Hezekiah said, "This day is a day of **pain**, rebuke, and disgrace, because children have come to the point of birth, but there is no strength for **giving birth**."

Micah 4:9-10 Why do you scream? Is there no king in you? Has your counselor perished that pangs have seized you like a woman **giving birth**? Cry out and groan, daughter of Zion, like a woman in **birth** pangs.

Now look! A huge red **dragon**,

Exod 15:8 **The dragons** were congealed in the heart of the sea.

Ps 74:13-14 You broke the heads of the **dragons**; you crushed the heads of Leviathan.

Ps 89:11 You crushed Rahab like a

having seven heads and **ten horns**. Upon his heads were seven crowns,

⁴and his tail swept **the third of**

the stars of heaven, and hurled

them down **to the earth. The dragon** stood before the woman who was about to give birth,

so that when she bore her child, he might **consume** [it].

⁵**She bore a son**, a male,

profaned creature. In that day Yehowah will visit **Leviathan** that fleeing serpent, with his great, hard, and strong sword, **Leviathan** that perverted snake (see Isa 27:1).

^(Dan 7:7)Look! I am against you, Pharaoh, king of Egypt; that great **dragon**, crouching in the midst of its channels. It [the fourth beast] was different from all the beasts that were before it; it **had ten horns**.

^(Zech 13:8-9)"It will happen in all the land," said Yehowah, "two thirds in it will be cut off and perish, but **the third** will be left in it. I will bring **the third** into fire, and I will refine them as refining silver and test them as testing gold.

^(Ezek 5:12)Your **third** will die of pestilence and be consumed with famine; **the third** will fall by the sword, surrounding you; and **the third** I will scatter to every wind and I will draw the sword after them."

^(Dan 8:10)It expanded as far as **the** troops **of heaven, and it made** some of the [heavenly] troops fall **to the earth**, as well as some **of the stars**, and it trampled on them.

^(Jer 51:34)Nebuchadnezzar, king of Babylon, has made us an empty vessel; he has **consumed** us like a dragon.

^(Isa 66:7)Before her **pain** came upon her **she bore a son**.

^(Jer 20:15)Cursed be the man who

announced the good news to my father, "Your **son** has been **born**.".

$^{\text{Isa 54:1}}$Sing, barren woman who did not give **birth**; break out in song and shout, you who have not **labored**, for the children of the desolate woman will be more than the children of the married woman.

$^{\text{Ps 2:9-10; PsSol 18}}$Ask me, and I will give you
the gentiles as your inheritance, the ends of the earth, your possession. You shall **rule** them
with an iron rod. You will shatter them like a potter's vessel.

$^{\text{Dan 12:11}}$From the time the daily offering was turned away until the provision of the abomination of desolations, **twelve hundred** ninety **days**.

$^{\text{Dan 10:13}}$Now look! **Michael**, one of the first officers to help me.

who was about to **rule** all **the gentiles**

with an iron rod. Then her son was taken up to God and to his throne, ^{6}and the woman fled into the wilderness where she had there a place prepared by God, so that they nourish

her there for **twelve hundred,** sixty **days**. ^{7}There was a war in heaven.

Michael and his angels [were there] so that they could fight with **the dragon**. The dragon and his angels fought, ^{8}but they were not strong [enough] for him, nor was their place still found in heaven.

COMMENTARY

A great sign appeared in heaven, a woman. The contract God made with his chosen people was a wedding contract. In ancient Israelite law, the husband was bound by contract to love his wife, which meant he was required to provide for her, as her father had done previously. She, in turn, was obligated to obey and be subject, as she had done for her father. The contract Israel signed with the lord was a wedding contract in which God was the husband and was obligated to love Israel, just as a husband is required to love his wife. The whole body of Israelites constituted the wife, because they were all members of a legal corporation, a legal body. A corporation in court is treated the same way an individual is, legally. Here, the **woman** that appeared was the wife, Israel.

The **signs** for which Jews and early Christians were looking were clues that would help them understand the future. These were usually discovered in terms of typology and fulfillment of Scripture. Because they thought time moved in predestined cycles, they could predict that which would happen next if they could only learn at which point of time they were in the cycle. Just as Tuesday had to follow Monday, and Thursday would follow Wednesday, if they knew which day of the week was current, they could know what the next day would be. In a similar manner, if they experienced events similar to those which took place in some period of their earlier history, like the wilderness, they would know that the conquest of Canaan would follow. They were constantly studying their history and their current experiences for matches. These matches were **signs.** In Rev 12 one of the **signs** recognized was dramatized and interpreted. That which happened in one cycle also was expected in every parallel cycle. That which happened in the Spring of the year that the Persians released the Jews from Babylon would happen every later Spring, every later Jubilee, and every later era, Jews expected signs that resembled the Spring when Persians released the Jews from Babylon. They would have studied that particular Spring very carefully to find details of resemblance with their own. If they could just find one or two, they would anticipate all the rest.

The **sign** given here of **a woman** giving birth was intended to call attention at the very introduction of the narrative of Isaiah's prophecy that **a woman** would become pregnant and bear a son who would be the Messiah, the next king of Judah. In the Isaiah passage, **the woman** involved was the wife of King Ahaz. The reader was expected to understand that **the woman** in the Revelation was also going to produce the next Messiah. This drama had its origin **in heaven**. Like other dreams, it was not limited to ordinary conscious experiences. The **woman** had cosmic proportions. Like God, she wore daylight as a garment (Ps 104:2). Therefore, her children would be the "children of light." Zion has been personified earlier as a **woman** stripped of her clothing (Ps 137:7; Lam 1:8-9; Isa 60:14-16). Fourth Ezra describes Zion as a mother who has sons and whose people were clothed in white (4Ezra 2:1-48). In one of his visions Ezra saw a **woman** but then she vanished and was replaced by a city which had huge foundations (4Ezra 10:26-27; Heb 11:10).

A woman wearing the sun [disk]. In ancient art, etched in stone are pictures of kings returning from victorious battles with **sun** disks in the air just above and just ahead of the king in his chariot. The sculptor sometimes incased **the sun** disk and the king with his bow and arrow drawn within the same frame. **The sun** disk was a divine symbol that indicated the deity was on the side of the victorious king. **The sun** disk flew ahead of the king in battle and terrorized the enemy. In early Israelite symbolism, the angel or the pillar of fire had nearly the same significance. **The sun**, however, did not lose its importance to Israelite and Jewish symbols. "The Song of Deborah" concludes,

> **So may all of your enemies perish, Yehowah, but his friends, like the sun [disk] going out in its power** (Judges 5:31).

The image of the **woman** clothed in **the sun** may have had some of the same significance. The divine power was all around her, defending her from the enemy. The heroine was a **woman** who was Zion, Judah, and the corporation of Jews--all at the same time. The **twelve stars** of her **crown** might represent the zodiac, but in this context they more likely represented **the twelve** tribes of Israel. This is a real melodrama (Gen 37:9-10).

Look! A huge red dragon. The **dragon** was an enemy figure for Israelites, Jews, and Christians. It was old Tiamat, the **dragon**, who provided obstacles at the sea when Israelites wanted to cross. It was also the **serpent** that tempted Eve (Gen 3:1-24). In other cultures, like the Chinese, the **dragon** was a good symbol, because it represented the empire. This may have had a side effect with Judaism, because the empire involved with Palestine would have been—not Zion—but Rome.

The Lord had to overpower this dangerous **dragon** before it was possible for the Israelites to cross from Egypt to the wilderness when they were fleeing from Egypt on Passover night. It was identified with Rahab and Leviathan. All of these **dragon** figures were then applied to political enemies of Israel. In NT times the **dragon** represented the Roman Empire. This huge **dragon** seemed invincible. The small group of Jewish guerrilla warriors in Palestine was no match at all for the Roman military might, but the point of the drama was that there was a secret invisible power fighting in behalf of the Jewish troops. The Lord was acting from heaven to overpower the Romans, and he was certain to win.

Jews could watch the play with confidence, knowing how it all was destined to turn out. Düsterdieck was correct in arguing that **the twelve stars** did not represent **the twelve** apostles, but he was just as badly mistaken when he held that **the woman** was the mother of Christ.[1] Weiss said **the woman** represented the Old Testament (OT) theocracy--not empirical Israel.[2] He thought the flight of **the woman** into the wilderness was the flight of the early church to Pella.[3] Petrement argued that **the woman** was the Holy Spirit.[4] Zahn correctly held that the idea that the son born was intended to be Christ was incredible.[5] He also denied that this drama could apply to the flight of Mary and Joseph to Egypt with Jesus or of the flight of Christians to Pella in 68 IA.[6]

---

[1] F. Düsterdieck, *Critical and Exegetical Handbook to the Revelation of John*, tr. H. E. Jacobs (Winona Lake: Alpha Publications, 1884), p. 336.
[2] B. Weiss, "ΑΠΟΚΑΛΥΨΙΣ ΙΩΑΝΟΥ," *Das Neue Testament* (Leipzig: J. C. Hinrichs, 1902) p. 474.
[3] Weiss, ΑΠΟΚΑΛΥΨΙΣ, p. 476, 479. Weiss was correct in trying to find a historical situation that has been mythologized here and then trying to demythologize it. He was also correct in recognizing its relationship to the three and a half years of Daniel's report.
[4] S. Petrement, "Une Suggestion de Simone Weil a Propos d'Apocalypse," *NTS* 11 (1964/65):291-96.
[5] T. Zahn, *Die Offenbarung des Johannes* (Leipzig: A. Deichert, 1926), p. 442.
[6] Zahn, *Offenbarung*, p. 444.

Having seven heads and ten horns. As in Rev 13 the **seven heads** seem to be the Herods, and the **ten horns** seem to be the Roman emperors. There were **seven** Herods: 1) Antipater, 2) Herod the Great, 3) Archaelaus, 4) Antipas, 5) Phillip, 6) Herod Agrippa I, and 7) King of Chalcis. Once a person decides he or she wants **seven** people to fit a myth it is possible to add and subtract in all sorts of ways to come out right. If someone chose to leave out Antipater, for instance, Agrippa II could be substituted. People have tried hard to find the ten Roman emperors to fit this claim, but few agree. The point is only one of matching an antitype with a type. The type was the Seleucid dynasty of **ten** kings. Both the Roman dynasty and the Herodian dynasty formed suitable anti-types whether there were eight emperors or Herods or fifteen, since the number is not the main point of the typology.[1]

Believing that the **seven** must match the **ten** in some way, scholars have made some of the following conjectures: the middle head (Diocletian) bore all **ten horns** which meant he governed **ten** provinces; three heads had double horns so that the heads match the **horns**; or the seventh head bore all **ten horns**.[2] Like many others Düsterdieck took the **ten horns** to mean the following ten Roman emperors: 1) Augustus, 2) Tiberius, 3) Caligula, 4) Claudius, 5) Nero, 6) Galba, 7) Otho, 8) Vitellius, 9) Vespasian, and 10) Titus.[3] He also thought that the **seven heads** corresponded to **seven** of these emperors, leaving out the three (Galba, Otho, and Vitellius) whom he said were never really settled in their power.[4]

Since the seven heads had seven crowns, scholars have assumed that they were all emperors. One of the new possibilities is that they were all Herods, a total of **seven** if counted suitably. Another possibility is that they were all kings who ruled at the same time and wore crowns in the Roman Empire. For example, at the same time one king wore a crown in Palestine another was wearing a crown in Parthia, a third in Egypt, etc., but it may be that they only attempted to identify the Roman dynasty or the Herodian dynasty with the Seleucid dynasty, typologically, without trying to match individual emperors.

His tail swept the third of the stars of heaven. This description was given to identify the **dragon** with Antiochus Epiphanes who became so violent that he even fought with **the stars of heaven** and threw some of them to the ground and trampled on them (Dan 8:10). John of Patmos called the officers of the churches **stars.** The fallen **stars** in Hasmonean times were probably the Hasmonean leaders who were killed in battle with the Syrian Greeks. In NT times **the stars** were probably Jewish and/or Christian saints who were killed by the Romans. The author made this identification to alert the readers that, just as the Greeks were defeated only 3½ years after all of

---

[1] See J. B. Pritchard, *The Ancient Near East in Pictures Relating to the Old Testament* (Princeton: Princeton U. Press, 1969), p. 121, #691, for a picture of a seven headed dragon.
[2] Pritchard, *Ancient*, 337.
[3] Düsterdieck, *Revelation*, p. 338.
[4] Düsterdieck, *Revelation*, p. 339.

the suffering saints faced, so also NT saints would be delivered in a short time. That would come after the Romans had been overthrown as the Syrian Greeks had been.

The heavenly court scene began in which the Son of man (Judas) and the **saints of the Most High** (Jews contemporary with Judas) were vindicated against the four beasts. That was related to the king's dream of an image of four parts that represented the four foreign countries that ruled the Jews. These countries were broken into pieces and blown away like chaff so that no trace could be found. Also the battle in heaven concluded with **the dragon** and his troops hurled down from **heaven** so that their place in **heaven** could no longer be found. In the meantime, the Messiah had been born and taken up to **heaven** to be protected by God, but he was destined **to rule the gentiles with a rod of iron**.

The dragon stood before the woman. Other scholars have noticed the close relationship between the vision here and the Greek myth of Leto.[1] Collins concluded:

> The similarity between Revelation 12 and Hyginus' version of the Leto myth is striking. Both depict the attack of a serpentine monster on a woman big with child. The flight of the woman in Rev 12:14 with the two wings of the eagle is analogous to Leto's flight from Python with the help of the north wind. The aid of the personified earth in vs. 16 is analogous to that afforded Leto by Poseidon, god of the sea. The ultimate source of the woman's aid in Revelation 12 is God himself, as the reference to "a place prepared for her by God" shows (vs. 6). This motif is analogous to Zeus' role in the Leto myth: she is rescued *Jouis issu* (140:3).[2]

The **dragon** in Chinese mythology represents the empire and is a good image. It can spew water out of its mouth and provide water for all of the springs and streams. Using this character, the author of the myth in Rev 12 presented **a dragon** that represented an evil empire that poured out water to destroy the woman who personified Judaism. The flash streams of water in the wilderness are not out of character. Stream beds that are dry six months of the year sometimes become several feet deep very suddenly, just as if some great **dragon** had poured it out. When the **dragon** was defeated, it just left the Palestine area to destroy Jews in the diaspora, other children of the **woman.** There was then a war in heaven between the **dragon** and its angels on the one side and Michael and his heavenly troops on the other. The result was that the **dragon**, who was identified with the serpent who tempted Eve and who was also the devil and Satan together with its troops, was thrown out of **heaven**.

---

[1] W. K. Hedrick, *The Sources and Use of the Imagery in Apocalypse 12* (Unpublished Th.D. dissertation, Graduate Theological Union, Berkeley, 1971); A. Y. Collins, *The Combat Myth in the Book of Revelation* (Missoula: The Scholars' Press, 1976).
[2] Collins, *Combat*, p. 67.

She was pregnant, and she cried out in birth pangs. The heroine **was pregnant**, and her gestation period was almost over. She was in the midst of **birth** pangs when the **dragon** appeared, prepared to consume her child as soon as it was born. These were the "**birth pangs** of the Messiah." "The **birth pangs** of the Messiah" was the name given for the antitype of the Hasmonean Revolt against the Syrian Greeks. That revolt lasted for 3½ years (167-64 BIA). Before these Hasmonean birth pangs there had been a national **pregnancy** that had lasted from the beginning of the Babylonian captivity until the temple was defiled by Antiochus Epiphanes. During this whole time the nation was struggling like a **pregnant** woman to **give birth** to a new leader who would rule the nation. With the defilement of the temple the real "**birth** pangs" began. They lasted 3½ years, after which the temple was cleansed, and Judas the Maccabee appeared as the national leader who had been legally "**born**" during this painful period. Once Judas appeared as a national leader prepared to finish throwing off the yoke of the Greeks, the nation began to appear as an independent entity like a proud mother with her new-born son.

In NT times Jews thought the Roman captivity was a time during which the nation was engaged in a period of gestation, waiting to **give birth** to a new Judas the Maccabee, a new Messiah, who would bring pride to his new national mother. They thought this gestation period would end with a 3½ year war with the Romans, which they referred to as the "**birth** pangs of the Messiah." At the end of this war the Messiah would appear on the throne at Zion and the nation could be proud and independent again. The Hasmonean history would have to be lived again. This was the length of the war against Rome in 66-70 IA and the Bar Cochba Revolt (132-35 IA).

There were many times when Jerusalem had no king, when Jews longed for a new messiah to be born. Micah had predicted that at such a time as that Zion would groan in **birth** pangs like a **woman** bearing a child. When that happened the **woman** would go out from the city into the open country, even as far as Babylon, but from there she would be rescued. The Lord would redeem her from her enemies (Micah 4:10). This is a mythical description of the significance of the Babylonian captivity. The woman in Rev 12 was some sort of antitype of earlier Zion. She did not flee to Babylon, but to the wilderness, and as Micah prophesied, she would be redeemed. The author of this narrative filled in the picturesque details.

Second Isaiah also prophesied that **pregnant Zion** would **give birth** to a new nation. Then Jerusalem would rejoice, and the Lord would comfort her. The new nation would prosper from the wealth of the nations (Isa 66:7-13).

The **woman** dramatized in Rev 12 **gave birth** to a son who was destined to be the Messiah, and Rome was expected to try to destroy the new Messiah just as Herod had killed various Hasmonean heirs to the throne, but Rome would not succeed. Characterized as a great dragon prepared to swallow the new Messiah, Rome was constantly being frustrated. Before the **dragon** could eat the Messiah, the Messiah was taken up to **heaven**. Then **the woman** fled to the wilderness where she stayed for a time, two times, and half a time--the predestined 3½ years.

There was scriptural typology and symbolism in all of this. The **dragon** was the monstrous obstacle that prevented Israelites from crossing over from Egypt to the wilderness. When the **dragon** was overpowered, the waters opened up and the Israelites crossed over to the desert. The desert was the place where Israelites survived while preparing to enter the Promised Land. It was in the wilderness where they were tested, but it was there that the testing ended. When the author visualized Jews in Palestine being tested, he pictured them being tested in the wilderness just before being admitted to the Promised Land under their own messiah.

The **woman,** groaning to **give birth,** follows either the type of the daughter of Zion whom the Lord promised that he would rescue and provide her with equipment to beat many peoples to pieces (Micah 4:9-13), or she symbolized Zion itself who produced sons without **birth pangs** when the Lord chose to comfort his people (Isa 66:7-13). Düsterdieck thought this conflict must represent the **birth** of Jesus in Bethlehem with the following flight to Egypt and the slaughter of the infants.[1] This is almost an inevitable conjecture for anyone who assumes that the Messiah involved was Jesus. Christians interpreted Rev 12 in this way after the **birth** narratives of Jesus were known, but that was not the only possibility. The original author may have identified the child with some other Jewish leader, but when the prophecy (Rev 4:1-22:5) became Christianized the Messiah became identified with Jesus. This is the normal kind of updating of images in literature of this kind.

When he fell to the earth the **dragon** chased **the woman** in the wilderness where he belched up a great river of water after **the woman**, but the land came to her aid. It opened up and swallowed the stream, and the woman was given an eagle's wings to fly away. Then the **dragon** became angry and left **the wilderness** to chase the **woman's** other children in other places (Rev 12:1-17). The other places would have been all over the civilized world. There were many thousands of Jews in the Roman Empire—so many that 8,000 appeared in Rome after the death of Herod the Great to influence Caesar in his determination of the choice of a successor to Herod. After the war of 66-72 IA was apparently over in Palestine, there continued to be Jewish rebellions in other parts of the Roman Empire. These other children continued to provide a security threat to Rome.

She bore a son, a male. Schüssler-Fiorenza said, "In Revelation, this child without question represents Jesus Christ."[2] This was true for John of Patmos, but in its earlier form, this unit may have applied to some other Jewish messiah. These nationalistic narratives were updated to suit contemporary situations. In Fourth Ezra there is a vision of **a woman** weeping because after her long period of barrenness, **she** finally **bore a son. She** reared him to adulthood, and prepared a marriage for him, but he died at the ceremony. The wedding ceremony was to have been a renewal of the contract God had made with his people at Mount Sinai. When the Messiah appeared as the new Moses, there was to be a new wedding contract, as Jeremiah promised, and Israel would again be free to live under the rule of its own king--but those plans

---

[1] Düsterdieck, *Revelation*, p. 342.
[2] E. Schüssler-Fiorenza, *Revelation: Vision of a Just World* (Minneapolis: Fortress Press, c1991), p. 81.

failed. The angel told Ezra that the **woman** was Zion who had been destroyed (4Ezra 10:19-54). Cities were frequently characterized as **women**. For example, Ps 37 described the Edomites cheering at the destruction of Jerusalem as if Jerusalem were a disgraced **woman** put on display, with men shouting, **Strip her! strip her, down to her skin [foundation]** (Ps 137:7)!

This portion of the Book of Revelation was composed before the fall of Jerusalem, and not afterward, as was true of Fourth Ezra. After Zion had been burned, Fourth Ezra lamented the death of the Messiah--probably one of the three pretending messiahs, John, Simon, and Eleazar, who had been killed in the war with Rome (66-70 IA). The author of this part of Revelation, however, still expected the son to become the new Messiah and to introduce a new contract between the Lord and his people.

Who was about to rule all the gentiles with a rod of iron. The one expected **to rule the gentiles** was the Messiah who **would rule** from Jerusalem. Shepherds usually carried staffs with hooks on one end, so that they could hook the leg of a sheep and capture it. Sometimes they also carried iron rods to fight off dangerous beasts. The king who shepherded a nation with **an iron rod** had a strong military force.

There were many stories related to the **birth** and anticipation of messiahs. Two of these, of course, are the narratives in Matthew and Luke of the **birth** of Jesus. Another pictures Elijah receiving a voice from **heaven** telling him that the temple had been destroyed. Later he found a **woman** with her newly **born son. She** was mourning the destruction of the temple. Elijah told her to rejoice because her **son** would be the salvation of Israel. When he returned to see the national deliverer Elijah found **the woman** alone. **She** said her **son** was not able to walk, hear, see, or talk. While she was talking a wind came and took her **son** away to the Great Sea (the Mediterranean). Elijah tore his clothes and complained that the salvation of Israel had perished. Then Elijah received another voice from **heaven** telling him that the Messiah would dwell in the Great Sea for 480 years. Then he would wait until the predestined time of the end.[1]

Another story is a midrash on Lam 1:2. A man was plowing in his field when his ox started to moo. An Arab came by and told him to unharness his ox, because the temple had been destroyed. Then the cow mooed a second time, and the Arab told the Jew to harness his ox again, because the Messiah, whose name would be Menahem, had been **born** in Bethlehem of Judaea. The Jew sold his ox and began to sell clothing for children. All women bought clothing from him except one. **She** refused, because, **she** said, it was because of his **birth** that the temple had been burned. He told her to take clothing for him, but **she** had no money. He told her to take them, anyway. **She** said her **son** had fallen, and the winds later came and took him away. The Jew said that it was because of her **son** (at his feet) that the temple

---

[1] The Hebrew text is from Ch. Albeck, *Midras Beresit Rabbati* (Jerusalem: Mekitse Nirdamim, 1940), *daf* 84-85, pages 130, line 25-131, line 26. English translation Buchanan, *Jewish Messianic Movements from AD 70 to AD 1300* (Eugene, Oregon: Wipf and Stock Publishers, 2003), pp. 452-54.

had been destroyed, and it would be because of him (at his feet) that it would be rebuilt.¹

The woman fled into the wilderness. The wilderness had two special meanings for Jews and Christians.

1) It was a place of testing and punishment, and
2) it was a place of refuge.

Israelites fled to the wilderness from Egypt. They tested the Lord there so they were punished for 40 years. When Elijah fled from Jezebel, he found refuge in the wilderness. When the Hasmoneans led a guerrilla attack on the Syrians, they established their base in the wilderness (1Macc 2:28-29). After the temple had been burned, those Jews who survived asked the Romans for permission to go to the wilderness. The Romans knew enough about the situation to prevent that from happening again.

They nourish her there. The Sinaiticus scribe made two mistakes here. He left out the initial epsilon in the word for **there**, and he put the present indicative form of the word for **nourish**, rather than the present subjunctive as NA reports; i.e., God (= **they**) might **nourish her** in the wilderness as he had nourished the Israelites for forty years in the wilderness before they entered the Promised Land.

Twelve hundred, sixty days. This is basically the same period of time the Hasmoneans led a guerrilla war (167-164 BIA) against the Syrian Greeks from the caves in the wilderness before Jews won the Battle of Beth-horon and cleansed the temple. It was the same as 42 30-day months or 3½ years. These were not understood as "prophetic days" which were really "657 full ordinary years," as Bengel claimed.² He thought these years should be counted from 864 to 1521 IA. The Book of Revelation has a long history of such imaginative and erroneous interpretations as this. The 1,260 days are exactly 3½ years on the basis that there are 42 30-day months in three years. This almost corresponds to the 1,290 days of Dan 12:11. It was just a month short of fulfilling the time of the Hasmonean Revolt. The revolt was followed by the liberation of Palestine to the Jews contemporary to Judas the Maccabee. It was not the last days of history, and the author of this Revelation passage did not expect the end of history either.³ There have been many inventive calculations made

---

¹ Hebrew text from Lamentations Zuta 452-62 (45a-45b). English translation, Buchanan, *Jewish Messianic Movements*, pp. 454-458.
² J. A. Bengel, *New Testament Word Studies*, tr. C. T. Lewis and M. R. Vincent (Grand Rapids: Kegel, 1971) II, p. 891.
³ M. E. Boring, *The Continuing Voice of Jesus* (Louisville: Westminster Press, c1991), p. 168, thought the author of Revelation 12 believed he was living in the last days of history.

that are designed to make all of these periods prophesied point to the current time of the calculator. Bengel, for example deduced the following scheme:

A Half-time is in ordinary years	111 1/9
A time (*kai-ráws*, καιρός)	222 2/9
The number of the beast	666 6/9
Time, Times, and Half-times	777 7/9
A Short Time	888 8/9
A Millennium,	999 9/9
A Chronos (*period*)	1111 1/9
An age	2222 2/9, etc.[1]

Mazzaferri said,

> The patent possibility of the eschaton in John's very own day forcefully implies that even the time periods borrowed from Dan (42 months, 11:1; 13:5, or 1,260 days, 11:3; 12:6, or 3½ years, 12:4; Cf. Dan 7:25; 12:7) are literal. This is frequently apparent in its own right as well. For example, the two prophets of Rev 11:6 have power to curtail rain for the entire 1,260 days of their ministry.[2]

On this Mazzaferri differs from Collins who said none of these time periods in the Book of Revelation make sense taken literally, so she gave them all symbolic interpretations. Peake correctly said,

> The interpretation of the Bible has suffered much from modernizing, from that treatment which will not let the writers mean what they say but insists on making them mean something much more in harmony with modern thought, sentiment, and taste.[3]

Shea believed that there was an *inclusio* relationship between Rev 12:6 and Rev 12:14, and they both refer to the same phenomenon. An *inclusio* is a literary form whereby the end repeats parts of the beginning statements to show the reader that the unit is completed at that point. Shea is probably correct, but the term **the woman** is not the principal basis. This term also occurs in Rev 12:4. The two references to the same time period, however, are persuasive. Shea also understood the unit, Rev 20:3-7 to be in some way reciprocal to Rev 12:6-14. Rev 20:3-7 is also enclosed within a time period *inclusio*, the millennium.[4] These similarities between chapters and other units should surprise no one familiar with redemption literature. Redemption

---

[1] Bengel, *Word Studies*, II, p. 898.
[2] F. D. Mazzaferri, *The Genre of the Book of Revelation from a Source-critical Perspective* (Berlin; New York: W. De Gruyter, 1989), p. 83.
[3] A. S. Peake, *The Revelation of John* (London: Holborn, 1919), pp. 179-80.
[4] W. H. Shea, "The Parallel Literary Structure of Revelation 12 and 20," *AUSS* 23 (1985):37-54.

literature represents the theology of the people. They longed for the restoration of the Promised Land. On the basis of Scripture and typology they deduced themes by which this might take place, and then they created numerous images and myths that expressed the same doctrines over and over again in slightly different ways. Another example of parallelism is the occurrence of the words "souls," "word of God," "their testimony," or "word of their testimony," in Rev 6:9, 12:17, and Rev 20:4.

There was a war in heaven. The heavenly force that stands opposed to the **dragon** was Michael the great prince (Dan 10:13, 21; 12:1). According to Daniel, Michael defended the Jews against their Persian and Greek enemies. Pieters correctly noted that these picturesque events that take place in heaven are only cartoons that describe some author's imagination. They never really took place.[1] He is correct, of course, but there is a certain validity about cartoons. They do not always describe events, but they usually point out notions, feelings, convictions, and character of individuals in such a way that nearly all of the readers get the point, even though no interpretation is given. There is no evidence at all to support the notion that there was **a war in heaven**, but there was a war taking place on earth. People who were engaged in that war conjectured the way God and his angels were involved. The Sibyl said,

> In the cloud you will see a battle of foot [soldiers] and horse[men],
> like a hunt for wild animals, like misty clouds. This is the end of the
> war which God, who dwells in heaven, is finishing (SibOr 804-806).

Shortly before the Maccabean Revolt for almost 40 days citizens of Jerusalem reportedly saw military action in heaven, with robed soldiers, armed troops and cavalry (2Macc 5:2-3).

There may not have been a dragon in heaven that was thrown down to earth, but there was a Roman empire that the Jews hated and thought of as a monstrous beast. Cartoonists often have a perverted sense of humor, and they are seldom even-handed or fair in their pictures, but they represent a viewpoint of some group of people. The authors in Revelation who cartooned events in heaven may have been completely wrong, but those of us who live later and are trying to learn what early Jews and Christians believed and thought need to read the "cartoons" that were given in the form of parables and myths, such as those in the gospels and the Book of Revelation.

There may not have been **a war in heaven**, but there was a war taking place on the earth that the cartoonist was dramatizing. The wars of Israel were thought to have been holy wars in which the God of armies was responsible for the victories (Josh 5:14; 2Kings 6:17; Dan 10:13, 21; 12:1; 2Macc 2:21; 3:25-26; 5:2-4; 8:19-20; 11:6; 15:22-23; 1QM9:5-6; 11:11-13). Rev 12 is filled with conflict that dramatizes

---

[1] A. Pieters, *The Lamb, the Woman, and the Dragon* (Grand Rapids: Church Press, 1946), pp. 172-73.

military events and action. There was conflict between the woman and the dragon and between Michael and the dragon.

Michael and his angels [were there] so they could fight with the dragon. The Greek from which this is translated is awkward. Charles was correct in holding that the problem was with the Hebraism. He chose to translate it **Michael and his angels had to fight with the dragon**.[1] That is also a possible translation. **Michael**, which in Hebrew means "Who is like God?" was the guardian angel for the Jews (Ber 46a; Yom 20a). **Michael** was referred to only twice in the NT (Jude 9; Rev 12:7). He was recognized as the highest general among the heavenly military angels (Rev 12:7-9).

Nor then was found there. This is not a very certain arrangement of words. There are several textual variants. NA accepted the reading that could translate, **Nor was a place found there**. Preceding these words Sinaiticus adds two words: **They were not strong** [enough] *for him*, not accepted by NA. **Michael and his angels** had overpowered **the dragon and his angels**, so that they were forced to retreat from heaven. Not a single one of **the dragon's** agents was allowed to remain in heaven.

TEXT

Revelation	First Testament
	Isa 27:1 On that day Yehowah will visit over Leviathan, the fleeing **serpent**, over Leviathan the twisting **serpent** with this large, hard, and strong sword, and he will kill **the dragon which is** in the sea.
[9]but **the large dragon,**	
the old **serpent**	Gen 3:1; also 14-15 Now **the serpent** was more clever than any other beast
which is	**which** the Lord had made.
called the devil, **Satan**, the one who led the whole world astray, was	Zech 3:1-2 Now he showed me Joshua, the high priest, standing before the messenger of the Lord and **Satan**, at his right hand to accuse him. Yehowah said to **Satan**, "Yehowah rebuke you, **Satan**! Yehowah, who has chosen Jerusalem, rebuke you."

---

[1] R. H. Charles, *A Critical and Exegetical Commentary on the Revelation of St. John the Divine* (Edinburg: T. & T. Clark, 1963) I, p. 322.

thrown **to the earth**, and his angels were thrown with him.	Isa 14:12 How have you fallen, Day Star! How you have been cut **to the earth**, conqueror of the nations.

COMMENTARY

The old serpent which is called the devil and Satan. NA text placed a conjunction **and** (*kai*, καί) between **devil and Satan**.

This is one of two places in the Book of Revelation where the **dragon** was identified with the devil, Satan, and the ancient serpent in the Garden of Eden. The other place is Rev 20:2. Shea has shown many ways in which there are reciprocal relationships between Rev 12 and 20.[1]

The **dragon** followed the typology, not only of the tempting **serpent** in the Garden of Eden, but also Satan acting as attorney for the opposition in a court session, arguing against Joshua being established as high priest and Jerusalem being reestablished (Zech 3:1-5). **The dragon** was also the prosecuting attorney in the council of heaven, according to Job's understanding (Job 1:6-2:9), and Leviathan, the monster of the great deep; but it specifically followed the typology of Antiochus Epiphanes, the Greek king who defiled the Jerusalem temple and opposed Judas in the Maccabean rebellion. It was Antiochus who came forth from the fourth beast as **a little horn** (Dan 7:7-8; 8:9-14), and it was Antiochus who hurled down **the stars from heaven** (Dan 8:10) and kept the temple desolate for 3½ years (Dan 8:13-14).

In the Hasmonean cycle, there was a 3½ year period between the defilement and the cleansing of the temple. The author of this passage in Revelation understood this to be the equivalent of the wilderness period in the earlier Moses-Joshua cycle. Therefore he portrayed the Jewish people, being nourished in the wilderness again as the Lord had earlier fed his people manna from **heaven.** They also would go through a temptation experience again, with **birth pangs** and torments, as they groaned to produce a new nation. This wilderness drama came from the Exodus from Egypt, but the 3½ year period of torture came from the Hasmonean cycle (Dan 12:11), although there was a variant of 30 days.

Another important contact this verse has with FT is with Isa 27, where Yehowah killed the dragon, which was also the serpent and Leviathan. This was the introduction to a chapter which concluded with the great Jubilee trumpet which would beckon all of the North Israelites to return to the Promised Land from Assyria and Egypt after they had fulfilled their obligation of punishment in foreign captivity (Isa 27:13). The author of Rev 12 used this passage to relate the death of the **dragon** to the Jubilee release and the restoration to the Promised Land. Rissi called Isa 27:1 "the bud which has blossomed out in Rev 12."[2]

---

[1] Shea, "Literary Structure," p. 45.
[2] M. Rissi, *Time and History* (Richmond: John Knox Press, 1965), p. 37.

The large dragon. . . was thrown to the earth. This statement has two implications:

1) The divine judgment had already been given. It was only a matter of time until Rome would be finished. Jewish forces were winning. If the dragon, Satan, or **the large dragon** were losing, then **the Dragon's** enemies were winning. When the missionaries returned with a victorious report, Jesus said, **I saw Satan fall like lightning from heaven** (Luke 10:18).
2) If **the dragon was thrown to earth,** then he could cause almost unlimited trouble there. That is the place where the Jewish-Roman war was being fought. This dragon was the one **who led the whole world astray.** The **whole world** (*oi-koo-méh-nay,* οἰκουμένη), as the term was used here, referred to the Roman Empire.

Rev 12 is a nationalistic drama. The two main actors are:

1) **the pregnant woman** and
2) the huge **red dragon**.

The woman symbolizes either Zion or the Palestinian Jews, suffering to produce a Messiah who would lead them to liberty from the **red dragon.** The huge red dragon is Rome, trying to suppress Jewish nationalistic attempts.

At this place in the drama, Americans would expect a pause for station identification, but first century Jews and Christians understood that they were just waiting until this 3½ year wilderness period was over before the Messiah would be revealed from heaven. They would subsist on wilderness fare for a while, but later they would march alongside God's **son** as they overthrew that Roman **dragon.** Instead of a pause for station identification, the author provided a salvation hymn.

TEXT

Revelation

¹⁰**Then** I heard a loud voice in heaven saying, "Now has come salvation and power, the Kingdom of our God, and the authority of his Messiah, because **the accuser** of our brothers was evicted, the one who **accused** them before God, day and night. ¹¹They conquered him through the blood of the Lamb and because of the word of their testimony. They did not love their souls until death.
¹²Therefore, **rejoice, heavens** and all those who dwell in them! Woe to the

First Testament

Zech 3:1**Then** he showed me Joshua, the high priest standing before the angels of

Yehowah, and **Satan** standing at his right hand to **accuse** him.

Isa 44:23**Rejoice, heavens**, for Yehowah has acted! Shout, foundations of the

land and the sea, because the devil went down to you, having wrath, knowing that he has [only] a little time."

Isa 49:13 **Rejoice, heavens**! Be glad, earth! Break out into singing, mountains, forest, and every tree in it .

Isa 49:13 **Rejoice, heavens**! Be glad, earth! Break out, mountains into singing.

COMMENTARY

I heard a loud voice in heaven. The author of this hymn obviously heard the **voice from heaven** while he was reading Second Isaiah, because many of the words he **heard** came directly from that document. **Heaven** is another name for God, and the Scripture was understood to be God's word. The word **heaven** is used 52 times in the Book of Revelation, 51 of which are singular. As it is structured here, the poem which follows was made to fit into the author's drama at precisely this point, just as leading soloists are given key positions in an opera. Chronologically, however, it is out of place. Historically, the song at the sea was given just after the Israelites crossed the sea. The wilderness flight and temptations came later. Here **the woman** in the wilderness came before the song at the sea. The editor could have organized the units differently, but he did not. He made his own decisions of organization for his own reasons. Whatever the basis for his choice, he was not the only editor to have put things out of place chronologically. There are enough examples of this in the Scriptures that rabbis prepared a special rule to justify it. They said, "There is no before and after in Scripture."

The author probably had at his disposal this hymn, announcing the imminence of **salvation** and **the kingdom of God** and promising vindication for the martyrs who were faithful in their resistance against the enemy. With the arrival of **salvation** came the overthrow of the enemy. There was rejoicing **in heaven** as the devil descended to the earth where he had a predestined **little time** in which to function. That **little time** is something less than 3½ years. With this motivation, the author prepared the drama of the battle in **heaven** and the contest between **the woman** and **the dragon,** all properly supported with typological identifications and scriptural proof. The **little time** the devil had to accomplish his goals was interpreted as 1,260 days, which is roughly the equivalent of 42 months or a time, two times, and a half a time.

Salvation and power. This could be translated **Victory and power**.

The Kingdom of our God and the authority of his Messiah. Instead of **authority** (*ehx-oo-seé-ah*, ἐξουσία) Beatty papyrus has **salvation** or **victory** (*soh-tay-reé-ah*, σωτηρία).

This is the second occurrence of the term **Messiah** with the definite article. This **Messiah,** like the others, is an official title. Like the expression in the FT, **the**

Messiah here refers to a king who will rule **the Kingdom of God,** which is the Promised Land. The Messiah has the authority to rule this land. As an agent of the Lord, he has **authority** God has given him.

Their accuser before God. The author or editor of Rev 12 used this hymn with the understanding that the **accuser before God** was **the dragon**, **Satan**, the **old serpent** who was thrown down to the earth. The victory hymn was sung after that happened. Following the role of Zech 3 and Job 1 and 2, **Satan** was the prosecuting attorney in **heaven**. He was the one who **accused** the defendants and offered evidence for their prosecution. In Zech 3, Joshua was the defendant, and **Satan** was rebuked. He lost his case, and Joshua was vindicated. In Job he was permitted to put Job "on the rack" to force a confession from him. This was often permitted in ancient courts when the opposing party suspected the party was lying. In the anticipated heavenly court trial Christians and Jews normally assumed that Satan was the one whom saints would confront in this trial. Without a prosecuting attorney in heaven to oppose them, believers had a good chance of winning their trial.

They conquered him. Düsterdieck was probably right in holding that the victory involved was not just a court conflict.[1] The brothers who conquered probably won a religious victory by overpowering the force of the devil, but the devil was probably not as individualistic as Düsterdieck thought. Jews usually thought, not in individualistic, mystic terms, but in community, nationalistic concepts. Judaism was a religion of the nation Israel. Therefore the devil and **Satan** for Jews and most early Christians was the enemy of the nation. The devil was also **the dragon** that was in armed conflict with Palestine.

Through the blood of the Lamb. **The blood** functioned as ransom money. It was the price required for victory to be granted by God. The blood by which the brothers conquered was **the blood** of whatever messiah the author intended. It could have been Judas the Maccabee, King Antigonus, Eleazar, Simon, John, or Athrongeus--all of whom died as martyrs for the nation.

The word of their testimony. This passage could be translated either **the testimony which they spoke** or **the word of their testimony.** The latter possibility is chosen here, following De Jonge, because of the similar construction which should be rendered, **The word of God and the testimony of Jesus** (Rev 1:2, 9; 20:4),[2] where **the word of God** is paralleled by **the testimony of Jesus**. This follows, because Jesus was the Messiah, and by virtue of his office was God's legal agent, so his **testimony** was identical to **the word of God** from a legal point of view. Like **the blood** shed by **the Messiah**, the **testimony** which the brothers gave, was considered

---

[1] Rissi, *Time*, 348.
[2] M. De Jonge, "The Use of the Expression ὁ Χριστός in the Apocalypse of John," *L'Apocalypse johannique et l'Apocalyptique dans le Nouveau Testament*, ed. J. Lambrecht (Gembloux: Duculot, c1980), p. 274.

meritorious, and sometimes it, too, resulted in **blood**shed. It would add to the merits in **heaven** which would be used in the **heavenly** court on the judgment day to counter-balance crimes. It would perform as Christians claimed was also true of Paul's sufferings that completed what was lacking Christ's afflictions (Col 1:24).

They did not love their soul until death. This means they were willing to testify openly even though it meant they would be put to death.

Woe to the land and the sea. NA omitted the word **to**. In the same verse, NA has the adjective **great** to modify **wrath**, which is not part of the Sinaiticus text. When Satan was thrown out of **heaven**, his place of operation was limited **to the land and the sea.** Therefore it was these areas of the universe which had reason for lamentation.

Rejoice Heavens. This is the only time the word **Heaven** is used in the plural in the Book of Revelation. This further supports the notion that Rev 12:10b-12 is a separate poetic unit, composed by someone other than the author who wrote that which appears before and after it. Even the introductory sentence (Rev 12:10a) used the word **heaven** in the singular. The author of this unit found his inspiration from Second Isaiah who called on earth, **heaven,** forests, and mountains to rejoice. This author, however, limited his rejoicing to **heaven**, because **Satan** was left to continue his destructive activity on earth.

He has a little time. This **little** time was less than 3½ years, the length of time the Seleucids had control of the temple before Judas regained control of it in 164 BIA. It was also called the tribulation, the end of days, or the birth pangs of the Messiah. Among the fantastic calculations is the one of Bengel:

> *A short time* (καιρός, [*kai-ráws*]). **Time**, in this place, has a peculiar signification, a **time** of 222 and two-ninth years; and *aw-leé-gaws kai-ráws,*(ὀλίγος καιρός), *a short time*, is the period next greater than the 3½ times, which are the subject of ver. 14; and therefore the **little time** is four times, or 888 and eight-ninths years, are from 947 IA to 1836 IA, as is collected from the proportions of the other periods, with which this is connected.[1]

Bengel published these conclusions in 1741 IA. In 1991 IA Boring held that this meant the author was living in the last days of history.[2]

The Greek word for time here is *kai-ráwn* (καιρόν), and some scholars have thought that this word always indicates a special kind and quality of time. That is often the case in classical Greek, but biblical Greek cannot be categorized that

---

[1] Bengel, *Word Studies*, II, p. 893.
[2] Boring, *Continuing Voice*, p. 168.

precisely. In the Old Greek translation (OG) *kai-ráws* (καιρός) most often renders the Hebrew word *ayt* (עת) a space of time, whereas *khráw-naws* (χρόνος). renders the Hebrew *moh-aíd* (מועד)--feast or special time. It is necessary in biblical Greek to determine the kind of time involved from the content of the sentence in which the word is written.

A little time here is **a little** space of **time**. In Rev 20:3, the same expression, **a little time**, with the same meaning, used a different word for time, *chráw-nawn* (χρόνον). Furthermore, in Rev 12:14, just two verses from this expression the word *kai-ráws* (καιρός) is used for the Danielic expression, **a time, two times, and half a time**, an idiom that means, "a year, two years, and half a year." This is simply an expression for a space of time in history.

TEXT

Revelation

First Testament

¹³When the dragon saw that it was thrown to the earth, it pursued the woman who bore the son.
¹⁴There was given to **the woman** [i.e., God gave the woman] two **wings** of the great **eagle** in order that she

Exod 19:4 I carried you on **eagle's wings** and brought you to myself.

Isa 40:31 They shall mount up with **wings** like **eagles**.

Ps 91:4 With his **wings** he will cover you, and under his **wings** you will take refuge.

might fly into **the wilderness**, to her place where she is

Deut 32:10-11 He found him in **the wilderness** land, in a waste, howling desert. He surrounded him and cared for him; he kept him as the apple of his eye. Like an **eagle** he stirred up his nest, fluttered over his young; he spread out his **wings**; he took him, raised him up on his wings.

nourished there **for**

Dan 7:25; also 12:7 He will plan to change the calendar and the religion, and they will be given into his hand **for a time,**

two times, and half a time from the presence of
the serpent. ¹⁵Then **the serpent** poured out from his mouth behind

two times, and half a time.

Gen 3:1 **The serpent** was more clever than any other beast of the field that

the woman	Yehowah God had made. He said to **the woman**, "Did God say, 'You shall not eat of any tree of the garden'?"
water, like a **river**, so that he would make her **river** borne. ¹⁶The land, however, helped **the woman**.	^{Isa 8:7-8}Therefore, look! The Lord will raise up over them **water** of the **river**, strong and large. The king of Assyria and all of his glory will rise up over all its channels and continue over all its banks. It will sweep into Judah, flood and spread out until it reaches the neck. Its outspread **wings** will fill the width of your land, Immanuel.
The land opened its mouth and swallowed the river which the dragon poured out of its mouth.	^{Num 16:32}**The land opened its mouth and swallowed** them. ^{Ps 106:17}**The land opened and swallowed** Dathan.

COMMENTARY

When the dragon saw that it was thrown to the earth. When Satan **was thrown to the earth**, this was believed to be the beginning of his defeat. When Jesus heard the joyful report of the success of the 70 missionaries whom he had sent out, he said, **I saw Satan falling from heaven like lightning** (Luke 10:18)! The success of Jesus' mission was a sign that Satan's mission was failing.

It pursued the woman. The word rendered **pursued** might also be rendered "pursued," "persecute" or "prosecute," but since the **dragon** chased **the woman**, it is translated **pursued**. The same word was used by Greek and Latin rhetoricians for prosecuting a case in court. The plaintiff was called the **pursuer**, and the defendant was called the "one who flees." This pictures a court case as a chase whereby the plaintiff was chasing the defendant, and the defendant was trying to run away.

The drama continued, still structured in dream imagery, unhampered by real life limitations. Just as **the son** was snatched magically and taken up to **heaven**, so **the woman**, just as magically, was given **wings** to escape from **the dragon**.

Two wings of the great eagle. The **eagle** symbolized power. The Lord brought Israel out of Egypt on **eagles' wings** (Exod 19:4). The Lord found Israel in the wilderness, just as this **woman** was chased in the wilderness by **the dragon**. Just as an **eagle** protects its young, bearing them up on its **wings,** so the Lord led Israel, bringing them to the land where there was ample provision (Deut 32:10-14). On the basis of Exodus and Deuteronomy, Second Isaiah promised that the exiled Jews in Babylon would mount up with **wings** like **eagles** (Isa 40:31). The **eagle** also symbolized Rome (TMoses 10:8), but that was not the case here. Here the **eagle's wings** symbolized the way the Lord would rescue the Jews in Palestine just as he rescued Israel from Egypt and Babylon.

She might fly into the wilderness. Militarily, Jews often fled to the wilderness where guerrilla warfare could be successful. Historically, the wilderness provided a place where Israelites could flee for protection and guidance. The Lord always provided for them there.

From the presence of the serpent. This is a Semitic expression. The Greek *ah-páw praw-sóh-pooh* (ἀπὸ προσώπου) reflects the Hebrew *meé-peh-náy* (מפני), which means, literally "from the face of." Idiomatically it means either "because of" or **from the presence of.** Either rendering would be possible here.[1]

The serpent poured out. The place to look for the **river that the serpent poured out** is not in Asia Minor, as Caird has done.[2] The area involved is Palestine, where there are many wadies and an adequate desert space. This image is fantastic but not ridiculous. There is an ancient tradition relating **the dragon** to the water supply. In China the dragon represented both the government and the source of water. **The dragon** belched out **water** to fill up the streams and springs, providing the necessary **water**. It was a good image. For Jews in Palestine it also represented a government, but not a good one. It was a foreign enemy--Rome. Its provision was not helpful, but destructive. Instead of providing, it damaged.

The idea of **water** suddenly pouring down a dry wady (i.e., creek bed) in the Near East is ordinary. It happens frequently. There is normally about half a year of completely dry weather which is followed by another half year of very wet weather. When the rains first come, they come with violence. It does not require a dragon to bring about a sudden flood. Nor does it require a miracle to assimilate it. When the rains cease the wadis dry up quickly. Furthermore, there is the scriptural picture of Korah and his followers being swallowed up by the earth, suddenly (Num 16:1-35). Isaiah prophesied that the king of Assyria and all of his troops and glory would come against Judah like a mighty **river** sweeping through the land (Isa 8:5-8).

In dream drama it is possible to change scenes and magically bring about miracles that would be inconceivable in conscious reality. In the imagination, the **serpent** could create a **great river** at a moment's notice, when it needed it. **The dragon's** action is dramatic symbolism for Rome's power. Rome seemed to have been able to pour unlimited amounts of arms, troops, horses, and weapons into the

---

[1] So also K. Newport, "Semitic Influence on the Use of Some Prepositions in the Book of Revelation," *BT* 37 (1986):328-34.
[2] G. B. Caird, *A Commentary on the Revelation of St. John the Divine* (London: Black, c1966), pp. 158-59.

Promised Land. It could saturate the land with warfare when it needed to. The land, however, seemed able, just as magically, to provide openings that would drain away all of Rome's efforts to control or destroy Jewish sabotage and underground work.

Palestinian mountains are honeycombed with caves, so whenever Rome brought out its huge armies, **flooding** Palestine the way Isaiah said the king of Assyria would **flood** Judah (Isa 8:5-8), Jewish guerrillas vanished into the caves and rocks of the mountains. They seemed to absorb all of Rome's power without letting Rome accomplish anything by its efforts. The following photograph was taken of caves near Tekoa, south of Bethlehem, by the author in 1957. The cave shown here, which is near Mount Herodium, is so large inside and has so many "halls" and "rooms" that local Bedouin said people had become lost inside and died. Hundreds of troops could be hidden here with only a few guards at the openings for defense. A photograph of this cave is found at the end of this chapter.

The river "cartoon" was apt. It illustrated the threat that the Jewish nationalists faced constantly, but it also pointed out the frustration Rome felt as it tried to bring this little country under its dominance. Although this seems like an unrealistic day dream, it was consistent with the faith of early Jews and Christians, who believed that the Lord controlled all of nature and could open the sea at the border of Egypt or the Jordan **River** when he chose. He could also make the sun stand still for Joshua and cause the **stars in their courses** to fight against Sisera. At Moses' command, the land could open and swallow rebels, like Korah and his followers (Num 16:23-35). Not only was the vision apt; it was motivated by Scripture.

Two times and half a time. Sinaiticus apparently omitted the initial word, **a time**, which is a standard part of the phrase reported first in Daniel. He may have omitted this word by neglect. The other possibility is that he was aware of the reality of his situation. There was still one year left of the 3½ year period of warfare.

In Daniel the 3½ years represented the period Judas the Maccabee fought with the Greeks before he won the famous battle of Beth-horon, and cleansed and rededicated the temple. The author may have written this narrative after the war with Rome had been going on for about 2½ years, between 66 IA and 69 IA.

TEXT

Revelation	First Testament and Targumim
[17]**The dragon** became angry at the woman,	Gen 3:14-15 Yehowah God said to **the serpent**, "Because you have done this, you will be cursed more than all the beasts and all the livestock. . . I will set enmity between you and **the woman**

and it went away **to make war** with	and between your children and **her children**."
	Dan 7:21 I was watching, and that horn **made war** with the saints of the Most High, and he overpowered them.
the rest of **her children**, those who **keep**	TgNeofGen 3:15 I will put enmities between you and **the woman** and between your **children** and **her children**. It will happen when **her children keep** the law and fulfill
the commandments of God (and hold the testimony of God), ¹⁸and it stood on the sand of the sea [shore].	**the commandments** they will aim at you, strike your head, and kill you.
	TgPsJonGen 3:15 I will set enmities between you and **the woman**, between your children and **her children**. It will be when **the children of the woman keep the commandments** of the Torah they will aim and strike your head, but when they leave **the commandments** of the Torah you will aim and strike their heels.

COMMENTARY

The dragon became angry. After **the dragon** had been frustrated in all of his efforts to kill the woman and her child, he then **became angry**. This is an excellent example of understatement. This dream or vision was probably a general description of the attitudes and actions that existed between Rome and Palestine, but the retreat of **the dragon** from the wilderness might also have been directly applied to the retreat of Cestius from Mount Scopus in 66 IA (War 2:513-68) or of Vespasian's withdrawal of Roman troops in 69 IA (War 4:498-502; 601-604), more likely the latter than the former.

To make war on the rest of her children. Minear was correct in observing the close verbal relationship between the conflict of the woman and the dragon here and the conflict in the Garden of Eden story. The enmity promised there is dramatized here.[1] There is obviously reflected here not only a familiarity with the text but also with the targumim of Genesis.[2] The targum had already woven together the themes of 1) the

---

[1] P. S. Minear, "Far as the Curse is Found: The Point of Revelation 12:15-16," *NovT* 33 (1991): 71-77.
[2] There are two other stories of the birth of the Messiah in rabbinic literature. Both relate the birth

woman, 2) **her children**, and 3) those who keep the commandments of God, an expression that appears many times in the Book of Revelation. The Genesis story is the first temptation narrative in the Bible, and the author intentionally wove together the temptation of the woman by the serpent, the temptation of the Lord by the Israelites in the wilderness, and the testing experience that **the woman** endured in the wilderness. **The serpent** here is at once **the dragon** and Rome. The 3½ year period of testing that **the woman** was expected to endure was later called the "birth pangs of the Messiah" or "the tribulation."

There were Jews throughout the Roman Empire. These were prominent, influential, and from Rome's point of view, sometimes threatening. After the death of Herod, for example, Archelaus went to Rome to claim his right to the throne, but 8,000 Roman Jews appeared to express their views of his possible appointment (War 2:80). Whenever Rome engaged in war with Palestinian Jews it always had to reckon with Jews in other parts of the Roman Empire. This was also true when Vespasian was involved in an all out war with Jews in Palestine. When he left Palestine to fight Vitellius in Rome, he also had to be fighting against other Jews there. They were part of the population, and they would have been involved in the civil war in some way—possibly, some on one side and some on the other, or more possibly, all were taking part on one side. The suggestion that Vespasian was going **to make war on** Jews outside of Palestine implies that the Jews in Rome favored Vitellius. This also seems like the most reasonable case. Jews in Rome supported Jews in Palestine. Palestinian Jews were fighting Vespasian. Therefore Roman Jews would oppose Vespasian in their civil war there. These Roman Jews, then, were **the rest of the woman's children** outside of Palestine with whom **the dragon** would **make war** after he failed to subdue **the woman** in the wilderness.

By the time John of Patmos received the prophecy that contained this document, he may have thought of **the rest of the woman's children** as being the members of the Christian church, as Caird suggested,[1] but the original author probably intended the Jews of the diaspora.

Those who keep the commandment of God. NA has **Those who keep the commandment of God (and hold the testimony of *Jesus*)**, consistent with Rev 1:2 and 17:6. **The commandments of God** were the rules of the contract between **God** and his people. To the person who asked Jesus what he must do to inherit life, Jesus said, **Keep the commandments** (Matt 19:17). This was the minimum requirement for membership in the contract community.

If the reading **Jesus** is correct here, then this is the first time since the beginning of the prophecy (Rev 4:1) that the name, **Jesus**, has occurred. Here it seems to enter the text as an intrusion.[2] The woman's children were **those who keep**

---

of the Messiah to the destruction of the temple.
[1] Caird, *Revelation*, p. 149.
[2] J. F. Whealon, "New Patches on an Old Garment: The Book of Revelation," *BTB* 11 (1981):55, lists the words, "and having the testimony of Jesus," as a later Christian interpolation to a Jewish

the commandments of God. These were the pious diaspora Jews, but it was probably some Christian who expanded the text before John of Patmos read it to show that the diaspora included also those **who hold the testimony of Jesus**. If the Sinaiticus reading is correct, then some later scribe only changed the word **God** to **Jesus** to conform to other similar statements in the Book of Revelation. This Christian scribe considered Christians to be part of this contract faith that was closely bound to the Scripture and the Promised Land. Holtz correctly compared this saying with that of Rev 6:9: **The testimony which they held**. This supports the conclusion that the genitive involved is objective rather than subjective.[1]

Paulien said, "**Jesus** Christ is present everywhere, both explicitly (1:1, 2, 5, 9; 11:15; 12:10, 17; 14:12; 17:6; 19:10; 20:4, 6; 22:16, 20, 21) and in symbol . . ."[2] This is a bold claim in a research project that is otherwise skillful and judicious. "Everywhere" means only a few places, and most of these are in the introduction and conclusion, apparently the only part composed by John of Patmos. In the prophetic section (Rev 4:1-22:5) the word **Jesus** does not appear at all from Rev 4:1-12:9—8½ chapters! Rev 11:15 quotes one of the Psalms, where the word "Christ" or "Messiah" is mentioned: **The kings of the earth take counsel together against *the Lord* and against *his Messiah*** (Ps 2:2). This, however, in no way identifies **Jesus** as the Messiah. John of Patmos probably understood Jesus to be intended here, but there is no evidence to show that the authors and editors of the text originally meant **Jesus** was the Messiah.

Rev 12:10 includes the term **Christ** or "Messiah" in part of a liturgical quotation which does not identify the messiah intended. The same is true of Rev 20:6. This means that in the prophetic section (Rev 4:1-22:5), the name **Jesus** occurs only in Rev 4:12; 12:17; 17:6; 19:10; and 20:4--5 verses, mentioning the name **Jesus** a total of six times in more than 18 chapters--only five times if the Sinaiticus reading of Rev 12:17 is accepted. Furthermore all of these places are those in which the half sentence including the name **Jesus** might have been added, interpretatively. For example, **those who keep the commandments of God *and the testimony of Jesus***. On the other hand, the introduction, writtten by the Christian John, mentions the name **Jesus** eight times in only two chapters (Rev 1:1, 2, 5, 9; 22:16, 20, 21).

Paulien went further and said, "There are scores if not hundreds of echoes of New Testament themes, vocabulary, and theology in the book."[3] Of course there are similar words and theology in the NT and the Book of Revelation. That is because most NT vocabulary and theology came directly from Judaism. These are most evident in the so-called "apocalyptic" sections of the Gospels (Matt 24; Mark 13; Luke 17), which quote some of the same FT passages and reflect some of the same redemption themes as the Book of Revelation. These are also found in the Pauline and deuteroPauline works, the apocryphal NT, and rabbinic literature. None of these

---

document.
[1] T. Holtz, "Gott in der Apokalypse," *L'Apocalypse johannique et l'Apocalyptique dans le Nouveau Testament*, ed. J. Lambrecht (Gembloux: Duculot, c1980), p. 254.
[2] J. Paulien, *Allusions, Exegetical Method, and the Interpretation of Revelation 8:7-12* (Ann Arbor, MI: University Microfilms International, 1987), p. 38.
[3] Paulien, *Allusions*, p. 40.

shows any direct literary relationship between the Book of Revelation and the rest of the NT

It stood on the sand of the sea [shore]. Schüssler-Fiorenza was correct in thinking that **the sea shore** involved was the Mediterranean, but because she thought John of Patmos wrote the entire book, she pictured the shore as one in Asia Minor rather than Palestine.[1]

The drama concluded with **the dragon standing on the** shore of **the sea** on its way **to make war with the woman's other children.** This may have been only a transition sentence to prepare the reader for the beast coming up out of the sea in the next paragraph, but there are also other possibilities. Just before he pillaged the temple, Antiochus Epiphanes was stationed with his troops on the shore of the Mediterranean Sea. He had successfully conquered Egypt and was returning, victorious, when, along the shore, came the Roman general, Popilius, with his army. He ordered Antiochus to go home and leave Egypt as a free nation. Antiochus asked for time to decide. The general took a stick, made a circle in the sand around Antiochus, and told Antiochus not to step out of the circle before he made up his mind (Livy 45:12,1-6; Ant 12:249). He yielded to the Roman power, but he was very angry. This drama may have been an intended attempt to typify the Romans as if they were in the same situation at the time the author composed this midrash as the Greeks had been after Antiochus III first conquered Egypt. There is still another possibility.

There was a period of about three years between the retreat of Cestius and the retreat of Vespasian. The author may have painted this entire drama to describe the war that went on in Palestine between Rome and the Jews from IA 66-70. This war went on for about 3½ years, or 1,260 days (Rev 12:6) or a time, two times, and half a time (Rev 12:14). By leaving **the woman** to **make war on the woman's other children**, the author probably meant Vespasian left Jerusalem, moving his troops to Caesarea, where some of them remained, at the sea shore, while others followed Vespasian to Egypt, from which point he directed the civil war in Rome. That may have been the event which the author called **the dragon** leaving **the woman** in the **wilderness** and making **war with the rest of her children** (Rev 12).

Vespasian and his troops might also represent **the dragon standing on the sand of the sea** shore. Vespasian left Palestine, temporarily, to concentrate on Jews of the diaspora in other parts of the Roman Empire. The Jewish and Christian problems for Rome were not simply localized in Palestine. Believers from all over the world in various ways were supporting the resistance movement in Palestine. Rome could not solve the problem in Palestine alone. This drama must have been written before the fall of Jerusalem (70 IA), because it would not make sense, after the fall of Jerusalem to envision Rome leaving the situation in Palestine after it had been unsuccessful in putting down the resistance movement, without ever returning.

---

[1] E. Schüssler-Fiorenza, *Revelation: Vision of a Just World* (Minneapolis: Fortress Press, c1991), p. 83.

Court's suggestion that the woman's flight was to Jabneh after the fall of Jerusalem has some serious problems. The first is that the woman fled to the wilderness--not to the sea shore. The second is that the **dragon** did not give up and leave in disgust after it had successfully swallowed up Jerusalem.[1] Peake assumed that this was part of the composition of John of Patmos and that John had pictured **the dragon** standing on the shore of Patmos Island, but that misses **the wilderness** imagery.[2]

Caricatures, such as **the dragon** and **the woman,** were intended to have the same effect as cartoons. Cartoons are drawn to point vividly to some peculiar contemporary event. Without ever writing anything to identify the person involved or the situation burlesqued, the cartoonist draws a picture that nearly all the readers can understand, because they know the peculiarities involved. The stories redemption authors composed accomplished the same result. Like cartoons, these pictures in words also were written so that only a certain select group of people would recognize the meanings hidden behind the pictures. This was subversive literature. Today we have to conjecture the situation from all the sources we can learn about the events and the location represented. It is like reading cartoons drawn a few hundred years ago without knowing the local situation. The same problem arises in the next chapter where the individuals involved have been "cartooned" as beasts.

---

[1] J. M. Court, *Myth and History in the Book of Revelation* (Atlanta: John Knox Press, c1979), p. 120.
[2] Peake, *Revelation*, p. 309.

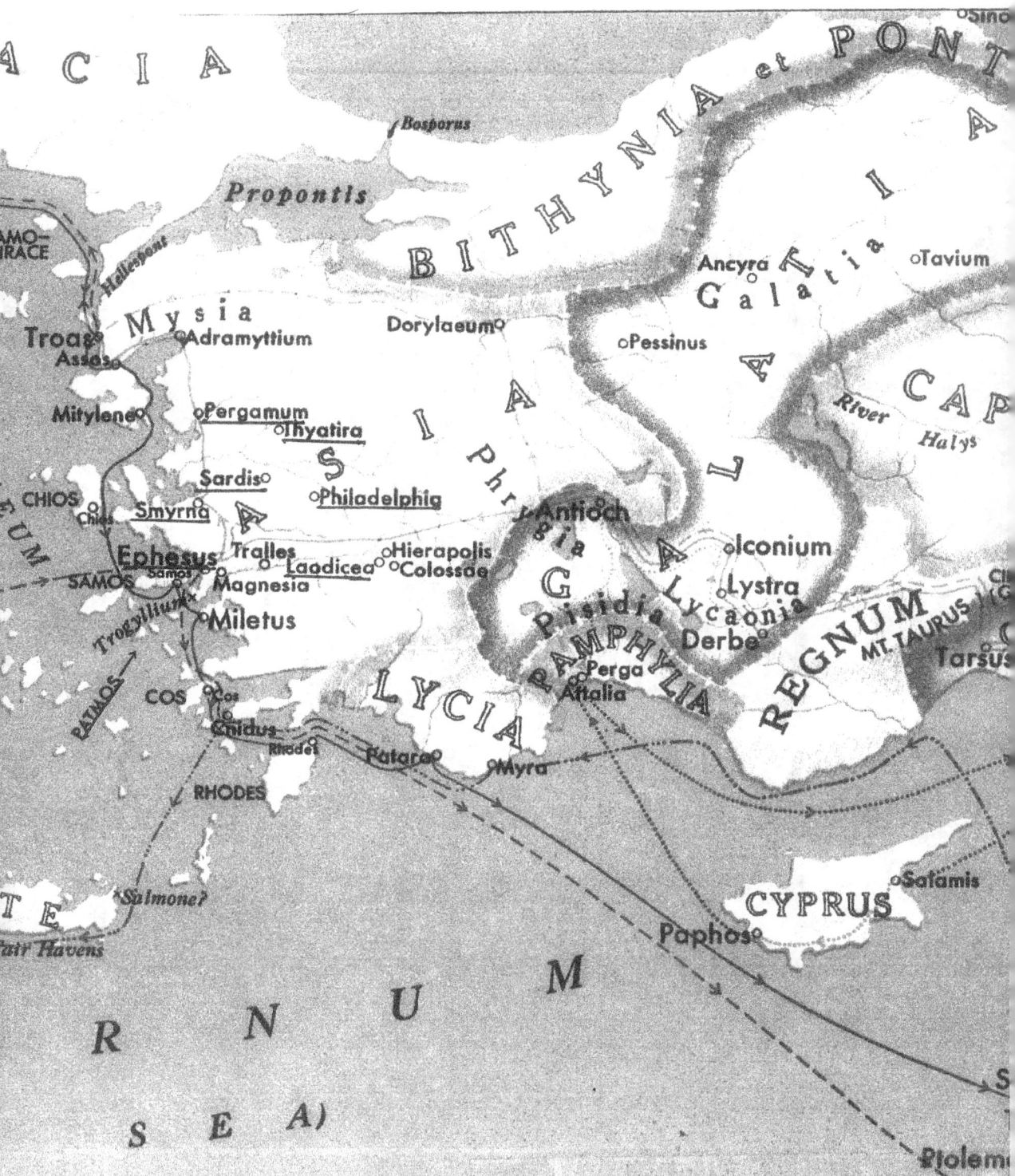

Plate XV of *Westminster Historical Maps of Bible Lands* (Philadelphia: Westminster Press, n.d.) ed. G. Ernest Wright and Floyd V. Filson. The seven church cities have been underlined. Patmos Island is one of the little islands between Ephesus and Athens.

An aerial photograph of the City of David, showing the Spring of Siloam. The large walled area, which now contains the Dome of the Rock and Al Aqsa Mosque, north of the spring, was the Roman Fortress of Antonia in NT times. The line across the ridge has been made at the approximate place of the north wall and the moat that Aulde and Steiner discovered. Photo by Dr. Richard Cleave, Rohr Productions, Ltd.

Mount Megiddo (Armageddon) and the Plain that was Formerly a Swamp

A scroll Sealed with Seven Metal Clasps

3. Papyrus 1 before its seven seals were cut and the papyrus unrolled. Photo: Palestine Archaeological Museum.

Sardis: One of the Seven Cities

The round altar at Megiddo, with steps leading to the top. This is the approximate size of Herod's altar (75 feet X 75 feet X 22½ feet) at the City of David.

A cement fountain and basin at the Court of the Lions in the Alhumbra, Spain. This suggests the kind of bronze sea in the temple at Zion, held up by beasts.

An important key for understanding the static character of the vision of the whore and the beast in Rev 17 may lie in a coin minted in A.D. 71 in the Roman province of Asia during the reign of Vespasian (A.D. 69–79); see plate 1.

Plate 1. IMP CAESAR VESPASIANVS . . . (Cohen, *Description* 1:398 [no. 404]).

Scanned from D. E. Aune, *Revelation 17-22* (Nashville: Thomas Nelson, c1998)

The artist's Mosaic drawing on a synagogue floor at Beth-Alpha. At one end of the floor is this picture of the holy of holies in the temple

The central figure on the Mosaic of the synagogue floor at Beth-Alpha. These signs of the Zodiac were also on the floor of the temple at Zion.

South of Bethlehem, near Tekoa, is this cave which can hold an entire troop of soldiers

At Wadi Zaraniq, about half way between Bethlehem and the Dead Sea, Prof. Buchanan is shown letting himself down from the top of the cliff, hand-under-hand, to examine a cave. There were no scrolls in the cave. The cave was an abandoned eagle's nest, but it shows the kind of caves that honeycomb the Palestinian terrain (1957).

The kind of bowl ancient people used to contain demons and prevent them from damaging certain people. Lids were sealed on top of bowls to keep the demons from escaping. This was probably the concept that is reflected in the Book of Revelation, picturing bowls of curses that were unsealed and poured out upon the Land.

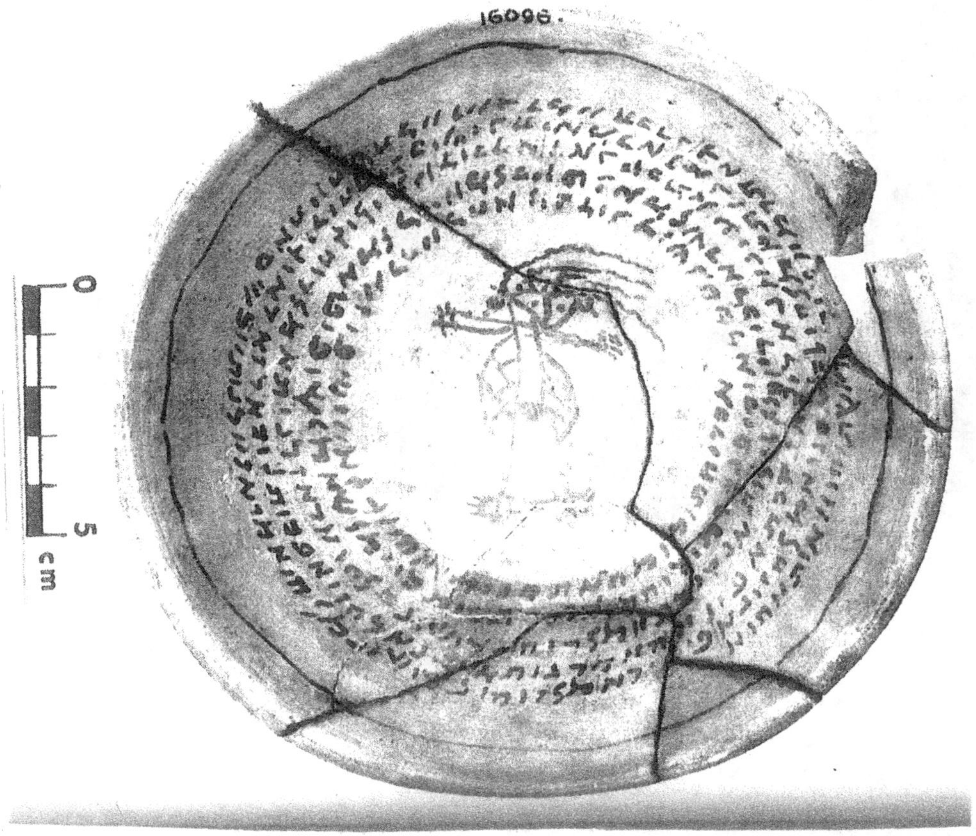

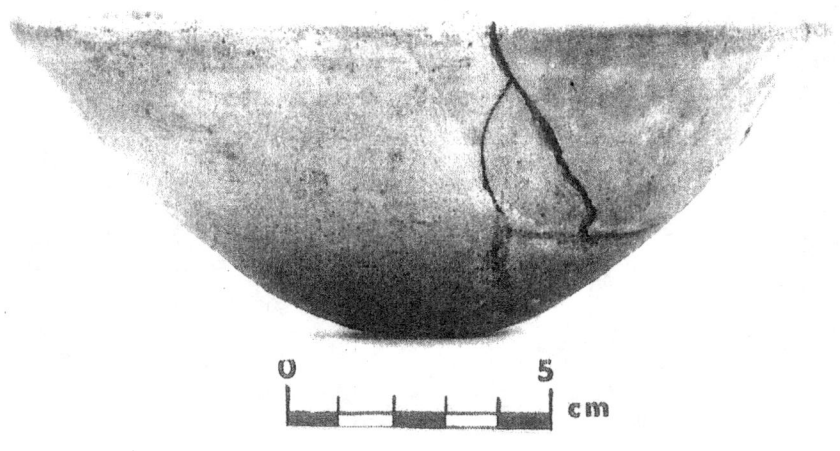

1957 carrying water from the Spring of Siloam

Boys swimming in the Pool of Siloam

A side-view of the temple at Lachish, showing the steps that lead from the court to the holy place and also the door that leads from the holy place to the holy of holies.

The upper and lower parts of a grindstone, showing the places where poles were inserted to which were fastened a donkey at the end of each pole to turn the upper mill stone around on the lower mill stone to grind the grain. Taken in the Rockerfeller Museum in 1957.

CHAPTER THIRTEEN

FIRST DIVISION

TEXT

Revelation	First Testament
¹³:¹I was watching	^{Dan 7:2-3}Daniel said, "**I was watching** in my vision in the night--Look! Four winds of heaven were stirring up **the** Great **Sea**, and four huge **beasts came up from the sea**, each different from the other."
from the sea a beast was coming up,	^{Dan 7:7}After this **I was watching** in my visions of the night--Now look! A fourth **beast**, terrible, frightful, and very strong. It had huge teeth of iron. It consumed and shattered [most of its victims], and trampled the rest with its feet. It was different from all other beasts that were before it.
having ten horns and seven heads. Upon its **horns** were **ten** crowns, and upon its heads were blasphemous names. ²**The beast** which **I saw** was **like a leopard,**	It **had ten horns**.
	^{Dan 7:6}After this **I was watching**--Now look! Another [**beast**] **like a leopard**, and it had four wings of a bird on its back, and **the beast** had four heads, and dominion was given to it.
and its feet were **like a bear**.	^{Dan 7:5}Look! Another **beast**, a second one, **like a bear**. It raised up on one side. It had three ribs in its mouth between its teeth. Thus they [=God] said to it, "Get up and eat a lot of meat."

and its **mouth** was **like** the **mouth** of **a lion**. A **dragon gave to it** its power, its throne, and great authority. ³One of its heads was as if slaughtered to death, but its mortal wound was healed. All the land was appalled because of the beast,

^{Dan 7:8}Now look! The eyes were like the eyes of a man in this horn, and a **mouth** [that was] talking excessively.

TECHNICAL DETAILS

The Units. Rev 13 consists of two units. Rev 13:1-10 is one unit which quoted parts of Dan 7 six times, supplemented by quotations from Ps 69, Isa 53, and Jer 15. It was given a literary conclusion, **Here is the patience and faith of the saints** (Rev 13:10). Rev 13:11 begins a new unit with the introduction **I was watching** and concludes with **Here is wisdom . . .** (Rev 13:18).[1] In this second group of eight verses there is only one quotation from the First Testament (FT) (Rev 13:15; Dan 3:5-6). The second unit seems to have been attached to the first, because its author used some of the same expressions as the first: dragon, beast, mortal wound that was healed, migrants of the land, and the authority of the dragon given to the beast. The second unit also seems to have been built on the first unit, referring to a **first beast** and **another beast**, but it does not distinguish beasts from horns and heads as the first unit does.

Jewish and Christian editors tended to organize material together that belonged to one subject classification. For example, in Matt 13 all of the Kingdom parables of that document are presented. In Luke 14, except for the last supper, all the stories about meals in that gospel are classified. Luke 15 consists of a collection of parables dealing with lost and found situations. Here in the Book of Revelation, Rev 12 dealt with **the woman** in the wilderness and **the dragon**. Rev 13 deals with **the dragon** and **the beasts.** They were organized so that Rev 13 properly followed Rev 12.

Jewish Use of Imagery. Jews frequently associated many metaphors and myths together in ways that were suggestive and closely associated with some **Jewish** tradition or Scripture. For example, **beasts** in Revelation were intended to call the reader's attention to the **beasts** in Daniel. In Daniel the **beasts** were kings of enemy countries. Once one of these images became well-known it could be used over and over again, alluding to some contemporary person or situation. These metaphors were not always precisely the same every time they were used. For example, in medieval Judaism there was a mythical character, called "Armilos." This was

---

[1] R. H. Charles, *Critical and Exegetical Commentary on the Revelation of St. John* (New York: Charles Scribner's Sons, c1920) I, pp. 339-44, followed J. Wellhausen, and J. Weiss in holding that there were two units in chapter 13:1-10 and 11-18. Many have followed these with some variations.

probably a mythical name taken from "Romulus." The story of Armilos' origin was repeated many times in medieval Jewish literature, but not always with exactly the same details. For instance, Saadia Gaon introduced him as one who originated from a stone in Rome.[1] He was destined to fight against the Jews under the leadership of their messiah, son of Joseph. At that time Armilos would kill the Messiah of Joseph. Afterward, the Messiah, son of David, would kill Armilos in the temple area at Jerusalem.[2] Saadia said Armilos would be ruler of Edom (meaning Rome). He would go out from Rome and rule the world and would be especially cruel to Jews, but later Elijah would return and the dead would be raised to dwell at Jerusalem.[3] These details were repeated many times in other literature.

An anonymous poem indicated that Armilos would kill Menahem, son of Amiel, the Messiah of Joseph,[4] but that the Messiah, son of David, would raise him up, and destroy the gentiles.[5] Wertheimer's text from *Pirke Hecalot Rabbati* of *The Book of Zerubbabel*, added some details. The stone from which Armilos had been born had the appearance of a beautiful virgin. Beliel had intercourse with this statue, and she bore Armilos, who was the chief of idolatry. Half of him was from the stone and half from Beliel.[6] Armilos was a king of fierce countenance, the son of Satan.[7] Jellinek's text and that of the Bodleian Library both note that all the gentiles would follow Armilos,[8] and that the son of David would blow into the nostrils of Armilos and kill him.[9]

Part of those texts related Armilos to the seventh century IA and to Shiroi, king of Persia. Up to that time Armilos was pictured as a human being who was a Roman and led armies against Palestine. After the division of the Christian church into the Greek branch whose headquarters were in Constantinople and the Latin branch which was centered in Rome, a caricature of Armilos said he was eighteen feet tall, had hands that reached to his feet, had yellow hair, and the soles of his feet were green. One of his arms would be about six inches long and the other, four and a half feet long. He would have two heads, and all who saw would shudder.[10] Still another text held that he would be bald with small eyes. He would have leprosy on his forehead, and his right ear would be deaf.[11] Another narrative said he claimed to

---

[1] Buchanan, *Jewish Messianic Movements from AD 70 to AD 1300* (Eugene, Oregon: Wipf and Stock Publishers, 2003), pp. 131-32.
[2] *Jewish Messianic Movements*, pp. 46-48.
[3] *Jewish Messianic Movements*, pp. 122-30.
[4] The names of the messiahs are sometimes confused. Sometimes the Messiah of Joseph was called Nehemiah, son of Hoshiah, and the son of David was called Menahem (*Jewish Messianic Movements*, pp. 364, 381, 456-57, 584-85, *et passim*.
[5] *Jewish Messianic Movements*, p. 243.
[6] *Jewish Messianic Movements*, pp. 351-52; see 362.
[7] *Jewish Messianic Movements*, p. 357.
[8] *Jewish Messianic Movements*, p. 364.
[9] *Jewish Messianic Movements*, p. 373.
[10] *Jewish Messianic Movements*, pp. 381, 415, 446.
[11] *Jewish Messianic Movements*, pp. 400-401.

be the Messiah of the Jews and God, and he proclaimed good news, and all the gentiles believed in him, but the Jews did not.[1]

With variations, the story of Armilos was told and written over and over always in a way that would ridicule the Christians, the church, Rome, or Jesus. The figure of two heads represented the Eastern and Western branches of the church; the mixture of a pure virgin and Satan was composed to ridicule Jesus and his association with pure Judaism and wicked gentiles. Armilos was also the king of Rome. In the Middle ages, Jews hated all of these and grouped them together under the title, "Armilos."

The story of Armilos may not have arisen independently. It may have been composed in reaction to a Christian myth that circulated widely and over many centuries. The Christian myth tells of its own origin in a favorable way. According to Eusebius, in the beginning the Lord made a contract with his people, agreeing to be their God and they would be his people, just as a groom enters into a contract with his bride. This bride was initially a pure soul, but she chose to leave her faithful groom and took for herself a sensual and evil demon. Then the Lord departed from her. When this happened, this bride fell to the ground, absolutely dead. Weapons of war were leveled against her so that not one stone was left upon the other. It was not a boar out of the wilderness but some demon and spiritual wild beasts who inflamed her with their passions. This set the sanctuary of God on fire, and the dwelling place of his name fell to the ground, and she lost all hope of salvation, but after she had paid double for all her crimes the Lord restored her and rebuilt the temple of precious stones (HE 10:4, 56-62).

This parable of Eusebius was a mythological way of telling of the events in history between the fall of the temple in Jerusalem in 70 IA and the establishment of the church in the time of Contstantine in the fourth century IA. The bride who had been polluted, thrown to the ground because of her intercourse with evil demons, was the Judaism that fell when the temple was burned in 70 IA, and finally so fully removed that not one stone was left on top of another in 135 IA. The restored bride was the Christian church after the victory of Constantine. This parable may have been circulated widely to the satisfaction of Christians, but to the dissatisfaction of Jews. In retaliation, Jews composed their own parable of Armilos which pictured Christianity as the polluted Judaism rather than the restored, forgiven bride. Another clue that Jews derived their caricature of Armilos from Christians is reported in the fifth century Apocalypse of John:

> I heard a voice saying to me, "Listen, righteous John! At that time the denier will appear, the one excommunicated in the darkness, the one called Antichrist." Again I said, "Lord, disclose to me what he is like." Then I heard a voice saying to me, "The appearance of his face is gloomy; the hair of his head is sharp-pointed, like arrows; his brows are wild; his right eye is like the morning star rising, and the other is like [the eye] of a lion. His mouth is eighteen inches wide,

---

[1] *Jewish Messianic Movements*, pp. 415, 496, 500.

and his teeth are seven and a half inches long. His fingers are like sickles; his feet are fifteen inches long; and on his forehead is the inscription, 'Antichrist'" (ApocJohn 4:6-7).

There are several points at which Christian description of the Antichrist was like the Jewish description of Armilos. Both are hideous.

After 600 years of telling and retelling the story Eusebius told, the tenth century Adso told the same story reported by Eusebius, but he added many homiletical details, pausing to compare Antichrist adversely to Jesus. He spelled out in detail the complete control the devil had over the woman, said he was born from the Jews, was born in crime rather than virginal purity and continued in complete subjection to the devil.[1] Jews also told and retold the story of Armilos, varying the details as the local need demanded. Both "Armilos" and the "Antichrist" were used over many centuries, varied somewhat according to current needs, and were caricatures of the authors' enemy leaders. Jews used Armilos to insult Christians, and Christians used Antichrist to insult Jews, Christian heretics (MPL 84, 381D), and Moslems.[2]

In the same way that Jews could use terms like "Armilos" they could also use terms like **beast**, **dragon**, and **harlot** sometimes to refer to Rome, sometimes to Rome's agents, and sometimes to Rome's kings. Likewise just as Christians could use the term "Antichrist" sometimes to mean Jews, at other times to mean Moslems, pagans, or some Christian sect, so they were able to use terms like **dragon**, **beast**, and **harlot** to apply to different entities at different times.

Just because the word **beast** was used does not mean that the same author wrote all the narratives where the name occurs or that all usages intend the same identity. Redemption anthologies were notoriously composite, consisting of small units taken from many sources. In order to understand a chapter like Rev 13, it will be necessary to segregate the units to the best of our ability, and try to understand the meaning of each unit separately and the way the editor worked when he put them all together. The place to begin is with the typological insights gained by comparing Rev 13 with earlier scriptural sources that it quotes.

COMMENTARY

I was watching. The word "redemption" is a financial term that has been used metaphorically in Christian and Jewish theology. When a person borrows money and later pays the loan, he or she "redeems" the note and no longer has to pay either principal or interest on it. When Jews and Christians committed crimes they realized that there was a necessary fine to be paid both to the victim and to the government. In a theocracy that also meant a fine to God. Unpaid fines accumulated and were called "iniquities." The redemption of Israel involved repaying all of the iniquities for Israel's crimes, so that the punishment could be concluded and the land restored

---

[1] B. McGinn, *Visions of the End* (New York: Columbia U. Press, 1979), pp. 84-85.
[2] Joachim of Fiore. See McGinn, *The End*, p. 137.

to the chosen people. Literature dealing with methods necessary for punishment and restoration of the land has been called "redemption literature." Because it sometimes is written in the literary forms of dreams and visions, those forms are also sometimes called "apocalyptic" literature. The word "apocalyptic" refers to something that has been closed that is now opened, such as a door, window, or a book or scroll. When a scroll is opened, it is possible to read it and learn its contents.

The words **I was watching** constitutes a typical redemption literature introduction. Literally the Greek is *kai áy-dawn* (καὶ εἶδον) "and I saw." It is frequently followed by, "Now look!" to point out to the reader what the author saw when he looked. Although the Greek is aorist, it is a translation of the Aramaic in Daniel of *kháh-zeh hah-wáyth* (חזה הוית) which is the imperfect tense, very literally rendered, **I was watching**. This idiom in Aramaic, like rabbinic Hebrew, is reflected in the New Testament (NT) by a periphrastic imperfect, using some form of the verb, "to be," as a helping verb, even though it is unnecessary in Greek.

The image given is that of the prophet watching, as if at a theater, when suddenly something appeared which prompted him to encourage the reader also to look. This, however, was not a vision in the sky that came to him. The place where he was directing his attention was not to the sky nor to a stage in the theater but to the FT where he read about the four beasts in Dan 7. He immediately saw the relationship between the picture Daniel had painted and the historical situation in his own day. He knew that Dan 7 was a mythicized history of the Maccabean victory. He believed that time cycled so that the same occurrence appeared in history again and again. Therefore he began to call the readers' attention to the mythicized scene of current history so the readers could understand what was then happening in Palestine.

A beast coming up from the sea. This text was taken directly from Dan 7:3, calling attention to the kings of four gentile countries that oppressed Israel before the Hasmonean Revolt. Instead of four **beasts**, however, this author was interested in only one **beast,** which was worse than any of the four **beasts** that oppressed the Jews in Hasmonean times. The author pictured this particular **beast** as a composite of all four of the **beasts** of Hasmonean times. This **beast** was an agent of Rome.

Düsterdieck argued against those who denied that the **beast** was the precise form of Roman secular power. He held that they were only guessing arbitrarily and were able to guess further that the heads and horns could represent seven periods of the world, the tenfold division of the government of the world; the seven secular powers; the final future power with its ten divisions; the seven persecutions of Christians; the seven powers hostile to Christianity; and the seven small powers that were united with the Antichrist.[1] There are no controls to this type of allegorization. Fourth Ezra also described a monster who came up from the sea who was an eagle, apparently symbolizing Rome (4Ezra 11:1-2).

---

[1] F. Düsterdieck, *Critical and Exegetical Handbook to the Revelation of John*, tr. H. E. Jacobs (Winona Lake: Alpha Publications, 1884), pp. 365-66.

THE HERODIANS AND THE BEASTS

No one has satisfactorily identified **the beasts**, horns, or heads in Rev 13. The reason is that Rev 13 is composed of coded terms which Jews that were contemporary with their author knew, and at this distance we can only guess. There are some clues--although not enough--that help with the identification. These will be shown here, some of which earlier scholars have not seen, but conclusions possible will not be absolute here, either. The problem is the identification of the characters in the drama (*dramatis personae*), with historical human beings of the author's time. This would be easier if that time were certainly known, but that too is a deduction. Customarily redemption anthologies were composed of many earlier units that some editors collected and organized into coherent documents. These units were used over and over again as is evident from medieval Jewish redemption literature.

The author of Rev 13:1-10 clearly patterned his image of **the beast** from Daniel. In Dan 7 and 8, however, there were four **beasts** that came up out of the sea. These represented the kings of the four nations that ruled the Jews from the time of the first destruction of Jerusalem (586 BIA) until the temple was defiled in the time of the Hasmoneans (164 BIA). Each of these four **beasts** represented kings of Babylon, Media, Persia, and Greece, respectively (GenR 42:2). Each of these **beasts** was more terrible than the previous one. The author of the drama in Rev 13, however, pictured only one **beast** in detail, which he caricatured as being the epitome of everything that was evil in all four ruling powers prior to the Maccabean Revolt. Not only was **the beast** more monstrous even than Antiochus Epiphanes, but he was an agent of the **dragon** caricatured in Rev 12. NA has **The dragon**, which is probably correct, because **the dragon** involved was not just any **dragon**; it was *the* **dragon** described in Rev 12. This sentence means

1) that **the beast** was a ruler or judge of some kind who had a throne and
2) that **the beast** did not act on the basis of its own authority and power. It acted on the basis of authority that belonged to another.

The beast evidently was a legal agent of some principal. An agent or apostle has the authority of the one who sent him to act in his interest, in his name, and at his responsibility. Here the principal or sender was the **dragon**. When the dragon commissioned **the beast** to fulfill some responsibility, **the beast** was legally identical to **the dragon**.

The dragon was required by law to uphold whatever agreements and promises **the beast** made. Ambassadors and governors or rulers appointed by a monarch functioned as agents of the monarch. They received their authority from the monarch, and, if they were loyal, they administered all of their business with the principal's interests in mind. Düsterdieck correctly said that when **the dragon** gave **the beast** a throne, he also gave it a kingdom.[1] He probably confused his pronouns,

---
[1] Düsterdieck, *Revelation*, p. 369.

however, when he took this to mean that **the dragon** gave his own throne to **the beast**. The pronoun "his" belongs to **the beast**. **The dragon** gave **the beast** the throne belonging to **the beast**, and he gave **the beast** whatever authority **the beast** had. This does not mean that **the dragon** no longer had a kingdom, a throne, or any authority.

BEASTS AND SCHOLARS

The beasts in Rev 13, like **the beasts** in Daniel, represent kings of countries. Those in Daniel are well understood, because Daniel interpreted them. Those in Rev 13 were not so identified, so they have been interpreted various ways over the years. Zahn said **the beast** was the Antichrist, and **the dragon** was Satan.[1] Erbes, Spitta and Vischer all believed **the beast** with ten horns and seven heads was Caligula who became seriously ill at one time in his career. Sweet followed Wellhausen in thinking that **the beast** represented the Roman empire and should not be identified with any individual.[2] Although there is no textual evidence for his position Charles concluded that the first beast was the personification of the Antichrist, and the second **beast** was the false prophet.[3] Weiss said it represented the entire Julian dynasty which came to an end, and the healing was the ascension to the throne of Vespasian. He argued that the identification of **the beast** with the mortal wound as Nero was altogether impossible.[4] Collins and Giblin both thought Nero was the only possibility.[5]

In Collins' opinion,

> Nero is depicted as an Antichrist. He fits that role exactly, although the name is not used.[6]

Others also fit the role exactly. Collins also made it easier for herself by deciding that it was not necessary to include all of the emperors on the list.[7] That methodology allows the person interpreting to pick and choose whichever emperors he or she wants and omit the rest. One of the best explanations for thinking that Nero would return to Rome and rule again was given by Peake.[8] He argued that people in antiquity did not think that Nero really died and came back to life any more than Herod thought John the Baptist had been raised from the dead. Instead he may have

---

[1] T. Zahn, *Die Offenbarung des Johannes* (Leipzig: A. Deichert, 1924), p. 451.
[2] J. P. M. Sweet, *Revelation* (Philadelphia: Westminster Press, c1979), p. 208. For Wellhausen, see Charles, *Revelation* I, pp. 338-39.
[3] Charles, *Revelation* I, pp. 341-42.
[4] B. Weiss, "ΑΠΟΚΑΛΥΨΙΣ ΙΩΑΝΟΥ," *Das Neue Testament* (Leipzig,: J. C. Hinrichs, 1902), pp. 481, 485.
[5] C. H. Giblin, *The Book of Revelation* (Collegeville: The Liturgical Press, c1991), pp. 133, 135.
[6] A. Y. Collins, *Crises and Catharsis: The Power of the Apocalypse* (Philadelphia: Westminster Press, c1984), p. 59.
[7] Collins, *Crisis*, pp. 60, 62, 63.
[8] A. S. Peake, *The Revelation of John* (London: Holborn, 1919), pp. 123-33.

fled to Parthia and there might have found support to return and reclaim his kingdom. His death would have been political rather than physical. Some thought Domitian was "a bald Nero," and compared him with Nero for his cruelty. Bodinger thought the myth of Nero's return was a natural one to develop, given Jewish and Christian eschatology and the events of the first century IA.[1]

Lilje held that the **first beast** represented "the imperial world power as a perverted political institution," and refused to identify the second beast at all.[2] Ford gave arguments for supporting either Caligula or Nero as the first beast without committing herself to either. She thought the second beast might be the religious Antichrist, including false cults and philosophers.[3] Mounce favored Caligula as the first beast and the false prophet as the second, but did not venture to guess who the historical character might be who fit both roles.[4] Zahn presented many arguments offered by the early church for identifying the beast with either Caligula or Nero and concluded in favor of Caligula.[5] Aune thought the first beast was the monster Leviathan and the second was Behemoth.[6]

THE BEASTS AND THE DRAGON

Most scholars identify **the beast** with Rome or its emperors, but that is the function of **the dragon**. In Rev 12 **the dragon** seems to have been represented by Cestius or Vespasian. The dragon was the principal in this narrative, so it would not be likely that it was also **the beast** in the same literary unit. From the standpoint of Jews in Palestine, the agent that carried out Rome's decrees was one of the Herods or one of the Roman procurators, both of whom were agents of Rome. This unit in Rev 13 was placed after Rev 12, because it was a continuation of **the dragon** theme of Rev 12. In Rev 12, **the dragon** was an antitype of the Hellenic Alexandrian empire. The ten horns in Daniel represented the Seleucid dynasty. Here there must be a similar antitype. **The dragon** is Rome, and the ten horns must be some successsion of leaders. Rev 12 presents the principal, **the dragon**, and Rev 13 shows **the dragon's** extension through its agents, **the beasts**. Like **the dragon** in Rev 12 **the beast** in Rev 13 had seven heads and ten horns, implying that in some way the two were equivalent.

Having ten horns.[7] In Daniel **the ten horns** represented the Seleucid dynasty. In Revelation an antitype of the Seleucids would either be the Caesars or the Herods. In

---

[1] M. Bodinger, "Le Mythe de Néron de L'Apocalypse de Saint Jean au Talmud de Babylon," *RHR* 206 (1989):21-40.
[2] H. Lilje, *The Last Book of the Bible*, tr. O. Wyon (Philadelphia: Muhlenberg Press, c1957), pp. 189-97.
[3] J. M. Ford, *Revelation* (Garden City: Doubleday & Co., 1975), pp. 211-14.
[4] R. H. Mounce, *The Book of Revelation* (Grand Rapids: Eerdmans, c1977), pp. 252-65.
[5] Zahn, *Offenbarung*, p. 550. See also pp. 450-500.
[6] D. E. Aune, *Revelation 6-16* (Nashville: Thomas Nelson Publishers, c1998), p. 779.
[7] The horn symbolizes weapons, military defense, power, success, dignity, and victory. See also I.

neither case does the number **ten** cohere perfectly, but that is not necessary for a typology. It is not the number that is important but the identity. The Seleucid dynasty had an antitype dynasty at the time the author wrote. The **ten** was used only to identify the dynasty.

Seven heads. Although this beast had seven heads, like **the dragon** (Rev 12:3), it had only one mouth (Rev 13:2). This was not simply careless forgetfulness on the part of the author, as Loisy thought,[1] but rather part of the author's faithfulness to the text. In Dan 7:8 was a "**horn** who had a mouth that was talking excessively." This horn was a caricature of Antiochus Epiphanes; it had only one head and therefore only one mouth. The author of Rev 13 created a beast with seven heads, but he wanted also to allude to Antiochus Epiphanes, so he mentioned **the mouth** as **one mouth** rather than seven. This is a *caricature* or a cartoon of a historical figure, not a real description of a historical figure.

If the author intended **the beast** to be the Herodian dynasty, then hypothetically one of its heads might initially have been Herod the Great, Archelaus, Antipas, or Agrippa I. It could later, then, have been updated by later editors to fit another of the Herods, just as Judaism did with Armilos and the church did with Antichrist. If, on the other hand, the royal succession of the Caesars was chosen as the antitype, then the narrative might first have begun with Augustus as one of the heads and then been updated to Tiberius, Gaius, Claudius, Nero, or any later emperor. In Rev 13, the heads seem to have been Herods rather than Caesars, because both Herod the Great and Agrippa I seem to fit the qualifications of political leaders who suffered mortal wounds and were revived. No scholar has succeeded in finding any of the Caesars who qualifies as one who received a mortal wound and was later healed.[2] Although the Herods fit the roles of beasts or heads better than Caesars, they do not conform to the pattern perfectly, either. Here we will give the evidence that supports Herod the Great as the first beast and Herod Agrippa as the second beast.

As if slaughtered to death. Since the word for "heads" in Greek is feminine, and the word for **beast** is masculine, the possessive pronoun **its** (*ow-toó,* αὐτοῦ) (neuter or masculine) refers to **the beast** and not to one of the heads. Zahn correctly observed that it was hardly possible to kill some animal's head without killing the entire

---

Scheftelowitz, "Das Hörnermotif in den Religionen," *ARW* 15 (1912):451-87.

[1] A. Loisy, *L'Apocalypse de Jean* (Paris: Emile Nourry, 1923), p. 247.

[2] The two examples scholars usually give are Gaius, who became very ill at one time and recovered, and Nero, who committed suicide, but who, some Romans thought, really escaped to Parthia and would return some time alive. Ford holds that the beast was the Roman empire and the wounded head was Vespasian (Ford, *Revelation*, p. 221). Nero (*Néh-rawn káy-sehr,* נרון קיסר) was suggested as the 666 by Irenaeus, *AdvHaer* 5:30, 1. Ford identified the first beast with Rome and the second beast with Josephus (Ford, *Revelation*, p. 227). Beagley's only refutation for this was that Ford's theory that Revelation is basically Jewish with some Christian interpolations is "unfounded" (A. J. Beagley, *The "Sitz im Leben" of the Apocalypse* [Berlin: W. De Gruyter, 1987], p. 79). Josephus did not qualify as an agent of Rome, but Ford's recognition that the Book of Revelation is basically Jewish is correct.

beast.[1] Two of the Herodian beasts were mortally **wounded** and survived. Although they were not *physically* **wounded** to the point of **death,** both Herods were at one time *politically* dead. They had been fatally **slaughtered,** but they recovered: One of these was Herod the Great, and the other was Herod Agrippa I.

In a style that is notorious for its code, it is not necessary to take every word literally, but this does not give exegetes the right to impose upon the Scripture any meaning they desire upon any scriptural term. If a word or expression makes no sense, literally, then it is the responsibility of the exegete to try to discover what, precisely, the term might mean. For example, even in the prophecy of Jeremiah, which is not coded, Jeremiah wrote of his experience in "eating" a scroll (Jer 36:2). This does not mean that he actually chewed a scroll with his teeth and swallowed it; it means he read it very carefully and "consumed" it mentally. The scroll which he "ate" was probably the Torah and such earlier prophets as Hosea. This is obvious from his extensive use of these documents.[2] In dealing with the physical or political death of certain **beasts** it is necessary to ask whether or not any one really **died** physically and came back to life. If not, then how was the term "slaughtered" intended? A careful study of two of the Herods shows that they both had been "killed?" politically, just as Jeremiah "had eaten" a scroll mentally.

Since Herod the Great was chronologically first, he will be examined first here. Herod's father, Antipater, appointed Herod to gain control of Galilee. He was successful in capturing Ezekias, the leader of a group of zealots, and killing both Ezekias and many of his followers (War 1:204-205). From this Herod gained wide acclaim. When he was brought to court to be tried for illegally killing many Jews, Sextus Caesar interfered and had the case dismissed (War 1:208-211). Herod's political power was so great that he acted as if he were king. He further strengthened his position by becoming engaged to Mariamme, a Hasmonean of royal Jewish blood, thus making him a prospective relative to the king, John Hyrcanus (War 1:240-41). After the engagement, but before the marriage to Mariamme, Jews persuaded the Parthians to invade Palestine, drive out the Romans and followers of Herod, and install another Hasmonean, Antigonus, as king (War 1:248-260). With strong Jewish support the Parthians captured Jerusalem and installed Antigonus as master of Jerusalem. They took Hyrcanus captive, brought about the **death** of Herod's brother, and planned to arrest Herod (War 1:261-62).

Herod escaped at night with Mariamme and his immediate family. The Parthians followed, with local Jews and Idumaeans harassing Herod every step of the way. He counted on military support from the Arabs, but the Arabs had become alienated from Herod, so he had to leave his family and friends at Masada and flee to Egypt. From there he took a ship to Rome (War 1:263-79). At that point it looked as if Herod were politically **dead**. He had lost military control of Palestine; his father and brother had been killed; he had found no allies in Arabia. He was almost killed

---

[1] Zahn, *Offenbarung*, p. 452.
[2] On this see further Buchanan, "The Function of Agency and the Formation of Canon," *Explorations* 8 (1990):63-79.

in a shipwreck on the way to Rome. From the patriotic Jewish point of view, Herod was **dead.** A Hasmonean was again on the throne at Jerusalem; the Romans had been overpowered--both the principal and the agent; Herod had been forced to flee; and the Jews were supported in their rule by the Parthians.

Rome liked Herod because he was strong, but he could expect little support when he came to them after all of these military failures. Herod, **the head of the beast,** had been inflicted with a **mortal wound**. When Herod reached Rome, however, the tables began to turn. The Roman senate was well aware of the seriousness of the Parthian invasion--not just to Herod's empire--but to the eastern border of the Roman empire. Instead of chastising Herod for his incompetence, they made Herod king and sent him back with Roman troops and supplies (War 1:280-85). After about three years of warfare (42 months), he gained complete control of the country again, drove out the Parthians, and killed Antigonus (War 1:343-57). By this time Herod the Great had recovered from his **mortal wound.**

Blasphemous names. These were titles a king might wear on his helmet that would give him honor, such as "son of God," "lord," "savior," or other praiseworthy titles that would not seem **blasphemous** to the king's loyal supporters. They seemed **blasphemous** to Jews and Christians who thought only their Messiah deserved such titles as these.

All the Land was appalled because of the beast. This is a Greek translation of a Semitic original. The word rendered "appalled" (Greek *eh-thow-máhs-thay*, ἐθαυμάσθη) reflects the Hebrew root *shah-máhm* (שמם), "to be appalled" or "to be shocked."[1] **Because of** translates the Greek *aw-peé-soh* (ὀπίσω, and suggests *the* Hebrew *ah-khah-ráy* (אחרי) which can mean "after," but also "on account of," "concerning," or **because of**.[2] This was not a friendly **beast,** from the Jewish point of view. The situation was not one that involved either "all the earth" or "all the people of the earth."[3] The area around which these **beasts** functioned, and the people whom they frightened were those who lived in the **Land,** namely the Promised Land. The Hebrew word *áh-rehtz* (ארץ) can mean either **Land** or "earth," depending upon its context. In the FT it nearly always means **Land.**

TEXT

[4]and they worshiped the dragon, because it gave the authority to the beast. They worshiped the beast, saying,

---

[1] So S. Thompson, *The Apocalypse in Semitic Context* (New York: Cambridge U. Press, 1985), p. 12.
[2] So also K. Newport, "Semitic Influences on the Use of Some Prepositions in the Book of Revelation," *BT* 37 (1986):333.
[3] Aune, *Revelation 6-16,* p. 737.

Revelation	First Testament and Targumim
"**Who is like** the beast, and **who** is	Exod 15:11**Who is like** you among the gods, Yehowah? **Who** is like you, majestic in holiness?
	TgNeof Exod 15:11**Who is like** you among the gods of the heights, Yehowah? Who is like you, majestic in holiness, feared in praises. All ages, working miracles and wonders for your people, the house of Israel.
	Ps 35:10Yehowah, **Who is like you**, delivering the poor from the one who is stronger than he?
able to **make war with** him?"	Dan 7:21I was watching and that horn **made war with** the saints, and he conquered them.
	Dan 7:8I was thinking about the horns when, look! Another small horn shot up among them, and the three first horns were uprooted before him. Look! Eyes like human eyes were in this horn, and **a mouth talking excessively**.
⁵There was given to it **a mouth talking excessively** and [speaking] blasphemy.	
Authority **was given** him **to act** for **42 months**.	Dan 7:25He will plan to change the times and the religion, and they **will be given** into his hand until **a time, two times, and half a time** [are over].

COMMENTARY

The dragon who gave authority to the beast. The word **worship** was given a much wider meaning in antiquity than it is given today. Whenever a citizen approached a judge or anyone else of higher authority it was normal to bow to show respect. This deference was called **worshiping.** For example, after Daniel's display of wisdom in interpreting dreams, King Nebuchadnezzar fell down on his face and **worshiped** Daniel (Dan 2:46). For years in England, some judges have been addressed as "Your worship."

The Jews in Palestine who **worshiped** the Roman principal that gave authority to its legal agent, Herod the Great, were the ones who faced the facts of life and cooperated with Herod in his function of enforcing Roman rule in Palestine. After he had gained control of Jerusalem Herod killed many of the supporters of Antigonus, demonstrating the way he could treat opponents. He also arranged to have Antigonus crucified (Dio, *Roman Hist.* 49:22, 6). This is probably the incident in Rev 11:7-8 in which the **beast** made war on **the witnesses,** killed them, and left their dead bodies on the street of **the great city, where their Lord was crucified**. If so, **the beast** was Herod the Great, and the martyrs supported Antigonus, who was **their Lord**. Recognizing Herod's power, many **worshiped** Roman authorities.

The Jews who **worshiped** the Roman principal were not the zealots but the tax collectors and other business magnates who found it profitable to cooperate. Although contemporary Jews worshiped both the beast and the dragon, the zealous author of this narrative in Revelation considered both of them mortal enemies. It was obvious to all Palestinian Jews that Herod functioned with Roman authority. If Herod had not had Roman troops and financial support he could never have returned after the Parthians conquered Jerusalem, and he had been forced to flee. The principal in this relationship was the Roman Caesar, and the legal agent was Herod the Great. When he spoke Rome spoke. That is what the author meant when he said God gave the beast **a mouth to speak great things** (Rev 13:5). Herod was Caesar's "mouthpiece." The author of Revelation realized this when he identified **the beast,** legally, with **the dragon** who gave him **authority** to rule.

Who is like the beast, and who is able to make war with him?. Morris has astutely related this expression to Exod 15:11 (*mee kah-móh-kah,* (מי כמוך)), Ps 35:10 (*mee kah-móh-kah*) "**who is like** you," and the name, "Michael," which means **Who is like** God (*mee khah-áyl?*)[1] People expressed amazement about the accomplishments of **the beast** in the same way they were astounded by the achievements of the Lord at the border of Egypt. This was a rhetorical question that many Jews asked, because they disliked both **the dragon** and **the beast,** but they did not believe they could do anything to stop them. **The beast** was not just a figment of the imagination. He was one who could lead troops and **make war**. This was true of Herod the Great. Herod had overpowered every resistance movement that occurred, including the guerrilla movements that had their hideouts in the caves of the cliffs and mountains. However much they disliked Herod, Jews had to recognize the tremendous power he had at his disposal.

Talking excessively and [speaking] blasphemy. By quoting from Daniel's description of the horn the author intended the reader to realize that this **beast** was the antitype of Antiochus Epiphanes. **The beast** not only **spoke** a lot, but the things he said had a lot of **authority**, because the beast was a legal agent of **the dragon**--Rome. The author also added some words to make **the beast** even worse than Antiochus--he also **spoke blasphemy**. This meant that he said something that Jews

---

[1] L. Morris, *The Book of Revelation* (Grand Rapids: Eerdmans, c1987), p. 168.

would have thought was degrading to God or their religion. All of the Herods and some of the procurators and Roman officers committed acts that Jews considered **blasphemous**.[1] Herod the Great had Roman eagles placed over the gate of Jerusalem, and he built pagan temples in Palestine. Pilate used temple funds to build an aqueduct to Bethlehem. Pompey had actually entered the holy of holies when he captured Jerusalem.

When trying to decide whether the claims made by the author for **the beast** were the kind Jews could have said of Herod the Great, Agrippa, or someone else, it is not necessary to ask if the insults were objectively valid. When religious people insult others they do not confine themselves to facts that could be proved in court. It is enough to ask whether a very religious, patriotic Jew or Christian might feel this way about some enemy. Jews and Christians were not always just in condemning their leaders as beasts. People can insult without having to prove in court that their accusations are just. By almost any standard, however, Herod the Great would have been accused of **blaspheming** God.

Authority was given . . . for 42 months. NA has **Authority was given him to act for 42 months**, omitting **whatever he wanted**. The passive voice was used here to avoid **blasphemy** by mentioning the name of God, but it means that God gave the beast **authority** to act. Of course Rome or one of its emperors gave Herod the **authority** to rule Palestine, but the author understood that it was God who controlled the rulings of nations. A few late manuscripts read, **make war** (*páw-leh-mawn poi áy-sai*, πόλεμον ποιῆσαι) instead of **act** (*poi-áy-sai*, ποιῆσαι). This is taken from Dan 7:21, *ahv-dáh kah-ráhv*, (עבדא קרב). The best readings (P^{27}ACP 1*pm*) all omit the word **war**. According to these texts the author evidently intended to ascribe the 42 months to the beast's activity in general and not limit it to its military activity. The same would be true of Sinaiticus.

If this **beast** were Herod the Great, then the 42 months probably were applied to the period between the time he was appointed king at Rome and the time he began to rule after he had reconquered Palestine. Three years elapsed between the time he was made king until he conquered Jerusalem. The additional six months were required to avenge his enemies, including killing **the witnesses** reported in Rev 11:7-8, settle affairs with the Roman soldiers, and establish himself in his palace. These 42 months constituted a time when Herod **acted**, but his action was basically that of making **war**, so it is easy to see why, in addition to the text in Daniel, some later manuscripts added the word **war**. This action identified him with Antiochus Epiphanes, the horn that grew out of the head of **the** fourth **beast** in Daniel.

---

[1] One of the things possible for Jews to do that was considered blasphemous was to take an oath by the name of any deity except Yehowah. But Herod was also expected to be loyal to the Roman emperor, and Romans had a law that prohibited anyone from taking an oath to anyone except the Roman emperor (Dio, *RomHist* 58:12, 6).

TEXT

Revelation

⁶**He** [the beast] **opened his mouth** for blasphemies **against** God, blaspheming him and his tent,

and those who dwell in **heaven**.

⁷[Authority] was given him **to make war with the saints and to conquer them**. Authority was given him over every

tribe, people, language, and nation, ⁸and all the migrants of the land worshiped him--

whose names **have been written in the book of life** of the

Lamb who was slaughtered from the foundation of the world. ⁹If anyone has an ear, let him hear.

First Testament

Dan 7:25**He** [the horn] **will speak words against** the Most High; he will wear out the saints of the Most High; and he will plan to change the calendar and the religion.

Dan 8:10It expanded to the army of **heaven**, and it made some of the army and some of the stars fall, and it trampled them.

Dan 7:21I was watching, and this horn **made war with the saints, and he conquered them**.

Dan 3:4The town crier announced with a loud voice, "You are informed, **peoples, nations, and languages**."

Isa 4:3Those who are left in Zion and those who remain in Jerusalem will be holy--everyone **who has been written in the book of life** in Jerusalem.

Ps 69:29Let them be blotted out of **the book of life** with the righteous **let them not be written**.

Jer 11:19I was like a gentle **lamb** led to be **slaughtered**, and I did not know that they had devised plots against me, [saying], "Let us destroy the tree with its fruit; let us cut [him] off from the land of life, so his name will not be remembered again."

Ps 44:12You have given us as **sheep** to be eaten.

Ps 44:23We are being murdered all the

day; we are counted as **sheep** to be **slaughtered**.

^{Isa 53:7}Just as a sheep that is led to be **slaughtered** and as a **lamb** before his shearers is dumb, so he did not open his mouth.

COMMENTARY

Blaspheming him and his tent. Instead of **him** (*ow-toó*, αὐτοῦ), NA has **his name** (*taw áh-naw-mah ow-toó*, τὸ ὄνομα αὐτοῦ). These both have the same meaning. **His name** is another way of saying "God," or the pronoun meaning God. **His tent** was either the holy or the holy of holies, the sanctuary of the temple. In the time of David there was no temple--only an altar and **a tent** that held the chest, containing the contract.

Defamation of character is sometimes called **blasphemy.** Even using the very word of God, while speaking, was held to be defamation of his character. This verse spells out in more detail the meaning of **blasphemy**, mentioned in the preceding sentence. Although Antiochus was not accused in Daniel of speaking **blasphemy**, that which Daniel reported amounted to **blasphemy,** and the NT exegete wanted his readers to understand what that was. Antiochus was the "horn" who had been in conflict with the Hasmonean saints. The words he spoke against the Most High constituted an offense of **blasphemy** (Dan 7:25).

Antiochus Epiphanes was also the **little horn** described in Dan 8. Antiochus was accused of expanding even to the army of heaven and throwing down some of the heavenly army and some of the stars (Dan 8:9-10). The NT commentator said this was **blasphemy**, and **the beast** of NT times was an antitype both of the **horn,** and the **little horn**. Like the **little horn** he **blasphemed** the name of God, his temple (literally **his tent**) at Jerusalem, and **those who dwell in heaven,** the author's paraphrase of some of **the army of heaven and some of the stars**. In addition to stars, angels, and heavenly troops, in **heaven** was also the Lord's council of 24 elders (Rev 4:4; 5:5-6; 7:11-13; 11:16; 14:3; 19:4).

To make war with the saints and to conquer them. This was a repetition and antitype of the event the Jews had suffered under the domination of Antiochus Epiphanes (Dan 7:21). In the new drama Herod was the new Antiochus Epiphanes. The **authority** given Herod was given both by **the dragon** (Romans), who furnished him with arms and troops, and God, who permitted him to torture the saints. The primary time when Herod the Great **made war with the saints** was the time he returned from Rome as king and spent more than three years overpowering the Palestinian Jews and their Parthian supporters. He also put down every rebellion that occurred afterwards. From the rebellion of Judas the Galilean and Zadok the Pharisee, at the end of Herod the Great's rule, until the destruction of Jerusalem in 70 IA there was a constant state of **war** between Jews and Romans. At nearly every feast, Jews assembled from all over the civilized world to Jerusalem. They came armed and were prepared to participate in any messianic rebellion that seemed scheduled to occur (War 1:88, 253). In all of these the Jews were suppressed by Roman arms, and Jews went back to their homes to prepare for another battle at the next feast.

Every tribe, people, language, and nation. This is an appropriation of a FT passage from Dan 3:4, mentioning **every people, language, and nation**. This was a summary statement meaning everyone *in the kingdom*. It was no more extensive than the Kingdom of Babylon, because the town crier went through the country making an announcement to these people. The same was true of its use in Rev 13:7, so its use does not mean the beast had authority over the entire civilized world. The kingdom first given to Herod the Great and later to Agrippa I would be large enough to attribute this kind of authority to its ruler.

The migrants of the land worshiped him. Sinaiticus has the dative for **him**. NA has the accusative. Both are grammatically approved. The dative is the pronoun used most frequently with this verb.

  The migrants of the land were the non-Jews who lived in Palestine. They were Romans, Greeks, Canaanites, Syrians, and others whom Jews believed had no right to live there--i.e., those of **every people, language, and nation.** These people were easily led into supporting any foreign group who wanted to control Palestine. They were hated by the author or authors of the Book of Revelation. Needless to say, they were supporters of the Herods as well as the Caesars. They could not really be *Erdbewohner* (earth dwellers), as Weiss calls them throughout the document. All living human beings are earth dwellers, but these are distinguished from other human beings who dwell on the earth as well. Their identity has to be learned from the way their name is used in the narratives in which it appears and the way the expression was used in FT and the Old Greek (OG) text.

Whose names have been written. NA has **whose name has *not* been written**. Sinaiticus is correct in having plural names and pronouns to go with the plural **migrants,** but his omission of the negative seems like a mistake. The **migrants of the land** were non-Jews who lived in Palestine, whom the Jews hated. They would not have been included in the list of meritorious people.

In the Lamb's book of life . . . from the foundation of the world. **The book of life** was the membership roll of the saints who were predestined to live in the age to come as citizens of the new kingdom. It was understood that no pagan would belong to this membership, so none of the procurators or Caesars would even be considered for this qualification. The fact that the issue was even raised speaks in favor of one of the Herods and against the Caesars for the role of **beasts**. Since Herod the Great was a half breed Jew he might have been a possibility, but Jews always considered him an outsider and an enemy. Even his marriage with Mariamme did not persuade Jews that he was a true member of their religion or race.

The book of life had its origin **from the foundation of the world. The Lamb was [not] slain from the foundation of the world** (See Rev 17:8). **The Lamb was slain** only once, and that happened at a specific time in history.

The Lamb that was slain. This is not such an obvious Christian addition as Loisy thought.[1] The Lamb throughout this scroll was the Messiah, but he was not always presented as a messiah **who had been slain**. This may be an addition made by a Christian editor as Whealon and Loisy suggested.[2] Those who had ears to hear may have understood that the Messiah involved was the one who had been crucified, namely Jesus, but Jesus was not the only Jewish messiah to die for his nation. Others include Judas the Maccabee who was killed in battle (War 1:47) and Antigonus, the last king of the Hasmoneans, who was crucified by the Romans.

The most likely candidate during the time of Herod the Great was the Hasmonean, Antigonus, whom the Parthians appointed king but whom Herod deposed and crucified. He would have qualified as the Messiah and therefore **the Lamb**. Since he was killed by Herod he would have been **the Lamb who was slain**. Others whom Herod killed were Judas, son of Ezekias, Simon, and Athrongaeus (War 2:55-65). Followers of any of these leaders might have thought of their leader as **the Lamb that was** led to the slaughter, one who had sacrificed his life for his nation. The servant in Second Isaiah was believed to have suffered, and through his suffering to have paid off all of the iniquities that had been added to the heavenly debt against the Jewish nation. The Messiah, **the Lamb**, whatever his identity, was held to be the antitype of the suffering servant. Like the servant, he was led like a sheep to be slaughtered. He had been sacrificed for his nation.

TEXT

Revelation	First Testament
[10]If **anyone** [takes others] away into **captivity**, will [himself] go away [into captivity]; **If anyone** will kill **by the sword** it will be necessary for him to be killed **by the sword**. Here is the patience and faith of the saints.	Jer 15:2, [11]**Whoever** [is predestined] for pestilence [will be given over] to pestilence; **whoever** [is predestined] **for the sword** [will be given over] **to the sword**; **whoever** [is predestined] for famine [will be given over] to famine; and **whoever** [is predestined] for **captivity** [will be given over] to **captivity**.

---

[1] Loisy, *L'Apocalypse*, p. 252.
[2] J. F. Whealon, "New Patches on an Old Garment: The Book of Revelation," *BTB* 11 (1981):55.

> ^{Jer 42:11}Whoever is predestined for pestilence [will be given over] to pestilence; whoever [is predestined] for captivity [will be given over] to captivity; whoever [is predestined] for the sword [will be given over] to the sword.
>
> ^{Gen 9:10}The one who pours blood of a man, by a man shall his blood be poured out, because in the image of God he made man.

COMMENTARY

If anyone [takes others] into captivity. On the basis of Lev 26, Jeremiah interpreted the word of the Lord to mean that the primary evil situations would come upon Judah--pestilence, sword, famine, **captivity**, dogs, birds, and beasts (Jer 15:2-3). The author of this portion of Revelation, however, changed Jeremiah's text in an important way.

Will himself go away. NA adds **into captivity,** consistent with Jer 15:2 and therefore easily implied.

If anyone will kill by the sword. The second line does not say, **If anyone is predestined to be killed by the sword, he will then be killed by the sword**, but **If anyone *will kill* by the sword, he will then *be killed* by the sword**. Since the first line does not have a verb, the author seems to have intended that the first line read, "If anyone *takes captive*, it will be necessary for him to go **into captivity**." This changes the prophecy from a threat to a promise. This would assure the readers that those who had been torturing Jews and/or Christians would be justly punished. Jeremiah told the people of Judah that God would punish *them*. The author of the text changed the implied verbs to mean God would punish *their enemies*--the ones who kill and take [Jews] captive, namely **the migrants of the land--those of every language, nation, tribe, and people.** This is **the patience and faith of the saints**. They can afford to be patient and wait, because they are confident of their future. They know God will punish the gentiles for their **crime** against his chosen people, and they can prove this from the text in Jeremiah.

SECOND DIVISION

TEXT

Revelation

¹¹I saw another **beast coming up from the land**. It had two horns like a Lamb, but it was speaking like a dragon. ¹²It exercised all the authority of the first **beast** which was before it, and it was making the land and those who dwell in it to worship the first **beast** whose mortal wound was healed.

First Testament

Dan 7:17-18 These huge **beasts**, of which there were four, [these represent] four kings will **come up from the land**. ¹⁸They will receive the kingdom of the saints of the Most High.

COMMENTARY

Another beast. The first unit (drama) has come to an end with Rev 13:10, and the second unit begins with Rev 13:11. With the new drama comes a new period of history and a new set of characters (*dramatis personae*). The **beast** mentioned here was distinguished from some **beast** that was considered **first**. Jacobs correctly said, "There can be no doubt that the beast stands in the closest relation of nature to the dragon," but he thought the **beast** was not a person but an empire.[1] Loisy thought the second **beast** was Nero redevivus.[2] Sweet said the second **beast** "could be simply a mock-up to ape the Holy Spirit."[3] Boring identified the second **beast** with the false prophet (Rev 16:13; 19:20; 20:10) and said he "rose out of the earth."[4] Topham correctly concluded that this **beast** was not just a foreign intruder. It "is presented as a snake in Lamb's clothing (Rev 13:11)."[5] The text made no mention of this other **beast's** ten horns or seven heads. The only *other* Herod to rule Herod the Great's entire kingdom and to hold the title "king" was Herod Agrippa I. He actually exercised the same authority as Herod the Great.

The beasts in Daniel's vision came from *the sea*. This indicates their demonic or foreign origin (Dan 7:3), but the interpretation of the vision said **the beasts** were four kings who came up *from the earth* (Dan 7:17), noting that they were real, earthly kings. Rev 13, however, seems to have taken the Aramaic *ah-ruh-áh*,

---

[1] Düsterdieck, *Revelation*, p. 386.
[2] Loisy, *L'Apocalypse*, p. 256.
[3] Sweet, *Revelation*, p. 214.
[4] M. E. Boring, *Revelation* (Louisville: John Knox Press, c1989), p. 156.
[5] M. Topham, "Hanniqola'ites," *ET* 98 (1986):44, opposed the idea that the beast was Nero. He thought the way to explain the phenomena was to assume that the beast represented a whole sect, namely the Nicolaitans. Agrippa I, however, would also qualify as a snake in sheep's clothing.

(ארעא), which can mean either "the earth" or "the land," to mean "the land"; i.e., the Land of Palestine. The author of Rev 13 associated the first **beast** with "the sea," and the second with **the land**. Ancient exegetes often used texts in this way.[1] By this he may have meant that the first **beast** was of demonic or foreign origin, but the second was of Palestinian origin. Herod the Great was born in Edom, which was used as a code term for Rome. Ever since the Edomites supported the Babylonian destruction of Jerusalem in 586 BIA, Jews had hated Edomites (Ps 137; Obadiah). They also hated Herod the Great and his sons.

Fourth Ezra also made a distinction between the monster who came up out of the sea and was the Roman eagle, the antitype of the fourth **beast** in Dan 7 (4Ezra 11:1-2; 12:10-11) and the lion who came out of the forest. The latter was the Messiah who arose at the end of the Lord's [evil] times. He rebuked the eagle, and the eagle was burned (4Ezra 11:36-12:3; 12:31). In another vision, however, the one who came up out of the sea, fought againsth the **migrants of the land**, gathered the tribes of Israel together, and then stood on Mount Zion--obviously the Messiah--was called the Lord's son (4Ezra 13:1-40, 51-52).

Weiss held that this whole experience reported in the Book of Revelation was related to Asia Minor, so pictured the **beast** that came up from the sea to have come from Rome, to the west of Patmos Island. The second **beast** came up from the land. This meant he came up from the western coast of Asia Minor, facing Rome. Weiss also thought the beast narratives were originally two different narratives written by different people. The final editor was Christian, and he put the two narratives together to form a unit.[2]

The Jews did not claim the half-breed Jewish Herodians as brothers--with one exception--Herod Agrippa I. Agrippa I, like other sons of Herod, was born in Palestine, even though he had been educated in Rome. Therefore, from the standpoint of origin, he could qualify as the second **beast.** The second **beast** could not have been any of the foreign procurators or Caesars, because none of them came from **the land**. Furthermore they would not have given even the appearance of a Lamb. Presumably, neither would any of the sons of Herod, but Herod Agrippa I, evoked a different feeling from many of the Jews, because he identified with them, and because he was of Hasmonean ancestry as well. At the Feast of Tabernacles he read the portion of Scripture that the king was supposed to read. That means the Jews present accepted him as the Messiah or the Lamb.

When he came to the portion in Deuteronomy that said no foreigner should ever rule over them, he wept, because he was of Idumean descent. Jews, however, assured him that they considered him, not a foreigner, but a brother (mSot 7:8). He was sympathetic to the revolutionaries' demands, and he began to build a huge wall around Jerusalem. Josephus said if the wall had been completed it would have made

---

[1] B. Weiss, ΑΠΟΚΑΛΥΨΙΣ, p. 483, said this meant he came from the Orient rather than from the west. This identified the second beast with the Parthians rather than the Romans. This at least recognized the existence of two different beasts, one from the land and the other from the sea. Some explanation is required for these phenomena.

[2] J. Weiss, *Die Offenbarung des Johannes* (Göttingen: Vandenhoeck und Ruprecht, 1908), p. 658.

any future attempt of Rome to lay siege to the city useless (War 2:218-19). When Claudius learned of its extent, he foresaw the problem that it might create for Rome in the future, so he required Agrippa to stop the construction. He correctly suspected that a wall of this dimension would be the basis of a revolution (Ant 19:326). Consequently Agrippa died without ever having finished the undertaking.

Agrippa made an effort to appoint an appropriate and well-qualified high priest; he reduced taxes; he, reportedly, put a stop to action taken to bring an image into a synagogue; and he dealt with the Jews more gently than his grandfather had. Both Herods built Greek buildings and temples, and Herod the Great even constructed the beautiful Jewish temple in Jerusalem. He hoped that this would bring him recognition for his piety, but Jews never gave him any credit for being pious.[1] Many Jews thought it was a pagan temple, a temple made with hands.

Agrippa also tried to observe the traditions of the Jews (Ant 19:286-331)--an effort never attributed to Herod the Great, even though he wanted recognition for his piety. Compared with Herod the Great and the procurators, Agrippa may have seemed like a true Jewish ruler. In fact Cohen speculated,

> Had Agrippa reigned a long time, perhaps the disaffected elements in Judea would have been reconciled again to foreign dominion.[2]

After his beneficent rule, however, the Roman procurators that followed seemed monstrous in comparison, and Jews were unwilling to become satisfied with the rule of procurators again. There was enough good feeling toward Agrippa I, that he might have been considered a **Lamb** as well as one coming from **the land**.

He had two horns like a Lamb. Although many Jews were fond of Agrippa I for his kindnesses, the author of Rev 13 thought all of this apparent supportiveness was deceptive. He really was not the Messiah Jews expected. He appeared to be **a Lamb,** but he was really a **beast**. This confusion of identity was intended to remind the reader of the time Jacob cheated Esau out of his father's blessing by covering his arms and part of his neck with goat skins and dressing in Esau's clothing. When he came near to Isaac, Isaac reacted: **The voice is the voice of Jacob, but the arms are the arms of Esau** (Gen 27:22). The author of the narrative of Rev 13 applied this to **the beast.** He appeared to be a messiah or **a Lamb** (he had two horns), but he spoke like a legal agent of Rome. As in the case of Jacob and Esau, the truth was in the

---

[1] Herod did several things to gain recognition for piety. He refused to allow his sister, Salome, to marry a Nabataean unless he was first circumcised and adopted the Jewish faith. He refused to eat pork, a characteristic that prompted Macrobius to tell Augustus, after Herod had had some of his sons killed, "I would rather be Herod's pig than his son." Furthermore, Herod did not mint coins with protraits. He was, in fact, a religious Jew, but those he ruled did not accept him. On this see further D. M. Jacobson, "King Herod's 'Heroic' Public Image," *RB* 95 (1988):386-403.
[2] S. J. D. Cohen, "Roman Domination," *Ancient Israel* ed. H. Shanks (Washington, D.C.: Biblical Archaeological Society, c1999), p. 215.

voice rather than in the appearance. The author may have had Agrippa I in mind when he made this comparison.

Even though Agrippa was a faithful Jewish leader in many ways, he was also a loyal supporter of Gaius and Claudius. He **had horns like a Lamb**, **but he spoke like a dragon**. He had the authority of Rome, and he acted as Rome's agent; he spoke and acted on behalf of Rome, in the interests of Rome, and at the responsibility of Rome. Therefore, in the final analysis, it was clear to the author that Agrippa I was excluded from the book of life from the foundation of the world (Rev 13:8). It is true that some Jews considered Agrippa to be their brother, but the author of this narrative did not.

The Lamb's horns were not little "lamby" horns that only designated the appearance of innocence, as Weiss claimed.[1] Horns represented military weapons, and the Lamb represented the Messiah, a king who was expected to conduct war to defend his nation.

He exercises all the authority of the first beast before him. Since Claudius gave Agrippa I all of the kingdom formerly ruled by Herod the Great, it seems that the author of Rev 13:11-18 wrote with the idea that **the beast** mentioned in Rev 13:1-10 was Herod the Great, and the **other beast** was Herod Agrippa I. Josephus compared Agrippa I with Herod the Great **who was king before him** (*toh pro heh-ow-toó bah-see-láy*, (τῷ πρὸ ἑαυτοῦ βασιλεῖ) (Ant 19:328). Herod the Great did not come from Judah but from Edom, and Edom was a Jewish code name for Rome. Jews felt very different toward Agrippa I from Herod the Great. Although in the first section Herod the Great was one of the heads of the beast, here he was called the first beast. In this second narrative, there is no division among the **horns**, **the heads**, and **the beast** as there was in the first narrative. The distinction is between the **first beast** and the **other beast**. The **other beast** was not an agent of the **first beast**, but he exercised the same authority as the **first beast**. This means Herod Agrippa had the same authority as Herod the Great, which was true. Both Herods received their authority from the same principal, the great red dragon, Rome.

He makes the Land . . . worship the first beast. NA left out a few letters in the Greek word for **worship**. This statement seems to imply that Herod Agrippa I upheld the work of Herod the Great. There is no direct literary support for this claim, unless the author meant that Herod Agrippa I continued the work and program of Herod the Great. According to Josephus, Claudius announced his close friendship both to Herod the Great and to Herod Agrippa I and praised them both for their loyalty to the Romans (Ant 19:286-89).

After Agrippa became king, he followed the example of his grandfather, Herod the Great, and constructed many public works. One of these was the beginning of a great wall of defense on the north side of Jerusalem. These may have been the so-called **great signs** he did. This may have been compared satirically to the works of Elijah who called down fire from heaven. The one who gave **the beast** the

---

[1] B. Weiss, ΑΠΟΚΑΛΥΨΙΣ, p. 483.

signs was God--not Rome. The passive voice was used to avoid blasphemy. The many public works that Agrippa I did that were like those of his grandfather may have reminded Jews of his grandfather and have seemed the basis for his urging **the migrants of the land to worship** Herod the Great even more than they already did.

Whose mortal wound was healed. This seems to be another reference to the political recovery of Herod the Great, but Agrippa I also suffered a **mortal wound and was healed**. When Berenice, Agrippa's mother, died Agrippa spent money lavishly until he was hopelessly in debt and contemplating suicide when his brother Herod Antipas appointed him to a position in Tiberias and paid him a regular salary (Ant 18:139-150). This salary, however, was not enough to provide Agrippa with all the money he wanted to spend, so he was soon hopelessly in debt again, and he finally fled from Palestine to escape his many debts (Ant 18:151-165). He went to Rome where he became a close friend of Gaius.

According to the War, Josephus said that at one of Gaius's banquets, Agrippa drank a toast to Gaius, saying that he hoped Gaius would soon be emperor. According to Antiquities, this hope was expressed to Gaius when he and Herod were riding together in a horse drawn vehicle and was overheard by the driver (Ant 18:168-204). This meant Agrippa wished Tiberius, who was old and in failing health, would soon die. When this word got back to Tiberius, he had Agrippa put in prison (War 2:178-80). This might be interpreted as Agrippa's **mortal wound.** Agrippa had been a close friend of the Tiberius family, but others who had once been close friends of Tiberius had later been imprisoned, exiled, or killed before this event.

One notable case was that of Sejanus who had acted for many months as if he were really the emperor. Busts of Sejanus had been **worshiped** in Rome; Sejanus had represented Tiberius in the Senate. No other citizen had ever before been given such great honor as Sejanus without becoming emperor himself. Yet, only a few years before Agrippa's imprisonment, Tiberius had Sejanus accused in the Senate, imprisoned, and later killed and his body thrown down the stairway, left exposed for three days, and later thrown into the river (Dio, *RomHist* 58:3, 1-9, 5). Agrippa, once in jail for an offense against Tiberius, had little hope for any better treatment.

Herod Agrippa's political and economic future seemed very bleak. He was hopelessly in debt; and he was also in prison, but after about six months, Tiberius died, and Gaius was made emperor. He immediately released Agrippa from prison and not only made him tetrarch of Phillip's tetrarchy, but he appointed him *king*. He removed Agrippa's chains and replaced them with a gold chain of the same weight (Ant 19:292-96).

Agrippa's new rank as king was higher than the rank Antipas held. When Antipas tried to appeal to Gaius for a similar privilege, he was exiled, and his tetrarchy was added to Agrippa's. Agrippa, like a new Joseph of Egypt, Moses, or Nehemiah, had ingratiated himself into the Roman imperial families of Tiberius, Gaius, and Claudius. Roman citizens were troubled because Gaius had Agrippa with him as an advisor much of the time. They suspected that Agrippa had been influential in persuading Gaius to kill as many Roman leaders as he had (Dio, *RomHist* 59:24, 1).

After Gaius died, Agrippa acted as an agent for Claudius, negotiating with the Senate. After Claudius became emperor, he repaid Agrippa by making him king over the entire country over which his grandfather, Herod the Great, had ruled, adding Judaea, Samaria, Caesarea, and some territories northeast of the Golan Heights (War 2:181-83; 204-17; Ant 19:274-77). After his poverty and imprisonment Agrippa's return to Jerusalem as king of Herod the Great's entire kingdom might have been interpreted as Agrippa's **recovery** from his **mortal wound**. From then on he exercised the same power as Herod the Great (the beast) had managed.

Although Agrippa I would qualify as one who suffered **a mortal wound and was healed**, so also would Herod the Great, and up to this point the identity of Herod the Great with the **head** of the **first beast** and also the **first beast** itself makes good sense. Agrippa also qualifies as the **other beast**. The author of this portion of Rev 13 knew there were Jews who thought Agrippa was **a Lamb,** but he thought he was a **beast**, and he spent the rest of the chapter telling what he had done that made him like a **dragon**.

TEXT

Revelation

¹³**He performs** great **miracles** so that he makes **fire come down from heaven** to the land before the people ¹⁴and makes the migrants of the land to go astray because of **the signs** which have been **given** him to perform before the beast, telling the migrants of the land to make an image of the beast ¹⁵who has the wound of the sword and lived. There was given to him [authority] to give breath to the image of the beast so that the image of the beast might

First Testament

Deut 13:2-4 If there arises in your midst a prophet or a dreamer of dreams, and **he gives you a sign or a miracle**, and **the sign** and the **miracle** come to pass which he has spoken to you, and he says, "Let us walk after other gods" . . . you shall not listen to the words of that prophet.

2Kings 1:10 If I am a man of God, let **fire come down from heaven** and consume you and your fifty. **The fire came down from heaven** and consumed him and his fifty.

1Kings 18:38 The **fire** of Yehowah fell, and it consumed the whole burnt offering, the wood, the stones, the dust, and the water.

Dan 3:5-6 People, nations, and languages, whenever you hear the sound of the horn, pipe, lyre, trigon, harp, bagpipe,

talk, and he will act so that **whoever does not worship** the image of the beast would be killed.

and every kind of music, fall down and **worship** the gold image which King Nebuchadnezzar has set.

^{Dan 7:8}Now look! in this horn was a mouth that **talks** excessively.

^{Dan 3:6}**Whoever does not** fall down **and worship** at that time will be thrown into a burning fiery furnace.

COMMENTARY

He performs great miracles. This paragraph is a midrash on a narrative in Daniel and on the commandment in Deuteronomy that Israelites should not pay any attention to anyone who prophesies, even if his prophecies come to pass, if he also encourages them to leave their traditional faith and worship other gods. The author of this section of Rev 13 pictured false prophets who had actually performed miracles who were testing the Israelites for their faithfulness.

In addition to calling attention to the commandment the miracle performer had broken, the author of this narrative based his message on Dan 3 and 2Kings 1:10. Dan 3 is a story of Shadrach, Meshach, and Abedneggo who lived in Babylon when Nebuchadnezzar was king. The king made a golden statue and decreed that everyone in his kingdom must **worship** this statue whenever all of the musical instruments sounded. These three Jewish Babylonians refused to comply so they were brought to trial and thrown into a fiery furnace. In the furnace none of the Jews was injured, so they were brought out and their accusers thrown in. The accusers were burned at once. This proved to Nebuchadnezzar that these Jews **worshiped** the true God, and he decreed that anyone who spoke against the Jews should have his house laid in ruin and would himself be torn limb from limb.

In North Israel, the prophet confronted 400 priests of Baal on Mount Carmel (1Kings 18:20). There a large sacrifice was prepared, but the priests of Baal could not call down fire from heaven to consume it, but Elijah was successful. Elijah was also able to call down fire to consume groups of 50 soldiers each that had been sent against him (2Kings 1:10). Elijah was able to do this because he was a man of God.

In some coded way, these messages were reapplied to a situation in Palestine when Jews either were rescued or needed to be rescued in the same way. The author listed the following facts:

1) The miracle that brought **fire down from heaven** was the equivalent of the **fiery** furnace or was related to Elijah's experience in some way.
2) It was not a man of God but the beast who brought **down fire from heaven.**

3) The beast also persuaded **the migrants of the land**--the foreigners in Palestine--to create the image.
4) The image was to be a statue of some **beast.**
5) The purpose of noting that the image was given a spirit so that it could speak was to identify it as an antitype of Antiochus Epiphanes, **the little horn**.
6) All Jews were forced to **worship** this statue.

Codes allow for generous fulfillment of natural events. Only a hint is required. For example in the report of the Pentecost experience, Joel's prophecy that God would provide miracles and signs both in heaven and on earth--blood, fire, and vaporous smoke, with the sun being darkened and the moon changing into blood--was considered fulfilled by the miracles Jesus had performed in their midst (Acts 2:19-22), none of which involved blood, fire, or vaporous smoke.

Therefore it is not necessary to find an exact event when some **beast** actually brought **fire down from heaven** to identify the situation. There is a broad range of possibilities, but this knowledge does not make the task any easier. It may be necessary to leave the original situation unknown and work instead to discover how the editor understood it. Since he put it together with a literary unit that was related to Agrippa I, it is possible that he understood some event in Agrippa's time where this midrash could apply. Such an event is not hard to find.

When Caligula (Gaius) insisted that a bust of himself be set up in every city in the Roman empire, he sent one of his army officers, Petronius, with an army to install statues of Caligula in the temple at Jerusalem.[1] Petronius entered Judaea with three legions of soldiers. Josephus said there were some who feared a war with Petronius, but they did not believe there was any defense. **Who could make war against the beast** (War 2:187)? Nevertheless, many tens of thousands of Jews left their farming tasks, took their wives and children, and came to Ptolemais (Acre) to persuade Petronius not to attempt this task. Ptolemais is near Mount Carmel where Elijah called **down fire from heaven** to overwhelm the priests of Baal. The proximity of locations would call the reader's attention to Elijah's miracle.

Petronius warned the Jews of the tremendous power of the Roman army. This was similar to the crisis Elijah faced when he alone was left a prophet of the Lord and military troops had been sent to have him killed. None the less, Elijah held out and confronted the whole danger, because he trusted the Lord for whom he was a man of God. Similarly, the Jews said Petronius would have to destroy the entire nation before he could set up the statues. He finally agreed to face the death that was almost inevitable rather than kill so many Jews as this. He sent a message to Gaius, telling him why he did not fulfill his orders. Gaius sent a message to Petronius ordering his self-murder, but before this message could reach Petronius, Gaius had been murdered, so the order was never fulfilled (War 2:184-203).[2] Like the 400

---

[1] Setting a statue of an emperor in a temple was not a unique event. Other emperors did the same. For example Antiochus III had a statue of himself set up in the temple of Athena in the territory of Coronea.

[2] Was this just a coincidence? How did the Jews persuade Petronius to risk a death sentence? Is it

priests of Baal, Petronius and his troops had to acquiesce before the committed servants of the Lord.

According to Josephus Agrippa I was in Rome while all of this was going on. When he heard of it he planned a fantastic banquet honoring Gaius. When afterward Gaius asked what he could do to repay, Agrippa I said he might withdraw the commission he had given to Petronius. This may have been true, but the story seems so much like the banquet of Esther that its veracity is questionable. In this narrative Gaius first granted Agrippa's wish and then reconsidered it (Ant 18:289-300). Some group of men killed Cestius before he could kill Petronius so that Petronius would decline his order to kill all of those Jews. Who were his murderers? Who wanted relief from Roman soldiers? Was the Jewish king Agrippa, who lived then in Rome involved? There were also many thousands of Jews in Rome at that time. This entire event was interpreted as the fulfillment or reenactment of scripture, but there were also some events on the ground that are suspicious.

Josephus attempted to present Agrippa I in a favorable way, but there may have been some negative aspects to Agrippa's rule which Josephus left out. Jews knew of the cruelty both of Gaius and of Claudius. They also realized that Agrippa was Caligula's and Claudius's agent. He had all the Roman forces to back up his position. No one of the Herods had possessed authority like Agrippa since Herod the Great. Agrippa's whole royal status depended on his favor with Gaius. Gaius saved Agrippa's life, released him from prison, gave him a kingdom together with enough money and authority to rule it. Gaius had a right to expect cooperation from his legal agent, Agrippa I, and he probably had it.

It is not likely that Agrippa would have challenged Gaius openly or taken issue with Petronius and his three legions of Roman soldiers. While Agrippa was king of Palestine a religiously scrupulous Jew, named Simon, said Agrippa should not be allowed in the temple, because he was ritually unclean (Ant 19:332-334). When Agrippa I died, people from Caesarea and Samaria took the images of Agrippa's daughters to brothels and treated them very disrespectfully (Ant 19:354-59). There were obviously people in Agrippa's kingdom who resented him. They thought he should have given total support for Jewish needs, the way Moses, Daniel, Nehemiah, Esther, and Judith had done when they were dealing with foreign powers, but even if he had, they would never have found out, because he would have had to perform such an act in a way that was secret.

---

possible that some of the Jews who negotiated with Petronius promised him that Gaius would soon be killed if he refused to carry out his orders? We will probably never know, but it is an interesting speculation. Jewish mythology includes as heroines such nationalists as Judith who saved her people by killing the king. The Jew who brought the message from Petronius to Caligula may have had other messages to deliver to other Jews in Rome. Agrippa was in Rome at the time, and Philo had been there just before with an embassy sent from Egypt to persuade Caligula to abandon his project in Palestine (*ad Gaius*). There was a strong feeling of hostility among Jews all over the Roman Empire against Gaius for his attempt to defile the temple with his statue. Some of them may have either directed the project or have been involved in some way with Gaius' assassination.

Even if Agrippa had been secretly involved in Caligula's assassination, its success and his survival depended on his ability to keep his deeds from becoming known. He obviously had a conflict of interests--loyalty both to Rome and to Palestinian Jews. He had to keep his loyalty to Jews suppressed in his relationship with Rome. Any zealot or scrupulously religious Jew might justly have thought he was a committed agent of Caligula and Rome, no matter what the secret facts were. Jews knew that anyone who fought openly with Rome would also have to fight with Agrippa I

Telling the migrants of the Land to make a statue of the beast. This probably meant that **the migrants of the Land** were expected to cooperate with Petronius and use their influence to accomplish Gaius' desires. It is difficult to understand this action if the expression **migrants of the Land** were mistranslated as "inhabitants of the earth" as most scholars do.[1]

Who has the wound of the sword and lived. In this situation, it was Petronius who was given the death sentence by Gaius, but survived the ordeal. This is not the same as having **a mortal wound that was healed**. That could have been interpreted politically, but Gaius had ordered a physical death sentence for Petronius. This was not just a **wound**; it was a **wound of** *the sword*. Gaius was also the image which was given the spirit so that it could speak, just as the little horn in Daniel was allowed to speak excessively (Dan 7:8). The spirit was the legal authority given to Petronius. Petronius was Gaius' legal agent who, with Gaius' spirit (=authority), did spoke in behalf of Gaius' image. For many days Petronius spoke extensively, just as the little horn did (Dan 7:8), defending Jews while they objected to the image of Gaius being installed in the temple at Jerusalem. At the same time Gaius' statue was the image of the same **beast**. This alternation between Gaius' statue and his military officer, Petronius, was possible because both were identified with Gaius--one as his physical identity and the other as his legal identity, his legal agent, Petronius.

He will act so that whoever does not worship. Instead of the future, **he will act,** NA has the subjunctive, **he might act.**

TEXT

Revelation	The First Testament
[16]He makes all--the small and the great, the poor and the rich, the free and the slaves, to wear his mark on their right hands and **on their foreheads**, [17]so that no one would be able to sell or buy who does not have the mark of the beast or	Ezek 9:4 Go through the midst of the city, in the midst of Jerusalem, and place a *tau* (ת = X) **on the foreheads** of the men who mourn and groan over all the abominations that have happened in its midst.

---

[1] Aune, *Revelation 6-16*, pp. 760-61.

his name. ¹⁸Here is wisdom: He who has a mind to decipher the number of the beast, for the number is of a man, and the number is **666**.

¹ᴷⁱⁿᵍˢ ¹⁰:¹⁴; ²ᶜʰʳᵒⁿ ⁹:¹³Now the weight of gold that came to Solomon in one year was **666** talents of gold.

ᴱᶻʳᵃ ²:¹³The sons of Adonikam 666.

COMMENTARY

All--the small and the great. Instead of **the poor and the rich** NA has **the rich and the poor.** Sinaiticus has better balance. These are all examples of *merismus*, a literary form in which both extremes are given, each as one half of the situation which includes all that are in between. "Everyone" is a synonym for each of these pairs.

To wear his mark. NA has **to wear their mark.** The difference is whether the mark is for **the beast** or for the subjects. Some wore their own **mark**. These were the followers of **the Lamb**. The **mark** was obviously on the hands and foreheads of the people, but it was the **mark** required by **the beast.** He may have required them to wear *their own* identifying mark, such as the sign of the *tau* (X) on their foreheads, to distinguish them from law-abiding Roman citizens. If he required them to wear *his* mark, that would have indicated that they were loyal Roman law observers. There is no record of Romans requiring any **mark** of identification, although this is possible. Weiss thought there must have been some requirement by the Roman government to tattoo its citizens.¹ The patriotic zealots would not have worn a Roman badge of this kind, but those who mingled with the Romans would have.

Romans may have required identification cards, something like American social security cards, for conducting legal transactions. Some countries required soldiers whom they had defeated in war to wear a brand as a sign of disgrace before their victors (Herod. Hist 7:233; Plut. *Per* 26).

The mark of the beast or his name. NA has **The mark [which is] the name of the beast.**

Six hundred, sixty-six. The number **666** has been a problem from a very early date. Victorinus (d. IA 304) offered the following possible solutions: Greek: *táy-tahn* (τείταν), *áhn-teh-maws* (ἄντεμος), *gehn-sáy-ree-kaws* (γενσήρικος). That which is important, said Victorinus, is that this symbol signifies the Antichrist, which is Rome (*Commentary on Revelation* 12:13).

666 has been most generally accepted as being Nero. This does not refute the identification of **the beasts** and heads with Herod the Great and Herod Agrippa. These identifications might have been changed by later generations who updated the political leaders called **dragons**, **beasts**, or **"heads"** of beasts. The number is

---

¹ J. Weiss, *Offenbarung*, p. 659.

certainly a code term, and it may follow some system of *gematria*, putting certain numerical values to certain letters of some alphabet. One such system is called the *atbash* system. This is described as follows by Fishbane:

> Most notable among inner-biblical cryptographic techniques is the deliberate permutation of letters to produce cryptic ciphers of the '*atbash*' type. This technique, known particularly from later Jewish sources, exchanges the first letter of the alphabet with the last, the second with the penultimate, and so forth (thus:, ש"ב,ת "א [like a"z b"y in English], Guided by this code, the meaningless [*shayshahk*] ששך in Jer 25:26 and 51:41 can be deduced to 'stand for' [*bah-vehl*] בבל [= Babylon]. Similarly, an application of '*aht-bash*' permutations to [*layv kuh-mai*] לב קמי in Jer 51:1 yields [*kahs-deem*] כשדים (Chaldaeans), as was first correctly deciphered in the ancient Targum--though its sense is also disclosed by the parallelism and in Jer 51:1.[1]

Gematria was not a unique code for Jews and Christians. Non-Christian, non-Jewish Greeks communicated to one another through this code. On the walls of some of the ruins of Pompey is preserved among the graffiti a note, "I love her whose number is *psme* (ψμε)." These three letters add up to 545. Some girl whose name also totaled 545 probably recognized this message when she saw it, but others would not.[2] The following is a brief portion of a long quotation in Sibylline Oracles. It illustrates some of the coded ways Jews wrote in NT times:

> 5:12The first one to rule [is one] whose beginning letter totals twenty [καισαρ = Caesar]. 13In war he will be very strong. 14He will have a first initial of ten (*I* for Julius), so that after him 15one will rule who has the first of the letters [*A*ugustus] who will terrify Thrace, Sicily, and Memphis.

This is very easy code with clues for interpretation. Revelation does not always give such extensive or easy clues. A simple 666 is given in Revelation without any other hints. The readers obviously did not need any interpretation.

Bergmeier was right when he said there was no Greek hypothesis for this name that is satisfactory.[3] He might have gone even further and said that no one has

---

[1] M. A. Fishbane, *Biblical Interpretation in Ancient Israel* (New York: Clarendon Press, 1985), p. 464.
[2] So Zahn, *Offenbarung*, pp. 460-61. Zahn has made a careful and extensive analysis of the attempts of early Christians to identify 666 (pp. 445-507). Their early identification was mostly with Gaius Caesar, whose letters total 616 rather than 666, or Nero Caesar. The change of text to 616 posed a problem, but Zahn thought Gaius was the most likely person to have been intended by the number (p. 550).
[3] R. Bergmeier, "Die Erzhure und das Tier: Apk 12 18-18 18 und 17 f. Eine quellen-und redaktionskritische Analyse," *ANRW* II.25.5, p. 3902.

been able to apply these techniques satisfactorily to decode 666 on the basis of any language. Weiss correctly said, "A certain meaning is for us impossible."[1] Schüssler-Fiorenza also correctly said,

> Despite centuries of puzzling over this problem, scholars have yet to agree on whether 666 refers to Nero, Caligula, Domitian, or any other historical referent. The number 666 is a polysemous symbol that defies referential analysis.[2]

It may be that the number 666 does not spell any person's name at all. It might have spelled in *gematria* fashion some insulting term that applied to any person the group involved wanted. It may have been a code term for an insult, just as the term Armilos was probably derived from Romulus and therefore could be applied to Rome, the Roman Christians, Jesus, or other enemies associated with Rome. The only reasonable way to proceed with the data we have is to identify the beast to the best of our ability on other bases and forget about the 666 as a clue.

Nevertheless, many have tried to identify 666 over the years. The number 666 was thought to be the number of years after the birth of Christ, the invasion of Pompey, the reign of Domitian, or some other early date so as to identify the beast with King Pepin III, father of Charlemagne, or the establishment of the papacy. When that date had long passed some tried adding 1,290 years, a year for a day from Daniel's prophecy. Through *gematria*--counting the number values of letters in a word, Protestants concluded that the beast was the Roman Catholic Church or one of the popes. Luther, Calvin, and Melanchthon all identified the papacy with the Antichrist.[3] Many lay Protestants also added to the list of accusers. Correspondingly, Roman Catholics identified the beast with Martin Luther (*Luther*, לולתר in Hebrew or *martin lutera* in Latin) or other reformers. Franciscans deduced that 666 meant *Benedictus*.[4] Another conclusion was Pope Innocence (*papa Innocencius*).[5]

Brady has collected hundreds of such examples as these in his 319 page book that deals only with English authors on the subject over a period of fewer than 300 years![6] He did not consider the imaginative suggestions offered earlier, at the

---

[1] B. Weiss, ΑΠΟΚΑΛΥΨΙΣ, p. 485.
[2] E. Schüssler-Fiorenza, *Revelation: Vision of a Just World* (Minneapolis: Fortress Press, c1991), p. 16; J. Weiss, *Offenbarung*, p. 661, thought the best explanation was that Nero was revived as Domitian in the tenth decade. W. G. Baines, "The Number of the Beast in Revelation 13:18," *HJ* 16 (1975):195-96, not only argued for the identification of 666 with Nero, but he also thought the first beast was Vespasian and the second beast was Titus.
[3] So C. Hill, *Antichrist in Seventh-Century England* (London: Oxford U. Press, 1971), p. 9. For only a few of the major works on the Antichrist, see E. Renan, *The Antichirst* (Boston:Roberts Bros., 1897); W. Bousset, *The Antichrist Legend* (Atlanta: Scholars Press: 1896; 1999); H. Preuss, *Die Vorstellung vom Antichrist im später Mittelalter* (Leipzig: J. C. Hinrichs, 1906).
[4] McGinn, *The End*, p. 214.
[5] McGinn, *The End*, p. 170.
[6] D. Brady, *The Contribution of British Writers between 1560 and 1830 to the Interpretation of Revelation 13.16-18* (Tübingen: J. C. B. Mohr, 1983). The examples given here were taken from

same time, or later by Continental Europeans or Americans. The calculations of authors in none of these countries stopped with 1830 IA They have continued right up to the present under the hands of both Christian and Jewish millennialists. Millennialists are people who relate the **thousand years** of Rev 20 to their own current time. Lindsey, for example, predicted that in 1990 the forces of China, Europe, Russia, and Arab countries would be led by the Antichrist to fight the great war of Armageddon.[1]

Robertson predicted this war in 1982.[2] White said the ten nations of the European Common Market represent the ten toes in Dan 2:41-45.[3] The dictator who will lead this group of nations may be King Juan Carlos of Spain who could qualify as the Antichrist.[4] The Israeli redemption calculator, Shiloh, promised that redemption would happen in 1973.[5] We can be sure that none of these calculators was correct. They misidentified the dragon, the beast, and 666. We can also be sure that the author of Rev 13 identified 666 with some one of his contemporaries, but we do not know who it was or by what code he labeled the beast as 666.

Sometimes all of this redemption literature identification was little more than a means of insulting enemies. For example Frederick II, after the pope had called him the Antichrist, returned the compliment,

> We maintain that he [the pope] is the monster of whom we read: "Another horse arose from the sea, a red one, and he who sat thereon took away peace from the earth so that the living slaughtered one another" (Rev 6:4). From the time of his election he has been not a Father of mercy, but of discord, an eager promoter of desolation rather than consolation. He has scandalized the whole world. Construing his words in the true sense, he is that great dragon who leads the world astray (Rev 12), Antichrist, whose forerunner he says we are . . . He is the angel coming from the abyss bearing vials full of bitterness to harm the sea and the earth (Rev 16:1-3).[6]

Newman opposed those, like Rist, who assumed the origin of Revelation during the persecution by Domitian in Asia Minor. He said there was no evidence outside the NT that would show a persecution of Christians by Domitian and that Irenaeus

---

only the first forty pages.
[1] H. Lindsey, *The Late Great Planet Earth* (Grand Rapids: Zondervan, c1970), pp. 14-41; *The Countdown to Armageddon* (New York: Bantam Books, c1980); and *The Rapture: Truth or Consequences* (New York: Bantam, 1983), pp. 7-21.
[2] W. E. Cox, *Biblical Studies in Final Things* (Philadelphia: Presbyterian & Reformed Publishing Co., 1967), p. 1.
[3] J. W. White, *Arming for Armageddon* (Milford: Mott Media, c1983), pp. 152-53.
[4] White, *Arming*, pp. 154-55.
[5] S. Shiloh, *The War of the Russians in Israel; The Year 1973* [Hebrew] (Jerusalem, 1973), pp. 8, 10, 17, 27.
[6] McGinn, *The End*, p. 175.

opposed those who identified 666 with Nero. Many of these conjectures, he said, have been erroneously accepted as if they were facts.[1]

666 and the End of the Common Era. Prof. Skehan once noticed a footnote appended to the text of Rev 13:18 in the Confraternity New Testament, which he correctly labeled "admirable." The anonymous author of this note said,

> The most probable interpretation of the number is that it represents the name Caesar Neron, which in Hebrew characters make up the number 666. It symbolizes imperfection, for each digit is one short of seven, the number that signifies perfection.[2]

This inspired Msgr. Skehan to deduce that by leaving out the "and" the title "King of Kings (and) Lord of Lords" (Rev 19:16) in Aramaic would be, מלך מלכין מרא מרון the number of whose letters adds up to 777, the perfect trio![3]

The number six, however, is not just extreme imperfection; it represents the end of the week, just before the Sabbath day. Early Samaritans, Jews, and Christians worked six common days every week; then they rested on the Sabbath holy day.[4]

---

[1] B. Newman, "The Fallacy of the Domitian Hypothesis," *NTS* 10 (1963/64):133-39.

[2] This insight was not first acquired or published by the editors of the Confraternity New Testament. It was proposed as early as 1895: C. A. Briggs, *The Messiah of the Apostles* (New York: Scribner's, 1895), p. 324. Others reaffirmed it, most of them using the very same words. For example, Eberhard Vischer, "Die Zahl 666 Apc 13,18," *ZNW* 4 (1903):167-79; F. C. Porter, *The Messages of the Apocalyptical Writers* (New York: Scribner's, 1916):47-48; A. S. Peake, *Revelation*, p. 318; F. C. Eiselen, E. Lewis, & D. G. Downey, *Abingdon Bible Commentary* (New York: Abingdon, 1929), p. 1388; R. H. Preston and A. T. Hanson, *The Revelation of Saint John the Divine* (London: SCM, 1962) 26-27; J. F. Walvoord, *The Revelation of Jesus Christ* (Chicago: Moody, 1966), p. 210; and G. R. Beasley-Murray, *The Book of Revelation* (Greenwood: Oliphants, 1978), p. 220.

[3] P. W. Skehan, "King of Kings, Lord of Lords (Apoc. 19:16)," *CBQ* 10 (1948):398. The note to which Skehan referred can be found in *The Holy Bible: Confraternity Text; Douay-Challoner Text* (Chicago: Good Counsel, 1956), p. 290. This is not the first insight or inspiration I have received from Msgr. P. W. Skehan, whose friendship I have treasured.

[4] The priests were commanded to discriminate the holy from the common, the clean from the unclean (Lev 10:10). Ezekiel criticized the priests for not making these distinctions and for not keeping the Sabbath (Ezek 22:26). He ordered that these distinctions be observed (Ezek 44:23). According to Acts 10:14, Peter refused to eat anything common (*koi-náwn*, κοινόν) or unclean. Consistent with Levitical concepts, the author of Rev 21:27 said the new Jerusalem would be holy; that meant that there would be nothing common (*koi-náwn*, κοινόν) in it.

Distinctions between common and holy have been retained throughout the centuries. For example, one of the prayers Jews recite at the conclusion of the Sabbath day is: "Blessed are you, Lord our God, king of the age, who discriminates between the holy (*kóh-dehsh*, קודש) and the common (*khól*, חול), between light and darkness, between Israel and the peoples [of other nations], between the Sabbath and the six working days (*yuh-máy hah-mah-ah-sáy*, ימי המעשה). Blessed are you, Lord, who discriminates between the holy and the common." The Hebrew text of this prayer is found in S. Singer (ed.), *The Authorized Daily Prayer Book of the United Hebrew Congregations of the British Empire* (London: Eyre and Spottiswoode, 1960), pp. 216-17.

They farmed the land six common years; then they let the land rest on the sabbath year. If a believer loaned money to another believer, no interest was allowed, but if the debtor had not paid the debt on time, the creditor was allowed by law to require the debtor to work off the debt at half wages (Deut 15:12-13, 18). This means he or she paid double for the debt, unless the Sabbath year came before the debt was paid. If that happened the creditor was required to cancel the debt and set the debtor slave free, because he or she had worked at half wages.

If a person sold his or her land to obtain necessary money, the one who purchased the land would have to return it to the debtor's family on the Jubilee year. The Jubilee year was the fiftieth year, the year after seven weeks of years had passed. This was the year of liberation *par excellence*, the year when the debtor slaves were set free, and the land was restored to the original owners (Lev 25:8-12).

Of course, creditors and debtors both knew when the Sabbath and Jubilee years occurred. Creditors normally paid only as much money for the property as it would be worth between the time of the purchase and the Jubilee. Very few would loan money when the Sabbath year was near, because there would not be enough time to work off the unpaid debt. This created a hardship for the poor. Therefore the Sermon on the Mount commanded potential creditors to loan money anyway, considering it really to be a gift (Matt 5:42).

These rules were later interpreted as those the Lord followed in relationship to his chosen people. Crimes were offenses that deserved punishment. Punishment could be paid by receiving similar injury, such as a hand for a hand and foot for a foot, or they could be paid with money or goods. Unpaid fines accumulated and were considered "debts." Among fellow citizens this could be worked off in terms of debtor slavery. When Israel was driven off the land into exile into a foreign country, the exile from the Promised Land was interpreted in terms of debtor slavery, when people were taken away from their homes and required to work for some master. The master was the king of the foreign nation where they had been exiled. Isaiah, Jeremiah, Second Isaiah, and Daniel were all sabbatical eschatologists. That means they thought all common days concluded with sabbath days of rest, and common eras ended with jubilees. Common eras were eras of slavery, and holy eras were eras of liberation. Jubilees were times of release when common eras were concluded, captives were set free and the land was restored to the original owners. Nationally, that meant the exiled "captives" were to return to the Promised Land.

Jeremiah said the Lord sent the Samaritans to Assyria (Jer 3:6-11). Jeremiah further warned that the nation, Judah, which had accumulated such a large debt of crime that it could not repay, would also be enslaved, or go into captivity, until it had paid double for all its crimes (Deut 15:18; Jer 16:18). Jeremiah's original prophecy was made in terms of Sabbath years and Jubilees. Some Isaianic author, during the seventh or eighth century BIA,[1] probably nearly 50 years after the North Israelites

---

[1] C. van Houten, *The Alien in Israelite Law* (Sheffield: JSOT, 1991), p. 128, overlooked Isaiah when she followed H. T. C. Sun in concluding, "Furthermore, there are no references to the Year of Jubilee in pre-exilic literature."

had been taken into captivity to Nineveh, expected the Lord to sound a great Jubilee trumpet at the end of the common era of 49 years to recall the Samaritans from Assyria to return to their land. He looked forward to the New Year's Day of the next Jubilee (Isa 27:13). Second Isaiah announced to the Jews in Palestine that the debtor's imprisonment was over; they could expect release, because they had fulfilled the debtors' requirements; they had paid double for all their **crimes** (Isa 40:1). He announced release to the captives (Isa 61:1-4) on the holiest of all years-- Jubilee. Daniel calculated the Hasmonean victory in terms of Jubilee justice, at the end of ten Jubilee years or 70 weeks of years (Dan 7).

The last week of the tenth Jubilee began with a treaty between Antiochus Epiphanes and the Jews; one half week of years later Antiochus broke the treaty, defiled the temple, and stripped it of its treasures. At that point (168/67 BIA), the sacrifice was stopped (Dan 9:24-27). Before the second half week of years was over (164 BIA), Judas had fought the famous Battle of Beth-horon, and the temple was cleansed and rededicated (Dan 7:25; 8:14; 9:27; 12:7; 1Macc 1:45-54; 4:54).[1]

This was the national Jubilee when the Promised Land was restored to its "original" owners, the Jews. With the Maccabean victory, the land had "rest," and freedom was proclaimed. Other authors followed a typology similar to Daniel's in constructing their literature. Pseudo-Jonathan and the Book of Jubilees, for example, narrated the history of Israel from creation until the "anticipated" entrance into the Promised Land in terms of Jubilees. The Testament of Moses followed the same type of eschatology. Zechariah announced that Israel's enemies would be defeated and her king ride in procession when the Lord sounded the trumpet, when he set the captives free, and when he restored them double, as at Jubilee (Zech 9:1-14). One of the Dead Sea Scrolls was obviously patterned after the tenth Jubilee Day of Atonement release of Daniel's doctrine:

> . . . which he will restore to them, and he will announce liberty to them, to abandon for them [their guilt] and atone for their iniquities . . . this word on the year of the last Jubilee . . . it is the Day of Atonement . . . the tenth Jubilee, to atone on it for all the sons of light and the men of the lot of Melchizedek (11QMelch 5-8).

By having three sixes, the author probably intended to mean that this was the ruler of the sixth Pentecost of the sixth year of the sixth week of years.

---

[1] The Book of Daniel "predicted" no messiah, son of David. That would have been a normal expectation before the Maccabean rebellion, but not after the Hasmonean dynasty had been established. J. Klausner, *The Messianic Idea in Israel* (New York: Macmillan, 1955), p. 232, upheld the usual view that Daniel was written just before the Maccabean revolt. For details counting years for these books see E. Weisenberg, "The Jubilee of Jubilees," *RevQ* 3 (1961):3-40.

    6 = sixth Pentecost (the end of the seventh concludes the year)
    6 = sixth year (the seventh is the sabbath year)
    6 = sixth week of years (at the end of the seventh is the Jubilee)

The six working days of the week were "common" days, followed by the Sabbath day which was a "holy" day. Pagans, idolators, and gentiles were all idenified with that which was common, in contrast to the Israelites and Jews who were the chosen and holy people (Deut 14:21).[1] Six, six, six, therefore, marked the end of the "common" era when gentiles ruled the Promised Land just as Friday afternoon was the end of the common days of the week. The end of the common era was the end of the age just before the liberation and the restoration of Jewish people to the "holy" land (Zech 2:12; 7:13). The "common era" was the evil era that Jews wanted to end. It would be followed by the "holy era" when Jews would enjoy their "rest."

The term "rest" in eschatological terms referred to the situation when the wars of conquest had been fought; the land had secure borders with its own king ruling the Promised Land (1Kings 8:56; Ps 95:11); and when gentiles would become slaves to Jews (Isa 60). Just as the Sabbath was a day or year of rest, so Jews and North Israelites considered the secure establishment of the Promised Land to be "rest."[2] After the holy land had been taken from Israelites or Jews, they would have realized that they were not enjoying their promised rest, so they were living in the "common" era. In Rev 13 the 666 was identified with the foreign leader who governed the Promised Land during the common era at a time the author hoped would soon come to an end.

After six weeks of years (42) have elapsed there would still be one more week of years (7) before the Jubilee. After six of these years have passed there would still be one year of seven Pentecosts (of 7 weeks each). Six of these Pentecosts would still belong to the common era before the holy Jubilee and the beginning of the new age. All of these sixes belong to the common era, but the worse the age becomes, the closer it is to the end, just as in the case of the ten Jubilees before the Battle of Beth-horon and the rededication of the temple in 164 BIA. Those last 3½ years constituted the birth pangs of the Messiah during which Judas and his following were engaged in war with the Syrian Greeks. 666 represented Antiochus Epiphanes and all of his later antitypes. After 666 was over the "captives"

---

[1] Van Houten, *The Alien*, p. 124, followed G. J. Wenham, *The Book of Leviticus* (Grand Rapids: Eerdmans, 1979), pp. 18-25, in holding, "The priest is the most holy, and can come the closest to God, while the infirm, the foreign and the female are furthest from God."

[2] For the use of "rest" to mean reestablishment of the land under Israel's messiah, see Deut 3:20; 12:9; 25:19; Josh 1:13, 15; 21:44; 22:4; 23:1; 2Sam 7:1, 11; 1Kings 5:4; 2Sam 7:1; cf. 1Kings 8:5; 1Chron 23:25; 2Chron 6:41; Ps 132:8, 13, 14; Isa 14:3; 66:1; and 4Ezra 8.52. See also Buchanan, *The Consequences of the Covenant* (Leiden: E. J. Brill, 1970), pp. 13-14 and G. Von Rad, *The Problem of the Hexateuch and Other Essays* (London: Oliver & Boyd, 1966), pp. 94-102. J. Daniélou, "La Typologie millanariste de la semaine dans le christianisme primitif," *VC* 2 (1948), pp. 2, 4. Rabbi Judah said rest means the land of Israel (*Sifre* Deut 1.2, #2; 65a). In Mark Anthony's declaration to the Jews he said that whatever was sold belonging to the Jews should be returned, slaves should be set free, as they were originally, and possessions restored to their former owners (Ant 14:321).

would be set free, and the land would be restored to its "original" owners, the Jews. This common era ruled by 666 was followed by the holy era ruled by Judas the Maccabee on the holy land, ruling the holy people from the holy city of Jerusalem. During the holy era gentiles would become slaves of the Jews, but before that happened 666 would have to come to an end.

It is only of secondary importance that Nero might have been identified with the number that marked the end. This number could have been applied frequently to other leaders associated with the end of the captivity. Ancient qualified people may have been Antiochus Epiphanes, Pompey, Herod the Great, Herod Agrippa, and any of the Caesars, including Gaius and Nero. Nero was probably called 666 even if contemporary Jews had not tried to spell Caesar Nero without a *yodh* and with a final *nun*, as some Christian scholars have done ever since the German scholar Heinrich Ewald thought of that identification in 1828.[1] This poses some difficulty

---

[1] So Peake, *Revelation*, p. 323. Peake also surveyed well the reaction of early scholars to the suggestion that 666 spelled *Neh-rawn kay-sahr*, נרון קיסר and identified Nero. The value of the name Nero *in Hebrew* totals 666. Milik renders a papyrus fragment among those found in the caves at Murabba'at as

... *tarte[en] leNeron kay[sar...* (תרתין] לנרון קנסר)

There are an uncertain number of spaces both before and after these letters. If read correctly, this would be rendered in to English as follows: "seco[nd] of Nero C[aesar]," suggesting that Caesar was normally spelled in Hebrew without the *yodh*. That is not certain, because the part of the word that would determine whether or not the word included a *yodh* is missing [P. Benoit, O.P., J.T. Milik, and R. de Vaux, O.P., *Les grottes de Murrabba`ât*, 2 vols.; *Discoveries in the Judaean Desert II*; (Oxford: Clarendon Press, 1961), Texte, p. 101; Planche 29]. If the word following Neron is correctly conjectured as "Caesar," then D. R. Hillers, "Revelation 13:18 and a Scroll from Murraba'ât," *BASOR* 170 (April, 1963):65, is probably correct in holding that there is not enough room for an additional *yodh* between the *qoph* and the next letter, which would be part of a *samek* if the word is קסר The only letter that is certain in that word is the *qoph*. The rest of the word is conjectured. Because of the space that follows, no one can be sure that the word was even intended to spell Caesar, or even how many letters belong to that word, although Milik's guess is as good as any. Hillers put too much confidence in M. Jastrow, *A Dictionary of the Targumim, the Talmud Babli and Yerushalmi, and the Midrashic Literature*, 2 vols. (New York: Pardes Publishing House, Inc., 1903), however, when he said there were other examples of Caesar spelled without the *yodh*. Jastrow lists both spellings as possible, but he conjectured only one. His examples are only those with the *yodh* (JBer 8:12b [J. mistakenly lists this as 9.12b]; bAbodZar 10b; bSan 98b). There are, in fact, 33 examples of Caesar in the Babylonian Talmud alone that are spelled with a *yodh*. The reason Jastrow gave no examples from the Babylonian or Jerusalem Talmuds, the Mishnah, Tosephta, or the Tannaitic Midrashim that are spelled without a *yodh* is that there are none. This can be checked from the concordances to these rabbinic documents. This means that *if* this Murraba'at fragment really had Caesar spelled *káy-sahr* (קסר), rather than *kai-sahr*, (קיסר) this would be the only example in all extant literature. Another problem with the Hebrew-Nero identification is that the authors and editors of Revelation called attention to the fact that the place where a great battle was to be fought was "in Hebrew" Har Maggedon (Rev 16:16). In Rev 13:18 it does not say "in Hebrew" 666.

There were people in the time of Irenaeus who also said 888 totaled the same number as the name, "Jesus," but Irenaeus argued that the name Jesus was only a Greek translation of the real name which had only three letters (*Yáy-shoo*, ישו) in Hebrew (AdvHaer 2:24, 1-2). Irenaeus thought this whole method was faulty. Nevertheless, others continued to call attention to the four vowels and two consonants in the Greek word for Jesus, noting that the total reached 888 (SibOr 1:325-29). Since

for scholars whose interpretation of Revelation depends on the theory that 666 represented *only* Nero.[1] The beasts of Rev 13 must be identified on some other basis first and afterward awarded the epithet "666."

There were at least two people involved in the composition of Rev 13. When the second author began to write he already was acquainted with the first narrative and probably knew perfectly well that the first beast was Herod the Great. When he wrote about Herod's grandson, he was not disturbed by the fact that this would mean there were more beasts than one, identified as more people than one, and applicable to more periods of history than one. When he read about the first beast, the narrative may originally have contained the verse about 666 as its conclusion. If that were so, he just removed it and placed it at the end of his narrative about the second beast. That is only a guess. That which is certain is that beasts, dragons, Antichrists, and Armiloses were updated from one historical crisis to another. Those who try to make them all fit the same individual at the same period of history provide more confusion to the literature than the literature requires.

There is nothing in this chapter to identify either of the beasts in Rev 13 with the false prophet of Rev 19:20. That is apparently a separate mystery.

Jesus reportedly was raised on the eighth day--the day after the seventh--later Christians anticipated an eighth age, a Christian age.

[1] To mention only a few, A. Y. Collins, *Crisis*; Giblin, *Revelation*, p. 135; and J. W. Bowman, "Revelation," *The Interpreter's Dictionary of the Bible* (4 vols.; New York: Abingdon, 1962) IV, pp. 61, 67. Even if 666 had been applied to Nero it might have been applied to other enemy leaders, like Gaius Caesar, first.

CHAPTER FOURTEEN

TEXT

Revelation	First Testament and Other Literature
14:1I was watching--Now look! The Lamb **standing on Mount Zion**, and with him 144,000,	4Ezra 13.36, 39-40He [God's son] **will stand on the top of Mount Zion** . . . and when you saw him gathering to himself another peaceful multitude, these are the ten tribes.
	Ps 48:3**Mount Zion** in the far north, the city of the great king.
	Ezek 9:3-6The glory of the God of Israel went up from over the cherubim upon which it was to the threshold of the temple. It called to the man dressed in linen who had the writing case at his side. Yehowah said to him, "Go over into the center of the city in the midst of **Jerusalem,**
having his name and the name of his Father **on their foreheads**.	and mark a *tau* **on the foreheads** of the men who mourn and sigh for all the abominations committed in its midst."
	To the others he said, so that I could hear, "Go through the city after him, and strike! Your eyes shall not spare; you shall show no pity. Kill the old men, young men, maidens, children, and women, but do not touch any man upon whom is the *tau*. Begin at my temple."
²**Then I heard a noise** from heaven **like the noise of much water [running]**,	Ezek 1:24**Then I heard a noise** of their wings **like the noise of much water [running]**.

like the sound of loud thunder. The sound which I heard was like harpers **playing** on their **harps**, ³and they were **singing a new song** before the throne and before the four beasts and before the elders. No one was able to learn
the **song** except the 144,000 who are

the redeemed of the land. ⁴These are the ones who have not defiled themselves with women, for they are celibate. These are those who follow the Lamb wherever he goes. They have been redeemed from human beings
the first [of the first fruits with respect] to God and to the Lamb.

⁵**In their mouth was not found** anything **false**; they were blameless.

^{Ezek 43:2}Look! The glory of the God of Israel came from the way of the east, and his voice was **like the noise of much water [running]**.

^{Ps 33:3}**Sing** to him **a new song**; **play** skillfully on a **harp** with ten strings.

^{1Chron 16:23} **Sing** to Yehowah, all the land; announce the gospel of his salvation from day to day.

^{Ps 96:1}**Sing** to Yehowah **a new song**; **Sing** to Yehowah, all the land.

^{Ps 40:4}He will put in my mouth **a new song**, praise to our God. Many see and fear and trust in Yehowah.

^{Ps 144:9}God, I will **sing a new song** to you; I will **play** for you with a **harp** with ten strings.

^{Isa 42:10}**Sing** to Yehowah **a new song**, his praise from the borders of the land.

^{Isa 35:8-10}It will be called a holy way. Nothing unclean will pass over it . . . there **the redeemed** will walk, and the ransomed of Yehowah will return.

^{Exod 23:19}**The first** of **the first fruits** of your ground you shall bring to the house of Yehowah your God.

^{Zeph 3:13}They had done no wickedness; they did not speak **falsehood**; a deceitful tongue
was not found in their mouth.

^{Isa 53:9}He had done no violence; there was no deceit **in his mouth**.

TECHNICAL DETAILS

The Book of Revelation has long been understood to have been written in some kind of code that most people find impossible to decipher. Because this is true, scholars have felt free to inject their own preferred meanings to the text without any controls. Many, like Caird, hold that "Like everything else in his book this is symbolical."[1] While explaining the meaning of Armageddon, Beasley-Murray concluded,

> Whatever the origin of the term, we are not to think in terms of a geographical locality in Israel (the Holy Land does not really feature in John's prophecy).[2]

Since the messages are not to be taken literally, they can be taken to mean almost anything, and very few people can prove that scholars who create fanciful interpretations for geographical and historical allusions are mistaken. Preston and Hanson gave the following reason for this use of symbolism. While examining the doctrine of hell in the Book of Revelation, they conceded,

> It certainly *sounds* vindictive and unchristian to a degree, but it is only fair to examine it more closely before we let our immediate feelings determine our judgment. The first thing to do is to discover the meaning of the *very symbolic* [emphasis added] language which John uses.[3]

---

[1] G. B. Caird, *A Commentary on the Revelation of St. John the Divine* (London: Black, c1966), p. 179.
[2] G. R. Beasley-Murray, *The Book of Revelation* (Greenwood: Oliphants, c1978), p. 246.
[3] R. H. Preston, and A. T. Hanson, *The Revelation of Saint John the Divine* (London: SCM Press, c1951), p. 101. A. Y. Collins, "Reading the Book of Revelation in the Twentieth Century," *Int* 40 (1986):229-42, in her survey of modern interpreters of the Book of Revelation, divided them into two groups: 1) those who interpret the book symbolically and 2) those who interpret the book literally. The former assume that the end is implied but they do not specify it. The latter expect the end to take place on earth in relationship to current events. These, however, are not the only possibilities. As early as 1886 Vischer set out to show that the Book of Revelation was a Christian adaptation of a Jewish original. So H. B. Swete, *The Apocalypse of St. John* (London: Macmillan, 1909), and J. P. M. Sweet, *Revelation* (Philadelphia: Westminster, c1979), p. LIII, correctly observed that there was no book in the NT so steeped in Hebrew thought and imagery from the FT as the Revelation of St. John, but this does not mean one is free to interpret this imagery in any way the scholar chooses. F. Düsterdieck, *Critical and Exegetical Handbook to the Revelation of John*, tr. H. E. Jacobs (Winona Lake: Alpha Publications, 1884), p. 245, correctly said, "But every kind of allegorizing is without the least foundation in the text."

Caird said, "Like everything else in his book this is a symbol."[1] That is one way to avoid an embarrassing problem by escaping into eisegesis, allegory, and fiction. It leads the reader away from the intended meaning of the text.

This redemption midrash is not nearly as confused or confusing as many have thought or desired. The authors wrote so that some people could understand them while others could not. Those who could understand them knew Jewish history, Jewish customs, and the First Testament (FT). Since many Western scholars are not very familiar with Jewish literature and thought-form, they have given up any attempt to crack the code and find its real meaning. Instead they have examined this document from a different perspective altogether. This chapter will show the kind of knowledge that is necessary to crack the code and find the authors' intended meaning for those still interested in that goal. This text will show the necessity of finding the existing FT types before trying to understand Revelation antitypes. This study will, at the same time, call attention to the mistakes other scholars make when they overlook this necessary procedure.

Prof. Schüssler-Fiorenza has written an article in which she sets forth her basic understanding of the Book of Revelation, concentrating on Rev 14:1-5.[2] She argued

1) that the poetic-symbolic language of the Book of Revelation has different layers of meaning rather than one single definite one,
2) that Revelation is a rhetorical work composed as a rhetorical response to the rhetorical situation of Asia Minor.

She presumed that the entire book was composed by John of Patmos for the Christians of Asia Minor, so she tried to evoke the meaning of the book from the situation she understood to have existed there at the time the book was written. After surveying and evaluating the scholarly works on Rev 14:1-5, she set out to interpret the text. Our first response will be to discuss the location of the composition, and later, her interpretation.

PALESTINE AND ASIA MINOR

Once Schüssler-Fiorenza began with the supposition that the entire Book of Revelation was composed by John in the area of Asia Minor, she overlooked the

---

[1] Caird, *Revelation*, p. 179.
[2] E. Schüssler-Fiorenza, "The Followers of the Lamb: Visionary Rhetoric and Social-Political Situation," *Semeia* 36 (1986):123-46. Schüssler-Fiorenza has been chosen as an illustration because she best represents this school of thought in scholarship today. This article was chosen because it clearly defines her position and methodology. This position is also published in *The Book of Revelation: Justice and Judgement* (Philadelphia: Fortress Press, 1985). There are other modern scholars, like M. Karrer, *Die Johannesoffenbarung als Brief. Studien zu ihren literarischen, historischen und theologischen Ort* (Göttingen: Vandenhoeck & Ruprecht, 1986), who, like Schüssler-Fiorenza, argue that the entire Book of Revelation is a letter.

biblical situation in Palestine and looked instead for a "rhetorical situation" in Asia Minor and for historical clues from Pliny's letters rather than the FT (Pliny, *Letters* 10:96).

Rhetoric is not a historical method. It is a legal technique for arguing cases, primarily in court. The rhetorician does not try to find new interpretations or new data to use for reconsideration. The rhetorician begins with a conclusion and finds all of the arguments possible for upholding it, dismissing all evidence that argues against it.

Hypotheses are designed primarily by and for rhetoricians to limit the extent of data allowed to be brought into consideration. Historians can study the work and technique of rhetoricians but their goal is different. The goal of a historian is to learn the truth and to uncover as much data as possible to reach that end. When more data is brought into the picture the historian is forced to reconsider the tentative conclusions accordingly. There is no direct relationship between rhetorical proof and historical fact.

Except for the geographical references in the first three chapters of Revelation, the geography that was given is either from some place in Palestine or some place, like Egypt or Babylon, that had some typological significance to Jews. Therefore it requires a real effort to ignore the geography and history of the Promised Land when reading the Book of Revelation. The very style of the book is one which indicates that Rev 1 is an introduction to a prophecy that John of Patmos acquired; Rev 2-3 consists of letters to the leaders of seven churches; Rev 4:1-22:5 is the prophecy about which John spoke in his introduction and conclusion; and Rev 22:6-21 is John's concluding recommendation of the prophecy for the serious reading of the Christians in Asia Minor.[1]

In assuming, rhetorically, that the entire Book of Revelation was written by a Christian and for Christians Schüssler-Fiorenza failed to notice that the word "Jesus" occurs five times in Rev 1 (Rev 1:1, 2, 5, 9) and three more times in Rev 22 (Rev

---

[1] See Buchanan, "John of Patmos and the Angel of Revelation," *The Proceedings of the Sixth World Congress of Jewish Studies* (Jerusalem, 1977) I, pp. 35-50. Scholars like Collins and Schüssler-Fiorenza, in presuming that the entire Book of Revelation was written in Asia Minor, have to take all of the geographical references in the book except Rev 1-3 and 22 to be symbols and not actual geographical sites. Many scholars have observed that the language in Revelation is Semitic, translated Greek. For example, see E. B. Allo, *S. Jean L'Apocalypse* (Paris: F. Gabalda, 1933); W. Bousset, *Kritisch-exegetischer Kommentar über die Offenbarung Johannis* (Göttingen: Vandenhoeck & Ruprecht, 1906); R. H. Charles, *International Critical Commentary on the Revelation of Saint John* (New York: Charles Scribner's Sons, c1930) II; T. C. Laughlin, *The Solecisms of the Apocalypse* (Princeton: C.S. Robinson Co., 1902); G. Mussies, "The Greek of the Book of Revelation," *L'Apocalypse johannique et l'Apocalyptique dans le Nouveau Testament*, ed. J. Lambrecht, *BETL* 53 (1980); K. G. C. Newport, "The Use of *Ek* in Revelation: Evidence of Semitic Influence," *AUSS* 24 (1986):223-30; Newport, "Semitic Influence on the Use of some Prepositions in the Book of Revelation," *BT* 37 (1986):328-34; R. B. Y. Scott, *The Original Language of the Apocalypse* (Toronto: U. of Toronto Press, 1928); Steven Thompson, *The Apocalypse and Semitic Syntax* (Cambridge:Cambridge U. Press c1985); and C. C. Torrey, *The Apocalypse of John* (New Haven: Yale U. Press, 1958).

22:16, 20, 21), but only six times altogether in the prophecy that is more than 19 chapters long. Furthermore, none of the references to Jesus in the prophecy seems integral to the context. In the following examples, the underlined portions seem to be glosses, probably added by some Christian to Christianize an otherwise Jewish prophecy:[1]

> 1. . . . on those who keep the commandments of God
>   *and the testimony borne by Jesus* (Rev 12:17).
> 2. . . . those who keep the commandments of God
>   *and [uphold] the faith [instigated by] Jesus* (Rev 14:12).
> 3. . . . drunk with the blood of the saints
>   *and the blood of the martyrs of Jesus* (Rev 17:6).
> 4. . . . *I am a fellow servant with you and your brothers who
>   uphold the testimony borne by Jesus, for the testimony
>   borne by Jesus is the spirit of prophecy* (Rev 19:10; cf 22:9).

The paragraphs that contain these sentences all make sense if the italicized portions are omitted. These were probably added by some Christian before the document came to John, because through the prophecy he received a revelation of Jesus Christ (Rev 1:1), and it was sent in Jesus' name (Rev 22:16).

The belief that the Book of Revelation is written in Hebraic Greek has long been accepted as valid. It has obviously been translated. Charles thought it was composed by one author, because the Greek style was the same throughout, but this would be true if John had composed the introduction, letters, and concluding recommendation and translated the prophecy, since his style and vocabulary would be evident either in his composition or his translation.[2]

One of the reasons many scholars have not recognized the distinction between the author of the introduction, letters, and concluding recommendation and the prophecy itself is that the first verse of the book mentions an *áhn-geh-laws* (ἄγγελος). Since there are many references to angels in the Book of Revelation, it is easy to assume that all *áhn-geh-loi* are of the same kind, even though most New Testament (NT) scholars realize that the term *áhn-geh-laws* is a very general, non-technical term for "messenger." It can refer to a heavenly or an earthly messenger.

Anyone who carried some parcel or message was an *áhn-geh-laws*. John thought it was God who sent him a message through a messenger. With the message came the blessing on the one who read this prophecy and the others who heard it read, probably in a synagogue (Rev 1:3). This shows that the message which John saw was something at least later Christians could read. John then sent this prophecy to officers of the seven churches, with a special personal message to the officer

---

[1] These four statements are quoted from Buchanan, "John of Patmos," p. 47.
[2] Charles, *Revelation* I, pp. lxxxiii-lxxxviii.

(*áhn-geh-laws*) of each church. His dialogue with the messenger which began in Rev 1 was not continued until the final recommendation in Rev 22.[1]

After the entire prophecy had been read, the messenger told John, **These words are faithful and true . . . Blessed is he who keeps the words of the prophecy of this book** (Rev 22:6). After that, John fell down to worship the messenger who showed him these things (Rev 22:8). The messenger, however, said,

> **Do not do that! I am a fellow servant of you and your brothers, the prophets, and those who keep the words of this book. Worship God** (Rev 22:9).

The messenger evidently did not want to be mistaken for a heavenly messenger. He was a human being, like John. Both referred to themselves as **servants** (Rev 1:1; 22:9). The words that were to be kept by John and his fellow **servants** were **the words of this book** or **the words of the prophecy of this book** (Rev 22:9-10). **The book** or **the prophecy** was probably the document that was included in Rev 4:1-22:5. This prophecy ends with a word of triumph, **. . . and they shall rule for ages of ages** (Rev 22:5). Then John added the words, **And he [the messenger] said to me, "These words are faithful and true"** (Rev 22:6), obviously meaning the words that had just been quoted extensively.

The messenger apparently brought John a scroll which he saw, read, and with which he was impressed. He translated it and sent it out to the churches in Asia Minor, but the prophecy itself had its origin in Palestine, so the geography and history of the prophecy have very little to do with Asia Minor, and if they have a "rhetorical situation," it is not to be found in Asia Minor but Palestine. The thought-form involved is not that of Asia Minor Greeks but Palestinian Jews. The literary background is not that of Pliny but of the FT. Although John understood **the Lamb** to be Jesus, the local context simply indicates that initially **the Lamb** would have been some messiah who had monastic followers. These followers were real, genuine celibate males, members of one of the monastic orders, who kept themselves from levitical defilement of real women. Mount Zion, where **the Lamb** and his followers were gathered, was the temple mount at Jerusalem. No further layers of symbolism are necessary to understand the text.

Rev 14 is a complex chapter composed of four separate units: Rev 1-5, 6-12, 13, 14-20. These units are introduced by **I was watching. Now look!** The chapter contains several parallels with other chapters of Revelation, implying that these are favorite sayings of the final editor who inserted these statements in several places he considered appropriate.

---

[1] Except for the apparent intrusion in 19:10.

COMMENTARY

¹*I was watching*. In Rev 14 these words always introduce a new subject (Rev 14:1, 6, 14). In Greek they should be rendered **I saw** (*áy-dawn*, εἶδον) and they are translated that way in Rev 14:6, but they require a different translation in Rev 14:1 and Rev 14:14. The words are taken from the Aramaic of Dan 7:13, *kháh-zeh hah-véyth* (חזה הוית), a periphrastic imperfect, showing continued action. Therefore it should be frequently translated in Revelation as **I was watching**.

The Lamb is standing on Mount Zion. The king normally sat at the Lord's right hand, so why was **the Lamb standing** (Ps 2:6; Acts 7:56)? That is because **the Lamb** was not the Lord's presence in heaven. He was on **Mount Zion** where he **stood** up to undertake his assignment as king.

1) Geographically, the events of Ezekiel, Fourth Ezra, and Rev 14, all took place in **Zion,** the City of David, which existed as a small town on the rocky ridge above the Spring of Siloam. Nothing in the text supports Loisy's claim that this Jerusalem was in heaven.¹ **Zion** was a strategic site. It was a fortress, the citadel for the city of David (2Sam 5:7; 1Chron 11:5), or the city of the great king (i.e., David) (Ps 48:2). Both the temple and the king's palace were **on Mount Zion**, the ridge immediately west of the Spring of Siloam. The Lord was thought to be present in both places. He was present through the smoke and the fire on the altar (Ps 9:11; 135:21; Isa 8:18; Joel 3:17 [4:17]). He was also present through his legal agent or apostle, the king. **Zion** was identified with Jerusalem, the capital city of Judah. **Mount Zion** is the fortress David took from the Jebusites. It is the holy hill on which God placed his king (Ps 2:6). **Zion** is the place where God would situate his messianic king (Ps 2:6) and from there the Messiah would exercise his authority (Ps 110:2). The regular feasts were held there, and Jews from all over the world assembled at **Zion** for festivals. There were deep nationalistic, and religious ties to **Zion** for all Jews in every part of the world.

The **Zion** to which **the ransomed** Jews expected to return (Isa 35:10) was not distinguished from Jerusalem as being "spiritual **Zion**." Hailey called **Zion** "spiritual **Zion**," but he correctly argued that this city was *the* **Mount Zion**, located here on earth on the Promised Land.² For Jews of NT times geographical **Zion** *was* spiritual **Zion**. When the author of Heb 12:22-24 told his congregants that they had **come to Zion, city of the living God, heavenly Jerusalem**, he did not mean that both they and he had gone to heaven. He meant that they were all gathered together to celebrate one of the festival days of the Jews in Jerusalem. **Zion** was not only called **heavenly Jerusalem**, but also "the city of God" (Philo, *Dreams* 2:250), and **the beloved city** (Rev 20:9).³ When Obadiah looked forward to the arrival of the day of Yehowah he thought that when that day came **Zion** would be restored to

---

¹ A. Loisy, *L'Apocalypse de Jean* (Paris: Emile Nourry, 1923), p. 260.
² H. M. Hailey, *Revelation: An Introduction and Commentary* (Grand Rapids: Baker's Book House, c1979), pp. 301-302.
³ See further Buchanan, *To the Hebrews* (Garden City: Doubleday & Co., 1972), pp. 222-23.

power; Israel's enemies would be punished; and the Kingdom would become the Lord's (Obad 15, 21). Obadiah referred to the same "spiritual" **Zion** as Rev 14:1. This was not only the **heavenly** Jerusalem, but also the geographical capital city of the Promised Land.

Rev 14 and Fourth Ezra both have the crowd gathered around the Messiah (**Lamb** or Son). In Rev 14 it is not "the heavenly counterpart of the earthly Jerusalem,"[1] as Sweet thought. **Mount Zion** is a location in the City of David and is often used synonymously with Jerusalem. To be sure, Jews and Christians believed there was a Jerusalem in heaven, but there is nothing in the text here to suggest that this was a description of heaven. Throughout his commentary Caird insists that **the Lamb** is different from the Lion of Judah. His commentary on this verse says,

> Now he is ready to describe the decisive battle, and, with a characteristic twist for which we should by now be prepared, he sees *on Mount Zion*, not the terrible warrior king of the psalmist's hope, but *the Lamb*.[2]

The twist is the one Caird made, rather than the author of the text. The title **Lamb** in the Book of Revelation obviously means the Messiah. Comparing Rev 14 with Ezek 9 shows that the author of Rev 14 understood **Zion** to be located in the city of Jerusalem, and not in some "meta-historical, supra-terrestrial place equivalent to heaven itself," as Giblin held.[3]

Rev 14 was purposely placed after Rev 12 and 13. In the Book of Daniel the four beasts were followed in sequence by the Son of man. The beasts were the leaders of the old age of gentile rule, between the destruction of the temple in 586 BIA and the rededication of the temple in 164 BIA This was the age of the beasts, which was followed by the new Hasmonean age, the age of Jewish rule. The editor or author responsible for the organization of chapters in the Book of Revelation followed Daniel's order typologically. He put the section of the beasts before the section dealing with the cleansing of Jerusalem and the movement of **the Lamb** with his followers. This was to be the new change of the ages and the new installation of the Son of man. The Son of man in Daniel cleansed the temple in Jerusalem; **the Lamb** in Revelation also stood on **Mount Zion** in Jerusalem.

His name and the name of his Father. **The name** involved is that of **the Lamb,** the designated Messiah, and his **Father** is God. The Messiah was understood to be God's son and God's legal agent. Those who were with him were **the 144,000** who **had both his name and the name of his Father.** These were the two **names** they had **on their foreheads.** Monks called God their Father. Since they had rejected the

---

[1] Sweet, *Revelation*, p. 221.
[2] Caird, *Revelation*, p. 178.
[3] C. H. Giblin, *The Book of Revelation* (Collegeville: Liturgical Press, c1991), p. 137.

families into which they were born, they called no man **father**. The other monks were their legal brothers, and God was their legal Father. Jesus fit this pattern. He was celibate; he called God **Father**; and he referred to his apostles as his **mother and brothers** (Matt 12:46-50; 23:5-10).[1] This does not necessarily mean that **the Lamb** in Rev 14 was initially written about Jesus. Any celibate Jewish Messiah could qualify for this role. By the time, however, that John of Patmos read the manuscript, he understood that **the Lamb** involved was Jesus.

Like the sound of much water [running] **Mount Zion** was located near Ain Gihon, the huge spring of Siloam, from which **much water ran** through Hezekiah's tunnel under the threshold of the temple. The author was pictured as one stationed at a place where he could see **Mount Zion** and **hear** the **water** of the spring charging through the tunnel. The reference to **much water** does not imply a "sea," as Aune suggested. This report has a parallel in Rev 19:6a.

They were singing a new song. There are many exhortations in Scripture to **sing a new song** (Ps 33:3; 40:4; 96:1; 98:1; 144:9; 149:1; Isa 42:10). It is not clear whether or not the **song** mentioned here is also the song in Rev 15:3-4.

The redeemed of the Land. Both groups were **redeemed** or saved. Those in Ezekiel were actually saved from being slaughtered like the rest of the inhabitants of the city. Those in Revelation were said to be **redeemed.** Those gathered around God's Son in Fourth Ezra were the ten tribes returning from Assyria. Josephus said,

> Until now there have been ten tribes beyond the Euphrates, countless myriads whose number cannot be determined (Ant 11:133).

In Rev 7 and 14, **the redeemed** included all twelve tribes. *Hoi ay-gaw-ras-méh-noi apáw tays gays* (οἱ ἠγορασμένοι ἀπὸ τῆς γῆς (Rev 14:3). They were not those who were "liberated from the earth," as Prof. Schüssler-Fiorenza holds.[2] They are "the redeemed ones of the land."

This is a Greek translation of the Hebrew, *geh-oo-leém* (גאולים) or *peh-doo eém min hah-áh-retz* (פדוים מן הארץ) **the redeemed** or **ransomed of the land**. In this case, which is dealing with a group of men selected from the twelve tribes of Israel (Rev 7:1-8) in the temple area of the capital city of the Promised Land, there can be little question that *hay gay* (ἡ γῆ) = *hah-áh-retz* (הארץ) and means **the**

---

[1] See Buchanan, *Jesus: The King and his Kingdom* (Macon: Mercer U. Press, 1984), pp. 171-90, for more insights into monasticism in early Christianity and Judaism.
[2] Schüssler-Fiorenza, "Followers," p. 132; ." J. B. Smith, *Revelation of Jesus Christ*, ed. J. O. Yoder (Scottdale, PA,: Herald Press, c1961), p. 209, thought this expression meant they had been taken up from the earth into heaven. He acknowledged, however, that the word for "redeem" really meant "buy" rather than "take up." Equally off target was F. D. Mazzaferri, *The Genre of the Book of Revelation from a Source-critical Perspective* (Berlin; New York: W. De Gruyter, 1989), p. 335; "They are οἱ ἠγορασμένοι ἀπὸ τῆς γῆς], so they are no longer on earth."

Land rather than "the earth." These were not the ones **redeemed from** the earth but those chosen few who belonged to the land and were redeemed.

They were called **redeemed**, because they belonged to a group of "debtors," who had a large collection of unpaid fines for crimes committed by the group. They were **redeemed** when the note was paid, the debt was cancelled. Either it had been forgiven, paid up, or ransomed by someone else.

The **redeemed** Rev 14 corresponded to the ransomed or **redeemed** of Babylon who were to return to **Zion** (Isa 35:9-10). Morris' suggestion that they are **redeemed** from "worldly things and worldly men"[1] was not the author's intention. Redeeming financial notes and getting debts paid is rather worldly. Ask any banker or mortgage company officer. Hailey correctly said, "They are God's **redeemed** on earth,"[2] but the group was more restricted in scope than Hailey allowed. They are the **redeemed** of the Jews and\or Christians who return to **Zion.** Hailey was correct in concluding,

> The one hundred forty-four thousand are those on earth who have come unto Mount Zion and the Lamb (Heb 12:22ff).[3]

Because they were **followers of the Lamb,** Aune concluded that they were Christians.[4] That is only one possibility. There were many Jewish messiahs all of whom would have had **followers,** who would have been Jews. This context does not require either that the **Lamb** was Jesus or that the **followers of the Lamb** were Christians.

For they are celibate. Usually the term "virgin" refers to women, but there are other instances when the same term is used for males. For example, Epiphanius, (*Pan.* 28.7, 5) called the Apostle John, "the holy virgin John."

Schüssler-Fiorenza concluded that the correct translation of Rev 14:3 meant that the 144,000 were "separated out," or "liberated from the earth."[5] She could not

---

[1] Morris, *Revelation*, p. 176.
[2] Hailey, *Revelation*, p. 303.
[3] Hailey, *Revelation*, p. 304.
[4] Aune, *Revelation 6-16*, p. 448.
[5] Schüssler-Fiorenza, "Followers," p. 132. In this she has the support of E. Lohmeyer, *Die Offenbarung des Johannes* (Tübingen: J. C. B. Mohr, 1953), pp. 121-22, who rendered the pertinent phrase, *von der Erde*, and H. Kraft, *Die Offenbarung des Johannes* (Tübingen: J. C. B. Mohr, 1974), pp. 186, 190, who translated it *weg von der Erde*. R. H. Mounce, *The Book of Revelation* (Grand Rapids: Eerdmans, c1977), p. 267 and A. J. Beagley, *The "Sitz im Leben" of the Apocalypse* (Berlin: W. DeGruyter, 1987), p. 81, concurred. Beagley said that since the 144,000 had been redeemed from the earth, they were obviously gathered around Mount Zion in heaven. Sweet, *Revelation*, p. 221, also thought Mount Zion was a heavenly location and rendered the passage, *from the earth*, even though this is incoherent with his further analysis of the followers as being celibate, earthly priests (pp. 222-23). Düsterdieck, *Handbook*, p. 257, said they were purchased from among men or from humanity, "not merely from the Jewish nation." G. E. Ladd, *A Commentary on the Revelation of John* (Grand Rapids: Eerdmans, c1972), pp. 189-90, thought Mount Zion was not to be taken

believe that the *pahr-théh-noi* (παρθένοι) could really refer to **celibate** monks, as the text says. She admitted that this word created some difficulties. This was further accentuated by the claim that these **celibate males** had not **defiled themselves with women** (Rev 14:4), but she got around that difficulty by saying that this statement, **For they are celibate** (Rev 14:4), did not have to be taken literally, any more than words *ah-gaw-ráhd-zayn* (ἀγοράζειν) (buy, ransom, redeem), **Mount Zion,** *hoo-páh-gayn* (ὑπάγειν (lead or go away), *ah-par-kháy* (ἀπαρχή) (first fruits), or *áh-moh-moi,* ἄμωμοι (blameless, guiltless, innocent), should be taken literally.[1] The

---

spiritually but understood as the heavenly dwelling place of God himself (189-90), J. F. Walvoord, *The Revelation of Jesus Christ* (Chicago: Moody Press, c1966), pp. 213-14), rendered the text, "from the earth," but he also held that Mount Zion was the earthly Jerusalem where the saved Jews would be gathered at the beginning of the millennial rule. Kraft justified his translation as having been influenced by Isa 53:8, which, correctly translated would be "cut off from the land of life" (= Palestine) (*neeg-záhyr may éh-retz khai-yeém,* (נגזר מארץ חיים). Kraft evidently misunderstood the expression "the land of life" to mean the earth. On this see Buchanan, *The Consequences of the Covenant* (Leiden: E. J. Brill, 1970), pp. 123-31. Caird, *Revelation,* p. 180, said "ransomed from the earth" means "they have been called to share Christ's royal and priestly office." L. Morris, *The Book of Revelation* (Grand Rapids: Eerdmans, c1987), p. 171, said, "Redeemed *from* the earth indicates redemption from worldly things and worldly people." J. B. Smith, *Revelation of Jesus Christ,* ed. J. O. Yoder (Scottdale, PA: Herald Press, c1961), p. 209, took the term "from" as further proof that the scene took place in heavenly Mount Zion rather than earthly Jerusalem.

[1] Schüssler-Fiorenza, "Followers," F. F. Segoreia, *Discipleship in the New Testament* (Philadelphia; Fortress Press, c1985), pp. 132-33. Kraft, *Offenbarung,* p. 189, also thought it was strange that celibates appeared in the Book of Revelation. He "solved" the problem, however, by claiming that it was an intrusion, not being integral to the work of the author. R. H. Preston, and A. T. Hanson, *The Revelation of Saint John the Divine* (London: SCM Press, c1951), p. 100, followed Charles in making the same judgment even though they acknowledged that there was no textual basis for their conclusions. They exclaimed, "If taken literally it means that only male celibates can be saved!" They suggest a late intrusion. None of these scholars realized how prominent celibacy was in Judaism in NT times. Ladd, *Commentary,* p. 191, said it could not mean real celibates, because that would be in violation of all biblical theology which nowhere looks upon sexual relations as criminal or defiling. It is therefore taken to be understood as a spiritual condition. Walvoord, *Revelation,* p. 116, concurred. Düsterdieck, *Handbook,* p. 257, says the "sons of Israel" mentioned here are "ancient Israel as little as Jerusalem in the Apocalypse is ancient Jerusalem." He did not seem to realize that his "symbolical" interpretation was no different from the allegorization he earlier criticized. Sweet, *Revelation,* p. 222, however, noted that celibacy was practiced by Israelites in times of war and by the authors of some of the literature found at Qumran. Morris, *Revelation,* pp. 171-72, found the idea of celibacy and women being defiled to be repulsive and held that it was not basically a NT concept. He acknowledged, however, that there was some First Testament (FT) basis for celibacy. He suggested that the term be taken symbolically to mean Christians should not have intercourse with the pagan world system.

Caird, *Revelation,* p. 179, thought this, like everything else in the book, should be understood symbolically. It was only in an unguarded moment that the author allowed his predilection for asceticism to creep into the text. Beasley-Murray, *Revelation,* p. 223, thought that the 144,000 meant the whole church and therefore the word "celibacy" must be understood symbolically to refer to abstention from fornication with "Babylon." Apostolos Makrakis, *Interpretation of the Revelation of St. John the Divine,* tr. A. G. Alexander (Chicago: Hellenic Christian Education Society, 1948), p. 353, thought Mount Zion should be understood spiritually as "the exalted truth constituting the foundation of the church and the spiritual temple of God," but the 144,000, he said were actual Christians who "espouse celibacy and virginity, deny their own will, and follow '*the Lamb*

women with whom the **followers** of **the Lamb** were **not defiled** must refer to false prophetesses, according to Schüssler-Fiorenza. The **celibates** probably refer to the representatives of the **bride of the Lamb**.[1]

Zahn was also shocked into finding some other explanation for the plain meaning of the text. Since he believed Revelation was composed by the apostle John, he said that the same apostle who became the substitute son for Jesus' mother, Mary, could not advocate marriageless existence in the church.[2] Rissi said, "*Parthenoi* cannot indicate asceticism," because one of the highest points of the document is the marriage of **the Lamb**. Therefore the word must indicate the pure people of God.[3] He did not relate the marriage of **the Lamb** to the contract of the Lord with his people. He took the marriage literally and the *parthenoi* (celibate males), metaphorically, when he should have reversed the process. Caird said,

> The *hundred and forty four thousand*, marshalled for the great battle from which they are to emerge as victors, these are not just heads of families but the whole army of martyrs with no distinction of age or sex.[4]

How could these dead martyrs march into battle? and how could they be of every age and sex and still be **celibate** males? That was no problem for Caird. All he had to do was declare that servants and prophets are automatically martyrs in the Book of Revelation.[5] On the same basis he could just as well declare that all **celibate** males were automatically martyrs of every age and sex. Of course this distorts the text, but it was an interesting declaration.

Collins thought the author referred to real **celibate** males, and she knew about the early Jewish Essenes, but she ignored all of that and declared that monasticism did not become generally practiced until several centuries later. Therefore these virgins were males who became continent in their later years of life. Collins noted that Essenes were monastic and raised other people's children, and she thought there were other exhortations in the Book of Revelation to continence. She

---

whithersoever he goeth' according to the Gospel text" (p. 355).

M. Rissi, *Time and History* (Richmond: John Knox Press, 1965), p. 91, however, acknowledged that the text really refers to celibate men and that women were excluded. Nevertheless, he concluded that the 144,000 constituted the pure people of God without saying further who these people were. Scholars like N. Perrin, followed by J. Butts, "Probing the Polling. Jesus Seminar Results on the Kingdom Sayings," *Forum* 3 (1987):98-128, extend this symbolism beyond apocalyptic literature to apocalyptic terms, like "the Kingdom of Heaven," which they accept as a symbol, without saying what it symbolizes. Smith, *Revelation*, p. 210, thought the "virgins" meant the Israelites, because Israel was sometimes referred to as "the virgin daughter of Zion" (2Kings 19:21; Isa 37:22; Lam 2:13).

[1] Schüssler-Fiorenza, "Followers," pp. 132-33--Whatever that could mean.
[2] T. Zahn, *Die Offenbarung des Johannes* (Leipzig: A Deichert, 1924), pp. 513-16.
[3] M. Rissi, *Time and History*, pp. 90-91.
[4] Caird, *Revelation*, p. 96.
[5] Caird, *Revelation*, p. 95.

even noted that Jesus praised those who made themselves eunuchs for the Kingdom of Heaven. She called attention to many teachings and reports in the NT that indicate monastic organization and practices,[1] and she might have cited still more.[2] These were things that had not waited to happen several centuries later. Origen had himself emasculated for the Kingdom of God. Jesus and Paul were both celibate. There were monks, like the Essenes, in pre-Christian times. Why, then, did Collins think monasticism did not become a Christian practice until several centuries later? She did not say.

It is not necessary to be as inventive as some scholars have been to understand the meaning of Rev 14:1-5. When seen within the normal context of its Hebrew Scriptural background, these words make sense in their normal usage. Only a casual reading of Ezek 9:1-6 in relationship to Rev 14:1-5 will show that the NT text is an intentional antitype of the FT text. There are the following similarities between these two passages:

> 1) Geographically, both take place in the temple area in Zion--not in Asia Minor or in heaven.
> 2) Both groups were redeemed or saved.
> 3) Both groups are marked with the sign of the *tau*.
> 4) Both groups are singled out for their righteousness.

These parallels will be spelled out in greater detail. This obvious interpretation of Rev 14:1-5 is one Schüssler-Fiorenza overlooked, because she had not learned the wealth of valuable material there is in the FT that is necessary for understanding the Book of Revelation nor the way Jews and Christians of NT times used the Scripture in secret communications. The authors of the Book of Revelation were very familiar with the FT, and anyone who wants to understand the meaning of that document will have to recognize every FT passage and discover how the author used the text in composing the Book of Revelation. Because Schüssler-Fiorenza overlooked this source, she went astray, looking for some religious, poetic-rhetorical symbolism that had no real validity in the text. She is not the first, however, to have overlooked this important passage in Ezekiel when interpreting Rev 14. She is preceded by Bowman,[3] Beasley-Murray,[4] Caird,[5] Charles,[6] Corsini,[7] Düsterdieck,[8] Ford,[9] Hailey,[10] Kraft,[1] Lilje,[2] Morris,[3] Mounce,[4] Preston and Hanson,[5] Rist,[6] Smith,[7]

---

[1] A. Y. Collins, *Crisis & Catharsis: The Power of the Apocalypse* (Philadelphia: Westminster Press, c1984), pp. 129-37.
[2] See further, Buchanan, *Jesus*, pp. 184-90.
[3] J. W. Bowman, *The Drama of the Book of Revelation* (Philadelphia: Westminster Press, n.d.).
[4] Beasley-Murray, *Revelation*.
[5] Caird, *Revelation*.
[6] R. H. Charles, *A Critical and Exegetical Commentary on the Revelation of St. John the Divine* (New York: Charles Scribner's Sons, c1966), II.
[7] E. Corsini, *The Apocalypse*, tr. F. J. Moloney (Wilmington: Michael Glazier, c1983).
[8] Düsterdieck, *Handbook*.
[9] J. M. Ford, *Revelation* (Garden City: Doubleday & Co., 1975).
[10] H. M. Hailey, *Revelation*, pp. 300-305: "The answer to the difficulties seems that here, as so

Terry,[8] and many others, but this error need not be extended further. Glasson acknowledged that the Rev 14:4 was problematical and the whole idea of defilement in association with women seems to be inappropriate language, but he did not look for a way to escape just because he did not like it. He said,

> We can only conclude that the reference is to men vowed to celibacy; for them marriage would be defiling for it would involve the breaking of their vow.[9]

Zahn, however, observed that the **144,000** would have been carrying out the example set by Jesus who evidently practiced sexual purity and separation from the family into which he had been born (Matt 10:35-38; 12:48-50; 22:30; Mark 12:25; Luke 9:59-62; 20:30-31; John 2:4; 19:26).[10] His followers had left homes and families. This means they abandoned brothers, sisters, parents, children, wives, and fields (Matt 29:27-29; Luke 20:34-36).

Düsterdieck said the **144,000** must be departed believers, but he objected strongly to those who spiritualized Zion, holding that it was heaven rather than Jerusalem. He also objected to those who tried to modify **celibates** to mean "faithful" or "those opposed to idol worship," or "those spiritually pure." He said the interpretation of the **celibates** as those **who had not defiled themselves with women** precluded any spiritual or figurative interpretation.[11] When he translated and edited Düsterdieck's book, however, Jacobs took issue with Düsterdieck. He said this would be inconsistent with Heb 13:4.[12] He found no difficulty in the fact that a different author wrote Hebrews 13 from the one that wrote Rev 14:1-5, evidently assuming that all Christians were of one opinion on the question of celibacy. Even before the Dead Sea Scrolls were found, Moffatt said, "The prevailing Jewish respect for marriage did not check a tendency to celibacy which was by no means confined to the Essenes or Therapeutae. He gave as an example, Methodius, who

---

often, John is using symbolism."

[1] Kraft, *Offenbarung*.

[2] H. Lilje, *The Last Book of the Bible*, tr. O. Wyon (Philadelphia: Muhlenberg Press, c1957).

[3] Morris, *Revelation*, pp. 257-63: "The answer to the difficulties seems that here, as so often, John is using symbolism."

[4] Mounce, *Revelation*.

[5] Preston and Hanson, *Revelation*.

[6] M. Rist, "The Revelation of St. John the Divine," *The Interpreter's Bible* (New York: Abingdon Press, c1957).

[7] Smith, *Revelation*, pp. 208-11.

[8] M. S. Terry, *Biblical Apocalyptics* (New York: Eaton & Mains, 1898).

[9] T. F. Glasson, *The Revelation of John* (Cambridge: Cambridge U. Press, 1965), p. 85.

[10] Zahn, *Offenbarung*, p. 378.

[11] Düsterdieck, *Handbook*, pp. 389-93. He also noted that the Greek term *parthénoi* (παρθένοι), used almost always for female virgins, was used for Joseph in Egypt (p. 393, fn. 3).

[12] Düsterdieck, *Handbook*, p. 404.

allorgized other parts of Revelation, but nevertheless took the reference to celibacy in Rev 14 literally (Epiph, *Haer* 30:2).[1] Aune said,

> The virginity of the 144,000, an allusion to the celibacy requirement for participants in holy wars, should be understood as symbolizing obedience to the commands of God and to the witness of Jesus.[2]

Anyone looking for background materials for understanding the Book of Revelation should begin with the FT.[3] The author or editor who put these chapters of Revelation together believed that he was reliving earlier Hebrew, Israelite, and Jewish history. From the time of the Babylonian captivity to the rededication of the temple in the time of Judas the Maccabee, Jews had been living under the rule of the **beasts**. These **beasts** influenced and corrupted every aspect of Jewish life. By the time of the Hasmoneans there were many local Jewish collaborators with the Syrian Greeks, such as the high priest, Alcimus (1Macc 7:1-9:58). In the midst of all of this corruption, however, there were a few who had remained pious and faithful. These were the ones in Jerusalem who lamented the crimes of the Jews in the city. Ezekiel, reinterpreting the Passover, visualized the Lord commissioning a scribe to mark them on their foreheads so that they could be saved from the devastation that was sure to come to destroy all the rest of the Jews in Jerusalem.

In Rev 12 and 13, the author mythicized the contemporary counter-parts of the earlier Alexandrian empire with its corresponding beasts and local collaborators in terms of a dragon and its legal agents, the beasts. The new antitype of Alexander's empire was Rome, and the new local agents were the Herods. The first was **the dragon** and the second constituted the **beasts**. Like Jerusalem before the Hasmonean Rebellion, the Roman Jerusalem was saturated with foreign influence and control. This was described in Rev 12 and 13. Rev 14 provides the good news! In the midst of all this corruption there was a new scribe who had marked the foreheads of a new group of righteous saints who lived in Jerusalem. These were the faithful monks who were true followers of the Lamb.

MONASTICISM IN NT TIMES

There was a much greater monastic movement in NT times than NT scholars have ever acknowledged. Monasticism probably began after the destruction of the temple in 586 BIA and the beginning of the Babylonian exile. Jeremiah had interpreted this event as a cancellation of the contract God had made with his people. Following the rules for divorce, God had sent his wife (the chosen people) out of his house (the temple) (Jer 3:1-10; 16:18). The temple had been the place that had been kept ritually pure so that the Lord could be present there to live with his people. To

---

[1] J. Moffatt, *The Revelation of St. John the Divine* (Grand Rapids, cEerdmans, 1979), p. 436.
[2] Aune, *Revelation 6-16*, p. 445.
[3] Kraft, *Offenbarung*, p. 187, was one of the scholars who realized that, and he interpreted Rev 14:1-5 in relationship to Ezekiel and Joel.

provide another temporary dwelling place for the Lord until the temple could be restored, very deeply committed male Jews set aside buildings that were kept as undefiled as the temple and those who lived there would keep themselves as ritually pure as the high priest in the temple. Since no woman ever entered the holy or the holy of holies in the temple, no woman was allowed in the monastery, and all members took vows of poverty, celibacy, and obedience. They ate only holy meals with extreme care to see that no dietary or purity rules were broken in their temples.

The laws of 1QS or those of the Essenes could apply only to groups of monks. The same is true of parts of the Sermon on the Mount and the exhortation in Heb 1:1-22:29. The author of the Habakkuk Commentary evidently belonged to a monastery where the teacher of righteousness performed necessary temple rites

Monks of NT times were not homosexuals who gathered for mutural sexual satisfaction. It was just as defiling to have intercourse with another man as with a woman. Monks had to learn to manage their lives without nocturnal emissions, and that was not easy. Paul told of the difficulties he had with this problem after he had passed his Bar Mizwah examination (Rom 7:9-24). Commenting on the commandment against adultery, Jesus reportedly said, "Everyone who sees a woman to lust, has already committed adultery in his mind.

If your right eye makes you stumble, take it out and throw it away from you,
> for it is to your advantage to lose one of your members
>> and not have your whole body thrown into Gehenna.
If even your right hand makes you stumble,
> Chop it off and throw it away from you,
>> for it is beneficial to you that one part of your body is
>>> destroyed but not your whole body
>>> go away to Gehenna (Matt 5:27-30).

Adultery in the FT involved intercourse with another Jew's wife, and the offense was against the husband of that woman. In NT times monastic adultery involved a nocturnal emission, for any reason. It was an offense against the monk himself, because he became defiled in the process. Looking at a fully clothed woman without touching her would be no offense either to her or to her husband, but it would be to the monk, because it might stimulate a nocturnal emission. Touching one's genitals would be no offense to anyone else, but it would be masturbation for the monk. These offenses were so terrible that they had to be avoided at any cost. Rabbis said,

> Whoever looks at a woman's heel is like one who looked at her genitals, and whoever looked at her genitals is like one who committed adultery with her (pHalla 2.41[58c]).

Rabbis said further that a woman who examined herself frequently was meritorious, because in this way she learned when her period began and could stay away from others. But with a man, "let his hand be chopped off." That would be masturbation (mNed 2.1; 5.2). These were some of the monastic rules that indicates the zeal with which some Jews of NT times acted to enable the Lord to be present in their midst. Without his presence, they believed the Kingdom could not be restored.[1]

Jesus himself was obviously a monk, as Paul recognized when he took up his collection in Corinth. On that occasion Paul sent Titus to Corinth to help with the fund raising campaign and encouraged them to give generously and willingly. He reminded them of the sacrificial giving of the Macedonians (2Cor 8:6-8). Then he reminded them of "the grace of our Lord Jesus, that on account of you, became poor when he had been rich" (2Cor 8:9). He also sent another brother to assist with the project (2Cor 8:18).

Paul set before the Corinthians two examples of generous giving: 1) the Macedonians, who had given money, and 2) Jesus, who had given up all of his money just as all other monks did. On this basis Paul encouraged Corinthians also to give money.

As a monk Jesus had denied the parents who gave him physical birth, did not even call the woman who gave him birth "mother" (John 2:4), and he considered his apostles his new legal family (Matt 12:56-50). He rejected an intended blessing on the woman who bore and whose breasts nourished him (Luke 11:27-28). He told his apostles to call no man "**father**" on earth (Matt 23:9). Everyone who was to be admitted into Jesus' order was required to **hate his father, mother, children, brothers, and sisters, and even his own soul** (Luke 14:25-26). This means he was required to deny his entire family and join a monastery, taking vows of poverty, chastity, and obedience. When the Pharisees asked Jesus about the marital relationship of a man and his former wives in the age to come, he said there would be no marrying or giving in marriage, but all would be like the angels of God in heaven, that were celibate (Matt 23:23-30). When asked the terms of admission into life, Jesus told him he first had to take all he had and give it to the community that called itself the poor, because individuals in the monastery owned no property. Then he could follow Jesus (Matt 19:16-21).

With such an extensive movement as this in NT times it is reasonable to consider **144,000** monks who constituted the minority of righteous members of the nation. It also implies that the author of this chapter was himself a monk.

These are those who follow the Lamb wherever he goes. **Following** begins as a rural term. When a shepherd rides on a donkey and plays his flute, sheep will **follow** him wherever he goes in single file. If there is an object in the path, the first sheep will jump over it. After that every **following** sheep will jump there, even if the object is removed. In a manner just as precise, soldiers will march to the direction of a commander, **following** every order. The term is extended to include the manner in which a student learns from a teacher, by imitating and **following** the teacher's example. The Lamb is a king, who not only leads his troops, but he leads his entire nation, and all soldiers and citizens obey his commands and **follow** him wherever he

---

[1] Buchanan, *The Gospel of Matthew* (Lewiston: Mellen Biblical Press, c1996) 1, pp. 256-63,

goes. The man who was interested in becoming one of Jesus' disciples said, **I will follow you wherever you go** (Matt 8:19-20; Luke 9:57-58). On another occasion, Jesus said, **If anyone would serve me let him follow me, and where I am there my servant will be also** (John 12:26). Jesus' apostles were those who had **followed** him (Matt 19:28). Those who were **with the Lamb** on Mount Zion were his apostles and **followers**.

The first [with respect to] God and to the Lamb. The text from Exodus said, **the first of the first fruits**. Sinaiticus has the word **the first** and NA has **the first fruits**. There are several possibilities for the variants. Initially, this text may have said, "**the first** of the **first fruits,**" and one text dropped out the word **the first,** but the other dropped the word **first fruits**. This is the most likely explanation. It could have happened because the two words, which are different in Hebrew, are very similar in Greek, so scribes thought the same word was mistakenly put in twice. The other possibility is that the text originally said **first fruits**, but the Sinaiticus scribe mistakenly copied **the first.** This is an easy mistake. The Greek sounds almost the same for both words. Sinaiticus has *ahp ahr-kháys* (ἀπ ἀρχῆ) which means "from the first." *Ahp-ahr-kháy* '(ἀπαρχή), however, means "first fruits." The problem arose because of a dictation error. Furthermore, either word makes sense in the context. If only one might be used, the larger context of the land and redemption speaks in favor of "first fruits." In the Book of Revelation there are many other examples of hearing error. In all of these instances, it is Sinaiticus who made the mistake, indicating that this scribe was writing from audible dictation. Therefore, it is likely that he was the one who made the same kind of error here. The Exodus text argues in favor of the full reading being originally **the first of the first fruits**.

According to NA, the followers were also called **first fruits** (Rev 14:4). **The first fruits** were the seven main products of the Land of Canaan--wheat, barley, grapes, figs, pomegranates, olive-oil, and [date] honey (Deut 8:8; *mBer* 6:4; *mBik* 1:2-3). Israelites were commanded to give **the first fruits** of all of these products *only* that were raised *only* in their land (*kol áh-shayr beh-áht-zam*, (כול אשר בארצם) (Num 18:13; see also Exod 23:16; 34:26). *Only* these products and *only* when they were raised in the land--not all the products that were raised in all of the earth. Since the term, **first fruits**, was used as a name for the followers of **the Lamb,** it is even more obvious that the author was concentrating his attention on the land of Palestine rather than the entire earth.[1] Therefore when the same people were called the **redeemed** they were **the redeemed** of the **land**--not of the earth. Not realizing the local, geographical significance of **first fruits**, Sweet followed Rissi in saying, "'It designates the Church as a promise for *all* [emphasis added] men.'" Morris said the

---

[1] Although the expression "first fruits" was also used of new converts outside of Palestine, such as the household of Stephanas that was the first fruits of Achaia (1Cor 16:15). Epaenetus was the first fruit of Asia for Christ (Rom 16:5).

144,000 stood "for the whole church of Jesus Christ." Beasley-Murray and Caird concurred.[1]

Both the groups of Ezekiel and that of Rev 14 had been stamped **on their foreheads**. Of course, the reader realized that this ritual was an antitype of the vision of Ezekiel, the author of Rev 14 quoted the passage, **on their foreheads** (Ezek 9:4; Rev 14:1).[2] For further confirmation, the author of the antitype also quoted from Ezekiel 1:24: **I heard the sound** of their wings **like the sound of much water [running]** (Rev 14:2).[3] He also mentioned **the throne** and **the four beasts** in the temple (Ezek 1; Rev 14:3). These were conditions found on Mount Zion where the Spring of Siloam roared under the threshold of the temple.

They had not defiled themselves with women. Both the audience of Ezekiel and that of Rev 14 were singled out for righteousness. They were undefiled. In Ezekiel those separated for salvation were distinguished from the rest who committed abominations and were defiled with idols and ritually unclean beasts (Ezek 8:9-10). The destroyers who were to follow the one dressed in linen who made marks on the saints were ordered to kill every **old man, young man, virgin woman, child, and woman, as well as every man who did not have the mark of the** *tau* **on his forehead** (Ezek 9:6). This means those marked with the *tau* were all pious males. Those in Revelation were described as **celibate**. Loisy was rather shocked by the apparently obvious meaning of this passage. He did not think the Messiah, whom he took to be Jesus, would have had such a narrow point of view as to limit the saved to **144,000** males. He correctly presumed that this came from a Jewish source, as did most of the prophecy of this book (Rev 4:1-22:5).[4]

---

[1] Sweet, *Revelation*, p. 223; Morris, *Revelation*, p. 170; Beasley-Murray, *Revelation*, pp. 222-23; Caird, *Revelation*, p. 180. Also A. Feullet, "Les 144,000 Israelites Marques d'Un Sceau," *NovT* 9 (1967):191-224, who argued that they did not constitute only Jewish Christians, but the whole church. Like many others, R. Divine, "The Virgin Followers of the Lamb," *Scripture* 16 (1964):1-5, did not rule out virginity entirely, but he emphasized that the 144,000 were called virgins, because they had not yielded to idolatry. Smith, *Revelation*, p. 210, said the 144,000 must mean the first small portion of the believers who would follow later. Jews and Christians were not the only religions to offer first fruits. Pagan religions also offered first fruits in pagan countries (Polybius 31:12, 12), but Jews and Christians would not have participated or promoted pagan sacrifices, and the author of Revelation 14 would not have had pagan first fruits in mind.

[2] Cyril of Jerusalem put together allusions to Ezekiel, Ps 121, and Deuteronomy in an exhortation to Christians for faithfulness. He said, "Then let us not be ashamed to confess the crucified one. Upon the forehead (Ezek 9:4) with boldness let the seal be [made] with the fingers, and upon everything let the cross be present--over the bread being eaten, over the cup being drunk, while entering and leaving (Ps 121:8), before sleep when going to bed, when rising, or going on a journey (Deut 6:7-9). Great is the phylactery (safeguard), free of charge, because of the poor without labor, because of the ill, since grace is from God. It is a sign for faithful people and a terror for demons, because it conquers them when [someone] displays it boldly, for whenever they see the cross they are reminded of the crucified one, and they become afraid of the one who broke the heads of the dragon" (MPG 13, 3:816).

[3] A medieval Amharic commentary on the Book of Revelation said the sound of much water meant the sound of a waterfall (So R. W. Cowley, *The Traditional Interpretation of the Apocalypse of St. John in the Ethiopian Orthodox Church* [Cambridge: Cambridge U. Press, c1983]), p. 306.

[4] Loisy, *L'Apocalypse*, pp. 263-65.

It is true that Jesus was not quoted in the gospels as limiting the elect to as few as this, but it is also true that John of Patmos understood this passage to refer to Jesus and did not remove it from the prophecy. Hailey said, "This quality refers not to physical celibacy, but to spiritual virginity."[1] How would a person become a "spiritual **virgin**" without being **celibate**? Sweet called these "chaste" and said it referred to their fidelity in contrast to idolatry.[2] The intention of the text is more specific than that. The Greek is *pahr-théh-noi* (παρθένοι)--masculine **virgins** or monks. To make sure that this was not intended metaphorically, as Hailey and Sweet suggest, the text describes these males further as those who **had not defiled themselves with women**. This was the seer's interpretation of the condition of those who mourned and lamented for the abominations committed in Jerusalem.

In NT times, those least defiled, whom the author of Rev 14 selected as an antitype of the undefiled in Ezekiel, were blameless monks, like the Essenes, those governed by the Community Rule (1QS), the Sermon on the Mount, or Heb 1:1-12:29. The main reason for monks' discipline was to be legally blameless, doing works of supererogation so as to remove crime from the land, so this word **blameless** should also be taken literally, *contra* Schüssler-Fiorenza. Kraft's Protestant persuasion prevented him from noticing that. He said they could only be **blameless** if the Lord had covered their crimes.[3] The word **blameless** probably came from Isa 53:9, describing the suffering servant who **had done no violence** (*khah-máhs* (חמס)) and was therefore innocent, or from Zeph 3:13, describing people who **had done no wickedness; had spoken no falsehood; and in their mouth was found no deceitful tongue**. There was also no deceit or falsehood (*mee-reh-máh*, מרמה) in the mouth of the Messiah. Those who followed the Lamb were described as those **in whose mouths was found no deceit, because they were blameless** (Rev 14:5).

A medieval Jewish narrative on the Garden of Eden includes a commentary on Prov 8:21: **To cause those who love me to inherit substance** (*yehsh*, יש)

> **Substance** (*yehsh*, יש) in *gematria* is 310, and in its midst are seven houses of righteous ones. . . . The sixth group [are composed] barren = celibate ones (*reh-vah-keém*, רווקים) who have never tasted crime in their days.[4]

Like the followers of the Lamb, these had **not defiled themselves with women**. They had not committed the crime Adam committed that caused him and Eve to be evicted from the Garden of Eden.

---

[1] Hailey, *Revelation*, p. 304.
[2] Sweet, *Revelation*, p. 221.
[3] Kraft, *Offenbarung*, pp. 190-91. For the purpose and practices of monasticism see Buchanan, "Essenes," *International Standard Bible Encyclopedia* (Grand Rapids: Eerdmans, c1980) II, pp. 147-55, and "The Role of Purity in the Structure of the Essene Sect," *RQ* 4 (1963):397-406.
[4] "The Order of the Garden of Eden," A. Jellinek (ed.), *Bet ha-Midrash* [Hebrew] (Jerusalem: Wahrman Books, 1967), II, p. 53.

Both the Zionists of Ezekiel and those of Rev 14 were branded with **the sign of the *tau* (ת = Χ** *chi* in Greek) **on their foreheads** (Rev 7:4). They alone were marked to be saved from the great destruction that was to come. For Rev 14, these were the **144,000**. They are distinguished as those **having the name of the Father on their foreheads** (*meh-tóh-pohn*, μετώπων). They are further described as a group of monks. They were **celibate**; they had **not defiled themselves with women**. Monasticism was considered the highest type of righteousness long before the time of Christ.

Monasticism probably began with either the Assyrian captivity or the Babylonian captivity, when members of the posterity of Abraham were removed from their land, and there was no priesthood functioning in the temple. After the temple had been burned, some of the laity took upon themselves the duties of the priesthood. Since there was no undefiled place in the temple for the Lord to be present, they endeavored to keep their homes as undefiled as the temple and their hearths as pure as the altar. The most pious of these organized themselves into celibate groups, so that their meeting place would not be defiled by women or men who had been motivated by the women to become defiled. The author of this document believed that in the age to come, the new Jerusalem would have only **celibate** monks as inhabitants.

These monks would keep the holy city holy. They were faithful **followers of the Lamb** (the Messiah). They had been singled out--not only from human beings--but also from other Jews, for redemption, which means that their crimes had been canceled. In his poem of rejoicing at the return of the Babylonian Jews to Jerusalem, Second Isaiah dreamed of a highway built just for this purpose. The Babylonian Jews would have no obstacle to hinder their return, because this was a select highway. Like the marked monks in the temple at **Zion**, only segregated, **redeemed** Jews were allowed to use this highway (Isa 35:8-9). **Redeemed** Jews were those whose iniquities had been paid in the heavenly treasury, so that they had a balance on hand. There were no outstanding bills left unpaid, from the standpoint of financial terminology. This same thing is said also from the legal point of view--they were blameless in the eyes of the court. They had not perjured themselves with falsehood. They were guilty of no crimes. Therefore they were considered **first fruit** offerings who had been singled out before the "harvest."

First fruit offerings were brought to the temple at Jerusalem between Pentecost and the Feast of Tabernacles; they might only be brought from production within the boundaries of the Promised Land. This did not include the territory beyond the Jordan. They were the **first** ripened **fruit** of the seven products best known to the land of Palestine. They are not permitted to be brought by slaves or tenant farmers, because those who brought them were required to bring them from their own land (mBik 1:2-10). These **first fruits** had to be marked and set aside before they were picked as **the first** to become ripe. **First fruits** were closely associated with the Promised Land--not Asia Minor. The same was true of the monks on Mount Zion. Jews who gave the first fruits of their harvests to the priests were then free to consume the rest of the produce. The first fruits sanctified all the rest. The same was implied for **the Redeemed** at **Mount Zion**. It was their works that would atone for the rest of Israel (Lev 23:14; Prov 3:9-10).

The author of this **redemption** midrash evidently had **the first fruits** procession in mind when he pictured the marked monks before the altar. They were like marked **first fruits.** They were distinctive products of the twelve tribes from the Promised Land. No foreigners were included. As they appeared before the heavenly altar at **Zion** there were loud natural noises, accompanied by harps playing and people singing. When **first fruits** were brought to the temple, neighborhoods gathered their supplies together and went up in procession with a flute playing before them until they reached the temple mount. At that point the Levites sang the song, **I will exalt you, Lord, for you have drawn me up and not allowed my enemies to laugh at me** (Ps 30:1). The Psalm continues to exhort the saints to **sing** to the Lord and give him thanks. In the temple in heaven the beasts and elders were also expected to function like Levites, **singing to the Lord a new song**.[1]

In their mouth was not found anything false. This is an allusion to the prophecy in Zephaniah when the Lord promised to hold judgment in which he would punish all of the gentiles and remove all the proud exultant ones from the midst of Israel. Then there would be left a pure remnant in Israel who were not fraudulent; they would tell no lies; they would not be deceitful; they would be humble. They would lie down and no one would make them afraid (Zeph 3:9-13). According to the author of this unit, the celibate followers of the Lamb on Mount Zion filled these qualifications.

TEXT

Revelation

First Testament

⁶I saw another angel flying in mid-heaven having

the gospel of **the age to proclaim** to the migrants of **the**

1Chron 16:23; Ps 96:1 **Proclaim the gospel** of his salvation from day to day.

1Chron 16:17 He will make it stand for Jacob, as a statute for Israel, a contract of **the age** [to come].

1Chron 16:34 To **the age** is his mercy.

---

[1] Like many others who symbolized the geographical references in the Book of Revelation, E. Schüssler-Fiorenza, *Revelation: Vision of a Just World* (Minneapolis: Fortress Press, c1991), pp. 87-88 held that Mount Zion meant neither heavenly nor historical Zion, but rather "an eschatological place of protection and liberation." Jews and Christians of NT times would have thought Jerusalem was the eschatological place of protection and liberation.

land [namely Palestinian residents] of every **nation**, tribe, **language and people**, ⁷saying in a loud voice,	Dan 3:7 All **peoples, nations, and languages** will **worship** the golden statue.
"**Fear God** and give him **glory, because**	1Chron 16:36; Ps 96-48 **Bless Yehowah, the** God **of Israel, from** age **and to** the age.
	1Chron 16:24-26; Ps 96:2 Tell among the **nations** his **glory**, among all **peoples**, his wondrous deeds, because great is **Yehowah** and very much praised. He is **feared** more than all the gods, **because** all the gods of **the peoples** are idols, but Yehowah **made the heavens**.
	Eccles 13:13-14 Everything has been heard; **fear God** and keep his commandments, for this is everything man [has to do]. For every deed, God
the hour of his **judgment has arrived**.	**comes in judgment** over everything hidden, whether good or evil.
	1Chron 16:33; Ps 96:13 He has come to **judge the earth**; he will **judge the earth** with righteousness.
	Ps 96:8 Give to Yehowah **glory** and strength; give to Yehowah **glory** of his name.
Worship the One who **made heaven, earth, the sea**, and springs of water."	Exod 20:11 For [in] six days Yehowah **made heaven, the earth, the sea** and all that is in them, and he rested on the seventh day.

SCRIPTURAL CONTEXT

This is the beginning of a new unit (Rev 14:6-10). Altink has demonstrated the importance of the background from First Chronicles to this passage in Revelation. This so-called Psalm of David is related there to the time when the chest containing the contract was brought back from the Philistines and placed in the tent David prepared for it, before the altar near Ain Gihon. The Philistines were instantly stricken with fear when the sons of Eli brought this sacred object into the battle. After the Philistines captured it they experienced bad luck, so they sent it back to Judah because of their fear. Even the Israelites were so much afraid of this holy object that they left it in a field for 20 years before trying to move it (1Sam 4:2-7:2).

When David ordered it to be brought to Jerusalem, Uzzah touched the cart that hauled the chest and was stricken dead. This put so much fear into the Israelites that they left the cart there with Obenedom the Gittite until they learned what luck he had with it on his property. When he had good fortune, it was brought the rest of the way to Jerusalem (2Sam 6:1-19). Terms like **fear**, **glory**, **judgment**, and **worship**, that are associated with the chest that contained the contract of the Lord (called the contract of the age, 1Chron 16:17) with his people are used midrashically by the author of this pericope in Rev 14. Altink has shown further that 1Chron 16 and Rev 14 both echo portions that are normally literary parts of ancient treaties and contracts:

1) preambles,
2) historical prologues,
3) stipulations,
4) witnesses, and
5) blessings and curses.[1]

First Chron 16 is itself a midrash on Pss 96, 105, and 106. John of Patmos evidently noticed the contractual terms in this prophecy, because he introduced the prophecy (Rev 1-3) as if he were presenting his readers a new contract.

Another angel. In a similar parallel, instead of an angel, there is an eagle (Rev 8:13). Rev 14 does not have a first **angel** to come before this one. The fact that the **angel** list begins with **another angel** suggests that this unit was once a part of a longer narrative which had **another angel** earlier in the story. The problem, however, is more complicated than that. The expression **another angel** occurs six times in Rev 14. All of these **angels** were destructive. One announced a gospel that was destructive to the **migrants of the land** (Rev 14:6), the second announced the fall of Rome (Rev 14:8), **the third** announced that fire and sulfur would await those who were loyal to the **beast** (Rev 14:9); the fourth told the Son of man to start the curses promised in Joel to the foreigners; the fifth started the curses to function (Rev 14:17); and the sixth told the **angel** with the sickle to start the action. This portion seems unified, but it once may have been part of another document.[2]

---

[1] W. Altink, "Theological Motives for the use of 1Chron 16:8-36 as Background for Revelation 14:6-7," *AUSS* 24 (1986):211-21.
[2] See further A. P. van Schaik, "*Allos Aggelos* in Apok 14," *L'Apocalypse johannique et l'Apocalyptique dans le Nouveau Testament* ed. J. Lambrecht (Gembloux: Duculot, 1980), pp. 217-28.

Having the gospel of the age. Aune rendered this verse:

> With an eternal message to proclaim among those who dwell on earth and among every nation and tribe and language and people.[1]

That is a reasonable translation when all of the Jewish idioms involved are ignored. In context, this is not an "eternal" **gospel**, as many have thought. And it is not directed to all those who dwell on earth. Neither is it an allusion to Mark 13:10, as Schüssler-Fiorenza holds.[2] Its allusion is to 1Chron 16, which is the basis of this entire midrash.[3] That passage refers to the **contract of the age** (1Chron 16:17), **proclaiming the gospel** (1Chron 16:23), God's mercy **for the age** (1Chron 16:41), and blessing Yehowah **from the age** [this one] **until the age** [to come] (1Chron 16:36). It is not "super temporal" or "timeless," as Zahn believed.[4] The **gospel of the age** (*yoo-ahn-géh-lee-awn ai-óh-nee-awn*, εὐαγγέλιον αἰώνιον = *buh-soh-ráht oh-láhm*, (בסרת עולם)) is **the good news of the age to come**, the news that the old **age** is finished and the new **age** is beginning. This verse should not be rendered, "holding an everlasting gospel to proclaim (as good news) to those dwelling on earth," as Giblin translated it.[5] It is also not the opposite of the woes pronounced in Rev 8:13, as Schüssler-Fiorenza suggested.[6] Caird said,

> Having written the word, gospel, he [the author] expected his readers to fill it with the full rich content of the apostolic preaching.[7]

That does not follow, automatically. This was good news only to faithful Jews and/or Christians. **The gospel** would be announced--not to "those dwelling on earth"--but to **the migrants of the land**, the enemies of the faithful nationalists in Palestine. This **gospel** would not be **good news** to them. They belonged to the old **age** of the Roman administration. This was not a winsome invitation to them; it was not even helpful counsel, such as the Preacher provided, saying it is wise to fear God and keep his commandments, **because God brings every deed to judgment** (Eccles 12:13-14). This was a threat. **The migrants** were told, "Either fear God or else!" The one who created all things also gave the ten commandments, and he was about to judge the secret thoughts of human beings. Jacobs overlooked this reality when he said this was a message of joy and salvation brought to **the migrants of the land**.[8]

---

[1] Aune, *Revelation 6-16*, p. 825.
[2] Schüssler-Fiorenza, *Vision*, p. 48.
[3] On this see further W. Altink, "1 Chronicles 16:8-36 as Literary Source for Revelation 14:6-7," *AUSS* 22 (1984):187-96.
[4] Zahn, *Offenbarung*, p. 518.
[5] Giblin, *Revelation*, p. 139. Also Caird, *Revelation*, p. 182.
[6] Schüssler-Fiorenza, *Vision*, p. 89.
[7] Caird, *Revelation*, p. 183.
[8] Düsterdieck, *Revelation*, p. 405.

To proclaim to the migrants of the land. From a literal point of view, Prof. Ford has accurately translated the expression here called **migrants of the land,** "those enthroned upon the earth."[1] Literally, that is what the Greek says, but it makes no sense in this context. The Hebrew root *yah-sháhv* (ישב can mean either dwell or sit). Morris seems to have missed several points. He said:

> *Everlasting* points to a message that is permanently valid, while *them that dwell on the earth* (see note on vi.10) and *every nation* (see note on v.9) show that it is universally applicable.[2]

The Greek translator (probably John of Patmos) mistakenly translated *tóh-sheh-váy hah áh-retz* (תושבי הארץ) to mean those who sit either on the Promised Land or on the earth. This is an idiom, overlooked, not only by John of Patmos, but by most NT scholars ever since. The *tóh-sheh-vay hah áh-retz* were **the migrants of the land,** those foreigners **of every nation, tribe, language, and people** (Rev 14:6) who lived *temporarily* (in Jewish judgment) in the Promised Land.[3] From the point of view of the author of this document, they were enemies of the faithful and had no business there. Beagley, mistakenly, thought this group of people were *Jewish* inhabitants of Palestine and therefore enemies of Christians.[4]

TEXT

Revelation	First Testament
[8]Another, a second, followed them, saying, ["**Fallen, fallen** is great **Babylon**.	[Isa 21:9]Look! A rider comes; horsemen in teams; he answered and said, "**Fallen, fallen, Babylon**! All the idols of her gods he shattered to the ground."
	[Jer 51:8]Suddenly, **Babylon has fallen** and been shattered. Wail for her.
Who **from the wine** of the anger of	[Jer 51:7]The gentiles drank some of her **wine**.
	[Jer 51:7]Therefore **the gentiles** went crazy.

---

[1] Ford, *Revelation*, p. 231.
[2] Morris, *Revelation*, p. 184.
[3] See Buchanan, "Sojourners in the Land," *The Answers Lie Below*, ed. H. O. Thompson (Lanham: The University Press of America, 1984), pp. 187-96.
[4] Beagley, *Sitz*, p. 86.

her sexual indecency **has made all the gentiles drunk.**"⁹Then another angel, a third one, followed them], saying in a loud voice, "If anyone worships the beast and its image and takes a mark upon his forehead or on his hand,

Babylon is the golden cup in the hand of Yehowah, **making every land drunk** from it.

COMMENTARY

Another, a second [angel]. NA adds **angel.** This is the obvious noun which the adjective **second** modifies.

The Bracketed Text. The bracketed text is taken from NA. Sinaiticus either omitted this portion or other texts added it. Because there is no further numbering of **angels** in this series, the context does not tell whether the angel after the third should be considered another third or the fourth. It seems more likely that Sinaiticus omitted the bracketed text by a homeoteluton error. A homeoteluton error is one that happens at the end, the *teh-laws* (τέλος), of a sentence. When two lines in a narrative end in the same word, it is easy for the copyist to drop from the first to the second and omit the line in between. Since there are other indications that the Sinaiticus scribe copied from spoken dictation, the error must have been made by the person who read the text to him.

Fallen, fallen is great Babylon. This is a quotation from parts of sentences prophesied earlier by Isaiah and Jeremiah. It is also quoted in Rev 18:2. **Babylon** in Revelation is always referred to as **great** (Rev 14:8; 16:19; 17:5; 18:2, 10, 21). Isaiah and Jeremiah prophesied the fall of the city of **Babylon** located on the shore of the Euphrates River. That city, however, had been destroyed centuries earlier than NT times. In NT times **Babylon** was used by Jews and early Christians as a code word for "Rome" (2Bar 11:1; SibOr 5:143, 159, 434). One of the reasons that Jeremiah knew **Babylon** was going to **fall** and be shattered was that Isaiah had prophesied it. Jeremiah was accepted as a reliable prophet of the Lord, because he prophesied both the **fall** of Jerusalem at the hands of the **Babylonians** and the later **fall of Babylon** itself. Both of these prophecies came true. The same was true for Isaiah of Jerusalem. He foretold the fall of North Israel and the later collapse of **Babylon**.[1] The author of Rev 14 adapted both of their prophecies to predict the downfall of Rome (2Bar 11.1; SibOr 5.143, 159, 434).[2]

---

[1] These events did not take place precisely as Isaiah and Jeremiah predicted. They prophesied that Media would destroy Babylon. That never happened.
[2] Zahn (*Offenbarung*, p. 520), however, insisted that the author of this part of Revelation also meant nothing other than the geographical Babylon, just as Jeremiah did. This is true even though he argued strongly in his commentary on Rev 16 that Rome was intended. He said Babylon had been destroyed by NT times (pp. 648-553).

Under the surveillance of Rome, the author could not openly predict Rome's destruction, but most Jews knew the religious significance of **Babylon** as a type for Rome, just as Edom was. Romans were also called the Kittim (1QpHab; 1QM). These were all code names. The author composed narrative that all Jews could understand--the downfall of **Babylon!** He also quoted Jeremiah to tell why **Babylon** should **fall**. It is not necessary to posit, as A. Yarbro Collins has, that Jews would not have identified Rome with Babylon before Rome had destroyed Jerusalem as Babylon had. Rome had oppressed Jews as the Babylonians had, and Jeremiah had predicted the fall of Babylon before it happened. Jews wanted Rome to fall long before Rome destroyed Jerusalem. They just applied Jeremiah's prophecy to their own desire for Rome.

Rome did not really make Jews drunk with wine, nor did she lure them into sexual promiscuity, but Jews were lured into Roman business and cultural life, and this mingling with foreigners was called "adultery" by pious, segregationistic Jews and Christians. Not only did the author of the prophecy fit that category, but so did John of Patmos (Rev 17:2; 18:3).

During the Crusades Rome was not only identified with **Babylon**, but also Nineveh, for the same purpose. One document reports the following: **This is Nineveh, the city of blood,** and it is **great** Rome (Jonah 4:11; Ezek 22:2; 24:6, 9; Nah 3:1).[1]

Takes a mark upon his forehead or on his hand. This is an often repeated expression (Rev 16:2; 19:20; 20:4). This was evidently some mark, like a social security card, that meant that person was not a security risk. He or she was a faithful citizen of Rome.

TEXT

Revelation	First Testament and Habakkuk Commentary
	Jer 51:5-7 Flee from the midst of Babylon, and rescue each man his life; do not keep still in her iniquity, because it is a time of vengeance for the Lord, the repayment he is paying her. A golden **cup** in the hand **of** the Lord was Babylon.
	Jer 25:15 Thus said the Lord God of Israel to me, "Take this **cup of** the

---

[1] "The Book of Zerubbabel," Buchanan (ed. and tr.), *Jewish Messianic Movements from AD 70 to AD 1300* (Eugene, Oregon: Wipf and Stock Publishers, 2003), p. 362.

¹⁰and he also **drinks from the wine of God's anger**,

poured **unmixed** in the **cup of his anger**,

and they will be tortured with **fire and sulfur** before the holy angels and the Lamb,

¹¹and **the smoke** of their torture **will go up for the ages** of ages, and they **will not have** rest **day or night**--those who worship the beast and its image or anyone who takes the sign of his name.¹²Here is the patience of the saints--**Those who keep the commandments of God** (and the testimony of Jesus).

wine of **anger** from my hand and **drink it**."

^(Hab 2:16)You will get your fill of contempt, rather than glory; for you **will drink** and stagger. **The cup in Yehowah's** right hand will circle over you, and shame will [cover] over your glory.

^(PsSol 8:15)God mixed for them a spirit of wandering; he made them **drink the cup of wine unmixed** so they would become drunk.

^(Ps 75:8)In the hand of Yehowah there is a cup; it is full of strong **wine**, mixed. He will pour from this its very dregs, and all the wicked of the land will **drink**.

^(Gen 19:24)The Lord made rain over Sodom and Gomorrah **sulfur and fire** from the Lord from heaven.

^(Isa 34:8-10)For it is a day of vengeance for the Lord, the year of retaliation for conflict of Zion; its [Edom's] streams will be changed to pitch and its soil to **sulphur**, and its land will become burning pitch. It **will not** be quenched **day and night. Its smoke will go up for the age** from generation to generation it will be destroyed. No one will ever pass through.

^(1QpHab 8.1-3)Its interpretation is concerning all **those who perform [the teachings of] the Torah** in the house of Judah, whom God will save from the house of judgment through **their work** and faith in the teacher of righteousness.

COMMENTARY

If anyone worships the beast and its image. The conditional sentence with which this passage begins is repeated almost word-for-word in Rev 14:11b. The word for **beast** is *thay-reé-awn*, (θηρίον) a diminutive form but not in force. This is a term used even for elephants. Here, of course, **the beast** is a caricature of a human being who demands and deserves respect from some people. The word, **worship**, in antiquity was not limited to God, except as national leaders were legal agents of the deity. People normally **worshiped** their leaders. Since the leader has been called a **beast**, insultingly, it means that the author did not like this particular leader.

There is no clue here to direct the reader to the first **beast**, the second **beast**, or the third **beast**. Nor is there any guidance to help understand the meaning of the **image** of the **beast**. The bust of Gaius' **image** was never set up, so it would not refer to that. The **image** may have meant such things as the eagle over the gate of Jerusalem which symbolized Roman authority. There is also no record of Rome requiring its colonists to wear signs on their hands or foreheads, but it may have been done. It is more probable that the author was not thinking either of Herod the Great or Herod Agrippa I when he composed this narrative about **beasts** and **images**. He was probably simply pointing to an antitype of Daniel where the **image** was made by a foreign king and Jews, like others, were forced to **worship** it (Dan 3). The fourth **beast** (Dan 7) was also the one who led the kingdom that Judas repelled when he reestablished the Davidic and Solomonic kingdom in the second century BIA. Almost anything Romans might do to interfere with Jewish independence or worship might be considered the image of the beast. The editor of Revelation may have put together Rev 12, 13, and 14, because they all dealt with **dragons** or **beasts** even though they were originally written by different authors with different identifications for the beasts involved.

While the Hasmonean rebellion was taking place, Jews in Palestine were forced to make choices. They could become a part of Judas' forces and fight against the Syrian **beasts**, or they could become collaborators with the **beasts** and support the pagan ruling power. Typologically, the author of this passage followed the same plan. He described the Roman agents who were the new equivalents to the Syrian Greeks and their Palestinian followers. Then he described the appearance of the new Son of man as the **Lamb**. His next step was to point out the choices Jews of Palestine had in the first century. They could become collaborators and tax collectors for the Romans, or they could join the zealots who were organized for war against the Romans. They had the mark of the Lord on their foreheads, or the sign of the **beast**. They **worshiped** either the Roman agents or the Lord's anointed agent.

He also drinks from the wine of God's anger. This expression is also paralleled in Rev 18:3. The comparison of **wine** to **anger** was used earlier by Jeremiah. In a land like Canaan, famous for its grapes and **wine** presses, people knew what happened to those who **drank wine**. At first they liked it; then they became **drunk**, sick, and crazy. The end result was destruction. Those who **drank from the** cup **of God's anger** were also taking serious risks, but this was "**wine**" that they did not literally **drink.** They were lured by Roman customs and opportunities to participate in gentile activities. The end result of this inebriation was torture with fire and sulfur. This torture took place before the Messiah and his holy angels. This pictures the "inebriant" being taken before a judge and condemned in court and sentenced to death by fire and sulfur. This type of torture pictures someone being thrown into a volcanic crater when the lava is boiling in accompaniment with sulfuric fumes.

The images of fire and sulfur were in the Scripture in the story of the destruction of Sodom and Gomorrah. The fire image was probably also suggested by Dan 3 where the enemies of the three pious Jews were burned in the fiery furnace they had designed for the Jews who would not **worship** the foreign image.

The smoke of their torture. This might possibly refer to the burning of Rome in 69 IA, as in Rev 19:3-4, which made the saints rejoice. More likely, however, this is just a fuller expression of the volcanic pit that produces smoking sulfur.

They have no rest day or night. In terms of sabbatical eschatology, **rest** does not mean sleep or relief from work. It refers to the security that comes with being a part of the kingdom when Israel's messiah is ruling over an independent country (1Kings 8:56; Ps 95:11). Those who were loyal would participate in this **rest**, whereas those who mingled with the Romans would never be admitted. To be a Jew and not be allowed to become a citizen of Israel in the age to come was the worst kind of torture. It was like being thrown into fire that burned with sulfur. Before the **rest** or torture, individuals would be brought to court where the Messiah was the final judge with his holy angels acting as assistants. Those who **drank of the wine of God's anger** would have no **rest** but only torture.

Here is the patience of the saints. This statement parallels a similar statement in the previous chapter. **The patience** and faith **of the saints** (Rev 13:8-10) was their confidence that crime would be punished and virtue rewarded. The ones who took captives would go into captivity; the ones who killed would be killed. The same message is here. The **144,000** saints were ushered before **the throne of God** and the Lamb as the **first fruits** of the Promised Land, while heavenly **beasts** and **elders** all **worshiped** and **sang a new song**. The ones who worshiped the political **beast** and its **image**, however, would receive the same punishment as had been promised years before to **Babylon** and Edom. **The saints** could be **patient** even in the midst of torture, because they knew this was accomplishing that which had to be done before redemption. The suffering they endured was canceling debts in the heavenly record. When all of these debts were canceled, the Lord would return the Promised Land to the chosen people. There was a predestined pattern to all of this, and Jews knew what it was. They had only to wait it out and watch the signs to learn what stage of development was currently in process. At the end of the process, the Messiah would come, and Jews would recover the Promised Land. This was the salvation for which they waited patiently.

The commandments of God (and the testimony of Jesus). **Those who keep the commandments of God** were the same as those reported in the Habakkuk Commentary who performed the teachings of the Torah. These were the meritorious ones who would be saved from future punishment. This is only the second time the name **Jesus** has appeared in this prophecy which began at Rev 4:1. The term was used only twice in ten chapters. It seems to be an intrusion into the text, which makes good sense without the phrase in parentheses. It was either John of Patmos or some earlier Christian who added this expression to Christianize the document.[1]

Summary. Rev 14:6-12 is another one of those passages where the author has disclosed his vast knowledge of Scripture and his ability to weave parts of it together in such a way that those familiar with Scripture would understand more than the mere words themselves say. He had previously described the kind of people who wore the sign of the Lord on their foreheads and the future that was in store for them. He then turned to those who, like the gentiles of Babylon when Daniel was there, **worshiped the image** and **the beast** and wore his mark on their right hands. He also began to tell what was in store for them. In describing these enemies of the faithful, he relied on six passages of FT:

1) Jer 51,
2) Jer 25,
3) PsSol 8,
4) Gen 19,
5) Ezek 38, and
6) Isa 34.

Jer 51 tells of the downfall of Babylon, together with the restoration of Judah and Israel. 2) Jer 25 foretells the punishment that awaits those who hurt Israel. 3) PsSol 8 reports the downfall of Jewish character before Pompey entered Jerusalem. 4) Gen 19 narrates God's destruction of Sodom and Gomorrah. 5) Ezek 38 is an account of Gog's attack on Israel with hordes of soldiers, set out to plunder a quiet and peaceful people; but Gog was in for a surprise, because the Lord released all the forces of nature against these foreign troops, raining down fire and brimstone to defeat Gog utterly and show forth the Lord's glory. 6) Isa 34, like Ezek 38, predicted the Lord's use of fire and sulfur to destroy his enemies on the day of vengeance when the Lord called others to account for their crimes against Zion. Fire and brimstone are the normal products of a volcano.

These themes of judgment, vengeance, defeat of enemies, and the use of smoke, fire, sulphur, and other natural catastrophes to destroy the enemies is a common theme throughout these passages. Although the enemy for Jeremiah was

---

[1] So also J. F. Whealon, "New Patches on an old Garment: The Book of Revelation," *BTB* 11 (1981):55.

Babylon, the author of the prophecy thought that Babylon was only an archetype for his contemporary enemy, Rome. The author used code terms throughout so that Romans who happened to read this document would find no reason for alarm. To the one who had ears to hear, however, this was revolutionary.

The Isaiah passage predicted the downfall--not of **Babylon**, but of Edom, which meant Rome. Because Jews hated Edom, especially since Edomites assisted the **Babylonians** in conquering Jews when Jerusalem was overthrown, Jews vowed that they would avenge Edom (Ps 137; Obadiah). Since Jews hated Rome in the same way, and because Jews also hated Herod and his family (Edomites) who supported Rome in suppressing Jews, Jews called Rome "Edom" and "Esau." By using references both to **Babylon** and to Edom in predicting the destruction, those who had ears to hear could have no question that it was Rome and Roman sympathizers, like the **migrants of the land,** who constituted the antitype of **Babylon** and Edom. Those who sided with Edom and **Babylon** in wearing the mark of the beast rather than the sign of God on their foreheads could expect the consequences the author indicated were in store for contemporary "**Babylonians**" and "Edomites." Throughout all of the terror, the patience of the saints who keep all of the commandments were destined to survive, in the author's judgment.

TEXT

Revelation	Habakkuk Commentary
[13]Then I heard a voice from heaven saying, "Write! Blessed are the dead who have been dying in the Lord until now. 'Yes,' says the Spirit, 'so that they may rest from their labors, for **their works** will follow them.'"	1QpHab 8.1-3 Its interpretation is concerning all **those who perform [the teachings of] the Torah** in the house of Judah, whom God will save from the house of judgment through **their work** and faith in the teacher of righteousness.

COMMENTARY

Dying in the Lord until now. Being **in the Lord** meant being a member of the community of the new contract. They were legally members of the corporation and were therefore identified with the Lord who was legally present in this community. Those who died in the Lord were those who were faithful participants in the contract, who did not deny their faith, even in the face of persecution. Everything was paid up and they were fully covered by their contract at the time of their deaths. They could not take their silver and gold with them, but they took their credit rating and their treasures in heaven. Their greatest **works** were **the works** of supererogation that accompanied martyrdom. A special time when Jews were willing to be martyred for their faith was when Petronius threatened to install a statue of Gaius in the temple at Jerusalem. Although the statue was never installed, there was a vocal demand for sacrifice at that time.

Another time would have been after 70 IA while three pretending messiahs were engaged in civil war in the city of Jerusalem. At that time many Jews were slaughtered and starved. This kind of literature might have been written to meet one occasion and later also have been used to meet another occasion. The sacrifice Jews were asked to provide would have laid up many merits in the heavenly treasury which continued to draw interest after their **deaths**.

Their works will follow them. This means that their merits have been invested in the treasury of merits, and because of this additional credit, God would support their cause and avenge them against their enemies, even after their deaths. When the seer said their **works will follow after them** he meant the same as the Habakkuk commentator who said God would save them from the house of judgment through their **works**. Those who kept **the testimony of Jesus** probably had about the same relationship to **Jesus** as those who were saved through their faith in the teacher of righteousness had to that teacher.[1]

TEXT

Revelation	First Testament
¹⁴**Now look!** A white **cloud**,	Dan 7:8**I was watching** the horns--**Now look!** Another small horn came up.
	Dan 7:13**I was watching** in my visions in the night--**Now look!**
and upon the **cloud** seated was **one like a Son of man**, having on his head a gold crown and in his hand, a sharp **sickle**.	with the **clouds** of heaven came **one like a Son of man**.
¹⁵Another **angel went out** from the temple, crying in a loud	Isa 37:35; 2Kings 19:35It happened in that night that the **angel** of Yehowah **went out** and struck in the camp of the Assyrians 185,000.
voice to the one seated upon the **cloud,**	Joel 4:13Let the gentiles arouse themselves and come up to the Valley of Jehoshaphat, because there I will sit to judge all the surrounding nations.
"**Put in your sickle and harvest, because the** time to **harvest has**	**Put in the sickle, because the harvest**

---

[1] See also O. Böcher, "Die Johannes-Apokalypse und die Texte von Qumran," *ANRW* II.25.5:3895. Böcher said, "The expectation of a--real, not some ethical-symbolic--final war (Rev 19:11-21; cf. Ezek 39:17-24) is found running through the Qumran texts (1QM *passim*; cf 1QS 3:24-25; 1QSa 1:21, 26; CD 4:13)."

come, because ¹⁶**the harvest** of the land **is ripe**." Then the one sitting on the **cloud put in his sickle**, and he **harvested** the land.

is ripe.

Jer 51:33 The daughter of Babylon is like a threshing floor at the time [the grain] is being trampled; just a little longer and the time of her **harvest** will come.

COMMENTARY

I was watching. This expression occurs three times in Rev 14, always as the introduction of a new subject (Rev 14:1, 6, 14). In Greek the expression should be rendered **I saw** (*áy-dawn*, εἶδον) and is translated that way in Rev 14:6, but it requires a different translation in Rev 14:1 and Rev 14:14. The expression is taken from the Aramaic of Dan 7:13, *kháh-zeh hah-véyth* (חזה הוית) which is a periphrastic imperfect with the helping verb "to be." Therefore it should be frequently translated in Revelation as **I was watching**.

Another angel went out from the temple. It is not as clear as Loisy thought that the **angel went out from the temple** in heaven rather than the temple at Zion.[1] This **angel** was followed by **another angel** who **went out from** the altar, and commanded **the angel with the sickle to harvest the land**. That was the place where the Lord reportedly killed 185,000 Assyrians in one night (Isa 37:36-37; 2Kings 19:35-36), and both Joel and Zechariah thought he would do it again. It was the angel of the Lord who got credit for killing the Assyrians, and the author of this unit in Revelation expected an angel to put in the sickle and do it again. It was normal in early Judaism and Christianity for believers to anticipate the future on the basis of what had happened before. For example, Joel (Joel 4:13) and Zechariah (Zech 14:4) prophesied that a famous battle would be fought in that same valley with the same amount of success.

When the Assyrians first gathered in the Kidron Valley and the two mountains to the east, the Rab-Shekah made an announcement to all the people of that little town, the City of David. It is now only 10-12 acres in size but it was probably three times as large in the days of Hezekiah and Isaiah—still a small town. The Rab-Shekah told the people that he would come down the next day and kill them all. Isaiah told Hezekiah the situation was well in hand, and all of those Assyrians would be gone in the morning. How did Isaiah know that? The Scripture does not say, but all those soldiers depended on the Spring of Gihon at the border of Zion for their water. All the Jews had to do was poison their water and the effect would have been tremendous. The angel may have had a little help from the Jewish military intelligence. It was probably not a sickle that cut the Assyrian soldiers down, but the effect was the same. The victory was never forgotten. Joel, Zechariah,

---

[1] Loisy, *L'Apocalypse*, p. 274-75.

and the author of Rev 14 may never have learned the military plot that brought about the victory, but they all wanted another just like it.

There never was another victory in that valley like the one in Isaiah's time. The reason may have been that the facilities at the spring changed when Hezekiah diverted the spring to run through the tunnel. Somehow any army attacking Zion would have to gather on the Mount of Olives and Mount Scopus and depend on the water from the spring that flowed out from the temple at Siloam. They probably had to get it from the overflow, near the Valley of Hinoam, and there may never have been access there for the water to be poisoned. This is all guesswork and supposition. That which is likely is that the report of the Assyrian victory motivated the author of Rev 14 to predict a great victory in the Kidron Valley again.

Modern scholars can argue about whether the angel had been expected to fly out from the earthly or the heavenly temple. Early Jews and Christians, however, did not make such a sharp distinction between **the temple,** city, and altar in heaven and **the temple,** city, and altar on earth, as twentieth century Westerners do. Zion, itself, was called **heavenly Jerusalem** (Heb 12:22). The Lord was believed to be legally present both in heaven and in the temple at Zion, so angels could be sent from both places. Whenever the two were distinguished, they were at least located in the same geographical area so that an **angel** could appear from **the temple** in heaven and be situated precisely at the same place he would have reached if he had come from **the temple** at Jerusalem.[1]

Upon the white cloud was seated. The king was normally pictured as **seated**, while those around him were standing. That was a symbol of his royal power. This line was designed to prepare the reader for a situation like the judgment scene of Dan 7 which mythicized the Hasmonean victory over the Syrian Greeks. In that scene, Antiochus Epiphanes (the horn) was given the death sentence and Judas the Maccabee (the **one like a Son of man**) was given the Kingdom, the power, and the governing authority over Palestine. Dan 7 was used by the author of Rev 14 to show his anticipation of a new judgment scene, a new **Son of man**, a new victory over the enemy, and a new kingdom established under the authority of the new Messiah, the new Lamb, the new **Son of man**. Zahn acknowledged that this passage reminded the reader of the second coming of Christ, but he insisted that the being **sitting on** the **cloud** was not Christ but an **angel**.[2] Morris also supposed that the **Son of man** was an **angelic** being,[3] but both are wrong.

The author of this literature used the term **angel** enough that he could have used it again if he had intended to speak of an **angel**. Rabbis thought that the Messiah might either come with **the clouds** of heaven (Dan 7:13) or riding on a donkey (Zech 9:9), but in either case he would be a human messianic king, the son

---

[1] See further Buchanan, *Hebrews*, pp. 221-24.
[2] Zahn, *Offenbarung*, p. 524.
[3] Morris, *Revelation*, p.184.

of David, entering Jerusalem.[1] Some rabbis said the Messiah would come with **the clouds** of heaven, and some even thought that meant he would come as an **angel,** but that did not mean he was an **angel** or would function only in heaven. That meant he was of heavenly origin, but he was expected to rule as king over all countries, because he would be given the **kingdom, glory, and the greatness** (Dan 7:14).[2]

The sixth vision of Fourth Ezra pictures something like the figure of a man who came up out of the sea and flew with **the clouds** of heaven. When foreign nations gathered against him he destroyed them with the breath of his mouth. Then he called to himself a peaceable group, who turned out to be the ten tribes of North Israel. This man was from the sea, on **the clouds**, and also on **Mount Zion.** This was the Messiah whom the Lord had been keeping for many ages. He was also identified as God's Son (4Ezra 13:1-40). Likewise, **the Lamb** in Rev 14 was **standing on Mount Zion** at the same time one like **a Son of man was seated on a cloud** (Rev 14:1, 14). The **cloud** was the symbol of God's presence. The chair was a symbol of royal or judicial authority. **Standing** probably implied the acceptance and maintenance of an office. The cloud went before and after the Israelites as they left Egypt; it accompanied Jesus, Peter, James, and John on the Mount of Transfiguration (Matt 17:1-8) where Jesus was recognized as God's son.

Since it took two or more witnesses to prove a case in court, the author of this narrative introduced a second witness (Joel), a second judgment scene during which God judged the enemy adversely. This was to take place in the Kidron Valley east of the temple area in Jerusalem and was prophesied by Joel. From these two prophecies (Joel and Daniel) the author obtained the same message; namely, that God was just about to judge Jewish enemies adversely and Israel favorably. As a result of this verdict, the kingdom was soon to be restored and Israel would soon have its own messianic ruler. According to the old Pentacontad calendar that was still observed in NT times by some Jews, each year the old year came to an end a few days before the new year began. During the period between the years unleavened bread was eaten after the end of the old year, right up to the time of the New Year, which occurred on the very day that later became Christian Easter.[3]

Schüssler-Fiorenza argued ineffectively that the author of this midrash in Rev 14 was using a harvesting scene to picture the Lord gathering in the gentiles from the ends of the earth as converts to Christianity, those who accept the eternal gospel.[4] She overlooked the fact that the author of this midrash used two important passages to prove the point that he had in mind:

---

[1] Buchanan, *Jewish Messianic Movements from AD 70 to AD 1300* (Eugene, Oregon: Wipf and Stock Publishers, 2003), pp. 317, 536.
[2] Buchanan, *Jewish Messianic Movements,* p. 505.
[3] See Julius and Hildegard Lewy, "The Origin of the Week and the Oldest West Asiatic Calendar," *HUCA* 17 (1942/43):1-152; J. Morgenstern, "The Calendar of the Book of Jubilees," *VT* 5 (1955):34-76; Morgenstern, *Some Significant Antecedents of Christianity* (Leiden: E. J. Brill, 1966), pp. 20-22; R. M. Johnson, "The Eschatological Sabbath in John's Apocalypse: A Reconsideration," *AUSS* 25 (1987):47.
[4] Schüssler-Fiorenza, *Visions*, p. 90.

1) The passage from Dan 7 described a court scene, in which the **Son of man** was awarded **the kingdom, the power, and the greatness of the kingdom.** This was a mythicized historical account of Judas the Maccabee, receiving **the kingdom** of Judah after he had defeated the Greeks in the battle of Beth-horon. In that battle, he and his troops cut down the Greeks like grain at harvest time. It was not the converts but the enemies who were **harvested.**

2) The same is true in the text from Joel. He envisioned the enemy gathered in the Kidron Valley prepared to attack Jerusalem but instead were cut down like grain harvested with **a sickle.** Both Christians and Jews expected the Lord to gather in the elect at the end of the age. In one Christian redemption prophecy the author promised that God would send his **angels** to gather in the elect from the four corners of heaven (Mark 13:27). A later Christian prayed that the Lord would gather in the faithful as bread scattered on the mountains (Did 9:4). On the basis of Deut 30:1-5, Jeremiah prophesied that the Lord would first push his people off the land into the diaspora, then, after he had punished them there; he would finally bring them back to Jerusalem (Jer 30-31; Zech 2:6-12).

If the author of the midrash in Rev 14 had wanted to picture the Messiah gathering in the elect or the converts, there were other texts he might have used. He chose, however, to use texts that **harvested** the enemy in war and not those who gathered the saints or the converts to Jerusalem for salvation. That is because these texts expressed his intended meaning.. The term **son of man** is normally applied to the Messiah. Here that is confirmed by the **golden crown** worn by that **Son of man**. **Golden crowns** were reserved for royalty alone.[1]

Another angel. This **other angel** seems to be the fourth, because in the text before there are three **other angels** (Rev 14:6, 8, 9). The first one is also called **another angel**, but it was understood to be the first, because the next two are called **another angel**, "the second" and **another angel**, "the third." At one time Rev 14 was probably part of another document which had more **other angels**. When this part was separated from the rest, the editor added the words "the second" and "the third," implying that the preceding **other angel** was the first. The **other angel** in Rev 14:15 is now fourth in the list, and the same expression in Rev 14:17 and 18 would be fifth and sixth. The fact that there are six **other angels** in Rev 14 suggests that once there may have been only one other **angel**, a first, making the total come out to seven. The expression **another angel** in Rev 14:15, following the **Son of man** in Rev 14:14 does not imply that the **Son of man** is **an angel**, as Giblin thought,[2] or that the **one seated on the cloud** was an angel, as Aune thought[3]. The **Son of man** was the equivalent of **the Lamb** or the Messiah--not an **angel**.

---

[1] Josephus said that the golden crown Israelite kings wore was always called a *stéh-phah-naws* (στέφανος), rather than a *deé-ah-day-mah* (διάδημα) (Ant 7:50; 17:196-97).
[2] Giblin, *Revelation*, p. 143.
[3] Aune, *Revelation 6-16,* pp. 842-43.

The time to harvest has come. The **time to harvest** does not mean the end of the world, as Morris thought.[1] On the first day of each new year, there was a ceremony of cutting the first of the New Year's grain. This ceremony was so important to tradition that it was preserved even after the lunar calendar was accepted, and New Year's Day changed to September or October. According to the Pentecontad calendar New Year's Day always happened the day after a Sabbath. This was not true of the lunar calendar which was not structured according to Sabbaths. Even if, according to the lunar calendar, the old New Year's Day happened on a Sabbath, Pharisees still conducted the ceremony.

People from the neighboring towns gathered, and when it was dark, and the new day had begun, one of the messengers of the court said, "Is the sun set?" Then the crowd answered in unison, "Yes!" This was done responsively three times. The same liturgical procedure followed identifying the basket. Finally, he asked, "Shall I reap?" and the crowd answered in unison, "Yes!" This also happened three times before he put the sickle into the new grain (mMen 10:3). Then they cut the grain and brought it into the temple court in baskets. There it was parched, ground into flour, and consumed after it had been properly tithed, and the priests had received their portions (mMen 10:4).

Also on the Pentecost New Year's Day the Lord was believed to open the books and judge the people. If they were judged meritorious, then they would be given back the land, and the enemy nations would be subdued. If they were still in their crime, they would continue in captivity to pagan nations. Judgment was to take place in the land of Israel when enemy nations would be gathered and utterly defeated by God's judgment (Ezek 38:19-36).[2] God's judgment day was described metaphorically as a harvest scene--an appropriate metaphor for the season in March or April when grain is harvested in Palestine. March would be early for some grain in Palestine. Therefore, Jews parched their grain before they made it into flour, because it would not have been completely ripe. In September or October, however, when New Year's Day was established according to the lunar calendar, harvest would have been finished months before.

The author of Joel probably had the judgment day associated with New Year's Day in mind, as well as the destruction of the Assyrians in the time of Hezekiah, when he wrote the following poem describing a war in terms of a harvest scene.[3] This poem is basic to the author's narrative:

---

[1] Morris, *Revelation*, p. 185.
[2] See L. Landman, *Messianism in the Talmudic Era* (New York: KTAV Publishing House, 1979), p. xii, and H. J. Kraus, *Die Königherrschaft Gottes im Alten Testament* (Tübingen: J. C. B. Mohr, 1951), pp. 50-57, 69-70, 106. Also see *mRoshH* 4.5; *tRoshH* 1.11-13; *LevR* 19.1. Düsterdieck, *Handbook*, p. 401, missed the local significance of this prophecy and said, "The whole earth is the harvest-field."
[3] Although this seems to be an obvious allusion to a New Year's Day judgment scene, the following commentaries on Joel overlooked it: L. C. Allen, *The Books of Joel, Obadiah, Jonah, and Micah* (Grand Rapids: Eerdmans, c1976); A. Cohen, *The Twelve Prophets* (Chesham: Soncino Press, c1948); F. W. Farrar, *The Minor Prophets* (New York: Fleming H. Revell, n.d.); Mag. H. Frey, *Das Buch der Kirche in der Weltwende; Die Kleinen Nachexilischen Propheten* (Stuttgart: Calwer Vereinbuchhandlung, n.d.); H. Henderson, *The Book of the Twelve Minor Prophets* (London:

> Sanctify war, stir up the mighty men . . .
> beat your plowshares into swords,
> and your pruning hooks into spears. . .
> Let the nations arouse themselves
> and come up to the Valley of Jehoshaphat, . . .
> for there I will sit to judge
> all the nations round about.
> **Put in the sickle, because the harvest is ready**.
> Come, **trample [the grapes]**, for **the wine press** is full,
> and the vats overflow . . .
> Mobs, mobs in the Valley of Verdict.
> The Day of the Lord is near in the Valley of Verdict
> . . .
> The Lord roars in Zion and utters his voice from
> Jerusalem . . .
> The Lord is a refuge to his people,
> a stronghold to the people of Israel.
> So you will know that I am the Lord your God,
> who dwells in Zion, my holy mountain.
> Jerusalem will be holy,
> and foreigners will never again pass through it (Joel 3:9-17 MT 4:9-17).[1]

New Year's Day was followed every year by the Day of Atonement. This took place just ten days later, according to the modern lunar calendar. Like the ten days of testing for Daniel and his friends in **Babylon** (Dan 1:12-21), this was a ten day period of testing between New Year's Day and the Day of Atonement for those who observed the new lunar calendar with New Year's Day in September or October. According to Lev 16:29 the Day of Atonement fell on the tenth of the seventh month, counting from the Pentecost New Year's Day. Those who observed the old Pentacontad calendar, evidently had seven months, ten days, between these two holidays.

Whatever the length of time scheduled between these two special days, this was a period when Jews might repent and do works of supererogation. If there happened to be only a few iniquities that needed to be canceled, repentance during that time might be enough to cancel them. Jews understood that God would not restore the kingdom to them so long as there were still unforgiven iniquities on file. Iniquities were the accumulated unpaid fines for crimes committed in the past. These

---

Hamilton, Adams, 1845); K. Marti, *Das Dodekapropheton* (Tübingen, 1904); C. Von Orelli, *The Twelve Minor Prophets*, tr. J. S. Banks (Edinburgh: T. & T. Clark, 1897); E. B. Pusey, *The Minor Prophets* (New York: Funk & Wagnalls, 1886); G. L. Robinson, *Die Zwölf Kleinen Propheten: Nahum bis Maleachi* (Tübingen: J. C. B. Mohr, 1954).
[1] Düsterdieck, *Handbook*, p. 402.

had either to be paid or forgiven before the kingdom could be restored. Judgment took place on New Year's Day.

The only way Jews could find out what the verdict was on New Year's Day was to wait until the Day of Atonement had come and gone. If the kingdom was restored then, it proved that all of Israel's crimes had been forgiven. For example, in 164 BIA the Battle of Beth-horon was fought and won by Judas the Maccabee just after the Day of Atonement, and the first Hanukkah was celebrated just a few months after that. That was when the temple was cleansed, and Jews were confident that it would be only a matter of time before the land was restored completely, and Jews would be ruled by their own Messiah. It was this victory celebration which is the central point of the entire Book of Daniel.

During that year, the Battle of Beth-horon was the liturgical equivalent of the Battle of the Valley of Verdict fought in the Kidron Valley, east of the temple area. The sharp sickle was the harvest metaphor used to describe the weapons used against Israel's enemies. It was the hand of the Lord that cut down the enemy like grain on that judgment day. While the Lord was judging, the Jews were fighting, and the Lord was acting in their behalf with a sharp sickle. This whole mythical concept would make no sense on a Day of Atonement that took place in September or October. Grain is harvested in the Near East in late April or May, beginning on the old New Year's Day which was the same as modern Christian Easter.

The author of Rev 14 anticipated a new Battle of Beth-horon, a new dedication of the temple, a new establishment of the kingdom, and the installation of a new Messiah as king at Jerusalem.

The harvest of the land is ripe. The imagery is that of a farmer **harvesting** his field with a sickle, but the "field" in this case is the Promised Land. The "grain" that was destined to be harvested consisted of all the surrounding enemy nations together with local collaborators. At the time of this writing, the enemy involved was Rome. This is not a new symbol for divine judgment (Jer 51:33; Hos 6:11; Lam 1:15).

The word for **ripe** is "dried." There was a ceremony of cutting grain on New Year's Day. They began to cut grain on New Year's Day even if it was on the Sabbath and even if the grain was not completely **ripe**. They cut it and dried it over the fire in the temple area, gave the proper offerings, ground the dried grain into flour and baked it (mMen 10:3-5).

TEXT

Revelation

[17]Another angel went out from the temple which is in heaven, having also himself a sharp **sickle**. [18][Still] another angel went out from the altar, who had authority over the fire. He called in a loud voice to the one who

First Testament

Joel 4:13 Let the nations arouse themselves and come up to the Valley of Jehoshaphat, because there I will sit to judge all the surrounding nations.

was seated on the cloud, saying, "**Put in** your sharp **sickle** and **harvest** the **clusters** [of grapes] of the vine of the land, **because** its grapes **are ripe**."

Put in the **sickle**,

because the **harvest is ripe**.

Deut 23:25-26 When you go through your neighbor's vineyard, you may eat as many **clusters** [of grapes] as you want, but you shall not put [any] in your container [to take with you]. When you go through your neighbor's standing grain you may pick the grain with your hand, but you shall not use a **sickle** on your neighbor's standing grain.

¹⁹Then the angel put his **sickle** to the land, and he **harvested** the vine of the land, and he threw [the grapes] into **the great wine press** of the anger of God. ²⁰He **trampled**

Isa 63:3 I have **trodden the wine press** alone . . .
I **trampled** them in my anger, for the day of vengeance was in my heart; the year of my redemption has come.

Joel 3:13 [MT 4:13] Come **trample**, because **the wine press** is full.

the wine press outside the city, and blood went out from **the wine press** until the bridles of the horses, from sixteen hundred stadia [about two hundred miles].

TECHNICAL DETAILS

Mulholland has correctly noted that there are two **harvesting** scenes in Rev 14 which are very similar. He explained the phenomenon by supposing that the first one **harvested** Israel (Rev 14:14-16) and the second one **harvested** Israel's enemies (Rev 14:17-19).[1] This is one possibility, but not the only one. There are some slight differences between the two scenes. The first one employed Daniel and Joel; the second used Joel, Second (or third) Isaiah, and Deuteronomy. The first simply **harvested** the land; the second **harvested** the grapes of the land and **trampled** the grapes in the wine press. Since both were dependent upon Joel, which was a battle whereby only Israel's enemies were killed, both may be different versions of a similar kind of midrash. The author of this chapter may have had at his disposal two different narratives that belonged in this chapter. Instead of choosing which was the

---

[1] M. R. Mulholland, Jr., *Revelation* (Grand Rapids: Francis Asbury Press, 1990), p. 36.

better, he included them both. He observed the same technique in dealing with the two narratives about the **144,000** that are now in Rev 7 and 14.

This was not a novel way of editing sources in the ancient Near East. For example there are two stories of creation in Genesis; there are doublets in Matthew where the same saying is used in different parts of the Gospel. There is much repetition in rabbinic midrashim. Early Semites tended to collect material that was similar and put it together into organized units without always editing out duplicate data to avoid repetition. In many kinds of literature, such as running commentaries (Mekilta, Sifra, Sifré), material is duplicated, because people seldom read the whole document, so that which is needed to interpret each verse is placed there. Later, material is gathered from the original commentaries and anthologies and collected in one place. Here in Rev 14 there were slight differences in the units, so the editor chose to include them both.

The poem of Joel was probably motivated by the destruction of 185,000 Assyrians in the Kidron Valley in one night, during the reign of Hezekiah, while Isaiah was his chief military intelligence officer (Isa 37; 2Kings 19). Joel expected it to happen again. So did the author of the units in Rev 14.

COMMENTARY

Another angel went out. **The temple** of Jerusalem and **the temple in heaven** were so closely identified that it is not clear whether the first **angel** (Rev 14:15) left **the temple in heaven** as the second **angel** did (Rev 14:17) or not. Even the second **angel,** who was said to have left the altar, appeared right there in the Kidron Valley (the Valley of Verdict) when he left the **temple.** It is far from certain whether he left the altar of **the temple** in Jerusalem or whether, like the first **angel**, he also left the altar **from the temple in heaven**. An anonymous medieval Jewish author said a throne on earth is prepared over against a throne in heaven and the holy of holies which is below is a counterpart for the holy of holies that is above.[1]

The One who was seated on the cloud. The one seated on the cloud was the Son of man, the Messiah, the Lamb as in Dan 7. The Son of man, also called the Son of God and the Messiah, was God's legal agent on earth. God was the principal who was responsible for all of the Messiah's actions and speech. When Jesus was directing his apostles, they asked him for a sign from Heaven, but he, himself, was waiting for a sign from God. He did not want to act without divine orders. One of the places he looked for direction was the Scripture. There Ezekiel promised that in the new age there would be fruit trees bearing fruit in the Kidron Valley every month of the year (Ezek 47). Jesus did not want to begin his program until the new age began. He would not act without God's direction. He and God had to be acting on the same time schedule, so he checked in the Kidron Valley so see if any of the fig trees were bearing ripe fruit out of normal season, as Ezekiel prophesied would be the case in the new age (Ezek 47). When there was none, he cursed the tree, and

---

[1] Buchanan, *Jewish Messianic Movements*, p. 551.

postponed his program. He needed **an angel** to come down **from Heaven** to tell him what to do. Here in Rev 14, the picture is given of the **angel coming down from the temple in heaven**, to tell the Messiah that it was time to begin the great war in the Kidron Valley that Joel and Zechariah prophesied.[1] This was **the day of vengeance** of which Second Isaiah spoke, **the year of** God's **redemption had come** (Isa 63:2-3).

The vine of the Land. Like the harvest **of the land,** the **vine of the land** is symbolic. In one case it was **the land** that was to be **harvested,** supposedly the grain or other crops in the field; in the other case it was a vineyard, but the "grapes" and the "grain" were not really food products. Instead of grape juice, **blood** poured out from this particular wine press. The "grapes" and the "grain" were enemies that needed to be cleared off **the** Promised **Land,** in Jewish and/or Christian judgment.

Put his sickle to the Land, the clusters, [of grapes]. Sickles are better known in the West as instruments for harvesting grain, but sickles are used for both purposes in some countries. For example the Swiss used an instrument for pruning and harvesting grapes that looked like a sickle. It was called a "heppe." In this chapter, however, harvesting grain and harvesting grapes were all in order, because the real objects were enemy soldiers. From Joel the author took the image of someone conducting a war in the Valley of Jehoshaphat the way someone would **harvest** grain with **a sickle,** but in Deuteronomy there were rules about picking grain in your neighbor's field and picking **grapes** in your neighbor's vineyard. The seer used both the image of picking **grapes** and of cutting grain with a **sickle.** The grapes were more vivid for the picture of a war, because **the blood** shed in a battle was like the juice of **grapes** in a **wine press**. The seer already had a pattern for this mixture of **grapes** and grain. He took passages from Ezekiel, Daniel, Zephaniah, and Joel and put them all together. Joel may have used Deut 23:25-26 as a basis for his poem of the great **harvest of grapes** in **the Valley of Jehoshaphat**. He also had the memory of the 185,000 Assyrians whose bodies were left dead in the Kidron Valley during the leadership of King Hezekiah and Isaiah (2Kings 19; Isa 37).[2]

The great wine press of the anger. An expression parallel to that of Rev 14:10; 15:7; 16:1, 19; 19:15), a vivid image of a great war that God would conduct in the Kidron Valley. Since God was known as the "Yehowah of the armies" (*Yeh-hoh-wáh tseh-vá-ohth,* יהוה צבעות), all of Israel's wars were believed to be God's wars, through which he expressed his anger against the enemies of Israel.

---

[1] Buchanan, "Withering Fig Trees and Progression in Midrash," C. A. Evans and W. R. Stegner (eds.), *The Gospels and the Scriptures of Israel* (Sheffield: Sheffield Academic Press Ltd, c1994), pp. 249-69.
[2] For details see Buchanan, "The Tower of Siloam," *ET* 115.2 (2003): 37-45.

Outside the city. **The city** involved was Zion, and **outside this city** was the Kidron Valley, the mythical Valley of Verdict. In Joel 3:16-17 [4:16-17] the **harvesting** scene is related to Zion and Jerusalem. The Kidron Valley (The Valley of Jehoshaphat) is **outside the city.** This is not a reference to the crucifixion of Jesus. It is just an accurate geographical location. Düsterdieck correctly said,

> . . . not heavenly Jerusalem, also not Jerusalem so far as the holy city represents the Church, but the real, earthly Jerusalem.[1]

The author of Rev 14 expected this battle to happen all over again on this special New Year's Day. The way to celebrate was to destroy the enemy in the Kidron Valley just outside of Jerusalem. This is obvious, because **the angels came out from the temple** with commands to **put in the sickle**, right there in that valley.

Not only Joel, but also Ezek 38-39 and Zech 14 report the expectation of a famous battle at Jerusalem when God would judge the enemy nations who would come against Israel and be destroyed there. **The wine press** that was **trampled** by this **bloody** war was just **outside the city** of Jerusalem. **The angel** was commanded to **harvest the vine of the land**, meaning the Promised Land. The first passage was introduced with an allusion to Dan 7 and the appearance of **the one like a Son of man** before the Ancient of Days in a **judgment** scene described by another myth. The images related to the Pentecost New Year's Day festival, **the harvesting of first fruits** of the land of Palestine, the Valley of Verdict was to be done with the sickle by **the new Son of man,** and the events destined to occur **outside the city** of Jerusalem all point to a Palestinian origin for Rev 14. There are no clues that point to an Asia Minor origin as Schüssler-Fiorenza and others have thought.

From sixteen hundred stadia. Ford has noticed that 200 miles is about the distance from the city of Tyre in the north to Wadi El Arish in the south. This was the full dimension of the Promised Land after the conquest of Joshua. It was an exaggeration, to be sure, but there was a tremendous amount of **blood** shed throughout this land before Vespasian drew up his legions to surround Jerusalem in 66 IA.[2] Even though exaggerated, it was not a description of the end of the world or **the harvest** of the entire earth, as Morris thought.[3] The word Morris translated "earth" should be rendered "land," meaning the Promised Land, whose capital city was Zion, Jerusalem, the city of God, outside of which was the Valley of Decision, the Valley of Jehoshaphat. The author of this narrative was not the only one given to exaggeration. Some of the rabbis described the battle at Betar (IA 135) as follows:

> [The Romans] continued to kill them [Jews] until the horses sunk into blood up to their nostrils. The [force of] the blood [pouring out]

---

[1] Düsterdieck, *Handbook*, p. 402.
[2] Ford, *Revelation*, p. 250.
[3] Morris, *Revelation*, p. 185.

rolled stones weighing forty seahs (about 15 bushels) until the blood flowed to the sea, 40 miles away (pTaan 69a).

In a medieval Jewish document the author "prophesied," after the event, "Legions of Edom [Rome] will be tested with them, and they will come and make war in the Valley of Acre, until the horse sinks up to his thigh in blood." A poetic account of that event is as follows:

> The Edomites and the Ishmaelites[1] (7) will fight in the Valley of Acre
> until the horses sink (8) in blood and whinny [in panic].
> Gaza and her daughters will be stoned (9),
> and Ascalon and Ashdod will be confounded.
> Then Israel (10) will go out from the city and advance.[2]

The blood poured out of the wine press. This is not a vision the author constructed *de novo* and used for the first time. Joel pictured a battle in **the Valley of Jehoshaphat,** at the border of Jerusalem, where **blood** of Israel's enemies would flow like **grape** juice from a **wine press** (Joel 4:11-15). Enoch described a battle scene where the horses waded in blood up to their chests 1Enoch 100:3-4). Fourth Ezra said **the blood** from the sword would flow up to the horses' bellies, to the hips of men, and to the hocks of camels (4Ezra 15:35-37). The triple designation was for rhetorical effect. The same measurement would reach the places indicated from the three different creatures. There probably never was a battle fought where **blood** ran so freely, but the exaggerated expression was evidently a familiar one in Jewish circles. Interpreting the promise that there would not cease to be an authentic ruler from Judah, the targumist said,

> How beautiful is the king the Messiah who is destined to arise from the house of Judah! Binding [his armor around] his waist, he will go out to engage in battle with those who hate him. He kills kings and rulers; he makes the mountains red with the blood of their corpses; the valley becomes white from the fat of their soldiers, his clothing is rolled in blood. He is like one who crushes grapes (TgNeof Gen 49:11).

Boring observed the exaggerated nature of these expressions and called them "pictures." They are not *just* pictures, but they are pictures, nevertheless, in his

---

[1] Christians and Muslims.
[2] From a unit that is a part of "The Prayer, Secrets, and Mysteries of Rabbi Shimon Ben Yohai," tr. by Buchanan, *Jewish Messianic Movements*, p. 412. This reflects the famous battle of Acre in IA 1291, when the Moslems drove the Christians from that city. The poetic lines are from "That Day," p. 292.

opinion. He calls them also "metaphors."[1] They are more realistic than that. In Exod 14 the water probably did not pile up like walls on either side of the Israelites as they crossed the sea bed, but Israelites were able to get across. **The stars in their courses** may not have **fought against Sisera**, but the Israelites won the battle, and **Sisera** was killed (Judges 5). The hyperbole was rhetorically and sometimes poetically effective, but the authors were describing real military battles and real crossings of bodies of water. The purpose of hyperbole is not to describe a situation scientifically accurately. It is intended to express the way the author felt about the situation.

Jewish and Christian tradition is not always passive and kind. It also includes such practices as apartheid and holy war conquest theology that reportedly takes glee in the suffering of enemies. It does not help either Judaism or Christianity to deny this part of our heritage and history. Commenting on the text **Rejoicing, I will rejoice in the Lord** (Isa 61:10), medieval rabbis said,

> **Rejoicing** in the days of the Messiah; **I will rejoice** with the down fall of wicked Rome. **My soul will delight in my God** (Isa 61:10). This is the war of Gog and Magog (PesiqR 37 [162b]).

None of the Jewish or Christian sources--Joel, Ezekiel, Zechariah, 1Enoch, Targumists, Talmudists, Pesikta Rabbati, or Rev 14-- intended readers to think they were describing or anticipating blood from Jewish or Christian martyrs to provide all the blood they described, as Caird and Boring hold.[2] The blood of the enemies filled the Kidron Valley, not the blood of believers. Believers would rejoice in the event.

There were two important victories in antiquity that later Jews and Christians continued to want relived more than 2,000 years later.
1) One of these was the incident where 185,000 Assyrian soldiers were killed in one night in the Kidron Valley (Isa 36-37; 2 Kings 18-19). This was probably poetized in Joel 3: 2 [MT 4:2].
2) The other was the victory of Judas over the Syrians in the Valley of Beth-horon, prior to the cleansing of the temple and the celebration of Hanukkah. This was reported mythically in Dan 7. Later literature reviewed these hopes again and again, believing that time moved in cycles and at the strategic time, they would recur. The authors of Rev 13 and 14 worked both events into their documents.

---

[1] M. E. Boring, *Revelation* (Louisville: John Knox Press, c1989), p. 116.
[2] Caird, *Revelation*, pp. 188-95; Boring, *Revelation*, p. 171.

CHAPTER FIFTEEN

TEXT

Revelation

$^{15:1}$I saw another sign in heaven, great and marvelous--**seven** angels having the **seven** last plagues--because through them **the anger** of God was completed. ²I saw [something] like a glassy sea mixed with fire. [I also saw] those who conquered [troops] belonging to the beast, its image, and the number of its name standing alongside the glassy sea, having harps of the Lord God.

³**They sang** the **song** of

First Testament and Targumim

$^{Lev\ 26:27\text{-}33}$If, even with this, you do not pay attention to me, and you walk contrary to me, then I will walk in **anger** contrary to you. I, myself, will punish you **seven times** for your sins: 1) You will eat the flesh of your sons and daughters. 2) I will destroy your high places and cut down your incense altars. 3) I will put your corpses on top of the corpses of your idols, and my soul will despise you. 4) I will lay your cities in ruin and destroy your sanctuaries. 5) I will not smell your pleasing odors. 6) I will desolate your land so that your enemies who live in it will be appalled, and 7) I will scatter you among the nations and I will unsheath the sword after you. Your land will become desolate and your cities, a ruin.

$^{Exod\ 15:1}$Then **Moses** and the children of Israel **sang** this **song**.

$^{Deut\ 31:30}$Then **Moses** spoke in the ears of the whole congregation of Israel the words of **this song**.

$^{1Chron\ 16:23\text{-}24}$**Sing** to Yehowah, all the land; announce the good news of his salvation from day to day; tell among the nations his glory, among the peoples his **marvelous deeds**.

$^{Josh\ 14:7}$I was forty years old when

Moses, the servant of God, and the song of the Lamb, saying,

"**Great and marvelous**

are your **works**,

Lord God of armies.

Just and **true are** your **ways**,

King of the ages.
⁴**Who will not fear**, Lord, **and glorify your name?**
because you only are holy, because

Moses, the servant of God, sent me from Kadesh-barnea to spy out the land.

Ps 86:10 You are **great and** you do **marvelous** things.

Ps 111:2-4 **Great** are the **deeds** of the Lord, searched out by all who desire them, glorious and majestic **are** his **works**; his justice stands continually. He has made a memorial to his **marvelous works**.

Isa 3:15 . . . says the **Lord God of armies.**

Isa 22:15 Thus said the **Lord God of armies**.

Deut 32:4 The Rock--his works are perect, because all his **ways are just**. A God of **truth** is he without evil; he is righteous and fair.

Ps 145:17-18 **Just** is **the Lord** in all his **ways**, pious in all his **works. The Lord** is near to all who call upon him in **truth**. Yehowah is the **true** God. He is the God of life and **king of the age**. At his anger the earth quakes, and

Jer 10:7 **Who will not fear you, King of the nations?**.

Jer 10:10 **gentiles** cannot endure his wrath.

TgPsJon Exod 15.18 His is the crown of the kingdom, and he is **King of** kings in this world and his is the kingdom for the age to come. It is his and [his] it will be for ages of ages.

all the gentiles will come and prostrate themselves before you, because just deeds before you have become publicly known."

Ps 86:9 **All the gentiles** which you have made **will come and prostrate themselves before you and glorify your name**.

Zech 14:16 It will happen that all who are left of **all the gentiles will come** up to Jerusalem. They will go up year after year to **prostrate themselves before** the King Yehowah of armies and for the feast, namely the feast of Tabernacles.

COMMENTARY

I saw. There are three units in Rev 15. Each begins with the words **I saw** (Rev 15:1, 2, 5. The unit continues through Rev 16. The entire unit deals with the bowls that are poured out from heaven which cause curses on earth.

Another sign in heaven, great and marvelous. This is the fourth scene of the prophecy brought to John at Patmos (Rev 4:1; 8:1; 11:19). Like the other scenes, this one takes place **in heaven**, but it is closely related to the earth. Action that was seen here was to remind the reader of the Exodus from Egypt and anticipate a new Exodus.

The plagues themselves were **great and** terrible. Worse than that, they were not directed against Israel's enemies, but against Israel itself. That which was **marvelous** about this vision is that the angels had the *last* plagues to release. That means that God's anger would soon be *over*. The end was in sight. Once these plagues had taken place, God's punishment against the Israelites would be finished. The Lord promised that if, after all of these afflictions, the Israelites repented and confessed their iniquity and the iniquity of their fathers (Lev 26:40), the Lord would remember the contract and the land and would again be their God (Lev 26:42-45). At the time of this writing, the author believed that the Lord was still angry with his people. He had already punished them, but not enough to satisfy his anger. He would still fulfill all of the promised curses of the contract enumerated in Lev 26, but whenever they had all been fulfilled, his anger would come to an end. This was good news!--not that God was still angry, but that he was about to bring all of his anger to an end. These seven plagues were the last plagues to be suffered before God would restore the kingdom.

Angels having the seven last plagues. **The seven plagues the angels** had were associated with the contract. When Israel made a contract with the Lord the terms were that if ever Israelites broke the contract they would be punished with **seven plagues**

for their sins. This warning was given four times, each accompanied with a list of **plagues** (Lev 26:18, 21, 24, 28). Only the fourth list seems to have **seven** actual **plagues** listed:
1) Eating sons and daughters;
2) religious places destroyed;
3) dead bodies cast on dead idols;
4) cities and sanctuaries desolate;
5) sacrifices rejected;
6) land devastated;
7) scattered among the nations (Lev 26:29-33).

These are probably the **seven plagues** that the **seven** angels had. The **plague**s were not those to be afflicted on the enemies of Israel. These were directed to the Israelites themselves, because the contract was made with the Israelites--not the gentiles.

The anger of God was completed. The plagues themselves were the means by which God could give the very last vent to his hostilities and become satisfied with his punishment.

A glassy sea mixed with fire. This vision in heaven was an antitype of the **sea** which the Israelites crossed when they left Egypt. The **fire** that was present at the **sea** may have represented the pillar of **fire** and smoke that went before the Israelites and went behind them as they crossed the **sea** and later into the wilderness. It might have been a vision of the bronze "**sea**" that was part of the temple, probably used for ablutions (2Chron 4:6; 1Kings 7:23), as Sweet thought.[1] The same **glassy sea** was also mentioned in Rev 4:6.[2]

This was a heavenly *temple* vision, but it reflects the situation of the temple at Zion as well. There was a **sea** in the heavenly temple, because there was also a **sea** in the temple at Jerusalem. Medieval rabbis said God willingly left the things that were in heaven to dwell among those who lived on earth (ExodR 23:4). Ancient prophets had a way of mixing images in visions so as to reflect Scripture, heaven, Jerusalem, and also some contemporary historical and geographical situations. Heavenly and earthly situations in visions were not mutually exclusive. This vision of the **sea** in the temple in heaven also pictured the Exodus from Egypt, and also either another Exodus or a desired new Exodus in New Testament (NT) times. The vision probably did not apply to the body of water at the border of Egypt, because that was no longer a barrier of resistance to Palestinian Jews or Christians of NT times. It probably meant the Mediterranean **Sea** for the following reasons.

Those who conquered. Rev 15 may have been composed by a different author from those who wrote parts of Rev 14. Therefore, it cannot be presumed that the conquerors here were initially the same as the 144,000 in Rev 7 and 14, as some

---

[1] J. P. M. Sweet, *Revelation* (Philadelphia: Westminster Press, c1979), p. 239.
[2] The photograph of a similar "sea" is found between chapters twelve and thirteen.

hold.[1] The final editor of the prophecy (Rev 4:1-22:5) and/or John of Patmos may have understood them to have been identical, but that is not certain.

The author envisioned himself and his contemporary Jews as those who were reliving the Exodus. Just as the Israelites crossed the **sea** safely, and the troops of the Pharaoh followed only to be destroyed, so contemporary Jews had just been rescued. Just as with the Israelites, there was a **sea** of water and **fire** between Jews and their enemies. The beast was just as dead as the troops of Pharaoh who had been drowned in the sea. The impossible had happened. Just as God had rescued the Israelites miraculously, so the Jews had been miraculously rescued from the **beast** *and its statue*. This evidently refers to **the beast** and **the statue** mentioned in Rev 13:13-18 and 14:11. This **beast** told **the migrants of the land** to make an image [**statue**] of **the beast,** and **the beast** required that everyone worship the image. The most likely incident mentioned here was the time when Caligula (Gaius) sent Petronius to Palestine to set up Caligula's statue in the temple and require everyone to worship it.

The joy Jews felt when Petronius withdrew his demands was like that felt by Israelites after the Egyptians had been overcome, and the Israelites were safe on the other side of the sea. Like the Israelites with **the sea** between them and the Egyptian Pharaoh and his troops, Jews who confronted Petronius had the Mediterranean **Sea** between them and the Roman emperors and their troops, after Petronius and his troops had left. They were conquerors even though they never engaged in battle.

The number of its name. There is no 666 here, as in Rev 13, so there is no certainty what **the number of its name** was. The original readers, however, would have known. Otherwise the author would not have used this code expression. His purpose was to communicate a message to the readers for whom this was intended.

The historical situation that prompted this chapter also prompted the narrative of the second beast in Rev 13, but the beast seems to have been different. Here **the beast** was one who had a **statue. The beast** and his troops were conquered by those who stood alongside **the sea**. This situation fits Gaius, his troops directed by Petronius, the statue of Gaius, and the courageous unarmed Jews who resisted him against all odds and were delivered. There is an intentional continuation of themes among chapters 12, 13, 14, and 15.

Having harps of the Lord God. NA omits **Lord.**

The song of the Lamb. Aune has observed the following:

> Note that there are several passages in Revelation in which "Lamb" has been added: (1) "and before the Lamb" (7:9), (2) "and to the Lamb" (7:10), (3) "and the Lamb" (14:4), (4) "and before the Lamb"

---

[1] G. B. Caird, *A Commentary on the Revelation of St. John the Divine* (London: Black, c1966), p. 197.

(14:10) (5) "and the Lamb" (21:22); (6) "and the lamp of the Lamb" (21:23), (7) "and the Lamb" (22:1), (8) "and of the Lamb" (22:3).[1]

He correctly deduced that some later editor inserted these expressions to unify and tie together the entire document. This is probably the work of the final editor who gathered together many redemption pieces and organized Revelation into a coherent anthology. All of these additions were included in the prophecy section (Rev 4:1-22:5). Similar additions were made to Christianize the document:

"having the testimony of Jesus" (12:17),
"and the faith of Jesus" (14:12),
"and from the blood of the witnesses of Jesus" (17:6),
"those who have the testimony of Jesus" (19:10).

Without these Christianizing additions, the prophetic section appears to be a Jewish document.

Moses was often called **the servant of God** (Exod 14:31; Num 12:7; Josh 14:7; 22:5). Both **songs** (Exod 15 and Rev 15:3-4) were victory **songs**. The type was sung for the deliverance at **the sea** that bordered Egypt, and the antitype was sung at the Mediterranean **Sea** after the demands of Petronius had been withdrawn. The seven plagues not only fulfilled the demands of the contract, but they also took the place of the plagues of Egypt, typologically. Once these plagues were over, the Israelites started to leave Egypt and begin their trek to the Promised Land. They came to the body of water at the boundary of Egypt; it opened up before them and closed after them, destroying all of the Egyptian troops. Then Moses and the children of Israel sang the victory **song** recorded in Exod 15. Therefore, as an antitype, the author's vision followed the last plagues with the saints gathered again before **the sea**, playing harps, and singing a **new song of Moses** with the addition that this was also **the song of** the Lamb.

The song that is quoted is comprised almost entirely of words and phrases taken from the First Testament (FT). Since Exod 15 was a **song of** praise to God for his mighty works of deliverance, this **song** also begins eulogizing **God's great and mighty works** but not only those listed in Exod 15.[2] The first words draw attention to Ps 111 which is a complete poem of praise to God for his mighty deeds, mercy, generous provision, redemption, loyalty to his contract, and power in overthrowing other nations. Exod 34 narrates Moses' second reception of the law. He provided it after he narrated the marvelous deeds the Lord had done in their behalf together with many promises and commandments. Shadrach, Meshach, and Abednego were also called **servants of God** (Dan 3:26) when they refused to worship the statue set up by Nebuchadnezzar and were rescued from the fiery furnace.

---

[1] D.E. Aune, *Revelation 6-16* (Nashville: Thomas Nelson Publishers, 1998), p. 873.
[2] Evidently it was the term "Song of Moses" that prompted T. Zahn, *Die Offenbarung des Johannes* (Leipzig: A Deichert, 1924), p. 531, to conclude that the song was not that of Exod 15 but rather Deut 32:3-4, 7-14.

Great and marvelous are your works. The **works** would have been miracles of various kinds, including natural miracles. The **works** this author was interested in were the ones that would aid in defeating the enemy, such as the time when the sun stood still for Joshua (Josh 10:12-13), or when rain fell along the Carmel Mountains and **the stars in their forces fought against Sisera** (Judge 5:20).

Just and true are your ways. Ps 145 is a praise to God for all his mighty works which are narrated from generation to generation. His kingdom is glorious; all of his **ways are just**; he preserves those who love him, but he destroys the wicked. The author of this narrative took some words from that Psalm to remind the reader of the two-fold nature of God. The author has alternately told of the punishment God has for the wicked and the **just** rewards he has for the faithful after they have paid for all of their sins. His allusion to Ps 145 with its alternating rewards and punishment was a reassertion of his convictions. To be delivered at the Mediterranean Sea from the Roman troops and **the beast** meant real punishment for the Romans and real victory for the Jews. The Jews who were threatened with complete extermination were saved, and **the** threatening **beast**, Gaius, was killed. This was not theoretical salvation and punishment; it was very practical from a Jewish point of view.

King of the ages. NA has **king of the nations**. Sweet might be right in saying that **ages** is the more difficult reading, because it might easily be corrected to adjust to Jer 10:7.[1] The counter argument is that since the rest of the sentence is from Jeremiah, it is likely that the entire passage was initially taken from Jeremiah. The possibility, of course, is that at one time there may have been variants of this passage in Jer 10:7 itself. Both readings could apply. As **King of the ages**, God is the one who created **the ages** and put them in their stable arrangements (So Heb 1). As **king of the** nations, he rules the world and is in control over even the hostile nations. Rissi thought the term **ages**, used here could be intended in a temporal sense. It means "an immeasurably long time."[2]

Who will not fear you? **Instead of** *dawx-áh-say* (δοξάση) **for glorify**, NA has *dawx-áh-say* (δοξάσει). Both words are pronounced alike in Greek, so this error is another made from hearing the text read.

Ps 145 tells of God's glorious kingdom, but it was Jeremiah who spoke of him as **King of the nations** and asked, **Who will not fear you**? This is in a context of praise to God for his greatness and wisdom in creating in contrast to the idols that perish. The author of this poem concluded with an appeal to God to pour out his wrath upon the gentiles who had abused the sons of Jacob. This background was also understood as the author picked only two phrases of eulogy to become a part of this hymn.

---

[1] Sweet, *Revelation*, p. 240.
[2] M. Rissi, *Time and History* (Richmond: John Knox Press, 1965), p. 31.

All the nations will come. Ps 86 praises God for his mighty works, echoing a note of praise from Exod 15: **Who is like you among the gods, Lord** (Exod 15:11) with his line, **There is none like you among the gods, Lord** (Ps 86:8). The Psalmist claimed further that **all the nations** would bow down **before** the Lord and glorify his name, and he concluded by asking God to embarrass those who hated the Psalmist while comforting the Psalmist himself. It is also coherent with the picture Zechariah imagined of all the gentiles coming to Jerusalem year after year, **prostrating themselves before** the Lord at the temple. The occasion for this would have been the feast of Tabernacles. These were all ideas the author of the prophecy would approve, and he echoed them in the poem. The song was placed where it occurs, however, as a *hysteron proteron*. That is a literary form in which the last was placed first in order. Typologically, the plagues all come first and then the victory hymn was destined to follow, but here a victory **song** was sung and the plagues were only introduced. The angels had not yet released these seven last plagues. This means the believers had to endure the birth pangs of the messiah before the victory song could be sung with confidence.

The just deeds before you. NA has **your just deeds**. The meanings of the two readings are different. **Your just deeds** are the **deeds** God does. **The just deeds** before him are the **deeds** of others that come before his judgment bench for judgment and to be recognized as virtuous.

TEXT

Revelation	Hebrew Scripture
⁵After this **I was watching**, and the temple of **the tent of testimony** in heaven **opened**, ⁶and the seven angels who had the seven plagues went out from the temple, **wearing** clean bright **linen** [coats], and gold [armored] vests around their chests. ⁷One of the four [heavenly] beasts gave to the seven angels seven golden bowls full of the anger of the God who lives for ages of ages. Amen. ⁸**The temple was filled with smoke**	Exod 40:34 **The cloud covered the tent of testimony** and the glory of the Lord filled the dwelling place. Ezek 1:1 **The heavens were opened**, and **I saw** an appearance of God. Lev 16:4 He shall **wear** a holy **linen coat**. Isa 6:4 The bases of the thresholds shook at the voice of the One who called, and **the smoke filled the temple.** 1Kings 8:11 When the priests went out from the sanctuary, the cloud **filled the temple** of Yehowah, and the

of **the glory of God** and of his power, and no one **was able** to enter into **the temple** until the **seven** plagues of the seven angels were completed.	priests **were not able** to stand to minister before the cloud because **the glory of Yehowah** filled **the temple** of Yehowah. Lev 26:21 If you walk contrary to me, and do not want to pay attention to me, then I will add more **plagues** upon you, **seven** times as many as your crimes. Lev 26:28 I, even I, will punish you **seven** times as many as your crimes.

COMMENTARY

The temple of the tent of testimony in heaven. This could be the beginning of a fifth scene, although Strand considered it only a part of the fourth of the scenes belonging to the prophecy brought to John.[1] In support of Strand's position is the content of the entire material from Rev 15:1 to 16:21. It is all directed to the Exodus from Egypt and the affliction of plagues. Furthermore, Rev 15:1 says the sign **in heaven** was about the angel having the **last plagues**. On the other hand, Rev 15:1-4 is all directed to the Exodus, whereas Rev 15:5 begins a new section dealing with **the plagues**, and it starts with a new introduction calling attention to **the temple in heaven** being open.

A later editor probably put two units together, because they contained subject material that was related. As it now stands, Strand is probably correct in considering the two parts as one unit, but he may have been mistaken about the end of the unit. He thought the next scene began with the seventh plague (Rev 16:18), which seems to be part of the narrative that contains the other six **plagues**, concluding with Rev 16:21. The conclusion of the unit with both noises associated with the confirmation of the contract at Sinai and the destruction of enemy locations is appropriate to the unit. The precise division of units in the Book of Revelation cannot be set with absolute certainty. Scholars will continue to disagree about these.

The description of **the temple of heaven** here as elsewhere in this document is based on descriptions of **the temple** at Jerusalem or **the tent of testimony** in the wilderness, which continued to be valid in Zion before Solomon's temple was built. David had a large altar and a tent adjacent to it which sheltered the chest containing the contract. In heavenly scenes the tent, rather than the temple often appears.

---

[1] K. A. Strand, "The 'Victorious-Introduction' Scenes in the Visions in the Book of Revelation," *AUSS* 25 (1987), 274-76. Strand started his division of visions with Rev 1:1, considering John's introduction to be itself part of the total unit.

The tent of testimony is that which Moses directed for Aaron and his sons to manage. The angels were dressed like priests, ministering at feasts. The vest of gold was probably something like armor made of small plates. Armored vests were usually made of iron or steel, but these were primarily for decoration, so they were of gold. **The temple in heaven** was filled with smoke just as the Jerusalem **temple** had been when Isaiah saw the Lord and when Solomon dedicated **the temple**. The smoke was the "glory" of the Lord. When the high priest entered the holy of holies on the Day of Atonement, he always threw incense ahead of him, filling the area with smoke, so that he would not see the Lord with unclouded vision (mYoma 5:1).

The seven angels who had the seven plagues. **The plagues** were those promised (Lev 26) to Israelites as punishment if they failed to keep the contract they made with the Lord.

God who lives for ages of ages. Amen. NA omits the **amen**.

The four [heavenly] beasts. **The beasts** who gave the angels the bowls should not be confused with **the beasts** who were antitypes of Antiochus Epiphanes. The latter were human politicians who were under the jurisdiction of the enemy. **The beasts** related to the altar were heavenly beings that looked like sphinxes. They were cherubim and seraphim; they were good monsters that looked like bats. They had six wings, a head like a human being or a lion; they had hooves like goats and super-human senses.

The seven gold bowls. **The bowls** were full of the anger of God who was sometimes reported to "pour out his anger" on his enemies (Jer 10:25; Ps 69:25; Zeph 3:8). The action of the angels, pouring out God's anger, may simply have been dramatized by having angels pour out **bowls** of different kinds of anger. Pouring out God's anger was involved in any case, but there may have been some magic involved. When they were emptied, certain prescribed actions began. There was evidently something in **the bowls** that caused the succeeding action. Ford's interpretation of this situation is thought-provoking, and probably correct. She argued that the bowls involved were like modern cereal **bowls**, but they had a very different purpose. These had texts engraved on them which were designed to bind and seal specified demons and liliths and prevent them from functioning in certain specific ways. Some scholars have argued that these **bowls** are of the wrong shape for such use. Demons, they say, would be closed up in bottles with lead seals at the top,[1] but bowls were used in ways like this, as the following example shows:

    Solomon was reported to have overpowered a demon that caused shipwrecks and other problems at the sea by having the demon cast into a broad, flat **bowl**--not a bottle. Then he had sea water poured over it; he strengthened it with marble, pitch, and hemp rope around the mouth of the vessel. Then he sealed it with a magic ring and stored it in the temple (TSol 16:6-7). Charm **bowls** like this that were used in

---

[1] C. D. Isbell, *Corpus of the Aramaic Incantation Bowls* (Missoula: Scholars Press, c1975), pp. 13-15.

antiquity to overcome evil forces have been discovered by archaeologists. Some of them have been found in pairs with their rims sealed together with pitch or tied together. As long as these **bowls** were sealed and stored in temples, as Solomon's was, in foundations of houses, or in tombs, as some were that archaeologists found, the demons were supposedly under control. One example of the text for an incantation bowl is the following:

> Bound and sealed are the house and the life of Ishpiza, son of Archa, and Yandundishnat, son of (2) Isipandarmed, and . . . daughter of Simkoi, from Sun and heat, from the devil, Satan, and both male demons 3) the female lilith, evil spirits, and impious Amulet-spirit, male or female lilith-spirits, the eye of man (or) (4) woman; the eye of contumely; the eye which looks right into the mind; the mystery which belongs to the evil power, that impious lord; from the evil, power (5) [which is] hateful; from disturbing vision; from evil spirits; from that impious lord, in the name of . . ..[1]

In one of Zechariah's visions, he saw a container which held all of the wickedness of the land of Palestine, and it was sealed with a lead cover. Two women with wings came and carried the container away from Palestine to Babylon where they planned to leave it. "Wickedness" in the container was personified as a woman. Once this wickedness was removed to Babylon, the Promised Land that was about to be restored would be free from evil (Zech 5:5-11). The idea that wickedness might be sealed in a container and removed from a place seems to reflect the same thought-form illustrated in the bowls that seal demons inside to keep them from being effective. The idea that the devil and Satan might be thrown into a bottomless pit and sealed for a thousand years may reflect the same belief (Rev 20:1-3).

The bowls used by angels here in Rev 15 and 16 may have been designed initially to seal in God's anger, just as other incantation bowls were created to seal in the demonic forces. These **bowls** had been sealed to prevent plagues like those of Egypt from taking place. These plagues differed from the plagues in Egypt to the extent that they were directed to the Promised Land and its surrounding area. They were directed against the unrighteous gentiles and Jews on the land, thereby cleansing the land from all wickedness so that the Kingdom of Heaven could be established there. When the angels broke the charm and poured out the anger of God, they allowed the plagues to take place.[2] When demons are released people are injured. Here, God's anger was released for the same purpose. Between chapters

---

[1] Slightly modified translation from that given by J. A. Montgomery, *Aramaic Incantation Texts from Nippur* (Philadelphia: University Museum, 1913), p. 221, on the basis of the Aramaic text given there.
[2] J. M. Ford, "The Structure and Meaning of Revelation 16," *ET* 98 (1987):329-31. H. P. Millere, "Die Plagen der Apokalypse," *ZNW* 51 (1960):268-78, observed the magic, not only in Revelation but also in the Book of Exodus. He held that Moses and Aaron also used magic to bring about the plagues.

twelve and thirteen are two photographs of one of the **bowls** archaeologists have discovered that were used to prevent demons from damaging people.[1] Incantation bowls like this had curses written inside. Two bowls were then sealed together with the rims touching, sealing in the curses so that they could not be effected. Wheneveer the seals were broken the curses would be released. That was the picture the author of this section of Revelation intended to portray, when the angels broke the seals and poured out God's anger, releasing all of the plagues upon people on earth.

Ford was correct in thinking that, according to Revelation, God would have to punish Israel before the contract could be renewed,[2] but that was done when the seven seals were broken (Rev 6:1-17; 8:1-5). Why is there a second instance of the seven last plagues being given in the Book of Revelation? The probable reason is that the editor had in his possession two narratives devoted to the plagues that come as a result of the curses of the contract. Not only did both narratives direct punishments to the Promised Land, but they both required seals to be broken before they could happen. The editor chose to use both narratives.

The seven seals that were bound around the scroll kept the contract between the Lord and his people from being made (Rev 5:1-6:17; 8:1). When those seals were broken the contract could be renewed. When the angels of Rev 15 and 16 took the **bowls**, they broke the seals, releasing all of the evil powers that were sealed there. Prior to this event, the seals prevented the chosen people from receiving the curses of the contract. The contract, however, had been broken, and the prescribed curses had to be put into action before the contract could be renewed. Although both narratives included curses, the first narrative (Rev 5, 6, and 8) punished people; the second (Rev 15-16) punished the situation around the Promised Land--the land, the sea, the springs, the sun, the Euphrates, Jerusalem and Megiddo.

No one was able to enter the temple. This is understood as an antitype of the Hasmonean revolt. That revolt began with the defilement of **the temple** by Antiochus Epiphanes. At that point the Hasmonean brothers led a guerrilla war against the Syrian Greeks. For 3½ years **the temple** had been defiled, and Jews were not permitted to worship there until Judas won the famous battle of Beth-horon, and **the temple** was cleansed, rededicated, and functions continued. The 3½ year Hasmonean war functioned as the seven last plagues required by Leviticus to pay for all the sins committed which broke the contract God made with his people. When the temple was cleansed, Jews understood that the sins had been cancelled; the Jews had suffered the required plagues; and the kingdom was in the process of being restored.

At the time when Rev 15 was written, some Jews, at least, considered **the temple** defiled. This could have been the case any time during the first century. There were communities, like those reflected in some of the Dead Sea Scrolls, that

---

[1] These pictures were taken, and permission for their use was granted by The University Museum, University of Pennsylvania (Negative numbers S4-140948 CBS 16096: interior view of Bowl from Nippur and S4-140949 CBS 16096: Side view of Bowl from Nippur).
[2] J. M. Ford, "Structure," p. 329.

performed their own religious activities apart from the temple at Zion, because they thought **the temple** and its priesthood were improper. Near the end of the war of the Jews against the Romans in 66-70 IA **the temple** was in control of the Jewish zealots who alone worshiped there. It was not accessible to others most of the time.

Until the seven plagues of the seven angels were completed. The word **complete** was used both in the first verse (Rev 15:1) and in the last verse (Rev 15:8), showing that this chapter was composed as a unit. It was probably composed, however, after the **song** (Rev 15:3-4) had already been a standard part of Jewish liturgy.

The angels obediently took their golden **bowls** and went out to **start the seven last plagues**. Although these **plagues** were like **the plagues** in Egypt, they seem to have been directed against Palestine rather than against any foreign land. These were the **plagues** inflicted on the Israelites because of their sin in breaking the contract rather than the Egyptians because they refused to allow the Israelites to return to the Promised Land. The author of this document wrote when he believed that **the plagues** were taking place, but at a time when they were not yet over.

The seven plagues which were first mentioned here continue through Rev 16. These are the punishments directed to Israel. The first of these **angels,** however, appeared again in later chapters. In Rev 17:1 he announced the destruction of the harlot, and in Rev 21:9 provided a vision of the new Jerusalem coming down from heaven.

CHAPTER SIXTEEN

INTRODUCTION

Rev 16 is an important chapter that has often been misinterpreted because it mixes important history with coded terms and a great deal of scriptural references. This is an attempt to untangle all of this and expose the strategic history involved.

TEXT

Revelation	First Testament
	$^{Isa\ 66:6}$A noise of tumult from the city; **a voice from the temple**, the **voice** of *Yehowah*, paying back his enemies.
$^{16:1}$I heard **a** loud **voice from the temple** saying to the seven angels,	
"Go and **pour out** the seven bowls **of the wrath** of God toward the land." [^{2}Then the first angel went away and poured out his bowl toward the land]	$^{Jer\ 10:25}$**Pour out** your **wrath** upon the gentiles who do not know you.
	$^{Ps\ 69:25}$**Pour out** upon them your **anger**! Let the burning **of your nostrils** overtake them.
	$^{Zeph\ 3:8}$To gather the kingdoms together, to **pour out** upon them my **wrath**--all the burning **of my nostrils**.
	$^{Ezek\ 22:31}$I **poured out my anger** upon them; with the fire of my wrath I consumed them.
	$^{Exod\ 9:10}$They took the ashes of the furnace, and they stood before Pharaoh,

and there appeared an **evil** and a bad **boil** upon the people who had the mark of the beast and those who worshiped his image.	and Moses sprinkled them toward heaven, **and there appeared** inflammation producing **boils.** Deut 28:35 The Lord will strike [you] with terrible **boils** on your knees and on your legs which cannot be healed from the sole of your foot to the top of your head.
³[The second (angel) poured out] his bowl toward the sea, **and it** became **blood** as dead, and every soul **living upon the** sea **died**.	Exod 7:17 Look! I will strike with the wand which is in my hand the water of the Nile, **and it will** change to **blood**. Exod 7:21 The fish **that were in the** Nile **died**; the Nile became polluted; and the Egyptians were not able to drink water from the Nile.
⁴The third [angel] poured out his bowl upon **the rivers** and **their** springs **of water, and it became blood.**	Exod 7:19 Take your wand and reach out your hand over the waters of Egypt; over **their rivers**, their canals, their ponds, and **their** pools **of water, and they will become blood.**

COMMENTARY

A voice from the temple. This means the events reported and anticipated mythologically were designated to take place when **the temple** was still standing--sometime before 70 IA. **The voice** from **the temple**, where God was present, is assumed to have been the **voice of God**. There is a report that just before the temple was burned, from **the temple** the sound of a crowd was heard, saying, "We are leaving here" (War 6:300). Since the plural subject is used, it may mean that God and all of his ministering angels had spoken. The message from **the temple** meant that God was no longer present. **The voice from the temple** in this case was an order from God to **the seven angels** under his command.

The seven angels. This was a different group of **angels** from those who broke the seals around the scroll. These were directed to the physical situation of the Promised Land. In the two previous series, the seals and the trumpets, there was an interruption between the sixth and the seventh item. That is not true of this third series.

Pour out the seven bowls of the wrath of God. **The bowls** used here were normally used for libation or drinking. Isa 66 predicted the Lord punishing his enemies as he restored Zion. Ps 69 is a plea to the Lord to save the poet from his enemies by **pouring out** his anger upon them. Zephaniah promised that the Lord would destroy Nineveh, that city which North Israelites hated as much as Jews hated Babylon. Israelites had only to wait for the Lord until the day when he would **pour out** his anger upon his enemies. As these angels **poured out** their **bowls**, different types of the Egyptian plagues came upon the people. The new Exodus, described in Rev 15, was the victory over the foreign enemy.

The bracketed words. The bracketed words in Rev 16:2 and 3 are included by NA, but are not part of the Sinaiticus text. The words omitted in Rev 16:2 represent a homeoteleuton error on the part of the Sinaiticus scribe. The word **homeoteleuton** comes from the Greek "same end." When a person is copying a text and finds two lines that end with the same word, it is easy to make a mistake and take the second for the first and omit all of the words in between. That is a homeoteleuton error. In this case the reader dropped from **the land** in Rev 16:1 to a second reference to **the land** in the same place in the line in Rev 16:2, leaving out the words in between. The second omission is more confused. In its present form it makes no sense. It says, ... **who had the mark of the beast and those who worship his image into his bowl toward the sea, and it became blood**. The best solution in this case is to follow the texts approved by NA.

Evil and bad boil. This was the antitype of one of the plagues of Egypt (Exod 9:10-11).[1]

It became blood as dead. In Egypt, the *rivers* **became blood** (Exod 7:17-21), but here, it is the **sea**, first of all, where every living creature **died**. Corpses were defiled so that anyone who touched one would be defiled for eight days and would have to be cleansed by a special liturgy afterward. **Blood** from someone **dead** (a corpse) would be extensively defiling. Since Rome was the enemy, the **sea** involved may have been the Mediterranean **Sea**. In one way or another the damage was intended to hurt Israel's enemies, just as the plagues in Egypt injured the Egyptians rather than the Israelites.

Every soul living on the sea died. Sinaiticus has a different meaning from that accepted by NA. According to NA **Every living creature that was in the sea died**. That meant all of the fish, turtles, alligators, and other sea creatures. Sinaiticus understood that the plague fell only on those who sailed or worked on ships on the sea.

The NA text would not apply to the Dead Sea where there would have been no living creatures, except a few small fish at the spots where the water from the

---

[1] See S. H. Kio, "The Exodus Symbol of Liberation in the Apocalypse and its Relevance for Some Aspects of Translation," *BT* 40 (1989):120-35, for a discussion of the extent of influence the Book of Exodus has had on the Book of Revelation.

springs of Ein Feshka and Ein Gedi flowed into the sea. The sea involved would either have been the Mediterranean Sea or the Sea of Galilee.

Upon the rivers. NA has **toward the rivers**. It was the third plague (Exod 7:17-21).

TEXT

Revelation

⁵Then I heard the angel of the waters saying, "**Righteous are you**

who is and **who was**,

the holy One, because you have judged these things, ⁶because
**they have poured out the
blood** of the saints and the prophets,

and you have given
them blood to drink. which [saints and prophets] are worthy." ⁷Then I

First Testament

ᴺᵉʰ ⁹:⁸You upheld your word, because **righteous are you**

Ps 119:137**Righteous are you, Yehowah**, and just are your judgments.

Ps 145:17**Righteous is** the **Lord** in all his ways, merciful in all his acts.

MTExod 3:14God said to Moses, "I am **whoever I am.** Thus you shall say to the children of Israel, `I am' sent me to you."

OGExod 3:14God said to Moses, "I am the one **who is.**"

OGPs 144:17**Righteous is** the **Lord** in all his ways, **holy** in all his acts.

2Kings 19:22Against whom have you raised your voice and arrogantly raised your eyes? Against
the holy One of Israel.

Ps 79:3**They have poured out their blood** like water around Jerusalem, and there is no one to bury [them].

Isa 49:26[Your oppressors] will be **drunk** with their own **blood.**

heard the altar saying,

"**Lord, God of armies**.

True and just are your judgments."

^(Amos 3:13)Hear and bear witness against the house of Jacob, says **the Lord God of armies**.

^(Ps 19:10)The **judgments** of Yehowah are **true [and] just** altogether.

COMMENTARY

Righteous are you. One of the things Greek rhetoricians, such as Aristotle and Quintillian, taught their students in trial techniques was how to control the judge. Attorneys were taught to learn about the judge, his prejudices, interests, and weaknesses. Then they were expected to flatter the judge judiciously to gain his favor before the trial began. It is a judge's responsibility to establish justice and be righteous in his or her judgments. Each attorney would tell the judge what it meant to be righteous as, of course, the judge was. This is the technique applied here in the prayer to God.

The author of this prophecy blamed the enemies for the sins they committed against the **righteous** ones, but just as with the hardening of Pharaoh's heart, he thought everything was part of God's plan. God's judgment was **righteous,** and his punishment was just. It was God who gave the enemy permission to drink the blood of the saints and prophets, but they were Jewish prophets and saints, and it was the Jews who had broken contract. Just as in Egypt the Israelites had to be afflicted before God sent plagues to the Egyptians, so here the prophets and saints were killed before God would pass judgment upon the enemies of Israel. Their injury made martyrs of the prophets and saints; it also helped fill up the deficit that was on record. Before this, the saints had their blood shed at the altar in heaven. The prophets and saints were citizens of Israel, the Promised Land. They were the ones required to pay off some of the seven last obligations owed to the Lord because Jews had broken contract. The martyrs were probably those Jews who had been killed in rebellious conflicts with the Romans.

Nehemiah called the Lord **righteous** because he fulfilled his contract with his chosen people and gave them the land he promised them (Neh 9:7-9, 33; see also Jer 12:1; 2Chron 12:6; Ezra 9:15). The expression **Righteous are you!** is at once a confession and a reminder. Because of their status judges are always **righteous** no matter how unfair they are. Whatever they decide is legally correct. This is especially true of the highest court of appeals. After a court trial is over, both the plaintiff and the defendant are expected to address the judge with the formal expression, "Thank you, your honor." Even the losing party has to acknowledge the judge's authority and admit that his decision was **righteous.** Part of the technique, recommended by both famous rhetoricians, Aristotle and Quintillian, and used by lawyers ever since in obtaining a verdict that meets their needs is to flatter the judge, as the angel of the waters is reported here as doing. While admitting that God, as judge, was legally **righteous**, the angel also hoped to remind the judge that it was his duty to function fairly, which the angel thought was to act as the angel advocated.

The content of the situation does not necessarily point to Hellenistic influences, as Betz suggests.[1] To be sure, there were Hellenistic influences on Jewish thought-forms from the time of Alexander the Great, but the fact that pagans also worshipped deities they believed controlled the powers of nature does not mean these notions came only from Hellenism. They were part of Israelite, Samaritan, and Christian beliefs as early as the Exodus from Egypt.

Which [saints and prophets] are worthy. NA does not have the word here translated as **which** (*háw-payr,* ὅπερ).

The saints and the prophets are worthy--not the ones **who poured out** their **blood**. Because they were faithful to death, the prophets and saints were considered **worthy**. They were blameless, accepted, meritorious, etc. The altar, where their **blood** had been **poured**, recognized God's justice in allowing this to be done. The crime that the Jews had committed had to be punished; the debts had to be paid. This would require unrewarded merit. Sooner or later, this debt would be paid up, and there would be a balance on hand of Jewish merit. When that happened the tide would turn, and foreign criminals would be punished. Also the fourth [angel] **poured out his bowl** upon the sun, and there was given it [permission] to scorch human beings with fire, and people were scorched [with] burning heat. They blasphemed the name of the God who has authority over these plagues, but they did not repent and give him glory.

Then I heard the altar saying. Hebrews frequently personified inanimate objects, especially in praise. For example, the heavens, the earth, the desert, the fields, the trees, Mount Tabor, Mount Hermon, Mount Zion, and the land, were all ordered to rejoice (1Chron 16:31, 32; Ps 97:1; Isa 35:1; 1Chron 16:32; Ps 96:12). In Rev 3:12 the one who conquers is promised that he or she would become a pillar in God's temple--evidently an animate pillar.[2] Rev 9:13-14 pictures the altar speaking.

Lord God of armies. Literally, this renders the Greek **Lord, God, the almighty one**, but the Greek renders the Hebrew *ah-doh-naí Yehowáh eh-loh-háy hah tseh-váh-ohth* (אדוני יהוה אלהי הצבעות), Lord, **Yehowah, God of the armies** (Amos 3:13). This is the title given most often to the Lord in the Scripture. This is the response given by **the altar.**

---

[1] H. D. Betz, "Zum Problem des religionsgeschichtlichen Verständnisses der Apokalyptik," *ZTK* 63 (1966):591-609. See also P. Staples, "Rev XVI 4-6 and its Vindication Formula," *NovT* 14 (1972):280-93.
[2] So D. C. Allison, Jr., "4 Q 403 Fragm. I, Col. I, 38-46 and the Revelation to John," *RQ* 47 (1986):412-13.

TEXT

⁸Then the fourth [angel] poured out its bowl upon the sun, and there was given to it [authority] to burn human beings with fire. ⁹The human beings were scorched with a great heat, and they blasphemed the name of God who has the authority over these plagues, but they did not repent and give him glory.

COMMENTARY

The fourth bowl caused a tremendous heat wave. In the Near East a heat wave is called a *hahm-seén*, from the Arabic word for "five," because *hahm-seéns* usually last five days. This happens when the winds change so that instead of receiving the cool breeze from the Mediterranean Sea, the land is blistered by the hot desert winds. The author did not say that this plague had any limitation to its time nor the direction of the wind, but the bowl poured on the sun. The awkward phrase **there was given to it** is set in the passive voice to avoid using the name of God. It means God gave the sun permission to scorch people with this terrific heat wave. This was a judgment scene during which the divine judge decreed that the people would be tortured until they gave him glory, but that objective was not achieved. People still blasphemed God for causing the plagues.

TEXT

Revelation	First Testament
¹⁰The fifth [angel] poured out his bowl on the throne of the beast, and his kingdom **became dark**.	$^{Exod\ 10:21}$Then the Lord said to Moses, "Extend your hand over the heaven, and the Land of Egypt will become dark."
	$^{Isa\ 8:21-22}$He will look to the earth, and look! Hardship, **darkness** of oppresssion, and gloom of anguish.
[People] chewed their tongues from the suffering, ¹¹and they blasphemed **the God of heaven** because of their grief, but they did not repent.	$^{Dan\ 2:19}$Daniel blessed **the God of heaven**.

COMMENTARY

Caird observed that the last three plagues of trumpets and the last three **plagues** of the **bowls** had similar peculiarities. The fifth introduced darkness, the sixth, an army from the Euphrates, and the seventh, earthquakes and thunder.[1] There are even more resemblances between the two series, as the following comparison shows:

Trumpets	Bowls
1.--Hail and fire mingled with blood.	Sore.
2.--Sea turned into blood.	Sea turned into blood.
3.--Rivers and fountains made bitter.	Rivers and fountains turned into blood. Scorching heat
4.--Darkness.	Darkness in the kingdom of the beast.
5.--Demon locusts.	Drying up of Euphrates and gathering of kings at Har-magedon.
6.--Demon horsemen from Euphrates.	
7.--Lightnings, voices, thunders, earthquake, hail.	Lightnings, voices, thunders, earthquake, fall of cities, hail.

The fifth plague was to recall the event in Egypt when Moses raised his wand to heaven and the sun **became dark** for three days--so **dark** that people could not see one another, but in the homes of the Israelites it was light (Exod 10:22). All of these afflictions, weather conditions, health problems, and damage to natural resources caused much pain and hardship, but those unsaintly people cursed God rather than repenting. The author did not say which "beast" was involved. It might have been either Herod the Great or Herod Agrippa I. In either case the throne would have been in Jerusalem rather than Rome.[2] There were seven *last* plagues to be afflicted as punishment before the **kingdom** was restored. A later medieval Jewish redemption document is coherent with the idea that Israel must be punished before it is redeemed. It is called "The Signs of the Messiah."[3]

TEN SIGNS WILL COME TO THE WORLD BEFORE THE END

The first sign

---

[1] G. B. Caird, *A Commentary on the Revelation of St. John the Divine* (London: Black, c1966), p. 204; G. Bornkamm, *Studien zu Antike und Urchristentum* (Munich: Kaiser, 1963), p. 206.

[2] Contra M. E. Boring, *Revelation* (Louisville: Westminster Press, c1989), pp. 175-77.

[3] There are three Hebrew texts for this document. They are parallel, but not identical. The text translated here is that of M. Higger, *Halakah and Haggadah* [Hebrew] (Brooklyn, 1933), pp. 127-30. Other texts are A. Jellinek, *Beth Ha-Midrasch* [Hebrew] (6 vols: Jerusalem: Wahrman Books, 1967) II, pp. 58-63 and A. Marmorstein, "Le Signes du Messie," *REJ* 52 (1906):176-86. These have all been translated into English and shown in parallel relationship in Buchanan, *Jewish Messianic Movements from AD 70 to AD 1300* (Eugene, Oregon: Wipf and Stock Publishers, 2003), pp. 486-506.

The holy One blessed be He is destined to send three angels with the three winds of the world. They will deny the [very] existence of God and show themselves to the sons of man as if they were serving him, and they will subdue human beings. At *the end of days* (Dan 2:28; 12:13), all gentiles will deny the [very] existence of God, as it is said, **The idols shall utterly be cut off,**[1] and **the idols will utterly pass away** (Isa 2:18), because the holy One blessed be He will display troubles in the world, each different from the other.

The second sign

The holy One blessed be He will bring out the sun from its sheath, and with it he will burn each day millions of gentiles until all the gentiles will weep and say, "Woe to us! Where can we flee?" They will dig up all the caves in the land to find relief for themselves, as it is said, **They will go into caves and rocks** (Isa 2:21). One will say to the other, "Come into the rock and hide in the earth!" Concerning that sun, Malachi prophesied, as it is said, **For look! the day of the Lord [is coming], burning like an oven** (Mal 3:19), but that sun will bring healing for the Israelites, as it is said, **For those of you who fear my name, the sun of righteousness will rise, and healing will be in its wings** (Mal 3:20). Concerning those hardships, the wicked Balaam prophesied, as it is said, **Also, who will survive after God has appointed him** (Num 24:23).

The third sign

The holy One blessed be He will cause dew of blood to descend for three days.[2] It will appear to the gentiles to be a dew of water, so they will drink of it and die.[3] Even the transgressors of Israel will drink of it and die. The moderate [criminals] will become ill, and the world

---

[1] This text is apparently not from the Scriptures, but the author thought it was.
[2] The three days was probably taken from David's choice of three days of pestilence as his punishment for having taxed Israel (2Sam 24:13).
[3] M. L. Margolis and A. Marx, *A History of the Jewish People* (London: 1927), p. 404, told that during the "Black Death" epidemic that was imported into Europe from India and carried off more than one third of the population, the notion arose that Jews were causing the disease by poisoning the wells and rivers that supplied the drinking water. This idea was probably based on the report that Moses was able to change the waters of Egypt into blood (Exod 7). Since Jews drank the same water, theological views such as these may have given rise to such suspicions. If Jews believed God would provide water that would cause gentiles to die and Jews to survive, a serious plague might suggest to Jews as well as to Christians that this was actually happening. Since Jews were international merchants, they were probably some of those who brought the disease to Europe from India, but they also died from it. In that age when all people were superstitious, it is not reasonable to expect that people could have deduced the real cause of the disease. It was normal both for Jews and Christians to find religious explanations for the disease.

will be in great distress during those three days, as it is said, **I will provide wonders in heaven and on earth, blood, fire, and pillars of smoke** (Joel 3:3).

The fourth sign

The holy One blessed be He will bring down healing dew for three days and three nights to heal the blood. All moderate [criminals] will drink from it. The sick will be healed, as it is said, **I will be as dew to the Israelites. They will blossom as the lily, [and cast forth their roots like a (cedar of) Lebanon]** (Hos 14:6).

The fifth sign

A king will arise in Rome, and he will destroy great states, and he will conquer Egypt, as it is said, **He will stretch out his hand against the North** (Zeph 2:13).[1] In his anger, he will turn against the Israelites and impose a heavy tribute upon them, and he will wish to destroy them from the world, as it is said, **He will turn his face to the strongholds of the land** (Dan 11:19). These [the strongholds] are the Israelites, because they are the strongest among the nations, and **his face** refers to his anger and wrath which he will place upon them.

The sixth sign

The holy One blessed be He will in that hour bring out the Messiah son of Joseph, whose name is Nehemiah ben Hoshiel, and with mighty men from the sons of Zerah, son of Judah, as it is said, **"Suddenly, the Lord for whom you are looking will come to his temple. [The messenger of the contract in whom you take delight, look! he is coming," says the Lord of armies]** (Mal 3:1). All the armies of Israel who are in those places will accompany him and war will be waged against the king of Edom. The rest will flee and come to Jerusalem and capture it. All the Israelites will hear and gather themselves to him. The king of Egypt will make peace with him, and he will slay all the gentiles that are around Jerusalem. Then the nations will hear, and great dread will fall upon them.

---

[1] This text is difficult or impossible to follow. Egypt was not from the North, either for Roman Christians or Arabian Moslems, although it more nearly applies to the latter, particularly with reference to the Fatimids who began in Yemen (901 IA), conquered Tunisia (908 IA), and finally Egypt (969 IA). From there, they moved still farther north and east until they conquered Baghdad itself, taking Palestine on the way.

The seventh sign

Armilos will come forth from that stone of a woman which is in Rome, and they will say of him that a great stone gave him birth. His length will be eighteen feet and his width, three feet. There will be a distance of a span between his eyes. He will be the Messiah of the sons of Esau. He will gather all the nations and say to the sons of Esau, "Bring me the Torah which I gave you." At once all Israelites will be startled. Nehemiah ben Hoshiel will rise up, he and thirty [thousand] mighty men with weapons of war under their garments. They will take the Book of the Torah, and they will come and read to him, **You shall have no other gods before me** (Exod 20:3). He will say to them, "Is this nothing at all?" Nehemiah will say to him, "You are not god, but Satan!" He will take to flight, and [Armilos] will say to those who serve him, "Look for him and hang him!" [Nehemiah] will make war with him and strike down many of them.

Immediately the anger of Armilos will kindle, and he will gather all the gentiles and come to fight with Israelites between the sea . . . and the holy . . . The Israelites will strike them mightily, and he [Armilos] will kill the Messiah. When the Israelites see the Messiah has been killed, their hearts will melt, and they will flee.

The world will be in great distress. For twenty-five days, there will be those who will hide themselves in caves and holes. Those who are left will be locked in the midst of Jerusalem. He will set his face to fight against it and destroy it a second time, but he will not be successful.

The eighth sign

At that time Michael, the great prince, will arise (Dan 12:1). Then Elijah will come with the Messiah son of David to fulfill that which was said, **He will turn the hearts of the fathers to the children and the hearts of the children to the fathers** (Mal 3:24). The Messiah will not be required to fight. He will fix his gaze on Armilos and destroy him from the world, as it is said, **With the breath of his lips he will slay the wicked** (Isa 11:4).

The ninth sign

The Messiah will ask from the holy One blessed be He to restore life to the dead, and the Messiah son of Joseph will be the first to come to life again. He will be the agent of the Messiah son of David. [The son of David] will send him [the son of Joseph] into all the lands where there are Israelites. They will be gathered from all the corners, and he [the son of David] will send him [the son of Joseph] beyond the river Cush, and he will bring out the ten tribes,[1] and he will bring out the vessels of the temple of the Lord from Rome. Every place where the Messiah son of Joseph enters there will be dead Israelites. He will revive them. All of them will come with him, as it is said, **Look! these will come from afar** (Isa 49:12).

The tenth sign

The coming of Gog and Magog, as it is written in the Book of Ezekiel (Ezek 38-39). May the holy One blessed be He grant us merit to see [him]. Amen! and quickly, in our days! May this be his will. Amen.

These ten signs provide injury and damage both for Israelites and for their enemies, but the final affliction will be to the gentiles. Just as in Egypt, Israelites suffered before the Egyptians were plagued, and Israelites were redeemed, so Jews expected to suffer again just before being rescued from their enemies.

Because of their grief. NA adds **and from their boils**.

They did not repent. NA adds **of their deeds**. In Egypt it was the Pharaoh and his gentile associates whose hearts were hardened after each of the curses. Here, of course, it would also be the enemies of Israel--the beast, the migrants, and their supporters.

TEXT

Revelation	First Testament and Other Jewish Literature
	Gen 15:14-15; see also Deut 1:7; Josh 1:4; Isa 11:15-16; 44:27; Jer 50:38 On that day Yehowah made with Abraham a contract, saying, "To your descendants I will give this land, from the river of Egypt to **the Great River, the River [Euphrates]**."
[12] The sixth [angel] poured out his bowl upon **the Great River Euphrates**,	
	4Ezra 13:43-44 [The ten tribes] entered by

---

[1] There was a deeply imbedded belief in medieval Judaism that the ten lost tribes were hidden in Africa and the East. In the days of the Messiah they would present themselves with thousands of well-trained and armed troops to defeat the gentiles, thus running interference for the Jews.

and its water
was dried up so that the way might be prepared for the

kings **from the East**. ¹⁶He will gather them together to a place called Armegiddo in Hebrew.

the narrow passages of **the Euphrates River**, for then the Most High performed signs for them. He stopped the channels of the river until they crossed over.

$^{Jer\ 50:35}$"A sword upon the Chaldeans," says Yehowah...
³⁸a sword upon **its water, and it will dry up**.

$^{Isa\ 41:2}$Who stirred up one **from the East**?
Victory meets him as he walks.

$^{Isa\ 41:25}$I stirred up one **from the** North, and he has come **from the rising of the sun.** He will call on my name.

COMMENTARY

The great river Euphrates. **The Euphrates River** was one of the northern borders of the Promised Land in the judgment of Jews of New Testament (NT) times.[1] This angel prepared the situation to receive help from a foreign nation. This was nothing new for Israelite and Jewish tradition. Although the prophets warned against entangling alliances with foreign nations and spoke of these alliances as "adultery" and "harlotry," nonetheless, Jewish recovery and maintenance of the Promised Land had depended heavily on outside military and financial support. The author of this document alluded to **the one from the East,** who, during the Babylonian captivity when Second Isaiah wrote, was Cyrus of Persia.

Cyrus was a friend of the Jews who helped them obtain their freedom to return to the Promised Land. Jews had negotiated with Cyrus, while they were in Babylon, to assist him from the inside in his attempt to overthrow Babylon if he would support them in their plans to reestablish the Promised Land. During the first century IA Jews expected another "Cyrus" to come to their aid from the East. Some have suggested that since Babylon is a code name for Rome that probably **the Euphrates** was also a code name for the Tiber, but that does not follow. **The Euphrates** was the **river** that was east from a Palestinian point of view, and it was expected to dry up so that the kings of the East could cross it. This makes no sense in relationship to the Tiber.

---

[1] Initially, the Great River was not the Euphrates but *Náh-hahr eel kah-beér,* "The Great River," at the northern border of Lebanon. See Buchanan, *The Consequences of the Covenant* (Leiden: E. J.Brill, 1970), pp. 91-109.

The kings of the East. This was not a frivolous expectation. There were reports of similar natural miracles having taken place before. For example, the Pamphylian Sea was said to have receded before Alexander the Great when he set out to overthrow the Persian empire (Arrian 1:26; Strabo 14:666-67; Ant 2:347-48).

When Cyrus of Persia captured Babylon he diverted the Euphrates, drying up the river bed so that Cyrus and his troops could enter Babylon on a feast day, taking Babylon without a serious conflict, because the Babylonians were drunk (Herodotus, *Hist* 1:189-91). Shea argued, on the basis of Isa 44:24-45:6 that the river dried up without any diversion.[1] At the right season, the Euphrates might have been low, so that there would not have been much diversion required. Herodotus probably reported the event more accurately than we can conjecture today, but either way, it would seem miraculous, in any event, because it provided an opportunity for Jews of Babylon to return to Palestine. It might have been one of the bases upon which the author of this pericope reasoned when he wrote the unit. Second Isaiah knew in advance that Cyrus was planning this event. Apparently Cyrus was not just responding to a coincidental dry period. If the river had been low, it would have been easier to divert.

Not only in the Greek tradition was there a famous miracle of nature, but there was an important miracle performed for the Israelites when they escaped from Egypt. The water receded, and Israelites crossed over on dry ground (Exod 14-15). When Joshua led the Israelites into the Promised Land, the waters of the Jordan River stopped their flow until the Israelites had crossed over (Josh 3:7-17). A Jewish contemporary of the author anticipated the Lord drying up **the Euphrates** so that the Israelites could cross over (4Ezra 13:43-44). This shows that the author of this passage in Revelation was not the only one in his day who expected the Euphrates, like the Jordan River, to dry up when the chosen people needed it.

During the Maccabean Revolt, it was Rome that supplied the Hasmoneans with financial and military aid in their attempt to overthrow the Syrian Greeks. During the first century IA, Jews expected the Parthians from the East to come to their rescue and help them to overthrow Rome. The author here expected a divine miracle, like the one whereby an angel dried up the Euphrates to expedite the Parthian entrance into the Promised Land.

Although the miracle expected for the Parthians seems inconsistent with the author's anti-gentile view, it really is not. Chosen people have always been willing to use individual gentiles as slaves and servants (Isa 61:5) and individual alien nations to finance their construction and fight their battles (Isa 60:10-18). Here the real help was not to the Parthians but to the Jews whom the Parthians were expected to deliver.

---

[1] W. H. Shea, "The Location and Significance of Armageddon in Rev. 16:16," *AUSS* 18 (1980):157-58.

GEOGRAPHY AND HISTORY IN REVELATION SIXTEEN

The geographical references in Rev 16 have been treated in many ways but they still raise questions:

1) What was the relationship of these sites to the reader?
2) Were the kings of the East friends or enemies?
3) Was the great city Jerusalem or Rome? Was the author a Palestinian Jew or a gentile Christian?
4) Were the locations mentioned actual or mystical?

The first examination of the text will presume that geographical names are accurate until proved otherwise. When the sixth angel poured out its bowl, the **Euphrates River** dried up. This happened so that the way was prepared for the kings of the East to travel over **the river** without obstacle to Palestine, just as Hebrews crossed over the body of water between Egypt and the wilderness (Exod 14-15) and the Jordan River (Joshua 3) in the Exodus from Egypt and conquest of Canaan. This was the kind of sign or miracle the author of Fourth Ezra thought had been performed to allow the North Israelites to escape from the multitude of nations to a desolate place where they might keep their religious laws the way they could not keep them in Samaria (4Ezra 13:39-45). The kings of the East were necessary to Jews of NT times if Jews were to overthrow Rome.

Long before the Book of Revelation was composed or even before Alexander the Great had conquered the East, there was tension between Europe and Asia, with efforts made to extend empires into Europe or North Africa from Asia or vice versa. Not only are there biblical reports of attempts in the past for Babylon, Assyria, or Persia to apply military force to annex Egypt and for Egypt to attempt to extend its borders eastward, but there are also secular histories, such as those written by Herodotus, Thucidydes, Polybius, Livy, Ugaritic documents, Josephus, and Tacitus, that report these activities.

Alexander's Empire. In the fifth century BIA, for example, Xerxes, after he had already taken possession of Egypt, made a strong, but unsuccessful attempt to conquer Greece (Herodotus, *Hist* 7-8). Alexander the Great was the first to join into one empire all of the territory from Macedonia to India. After his empire had been divided among his generals, each of these tried to gain control of Alexander's complete empire. Ptolemy began at once to annex part of Libya to Egypt and claimed Palestine. Seleucus quickly conquered Lysimachus, after which he added to his kingdom most of the territory between Babylon and Europe, including Thrace and Asia Minor. He then moved his capital to Antioch, Syria, which he considered central to his kingdom. While Rome was busy fighting for its existence against Hannibal, Antiochus III, descendant of Seleucus I and heir of his throne, took over many of the islands between Asia Minor and Greece. He also gained as allies many of the Greek cities.

The Roman Heritage. None of these kings whose ancestors were Macedonian generals was successful in reestablishing the unified empire of Alexander under his own rule. Rome was the real successor to Alexander. Rome not only ruled Alexander's empire; it finally gained control of all North Africa, southern Europe, and the British Isles as well. Before this Roman achievement, however, when Antiochus III was king of the eastern branch of Alexander's empire, his country extended through Asia Minor, across the Hellespont into Europe, and he had succeeded in taking Palestine from Egypt. While Hannibal was aggressively adding more of Europe to Carthage, Rome was on the defensive and could do little to limit Antiochus' westward expansions. Hannibal had taken all of Spain and moved through the Alps from the north into Italy. At one time he had possession of most of Italy and was at Rome's doorstep when Scipio began to turn the tide. After many battles, Scipio finally forced Hannibal to a showdown and made Carthage surrender unconditionally to Roman rule.

Rome and the Seleucids. While Rome was occupied with this war, Antiochus III was swallowing up the islands of the Mediterranean Sea, stretching his boundaries across the Hellespont to the northern borders of Thrace, and gaining influence among the cities of Greece. He was in the process of getting control of Egypt when Scipio became free from Hannibal to turn his attention eastward. Scipio first conquered Greece and ordered Antiochus to withdraw from Europe and certain cities in Asia Minor. Antiochus refused, and there was a battle fought both at sea and at the Meander River in Asia Minor. Antiochus was badly defeated and forced to accept severe terms of peace. He had to withdraw from the islands of the Mediterranean Sea and move his western border to the Taurus Mountains (Polybius 18:49, 2-51, 10; 21:13, 1-16, 12).

Scipio and Pompey. It was not Scipio but Pompey who finally brought down the Seleucid rule. He was sent to Asia Minor to destroy the pirates who were operating from Celicia and oppose Mithradates, who had been distressing Rome with his guerrilla attacks for 40 years. In 63 BIA, Pompey entered the City of David by filling in the moat at the northern border of the City of David and stretching ladders across it. In the same year, Mithradates died, and the Seleucid rule came to an end, with all Asia Minor under Roman rule. By that time Rome ruled all of Alexander's empire as well as North Africa and much of Southern Europe but that did not bring the tension between Europe and Asia to a close. Throughout the empire, individual cities and peoples tried to regain their former independence. When Rome's troops were concentrated in one part of the empire, countries in other corners rebelled. By the seventh decade IA Parthia was the force in the East that replaced the Seleucid Syrians as a nation that could challenge Rome. Syria and Palestine were some of the lands that became involved in these shifts of power.

Jews and the Super Powers. **Jews** and Samaritans had learned to capitalize on these major shifts of **power**. Before the Maccabean Revolt began (167 BIA), **Jews** had observed that the Romans had only to send a letter to Antiochus IV through the agency of Popilius Laenas to force Antiochus IV Epiphanes to withdraw after he had taken control of Egypt (Polybius 29:27, 1-13). As soon as Judas the Maccabee had his guerrilla movement well underway, he began negotiations with Rome, realizing that Judah and Rome had the same goal--that of suppressing the Syrian Greeks. Rome was glad to furnish arms, guidance, and if necessary, troops to assist in this movement. Without Rome's support the Maccabean Revolt would never have been successful. By the time the Maccabean Revolt began, Rome had settled its conflict in Greece by bringing the Macedonian kingdom to an end. After that it could devote more attention to the East than it had given previously (1Macc 8:1-32; War 1:38).

Jews had a long record of playing two superpowers against one another in order to gain advantages, and they were not hesitant to change sides when it became beneficial. They had negotiated with Cyrus of Persia to become liberated from Babylon; they supported Antiochus when they were under Egyptian control; when they wanted to become liberated from Syria, they negotiated for support from Rome. When they had gained all they could from Rome and wanted to be liberated from this superpower, they turned to the Parthians. During the time when Herod was trying to gain power in Judah with the support of Rome, the Parthians helped one faction in opposing Herod and gaining control of Jerusalem, forcing Herod to flee for his life.

The Parthians. The kings from the East were **the Parthians.** The Sibyl said, **The dread Parthians have made you [Rome] rattle through and through** (SibOr 5:38-39). To be sure, **the Parthians** had been enemies of Rome for a long time. They threatened Rome's eastern border. In order to be able to lead a war against **the Parthians**, the Roman general, Crassus, stripped the temple at Jerusalem of all its gold, taking 2,000 talents that had been left by Pompey (War 1:179-82).

Rome and the Parthians. Sometimes **Parthia's** western border included Armenia and came right up to the Mediterranean Sea. Most of the time Armenia was a buffer state between **Roman** forces and **Parthia**. In 53 BIA, for example, **the Parthians** broke through the Commagene buffer and threatened Syria and Cilicia.[1] At Carrhae **the Parthians** destroyed Crassus and a **Roman** army. Shortly after Marcus Aurelius came to power (161 IA), **the Parthian** Shah Vologeses III crossed the frontier into Armenia, destroyed the **Roman** legion, and installed a new king. Another **Parthian** army also defeated the **Roman** army in Syria.

Later **Romans** regained both territories, but **Parthia** continued to exist. **Rome** brought it to its knees in some bitterly fought battles (197-99 IA). After the death of Caracella, **the Parthian** Artabanus V slaughtered the **Romans** until they

---

[1] L. Morris, *The Book of Revelation* (Grand Rapids: Eerdmans, c1987), p. 191, was not completely accurate in saying that the Euphrates was the boundary of the Roman Empire. The border was sometimes east and sometimes west of the Euphrates.

were forced to sue for an expensive peace. It was not **Rome** but local eastern battles that cost Artabanus his life and brought an end to **the Parthian** rule. This was in 225 IA and only after 300 years of animosity to **Rome**. **Jews** and Judah were involved in many of these conflicts. When Mark Anthony attempted to add their country to **Rome** his troops were nearly annihilated. **Parthians** were powerful adversaries to **Rome**, but for that very reason they were usually friends of the **Jews**.

Jews and the Parthians. When Herod was just beginning to gain control of Palestine, the Parthian satrap, Barzapharnes ruled Syria and had organized troops to restore Antigonus to the throne at Jerusalem (War 1:248-49). **Jewish** nationalists hurried to give him support, gathering at Mount Carmel, near Megiddo, to volunteer into the **Parthian** army. At the Feast of Pentecost **Parthians** captured Jerusalem, appointed Antigonus, a Hasmonean, to be king, and forced Herod to flee for his life (War 1:250-70).

When Herod got to Rome, he found Rome more than eager to provide the necessary military supplies, troops, and financial means to regain possession of Jerusalem. Romans realized that **the Parthians** constituted a serious problem, not only to Palestine, but to Rome, and they did not want **Parthians** in control of Rome's eastern-most part of the empire. With Rome's heavy military support Herod was successful in recapturing Jerusalem and having King Antigonus killed, but **Parthians** did not cease to watch for a chance to regain this strategic position, and they continued to have **Jewish** supporters in Jerusalem eager for an opportunity to cooperate with the **Parthians** in an effort to expel Rome from the Near East.[1]

Seventh Decade Conflicts. It seemed as if this opportunity was coming. In 63 IA, Paetus relieved Corbulo as commander in charge of the legions of the East, and Corbulo was moved to take charge of Syria, stationed near the bridge crossing the Euphrates River. Then Vologeses, king of the Parthians, won an overwhelming victory against the Romans, forcing Paetus to surrender, withdrawing his troops completely from Armenia, and Corbulo was required to remove Roman troops west of the Euphrates River (*Annals* 15:7-12). Soon after, the Roman Senate sent Corbulo back with more troops and equipment and was able to negotiate a treaty with Vologeses which returned the land without a conflict, and established Vologeses as ruler of the territory under Roman domination. Nevertheless Parthians continued to be a threat to the eastern border of Rome--especially during the sixties, when Rome had weak imperial leadership.

Before leaving his troops in Palestine to undertake a civil war against Vitellius in Rome, Vespasian knew it was necessary to make a treaty with Vologeses to assure himself that there would be no Parthian invasion of Palestine while he was

---

[1] David E. Aune, *Revelation 6-16* (Nashville: Thomas Nelson Publishers, c1998) p. 891, noted, "In the view of many commentators, the phrase, 'the kings of the east' refers to Nero *redivivus* myth included the belief that Nero would return from the east leading a vast Parathian army."

gone (Tacitus, *Hist* 2:82).[1] At that time Vologeses volunteered to provide Vespasian 40,000 horses with armed riders if he needed them (Hist 4:51). Although that assurance satisfied Vespasian that Vologeses would not start a revolt in Palestine while Vespasian was engaged in a civil war in Rome, Jews in Palestine may not have known of the treaty, because they continued to count on Parthian support at the crucial time.

After the Jewish-Roman war of 66-70 IA was over Josephus knew that the Parthians had been secured by treaty not to make invasions into Palestine during the civil war in Rome, so he wrote as if Herod Agrippa II also knew this *before* the end of the war. Josephus pictured Agrippa II warning Jews that they could not expect Jewish support from outside Palestine. He specifically refuted their expectation that there would be Jews in Adiabene who had enough power and influence to obtain military support from that area. He said the Parthians would not cooperate and let themselves become involved in this war, since they were bound to the Romans by treaty (War 2:388-89).

Diaspora Jews were always considered necessary for support in any international event in which Jews were effected. Josephus said there was not a city in the world where there were no Jews (War 2:399). Indeed, when Archelaus went to Rome to secure the kingdom for himself more than 8,000 Jews appeared to influence Caesar's decision (War 2:80).

INTERNATIONAL JEWISH PATTERNS

Previous victories of Jews over large enemy nations have always happened with the financial and military support necessary provided by some other strong power that also wanted to overthrow Jewish enemies. For example, Jews in Babylon negotiated with Cyrus of Persia to bring about their liberation from Babylon.[2] Without the support of Rome, the Hasmoneans would never have been successful against the Greeks. Before the Maccabean movement began, Rome twice interfered to stop the expansion of the Seleucids:

1) One Roman interference was a thorough defeat of Antiochus the Great by Scipio at Magnesia on the Meander river in Lydia (Livy 37:39-44), forcing Antiochus to abandon all of the territory he had previously claimed west of the Taurus Mountains, limit his navy, pay heavy financial fines, and make promises against other expansion attempts.

---

[1] At that time Vespasian was leading a rebellion against Rome, and Vologeses was willing to lend it his support.

[2] This is conjecture based on the fact that Cyrus had informers in Babylon who enabled him to take the city without an open battle (Herodotus, *History* 1:191; Xenophon, *Cyropaedia* 7:5, 1-57; A. L. Oppenheim [tr.], "Babylon and Assyrian Historical Texts," J. B. Pritchard [ed.], *Ancient Near Eastern Texts* [Princeton: Princeton U. Press, 1969], pp. 315-16). Since, before the event, the author of Second Isaiah expected Cyrus to do this and to release the Jews to return to Palestine afterwards, it is reasonable to suspect that there were Jews among Cyrus' informers who made Babylonia's capture possible.

2) The other occasion was the embarrassing submission of Antiochus Epiphanes to the Roman commander, Gaius Popilius (Livy 45:11, 1-12, 6; Polybius 29:27, 1-13) after Antiochus had just over powered Egypt.

It was by stimulating war between large nations that Jews were able to expand and gain power. In the fourth century IA Christians followed this pattern and negotiated with Constantine to overthrow Maxentius. During the Crusades Jews provided support and guidance to the Muslims in an attempt to overthrow the Christians. They really hoped that both would destroy the other, leaving Jews alone in control.[1]

This was the pattern of Jewish participation in international negotiations which was used over and over. Jews always counted on support from diaspora Jews in strategic positions in foreign countries and the intervention of God to bring large foreign countries to their military support. In the first century the great harlot was Rome, and Jews expected help from the Parthians, east of the Euphrates River. They had good reason for thinking they could count on this. Although Rome and Parthia had made a treaty after the battle in IA 63, Parthia did not stop wanting to have complete control over the territory it then held only under Roman domination.

PARTHIA AND MEGIDDO

Parthians and Megiddo. Armageddon is the transliterated form of the Hebrew for Mount Megiddo. If Parthians had come to rescue Palestine from the Romans during the war between Vitellius and Vespasian, there would have been Jewish volunteers to meet them at Mount Carmel, just as there were at the beginning of Herod's rule, because Megiddo was one of the most strategic fortresses in Palestine, and it was the first one the Parthians would have reached as they came to Palestine from the north (War 1:250).

Megiddo as a Fortress. Megiddo was an ancient town. It was mentioned in Josh 17:11, Judges 1:27; 5:19, 2Chron 35:22, and Zech 12:11. A famous victory was won against Sisera near there (Judges 4:5). Gideon's 300 soldiers drove out the **Midianites** from the Valley of Esdraelon, east of Megiddo (Judges 7:1). In the same plain Saul and Jonathan were killed (1Sam 31:1-6). King Ahaziah and King Josiah were both killed at **Megiddo** (1Kings 9:27; 23:29-30; 2Chron 35:22). It was situated at a strategic location where important international battles were destined to be fought. It held its place at the southeastern end of the Carmel range, which was about twenty miles in length. Medicddo was bordered by a swampy plain to the east, about six miles wide at its widest point. East of that swamp was Mount Tabor. When armies marched either north or south along the Mediterranean shore, they had to follow the roads above the swampland, either on the Megiddo side or the Mount Tabor side.

---

[1] For examples of this see the index on "Magog" in Buchanan, *Jewish Messianic Movements*.

Many scholars have noticed that **Megiddo** is not really a mountain. It is a fortress on the edge of a mountain range just as Gezer, Hazor, and Dan are placed at the edge of their respective mountain ranges. It was not just a little town on a plain. It was built well above the level of the plain and constructed on a pattern by which fortresses were built. Judges 5 locates the waters of **Megiddo** as the Kishon torrent, in the Jezreel Valley. The mountain of **Megiddo**, then, is the Carmel mountain that is adjacent to the stream.[1]

Fortresses normally have towns built around them, where people live in time of peace, but in time of war they move up to the high and fortified place of the village or city fortress. As early as the fifteenth century BIA Megiddo was known as a town, but it was also known as a well defended fortress. It does not require much imagination to understand why it was called a mountain.[2]

Jewish History. Most of the year the Esdraelon plain was a swampland, impossible to navigate. The roads that joined Egypt and the nations in the East ran along the edge of the mountain ranges on both sides of the swamp. This is the reason the armies of Deborah and Barak were successful against Sisera at this point (Judges 5). All they had to do was to use stones and clubs to drive the horse-drawn chariots into the swamp, and the troops were helpless. King Josiah was seriously wounded from an Egyptian arrow when he confronted Pharaoh Necho at Megiddo while he was attempting to stop the Pharaoh from crossing Palestinian land with Egyptian troops to fight the king of Babylon. After he was wounded King Josiah called a retreat and returned to Jerusalem where he soon died. (2Kings 23:29; Ant 10.74-78; see also Zech 12:11). King Ahaziah also died from an arrow wound at Megiddo (2Kings 9:27-28).

Megiddo was a strategic fortress for controlling the march of armies from one end of the Fertile Crescent to the other. Scholars like Beckwith, who thought the term was used for no geographical reason but had only a mystical or symbolical meaning,[3] failed to understand its significance to Israel's defenses and nationalistic expectations. Others, like Düsterdieck, thought the word **Megiddo** had a typological meaning for the church. The antitype was the victory of the Israelites over Sisera and

---

[1] So also Shea, "Armageddon," pp. 158-61.
[2] Boring, *Revelation*, 177, mistakenly said, "Probing of John's meaning of the 'battle of Armageddon' thus reveals that we should not be concerned to locate it on a map or give it a date. It is not the prediction of some historical battle." This anticipated battle was not a vague mythical, philosophical, or poetic fairy tale. The hope was to destroy Israel's enemies and liberate the Promised Land from real foreign military and political powers.
[3] G. R. Beasley-Murray, *The Book of Revelation* (Greenwood: Oliphant, c1978), pp. 245-46; I. T. Beckwith, *The Apocalypse of John* (New York: The Macmillan Co., 1919), p. 685; Caird, *Revelation*, p. 207; H. M. Hailey, *Revelation: An Introduction and Commentary* (Grand Rapids: Baker's Book House, c1979), p. 336; Morris, *Revelation*, p. 193. J. P. M. Sweet, *Revelation* (Philadelphia: Westminster Press, c1979), pp. 249-50, and J. B. Smith, *Revelation of Jesus Christ*, ed. J. O. Yoder (Scottdale, Pa: Church Publishing Co., c1961), p. 236; all noted the geographical significance and important history of this location, but Smith also mistakenly identified Armageddon with the Valley of Decision which is the Kidron Valley on the border of Jerusalem, and Hailey insisted that the term was used in Revelation only symbolically.

his armies (Judges 5:10). He correctly thought the expectation involved victory, rather than defeat, for the Israelites, but he was mistaken in thinking that it had no original geographical or political significance.[1]

Megiddo and Fertile Crescent History. Palestine was an important land bridge, connecting Egypt with Syria, Assyria, Babylon, Persia, and Parthia. Controlling this bridge was important for taking charge of military defenses and the flow of commerce. **Megiddo** was in the Near East what the Rock of Gibraltar was to Mediterranean traffic. This had been the situation for centuries. Pharaoh Thutmose III (15th century BIA) learned that the king of Kadesh had organized all of the countries north of **Megiddo** and gathered their troops at this pass. In consultation with his military leaders, the Pharaoh realized that this was a difficult place to fight. If he should take his entire army there, only the front lines could fight, while the rest of the army was out of range.[2] Even after the Egyptians had successfully overpowered these forces, the enemy gathered inside the fortress at **Megiddo**, and it took seven months to overthrow the fortress. The Pharaoh correctly deduced that "the capturing of **Megiddo** is the capturing of a thousand towns!"[3] He was right both from the standpoint of difficulty and importance.

This was neither the first nor the last battle fought there, and anyone acquainted with Palestinian defenses would have expected the Parthians and the Romans to engage in a serious confrontation there if the Parthians should come to Jewish rescue. Jews counted heavily both on the assistance of other powerful nations and the miracles of God to win their battles. If the Parthians should come, the Lord would dry up the Euphrates to expedite their movement, just as another author expected the Lord to dry up the Euphrates for the Northern tribes of Israel to return (4Ezra 13:43-44), and the stars in their courses would again fight for them at **Megiddo** as they had against Sisera (Judges 5). The author of this narrative expected an angel from heaven to empty a bowl into the air to release God's anger and get this whole process started. He believed that the events on earth were predestined and controlled from heaven, but they were realized in identifiable time and space. The deliverance the author expected at **Megiddo** was no more mystical or symbolic than the salvation from Sisera or the crossing of the sea by the Israelites after the Exodus from Egypt. Mount Megiddo (*hahr-meh-geé-dawn* = *A*rmegiddon) is no more mystical than Jerusalem, London, or New York City.

---

[1] F. Düsterdieck, *Critical and Exegetical Handbook to the Revelation of John*, tr. H. E. Jacobs (Winona Lake: Alpha Publishing Co., 1884), p. 423. There were, however, scholars like E. Lohmeyer, *Die Offenbarung des Johannes* (Tübingen: J. C. B. Mohr, 1953), p. 137, and Sweet, *Revelation*, p. 250, who thought Armageddon was the fortress at Megiddo that had historic roots in the defense of Israel.

[2] J. Wilson (tr.), "Egyptian Historical Texts," J. B. Pritchard, *Ancient*, pp. 234-35.

[3] Wilson, "Historical," p. 237.

Opinions of Scholars. Allo[1] mistakenly followed Bousset in thinking that the nations of the East were allies of the beast, and that Rev 16:12 is a sort of introduction to the harlot of Rev 17, 19, 20. Beasley-Murray concurred.[2] Weiss reached a similar conclusion. He said these were not Parthian kings but kings that were not Roman. They would cross the Euphrates River and join forces with the Romans to overpower the community of God's people.[3] Loisy and Ford also held that the drying up of the Euphrates was to provide a way for the enemy, not the chosen people.[4] Lohmeyer denied that the river Euphrates had any geographical identity, and he thought the kings of the East were really demons and not human forces.[5] Beasley-Murray said the Euphrates would be dried up so that the Israelites from the Assyrian captivity could return, and the kings of the East would just happen to cross over as well.[6] Terry argued that the Euphrates River symbolized the source of God's anger to be used against Israel.[7] Caird erroneously concluded,

> ... this much at least is clear, that, like John's other names, it [the Euphrates] is a symbol. He was not expecting a battle in northern Palestine, but Rome.[8]

Schüssler-Fiorenza was of the same opinion.[9] Caird was led astray by the letters to the seven churches in trying to locate the scene of operations near Rome and Asia Minor. Farrer thought that if the author had been speaking geographically, he would have intended the kings of the East to have arrived to help the Romans in their war against the Holy Land, but Farrer did not believe the message was for Palestinian Jews or Christians. It was written instead to the Western church and therefore all of this was symbolism and not geography.[10] Farrer also overlooked the relationship between Parthia and Rome when he presumed Rome could have expected Parthia's support in a war against Palestine. Although Beckwith knew that Parthians were

---

[1] E. -B. Allo, *Saint Jean L'Apocalypse* (Paris: F. Gabalda, 1921), p. 236. Düsterdieck, *Handbook*, p. 419, held the same basic opinion. H. Kraft, *Die Offenbarung des Johannes* (Tübingen: J. C. B. Mohr, 1974), p. 208, thought the expression, "the kings of the East," was simply some mythical designation with no relationship to real politics.
[2] Beasley-Murray, *Revelation*, c1978), p. 244.
[3] B. Weiss, *Die Apostelgeschichte Katholischen Briefe Apokalypse* (Leipzig: J. C. Hinrichs, 1902), p. 496.
[4] A. Loisy, *L'Apocalypse de Jean* (Paris: Emile Nourry, 1923), pp. 290-92; J. M. Ford, "The Structure and Meaning of Revelation 16," *ExposTim* 98 (1987):328.
[5] Lohmeyer, *Offenbarung*, p. 135.
[6] Beasley-Murray, *Revelation*, p. 244. J. F. Walvoord, *The Revelation of Jesus Christ* (Chicago: Moody Press, 1966), p. 236, studied a hundred commentaries and found as many as fifty different interpretations of the kings of the east.
[7] M. S. Terry, *Biblical Apocalyptics* (New York: Easton and Mains, 1898), p. 421.
[8] Caird, *Revelation*, p. 207.
[9] E. Schüssler-Fiorenza, *Revelation: Vision of a Just World* (Minneapolis: Fortress Press, c1991), p. 94.
[10] A. Farrer, *The Revelation of St. John the Divine* (Oxford: Clarendon Press, 1964), pp. 176-77.

dreaded in the Roman world, he reasoned that Nero would return, leading the Parthian troops against Rome.[1]

This presumes that the very Caesar who had recently forced the Parthian, Vologeses, into subjection could count on him for rescue and military support. Although Vologeses gave Rome trouble on the eastern border, he was not as strong as Hannibal when the latter came down the Italian Peninsula toward Rome itself. Terry believed the kings of the East symbolized the kings of the whole world which would come to attack Israel,[2] but Makrakis offered a different symbolism. He said they symbolized the Moslems of Japan, China, and India. The drying up of the Euphrates symbolized God's plan to exterminate the Moslems by starvation to make way for a new social order.[3] Beagley thought Megiddo really meant Jerusalem.[4] That is like thinking someone meant London when he or she said New York! Halver said the whole event was a myth and not a geographical reality. There was no expectation that a real battle would be fought on earth.[5] Scholars who abandon the normal restraints of geography and history to escape into a vague "symbolism" employ a methodology that is very similar to allegory and equal in validity.

Like many other scholars Düsterdieck confused **the migrants of the land** with the "inhabitants of the earth" and the kings of the East with the ten kings who were ten horns. He also confused the typology related to Jerusalem and the Kidron Valley given by Isaiah, Ezekiel, Joel, and Zechariah, with the typology associated with Mount Megiddo.[6] It is important to keep all of these expectations separate. Rev 16 begins a new topic. It does not mention the dragon, the Valley of Decision, the ten horns, or **the migrants of the land**. It does, however, mention **Mount Megiddo, the Euphrates**, and **the kings of the East**. Therefore the history of **Megiddo** and its typology are important for understanding this unit of literature.

Dio acknowledged that even down to his day (2nd century IA) **Parthians** were able to hold their own against the **Romans** in war (*RomHist* 40:14, 4). They were skillful in overpowering other troops in the hot, dry, **Parthian** climate, where westerners were at a disadvantage, but they had never learned to fight except in their own desert climate and topography. They were restricted, therefore, from expanding their borders extensively westward (*RomHist* 40:5-6). **Parthians** were lucky in 63 IA to have been able to overthrow some **Roman** troops in an important battle in Armenia, but they were ready to negotiate with **Rome** rather than fight a second battle with renewed **Roman** troops. The **Parthian** way of weakening **Rome** was to

---

[1] Beckwith, *Apocalypse*, pp. 682-83.
[2] Terry, *Apocalyptics*, p. 421.
[3] Apostolos Makrakis, *Interpretation of the Revelation of St. John the Divine*, tr. A. G. Alexander (Chicago: Hellenic Christian Education Society, 1948), pp. 401-402. Smith, *Revelation*, made a reasonable deduction. He said the kings of the East would come from the east side of the Euphrates. J. O. Yoder, however, who edited Smith's book, added that the kings were probably representing Red China or Japan (Smith, *Revelation*, p. 233).
[4] A J. Beagley, *The "Sitz im Leben" of the Apocalypse* (Berlin: W. De Guyter, 1987), pp. 88-89.
[5] R. Halver, *Der Mythos im letzten Buch der Bible* (Hamburg: H. Reich, 1964), p.89.
[6] Düsterdieck, *Revelation*, 419.

irritate and increase **Rome's** eastern problems. **Parthians** were willing to support a Jewish rebellion when the conditions were right in order to take a part of **Rome's** territory that was adjacent to **Parthia**, but they did not even try to move into Asia Minor, let alone move far enough westward to overthrow **Rome** at any time.

Scholars who have tried to interpret these geographical locations mystically have overlooked some important points in Israel's history:

1) The plagues, which are types for these dramatic events, were injurious to Israel's *enemies*--not Israel.
2) Parthia had played a beneficial role in relationship to Jews in the past. **Parthia's** enmity with **Rome** was encouraging to Jews in Palestine. Jews wanted the **Parthians** to come to their rescue. They were not expecting them to join forces with the **Romans**--especially after the famous **Roman-Parthian** battle in IA 63.
3) When God opened the sea at the border of Egypt and the Jordan River the miracles were for *Israel's* deliverance--not for the benefit of the Egyptians or the Canaanites.

Therefore the later antitype of this miracle would not have been created to enable Israel's enemies to succeed at Israel's expense. The Book of Revelation has many signs to show that the author of this book expected Israel's history to be relived. This was more than a mystical feeling; it involved history. There would be plagues again as in Egypt; hardship as in the wilderness; suffering as in Palestine before the Maccabean victories, but from it all Israel would emerge victorious. Tragedy was to be only temporary.

Parthian-Rome Symbolism. Even though the Parthians gave Rome trouble on the eastern border, the battles they won were always in the East, near **Parthia's** borders. They never gained enough power to challenge the Roman Empire itself for rule of the entire civilized world. The battle the Parthians won in 63 IA was not a stepping stone to other battles. The Parthian way of weakening Rome was to irritate and increase Rome's distant problems. They gladly cooperated with Vespasian in his war against the current emperor of Rome; they were willing to support a Jewish rebellion when the conditions were right in order to take a part of Rome's territory that was adjacent to Parthia; but they did not try to overthrow Rome at any time. When the angel emptied the bowl, a voice went out from the temple (Rev 16:17) reminding Jews of the voice that Trito-Isaiah prophesied (Isa 66:6), a voice from God rendering recompense to his enemies and providing comfort to Jerusalem. The loud natural noises were associated with the revelation of the ten commandments at Mount Sinai.

Nebuchadnezzar referred to the country he ruled as **great Babylon** just before his sanity was removed. The cup of the wine of God's wrath was an expression Jeremiah used to refer to God's punishment to be inflicted on the Babylonians after the Jews had worked off their allotted 70 year prison term in payment for their crimes. The large hail stones were intended to remind readers of one of the plagues of Egypt, but these were still bigger (Rev 16:21). A talent is about 75 pounds or 30 kilograms in weight.

THE GREAT CITY

Contrary to Allo,[1] Beasley-Murray,[2] Caird,[3] Charles,[4] Corsini,[5] Düsterdieck,[6] Hailey,[7] Holzmann,[8] Mounce,[9] Preston and Hanson,[10] Swete,[11] Terry,[12] and others, **the great city** is not Rome. Nor were Sweet and Kraft correct in assuming that the author of this passage intended the title here to allude both to Rome and to Jerusalem.[13] Still further off course was Morris, who said the great city was only a symbolic term that stands for civilized man.[14] Preston and Hanson said Babylon's being divided into three parts probably signifies the crumbling of the Roman Empire.[15] Hailey and Ladd concurred.[16] Makrakis thought the great city referred to Constantinople which had been divided into three groups of people--the Greeks, the Slavics, and the Turks.[17] Wetstein suggested that this passage represented the period of history when Vespasian was fighting Vitellius in a civil war and the three parts were

1) The Vitellians,
2) The Flavians, and
3) The Roman people.[18]

---

[1] Allo, *Saint Jean*, p. 241.
[2] Beasley-Murray, *Revelation*, pp. 244.
[3] Caird, *Revelation*, p. 209.
[4] R. H. Charles, *A Critical and Exegetical Commentary on the Revelation of St. John the Divine* (New York: Charles Scribner's Sons, c1966), vol. 2, p. 52.
[5] E. Corsini, *The Apocalypse*, tr. F. J. Moloney (Wilmington:Michael Glazier, c1983), p. 308.
[6] Düsterdieck, *Handbook*, p. 424.
[7] Hailey, *Revelation*, pp. 338-39.
[8] H. J. Holtzmann, *Briefe und Offenbarung des Johannes* (Tübingen: J. C. B. Mohr, 1893), p. 348.
[9] R. H. Mounce, *The Book of Revelation* (Grand Rapids: Eerdmans, c1977), pp. 303-04.
[10] R. H. Preston and A. T. Hanson, *The Revelation of Saint John the Divine* (London: S.C. M. Press, c1951), p.109.
[11] H. B. Swete *The Apocalypse of St. John* (London: Macmillan, 1906), p. 208.
[12] Terry, *Apocalyptics*, pp. 424-25.
[13] Sweet, *Revelation*, p. 251; Kraft, *Offenbarung*, p. 211.
[14] Morris, *Revelation*, p. 195.
[15] Preston and Hanson, *Revelation*, p. 109.
[16] Hailey, *Revelation*, p. 338; G. E. Ladd, *A Commentary on the Revelation of John* (Grand Rapids: Eerdmans, 1972), p. 218.
[17] Makrakis, *Interpretation*, pp. 413-14.
[18] J. J. Wetstein, *Novum Testamentum Graecum* (Amsterdam: Ex Officina Dommeriana, 1752, 1962) II, p. 819.

This is forced. There were really only two divisions in that civil war, and Rome was divided into only two parts. The Roman people were divided between the two. Anyone wanting to force the issue still further might say Rome was divided into four for five parts, separating the men from the women and children.

The author of the Sibylline Oracles called Jerusalem **the great city** which held the temple that God protected--the temple that had been built with holy hands. Nevertheless a wicked king threw it down. Jerusalem was the city God loved, the jewel of the world, and the one in which God made a temple (SibOr 5:395-433). It was the **city of God** at the center of the earth (SibOr 5:250). It was the city where the godlike, heavenly race of blessed Jews lived (SibOr 5:249-50). In the Book of Revelation Jerusalem was sometimes called **the great city** (Rev 11:8; 21:10), but so also was Rome (Rev 14:8; 17:18; 18:10, 16, 18, 19, 21), so the title itself cannot be a determining factor in deciding which city was intended. This was a title of approval when Jerusalem was meant.

Jerusalem was also called **the holy city** (Rev 11:2; 21:2, 10), and **the beloved city** (Rev 20:9). When applied to Rome, it was the enemies of the author who made the designation, or it was applied satirically. Rome was also called **Babylon** (Rev 16:19; 17:5; 18:2, 10, 21). Here in Rev 16:19 **the great city** seems to be the designation the author intended favorably, but that is not certain. Kraft thought the great city here applied both to Rome and Jerusalem. He thought that the divisions intended were:

1) the fore city,
2) the upper city, and
3) the lower city.

He did not relate the division to any period of history.[1] In response to Carrington's claim that the city divided was Jerusalem divided by three factions during the Jewish war with Rome, Beagley, simply dismissed the suggestion with the comment, "but this is improbable."[2] Weiss correctly said the great city could be only Jerusalem.[3]

Ruiz correctly concluded that the city which was divided into three parts was Jerusalem and Babylon referred to Rome, but his reasoning was not related to any special historical event. Since these consequences all came when the seventh angel poured his bowl into the air, Ruiz thought everything fell in chronological order: first the pouring by the angel, second the lightning, thunder, and earthquake, and third, the division of Jerusalem and the destruction of gentile cities, including Rome. Since they were reported in that order, the earthquake caused Jerusalem to be divided into three segments by geological splits. This earthquake was so big, he thought, that it reached all the way from Rome to Jerusalem and the Mount of Olives, splitting the mountain into two, as Zech 14 prophesied, and then destroying

---

[1] Kraft, *Offenbarung*, p. 211.
[2] Beagley, *Sitz*, p. 90; P. Carrington, *The Meaning of Revelation* (London, 1931), p. 266.
[3] B. Weiss, *Apostle geschichte-Katholische Briefe-Apokalypse* (Leipzig, 1902), p. 498.

Rome and other cities of the nations.[1] Although there is logic to his interpretation, that is not the only, or even the most likely, possibility. These disasters did not all happen, each one as a result of the preceding one, something like dominoes. These were events that were happening at the same time and were all caused when the angel poured out his bowl into the air.

Although the events were all bad, the catastrophes were intended to show that good things were designed to happen for Israel:

1) The natural events of the Sinai revelation were reenacted. This meant there would soon be a new contract between the Lord and his people, like the one given to Moses.
2) The cities of enemy nations were actually falling at that time, relieving Jews of much of their adversity.
3) All of the evils of Rome were going to be called to God's attention so that he would punish Rome for all of them.
4) The city of Jerusalem was divided into three parts, as it actually was, but the civil war would soon be over, and one of the conflicting generals would become the Son of man to rule over God's chosen people from Jerusalem. The divisions were political rather than geological. The prophecy was based on specific historical events and Scripture rather than general application of curses.

There may be an intended allusion to the three kinds of punishment Ezekiel prophesied against Jerusalem (Ezek 5:1-12), because its inhabitants had been unfaithful to the contract made with the Lord, but the relationship is not at all clear. This narrative (Rev 16:12, 16-21) is still part of the mythological report of the seven angels with the seven plagues. These plagues were all directed against Jews--not Romans. They were all directed to the Promised Land--not some other foreign territory. Therefore, the city involved would be within the Promised Land. The great Palestinian city was Jerusalem.

Aune, assumed that the city "fell" apart into three parts as a result of the earthquake mentioned in Rev 16:18. Therefore he concluded,

> "The great city" should probably be understood as Babylon-Rome, however, for the fact that the city was split into three parts by the earthquake does not mean that it had yet been adequately punished. Further, Babylon-Rome is certainly referred to as "the great city" in Rev 17:18; 18:10 (2x), 16, 18, 19, 21 (μεγάλη πόλις). The phrase

---

[1] J. P. Ruiz, *Ezekiel in the Apocalypse: the Transformation of Prophetic Language in Revelation 16,17-19,10* (Frankfurt am Main: Peter Lang, c1989), pp. 265-91.

is used once of Jerusalem (11:8), but the context here cannot refer to Jerusalem.[1]

Lightning, thunder, and other phenomena of great violence are associated with the provision of the contract at Mount Sinai. One of the ways later authors show that they are expecting a restoration of the Promised Land together with a renewed contract was to list these again. In the midst of these literary phenomena are inserted some geographical locations, such as Megiddo, Euphrates, and the city that is divided into three parts. Megiddo and the Euphrates belong to an expectation that the Parthians would come to help Jerusalem in some war situation. That happened most vitally between 69 and 70 IA. At that time Jerusalem actually was divided into three parts, without any influence of an earthquake. An attempt to relate some of these curses to historical events that are reported with them is in order.

Aune rendered the Greek *eh-géh-neh-taw* (ἐγένετο) by "fell." In this commentary it is rendered "divided" into three parts. The Greek requires some implied verb. It literally says, "The city happened into three parts" or "The city was in three parts," meaning that the city was divided into three parts. The question is, "How did it get that way?" Aune thought, since the verse above tells of an earthquake, that the earthquake actually split the city into three physical units, but the earthquake is only a part of a number of natural phenomena, like those at the provision of the commandments at Sinai, and there is no report that Rome suffered any such affliction. Without an earthquake, Rome was divided into *two* parts during a civil war that was going on at the time. Megiddo became an important issue. That happened at precisely the time when Jerusalem was a city that was divided into *three* parts.

Gentile Cities. Josephus described the situation in Jerusalem at the beginning of 70 IA. That was the time when Vespasian had withdrawn the troops he had gathered around Jerusalem to capture it. He went to Egypt, from which to conduct a civil war against Vitellius in Rome. He finally won this war and was made emperor of Rome. During this time, however, Jews thought their problem with Rome was nearly over, and three pretending rulers, Simon, Eleazer, and John fought in armed combat over control of the country. Each controlled a section of the city (War 5:1, 1-5).

The temple was stationed just south of Herod's fortress, Antonia. It was attached to the fortress by a bridge about 600 feet long. There was also a bridge connecting the temple to the upper city to the west. Eleazar controlled the temple. John was stationed in the lower city, near the spring of Siloam. Simon was evidently located west of the temple where he could fight with Eleazar from the bridge (portico). He was exposed to John's attack from the south and Eleazar's, from the east. John could attack the temple area from the south and also Simon's position. In this way the three could continue in warfare with one another. This continued until Vespasian's son Titus returned to surround Jerusalem with Roman soldiers

---

[1] Aune, *Revelation 6-16*, pp. 900-901.

While all of this was going on in Jerusalem, Rome was deeply engaged in another civil war in which Rome burned, but the city survived. Tacitus described this period as one

> rich in disasters, terrible in battles, torn by civil struggles, horrible even in peace. Four emperors fell by the sword; there were three civil wars, more foreign wars, and often both at the same time (*Hist* 1:2).

The Roman civil war was not over before Rome burned, and the Capitol with its temples was burned. This was a time when **God remembered great Babylon.** Rome, however, was not the only city of the nations suffering destruction. Tacitus further reported that there were cities on the rich fertile shores of Campania that were swallowed up or overwhelmed (*Hist* 1:2). Rome had been involved in battles from Britain to Armenia. While civil war was going on in Rome, there were rebellions in Britain, Germany, Pontus, and Byzantium. In addition there were barbarian pirates who roamed the seas with specially built boats that could withstand waves (Tacitus, *Hist* 3:45-47).

Jerusalem. The period when all of this was taking place is very precise. It happened at the last of 69 IA or the first of 70 IA. This joyful period took place when the cities of the nations were falling, Rome was being punished, and Jerusalem was divided into three parts--all at the same time. Only a few months later, the civil war was over in Rome; Titus returned to **Jerusalem** to complete Rome's campaign there; the three pretending messiahs had successfully burned the grain stores in **Jerusalem** so that **Jerusalem** was forced to starve. Before all of these conditions had been reversed, this part of Revelation was composed. Because the context seems to fit the international situation of the time better with **Jerusalem** as the **great city**, this title seems to apply to **Jerusalem** rather than Rome, and the author referred to three events instead of one.

1) The city (Jerusalem) was divided into three parts;
2) the cities of the nations were falling;
3) God remembered the great harlot (Rome).

From the author's point of view, the gentiles were bad, and the Jews were good. Therefore, he distinguished **the great city** from the **cities of the gentiles** or **nations**. Had the great city been Rome, it also would have been one of the cities of the nations. Rome was clearly insulted by the title **Babylon**. The only city not insulted is **the great city,** which obviously means **Jerusalem**--not just a symbol, but a real city, located on a mountain west of Jericho, the city David chose as his capital city on the Promised Land.

Plagues. The seven last **plagues** which these angels instigated were intended as antitypes of the **plagues** in Egypt before the Exodus from Egypt and the contract renewal at Sinai. In the first century IA the angels' bowls brought about the following results:

1) boils affected the enemies in Palestine;
2) the sea became blood, and all of the creatures in it died;
3) rivers became blood, and God allowed the heathen to drink the blood of the saints and prophets to make the latter worthy;
4) the sun scorched people;
5) the beast's kingdom became dark;
6) the Euphrates River dried up to permit the kings of the East to come to Palestine and gather at Megiddo; and
7) great hail stones afflicted human beings. At that time, Jerusalem was divided into three parts; cities of other nations were falling; and God was punishing Rome. The progression of this narrative was interrupted and confused by Rev 16:13-15, which is a separate vision. This becomes obvious when the text is shown with these verses separated:

TEXT

Revelation 16:12, 16-21

¹²**Now** the sixth [angel] poured out its bowl upon **the Great River Euphrates** (Gen 15:18) and its **water was dried up** (Jer 50:38) so that the way of the kings of the East may be prepared. ¹⁶He brought them together to the place called in Hebrew "Har-Megiddo." ¹⁷Now when he [the angel] poured out his bowl upon the air, and a loud **voice from the temple** of God (Isa 66:6) went out, saying, "It has happened." ¹⁸Then there occurred **bolts of lightning, noises, peals of thunder** (Exod 19:16; Ps 77:16-18; Hab 3:10), and there was a great earthquake, **such that there has not been from the time** human beings **appeared to the earth** (Dan 12:1) an earthquake so great as this. ¹⁹Then the great city was divided into three parts,

Revelation 16:13-15

¹³**Now** there was given from the mouth of the false prophet three unclean spirits like **frogs** (Exod 8:2), ¹⁴for they are spirits of demons, performing great signs to go out toward the kings of the whole civilized world, to gather them together to the war of the great day of the almighty God. ¹⁵Look! he is coming like a thief. Blessed is he who stands guard and keeps his garments [clean], so that he may not walk naked, and they see his shame.

the cities of the nations fell, and **Babylon the great** (Dan 4:27) was remembered before God for the purpose of giving to her **the cup of the wine of the wrath of his** anger (Jer 25:15). ²⁰Every island fled, and the mountains were not found.

²¹**Huge hailstones** (Exod 9:23) came down from heaven upon human beings, and people blasphemed God because of the pain of the hailstones, because its plague was **exceedingly great** (Exod 9:11).

COMMENTARY ON THE UNIT

Variants in the Main Text. Before reading further, look again at the two columns above. Notice the difference in the proportion of quotations in the two columns. This in itself suggests that the two columns are of different composition. Several scholars have raised textual integrity questions. Rev 16:12, 16-21, forms a complete unit. There are a few variants that seem like explanatory additions on the part of the NA scribe. For example, Sinaiticus has only **when he poured out**. NA clarifies the sentence by saying, **Now the seventh [angel] poured out.** Sinaiticus has **from the temple of God.** NA has **from the temple, from the throne, of God.** Sinaiticus has an extra **peals of thunder.** Mealy also saw a division of sources here, but he divided them differently. He thought Rev 16:12-14, 17 was one unit, omitting verses 15-16. He did not say why he made this division. Steinmann also considered Rev 16:15 as an intrusion.[1]

Variants in the Separated Passage. Rev 16:13-15 seems to be a complete unit with a different subject.[2] There are many variants between Sinaiticus and NA. NA seems to have elaborated on the Sinaiticus text homiletically, filling in details and modifying the style accordingly. Sinaiticus has **there was given.** NA reports **I was watching**. Sinaiticus said, **from the mouth of the false prophet.** NA expanded, **from the mouth of the dragon, from the mouth of the beast, and from the mouth of the false prophet.** Sinaiticus has **performing great signs to go out to the kings**. NA text is **performing great signs which go out to the kings**. According to Sinaiticus, the one coming like a thief is reported in the third person. According to NA it is first

---

[1] J. W. Mealy, *After the Thousand Years* (Sheffield: JSOT Press, c1992), p. 76. A. E. Steinmann, "The Tripartite Structure of the Sixth Seal, the Sixth Trumpet, and the Sixth Bowl of John's Apocalypse (Rev 6:12-7:17; 9:13-11:14; 16:12-16," *JETS* 35 (1992):69-79.

[2] Boring, *Revelation*, p. 178, disagreed with other scholars who thought (correctly) that Rev 16:15 was an intrusion, added by some later scribe.

person. Both versions are stylistically acceptable, and the basic meaning of both texts is the same.

The false prophet. This is the only place this character is mentioned in Revelation. It is probably impossible to identify him.

Unclean spirits like frogs. **Frogs** are not normally described as **spirits.** Frogs are introduced here, probably, just because they were some of the plagues of Egypt and are classed along with the other plagues.

Keeps his garments [clean]. The **garments** mentioned here are legal **garments**. When a person became a Christian, he or she was baptized. This involved putting off the old **garments** of the gentile religion and putting on the new **garments** of Christ. Physically, that meant removing the old clothing and putting on a new white robe to symbolize the new legal condition that the **garment** represented. Keeping the legal **garments** clean meant keeping the faith.

The Kings of the East. In Rev 7:2, an angel came up from **the East**, having the seal of the God of life. Four other angels were standing at the four corners of the land, one of which was probably at the Euphrates. The boundary between **the East** and the West seems to have been thought to have been the Euphrates River. It was at the Euphrates River that the four angels were tied until the sixth angel was commanded to release them (Rev 9:13-14).

The passage, Rev 16:12, 16-21, forms a complete unit. The topic deals with the effects of the sixth angel, whose bowl caused the Euphrates River to dry up so that the way might be prepared for **the kings of the East** to cross. This bowl also gathered these **kings** together at Megiddo, about three or four hundred miles southwest of the Euphrates. The seventh bowl caused all sorts of natural disasters to happen, such as those that occurred when the ten commandments were given. The consequences of these phenomena were to bring pain and destruction upon human beings. The geography involved included the Euphrates, **the kings** from the territory east of the Euphrates, and Mount Megiddo. Only the voice went out from the temple at Jerusalem. The destruction took place at Megiddo. No location in Asia Minor was mentioned.

Mealy ignored geographical factors and lumped together the battle of Mount Megiddo (Rev 16:12, 16-21) with the Battle in the Valley of Decision outside Jerusalem (Rev 19:15-19), which is an antitype of the battle there prophesied by Ezekiel and Joel. By making one battle out of two he had to add to the kings of the East also the kings, generals, and armies of all the earth.[1]

The Characters. The narrative (Rev 16:13-15) begins with the introductory formula, **There was given . . .** (Sinaiticus) or **Now I was watching . . .** (NA). That which was given or seen was the three spirits that went out from the three hated

---

[1] Mealy, *Thousand Years*, pp. 76-77.

representations of the enemy--**the dragon**, its agent, **the beast**, and the **false prophet**. This was a different gathering of the enemy at a different place. This was to take place on the day of the Lord, which was destined to happen in the Kidron Valley, east of the temple area following the typology of Ezek 38-39, Zech 14, and Joel 3. The passage concludes with a warning to watch (Ezek 33).

Although the unit begins as with a new paragraph, it speaks of the mythical beings as if they were known to the reader and had been mentioned in the paragraph just above, but this is not so.[1] This is the first time the term **false prophet** occurs in Revelation (also Rev 19:20 and Rev 20:10).[2] **The dragon** was introduced in Rev 12, and **the beast** in Rev 13. **The dragon** was described as the one who gave authority to **the beast** (Rev 13:2, 4, 11). That is the last time it was mentioned until Rev 16:13, and only then in texts other than Sinaiticus. **The beast** appears only in Rev 13:1-4, 11-12, 14-15, 17; 14:11, and 15:2. This means the last reference to **the dragon** was 49 verses before the expression appears in Rev 16:13 (NA) as if it were a continuation of the previous paragraph or sentence.

The characters were described as spirits that were like **frogs**, but **frogs** are not well known as a synonym for spirits. **Frogs,** like other beings that live around water but have no scales or fins, are considered unclean from a ritualistic point of view. **Frogs** are also some of the creatures Aaron produced with his famous wand as the second plague brought upon the Egyptians (Exod 8:3). If the identity of the three characters with **frogs** had already been made, then the editor who put together Rev 16 added it to the rest of the narrative, because the subject was **plagues**, and one of **the plagues** of Egypt was frogs, so the topic belonged to this category even if it interrupted the narrative into which it was inserted. The only way Lohmeyer could make sense out of these **frogs** that were spirits that might be coherent with the entire unit was to identify the spirits with the kings of the East (Rev 16:12).[3]

There is enough information given about **the dragon** and **the beast** in Rev 12 and 13 to identify **the dragon** as Rome and **the beast** as Rome's local agent. Rome's legal agents in Palestine were either the Herods or the Roman governors and procurators, but there is no data given about the **false prophet** to allow for its demythologization. If we still possessed the document from which Rev 16:13-15

---

[1] Contra Swete, *Revelation*, p. 249. Lohmeyer, *Offenbarung*, pp. 136-37, and Kraft, *Offenbarung*, pp. 208-09 were probably correct in thinking that Rev 16:15 was a later intrusion. It seems to interrupt the flow of the narrative. They both failed, however, to see that verses 13 and 14 also constitute an intrusion. There is obvious editorializing in this unit. Walvoord, *Revelation*, p. 237, said, "In verses 13-16 John has an additional vision introduced by the phrase 'and I saw' which is parenthetical in nature but a commentary upon the sixth bowl and somehow related to it." Walvoord was not precisely correct in his boundaries, but he at least observed that there was an interruption here. Ladd, *Commentary*, p. 213, also noticed that the kings of the East suddenly disappeared from the narrative, "and equally suddenly the *dragon and the beast* appear."

[2] Caird, *Revelation*, however, assumed that the false prophet was the same as the second beast of Rev 13:11-18.

[3] Lohmeyer, *Offenbarung*, 135-36.

was taken, the **false prophet** might also have been described in ways that could be understood by Palestinian Jews.

CONCLUSIONS ON THE UNIT

Although there are some unknown quantities, such as the identification of the **false prophet**, this examination has shown that the probabilities are the following:

> 1) Rev 16:13-15 was a separate unit, not composed by the same author as Revelation 16:12, 16-21, but added to Rev 16, because it dealt with plagues.
> 2) The kings of the East were the Parthians, who were friends of the Jews.
> 3) The author believed the Parthians would come to Megiddo to help the Jews overpower Rome.
> 4) The drying up of the Euphrates was an antitype of the Exodus from Egypt and the entrance into Canaan.
> 5) The great city in this context should be distinguished from the cities of the gentiles and Babylon. It is Jerusalem that was really divided into three parts.
> 6) Babylon is a mythological term for Rome.
> 7) The date for the composition of Revelation 16:12, 16-21 is the ending of 69 IA or the beginning of 70 IA--after Vespasian had left Jerusalem for Rome and before Titus returned to complete the destruction of Jerusalem.[1]
> 8) The plagues associated with the bowls were directed primarily at Israel's enemies--not Israel. This was also true of the plagues activated by the trumpets in Rev 8, 9, and 10. The curses that were initiated when the seals were opened were directed at the Jews themselves. They were the curses that were promised if Israelites broke their contract with the Lord, which they did.
> 9) The text accepted by NA seems to include homiletical expansions added to the text preserved by Sinaiticus.

TEXT REPEATED

Revelation 16:12, 16-21	First Testament
[12] Now the sixth [angel] poured out	Gen 15:18 On that day Yehowah made a contract with Abram which said, "To your seed I have given this land
its bowl upon **the**	from the River of Egypt to **the Great**

---

[1] B. Newman, "The Fallacy of the Domitian Hypothesis," *NTS* 10 (1963/64):133-39, argued that there is no real basis for assuming that the Book of Revelation was written in the time of Domitian.

Great River Euphrates. and **its water was dried up** so that the way of the kings of the East may be prepared. ¹⁶He brought them together to the place called in Hebrew "Har-Megiddo." ¹⁷Now when [the seventh angel] poured out his bowl upon the air, and **a** loud **noise from the temple** of God went out, saying, "It has happened." ¹⁸Then there occurred **bolts of lightning, noises, peals of thunder**, and there was a great earthquake,	**River,** the River **Euphrates**." ᴶᵉʳ ⁵⁰:³⁸A drought to **its water** and **it was dried up**.
such that there has not been from the time human beings appeared on the earth an earthquake so great as this. ¹⁹Then the great city was divided into three parts, the cities of the	ᴵˢᵃ ⁶⁶:⁶The noise of an uproar from the city, **a noise from the temple**, the sound of Yehowah paying back his enemies. ᴱˣᵒᵈ ¹⁹:¹⁶There were **noises, bolts of lightning** and heavy clouds over the mountain--the very strong blast of a trumpet, and all the people in the camp trembled. ᴰᵃⁿ ¹²:¹It will be a time of hardship **such that there has not been from the** origin of the nation until that **time**. ᴶᵒˢʰ ¹⁰:¹⁴**There has not been** a day like that one, either before or since, when Yehowah listened to the voice of a man, because Yehowah fought for Israel.
nations fell, and **Babylon the great**, was remembered before God for the purpose of giving to her **the cup of the wine of the wrath** of his anger. ²⁰Every island fled,	ᴰᵃⁿ ⁴:²⁷Then he said, "Is not this **Babylon the great** which I have built?" ᴶᵉʳ ²⁵:¹⁵Take this **cup of the wine of the wrath** from my hand, and drink it. ᴵˢᵃ ⁵¹:¹⁷Stand up, Jerusalem--you who **have drunk** at the hand of Yehowah **the cup of his wrath.**
and **the mountains** were not found.	ᴱᶻᵉᵏ ³⁸:²⁰**The mountains** will be thrown down, and the cliffs will fall.

²¹Huge **hailstones came down** from heaven upon human beings, and people blasphemed God because of the pain of the **hailstones**, because its plague was exceedingly great.

Exod 9:23 Moses extended his wand to heaven, and Yehowah produced noises, **hail**, and fire **came down** to earth, and

Yehowah rained **hail** on the land of Egypt.

COMMENTARY ON TEXT

The great river Euphrates. **The Euphrates River** runs roughly parallel to the Tigris River. At times it was Rome's eastern border. Scholars, like Hailey, interpret this river as being only a barrier symbol with no geographical reality.[1] Jewish and Christian theology, however, was vividly related to geography. Zion, the Promised Land, Egypt, Babylon, Assyria, Jerusalem, the Wilderness of Zin, and other locations mentioned in the Bible were more than symbols. That is also true of Mount Megiddo and **the River Euphrates**.

Called in Hebrew "Har Megiddo." Many scholars have tried to claim that **Megiddo** comes from the Hebrew word meaning "assemble." Therefore it means Mount of Assembly and is Mount Zion rather than a place near the Carmel Mountain Range. LaRondelle, however, noticed an old Greek (OG) text of Zech 12:11 for Megiddo, which means "the plain of the *cut down*."[2] This might mean the plain where grain has been cut down or where soldiers have been cut down in battle, but it does not mean "assemble." There are still those who want to modify the text to suit their theology,[3] but this effectively refutes any etymological basis for identifying **Mount Megiddo** with Mount Zion. Caird said that, like John's other names, this name is a symbol. He was sure that there was no expectation of battle here in northern Palestine, but rather, in Rome.[4]

Bolts of lightning, noises, and peals of thunder. All of these natural phenomena and sound effects allude to the contract made at Mount Sinai together with the commandments given to the Israelites (Exod 9:24; 19:16-19; also Rev 4:5; 6:12; 8:5; 11:13, 19). The seventh angel not only concluded with the destruction of the enemy, but it also prepared the way for the renewal of the contract. Bauckham has shown the effective role these natural catastrophes have played in the Book of Revelation:

---

[1] Hailey, *Revelation*, p. 333.
[2] H. K. LaRondelle, "The Etymology of Har-Magedon (Rev 16:16)," *AUSS* 27 (1989):69-73.
[3] Such as R. E. Loasby, "'Har-Mageddon' according to the Hebrew in the Setting of the Seven Last Plagues of Revelation 16, *AUSS* 27 (1989):129-32.
[4] Caird, *Revelation*, p. 207.

4:5--bolts of lightning, noises, and peals of thunder,
8:5--peals of thunder, voices, bolts of lightning, and an earthquake,
11:19--bolts of lightning, noises, peals of thunder, an earthquake, and huge hail stones,
16:18-21--bolts of lightning, noises, peals of thunder, a great earthquake, and huge hail stones.

These have been organized in a crescendo effect with one more natural event added by each additional use.[1] Both the trumpets and the bowls provided the appropriate reinstitution of the sufferings and plagues that had once occurred in Egypt. These were followed by the establishment of a contract between God and Israel. The outline of the narrative of the seven trumpets is similar to the one of the seven bowls. Both began with plagues and ended with the reinstitution of the contract on the new Mount Sinai. The reestablishment of the contract was an important theme for the Book of Revelation. It was indicated by the noises at Sinai, the sealed and unsealed scrolls, and the books that were involved in judgment scenes, resembling Dan 7. Rabbis said God revealed himself to Israel when he gave them the contract at Mount Sinai (Sifra Deut, bBer, #343, 142b; ExodR 27:9, 209-10; LamR, Intro 24, 6b), just as John of Patmos said God gave him a revelation when the messenger brought him a prophecy. The Sinai revelation was accompanied by many kinds of natural sounds. The provision of a contract here is also accompanied by many kinds of noises and is understood to be a revelation.

This reinstitution of the Sinai scene differs from the seven seals which released curses of the contract that were directed at those who were parties to the contract with the Lord. Instead of being aimed at the chosen people who had broken the contract, these natural phenomena were directed against Israel's enemies, just as Ezekiel promised:

> **"I will call up against him [Gog]** (Ezek 38:18) **a sword in all my mountains," said the Lord Yehowah . . . "I will judge him with disease, blood, torrential rains, hail stones, and I will rain upon him fire and brimstone"** (Ezek 38:21-22).

Peake noticed long ago that there was a similarity between the series of trumpets and the series of bowls,[2] but there is a difference in the goals. Attributing the saying to Rabbi Hama ben Rabbi Hanina, Rabbi Levi said, "Just as he punished some of the first ones, in the same way he will punish some of the last ones" (Pesikta Rabbati 17:8 [70a]). He expanded this conclusion by noting who those of the first and the last would be. The ones punished of the first ones were the Egyptians and the last ones to be punished would be Romans. Rabbi Levi listed the plagues brought against

---

[1] R. Bauckham, "The Eschatological Earthquake in the Apocalypse of John," *NovT* 19 (1977):226-27.
[2] A. S. Peake, *The Revelation of John* (London: Holborn, 1919), p. 343.

Egypt before the Exodus and argued that God would punish Edom (Rome) in the same way--with blood, frogs, boils, wild beasts, gnats, disease, hail, locusts, darkness, and slaughter.

The Sibyl prophesied that after the barbarian empire (=Rome, SibOr 3:638) had ravaged other lands that God would send a king (the Messiah) to provide relief (SibOr 3:652) through war. God would accompany the Messiah's efforts with natural calamities, judging all people with war, sword, fire, rain, and flood (SibOr 3:689). Then the sons of the great God would live quietly around their temple (SibOr 3:702). This would be Eden and the age to come.

The cup of the wine of his wrath. Ruiz correctly disagreed with those scholars who thought this represented an ordeal by bitter water. **The cup** did not contain poison or a bitter potion but wine. The wine was intended to represent punishment but not trial.[1]

Every island fled and the mountains were not found. This is part of the natural disaster destined to take place when the contract is renewed between God and his people. The way islands flee is that the water rises up so high that they are covered. The water would have to flood much more before the mountains disappeared. The same destruction was to have happened to the mountains and islands in association with the sixth seal (Rev 6:14). Although the seventh seal introduced many natural disasters, Caird was correct in saying that it was impossible to maintain that the author

> included in these immediate expectations the end of the world. The utmost limit of his prophetic vision was the end of Rome's world.[2]

Babylon the Great was remembered before God. The visual image implied here is that of an attorney coming **before** the great king as he sat on his judgment bench. The legal plaintiff reminded the king of something that he needed to know at that precise time. In this case the king was **God,** and the plaintiff was one of God's intelligence agents, calling God's attention to things he had learned about **Babylon.** The author assumed that when this case was presented to the judge, God would apply punishment to Rome just as soon as he learned the facts of the case.

After Nebuchadnezzar had boasted of **Babylon** being **great** he lost his sanity and was punished for seven years. With the seventh bowl two things happened:

1) on the one hand all the noises and natural phenomena that were associated with the establishment of the contract at Sinai reoccurred, and
2) at the same time the enemies of Israel were punished.

---

[1] Ruiz, *Ezekiel in the Apocalypse*, p. 277.
[2] Caird, *Revelation*, p. 209.

The **Babylon** that **was remembered** was Rome. The passive voice was used to avoid mentioning the name of God. It means that God remembered Rome for some incident, evidently something evil. Rome would be **remembered**--not for blessing-- but for punishment. He would then give her the cup of the wine of his anger. Roman islands would vanish and mountains would disappear as huge hail came down upon Rome. Rome was to be the antitype of ancient Egypt and correspondingly, Rome would receive the same plagues Egypt had received while Israelites were in the process of escaping and receiving their contract with the Lord.

TEXT REPEATED

Revelation 16:13-15

First Testament

¹³Now there was given from the mouth of the false prophet three unclean spirits like **frogs** ¹⁴for they are spirits of demons, performing great signs to go out toward the kings of the whole civilized world, to gather them together to the war of the great day of the almighty God. ¹⁵Look! he is coming like a thief. Blessed is he who stands guard and keeps his garments [clean], so that he may not walk naked, and they see his shame.

Ps 78:45 He sent among them flies, which consumed them, and **frogs**, which destroyed them.

Exod 8:1-2 Then Yehowah said to Moses, "Tell Aaron, 'Stretch out your hand with your wand over the rivers, the canals, and the pools, and bring up **frogs** over the land of Egypt.'" Aaron stretched out his hand over the waters of Egypt and brought up **frogs**, and covered the land of Egypt.

COMMENTARY

The false prophet. Again the passive voice was used to avoid mentioning God as the subject. It means that God provided **the false prophet** with **three unclean spirits**. Loisy wondered if this character might be Simon Magus.[1]

Unclean spirits like frogs. At least the first two of these three verses constitute a small midrash on Exod 8. Although the **frogs** are interpreted as unclean demons, their task was constructive so far as Israel was concerned. They were commissioned to go out to the kings of gentile nations, just as they once had done to the Pharaoh in the land of Egypt. Their value was in becoming nuisances to Israel's enemies.

He is coming like a thief. This is a sudden change of subject, as many scholars have noted, but it is not necessarily a *Christian* interpolation, as Whealon thought.[2] The

---

[1] Loisy, *L'Apocalypse*, p. 291.
[2] J. F. Whealon, "New Patches on an Old Garment: The Book of Revelation," *BTB* 11 (1981):55.

only association between this verse and the one preceding has to be inferred. At the same time the unclean spirits went out and infected the kings of foreign nations the Messiah would suddenly appear to lead Israel in her war against all the nations involved. This would happen on the great day of God when Gog and Magog would lead all gentile nations against Israel--not at Mount Megiddo, as the unit, Rev 16:12, 16-21, describes, but in the Kidron valley outside the temple area at Jerusalem. This suggests that this verse was at one time associated with a different context.

Keeps his garments clean. This is not a discussion of laundering cloth garments. The "cleanliness" involved is ritual cleanliness. The **garments** involved were legal **garments.** Those who kept these **garments** clean were themselves rigorously orthodox observers of Levitical laws.

CHAPTER SEVENTEEN

TEXT

Revelation

First Testament

^{17:1}**Now** one of **the** seven **angels** having the seven bowls, came to me **and spoke to me, saying**, "Come, and **I will show you** the judgment of

^{Zech 1:9} **Now the angel** who

spoke to me, **said** to me, "**I will show you** what these things are."

^{Isa 23:17}At the end of 70 years Yehowah will visit Tyre, and she will return to her [work for] salary and her **prostituting** all the kingdoms of the earth on the surface of the ground.

the great harlot,

^{Nah 3:4}**Of the great** harlotries of **the harlot** the beautiful grace, a mistress of witchcraft.

the one who is **sitting on much water**

^{Jer 51:13}Yehowah has both planned and done that which he said to those who live (*sit*) in Babylon, **you who sit on much water**, rich in treasures, your end has come.

^{Isa 23:17}She **acted indecently** with all the **king**doms **of the earth**.

²**with** whom **the kings of the earth acted indecently**, and the migrants **of the Land**

became **drunk** from **the wine of** her **sexual indecency**."

Jer 25:15God of Israel, said this to me, "Take this cup of **the wine of** anger from my hand, and make all the nations to whom I send you drink it."

Jer 51:7A golden cup is Babylon in the hand of the Lord, making all the earth [or land] **drunk** from its **wine**.

COMMENTARY

One of the angels . . . spoke to me. The words **spoke to me, saying, "Come, and** I will show you" **appears also in Rev 21:9. At that point** one of the seven angels, who had the seven bowls **was prepared to show** the bride, the wife of the Lamb.

This vision begins like the first vision of Zechariah, with an **angel** present to provide the necessary answers to questions. Throughout Rev 17 there continues to be **the angel** there answering questions and interpreting visions: 1) **I will show you the judgment of the great harlot** (Rev 17:1); 2) **I will tell you the mystery of the woman** 3) **The beast that you saw was** (Rev 17:8)**;** 4)**; Here is the mind that has wisdom** (Rev 17:9); 5)**The ten horns that you saw are** (Rev 17:12); 6) **The water that you saw is** (Rev 17:15); 7) **The ten horns that you saw** (Rev 17:16); 8) **The woman that you saw is** (Rev 17:18). The answers to the questions waere designed to demythologize the mythical terms.

The interpretations of visions here are similar in method to those of the Habakkuk Commentary among the Dead Sea Scrolls. There the author quoted passages of Scripture and then told their meaning for the contemporary situation. Following a text he would write "Its interpretation is". . . (*peesh-róh*, פשרו). "Its interpretation is concerning the Kittim" (1QpHab 2:12; 3:4, 11); **The wicked one**. "Its interpretation is the wicked priest" (1QpHab 1:13).

The methodology of the exegete was to start with a message he wanted to deliver. Then he or she found some text to support the argument and give it authority. It was not necessary for the text to be logically related to the message. All that was needed was a few words that could be exploited. For example, Rabbi Eleazar of Modi'im selected for his text,

> **Tomorrow I will stand on the top of the hill** (Exod 17:9). He said Israel should fast and rely on the deeds of the fathers. "**Top**--These are the deeds of the fathers. **The hill**--These are the deeds of the Mothers" (Mek. *Amalek* 1:96-98.

Of course, the deeds of the mothers and fathers hundreds of years after Moses stood on the top of the hill had nothing to do with the text in Exod 17:9, but it did not have to. Like many twentieth century scholars, the author demythologized that which was not myth, inventing a meaning he wanted. More often there is a way in which an ancient text can be applied to a contemporary situation: The text in Habakkuk is **It is terrible and dreadful. Its justice and greatness proceed from itself** (Hab 1:7). The exegete said, "Its interpretation is concerning the Kittim, fear and dread of whom will reach over all the nations." (1QpHab 3:4-5).

Daniel had a vision of a beast that had **ten horns** (Dan 7:7). He interpreted the **horns** to mean **ten kings** (Dan 7:24). **The ten horns** (Dan 7:20) were interpreted by the author of Rev 17 as **those who had not yet received the kingdom** (Rev 17:12). This is a well-known way of explaining earlier texts. There were eight interpretative passages in Rev 17.

It is probably the beginning of the fifth victorious vision, although that judgment is almost an arbitrary choice. Strand held that the vision begins with Rev 17:3, and Rev 17:1-2 belongs to the fourth vision of the prophecy.[1] The fourth vision, however, seems to conclude with Rev 16:21. Rev 17:1-2 is not a part of that vision. This passage either constitutes the beginning of the fifth vision, or it forms an introduction to the fifth vision. As Ladd observed this is the first instance in the book where an **angel** provided the vision.[2] There were many instances where **the angels** were active and also situations in which **angels** were parts of the visions, but this is the first case where **the angel** brought the vision. The vision of the great harlot in Rev 17 is enough like the beast in Rev 13 that Bergmeier thought Rev 13, 17, and 18 once belonged together as part of the same document.[3] Rev 13 and 17 are both based on earlier Scripture passages, so their similarities may be accidental.

Come, and I will show you. This is an introductory expression, used also in Rev. 21:9. In this latter passage, the object of view is **the bride, the wife of the Lamb**. In contrast, this new discovery is **the judgment of the great harlot.**

The judgment of the great harlot. **The harlot** here is Rome, personified as a woman. This is a different way of dramatizing and cartooning Rome. It was done earlier in Rev 13, where Rome was characterized as a dragon. Personifying a city as a woman was frequent in antiquity (Isa 23; 37:22; 66:7-14; Ezek 16; Nah 3:1-7; Lam 1). Once the reader recognizes that the author of Rev 17 was quoting from Jer 51:7-13, he or she will know at once what the judgment will be. This was not a judgment which **the great harlot** made but a court situation during which **the great harlot** was a defendant to be judged. The old Babylon had lived on much water,[4] having lived on the Euphrates, and the next phrase was **whose end has come**. The new "Babylon" mentioned here in Rev 17 also lived on much water, right there on the Tiber River, just as the old Babylon had. By typological transfer, the reader was expected to

---

[1] K. A. Strand, "The 'Victorious-introduction' Scenes in the Visions in the Book of Revelation," *AUSS* 25 (1987):275.
[2] G. E. Ladd, *A Commentary on the Revelation of John* (Grand Rapids: Eerdmans, 1972), p. 23.
[3] R. Bergmeier, "Die Erzhure und das Tier: Apk 12 18-18 18 und 17f. Eine quellen-und redaktionskritische Analyse," *ANRW* II.25.5. p. 3905.
[4] C. H. Dyer, "The Identity of Babylon in Revelation 17-18," *BibSac* 144/575 (1987):305-16; 433-49, argued that Babylon in these verses was really Babylon and not Rome.

recognize that the judgment on Rome would also be that **her end had come.** Like the horn in Dan 7, the verdict of this judgment would be negative for the enemies of the Jews. Schüssler-Fiorenza depoliticizes the harlot figure by calling it

> a symbol of the archetypal enmity against God or the sign for the general decadence of all civilization.[1]

The texts of Revelation, however, are so clearly localized and related to geography and history, war, conquest, destruction, and military strategy that it is impossible to dismiss it all without writing a new fiction.

Beauvery related Rev 17 to a Vespasian coin, evidently minted about 71 IA. That year was a good year for Rome. After years of civil war and change of emperors, Vespasian finally overthrew Vitellius and began a new move to governmental stability. There had been four emperors in one year. During the last civil war Rome burned, and the Capitol was destroyed. Vespasian had surrounded Jerusalem, after taking the major fortresses in the other parts of Palestine. Because of the critical problems in Rome he was forced to withdraw his troops from Jerusalem and direct a war in Rome. The reaction of nationalistic Jews in Jerusalem was one of great rejoicing (Rev 18-19). Between chapters twelve and thirteen there is a sketch made of both sides of the Vespasian coin.[2] The coin was minted after the Jewish rejoicing had ceased, and Jerusalem had been burned. Beauvery conjectured that the Vespasian coin was minted as a victory celebration in Rome. Jerusalem had been destroyed, the civil war had been won, and the Capitol temples had been rebuilt. The coin pictured the goddess Roma, seated on the seven hills, with her right foot in the Tiber River. She was seated restful and confident, with her left hand holding the top either of her staff or of a small sword that rests on her knee.[3] At her right side is the mother wolf nursing Romulus and Remus, the mythical founders of Rome. On the reverse side of the coin is an image of the head of Caesar Vespasian, with these words IMP CAESAR VESPASIANVS AVG PM TP PP COS III. This is "Emperor Caesar Vespasian Augustus, PM, Pontifex Maximus (head of the college of priests), TP, Tribunal Power, PP, Pater Patriae (Father of the Fatherland). S C stands for *senatus consultum* (resolution of the senate), "decree of the senate." The coin is dated at 71 IA, very shortly after the destruction of Jerusalem. In the opinion of the Roman who made the coin this showed Rome as a goddess, a queen, sitting in all of her glory and power. Rev 17, however, cartooned her as a harlot. The Latin word for a female wolf (*lupa*), like the one that nursed Romulus and Remus. Pictured on the coin is *lupa*. The same word means "prostitute," so this stimulated Jewish minds to distort the picture on the coin. That which Roman citizens proudly called a goddess,

---

[1] E. Schüssler-Fiorenza, *Revelation: Vision of a Just World* (Minneapolis: Fortress Press, c1991), p. 98.
[2] The sketch was made for the use of D. E. Aune, *Revelation 17-22* (Nashville: Thomas Nelson Publishers, c1998), p. 920. It was copied from that sketch for use here.
[3] R. Beauvery, "L'Apocalypse au Risque de la Numismatique," *RB* 90 (1983):243-60+Planche I.

nationalistic Jews called a prostitute. This Roman queen expanded her power and wealth by conquest and colonizing.

Kim correctly noted that Rev 17 was written from a masculine point of view. The picture of a harlot was defaming.[1] It was also from the point of view of an isolationist who believed it was wrong to mingle with foreign nations and engage in trade with them. Biblical concepts usually pictured the whore as an enemy nation, like Nineveh (Nah 3:4) and Tyre (Isa 23: 15-18), but it also describes Jerusalem and Israel when they engage in foreign trade and treaties (Hos 2:1-13; Jer 13:20-27; Ezek 16:35-38). When Jerusalem was isolationistic, it was like a pure, innocent bride (Jer 2:1), a princess (Lam 1:1), but when she mingled with foreign nations she became a prostitute and was finally stripped of her glory and left a desolate widow (Lam 1:2-22; Ps 137:7-8).

The passion between the sexes is powerful; so is the lust for power, wealth, and expansion among nations. Therefore sexual relationships provide an excellent metaphor to describe international relationships. Describing cities as feminine is not necessarily pejorative. For the expansionistic native the city sits like a glorious queen, princess, or bride. For the enemy isolationist the same city is a harlot sitting on a prostitute's stool.

The author of Rev 17 did not recognize Roma as a true, glorious goddess and was not rejoicing at her success. In his opinion, that scantily clad goddess was really a harlot who had gained prosperity and status at the expense of other nations that had mingled with her. This author was an ancient Rudyard Kipling. Kipling lived during the extravagant celebration in England for the prosperous reign of Queen Victoria. During her reign England ruled the seven seas. Kipling, however, predicted her downfall:

> The tumult and the shouting dies
> The captains and the kings depart
>
> . . .
>
> Far flung her navies melt away.
> In dune and headlands sinks her fire.
> Lo, all our pomp of yesterday
> Is one with Nineveh and Tyre.

In a similar vein, a Jewish nationalist, visualized Rome's great prosperity and political success as temporary. At that point in history, Jerusalem had fallen; Rome had apparently recovered, but the game was not finished. There were Jews in nearly every country whose primary loyalty was to Jerusalem. Thousands of these were in parts of the Roman Empire. After the fall of Jerusalem there continued to be rebellions in other parts of the Roman Empire in which Jews and Christians were

---

[1] J. K. Kim, "'Uncovering Her Wickedness': An Inter(con)textual Reading of Revelation 17 from a Postcolonial Feminist Perspective," JSNT 73 (1999):61-81.

involved. Rome was normally able to suppress these, providing Jews and Christians with martyrs.

There were many Jewish and Christian leaders engaged in important parts of the Roman government, business, shipping, banking, and other positions that they could use, if necessary, to support Jerusalem in any rebellion against Rome. They were in strategic positions that made sabotage possible and threatening to Rome. If this had not been so, Christianity could not have been in a position to negotiate with Constantine in the fourth century. From a Roman point of view, Christians behaved just about the same way other Jews did and were only a part of the entire Jewish security threat. These were not just idle threats. Jews and Christians had a lot of underground power. The promise given by the author of Rev 17 that the old harlot, Rome, would fall, was much slower in happening than that author expected.

Living on much water. A literal translation would be, **sitting on much water**, but this is a quotation from Jeremiah, where Babylon was depicted as **living** on much water. In Jeremiah the Hebrew was *shah-kahn-táy* (שכנתי),[1] which is in synonymous parallel with *yoh-sheh-váy* (ישבי). *Shah-káhn* (שכן) unquestionably means **dwell, live,** or **be present** in a tent. The parallel synonym for **living** or **dwelling** is *yah-sháv* (ישׁב). *Yah-sháv*, however, also means **sit**, so it is possible that the translator of the text in Jeremiah had the word *yah-sháv* before him rather than *shah-káhn*. If that is not the case then the author of Rev 17 intentionally changed the term to suit his own needs.

Of course, Rome **lived** right there on the Tiber River, where there was much water, but the coin showed the goddess Roma, **sitting** on the seven hills with her right foot in the Tiber River. The author of Rev 17 may have chosen to emphasize the **sitting,** rather than the **living** or **dwelling** role of Roma. In a subversive atmosphere, the author did not mention the name Rome at all. His code terms directed to Jews and Christians were the existence of the coin, the role of Babylon and Tyre in Jewish history, and the Scripture. With these he continued to direct his defamatory attack against Rome.

Most English translations render **much water** as "many waters," implying that there were many streams, lakes, seas, or springs on which the city was situated. The word for water in Hebrew has a dual or plural form (*máh-yeem*, מים), but its meaning is singular. There is no separate plural distinguished from the singular. Used with the adjective, **great,** it refers to a large body of **water** rather than many bodies of **water**. Beagley took **many** literally, and then concluded that Rome did not sit on **many waters**, so the wicked city represented must be Jerusalem instead,[2] even though Jerusalem is not a sea port or located near a river. Morris even interpreted the **water** symbolically to mean "many peoples."[3]

---

[1] There is a textual problem here: *Shah-kahn-táy* is an impossibility. It may once have been *shah-káhn-ty,* "I have dwelled" or *shoh-kahn-áy,* "those who dwell" The latter possibility makes sense in the sentence.

[2] A. J. Beagley, *The "Sitz im Leben" of the Apocalypse* (Berlin: W. De Gruyter, 1987), pp. 107-108.

[3] L. Morris, *The Book of Revelation* (Grand Rapids: Eerdmans, c1987), p. 204.

This Revelation narrative is composed of a combination of imagery directed at Rome from the typology of Babylon. It was Babylon who sat on a large body of water whose end had come, according to Jeremiah. Jeremiah was ordered to make all the gentile kings drink the wine of the Lord's anger before the Lord would send his sword into their midst. Babylonians did not know, as Jeremiah did, that Babylon was only a cup in the Lord's hand. From this intoxication other nations would go mad and Babylon would fall. The author also quoted from Isaiah's song of the harlot, which Isaiah attributed to Tyre. The author also transferred that designation to Rome. Rome made an easy antitype both for Tyre and Babylon. It was Rome during the author's time that ruled Jews the way Babylon did during Jeremiah's time.

Like Babylon and Tyre, Rome was a commercial city, located on the Tiber River, not far from the sea. The author also followed the clue of a Roman Vespasian coin, made in 71 IA, which every contemporary Jew would have recognized. It was the coin of the realm. It showed a woman, obviously the goddess, Roma, sitting on seven hills and also over the water of the Tiber, with the wolf and her cubs nearby. The author's use of **sitting**, rather than living, would identify the woman on the coin with Jeremiah's prophecy concerning Babylon. It did not require much hostile imagination to interpret this scene as if the woman were a harlot whose commerce was with male lovers rather than countries with whom Rome traded.[1] This was especially true since the author of Revelation was able to find prophets who foretold the doom God had destined for cities, like Nineveh and Tyre, that the prophets described as **harlots** who made nations drunk from her wine.

Two prophecies plus an identifying coin clearly proved to the author that God intended these prophecies to be fulfilled in his day in relationship to Rome. The date of the coin also helps date the final composition of this unit. Vespasian's coin would not have had much modern significance during the time of Domitian, twenty years later. There were three groups of people who depended heavily on Rome's prosperity and success: 1) Kings of other countries, 2) Business magnates, and 3) Shipping firms. The author dealt with all three and the misery they suffered when Rome was threatened to fall.

With whom the kings of the earth acted indecently. Rome, with her extensive international commerce, was described disrespectfully here as a **harlot** who was engaged in sexual prostitution with all these **kings**. Because Rome did business with all the nations of the known ancient world. Rome, then, was like a **harlot** who mingled with all customers. This, according to the author, was not only true of the kings, but also of those special enemies of his, **the migrants of the land**. These were the foreigners in Palestine, the people of **every language, tribe, nation, and people** who Jews thought did not deserve to live there. The author mixed his metaphors in accusing **the migrants of the land** of being drunk with sexual promiscuity. All this really meant was that they were pro-Roman and were having business and social intercourse with Romans. They bought from them, sold to them, attended the same

---

[1] See Beauverry, "L'Apocalypse," pp., 243-60 et Planche I.

country clubs, and associated with them in other non-sexual ways. Jewish mingling with Romans, however, was like Jewish mingling with Babylonians. Prophets objected to their behavior (Hos 2:5; Isa 1:21; Ezek 16:36-37; 23:2-10; Nah 3:4).

Like Babylon and her supporting nations, Rome would become **drunk** and then stagger and fall. Since the attitude of **the migrants of the land** was the same as **the kings,** from an orthodox Jewish point of view, the correct translation of the latter may have been intended to be **kings** of the **land** rather than **the earth**, as in Jeremiah. If this were the case, **the kings** would have been the Herods, primarily Herod the Great and Herod Agrippa I.

Ezekiel used the **harlot** metaphor in relationship to the city of Jerusalem who traded with Egypt and Assyria. He accused Jerusalem of being a **harlot** for Egypt and Assyria (Ezek 16:26, 28). He followed his metaphor further to say Jerusalem was not only a prostitute, but she paid her customers for the privilege of mingling with them (Ezek 16:30-34).

TEXT

Revelation

³He took me away
to the wilderness, in the spirit, and I saw a woman

seated on **a crimson beast**, filled with blasphemous names,

having seven heads and **ten horns**.
⁴The woman was wearing purple and crimson, also gilded with gold, precious stones, and pearls, having
a gold cup in her **hand**, full of abominations and the defilements of her sexual indecency. ⁵On her forehead, a name was written, a mystery,

"**Great Babylon**, the mother of **harlots** and those who abominate the land."

First Testament

$^{Ezek\ 20:35}$I will bring you
to the wilderness of the nations, and I will try you in judgment there, face to face.

$^{Dan\ 7:7}$Now look! **A beast**, a fourth one--terrible, dreadful, and stronger [than the others]; it had teeth of iron. It ate and shattered [most of its victims], and trampled the rest with its feet. It was different from all the beasts that were before it;
it **had ten horns**.

$^{Jer\ 51:7-8}$Babylon is
a gold cup in the Lord's **hand,**
making all the land drunk. . . .
⁸Suddenly, "**Babylon** is fallen and broken."

$^{Nah\ 3:4}$From the **great** harlotries of the **harlot**, her beautiful grace, a mistress of witchcraft.

$^{Hos\ 2:4}$Argue with your mother [Israel].

. . and let her turn her **harlotry** away from before her face and her prostitution from between her breasts.

Ezek 16:8"I covered your nakedness, and I took an oath with you [Judah]; I entered into a [marriage] contract with you," said the Lord Yehowah, "and you became mine."¹⁵ . . . but you trusted your beauty and you engaged in **harlotry**."

Ezek 23:17Babylonians came to her in a lover's bed; they defiled her with their **harlotry**, and she became unclean through them.

COMMENTARY

He took me away to the wilderness. The mention of **the wilderness** was to alert the reader that the stage was being reset for a continuation of Rev 12. There the **dragon** (Rome) tried to consume the woman (Jews). Here the **dragon** was identified with **the great harlot**--also Rome. Although the vision was about **the wilderness**, it was interpreted as **the judgment of the great harlot.** This was intended to remind the reader of the judgment scene of Dan 7 where the **horn** (Antiochus Epiphanes) was given the death sentence, and the Son of man (Judas, the Maccabee) was appointed leader over Palestine.

The wilderness was the great refuge for Israelites and Jews. They had to go through **the wilderness** to get from Egypt to the Promised Land. When Israel became unfaithful so that Yehowah divorced her, Hosea predicted that the Lord would lead Israel through **the wilderness** again to prepare her for a new marriage contract. Israelites tested the Lord in **the wilderness**; the Lord punished them there and prepared them to enter the Promised Land. In New Testament (NT) times, Jews interpreted their struggle with Rome as a **wilderness** testing, and they looked forward to a new restoration. **The wilderness** struggle was difficult but it provided the necessary discipline for the Promised Land. It was also the place where the Lord judged his people. Here the judgment was with the Jews, but also with Rome, and the author of this literary unit expected Jews to be vindicated.

In the spirit. It was still one of those seven angels who **took** the author **in the spirit** to **the wilderness**. By **in the spirit** he meant "in his imagination" or "in his mind's eye." He "visualized" the following spectacle. He did not see it with his human, physical eyes. The trip the author took was not in a chariot. It was **in the spirit**.

Instead of "day dreaming" Aune said the author "fell into a prophetic trance,"[1] by which he may also have meant, "he started day dreaming." That is what happened. The "vision" which came to him should not have surprised the reader. He came to the same realization that he had held all along. He became convinced that Rome was a wealthy, gentile country, the chief of all countries to promote gentile commerce.

Having seven heads and ten horns. **The seven heads and ten horns** attributed to the dragon and the beast (Rev 12:3; 13:1) were also applied to **the beast** in Rev 17:3. The dragon was Rome, the devil, or Satan. It was the principal responsible for all the wickedness that was happening. **The beast** was the legal agent of Rome that dealt with the Jews in Palestine. **The beast** or the **heads** probably refer to Herod the Great or Herod Agrippa I. **The ten horns** may allude to the Caesars, the latter being an antitype of the Seleucids prior to the Maccabean Revolt and also an antitype of Tyre in the time of Isaiah. **The seven** and **ten** are typological equivalents rather than numerical equivalents. The **ten horns** are taken from Daniel. The **seven heads** could have been deduced from the actual number of Herods, but so also could six or eight. **Seven** was chosen because it was a magic number. The horn of the **fourth beast** in Dan 7 received a death sentence at the same time Judas the Maccabee received a favorable verdict.

Having a gold cup in her hand. The woman held **in her hand a gold cup**, which should remind the reader that Rome, like Babylon, was only **a gold cup in** the Lord's **hand**, and the Lord determined what the **cup** contained. When Jeremiah spoke of the gold cup in Babylon's hand he followed with the words, **Babylon is fallen and broken** (Jer 51:8). The author knew that wine made people crazy, senseless, out of control, and led many people to ruin. So he visualized Rome as a woman who, in the midst of her debauchery and promiscuity, was destined to fall. The title on **her forehead** simply announced that which the author had revealed in many ways--Rome was the epitome of wickedness, the enemy of God's chosen people. The mystery which the author disclosed to those Jews who had ears to hear was that Rome was the antitype of Babylon in its relationship to Jews.

On her forehead a name was written--a mystery. Just as the saints at Mount Zion had the sign of a *tau* (X) written on their **foreheads**, so the dragon had a name written **on her forehead**. The author evidently knew of the practice in Rome for prostitutes, who serviced upper class men, to wear their names on headbands (Seneca, *Controv* 1:2; Juvenal 6:123). This name, however, was a mystery. The word **mystery** was to alert the reader that the author was writing in code. The name that followed was not the mythical woman's real name; it was the author's insulting title given to inform the reader of the character of this woman. Jews understood the code. Babylon was the place where Jews had been in "captivity." Therefore this **woman** was an antitype of old Babylon, from a Jewish point of view. The current **Babylon** was Rome. This also meant that contemporary Rome was holding Jews in

---

[1] Aune, *Revelation 17-22*, p. 933.

the same kind of captivity experience that Babylon had provided several centuries earlier.

Collins and Boring were both mistaken in assuming that Rome could not have been called **Babylon** until it had destroyed Jerusalem, as **Babylon** had done earlier.[1] As soon as Jews began to feel under the same kind of "captivity" under Rome as they had under **Babylon**, Rome began to be labeled **Babylon.** Nineveh did not burn the temple at Jerusalem, but later rabbis identified Rome, not only with **Babylon**, but also with Nineveh. The primary basis for both names comes from Scripture. On the basis of Jer 51, Rome was called **Babylon**; on the basis of Nah 3:1; Ezek 22:2; 24:6, 9; and Jonah 4:11 it was called **Nineveh**.[2] The destruction of the temple would have added an additional dimension to the insult, but the title probably was applied before 70 IA as well as afterward.

TEXT

Revelation	First Testament
⁶I saw the woman becoming drunk from the blood of the saints (and from the blood of the witnesses of Jesus). I was tremendously appalled when I saw her. ⁷Then the angel said to me, "Why are you horrified?" I will tell you the mystery of the woman and of the **beast** with seven heads and **ten horns** who carries her.	Dan 7:7 . . . a fourth **beast** . . . it had **ten horns**.
⁸The **beast** which you saw was, is not, and is about to **come up from the** abyss and go away to destruction.	Dan 7:3 The four great **beasts came up from** the sea.

COMMENTARY

The blood of the witnesses of Jesus. This is one of the few Christianizing phrases added to the prophecy (Rev 4:1-22:5) to make it acceptable to Christians.[3] This was made either by John of Patmos when he translated the document into Greek or, more

---

[1] A. Y. Collins, *Crisis & Catharsis* (Philadelphia: Westminster Press, c1984), p. 76; M. E. Boring, *Revelation* (Louisville: John Knox Press, c1989), p. 180. Boring claimed that the title "Babylon," would have been applied to Rome only after the fall of Jerusalem, even though he also said Jerusalem could also be Babylon (p. 187). Does that mean Jerusalem also destroyed Jerusalem?
[2] Buchanan, *Jewish Messianic Movements from AD 70 to AD 1300* (Eugene, Oregon: Wipf and Stock Publishers, 2003), pp. 339, 351-52, 362-63.
[3] So also J. F. Whealon, "New Patches on an Old Garment: The Book of Revelation," *BTB* 11 (1981):55.

likely, by some earlier Christian scribe. The Christian who added it wanted Christian martyrs as well as Jewish martyrs to be thought of as the contemporary equivalents of the saints of the Most High in Hasmonean times. Jews and Christians were both involved in the same kind of political activities in the first century and both suffered the same consequences from Rome. From the Roman point of view they were terrorists, saboteurs, and insurrectionists; from the Jewish and Christian point of view they were heroes, true patriots, and martyrs.

The mystery of the woman. This is another interpretation. This time giving the significance **of the woman and the beast who was carrying her. The woman** was **great Babylon, the mother of harlots and the abomination of the land.** For those who did not understand the code, this answer would still remain a mystery.

I was tremendously appalled. Literally, I marveled a great marvel. This appears to be a literal Greek translation of a Semitic construction, a finite verb with an infinitive absolute.

The beast with seven heads and ten horns carries her. Boismard correctly said the author described

> the beast as if he were speaking for the first time, as if Rev 13 did not exist.[1]

Rev 13 and Rev 17 apparently belonged to different bodies of literature, initially, but they all grew out of an environment where **beasts** were understood code terms,[2] and where identities of **beasts** could be updated to suit new situations.

The beast with the ten horns[3] in Daniel was Alexander's empire. **The beast** of Rev 17, however, varied somewhat. It also had **seven heads** which may have typologized the Herodian dynasty. The author may have intended **the beast** to be the Roman Empire represented both by the Herods (**seven heads**) and by the Caesars (**ten horns**). In the Danielic judgment scene (Dan 7) the fourth beast, represented by the little horn, lost the case and was sentenced to burning.

The Revelation **beast**, however, seemed to be more than the Danielic fourth **beast.** It supported or carried the harlot. This may be just a way of identifying Rome with Greece, typologically, or it may be a mythological way of saying that Rome (**the harlot**) came on the back of Greece (**the beast**), chronologically. The last of the Syrian Greek leaders to trouble Israel before Hanukkah was Antiochus Epiphanes, whom Judas defeated at Beth-horon. With only a few years of liberation, Rome replaced Syria as the oppressor. A similar vision interpreted the births of Jacob and Esau (Rome).

---

[1] M.-E. Boismard, "'L'Apocalypse,' ou 'les Apocalypses'"de s. Jean," *RB* 56 (1949):513.
[2] Contra Bergmeier, "Die Erzhure," p. 3905.
[3] The horn, all by itself, is a symbol of power, dignity, success, or victory. On this see further I. Scheftelowitz, "Das Hörnermotif in den Religionen," *ARW* 15 (1912):451-87.

> Jacob's hand held Esau's heel from the beginning. The heel of the first age is Esau (Rome); the hand of the second is Jacob. The beginning of a man is his hand, and the end of a man is his heel (4Ezra 6:7-10).

This was Ezra's mythological way of saying the Roman age (Esau) was about over, and the Jewish age (Jacob) was about to begin. In a similar way the author of this Revelation may have intended to picture Rome riding **on the back of a beast** that was destined for destruction. Just as the fourth **beast** came up **out of the sea**, and was finally destroyed, so this **beast** came up out of the abyss and would be destroyed. The word **appalled** renders the Greek *thau-mahs-tháy-sawn-tai* (θαυμασθήσονται) sometimes translated "marveled," "astonished," or "surprised," but it also renders the Hebrew *shah-máhm*, (שׁמם), **appalled,** "shocked," or "horrified" (Dan 8:13; 12:11; Lev 26:32).[1]

The author probably intended the reader to think of the dragon **in the wilderness** and **the beast** mentioned in Rev 12 and 13 when he pictured **the harlot** riding on **a beast.**[2] There the **dragon** was Rome, and **the beast** either the Herodian dynasty or one of the Herodians, either Herod the Great or Herod Agrippa I--the two Herodians who were kings. Palestinian Jews thought of Rome as a burden, carried by Jewish taxes, so here, at an earlier time, it was the Herods who **carried** Rome. Later Rome was upheld by the Roman procurators. Both were financed by Palestinian Jews.

The beast . . . is about to go away to destruction. This is the beginning of another interpretation section. Answering the question, "Who is this beast?" The author here provides the answer in code.

Like Babylon and Rome, **the beast** was destined to **fall and be broken** (Jer 51:8). This statement is probably made in intentional contrast to the Lord, **who is, who was, and who is coming** (Rev 1:4, 8). This **beast,** on the contrary, is the one who is *not* and is *not* about to come but rather is about **to *go away* to destruction.** This means **the beast** is a negative force, a satanic figure. By the time the author wrote, both Herod the Great and Herod Agrippa I were past tense. They **had been,** but they no longer were alive, and they would not exist in the future. The author who wrote this document lived at a time when **the beast was not. The beast** constituted the antitype of the four **beasts who came up from the abyss** (Dan 7:3). Like the

---

[1] So S. Thompson, *The Apocalypse and Semitic Context* (New York: Cambridge U. Press, c1985), p. 12.

[2] Although some scholars have held that the beast of Rev 17 was different from the beasts of Rev 13, there seems to be a relationship between the two Revs. Scholars are correct, however, in questioning every point. It is not good scholarship to presume that every time a term is used it has the same meaning. This is especially true of a composite document such as is typical of anthologies. See F. Düsterdieck, *Critical and Exegetical Handbook to the Revelation of John*, tr. H. E. Jacobs (Winona Lake: Alpha Publications, 1884), p. 431.

horn of the fourth **beast** this dynasty was destined to **go away to destruction** (Dan 7:11). On the great day of judgment they would **go away to** the abyss from which they came.

The destruction Herod Agrippa I would face was more than death. The author needed to make this clear, because many Jews respected this leader who was a descendant of the Hasmoneans as well as Herod the Great. They may have expected him to be raised from the dead in the new age and rule again as Messiah. The author disagreed with this point of view and insisted that Herod Agrippa would share the destiny of the dragon. Rev 17 is directed to the **judgment of the great harlot** (Rev 17:1). This would be the divine future judgment, the antitype of the divine judgment in Dan 7 where the Ancient of Days pronounced the death sentence on Antiochus Epiphanes and decreed that the Son of man (Judas) would receive the kingdom, authority, and glory that goes with royalty (Dan 7:12-14).

The two groups were intentionally set against each other before a judge in a divine court scene. On the one hand, the Hasmonean victors were Judas (**the Son of man**) and the contemporary Jews, called **the saints of the Most High**. The defendants who lost the trial were the horn (Antiochus), the other **beasts,** and the contemporary Greeks. The author of this narrative in Revelation placed as corresponding participants in the new judgment the vindicated plaintiffs who were the Messiah (the Lamb) and the contemporary Jews (**saints and witnesses** of Jesus). Enemies of the Messiah were the defending dragon, harlot, and beast. In opposition to the saints and the **witnesses** of Jesus were **the migrants of the land.**

The verdict would favor the Messiah, **the saints**, and **the witnesses** of Jesus just as it had done for Judas **and the saints of the Most High** in Hasmonean times. Just as the horn and his supporters were condemned in Daniel, so **the dragon, harlot, beast,** and **migrants of the land** would be condemned in the author's day. All of these enemies of the Jews originally came from the abyss in the first place, and so they were destined to go back to the abyss. This follows the same pattern of **the beasts** in Daniel that came up out of **the sea** and in Dan 7 were condemned in judgment--the horn to death by fire and his supporters to existence without political power (Dan 7:11-12, 26-28).

During the generation of the author, Herod Agrippa I had functioned as king or Messiah in Jerusalem under Rome's authority and was probably still held in respect by many Palestinian Jews. The author wanted his readers to understand that this would not continue in the new age when Jews regained political power. Then they would have a new and proper messiah, and Agrippa would be identified with those who were destined for the abyss.

TEXT

Revelation	First Testament
The **migrants of the land,** those whose names are **not written** in **the book of life** from the foundation	Let them be blotted out from **the book of life**; with the righteous,

of the world will be appalled when they see the beast that was, is not, and will appear. ⁹Here is the mind which has wisdom. The seven heads are seven mountains where the woman sits on them. There are seven kings; ¹⁰the five fell, the one is, and the other has not yet come. When it comes it will be necessary for it to remain a short time. ¹¹The beast which was and is not is also the eighth, but it is one of the seven, and he goes away to destruction.

let them **not** be **written** (Ps 69:29).

$^{Isa\ 4:3}$The remnant in Zion, the one left in Jerusalem will be called holy, everyone **written** for **life** in Jerusalem.

COMMENTARY

The book of life. This was the membership roll of the elect who were destined to survive the great judgment. These were the righteous Jews and/or Christians. It did not include those **migrants of the land** whom the author hated. These were foreigners who lived in **the land**, but in the age to come the land would be restored to Davidic control. At that time the land would include only those whose names were written in **the book of life**. This would exclude all foreigners, even though they once lived on the land. According to the Gospel of Phillip 87 gentiles could not die, because they have never lived, since they did not believe the truth, a necessity for **life**. **The Book of Life** would also not include half-breed Jews like the Herods, in the author's judgment. Of course the Roman non-Jews would not even be considered (Rev 13:7-8). Many claimed Agrippa I as a true party to the contract between Jews and the Lord. He was a descendant of the Hasmoneans and tried to provide Jews with an acceptable government. The Herods, however, were all pro-Roman; and Rome depended on their support. They were also the seven mountains on which Rome was located. Without the Herods, Rome could not exist, according to the author.

Here is the mind which has wisdom. Another of the six interpretation sessions begins here. Those who have not understood the message up to this point should listen carefully and the coded message will become clear only for those who know the secret code. That requires special training to obtain **the mind who has wisdom.**

The seven heads are the seven mountains. Rome is known for being the city of **seven** hills (*Róh-mays hehp-tahl-áw-phoi-aw* (Ῥώμης ἑπταλόφοιο) (SibOr 2:18; 13:45; 14:108; Suetonius, *Dom* 4; Vergil, *Georg* 2:535; Horace, *Carm* 7).

There are seven kings. The earlier mention of **the beast had ten horns and seven heads** (Rev 13:1). Many scholars have strained to identify this **beast** and the **seven** kings, but none has been clearly successful. Most take one of the heads to be Nero, but, as Sweet noticed, "There is no agreement where to begin--Julius Caesar? Augustus? Caligula?" Sweet thought the author wrote during the time of Domitian, composing early history of the time of Vespasian as if it all were prophecy.[1] One scholar held that the **seven kings** were primates of the churches in Alexandria, Jerusalem, Antioch, Constantinople, Rome, France, and Spain. Some churches were in cities and others only somewhere in countries. Düsterdieck and Weiss both said they were **seven** of the kings of Rome:

1) Augustus,
2) Tiberius,
3) Caligula,
4) Claudius, and
5) Nero,
6) Vespasian
7) Titus, and
8) Domitian.

Domitian was the son of Vespasian. He was not one of the **seven**, but he was fathered by one of the **seven**.[2] The author of Rev 17 wanted this coded message to be understood only by his intended readers, those who had "wisdom," and that has been the case. Most, like Düsterdieck and Weiss, presume that the kings were Roman emperors. Another possibility is that they were not kings of the "earth" (Rev 17:2), but kings of **the land**. In this case, they would have been Herods:

1) Antipater,
2) Herod the Great,
3) Archaelaus,
4) Antipas,
5) Phillip,
6) Agrippa I,
7) Herod king of Chalcis.

---

[1] J. P. M. Sweet, *Revelation* (Philadelphia: Westminster Press, c1979), pp. 256-57. E. Lupieri, "The Seventh Night: Visions of History in the Revelation of John and the Contemporary Apocalyptic," *Henoch* 14 (1992):113, said, "The verses that seem to be the most closely related to known historical events in the Book of the prophecies of John are Rev 17:9-11." He is correct in thinking that material in Revelation is not easily datable, but some chapters are at least as datable as Rev 17: For example Revs 12, 13, 16, and 19, but these also require decoding.

[2] Düsterdieck, *Revelation*, 434-37; B. Weiss, *Apostle geschichte-Katholische Briefe-Apokalypse* (Leipzig: J. C. Hinrichs, 1902), p. 503; Morris, *Revelation*, p. 211; J. Weiss, *Die Offenbarung des Johannes* (Göttingen: Vandenhoeck und Ruprecht, 1908) II, p. 668; and M. Rissi, *The Future of the World* (Naperville: Allenson, n.d), pp. 3, 6, thought the seventh was Vespasian and the eighth was Domitian, whom many Romans compared to Nero and considered him as a sort of Nero redivivus.

In some way Jews of the author's time were able to follow the author's logic, even if they had to force the facts to conform to the pattern desired. **Seven kings** were intended to correspond to **the seven** hills of Rome. These **seven** Herods were believed by Palestinian Jews to have been genuine Roman agents--as integral to Rome as its **seven** hills. Forcing facts to fit doctrine is at least as old as Daniel. Daniel forced the number of weeks of years between the first Jubilee and the last week between 586 BIA and 164 BIA to be 62. He wanted the total to be 70 weeks of years, so he overlooked some facts and used only those that supported his case, upholding his doctrine. The author of this unit did the same. How did he come to **seven** in identifying the Herods? He could have accepted the list above, beginning with Antipater, or he might have begun with Herod the Great and included Agrippa II. Many possibilities are available for apologists, so long as they understand one another. We can be sure that the readers and the author of this document understood each other, but at this distance we can only deduce some solution, even though it may not be the right one.

It will be necessary for it to remain a short time. Instead of *day* (δεῖ) **it is necessary,** Sinaiticus has *dzay* (ζει), which is simply a misspelling of *day*, based on mispronunciation. This is a dictation error.

Boring took the **short time** statement to mean the author was living in the last days of history.[1] This makes no sense. The author never mentioned the end of history--not even once! Moberly argued that all of Revelation except the letters to the churches was written in 69 IA. Of the five Caesars **who had fallen,** three (Nero, Galba, and Otho) had fallen in rapid succession. The **one who is,** was Vitellius, and the **one who was still to come** was Vespasian who was old and not well known. He appeared to be coming, but he could not last long, because he was so old. This would have been the case in 69 IA, before Vespasian was declared emperor.[2]

The beast who was, is not, and is himself the eighth. Herod Agrippa I might fit into the author's logic here as a second ruler, since he was politically dead and in prison at the end of Tiberius' rule and later returned to Palestine to rule the entire kingdom his grandfather Herod the Great had ruled. This would correspond to the beast or the head whose wound was healed (Rev 13:3, 12).

His imprisonment might be considered the time when Agrippa was not. Afterwards, when Gaius became king, Agrippa at first became king of former territory of Herod Philip and, before he died (a little while), he ruled all of Herod the Great's kingdom. His political revival may have been called restoration from death by code-conscious Jews of NT times. Mythologically he was, was not, and then was

---

[1] M. E. Boring, *The Continuing Voice of Jesus* (Louisville: Westminster, c1991), p. 168.
[2] R. Moberley, "When Was Revelation Conceived?," *Bib* 73 (1992):376-77. Moberly challenged the basis for accepting Irenaeus' testimony as accurate, and he thought the letters were written by John at a much quieter time in his old age (pp. 380-93).

again. In a similar metaphor Herod referred to Jesus as John the Baptist raised from the dead (Matt 14:2). This interpretation is only one more guess, but the way of guessing was to find a king who fit the circumstances without trying to find out how all of this fit into the mathematical details. Like the myth in Dan 7, this was probably written after all of this was over, and **the eighth** king had finished his rule. The other possibility is that Agrippa II, the eighth, might have been thought to be Agrippa I all over again. These are code terms, and those who spoke them also understood them. We cannot be sure that we do.[1]

The five have fallen. When Agrippa I became king he displaced all the tetrarchs who had ruled before that time, just as Antiochus Epiphanes displaced three other Seleucids who really deserved his position (Dan 7:24). Agrippa I was the sixth, **the one who was**, and Herod king of Chalcis was the one Agrippa I persuaded Claudius to appoint as king. Agrippa I ruled at the same time as Herod of Chalcis and was therefore both the sixth (one of the seven) and the eighth. Like Antiochus Epiphanes, he was destined to go away to destruction. Rissi, arguing against Strobel, said, "Moreover, it cannot be proved that *epesan* [*éh-peh-san*, ἔπεσαν] (17:10) can refer only to violent death."[2]

TEXT

Revelation	First Testament and Other Jewish Literature
	Dan 7:7 Look! A fourth **beast** . . . and it had **ten horns.**
[12]Now **the ten horns** which you saw are **ten kings** who have not yet received a kingdom, but they receive authority as kings for a short time together with the beast. [13]These [all] have one opinion, and they give their power and authority to the beast. These will join battle with the Lamb, [14]and the Lamb will conquer them, because	Dan 7:24 Now **the ten horns**--from the kingdom **ten kings** will arise, and after them another will arise.
he is **Lord of lords**	Deut 10:17 Because Yehowah, your God, is God of Gods and **Lord of Lords**, the great, mighty, and fearful God

---

[1] Collins, *Crisis*, p. 76, for example presumed that the "one who is" was Domitian, and she started counting with Caligula (Gaius).
[2] Rissi, *Future*, p. 5.

and **King of kings**, and those with him are called "elect" and "faithful."

who will not show favoritism and will not take a bribe.

OG Dan 4:37 He is God of Gods, **Lord of lords, and King of kings**

Dan 7:20 Concerning the **ten horns** which were in his head and the other [horn] which grew up and before which three [horns] fell, the horn which had eyes and a mouth that talked excessively and which appeared bigger than the others.

2Macc 13:4 The **King of kings** raised the anger of Antiochus against the criminal.

3Macc 5:35 When the Jews heard the things that had happened with the king they praised the God manifest, the Lord, **the King of kings**, having also received this help from him.

1Enoch 9:4 They said to the Lord, "You are **Lord of Lords**, God of gods, **King of kings**, and God of the ages, your glorious throne is for generations of the age."

COMMENTARY

The ten horns which you saw. Again the author has stopped to explain the meaning of that which he has already. The following will be words of explanation.

They receive authority as kings . . . together with the beast. In the story in Daniel, **the ten horns** represent **the ten** members of the Seleucid dynasty, the last of which was Antiochus Epiphanes. The author of this document also considered them to be **kings**, but obviously not the same **ten**. These would have been **kings** associated with this antitypal situation. **The ten horns** were the Caesars who ruled at the same time the Herodians ruled. Jointly the Caesars and the Herodians kept the Jews under Roman control. The Caesars (horns) ruled in succession but from the Jewish point of view they were all the same; they had one goal; they all treated Jews very much the same way. They were the ones who gave the Herodian kings their power and **authority** to suppress the Jews in Palestine.

It is difficult or impossible to make the count of **ten** plus one to fit any chronology. The numbers are not important. Instead of the Seleucids there are the Roman emperors, **ten** or not. This group of kings of NT times **received authority** from God to rule for one hour with the Herods as some of their subordinate leaders. They were all of one opinion, from an outsider's point of view, and they all gave **authority** to the Herods.

The Lamb will conquer them. **King of kings** was a title originally given to **the king** of Persia, but it was later transferred to the **kings** of Parthia (Suetonius, *Lives* 4:5). This is a normal Hebrew way of dealing with a superlative. It was applied to **King** Nebuchadnezzar (Dan 2:37), God (Dan 4:37),[1] and the Messiah (Rev 19:16). Slater and Beale were both probably right in holding that this text is primarily dependent upon Dan 4:37 rather than 1Enoch 9:4,[2] but 1Enoch 9:4 is also probably dependent upon Daniel.

Applied to **the Lamb** this designation meant that **the Lamb** ruled over kings of all smaller countries the way the king of Babylon and the Roman emperor ruled over all leaders of subordinate countries. Like many contemporary Jews the author of this chapter of Rev genuinely believed that Israel could overpower Rome and become a greater power than Rome had ever been. After all, at one time Alexander the Great's kingdom consisted of only the small state of Macedonia. Less than three hundred years earlier Rome had been only a city state, not even controlling the peninsula of Italy. With their strong belief that their God was a God of war, Jews believed that they could make the same world-wide expansion movements other nations had done--only greater and more extensive.

Sooner or later, Jews thought, the Roman regime would have to come to an end, and that would involve a great war between **the Lamb** and his faithful followers against the Roman forces, just as Judas and the saints of the most High fought the Greeks two centuries earlier. **The Lamb,** or the Messiah, would conquer the Romans, just as Judas had conquered the Greeks, and then the Messiah would be greater than the Roman emperors. At the time of this writing, it was the Roman emperors who were over such **kings** and lords as the Herods and rulers of many subordinate countries, all the way from Britain to the Euphrates River. After this war, the Messiah would be **King of kings and Lord of lords**, and the Roman emperor would be no more than one of **the Lamb's** subordinate rulers.

Although Jews did not succeed in overpowering Rome during the first century IA, nor in their second revolt against Rome in 132-35 IA, they continued to believe that some day they would overpower Rome. Christians believed this anticipation had been fulfilled with the victory of Constantine and the establishment of the

---

[1] See G. K. Beale, "The Origin of the Title 'King of Kings and Lord of Lords' in Revelation 17.14," *NTS* 31 (1985):618-19, and T. B. Slater, "'King of Kings and Lord of Lords' Revisited," *NTS* 39 (1993):159-60.

[2] Beale, "Origin," pp. 618-20, and Slater, "King of Kings," pp. 159-60.

Holy Roman Empire. During the Crusades, especially, there were many messianic movements led by Jews who believed, as the author of this Rev 17 believed, that God would soon bring Rome to submission and exalt Israel as the greatest of all earthly kingdoms. During the Crusades some rabbis believed that it was God's design to allow the Christians to get the world all organized into one unit so that Jews could overtake only one country in order to rule the world.

The title **King of kings and Lord of Lords** in Scripture is a title given to God. Here it is given to **the Lamb**. This means the author believed **the Lamb** was a legal agent of God with authority to act and speak in his name.

Elect, and faithful. These were the contemporary equivalents of the Maccabean saints of the Most High.

TEXT

Revelation

[15] He said to me, "These things which you saw, where the **harlot** sits, are peoples, crowds, nations, and languages. [16] The ten horns which you saw, and the beast--these **hate** the **harlot**, and they will

make her devastated and **naked**.

First Testament

[Jer 51:12] You who dwell on much **water**, rich in treasures, your end has come.

[Ezek 23:29; see 16:39] They will act with you in **hatred**; they will take the products of your labor and leave you **naked**.

[Ps 137:7] **Make her naked! Make her naked**! [Strip] her down to her foundation!

[Hos 2:4-5] Let her turn her **harlotry** away from before her face . . . lest I strip **her naked** and make her as the day of her birth.

[Nah 3:5] Look! I am against you, said Yehowah of armies. I will uncover [your private parts, raising] your skirts over your face. I will show the

gentiles your **nakedness**, kingdoms, your shame.

[2Kings 9:36] In the region of Jezreel the

They **will eat** her **flesh** and **burn** her **with fire**, ¹⁷for God has put a [desire] in their minds to do his will, to reach one opinion, and to give their kingdom to the beast, until the words of God are carried out.

¹⁸Then the woman which you saw is the great city which has a kingdom over **the kings of the earth (land).**"

^(Ps 27:2)When wicked people come against me to **eat** my **flesh**, my foe

dogs **will eat the flesh** of Jezebel.

and my enemy, they will stumble and fall.

^(Micah 3:2-3)[You who] steal their skin from them, their **flesh** from their bones, who **eat** the **flesh** of my people, who strip off their skin from them and crush their bones.

^(Lev 20:14)If a man takes a woman and her mother as wives he is lewd, and they shall **be burned with fire**. There shall be no lewdness in your midst.

^(Lev 21:9)If the daughter of a priest profanes herself for **harlotry**, she profanes [also] her father; she shall **be burned with fire**.

^(Ps 2:2)**The kings of the earth (land)** and leaders have established themselves; they have held council against Yehowah and against his Messiah.

^(Ps 89:27-28)He [the son of David] will say to me, "You are my Father, the Rock of my salvation." I will make him my first born, the highest of **the kings of the earth**.

COMMENTARY

These things which you saw. This is the beginning of another interpretation session. Instead of **the things** NA has **the water which you saw**. The author was still commenting on Jer 51:13 and Isa 23:17. Jeremiah spoke of Babylon that sits on much **water**. The author was preparing to explain either what **these things** or **the water** of which Jeremiah spoke involved. Most texts favor **water**. If that was the case, then the author was taking that word to tell what it meant. It obviously meant something much more than H_2O. **The water** of which he spoke was **the water** of the Tiber where **the** harlot sits amounts to **peoples, crowds, nations, and languages.** He also included a few more texts that would apply to Rome the kind of punishments that Jews and Israelites applied to harlots and those who break contracts--nakedness and burning with fire. Like harlots, cities could be destroyed, left barren, and burned. Therefore the metaphor was appropriate.

The water which Jeremiah mentioned was that near the mouths of the Tigris and Euphrates rivers. The city situated there was Babylon. The water about which the author of this prophecy wrote, on the other hand, was the Tiber, that **water** which was near the place where the people of Rome sat. Since this was an international city, all different kinds of people could be found there--**people, crowds, nations, and languages**.

The ten horns which you saw. These were the **ten horns** already mentioned. They were not really **horns**. They were **kings**, according to the author's interpretation.

The ten horns . . . and the beast . . . hate the harlot. The Caesars and the Herods all owed their power and prosperity to Rome. Therefore they would be expected to love Rome, but the author had some basis for his judgment. The Caesars--Augustus, Tiberius, Gaius, Claudius--were cruel leaders. They fought civil wars; they punished many citizens with torture, banishment, and death for no valid reasons (Seutonius, *Lives*). They wasted money in self-indulgence and confiscated the money of wealthy Romans to cover their extravagances. There was an expensive war between Mark Anthony and Augustus. Rome was burned twice in the seventh decade. During the year 69-70 IA there were four different emperors in Rome, and there was nearly constant civil war.

Many people thought Rome had fallen permanently when Rome burned the second time--this time by Roman citizens who, under the leadership of an emperor and a pretending emperor, burned the Capitol and its temples. With such emperors as these it is not surprising that anyone might think these emperors hated Rome. **The beast** or one of the heads of **the beast,** Herod Agrippa I and Herod the Great, were both deeply involved in these Roman political moves, although neither survived until the war of 66-70 IA. Herod the Great first supported Anthony in his war against Augustus and later supported Augustus. Herod Agrippa I was a close friend of Gaius, and he helped Claudius become emperor. Therefore these intrigues that were destructive to Rome were caused both by the Caesars (**ten horns**) and the Herods (head or **beast**). It seemed that both **the horns** and **the beasts** hated the harlot.

They will make her devastated and naked. A city that has been destroyed was sometimes described as a woman who had been stripped of her clothing and displayed for public viewing in her shame. The bitter Psalmist, for instance, reporting his complaints against the Edomites for assisting the Babylonians in destroying Jerusalem in 586 BIA, described Jerusalem as a disgraced woman. These neighbors cheered as they saw Jerusalem burn, saying, **Strip, strip! down to her skin** (Ps 137:8), or literally, **Make naked! Make naked! down to her foundations.** There is nothing like an extended civil war to leave a country impoverished. When the author of Rev 17 accused the very **kings** and agents of Rome as hating the city, he was probably taking into account the treatment Rome had had during the decade of 60-70 IA. During that time there had been many civil wars, and Rome had been burned twice in the process, leaving the city the author called a **harlot naked,** desolate, and burned with fire (Rev 16:16).

Burn her with fire. Tacitus lamented the destitute condition of Rome during the civil war between Vitellius and Vespasian. When the Capitol burned he said this was the most shameful and saddest crime that had ever happened to Rome. Rome was **burned** in a civil war led by the Roman leaders themselves (Hist 3:72). Tacitus mourned the situation dramatically:

> Thus the Capitol burned with its doors closed. None defended it; none plundered it (Hist 3:71).

Without taking these facts into consideration, Beagley asked rhetorically,

> In what sense can it be said that the Empire or one specific Emperor turns against the capital city and destroys it? How can Rome destroy Rome?

Beagley's answer to his own question is that it could not happen. Therefore, he argued, the **harlot** cannot represent Rome. Instead it should be applied to Jerusalem.[1] This identification is essential to his theory that the enemies of Revelation were not Romans but Jews.

The word "**harlot**" is such an insulting term that there are many reasons why Jews chose to give it to Rome. One might have come after Rome began to burn, because burning was a punishment set for harlots (Lev 21:9; see also Lev 20:14; Jer 38:18-23). On the basis of Lev 20:14 the author may have interpreted Rome's **burning** as her just punishment. Just as harlots were **burned** to death, so Rome would be finally destroyed.

God has put a desire in their minds to do his will. NA has **their hearts**, a better construction, since one person has only one **heart**, but the Hebrew word, usually rendered **heart** is really the instrument for thinking, so it should be rendered, **minds.** One of the Dead Sea Scrolls told of the teacher of righteousness who was the priest into whose mind **God had placed** understanding (1QpHab 2:8). The author believed that it was God who put wisdom **into the mind** of the teacher of righteousness and also prompted the Caesars and the Herods to sabotage Rome and destroy it, just as he had hardened Pharaoh's mind before the Exodus. It was God's **will** that Rome be destroyed.

---

[1] Beagley, *Sitz*, pp. 92-93.

To give the kingdom to the beasts. The purpose of all this was to transfer the power and authority of Rome to the **beast**, probably Agrippa I. Agrippa had begun to encircle Jerusalem with a huge wall. This would have made it impossible to overthrow. It was God and not Claudius, in the author's opinion, who had given all of Herod the Great's kingdom into the hands of Agrippa I. In the author's point of view, this was only the beginning. Before **the beasts** finished ruling, God would put the entire Roman empire under his control. At that time the words of God would be finished, and **the Lamb** would take control.

The woman which you saw. This was probably the harlot that was the main topic of this chapter. The **woman**, according to the code, was not a female human being, at all. It was a **great city which has a kingdom over the kings of the land**. This identification may mean that the woman was Rome whose kingdom was over all the **kings of the** earth, or it may have been a more provincial statement. The kingdom of Herod Agrippa I was also a kingdom which Rome had under its control. Herod Agrippa I was only Rome's agent. This description of the woman would remind the Jewish reader of Jezebel, the queen of North Israel. She was Ahab's wife, and she obviously ruled him.

When Jehu came to Jezreel he commanded Jezebel's own servants to throw her down into the street. Jezebel was then thrown out of a window by her own eunuchs where the dogs could eat her flesh (2Kings 9:30-37). The Roman harlot controlled Agrippa I the way Jezebel controlled Ahab. The author reasoned that she would suffer even a worse fate than Jezebel. Her own kings would eat her flesh and **burn her with fire**. This probably referred to the impoverishment and **burning** caused by the civil wars. This woman, the author held, was the city (Rome) who ruled over the kings of the land. These were first the Herods and later the Roman procurators.

Summary. Rev 17 was written as a unit, marked off by an inclusion. The first verse introduces the reader to the great harlot and the last verse (Rev 17:18) closes with a definition of the woman. The author may have used sources, such as a unit about beasts which at one time applied to one or the other of the Herods, but which the author of this Rev understood to apply to someone of the Roman procurators of Palestine, such as Festus or Felix, who ruled during the seventh decade, or possibly Herod Agrippa II, who also functioned during that decade.

CHAPTER EIGHTEEN

INTRODUCTION

Rev 18 is a continuation of the interpretation of the fall and burning of Rome given in Rev 17. Rev 18 is a midrashic chapter that reflects a wide knowledge of the First Testament (FT). The first three verses alone employed Daniel, Amos, Ezekiel, Nahum, Isaiah, and Jeremiah. Throughout the chapter, however, it is Jer 50-51 and Ezek 25-27 that constitute the basic text upon which the narrative was based. The allusions to Isaiah and Jeremiah all are intended to show that Rome is the antitype of Babylon and, like Babylon, would fall. Following Jeremiah Ezekiel directed his hostility to Tyre. Isaiah first pictured himself as a watchman, announcing what he had seen. When he saw horsemen in pairs he quickly announced that Babylon had fallen. Coming in pairs would be in military formation to attack the city. The Lord told Jeremiah to make the nations, including Jerusalem, drink from the wine of his wrath. After this the Lord would punish them all severely. Jeremiah also pictured Babylon as a cup in the Lord's hand, making the nations drunk with her wine, until suddenly Babylon had fallen. She was burned, and her land became a wilderness or a threshing floor. The author thought of Rome in the same light--a huge, wealthy country, that soon would become a victim of pillage. Her land would be destroyed.

Provan correctly insisted that NT scholars needed to consider carefully the role the FT played in forming New Testament (NT) texts. He correctly confronted objections that

> rest on implicit and explicit distinctions between a theologically/morally inferior Old Testament and superior New Testament, or between zealous Jews and (moderate? Loving?) Christians.[1]

He also correctly noted that Rome is not mentioned by name in the entire chapter, and argued that,

> The Babylon that John is denouncing is no more Rome than any other city of biblical times, indeed of any time.[2]

---

[1] I. Provan, "Foul Spirits, Fornication and Finance," *JNTS* 64 (1996): 83.
[2] Provan, "Foul Spirits," p. 99.

He called attention to the fact that insulting names, like "harlot," were also applied to Jerusalem. That which he overlooked was the political and international situation that existed in the first century IA and the necessity for Jews and Christians to apply typological names to current situations and to speak in code. To understand the code the person receiving the message would have to understand the FT and Jewish traditions, to be sure, but he or she would also have to understand the local, current situation to which that applied. To learn to deduce that code it would be necessary today, not only to read the FT as Provan suggested, but also Josephus, Tacitus, the NT, the apostolic fathers, the Dead Sea Scrolls, and rabbinic literature. The Vespasian coin, reflected in Rev 17, could not apply to Jerusalem or "any other city of biblical times, indeed of any time."[1] The "Babylon," "Nineveh," and "Tyre" of FT times apply in Rev 18 only to the Roma of the Vespasian coin reflected in Rev 17 and called the "harlot."

Strand has accurately noticed that there is a chiastic structure to Rev 18, organized as follows: A: situation in Babylon (Rev 18:1-3); B: an appeal (Rev 18:4-8): C: mourning at the judgment (Rev 18:9-19); B': an appeal (Rev 18:20); A': situation in Babylon (Rev 18:21-24).[2] Inspired by Strand, Shea sharpened the chiasm by pointing out poetic units, separated by prose introductions. His pattern is as follows:

>A. Prose--angel calls.
>>B. Prose--another voice from heaven.
>>>C. Prose--kings stand off and weep.
>>>>D. Prose--merchants weep.
>>>>D'. Prose--merchants weep.
>>>C'. Prose--sailors cry out.
>>B'. Prose--another voice.
>A' Prose--angel speaks.

In between these prose introductions there are poetic units.[3] This shows Rev 18 as a unit, even though it blends in well with Rev 17 and 19. Charles observed that this unit contains a number of words not found in the rest of the Book of Revelation, and the word order of its sentences is less Semitic than other chapters.[4] Rev 18 was probably composed independently and later organized by some editor into its present position in the Book of Revelation.

---

[1] Provan, "Foul Spirits," p. 99.
[2] K. A. Strand, "Two Aspects of Babylon's JUDGMENT Portrayed in Revelation 18," *AUSS* 20 (1982):53-60.
[3] W. H. Shea, "Chiasm in Theme and by Form in Revelation 18," *AUSS* (1982):249-56.
[4] R. H. Charles, *A Critical and Exegetical Commentary on the Revelation of St. John the Divine* (New York: Charles Scribner's Sons, c1920), p. 88.

TEXT

The Poetry

¹⁸:¹After this I saw another angel coming down from heaven, having great authority, **and the land shone from his glory**. ²He cried out in a loud voice,

> **"Fallen is Babylon the great**.
> It has become a **dwelling place** of demons,
> a prison of every unclean and hated spirit,
> a prison of every **unclean** and hated bird,
> ³because from **the wine of the anger** of her harlotries
> **all the nations** have fallen."
> The kings of the earth have had sexual intercourse with her,
> The merchants of the land have become rich
> from the power of her licentiousness.

⁴Then I heard another voice from heaven, saying,

> **"Go out from her, my people**,
> so that there may be no sharing in her crimes,
> and no receiving of her afflictions
> ⁵**because her crimes have been glued to heaven**,
> and **God has remembered her unjust deeds**.
> ⁶**Give back to her as she has given**!
> Pay her double according to her deeds;
> In the cup she mixed for others, give her double!
> ⁷**However many things** glorified her and made her strong,
> **give back this much** torture and lamentation to her.
> **She says to herself, 'I sit** a queen;
> I am not **a widow**;
> **I shall never** see mourning.'
> ⁸Because of this, her **plagues will come in one day**,
> pestilence, mourning,¹ famine,
> and she **will be burned with fire**,
> because **strong is** God,
> **the Lord**, who has judged her."

⁹**The [above mentioned] kings of the earth**, who **had sexual intercourse** and became uncontrolled with her, **will weep and mourn over her** when they see the smoke of her fall.¹⁰Standing at a distance from fear of her torture, they say,

---

¹Charles, *Revelation*, p. 100, renders this word "destruction." Famine and pestilence are both curses promised if the contract were broken. The other two are wild beasts and the sword. Either destruction or mourning would fit well in this context.

"Woe! woe! **the great** city,
 Babylon the strong city,
  because in one hour your judgment has come."
¹¹**Merchants** of the land **weep** and mourn **over** her,
 because no one buys their cargo anymore--
  ¹²cargo of gold, silver, precious stones,
   pearls, linen, purple, silk, crimson,
every [kind] of scented wood,
 every vessel of ivory,
  every **vessel of** very precious wood,
bronze, iron, marble,
 ¹³cinnamon, spice, incense, myrrh,
  frankincense, wine, oil, fine flour,
wheat, cattle, sheep,
 horses, mules, and human slaves.

⁹**The [above mentioned] kings of the earth**,
 who **had sexual intercourse**
  and became uncontrolled with her,
¹⁴The products of the lust of your soul have left you,
 and all the bright and shining things have vanished from you;
  they can no longer find them.

¹⁵**The merchants** of these [products],
 who have become rich from her,
stand at a distance, **weeping and mourning**,
 ¹⁶saying, "Woe! woe! *the* city,
  [which is dres]sed in fine linen,
purple, and crimson, and gilded with gold,
 precious stones, and pearls,
  ¹⁷because in one hour such wealth as this has dried up."

Every **skipper**, everyone who sails somewhere,
 the **sailors**, and those employed [in labor related] to **the sea**
  stood at a distance ¹⁸and **cried out**
when they saw the smoke of her burning, saying,
 "**who is like** the great city?"
¹⁹**They will put dust over their heads**,
 and they will cry out,
  weeping and mourning, saying,
   "Woe! woe! **the great** city
in which all those who have boats in the sea

became rich from her prestige,
> because in one hour she was destroyed."

²⁰**Rejoice** over her, **Heaven,**
> saints, apostles, and prophets,
>> **because** God has decided your case against her.

²¹Then a strong angel took **a stone,**
> as big as a mill **stone,**
>> **and he threw it into the** sea, **saying,**

"**Thus** with force **shall Babylon** the great be thrown,
> **and she will not be found again any more.**
²²**The sound of harp** players and musicians,
> flute and trumpet players
>> **will no longer be heard.**
Every craftsman will no longer be found in you.
> ²³The light of the lamp will no longer shine in you;
>> **The sound of the bridegroom and the bride**
>>> will no longer be heard in you,
because your **merchants** were
> the great people of the earth,
because **through your witchcraft**
> all the nations have been led astray,
>> and through it the blood of prophets and saints
>>> have been found
²⁴and [the blood] **of all of those slain** upon **the land**
> **will weep and mourn over her**
>> when they see the smoke of her fall.
The kings of the earth had sexual intercourse with her, and
> have become rich from the power of her licentiousness."

TEXT

The Midrash

Revelation	First Testament and Other Jewish Writings
¹⁸:¹After this I saw another angel coming down from heaven, having great authority, **and the land shone from his glory.** ²He cried out in a	Ezek 43:2-3 Look! The glory of the God of Israel comes from the way of the East. His voice is like the sound of much water [running], and **the land shone from his glory.**

loud voice, **"Fallen is Babylon the great**.	Isa 21:9Suddenly, **"Fallen! fallen is Babylon**, and all the statues of her gods he has shattered to the ground."
	Dan 4:26; RSV 4:30The king said, "**Is** not this **Babylon the great** which I have built?"
	Jer 51:8Suddenly, **"Fallen is Babylon** and shattered. Mourn for her."
	Jer 51:49For **Babylon is to fall** for the slain of Israel; it **will fall** for the slain of all the land.
	Amos 5:2 **Fallen**, no more to rise is the virgin Israel; abandoned on her ground-- no one raises her.
It has become a **dwelling place of demons**, a prison of every unclean and hated spirit, a prison of every	Bar 4:35Fire will come upon her [Jerusalem] for many days, and she will be **inhabited by demons** for a long time
	Jer 50:39Therefore wild beasts of the desert with jackals will **dwell** [in Babylon]. Ostriches will **dwell** in it, but [people] will never inhabit it again.
unclean and hated bird, ³because	SibOr 5.167Woe to you, completely **unclean** terrible Latin land.
from **the wine of the anger** of her harlotries **all the nations** have fallen."	Jer 25:15-16For thus said Yehowah, God of Israel to me, "Take this cup of **the wine of anger** from my hand and make **all the nations** to whom I am sending you drink it. They will drink, stagger, and become crazy because of the sword which I am sending among them."

The kings of the earth had sexual intercourse with her, and the merchants have become rich from the power of her licentiousness.

^(Jer 25:27)You shall say to them, "Thus said Yehowah of armies, God of Israel, 'Drink and become drunk; vomit and fall, and you will not rise because of the sword which I am sending'"

^(Jer 51:7)**Babylon** is a gold cup in the hand of Yehowah, making all the land drunk from it. The gentiles have drunk; therefore, the gentiles act foolishly.

^(Isa 23:17)It will happen after the end of seven years Yehowah will visit Tyre, and she will return and play. She will **have sexual intercourse** with all **the kingdoms of the earth** on the face of the ground.

^(SibOr 5:165-67)**Adulteries** are **with** you, and unlawful mingling with children; effeminate and unjust, evil city, most ill-fated of all. Woe, woe to you, terrible, most **unclean**, Latin land.

^(Nah 3:1)Woe to the bloody city [Nineveh]. . . . ⁴From the many **harlotries** of **the harlot**; graceful charms, a mistress of magic, delivering the nations for the price of her **harlotries** and families for the price of her magic.

COMMENTARY

After this I saw another angel. **After this** means **after** the things that happened in Rev 17. There have been many **angels** introduced in the prophetic section of Revelation. To distinguish one from the other, the author calls the next angel **another angel.**

The land shone from his glory. Rev 18 is introduced with an antitype of Ezekiel's vision when he saw the **glory** of God fill the temple at Jerusalem just before Ezekiel learned that God would return to Jerusalem and there dwell with his people. Instead of God, the mediator of the message was a heavenly **angel,** but he was associated with the **glory** of the Lord, which was present in the flame and smoke from the altar that joined earth to heaven. It was the light from the flame of the fire that made **the land shine**. With the **glory** of the Lord came the downfall of Rome.

Fallen is Babylon. NA has a second **fallen**. Sinaiticus is consistent with Jer 51:8. NA follows Isa 21:9. The **fall** of **Babylon** is also mentioned in Rev 14:8; 16:19; 17:5; 18:10, 21. **Babylon** is always expressed with a negative connotation, and always as a code name for Rome.

The funeral dirge of Rev 18 gets its initial impetus from Isaiah, Amos, and Jeremiah. Amos confronted the Israelites after the separation of North Israel from Judah. While Israel was still a great country, Amos prophesied, in the form of a funeral dirge, that Israel would be a **fallen** nation. Centuries later, in 1897, Rudyard Kipling wrote "Recessional" in the same way, based on Nahum and Ezekiel. The occasion was the celebration of Queen Victoria's reign of 60 years, when England boasted of ruling the seven seas. After the famous processional was over, Kipling wrote:

> The tumult and the shouting dies;
> > The Captains and the Kings depart
> . . .
> Far-called, our navies melt away;
> > On dune and headland sinks the fire:
> Lo, all our pomp of yesterday
> > Is one with Nineveh and Tyre!

Amos described Israel's **fallenness** like that of a virgin that had become a prostitute. She had **fallen** from grace--not from a cliff or a building. Once she had lost her virginity she would never again rise to a position of dignity. Isaiah and Jeremiah pictured **Babylon** in the same way. Jeremiah not only said **Babylon** would **fall**, but, possibly because of his dependence on Amos 5:2, he also foretold that she would not rise again. In one of his prophecies, Isaiah said,

> **Babylon, the glory of the kingdoms, the beautiful pride of the Chaldeans, will become like Sodom and Gomorrah, when God overturned them** (Isa 13:19).

The author of Rev 18 was not only influenced by these three prophets, but he also borrowed the adjective, **the great**, from Daniel. This author, however, wanted Rome, not **Babylon**, to **fall.** Another Jewish author felt the same way: **Woe to you, completely unclean Latin city** (SibOr 5:168).

The dwelling place of demons. From Jeremiah this author learned that **Babylon** was destined to become uninhabitable for human beings. From Baruch he learned that it would become inhabited by **demons.** It would become like a wilderness where wild animals howled. The author of Rev 18 was eager to think of Rome as also becoming uninhabitable for human beings, especially for those who tried to keep dietary and purity rules.

The wine of the anger of her harlotries. **Wine** and sexual lust were the idioms the author of Rev 18 used to describe the potent influence of Roman sectarian culture upon Jews. The positive effect of foreign culture on Jews did not seem reasonable to the author of Rev 18 at all; Jews were under the influence of this culture just as if they were drunk from alcohol, and their drive to conform to Roman practice was like an uncontrollable sexual lust. The harlotries and drunkenness mentioned here, however, did not at all mean the chief object was sexual indecency and drunkenness from **wine.** The real problem was that orthodox Jews were made to stumble and **fall** for this new culture, leaving the Jewish practices in which they were trained.

Some ancient texts read "drunk" (*péh-poh-kahn*, πέπωκαν) whereas others read **fallen** (*péhp-toh-kan*, πέπτωκαν). Drunk is consistent with the metaphor of drinking **wine** (Rev 18:3), but **fallen** is also coherent with the reference to **Babylon** having **fallen** (Rev 18:2). In either instance the offense was intended to be understood metaphorically. Commenting on a passage from Isaiah,

> **Come down and sit in the dust, virgin daughter of Babylon.**
> **Sit on the ground without a throne** (Isa 47:1),

Rabbi Hunia said Isaiah meant,

> Sit on the ground, you old harlot. You think you are a young virgin,
> but really you are an old woman (CantR 3:4, 2).

The practice of describing a gentile city as **a harlot** who lured kings and merchants was not something the author of Rev 18 invented. The prophet, Nahum, described Nineveh that way, and both Isaiah and Jeremiah pictured **Babylon** as a harlot. Even Zion was described as an abandoned wife (Isa 54:6; 60:15; 62:4; Jer 4:29); Gaza was prophesied to become a woman who was abandoned (Zeph 2:4); and Ashdod was to be a woman who would be divorced and sent out [of her husband's house].[1]

The merchants have become rich. **Merchants become rich** by trading in large, prosperous cities, like Rome. They come to such cities and stay as long as they can prosper there.

According to Sinaiticus, the kings are the subject of this sentence. NA has another subject added: **The merchants of the land.** The **merchants of the Land**

---

[1] See further L. Zalcman, "Ambiguity and Assonance at Zephaniah II 4," *VT* 36 (1986):365-70, for an analysis of Zeph 2:4.

could mean just those **merchants** that came from the Promised **Land**. There were many Jewish businesses in Rome in NT times, and those would have been the ones in which the author would have been the most interested. **Licentiousness** is used here metaphorically and insultingly. It refers to the luring ability of the big city, not just sex. It involves business, society, and entertainment.

TEXT

Revelation

⁴Then I heard another voice from heaven, saying, "**Go out from her, my people**, so that there may be no sharing in her crimes, and no receiving of her afflictions

⁵**because her crimes have been**

First Testament

Jer 51:45**Come out from her** midst, **my people**; let each man himself escape from the burning anger of Yehowah.

Jer 50:8Flee from the midst of Babylon; **go out from** the land of the Chaldees. Become like male goats in front of the flock.

Jer 51:6**Flee from** the midst of Babylon. Let each one himself escape! **Do not stand still in** her punishment, because it is a time of vengeance for Yehowah; it is the wage he is paying her.

Isa 52:11Leave! Leave! **Go out from** there. Do not touch defilement! **Go out from her** midst.

Isa 48:20**Go out from** Babylon, flee from Chaldea.

Ezra 9:6My God, I am ashamed and embarrassed to raise my face to you, **because** our **iniquities** have multiplied higher than [our] heads, and our guilt has grown **to heaven**.

Jer 51:9Let us walk, each man to his land, **because her** judgment **has**

glued to heaven

and **God has remembered her unjust deeds**.

⁶**Give back to her**

as she has given! Pay her double according to her deeds. In the cup she mixed for others, give her double! ⁷**However many things** glorified her and made her strong, **give back this much** torture and lamentation **to her**.

reached heaven; it has gone up to the sky.

Ps 137:7-8 **Remember, Yehowah**, the sons of Edom, the day of Jerusalem, who said, "Strip [her]! Strip [her]-- down to the skin! Daughter of Babylon, who is to be destroyed, happy is the one who **pays you back** your punishment **as you have punished** us."

Jer 50:29 Take vengeance against her [Babylon]! **As she has done, do also to her**.

Deut 32:41 I will return vengeance to my enemies; I will **pay back** those who hate me.

COMMENTARY

A voice from Heaven. The word **Heaven** is used here as a name for God. This **voice from God**, however, did not come audibly. Any word of God was held to have come **from heaven**, but one of the chief ways it reached God's people was from reading the Scriptures. In this case word of God came to the author when he read Jer 50 and 51. In a similar warning, the Sibyl said,

> When the anger of the great God comes upon you,
> then, of course, you will acknowledge the face of the great God.
> All human souls will groan heavily, and,
> stretching out their hands to the wide heaven,
> begin to call upon the protector, the great king
> (SibOr 3:556-60).

Come out from her, my people. Jeremiah issued this to the Jews in **Babylon,** urging them to leave **Babylon** as soon as possible. God would punish **Babylon** with pestilence, war, famine, wild beasts, and other types of destruction. Her crimes had accumulated in God's heavenly record until God was about to foreclose. If Jews were in **Babylon** when all of this happened, they, too, would share in **Babylon's** punishment. When **Babylon's** stock market crashed, Jews would also lose their investments. When the war broke out, Jewish homes and business could also be destroyed. Jews should sell everything, take their possessions and avoid all of that tragedy.

The author of Rev 18 told his readers that the message of Jeremiah in relationship to Babylon applied to them in relationship to Rome. At that time there were thousands of Jews living in Rome. The author warned that they must leave Rome immediately. This would have been excellent advice to Jews in Rome during the civil wars of Rome in 69-70 IA. It was not during the time of Jeremiah, but later, that Jews in Babylon corresponded with Cyrus of Persia and enabled him to enter **Babylon** during a feast without an all-out war. At the time of this writing there were thousands of Jews in Rome in communication with Jewish leaders in Palestine, keeping each other informed about their mutual plans.

No sharing . . . no receiving. NA has these verbs in the active voice and second person plural: **you may not share . . . you may not receive**. This may be the work of an editor improving the text. The counsel given was to protect Jews from receiving the punishment destined to fall upon Babylon.

For her crimes have been glued to heaven. This statement probably has a double meaning. On the one hand Rome's crimes have been so extensive that they have piled up to heaven. The other point is that these crimes have not escaped God's notice. They are there, firmly glued to the recording system, so that there is no way that Rome can get by with all of these crimes. punishment is certain to come. **God has remembered her unjust deeds**.

Give back to her as she has given. This is not the only vengeful, biblical expression. One of the Psalmists said,

> Daughter of Babylon, who [is destined to be] devastated, blessed is the one who pays you back for that which you have done to us! Blessed is the one who seizes your little children and strikes [them] against the rock (Ps 137:8-9)!

The vengeful cry given here has embarrassed many twenty-first century Christians who have thought that Paul represented true Christianity when he encouraged Christians to render no one evil for evil, because vengeance was God's responsibility (Rom 12:17-19). Like Jews, Christians differed on this point. Some advocated active, militant theology and others taught passive suffering as a means by which they might regain the land. The argument given here is that of a plaintiff in court. The plaintiff was not in a position to avenge the defendant, personally, but he was appealing to the judge (here the judge was God) to punish the defendant to the extent of the law. A little study of history will show that Jews and Christians have learned to hate as well as to love, and there are biblical bases for both attitudes. The most wholesome thing for us all to do is to acknowledge our checkerboard past and try to improve our character.

Pay her double. NA adds **and** before this clause. The text literally says, **Double the doubles,** which may be a Greek translation of a Hebrew infinitive absolute. An infinitive absolute strengthens the verb, meaning something like "at least" **double**. The other possibility is that the author argued that the defendant had committed a crime that would normally require a fine of twice the cost of the offense, and the plaintiff asked that the defendant be required to pay double that amount, or four times the cost of the offense. Jeremiah predicted the fall of Babylon. At that time he urged Jews to leave Babylon as fast as they could. The author of Rev 18 quoted Jeremiah, indicating that these were the words of God which he thought were applicable to Rome.

The author wanted Rome not only to receive the payment that Rome had given Jews, as Jeremiah and the author of Psalm 137 requested for Babylon, but **double** or quadruple that amount. **Double** punishment was normally assigned by courts in antiquity as for debtor obligations. Some types of injury required quadruple or quintiple payment. That means if a person damaged someone else to the extent of $100.00 he or she would have to repay $400.00 or $500.00 as punishment. **Double** payment was required in court for certain crimes, including that of a malicious witness (Deut 19:16-19). A thief who had stolen a sheep was required to pay the victim four sheep; for stealing a cow, the thief would repay five cows (Exod 21:37). The terms "sheep" and "cow" covered crimes of deception, thievery, fraud, or misrepresentation, depending on the extent of the crime (Exod 22:3, 6, 8).

The sheep was equivalent of petty thievery. The cow dealt with large company fraud. Double payment was the normal demand made against a debtor if the accepted loan were not paid on time. The debtor would have to work off the debt at half normal wages. Just as the Lord allowed Rome to become glorious and strong, now the author wanted her to become miserable and tortured. The reason for this, theologically explained, was that Rome's crimes had piled up **to heaven.** On this day of reckoning, she would come up short; she would be in debt; so the Lord would foreclose. It was the Lord who had made **Babylon** powerful in the first place, and now it would be the Lord who would punish her. The same was true of Rome. This message would have been written at a time when the international situation looked bad for Rome, the way it did during the civil wars of 69-70 IA.

TEXT

Revelation   First Testament

^{Jer 50:31-32} "Look! I am against you, proud one," says the Lord, Yehowah of armies, "because your **day is coming** the time when I will visit you [with punishment]. The proud one will stumble and fall, and there will be no rising for him. I **will start a fire** in his cities, and I will destroy all his

She says to herself, 'I sit a	surrounding territory."
	Isa 47:8 Now listen to this, luxurious woman, who dwells in confidence, **who says to herself**, "I am, and there is no one else. **I shall not sit**
queen; I am not **a widow; I shall never** see mourning.' ⁸Because of this, her **plagues will come** in **one day**, pestilence, mourning, famine, and she **will be burned with fire**, because **strong is God, the Lord**, who has judged her."	as **a widow; I shall** not know childlessness." **These two things will come** upon you instantly, **in one day**.
	Jer 50:34 Their redeemer **is strong. Yehowah** of armies is his name. He will surely contest their case [in court], so as to give rest to the land but to disturb the inhabitants of Babylon.
	Isa 23:17 It will happen after the end of seven years Yehowah will visit Tyre, and she will return and play. She will **prostitute** all
⁹**The [above mentioned] kings of the earth**, who **had sexual intercourse** and became uncontrolled with her,	the **king**doms of the earth on the face of the ground.
	Ezek 27:33 You satisfied many peoples with your great wealth, and your commerce made **the kings of the earth** rich.
	Ps 2:2 **The kings of the earth** have established themselves; they have taken counsel together against Yehowah and against his Messiah.
	Ezek 27:35 All the inhabitants of the islands are appalled over you, and their **kings** will shudder and grimace in fear.
	Ps 48:5-8 Look! Their **kings** assembled;

	they crossed over together. They saw; they were accordingly astounded. They were frightened and hurried. Trembling seized them there, anguish as a woman giving birth.
	With the east wind the ships of Tarshish were broken.
	Ezek 27:30-31 They will announce with their voices concerning her; they will shout bitterly, and they will put dust over their heads and wallow in ashes. They will cut their hair and wear sack cloth.
will weep and mourn over her when they see the smoke of her fall. ¹⁰Standing at a distance from fear of her torture, they say, "Woe! woe!	They **will weep for you** with bitterness of soul, **mourning** bitterly.
	Ezek 26:16-17 All **the princes of** the sea . . **will raise a lamentation over her**, and they will say to you: How you have perished, inhabitant of the seas, the praised city who has been strong in the sea.
the great city, **Babylon** the strong city, because in one hour your judgment has come."	Dan 4:27 Is not this **Babylon the great** which I have built.
	Jer 51:8 Suddenly, "**Fallen is Babylon**, and she is shattered. **Mourn** for her."

COMMENTARY

She says to herself, "I sit a queen." The author thought Rome had a big surprise coming. Rome did not realize that God was getting ready to punish her extensively. While Rome was enjoying a false security the author foresaw quite a different future for Rome, based on the prophecy of Jeremiah. That which the author knew, which Rome did not, was Isaiah's prophecy against **Babylon** (Isa 47:8). Even if Romans knew of this prophecy, they would not have known that Rome was really the **Babylon** that the prophecy attacked.

Jeremiah first described the attitude of **Babylon** about herself at the height of her power. **She** thought this condition would continue forever, but Jeremiah prophesied that **Babylon** would be severely punished. His feeling was similar to that of Kipling when **Queen** Victoria's power was at its height. While England ruled the seven seas, and all its celebration was a processional, Kipling wrote the hymn "Recessional." He foresaw the tumult and the shouting, dying and the military forces retreating as England's glory faded. In a similar way, at the time when **Babylon** was at her height and believed it would always be thus, Jeremiah foresaw her destruction and burning. The author of Rev 18 believed **Rome** was an antitype of **Babylon** and that Jeremiah's prophecy would also apply to **Rome.**

Strong is God, the Lord. NA has **the Lord God**.

The kings of the earth . . . will weep and mourn for her. NA adds **and became uncontrolled** after **intercourse**.

Jeremiah described the way people would respond when they learned that Great **Babylon** had been burned and destroyed. The kings who used to mingle with her would weep as they realized this relationship was forever gone. The author of this document believed **Babylon** was just a preview of the situation in **Rome** and that God would destroy Rome as he had **Babylon,** Tyre, and other great cities. The kings did not really have sexual **intercourse** with Rome or **Babylon.** Both were great countries that were involved in commerce. Rome and **Babylon** both bought produce from other countries and sold products to other countries. Merchants made money from this business, and other kings depended on Rome for their economies. These subordinate **kings** were dependent upon Rome for their financial and military security. The author of this passage was advocating economic sanctions against Rome. He thought all Jews should boycott Rome, avoiding all business contacts. Those who refused to do this were considered "minglers" and accused of "adultery."

The allusions to passages in Ezekiel were all directed to **Tyre,** originally, but the same kind of prophecy was given as to **Babylon,** and the author of the apocalypse understood that all of this applied to Rome. All three of these cities were commercial centers that bought and sold the products listed here. The economies of other countries were not dependent upon Jerusalem in the same way. Jerusalem was not primarily a commercial and shipping city the way **Tyre, Babylon,** and Rome were. Jerusalem had no seaport. Those, like Ford and Beagley, who hold that Jerusalem was the great harlot have overlooked this fact. The intercourse kings had with Rome was commercial and not sexual. Isolationistic Jews, however, described this activity insultingly. The kings Jews accused of this activity may have been the kings of the *land* rather than the kings of the earth. These would have been Herodian kings, Herod the Great and Herod Agrippa I.

The smoke of her fall. NA has **the smoke of her burning.** This is another confusion caused by hearing dictation. The Greek for **fall** (*ptóh-seh-ohs*, πτώσεως) sounds very much like **burning** (*poo-róh-seh-ohs*, πυρώσεως) Smoke is caused by **burning** and not by **falling,** so the correct reading is **burning**, just as Sinaiticus has in Rev 18:18.

Although Rev 18 is heavily dependent upon Ezek 27, Ezekiel pictures **Tyre falling** like a ship that has been wrecked in the sea. This is not mentioned in Rev 18, but Revelation, unlike Ezekiel, describes Rome being **burned**. The reason for this is obvious. **Rome** was not destroyed in a ship wreck. She was **burned with fire.** The author of this dirge took from FT only those passages that applied to the description of the **fire** at Rome. This involved many of the same tragedies that Ezekiel foresaw for Tyre, but not all.

Rome **burned** during the time of Nero (66 IA) and again during the civil war at the end of 69 IA. It was probably this latter fire that was described as being a tragedy. During that **fire** the Capitol burned with its temple. After that all of the Roman empire feared that Rome was finished. Tacitus said Rome had been sacked before but this time Rome was burned by its own citizens, and Romans feared this was the punishment of the gods.

In one hour your judgment has come. **One hour** was an expression that meant a very short time (Rev 17:10; 18:10, 17, 19). According to Josephus, the Jews burned the Roman siege weapons "in one hour" (War 3:227-28). The residents of Caesarea slaughtered the local Jews " in one hour" (War 2:457).

TEXT

Revelation	First Testament
¹¹**Merchants** of the land **weep** and mourn **over** her,	Ezek 27:36**Merchants** among the peoples whistle **over** you. You have become exhausted, and you will not survive until the age.
because no one buys their cargo anymore--¹²cargo of gold, silver, precious stones, pearls, linen, purple, silk, crimson, every [kind] of scented wood, every vessel of ivory, every	Ezek 27:30-31They will announce with their voices concerning her; they will shout bitterly, and they will put dust over their heads and wallow in ashes. They will cut their hair and wear sack cloth. They **will weep for you** with bitterness of soul, **mourning** bitterly.
	Ezek 27:13-14Greece, Tubal, and Meshech traded with you **human slaves** and
vessel of very precious wood, **bronze**, iron, marble, ¹³cinnamon, spice, incense, myrrh, frankincense, wine, oil,	**vessels of bronze** for your merchandise. Bethtogarmah gave
fine flour, wheat, cattle, sheep, **horses, mules, and human slaves**.	**horses**, war **horses and mules** for your wares.

COMMENTARY

Merchants of the Land. Like **the migrants of the land**, these were people the author hated. They did business with Rome. They mingled and ate with those whom orthodox Jews would not approve. Like Jewish tax collectors, they compromised their orthodox principles. Rome, like **Babylon** before her, was the greatest of nations in her day. The emperor of Rome was the king over the kings of all other nations around the Mediterranean Sea area.

Merchants from Palestine, like those from all over the world, would lament at the fall of Rome, because it meant the stock market would crash, and their businesses would fail. **Merchants** bought and sold all these products--[12]**cargo of gold, silver, precious stones, pearls, linen, purple, silk, crimson.** Rather than summarizing all kinds of products for the wealthy, the author listed them for literary effect. This method was practiced several times in Rev 18. Those merchants who became rich from Rome did not stay there and wait to be destroyed. **They stood at a distance** and watched the city burn, **because of the fear of her torture**, weeping and lamenting, saying, **Woe, woe! the great city**.

In listing the products **merchants** could buy and sell with Rome the author intentionally included some of those listed by Ezekiel, so that the reader could realize that this was an antitype of an earlier prophesied destruction. When Jerusalem fell many pious Jews and Christians wept, but not **the merchants**. These were dependent, not upon Jerusalem, but Rome for their financial success. Before Rome's ascension to power, Jerusalem was dependent on Egypt, Babylon, Assyria, Syria, and Parthia. Jerusalem gained its role among the nations as a land bridge—not a seaport.

Ford and Beagley have tried in various ways to account for these difficulties by saying that Jerusalem really was a commercial city. The things listed in Rev 18 include some of the things needed either in the temple or in other ways by Jews in Jerusalem. The sailors might be those who managed boats on the Sea of Galilee.[1] Of course Jerusalem, like every other city in the world, imported goods from other places, but that does not make it a commercial city upon whom merchants and sailors would be heavily dependent for their livelihood.

Collins followed Harold Fuchs in holding that the resistance of the East to the West was largely verbal, intellectual, or spiritual.[2] That conclusion overlooks many wars and a great deal of rebellion. Antiochus III, the Great, moved militarily westward until he had control of all of modern Turkey, part of Europe (Thrace), and all of the islands in the eastern Mediterranean Sea. He had also made treaties with many Greek cities. It required strong military action on the part of Rome to force him to retreat as Rome moved successively eastward. These were not just

---

[1] J. M. Ford, *Revelation* (Garden City: Doubleday, 1975), p. 240; A. J. Beagley, *The "Sitz im Leben" of the Apocalypse* (Berlin: W. DeGruyter, 1987), p. 109.
[2] A. Y. Collins, *Crisis & Catharsis* (Philadelphia: Westminster Press, c1984), p. 89.

intellectual or verbal debates. After Rome had finally overthrown the Seleucids it still had to deal with the Parthians who had defeated the Roman army in the seventh decade IA.

Alexander the Great introduced a one-world concept that never vanished. When it became known that a small country like Macedonia could conquer the world from Macedonia to India, other cities, like Carthage and Rome, set out to make similar conquests. Palestine was not exempt from this lust for power. Jews and later Christians adopted a world conquest policy that neither ever abandoned. If the conflicts between the East and the West had been only spiritual or verbal there would have been no expansion of Islam, no Holy Roman Empire, no Crusades, no Spanish Inquisitions, no European conquest of the Americas, and no Middle East wars in the twentieth and twenty-first centuries.

Very precious wood. Probably ebony.

And human slaves. Literally, **bodies and souls of men**. Like Ezek 27:13, the context here requires that **the souls of men** here were being sold like livestock. **Souls and bodies** were different. **Souls** were identities, commitments. **Souls** were established legally. A baby became Jewish or Christian by legal baptism. At that time he or she acquired a **soul.** A baby that died unbaptized and, for Jewish males, uncircumcised, was not a Jew or a Christian, and therefore had no Jewish or Christian **soul**. Roman Catholics and Jews still follow this formula. When a person gave up his or her religion, became apostate, was excommunicated, or surrendered his or her religious identities for monetary reasons, that meant **souls** were bought and sold. The sale of **bodies** was nothing other than **human slavery. Slavery** was standard practice in the ancient Near East of NT times. It was especially extensive in times of war. This is not necessarily a Christian addition, as Whealon thought.[1]

TEXT

[14]The products of the lust of your soul have left you, and all the bright and shining things have vanished from you; they can no longer find them.

Revelation	First Testament
[15]**The merchants** of these [products], who have become rich from her, stand at a distance,	Ezek 27:36**Merchants** among the peoples whistle **over** you. You have become exhausted and you will not survive until the age.
	Ezek 27:30-31They will announce with their voices concerning her; they will shout bitterly, and they will put dust

---

[1] J. F. Whealon, "New Patches on an Old Garment: The Book of Revelation," *BTB* 11 (1981):55.

weeping and mourning, ¹⁶saying, "Woe! woe! the city, [which is dres]sed in fine linen, purple, and crimson, and gilded with gold, precious stones, and pearls, ¹⁷because in one hour such wealth as this has dried up."

over their heads and wallow in ashes. They will cut their hair and wear sack cloth. They **will weep for you** with bitterness of soul, **mourning** bitterly.

Dan 4:27 Is not this **Babylon the great** which I have built?

COMMENTARY

The bright shining things have vanished. This entire sentence is a summarizing sentence, following all of the valuable products that have been listed. The author of this unit probably wrote the sentence. It is not necessary to assume that it is a later addition or something misplaced, as Charles and Loisy presumed.[1]

Woe! woe! the city. NA adds **great**, which is probably the correct reading. The Sinaiticus scribe not only omitted **great**, but also most of the words, **which is dressed** ([*hay pehr-ee-beh-blay]-méh-nay*, [ʽαι περιβεβλημέναι). Caird correctly reminded his readers that the fall of **Babylon** is not the end of the world, because **merchants** still stood at a distance to see her end.

In one hour. This is further and repetitious description of the tragedy that would be involved in the fall of Rome. Like **Tyre**, this great **city** would soon lie a rubbish heap. All of her **glory** and prosperity would perish. Of course, this which was tragedy for Rome, her agents, and the **merchants** dependent upon her business, was joyful good news for the author of this document, who wanted Israel to displace Rome as the world superpower.

TEXT

Revelation

Every **skipper**, everyone who sails somewhere, the **sailors**, and those employed [in labor related]

to **the sea** stood at a distance

First Testament

Ezek 27:27 Your **sailors, skippers**, those who repair holes, your merchants, and all your men of war, who are among you with all your crowd which are in your midst, will fall into the heart of **the sea** on the day of your destruction.

---

[1] Charles, *Revelation*, II, 105; A. Loisy, *L'Apocalypse de Jean* (Paris: Emile Nourry, 1923), p. 321.

¹⁸and **cried out** when they saw the smoke of her burning, saying, "**Who is like** the great city?"

^(Ezek 27:29)All the sailors who row, all the **skippers** of **the sea**, will come down from their ships and stand on the shore.

^(Ezek 27:32)They raise their lament to you; they **mourn** over you, "**Who is like** Tyre, a silent one in the midst of **the sea**?"

^(Dan 4:27)Is not this **Babylon the great** which I have built?

¹⁹**They will put dust over their heads, and they** will cry out, **weeping and mourning**, saying, "Woe! woe! **the great** city in which all those who have boats in the sea became rich from her prestige, because in one hour she was destroyed."

^(Ezek 27:30-31)**They will announce with their voices** concerning her; they will shout bitterly. **They will put dust over their heads and** wallow in ashes. **They** will cut their hair and wear sack cloth. They **will weep for you** with bitterness of soul, **mourning** bitterly.

^(Josh 7:6)Joshua tore his robe, fell on his face to the ground before the ark of Yehowah [and remained there] until evening, he and the elders of Israel, and **they put dust over their heads**.

COMMENTARY

Everyone who sails somewhere. Literally, **everyone who sails to a place**.[1] Most of the people wh**o sailed** the seas in those days were not on cruises or vacations. The sea was the great transport medium. Moving large quantities of produce over great distances on land meant by camel caravans or wagons and horses or donkeys. These moved slowly with very limited amounts. Ships, however, could travel from Spain to China, and the ship owners were mostly national or big business magnates.

The author has here continued his elaboration on the destruction of Rome, using all inclusive generalities, patterning his sentences after those Ezekiel and Daniel used either to describe the downfall of **Babylon** or **Tyre**. The destruction of a great commercial city has serious international and economic consequences. Not only do merchants face financial losses in business, but those involved in the

---

[1] H. Conzelmann, "Mizelle zu Apk 18,17," *ZNW* 66 (1975):288-90, renders this passage on basically the same premise--that *tópon* (τόπον) should be considered a place or location.

transportation business become unemployed--the sailors, pilots, ship builders, and shipping magnates.

The smoke of her burning. This applies to the **burning** of Rome. That city **burned** twice in the sixth decade. The first **burning** was at the time of Nero, and the second was in 69 IA. The second was the worst, because it was done by the Romans themselves and it included the burning of the Capitol with its temples. At that time Vespasian withdrew his troops from Jerusalem and began to participate in a civil war. All of these activities made Jews in Jerusalem rejoice. The mourning of the merchants and shippers would have taken place because it was Rome that burned, not Jerusalem. Jerusalem had no seaport. It also burned, and its destruction was tragedy, but not to the shipping industry.

TEXT

Revelation

[20]**Rejoice** over her, **Heaven**, saints, apostles, and prophets, **because** God has decided your case against her.

[21]Then a strong angel took **a stone**, as big as a mill **stone**,
and he threw it into the sea,
saying,

"**Thus** with force **shall Babylon** the great be thrown,

First Testament

Isa 44:23 **Rejoice, Heaven,**
because Yehowah has acted! Shout, earth beneath! Break out into song, mountains! Forest and every tree in it, because Yehowah has redeemed Jacob and will be glorified in Israel.

Deut 32:43 Praise his people, gentiles! **Because** the blood of his servants will arise.

Jer 51:48 "Heaven, earth, and all that is in them will sing for joy over Babylon, **because** the destroyers will come to her from the North," says Yehowah.

Jer 51:63-64 When you have finished reading this scroll you shall tie **a stone** to it

and throw it into the Euphrates, and you **shall say,**

"**Thus shall Babylon** sink and not rise because of the evil which I am bringing against her."

and she will not be found
again any more.

^(Ezek 26:21)I shall give you exhaustion, and you will no longer exist. You will be sought, **but you will not be found again for the age**.

²²**The sound of harp** players and musicians, flute and trumpet players **will no longer be heard**. Every craftsman will no longer be found in you.

^(Ezek 26:13)I will stop the noise of your songs; **the sound of your harps will not be heard again**.

^(Isa 24:8) The joy of the drums has stopped; the noise of those who rejoice has ceased; the joy of the lyre has stopped.

^(Amos 5:23)Take away from me **the sound of your songs**. I will not listen to the melody of your **harps**.

^(Jer 25:10; also 7:34 and 16:9)I will destroy from them **the sound of** joy, **the sound of** happiness,
the sound of the bridegroom, the sound of the bride,
the sound of the mill, and the light of the lamp.

²³**The light of the** lamp will no longer appear in you;
The sound of the bridegroom and the bride will no longer be heard in you,

^(Isa 23:8)Who has counselled this concerning Tyre, the one who crowns [kings],

because your **merchants** were
the great
people of the earth because

whose **merchants** were princes and whose traders are **the honored people of the earth**?

^(Isa 47:9)These two [widowhood and childlessness] will come upon you **through your** extensive **witchcraft** and your great personal charm.

through your witchcraft all the nations have been led astray, and through it the blood of prophets and saints have been
found ²⁴and [the blood]

^(Jer 51:49)Babylon [is destined] to fall for the slain of Israel for

of all of those slain upon **the land**."   **the slain of all the land** have fallen for Babylon.

COMMENTARY

Rejoice over her, Heaven. Jeremiah prophesied that **heaven**, earth, and all that is in them would rejoice at the fall of **Babylon.** The very pious, orthodox Jews who would lament the fall of Jerusalem rejoiced at the burning of Rome. These were of very different points of view from **the merchants** and those involved in the shipping industry. When Second Isaiah thought Jeremiah's prophecy was being fulfilled, he urged the heavens to sing and the earth to shout, because the Lord had redeemed Jacob and would be glorified in Israel. All of this would take place in the heavenly court when God would judge the believers' case against Rome.

Enoch also promised that there would be a great **rejoicing** on the day of judgment for the righteous who had no reason to hide. The criminals, however, would discover that all of their crimes had been recorded (1Enoch 104:4-7). The author of this literary unit believed that he was at the very point in the cycle of Rome about which Jeremiah and Second Isaiah wrote. This was the judgment day about which Enoch reported, so he called all Christians and/or Jews to rejoice over her downfall. He then relied heavily upon Jeremiah's prophecy of the downfall of **Babylon** and Ezekiel's prophecy of the downfall of **Tyre**. Like many others, Hailey has tried to justify the message. He said the author was not gleeful over the destruction of Rome, but only the defeat of evil and the victory of righteousness.[1] For Jews and Christians of NT times, Rome was evil and Jews and/or Christians were righteous in their own judgment. If Rome fell, evil would also fall. Barclay was correct in observing,

> It may be that we are far from the Christian doctrine of forgiveness;
> but we are very close to the beating of the human heart.[2]

It is the kind of reaction expected of people who cried out to the Lord, asking how long it would be before he avenged their enemies (Rev 6:9-10).

Saints, apostles, and prophets. Whealon believed that Jesus was the only one to have apostles, and therefore this is a later Christian addition to a Jewish document.[3] Aune concurs, saying,

> In each of these texts οἱ ἀπόστολοι is a technical term referring to the twelve apostles.[1]

---

[1] H. M. Hailey, *Revelation: Introduction and Commentary* (Grand Rapids: Baker's Book House, c1979), p. 369.
[2] W. Barclay, *The Revelation of John* (Philadelphia: Westminster Press, 1960) II, pp. 195.
[3] Whealon, "Patches," p. 55.

That would be true if the prophecy (Rev 4:1-22:5) had been written by and for Christians, as Aune assumes. That, however, does not seem to be the case. The Greek term for apostles, was widely used in antiquity. In both Greek and Hebrew, this word for legal agent occurs. The Hebrew word for agent is *shah-leé-akh* (שׁלִיחַ). In Greek it is *ah-páws-taw-laws* (ἀπόστολος) or **apostle**. Therefore this is a legal term that is not distinctively Christian.

The terms, **saints, apostles, and prophets** are near synonyms. All of these were legal agents of the deity. The author used all three for emphasis. He might have, instead, spoken generally and said "Christian holy offices."

As big as a mill stone. **Mill stones** were huge. Thrown into the sea **a mill stone** would make a tremendous splash. This expression does not indicate that the author of Rev 18 had access to Matt 18:6 or Mark 9:42. **Mill stones** were standard parts of ancient society. Everyone in ancient society would have known how big they were. Therefore they provided excellent images to illustrate something very large and very heavy. Two stones were required for grinding. The lower **mill stone** was conical in shape and sat on the ground with the point directed upward. The upper **mill stone** was much larger, and it was the one mentioned here. It fit on top of the cone. Grain was ground by rubbing these two stones together. The upper **stone** was so large that it required the leverage of two wooden tongues with a donkey at the end of each tongue to make the stone move for grinding. A photograph of a mill stone is shown between chapters twelve and thirteen.

Thus with force will Babylon the great be thrown. After Jeremiah had finished writing Jer 50-51 he sent Seraiah to **Babylon** and ordered him to read these words and then tie a **stone** to the message and throw it into the Euphrates, and say, **Thus Babylon shall sink, never to rise again.** The prophet varied this a little. Instead of Seraiah, he visualized an **angel** throwing the **stone** into the sea, with a message similar to that of Jeremiah, promising that this would be the end of **Babylon**, which here meant Rome. Jesus spoke protectively in defense of those "little ones," who believed in him. Anyone who was this offensive, it would be better if a great mill stone were tied around his neck, and he would be thrown into the depths of the sea (Matt 18:6). The violence intended was the same as reported in Rev 18. As in the case of **Tyre**, when she was to be destroyed, people would look for Rome but they would never again find her.

Jeremiah's action was more than the symbol that some scholars have claimed. Jeremiah expected his prophecy to function as a curse, such as the one given to the woman suspected of adultery (Num 5). He thought that his action would have caused the destruction of **Babylon**. In the same way, the author of Rev 18 thought the angel's action would have initiated cosmic action that would have caused the destruction of Rome. This was magic.

---

[1] Aune, *Revelation 17-22* (Nashville: Thomas Nelson Publishers, c1998) 3, p. 1007.

Will no longer be heard. The **mills** in antiquity were some of the best known factories. They ground all of the grain into flour and made a lot of noise doing it. Still expatiating on the finality of Rome's destruction, John quoted from Jeremiah's prophecy concerning Judah when Nebuchadnezzar would come against her. The Lord would put an end to gladness and mirth, to the voice of the bridegroom and bride, to the grinding of **millstones,** and the light of the lamp. The poetic, repetitive way the author said **no longer be heard. . . no longer be found . . . no longer appear** emphasizes the funeral dirge quality of Rev 18. In Semitic languages, the expression **is found** means it exists. That which cannot be seen, heard, or found no longer exists. See also Ezek 26:21 and 2Kings 2:17. Josephus described the destruction of the wall of the city of Jerusalem in similar terms. He said the wall was so completely destroyed that future visitors to the city would wonder where the wall had been (War 7:1[3-4]). That which Titus ordered for Zion is that which the author of Rev 18 anticipated for Rome.

Every craftsman. NA adds **of every craft.**

The light of the lamp. NA precedes this clause with **The sound of the mill** will no longer be heard in you. References to the bridegroom, **the mill,** and **the lamp**, all come from Jer 25:10. Sinaiticus may have accidentally omitted the **mill** or NA texts may have added it from Jeremiah. Following Jeremiah, the author knew that not only commerce depended upon Rome, but also business, crafts, factories, and all other economic enterprises.

The merchants were the great people of the earth. Isaiah told of **the merchants** who were princes whose business was respected all over **the earth,** but they would also be destroyed with **Tyre.** The author of this document attributed this fate also to the merchants whose witchcraft had caused all the nations to go astray. Jeremiah said **Babylon** would have to **fall** because of all the slain of Israel for which she was guilty.

The blood of prophets and saints. The author of this redemption piece said Rome was guilty for **the blood** of all the **saints, the prophets**, and all other Jews and/or Christians who had been slaughtered on the land. This included all of the Jews killed by Romans in the numerous rebellions that occurred from the time of Pompey (63 BIA) to the time of the war in which the author was involved, probably that of 66-70 IA.

At the suitable time, which the author of this prophecy anticipated very soon Rome would be repaid for all these crimes. Zahn asked who these **prophets and saints** were. He concluded that **the saints,** at least, were ordinary Christians who lived in the tenth decade and had been martyred for the faith.[1] Weiss thought this last

---

[1] T. Zahn, *Die Offenbarung des Johannes* (Leipzig: A. Deichert, 1924), p. 575.

verse was a Christian editorial addition to a Jewish narrative. The Christian added it after the deaths of Peter and Paul as martyrs.[1]

Palestinian Jews resented all the taxes they had to pay Rome and all the oppression Jews had received from Roman hands. Of course, there were many Jewish **merchants** and tax collectors who became rich in the process, but Rome was the one who was hated. Rome was the power behind all of this exploitation. The Sibyl looked forward to the time when God would avenge the Jews and punish Rome. At that time Rome would have to pay three times as many taxes as it had extracted from Palestine, and there would be 20 times as many Roman slaves serving Jews as there were Jewish slaves serving Rome at the time the author wrote (SibOr 3:350-55; also 4.145-48). The author of Rev 18 expressed the same kinds of hope and hatred. Collins observed that Rev 18 reflects Isaiah, Jeremiah, and Ezekiel, but nevertheless, she concluded,

> [I]t is still likely that the passage reflects the social situation of Asia Minor in John's time.[2]

Rev 18 alludes to **Babylon** as a type for Rome, but Rome and **Babylon** are the only two social situations the chapter mentions. There is nothing in Rev 18 to direct the reader to Asia Minor. This is an invented interpretation based on her conviction that John of Patmos wrote the entire Book of Revelation and that John lived in Asia Minor. Nevertheless, she noted so many allusions to Palestine in the Book of Revelation that she conjectured that John was a former resident of Palestine.[3]

SUMMARY

Rev 18 has a very simple message that has been written very eloquently and repetitiously to explain the emotion involved. It has only two points:

1) Rome (Babylon) has done unlimited wicked things to the Jews while she herself was prospering and being admired all over the world; and
2) God knows all of her deeds and is just at the point of destroying Rome completely as punishment.

---

[1] J. Weiss, *Offenbarung des Johannes* (Göttingen: Vandenhoeck & Ruprecht, 1908), p. 671.
[2] Collins, *Crisis*, p. 123.
[3] Collins, *Crisis*, p. 136.

CHAPTER NINETEEN

TEXT

Revelation

$^{19:1}$After this I heard [something]

like the loud **noise of a** great **crowd** in heaven, saying,

"**Hallelujah**! [Let there be] salvation and power of our God,
^{2}because true
and just are his **judgments**, because he judged the great harlot who defiled the land with her harlotry. **He has avenged the blood of his servants**

from her hand."

First Testament

$^{Dan\ 10:6}$His arms and his legs were like polished brass, and the sound of his words was **like the noise of a crowd**.

$^{Ps\ 104:35}$Let criminals be finished and the wicked no longer exist. Bless the Lord, my soul **hallelujah**.

$^{Ps\ 119:137}$Righteous are you, Lord, **and just are** your **judgments**.

$^{Deut\ 32:43}$Praise, gentiles, his people, for **he avenges the blood of his servants**. He returns **vengeance** on his adversaries and atones the land of his people.

$^{2Kings\ 9:7}$You have struck the house of your lord, Ahab, and I **have avenged the blood of my servants** the prophets and all **the servants of** Yehowah **from the hand of Jezebel**.

COMMENTARY

After this. This is an expression often used in Greek literature to connect two independent units. There is one unit before this expression and one after it. The unit that follows begins with **I heard [something].**

Like the loud noise. A loud noise of a great crowd in heaven. Like several of the earlier victorious scenes, this vision takes place in heaven. Its announcement, however, was not made by something seen, but by something heard

Hallelujah! **Hallelujah** often either begins or ends some Psalms. For example, Ps 104 ipraises God for his creative and providential acts. It concludes by asking that criminals be destroyed wicked no longer exist, followed by the **Hallelujah**! This expressed the author's feelings completely. Anyone reading this message and sensing the joy of the author will somehow miss the quality Rissi said was there:

> Even when he describes the destruction of Rome, we feel his deep regret for the beauty, wealth, and radiating world of art misled by godless powers.[1]

Where did Rissi find that? Just because he thought the author should have felt regret at the fall of Rome, it does not mean the victors who were trying to destroy Rome would feel that way. Giblin admitted that "Revelation never presents the faithful as coming closer to 'gloating' over just punishment." But he defended the action:

> even here, does so in reference to "institutional evil," not to specific human persons.[2]

The author here not only came close to gloating. He openly gloated. He was not the least bit sorry. He was as happy over Rome's misery as Second Isaiah was over Babylon's pain years earlier.

Let there be salvation. NA adds **and glory**. There were at least three ways in which Jews were concerned with **salvation:** 1) The individual who was a member of a group was **saved**. If he or she was expelled, that member was "lost" (Luke 15:24; Acts 16:30-31). This was like the Greek mystery cults where members were called **saved** (*soh-théhn-tehs*, σωθέντες) (Diogenes Laertius 6.59). Those who were legally members of the corporation had souls that were **saved**. Once they became apostate or were excommunicated, their souls were lost. 2) Those needing to be rescued from prison or crisis might be **saved**, physically; and 3) **salvation** could come to a nation that was delivered politically and militarily. The following events were called **salvation**:

---

[1] M. Rissi, *The Future of the World* (Naperville: A. R. Allman, 1966), p. 12.
[2] C. H. Giblin, *The Book of Revelation* (Collegeville: Liturgical Press, c1991), p. 174.

1. Exodus from Egypt (Exod 14:30; Mek *Beshallah* 7.139-42).
2. Conquest of Canaan (Deut 20:4; Josh 10:6; Judges 6:14-15, 31, 36; 7:7).
3. Restoration of the land after the Babylonian captivity (Isa 35:4; 43:1, 12, 22-23; 48:20: 52:9; 59:1; 63:9).
4. Restoration of the kingdom to the Hasmoneans (1Macc 3:18; 4:9; 6:44; 2Macc 2:17; 1Enoch 62:13).
5. Zealots in charge of the temple acted like saviors (*soh-táy-rehs*, σωτῆρες) of the city (War 4:146). When Simon was admitted to Jerusalem, people acclaimed him as savior (*soh-áyr*, σωτήρ) leader (War 4:575).
6. In *The War* alone, the Jewish historian, Josephus used the term *soh-tay-reé-ah* (σωτηρία) 83 times, 81 of which were related to Jewish **salvation**.

All but one of these referred to concrete, physical deliverance of human beings in this life. The exception dealt with military weapons that were on fire. Of the rest, one spoke of God's **salvation,** meaning his deliverance of Jerusalem (War 3:387), and another of Ananus as high priest and leader of their **salvation** (War 4:318), again meaning the **salvation** of Jerusalem from the Romans. Two references were to Herod's recovery from illness before death (War 1:657-58) and another for the welfare of the Roman people (War 7:65). One was deliverance from a storm at sea (War 3:424), and 12 dealt with royal or miliary court trials where individuals or groups were or were not **saved** from capital punshment (War 1:121; 3:534; 4:32, 259, 338, 390, 456, 504, 523, 616; 6:230; 8:379). There were two instances of signs that Jews thought were of divine deliverance, but this deliverance was military (War 1:332; 6:285). Two usages spoke of deliverance of a city (War 1:295; 3:194). The other 60 instances refer to individuals or groups in relationship to the Roman-Jewish war. Thackeray rendered these terms by such words as life, escape, safety, security, protection, preservation, pardon, welfare, deliverance, and **salvation**--words that reflect the clear context of **salvation** of human lives from physical dangers, mostly in war. Not one instance dealt with otherworldly soteriology.

In *The Antiquities*, Josephus used the term *soh-tay-reé-ah* 150 times--all of which were concrete: **Salvation** of Noah from the flood (Ant 1:76), Isaac from his father's sword (Ant 1:224), Jacob from Esau (Ant 1:327), Benjamin in Egypt (Ant 2:134, 139, 140, 141, 147, 159), Moses in the bull rushes (Ant 1:219, 221, 236), the Gibionites from Joshua (Ant 5:57), Saul from David (Ant 6:315), Jeremiah from the pit (Ant 10:123), Israelites at the Exodus (Ant 1:327, 331-33, 336, 339, 342, 345, 347; 3:1), Moses and the Israelites in the wilderness (Ant 3:6, 21, 23, 27, 36, 64, 65; 4:68; 8:190; 4:42; 5:89; 8:194; 8:268; 8:312; 13:297; 14:310;), Hasmoneans from the Syrians (Ant 12:292), and the deliverance of various kings from death or danger.

To be sure, people prayed to God for **salvation**, but this was not so that they could go to heaven, but that they might live longer on earth (Ant 10:11; 11:134).

Some scholars, like E. P. Sanders still think soteriology, the study of **salvation,** has to be free from historical rewards,[1] but that was not the standard for NT, Judaism, and Christianity. The Jews who were shouting, **Hallelujah!** thought the **salvation** they were about to receive was deliverance of the nation from subservience to the Romans and the reestablishment of the Promised Land under a Davidic king. There was rejoicing but no "rapture," and no one was reported as having been taken up to heaven.

Just are his judgments. Ps 119 is also a hymn of praise for God's handiwork in creation of the universe, and also for his provision of the law, **judgments,** and teaching that are perfect in all respects. The author then turned his attention from God's **judging** activity to the result of one of his important **judgments.** The only thing that was important to the author about God's **judgments** was that the verdict was "guilty" for Rome, and God would carry out his sentence with vengeance. Earlier, when the angels were delivering plagues to the Jews on the Promised Land, the author acknowledged that God's **judgments** were just. That is the normal confession for a defendant to make before a judge at the opening of a trial.

The Jews had broken contract with the Lord and therefore deserved the curses that accompanied the contract and were listed in Lev 26. Here the same affirmation is made but with more glee. Events in history led the author to believe that the plagues destined for the Jews had already been applied, and Jewish punishment was over. After that it was not the Jews who were destined to receive the predestined punishment but the enemies of the Jews--the Romans.

He has avenged the blood. Just as Elisha sent one of the sons of the prophets to anoint Jehu and command him to wreak **vengeance** on Jezebel for the blood of the Lord's **servants** the prophets, so the author reasoned God would **avenge** his contemporary **servants** from the harlot, Rome, whom he considered to be an antitype of the wicked Jezebel. Rissi argues that words like **vengeance** and "war" are only metaphorical terms used symbolically. Harmageddon (Rev 16:16) is only a mythical mount. Anger of the Lamb is really his divine love. When Revelation says Christ wages war that really means that Christ is **judging** his church.[2] If "anger" really means "love" and "war" means "judgment," what do the terms "love" and "judgment" mean?

TEXT

Revelation   First Testament

Ps 104:35 Let criminals be finished from

---

[1] E. P. Sanders, *Paul and Palestinian Judaism* (Philadelphia: Fortress Press, c1977), p. 198.
[2] Rissi, *Future*, pp. 13-15, 22.

³Then they said a second time, "**Hallelujah!**	the land and wicked be no more! Bless Yehowah, my soul. **Hallelujah**.
and **her smoke goes up into the ages** of ages!" ⁴Then the twenty-four elders and the four fell	ᴵˢᵃ ³⁴:¹⁰Her land has become like burning pitch . . . **her smoke goes up into the age**.
down and worshiped **God** who **sits on the throne**,	ᴵˢᵃ ⁶:¹I saw **the Lord sitting on the throne** high and exalted.
	ᴾˢ ¹⁰⁶:⁴⁸⁾¹Bless Yehowah, the God of Israel from the [present] age **to the age** [to
saying, "**Amen! Hallelujah!**" ⁵Then a shout went out from the throne, saying,	come]. Let all the people **say "Amen! Hallelujah."**
	ᴶᵉʳ ²⁰:¹³Sing to Yehowah! **Praise Yehowah**.
"**Praise to our God**, all **his servants**	ᴾˢ ¹³⁵:¹⁻³**Hallelujah! Praise** the name of Yehowah; **praise, servants of Yehowah** who stand in the temple of Yehowah, in the courts of the house of our God. **Hallelujah**, for Yehowah is good.
who fear him, both small and great."	ᴾˢ ¹¹⁵:¹³[The Lord] will bless those **who fear** the Lord, **both small and great**.
	ᴾˢ ¹¹⁵:¹⁶Heaven is the heaven of Yehowah, but the land he has given to human beings.

COMMENTARY

The smoke goes up into the ages of ages. This is usually rendered "for ever and ever," which sometimes means the same. Zahn correctly observed,

> Whoever opens a Hebrew lexicon would see that the words [*ace toos ai-óh-nahs tohn ai-óh-nohn*] εἰς τοὺς αἰῶνας τῶν αἰώνων] never corresponds with the idea of timeless eternity.[1]

Charles thought it meant 1,000 years.[2] The point of this translation is that the author was writing in both temporal and qualitative terms. An **age** is an unspecified length of time. It could be the length of a king's rule, the length of time a country is under the rule of another power, or some such period. The **age** under discussion here was the **age** when Jews would rule the world, and Rome's power would come to an end.

Ages of ages is first of all plural and secondly greatest. Normally one **age** was expected to be an **age** of gentile rule and the next **age** one of Jewish rule. Here the author expected Jews to rule more than one **age**. Furthermore, these Jewish **ages** were expected to be the greatest of all **ages**. For them this was superlative time—but it was time that was measured by days, weeks, and years.

This is not "only a grisly contrast to the incense of the heavenly worship (5:8; 8:3-4)," as Boring claims.[3] The occasion for the rejoicing was that Rome was burning. Its citizens had set the city on fire (IA 69), and the Jews in Palestine were glad. There was lamentation in Rome, but there was joy in Jerusalem, and Jews believed this meant there was joy in heaven. Jews expected Rome would continue burning until the new **age** began. It would burn into the Jewish **age.**

When Tacitus described the burning of Rome, he said it could not be determined which side of the civil war actually set fire to the roofs of the Capitol, but once the fire began it spread rapidly.

> Thus the Capitol burned with its doors closed; no one defended it, and no one plundered it (Hist 3:71).

Tacitus further noted that this was the saddest and most disgraceful crime Rome had ever suffered (*Hist* 3:72). Jews had different feelings about the incident. Rabbis said that whenever the Hebrew word *tsor* (צור) was spelled with the vowel *waw* (ו) in First Testament (FT) it meant the city Tyre, but when it was spelled without the *waw* (*tsar*, צר) it meant the wicked state (Rome). This was an important expression, because the word *tsar* (צר) means such adverse things as "assault," "oppress," "besiege," or "afflict," and Tyre was a Phoenician city which was one of Israel's enemies. Therefore, this has allowed Jews to play on the two words, applying the verb to the city and then transferring to Rome as an antitype the hostility attributed to both. Rabbis said also that God **avenged** himself on the city of Rome with fire that would never be quenched day or night, because the Romans burned the temple of God at Jerusalem. This fulfills the prophecy of Isaiah:

---

[1] T. Zahn, *Die Offenbarung des Johannes* (Leipzig: A. Deichert, 1924), pp. 606-608.

[2] R. H. Charles, *Critical and Exegetical Commentary on the Revelation of St. John the Divine* (New York: Charles Scribners, c1920) I, p. 120.

[3] M. E. Boring, *Revelation* (Louisville: John Knox Press, c1989), p. 193.

A sound of uproar from the city, a noise from the temple. The sound of Yehowah paying back his enemies (Isa 66:6; ExodR 9:13 [7:25]).

The rabbis overlooked the fact that Rome burned before the Jerusalem temple did, but there is enough similarity between this rabbinic interpretation and Rev 19 to arouse the suspicion that rabbis were familiar with the Book of Revelation. This is also true of the two messiahs of Revelation and the messiahs of Joseph and Nehemiah described by various rabbinic documents. The second Hallelujah was followed by a quotation from Isa 34 which was an expression of the Lord's anger against Edom and his promise that Edom would undergo a terrible destruction. The dress rehearsal for this bloody event had already taken place in heaven (Isa 34:5) against that doomed nation. The land would become soaked with blood, and the streams of Edom would be turned to pitch, so that the smoke from this burning pitch would go up for ages. This would happen on the Lord's day of **vengeance,** after which Edom would become a waste wilderness where only wild beasts and birds could dwell. For the author, Edom meant Rome, and that was the punishment he yearned for Rome to receive.

The 24 elders. These are referred to also in Rev 4:4. **The 24 elders** in heaven corresponded to the 24 courses of priests who functioned in sequence at the temple in Jerusalem (1Chron 24:7-18). They were the associate judges in the Lord's judicial council.

The four. NA identifies these **four** accurately as "beasts." These are also mentioned in Rev 4:6. These were not the same kind of **beast**s as those in Daniel that mythicized the four nations that ruled Palestine from 586-164 BIA. These were heavenly **beasts**--cherubim and seraphim. They were sphinx-like monsters that had wings like a bird, horns like a cow or goat, a head like a lion, hooves like a cow, sheep, or goat, etc. They were specially equipped to perform all sorts of functions that the Lord might command. As soon as this decree was made in heaven, then all the company of heaven worshipped God, according to the author, following the direction of an enthronement Psalm. The heavenly hymn was composed of a few lines from Ps 135:1-3 and from Ps 115:13. The latter Psalm is one that contrasts God with the idols of the gentiles. It further affirms that the heavens belong to the Lord but that he has given the earth to human beings. Although the Psalmist clearly used *áh-rehtz* (ארץ) to mean "earth" here, the author probably understood its allusion to have been made with reference to **the land,** which he expected the Lord to give to his children, the Jews, soon.

Both small and great. This is a literary form called a *merismus*. It comes from the Greek word that means "part." To list all of the parts means "the entire unit." To list the extreme parts has the same meaning. **Small and great** includes everything in between. In this context the **small and great** do not apply to size but to status. It includes all people of all economic classes. This expression was used frequently in Judaism and early Christianity (Rev 11:18).

TEXT

Revelation	First Testament
	^{Dan 10:5-6}I lifted my eyes and watched-- Look! A man dressed in linen; his loins were girded with the gold of Uphaz. His body was like beryl, and his face seemed like lightning. His eyes were like fiery torches; his arms and legs gleamed like polished brass, and the sound of his words was **like the noise of a crowd**.
⁶I heard something **like the noise of a** large **crowd,**	
like the sound of much water [running], and like the sound of loud thunder, saying,	^{Ezek 1:24; 43:2}I heard **the noise of** their [heavenly beasts] wings **like the sound of much water [running]**.
"**Hallelujah**! God,	^{Ps 104:35}Let criminals be finished and the wicked be no more! Bless the Lord, my soul. **Hallelujah**.
our Lord, the almighty One	^{Amos 9:5}**The Lord** Yehowah **of armies** who touches the earth and it melts, and all its inhabitants mourn.
has become king.	^{Zech 14:9}**Yehowah will become king over all the land**. On that day Yehowah will be one and his name [will be] one.
	^{Obad 21}The kingdom will belong to **Yehowah**.
	^{Ps 93:1}**Yehowah has become king**! He is dressed in majesty.

⁷**Let us rejoice and be glad**, and let us give them glory, because the wedding of the Lamb has come. His **bride** has prepared herself; ⁸she was given [permission] to wear bright, clean linen." (for the linen is the **righteous deeds of the saints**).

Ps 99:1-2 **Yehowah has become king**; let the peoples tremble. He sits [on] the cherubim [in the temple]; the land shakes. Yehowah is magnified in

Zion; he is exalted above all the peoples.

Ps 118:24 This is the day that Yehowah has made; **let us rejoice and be glad** in it.

Isa 61:10-11 I will greatly **rejoice** in Yehowah; my soul will **be glad** in my God, because he has dressed me [with] garments of salvation; he has covered me with a robe of **righteousness** just as a bridegroom decks himself with a garland, and as a bride adorns herself with her jewels . . thus the Lord Yehowah will shoot forth **righteousness**.

COMMENTARY

I heard. This is an introduction to the hymn that is quoted, but first the author of Rev 19 pictured himself as a new Daniel just before someone put his hand on him and told him, orally, about the events that would happen at the end of the gentile age.

Like the sound. Again as a preamble the author described **the sound** in which the poem was read. The main point of his description is that the message was read in a loud voice--**like the noise of a crowd, like the roar** of a waterfall, **like the sound of loud thunder** rumbling. Not just **the noise of the crowd**, as in Rev 19:1, but also two other loud **noises** at the same time, **thunder** and a waterfall. These similes were to remind the reader of heavenly announcements that had been made to Daniel and to Ezekiel and of **the thunder** that shook the earth when the ten commandments were given. All of this was introduction which the reader needed to understand before reading the hymn that followed. The poem begins with, **Hallelujah**! which means "Praise be to Yehowah!"

Hallelujah! . . . the almighty One has become king. Instead of **God, our Lord**, NA has **the Lord God.** Since this passage is well known and sung every year in Handel's *Messiah*, it seems to be going against the tide to render this verse in any way except, **For the Lord, God, omnipotent reigneth!**, but that is not the best translation. The word, which Handel rendered **omnipotent** is an accurate translation of the Greek, but the Greek has inaccurately rendered the Hebrew *tseh-váho-th* (צבעות) which means **armies** or **soldiers,** and is the single most frequently used attribute for God in the entire First Testament (FT). The Old Greek (OG) regularly rendered **armies** in Hebrew by **omnipotent** in Greek (see also *PssSol* 2:33-36; 5:21). This suggests that, in the view of early Jews and Christians, the one who ruled **the armies** was omnipotent or almighty. Military power was the greatest of all forces.

In antiquity, enthronement psalms were composed for use in ceremonies whereby some king was installed. The king was believed to be God's agent or apostle, legally installed as God's son at the moment of his anointing or coronation. A legal agent is legally identical to the principal who commissioned him. Therefore ancients believed that through his agent their God was enthroned whenever their king was crowned.

Rev 19:6 is related to Zech 14, a prophecy that anticipated the restoration of the land, when the Lord would stand on Mount Zion, and Jerusalem would be restored to the chosen people. Also as background was Obad 21, the conclusion of a passage that looked forward to the military destruction of Edom, the unity of Judah and Israel, and the recapture of the Davidic kingdom. When all of the land would be restored, there would be saviors who would rule all of this land from Jerusalem. When this took place, **the kingdom** would become God's (Obad 21). God was not **king** until he placed his legal agent on the throne in Jerusalem (see Sifre Deut 32:10). The author of Rev 19:6 expected the same events to be reenacted. This would be the conclusion of their experience. When Rome, which Jews called "Edom," was destroyed, the saints would again receive the kingdom under their own Messiah, the Lamb.

The poem that began with **Hallelujah!** was a messianic hymn, whereby the author anticipated the enthronement of the Messiah at Jerusalem. It is similar to other hymns of praise in Rev 7:9-12; 11:15-17. This enthronement of the Messiah was called the wedding feast of the Lamb or the messianic banquet. It was called a wedding feast, because it was related to the renewal of the wedding contract which the Lord was making with his people. The "bride" prepared to be united with the Messiah was the chosen people, either Judaism or the church. The permission that was granted her to wear these special garments was given by the Lord whose name was avoided to prevent blasphemy.

Let us give them glory. NA has **give him glory**.

The wedding of the Lamb. There are several instances in the FT where God's relationship to the Israelites was that of a marriage (Hos 2:19-20; Isa 49:18; 50:1;54:1-6; Jer 2:32; 3:20; Ezek 16:8-14). The people of Israel and the Christian church (Rom 7:4; Eph 5:22-6:9) each considered itself to be a body or corporation. In a corporation an entire group can function legally as a person. It can buy and sell; it can make contracts; it can defend itself in court. Since the chosen people believe that they have a contract with the Lord, they picture the Lord or his legal agent, the Messiah, as the bridegroom and themselves as the bride. The contract, then, is a marriage contract.

The wedding between the Lord and his people was a dramatic way of showing that the contract that had been annulled when the Lord sent his people out of his house (Deut 24:1) and off his land was being renewed (Jer 31:31). Just as at an ancient wedding the bride vowed to be obedient to her husband, and her husband vowed that he would provide for her adequately, at the contract between the Lord and his people, God swore that he would be the people's God and Israelites vowed that they would be his people. God would provide for the people's needs, and the people would obey his laws. When the land was restored the Messiah would appear, and the contract would be renewed.

The contract between Israel (the bride) and Yehowah (the groom) was set in terms of a **wedding** agreement so often in the FT that it is surprising that Aune thought it was unexpected for the expression to occur here in Rev 19. He noted that this was a First Testament (FT) concept, but believed it rarely occurred in later Judaism.[1] He overlooked the fact that the New Testament (NT) itself is Jewish literature and that the Book of Revelation depended heavily on the FT. Parables told about **weddings** are coded stories about the renewal of the contract (Matt 22:2-10). On Passover night it is customary for Jews to expect the Messiah to appear. Openly they do not say that, for political reasons. They say they are waiting for Elijah, but Jews know Elijah is expected to appear just before the Messiah. The expectation of one is the expectation of both. Another way of disguising this expectation is to tell about the anticipation of a bridegroom appearing at night (Matt 25:1). The **wedding** of the Messiah and Israel would happen whenever the new contract was reestablished. Jesus spoke of himself and his disciples in terms of a **bridegroom** and **the sons of the bridegroom** (Matt 9:15). **The wedding** of the Lamb fits into the same kind of expectation.

The bride has prepared herself. This means she was **prepared as a bride adorned for her husband** (Rev 21:2). **The bride** represents the people who are parties to this wedding contract. The whole nation is treated as one person, because it is a legal corporation. At **the wedding** the king would be enthroned, the foreigners driven out, and the land would be restored to Jewish rule. In order to **prepare** themselves for this **wedding** contract, the people would be engaged in warfare the way the Hasmoneans were for 3½ years before the temple was rededicated in 164 BIA. It would also require good deeds on Israel's part to cancel the crimes that had been committed by the nation earlier. When **the bride prepared herself,** she **prepared** her **wedding** garment.[2] In the Near East it was customary for girls to begin preparing a wedding dress when they were very small, so that by the time of their wedding

---

[1] D. E. Aune, *Revelation 17-22* (Dallas: Thomas Nelson Publishers, c1998), pp. 1029-30.
[2] So also D. A. McIlraith, "'For the Fine Linen is the Righteous Deeds of the Saints': Works and Wife in Revelation 19:8," *CBQ* 61 (1999): 525.

they would be magnificently dressed. These dresses were not only very beautiful, but they had a legal and symbolical significance. The more beautiful the dress the more capable and desirable **the bride**.

The clothes that people wore not only exhibited their wealth, but also their status. Uniforms were associated with people's positions. When a king or high priest was anointed each was clothed with a new garment and crown. Each became a new creature, legally. Christian baptism was called a "wedding garment," because through this legal ceremony, non-Christians removed their clothing, and with it their legal clothing—their former legal identities, their debts, and their crimes—stepped naked into the water accompanied by a church officer who recited the proper legal ceremony. Then the newly baptized Christian was reclothed with a white robe and became a new creature. Paul was speaking of initiation into Christianity, when he said, "Put off the old," and "put on the new" (2Cor 5:17; Col 2:11; 3:9-14; 4:22-24). This change involved not only a change of clothing, but also a change of legal identity. When Elijah chose Elisha for his successor as the national prophet, he put his own robe on Elisha's shoulders (1Kings 19:19). Joseph's brothers were jealous of him, because of the legal significance of the special coat that his father provided for him (Gen 37:3-4, 23, 30-33).[1]

Ever since the time of Hosea, the contract God made with his people was thought to have been a marriage contract. Like other marriage contracts, this **wedding** would take place in a legal ceremony, with the proper witnesses and legal officials presiding. With this ceremony God would become Israel's God and they would become his people. God would be the groom, and Israel would be the corporate bride. In preparation for this ceremony, Israel was expected to prepare a special **wedding** garment of fine linen.

The linen is the righteous deeds. This is a small midrash on **linen**. There are other explanatory commentaries in the Book of Revelation. For example, **The seven stars are the messengers of the seven churches and the seven lamp stands are the seven churches** (Rev 1:20); the seven horns and the seven eyes of the Lamb are **the seven spirits of God** (Rev 5:6); the seven lamp stands of fire, burning before the throne, **are the seven spirits of God** (Rev 4:5); and . . . golden bowls filled with incense**, are the prayers of the saints** (Rev 5:8). All of these small midrashim were probably written after the rest of the narratives to which they belong by someone who thought the code needed to be interpreted. In a Scripture passage devoted to the anointing of a king, the author said,

> [Yehowah] has clothed me with garments of salvation;
> He has covered me with a robe of **righteousness** (Isa 61:10).

White **linen** represented ritual cleanliness and **righteous deeds**. Here the discussion is about the **bride,** God's people, getting **prepared** for a **wedding** with the Lamb,

---

[1] See further Buchanan, *Biblical and Theological Insights from Ancient and Modern Civil Law* (Lewiston: The Edwin Mellen Press, c1992), pp. 92-96.

the Messiah of the Lord. The way this bride gets prepared is to perform many deeds of **righteousness** to lay up treasures of merit in the heavenly treasury, or to prepare a marvelous wedding gown for the renewal of the contract with God, through his legal agent, the Lamb.[1] McIlraith noted that Jesus was not pictured as the groom in any of the **wedding** symbolism of the main section of Revelation. Instead of Jesus, it is the Lamb that was the groom.[2] That is because Rev 4:1-22:5 was initially a Jewish prophecy in which the groom was the Lamb, which was any Messiah that happened to become king of Israel at that time. The prophecy was only slightly Christianized in four places.

The bride had been divorced after the temple was burned in 586 BIA because Israel's deeds had not been **righteous**. There would be no new **wedding** contract between the Lord and the Israelites until there had been enough **righteous** deeds to counter-balance the unrighteousness ones. These deeds were called the **wedding garment** necessary for **the bride** to wear at the conclusion of the marriage contract when God would take back his people and provide for them again on the Promised Land. The poem ended before this comment was added. This sentence is an interpretive midrash. Her wedding garment mythologically consisted of the acts of supererogation performed by the saints and martyrs whose blood was shed to pay off the debt of crimes that Israel had committed without paying the appropriate punishment at the times of the offenses. This all had to be canceled before the new **age** could be inaugurated.

The ones invited to **the wedding banquet of the Lamb** would be the same ones who **had washed their robes and made them white by the blood of the Lamb**. They were the 144,000 celibate saints who were considered the first-fruits to be included in the heavenly offering of **first fruits**. They were the ones whose names were written in **the Lamb's Book of Life** (Rev 14).

TEXT

Revelation

⁹Then he says to me, "Write: 'Blessed are those who are invited to the wedding banquet of the Lamb.'" And he said to me, "These are the true words of God." ¹⁰Then **I fell on my face** before his feet to worship him,

First Testament

Ezek 1:28-2:1 Such was the appearance that shone around, the appearance was like the glory of Yehowah. When I saw [it]
I fell on my face, and I heard a voice speaking. It

---

[1] McIlraith, *"Fine Linen,"* analyzed the use of the term "works" in the entire Book of Revelation. He found a few evil works, and organized the good works into categories, but all of the good works were works of supererogation.

[2] McIlraith, *Fine Linen,* p. 524. K. E. Miller, "The Nuptial Eschatology of Revelation 19-22," *CBQ* 60 (1998):301-318, argued that all of Rev 10-22 constituted a report of a marriage between the Lamb and the people. There are many marriage contract points in Rev 19, but the case does not extend as far as Miller claimed.

but **he said to me,** "Don't do that! I am a fellow servant of you and your brothers who have the testimony of Jesus. Worship God, for the testimony of Jesus is the spirit of prophecy."

said to me, "Son of man, stand on your feet, and I will speak to you."

COMMENTARY

He said to me. This renders the Greek, **He says to me.** The tense has been changed for clarity in English. The passage that begins here is an interruption of a long dissertation that began back in Rev 16, dealing with **the great harlot, the beasts**, and **great Babylon**. Some later editor inserted this pericope with the blessing (Rev 19:9) and Christian affirmation. Most scholars think the unit on the harlot ends with Rev 19:10, but that overlooks the interruption given by these two verses (Rev 19:9-10). Loisy, for example, held that this verse was copied from its original place in Rev 22:8-9.[1]

Those who are invited. These are the ones who will be members of the new contract, the 144,000 celibate monks. The bracketed passage is misplaced. It was originally composed by the elder John. John wrote it in the context where it belongs (Rev 22:6-9). Some later scribe copied it also here where it makes no sense. Weiss and Whealon both thought this was a Christian addition to an otherwise Jewish composition.[2] The contract the Lord made with his people when he gave them the commandments was held to be a wedding contract. The Lord was the groom; the nation or church was the bride. Therefore wedding imagery is frequently meant to dramatize the new contract which the Lord was expected to make with his divorced people. These invited ones were the new antitypes of the saints of the Most High (Dan 7:27).

The wedding banquet of the Lamb. This is not the kind of banquet Jesus ate together with tax collectors and criminals, as some scholars suggest. Those meals were recruitment celebrations. Whenever some wealthy businessman gave all of his money to the monastery that called itself the "poor," and took up vows of poverty, celibacy, and obedience as a follower of Jesus, then the apostles and Jesus met with that person at a special celebration meal.

The wedding banquet, however, was associated with the anointing of the Messiah. On that great occasion the Messiah would be anointed, the new contract would be established, and a great celebration feast would be planned.

The true words of God. All FT was understood to be **the word of God**, but prophecy that was fulfilled was also thought to be the word of God. The messenger assured

---

[1] A. Loisy, *L'Apocalypse de Jean* (Paris: Emile Nourry, 1923), p. 335.
[2] J. Weiss, *Die Offenbarung des Johannes* (Göttingen: Vandenhoeck & Ruprecht, 1908), pp. 671-72, and J. F. Whealon, "New Patches on an Old Garment," *BTB* 11 (1981):55.

John that the words written here in Rev 19 which were not taken from FT were nonetheless true words of God. He believed the author of this prophecy was a prophet. John accepted this analysis.

I fell on my face. Rabbis said people worshiped kings out of respect for royalty (ExodR 18:1 [12:29]). Worshiping was falling down before the object of worship with **the face** toward the ground. This posture is still a part of Moslem worship. The author of this verse pictured John of Patmos as an antitype of Ezekiel when he **fell on his face** before the **voice.** The similarities between Rev 19:10 and 22:8-9 are striking.

A fellow servant of you and your brothers. This is an attempt to disown any suggestion that the voice came from a heavenly angel. When Joseph's brother bowed down before him, he said, "Don't be afraid! Am I in the place of God" (Gen 50:19).

The testimony of Jesus is the spirit of prophecy. Vassiliadis rendered this passage, "What inspires the prophets is that they can witness (even unto death) to Jesus."[1] Another way of saying this is that those who have **the spirit of prophecy** are those who worship God and are willing to **testify** at the cost of death to their beliefs about **Jesus.** Many scholars think Rev 19:9b-10 are interpolations. Charles argued strongly that this was the stupid addition of an unintelligent disciple of John.[2] Longnecker has found fault with Charles' reasons for this conclusion. Although he did not deny that this was an interpolation, Longnecker argued that its insertion had good merit,

> Since it allows the visions of 17,1-19,10 and 21,9-22,9 to share both common introductions (cf. 17,1-3 with 21,9-10) and common conclusions (cf. 19:9-10 with 22:6-9), even on Charles' supposition that 19,10 is to be attributed to a redactor, that redactor was intelligent enough to incorporate an aesthetically pleasing structural feature into the text.[3]

TEXT

Revelation	First Testament
[11]**I saw the heavens opened.**	Ezek 1:1**The heavens opened**, and **I saw** the appearance of God.
Now look! **A white horse**, and the	2Macc 3:25For **a certain white horse**

---

[1] P. Vassiliadis, "The Translation of *martyria Iesou* in Revelation," *BT* 36 (1985):134.
[2] R. H. Charles, *A Critical and Exegetical Commentary on the Revelation of St. John* (Edinburgh: T. & T. Clark, 1920) 2, p. 129.
[3] B. W. Longnecker, "Revelation 19,20: One Verse in Search of an Author," *ZNTW* 9 (2000): 37.

one seated on it was called "faithful and true." **He will judge righteously** and make war	appeared to them, having a fearful rider and [the horse was] decorated with a magnificent harness.
	Isa 11:4[The son of David] **will judge** the poor **righteously** and examine the humble of the land justly. He will strike the land with the staff of his mouth, and with the breath of his lips he will kill the wicked.
	Ps 96:13**He will judge** the world **righteously**, and the peoples truthfully.
¹²**His eyes were like a fiery** flame, and he had upon his head many crowns, having a name written which no one knew except him,	Dan 10:5-6I lifted **my eyes** and watched-- look! A man dressed in linen; his loins were girded with the gold of Uphaz. His body was like beryl, and his face seemed like lightning. **His eyes were like fiery** torches; his arms and legs gleamed like polished brass, and the sound of his words was like the noise of a crowd.
¹³and he wore a **garment sprinkled** with blood, and his name was called	Isa 63:3I walked on top of them in my anger; I trampled them in my wrath; their [blood] was **sprinkled** on my **garment**, and I stained all of my clothes.
"The **Word of God**."	OGWis 18:15-16**Your** all powerful **word** attacked from heaven, **from the** royal throne, as a warrior with a sharp sword.

COMMENTARY

I saw the heaven opened. This is the beginning of a new vision which produced a new unit of literature. It is similar to the introduction at the beginning of the prophecy (Rev 4:1). It comes after the climax of a long dissertation on the victory over the great harlot. Originally, it probably was the beginning of some narrative. Whoever the collector was that edited the prophecy found this unit somewhere and inserted it into his anthology here. When Jacob was running away from Esau, he dreamed that he saw a ladder reaching **heaven** (Gen 28:11-13). This vision reportedly took place at Bethel. The entire prophecy of Ezekiel begins with his testimony that the **heavens were opened** and he saw a vision (Ezek 1:1). The vision that he saw turned out to be one, not of the sanctuary at Bethel, but rather of the temple in Jerusalem. This vision of the **open heaven** was designed to alert the reader to the fact that the scene which follows, like those before, would take place **in heaven**. It was normal for Jews to think of **heaven** in temple concepts. Jews and early Christians assumed that because God was present in the Jerusalem temple as well as **in heaven** that **heaven** was therefore constructed exactly like the temple.

The one seated upon it was called faithful and true. The rider on **the white horse** was identified through quotations with the Messiah, son of David (Isa 11:4-5) and the one who spoke to Daniel and told him about the end of the gentile rule (Dan 10:6). The **white horse** upon which the Messiah rode and the other **white horses** on which the **heavenly** soldiers were **seated** reflect the belief Jews held that there were heavenly soldiers that joined battle against the soldiers of Israel's enemies. One narration of that belief tells of the time Heliodorus attempted to invade the temple treasury and rob it of its contents. At that time, a fearful rider appeared on a horse, wearing what looked like golden armor. He was accompanied by two other young men also on horseback. These charged and overpowered Heliodorus, so Heliodorus had to be carried away in a litter (2Macc 3:22-30).

He will judge righteously and make war. These were two of the standard obligations of a king. The new ruler from the family of David who was expected to rule Israel in the future was believed to delight in the fear of the Lord. He was expected **to judge** the poor with **righteousness**. That means he would establish an efficient **judicial** system throughout the land, so that all people would have access to the courts. That was part of the responsibility of a national leader, so the author of this prophecy reasoned that the Messiah would fulfill that requirement. The other responsibility of the king was that he would also **make war**. He would extend the borders and establish a military force adequate to defend the nation against invaders. The further description of the Messiah **in heaven** as one with eyes like fiery flames was intended to remind the reader of the man who appeared to Daniel to tell him what would happen at the end of the gentile **age**. Rissi did not like the idea of the rider **on the horse**, whom he thought was Jesus, shedding blood or **making war**. He said the blood involved was only Christ's own blood, which had the metaphorical meaning of self sacrifice and forgiveness. Furthermore, he argued, there is no mention of **a war** being fought in this context.[1] Boring had the same problem, so he said,

---

[1] Rissi, *Future*, p. 24. O. Böcher, "Die Johannes-Apokalypse und die Texte von Qumran," *ANRW* II.25.5:3895, however, said, "The expectation of a real, not some ethical-symbolic--final war (Rev 19:11-21; cf. Ezek 39:17-24) is found running through the Qumran texts (1QM frequently; cf. 1QS 3:24-25; 1QSa 1:21,26; CD 4:13)."

> This conqueror destroys his enemies, not with the literal sword, but with the sword of his mouth . . . In contrast to the divine warrior of Isa 63:1-3, the source for this imagery, this blood is not the blood of his enemies but his own martyr blood . . . He uses the ancient *form* of portraying the ultimate victory of God as winning a great battle . . . But he fills this with a new *content*.[1]

The original Jewish author of this narrative did not picture Jesus as the warrior here, although John of Patmos probably interpreted it that way. Even though this is offensive to many twentieth century Christians, it was intended as it was said. There is no evidence that there was a new remythologization of FT here. It was Boring, and not the author of Rev 19 who infused the new content and gave the passage a new meaning the author never intended. Anyone who kills with **the sword of his mouth** either curses his enemies, and they fall dead, or he orders them killed, and someone else fulfills the command. In either case, the enemies are left dead, so the new content is no more humane than war.

He had upon his head many crowns. That is because he ruled many countries. He was not just a king of a small land. He was an emperor, a king over other kings. He wore one crown for each country he ruled. For example, Ptolemy VI Philometer entered Antioch wearing two crowns, one representing Asia and the other for Egypt (Ant 13:113).

Having a name written. **The name** which was **written** at first appeared as a mystery, but before the sentence was finished it was given as **The Word of God** (Rev 19:13). The **name** was **written**—not on his horse, but on himself. This means that it was **written** on his armor. He had been called **faithful and true** earlier (Rev 19:11), and he was later called **King of kings and Lord of lords** (Rev 19:16). The idea of having magic slogans on various parts of soldiers' armor seemed normal in Judaism of NT times. There are many slogans, such as these in the War Scroll among the Dead Sea Scrolls. For example: When soldiers went into battle they should write on their standards **truth of God, justice of God, glory of God, judgment of God** (1QM 4:6). On the javelin's pennant they should write **bloody darts to bring down the slain by the wrath of God** (1QM 6:3). These were magic expressions which were to give their bearers good luck and success in the same way a horse shoe above an entrance door would do. They should add strength to the warrior and drive off the demons and the enemy soldiers. Martin Luther's famous hymn, **A Mighty Fortress is our God**, expressed the same belief,

> The prince of darkness grim; we tremble not for him;
>   one little word shall fell him.
> Just ask who that may be. Christ Jesus it is he,
>   and he must win the battle.

---

[1] Boring, *Revelation*, 196.

A garment sprinkled with blood. Osbourn has shown strong textual support for the reading *eh-rahn-tees-méh-nawn* (ερραντισμένον, (sprinkle) in preference to the reading *beh-bah-méh-nawn* (βεβαμμένον) (dip).[1] It is more likely that the picture given here is one of a great warrior returning from battle where he received splatterings of blood on his garments than that he would have taken off his clothes and laundered them **with blood**. This is also closer to the reading of Isa 63:3 upon which the author depended for his textual support. Like others, Loisy had trouble thinking that the Messiah Jesus would be involved in any bloody activity.[2] Aune thought this meant Jesus was sprinkled with his own blood. He said this was a metaphor for "The atoning death of Christ,"[3] but the picture given here is that of a military general or king, riding a horse. He was very much alive himself, but had emerged from battle where many others had been killed, and their blood splattered on his clothing. The Messiah involved is unidentified, but it evidently was not Jesus.

His name was called "the word of God." **The word of God** may have been the secret **name** that was reported in the previous verse. This might be a later addition, because the person who wrote that this was the secret **name** was exposing the secret. The original author might have wanted that kept secret. But even if it is an addition, it is not necessarily a *Christian* addition, as Whealon thought.[4] The name "Jesus" nowhere appears in this context. Jews also thought of the Scripture as **the word of God**. A legal agent of God, which could be a properly authorized angel, a king, or a prophet, was legally **the word of God** incarnate, the word become flesh. He was authorized to speak in God's **name,** in his behalf, and at his responsibility. His **word** was **God's word,** legally. From the context it is apparent that the rider on this horse was the Messiah. Rabbi Manna, commenting on the verse telling about the way Josiah was killed (2Chron 35:21-22), said that Josiah confessed to Jeremiah, while dying, that he deserved his punishment, because he had **rebelled against** God's **word--against his word** and **the word** of his legal agent (*peé-hoo mah-reé-tee peé-hoo wuh poom seér-sawr-óh,* פיהו מריתי פיהו ופום סרסרו) (Lam 1:18; LamR 1 #53, 19a). In this case God's agent was the prophet Jeremiah. When Josiah rejected Jeremiah's advice he rejected God's **word**.

Describing the tragedy of the Egyptians on the Passover night when Israelites left Egypt, a Jewish author pictured the slaughtering angel as **your all powerful word** that came down **from heaven, from the royal throne. Although it touched heaven, it walked on the earth** as a warrior with a sharp sword, filling the Land of Egypt with death. It acted as God's agent, fulfilling his command (Wis 18:15-16). This is only one of the examples that show God's word being personified as his legal

---

[1] C. D. Osbourn, "Alexander Campbell and the Text of Revelation 19:13," *RQ* 25 (1982):129-38.
[2] Loisy, *L'Apocalypse*, pp. 338-39.
[3] Aune, *Revelation 17-22,* p. 1057.
[4] Whealon, "Patches," p. 55.

agent. Wisdom's picture of God's word, originating in heaven but carrying out its activity on earth as a destructive, mighty warrior, with a sharp sword to kill numerous members of enemy nations corresponds well with the description given here in Rev 19.

TEXT

Revelation

¹⁴The troops that were in heaven followed him on white horses, dressed in clean white linen. ¹⁵From **his mouth** went out

a sharp, two-edged sword, so that

he **will shatter** the gentiles;
He will rule them with an iron rod;

First Testament and Other Jewish Literature

^(Isa 11:4)He will hit the earth with the staff of **his mouth**; with the breath of his lips he will kill the wicked.

^(Isa 49:2)He set my **mouth** like **a sharp two-edged sword**.

^(Ps 149:6)Let high praises of God be in their throats, and **a two-edged sword**, in their hands.

^(Isa 49:2)You **will rule them with an iron rod**; you **will shatter** them like a potter's vessel.

^(PssSol 17:23-27)Look, Lord! Raise for them their king, a son of David, at the time you know, God, so as to rule over your children of Israel. Gird him with strength **to shatter** unrighteous rulers. Cleanse Jerusalem from the gentiles who destructively trample [it]. Wisely, righteously root out criminals from the inheritance. **Shatter** the pride of the sinner as a potter's vessel; **with an iron rod shatter** all their confidence. Destroy the law-breaking gentiles with the word of **your mouth**.

^(Joel 4:13; RSV 3:13)Go down, **trample**, for **the wine press** is full.

^(Isa 63:2-3)Why are your garments red? your

and he will **trample the wine press** of the wine of the **wrath** of

the anger of the God of armies. ¹⁶He has on his robe and on his thigh the name written,

"King of kings and Lord of lords."

clothes like one who **tramples the wine press**? I **have trampled the wine press** alone; no one of the peoples was with me. I **walked over** them **in my anger**; I **trampled** them in my **wrath**.

^{Deut 10:17}For Yehowah, your God, is God of gods and **Lord of lords**.

^{Dan 2:47}The king said to Daniel, "Certainly, your God is God of gods and **Lord of kings**."

^{Dan 2:37}You, king, are **king of kings**.

^{Dan 4:37} He is God of gods, **Lord of lords, and King of kings**.

^{2Macc 13:4}The **King of kings** raised the anger of Antiochus against the criminal.

^{3Macc 5.35}When the Jews heard the things that had happened with the king they praised the God manifest, the Lord, **the King of kings**, having also received this help from him.

COMMENTARY

A sharp, two-edged sword. This is probably a legal expression. It does not mean that **a sword** really darted **out of his mouth** like the tongue of a snake. One who could kill with the breath of his lips (Isa 11:4) was a king who had authority to order anyone killed, and it would happen. People who were killed by the word of someone's **mouth** were just as dead as if the person who issued the decree had, himself or herself, cut off the victim's head. Boring defensively modified this bloody scene by saying there was really no **sword** involved: "His only weapon is his word." The blood shed was not the blood of the martyrs, as Boring holds,[1] but of the enemies. The entire tenor of Rev 19 is one of rejoicing over the destruction of enemies. The **sharp two-edged sword** was intended to shatter the gentiles, one way or another. Many kings of NT times were notoriously cruel. To learn the ease with

---

[1] Boring, *Revelation*, p. 196.

which kings had friends, relatives, prestigious citizens, and others killed read Seutonius, *The Lives of the Caesars*.

There is another possible meaning. Although it seems physically weird for a military leader to have a sword for a tongue, when the artist painted a picture in words of a mystical rider who rode in the sky rather than on the ground, that author could paint any picture he or she chose. During the Maccabean Revolt, for example, people were reported to have seen a great apparition, showing that the Lord of spirits was present with the soldiers in battle. The scene pictured a white horse, having a fearful rider, riding on a horse that was decorated with a magnificent harness. The rider was wearing a suit of gold armor (2Macc 3:25-26). The man from the sea was able to pour out a stream of fire to defeat the enemy (4Ezra 13:5-11). The author of Rev 19 may have wanted the reader to visualize a Messiah who had a tongue like a sharp, two-edged sword coming out of his mouth.

He will shatter the gentiles. The quotation from Ps 2:9 is about a king whom the Lord established on Zion to take control of the ends of the earth, **shattering the gentiles** like a crock or a piece of china, after which he would rule them with **an iron rod** until they were submissive to him and would not stir up his anger. This kind of violence was offensive to Caird, so he said we must not take these expressions at face value. He thought this really referred to a king's judicial authority.[1] One of the things kings did with their judicial authority, however, was to send their troops out to shatter the enemy.

He will trample the wine press. The **wine press** about which Joel wrote was the Kidron Valley, east of the temple area in Jerusalem, where he expected the blood to flow like grape juice in a wine press, because the so-called **wine press** was really a battle field that would take place in the Kidron Valley. This would occur on a judgment day when the Lord would judge the conflict between Israel and the surrounding nations. The verdict would be in favor of Israel, of course, and the enemy would be cut down like grain before a sickle and **trampled** like grapes in a **wine press**. The author of this prophetic literary piece expected the **Lamb** or Messiah to treat **the gentiles** the way Ps 2, Joel, and PssSol 18 all prophesied. The allusions to Isa 63 were of the Lord who came up from Edom (Isa 63:1) after all this bliss of bloody **trampling**. The scriptural prophecy of this successful battle was probably motivated by the occasion when many thousands of Assyrian soldiers were waiting on Mount Scopus and the Mount of Olives to destroy Zion. The next morning 185,000 of them lay dead in the valley and on the hillsides (1Kings 19).[2] Jews looked forward to another time when the same thing would happen to other enemies in the same valley. In NT times, the enemy was Rome.

---

[1] G. B. Caird, *A Commentary on the Revelation of St. John the Divine* (London: Black, c1966), p. 245.

[2] The Scripture credits Hezekiah's prayer for this victory, but he may have had a little help form the local *Jewish* military intelligence agency. All the soldiers depended on the water from the Spring of Siloam. All Jews had to do was to poison the water. See Further Buchanan, "The Tower of Siloam," *ET* 115.2 (2003):41-42,

In NT times Edom was a code name for Rome, so the author of Rev 19 was visualizing Rome after the **trampling** was over. All of this was to happen on the day of vindication on the year of redemption (Isa 63:4). This would be on New Year's Day on a Jubilee year when captives were set free and the land was restored to its "original owners." This was to be the final battle before Rome was overturned--not before the end of the world as many scholars have thought.

On his thigh the name written. The idea of writing a slogan on some part of a warrior's gear was not unusual. This particular rider held such other titles as **Faithful and True** and **The Word of God**. Ancients evidently thought this would have a magic effect on the outcome of the battle. **Names** and slogans were written on various parts of the soldiers' armor, standards, banners, or trumpets (1QM 4:6, 8). It is not a custom taken from sculptors who fixed the stamp of their names on the **thighs** of statues they made, as Düsterdieck thought.[1] **The name written** on the **thigh** of the one who was riding on the horse was **King of kings and Lord of lords**. This was a title originally given to the king of Persia, but it was later used by Parthian kings (Seutonias, *Lives* 4:5). As early as the second millennium BIA monarchs were called **the great king**, with the same basic meaning as **King of kings**. This happened in Assyria, Babylonia, Parthia, and Egypt (see Deut 10:17; Dan 2:37, 47; 4:37; Rev 17:14).[2] After all of this victorious warfare, of course, the rider was recognized as the greatest of all kings and lords. As **king of kings,** he would have other **kings** as his subjects the way Roman emperors had in the author's time.

King of kings and Lord of Lords. Msgr. Skehan, in response to the suggestion of other scholars that 666 represented imperfection, observed that the expression **King of kings, Lord of Lords**, omitting the conjunction, would total 777, or perfection, according to the numerical value of letters in Aramaic.[3] This is not only perfection. According to sabbatical eschatological concepts it is the seventh day of the seventh year, of the seventh week of years--the Jubilee, when the "captives" are set free and the land is to be restored to the "original" owners (Lev 25). Weiss thought this entire unit was of Jewish origin and probably written about 70 IA, but he thought there were Christian intrusions. The reference to **King of kings and Lord of lords** was originally Jewish, but it was reidentified by Christians who already knew who the Messiah was.[4]

---

[1] F. Düsterdieck, *Critical and Exegetical Handbook to the Revelation of John*, tr. H. E. Jacobs (Winona Lake: Alpha Publications, 1884), p. 459.
[2] D. C. Duling, "'[Do Not Swear . . .] by Jerusalem because it is the City of the Great King,' (Matthew 5:35)," *JBL* 110 (1991):291-309.
[3] P. W. Skehan, "King of Kings, Lord of Lords (Apoc 19:16)," *CBQ* 10 (1948):398.
[4] J. Weiss, *Offenbarung*, p. 672-73.

EZEKIEL AND THE ORDER OF EVENTS

Lust has noted the following parallels of order between Ezekiel and the final order of events in the Book of Revelation:[1] The Scripture was the primary source for the author in determining that which would happen in the future.

Revelation	Ezekiel
1. The final battle against the beast: Rev 19:17-21.	1.**The final battle** against
1.a The first resurrection and the Messianic reign: Rev 20:4-6. **The final battle** against **Gog and Magog**: Rev 20:7-10.	1.a . . . . **Gog and Magog**: Ezek 38-39.
2 The second resurrection: Rev 20:11-15.	2.The revival of the dry bones: Ezek 37
3.The descent of the heavenly Jerusalem: Rev 21-22.	3.The vision of the New Temple and of the New Israel: Ezekiel 40-48.

Revelation	First Testament
[17]I saw an angel standing in the sun. He cried out in a loud voice, **saying to all of the birds** flying in the sky, "**Come, gather** yourselves **together** at the great dinner of God, [18]so that the flesh of kings, the flesh of chiliarchs, the flesh of mighty men, the flesh of horses and riders, the flesh of all free men and slaves, small and great might be consumed."	Ezek 39:17-18, [20]Thus **said** the Lord Yehowah, "**Say to the birds** '**Gather together**, every **winged creature** and every beast of the field, and **come** from around over my sacrifice which I am sacrificing for you--a great sacrifice upon the mountains of Israel. You shall eat **flesh**, and you shall drink blood. **You shall eat the flesh of mighty men** and you shall drink the blood **of princes** of the land . . . You shall be satisfied at my table [eating] **horses, riders, mighty men, and every man** of war,'" said the Lord Yehowah.

---

[1] J. Lust, "The Order of the Final Events in Revelation and in Ezekiel," *L'Apocalypse johannique et L'Apalyptique dans le Nouveau Testament* (ed.), J. Lambrecht (Gembloux: Duculot, 1980), pp. 179-83. This quotation is from p. 181.

COMMENTARY

The great banquet of God. After reading about the victory of the Lamb who had finished treating the gentiles the way Joel, Ps 2, and PssSol 18 prophesied, it does not take a great deal of imagination to visualize the appearance of the battlefield afterwards. It would be like the 185,000 Assyrians who were left dead in the Kidron Valley the day after the Rabshakeh's threat to destroy Zion (2Kings 18:19-19:37). The author called this battlefield a dinner of God, because he presumed that it was God who really killed all of the people and animals involved. Of course he had a little help from military religious believers. The angel issued the invitations to this **banquet** on behalf of the Lord. After all, God was a man of war, and the battlefield was described in God's written word as a sacrifice or banquet for the birds and beasts of the field. Years before Ezekiel described the way the valley east of the sea would look after **Gog** was defeated on the land of Israel. Ezekiel said it would take seven months just to find and bury the bodies of foreigners there. They could make their task easier by inviting vultures and scavengers to clean the bones of their **flesh** before burial. For **the vultures** this would be a **great banquet.**

The flesh of kings. Mulholland correctly noticed the plural noun. It is not just the **flesh,** but the **fleshes of kings.** Mulholland labeled this "corpses," to show the plural.[1] God provided **the vultures a banquet.** Repulsed by this bloody scene, Rissi dismissed Rev 19:9b-17 as a later addition. He inaccurately considered it foreign to the spirit of the rest of the Book.[2] There are other parts of the Book of Revelation that express more than affection and self sacrifice.

Might be consumed. NA has the verb for **consume** or **eat** in the second person plural active form. **So that you may eat . . .**

TEXT

Revelation	First Testament
[19]I saw the beast and **the kings of the earth** and their troops gathered **together** to make war with the one seated on the horse and with his army. [20]The beast was seized and with him the false prophet who performed the signs before him by which he led	Ps 2:2**The kings of the earth** have established themselves; the rulers take counsel **together** against Yehowah and against his Messiah. Isa 30:33 A place of burning has been

---

[1] M. R. Mulholland, Jr., *Revelation* (Grand Rapids: Francis Asbury Press, c1990), p. 303.
[2] Rissi, *Future*, p. 27.

astray those who received the mark of the beast and who worshiped his image. The two beasts were thrown into the lake of fire which **burns** with **sulfur**, [21]and the rest were killed by the sword which goes out of the mouth of the one seated on the horse, and **all the birds** **will be filled** from their **flesh**.	prepared for a long time. Furthermore, it has been prepared for the king. Its pyre is deep and wide with fire and plenty of wood. The breath of Yehowah, like a stream of **sulfur makes it burn**. Ezek 39:17, [20]Thus said the Lord Yehowah, "Tell the **birds, 'Gather, all the birds together, every winged creature** and every beast of the field, and come from around over my sacrifice which I am sacrificing for you . . . You will eat the **flesh** and drink the blood. . . . **You shall be filled** at my table, [eating] horses, riders, mighty **men**, and every man of war,'" said the Lord Yehowah.

COMMENTARY

I saw the beast. Loisy identified the beast here as in Rev 13 as Nero, brought back to life, and the kings of the earth as his allies.[1] It is difficult always to know the identity of the beast. In Revelation it was often one of the Herods. It is clearly an enemy leader and apparently associated, at least in concept if not in time, with the false prophet, whoever that was.

The kings of the earth and their troops. Not only were there mobs of gentiles killed in this great battle, but in the process, **the beast** and **the false prophet**, whom the author hated, were captured by the Lamb himself and thrown alive **into the lake of fire,** just as the enemies of Shadrach, Meshech, and Abedneggo were (Dan 3). The author knew his FT so well that he was able to join passages of different Scriptures together in a coherent way. For example, after using the banquet scene dramatized by Ezekiel, he turned to another feast, foreseen by Isaiah, in which the lord's anger interrupted the celebration, hurling great hailstones down upon the Assyrians, after which they were to have been burned in a place of **fire and sulphur**.

The **lake of fire and sulfur** was the equivalent of a volcanic crater, **flaming** with boiling lava and blowing off **sulfuric** gases, as volcanoes always do. Anyone thrown into such a pit would be dissolved instantly. Because there were volcanoes, springs, and wells, ancients assumed that there was an existence under ground where there were flames of fire and lakes of water. It is not clear where the author thought

---

[1] Loisy, *L'Apocalypse*, p. 344.

this lake of fire existed, geographically or geologically. **The lake of fire and sulfur** was a concept alluded to in later Jewish and Christian literature.

The beast was seized and with him the false prophet. **The beast** frequently fits the role of King Herod the Great. **The false prophet,** however, is no longer identifiable. Anyone who prophesied and his prophecy failed, was considered **a false prophet.** Josephus said **the prophets** who predicted the destruction of the Romans and the reestablishment of the Kingdom of God on Palestinian soil were **false.** The Messiah on the horse was obviously the one who captured both **the false prophet and the beast.**

When Daniel made the report, the death of **the beast** was Antiochus Epiphanes, who was killed with the sword of the mouth in a heavenly court trial. The trial was in heaven, but the death took place on earth (Dan 7:11). Rissi was able to ignore all the references to blood, slaughter, corpses, and enemy troops, and say gleefully,

> No trace of any battle! For him [John] there is only one battle and victory of Christ, which already lies in the past.[1]

The mark of the beast. This was evidently some identifying **mark** that functioned the way social security cards are used in the United States. Those who were loyal to the country in which they resided wore certain bodily marks or carried certain papers. Second Isaiah visualized Jews having written on their hands, **The Lord's** (Isa 44:5). Those who wore **marks of the beast** could do business with Rome, but loyal nationalistic Jews thought they were unfaithful. If they belonged to **the beast,** they could not also belong to **the Lord.**

All the birds will be filled. The author returned to **the banquet** scene of **the birds** to finish the destructive task he had planned for these two enemies. The author was acquainted with the customs of scavanger **birds** in the Near East. Whenever an animal dies in the desert it is left untouched for several days, as it swells up and begins to decay. At this time there will not be a crow, an eagle, vulture, or a hawk in the sky. Then, the corpse bursts, and scavengers come from everywhere and leave only the bones. They will then have had their **banquet.** This is the picture the author visualized after the war. Not only mules, donkeys, and horses would be left on the field to decay; there would be enemy soldiers, officers, and **king**s--all to the joy of the author. The author also knew earlier Scripture that reported a banquet for the birds, such as this (Jer 7:33; 16:4; 19:7; 34:20; 1Sam 17:44-46).

The ancients knew the consequence of war—famine, pestilence, wild beasts, and the sword. The sword killed, the damages of war destroyed the food, so there was famine. As the dead bodies decayed there was rampant disease. Also with dead

---

[1] Rissi, *Future*, p. 26.

bodies there were various kinds of wild beasts and birds as scavangers that would gather to clean up the bones.

Rev 19:17-21 seems originally to have been a separate unit based on Ezek 39:17-20. It may have come from the same document from which Rev 16:13-15 was taken. Both passages deal with **the false prophet** and **the beast.**

This great battle was to be fought in the Valley of Jehoshaphat at the border of Jerusalem, alongside the Springs of Gihon and Rogel, just outside the city walls and the temple area. It was not expected to put an end to all the inhabitants of the earth, as Mealy thought.[1] When the battle was over there would be animals and birds around to eat the corpses of the victims, piled up in the Kidron Valley, all of whom would be enemies of the Messiah and his followers. The followers of the Messiah would survive and eat of the tree of life from the Paradise of God (see Rev 2:7, 10-11, 17). These trees would grow right there in the Kidron Valley (Ezek 47).

Mealy supported his conviction that this destruction would be universal by quoting from Zeph 1. He misinterpreted that chapter by taking the Hebrew word, *ahretz* (ארץ) to mean "earth" rather than **Land.** The word can hold either meaning, but in Zephaniah the context shows that **the Land** involved Judah and Jerusalem (Zeph 1:4, 10-12). The inhabitants of this **Land** would be punished for wearing foreign clothing (Zeph 1:8). This would be no prohibition for people of other lands and cities--i.e., the foreigners.[2] The author of this unit in Revelation did not employ the text from Zephaniah, but if he had, it would not have helped to interpret his narrative to mean the destruction of all the people of the world. The author used principally Ezekiel, with some supporting texts from Isaiah and one of the Psalms. None of these texts prophesied the end of all the people of the world. Prophecies were locally oriented. The author of this midrashic unit wrote his narrative with the same local perimeters as his sources. The destruction was of the enemies of Israel. The victory would produce the deliverance of the faithful, and all of this would be finalized in the Kidron Valley outside Jerusalem.

The sword of his mouth. Weiss said this was no real **sword**. It was only a metaphorical expression alluding to judgment, such as that reported in the Fourth Gospel (John 3:18-20).[3] That, however, does not mean that **the sword** is harmless. When a judge uses this metaphorical **sword** he or she gives the defendant a death sentence. The **sword** is employed to chop off someone's head. The judge is saved from performing the ugly task himself or herself.

Chapter Nineteen and other Chapters. Mealy has correctly noted that there are many passages in Rev 19 that parallel other parts of Revelation. The author may have intentionally created this chapter as a summary unit while having other parts of the book before him. After the facts have been noted, scholars can only conjecture how

---

[1] J. W. Mealy, *After a Thousand Years* (Sheffield: JSOT Press, 1992), pp. 91-92.
[2] So also Marvin A. Sweeney, "Zephaniah: Prophet of his Time—Not the End Time," *Bible Review* 20.6 (2004):34-40, 43.
[3] J. Weiss, *Offenbarung*, p. 673.

these facts came about. Mealy's solution is one. Another possibility is that redemption literature had many basic texts and common ideas that were used by many authors so that these contacts are purely accidental to the literature.

CHAPTER TWENTY

TEXT

Revelation

²⁰:¹I saw an **angel** coming down having the key of **the abyss** and a huge **chain** in his hand. ²He overpowered the dragon, **the old serpent**,

who is the devil and **the Satan**, and he

bound him ³**into the abyss**, and closed

and **sealed [it]** over him, so that he could not make the gentiles wander

until the **thousand years** are complete. After

that it will be necessary for him to be released **for a short time**.

First Testament

Gen 3:1The man and his wife were naked, and they were not ashamed. Now **the serpent** was more clever than all the [other] beasts of the field.

Zech 3:1He showed me Joshua, the high priest, standing before the **angel** of Yehowah. **Satan** was standing at his right to try him.

1Enoch 54.4-5I asked . . . "For whom are these imprisonment **chains** prepared?" He said to me, "These are prepared for the armies of Azazel so that they may take them and cast them **into the abyss** of complete condemnation."

Dan 6:18A stone was brought and placed on the mouth of the den, and the king **sealed it** with his own signet and with the signet of his officers.

Ps 90:4A **thousand years** in our eyes are as yesterday, for it is past, or as [one] night watch.

Isa 26:20Hide **for a short time** until the wrath passes.

COMMENTARY

I saw. An expression to show that this is the beginning of a new unit, a new vision.

An angel coming down . . . overpowered the dragon. NA adds after **coming down** the explanatory words, **from heaven**.

The dragon that chased the woman in the wilderness, was also portrayed as a harlot who sat on the seven hills, and authorized the evil works of the first beast. This is the second version of **Satan** having been cast out of heaven. Also here **Satan** is identified with **the dragon.** The two versions (Rev 12 and 20) are not completely parallel, and they obviously were composed by different authors, but they reflect a prominent theme in NT redemption literature. They were both familiar with the same concepts. **The dragon** that chased the woman in the wilderness (Rev 12) was also portrayed as a harlot who sat on the seven hills (Rev 17) and authorized the evil works of the first beast (Rev 13). It is here identified with the serpent that tempted Eve, **the devil**, and **Satan.** All of these were insulting titles the Jews and early Christians gave to Rome. These terms enabled the Jews and Christians to express their hostility to Rome without mentioning the name "Rome."

The accusative case shows that the thousand years is the length of time involved. Trying to explain away the seer's vindictiveness, Rissi said,

> John is not concerned with the triumph of the believers over the unbelievers (although desired by the church time and again!), but rather with the revelation of the *kingship* of believers in the sense of an evidence of their absolute *freedom* from all human and superhuman forces.[1]

Of course, if the believers were as free and authoritarian as Rissi wanted them to be, the non-believers would be reduced to the role of slavery to the believers. In order to achieve this the seer would have to be concerned with the triumph of believers over the unbelievers. Kings and slaves did not belong to the same social and economic classes in NT times. Stadelmann criticized both the Lutherans and the Catholics for spiritualizing Rev 20. She said they were more concerned about interpreting their denominational doctrines than in interpreting the Scripture. She argued that this entire chapter coheres with the First Testament (FT) and Jewish literature contemporary with Revelation. These are all this-worldly and materialistic.[2]

The key of the abyss and a chain. Sinaiticus misspelled the words (*kleén-tays*, [κλίντης] "couch" for *klayn* [κλεῖν] "key") and "chain" (*loó-seh-seen*, [λύσεσιν] for *háh loo-seen*, [ἅλυσιν]). Enoch pictured the troops of Azazel bound with chains (1Enoch 54:4-5). The reference to the abyss also occurs in Rev 9:1.

Who is the devil and the Satan. Enoch called the equivalent of **the devil,** Azazel (1Enoch 54:4-6), and he presumed Azazel would receive the same kind of punishment that **Satan** receives here--only still more severe. It also involves burning the

---

[1] M. Rissi, *The Future of the World* (Naperville: Allenson, c1966), p. 33.
[2] H. Stadelmann, "Das Zeugnis der Johannesoffenbarung vom Tausendjährigen Königreich Christi auf Erden," *Zukunftserwartung in Biblischer Sicht*, ed. G. Maier (Wuppertal: R. Brockhaus Verlag, c1984), pp. 144-60.

troops of Azazel in a furnace. In addition to being a **dragon** who chased the woman in the wilderness or the harlot sitting on seven hills, this **dragon** was also **Satan,** the male prosecuting attorney in the heavenly council (*ha sah-táhn*, הסטן)--**the satan**, Job 1:7; Zech 3:1).[1] The narrative was structured so as to identify **the dragon** also with the heavenly prosecuting attorney who was prepared to prevent Joshua and Zerubbabel from returning to Palestine to reestablish Jerusalem and rule the Promised Land.

So far as the author was concerned, the **dragon** was the evil force behind the Roman emperors, the procurators, and the Herodian kings on the Promised Land. By dramatizing the heavenly trial so that Joshua won and **Satan** lost, the author was saying in a mythological way that Rome was overthrown, the gentile age was over, "the captivity" of the chosen people was completed, and Jews would again control the Promised Land, and possibly the whole Mediterranean world as well,[2] under the leadership of their own messiah. Just as the **angel** in Zechariah accompanied Joshua at the judgment, defending him against the prosecuting attorney, **Satan,** here the author also pictured an **angel** as the defense attorney who appeared and overthrew **the dragon,** the equivalent of **Satan** in Zechariah and the equivalent also of Rome in the author's day.

He bound him into the abyss. NA has **He bound him for a thousand years, and he threw him into the abyss.** Enoch also pictures the troops of Azazel being thrown into an **abyss** and burned in a furnace (1Enoch 54:4-6). Dan 6 tells of Daniel who refused to obey the king's order to stop worshiping any other god or being except the king. As punishment the king had Daniel thrown into a den of lions, covered the mouth of the den with a large rock and **sealed** the den with his own signet ring (Dan 6:17). Jesus reportedly said, **How can anyone enter a strong man's house and plunder his goods, unless he first binds the strong man** (Matt 12:29). The technique for burglary is the same as that employed for national conquest. If an angel would just intercede and handcuff Rome, then the chosen people could plunder to their hearts' content.

Sealing Satan into a pit may reflect a magical practice known in New Testament (NT) times of **sealing** all sorts of demons into incantation bowls by writing certain charms into the bowls themselves and sealing them together with rope and bitumen to keep the demons under control. This may be the practice shown also in Rev 15 and 16 where the charms were later broken and the demons were allowed to escape and become destructive when the **angels** emptied the bowls into the air.

---

[1] Satan has become identified with evil, because he is always presented in Scripture as the one who prosecutes believers. They confront Satan when they are defendants in the heavenly court.
[2] Saadia Gaon (892-942 IA) said God had promised that there would not be left one nation that was not under Israel's rule (Isa 60:12) (*Book of Convictions and Beliefs*, "Deliverance." English Translation Buchanan, *Jewish Messianic Movements from AD 70 to AD 1300* (Eugene, Oregon: Wipf and Stock Publishers, 2003), p. 47.

Until the thousand years are complete. There is no reference to a **millennium** (1,000 years) in any other book of the NT, but there are many allusions to it in later Jewish and Christian literature. There is an abundant Jewish and Christian literature about **millennium** theology during the Middle Ages, and it continues in both religions up to the present time. Both religions have tried to interpret contemporary events in terms of their beliefs about the **millennium**. Some of these will be shown here. Ulfgard objected that the binding of Satan for **a thousand years** could not be taken literally, because that would imply that the victory of Christ was only temporary.[1] Schüssler-Fiorenza claims that this **millennium** is "beyond space and time."[2] Morris said we should take this term symbolically. It is the cube of ten and means completeness.[3] Rissi argued that the numbers in the Book of Revelation have a qualitative, rather than a quantitative, meaning. We should not expect the term **1,000 years** to have any temporal value.[4]

Minear dismissed the **millennium** as unimportant because it appears only in Rev 20. He reasoned further that John, of course, did not have the same conception of time as we do, although he failed to say what John's concept was or why he would use the same terms for time--days, weeks, months, and years--and still think of time differently. In any event, Minear held, we must not think of John as a **false prophet** just because a **thousand years** have passed and the promises were not yet fulfilled. Furthermore human history was never meant to have concepts adequate to deal with the kind of end of which John spoke. Again, Minear did not say what kind of end that was or why it was not related to history.[5] Caird said **millennial** was not a Christian innovation; it was part of the tradition the author had accepted from Judaism. The author evidently used it because he needed it for his theory.[6] Hughes said **the thousand years** period

> covers the time from the destruction of Jerusalem to the end of this dispensation. So the **thousand-year** reign is going on now,[7]

But the **thousand year** period would have been completed by about 1070 IA, so it cannot be going on right now. Glasson said,

> It is difficult to believe that those who have lived and reigned with Christ for **1000 years** should be regarded as on trial at the close.

---

[1] H. Ulfgard, *Feast and Future: Revelation 7:9-17 and the Feast of Tabernacles*, (Stockholm: Almquist and Wicksell, 1989), p. 58.
[2] E. Schüssler-Fiorenza, *Revelation: Vision of a Just World* (Minneapolis: Fortress Press, c1991), p. 104.
[3] L. Morris, *The Book of Revelation* (Grand Rapids: Eerdmans, c1987), p. 235.
[4] M. Rissi, *Time and History* (Richmond: John Knox Press, 1965), p. 117.
[5] P. Minear, *I Saw a New Earth* (Washington, D.C.: Corpus Books, c1968), pp. 170-79.
[6] G. B. Caird, *A Commentary on the Revelation of St. John the Divine* (London: Black, c1966), pp. 450-51.
[7] J. A. Hughes, "Revelation 20,4-6 and the Question of the Millennium," *WTJ* 35 (1973):286.

He was also surprised by the contexts in Jewish literature and FT for the Day of Judgment. He learned that the Day of Judgment was not an all-inclusive forensic judgment at the end of the world. Instead, he discovered its relationship to battles fought in the Kidron Valley or some other Near Eastern location between Israel and her enemies.[1] He thought the judgment involved only the punishment, rather than the decision making process. He was right in discovering that there was military power and punishment on earth in relationship to the Judgment Day, but there was also understood to be a heavenly judgment scene that determined the outcome of battles on earth. This was dramatized in Dan 7 with the trial taking place in heaven before the Ancient of Days while Antiochus Epiphanes and Judas the Maccabee were engaged in military conflict on the Promised Land.

Furthermore there was more than one Judgment Day, and they were often less than **1,000 years** apart. For example, there was a Judgment Day in Egypt when Hebrews were vindicated in their court case against the Pharaoh. Following the decision, Hebrews left Egypt, came through the wilderness, and conquered Canaan. After that they built a temple and lived under their own kings for hundreds of years. Then, in 586 BIA. Jews lost the next Judgment Day; they were thrown into "prison" in Babylon to serve out their term. It was by observing, after the fact, the outcome of conflicts that early Jews and Christians learned the way the Lord determined judgments in his heavenly court.

When the many Judgment Days found in FT, 1Enoch, 4Ezra, Sibylline Oracles, 2Baruch, the Assumption of Moses, and Rabbinic literature are identified in context, the setting for Rev 20 can be understood correctly. The Judgment Day dramatized there was not thought to be the final judgment at the end of the world. It was the judgment inflicted upon Rome at which Jews and/or Christians would be restored to the Promised Land under the leadership of their own king. After a certain predetermined length of time, however, there would be still another Judgment Day with a different verdict.

Contrary to the opinions of many scholars, **the thousand years** of ordinary historical time is probably exactly the meaning intended by **the millennium**. The basis for making this judgment is not just that it would or would not seem logical to twentieth century westerners, but that there is no basis for thinking the Scripture meant anything else.

The thousand years (millennium) was based on the biblical passage which said that a **thousand years** in the sight of the Lord was as yesterday or a night watch (Ps 90:4). The author of 2Peter interpreted this to mean that with the Lord **a thousand years** is as one day and one day is as **a thousand years** (2Pet 3:8). This seems like rather far-fetched reasoning, but it had scriptural support, so that was accepted logic. Barnabas commented on Gen 2:2: "God did **in six days** the works of his hands, and **he completed** [it] on the seventh day" (Barn 15:3). Barnabas omitted several words and concentrated only on the word, **he completed** or **he made an end** and the words, **in six days**:

---

[1] T. F. Glasson, "Judgment Day," pp. 528-39.

> Observe, children, what the [expression] **he made an end in six days** means. This means that in six thousand years the Lord made an end to everything, for a day with him signifies a thousand years (Barn 15:4). **And he rested on the seventh day** means that when the Son comes he will destroy the time of the lawless and judge the impious (Barn 15:5).

The time of the lawless was the antitype of the time when the Syrian Greeks ruled before Hanukkah, which was the time when Romans ruled.[1] Those Jews and Christians who survived the wars of 66-70 IA and 132-135 IA and utilized rhetorical techniques to explain the failures of these wars did not think the defeat of the Romans would take place 1,000 years later. They did not explain where they thought they were in the extended millennium, but they would not have found encouragement if they had believed it would not have happened in their own lifetimes. **The millennium** was a rhetorical way of keeping their nationalist hopes alive during their current times of discouragement. The rhetoricians could not admit that their confident beliefs had been mistaken. The **millennial** explanation has been used in the same way ever since. The goal of rhetoric is not to reach new conclusions as a result of new evidence. It is to gather more arguments to support the conclusion with which the debaters began. That which has been proved rhetorically has no automatic relationship to truth.

When Jews were deeply engaged in the Crusades, they believed that they would be given back the Promised Land **a thousand years** after the fall of Jerusalem in 70 IA. In between the first and the tenth, eleventh, and twelfth centuries were many other time counts: Sabbaths of years, Jubilees of years, and other real, calendrically calculated units of time. When these occurred, messianic and military movements were organized according to the faith of the believers. The poet, Benjamin ben Zerah, complained to the Lord after 1070 IA had passed:

> **If my Strength were the strength of stones and my flesh [as tough as] brass** (Job 6:12),
> [would I be able] to stand and bear all of these hardships?
> This destruction and desolation has been mine for many years--
> a thousand, and yet [I am] bereaved and forsaken,
> fettered and in prison, **plowed up like a field** (Micah 3:12),
> disgraced like a thief, **head lowered** (Esther 6:12) like a mourner.
> My sanctuaries are defiled, and my saints profaned;
> my incense offerings are desecrated and soiled.[2]

---

[1] Saadia Gaon (892-942 IA) said the logic was a day for a year. Therefore the 1335 days mentioned in Daniel mean 1335 years. English translation of the Hebrew text in Buchanan, *Jewish Messianic Movements*, p. 43.
[2] Buchanan, *Jewish Messianic Movements*, p. 230.

Once this **millennium** had passed without redemption, ben Zerah thought all hope of deliverance was gone. He continued, "You have counted the times of redemption, and they are exhausted."[1]

Nevertheless, this did not put an end to the counting. When this measurement of **millennia** failed, they counted on the basis of the Jewish **millennial** calendar. Since there were six days of work and one day of rest in the Jewish week, and the Lord created the universe in six days, resting on the seventh, it follows that time was organized into seven units of **thousand**-year days. The term **rest** in biblical concepts referred to rule of the Promised Land. Therefore, Jews of NT times argued that they were at the end of the sixth **thousand-year** day, and God was just about ready to restore the Promised Land where they could rest by ruling the land for **a thousand** years (2Enoch 32.2; bSan 97a). Jews and early Christians calculated very carefully on the basis that the Scripture was the Lord's written contract with them, and they believed that he was obligated to fulfill their understanding and deduction of the Scripture.

The **thousand year** periods had not lost their temporal significance as Rissi argued,[2] nor was it intended to be taken symbolically, as Morris and Giblin held.[3] Neither did these Jews have a different concept of time from Westerners, as Minear thought was true of John.[4] Early Jews and Christians studied cycles to learn their position in the eternal time plan even more zealously than financial investors study stock market cycles today. The Crusades were fought by Christians and Jews who realized that it was the **millennium** of years after the crucifixion, and neither one had political control of Jerusalem.

One Jewish prophet of the Crusader period visualized the temple coming down from heaven and being relocated at Jerusalem, as the Holy Spirit (Scripture) promised (Exod 15:17). At the end of the two **thousand-year** period God would sit on the throne of judgment in the Valley of Jehoshaphat (Kidron Valley) just as he had done in the days of Hezekiah, leaving 185,000 enemy soldiers dead (2Kings 18-19). This would fulfill the Scripture which said, **After two days he will revive us** (Hos 6:2). These would be the "days" (**millennia**) of the Messiah. The rest of the verse said, **On the third day he will raise us, and we shall live before him** (Hos 6:2). This is the **millennium** of judgment when the gentiles would be burned while Jews passed through Gehinnom unscathed to fulfill the Scripture, **All your people will be righteous** (Isa 60:21).[5] In 1216 IA the poet, Judah Elharizi, speaking of Zion, said:

---

[1] Buchanan, *Jewish Messianic Movements*, p. 231.
[2] Rissi, *Future*, p. 34.
[3] Morris, *Revelation*, p. 235, said the thousand years was based on the symbolic significance of the cube of ten. H. G. Giblin, *The Book of Revelation* (Collegeville: The Liturgical Press, c1991), p. 186, said, "The entire description corresponds not to some temporal, clock-and-calendar perspective or even to some kind of symbolically temporal, earth-bound computation of time."
[4] Minear, *The New Earth*, pp. 170-79.
[5] From "The Prayer, Secrets, and Mysteries of Rabbi Shimon ben Yohai," tr. Buchanan, *Jewish Messianic Movements*, pp. 405-406.

Until now she has not become pure; she is still not clean.
It has now been one thousand, one hundred,
forty-eight [years] that she has been exiled from her home.
She is separated from the midst of her residence in Zion.
Until now, Zion has been expiating for her sabbatical years (Lev 26:34).
She is waiting for her time of favor . . .[1]

The poet, Benjamin ben Zerah, complained:

This destruction and desolation has been mine for many years--
a thousand, and yet [I am] bereaved and forsaken.
. . .
You have counted the times of redemption, and they are exhausted.[2]

Impatient Jews counted Sabbaths, Jubilees, and millennia. They called their anticipated redemption and political rule "the Sabbath rest." One unknown poet said:

To enjoy [the Sabbath] is like the age to come, the day of Sabbath rest;
all who enjoy themselves in it merit great joy;
from pre-messianic tribulations they will be delivered into well being;
our redemption will shoot forth, **and pain and sighing will pass away** (Isa 51:11).[3]

The "day of Sabbath rest" of which the poet spoke was the **millennium** of the age to come. According to one anonymous Jewish document,

Many of the Jews began to rejoice, and they imagined that they would see their Messiah coming and that their redemption would be drawing near in that very year, for it was the year 1241 IA when the [plan of] the Lord was to be realized. When suspicions were aroused that they were intending to stir up trouble against the Christians, they lost favor in the eyes of many [people], but they were protected by the ruling emperor.[4]

The excitement came, because 1241 IA was the beginning of the **millennium** of the Messiah. According to Jewish reckoning the fifth **millennium** began at 240 IA and would last until 1240 IA. This was the equivalent of Thursday in the week. Friday,

---

[1] Buchanan, *Jewish Messianic Movements*, p. 263.
[2] Quoted from "Out of the Depths," tr. by Buchanan, *Jewish Messianic Movments*, p. 230-31.
[3] Quoted from "Sabbath and Redemption," tr. by Buchanan, *Jewish Messianic Movements*, p. 212.
[4] A quotation from "Christian and Jewish Expectancy," tr. by Buchanan, *Messianic Movements*, p. 203.

the day before the Sabbath, had as its **millennial** equivalent the period beginning with 1240 IA and lasting until 2240 IA. This was the **millennial** day of the Messiah. During this **millennium** the Messiah was expected to come and lead the international war necessary to gain control of the world and govern for the next **millennium** from Jerusalem. It was the war the Jews were preparing to fight against the Christians that caused them to lose favor among Christians.

Following the logic of cyclical time, the author of Rev 20 believed that all time was predestined. Those who knew what position Jews were in the time cycle would know that which was certain to happen next. Nothing could keep it from happening. That which happened in one cycle would happen in the same order in the next corresponding cycle. After the captivity in Egypt, there was an Exodus, a wilderness wandering, a conquest, and a period of ruling. The author evidently thought Jews were, at the time he was writing, at the period of conquest and would soon have a **thousand** years of rule.

During this period **Satan** would be bound and thrown into captivity. This **satanic** captivity, like the Jewish captivity, was for **Satan's** punishment as well as for the Jewish liberation. This automatically meant also that Rome would be subject to Jewish rule for the same **thousand year** period. There seemed to be an equality in the design: at one age Jews were in captivity and gentiles ruled, and the next age the gentiles were in captivity and Jews ruled. When the Jews ruled, the Messiah, the Lord, and his angels also ruled. When the gentiles were in charge, **Satan, the devil, the old serpent, the dragon, and the harlot** had control. A complete cycle included one period of gentile rule and one period of Jewish rule.

After this it will be necessary for him [Satan] to be released. Isaiah foresaw a time when people all around were suffering and dying. This, Isaiah believed, took place because God was angry with these people. Isaiah encouraged the faithful to hide themselves from all of this danger during this time of wrath. The author of this Revelation passage may have identified this short time of God's anger with the short time when **Satan** would be **released** to injure the faithful. That short time was probably expected to be 3½ years, the length of time between the defilement and the cleansing of the temple in Daniel.

The author was consistent with the Near Eastern concept of cyclical time. There were alternating ages in these cycles, just as there were alternating periods of light and darkness in every day. Second Baruch said the time between Adam and the Messiah was divided into twelve periods of alternating good and bad fortune for Israel. These periods were probably considered 24 ages or twelve complete cycles of time (2Bar 53:12; 56:1-69; 4Ezra 14:11-12). While the gentiles were in the abyss,[1] Jews would rule; but when the Jewish age was completed, the gentile age would begin again. Since Satan ruled the gentile age, he would be bound during the Jewish age but **released** to rule the gentile age when his turn came. Jews did not like the idea of gentiles ever being in control, but the author eased the anxiety of this

---

[1] Of course 1Enoch 54:4-6 visualizes Azazel's troops being thrown into a furnace of fire. That author might not have had a return from the abyss in mind.

anticipation by suggesting that the gentile age would be short. According to Matthew, the evil days of the gentile age would be shortened for the sake of the elect (Matt 24:22). That means that the prison term would be reduced for good behavior or the mercy of the court.

Consistent with 4Ezra and 2Baruch, Hai Gaon, recognized the reality of the cyclical time. Jews would inevitably rotate into a position of rule, but at the predestined time, gentiles would also return to rule, and Jews would become "captives" again. Telling of the anticipated salvation of the Jews, he said,

> They will dwell in their kingdom until the end of the age. There are some who say until the completion of 7,000 years from the days of creation (3240 IA). There are [some who say] many thousands [of years] with no known limit.[1]

It was this **millennium** when Jews would be ruling that they understood **Satan** would be bound--but there were those, like the author of Rev 20, who thought it was only for a **thousand years**. A certain Samuel said there would be no difference between the age in which Jews then lived under gentile rule and the days of the Messiah except that in the days of the Messiah Jews would no longer be subject to the Romans (bSan 99a).

In between the evil gentile age, the common era, and the good Jewish age to come, the holy era, would be a messianic age (days of the Messiah) that would conclude with judgment and a decree that the times would change over believers for good, and they would see the consolation of Zion (2Bar 44:6-7). A medieval Jewish prayer asked,

> . . . that we may keep your statutes in this world and may merit life and inherit prosperity and blessing for the years of the days of the Messiah and for the life in the age to come.[2]

The order was correct:

1) this age,
2) the days of the Messiah, and
3) the age to come.

The messianic age was an antitype of the 3½ year war between the time Antiochus Epiphanes defiled the temple and the time when Judas the Maccabee defeated the Greeks at the Battle of Beth-horon and had the temple cleansed and rededicated (167-164 BIA). The messianic age came at the end of the old, common age, when

---

[1] Buchanan, *Jewish Messianic Movments*, pp. 129, 203.
[2] Buchanan, *Jewish Messianic Movements*, p. 249.

the Promised Land was under the rule of some foreign power. It was called the messianic age, because it was the period when the Messiah led a war against the enemy before gaining control of the country and ruling it as its leader.[1] During the messianic age from 167-164 BIA, Judas the Maccabee was the Messiah who led the revolt. Millennialists thought the messianic age would last a **thousand years**, followed by a **thousand years** during which the believers ruled the world and pagans would be subjects.

The judgment in heaven could coincide with the battle of Jews against Gog and Magog in the Kidron Valley. Commenting on the passage, **Rejoicing, I will rejoice** (Isa 61:10), one of the rabbis said,

> **Rejoicing** in the days of the Messiah; **I will rejoice** with the downfall of wicked Rome. **My soul will delight in my God** (Isa 61:10). This is the war of Gog and Magog (PesiqR 37 [162b]).

Maimonides said the Messiah would first be revealed. Then the war of Gog and Magog would be fought.[2] Jews expected the Messiah to lead the war, just as David and Judas the Maccabee had done. A Jewish poet described the Battle of Acre (1291 IA) where Christians were defeated by the Moslems. He interpreted this as the war of Gog against Magog--one of the participants was Gog and the other was Magog. He thought God was at work in this event, directing Gog and Magog to destroy one another before the Jewish Messiah arrived and took over the rule of the world:

Side 1

The king from the West with the king from the East
will beat each other to dust,
. . .
and the winds will blow in the land.
Gog and Magog (11) will each strike the other,
and panic will kindle in the heart of the nations.
The transgression of all Israelites will be removed.

Side 2
. . .
Then Israel (10) will go out from the city and advance.
. . .
Their Messiah will be revealed (12), and they will be comforted.
The secret mystery of their king they will enjoy, (13)
and they will sing praise to their king!

---

[1] See further M. Waxman, גלות וגאולה בספרות ישראל (*Gah-loót wah Geh-oo-láh buh Seef-roót Yees-rah-áyl, Exile and Redemption in Jewish Literature*) [Hebrew] (New York, 1952), pp. 215, 221-22.

[2] Maimonides, "Epistle to Yemen," tr. by Buchanan, *Jewish Messianic Movements*, p. 91.

But none of the wicked (14) will be acquitted in judgment.[1]
The poet Solomon ben Isaac Gerundi said,

> Do not rejoice, my enemy, about the crushing of my horn,
> For I have fallen; I will rise, and the Lord will help me!
> Look! My God who scattered me will gather me.
> My Rock who sold me will redeem me from you,
> for the cup which passed to me will pass to you.
> Then, *in the clefts* of your rocks, I will *smash your* little ones *to pieces* (Ps 137:9).[2]

Boring has tried to dehistoricize this concept by saying,

> By "Gog and Magog" we should not think of historical nations that have had a continuing existence during the preceding scene of the millennium.[3]

Like Boring, many Westerners would like to believe there were no such hostile thoughts in the minds of early Jews and Christians, but neither the author of Rev 20 nor any of his biblical sources thought this was a game of chess or a psychological exercise. The author and the people for whom he wrote were dead serious in their belief that God would destroy Rome and exalt Jews and/or Christians. This would require a great war, and the enemies were labeled "Gog and Magog." Jews and Christians who were prepared to fight against Gog and Magog believed they were living in the messianic age--the time just before the age to come.[4]

In the Mazdean understanding of time, the world would endure for six ages, during which "evil will conquer and triumph" on the earth. During the seventh age, the prince of demons would be chained, and humanity would have a **millennium** of years of rest and justice. After that **millennium**, the prince of demons would escape

---

[1] Author unknown, "That Day," tr. by Buchanan, *Jewish Messianic Movements*, pp. 291-93.
[2] Buchanan, *Jewish Messianic Movements*, p. 259.
[3] M. E. Boring, *Revelation* (Louisville: John Knox Press, c1989), p. 209.
[4] So Hai Gaon, "The dead in the days of the Messiah will live for life in the age to come by the merit of the perfectly righteous. A man, a hundred years of age will not die a certain death, but thus it will be in the time of salvation: Whoever dies at the age of one hundred will be like one who now dies at the age of twenty." (tr. Buchanan, *Jewish Messianic Movements*, pp. 128-29). Hai Gaon assumed, however, that this life would take place on this earth, and that even faithful Jews would ultimately die. To be specific, he said, "The people whom the messianic king will find will live long lives, and they will die" (tr. Buchanan, *Jewish Messianic Movments*, p.128). The order of expected events was:
  1) The Messiah would appear and begin the days of the Messiah;
  2) the Messiah would fight the war of Gog and Magog and defeat Israel's enemies;
  3) there would be a judgment day;
  4) the dead would be raised for judgment; and
  5) the righteous would live in the kingdom of the Messiah in the age to come.

for a **thousand years**, after which he would be vanquished.[1] This doctrine was clearly the basis for Rev 20. The Testament of Levi held that a new priest would arise who would bind Beliar. Then sin would cease, and the saints would be clothed in righteousness (TLevi 18:9-14). Another testament held that in the resurrection, after Abraham, Isaac, and Jacob had arisen, followed by their descendants, Beliar would be thrown into eternal fire, and his spirit of error would be no more. Then those who died in sorrow would arise in joy (TJudah 25:1-5).

Charles was of the opinion that the work of the elder John came to an end at this point (Rev 20:3) as an organized document. The rest of the Book of Revelation was composed by some stupid student of the elder who took the notes of the deceased John and put them together in a haphazard way.[2] Charles was forced to recognize John's style in these verses, but he did not think of the possibility of John being only the translator of the entire prophecy, thus leaving his vocabulary and style in evidence throughout. If Charles had seen the numerous examples of medieval Jewish literature that resemble Revelation he would have realized that many units of redemption literature were used over and over again. Major documents included many independent units, such as these. Whoever the messenger was who brought the document to John already had the complete prophecy with the separate units already organized as they are now.

TEXT

Revelation	First Testament
[4]**I saw thrones and** [elders] **sat** on them,	Dan 7:9 **I watched** until **thrones** were set up, **and** the Ancient of Days **took his seat**.
and the judgment was given to them. [I saw] Also to the souls of those who had been beheaded because of (the testimony of Jesus and) the word of God, which very ones did not worship the beast or his image, and did not take the mark on their foreheads	Dan 7:22 The Ancient of Days came **and he gave the judgment to** the saints of the Most High. Dan 7:27 The kingdom, ruling authority, and the greatness of the kingdom under all heaven **was given to** the saints of the Most High.
or on their hands. **They came to life** and ruled with the Messiah for a	Ezek 37:10 The Spirit will enter them and **they will come to life** and stand upon their feet--a very, very great troop.

---

[1] M. Eliade, *Cosmos and History, The Myth of the Eternal Return*, tr. W. R. Trask (New York: Harper, c1959), p. 126.
[2] R. H. Charles, *Critical and Exegetical Commentary on the Revelation of St. John the Divine* (New York: Charles Scribner's Sons, c1920) II, pp. 144-54.

thousand years

Dan 12:2-3 Many who sleep in the dust will jump up, some **to life** of the age and some to shame and rejection of the age, but the wise ones will shine like the light of the firmament, and those who make the many righteous, like the stars for the age and until [the next gentile age begins].

COMMENTARY

I saw thrones, and [elders] sat on them. This scene was patterned after the judgment scene in Dan 7, where **thrones** were placed, and the Ancient of Days sat on one of them. A **throne** in antiquity was a chair, but chairs were not very common. Most people did not eat at tables and sit on chairs. Instead they reclined around the food prepared on the floor. Still today, most Near Easterners are able to sit erect for long periods of time on the ground or the floor with their legs crossed in a way that is impossible for most Westerners. Chairs were provided only for people in positions of dignity—kings, queens, judges. One of the Greek words for chair is *kah-théh-drah* (καθέδρα). This was the chair on which a bishop or higher Roman Catholic officer sat when rendering judgment. The status of this chair was so important that the building in which judgment was performed was named the "cathedral"—the place of the chair. In the Western world there are many chairs today, but the chairs reserved for people of dignity are still called "**thrones**," to distinguish them from ordinary chairs.

Judgment was given to them. The pronouns have no clear antecedents. There is no direct way to discover who **sat on** these **thrones**. "They" who sat on **the thrones** might correspond to the **them** to whom the judgment was given. Since the judgment was given to the saints, in Daniel, and **the elders**, here, the saints might, hypothetically, also have been the ones who **sat on the thrones.** In Daniel, however, **the thrones** were for the assistant judges who were there in consultation with the Ancient of Days. In other places in the Book of Revelation it was the 24 **elders** who were seated on **thrones** in heaven (Rev 4:4; 11:16). In the court scene of Dan 7, the gentile beasts lost the case; Antiochus Epiphanes was condemned to be killed and his body burned, and the kingdom was given both to the Son of man (Judas the Maccabee) and the saints of the Most High (contemporary Jews).

In that judgment scene the saints were some of the contestants--not assistant judges. Therefore, it is not likely that contestants would be those seated on official **thrones**. Like the assistant judges in Daniel and the sons of God in Job 1:6, in Revelation the council of God was comprised of **elders**, and it was the **elders** who had official **thrones**. According to medieval rabbis in the age to come **the elders** would be honored, because when the Lord ruled from Zion there would be glory before his **elders** (Isa 34:23). The **elders** were political officers. Sometimes they were officials in a court and members of the Sanhedrin who assisted the chief judge in making court decisions (LevR 11:8; EcclR 1:11 #1; Prov 31:23; 1 Kings 22:10). Rabbi Jose the Galilean said,

> In the age to come the Holy One blessed be He will be seated, and the kings will give [their] thrones to officers of Israel, and they will be seated. Then the Holy One blessed be He will sit with his elders as the president of the court, and they will judge the nations of the world (Tanhuma, *Keh-doh-sheém* 1 [31a]).

Judgment was given to them [the elders]. This means the **judge** ruled in favor of the **elders.** They received the verdict of "not guilty," which means that for some reason they were in trial in court. These would not have been the only government officials who have been tried for breaking laws and breaching their fiduciary trust. Mealy interprets this to mean that the **elders** were given the authority to **judge**.[1] That is possible, but not likely. The situation seems more confusing than that. On the one hand the members of the councils (the **elders**) already had authority to assist in the **judgment** by virtue of their offices, and it was the **assistant judges** for whom the **thrones** were placed in Daniel (Dan 7:9). On the other hand, in the same chapter in Daniel, appears the words, **the judgment was given** (Dan 7:22) upon which the author was dependent. Dan 7 did not give authority to the council but gave a verdict in favor of the contestants in court, namely the saints. In order to make sense of these verses we must assume that the **assistant judges** were prejudiced Jews or Christians and that **the judgment** was prejudiced. Such a concept is possible.

In ancient courts **judges** themselves sometimes gathered information about cases and even acted as witnesses at the very time they were **judges**.[2] **The elders** seem to have been both Jewish and/or Christian defendants at the same time they were members of the **judicial** council helping to make decisions. They were in a legal position to help decide the case at the same time they had a conflict of interest (Ps 50:7, 21). This would be considered unfair in Western courts today, but some of those who composed the Scripture held two conflicting beliefs at the same time.

They believed, on the one hand, that God is an impartial **judge** who is no respecter of persons. This is only legally true. By virtue of the judge's authority, whatever he or she concludes in judgment is just, even if he or she has been bribed to make the decision. That which he or she decides is officially fair, whether or not it is actually fair. On the other hand, however, since the judge is also almighty, he or she can **judge** the way she or he wishes. Like many modern **judges**, ancient **judges**

---

[1] J. W. Mealy, *After the Thousand Years* (Sheffield: JSOT Press, c1992), p. 105.
[2] See further A. A. Trites, *The New Testament Concept of Witness* (Cambridge: Cambridge U Press, 1977), p. 27; L. Köhler, *Hebrew Man*, tr. P. A. Ackroyd (London: SCM Press, c1953), p. 96, fn. 1; and Buchanan, *Biblical and Theological Insights from Ancient and Modern Civil Law* (Lewiston: Edwin Mellen Press, 1992), p. 35.

were often influenced by bribes and political influence. Jews and Christians also assumed that God could be swayed by sacrifices and prayers of the "friends of the court," that can influence the court's decision. Since God always favors those who believe in him, Jews and Christians trust that he is prejudiced in our behalf, and we have wanted to receive favorable, rather than fair, decisions in the heavenly court. One of the oldest passages of FT asks God to show favoritism to the chosen people:

> May Yehowah bless you and protect you;
> may Yehowah look upon you with favoritism
>   and be kind to you;
> may Yehowah show you favoritism [when he judges],
> and declare you innocent (Num 6:25-26).[1]

The best explanation for the text (Rev 20:4), where the author has left the antecedents to the pronouns unclear to twentieth century readers, probably requires that we take these factors into consideration.

[I saw] also the souls of those who had been beheaded. Souls are legal identities that cannot be seen, visually, but can only be conjectured on the basis of membership rolls. Rabbi Judah thought the Roman governmental way of beheading people with a sword was very shameful. Jews normally laid the victim's head on a block and cut off his head with an ax (mSan 7:3). Jews also stoned people to death or even crucified them. Romans thought the sword was the most civil. It was used for people of dignity. Crucifixion was a humiliating type of execution. On the basis of Prov 6:22, Rabbi Jose ben Kisma was convinced that the Torah would watch over the faithful in the grave and awaken with them in the age to come (mAboth 6:9). **The souls** involved here were the current antitypes of the Hasmonean saints who were killed for practicing their faith and/or the soldiers who had been killed in the war against the Syrian Greeks (1Macc and Ant 12:242-13:227). This Revelation author evidently had two objects of his vision:

1) **the elders** on **the thrones** and
2) **the souls** of those who had been beheaded.

The souls of those who had been beheaded were not those who had sat on **the thrones,** as Mealy and Hughes thought.[2] The word for **souls** (*psoo-kháhs*, ψυχάς) is in the accusative case, as is the word for **thrones** (*thráw-noos*, θρόνους). It is not dative as is the **them** (*ow-toís,* αὐτοῖς) to whom the judgment was given. It is not completely clear how these two objects are related. The **elders** were the associate **judges** in the council, and they were given the favorable verdict. These **souls** also

---

[1] See further Buchanan, *Insights*, pp. 54-73.
[2] Mealy, *Thousand Years*, p. 109; Hughes, "Revelation 20, 4-6," pp. 288-89.

have received a favorable verdict. In the same way in Dan 7, the Son of man was given the kingdom at the same time the saints were given the kingdom. Here the ones **beheaded** were permitted to live and rule with the Messiah--apparently the same ruling as that received by the saints in Dan 7 and those who slept in the dust and jumped up in Dan 12:2.

The **elders** were not the final judges but rather assistants, which means they assisted in the court process. They may have functioned as lawyers, arguing a case in behalf of the martyrs.[1] When these lawyers won cases, so did their clients, so **elders** could be given a verdict at the same time and during the same trial as the martyrs, even though the text does not say that explicitly. The **elders** in the Revelation text may have been contemporary antitypes of those in Daniel who were wise and who made the many righteous (Dan 12:3). Making people righteous was a legal term that meant clearing them of guilt in court.

In this antitypal **judgment** scene, the new saints were to receive the kingdom again, just as the Hasmonean saints of the Most High had received it in the Maccabean rebellion. Because different authors wrote different parts of the Book of Revelation at different times, it is not certain that all of the parts have the same meaning. For example, there were martyrs under the altar in one unit (Rev 6:9-11); there were 144,000 followers of the Lamb who were celibate monks in another unit (Rev 14:1-5); and here in a third unit are those who **had been beheaded** because of their testimony (Rev 20:4). The editor who organized all of these parts obviously considered all three of these groups favorably. He may have intended all of them to be identified and all considered saints, but that is not certain. If they are all to be identified, then the 144,000 celibate saints were also those who **had been beheaded,** and their blood was poured on the heavenly altar. They wore the mark of God on their foreheads, but they refused to wear the sign of the **beast**. The first **beast** in Rev 13 seems to have been Herod the Great, and among the ones **beheaded** were King Antigonus and his chief general Pappus (ca. 37 BIA).

The author of Rev 20 placed **the elders** in the heavenly court, sitting on **thrones** alongside the **throne** of the Lord. They were in some sort of association with those who had been **beheaded** for their faith. The ones **beheaded** were destined to come back to life and live on the Promised Land with their messiah for the coming age of a **thousand years**. Baruch described this resurrection as follows:

> The earth will certainly restore the dead which it now receives in order to preserve them. It will make no change in their form, but as it has received, so it will restore them. As I delivered (*tradidi*) them to it, so it also will raise them, for then it will be necessary to show the living that the dead have revived, and those who had left have returned. Then after they have recognized those whom they now know, their judgment will be strong, and the things predicted will come to pass (2Bar 50:2-4).

---

[1] See futher Buchanan, *Insights*, p. 35.

Weiss correctly observed that this was an antitype from Dan 7 where the saints who were there promised world rule would receive the kingdom, but these were also Christian views. Paul said the (Christian) saints would judge the world (1Cor 6:2-3), and Jesus told his disciples that they would sit on twelve thrones, judging the tribes of Israel (Luke 22:29-30). The disciples would either be governors of the twelve tribes with thrones located within the geographical limits of the tribes or they might represent the tribes as members of the national Sanhedrin in Jerusalem, functioning as assistant judges.

On account of the testimony of Jesus. This is one of the few times Jesus was mentioned in the entire document, Rev 4:1-22:5. This is an explanatory addition by some Christian who understood the **word of God** to be the testimony of Jesus. All of these are Christian additions that were made to an otherwise Jewish redemption anthology. These Christianizing additions are all interpretative and not integral to the contexts. They were made either by John of Patmos when he translated the document or, more likely, by some earlier Christian who made them before John received the scroll. Whealon thought the whole phrase, **and the souls of those slain by the sword for the witness of Jesus and for the Word of God,** (his translation) was a Christian addition. He was correct in thinking that there was a Christian addition here to a Jewish document.[1]

Which very ones did not worship. Sinaiticus misspelled two words in this passage: **which very ones** was spelled *áy-teen-ehs* (εἴτινες) rather than *hoi-teen-ehs* (οἵτινες) and **therefore** *oon*(ουν) for **not** (*oo,* ου).

And the saints lived and ruled with the Messiah. In the Greek, the tense of these two verbs is in the past tense, **lived and ruled.** This might be understood as a Greek translation of a Hebrew text in which the Greek word for **and** comprised part of a *waw* consecutive construction, transforming a past tense verb into the future tense, but that is not required here. This sentence is part of the vision that began with Rev 20:4: **And I saw . . .** which means he saw all of this in his imagination *as if* it had already happened. Actually he was expecting it to happen in the future. He had in mind a recollection of that which had happened to the **saints of the Most High** and the **Son of man** in Dan 7, and he envisioned its antitype having happened again.

These antitypical saints were expected to come to life and rule with the Messiah in the same way that the second century BIA Palestinian Jews, as **saints of the Most High** (Dan 7), lived and ruled together with Judas the Maccabee after the death of Antiochus Epiphanes. This is the third use of the expression **Messiah** with the definite article.[2] In all three cases (but not only these) **the Messiah** functioned as

---

[1] J. H. Whealon, "New Patches on an Old Garment: The Book of Revelation," *BTB* 11 (1981):55.
[2] This is not a specially important observation. Rabbis were careless about definite articles, and so were NT scribes. Paul used words, like "law" and "the law" interchangeably with the same meaning. Messiah, and its Greek counterpart, Christ, is a title and should always have the definite article when

a leader of a nation who would **rule** as a king. The age when **the Messiah** ruled was the age to come. It came after the messianic age was over, and **the Messiah** ruled the Promised Land in peace. **The Messiah** was understood to be a political leader in the Book of Revelation, just as it was in the FT. De Jonge was correct in identifying **the Messiah** here with **the** Davidic **Messiah** of PssSol 17 and 18.[1] The following quotation from that Psalm will show the kind of **Messiah** that poet had in mind. It will also suggest the kind of **saints** and **Messiah** the author of Rev 20 expected.

> Look, Lord! Raise up for them their king, the son of David,
> at the time you choose, God, so that he will rule over your servant, Israel.
> Gird him with strength so that he may shatter unrighteous rulers,
> cleanse Jerusalem from the gentiles who trample [it] destructively.
> In just wisdom [let him] evict criminals from the inheritance,
> shatter the criminal's pride like a clay pot,
> break all their substance with an iron rod . . .
> Then he will gather a holy people which he will lead in righteousness (Ps. Sol. 17:21-24, 26).

Scholars, like Düsterdieck, Morris, and Boring, objected to any earthly kingdom concept. Düsterdieck said,

> For there is no reason for ascribing to John the play-work by which the Talmudists and the Church Fathers, combining such passages as Isa. lxiiii.4, Zech. xiv.7, Gen. i., with Ps. xc.4 have inferred that the Messianic reign will last a thousand years, or that the world will stand for six millenniums, and in the seventh millennium the eternal Sabbath will follow.[2]

Morris said,

> John is thus not simply repeating accepted Jewish ideas . . . He does not say that it takes place on earth and in fact it may well be located in heaven.[3]

Ulfgard held that the expressions, "first resurrection" and "second death" were obviously metaphorical concepts that had no physical or temporal significance. The

---

associated with an individual, such as Jesus *the* Christ. When a specific messiah is intended it should always be "the Messiah," but the definite article is often omitted.

[1] M. DeJonge, "The Use of the Expression ὁ Χριστός [*haw Christos*] in the Apocalypse of John," *Apocalypse johannique et l'Apocalyptique dans le Nouveau Testament* (Gembloux: Duculot, c1980), p. 279.

[2] F. Düsterdieck, *Critical and Exegetical Handbook to the Revelation of John*, tr. H. E. Jacobs (Winona Lake: Alpha Publications, 1884), pp. 470-71.

[3] Morris, *Revelation*, p. 234.

resurrection was expected to be a quality of life rather than a fact in history.[1] These scholars have not given good reasons, however, for ignoring the opinions of those Christians and Jews who were much nearer in time and geography to the thought forms of the NT than we are. Weiss thought "living" here had a double meaning. On the one hand it meant living again after the resurrection and on the other hand it meant those who would take part in the thousand year reign.[2] Caird was correct in saying that those who **lived and ruled** were not the only ones left in the world. Otherwise they would not be ruling over anyone.[3] Deere was also correct in holding that the kingdom involved here would be an earthly kingdom.[4] Following the type of Dan 7, the author anticipated a reestablishment of the Promised Land with still more grandiose conditions. Not only would the chosen people be saved from Roman domination. They would replace Rome as the rulers of Europe and the Middle East. **The Messiah** and the new **saints** would rule over the gentiles with an iron rod, fulfilling the prophecies of Second Isaiah, in which foreigners would do all of the manual work for the nation (Isa 61:5-7).

Jews and Christians of NT times knew of spiritual or quality values, to be sure, but these positions never removed them from practical, geographical, and political anticipations. They called existence within the community "life" and existence outside the community, "death." This did not prevent them from longing for national liberation in time and space. They were not aware of twentieth century Western cosmology. They deduced their belief in the resurrection as reasonable interpretation of Deuteronomic theology: God promised to bless his faithful with long life, prosperity, many children, and prominent status in the world. Those who gave up their lives in battle for the community, as Jews did during the Hasmonean rebellion and in the revolts of 66-70 IA and 132-135 IA, could be assured of God's future reward. They had not lived long enough to be rewarded in this world and in this life for their virtue. Jews and Christians believed that God would give them a second chance to live out their years. This was not eternal life in heaven but extended physical life on earth under superior conditions on the Promised Land.

While interpreting these difficult passages it is not necessary to make them seem reasonable to scientific twentieth century scientists. To be fair to the text it is necessary to interpret them in terms that are fair to Jewish and Christian concepts of 2,000 years ago in the Middle East. Somehow those believers reasoned that it would take both a first and a second resurrection to fulfill God's promises--not in a manner that is symbolic or qualitative only in spiritual time and space. Early Christians and Jews thought in terms of years that included summers and winters, with a **messiah** ruling from Jerusalem. This made sense in ancient terms of cyclical time and sabbatical eschatology, terms well-known at the time the Book of Revelation was

---

[1] Ulfgard, *Feasts*, pp. 62-64.
[2] B. Weiss, *Apostle geschichte-Katholische Briefe-Apokalypse* (Leipzig, 1902), p. 519.
[3] Caird, *Revelation*, p. 251.
[4] J. S. Deere, "Premillennialism in Revelation 20,4-6," *BibSac* 135 (1978):58-73.

written. Words written on paper are not the same as an ink blot into which people may infuse their own feelings and ideas.

TEXT

Revelation

⁵The rest of the dead will not come **to life** until the thousand years is completed. This is the first resurrection. ⁶Blessed and holy is the one who takes part in the first resurrection. Upon these the second death has no authority,

but they **shall be priests** both **of God** and of his Messiah, and they shall rule with him for the thousand years.

First Testament

Dan 12:2 Many who sleep in the dust will jump up--some **to life** of the age and some to shame for rejection of the age.

Isa 61:6 Foreigners will stand and herd your flocks, and gentiles will be your plowmen and vine dressers, but you **shall be** called **the priests of Yehowah**; "ministers **of** our **God**" will be your title. You will consume the wealth of the gentiles; in their glory you shall be transferred.

COMMENTARY

The rest of the dead will not come to life. These are the antitypes of those who would be raised to shame and rejection of the age, namely the Hasmonean age (Dan 12:2; also Matt 9:18; Acts 9:41). In this context, **the rest** seems to mean all the people of the world who had died, except those who **had been beheaded.** Only **the beheaded** ones would reign with **the Messiah** for **a thousand years.** This would be a more restrictive group than **the saints** in Dan 7.

Hai Gaon was less explicit, but he might have agreed. He said, "The dead in the days of the Messiah **will come to life** for **life** in the age to come."[1] By this he might have meant the martyrs who were killed in the 3½ year war, or he might have understood this to include all believers who died from any cause during this period of conflict, the days of the Messiah. He told further of the particulars necessary to bring this about:

> Then he will blast with a great trumpet, as it is said, **In that day a great trumpet will be sounded** (Isa 27:13). Some say that Zerubbabel will blow this trumpet. But why will there be a great earthquake? So that when the bones that have been trampled on in the land will arise and whoever is built into buildings and whoever is burned in the bricks, and whoever is buried under the debris, and bone will approach bone, just as it is written in the chapter on the valley (Ezek 37). Then the holy One

---

[1] Buchanan (tr.), *Jewish Messianic Movements*, p. 128.

blessed be He will stretch tendons on them, cover them with flesh, and wrap skin over them, but there will be no breath in them. Afterward the holy One blessed be He will bring down dew of life from heaven which contains the light of breathing life.[1]

Both the messianic age and the following age to come were expected to take place on this earth in historical time where human beings exist with bones, flesh, and skin, just as they do now. The age to come was to be an age of peace and Jewish or Christian rule at the end of the messianic age. Evidently the first resurrection would occur immediately after the **dragon** was thrown into the abyss. After that **the saints would** rule for a millennium. This would be a reign of peace when there would be no opposition to **the Messiah's** rule. All gentiles would be under Jewish control, and **Satan** would be **bound** and restrained. This would be the Sabbath day of **a thousand years.** Of course, there are scholars, like Hailey, who hold that resurrection has nothing to do with a resurrection of the body. This deals only with national triumph in battle.[2] That was part of the belief. With the resurrection would come the restoration of the nation to the faithful believers, but Jews and Christians also believed that the dead bodies would be raised from the ground and enabled to live in the new kingdom.

The first resurrection. Stadelmann said Rev 20 expected two **resurrections**, and they were both bodily. There is no basis for imposing a spiritual **resurrection** on the text.[3] Hughes concurred, arguing that there were two **resurrections** involved: 1) **The first was the resurrection** of Jesus. Through baptism Christians share in this **resurrection.** 2) The second was the general **resurrection** at the consummation of the age.[4]

The second death has no authority. **Second death** did not mean eternal hell, as Giblin held,[5] unless hell is understood in some meaning different from that portrayed by Dante. Loisy said it was eternal death.[6] **The second death**, like **the second** birth, is legal. People are born physically as infants. Whenever they make some radical change, legally, such as joining a church, synagogue, getting married, accepting some very high office, or becoming naturalized as citizens to a country into which they were not born, physically, they are born again. This is their **second** birth. Non-Jews or non-Christians who become Jews or Christians are said to be born again, legally. While they are members they are legally alive, but if members are excommunicated or become apostates they die, legally

---

[1] Buchanan (tr.), *Jewish Messianic Movements*, p. 126.
[2] H. M. Hailey, *Revelation: An Introduction and Commentary* (Grand Rapids: Baker's Bookhouse, c1979), p. 394.
[3] Stadelmann, "Das Zeugnis," pp. 153-55.
[4] P. E. Hughes, "The First Resurrection: Another Interpretation," *WTJ* 39 (1977):315-18.
[5] Giblin, *Revelation*, p. 185.
[6] A. Loisy, *L'Apocalypse de Jean* (Paris: Emile Nourry, 1923), p. 354.

According to Cyril of Alexandria coming "to judge the living and the dead" meant judging between the Christians (the living) and the apostates (the dead).[1] The distinction made here is not between the physically living and the physically dead. The death involved is legal or **second death.** Targumists said those who assisted in the destruction of Jerusalem before the Babylonian exile would die **the second death** and not live in the age to come (TgOnq Deut 33:6; Jer 51:39, 57; TgJon Isa 22:14; 65:6, 15).

The faithful **saints** who lived during the **millennium** after the first **resurrection** would never be excommunicated. **Second death would have no authority over them**. Not everyone is tried in every court trial. Trials are only for those suspected of being guilty of something. **The saints** were cleared of all possible felonies and misdemeanors, so they would not be tried. Their membership in the future community was guaranteed.

Priests of God. The Jews who were privileged to return to the Promised Land after Cyrus' victory over the Babylonians expected to have such glorious living conditions that they would never have to do any physical work. All of this would be done by gentiles. Jews, however, would be priests of God. The importance of being priests, here, is clearly one of status. In Judaism people were ranked as follows:

1) priests,
2) Levites,
3) Israelites, and
4) proselytes (CDC 14:3-4; 1QS 2:19-21).

Priests were prosperous. They received the choice cuts from all the animals slaughtered. Even the Levites had to bring tithes and offerings to the priests. Priests did not have to farm or raise sheep. The non-priests did all of this work and brought to the priests the choice of all their produce. According to Second Isaiah, all Jews would return to the Promised Land and be treated like priests (see also Exod 19:6). Gentiles would do all the hard demeaning work, and Jews would receive the benefits. The author of this portion of Revelation thought those who were part of the first **resurrection** would be treated like upper class citizens.

Priests both of God and of his Messiah. NA omits **both,** but it adds **for a thousand years**. Whealon listed the words **and of his Messiah** as possible Christian insertions. Of course, it is possible, but not at all necessary that the words constitute either an insertion or that they be understood as distinctly Christian.[2]

The pattern here follows that of Dan 7. There the Son of man was given the kingdom, authority, and glory of a monarch, and **the saints of the Most High** would also receive the kingdom, **ruling** authority, and the greatness of the kingdom. This

---

[1] R. W. Cowley, *The Traditional Interpretation of the Apocalypse of St. John in the Ethiopian Orthodox Church* (Cambridge: Cambridge U. Press, c1983), p. 147.
[2] Whealon, "Patches," p. 55.

means the Son of man would **rule** together with the saints. In Daniel **the Son of man** was Judas the Maccabee, and **the saints of the Most High** were his Jewish contemporaries. Following the same structure, the author of this prophecy claimed that the priests of God and his **Messiah** would rule together for **a thousand years**. This author replaced **the saints** with **priests.** This is one of the indications that the authors of several of these units in Revelation belonged to a **priestly** group. In Daniel **the saints** represented all of the Jews of the nation. Here, the author may have thought there should be only **priests** in the nation, or, more likely, he may have thought that the council of elders were **priests.** In neither instance does it mean either that **the saints** themselves in Daniel or **the priests** in Revelation **ruled** without **the Messiah**. They would rule with **the Messiah** either as members of the Sanhedrin or as citizens of a nation that **ruled** other countries the way the Roman Empire ruled over Palestine during the current evil age.

The second death would come, apparently, after the **thousand year** period of rest was over. Then the rest of the dead would be raised up for judgment, but **the saints** would escape this judgment and the **death** that would follow. Their status as guiltless members of the community had been established without any doubt. After the **thousand years** was over **the dragon** would be released and be allowed to **rule** again. This would be considered a rule of **death**, because only Jews and/or Christians belonged to the community where life was possible. Second Baruch said that the dead would be raised exactly as they died, without any change. This would prove to the living that those who died were identical to those who had been raised. They could be recognized (2Bar 5:2-4).

TEXT

Revelation	First Testament and Targumim
	Ezek 7:2 The word of Yehowah came to me, saying, "You, son of man, thus said the Lord Yehowah to the Land of
⁷When the thousand years are over, Satan will be released from his prison	
⁸and will **come** out to make the gentiles wander--those who are in **the four corners**, namely,	Israel, 'An end has **come,** the end ove **the four corners of the land.'"**
	Gen 10:2 The sons of Japeth were Gomer, **Magog**, Madai, Javan . . . .
	Ezek 38:2 Son of man set your face toward
Gog and Magog, lead them together	**Gog of** the land of **Magog**, the chief

into war,	prince of Meshech and Tubal, and prophesy against him.
	^{TgNeof Num 11.26}At the very end of days **Gog and Magog** will go out to Jerusalem, and they will fall into the hands of the king Messiah.
the **number** of whom will be	^{Jer 15:8}I have made their widows more in **number** than **the sand of the sea**.
as [great as] **the sand of the sea.**	^{Gen 22:17}I will multiply your descendants as the stars **of** the heaven and **as the sand** which is on **the seashore**.
	^{Hab 1:5-6}Look among the nations. Observe and be thoroughly astonished. I am accomplishing something in your days which you would not believe if it were told. Look! I am raising up the Chaldeans, that bitter and swift nation which
⁹They **went up over the breadth of the Land,** and they surrounded the camp	**comes over the breadth of the Land** to seize dwellings that do not belong to it.
	^{Ezek 38:11}You said, "I will **go up over** a level **Land**; I will come to a quiet people, all living in confidence."
	^{Jer 11:14-15}Do not pray for this people; do not raise up a lamentation or prayer in behalf of them, because I will not listen at the time they call to me in the time of their trouble. What [right] has **my beloved** in my house? Will her mechanistic deeds and holy flesh pass over your evil actions?
of the saints and **the beloved city**.	^{Sir 24:11}In **the beloved city** likewise he gave me rest; in Jerusalem was my authority.
	^{Ps 78:68}He chose the tribe of Judah,

Fire came down [from heaven and consumed them]. ¹⁰Then the devil, who leads them astray, was thrown into

Mount Zion, which he **loves**.

^(Ps 87:2-3)Yehowah **loves** the gates of Zion more than all the tents of Jacob. Glorious things in you are spoken, **city** of God.

^(Jer 12:7)I have abandoned my temple; I have forsaken my inheritance; I have given the soul of **my beloved** into the hand of his enemies.

^(2Kings 1:10, 12)Elijah answered and said to the officer of the fifty, "If I am a man of God, let fire come down from heaven and consume both you and your fifty [soldiers]." Then **fire came down from heaven and consumed** him and his fifty [soldiers].

^(Isa 26:11)Even **fire will consume** your enemies, but Yehowah, you will pour out peace for us, for all our deeds you have performed for us.

^(Ezek 39:6)I will send a **fire** into Magog and into the confident inhabitants of the coastlands, and they will know that I am Yehowah.

^(Amos 1:8)I will send a **fire** against the wall of Gaza, **and consume** its fortifications.

^(Amos 1:14)I will kindle a **fire** against the wall of Rabbah **and consume** its fortifications.

^(Amos 2:2)I will send a **fire** into Moab **and consume** the fortifications of Kerioth

^(Ezek 38:22)I judge him with pestilence

the lake **of fire and sulfur**, where the beast and the false prophet are, and they will be tortured day and night to ages of ages.

and blood. I will rain down upon him, his troops, and many peoples who are

with him flooding rain, hail, and **sulfuric fire**.

COMMENTARY

Satan will be released from prison. Apparently whenever the millennium was over, **Satan** would be **released from prison** and lead astray **the gentile nations** who had been there all the time. This seems incoherent to scholars who take literally all of the details of these various visions. In Rev 20:5, the report is that the rest of the dead will not come to life. If that means all those in the world except these few believers who had been beheaded, then there would be no nation for **Satan** to **lead astray.**

This assumption does not allow for Oriental hyperbole and imagination. When the tide went down at the border of Egypt just enough for the Israelites to escape across the water, the Scripture reported that the water was held back and became a wall on both sides of the path through which the Israelites crossed (Exod 14:22). When the Israelites needed to cross the Jordan when its banks were full, the water piled up in a heap at a distance so they could cross over on dry land (Josh 3:14-17). When Sisera attacked the Israelites in the Valley of Jezreel, it rained so that the horses and chariots of Sisera got stuck in the mud. The poet said, **The stars from their courses fought against Sisera** (Judges 5:20). The author of Daniel calculated, *after the fact*, that the temple had been cleansed and rededicated in 164 BIA--in perfect sabbatical logic, exactly 490 years after it had been burned in 586 BIA--even though only 422 years actually elapsed.

Early Israelites, Jews, Samaritans, and Christians had good imaginations and colorful vocabularies, but they were able to relate these dreams to practical facts that could take place in history. So, in one vision the seer anticipates the destruction of all the people of the world, but the surviving martyrs would live and rule with the Messiah. There seemed to be no problem with the idea that a ruling people have to rule some land and some other people.[1] When **Satan was released** there were the **gentiles** waiting for him to make them **wander**.[2] If Rome had been overthrown, or even seriously weakened, and Israel was able to **rule** Palestine under some

---

[1] Mealy, *Thousand Years*, p. 121, fn 1, was troubled with the thought that the author might ever dream of ruling some other people. He said that would connote despotism, which he could not accept. A brief study of the conquest of Canaan, the Hasmonean Revolt, the conquest of Constantine, and the Crusades should remind him that conquest theology is inherent to Jewish and Christian theology. He may have overlooked some of the glee attached to some chapters of the Book of Revelation, as well.

[2] Mealy, *Thousand Years*, p. 124, understands this passage to mean that those who were not martyrs would be raised after the millennium was over at the same time Satan was released. They would instantly become nations armed and ready to be led by Satan. During the millennium, however, there would only be those few martyrs alive on earth. This is possible logic in dealing with the passage, but it is not the only possibility.

reasonable conditions, believers would consider all of these prophecies fulfilled. Even if there continued to be nations around, and even if Israel did not **rule** all of them, they would believe that **Satan** was **bound**, because there was at least a short reign of peace. The Hasmonean reign lasted fewer than a hundred years (142 BIA-63 BIA.)--not nearly a **millennium,** but it qualified as a glorious age. Even history was described in hyperbolic detail. How much more colorful visions of the future!

Ulfgard held that the **binding of Satan** for a **thousand years** could not be taken literally, because that would mean that the *parousia* would be only a partial success, a temporary victory for Christ.[1] This means Ulfgard would not be satisfied with this arrangement, but it does not mean Jews and Christians of NT times thought it was faulty. They could stretch time spans and geography to fit dogma, but they did not prophesy in terms of time and space when they really meant some kind of philosophy, psychology, or something else.

The cyclical logic of the author was reasonably consistent. He believed that there were two mighty political forces in the world, the children of light, the Jews and/or Christians, and the children of darkness, the **gentiles.** Alternatingly, the powers took turns in ruling the world. At one period the gentiles ruled the world, and at the next age the Jews ruled the world. These two ages were predestined just as day is predestined to follow night. When the **gentiles** were ruling, the Jews were in captivity, prison, or slavery. When the Jews were ruling, the gentiles would be prisoners, slaves, or captives.

After the Jews and/or Christians had ruled for **a thousand years, gentiles** were predestined to rule during the next period. When the Jews were ruling, God was in his holy temple at Zion,. the Messiah was on his throne at Jerusalem, and **Satan** was in prison. When **Satan** was released, the **gentile** captivity was over, and **Satan** would promptly organize all of the **gentiles** to make war on the Jews and/or Christians to regain control of the world. Reportedly, the Lord told Baruch that the holy city would be taken away for a time, but the Lord would not remove it forever. Ever since the Lord created the Garden of Eden he had a constructed city in heaven, waiting to be brought down to earth (2 Bar 4:1-7).

The four corners, namely Gog and Magog. NA adds after "corners" the words, **of the earth.** Hailey followed others in thinking that the battle with **Gog and Magog** was to be only a spiritual and moral struggle, "far from a physical conflict."[2] Early Jews and Christians thought differently. Hai Gaon, for example, said the land of **Gog and Magog** was in the land of Edom, and Edom for him was a code name for

---

[1] Ulfgard, *Feast*, p. 58. Some scholars refer to the beginning of the age to come as the *parousia*, even though this word nowhere occurs in the Book of Revelation. See for example, Mealy, *Thousand Years, passim.*

[2] Hailey, *Revelation*, p. 397. For a list of others who thought Gog and Magog could not refer to people see Mealy, *Thousand Years*, p. 37, fn. 4. Mealy also concurs with these (see pp. 120-21).

"Rome."[1] Loisy thought **Gog** was the country whose ruler was **Magog.** The people of this country were Scythians and lived north of Asia Minor.[2]

The battle with **Gog and Magog** was to be fought during the messianic age, just before the age to come. In Rev 20:8 there can be no question: **Gog and Magog** are in parallel with **gentiles** who were **in the four corners**. Medieval Jews thought **Gog and Magog** were any two different enemy **gentile** countries that were destined to go to war with one another and reduce each other's military power so that it would be easy for Jews to conquer both. During the Crusades **Gog and Magog** were the Christians and Muslims, in rabbinic opinion.

Some argue that there were not any survivors left after Rev 19:21 for **Satan** to deceive in Rev 20:8. This logic presumes that the same author composed all of this literature and intended it all to follow chronologically. The same kind of questions could be asked of events in the Book of Exodus. Like Exodus, Revelation consists of units that have been spliced together. The new vision that begins with Rev 20:4 started *de novo*, without any dependence upon Rev 19:21. Some later editor put all of these units together in a way that satisfied him, even though it does not satisfy some Western scholars.

The author of Rev 20 spliced together passages from two places in Ezekiel as if they were synonymous. The four corners of the *land* in Ezek 2 had a different connotation from that which **Gog** from the land of **Magog** did in Ezek 38, but the author or editor of Rev 20 took *hah-áh-retz* (הארץ) in Ezekiel in both places to mean "earth," rather than the land of Palestine. This is evident, because his **corners** enclosed the territory of **Gog and Magog** which extended beyond the borders of Palestine. The midrashic author determined his message primarily on the text of Ezekiel, and he seemed to have at least a general idea of the locations mentioned by Ezekiel. He may have considered the northwest corner of the earth, for instance, to include the northern or western border of the Roman Empire. This would have been true, because the author both knew and hated Rome. He was sure that it was within the borders of the world, but he did not limit **Gog and Magog** to that area.

The author of Rev 20 seems to have thought that **Gog and Magog** represented all of the gentiles whom Ezekiel said would surround Jerusalem. That is why he paralleled **Gog and Magog** with the **four corners** of the earth. He took the names from Ezekiel and the concept from Ezekiel. Ezekiel began with the hordes from the north, because many people in the south, all the way from Rome to China, knew about the hordes of barbarians who lived north of the Caucasian Mountains and the Alps who made raids with their horses on the civilized southerners and took large quantities of booty. More people of more nations seemed to fear these northern barbarians than other neighboring enemy nations. To give his message more impact, Ezekiel started by telling of these hordes and then added to the threat by accumulating more troops from other nations as they approached Jerusalem.

Geographically, all of these references in Ezekiel--**Magog, Tubal, Tograma, Gomer,** and **Meshech**--seem to come from places northwest of Palestine,[1]

---

[1] Buchanan, *Jewish Messianic Movements*, p. 123.
[2] Loisy, *L'Apocalypse*, p. 355.

around the northern border of the Black Sea and north of the Caucasian Mountains. Since Ezekiel referred to **Gog from the Land of Magog** (Ezek 38:2) and also **Gog, chief prince of Meshech and Tubal** (Ezek 38:2; 39:1; also see Gen 10:2), he seems to have thought those cities or towns existed inside the borders of Magog. This same Gog might have been identical to the Lydian king "Gyges," although Lydia was located in Asia Minor, in the western part of modern Turkey and would hardly qualify as "the most distant regions of the North" (Ezek 39:2). The name is more likely to have come from "Gagaia," which is the name of a barbarian tribe mentioned in the El Amarna tablets.[2] Josephus and Second Maccabees identified **Gog and Magog** with the Scythians (Ant 1:123).[3] They symbolized the hordes of barbarians from the north.[4] Approximately six hundred years later the prophet Muhammad still identified **Gog and Magog** with distant enemies, whom he described in terms similar to the ways other southerners thought of the northern barbarians: "You will go on fighting against enemies until you fight **Gog and Magog,** who are the people with broad faces, small eyes, and reddish hair."[5]

Although Ezekiel thought **Gog** came from the North, he did not limit the enemies to the northern troops. To the northern hordes would be added armies from Persia in the East, and **Cush** in North Africa. That is the reason the author of Rev 20 paralleled this mob with people who came from the four corners of the earth, and he seemed to think the whole group--from northwestern Europe to southeastern Persia; from central Russia to southwestern Ethiopia--the equivalent of "Gog and Magog."

Ezekiel visualized, at the end of the prison sentence in Babylon "at the end of the days," (*buh-ah-khah-reét hah yah-meém,* באחרית הימים) (Ezek 38:16), or "at the end of the years" (*buh ah-khah-reét hah-shah-neém,* באחרית השנים) (Ezek 38:8), that Jews would be restored from the diaspora to the Promised Land, and there they would dwell securely until **Gog** came from the land of **Magog** with troops so great that they would cover the Promised Land like a cloud. This **Gog** would come with horses and riders who were armed and fitted in armor and helmets. When he attacked Israel he would have the support of troops from Persia, Cush, and Put, which include all the territory of the Fertile Crescent from Ethiopia to Babylon.

These troops, which include Bet-Tograma from the far North, would be so numerous that other places, like Sheba, Dedan, and the merchants of Tarshish, would feel threatened, because they would suspect that Gog's motive was to carry

---

[1] On this see Aare Lauha, "Zaphon: Der Norden und die Nordvölker im Alten Testament," *Annales Academiae Scientiarum Fennicae* 49 (1944):22-23. For a still more extensive study of Gog and Magog in relationship to other geographical locations see A. R. Anderson, *Alexander's Gate, Gog and Magog, and the Enclosed Nations* (Cambridge, 1932), pp. 5-14.
[2] Lauha, "Zaphon," p. 69.
[3] For an account of the way Medieval theologians used these terms see G. Cary, *The Medieval Alexander* ed. D. J. A. Ross (Cambridge, 1956), p. 130.
[4] For a careful analysis of the barbarians in relationship to the northern areas of central Europe and Asia see Denis Sinor, "The Barbarians," *Diogenes* 18 (1957):47-60; and "The Greed of the Northern Barbarian," *Indiana University Uralic and Altaic Series* 134 (1978):172-81.
[5] B. Lewis, *Islam* (New York, c1974) II, p. 197.

away spoil--that is what northern barbarians usually did when they moved south--and Spanish merchants did not think the mobs would stop with Palestine but would continue as far as Spain and plunder them also (Ezek 38:13). The author of Rev 20 thought the gathering of the gentile hordes around Jerusalem was the sign that Satan had been released from the abyss, and this battle that he would lead would be the equivalent of his rule for a short time. The Neofiti targumist was faithful to Ezekiel; he had Gog and Magog coming up against Jerusalem at **the very end of the days** (*buh sóhf ay-kéhv yoh-máy-yah,* בסוף עקב יומיא) and there fall into the hands of the Messiah (TgNeof Num 11:26). Both *sohf* and *ay-kehv* mean "end." They seem to have been joined here to mean "the very end."

They went up over the breadth of the land. Many scholars confuse the issue here by translating this "the plain of the earth," and picture the adversaries as demons who came up out of the abyss.[1] Those who approached the **camp of the saints** at Jerusalem **went up,** not because they were under the earth before, but, from a Jewish doctrinal point of view, Jerusalem is the highest place on the face of the earth. All those who come to Jerusalem **go up**. Even if they came from the top of the Himalaya Mountains, they would **go up** to Jerusalem. Actually most of those who travel to Jerusalem go up either from the Jordan Valley or from the sea coast plain, and go up from a topographical point of view as well, but the real point is theological, and that theology was assumed by the author of this passage. Going to Jerusalem from the diaspora, land where Jews lived away from Palestine, meant **going up** to the Promised Land. Once they got to the land they still **went up** to Jerusalem. This did not imply arising to the level of the earth from Sheol or Hades, underground.

In 1957, while participating in an archaeological excavation in Shechem, at the base of Mount Gerizim, a Samaritan told me that Gerizim was the tallest mountain in the world, I pointed to Mount Ebal just across the valley. The Samaritan could see that Mount Ebal was higher. Nevertheless, he responded that Gerizim was the tallest mountain "spiritually." By spiritual he meant by doctrinal definition. Jews and early Christians would have responded the same way about Zion, which is actually lower that Mount Scopus and the Mount of Olives, across the Kidron Valley. People went down to Egypt (Acts 7:15), to Capernaum (John 2:12), or to Caesarea (Acts 25:6). Leaving Jerusalem requires **going** down (Mark 3:22; Luke 2: 10:30; Acts 8:26; 25:7).

They surrounded the camp. This was obviously a military movement. They did not go to the country involved for a friendly visit. They came **to surround the camp** with soldiers, just the way Vespasian did in 69 IA.

The saints and the beloved city. Now the geography is clear. This was not just any camp. This was **the camp of the saints**, and its location was Zion, **the beloved City of God**. Since the harlot was Rome, the dragon was Rome, **the beast** was an agent

---

[1] See Mealy, *Thousand Years*, p. 51.

of Rome, **Satan** and **the devil** were the religious supporters of Rome, then it means that **Gog and Magog** were taken to be the enemy of Zion, Rome.

The author of this passage took his point of departure from Habakkuk who threatened that the Lord would send the Chaldeans to go across **the breadth of the Promised Land,** seizing dwellings that did not belong to it. This was expected as an act of war against the Jews and Israelites. This was the kind of behavior the Revelation author expected to happen again.

Herod the Great led the Romans troops over **the breadth of the land** when he overpowered the Parthians and troops of King Antigonus (40-37 BIA). This is also what the Romans did from 66-69 IA when they plundered all of the territory of Palestine before they concentrated on an attack against Jerusalem. They began in Galilee, then took Perea, then the Mediterranean coastal area and Idumaea before attacking Jerusalem.

This passage from Habakkuk was also used by the author of the Habakkuk Commentary in the Dead Sea Scrolls to describe the activity of the Romans. Weiss said there could be no doubt that this narrative was composed before 70 IA.[1] The author here apparently put together the Ezekiel passage, telling of the attack of the hordes from **Gog and Magog** against Jerusalem and the text from Habakkuk who visualized the Chaldeans coming from the East to attack Jerusalem. Any nation or group of nations who came against Jerusalem might qualify as the new Gog and Magog who came across the plain to get to Jerusalem for an attack--even if they came from the West, rather than the East.

They surrounded the camp of the saints. The tenses are a bit confusing here. First the text says Satan **will be released** . . . then **he will come** . . .. The next finite verb is **they went up** . . . **and they surrounded**. The last three verbs have conjunctions (*kaí*, καί)) before them. In Hebrew the last two might be *waw* consecutives. In this construction the past tense is transferred into the future. If this were followed, all tenses would be future. Even without that possibility the past tenses may be intended as future events. This entire passage is told as if it were part of a vision that began at Rev 20:4, **And I saw.** That which he **saw** may have been an expectation of the future even though it was told as if it were past. Of course, past tense might also have been intended to describe past events, so the message is not certain.

A factor in the judgment is the close identity of the description with the history that actually took place around Jerusalem in 69 IA. The camp of the saints was Jerusalem, **the beloved city**, where Vespasian brought many Roman troops, as numerous as **the sand of the sea [shore],** and **surrounded the** holy **city** in 69 IA. The author of this passage may have identified these Roman troops with the troops of **Gog and Magog.** Because of the civil war in Rome, Vespasian withdrew his troops in July, 69 IA, and he moved to Egypt from which he supervised troops in Rome that were fighting against the newly appointed emperor, Vitellius. This civil

---

[1] J. Weiss, *Die Offenbarung des Johannes* (Göttingen: Vandenhoeck & Ruprecht, 1908), p. 676.

war in Rome lasted only until Dec. 20-21 when Vitellius was killed after Rome had been taken by the troops of Vespasian (Tacitus, *Hist* 3:84-85).

When Vespasian withdrew his troops from **Jerusalem**, those Jews who were in **Jerusalem** thought the war with Rome was over. God had intervened, and Jews had only to pick out the right Son of man to be the new King of Israel. There were three candidates, John, Eleazer, and Simon, fighting militarily to make this decision. This inner conflict in **Jerusalem** continued until just before the temple was burned on August, 70 IA. The tide began to turn at the beginning of 70 IA. As soon as the civil war in Rome was over, Vespasian sent his son, Titus, to Palestine to finish the war there (Tacitus, *Hist* 5:1). It took less than eight months to complete the assignment. There is no certainty, when dealing with allusions such as these, that the historical identification is correct, but the description of this drama fits the history just before the fall of **Jerusalem** at least as well as any other historical period. This narrative may have been composed after Vespasian had gathered his troops around Jerusalem and then left, but before Titus returned. The same is true of the following:

Fire came down from heaven. Sinaiticus omitted the long bracketed passage here, obviously a homeoteleuton error. His eye dropped from one **fire and** to another **fire and.** After the word **fire**, NA has **from heaven, and [it consumed them. Then the devil, who leads them astray, was thrown down into the lake of fire, and . . .]**

Normally **fire** and smoke do not **come down**. They go up. The exception is lightning. Ancients thought lightning was the result of the Deity's anger which he expressed by hurling arrows to certain people on earth. The noise and damage of war reminded ancients of thunder and lightning **from heaven.**

Schüssler-Fiorenza was pleased that no war was mentioned here. It is **fire** that God sends **down** to destroy the enemy, so the killing was done by God rather than by military might.[1] Those who were killed probably did not take as much comfort in this distinction as Schüssler-Fiorenza did.

Ezekiel assured his readers that these gentile troops would be stopped at Palestine, because there the Lord would bring against them every kind of natural calamity--hail, earthquakes, **fire,** sulphur, and diseases. He would confuse them so that they killed one another and would lie slain on the mountains of Israel. For Elijah, his experience on Mount Carmel, near Mount Megiddo, was one of the times he destroyed enemy troops by calling **down fire** from heaven. For the author of Rev 20, this event may have already taken place--not at **Jerusalem**, but at Rome. The time was at the end of 69 IA when citizens of Rome, in the midst of civil war, set the Capitol with its temples **afire**. Historians were not sure whether it was soldiers of the Flavian (Vespasian) party or the Vitellians who started the **fire** (Tacitus, *Hist* 3:71), but it was considered a national tragedy. Tacitus said,

> So the Capitol burned with its doors closed; none defended it, none pillaged it (Tacitus, Hist 3:71).

---

[1] Schüssler-Fiorenza, *Revelation*, p. 107.

Tacitus said this was the greatest tragedy that had ever faced Rome since its origin. At a time when there were no foreign foes the Capitol was burned in a civil war. This temple had been destroyed by the mad fury of Roman emperors (Tacitus, Hist 3:72). Romans feared the consequences. Surely the gods would punish Rome for this. Although Romans did not know who started the **fire**, Jews in Palestine were confident that they knew--it was the Lord of armies who sent **down fire** from heaven to destroy Rome just as he sent **down fire** to destroy Elijah's enemies. While the merchants mourned, and the stock market crashed, Palestinian Jews shouted, "Hallelujah! Her smoke goes up for ages of ages" (Rev 19:3). This all took place between July and late December, 69 IA. When these events happened in history, the author of this passage in Revelation interpreted them as the fulfillment of well-known prophecy. To the famous prophecies of Ezekiel, the author also added another from Habakkuk about the Chaldeans who marched through the breadth of the land to seize dwellings that were not theirs, just as the Romans had done before they surrounded Jerusalem.

Following the prophecy of Joel, these troops all congregated around Jerusalem, in the Kidron Valley, called the Valley of Verdict. The troops of all these nations were destined to be destroyed, just as the troops of Ahaziah that had been sent against Elijah had been demolished when Elijah called **down fire** from heaven (2Kings 1:9-16). There was an earlier tradition that whenever Israelites crossed the Jordan to enter the Land, the land and the Israelites would be cleansed from sin, guilt, and defilement. Then Satan would be no more (Jub 50:5; also 4Ezra 6:25-28).

The author of this redemption literature was acquainted with all of these traditions, and he based his narrative on them. Ezekiel, commenting on the prophecies both of Amos and the report of Elijah, predicted that **fire** would **come down** from heaven and consume all of these enemy hordes. The author of this narrative in Revelation thought that had already happened in Rome. By the time this work was composed, the author thought it was only a matter of time until the final details of Ezekiel's prophecy would be completely fulfilled. The actual historical events surrounding Jerusalem and Rome certainly lent themselves to the belief that many of the FT prophecies were in process of being fulfilled during the period just before and during the destruction both of Rome and Jerusalem.

The devil was thrown into the lake of sulfuric fire. Mealy correctly called attention to the comparison of this text with another that promised that those who worshiped the beast would be tortured with **fire** and **sulfur** before the holy angels and before the Lamb. The smoke of their burning went up **for ages of ages** (Rev 14:9-11).[1]

By December, 69 IA, when Rome was burning, and **the devil was thrown into the lake of sulfuric fire, the beast and the false prophet** were already there to greet **the devil** when he arrived. This means these characters had already died before 69 IA. Herod Agrippa I (the beast) had been dead for many years, and, according to

---

[1] Mealy, *Thousand Years*, p. 139.

the author of this document, he had been **tortured day and night** ever since his death. If we knew who **the false prophet** was we would probably realize that he too was dead by 69 IA. The author assumed that both were suffering terrible punishment after their deaths.

If the author actually wrote at that time, Rome had already begun burning. The Roman troops had already **surrounded the camp** of the Jews at **Jerusalem** and had retreated in July, 69 IA. Rome burned before late December, 69 IA, and **the fire** was extinguished by Dec. 21, 69 IA. This redemption document, however, might have been written when the author still expected **the devil** to be **thrown into the lake of fire** while Rome was still burning, and all the rest of Jewish or Christian enemies were expected to be destroyed. In fact the burning of Rome was all the clue the author needed to deduce that the Lord had sent **fire down from heaven** and an angel had thrown **the devil into the lake of fire and sulfur. The fire** in Rome, however, was finally put out before all of the Jewish and/or Christian enemies had been destroyed. By August, 70 IA the holy city, **Jerusalem**, was also destroyed and the temple was burned instead. The author could never have written with the confidence he had if he had waited just one more year. This is also true of parts of Rev 16 and many other parts of the Book of Revelation.

There was never a time in the history of Judaism when the religious hopes of the people were as high as they were at this time (July, 69 IA-August, 70 IA). Events seemed like signs of previous victories. The author of this text may have been one of the prophets of whom Josephus spoke. Josephus told of numerous prophets who announced to the Jews at this time the certainty that they would receive help soon from God. At the very time when the temple was burning a **false prophet** told the people that they should go to the temple court and receive the signs of deliverance God would give them (War 6:285-87). These signs never came. Rabbis said,

> Gehinnom will be opened and there the holy One blessed be He will bring down his throne and set it in the Valley of Jehoshaphat, and there he will make every nation and its idols pass by. When the gentiles pass by there, they will fall into it, as it is said, **Like sheep appointed for Sheol; death will shepherd them, [and the righteous will dominate them in the morning, and Sheol will consume their form from his dwelling]** (Ps 49:15).[1]

The scene the rabbis pictured was the Lord, fulfilling his function as a circuit judge. He would come with his portable bench and hold court. In this court case, the gentiles would be defendants, and they would lose the case.

TEXT

Revelation   First Testament and Other Jewish

---

[1] Buchanan (tr.), *Jewish Messianic Movements*, p. 544.

597

	Literature
¹¹**I saw** a great white **throne** and the one **seated on** it,	^{Isa 6:1}In the year that King Uzziah died **I saw** the Lord, **seated on his throne.**
	^{Dan 7:9}I kept watching until the **thrones** were set up and the Ancient of Days **sat down.**
	^{1Kings 22:19}Then [Micaiah] said, "Hear the word of Yehowah: **I saw** Yehowah, **sitting on his throne**, and all the troops of heaven were standing beside him, at his right and at his left."
from whose face the earth and heaven **fled**,	^{Ps 114:3}The sea saw and **fled**; the Jordan turned back.
	^{Ps 97:4-5}**The earth** saw and the land trembled; the mountains melted like wax from the face of Yehowah, from the face of the Lord of all the land.
	^{Dan 2:35}Then the iron, clay, bronze, silver, and gold were all crushed at once, and they became like chaff on a threshing floor strong wind took it away,
and no place for them was found. ¹²Then I saw the dead, both famous and ordinary, standing before the **throne**,	**and no place for them was found**, but the stone which struck the statue became a great mountain and filled all the Land.
	^{Ps 37:36}I looked for him [the wicked man] and he was **not found**.
	^{Dan 7:10}A million served him, a hundred million stood up before him [out of

and the books were opened

and another **book was opened**,

which is **[the Book] of Life**, and the dead were judged from the things written in **the books**,

[superscript]13[/superscript]**according to their works**. The sea gave up the dead who were in it, and death and Hades gave up the dead who were in them. They were judged, each **according to his works**. [superscript]14[/superscript]Then death and Hades were thrown into the lake of fire.

This is the

second death, the lake of fire, [superscript]15[/superscript]and if anyone will be found written in the Book of Life [he or she] was thrown into the lake of fire.

respect]. The judge sat down, **and the books were opened**.

[superscript]Dan 12:1[/superscript]In that time your people will escape, all who are found written in the **book**.

[superscript]Ps 69:28[/superscript]Give them [punishment for] iniquity upon their iniquity. Let them not enter into your [verdict of] righteousness. Let them be blotted out of **the Book of Life**; let them not be listed with the righteous.

[superscript]Mal 3:16; RuthR 5:6[/superscript]In the past, whenever someone performed a good **work**, the prophet recorded it; but now when someone performs a good **work**, who records it? Elijah, the Messiah, and the holy One blessed be He put their seal to it. This is what the verse means:

". . . the Lord listened, heard, and a **book of remembrance** was written before him."

[superscript]Ps 28:4[/superscript]Give to them **according to their works. According to their** evil **deeds,**

according to the works of their hands give to them. Return to them their deserved punishment.

[superscript]TgOnq Deut 33.6[/superscript]Let Reuben live (in the life of the age [to come]), and let him not die (**a second death**).

[superscript]TgJon Isa 22.14[/superscript]The prophet said, "I have been listening with my ears when it was decreed before Yehowah of armies, '[May the following unmentioned curses come upon me] if this debt is forgiven you until **the second death**," said Yehowah, God of armies.

^{TgJon, Isa 65.15}He will leave your name for a curse to my chosen ones, and the God, Yehowah, will kill you a **second death** but the righteous ones, his servants, he will call by another name.

^{Isa 15:8}He will swallow up **death** forever, and the Lord Yehowah will wipe away the tear from all the faces. The disgrace of his people he will turn away from all the land, because Yehowah has spoken.

COMMENTARY

A great white throne and one seated on it. This is the beginning of a new unit. Like Rev 20:4-10, this is a judgment scene--a different one. The judgment that began in Rev 20:4 was completed in Rev 20:10. With Rev 20:11 a judgment begins all over again, just as if it had not taken place. The reason for this is the way the Book of Revelation was organized in the first place. Some editor took all of the materials now found in Rev 4:1-22:5 and put them together in the most coherent way he could, but he did not compose the units. He had two judgment scenes, and he decided to use them both, one after the other.

Rev 20:11-15 seems like a vision of heaven, similar to the vision Isaiah had in the temple when he received his commission to prophesy. It was like visions of Micaiah, Enoch (1Enoch 14:18), Levi (TLevi 5:1), and also like the vision of the Ancient of Days, **seated on the throne** on the judgment day when Judas and the saints of the Most High were awarded the Promised Land. In Enoch's version of that judgment, the Lord of the sheep (Jews) **sat on a throne** that had been erected on the pleasant land, namely Palestine (1Enoch 90:20). Rev 20:1-10 described conditions before the judgment; when the Lord approached the bench and took his **seat**, court was in session. Weiss and Hailey, however, said it is not possible to know whether **the throne** was envisioned in heaven or on earth, because no clear distinction was made. Hailey further held that it really made no difference, since both were one.[1] Legally, this was true, because **the Messiah** was the agent of the Lord. When **the Messiah** sat **on the throne** in Zion, legally the Lord also sat on the throne through his representative.

---

[1] J. Weiss, *Offenbarung*, p. 677; Hailey, *Revelation*, p. 400.

From whose face earth and heaven fled. The allegations given to describe God in this situation were from Psalm 114 which described the sea personified, **fleeing from the face** of the Lord, as the Israelites escaped from Egypt under the leadership of Moses. In this instance the sea was personified. It "saw" and **fled** the way a human being would do when frightened. This was a dramatic way of saying that the tide moved back. In the same context, the Jordan turned back when Joshua wanted to cross it, and the **mountains and hills skipped like sheep, and the land trembled** (Ps 114:3-7). The author of the Revelation midrash put together parts of two Psalms. Ps 114 held that the sea saw, **fled**, and the land trembled from the **face** of the God of Jacob; Ps 97 said that the earth saw, and the land trembled when the Lord ruled as king. These descriptions fit nicely into Rev 20 where the Lord sat on his **great white throne** and ruled as king.

In the Revelation version, the author replaced the sea from Ps 144 with **the earth** from Ps 97, and he added **heaven** for good measure. Nevertheless the same kind of poetic personification was in force. They **fled** because of their fear of the terrible judge in Rev 20, just as **the earth trembled** from fear of the king in Ps 97, but this was not literal, physical **fleeing** which would evoke most people to ask where they went when they **fled** or where the judgment could be held if there was **no earth or heaven**.[1] The exegete, however, did not fall into the category of "most people." Still picturing the situation as if the earth and heaven were people who could run and hide in caves or behind trees, the author of this unit in Revelation said, **no place for them was found.** He took this answer from Dan 2:35 which described the statue that was demolished, and the wind blew away all of its parts that were shattered into dust, so that they could not be found.[2] The earth and heaven vanished like dust in the wind.

No place for them was found. Like dust blown away by the wind, the heaven and the earth had been ground to bits, like the pagan statue in Babylon (Dan 2:35). Even though they **could not be found,** in the author's imagination, they actually went some place away from the judge. Poetic personification and literal details were confused. These were problems exegetes had, because they had to get all of their answers from the Scripture. Authors in the Book of Revelation, like those in FT, liked this kind of personification (See also Rev 6:12-17; 16:20).

None of this means that the **earth and heaven** would **flee** the moment the **great white throne** appeared and **one took his seat**. Following Lattimore and Mealy, the description given here was of the one who **sat on the throne**--not on his activity at that time.[3] The one who sat on that **great white throne** (Rev 20:11) was

---
[1] A question asked by L. Gry, *Le Millénarisme dans ses origines et son dévelopement* (Paris: Picard, 1904), pp. 53-54.
[2] The exegete of this passage from Daniel rendered the Aramaic *ah-táhr* (אתר), correctly, as "place," rather than "trace," as the RSV has it.
[3] R. Lattimore, *Four Gospels and Revelation* (London: Hutchinson, 1979), p. 284; Mealy, *Thousand Years*, pp. 164-65.

the same one who ruled as king (Ps 97:1) and the one who acted at the Exodus from Egypt and the entrance into the Promised Land (Ps 114:3-7).

On this judgment day, it was not Judas and **the saints** who were contesting the possession of the Promised Land against the Syrian Greeks, but it was all the dead who were being raised to face the judgment. When Antiochus Epiphanes was judged guilty, he was killed, **and his body was burned** (Dan 7:11). All the guilty ones were thrown **into a lake of fire,** and their bodies were burned. If Antiochus Epiphanes' body had not been burned in Dan 7 **the lake of fire** would not have been essential to the author (Rev 20). It was their deeds by which the defendants were judged. This was consistent with Hebrew justice (TgJon Isa 65:7), but some Jewish testimony also indicated salvation either by faith or by works (4Ezra 8).

Standing at the throne. NA has **before the throne**, *eh-nóh-pee-awn* (ενώπιον) rather than *eh-peé* (ἐπί).

The books was opened. Sinaiticus made another homeoteluton error: His eye dropped from **books opened** to **book opened**, omitting the words in between, which are **opened** (pl.), **and another book.** This produced the odd sentence, **The books** (pl.) **was opened** (s.).

These were the briefs prepared before the trial by the prosecuting and defense attorneys. They included the accusations, the depositions, the evidence, and the arguments. They are not identical to the other book, namely the **Book of Life** (see further 2Bar 24:1-4; 4Ezra 6:20).

The Book of Life. This was a different **book** from the ones first mentioned. This was the record of the membership. The only members of the true community were those who had already passed judgment, and their names were then recorded in **the book of life**. Since they had already been judged favorably, they would not be contested again. There were others whose membership qualification was in question that would appear in the judgment, even after they had died. God had kept accurate books, which were presented like lawyers' briefs to be used in judging which way each case would go (see 1Enoch 47:3; AsIsa 9:21-22; TAbr 10:11-16; 2Bar 24:1).

The Book of Life contained the Judge's verdict. Those whose names were included in this **book** were vindicated, but those excluded were considered guilty and would have to face sentencing and punishment. Judgment was made according to the works of those appearing in court. This is acknowledged by Rissi, who said,

> At any rate, John makes clear that "works cannot save us". He does not allow us to place our hope on our deeds.[1]

This is more of an affirmation of faith than an analysis of the text.

---

[1] Rissi, *Future*, p. 36.

The dead were judged. These **dead** were not necessarily the same **dead** as the ones who had been beheaded (Rev 20:4) or the rest of **the dead** (Rev 20:5), because this is a different unit, composed by a different author.

The sea gave up the dead who were in it. Not aware of the physical and geographical reality of early Jewish and Christian beliefs, Hailey said the sea should be understood "symbolically."[1] The eleventh century IA author of "The Book of Zerubbabel," was more practical. He pictured the Messiah, son of David, and the prophet, Elijah, reading the prophecies of the Lord (probably Zech 14) on the shores of the Mediterranean Sea. As they read, the waves brought up all of the Jewish corpses. Because the Mount of Olives had already split in two, in fulfillment of Zech 14, and the water pouring out from the tunnel under the temple would have been adequate to supply two streams. One would be a river joining the Kidron Valley to the Mediterranean Sea (Zech 14:4-8).

The waves of the Mediterranean Sea, then, would wash all of the corpses from the sea upstream throuh the river to Jerusalem and deposit them in the Shittim Valley, near the Mount of Olives. That would take some fantastically large waves! There the Lord would conduct a judgment between the Jews and gentiles (Joel 4:18). Of course this ignored the laws of gravity and the direction rivers flow, but early Jews and Christians counted on miracles to take care of those difficulties. The river which was expected to join the Mount of Olives to the Mediterranean Sea would be called the river Soter, which in Greek means "savior."[2] This kind of exegesis seems ridiculous to twentieth century Westerners, but it was accepted by dogmatic exegetes as the literal, fulfillment of the prophecies upon which they depended. They had to their credit the fact that they kept the vision around the area of Jerusalem.

Death and Hades gave up the dead. These were probably the corpses buried in the ground, but **death and Hades** were treated here as if they were people who could hand over corpses the way a merchant might deliver goods.

They were judged, each according to his works. This was the great court case that would determine whether Jews or gentiles ruled the next age and also the one that determined who would be members of the victorious group in the age to come. The targumist said the Lord would punish the wicked for their deeds, but he would do all of this the way he acted with Noah when he established a new world for him. He

---

[1] Hailey, *Revelation*, p. 402.
[2] See futher Buchanan, *Jewish Messianic Movements*, p. 371. There are four variant texts of this passage. Two seem to indicate that Elijah and the Messiah would draw up all the corpses and throw them into the Shittim Valley which seems to be identical to the Valley of Jehoshaphat (also called the Kidron Valley). No mention is made of carrying the corpses all the way from the Mediterranean shores to the Mount of Olives. Maybe they visualized them throwing the corpses all that distance. These are details that authors of imaginary fulfillments of Scripture can include or exclude as they choose.

would not destroy all of the people. He would preserve the sons of Jacob (North Israel) and Judah (the southern kingdom) who would inherit the mountains of Palestine and the plains of Sharon and Achor and dwell there (TgJon Isa 55:7-10).

Death and Hades were thrown into the lake of fire. Again, **death and Hades** were personified as if they were people who could be hurled into a pit.

This was the second death. Many, like Rissi, have trouble making sense of **the second death.** He said,

> The expression, "second death," must in this case mean something other than in the case of the godless (20:15), who have already died once.[1]

Rissi correctly thought that the same people would not die twice **physically.** The text does not refer to the two judgments in two units on judgment, either (Rev 20:4-10 and 11-15). The same people were expected to die twice. One death was physical, and the other was legal. The legal **death** occurred when the person was excluded from the community in which there was legal life. The physical death was when he or she stopped breathing. If a person became apostate, and was therefore dead, legally, **the second death** was physical. It was the great judgment day which determined which of those who had died physically were also to face **the second death** which was legal. When the legal **death** was **second** it would come after the dead had been raised up for judgment and condemned. The Targum of Isaiah held that the punishment would be given not only for the transgressions individual Jews committed, but also for the transgressions of their fathers. **The second death** would be the last resort after they had already been punished in Gehinnom, where the fire burns all day (TgIsa 65:5-7). This is the Targumist's equivalent of **the lake of fire.**

If anyone will be found. NA has **was found**, which is consistent in tense with the following verb, **was thrown**, but the meaning is the same, because this is all a vision, which begins at Rev 20:11. The author saw it as if it had already happened, but he really intended this report to show that which would happen in the future.

---

[1] Rissi, *Future*, p. 70.

CHAPTER TWENTY-ONE

TEXT

Revelation	First Testament and Other Jewish Literature
^{21:1}Then I saw **a new heaven and a new land for the first** heaven and **the first land** have passed away, and the sea exists no longer.	^{Isa 65:17-18}Look! I am creating **a new heaven and a new land**. **The first** will not be remembered; it will not come to mind. So, be glad and rejoice as long as this lasts which I am creating, because look! I am creating **Jerusalem**, a rejoicing, and her people, a joy.
	^{Isa 66:22} "For just as **the new heaven and the new earth** which I am making stand before me," says Yehowah, "thus your posterity and your name will stand."
²I saw **the holy city**	^{Isa 52:1}Awake! Awake! Dress yourself with strength, Zion. Dress yourself with beautiful garments, **Jerusalem, the holy city** because the uncircumcised and the unclean will never again enter you.
	^{TDan 5:12-13}Saints will rest in Eden, and the righteous will rejoice in
the new Jerusalem, coming down from heaven, from God	**the new Jerusalem** . . . because the Lord will be in its midst.
	^{Isa 61:10}I will earnestly rejoice in Yehowah; my soul will exult in my God, because he has dressed me with garments of salvation, with a robe of righteousness he has covered me, as a bridegroom decks himself with a

prepared **as a bride adorned** for her husband.

garland, and **as a bride adorns** herself with her jewels.

TECHNICAL DETAILS

Rev 21:1-22:5 is a complete unit, probably written before the fall of Jerusalem in 70 IA. Before the fall of Jerusalem there was a beautiful, large temple in the City of David with an altar that was 75 feet X 75 feet and 22 ½ feet tall. The temple itself was probably also 75 feet wide, because the earlier Solomonic temple was 30 feet wide, and so was the altar. The Herodian temple was larger than the earlier temples, but it was probably consistently larger, with the altar of matching width. It had been constructed under Herod's rule at Roman expense. It was stationed just south of the Tower of Antonia, a 35 acre city and Roman Fortress that now encloses the Dome of the Rock and the Al Aqsa Mosque. The Roman fortress was built so that Roman guards could look down on the Jewish temple south of it and control it. Rome appointed the high priests and controlled their official garments, so that they could not conduct any activities without Roman permission.

The first temple was constructed when Solomon was king. It was designed and built by King Hiram of Tyre's contractors just like other Baal temples. Many conservative Jews thought it was pagan and refused to participate in its services. They thought the true place of worship was the tent that was used in the wilderness and also in Jerusalem when David was king. This was called the tent of God. Monasteries developed in Palestine where there were true priests, according to the views of the orthodox. These priests also kept their quarters, their food, and all of their garments undefiled. These were as valid as the tents of the wilderness. Rev 21:1-22:5 visualized a return to the days of the tent which meant that the temple would have to pass away. When the temple was destroyed in 70 IA, it was the Jewish soldiers, rather than the Romans who set it on fire. According to Matthew, Jesus predicted the destruction of the temple (Matt 24:2). When the disciples called Jesus' attention to the beautiful buildings of the temple, he said, "I am able to destroy the temple of God and in three days rebuild it" (Matt 26:61), which probably meant that he could replace with it with the tent of God, as David had before Solomon's rule.

Aune correctly noticed that Rev 21:1-4 consists of an *inclusion*. This is a literary form that has basically the same introduction as conclusion. It is also a *chiasm*. The latter form is based on the Greek letter *chi* (X), with the parallel sentences holding subjects and objects at opposite ends. The following is Aune's analysis:[1]

A new [καινός] heaven and the new [καινή] earth (v. 1a)
   b) first [πρῶτος] heaven, earth, and sea have passed away [ἀφῆλθαν] (v.1b)
      c) the sea exists no longer [οὐκ ἔστιν ἔτι] (v.1b)
         d) the holy city descends from heaven (v 2)

---

[1] D. Aune, *Revelation 17-22* (Nashville: Thomas Nelson Publishers, c1998), p. 1114.

d') God dwells with his people (vv. 3-4a)
c') death exists no longer [οὐκ ἔσται ἔτι] (v. 4b)
b') former things [τὰ πρῶτα] have passed away [ἀπῆλθαν] (v. 4b)
a') God creates everything new [καινά] (v. 5a).

Structurally, it looks like this, forming a *chi* (X).

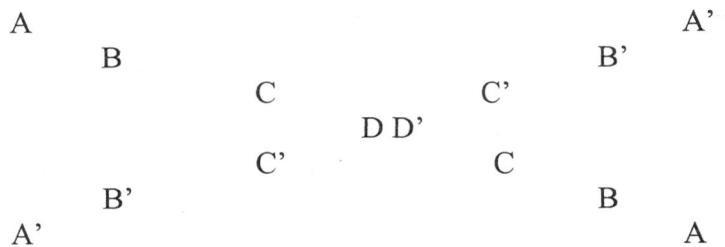

COMMENTARY

A new heaven and a new Land. The word here rendered **Land** is *áh-rehtz* (ארץ), which is sometimes rendered "earth." In most cases in the Scripture it means **land,** namely the Promised **Land** and has been mistranslated into English as "earth." There is another Hebrew word for "earth." It is *tay-behl* (תבל). Both in the quotation from Second Isaiah and for this entire chapter the subject is the Promised **Land** with its capital city, Jerusalem. The entire earth is not a concern. Therefore it is rendered here **a new land.** Even if it were translated "the earth" it would involve the earth only in the way that it changed the Promised Land.

Strand called attention to seven victorious introduction scenes in the prophecy which the messenger brought to John at Patmos. This vision of the **new heaven and the new Land** is the seventh of those. Others begin with Rev 4:1; 8:1; 11:19; 15:1; 16:18; and 19:1.[1] Hai Gaon said that in the new age the temple and Jerusalem would be revealed, and the *Sheh-kee-náh,* (שכינה) (God's legal presence or the Holy Spirit) would come down from **heaven** and be established as a pillar of fire that would reach **heaven from the earth.** He was speaking, of course, of the huge bon fire on the altar behind the Spring of Siloam, that made a pillar of fire by night and a pillar of smoke during the day. These joined earth to heaven in the City of David. Hai Gaon said further,

> In that hour they will see the heaven and the Land as if they had been renewed and as if [the] heaven and the Land of enslavement has

---

[1] K. A. Strand, "The 'Victorious-Introduction' Scenes in the Visions in the Book of Revelation," *AUSS* 25 (1987):267-88. Strand included also another victorious introduction scene (Rev 1:10b-20), but that scene would have been added by John of Patmos and would not have been part of the prophecy the angel brought him. There are some slight variations in boundaries of units. For example, Strand's second (third) unit begins with Rev 8:2 rather than 8:1. These are not significant changes.

passed away and were changed, and a new heaven and the Land were brought in their place, as it is said, **For look! I am creating a new heaven and a new Land** (Isa 65:17). Also they will see Jerusalem and Israel as if they were new, and as if Israel and Jerusalem of enslavement had been changed and passed away, and as if others were brought in their place, [an Israel and a Jerusalem] of joy and gladness, as it is said, **For Look, I am creating Jerusalem a delight and her people gladness** (Isa 65:18).[1]

Notice the number of times Hai Gaon said "as if." He expected the new **Jerusalem** to be exactly where it had been before. When the enslavement to foreign powers had disappeared, and Israel was ruled by its own king, the change was so great it was *as if* there were **a new heaven and a new Land**. He had no idea that history would come to an end, and the cosmos would be destroyed. That is an idea Westerners have invented.

Sweet asked, "How can the **new heaven and earth** beyond space and time contain all the material and measurable elements of 21:10 ff.?"[2] The answer is not the one he offered. **The new heaven and the new earth** were *not* expected to be beyond space and time.When the Lord created these he would also create **a new Jerusalem** (Isa 65:18). These new creations were expected to take place right here on earth with all of its normal geography, and that which was important was Jerusalem and the Promised Land. Neither Isaiah nor the author of Rev 21:1-22:5 believed that the earth was round. Their knowledge of the world was the Near East, and their concern for reconstruction was only the Promised Land. In order to introduce the tent of God to Jerusalem it would be necessary for Herod's temple, with its bronze sea (2Kings 25:13; 1Chron 18:8; Jer 52:17) and all of Rome's control to pass away. With a new heaven and a new Promised land, Jews would rule rather than Romans. That would make a tremendous difference. The dramatic and fantastic description of the new Promised Land is understandably hyperbolic.

When Third Isaiah spoke of the Lord making **a new heaven and a new Land,** he put it in a context where descendants of contemporary Jews would worship regularly on Sabbaths and new moons and where Jews would look on the battle field and see the corpses of the Lord's enemies, just as they actually saw them, scattered all over the Kidron Valley, Mount Scopus, and the Mount of Olives (Isa 66:22-24), after the syrians invaded Jerusalem, and 185,000 of them died in a single

---

[1] English translation: Buchanan, *Jewish Messianic Movements* (Eugene, Oregon: Wipf and Stock Publishers, 2003), p. 129.

[2] J. P. M. Sweet, *Revelation* (Philadelphia: Westminster Press, c1979), p. 297; C. Deutsch, "The Transformation of Symbols: The New Jerusalem in Rev 2:11-22:5," *ZNW* 78 (1987):115-16. For example F. Düsterdieck, *Critical and Exegetical Handbook to the Revelation of John*, tr. H. E. Jacobs (Winona Lake: Alpha Publications, 1884), pp. 476-77, said, "But in John the matter is different in a twofold respect; since, in the first place, he regards the new Jerusalem only after the history of the world, when the heaven and earth also are made new, and then regards the new Jerusalem as descending from heaven to earth."

night.¹ The whole **new creation** was expected to take place in such a way that posterity of family lines would continue intact, and physical bodies of human enemies would be killed. Remembering what happened to the Assyrians when they lined up on the mountains, looking down on Zion, Joel said,

> Let all the warriors come! . . . Hurry and come, all you nations round about! . . . Come up to the Valley of Jehoshaphat (Joel 3 [4]: 9-12).

Joel was boasting, taunting all the nations that thought they could take Zion, just as the Jebusites had taunted David many years earlier. The enemy nations could gather in the Kidron Valley, but they would then be mowed down like grain. Just look at what happened to the Assyrians! Whenever any nation threatened the holy city of David, it would learn that the streambeds of Judah flow with water. A fountain would pour out from the house of the Lord (Joel 3:18). It was this streambed, this fountain, this Spring of Siloam that poured out from under the threshold of the temple at Zion that provided Jews their security.

Like other Jews Joel thought that which God had done before he could and would do again. The author of the Book of Jubilees prophesied that in the recreation there would be a new sanctuary of the Lord established on Mount Zion, and there would be peace and blessing for all the elect of Israel (Jub 1:29). Whatever would happen to the rest of the world was of little interest. All of these practical events would take place in the creation of a **new heaven, a new Land,** and **a new Jerusalem**.

There are many poetic reports of cosmic disorder involved in the fulfillment of God's plans. When God gave Moses the ten commandments, the mountain was wrapped with clouds, and the event was heralded by thunder and lightning (Exod 19:18-19). When the Philistines and Israelites joined battle at Mount Carmel, **the stars in their courses fought against Sisera**. This meant that the rain poured down; the Brook Kishon flooded; the enemy's horses got stuck in the mud; and Israelites won a great victory (Judges 5). Later authors expected great signs in **the heavens** and on **earth** when the Lord would act in the future in a decisive way. One author expected a cosmic catastrophe when the sea would back off into the abyss as it had done for Moses in the Exodus (AsMos 10:6), and another expected the sea to dry up in the same way (SibOr 5:447).

These events were all expected while life on earth went on, just as they had at the Exodus, the revelation at Sinai, and at the defeat of Sisera near the Brook Kishon. Many modern scholars have overlooked the reality that was related to these poetic, hyperbolic descriptions and assumed they were all intended to be fulfilled literally in twentieth century terms.² Such exegesis is like analyzing Joyce Kilmer's

---

¹ On this see Buchanan, "The Tower of Siloam," *ET* 115.2 (2003):37-45; and "Running Water in the Temple of Zion," *ET* 115.9 (2004):289-92. This description implies that this portion of Isaiah was composed after the event of the Assyrian destruction at the Kidron Valley.
² J. W. Bowman, "A British Museum Arabic Eschatological Fragment," *The Muslim World* 38 (1948):198-217.

poem "Trees" literally. Trees do not really have hair and lips, but personification helps to tell how a person who loves trees feels about them. Trees do not really clap their hands, and mountains and hills do not really sing (Isa 55:12). Poets who describe mountains and trees this way do not expect readers to understand them literally.

The same is true when a nationalistic, religious person describes the great change that would take place in the world enabling his or her own country not only to become independent but to become the world superpower. Before events take place, imaginations of dreamers are not confined to physical facts. These dramatists do not tell what will happen to all of the other nations. That which is to become new was Jerusalem and the Promised Land. All the rest of the world would continue and bring huge gifts making Palestine wealthy and magnificent. There were no plans in the dream for a new Egypt, Rome, Spain, or any other country. This dream was for the prosperity and greatness of the Promised Land only.

Contemporary nationalists would all understand the poetic value of the hyperbole, but they really were mostly interested in the practical events that involved political independence in their own land. Less poetic and dramatic was Rabbi Johanan who said the Jerusalem of the age to come would be like the Jerusalem of this age with one exception. In this age any person might be admitted into the city. In the age to come Jerusalem would be an exclusive city. Only those invited might be admitted (bBBat 75b). The restriction policy would insure that no defilement entered the city.

Creating **a new heaven and a new Land** did not seem as cosmic or total to the ancients as it does to us. To them **the heavens** were not endless space in which are millions of galaxies, of which the earth is only one small unit. They thought of **heaven** as a huge tent roof, like those goat hair roofs used in Bedouin tents. They were not solid, like cement floors. They moved up and down, and they were changed with seasons. Biblical authors thought God spread out **the heavens** the way sheets are spread over beds, or like table cloths over tables. Of course, God spread them out (Job 9:8; Ps 104:2; Isa 40:22; 45:12; 51:13), and he could also roll them up (Isa 34:4) like a scroll or a tent roof. The Lord had hands, like human beings, and his hands were so big that he could put **the heavens** between his thumb and little finger (Isa 48:13).

Jubilees said the angel of the presence was commanded to write a document for Moses that told the events from creation until the sanctuary was built on Mount Zion. The angel of the presence was a legal agent who was currently present as a representative of someone else. The someone else here was God. Jerusalem was to be rebuilt. This would happen when **the Land** was renewed and a king was established on Mount Zion (Jub 1:27-29). The new creation did not destroy the geographical location of Jerusalem, or the palace of the king of Israel. Since Jubilees was written to report an interpreted history of the period between creation and the construction of Solomon's temple on the Promised Land,[1] the context shows that the author referred to the original establishment of the Kingdom in Palestine with a temple and a king as the renewal of the **Land and heaven**. There is no mention of the destruction of the cosmos or of time.

There are other contexts in which the renewal is associated with the temple and the establishment of the Promised Land, as if these nationalistic circumstances were hyperbolically called the renewal of the Land and heaven. For example, Second Baruch told of the development, during the time of Abraham, of the belief in a future judgment (feé-days yoo-dee-keé-ee foo-toó-ree, *fides iudicii futuri*), of hope for the renewal of the world (spays moon-dee kwee een-noh-váh-bee-toor, *spes mundi qui innovabitur*), and the promise of life that would come afterwards (proh-meé-see-oh veé-tai kwai póhs-tee-ah veh-née-eht, *promissio vitae quae postea veniet*). The author seemed to have based his message on the faith and hope that was initiated with the contract and promise God made to Abraham in Gen 15:1.

1) The promise involved the posterity of Abraham (Gen 15:5-6) and the Land (Gen 15:7, 18);
2) the future life was the return to the Land after the Exodus from Egypt (Gen 15:16);
3) the future judgment was the judgment promised against the Egyptians (Gen 15:14).

This means that the expression "renewal of the world" was used to indicate the conquest of Canaan, the establishment of the Davidic kingdom, and the construction of the temple. After the Babylonian Captivity and the promise of return, it was not difficult for Third Isaiah to update the concept with a promise that the Lord would create a new heaven and a new Land at the same time that he created Jerusalem (Isa 65:17-19). It was also reasonable for any Jew or Christian of NT times to describe the restoration of Jerusalem as something created in **heaven** and brought down to **earth** along with the creation of a **new heaven and a new Land.** By that time these were well established metaphors and were not actually expected to be implemented scientifically. If the land were restored, a new tent were built, and a new **Messiah** were to rule from Jerusalem, believers would consider that their expectations had been fulfilled. They would call this the creation of **a new heaven and a new Land.** Some Jews expected a new temple, but the author of Rev 21:1-22:5 looked for a new tent.

Cities in the Near East had been destroyed and rebuilt many times. When an attacking army destroyed a city, it burned the thatched roofs off all the buildings. This was easily done. To rebuild the city, some people had to lay another slab of cement over the ruins on the floors of buildings, add a foot or two of stones on top of the surviving walls, and construct a new thatched roof above the walls, and a new city was constructed. The authors probably had some concept such as that in mind

---

[1] For a modern, popular analysis of Jubilees see J. C. VanderKam, "Jubilees: How it Rewrote the Bible," *BibRes* 8 (1992):32-39, 60-62.

when they visualized the Lord creating a **new Land.** It did not involve dissolving the elements of the **earth,** because there continued to be a geographical place where **the new Jerusalem** could be established.

Some Muslim sects believed the world could talk, hear, and see. They thought further that, like human beings, the world grew old, and the angel of death would remove its breath.[1] Then everything would be restored to conditions before creation. It is difficult for twentieth century Westerners to think in such personified, cosmological terms as this, but it is necessary to be fair to the poetic language of a Near Easterner who expected **a new heaven and a new land** twenty centuries ago. Weiss reminded his readers that this vision was to direct believers to a paradise condition on earth rather than an ascension to heaven.[2]

At that time God would recreate the pure Land where no blood would be shed, and all people would always obey God's commands. These religious people did not think of the scientific details involved in destroying the cosmos with nuclear weapons and reconstructing the entire cosmos, *de novo*. The prophet who wrote this part of Revelation did not speculate about the way this would be done any more than the author of Gen 1:1-2:4 detailed the plan by which the world was created. God just gave the command, the way a monarch can do, and expected that it would take place. Like the king in *Camelot,* he could issue a decree and the weather would "be perfect all the year!"

The sea will be no more. This may not have had any effect on **the Sea** of Galilee, **the** Mediterranean **Sea,** or the Dead **Sea.** There was in the temple a huge bronze basin (1Kings 7:23-39; 1Chron 18:8; Jer 52:17), described in Ezek 1 and Dan 7 that was called **the sea.** It was supported by statues of beasts on whose backs the basin sat with their heads facing out. It was probably used for libations and washing sacrifices. It was part of the temple structure, which the author visualized as having vanished. Water from the Spring of Siloam was probably directed through this basin.

The author dreamed of a situation in which everything he disliked would be gone—especially the temple. There were other authors who expressed similar opinions. The Sibyl, for example, thought that at the last times the sea would be dry. If he had the entire Mediterranean in mind, this would destroy the shipping business of Italy, Cyprus, Crete, and Tyre--all enemies of Israel whose prosperity Jews and early Christians resented, but upon whose economy Israel also depended (SibOr 5:447-56). The Sibyl may have thought only of a temporary event, like the one that occurred when the Israelites escaped from Egypt.

Another Jewish author anticipated the coming of God's kingdom at a time when Israel would be happy after having overpowered Rome. All the gentiles would be thrown into Gehennom, and **Satan** would be no more. In association with these joyous events the mountains and hills would be removed; the sea would retire into

---

[1] "The Book of Elijah," A. Jellinek, *Bet Ha-Midrasch* (Jerusalem: Wahrmann Books, 1967) III, p. 67.
[2] J. Weiss, *Offenbarung des Johannes* (Göttingen: Vandenhoeck & Ruprecht, 1908), p. 681.

the abyss; and all the rivers and springs would dry up (AsMos 10). These authors evidently did not seem to have considered the practical consequences of this damage to Israel's economy.

The new Jerusalem coming down from heaven. The Testament of Dan (TDan) also anticipated a **new Jerusalem** where the saints would rest in Eden and the righteous would rejoice. At that time **Jerusalem** would no longer be desolate, and Israel would no longer be in captivity. God would provide peace for those who turn to the Lord and call upon him (TDan 5:9-13). Jews and early Christians never dreamed of a holy city that was permanently stationed only in **heaven.** The temple at **Jerusalem** had been built according to a plan received from God's own hand (Exod 25:40; 1Chron 28:19; Sol 9:8; Ps 78:69; Mek *Shirata* 10:29-42) and was constructed by God's hands (Exod 15:17). With all the cosmic activity related to **the New Jerusalem**, Paradise, or the Garden of Eden, it was generally assumed that this would all be related to an earthly condition where **the saints** would refresh themselves (1Enoch 90:33-36) and rejoice (TDan 5:12-13). God had made his name to dwell there (1Kings 8:29; Ezek 48:35). This meant that God was legally present there at the same time that he was physically presenting heaven.

When Adam and Eve were expelled from the Garden of Eden, they were driven east of the Garden of Eden (Gen 3:24). Once Jews were removed from Palestine to Babylon, east of Palestine, they may have thought of Palestine as the Garden of Eden and Babylon as the place where Jews, like Adam and Eve, were driven when they had eaten the forbidden fruit. Evidence for this is found in the prophecy of Ezekiel where **Jerusalem** and the surrounding area was described in terms like those of the Garden of Eden (Ezek 47). In behalf of the Lord, Ezekiel said, **This land which has been a desolation has become like the Garden of Eden** (Ezek 36:33-35).

In the Book of Revelation, Rome was really to the west of Palestine, but Jews and early Christians continued to contrast Babylon to the Garden of Eden. Typology was so much a part of their thinking that they had no trouble saying "east" when they really meant "west," any more than they had saying "Babylon" when they meant "Rome," and by the Garden of Eden they meant the Promised Land restored with **Jerusalem** as its capital. Restoration to the Promised Land meant being restored to the Garden of Eden from the world outside Eden. These were code terms that had historical, political, and religious significance for the people who understood the code. After the temple had been destroyed in 586 BIA, Ezekiel reportedly was given a vision of the ideal temple that he described in detail so that the temple might be built according to that plan when it was restored (Ezek 40-48).

Jerusalem was praised as **the highest of the mountains** (Isa 2:2); **the city of Yehowah, Zion, the holy One of Israel** (Isa 60:14). In reality Zion was a little town. The remnants of that city are now only about 10-12 acres in size on a ridge, just across the Kidron Valley from much taller mountains. In biblical times it was probably about three times as large, built out by the Jebusites and Solomon, but still a small city. Second Isaiah prophesied that the Lord would make Zion's wilderness become like **the Garden of Eden, the Garden of Yehowah** (Isa 51:3). That would involve it being populated with monks as prophesied in Rev 14:1-5. The restored Garden of Eden would have to be as it was before the curse of marriage, before Eve became pregnant and Adam had to work for a living to support his family. One of the medieval rabbis said,

> Elijah said, "I see a great and beautiful city, coming down from heaven just as it was constructed, as it is said, **Jerusalem, built like a city which is bound together**" (Ps 122:3).

Commenting on this Psalm, Rabbi Johanan said that the holy One blessed be He would not enter into the heavenly **Jerusalem** until he had entered the earthly **Jerusalem** (Mid Ps 122:4).[1] An anonymous Jewish author said,

> Then the holy One blessed be He will bring down the temple from heaven, just as the holy One blessed be He showed to Moses, as it is said, **You will bring them, and you will plant it in the mountain of your inheritance, the place of your residence, you have done the work, O Lord**.[2]

Rabbis thought of heavenly **Jerusalem** always in relationship to earthly **Jerusalem**. They understood that there would be a temple brought down **from heaven** and resituated at **Jerusalem,** but the first time that claim was made was in the Book of Revelation. There are also other traditions reflected in rabbinic literature belonging to the medieval period which are the same as those first recorded in the Book of Revelation. This may mean that rabbis had access to this document, or it may mean that the traditions were known in Judaism earlier but not recorded anywhere except in the Book of Revelation.

Even though no extant data shows an expectation of a temple brought **down from heaven** prior to the Book of Revelation, it was widely believed that temples were of divine origin. The temple built at Lagash was the result of a dream in which the goddess Nidaba revealed to the king the plan of the temple.[3] Like **Jerusalem** (2Bar 4:2-7; Tob 13:16; Isa 60:11-14; Ezek 40), other cities were built according to heavenly archetypes. This was true of cities such as Sippar, Nineveh, and Assur.[4]

---

[1] M. Eliade, *Cosmos and History: The Myth of the Eternal Return*, tr. W. R. Trask (New York: Harper Torchbooks, 1959), p. 7; E. Burrows, "Some Cosmological Patterns in Babylonian Religion," *The Labyrinth*, ed. S. H. Hooke (London: S.P.C.K., 1935), pp. 65 ff.; C. T. Fritsch, "TO ANTITYPON," *Studia Biblica et Semitica* dedicated to Th. C. Vriezen (Leiden: E. J Brill, 1966), pp. 100-07).
[2] Buchanan, *Jewish Messianic Movements*, p. 446.
[3] Eliade, *Cosmos*, p. 7-8.
[4] D. Flusser, "Two Notes on the Midrash on II Sam 7," *IEJ* 9 (1959):99-104; see also Y. Yadin, "A Midrash on II Sam 7 and Ps 1-2 [4Q Florilegium]," *IEJ* 9 (1959):93-98; R. Hummel, *Die Auseinandersetzung zwischen Kirche und Judentum* (München: Kaiser, 1963), pp. 106-07; Matt 26:61; 27:40; Mark 14:58; 15:29; John 2:9; Acts 6:14.

(see also Tob 13:9 ff; 14.5; Jub 4:26; 2Bar 4:3-5; 32:2-4; 4Ezra 7:26; 8:52-53; 10:26-27, 44-59; 13:36. Also 1Enoch 6-36; 83-90; TDan 5:12-13). Halver has shown that there were many countries in antiquity that believed their own capital city to be the center of the universe and the holy city.[1]

Plato was not the only author who had the idea that all earthly things were created according to a heavenly prototype. This concept was common in the ancient Near East. After the Babylonians destroyed the temple which had been built according to the pattern given on Mount Sinai, Jews looked forward to the time when the heavenly city and the heavenly temple would be reestablished on earth, still more luxurious than before in the same position where the type formerly stood--Zion (4Ezra 7:26; 8:52; SibOr 5:420-29). According to Pseudo-Philo, Joshua called the altar built across the Jordan by the 2½ tribes living there an **altar made with hands** (sahk-ráh-ree-oom mahn-oo-fáhk-toom, *sacrarium manufactum*) (Pseudo-Philo 22:5).[2] Some of the Dead Sea fragments seem to reflect an anticipation of the destruction of the then existing temple, built by the Romans, and the establishment of one built with God's hands (4QFlor).

Flusser compared this to the report that Jesus planned to destroy the temple and build another not made with hands. The expression "made with hands" (*khay-raw-poí-ay-taws*, χειροποίητος) frequently referred to idolatry in the Old Greek (OG) translation of the Scripture, rendering *eh-leél* (אליל) or *eh-lee-leém* (אלילים) The OG version of Daniel rendered these terms **gods** or **idols made with hands**; Stephen described both the temple and the golden calf as objects **made with hands**; and Paul was quoted in relationship to the pagan temples in Athens as saying that the Lord did not dwell in temples made with hands (*khay-raw-poi-áy-tois nah-oís*, χειροποιήτοις ναοῖς (Acts 17:24. See also Isa 2:18; 19:1; 31:7; LXX Dan 5:4, 23; 6:27 [28]; Acts 7:41, 48),[3] which meant God did not dwell in pagan temples. Enoch said the temple had been folded up and carried off. After that, however, the Lord of the sheep provided a new temple (*beht kháh-deesh*) which was bigger, but placed where the old one had formerly been (1Enoch 90:28-29). Fourth Ezra thought that when the Messiah appeared the city which had previously been hidden would be revealed (4Ezra 7:27, Arabic text). When the Son is revealed Zion will become visible to everyone, prepared and built **without hands** (see-nay máhn-ee-boos, *sine manibus*) *(*4Ezra 13:36).[4] The Sibyl referred to the **Jerusalem** temple as "the temple built by God" (SibOr 5:150). The author of Hebrews addressed people on earth when he reminded them that they had come to

---

[1] H. Halver, *Der Mythos im Letzten Buch der Bible* (Hamburg-Bergstadt: H. Reich, 1964), p.112.
[2] S. G. Sowers, *The Hermeneutics of Philo and Hebrews* (Richmond: John Knox Press, 1965), p. 110, n. 57.
[3] For this whole discussion, see Buchanan, *The Consequences of the Covenant* (Leiden: E. J. Brill, 1970), pp. 76-80, and *To the Hebrews* (Garden City: Doubleday & Co., 1972), pp. 135-36. R. Martin-Achard, "Esaie LIV et la Nouvelle Jerusalem," *VTSup* 32 (1981):238-262, argued that Isa 54:10-13 was integral to the entire message of Second Isaiah and the topic of discussion was the new Jerusalem.
[4] Buchanan (tr.), *Jewish Messianic Movements*, pp. 526-28. The text is from Ch. Albek, *Beresit Rabbati* (Jerusalem, 1967) [Hebrew], *daf* 89-90, pages 136, line 3-137, line 18.

Mount Zion, city of the living God, heavenly Jerusalem, myriads of angels, a national assembly, a church of first-born [people], enrolled in heaven (Heb 12:22-23).

This does not imply that all of these Christians were in **heaven**, but that they had come to **Jerusalem** for a national assembly at the occasion of a feast. Zion was not only called **heavenly Jerusalem,** but Philo called it "the city of God" (*Dreams* 2:250).The Sibyl called the godlike Jews who lived around the city of God (**Jerusalem**) "the heavenly race of the blessed Jews" (SibOr 5:49). The "heavenly race" was a group of people who lived on **earth** at a certain geographical site. Rabbis interpreted the text **And I brought you to myself** (Exod 19:4) to mean God brought them to the temple (*bayt beh-chee-ráh,* בית בכירה) (Mek., *Bahodesh* 2:24-25). Judah Halevy, in his poem, "Longing for Zion," wrote, "Your Creator opens your [Zion's] gates before the gates of heaven."[1] Jewish and early Christian expectation was not that all believers would be taken up to **heaven**, but that the Lord had condescended to come to earth and make his legal presence there, in one selected spot--Zion, the temple at **Jerusalem,** a house **not built with hands**, eternal in the **heavens,** but also firmly established at **Jerusalem**. Biblical authors had never heard of the nineteenth century concept of "the rapture." Some Jews thought the temple itself had been built with hands, but when the Son is revealed, Zion will become visible to all people, prepared and built without hands (*parata et aedificata . . . sine manibus*) (4Ezra 13:36).[2]

There is no doubt that Jews and Christians believed there was a tent type or a temple type in **heaven** after which the **Jerusalem** temple was patterned. Some Jews thought it was a temple type, but those, like the author of Rev 21:1-22:5, thought it had to be a tent type. Paul spoke of the **Jerusalem** above which was free (Gal 4:26), but the prayer on the hearts of nationalistic Jews was that this heavenly temple be brought down to the same location where Solomon's temple had been built. Rabbis said the holy One blessed be He said he would not enter **Jerusalem** which is above until he had entered **Jerusalem** which is below (bTaan 5a; see also 1Enoch 90:28-29; 4Ezra 7; bBBat 75b). Many people have been killed since 1947 because many Jews and Christians mistakenly believe the heavenly temple has to be located exactly on the very geographical earthly spot where the Moslem Dome of the Rock is now situated. That was the location of Herod's fortress, Antonia, which Jews of NT times hated. The following is a brief Jewish medieval sermon about the heavenly temple.

---

[1] Tr. Buchanan, *Jewish Messianic Movements*, p. 254. See further Buchanan, *Hebrews*, p. 222.
[2] For this whole discussion, see Buchanan, *The Consequences of the Covenant* (Leiden: E. J. Brill, 1970), p. 76-80.

HEAVENLY JERUSALEM

This is none other than the house of God (Gen 28:17).

Our rabbis said: "That day when the death of Moses, our teacher, had drawn near, the holy One blessed be He took him up to the exalted heavens and showed him his reward as well as that which was destined to take place. The attribute of mercy stood before Moses, our teacher (upon whom be peace), and said, 'I will announce good news to you in which you will rejoice. Turn your face toward the throne of mercy and look!' He turned his face toward the throne of mercy and saw the holy One blessed be He building the house of the sanctuary with precious stones and pearls, and among all the stones [as mortar] was the splendor of the Shekinah, which was better than pearls, and the Messiah son of David was standing in the midst with his brother, Aaron, standing up and wearing his robe. Aaron spoke at this time with Moses, 'Do not touch me, for I am afraid concerning you because of the Shekinah; since a man cannot enter there until he tastes the taste of death and gives his soul to the angel of death.'[1]

When he heard the words of Aaron, he fell on his face before the holy One blessed be He and said, 'Master of the age, give me authority to speak with your Messiah before I die.' The holy One blessed be He said [apparently to an angel], 'Go, teach him my great name, so that the flame of the Shekinah will not consume him, when he sees that Messiah son of David. Then inform Aaron, his brother, that the Lord has taught him his great name.' The Messiah and Aaron stood before him and said to him, **Blessed be he who comes in the name of the Lord** (Ps 118:26).

Moses asked the Messiah of David, "Tell me, will the holy One blessed be He build the house of the sanctuary on earth for the Israelites, and may I see him building the house of the sanctuary with his hand?' The Messiah said to Moses, 'Moses, your father Jacob saw the house which he will build on the land, and he saw the house which the holy One blessed be He will build in heaven with his hand, and he understood with all his might that the house which the holy One blessed be He will build with his hand in heaven will be with precious stones and pearls and with the splendor of the Shekinah. [This] will be the house which will exist for the Israelites for an age and for ages of ages[2] until the end of all generations."

---

[1] Since Aaron was a priest he was not permitted to defile himself by touching a dead person.

[2] Ages here refer to temporal units, like generations. A prime example of mixing concepts is that of M. Rissi, *The Future of the World* (Naperville: Allenson, c1966), p. 40: "Without doubt, the heavenly Jerusalem is for Paul 'the new aeon.'"

Thus he said at night when he was sleeping on the stone and saw Jerusalem built on the earth and Jerusalem built in heaven. While the holy One blessed be He was standing he saw Jacob our father and said to Jacob, 'Jacob, my son, I am now **stationed above** you and until your sons are established before me, as it is said, **Look! the Lord was stationed above him** (Gen 28:13). [Regarding] the Israelites, **they are stationed at the foot of the mountain** (Exod 19:17), and it says, **[all of] you are stationed this day**' (Deut 29:9). When Jacob saw Jerusalem, once on earth and once in heaven, he said, 'This is not anything at all which is on earth, as it is said, **This is nothing but the house of God** (Gen 28:17). **This** is not **the house** which will stand for my sons for generations of generations, but rather that **house of God** which he is building with his hands.' Should you say, 'The holy One blessed be He will build for himself **a house** of the sanctuary with his hands [in heaven],' thus will he build it with his hand on earth, as it is said, **The sanctuary, O Lord, your hands have established it** (Exod 15:17).

When Moses our teacher (upon whom be peace) heard these words [in the presence] of the Messiah son of David, he rejoiced greatly and turned his face toward the holy One blessed be He and said, 'Master of the age, when will you bring down this Jerusalem which is now being built?'[1] The holy One blessed be He said, 'That which I have not disclosed to any living being, neither to the first ones nor to the last ones, shall I tell you?' [Moses] said to him, 'Master of the age, give me a hint of which is being done.' The holy One blessed be He said to him, 'I will scatter the Israelites at first in a dispersion within the gates of the earth, and they will be scattered to the four corners of the earth among all the gentiles, so that in them the Scripture may be fulfilled, where it is written, **Even if your outcasts [are in the uttermost parts of the heavens, from there the Lord your God will gather you and from there he will bring you]** (Deut 30:4). My hand will gather a second time, and I will bring back those who went with Jonah ben Amiti[2] to the land of the Pathrosians and who will be in the land of Shinar, Hamath, Elam, Ethiopia, etc., as it is said, **[It will happen in that day that the Lord will set his hand again to receive the remnant of his people who will remain in Assyria, Egypt, Pathros, Ethiopia, Elam, Shinar, Hamath, and the isles of the sea]** (Isa 11:11).

Moses then came down from heaven, happy. The angel of death descended after him, but he did not give his spirit and his soul

---

[1] This is the burning, eschatological question. The important point of God's work in heaven is how it is related to Israel, the land, and the temple.

[2] This is probably an error for Yohanan ben Korah (Jer 43:5).

to the angel until the holy One blessed be He had revealed himself to him. Then he gave up his soul to the holy One blessed be He with a perfect heart and a longing soul. This is the meaning of [the verse] **This is none other than the house of God** (Gen 28:17)."[1]

Another medieval Jewish prophecy is the following:

RESTORATION OF THE TEMPLE[2]

Then a fire will come down from heaven and consume Jerusalem until [only] three cubits [are left], and he [the Messiah] will clear out the strangers, the uncircumcised, and the defiled [Jews] from its midst. Then the perfected, rebuilt Jerusalem will come down from heaven, in which will be seventy-two pearls which will shine from one end of the world to the other. All the gentiles will walk towards its shining, as it is said, **gentiles will walk to your light** (Isa 60:3). Then the [already] constructed temple will descend from heaven, for it is bound to the celestial abode, for this is what Moses (upon whom be peace) saw through the Holy Spirit,[3] as it is said, **You shall bring it, and you shall plant it [on the mountain of your inheritance; a place of your dwelling you have constructed, Lord; a temple, Lord, your hands have prepared it]** (Exod 15:17).

In one medieval Jewish document, the author said the Lord would bring down a rebuilt **Jerusalem from heaven**, Elijah was shown, coming and building the temple of the Lord in its position.[4] The poet, Judah Elharizi said:

Zion, which many governments have honored, // but no human eye has seen [anything] like her splendor .// I do not know if the heavens bent down before her, // or if she ascended beyond the heavens.[5]

---

[1] This conclusive allusion to the introductory text provides an inclusion to set this narrative apart as a separate unit, distinct from the surrounding literature. This unit was translated by Buchanan, *Jewish Messianic Movements*, pp. 526-28, from the Hebrew text of S. A. Wertheimer, *Peér-kay Hay-kah-lóht Rah-báh-tee* (פרקי היכלות רבתי) (Jerusalem, 1890), 6:3-7:2 [3b-4a].

[2] This paragraph is from a long redemption document which now appears in three Hebrew documents that are somewhat parallel: "The Prayer, Secrets, and Mysteries of Rabbi Shimon ben Yohai," translated from the text of A. Jellinek, בית המדרש (*Beht hah Meéd-rahsh*) (8 vols; Jerusalem: Wahrmann Books, 1967) III, 78-82. A similar text is "The Future Events of Rabbi Shimon ben Yohai," translated from the text of Ch. M. Horowitz, בית עקד האגדות (*bayt áy-kehd hah-ah-gah-dóht*) (Frankfort a. M., 1881), pp. 51-55. The third text is "The Prayer, of Rabbi Shimon ben Yohai," from the text of A. Jellinek, *Bet ha Midrasch* IV, pp. 118-26. They are translated into English in Buchanan, *Jewish Messianic Movements*, p. 404.

[3] The fact that it now occurs in the Torah means the Holy Spirit revealed it to Moses.

[4] From "The Story of Daniel (Upon Whom be Peace)," tr. by Buchanan, *Jewish Messianic Movements*, p. 474.

[5] Buchanan, *Jewish Messianic Movement*, p. 262, from Elharizi's Hebrew poem, "Jerusalem." There were other writings that showed that medieval Jews expected a new temple to be brought down from heaven. See *Jewish Messianic Movements*, pp. 446, 474, 486.

COMMENTARY

The new Jerusalem. When Paul spoke of the church members as members of the **Jerusalem** above (Gal 4:26) he probably meant that the **Jerusalem** of the future, which would be brought down to earth, would be one comprised of Christian citizens. Among the Dead Sea Scrolls was found an Aramaic document also describing **a new Jerusalem,** based on Ezek 48 but with more extensive measurements. It was to have twelve gates and streets made of precious stones (5Q 15). Baillet, Milik, and deVaux, after translating this document, were correct in saying,

> It is not impossible that the author of the Greek apocalypse of the NT knew our Aramaic description of the New Jerusalem. The enormous holy city of chapter 21 is encircled by a bulwark with twelve gates, exactly as that of the manuscripts of Qumran and not as the small city of Ezekiel.[1]

Prepared as a bride. **Jerusalem** was personified as a beautiful woman, adorned with fancy garments and jewels, the way a bride would be adorned before the wedding. This was a reasonable metaphor. **Jerusalem** was the capital city of the Promised Land. The people of Israel were also identified as a bride. This was legally based on corporation logic. A corporation can be legally treated as a human being. It can buy and sell, enter into legal disputes, and make contracts. The contract the people of Israel made with the Lord was considered to be a marriage contract. The parties to this contract were the bride and the groom. If **Jerusalem** was to be the bride, then the Lord was the bridegroom whose legal agent was the Messiah. The ceremony would be the establishment of the new contract between the Lord and his people that Jer 31:31 promised. Rabbis, commenting on Exod 19:17, said Yehowah came from Sinai to receive Israel the way a bridegroom comes to meet the bride at a wedding (Mek *Bahodish* 3:115-119). Therefore either the Israelites or their capital city, **Jerusalem,** could be pictured as the bride.

Cities were often personified as women, sometimes in less than glorious situations. When **Jerusalem** was destroyed, for example, the Edomites stood around and watched, as if they were watching a disgraced woman, saying, **Strip her! strip her! all the way down!** (Ps 137:7).[2] Zion was pictured as a divorced woman during

---

[1] M. Baillet, J. T. Milik, and Roland deVaux, *Les 'Petites Grottes' de Qumran* (Oxford: Clarendon Press, 1962), p. 186. See further pp. 184-192. See also M. Wilcox, "Tradition and Redaction of Rev 21, 9-22, 5," *L'Apocalypse johannique et l'Apocalyptique dans le Nouveau Testament* ed. Jans Lambrecht (Gembloux: Ducolot, 1980), pp. 212-13.

[2] Deutsch, "Transformation," pp. 112-13, said the point of the bride symbol suggests newness, ardor, beauty, and intimacy. The most important point of the symbol of the bride is the new contract. Just as the Lord made a contract with his people to be their husband at Sinai, so here the Lord will marry his people again, making with them a new marriage contract, as Jeremiah, Ezekiel, and Zechariah promised that he would do. For early Christian interpretations of Rev 21:1-22:5 see Justin Martyr, *Dial* 73; Ireneus, *AdvHaer* 5:35, 2; Tertullian, *AdvMarc* 3:25; Hermas, *Vis* 4:3,6-7.

the Babylonian captivity, but when Jerusalem was expected to be rebuilt, Second Isaiah described the city as "married." It was "married" to the Promised Land and married to the Lord. With **Jerusalem** in marriage were her sons, the Jews who returned to **Jerusalem** (Isa 62:4-5). The contract the Israelites made with the Lord was a marriage contract in which God was the groom and Israel was the bride.

Halver has shown that in many ancient religions and cultures, people believed that heaven was married to the earth. In India, for example, this was so apparent in the consciousness of the people that an ordinary wedding ceremony involved the husband saying to his wife, "I am heaven; you are the earth." In some cultures the victorious king, returning from battle, received the bride.[1] This myth implied that the king, as legal agent of the deity, received the kingdom in behalf of the deity as part of the marriage contract.

After Constantine conquered Rome, and Christians were placed in a position of prestige and power, Eusebius interpreted this whole event theologically as he rejoiced. With that victory, Jesus became the very Son of the God and was himself God (*HE* 10:4, 16)--legally, of course. Eusebius thought that prior to Jesus, the only way the word of God came to human beings was through the Scripture. With the incarnation of Jesus, however, God had a legal agent with authority to speak his word. That was God's *word* made flesh--not God made flesh. God's message was communicated to earth through a human agent. On this basis, Eusebius said,

> For what could resist the will of the universal king, ruler of the universe, (*pahm-bah-see-leh-ohs kai pah-nay-geh-máw-naws*, παμβασιλέως καὶ πανηγεμόνος and the word of God himself (*HE* 10:4, 20).

The fact that Jesus was called the word of God meant he was only legally God, according to Eusebius. He was the word of God made flesh the way the secretary of state is the word of the president of the USA made flesh. He is free to negotiate in behalf of the president and in his name. His resulting statement is the word of the president. As a legal agent Jesus was legally identical to the principal (God) who sent him.[2]

J. Fekkes, "'His Bride Has Prepared Herself': Revelation 19-21 and Isaian Nuptial Imagery," *JBL* 109 (1990):269-87, has shown how closely dependent these chapters in Revelation are upon Second Isaiah for bridal imagery.

[1] Halver, *Mythos*, p. 114.

[2] See further Buchanan, *Biblical and Theologial Insights from Ancient and Modern Civil Law* (Lewiston: Edwin Mellen Press, 1992), chapter six.

TEXT

Revelation	First Testament
³A loud voice from the throne was saying, "Look! **The tent of God** is with human beings.	Exod 40:34 The cloud covered **the tent of** meeting (*oh-hehl moh-áyd,* אהל מועד); the glory of Yehowah filled **the tent** (*mish-kahn,* משכן)
	Sir 24:10 In the holy **tent**
He will tentdwell with them, **and**	I **dwelled** before him; and thus I was established in Zion. Sir 24:4 My **tent-dwelling** place was in high heaven. My throne was in a pillar of cloud.
	Zech 2:14 "Sing and be glad, daughter of Zion, because look! I am coming, and **I will dwell** in your midst," says Yehowah.
	Joel 4:17 I am Yehowah, your God, who **dwells** in Zion, my holy mountain.
	Exod 25:8 They will make me **a sanctuary**, and **I will dwell** in their midst.
	Jer 7:3 Improve your ways and your works, and **I will dwell with** you in this place.
	Exod 29:45 **I will dwell** in the midst of the Israelites, and I will be their God.
	Ezek 43:7 **I will dwell** there in the midst of the Israelites for the age.

they themselves will be his people;
God himself **will be with them**

and he will
wipe away every tear from their eyes. **Death will** be no longer.

There will be neither **lamentation** nor **crying**, because the first things have vanished."

⁵The One **seated on the throne** said to me,

"Look! I am making all things **new**." He said, "Write, 'These words

Ezek 37:27 I will be their God and **they will be my people**.

Zech 8:8 I will deliver my people from the land of the rising sun. I will bring them, and **I will dwell** in the midst of Jerusalem. **They will be my people, and I will be their God**.

Jer 31:32-33 This is the contract that I will make with the house of Israel after those days . . . I will be their God **and they will be my people**.

Lev 26:11-12 I will put my **tent** in your midst, and I will not abhor you. I **will** walk in your midst. I **will** be your God, **and** you **will be my people**.

Isa 25:8 He has swallowed up **death** forever, **and the Lord Yehowah will wipe the tear from all their** faces. The disgrace of his people he will turn from all the land, because the Lord has spoken.

Isa 66:22 "For just as the new heaven and the new earth which I am making stand before me," says Yehowah, "thus will your posterity and your name stand."

Isa 65:19 I rejoice in Jerusalem, and I am glad with my people. The voice of weeping and the voice of **crying** will not be heard in it.

Isa 6:1 In the year that King Uzziah died I saw the Lord, **seated on the throne**, high and exalted. His train filled the temple.

Isa 43:19 **Look! I am making** [something] **new**. Now it is emerging.

are faithful and true.'" ⁶Then he said to me, "They have happened."

ᴵˢᵃ ⁶⁵:¹⁷Look! I am making a **new** heaven and a **new** Land.

COMMENTARY

A loud voice from the throne was saying. NA introduced this expression with the words **I heard**, and instead of **was saying** has **saying.**

The tent of God is with human beings. **The tent of God** was the *meésh-kahn,*(מִשְׁכָּן) (Exod 26:1-35; Num 9:15-22; and frequently) or the *óh-hehl* (אוֹהֵל) (Exod 31:7-9; 33:8-11; and frequently) which moved with the Israelites through the wilderness and was later moved to **Jerusalem** (1Sam 6:1-19). Wherever **the tent of God** went, **God** was understood to be legally present. **The tent** was the place in the wilderness where the contract was kept and where court sessions took place. The judges who functioned at this **tent** were legally **God's** agents, whose decisions were held to be God's decisions. Wherever **God's** agents functioned, **God** was legally present.

The Hebrew word for dwell is *shah-káhn* (שָׁכַן); the place to **dwell** is the *meésh-kahn* or tent; the act of dwelling is *sheh-kee-náh* (שְׁכִינָה) or presence. Therefore, when **God's tent** is pitched among human beings, it means that his presence is legally there, just as a plaintiff or defendant is legally present in court when the respective attorney is there. It was in **God's tent** or **the tent** of meeting where the marriage contract was kept, the contract that united the people of Israel with their God. It was in God's tent where Moses and subordinate judges met with Israelites to settle disputes. There is where they went to "see God." When Second Isaiah said,

> Look for Yehowah while he may be found;
> Call upon him while he is near (Isa 55.6),

He meant the Israelites should go to God's tent, and get their crimes pardoned, offenses vindicated, and defilements cleansed. That tent held the contract that contained the terms, both the demands made upon the people and the blessings they would receive if they observed them. The contract provided the terms of God's relationship with his people. The security of the relationship depended on the existence of that contract. The psalmist said,

> There is a river whose streams make glad the city of God,
> The holy tent (*meésh-kahn*, מִשְׁכָּן) of the Most High (Ps 46:4).

The city of God was Zion, from whose **holy tent** may have been the tent of God that David established beside the Spring of Siloam (Gihon) or it may have been the later temple that had a holy and a holy of holies inside, both of which were also called tents. This was **the very holy tent** where the **Most High dwelled**. This great spring was a rarity in the Middle East, where the streams flow in the winter, but become dry wadies in the summer. This was the **river** which **made glad the city of God**, David's **holy city** of Zion. It was King David who had **the tent** installed near the spring where the Jebusites may have had an altar before David's arrival. David had the chest containing the contract brought to Jerusalem and placed in that **tent.** This **tent** was the dwelling place of **the Most High**.

The contract that was kept in **the holy tent** also told of the curses the people would suffer if they broke the contract. As in other marriage contracts the terms for divorce were given. When the people were away from their land, their temple, and the holy city, and the land was controlled by another political power, then believers thought they were divorced (Deut 24:1). When the tent was to be reestablished, Israel would be restored to the Promised Land with her own king ruling from Jerusalem. When all of that took place, that was when the then they thought the contract would be renewed. Until then they were still expecting something which had not taken place.

When Israel was in the wilderness, there was always a fire burning on an altar near this **tent**. The fire signified the Lord's presence with human beings. It could be seen at night by its pillar of fire and in the daytime by its pillar of cloud, as the smoke and fire reached heaven. It was presumed that the Lord in the heavens could come down through this pillar of smoke to be with his people at the tent. This is one of the ways the Lord **dwelled** with his people in the desert.

In the Autumn, when the rainy season began, the sky in the Near East is frequently cloudy. At that season, ancient Israelites refused to move camp, because the smoke from the camp did not ascend to heaven like a pillar. Therefore there was no access route whereby the Lord could come through the pillar of smoke to **the tent** of meeting. When the rainy season was over, and the smoke again went straight up, Israelites were free to move camp.

This regularly happened after New Year's Day which, according to the old Pentacontad calendar, used by some Jews and Christians in NT times, took place exactly on the date every year that Christians now celebrate Easter. Fifty days after New Year's Day was the first Pentecost. This was the day that Jews of NT times celebrated the presence of God in their midst. This was the time at which God condescended to be present in the tent of meeting and dwell with his people as he had all of the summers before. The prophetic narrative given here is centered around the Jewish Shebuoth (*Sheh-voo-ohth,* שבועות)or Feast of Pentecost.[1]

The author Rev 21 anticipated, on the basis of Ezekiel, that there would be a new Pentecost in Palestine. Then the Lord would again dwell with his people at Jerusalem in the restored tent. When the temple and the associated Romans were gone, there would be God's tent, where people could come to have their offenses tried, crimes punished or pardoned, and defilements cleansed. Following Deuteronomic theology, God punished people for their wickedness through

---

[1] On the ancient pentecontad calendar see Julius and Hildagard Lewy, "The Origin of the Week and the Oldest West Asiatic Calendar," *HUCA* 17 (1942):1-152a and Julius Morgenstern, "The Calendar of the Book of Jubilees," *VT* 5 (1955):34-76; Morgenstern, *Some Significant Antecedents of Christianity* (Leiden: Brill, 1966), pp. 20-22.

sickness, pain, suffering, and hardship, but if all crimes and defilements were cleared at the tent, there would be no more pain or suffering. God would comfort his people and wipe away their tears, as Isaiah had promised. Rabbis said that in the wilderness there was no crime (*khah-táh,* חטא) and no record of unpaid fines (*ah-vóhn,* עון) (Mek *Vayassa* 3:76-77). That was thought to be true, because of God's tent that was there to rid the nation of its iniquity, crime, and defilement. That condition could not exist again, in the opinion of this author, until the Roman temple with its wicked priests were banished and replaced with God's tent. The tears, death, and mourning were part of the gentile age which would vanish like smoke as the Lord rolled up the heavens and replaced them at the same time he created a new Promised Land with Zion, David's holy city, as the central city. This was testified by Second Isaiah, who promised that the Lord would make something new.

He will tentdwell with them. Whenever God lived (**dwelled**) **with** his people (his wife), there was a marriage contract that bound the people to God. While this contract was in force, God would fulfill the duties of a husband: he would provide for **them**, give them a land in which to live and protect them from their enemies. If the people were faithful God would reward them with posterity, prosperity, and the Land. When he divorced his people because they had been unfaithful to their contract, he drove them away from his house (Deut 24:1) and no longer **lived** with them. The gentile age was the time during which God was divorced from his people. Jews and early Christians looked forward to the time Hosea and Jeremiah promised, when God would take his people back. Then there would be a new marriage ceremony and a new contract. This would be the age to come. If the promises were not fulfilled, Israel was still **living** in the old, gentile age.

  The age to come would be marked by the restoration of the land, and all the other promises of the contract being fulfilled. When the temple was dedicated, Solomon reportedly said that God's **dwelling** place was in heaven (1Kings 8:27, 39), but after he had a temple, his name would be there (1King 8:29). That meant that he would be there legally through the representation of his legal agents, the king and high priest. Yehowah promised that the Israelites would **dwell** securely in the place Yehowah had chosen that his name would **dwell** there (Deut 12:10-11, 21). Having his name to **dwell** there had the legal significance of establishing an embassy in Zion whereby the Lord could send a king as his legal agent, and there would be priests to communicate with the Lord in behalf of the people. When the Lord said he would **dwell** with the Israelites in this place (Jer 7:3), it meant that he would be present legally, the way a king is present in other countries at the same time he resides in his capital city.

  The Lord promised that the glory of Yehowah would fill all the land (Num 14:21). He had created the sanctuary, the place of his **dwelling**, from which he would rule for the age (*luh oh-láhm,* לעולם), meaning "for the age to come," "the age of the contract," or "the age of the Messiah," the age when the Lord will **live** with his people, or "for the age and until" (*luh oh-láhm vah ahd,. . .* לעולם ועד

(11QT 29:7-10), meaning "for the age [to come] and until [the gentile age is renewed, and the Lord divorces his people again]." These expressions, **dwelling,** "making his name **dwell,**" "making his glory **dwell,**" or calling attention to **the tent** where God **dwells**, all mean that God would not be in **Jerusalem** *ontologically.* Ontology is a philosophical term that defines some physical reality, as over against something that is legally or imaginatively real. *Legal* existence, however, is also real, but it is real in a different sense. Legal reality has to do with authority and political power. It does not require physical presence to be involved. God's presence in Jerusalem, while he was in heaven, was a legal presence. It is one in which his desire could be expressed through a legal agent, like a king. God's legal agent was the incarnation of his word through the action and speech of a human being. It is through a human agent—prophet, apostle, king—that his word could become flesh.

They themselves will be his people. NA does not have the emphatic pronoun, **themselves**. Some texts, including Sinaiticus, have **peoples**, and some have **people.** The plural text is one of the reasons Deutsch has given to propose a major shift in Rev 21:1-22:5 from nationalism to universalism. Her other reasons are:

1) Not only God, but also the Lamb would dwell in Jerusalem.
2) There is no reference to Jewish people as a national entity in this passage; and
3) the author of this passage was an anti-Jewish Christian.
   All of these will be considered.

Whichever text is approved, it does not mean that the author of the entire Book of Revelation, or even of this passage, was universal in the sense that there would be no distinction between Jews and gentiles, Christians and pagans.[1] The only way in which the new contract community would be universal was that all other nations would be

   a) destroyed,
   b) subject to the contract community as Isa 61 foresaw, or
   c) all gentiles would become Jews or Christians as Zech 8:23 proposed.

There was no plan for peoples of all nationalities and religious beliefs to exist in Jerusalem on the same footing as believers.

The new Jerusalem was not to be a democracy like that of the United States where people of all religious beliefs are expected to coexist and have equal protection of the law. Those within the city of Jerusalem would be those who were redeemed and undefiled (Isa 35:8-10). There would be no idolaters (Rev 21:8). Those who conquered would belong to the party to the contract (Rev 21:7), but not all were included. In the very next verse the author listed all those who would *not* be parties to the contract (Rev 21:8) but instead would be thrown into the lake of fire. The

---

[1] As Deutsch, "Transformation," p. 120, holds.

message of this homily is supported by quotations from various non-universal FT passages, like Isaiah, Ezekiel, Jeremiah, Zechariah, and some Psalms. To find the cosmic point of view of the author it is necessary to examine the points of view of these First Testament (FT) passages.

Deutsch acknowledged all of these nationalistic, ritualistic expectations of the passages quoted, but because there "is no reference to the Jewish people as a national entity" in Rev 21:1-22:5, therefore there must have been a "shift" from nationalism to universalism.[1] The word "universalism" also does not occur in those verses, so on the basis of the kind of logic Deutsch proposes, there is no reason to suggest a "shift" from one non-existent expression to another.

The presence of the Lamb in Jerusalem does not prove that he was universalistic. The Lamb was the Messiah or king. Most kings were neither democratic nor universalistic. There is nothing in his role that suggests universalism.

All of the new things listed here were expected to happen together. The Land would be restored; Jerusalem would be reconstructed; and God would renew his contract with his people--not with all the people of the world. The entire city of Jerusalem would exist as if it were the tent, with all the Levitical rules that applied to the tent observed throughout, just as if the whole city were a monastery. The new contract Jeremiah, Ezekiel, and Zechariah promised was a wedding contract, with Israel as the bride and God as the groom. God's legal agent in Jerusalem would be the Lamb, the Messiah, the king who would rule from **Jerusalem.**

As a husband lives with his wife after the marriage contract is performed, so God would **live** with his people after the new contract would be confirmed. His **dwelling** place would be in the tent, which would be in Zion. Since the ruling king was to be God's legal agent, wherever the Lamb was present, God was legally present. The tent would exist primarily to provide a ritualistically pure place for God to **dwell**. If a situation was provided in Jerusalem that was suitable for the Lamb to **live** there, then the purpose of the tent was fulfilled with the presence of the new king. The presence of the Lamb does not provide any basis for concluding that the author's point of view was universalistic, as Deutsch declared.[2]

Rev 21:1-22:5 nowhere used either the term "Christ" or the word "Jesus." Much less does it speak of Jews who either have or have not accepted Christ. Nevertheless, Deutsch proposed on the basis of her interpretation of Rev 2:9 and 3:9 that the author of Rev 21:1-22:5 was a universalistic Christian, rather than a nationalistic Jew. She mistakenly presumed that John of Patmos who wrote the introduction (Rev 1:1-3:22) and conclusion (Rev 22:5-21) also wrote the anthological prophecy in between (Rev 4:1-22:5), including all of its separate units. This allowed her to use material from the introduction to refute the message of the unit of the prophecy with which she was primarily concerned (Rev 21:1-22:4).

Even if, however, her use of Rev 2:9 and 3:9 had been legitimate, the words **synagogue of Satan** could not be fairly used to show that John of Patmos was a

---

[1] Deutsch, "Transformation," p. 122.
[2] Deutsch, "Transformation," p. 122.

universalistic Christian. It is much more likely that the expression **synagogue of Satan** was contrasted to the "**synagogue** of God," than "the universalistic Christian church of God." That is the kind of name one rigorous, law abiding sect would attribute to another sect of liberal Jews. The use of the term **synagogue** is itself a technical Jewish term. John's enemies--the Nicolaitans, false apostles, Jezebel, Balaam, those of the **synagogue** of Satan, and those who called themselves Jews but were not--were not Judaizers, as was true of Paul's enemies, but the liberal Christians, who were not true Jews. If John had not considered himself a true Jew why would he have criticized others for falsely calling themselves Jews? John was favorably impressed with the nationalistic prophecy he was brought (Rev 4:1-22:5), and he chose to send it out to the churches. This does not suggest that he was a universalistic, anti-nationalistic, anti-Jewish Christian.

Deutsch's article shows much careful and accurate research. It was only her conclusion that the author of Rev 21:1-22:5 had transformed the nationalistic symbols she used into universalistic symbols that was unsupported by evidence.

There will be neither lamentation nor crying. NA has, "There will **no longer be lamentation nor crying nor distress**." This is another instance in which later commentators seem to have expanded the text homiletically. This favorable situation would be the result of the presence of the tent to allow for justice and ritual purity.

The One seated on the throne said to me. NA omits the words, **to me.** The expression, **the One seated on the throne**, is a euphemistic name for God who was pictured as a great king. The Lamb, as the ruling king, was also thought to be **the one sitting on the throne.**

These words are faithful and true. This sentence seems to be an intrusion into the text. It may have been made by the elder John, emphasizing his agreement with the message of the prophecy he was translating. The word here translated as if it were the sign of a direct quotation is the Greek word, *háw-tee* (ὅτι). It can also mean **that** or **because.** The text could be rendered either, "**Write that these** things **are faithful and true**," or "**Write** [the following quotation]: '**These things are faithful and true**.'" The latter seems more reasonable. This recommendation may refer either to the message so far or to the poem which follows (Rev 21:6b-8). That which had happened (*géh-gawn-ahn*, γέγοναν) was probably the fulfillment of all of these passages either quoted or to be quoted in the poem. These words are probably not the very words of Christ as Weiss believed.[1]

They have happened. This means the author believed that the words of Scripture had been fulfilled according to the treasury of merits doctrine. Isaiah, like all other prophets, prophesied only for the days of the Messiah. That which had been anticipated for generations had taken place in the author's time.

---

[1] B. Weiss, *Die Apostelgeschichte Katholischen Briefe Apokalypse* (Leipzig: J. C. Hinrichs, 1902), p. 523.

TEXT

Revelation	First Testament
I am the Alpha and the Omega, the beginning and the end. I will give **to the thirsty one**	Isa 55:1 Ho! Every**one who is thirsty** come **to** the water! Whoever has no silver, come, buy and eat! Come and buy wine and milk **without money and without cost**.
from the spring of **water of life**	Zech 14:8-9 It will happen on that day that **Water of life** will flow out from Jerusalem, half to the Eastern Sea and half to the Western Sea. It will be [thus] in summer and in winter. In that day Yehowah will be king over all the land.
free of charge. ⁷He who conquers will inherit these things, and	
I will be his God, **and he will be my son**, ⁸but the cowards, the unfaithful, the defiled people, murderers, sexual minglers, magicians, idolaters, and all who are false [to the contract], their portion is the lake	2Sam 7:13-14 I will establish the throne of his kingdom for the age. **I will be his** [Solomon's] Father, **and he will be my son**.
	Ps 2:7 **You are my son**. Today I have given you birth.
	Isa 30:33 For Tophet it has been lined up for a long time; Also it is prepared for Molech. The pyre is deep and wide. **Fire** and an abundance of wood. The breath of Yehowah, like a stream of **sulphur** makes it **burn**.
which **burns with** **fire and sulfur**. This is the second death.	Gen 19:24-25 Yehowah rained upon Sodom and Gomorrah **sulfur and fire** from Yehowah, from heaven. He overthrew these cities and all the valley, and all the inhabitants of the cities--even the vegetation.

> Ezek 38:22)I will judge him [Gog] with pestilence, blood, flooding rain, hail stones, **fire, and sulfur**, I will rain upon him, his troops, and many peoples who are with him.

COMMENTARY

I am the Alpha and the Omega. **The alpha (Α) and the omega (Ω)** are the first and last letters of the Greek alphabet. This was probably originally written in Hebrew and the letters were the *aleph* (א) and the *tau* (ת). The **tau** in the Hebrew alphabet originally looked like the Latin X, and was understood as the sign of the cross. This expression was a periphrastic way of speaking of God without mentioning his name.

The Author's Use of Second Isaiah. The entire unit, Rev 21:6b-8, is a poem which contains quotations or allusions to passages from Second Isaiah, Ezekiel, Zechariah, and Psalms. The description of God as **the Alpha and the Omega, the beginning and the end** comes from Isa 44:6 and 48:12: **I am the first and I am the last.** This comes with the claim that God is the one who spread out the heavens with his own hand, would call Cyrus to overthrow Babylon, and he would redeem his chosen people. Second Isaiah also invited people to come to the fountain and drink water free of charge. God would provide for his people the water of life, which meant they would have running water to baptize initiates into the community of the contract where, alone, life was possible. The water that was special to Zion was that which flowed from the Spring of Siloam all the year around in a country that was normally dry half of the year. David's altar and all later temples were established just above and behind that great, everflowing spring.

The Second Death. There were two kinds of life and two kinds of **death**. When a person was initiated into the community he or she became legally alive for the first time so far as that community was concerned. This was true even at old age, chronologically. When a person became apostate, and therefore excluded from the community, that was legal **death.** Either **death** could come first. If a person was excommunicated, then physical **death** was the second **death.** After **death** there was a judgment on those members who had died, physically, but were considered members of the community. The final judgment might determine that they were really apostates. In which case, the **second death** was legal. Targumists referred to **the second death** as if everyone knew what it was.

> The prophet said, "With my ears I have been hearing when this was decreed from before Yehowah of armies, '[May the following unmentioned curses come upon me] if this crime will be forgiven you until the second death'" (TgJon Isa 22:14).

> Your [unrighteous Jews'] names will be abandoned as a curse to my chosen ones, and Yehowah God will kill you the second death, but for his servants, the righteous ones, he will call by another name (TgJon Isa 65:15). Let Reuben live in the life of the age [to come], and let him not die the second death (TgJon Deut 33:6).

The one who would not live in the age to come was permanently excluded from the community where life was possible. Therefore he or she died **the second death**. **The second death** is a legal **death** that brings an end to existence within the community. The one who belongs to this community will inherit the promises given in the FT and belong to the community in the age to come, which is another way of saying that his or her soul will be saved. All the rest will be thrown into the lake of sulfuric fire, which is **the second death**.

In order to get the picture of sulfuric fire, you have to visualize flaming lava, boiling in a crater, with the sulfuric smell bubbling up all over. Being thrown into the pit of sulfuric fire was like being thrown into a crater of boiling, smelling lava. Our religious ancestors had vivid imaginations. This is a vivid and dramatic way of saying that the **second death** is terrible and final. Rissi has tried to tone down the anger and vindictiveness expressed here. He explained that the author was "actually hoping for the redemption of the foes of Christ *par excellence*."[1] Quite different was the judgment of D. H. Lawrence:

> Resentment and not love is the teaching of the Revelation of St. John the Divine. It is a book without wisdom, goodness, kindness, or affection of any kind.[2]

There is no planned redemption for those who receive **the second death**. Medieval rabbis allowed forgiveness toward repentant Jews, but they had no more kindness or generosity toward gentiles than the author of Rev 21 had.

> Gehinnom will be opened and there the holy One blessed be He will bring down his throne and set it in the Valley of Jehoshaphat, and there he will [hold court and] make every nation and its idols pass by. When the gentiles pass by there, they will fall into it . . . When a man commits a crime against the throne of glory and repents, they [God] will forgive him, as it is said, **Return, O Israelites, to [the Lord your God]** (Hos 14:2), but the gentiles will pass into Gehinnom and will fall into it.[3]

---

[1] Rissi, *Future*, p. 78.
[2] Quoted from H. Bloom (ed. and intro.), *The Revelation of St. John the Divine* (New York, 1988), p. 4.
[3] The text is from Jellinek, *Midrasch* [Hebrew], tr. by Buchanan, *Jewish Messianic Movements*, p.

The one who conquers will inherit these things. **These things** were the new Jerusalem, the restoration of the tent so that God would dwell there, the removal of tears from his or her eyes, the removal of death, lamentation, weeping, and the privilege of drinking from the water of life without cost. Furthermore God would make a new contract with the community to which that person belonged; members of that community would be God's people, and he would be their God. These were all gifts which the early Israelites inherited during the reigns of David and Solomon when the kingdom was first established and the temple, constructed. The author of this passage expected all of that which happened with the establishment of the kingdom to happen again. This involved the renewal of the nation under Davidic rule.

The Unfaithful. These were not people who were uncertain about their faith, those who were **unfaithful** to their spouses, or those who were not trustworthy. The unfaithful here were those who had broken contract with the Lord and were therefore apostates.

TEXT

Revelation	Hebrew Scripture
⁹Then one of the seven angels who had the seven bowls which were filled with the **seven** last **plagues** spoke to me, saying, "Come, I will show you the bride, the wife of the Lamb." ¹⁰Then he **brought me in the spirit on a mountain, large and very high,**	Lev 26:21 Then if you walk contrary to me and do not want to pay attention to me, I will increase over you **seven plagues** for all your crimes
	Ezek 40:2 **In visions** God **brought me** to the land of Israel, and he set me **on a very high mountain**. On it was something like a constructed city from the south.
and he showed me	Isa 52:1 Awake! Awake! Put on your strength as garments, Zion. Put on beautiful clothes,
the holy city, Jerusalem, coming down from heaven, from God,	**Jerusalem, the holy city**, for the uncircumcised and defiled person will never enter you again.
	1Kings 8:11 It happened when the priests went out from the temple, the cloud filled the house of Yehowah. The

¹¹having **the glory of God**. Its light was something like a precious stone, as a crystallized jasper stone. ¹²It had great and high walls,

having 12 **gates**, and at the gates are 12 angels. **The names are written** [on the gates] which are of
the 12 **tribes of** the sons of **Israel**. ¹³There are **three gates**

on the east, three gates on the north three gates on

the south.

¹⁴The wall of the city has
12 foundation **stones** and upon them are

priests were not able to stand and minister before the cloud, because The **the glory of God** filled the house of Yehowah.

^{Ezek 43:5}The Spirit lifted me and brought me to the inner court [of the temple]. Now look! **the glory of Yehowah** filled the temple.

^{Isa 58:8}Your righteousness will go before you, and **the glory of Yehowah** will come from behind.

^{Isa 60:1}**The glory of Yehowah** has dawned upon you.

^{Ezek 48:30-35; cf. also 42:16-19}These are the exits of the city: On the north side, 4,500 cubits by measure. The **gates** of the city **are named**

for **the tribes of Israel**. The
three gates on the north: one gate of Reuben, one gate of Judah, and one gate of Levi. **On the east side**, 4,500 cubits, having **three gates**: one gate of Joseph, one gate of Benjamin, and one gate of Dan. **The south** side, 4,500 cubits by measure, with **three gates**: one gate of Simon, one gate of Issachar, and one gate of Zebulon. **The west side**, 4,500 cubits and their **three gates**: one gate of Gad, one gate of Asher, and one gate of Naphtali. The circumference shall be 18,000 cubits, and the name of the city from now on, *"Yehowah is there."*

^{Exod 38:21; 39:14}There shall be
12 stones according to **the names of the** sons of Israel. There will be engraved signets, each according to

the 12 names of the 12 apostles of the Lamb.   his **name for the 12 tribes.**

COMMENTARY

One of the seven angels who had the seven bowls. This refers back to **the angels** with **the seven** last plagues in Rev 15:1, 6-7. Rev 21:9 and 10 are almost verbatim quotes of Rev 17:1.

> **Now** one of **the** seven **angels** who had the seven bowls, came to me **and spoke to me, saying,** "Come, and **I will show you** the judgment of **the great harlot**" (Rev 17:1).

That which one of the angels showed in Rev 17 was the judgment of the great harlot. Instead of bringing the seer **in the spirit** to a high hill, in Rev 17 one of the angels brought him into the wilderness.[1] The succeeding narrative follows the prophecy of Ezekiel.

He brought me in the spirit. Just as Ezekiel was taken up from Babylon, in his imagination, to the Mount of Olives, from which point he could see the temple area, so the author of this apocalypse also was taken to the same place, also **in the spirit**.

I will show you the bride. Second Isaiah anticipated the return of Babylonian Jews to the Promised Land. When that happened the land that had once been desolated and abandoned, as a wife who had been divorced, would again be remarried. The land would be called "married" (*buh-oo-láh* בעולה), and Israel's God would rejoice over Israel the same way a bridegroom rejoices over a new **bride** (Isa 62:4-5). In this context, God was understood as the bridegroom and the people and the land were considered his wife. God and Israel would be married when these conditions existed. Whenever Jerusalem, Judaism, or the Christian church is pictured as a bride or the Messiah as the groom, the symbolism accentuates the importance of the new contract that Jer 31:31 promised. In antiquity marriage vows were required for marriage.

We do not have any report of the vows taken, but we might be able to deduce them from material available. For example, Paul said that husbands should love their wives, and wives should be obedient to their husbands. He may have only reminded them of their vows. When married, the husbands may have taken vows to love their wives, and wives may have vowed to be subject to their husbands (Col 3:18). Many times in the FT is given the promise that God would be Israel's God and Israel would be his people. Because the contract was a marriage contract, this would have been the marriage vows God took. This probably was taken from the same liturgical ceremony in which other husbands participated when they were married. This is only a deduction. That which is clear is that all of this marriage

---

[1] Wilcox, "Tradition," p. 205.

symbolism in the Book of Revelation is related to the renewal of the contract that Jeremiah promised. The Lamb, as God's legal agent, was the human representative commissioned to take vows and renew the contract in God's behalf, so this was a marriage between Israel and the Messiah (Lamb).[1]

The holy city, Jerusalem, coming down from heaven. This is a repetition of Rev 21.2. **Jerusalem** was normally thought by early Jews and Christians to have been sent from God as **a holy city**, **a heavenly city** of God (Heb 12:22). When it would be restored again it would be because God would restore it. This would be true even if the money raised for its reconstruction came from foreign countries. This belief was here dramatized in a beautifully picturesque fashion.

Scholars have had difficulties making sense of this passage in relationship to the earlier claim (Rev 21:2) that **Jerusalem** was seen **coming down from heaven**. Does this mean that **Jerusalem came down** once, went up to **heaven**, and then came down again? Or, that here were two **Jerusalems**? Probably not. It probably means that just as there are two judgment scenes in Rev 20 (20:4-10 and 20:11-15), there are two scenes in Rev 21 (Rev 21:1-8 and Rev 21:9-27). In both cases there is no chronological relationship between the two scenes. In each chapter there are two literary units which were composed by two different authors who had similar beliefs about **Jerusalem**, and then later these were spliced together by the final editor who organized all of these visions into one anthology. In Jewish and Christian literature it is normal for editors to put together units that have something in common. In the Mishnah, Tosephta, and talmuds, for example, material is organized under topics, such as "The Day of Atonement" or "Sanhedrin." In the Gospel of Matthew, all the parables dealing with the Kingdom of God occur in Matt 13; all the healing miracles are organized into Matt 8. Here the editor put the judgment scenes together into Rev 20 and the units on the descent from heaven of the new **Jerusalem** into Rev 21.

Babylon (=Rome) is always described in the Book of Revelation as a **great city** (Rev 14:8; 16:19; 17:5; 18:2, 10, 21). **Jerusalem** is also called a **great city**, but it was not only **great.** It was also **holy.** Ezekiel was shown the place where the temple would be restored; the prophet of Revelation was shown **the holy city** as it was **coming down from heaven** to the place where it formerly stood. Second Isaiah visualized the chosen people returning to Zion (Isa 59:20), which would then be called **the city of Yehowah, Zion, the holy one of Israel** (Isa 60:14). Micah promised that in the last days [of the gentile control of the land] the mountain of the house of Yehowah would be established as the highest of the mountains (Micah 4:1). The author of Hebrews told his hearers, **You have come to Mount Zion, the city of the living God, heavenly Jerusalem** (Heb 12:22). Weiss noted that this was the second time in Rev 21 that the holy city was pictured as **descending from heaven**. He correctly concluded that there were initially two separate documents here

---

[1] Although Deutsch, "Transformation," p. 112, was primarily interested in the symbolism of this portion of Revelation, she did not deal with the legal symbolism of the marriage ceremony at all.

which some editor put together into one--Rev 21:1-8 and Rev 21:9-27. He thought the second unit was Jewish and reflected the year 70 IA.[1]

The glory of God. The new **Jerusalem** displayed **the glory of God,** which meant the temple was functioning, and smoke was going up **to heaven** like a pillar, and the light from the bonfire provided a good light. The light and smoke (cloud) was **the glory of God.**

Twelve gates. The number **twelve**, like the number seven had a magical significance to the author. There were **twelve** gates, **twelve** angels, **twelve** tribes, **twelve** foundations, and **twelve** names of **twelve** apostles of the Lamb (Rev 21:12-14). Aune said,

> Rev 21:14 may also shed light on the *date* of Revelation. It is not usually recognized that the phrase of οἱ δώδεκα ἀπόστολοι, "the twelve apostles," is a rare phrase in the NT, occurring elsewhere only in Matt 10:2 in a closely parallel phrase (τῶν δὲ δώδεκα ἀποστόλων τὰ ὀνόματα, the names of the twelve apostles).[2]

Aune assumed that the Lamb mentioned was Jesus, and the twelve apostles written in Rev 21:14 were Jesus' twelve apostles. There is nothing certain about that. The Lamb in the prophetic section of Revelation represents some Jewish messiah—not necessarily, Jesus. More likely, this shows that the notion that any messiah that pretended the throne of Jerusalem would be expected to have a cabinet composed of twelve apostles, one for each of the twelve tribes of Israel. Jesus fit into that pattern.

Three gates on the north. Sinaiticus repeated this expression, mistakenly. After the next expression, **three gates to the south**, NA adds **and three gates to the west.**

The walls of the city, having foundation stones. Following Ezekiel's description, the city had large **walls** with three gates in each wall. These gates all had names, which Ezekiel listed, but Rev 21 did not. Josephus described the **foundation** which Agrippa I had constructed, planning to build an entire wall, but Claudius made him stop. Josephus said that this wall was so huge that if it had been completed Romans could never have broken it down (War 2:218-19; Ant 19:326-27). These may have been the same walls, but they also may not have been. The walls around the Dome of the Rock were not built in Ezekiel's time. Neither was Agrippa's wall, but there were walls around Zion that were there 3,000 years earlier than Josephus. Titus thoroughly had all of the walls and gates around Zion destroyed so thoroughly that they cannot be uncovered by archaeologists.

---

[1] J. Weiss, *Die Offenbarung de Johannes* (Göttingen: Vandenhoeck & Ruprecht, 1908), p. 680. Robert H. Charles, *Critical and Exegetical Commentary on the Revelation of St. John the Divine* (New York: Charles Scribner's Sons, c1920) I, p. 151, thought the first reference to a city in this chapter was to a heavenly city, whereas the second was to an earthly city. The second city was to take the place of Rome after it had been destroyed.

[2] David E. Aune, *Revelation 1-5* (Dallas: Word Books, c1997), p. lxiv.

The city that had the foundations was almost certainly Zion, but probably not Herod's Jerusalem, which was enclosed within the Roman fortress walls. South of Herod's walls was David's Holy City, Zion (Isa 52:1), where Solomon's temple had been constructed. There were tender religious ties to this city that had never been transferred to the city within Herod's walls. **The city which had the foundations** (*toos theh-meh-leé-oos*, τοὺς θεμελίους) was probably Zion. That city existed thousands of years before the time of Herod. It was recognized by Ezekiel before Herod built his fortress.

The psalmist (Ps. 87:1) said Zion's **foundation** (*yeh-soo-dah-taw*, יסודתו) was in the holy mountain (Ps 87:1). It was the city Yehowah had founded (Isa 14:32; 28:16). After the fall of Jerusalem in 70 IA, an unknown seer had a vision of a constructed city that had large **foundations** (foon-dah-méhn-tees máhg-nees, *fundamentis magnis*) which turned out to be Zion (4Ezra 10:26-27, 44)--**Zion, city of the God of life, heavenly Jerusalem** (Heb 12:22). The ridge upon which Zion was constructed was initially of natural rock, which slanted from the top to the east in the Kidron Valley and on the west to the Tyropoeon Valley. The Jebusites evidently built walls straight up from near the bottom of the valleys and filled in the triangular areas between the walls and the top of the ridge with large rocks. This was a carefully designed project that provided a very strong wall and foundation. It also made the city about three times its natural size. Nowhere in the Near East have archaeologists found anything like such exquisite building skills displayed as in these walls. They have been carefully and defensively made. These thick walls became the **foundations** of the temple which was built on top of the walls, which became its **foundations**.

It is no wonder that the City of David was called **the city which had the foundations**. The entire ridge was made of rock. The city was built on top of all of this construction, high above the valleys on both sides.

To be sure, Herod's fortified city, Antonia, just north of Zion, had notable **foundations** as well. but the **foundations** of Zion were reported in the Scripture, and the author of Hebrews based his most important arguments on Scripture, so the **foundations** mentioned by the psalmist were probably the ones intended (Ps 87:1). The practice of identifying something through some small detail, such as this, was typically Jewish, Christian, and Samaritan. It functioned as a code for those who knew the details. The author of Hebrews described Jerusalem as the **city which had foundation**s (Heb 11:10), and Fourth Ezra had a vision of a city which had huge **foundations** (4Ezra 10.26-27).

Twelve names of the twelve apostles of the Lamb. The description given of the priestly vest included **the twelve** stones which had the names of **the twelve** sons of Israel. Then the author relocated those stones, making them **foundation** stones for the **walls**, and instead of **the twelve** sons of Israel, they were given **the names of the twelve apostles**. This seems to have been the work of some early Christian scribe who made this change in order to Christianize the document. Whealon thought the entire verse (Rev 21:14) was a Christian insertion.[1] The Christian **Lamb** or Messiah, for Christians, was Jesus, but for Jews there is another possibility. The other possibility is that this alteration was part of the Jewish prophecy before John received it and that other Jewish messiahs were expected to have **twelve apostles.** Jesus fit that traditional role, but by the time of Paul, the church was divided into only three Palestinian divisions for three **apostles**, James, John, and Peter (Gal 2:9-14).

TEXT

Revelation

First Testament

Ezek 40:1-4 He brought me there [to Jerusalem]. Now look! A man whose appearance was like bronze

¹⁵The one who was speaking to me

had a gold **measuring stick** so that he could **measure** the city,

had a line of flax in his hand and **a measuring stick**. He was standing at the

its gates, and

gate. The man said to me, "Son of man, watch with your eyes, listen with your ears, and set your mind to all that which I am showing you, because it is for the sake of your vision that you were brought here. Tell all that you see to the house of Israel."

Zech 2:5-9 I lifted my eyes and watched-- Now look! A man with a **measuring** line in his hand. I said, "Where are you going?" He said to me, "I am going to **measure** Jerusalem to see what its width and length are." Look! The angel who was speaking to me went out, and another angel went out to meet him, and he said to him, "Run, tell this young man, saying, 'Jerusalem will dwell without **walls** because of the numerous people and livestock in it, for I will be to it,' says Yehowah, '**a wall** of fire outside and I will be a glory in its midst.'"

its walls.

Ezek 41:21-22 The temple doorposts were **square**, and the holy place looked like

¹⁶The city lay **square**, its length equal

---

[1] J. H. Whealon, "New Patches on an Old Garment: The Book of Revelation," *BTB* 11 (1981):55.

to its width. He measured the city with the stick, **12,000** stadia, its length, width, and height are equal.

¹⁷He measured its fodder, 144 **cubits**, human measure, which is of [the] angel.

a wooden altar, three cubits high, and two cubits long, and two cubits wide .

^(Ezek 43:16)The altar will be **square— twelve cubits** long

and **twelve cubits** wide.

^(Ezek 48:16-17)These are its measurements: The north side, 4,500 [cubits], the south side, 4,500 [cubits], the east side, 4,500 [cubits], and on the west side, 4,500 [cubits].

COMMENTARY

The one who was speaking to me. The angel.

So that he could measure the city. This was done in preparation for rebuilding **the city.** Since **the city** was built originally according to the perfect plan, in Jewish judgment, it must be rebuilt in the same way. The care with which ancients tried to follow exact prescriptions about building temples is evident from the excavations of Prof. Aharoni at Arad and Lachish. In both locations he found temple ruins and in both cities the temples had been constructed according to **the measurements** given in Chronicles. The concern for precision in **measurement is** evident from the number of instances in the Scripture where **measurements** are given. These two temples were parts of fortresses, and both were approximately the same size. The photograph of the temple at Lachish, shown between chapters twelve and thirteen, is a side view of the temple, showing the steps that lead up to the holy place and the door into the holy of holies. From the court there are steps up to the holy place where only priests were allowed. From the holy place is another door into the holy of holies, where only the high priest was allowed, and he entered this little room only on the Day of Atonement. These small temples constituted the first step up from the tent in the wilderness. Solomon's temple was much larger.

The city lies square. The idea of a **city** whose length and width are equal provides no problem. Ezekiel expected **the city** to be **square.** Ezekiel wanted nearly everything to be **square**—the door posts, **square**, the altar, **square** (Ezek 41:21), the altar hearth, **square,** the ledge, **square** (Ezek 43:16-17), the lot for the sanctuary, **square** (Ezek 45:2), and land allotted for general use of **the city, square** (Ezek 48:15).

Ezekiel, however, did not expect **the city** to be a cube, with its height the same measurement as its length and width. This is still more incredible. This would mean that **the city** would be 1,500 miles high with a wall that was only 210 feet tall.[1] That would be an impossibly tall skyscraper. The first instinct at the thought of a **city** that was as tall as it was wide is that it would be hideous and could not possibly be a real concept. The word **square** was sometimes used in antiquity to mean "perfect" or "excellent." It sometimes was applied to a man (Diogenes Laertes 5:82 of *Demetrius*). Therefore this could be applied as an approving term to describe a **city** that was not actually **square** from a geometric point of view, but there is other evidence that Jews intended **the city** to be built sometime in the future with the outside walls of equal length, just as Ezekiel directed and as the author of this document required. None of these, however, expected the city to be as tall as Rev 21 prescribes. They only expected it to be **square,** as Ezekiel and Zechariah indicated.

In the Temple or Torah Scroll the term **square** appears several times in relationship to the temple area.[2] Furthermore, Ms. G. M. Crowfoot, who studied the fabrics used at Qumran, reported 16 rectangular linen sheets with a pattern woven in blue linen thread. The pattern was one with a rectangle in the middle which was surrounded by three concentric rectangles. Each larger rectangle became more nearly square.[3] The most likely explanation of this data is that this was the design intended for the future **city of Jerusalem**, with the inner rectangle designed like Herod's temple[4] and the surrounding courts, each more nearly **square** until the final outside walls were intended to be **square.**

The Torah Scroll (11QT 29:8-10) reflects an expectation that a temple would be constructed on the day of blessing.[5] Enoch also expected the old temple to be destroyed and a new temple to be constructed to replace the first (1Enoch 90:29). Another one of the Dead Sea Scrolls (5Q 15) also gives measurements of **the new city** of Jerusalem, based on Ezekiel's measurements, but not exactly the same.[6] Rissi noted that Solomon's temple was not constructed **square**, but the holy of holies was[7] 20 cubits long, 20 cubits wide, and 20 cubits high (1Kings 6:20). Twenty cubits are about 30 feet. Solomon's altar was the same size as the holy of holies--30 feet by 30 feet. The Solomonic holy of holies was reportedly covered with gold (1Kings 6:20), and the author of this passage of Revelation said new Jerusalem would be all gold (Rev 21:18). Even the streets of the new Jerusalem were singled out to be constructed of gold (Rev 21:21).

---

[1] A. S. Peake, *The Revelation of John* (London: Holborn, 1919), pp. 364-65, was just one of the scholars who thought this was unreasonable.

[2] See Yigael Yadin, *The Temple Scroll* (Jerusalem: Israel Exploration Society, 1983) I, pp. 197-200.

[3] G. M. Crowfoot, "The Linen Textiles," *Qumran Cave I* ed. D. Barthélmy and J. T. Milik (Oxford: Clarendon Press, 1955) I, pp. 18-25.

[4] For diagrams of earlier temples excavated together with one of Herod's temple, see Buchanan, *Hebrews*, p. 142.

[5] Yadin, *The Temple Scroll*, p. 183, concluded that the day of blessing was the equivalent of the end of days. This is a misunderstanding of Jewish terms. The end of days were the last days of the *gentile* rule. The day of blessing was the *Jewish age* that followed. This would assume that a day is the same as a thousand years or an age.

[6] On this see Baillet, Milik, and De Vaux (eds.), "*Petites Grottes,"* pp. 184-93, and F. G. Martinez, *Qumran and Apocalyptic* (Leiden: Brill, 1992), pp. 180-213.

[7] Rissi, *Future*, p. 62.

Morris calculated that 12,000 stadia equals about 1,500 miles.[1] Such a radius as this would include the entire peninsula of Italy to the northwest and the entire Arabian Peninsula to the southeast. This seems so exorbitant that Morris thought it simply symbolized a number beyond the imagination. It certainly is larger than the circumference of 27,000 feet that Ezekiel envisioned (Ezek 48:35). There still remains a great deal of hyperbole, to be sure, in the image given, but it is more likely to have been a real notion Jews and Christians of NT times actually held. Figures varied, but early Christians and Jews aspired to world-wide domination with Jerusalem as the greatest city in the world. The theme of measuring Jerusalem and its temple was well-developed in Ezekiel and Zechariah. Both visualized the new Jerusalem as a much bigger city than it had been before. Bengel compared Revelation's measurement of the visualized Jerusalem (1200 stadia around) to **the** actual **city** of Alexandria (30 stadia long). Thebes had a circuit of 43; Nineveh was 400 stadia around the walls; Babylon, 480.[2] Josephus said the walls of Jerusalem were 33 stadia long (132 stadia around).

Exaggerated expectations for the new Jerusalem were normal for Jews and Christians. The Sibyl said that **Jerusalem** would be so great its walls would reach to Joppa on the Mediterranean Sea and its towers would pierce the clouds (SibOr 5:250-51). Medieval rabbis described it as follows:

> Jerusalem is destined to be built [with] 1,000 suburban castles, 1,000 defense towers, 1,000 country residences, 1,000 mansions, and everyone will be like Sepphoris in its prosperity. (Rabbi Jose said, "I remember Sepphoris in its prosperity when it used to produce 80,000 spiced puddings.")
>
> There is destined to be in Jerusalem 3,000 towers and every tower will have 7,000 stories [this would be more than 13 miles high]. (It will be perched on three mountains: Sinai, Tabor, and Carmel.) Every story will have 7,000 divisions, and every division will be 62 cubits. It will be perched on the top of 33 slopes, and the house of the sanctuary will be on top of them all. How will they be able to ascend it? Like clouds and winged doves and flying beings [they will become], as it is said, **Who are these, flying like a cloud of doves to their windows** (Isa 60:8). The house of the sanctuary will extend in width to Damascus, as it is said, **The word of the Lord is raised against the land of Hadrach and will rest on Damascus** (Zech 9:1). Seven walls will surround Jerusalem: of silver, gold, precious stone, puk, sapphire, carbuncle, and fire. Its brilliance will shine from one end of the world to the other.[3]

---

[1] L. Morris, *The Book of Revelation* (Grand Rapids: Eerdmans, c1987), pp., 250-51.
[2] J. A. Bengel, *New Testament Word Studies*, tr. C. T. Lewis and M. R. Vincent (Grand Rapids: Kregel, 1971) II, p. 925.
[3] Buchanan, *Jewish Messianic Movements*, pp. 543-44.

Some said the temple would be so large it would cover the tops of Lebanon, Mount Moriah [Jerusalem], Tabor, Carmel, and Hermon [Golan Heights].[1] When all the gentiles would gather into Jerusalem Rabbi Eliezer the Modiite said the holy One blessed be He would order Jerusalem to become greater to make room for all of these (PesiqR 21:8). Rabbi Levi held that Jerusalem was destined to become as large as the land of Israel and the land of Israel was destined to become as large as the whole world (PesiqR 1:3). Others claimed that the temple itself would fill up the borders of the land ruled by David and Solomon.[2] Rabbi Yohanan said Jerusalem was destined to extend its borders as far as Damascus (PesiqRK 20, p. 316; CantR 7:5 #37a). He said further that **Jerusalem** was destined to become the metropolis of all the lands (ExodR 21:10 [43d]). Some rabbis believed the new **Jerusalem** would include within its borders the city of Damascus, about 125 miles away. They also said its walls were to have a height of 700 miles (tSot 8:1-4; bSot 33b-34a; pSot 21d-22a). Other anonymous rabbis said **Jerusalem** was destined to expand and grow taller until it reached the throne of glory (CantR 7:5.3).

Where did the rabbis get the notions they wrote? They obtained them the same way NT writers--and even FT prophets like Ezekiel--got theirs. Some of them came from their imagination, and others they got from the Scripture, following the rules that

1) there is no prophecy prophesied except for the days of the Messiah, and
2) everything that is in the world is in the Scripture. Therefore they were free to apply anything they could find in the Scripture to **Jerusalem** and the temple to the age of the Messiah.
3) Time moved in systematic cycles, so that the end of one cycle would be like the end of another, and the beginning of one cycle would be like the beginning of another.

Cycles began with the creation of the Garden of Eden, the Exodus from Egypt, the Exodus from Babylon under Ezra and Nehemiah, and the Exodus from Greece in the time of the Hasmoneans. Each of these Exoduses marked the same point in the cycle of time. The author of this document thought he lived in the very point of the much larger cycle that began with the Garden of Eden.

From Rev 22 it is clear that the Garden of Eden was expected to be restored. Furthermore the throne of God and **the Lamb** would be there (Rev 22:3). The messianic throne was to be in Jerusalem, and the river described by Ezek 47 that was to flow out from the temple area in Jerusalem was to flow in this Garden of Eden. This means the author identified the Garden of Eden with **Zion**, and he did it all on the basis of Scripture. Since the Garden of Eden was the new **Jerusalem, Jerusalem** would be as big as the Garden of Eden. This makes no sense, rationally, but it does

---

[1] Buchanan, *Jewish Messianic Movements*, p. 377.
[2] Buchanan, *Jewish Messianic Movements*, p. 375.

doctrinally. The author of the relevant passage in Revelation was controlled by the doctrines that justified the prophecy.

Fourth Ezra also believed that in the age to come there would be a new **Jerusalem** which would be a new paradise where the tree of life would be planted. There would be plenty of provisions; the city would be rebuilt; and rest would be appointed (4Ezra 8:50-52).

The Garden of Eden was to be located in the Near East, reaching from the end of Ethiopia to the west and south, and to the Tigris and Euphrates rivers to the east (Gen 2:10-14). Rabbi Ishmael is quoted for saying,

> In the future the holy One blessed be He will call the Garden of Eden "Zion," as it is said, **The Lord loves the gates of Zion more than all the dwellings of Jacob** (Ps 87:2). . . **he will make her wilderness like Eden and her desert like the Garden of the Lord** (Isa 51:3).[1]

If **Jerusalem** were to be the new Garden of Eden, then **Jerusalem** would have to include all of this territory, as the author evidently intended--all the way to Italy, Ethiopia, Babylon, and Assyria. This may have been the biblical basis for his description of the new **Jerusalem**, from the geographical point of view. There is still another curious observation: The territory also had as its borders roughly the same as Gog and Magog or the four corners of the earth (Rev 20:8). There is a consistency in the measurements of the boundaries given in Rev 20, 21, and 22. The height of the city seems an especially unjustified mystery, either from the point of view of the rabbis (13 or 700 miles) or the author of Rev 21 (1,500 miles), but even this has a scriptural basis.

In order to understand how a prophet could visualize anything like this, it is necessary to realize that Jews and Christians of NT times believed that the Bible was the only source of knowledge that could be used in legal argument. If anything was in the world it was in the Scripture. This hypothesis seriously limited prophetic discussion. The following rabbinic illustrations will show how Rabbis deduced fantastic solutions on the basis of Scripture. That still seem incredible. At the time of the prophesy, the City of David was 10-12 acres in size.

Rabbinic interpretation. Interpreting the passage, **Let us make man** (Gen 1:26), rabbis reasoned that Adam filled the entire world. Where did they get their data for such a deduction as this? From the Scripture, of course.

1) First they said Adam reached from east to west. The proof text was Ps 139:5: **You have formed me behind** (*ah-khóhr*, אחור) **and before** (*kéh-dehm*,

---

[1] Buchanan, *Jewish Messianic Movements*, p. 517.

קדם). Since the Hebrew word for **before** can also mean "east," **behind** must therefore mean the opposite--"west."

2) The next proof required is to show that he reached from north to south. The text found was Deut 4:32:

> Ask, if you will, with respect to the early days which happened before you, from the day in which God created Adam on the earth, from one end of heaven to the other end of heaven if anything so great as this has happened or anything like it ever been heard.

The important words here are **Adam, behind, and before**, and **from one end of heaven to the other**. Put these together, understanding that **behind and before** means "east and west," and **one end of heaven to the other** means "north and south," rather than "east and west." You must further presume that the dimensions of the earth are the same as those of heaven, and you have proof that **Adam** was so big that he reached all the boundaries of the earth and heaven. This kind of logic allows a person to prove that a cat has ten tails. It may not seem good to twenty-first century westerners--even to rhetoricians--but it was accepted by medieval rabbis. Many years earlier FT prophets reasoned in a similar fashion. Just as if this did not produce a sufficiently exaggerated picture of the new Jerusalem, notice that in the new Zion the 144,000 inhabitants would all be monks (Rev 14:1-5). That would be a large monastery. Rabbi Judah said,

> Since [God] desires your redemption, he pays no attention to your calculations, but he **leaps over the mountains, [bounding over hills]** (Cant 2:8). **The mountains and hills** here mean only "end times" and "intercalations." He **leaps** over the calculations, over the end times and intercalations, and in this month you are to be redeemed, as it is said, **This month is for you the first of the month** (Exod 12:2).

The rabbi said nothing to justify his use of **mountains** and **hills**, which he took out of context to mean calculations, end times, and calendrical intercalations. These words were found in the Scripture. That was all the proof he needed. Some jurists and theologians still reason like this, but they realize that proof and truth are not identical.

He measured its fodder. This is clearly a hearing mistake. The Sinaiticus scribe heard *chee-láws* (χιλός) "fodder," which makes no sense, instead of *táy-khaws* (τεῖχος) "wall," which both the text from Ezekiel and the context requires. It is also the text accepted by NA.

The measure of a man, that is of [the] angel. This has always been puzzling verse. The **measure of a man** is not difficult. A cubit was a unit of **measure** based on a human being's forearm, from the elbow to the knuckles. It was not a human being, however, that was doing the **measuring**. It was one of the seven **angels**. Therefore it would be his forearm that determined the measurements--that is, of [the] **angel**. The most likely assumption is that the **angel** who did the measuring had an arm that was approximately the same length as anyone else.

TEXT

Revelation

^{18}Construction [material] of its walls was jasper, and the city was **pure gold** like clear glass. ^{19} **The foundations** of the **wall** of the city will be decorated with every kind of **precious stone**. The first foundation [stone] is **jasper**; the second, **sapphire**; the third, agate; the fourth, **emerald**; ^{20}the fifth, **onyx**; the sixth, **carnelian**; the seventh, **chrysolite**; the eighth, **beryl**; the ninth, **topaz**; the tenth, chrysoprase; the eleventh, **jacinth**; and the twelfth, **amethyst**. ^{21}The twelve gates were [made of] twelve pearls--each of the gates was [carved] from one pearl, and the street of the city was **gold, pure as transparent glass**.

First Testament and other Jewish Literature

$^{Isa\ 54:11}$Look! I will set your stones with bright colors; I will lay **your**

$^{Isa\ 54:12}$**foundations** with sapphires. I will set your battlements of sparkling gems, your gates of carbuncles, and your walls of **precious stones.**

$^{Ezek\ 28:13}$You [Tyre] were in Eden, the Garden of God. Every **precious stone** was your covering: **carnelian, topaz, jasper, crysolite, beryl, onyx, sapphire, carbuncle, and emerald**.

$^{Tob\ 13:16-17}$The gates of Jerusalem shall be constructed of **sapphire** and **emerald**, and all their walls of **precious stone**. The towers of Jerusalem shall be constructed of gold, and their battlements of **pure gold**. The streets of Jerusalem will be paved with **carbuncle** and **ophir** stones.

$^{5Q15:6}$Every market and village is paved with white stone.

$^{TgPsJon\ Exod\ 19.17}$Moses brought the people out to meet the Shekinah of Yehowah outside the camp, and at once the Lord of the age snatched the mountain, raised it into the air, and it became **clear as glass.**

^{Exod 28:15, 17-20}You shall make a breastplate of judgment with skilled work . . . You shall fill it in with four rows of stones. The first row will have a sardius, a **topaz**, and a **carbuncle**; the second row will have an **emerald**, a **sapphire**, and a **diamond**; the third row will have a **jacinth**, an agate, and an **amethyst**; and the fourth row will have a **beryl**, an **onyx**, and a **jasper**.

COMMENTARY

Construction [material] of its wall was jasper. The Sinaiticus scribe, while listening to dictation, heard *ayn* (ην) "was," instead of *ay* (η), "the." NA has "*The* construction [material] of its wall, jasper."[1]

The city was of pure gold. This was to fulfill the requirements of the sanctuary in Solomon's temple which was made in the form of a cube and was overlaid with gold (1Kings 6:20). The city would also have streets of gold (Rev 21:21).

The foundations of the wall of the city. Jerusalem has been associated with **foundations** in other documents. The Psalmist said Zion's **foundation** was in the holy mountain (Ps 87:1). It was probably Jerusalem to which the author of Hebrews referred as **the city which had the foundations whose builder and constructor was God** (Heb 11:10). In one of Fourth Ezra's visions he saw a city with large **foundations** (4Ezra 10:26-27, 44), which he identified as Zion. This probably refers to the entire City of David. Initially this was a stone ridge, but the Jebusites extended the city in width to nearly three times its original size. This was done by building perpendicular walls on both the east and west sides. Then they built walls at regular intervals of large rocks, joining the ridge to the walls. The spaces between these walls was also filled with rocks, making the entire city one solid, rock wall, on top of which were placed the temple, David's citadel, and the royal palace. This made Zion **the city** which was distinguished for its **foundations.** These foundations would have been more than forty feet deep and secured to solid rock footing.

Decorated with every kind of precious stones. The stones resembled those in the high priest's breastplate (Exod 28:17-20, supplemented by Ezek 28:13, or vice versa). Josephus (Ant 3:186) and Philo (Moses 2:124-26) both related the **precious stones** of the high priest's breastplate with the signs of the Zodiac. This seems

---
[1] Buchanan, *Hebrews*, p.188-89.

reasonable since Josephus also said that the floor of the temple was a mosaic of the signs of the Zodiac. Josephus' testimony is supported by the floors of the synagogues at Beth Alpha, Beth Shan, and Hamath. All had the Zodiac as the central design,[1] probably following the floor of the temple. Following Isa 54:12, Tobit 13:16-17 dreamed of a new Jerusalem whose gates were made of sapphire and emerald, whose walls were made of **precious stones**, whose towers were made of gold, and whose streets were constructed of carbuncle and stones of Ophir.

Each gate was [carved] from one pearl. These are the **pearly gates** which twentieth century Christians visualize as being in heaven where St. Peter stands to admit or reject people after death on earth. The author of this scriptural document, however, thought of them as being in Jerusalem on earth. Imagine the size of the oyster it would take to produce a pearl of this size! This is such a fantastic size for pearls that most people have held that there is no intended value to these measurements, but they do not seem as ridiculous as they did fifty years ago. When the walls of the Tower of Antonia in Jerusalem were excavated by Professor Mazar they were found to be precisely as large as Josephus had reported, and scholars are still trying to imagine how builders handled stones of that dimension 2,000 years ago.[2] Rabbis said that the holy One blessed be He would use **precious** pearls and **stones,** 30 cubits by 30 cubits in size. From these he would cut from them gate openings ten by 20 cubits (bBBat 75a). Archaeologists think this is approximately the way these huge stone blocks were made. The builders rolled the stones into place and then carved them there.

The street of the city was gold, pure as transparent glass. Compare Rev 21:21 with Rev 21:18. Christians traditionally visualize heaven as a place where there are streets of gold. This imagery comes from Rev 21, but in Rev 21 the picture is of Jerusalem that was once in heaven but was brought down to earth (Rev 21:10). Less extravagant is the picture of the restored Jerusalem with all of its market and village [streets] paved with white stone. These would have been like those stones used for the great Roman highway, going north from Petra. It is now called the King's Highway. The author of Rev 21 seems to have known Targum Pseudo-Jonathan which interpreted the Exodus report of Moses bringing the Israelites outside the camp to Mount Sinai. There the Lord picked up the whole mountain, raised it into the air, and the mountain became like transparent glass. The author of Rev 21 transposed this imagery from Mount Sinai to the mountain in Jerusalem where the temple was located. The author also used the description of the holy of holies in

---

[1] Hershel Shanks, "Synagogue Excavation Reveals Stunning Mosaic of Zodiac and Torah Ark," *BAR* 10 (1984):32-44; "The Philistines & the Dothans: An Archaeological Romance," *BibSac* 19 (1993):28-29.
[2] Benjamin Mazar, "Excavations Near Temple Mount Reveal Splendors of Herodian Jerusalem," *BAR* 6 (1980):44-59; E. -M. Laperrousaz, "King Solomon's Wall Still Supports the Temple Mount," *BAR* 13 (1987):34-44.

Solomon's temple which was both overlaid with gold and made of equal length, width, and height (1Kings 6:20).

TEXT

Revelation	First Testament and other Jewish Sources
²²I saw no temple in it, for	^(Isa 24:23)**The moon** will be confused, and **the sun** will be ashamed, because
the Lord God, the almighty One, is its temple, and the Lamb.	**Yehowah of armies** will become king on Mount Zion and in Jerusalem, and glory before his elders.
	^(Isa 60:1)Arise! Shine! For your **light** has come, and the glory of Yehowah has dawned upon you.
²³The city will have **no need** of	
the sun **nor** **the moon that they may lighten** it, but its **lamp will be** the Lamb.	^(Isa 60:19-20)**The sun** will no longer be your light by day **nor** for the brightness will **the moon give you light** [at night], but **Yehowah will be** your **light** for the age, your **God** your **glory**.
	^(Sir 24:4)My tent-dwelling place was in high heaven. My throne was in a pillar of cloud.
	^(Zech 14:7)One day it will happen. [At a time] known to Yehowah, there will be no day and no night. In the evening **there will be light**.
	^(TgJon Isa 60.19)You will **no** longer **need the sun** to shine in the day time or even for **the moon to shine** at night, but Yehowah will be for you a light for the age and your **God** your **glory**.
²⁴**The gentiles will walk** through its **light, and**	^(Isa 60:3) **Gentiles will walk** to your **light, kings** to the brightness of your dawn.

the kings of the earth	Ps 89:28He will address me, "You are my Father, my God, and the Rock of my salvation." Also I will make him the first born, the highest of **the kings of the earth**.
	Ps 138:4All **the kings of the earth** will praise you, Yehowah, because they have heard the words of your mouth. They will sing of the ways of Yehowah, because great is the glory of Yehowah.
	PssSol 17:34**Gentiles will come** from the end **of the earth** to see his glory, bearing as gifts her sons who have been cast out [from the Promised Land].
	Isa 49:23**Kings** will be your foster fathers, their queens, your nursing mothers. With their faces to the ground, they will worship you, and they will lick the dust of your feet.
bring their **wealth to** it, 25and	Isa 60:5Then you will see and **shine**; your heart will be afraid and expand, for the abundance of the sea will turn to you, **the wealth of the gentiles** will come to you.
	Ps 72:10-11**Kings** of Tarshish [Spain] and the [Mediterranean] islands will return their tribute; kings of Sheba and Seba **will bring** gifts. All **the kings**--all **the gentiles**--will serve him [the king of Israel].
the gates will **not be closed during the day,**	Isa 60:11Your **gates will** be open continually; **day and night**; they **will not be closed.**

for **there will be no night** there.

²⁶They
**will bring the
wealth** and the honor **of the gentiles
into** it.

²⁷Nothing **common**
will enter it,
nor [anyone] who commits abomination and is false [to the contract]--

^(Zech 14:7)It will happen on one **day**, which is known to Yehowah,
there will be neither day nor night.
It will occur that at evening time there will be light.

^(Isa 60:11)[They will] **bring to** you **the wealth of the gentiles**, and their **kings** will be led [in procession].
Kings of Tarshish and the islands **will bring** tribute; kings of Sheba and Seba will offer gifts; all the kings will prostrate themselves before him;

^(Ps 72:10-11)and all **the gentiles** will serve him [the king of Israel].

^(Isa 52:1)Awake! Awake! Dress yourself with garments of strength, Zion; put on beautiful clothes, Jerusalem, holy city, because the uncircumcised and **defiled will never again enter** you.

^(1QH 6:27-28)**No** foreigner **shall enter** its gates. Its doors will guard so that **no one will enter**, and its bars strong so that they cannot be broken. **No** military troops **shall enter** with weapons of war.

^(Isa 52:1)Jerusalem, the holy city, for the uncircumcised and **unclean
will no longer enter** you.

^(Ezek 42:20)There was a wall around it, five hundred cubits long and five hundred cubits wide to separate the holy from **the common**.

^(Ezek 44:9)No foreigner, uncircumcised of heart and flesh shall enter my sanctuary.

[no one] except **those written** in the Book of Life of the Lamb.	Isa 4:3 The one who is left in Zion, the one who remains in Jerusalem will be called holy--**everyone written** for **life** in Jerusalem.

Ps 69:28 Let them be blotted out of **the Book of Life**, with the righteous, not written down. |

COMMENTARY

I saw no temple in it. After all of the attention given in this anthology to the heavenly **temple** (Rev 11:19; 13:6; 15:5-8), the altar, the beasts, the cherubim, the lamp stands, and the throne, it comes as a surprise to find an expectation of a new Jerusalem without a **temple**, especially in a chapter where the glory of God is specified as being part of the city (Rev 21:11). The glory of God is normally associated with the smoke that goes up from the **temple** (Rev 15:8).

How can this be explained? Although this is inconsistent with other parts of this anthology in Revelation, it is consistent with this unit which begins with Rev 21:1 and continues to Rev 22:5. The new Jerusalem that comes down from heaven would not have a **temple**. The tent of God (*skay-náy too theh-oó*, σκηνὴ τοῦ θεοῦ) would be there on the land among human beings in the City of David, just as there had been before the time of Solomon, and God would **tent dwell there** (*skay-nóh-say*, σκηνώσει) (John 21:3). His presence would not be in a temple, but in the **tent of God**. Furthermore, the sea would no longer exist (John 21:1). The sea involved was not the Mediterranean Sea, the Sea of Galilee, or the Dead Sea. That sea was the bronze sea that was part of the furniture of he temple (1Kings 7:23-39; 2Chron 18:8; Jer 52:17). It would not be there, because the **temple** would be gone. There would be no place in **the tent of God** for a huge bronze basin.

This portion of Revelation was probably written before the fall of Jerusalem. This author was still dreaming of the destruction of that **temple** which was considered pagan by many orthodox Jews. It was only a dream of destruction, because at the time he wrote this message the temple was still standing.

Faithful Jews hated that Roman **temple** that Herod had built. In the war of 66-70 IA, it was the Jews themselves who started the **temple** on fire. The author of Heb 1-12 thought it was pagan. The huge altar that Herod built may have survived the destruction, and only a tent would have to be provided to have a tent of God again. If the altar had also been destroyed, it would not have been difficult to use the loose rocks that were available to construct another altar, like the one in the wilderness. With an altar for sacrifice, there could be enough light to lighten the entire 10-12 acre town of Zion. A tent could be reconstructed adjacent to the altar very quickly. None of these explanations is certain. This is one of the indications that the Book of Revelation is an anthology that has collected many documents dealing with the subject of redemption, some of which are contradictory.

The words, **I saw**, may indicate the beginning of a new unit. That which follows may not have been written by the same author as that which went before. This is a new vision. This unit anticipates the city restored to the time of David, when the chest containing the contract was in Jerusalem. At that time there was an altar near the Spring of Siloam, but **there was then no temple**. According to gospel reports, Jesus expected Herod's temple to be destroyed (Matt 24:1-2). Jesus was accused of having said that he could destroy Herod's temple and after three days rebuild it (Matt 26:61). He may have planned to restore only David's tent beside the an altar that either existed after the temple was destroyed in 70 IA or could be easily constructed from loose stones. Paul also regarded the community itself as **a temple of God** (1Cor 3:16; 2Cor 5:1-2; 6:16). One of the reasons Stephen was reportedly martyred was that he spoke against the temple and the law (Acts 6:13). The author of this discussion in Rev 21 still expected the prophecies of Isaiah and Second Isaiah to be fulfilled in Jerusalem.

The author probably also presumed that there would be only celibate priests in Jerusalem who would always be as free from defilement as the high priest on the Day of Atonement. This condition of holiness, where nothing unclean would ever exist (Rev 21:27) was a Utopian dream. It would have been very difficult to maintain, but the author of this portion of Revelation was not the only believer who thought that was the correct ethics to require in Jerusalem. In one of the Dead Sea Scrolls, the author expected a temple in Jerusalem, but he forbade any defiled person to enter any part of the city (*kol eer ha meek-dahsh,* כול עיר המקדש [11QT 45:11-12]). People were forbidden to defile "my sanctuary and my city" (meek-dash-eé va eereé, מקדשי ועירי [11QT 47:17-18; see also 46:16-18; 47:3-6]).

The Lord was thought to be enthroned between the cherubim in the holy of holies, but he also was legally present in the person of the king who was his legal agent. Therefore the Lord was seated on his throne whenever the Messiah was seated on the royal throne in Jerusalem. So long as the Lord could be present in Jerusalem it did not matter how this condition was achieved. Without a temple, the emphasis would be on the throne of the Messiah and the holiness of the city. The presence of the Lord was through his agent, the Lamb (Rev 21:22).

The idea of a holy city without a temple was not unique to the author of this chapter in Revelation. The author of the Rule of the Community expected that in the new age the council of the community would itself be the holy temple for Israel and a holy assembly. It would be a holy of holies for Aaron (1QS 8.5-6). Furthermore, the holy of holies in the New Jerusalem was to be the entire city, which was also the Garden of Eden. Therefore an additional temple was not needed. All Jerusalem would be a holy of holies, and all of its inhabitants would be as undefiled as the priests who served in the temples of Solomon and Herod. The author of 11QT expected a temple to fulfill Exod 25:8 and Lev 26:12.

I will be pleased with them, and they **will be my people, and I will be theirs** (Lev 26:12) for the age [to come]. **I will dwell with them** (Exod 25:8) for the age [to come] and until [the age ends].[1] I will sanctify **my temple** (Exod 25:8) with my glory when **I make** (Exod 25:8) my glory **dwell over it** (Lev 26:12-13) until the day of blessing when **I create my temple** (Exod 25:8) and establish it **for myself** (Exod 25:8) all the days, according to the contract which I made with Jacob in Bethel (11QT 30:7-10).

No need of the sun or the moon. The City of David, Zion, was a small town alongside the western edge of the Kidron Valley, closely attached to the Spring of Gihon. That which is now called "the old city," was primarily Antonia, the Roman fortress in NT times. The temple itself had been built by Herod, south of the fortress, but rigorous Jews did not recognize it as God's temple. Zion was the small town south of the fortress. The entire town was less than a mile in length .

Herod's temple was large and beautiful with a huge altar, 22½ feet tall, 75 feet long, and 75 feet wide. On this mammoth altar a large bonfire was kept burning day and night. The City of David is only ten or twelve acres in size, now. It was nearly three times that size in Biblical times, but the light from the bon fire would light up the whole city of Zion when the temple and altar were still standing. The author probably did not intend to see Zion lighted up as bright as if it had numerous electric street lights, but a huge bonfire on the top of an altar more than two stories high would have given lots of light to a little town. This fire would be so much brighter than the small oil lamps, that were not much brighter than birthday candles, that it would seem like daylight in comparison.

The column of fire by night and smoke by day, called the glory of the Lord, was visible from long distances. This promise came from Isa 60:19-20. The targumist for that passage understood the text to mean the kingdom would be enduring. The targumist added: "Your kingdom will never cease, and your glory will not pass away. Look, Yehowah will be your light of the age [to come]" (TgJon Isa 60:20). Zechariah promised that on the Day of the Lord there would be no difference between day and night, because there would be this artificial light at evening time (Zech 14:7).

Its lamp will be the Lamb. This is the author's interpretation of the passage, **Yehowah will be your light** (Isa 60:19-20). Since the Lamb, as the Messiah, is Yehowah's legal agent, the Lamb's light is also Yehowah's light. According to a medieval midrash on Exod 27:20.

---

[1] This translation presumes the author accepted the doctrine of the cycling of the ages. The good age was the one when Jews and their God ruled. The evil age was that period which preceded the good age and that which followed it. "for the age and until" . . . meant for the entire good Jewish age until that age would also come to an end, and the cycle continue to rotate.

The holy One blessed be He said to Israel, "In this age you have been purified by the light of the temple, but in the age to come, [you will be purified] by virtue of that **lamp** (Exod 27:20). I will bring you the messianic king, who is like a lamp, as it is said there, **I will make a horn sprout for David; I have prepared a lamp for my anointed one**" (Ps 132:17; Tanhuma, *Teh-tsah-váy* 31-32; #6, 50a).

During the rule of King David there was no temple, but David was already the anointed king. In the age to come, the temple would be unnecessary, but there would have to be an altar, a tent, and the Messiah. This would be all that would be necessary to be assured of God's legal presence.

The gentiles will walk through its light. Not only would the gentiles all around see the glory of the Lord, but they would come to Jerusalem, as Zechariah promised (Zech 8:20-23), and bring gifts to finance and enrich Jerusalem (TBenj 9:2). It is puzzling to understand how all these foreign kings would come to Jerusalem without allowing any defilement in the city, but that is the way the dreamer thought it would be. The author of this unit may not have been as much concerned about defilement as authors of other parts of Revelation were. Since he did not conceive of a new temple in Jerusalem he may have reasoned that Levitical rules would not apply in that city. A more likely possibility is that he may have expected all gentiles to become Jewish converts and therefore be undefiled, because he said no unclean thing would enter the city. Perhaps he meant only that the glory and honor that had formerly belonged to the gentiles would in that day belong to Israel.

Morris said, "It is hard to see what **the glory of the nations** could bring to the heavenly city."[1] He assumed that Jerusalem would be so great and glorious that no one could add anything more. Ancient Jews, however, were more materialistic and realistic than Morris. One Jewish author looked forward to the time when people from every nation would bring frankincense and gifts to the temple of the great God (SibOr 3:772). That author planned on lots of foreign aid! This heavenly city was to be firmly established on earth. Jerusalem would become great and glorious by receiving the gifts foreigners would bring to it. It would become the center of international commerce. That is the way Second Isaiah expected it to be, and the author of this document took Second Isaiah's message to be the word of God.

The foreign kings would give up their honor, glory, and material possessions, but they, themselves, would not be permitted to enter this exclusive city. Only faithful Jews who were free from criminal guilt, whose names were written in the Lamb's book of life, would be admitted. This was not any kind of desegregated universalism. One poet said that when God sent a messiah to be king over Jerusalem that king would purge Jerusalem of its criminals and gentiles, so that it would again be holy. After that there would be no migrant or foreigner in the city. As Second Isaiah promised, foreigners would come from everywhere bringing as gifts the diaspora Jews to the city, but only the saints would be admitted (PssSol 17:25-38). The

---

[1] Morris, *Revelation*, 255.

War Scroll, found in one of the caves at Qumran, also commented on Isa 60:3. It pictured the situation still more vividly.

> Glory will fill your land;
> > blessing, your inheritance;
> > > herds of cattle will be in your fields (portions);
> > > > silver, gold, and precious stones
> > > > > will be in your palaces.
> Greatly rejoice, Zion!
> > Come forth, singing, Jerusalem.
> > > Move in procession, all cities of Judah!
> **Open your gates continually**
> > **to bring in to you the booty of the gentiles**.
> Kings will serve you,
> > and all those who oppressed you will worship you,
> > > and **[they will lick] the dust of your feet**
> (1QM 12:12-15).

This heavenly city was obviously expected to be located on earth.[1] In his analysis of the messianic expectations reflected in the Dead Sea Scrolls Talmon corrrectly observed,

> The Anointed will not come at the *end of time* [emphasis his], but rather after a *turn of times* [emphasis his] after a profound crisis in history, marked by tribulations of cosmic dimensions (cf. Hag 2:20-22). Once these are overcome, the world shall settle down to experience "a time of salvation for the people of God" that is *eo ipso* "an age of [world] dominion for all members of his fellowship," *i.e.*, for the *Yahad* (1QM 1:5; contrast Zech 1:1ff.).[2]

Zechariah expected that Israel's reputation would become so great that ten gentiles would take hold of the robe of a Jew going to Jerusalem, saying, **Let us go with you, for we have heard that God is with you** (Zech 8:20-23). After the Day of the Lord when many of the gentiles would be killed, those gentiles who were still alive would recognize their inferior positions and learn that it was prudent to become Jews and worship regularly at the Feast of Tabernacles (Zech 14:16-19), when they would

---

[1] See further, Wilcox, "Tradition," pp. 210-11. After pointing out all of the earthly associations with various interpretations of Isa 60:3, Wilcox strangely still held that Revelation intended "non-earthly" meanings to his use of the same text, using many of the same words.
[2] S. Talmon, "Waiting for the Messiah: The Spiritual Universe of the Qumran Covenanters," *Judaisms and Their Messiahs at the Turn of the Christian Era*, ed. J. Neusner, W. S. Green, and E. Frerichs (Cambridge, c1987), p. 128.

wave their palm branches and sing, **Blessed is he who comes in the name of the Lord**.

According to the Sibyl they would worship in the temple of the Great God (SibOr 3:772-73). The expectation in Rev 21:22 that there would be no temple in the new Jerusalem was not the norm. Most Jews expected a glorious temple in the new age. The "universalism" described here is not the freedom to believe as one wished, equality among all peoples, or co-existence among peoples of all beliefs. It was only the right to accept Judaism or Christianity and become a part of *that* "universal" religion. Rabbi Jose said that proselytes would come to Jerusalem in the days of the Messiah, but they would not be accepted, because proselytes could not be trusted in times of stress (bAbodRA 3b; so also Matt 7:6; 2Peter 2:22).

The gates will not be closed. This was to permit the gentiles to enter with their gifts day and night, thereby increasing the wealth of the city. Light and darkness were terms that were used in relationship to Jewish or Christian and gentile or pagan rule. The Jews and Christians thought of themselves as the children of light and the gentiles or pagans as children of darkness. The picture given in Second Isaiah upon which the author of this text depended was that of people who had been sleeping through the night. Then someone came to wake them up from their sleep, because it was morning. They should get up and dress themselves. It was time for the Jews or Christians to wake up and rule. Most of the expectations in the Book of Revelation are based on prophecies that the author thought would be fulfilled in his own time.

Nothing common will enter it. The **common** era of the gentiles will be over. The holy age of the chosen people will begin. Part of the scriptural doctrine was that the holy was distinguished from the **common** (Lev 10:10). Jerusalem was the holy city; all the rest of the cities of the world were common, meaning that they were profane, pagan, gentile. Nearly every sect of Judaism and Christianity has thought of itself as being holy, whereas all of the rest of the people of the world are **common**. There are six working days of the week that are **common**. The Sabbath day alone is holy. When Peter reportedly had a vision at Caesarea he saw a table cloth spread before him with all kinds of meat from all animals and birds. He refused to eat anything that was **common and unclean** (Acts 9:14). Unclean foods would have been those that had become defiled by corpse uncleanness or contact with any of the Levitical defilements such as menstrual uncleanness, nocturnal emissions, or anything like that. That which was **common** was that which was pagan, idolatrous, food offered to idols, food not approved by biblical dietary laws which idol worshipers ate. This included such "**common**" foods as pork and shell fish, meat of animals that did not chew the cud and have cloven hooves or fish that did not have scales and fins.

Jews thought Christians also were pagans, so they labeled the age Christians called the "Christian age" (A.D.), the "**common** era (C.E.)." From a Jewish point of view, the era when any pagan nation ruled Jerusalem was a common era, but it was to be followed by a holy era in which Jews ruled, just as surely as the Sabbath day followed the sixth day of the week.

The author of this portion of Revelation envisioned a city which was holy; it included only the orthodox Jews or Christians. It was like the highway from Babylon to Jerusalem on which all orthodox Jews from Babylon would be permitted to return. That was to have been an exclusive, holy, highway--only the redeemed Jews would be allowed to walk there. The defiled were not allowed to walk on it (Isa 35:8-10). In the new Jerusalem all heretics, all those Jews and Christians who mingled and ate with pagans, and all gentiles would be excluded. The holy city was reserved for the holy people who observed all dietary and purity rules very rigorously. This seems to contradict the passage just before which said the gates would always be open for the gentiles to bring their contributions to Jerusalem. In some way all of this seemed reasonable to the author. This new city would have an altar with a fire burning night and day, so that the entire City of David was kept light. This required an altar, but it did not need a temple. The temple Herod built was thought to be pagan, "a temple built with hands." This would be destroyed so that one stone would not be left on another (Matt 24:2). It would not replaced. The priest who had functioned there was "a wicked priest" (1QpHab) and the entire pagan service was ineffective (Hebrews). The new city would be rid of such pagan institutions as this.

CHAPTER TWENTY-TWO

TEXT

Revelation	First Testament
^{22:1}He showed me **a river of the water of life**, clear as a crystal, **going out from**	^{Zech 14:8}It will happen on that day **water of life** will **go out from** Jerusalem, half to the Eastern [Dead] Sea and half to the Last [Mediterranean] Sea. It will be thus in summer and winter.
	^{Ezek 47:1}He returned me to the door of the temple. Now look! There was **water flowing out from** under the threshold of the temple eastward, because the temple faces east, and **the water** ran down from under the south side of the temple, south of the altar.
the throne of God and the Lamb.	^{Jer 3:17}In that time, they will call Jerusalem, **"the throne of Yehowah,"** and all the gentiles will be gathered to it, to name Yehowah at Jerusalem, and they will never again walk after the stubbornness of their evil heart.
	^{Joel 4:18}It will happen on that day the mountains will drip juice, and the hills will flow with milk. **Water** will run in all the wadies of Judah, and a spring will **go out** from the temple of Yehowah and **water** the Valley of Shittim.
²**In the midst of** its street and	^{Gen 2:9}There was a **tree of life in the midst of** the garden and a **tree of** the knowledge of good and evil.

659

on both sides of **the river** is the **tree of life**,	Ezek 47:12 Alongside **the river on both sides** on the banks, will grow up every kind of **tree** for food. Their **leaves** will not wither,
bearing fruit twelve [times a year], **producing its fruit** every **month** [of the year.	and its **fruits** will not fail **for the [twelve] months [of the year] It will produce [its fruits] because its water flows out from** the temple, so its fruits will be for food **and its leaves will be for healing**.
The leaves of the tree **are for healing** of the nations.	Ezek 47:7 Look! On the shore of **the river** were very many **trees on both sides** [of the river]. He said to me, "This **water goes out** to the eastern region, goes down over the Arabah, and comes to the [Dead] Sea. It **goes out into** the sea and **heals the water** [of the sea]."

COMMENTARY

He showed me a river. This chapter begins at the holy city of Zion, with the textual support of a prophecy of Ezekiel. Ezekiel had a vision of water flowing out from the temple, under the threshold, into the Kidron Valley. The author knew that the temple never existed on the dry hill, mistakenly called the "temple mount." He wrote hundreds of years before anyone had ever conjectured that the temple belonged inside of the Haram. The temple existed down the slope, south of Herod's fortress, behind, and partially on top of the Spring of Siloam.

Ezekiel was a good geographer. He knew the boundaries of Israel and he knew the true location of the temple and the geographical situation of the stream that flowed out from the Spring of Siloam, under the temple. That stream went down the Kidron Valley. Ezekiel probably thought of the situation in rainy seasons when dry wadies fill up and become rushing rivers. He told of that stream becoming larger and larger the farther it went until it was deep enough for swimming. Since the time of Hezekiah there actually was a Pool of Siloam that was deep enough for swimming, but that was probably not what Ezekiel had in mind. The stream he visualized continued in accurate topography and geography until it ran into Wady Qumran, through the Valley of Achor, and into the Dead Sea at Ain Eglaim, which is now Ain Feshka, just south of Qumran.

The water of that stream was supposed to nourish trees on both banks, produce fruit all the year around, and support all kinds of fish. Geographically that is all clear, but how about the **streets?** If the spring were to flow directly down into the

Kidron Valley, where would the **street** be? The City of David was up on the top of the ridge, and it had **streets.** It also had water, as many ancient witness testify.

Two centuries before the time of Herod, Aristeas saw the spring water flowing through the temple, flushing out the blood from sacrifices. When Yadin was editing the Qumran Temple Scroll, he quoted the text that gives directions for establishing a place where priests could change their garments, bathe, and change into priestly garments before participating in the temple services. This place for bathing required flowing water with a canal to direct the bath water away into a drain that escaped into the ground (1QT 32:11-15). The mixture of blood and water was forbidden to be touched before it vanished into the drain, because it would have been defiled with blood (1QT 32:14-15). Rabbis said it would flow into the brook Kidron (mMid 3:2). The canal which drained the bath water away may also have been the same canal that washed away the blood from the sacrifices.

Yigael Yadin noticed that there was a great deal of agreement among the sources regarding the necessity of flowing water for sacrifices, but he seemed not to wonder what the source of all this water was if the temple was up north on the platform of the Al Aqsa Mosque, where there is no water flowing.[1] Like Shanks, Yadin defined one situation without noticing how that insight effected other details. Warren knew that the temple required lots of water for sacrifices. He assumed that the area that contains the Dome of the Rock and Al Aqsa mosque was also the temple area. He did not know where all that water came from, but he thought there must be a spring somewhere north of the northern wall of the Al Aqsa area, although he was not able to find one.[2]

It is clear from the literary testimony that there had to be water flowing through the temple area. It is also obvious that there was no such water available in the area of the Dome of the Rock, but there was also no spring up on the top of the ridge in the City of David, either. There was the huge Spring of Siloam down in the Kidron Valley, but the temple was many meters away, up on top of the ridge where the City of David was located, far above the Spring of Siloam. How did the water get up to the temple area? There is an answer to that question.

There is a 40 foot shaft that still exists that goes almost straight up from the level of the spring to a platform area where it joins a tunnel that goes 130 feet horizontally to the west before it comes out of the ground. At the end of the war between the Jews and the Romans (70 IA), Simon, one of the messianic rebels that led that war, surrendered to the Romans by appearing out of the ground *at the very place where the temple had stood before it was destroyed.* He appeared dressed in royal garments of white and purple to show that he claimed royalty, and he demanded to see the top general. As a pretending king, he claimed royal respect. He had obviously been hiding in that tunnel under the temple, which had also been a fortress—the last defense of Jerusalem (War 7:28-30).

This shows the direct route from the spring to the temple area. The temple was also a fortress, and fortresses always have to be built where water can be made

---

[1] Y. Yadin (ed.), *The Temple Scroll* (Jerusalem: The Israel Exploration Society, 1983) I, p. 222.
[2] C. Warren, *Underground Jerusalem* (London: Richard Bentley and Son, 1876), p. 352.

accessible for a large number of troops. Fortresses, such as Megiddo, Gezer, and Hazor all have good water systems. It was no accident that the temple-fortress at Zion was built in relationship to the Spring of Siloam. The last of the war between Rome and Israel had been fought at the temple,[1] and Simon had evidently been in that fortress as the temple had begun burning. He took the normal route for refuge through the nearby tunnel. The temple had been built over that channel where, if it was dry, it might provide an escape route for the fortress. It was more important, however, that it provide the necessary water both for the fortress and for the temple sacrifices. Here was the place and the way that the water flowed out from under the temple. The water was flowing west when it ran under the threshold of the temple.

Faust argued that this huge shaft, sometimes called Warren's shaft, was used to dip water in buckets for the city.[2] After they had been pulled up to the tunnel level, they would still have to be carried through the tunnel to become accessible to the city. The city needed more water than could be provided in small buckets, dipped and pulled up long distances with ropes. Think of the number of ropes this would wear out as they rubbed along those rocky walls!

Faust recognized some problems with his conjecture. He knew that pulling water up by the bucketfuls was not easy, and he suggested that it would have been used only in emergencies. He also noted that in order for water to be reached by buckets on ropes that the water would have to have been dammed up at the bottom of the shaft so that water could have been forced several meters up the shaft to bring the water level closer to the reach of the platform on which the people stood when they drew the water.[3] He neglected only to consider the possibility that the dam could have worked to allow the water to be forced all the way up the shaft, through the tunnel, and out on to the top of the ridge in the temple area. It was after that that the water could run down **the middle of the street**, as the seer described (Rev 22:2).

It is more likely that the shaft was constructed originally to bring water up to the city by force. This shaft was known as the water channel (*tsee-nohr*, צנור) (2Sam 5:8) at the time that David took the city. A water channel is normally designed and used to allow water to flow from one place to another. There was no water up on the ridge to flow down to the spring, so the water must have flowed upward from the spring to the top of the ridge, where it poured out the way Aristeas and the temple scroll testified. It evidently had to be possible, because Josephus said that was the precise spot where the temple had been before it was destroyed, and Aristeas claimed to have seen the water flowing up on the temple level.

The next question is, "Where did the water get all of the power required to force the water up the channel?" There seems to be only one answer. The huge Spring of Siloam (Gihon) was blocked somewhere near the spring and diverted the water up the chimney-like channel where it could join the horizontal tunnel, taking

---

[1] Remnants of the war continued, however, for two more years until Machaerus and Masada were taken.
[2] A. Faust, "Yes, It Really Was Used to Draw Water," *BAR* 29,5 (2003):70-76.
[3] Faust, "Used to Draw Water," pp. 73-74.

the water to the temple area where Simon appeared. If this was actually functioning in David's time, as the evidence seems to show, it would mean that the Jebusites had a superb running water system operating in that little town, perched on a ridge, three thousand years ago! In the first century IA the seer anticipated the situation being restored so that the water would run down through the middle of the street in the City of Zion (Rev 22:1-2).

If this was really so, then the Jebusites were justly confident that their little city was secure. It was well defended and supplied with all the water it needed. That is why the Jebusites thought David could never conquer this town. They had steep walls on two sides of their triangular ridge. According to Strabo, there was a wall and moat that was 60 feet deep on the north side of the city at the time of the Hasmoneans. Strabo also said that the Hasmoneans had dug rock from that moat to build the wall and the tower of the temple, so it is likely that the moat was not 60 feet deep at the time of David, but some such defense was required to provide the Jebusites the military confidence they expressed.[1] The water channel was not an entrance into the city. It was filled with rapidly running water. How could anyone lead troops into this city?

The text says that David conquered the town by approaching through the water channel (*wuh yee-gáh buh tsee-nóhr*, ויגע בצנור). If the water was running at full speed, that would have seemed impossible. The walls would have been slippery, and the force of the water would have prevented any human movement through that large canal. David's team probably had to break into the channel and turn away the water first. If they diverted the water, they could have climbed up the shaft--still with difficulty-- but they also would have cut off the water supply for the city at the same time, forcing the Jebusites to surrender. One of the ancient techniques of conducting a siege against a city was to cut off its water supply. People would die of thirst before they would die of hunger.[2]

The spring was large and strong. It also swelled every day, just the way "Old Faithful" emerges in the state of Wyoming, U.S.A. That made the water level in Hezekiah's tunnel rise regularly. If Hezekiah's tunnel had been non-existent or dammed up, that water would have been forced to rise up and fill that shaft and then run through the tunnel to appear in the temple area. This is evidently the way it happened, and Josephus' testimony tells exactly where the temple was. This channel was a huge tube through which water could be channeled from the spring to the temple, just as Aristeas and the temple scroll testify. If there had been a rope ladder at the east end of the tunnel, and the water had been turned off, Simon could probably have escaped through the spring. The fact that he confronted the Romans from the west end of the tunnel means that he had no other exit.[3]

---

[1] M. Steiner, *Excavations by Kathleen Kenyon in Jerusalem* 1961-1967, Vol. III (London: Sheffield-Academic Press, 2001), p. 21, may have found that wall and moat.
[2] So P. B. Kern, "Under Siege," *Odyssey*, 7.1 (2003):44.
[3] For a different opinion see, H. Shanks, "I Climbed Warren's Shaft (But Joab Never Did)," *BAR* 25.6 (1999):31-35.

The topography and geography of Ezekiel's vision fit perfectly, once it is recognized that the temple was closely associated with the Spring of Siloam that provided all of that water. Ezekiel was learned in this geography. He would not have pictured a temple high on the dry hill north of the spring where there would have been no water to flow down to the Dead Sea. Enoch also claimed to have seen the holy mountain with a stream that flowed underneath that mountain toward the south (1Enoch 26:2-3). There is no such stream flowing underneath the platform of the Al Aqsa Mosque and the Dome of the Rock. All Warren could find was a sewage drain down the Tyropoeon Valley, but no water running into the Dome of the Rock area.

Hezekiah's tunnel does not flow north, but it had been constructed before Ezekiel's time. The holy mountain was obviously Mount Ophel, located just above the Spring of Siloam. This is the location which Josephus pin-pointed—600 feet south of the Roman city of Antonia and right at the western end of the water tunnel (War 6:144). It is also the location of which Ezekiel spoke, where the stream that flowed underneath the mountain also flowed underneath the temple near Siloam. That was either the water chute conducting water up to the temple or the reference to Hezekiah's tunnel.[1]

Before Hezekiah's tunnel, there would have been more water pouring through that canal than either the town or the temple required. Where did the water go? There are several possibilities.

1) It might have filled the defense moat at the north edge of the town that Strabo described (Strabo, *Geography* 7.16, 2, 40), and after it was full, the run-off might have run either
2) down the Tyropoeon Valley, where Warren found a huge sewage drain, or
3) it might have run into the Kidron Valley, as the rabbis held.

In the middle of its street. In most American and European roads, water that follows a road normally runs down gutters on the sides of the road, but in Jerusalem and other Near Eastern cities, the gutter is made in the center of the road, drawing water away from the edges. Depending on the demand, many streets have only small gutters, perhaps two inches deep and four inches wide, but in others, the gutter is deep and wide. For example the road leading into the city of Gezer has a large gutter **in the middle of the** road. This requires chariots that enter the cities to straddle the gutter with wheels on both sides of the gutter. It is not clear whether this gutter in Gezer was for water or for a drain, but that which is certain is that the gutter was built **in the middle of the street.** That is the custom in the Near East and it is apparently the situation the seer anticipated. He visualized a new Jerusalem in which there would be **crystal clear water,** like that flowing from the spring, which poured **out from the throne of God,** down **the**

---

[1] So E. Martin. *The Temples that Jerusalem Forgot* (Portland: ASK Publications, c2000), pp. 277-280.

middle of the street (Rev 22:1-2) on down toward the Dead Sea, just as Ezekiel said (Ezek 47:12). It is difficult to visualize a stream and street situation if the water did not flow up on top of the ridge into the City of David where there would have been streets. Somehow this water found its way back into the Kidron Valley, making an abundance of water available for those outside of the city, including foreign armies.

Hezekiah's tunnel was probably designed partly so that the amount of water that ran outside of the city could be controlled. The Chronicler said Hezekiah built that tunnel as part of his defense system against the Assyrians. He stopped up the water of the spring that was outside of the city (2Chron 32:3). He must have built the tunnel to prevent the run-off from existing. This would have involved a system whereby part of the spring could still fill the water channel and provide all the needed water in the city, but the rest would have been channeled through the tunnel to the Pool of Siloam. Kathleen Kenyon thought the Pool of Siloam would have had a roof over it so that no one outside of the city would have known that it existed.[1] Between chapters twelve and thirteen there is a photograph of the Pool of Siloam, with boys swimming in it. This pool no longer exists, but the picture was taken in 1973.

This meant that Hezekiah planned to have the spring controlled, without huge amounts of water pouring down the banks of the Kidron Valley to provide water for an attacking enemy. This would not have kept Hezekiah from having a special pond constructed outside the city wall, near the spring to provide water for the Assyrians when they gathered--a special pond that could be poisoned from inside the city. The Scripture does not say that the Jews poisoned the water the Assyrians drank, but it reports that Isaiah and Hezekiah were well informed about the threat of the Assyrians. They also knew what it would be like if the Assyrians completed their siege of the City of David. Kern described the horrors of siege warfare. After sieges Assyrians impaled prisoners on stakes and cut off their noses, ears and lips, skinned them alive, and built mounds of their skulls.[2] In the face of that, slavery would have seemed to have been a better alternative. If the Jewish plan had not worked, the future of the city would have been predictable—"Rape, baby killing, and splitting open the wombs of pregnant women. Such terrors suggest a morally chaotic world without limits or structure. Thucydides called war a harsh master because it reduced men to an elemental level in which survival was the only goal. Siege warfare was the harshest master of all."[3]

That was the threat that came to the City of David, but Hezekiah and Isaiah were sufficiently confident of their plan to ignore this threat. The day before the extensive slaughter of Assyrians, Isaiah knew that it was going to happen, and the military intelligence of the nation risked the lives of all the people in the city on the basis of their plan. True to their plan, there were 185,000 Assyrians dead in the Valley the next day.

---

[1] Kenyon, *Jerusalem*, pp. 70-77.
[2] P. B. Kern, "Under Siege," *Odyssey*, 7.1 (2003): 44.
[3] Kern, "Under Siege," p. 61.

CONCLUSIONS

None of us was there to see all of this happening, and there may be some flaws in this conjectured reconstruction of events, but there are several points that all come together to indicate the location of the temple behind the spring, in addition to all of the biblical testimony reported in the first article. Some of them are these:

1) The testimony of Ezekiel, indicating the water flowing out from under the temple to the Dead Sea,
2) the testimony of Aristeas and the temple scroll of the huge amount of water that flowed through the temple area to wash away the bath water and the blood from the sacrifices.
3) The testimony of Tacitus (Hist 11:2) and Enoch (1Enoch 26:2-3) of the relationship of the flowing water to the temple.
4) The anticipation of the Revelation seer that crystal clear water would flow down the middle of the street in the City of David (Rev 22:1-2).
5) The anointing of Solomon at the spring of Gihon, because that was where the anointing oil was kept in the Tent of God, near the altar.
6) Josephus told of a hand-to-hand battle that took place between Antonia and the temple and said the space was narrow for that purpose. It was only 600 feet wide a (*stah-dái-ahn*, σταδαίαν) (War 6:144). When he told that Simon appeared out of the ground at the very place where the temple had been (War 7:28-30), he provided still more specific information about the location of the temple.
7) When attention is called to the water channel in which Simon was hiding, it suggests the way all of the water was brought up to the temple from the spring.

These facts and conjectures provide possible answers to questions that have puzzled historians and archaeologists for many years. This fresh **crystal clear** water was to freshen (heal) the salty sea all the way from Ein Feshka to Ain Gedi, farther south on the same bank of the Dead Sea.[1] The vision of the stream of water that would flow from under the temple was known not only by Ezekiel, but also Joel, Zechariah, and the author of Rev 22--all of whom expected magical events to happen because of this sacred river. Zechariah and Joel probably took their authority from Ezekiel, and Ezekiel based his message on Ps 1 and Jer 17. Jer 17 contains a midrash on Ps 1, and Ezek 47 is a midrash on both of these passages.[2]

The author of this section of Revelation followed Ezekiel and expected fruit 12 months of the year--not 12 kinds of fruit, as Moffat held, or 12 times the normal

---

[1] On this see W. R. Farmer, "The Geography of Ezekiel's River of Life," *BA* 19 (1956):17-22.
[2] Buchanan, "Withering Fig Trees and Progression in Midrash," *The Gospels and the Scriptures of Israel*, ed. C. A. Evans and W. R. Stegner. (Sheffield: JSNT, c1994), pp. 249-69.

amount of fruit, as Mussies understood.[1] Furthermore, Ezekiel decided the tree pictured in Ps 1 was not just one, but several, and they would all grow on the banks of a stream that began at the new temple at Zion. The author of Rev 20, 21, and 22:1-5 constructed his narrative, not just on the basis of Ezek 47, but also the Garden of Eden narrative, which also had rivers and trees. The Garden of Eden included territory all the way from Ethiopia to Parthia (Gen 2:10-14). Jerusalem and the Garden of Eden were frequently identified. One ancient author said that in the future age Paradise would be opened, the tree of life would be planted; the city [of Jerusalem] would be constructed; and a rest would be appointed (4Ezra 8:52). Another Jewish scholar said:

> The saints will rest in Eden;
> the righteous will rejoice in the new Jerusalem (TDan 5:12).

In this parallel structure, Eden was the same as the new Jerusalem. The author of this passage (Rev 22) received his clue from Ezekiel to relate the trees and the rivers of Ezek 47 to the Garden of Eden, because Ezekiel portrayed the Lord promising that the land of Israel, which, at the time Ezekiel wrote, was desolate, would be restored so that it would become like the Garden of Eden. Its towns would be rebuilt and inhabited (Ezek 36:33-35). The author of Rev 22:1-5, like authors of some other Jewish literature, sharpened the focus from the entire land of Israel to the one city of Jerusalem, but its size would be greater than the entire land of Israel had been formerly.

Since Jerusalem was to be identical to the Garden of Eden, it would have to be 1,500 miles in every direction. It would reach as far as Gog and Magog (Ezek 38-39; Rev 20:8), the four corners of the earth. Rabbis thought of the Garden of Eden in huge proportions. Rabbi Joshua ben Levi reportedly said in the Garden of Eden there would be seven houses, and each house would be 120,000 miles long and 120,000 miles wide. This information came to him when he was about to die. Just before his death he requested the angel of death to show him the Garden of Eden, and the angel granted his request.[2] Jubilees did not identify the Garden of Eden with Jerusalem, but its author argued that it was the holiest place on earth, and all of its trees were holy (Jub 3:12). He also said the Lord had four places on earth:

1) The Garden of Eden,
2) The Mountain of the East,
3) Mount Sinai, and
4) Mount Zion. It was Mount Zion through which the land would be sanctified and cleansed from its pollution (Jub 4:26).

---

[1] G. Mussies, "DYO in Apocalypse 9:12 and 16," *NovT* 9 (1967):151-54.
[2] Buchanan, *Jewish Messianic Movements from AD 70 to AD 1300* (Eugene, Oregon: Wipf and Stock Publishers, 2003), p. 553-555.

In addition to being as large as the Garden of Eden, Jerusalem in the age to come was expected to be the most holy place in the world, equivalent to the inner sanctum in Solomon's temple, but much bigger. Solomon's temple had a holy of holies that was 30 feet long, 30 feet wide, and 30 feet tall--and it was overlaid with gold (1Kings 6:20). The new Jerusalem, however, would all be a holy of holies; it would be also golden (Rev 21:18, 21). Like Solomon's holy of holies, Jerusalem would contain nothing common. Ezekiel had said that Israel would be restored like the Garden of Eden, but that would happen only after the land had been cleansed of its inequities (Ezek 36:33), so that it would be perfectly holy. Like the original Garden of Eden it would be a new holy of holies.

That would require that it would resemble the holy of holies in Solomon's temple in other ways as well. Like the holy of holies in Solomon's temple, it would also be formed in the shape of a perfect cube; but it would be bigger--1500 miles long, 1500 miles wide, and also 1500 miles high! Why so big? Because it would have to be the size of the Garden of Eden. The words **river** and **tree,** occurred both in Ezekiel's prophecy of Jerusalem and also in the Garden of Eden story. The new Jerusalem was to be holy, so it would be a cube like the holy of holies in Solomon's temple. Put all of these together and you have the cubical Jerusalem of the size described in the Book of Revelation.

This is the logic of rhetoricians. The technique is to begin with a hypothesis and follow through with assumptions. Here hypothesis no. 1 is that in the future all Jerusalem will be like the holy of holies in Solomon's temple. The original meaning was that it would be like the holy of holies in purity. Hypothesis no. 2 is that in the future Jerusalem will be like the Garden of Eden before the fall. This meant that it would be free from crime and defilement. Then the questions arises, "How large will the New Jerusalem be?" The rhetorician turns at once to these two hypotheses:

1) It will be like the Garden of Eden—in size! The Garden of Eden is so large that it includes both the Tigris (*Hiddekel*) and the Euphrates River to the Northeast and the River Gihon in Euthopia (*Cush*) to the Southwest. Therefore Jerusalem must be that big.
2) It will be like Solomon's temple—four square. The same distance in width, length, and height. Therefore the city will be a fantastically huge cube. This logic is not unique. It is rhetorically sound, but no one should expect the conclusion ever to correspond with reality. Rhetorical proof and fact are often poles apart.

A similar deduction was made by Ezekiel. The Psalmist referred to a **tree** planted by streams of **water** (Ps 1:1).

1) It produces **fruit in its season,** and its leaf will not wither.
2) Jeremiah paraphrased this, mentioning a **tree** planted by water (Jer 17:8). In the year of drought it will not worry. It will **not cease** producing **fruit** (Jer

17:9). By this Jeremiah simply meant that it would produce fruit year-after-year. All of this was to explain the value of goodness.

3) Ezekiel used these texts to determine what the age to come would be around Zion. He applied these texts—not to the benefits of virtue, but to the geography and topography around Jerusalem.
   a) The **water** involved became that which flowed out from the temple at Zion, where the **water** gushes out from the Spring of Siloam.[1]
   b) The **tree** became **trees** that grew alongside the stream that flowed into the Kidron Valley, down the Wady Qumran and into the Dead Sea. Jeremiah said the tree would **not cease producing fruit**, meaning that it would **produce fruit in its season**, every year.
   c) Ezekiel took Jeremiah's claim that it would **not cease producing fruit** to mean that it would **produce fruit** twelve months of the year. (Ezek 47:12).
4) The implications that Ezekiel drew were much more than the Psalmist intended, but the author of the text in Rev 22 took all of these deductions into account when he tried to picture Jerusalem in the age to come.[2]

Some of this does not make practical sense, but it makes dream sense. It was based on solid geographical reality, and the dream was justified by Scripture in the same way the rabbis, Ezekiel, and Jeremiah used Scripture. Since this was all a dream, it did not have to make practical sense. The author believed all prophecy would be fulfilled in the days of the Messiah, and these were days of the Messiah. Jews and Christians expected a real messiah and a real Zion where the new age would be fulfilled. In the new age it was not the normal that would be expected but the miraculous. One anonymous Medieval Jew thought that in the new age, there would be so much productivity that every Jewish woman would produce a child every day. Chickens, of course, would be still more productive. Every vine would produce enough grapes to provide all a donkey could carry, and even barren trees would

---

[1] For more details see Martin, *Temples*. Y. Shiloh, *Excavations at the City of David* (Jerusalem: The Hebrew University, 1984), pp. 46-47; D. T. Ariel (ed), *Excavations at the City of David, 1978-1985, Directed by Yigal Shiloh* V (Jerusalem: The Hebrew University, 2,000), pp 1-21.

M. P. Germano, (ed), *BA,* said of Martin's book, "Not only a work of significant scholarly impact. It may well serve as the awaited stimulus for the building of Jerusalem's Third Temple." H. Shanks, "Everything You Ever Knew about Jerusalem is Wrong," *BAR* 25.6 (1999): 20-29, and "I Climbed Warren's Shaft," *BAR* 25.6 (1999):30-35; J. Sudilovsky. "Virtual Temple Mount," *BAR* 27.4 (2001):16. J. D. Tabor, *Locating the Herodian Temple: Old and New Theories in Light of Ancient Literary Evidence* (Video Tape made by Biblical Archaeology Society), summarizing parts of Martin's book, pointed out how visible Herod's camp was and still is. Following Martin, he also has shown how similar the large 35-acre fortress is to other Roman fortresses in other parts of the world. That little area in the northwest corner of the city could never qualify as Fortress Antonia. Josephus said Herod made Antonia so that soldiers could overlook the temple, but it would not be possible to see the temple through the high walls from that distant corner.

[2] Buchanan, "Withering Fig Trees," pp. 249-69.

produce fruit.¹ Just as rabbis proved that Adam was as large as the entire world and Ezekiel proved that the trees in the new Jerusalem would bear fruit all the year around, so the author of this narrative in Revelation proved that the new Jerusalem would be cubical in shape, 1500 miles long, 1500 miles wide, and 1500 miles high. All of this, of course, would be enacted on earth around Zion.

Wise has argued cogently that 4QFlor, CDC, 4QpPs 37, 11QT, and Ezekiel all expected a purified temple at Jerusalem where the glorified, redeemed Adam, and the Garden of Eden would co-exist.²

Medieval Jewish Expectations. By NT times prophecies of Ezekiel, Joel, and Zech 14 were well known. The expectation of their fulfillment was considered standard theology. An anonymous medieval Jewish author expanded Ezekiel's prophecy to say that the water would not only freshen the Dead Sea, but it would also cleanse the whole burnt offering of the temple, the sin offering, and the menstrual defilement. He also reasoned that all of this would take place at the time of the resurrection.³

Medieval Jews believed Ezekiel, Joel, and Zechariah would all be fulfilled at the resurrection, and they tried to deduce how it could all take place. The water would flow out from the temple and water the Valley of Shittim (Joel 4:18) which was either the valley that bordered the stream flowing from Jerusalem to the Dead Sea, or the whole valley surrounding the Dead Sea. At the resurrection the council of Korah and those who died in the wilderness would come to life at the Valley of Shittim. There would also be gathered the prophet Elijah, the two messiahs, and all Israelites, from everywhere. They would destroy Armilos, the Jewish Antichrist, and go up to Jerusalem and receive the kingdom.⁴

According to Lundquist, ancient temples generally were constructed on hills or mountains with lakes or springs from which four streams of water could flow to the four regions of the earth.⁵ Widengren relates water, trees, temple basins, and

---

¹Buchanan, *Jewish Messianic Movements*, p. 547.
² M. O. Wise, "4QFlorilegium and the Temple of Adam," *RevQ* 15 (1991):103-132. Wise was correct in holding that "wicked era" and "end of days" were technical terms (p. 114-15), but his distinction was not completely accurate. The wicked era was the era of the gentile rule, patterned after the period from the destruction of the temple in 586 BIA to 164 BIA when the temple was restored. The end of days constitutes the last portion of this wicked era, the antitype of the 3½ years from the defilement of the temple by Antiochus Epiphanes to its cleansing by Judas the Maccabee and his delegated priests. The new age began with the reinstitution of the temple functions and the repossession of the land.
³ Buchanan, *Jewish Messianic Movements*, pp. 542-43.
⁴ For English translations of these Jewish documents, see Buchanan, *Jewish Messianic Movements*, pp. 370-75, 380-82, 541-45.
⁵ J. M. Lundquist, "What is a Temple," H. B. Huffman, F. A. Spina, and A. R. W. Green, *The Quest for the Kingdom of God: Studies in Honor of George E. Mendenhall* (Winona Lake:), pp. 208-209.

sacred groves as parts of sacred sites.¹ Comblin relates this water to the liturgy of the Feast of Tabernacles.²

From the throne of God and the Lamb. **The Lamb** was the Messiah, the future king of Israel who would sit on **the throne** of David in Jerusalem. **The throne** belonged both to God, the principal, and **the Lamb**, his legal agent, because as God's legal agent, the Messiah, was legally God, so that which was God's belonged also to the Messiah or **the Lamb** (see 1Chron 17:13-15). From this point of view, **the throne of Yehowah** and **the Lamb** would be in the king's palace rather than the temple. That is one explanation. Another possibility is that the author followed Jeremiah and referred to Jerusalem itself as **the throne of God.** In any event, the water that left Jerusalem toward the Dead Sea went through the Kidron Valley. Rabbis said,

> When David comes and sits on that **throne** which is prepared for him, facing the throne of his Creator, all the kings of the house of David will immediately stand up and recite poems and praises which no ear has ever heard.³

Ezekiel's vision was accepted as the word of God by later writers who expected this to happen just as the nation was being restored. Joel and Zechariah both continued this expectation. The author of this unit of redemption literature changed the image just a bit. He expected no temple in the new Jerusalem. He probably expected the altar behind the Spring of Siloam to continue, as it did after the temple was burned, but instead of a temple, like the one Herod built, he expected a tent, like the one David built adjacent to the altar, before the days of the temple. Since he expected no temple in the new Jerusalem he was consistent in saying that the water flowed, not from the temple, but from Jerusalem, without mentioning the temple. The water, however, flowed out from the Spring of Siloam, whether there was a temple above it or not.

To the text, **Its street and the river there** (Rev 22:2), NA adds **on this side and on that side was the tree of life**. This was probably an omission on the part of Sinaiticus, because the following lines presume the reader knows that there was there a tree of life.

In the Garden of Eden, in addition to every kind of tree, there was a tree of life and a tree of the knowledge of good and evil. The Lord prohibited Adam and Eve from eating of the tree of the knowledge of good and evil (Gen 2:16), but they were not prohibited from eating of the tree of life. When they "ate," however, from the tree of the knowledge of good and evil, they were driven out of the garden and

---

¹ G. Widengren, "Early Hebrew Myths and their Interpretations," S. H. Hooke (ed.), *Myth, Ritual and Kingship* (London: Oxford U. Press, 1956), p. 168.
² J. Comblin, "La liturgie de la Nouvelle Jerusalem" *Ephemerides Theologicae Louvienses* 29(1953): 35.
³ The Hebrew text is from S. A. Wertheimer, *Peér-kay Hay-kah-lóht Rah-báh-tee* (פרקי היכלות רבתי) (Jerusalem, 1890). English translation Buchanan, *Jewish Messianic Movements*, p. 531.

prohibited from eating of the tree of life. This story is probably a monastic legend justifying celibate life. The knowledge of good and evil is the knowledge that comes with marriage at the age of twenty or older.[1]

The Garden of Eden was apparently understood to have been a geographical location that comprised all of the ancient Near East. It was circumscribed by the Tigris and Euphrates Rivers to the East, Pishon River which circumscribes the Land of Havilah, and Gishon which circumscribed Ethiopia (Gen 2:10-14). The author may have thought the new Garden of Eden would be of the same dimensions. That may account for the extensive borders around the city of Jerusalem in the new age. It was easy to exaggerate in an area where no one could prove the speaker was wrong.

Adam and Eve "ate" of this "fruit" and were expelled from the garden. At the same time Adam had to work for a living, and Eve became pregnant. They were also expelled from the tree of life, which meant they were "dead" from a legal or religious point of view, even though they continued to live physically and produce children. They were "dead," because they no longer belonged to the community where life was possible. The 144,000 saints of Rev 14 were celibate. The implication of Rev 22:2 is that in the new Jerusalem "life" would be restored, and the community would be monastic, just as it had been before Adam and Eve "ate" the forbidden "fruit."

The Garden of Eden would, of course, be Jerusalem, but it seems to include also all the area from the temple to the Dead Sea, following **the river** that flows out from the temple into the Kidron Valley. That **river** ends at Qumran, where the water of life from Jerusalem reached the Dead Sea and "healed" the water of the Dead Sea. A seventh century IA redemption document pictured Abraham, Isaac, and Jacob together with the righteous after the resurrection, reclining on the banks of this stream, enjoying the fruits.[2]

Jesus expected fruits to be produced along this **river** out of season (Matt 21:18-20) in the age to come, and he was checking to see if that was the case when he cursed the fig tree. A literal translation of Rev 22:2 is, **In the midst of its street is also the river** and **the tree** of life on both sides. This accurately described the situation on the ridge of Zion, where the gutter for water was in the center of the street, as is common in the Near East, and the place for trees would be on the sides of the street. The author took **in the midst of** and **tree of life** from the Garden of Eden story and **the river on both sides** from Ezekiel and combined these two. The orchard consisted of many **trees** in Ezekiel's picture but of only one **tree** in Genesis, so the plurals and singulars are confused in the Revelation narrative. Early Jews and Christians were accustomed to read this kind of literature and probably had no difficulty in understanding that the Garden of Eden would be reestablished in Jerusalem when Ezekiel's prophecy was fulfilled. Later rabbis also expected the Garden of Eden to be restored in the new Jerusalem. Rabbi Ishmael reportedly said,

---

[1] See Buchanan, "The Old Testament Meaning of the Knowledge of Good and Evil," *JBL* 75 (1956):114-20.
[2] For an English translation of this document see Buchanan, *Jewish Messianic Movements*, p. 440.

> In the future the holy One blessed be He will call the Garden of Eden, "Zion," as it is said, **The Lord loves the gates of Zion more than all the dwellings of Jacob** (Ps 87:2). The holy One blessed be He is destined to call Zion, "The Garden of Eden," as it is said, **The Lord will comfort Zion; he will comfort all her ruins; he will make her wilderness like Eden and her desert like the Garden of the Lord** (Isa 51:3).[1]

Second Baruch said that not all was lost when Jerusalem was destroyed. Jerusalem was preserved as Paradise with the temple intact and would be held until the last times (the end of the gentile era) when it would be restored (2Bar 4.1-10.19).

Its fruit. NA has **fruits**.

The leaves of the trees. NA has **tree**, referring back to the **tree** of life. Sinaiticus has **trees**, because there were **trees** on both sides of the stream, and therefore plural. This passage may have originally had only **trees** on one side of the stream, and it was called **tree**. The texts approved by NA may then have added the words **on both sides of the river**, following Ezekiel. Sinaiticus did not make that addition, but made **the trees** plural. This is only a guess. NA may have had the original text, part of which Sinaiticus omitted, but corrected the singular **tree** to make sense of the passage.

Saadia Gaon (IA 892-942) said that the Lord had promised through Ezekiel and Zechariah that he would split the Mount of Olives in two and that there would be a river flowing out from the temple. On either bank of the river would be trees bearing fruit continually with leaves that did not wither. Since these promises had never been fulfilled, Jews could be confident that they would still come to pass.[2] In tenth century Spain, this faithful Gaon, who had never been to Palestine, would not have known as much about geography, archaeology, or interpretation of Scripture as we do today. His vision probably involved the Mount of Olives that stood between the Spring of Siloam and the Jordan Valley as splitting in two, south and north, so that the stream that now flows down the Kidron Valley would then flow between the halves of the mountain into the Jordan Valley.

For healing of the nations. The author of this document, like Ezekiel, expected the **trees** would be unusually productive, producing harvests every month. Ezekiel said the leaves of the **trees** would be **for healing,** but the midrashic author added **of the nations** or **of the gentiles.** Since throughout most of the Book of Revelation, the gentiles and foreign nations were anathematized and consigned to the lake of fire or the abyss, it is surprising here to find leaves specially created for gentile **healing** when gentiles were not to be admitted into the new Jerusalem at all! The question is,

---

[1] Buchanan, *Jewish Messianic Movements*, p. 517.
[2] Buchanan, *Jewish Messianic Movements*, pp. 56-58.

"What did the author expect to happen to the nations when they were **healed**?" The salty water of the Dead Sea was also expected to be healed by the water of life that flowed out from the temple area. When it was **healed** it was no longer salty; fish could live in it safely. While it was salty, it was evidently thought to be "sick." In some way the gentiles were also thought to be "sick" and need healing. Of what would that **healing** consist?

Although it disagrees with Rev 11, **the healing of the nations** is consistent with the verse just before it. Jeremiah had promised that when people would call Jerusalem **the throne of Yehowah** that all the gentiles would become Jewish converts. They would gather at Jerusalem to name Yehowah there. They would never again walk after their evil hearts (Jer 3:17). Therefore they would be healed at the source of this stream that flowed out from Jerusalem just as the water of the Dead Sea would be **healed** at the mouth of the same stream, flowing from Jerusalem, and become **water of life.** This is also partially coherent with Rev 21. There the gentiles gave up all of their wealth to Jerusalem, and gentiles became slaves to Jews. Rev 22 followed through on the idea that gentiles would be so impressed with the Jewish God and Jewish success that they would not only bring their wealth, but they would beg to join **the nation** of the Jews. If that happened they would no longer be defiled and so would be allowed to enter Jerusalem. This may have been the **healing** the author anticipated.

A medieval Jewish author said the **leaves** in this promise were of an ethrog tree, because the ethrog leaves were suitable for eating as well as the ethrog fruit.[1]

TEXT

Revelation

There will not be any wool (*káh-tahg-mah*, κάταγμα),

³but **the throne of God** and of the Lamb **will be** in **it**, and his servants will minister to him, ⁴and

they **will see** his
face, and his name will be on their foreheads.

First Testament

$^{Zech\ 14:11}$They will dwell in it [Jerusalem]. **There will no longer be a ban** (*khéh-rehm*, חרם) and Jerusalem will dwell in confidence.

$^{Jer\ 3:17}$In that time, they will call Jerusalem, "**the throne of Yehowah**," and all the nations **will be** gathered to **it**, to name Yehowah at Jerusalem, and they will never again walk after the stubbornness of their evil heart.

$^{Ps\ 17:15}$In righteousness I **will see** your **face**; I will be satisfied with your form when I arise.

---

[1] Buchanan, *Jewish Messianic Movements*, p. 543.

	Ps 42:3When shall I come and **see** the **face of God**?
	Zech 14:7It will happen on one day, which is known to Yehowah,
⁵**There will be no night**. They will have no need of **the light** of the lamp or	**neither day nor night**. It will be at evening time there **will be light**.
the light of the	Isa 60:19-20 **The sun** will no longer be your **light** by day **nor** for brightness will **the moon give you light** [at night], but **Yehowah will be** your **light** for the age, your **God**, your **glory**.
because **the Lord God will shine upon** them,	
	Dan 7:18The saints of the Most High **will** receive **the kingdom**,
and they will rule **the kingdom until the ages of ages**.	**and they will** possess **the kingdom until the age** and until **the age of ages**.

TECHNICAL DETAILS

Rev 22:1-5 is clearly a summary paragraph. Many of the claims made here were made earlier in Rev 21. Rev 21:22-22:5 consists of some very skillful use of FT. The author has brought together passages from different Psalms and prophets that supplement each other and deal with the same subject in which the author was most interested--the restoration of the kingdom of Israel to the chosen people very soon. This paragraph also functions as the last part of an inclusion that begins with Rev 4:1. The beginning and the ending of this prophecy depict heavenly throne scenes with the Lord himself sitting on the throne. Both are also closely related to the temple area at Jerusalem. Charles thought the work of John of Patmos began with Rev 1:1 and continued to Rev 20:3. Rev 20:4-22:21, he thought, was a later addition made up of confused fragments.[1] There are more separate units in the Book of Revelation than Charles noticed.

---

[1] R. H. Charles, *Critical and Exegetical Commentary on the Revelation of St. John the Divine* (New York: Charles Scribner's Sons, c1920) I, pp. 144-53.

COMMENTARY

There will not be any wool. This sentence makes no sense here. NA has instead, **There will no longer be a curse.** The word for curse is *kah-táth-eh-mah* (κατάθεμα) and the word for wool is *káh-tahg-mah* (κάταγμα) Both words sound very much alike in Greek. Sinaiticus was apparently taking dictation as he wrote, and he misheard the word. The reading that makes sense is that of NA, dealing with curse.

The Hebrew word for **curse** used in Zechariah was a special kind of **curse**. When a general pronounced *khéh-rehm* (חרם) over a city, that meant he intended to destroy it completely. He would not spare any of the people, the livestock, or the booty. When the author of this text used Zechariah he evidently thought that *khéh-rehm* had been pronounced over Jerusalem when Nebuchadnezzar destroyed it in 586 BIA. The fact that Jerusalem would soon be restored meant that there was no longer a ban of destruction in effect over Jerusalem. In association with other Garden of Eden themes in this narrative, the celibate male author probably understood also that the **curse** that had been given Adam, because he had listened to his wife, would be removed:

> Cursed be the ground because of you;
> through labor you shall eat of it all the days of your life;
> thorns and thistles it shall produce for you.
> By the sweat of your face you shall eat bread,
> for you are dust, and to dust you will return (Gen 3:17-19).

That would be necessary for the Garden of Eden existence to be restored. With the curse came expulsion from the celibate community. With the removal would come the restoration of the celibate community and the removal of the curse. This is coherent with the restoration of the tree of life (Rev 22:2), a strategic part of the Garden of Eden.

There seems to have been a monastery in Zion with which Jesus was familiar. As he approached Jerusalem, Jesus sent his apostles to the city to wait for a man who would be carrying water. The city was obviously Zion, and the place where they waited would have been either near Ain Gihon or near the other end of Hezekiah's conduit at the Pool of Siloam, where people came to get water. In those days women carried most of the water. The exception was the monks who did all of the necessary household chores. Any man carrying water would have been a monk. The man who carried the water did not lead the apostles to his own house to meet with his wife and children, as he would if he had been an ordinary husband.

Instead he led them to a monastery where the manager was equipped to prepare a place for Jesus and twelve other guests to celebrate the Passover. Monasteries have traditionally been prepared at all times to provide hospitality for qualified guests. This monastery would have to have been near enough either to Ain Gihon or the Pool of Siloam to make carrying water in a ceramic jar practical. That was most likely at Zion, David's holy city, near the spring (Mark 14:12-16).

Zion is the choice place for a monastery. The new Zion was to be the new Garden of Eden before the fall. The fall came when Eve became pregnant, Adam had to work to support the family, and the couple was expelled from the Garden of Eden (Gen 2:4-3:24). This was the curse of marriage. Conditions without families would be monastic. If monastic conditions were to be restored, the curse removed, the Garden of Eden established in Zion, there would have to be a monastery there, and there evidently was. Zion is the place where the Messiah was expected to gather with his 144,000 monks. These were the redeemed of the Land. They were celibate males who had not defiled themselves with women (Rev 14:1-5). Like other monks on Mount Zion, they were there to provide a temporary temple in which the Lord could dwell in purity and where they could remove the curse applied to Adam and Eve, so that Zion could be reestablished as the new Garden of Eden.

The throne of God and the Lamb is in it. Here the author departed from Jeremiah. He did not identify Jerusalem itself with the throne, but he said Jerusalem was the place where **the throne of God** was located. The throne of God is either the temple or the throne of the king in Jerusalem. The temple and the king's palace were buildings that were close to one another located behind the Spring of Siloam. The Messiah (king), was God's legal agent by virtue of his office. As such he was legally identical to God. Therefore the throne of God is also the throne of the Messiah or the Lamb.

They will serve him. There are two possible antecedents for the pronoun, **him**. It seems as if the servants would belong to the Lord rather than the Messiah. Since these servants minister to **him** and see his face, these may be priests or Levites who minister to the Lord in the worship service. Normally it is only the high priest who sees the Lord in the holy of holies and only on the Day of Atonement through the smoke of the incense. This redemption document strongly favored priests, and its authors might have thought that all of the elect who would be raised to live in Jerusalem would be priests. These would be the 144,000 who had the Lord's sign or name upon their foreheads. On the other hand, it is possible that the author intended that the servants would belong to the Lamb, because the reference in Dan 7:27 pictures the saints of the Most High receiving the kingdom and governmental authorities of all other nations serving and being subject to the Saints, and, of course, also to their leader, the Son of man, who is here called the Lamb. One of the Dead Sea Scrolls testifies that in the age to come heaven and earth would obey the Lord's messiah (4Q521:1).[1] In a relationship between principal and legal agent, the agent (the Messiah) was expected to receive the same deference as the principal (God). This exalted claim reflects that understanding.

---

[1] M. O. Wise and J. D. Tabor, "The Messiah at Qumran," *BAR* 18 (1992):62.

They will see his face. To **see** God's **face** was a privilege not even Moses was allowed (Exod 33:20), but this text pictures a court scene on judgment day with the believers on trial before God. In antiquity it was customary in a court session for the defendant to wait for the verdict of a judge while lying prostrate before him. If the judge asked the defendant to rise so that **he could face** of the judge that would be an indication that the judge's verdict would be favorable to the defendant. The defendant would then stand up and **see** the judge's **face** and be satisfied with the outcome of the trial.[1]

A medieval Jewish author interpreted Hos 6:2 as a judgment scene. He understood "days" to mean "millennia." After the prescribed number of millennia had passed, he expected to **see** the Lord, sitting on his throne of judgment in the Valley of Jehoshaphat (the Kidron Valley). Then gentiles and Jews would lie prostrate before him, awaiting his verdict. There would be two gates opened, one to Gehinnom and the other to the Garden of Eden. Rabbi Shimon ben Yohai, reportedly said,

> **After two days he will revive us.** These are the days of the Messiah, which [will last] for two thousand years. **On the third day he will raise us, [and we shall live before him]** (Hos 6:2). This is the day of judgment. Woe to everyone who dies in it![2]

Those who "lived" would live in the Garden of Eden; those who "died" would suffer in Gehinnom, in this author's opinion. The bad thing about Gehinnom was that it was outside of the holy city. The City of David had a wall around it which excluded the Valley of Gehinnom. This is the implication of Ps 17:15 upon which the author of this passage in Revelation relied for authority, and that may have been the meaning intended by the author of Rev 22 as well.

In such case it would be the Lamb, as judge, to whom the servants would minister. Those who wanted to become members of the king's country also appeared before him and pledged their allegiance to him. If he agreed to accept them, he performed some rite, such as placing his sword on the applicants' heads, giving them individually some seal, or something like that. The author said that those involved would *see* the judge's *face* and the judge's name would be placed on their foreheads. This means a favorable judgment. The judge, which in this instance was God, functioned through his legal agent, the Messiah, who was the king.

There will be no night. This is a reaffirmation of Rev 21:25, **For there will be no night there** [in Jerusalem]. With the large bonfire burning night and day, all of the surrounding area would be so well lighted that there would be no dark period at any time. The altar on which this fire was lighted was 22½ feet tall, 75 feet long, and 75

---

[1] For a discussion of this custom see Buchanan, *Biblical and Theological Insights from Ancient and Modern Civil Law* (Lewiston: Edwin Mellen Press, c1992), pp. 57-61.

[2] Quoted from "The Prayer, Secrets, and Mysteries of Rabbi Shimon Ben Yohai," tr. Buchanan, *Jewish Messianic Movements,* pp. 405-406.

feet wide. The entire City of David was a little town. A huge bonfire, more than two stories above the city would make the entire city shine. The City of David was only, about ¾ of mile long. The huge bon fire would light up this little town like streetlights.

This flame and smoke was called the glory of the Lord, and this was that which lightened up the city. Therefore, it was reasonable to say that the Lord would make his light shine upon them, but that was not the only reason. The assurance came from the Scripture. This promise is taken from Isa 60:19-20, which is interpreted by the targumist:

> You will no longer need the sun to shine during the day or even the moon to shine by night. Yehowah will be your light of the age and your God your glory. Your kingdom will never cease and your glory will not pass away.

Zech 14:7 also said there would not be alternate night and daytimes in the new age. On that day the light would appear continuously--not overly dark or light, but about the way the light appears near sun down.

They shall rule as kings. The pronoun **they** has as its antecedent the noun **servants**. This means the "servants" were not household slaves. The Greek *doó-laws* (δοῦλος) means, not only slave or servant, but any subordinate officer. For example, a general, a governor, or an ambassador was a servant of the king. Here the servants were subordinate to the Lamb or to God, but they were also citizens who had ruling authority. The conclusion that the elect would rule for ages of ages is the same as the judgment given to the saints of the Most High with the cleansing of the temple after Judas' victory at Beth-horon. It does not mean that they would all be kings, but it means they would all be citizens of a kingdom that controlled other countries and received tribute from them as colonies. According to Rabbi Ishmael,

> [With respect to the] righteous who are left in Zion and the pious ones who remain in it, the holy One blessed be He is destined to place each of them on the throne of glory, as it is said, **He will make them inherit a throne of glory** (1Sam 2:8). There will be a crown on the head of every one of them and the brilliance of the Shekinah on their faces, as it is said, **Those who love him [will be] like the sun when it goes out in its might** (Judges 5:31).[1]

This seems to be the conclusion of the prophecy which the messenger brought to John, and this summary paragraph concludes the entire message from Rev 4:1. The rest of Rev 22 is given to explain John's reaction to this prophecy after he had read it.

---

[1] Buchanan, *Jewish Messianic Movements*, p. 517.

SUMMARY

The final editor of Rev 4:1-22:5 brought together the best of the literary pieces he knew that prophesied a glorious future for Israel, and he put them altogether at the end of his document (Rev 21:1-22:5):

1) The first of these (Rev 21:1-8) described the new Jerusalem coming down from heaven, decorated like a bride prepared for her husband. Here is where God would dwell legally with human beings on earth.[1] He would remove all sadness and weeping and make all things new. The righteous would be blessed and the evil ones would be thrown into the lake of fire and sulfur, which would resemble a boiling volcanic crater.

2) The second (Rev 21:9) is another vision of Jerusalem coming down to earth from heaven. This vision described the city in terms of walls, foundations, gates, and measurements--all of which were magnificent and enormous. This new city would be lighted up so well by the huge bonfire that he would not need the sun or moon. Although the author dreamed of a huge Jerusalem, the picture of a city that would be completely lighted up by the bonfire on the altar would have been the small City of David, west of the Spring of Siloam, south of the current "old city." This was David's Zion, city of the God of life, which archaeologists recently determined, did not include Herod's walled-in military stronghold. The gates would be open continually to admit gentiles who would come bringing gifts. Nevertheless, only the undefiled righteous Jews would be admitted into the city. The city would be holy without a temple

3) The third vision (Rev 22:1-5) was based primarily on Ezek 47 and Gen 2:5-3:22. The glorious future would be like the restored Garden of Eden and also the fulfillment of Ezekiel's vision of the water flowing out from the temple area and flowing down to the Dead Sea, providing productive fruit trees all along the way. The throne in Jerusalem was for God and his Messiah, the Lamb.

People would worship both. According to Isaiah's promise there would be no night in the new Jerusalem and the believers would rule with the Messiah for ages of ages. There are conflicts among these three visions. They do not agree on the status of the temple, but they are all based on biblical prophecies and typologies. Prigent correctly observed that the kingdom pictured here is neither the Christian church nor the Christianized land.[2] It is based completely on Palestinian geography and FT prophecies and typologies. No mention was made of Jesus as the Messiah, the resurrection, or any other distinctively Christian theme.

This glorious future was expected to take place on earth and in history, just as was true of the Jews of NT times who wrote the Dead Sea Scrolls. At the

---

[1] J. Weiss, *Offenbarung des Johannes* (Göttingen, 1908), p. 681, reminded his readers that the final goal of the author was a new paradise on earth rather than an ascension to heaven.
[2] See also P. Prigent, "Le temps et le Royaume dans l'Apocalypse," *L'Apocalypse johannique et l'Apocalyptique dans le Nouveau Testament,* ed. J. Lambrecht (Gembloux: Duculot, 1980), pp. 23-45.

conclusion of his analysis of messianic expectations of the Qumran community, Talmon correctly said,

> The expected *New Aeon* will unfold as an age in which terrestrial-historical experience coalesces with celestial-spiritual utopia. Salvation is viewed as transcendent and imminent at the same time. The New Order to be established by the Anointed is not otherworldly but rather the realization of a divine plan on earth, the consummation of history in history. Qumran Messianism reflects the political ideas of the postexilic returnees' community. It is the *politeia* of the New Commonwealth of Israel and the New Universe.[1]

Loisy correctly observed that the major part of the Book of Revelation ended with Rev 22:5. The rest of the document was the work of an editor. Loisy called the beginning and conclusion of the book (Rev 1:1-3:22; 22:6-21) the work of some editor, which he did not try to identify, even though a certain John said he wrote it. Both the first and the last of the work are editorial, in Loisy's opinion.[2] He considered this to be a Christian book, but that it was a compilation of sources, some of which were of Jewish origin.

JOHN'S CONCLUSION

TEXT

Revelation	First Testament
⁶Then he [the messenger] said to me, "These words are faithful and true, and **the Lord God of the spirits of** the prophets sent [to] me his messenger to show his servants	Num 27:16-17 Moses said to Yehowah, "Let **Yehowah, God of the spirits of** all flesh appoint a man over the flock, who will go out before them and who will come in before them, one who will lead them out and bring them in, so the flock of Yehowah will not be like a flock that has no shepherd."
	Dan 2:28 But the God in heaven revealed to me a mystery. He made known to
what things **are necessary to happen** quickly.	me **what is necessary to happen** in the last days.

---

[1] S. Talmon, "Waiting for the Messiah: The Spiritual Universe of the Qumran Covenanters," *Judaisms and Their Messiahs at the Turn of the Christian Era*, ed. J. Neusner, W. S. Green, and E. Frerichs (Cambridge: Cambridge U. Press, c1987), p. 131.

[2] A. Loisy, *L'Apocalypse de Jean* (Paris: Emile Nourry, 1923), p. 387.

⁷**Look!**
I am **coming** quickly.

Blessed is he who keeps the words of the prophecy of this book."

^(Isa 40:10)**Look!** Your God! Look! Yehowah with strength **will come**,

and his right arm will rule.

TECHNICAL DETAILS

The inclusio. An *inclusio* is a literary form that acts as the slices of bread for a sandwich. It marks both the beginning and the end of a literary unit, including all the basic message in the unit included in between the two parts of the *inclusio*. Although there is a great deal of agreement in vocabulary throughout the document, the conclusion (Rev 22:6-21) includes a number of the same terms as the introduction (Rev 1:1-3:22). These remind the reader that he or she has just finished reading **the words of the prophecy of this book** that are included between the introduction and the conclusion. This author wrote also the conclusion. The use of the very same words in the beginning as in the ending means that the belief that same author who wrote the two is required by the context, and they also circumscribe the entire document with an *inclusio*.

Hartman has correctly said, "It is commonplace among authors dealing with Rev that there is some kind of relationship between the beginning and the end of the book."[1] Many scholars think this is the work of a redactor (= editor). If they are willing to think of John of Patmos as a redactor or editor, that would make sense. The author seems not to have been anonymous. Schüssler-Fiorenza holds that there is a chiastic structure in the Book of Revelation in which Rev 1:1-8 and Rev 1:9, 22 correspond to Rev 22:10-21 and Rev 19:11-22:9, respectively.[2] There are at least some very obvious relationships between the two units:

1) God, Jesus, the angel, and John are members of the cast in both.
2) Both recommend the message of the book under discussion.
3) Both recognize John as a member of a group of prophets.
4) Both are heavily documented with FT.
5) One is the introduction of the book involved and the other is the conclusion.

---

[1] L. Hartman, "Form and Message: A Preliminary Discussion of 'Partial Texts' in Rev 1-3 and 22, 6 ff.," *L'Apocalypse johannique*, p. 144. So also M. Wilcox, "Tradition and Redaction of Rev 21, 9-22, 5," *L'Apocalypse johannique* p. 206. Many scholars take Rev 22:6-22 to be an epilogue. So, for example, Prigent, "Le temps," p. 231.
[2] E. Schüssler-Fiorenza, "Composition and Structure of the Revelation of John," *CBQ* 39 (1977): 344-66.

Weiss considered the conclusion of the book to be Rev 22:6-21. He did not notice that the same hand that wrote Rev 1-3 also wrote Rev 22:6-21, but he observed, as many other scholars have, that one unit comes to an end at Rev 22:5 and another begins with Rev 22:6. The one that begins with Rev 22:6 is also related to the unit that begins with Rev 1:1.[1]

COMMENTARY

Sent [to] me his messenger. NA omits **[to] me** (*me*, με).

What things are necessary to happen. This is a partial quotation from Dan 2:28. That which John of Patmos called quickly was that period of time which Daniel called **in the last days**. **The last days** for Daniel were the last 3½ years of the old pagan age before the battle of Beth-horon and the establishment of Hanukkah. John evidently thought they would happen at a time no more distant than 3½ years. Both Daniel and John thought time was destined to follow in a certain prescribed course whose pattern was evident from the Book of Daniel. Neither Daniel nor John had any idea about the last days of history, as Boring thought.[2] Boring held that

> The author of Revelation does not predict the future in the normal sense of this expression because in this sense the future did not exist for him. The series of catastrophes that he announces are not predictions of events in history but those which form the end of history.[3]

This presumes a philosophy of history that was unknown to Judaism and Christianity of NT times. The author of this unit of Revelation knew about the Book of Daniel. It predicted **the last days** when the Greeks would be overthrown in history and Jews would rule over Palestine in history. The author of Rev 22 expected the same kind of an end to the Roman rule with the same kind of Jewish rule from Jerusalem as the Hasmoneans had enjoyed 200 years earlier--in time, geography, and history.

TEXT

Revelation 1:1-3	Revelation 22:6-21
$^{1:1}$The revelation of Jesus Christ which God gave him **to show to**	$^{22:6}$The Lord God of the spirits of the prophets sent his messenger **to show to**

---

[1] J. Weiss, *Offenbarung*, p. 683. H. Hailey, *Revelation: An Introduction and Commentary* (Grand Rapids: Baker's Book House, c1979), p. 424, was one who realized that there was a structural change between Rev 22:5 and 22:6.
[2] M. E. Boring, *The Continuing Voice of Jesus* (Louisville: Westminster, c1991), p. 168.
[3] Boring, *Continuing Voice*, pp. 177-78.

his servants the things that are necessary to happen quickly.	his servants the things that are necessary to happen quickly.
^{1:3}**Blessed is the one who** reads and those who hear **the words of the prophecy of this scroll**	^{22:7}**Blessed is the one who** keeps **the words of the prophecy of this scroll**.
	^{22:9}I am a fellow servant of you and your brothers, the prophets, and those **who keep the words of this scroll**.
and **keep** the things written in it.	^{22:18}I testify to everyone **who hears the words of the prophecy of this scroll.** If anyone adds to them, God
	will add to him the plagues that are written in **this scroll**.

COMMENTARY

These words are faithful and true. Some scholars, like Hailey, have thought that **these words** refer to **the words of the entire revelation,**[1] including the ones that made this affirmation. That makes no sense. Instead **these words** designate the words written in the prophecy included in this scroll (Rev 4:1-22:5). **These words** are the words contained in the message brought to John by a messenger, like the expression: **These are the true words of God** (Rev 19:9). Both statements may reflect Dan 10:21: **But I will tell you what is written in the book of truth**. Rev 22:6 refers to the prophecy contained in Rev 4:1-22:5. The introduction to the Book of Revelation concluded with the following benediction: **Blessed is he who reads the words of the prophecy, and blessed are those who listen and keep that which is written in it, for the time is near** (Rev 1:3).

This followed John's testimony that he had received a revelation which God had sent through a messenger, when John was an exile on the Island of Patmos and was inspired to write what he had seen and send it to the seven churches (Rev 1:1, 9-10). This he did with an accompanying letter to each of the seven churches. The revelation he received seems to have been an insight that he obtained by reading the prophecy which the messenger brought him. This evidently consisted of Rev 4:1-22:5. Except for a very few Christian interpolations, this was a Jewish prophecy. Since the same basic vocabulary appears in Rev 1:1-3:25 and 22:6-21 as in Rev 4:1-22:5, it is likely that John translated a slightly Christianized Hebrew prophecy into Greek and sent it with the accompanying letters, also in Greek.

---

[1] Hailey, *Revelation*, p. 425.

Look, I am coming quickly. Whealon thought the prophecy went from Rev 4:1 to 22:8, took Rev 22:7 to be an interruption to the text and therefore a later Christian addition.[1] It makes much more sense to recognize the end of the prophecy to come at the end of Rev 22:5. Then the verses, Rev 22:6-8, are also part of the Christian conclusion of John of Patmos.

The subject of this sentence can be either God, as in Second Isaiah, or the Lamb. Since the Lamb, as Messiah, was legally identical to his principal, God, there is no distinction, legally. This is an interruption in the continuity of the message. The author of this part of the message, apparently John of Patmos, was favorably impressed with this document and also the messenger, who attested to the value of the document. John spoke in Rev 1 about the revelation God gave him when the messenger brought him a prophecy to read, and he offered blessings for those who read, heard, and kept it. At the conclusion (Rev 22:7) he again mentioned the messenger and renewed the blessing. The expression, **Lord God of the Spirits** not only reflects a passage in Numbers, but it also is similar to the expression **Lord of spirits** often used in the Book of Enoch. Most scholars have assumed that the messenger was a heavenly messenger who communicated this prophecy to John through the spirit, but John's testimony is as follows:

TEXT

⁸I, John, am the one who hears and sees these things, and when I heard and saw, I fell down to worship before the feet of the messenger who showed me these things, but he said to me, "Don't do that! ⁹I am a fellow servant of you and your brothers, the prophets, and those who keep the words of this book. Worship God!"

COMMENTARY

Who hear and see these things. That which John **heard** was told to him by the messenger who brought him the scroll of prophecy included in Rev 4:1-22:5. That which he **saw** was the scroll of prophecy which he promptly read and with which he was very favorably impressed.

Don't do that! I am a fellow servant of yours. After John had seen the prophecy and talked with the messenger about it, he was so positively impressed that he fell down to **worship** the messenger. This was not completely surprising behavior. In the ancient Near East it was not considered idolatry to **worship** a human being. It was customary to prostrate oneself before a king or a person who deserved special respect, just as a matter of deference and acknowledgement of the other person's superior rank. The Scripture reports that Nebuchadnezzar **worshiped** Daniel, and Daniel did not object. Heavenly angels would not have objected to this deference, but this human messenger did. He believed that only God was worthy of **worship.** He called himself a **fellow servant.**

---

[1] J. F. Whealon, "New Patches on an Old Garment: The Book of Revelation," *BTB* 11 (1981):56.

Almost all people **worshiped** a king. This is the place where Jews and early Christians drew the line. To worship a gentile king was an act of submission to a foreign ruler. Since a king was recognized as an apostle of his deity, worshiping him was believed to be the same as worshiping other gods. Because religion was closely related to the state, such an act as this would be considered high treason. With a fellow believer, however, this would not normally be the case. The messenger, like Paul and Silas, objected. The messenger considered himself a colleague of John and his fellow Christians who were committed to keep the same prophecy as he kept. Especially in monastic orders, where all members were considered brothers, it would seem improper to defer to one another. The messenger worshiped God and commanded them to worship God as well. Prigent said, "The angel was not able to pretend to a dignity superior to that of a prophet or a Christian."[1]

A Jewish or Christian pseudepigraphical document, "The Apocalypse of Zephaniah," seems to have been composed after the Book of Revelation and also later than the Gospel of Luke and the Gospel of Matthew. It reflects more association with the Book of Revelation than any other NT document. In one passage the author claimed to have been encountered by an angel. At once he fell down to worship the angel, but the angel objected, saying,

> Don't worship me. I am not the Lord Almighty, but I am the great
> angel Eremiel, who is over the abyss and Hades (ApocZeph 6:15).

The author of this document evidently understood the angel who conversed with John to have been a non-human angel and provided an exegesis of the text to explain why the angel involved should not have been worshiped. The author used several scriptural sources, working in phrases from Revelation just as he had from Daniel and other FT and NT passages.[2]

Your brothers, the prophets. **Prophets** sometimes predicted future historical events (Isa 7:1-8:15), but they did not prophesy the end of history, as Boring thought.[3] They were sometimes mistaken, so Deut 18:15-22 warned the Israelites not to believe self declared prophets, until their predictions came true. If they did, they were to be recognized as true **prophets**. If not, they were false **prophets**. True **prophets** were considered legal agents for the deity, and, after their prophecies had been fulfilled, they were accepted as messages from God. Boring said,

> The authority behind the prophet's message is not empirical observation, common sense, human experience, religious tradition, or

---

[1] P. Prigent, "Apocalypse et Apocalyptique," *RSR* 47 (1985):287.
[2] J. H. Charlesworth, *The Old Testament Pseudepigrapha* (Garden City: Doubleday & Co., 1983), I, p. 513.
[3] Boring, M. E. Boring, "The *Apocalypse* as Christian Prophecy: a Discussion of the Issues Raised by the Book of Revelation for the Study of Early Christian Prophecy," *SBLSP* 2 (1974): 24.

interpretation of Scripture, as is the case with scribes, rabbis, and teachers. The prophet is one who speaks because he or she has been given his or her message directly from God.[1]

This is not completely true. Prophets, like Isaiah, Jeremiah, Ezekiel, and Zechariah, often based their prophecies on current international events and Scripture that they considered to be the word of God.[2] They were sometimes wrong. Jeremiah, for example made more than 20 mistaken predictions. One of these was that Media would destroy Babylon. That never happened, and since neither country now exists, it is clear that these prophesies will never be fulfilled. Boring said further,

> On the one hand, there is no reason to doubt that John had real visions. Ecstatic experience of various kinds is an aspect of human religion generally.[3]

This claim is also vulnerable. There are several places in the Book of Revelation where the author said, **And I saw** (Rev 9:1-12; 11:1-13; 13:1-10; 14:14-20; 15:1-4) leading most readers to think that he was observing a vision, when the next few sentences show that he was looking into the Scripture when he was seeing that which inspired him.[4] Instead of ecstatic experiences, the prophets used good judgment. They were legal consultants who were well versed in Scripture and government.

TEXT

Revelation	First Testament
[10]Then [God] said to me [through the messenger], "Do not **seal up the words** of the prophecy of this scroll, for **the time** is near."	Dan 12:4You, Daniel, roll up [the scroll] and **seal up the words**, until **the time** of the end.
	Dan 8:26The vision of the evening and the morning which has been told is true. Now **seal up** the vision, for it is [a revelation that will not be fulfilled] for many days.

---

[1] Boring, *Revelation*, p. 24.
[2] For a partial demonstration of this see Buchanan, "The Function of Agency in the Formation of Canon," *Explorations* 8 (1990):63-79.
[3] Boring, *Revelation*, p. 27.
[4] Buchanan, "The Word of God and the Apocalyptic Vision," *SBLSP 1978* (Missoula, 1978), pp. 183-92.

COMMENTARY

He said to me. This was obviously the messenger who was continuing to speak. The only reason for conjecturing that it was God speaking through the messenger is that the messenger began his conversation with a quotation from Scripture, the understood word of God, **Do not seal up** (Dan 12:4), and he continued to quote from Scripture (Rev 22:1-14).

Do not seal up the words. **The words** involved were those written on the scroll that the messenger brought to John. He was saying in essence, "Do **not** roll up this scroll and put it away for future reference. Keep this scroll open for instant reference, because it is applicable for our day, right now!" The message Daniel received was to seal up the vision for 3½ years before the end would come. John received the message that he should *not* **seal up** this prophecy. There would *not* be 3½ years to wait before this old, common age would come to an end. That 3½ year period was already over. This **prophecy** was **not to be sealed** and stored; it was to be kept open and read--revealed. When John read it, it was to him a revelation, which he set out to reveal to other Christians.

That is why **the prophecy** itself, and even the introduction and conclusion composed by John, have all been credited with the title "apocalypse." The message John heard at first was that he should send this **prophecy** out to the churches (Rev 1:11) so that other readers might also receive the revelation. This was again reinforced. The time was too short to do anything about it. Instead of being at the beginning of the 3½ year period, as in Daniel, this was the end.

The prophecy of this scroll. John of Patmos began his introduction by offering a benediction for the one who read and all those who heard the words of **the prophecy** he was sending to them. At the conclusion he repeated this description of the text. He took the word **scroll** from Dan 12:4, but he interpreted the nature of **this scroll** as a **prophecy.** He knew this was a **prophecy** because he had seen it; he read it; and later he translated it and sent it to the churches. He probably believed that all who read or heard this **prophecy** would also receive the appropriate insights.

The time is near. **The time** involved is **the time** when the gentile age would be over, **the time** when the Son of man would be given the kingdom, power, and authority over a kingdom, a **time** when there would be a new Battle of Beth-horon and a new Hanukkah. This would be **the time** when the age to come would come, and the Jewish rule would be restored to the throne at Jerusalem. Judgment would be almost immediate. There was no time for repentance before judgment. The wicked would be punished. It was too late for them to change their ways and be declared "innocent" at the great judgment day. The readers were not to try to evangelize any more. It was too late for that. The author of this unit had no idea that Christians and Jews would still be expecting that judgment day 2,000 years later.

TEXT

Revelation

First Testament

¹¹Let the unjust be unjust still; let the filthy be filthy still; let the righteous one still act justly; and let the holy one be holy still.

Dan 12:10The wicked ones will act wickedly; none of the wicked ones will understand, but the teachers will understand.

¹²**Look!**
I am coming quickly, and

my **reward is with** me

Isa 40:10**Look!**
the Lord Yehowah is coming, with strength, and his right arm rules for him. Look! his **reward is with** him.

Ps 62:12-13Power is God's, and to you, Lord, is faithfulness to contracts, because you **pay to each according to his work**.

to **pay to each as his work** is [valued],

Jer 17:10I, Yehowah, search the minds and test the hearts and give to each according to his way, **according to the fruit of his work**.

Ps 28:4**Give to them according to their work, according to the evil of their deeds and the work of their hands give to them. Pay them back** their just punishment.

Isa 44:6; cf. also 48:12Thus says Yehowah, King of Israel and its redeemer, Yehowah of armies, "**I am the first and** I am **the last**. Apart from me there is no god."

¹³**I am** the Alpha and the Omega, **the first and the last**, the beginning and the end. ¹⁴Blessed are those who

wash their robes so that their authority will

Gen 49:11 [Judah] **washes his robe** with wine, with the blood of the grape, his garment.

Gen 2:9Yehowah God produced from the ground every tree that was beautiful to see and good for eating,

be over **the tree of life**, and they shall enter the gates of the city. ¹⁵Outside are the "dogs," the magicians, the "harlots," the murderers, the idolaters, and everyone who acts and loves falsely [with respect to the contract].

and **the tree of life** in the midst of the garden as well as the tree of the knowledge of good and evil.

COMMENTARY

Let the unjust be unjust still. The time is too short to repent. Even the ten day period between popular New Year's Day and the Day of Atonement provided some time for repentance. There was not even enough time to be reconciled to one's adversary before the court session would begin (Matt 5:25). Either the author thought the time was shorter than that or that the crimes were too great and too numerous to find reconciliation and to be atoned in the short time that was left before the great divine court session. There is the possibility that the author still observed the old Pentacontad calendar that was still followed by the author of Enoch and some of the Dead Sea Scrolls. According to that calendar New Year's Day began the first day of the week after Passover. In that case, there would have been a few months before the Day of Atonement, but it still would have been a very short time.

I am coming quickly. From the FT the author found the proof that the Lord was coming. The word **quickly** was his own addition. **Quickly** always means fewer than 3½ years, a figure he obtained from Dan 7. Judging from the fact that there was no longer time enough to repent before the day in court, the author thought it was much shorter than 3½ years. Also from the Psalms the author obtained the evidence that when the Lord came he would bring rewards--good rewards for the good--Jews and/or Christians--and bad rewards for their enemies, each according to his or her works.

I am the Alpha and the Omega. This is a euphemism for the name of God. It was one of the terms used to avoid blasphemy by misusing the name of God. It was also used in Rev 1:8, in the section attributed to John of Patmos. This euphemism is also a literary form called a "merism." Merism comes from the Greek word that means "part." Instead of saying the whole thing, a person can mention both halves or all four parts. This has the same meaning as saying the whole. The first and last letters of the alphabet form the two ends, meaning the entire alphabet. When attributed to God it emphasizes God's greatness.

Blessed are they who wash their robes. These are the ones who are vindicated in the divine court session. The ones who passed judgment would again be admitted into the **Garden of Eden**, which is the new Jerusalem and the associated **Garden of Eden** between Jerusalem and the Dead Sea. Those not admitted, the ones left "outside," would be the gentiles (**dogs**), those magicians who trust in drugs, the Jewish people who have not kept their traditional laws, the "harlots" who mingle with gentiles, and others who commit crimes and are unfaithful to the contract.

These would be especially those who belong to **the quadrangle outside the temple** (Rev 11:2), the Roman fortress, called Antonia. This 35 acre military court that housed Roman soldiers was not to be included in the holy city, the true temple, or the Garden of Eden. It was to be excluded together with its inhabitants, who would not have clean garments.

This is about the same division that has been given before. It applies first of all to Zion in contrast to Antonia and after that between the chosen people and the rest of the world. The chosen are to be given control and status in the Promised Land; the rest will be thrown into the lake of sulfuric fire. Düsterdieck was mistaken in holding that the name **dogs** referred to moral impurity.[1] Swete and Morris are also mistaken in thinking the word **dogs** means "abominable."[2] The concern in this context was for liturgical purity rather than moral purity.

Their authority will be over the tree of life. **The tree of life** was a metaphor for the existence within **the Garden of Eden** before crime had ever been committed. In the age to come Jews and Christians looked forward to a new Jerusalem which would be **the Garden of Eden** before crime. It would be a city without crime. From a purity standpoint that would be a monastic community where there would be no procreation of children and no marriage. This community had control over **the tree of life.** It had the authority to prevent others from "eating of the forbidden fruit."

And they shall enter the gates of the city. **Enter** was a term not only used, as here, to refer to the process of entering Zion, physically. The **city** involved was Zion. It had **city gates** that could be opened or closed to control the people who were allowed to exist in that **city**. There was also a related theological concept: "entering the Kingdom of God" (Matt 5:20; 7:21; 18:3; 19:23-24; 23:13; Mark 9:47; John 3:5; Acts 14:22). These were not separate concepts. Those who entered the new Jerusalem in the age to come were also entering the Kingdom of God.

Outside are the dogs. As Charles has observed the **dogs**, in Jewish and early Christian thought referred to male prostitutes in a fertility cult. Israelites were forbidden to bring the salary of a harlot or the wages of a **dog** into the house of the Lord. This was the same as a female prostitute and a male prostitute (Deut 23:18). In NT times **dogs** meant gentiles who mingled with Jews, and **harlots** were Jews who mingled with gentiles (Exod 22:30; Matt 7:6; 15:22-27; 1Enoch 90.4; bMeg 6b).[3] The new Jerusalem would be free from any kind of defilement. It would be a haven

---

[1] F. Düsterdieck, *Critical and Exegetical Handbook to the Revelation of John*, tr. H. E. Jacobs (Winona Lake: Alpha Publishers, 1884), p. 491.
[2] L. Morris, *The Book of Revelation* (Grand Rapids:Wm. B. Eerdmans, c1987), p, 260.
[3] See further Buchanan, *The Consequences of the Covenant* (Leiden: E. J. Brill, 1970), pp. 184-88.

of refuge for only the rigorously faithful. The **outside** referred specially to those in the Roman military court, which would be left out.

Acts and loves. NA has **loves and acts**.

TEXT

Revelation

¹⁶I, Jesus, sent my messenger to testify these things to you for the sake of the churches. I am **the root** and the offspring **of David**,

the bright and early morning **star**.

First Testament and Christian Didache

^{Did 9.2}We give thanks to you, our Father for the holy vine **of David** your servant.

^{Isa 11:1}There shall come forth a shoot from the stump of Jesse; a branch will grow out of its **roots**.

^{Isa 11:10}In that day there will be **the root** of Jesse which will stand as an ensign to the peoples.

^{Num 24:17}A **star** stepped forth from Jacob; a staff arose from Israel. He will beat down the corners of Moab, and trample all the sons of Seth.

COMMENTARY

I, Jesus. This was obviously not written by **Jesus** himself, but the author believed that he was a legal agent of Jesus and therefore had a right to speak, write, and send messengers in **Jesus'** name. This unit was composed to show that the messenger was a Christian and that the message he brought was a Christian revelation. It had the legal authority of **Jesus**. **Jesus** was here identified as the Messiah from the line of David. The term **star** (Num 24:17) was used to mean the Messiah.

The root and the offspring of David. In NT times sons of David were not the only potential messiahs. The most recent messiahs were the Hasmoneans who had ruled Israel from the time of Judas the Maccabee (164 BIA) until Herod (38 BIA). All the while the Hasmoneans ruled, however, there continued to be Jews who thought that they were invalid rulers. The true Messiah was expected to be a son of David. Jesus fulfilled that requirement.

For the sake of the churches. The Greek *eh-peé* (ἐπί) here translated "For the sake of," reflects the Hebrew *ahl* (על) "concerning," **for the sake of,** "because of."[1] Aune noted that the **you** to whom this letter was written could not be the same indirect object as **the churches**.[2] The recipients of this letter then were not the churches, but certain individuals at the churches, either the readers or the officers (*áhn-geh-loi*) at each of the churches (Rev 2:1, 8, 12, 18; 3:1, 7, 14). These were the legal agents responsible for the individual churches. They all received this message **for the sake of the churches**, for whom they were leaders, and they were also probably the ones who would have read this message to their respective congregations.

The discussion about churches occurred in this document 19 times in the first three chapters (Rev 1:4, 11, 20; 2:1, 7, 8, 11, 12, 17, 18, 23, 29; 3:1, 6, 7, 13, 14, 22) and once in chapter 22 (22:16). In between, the word was not mentioned at all. Hodges argued that this means that the church has been translated.[3] A much more reasonable answer is that Rev 4:1-22:5 was not composed initially by any member of the Christian church. It was the author of Rev 1-3 and 22:5-22 who was writing to and about churches. This was evidently John of Patmos.

TEXT

Revelation	First Testament and Christian Didache
[17]The Spirit and the bride say, "**Come!**" Let him who hears say, "**Come!**" Let **him who is thirsty come**. He who wishes let him receive **the water of life without charge**. [18]I bear witness to everyone who hears the words of the prophecy of this book.	Isa 55:1 Ho! **Everyone who is thirsty come** to the **water**. Whoever has no money **come**, buy and eat. **Come**, buy without money, **without charge**. Zech 14:8 It will happen in that day **water of life** will go out from Jerusalem. Did 10.6 Let grace **come** and let this world pass away. Hosanna to the God of David. If anyone is holy **let him come**; if anyone is not let him repent.

---

[1] In agreement with K. Newport, "Semitic Influence on the Use of Some Prepositions in the Book of Revelation," *BT* 37 (1986):330.

[2] D. E. Aune, "The Prophetic Circle of John of Patmos and the Exegesis of Revelation 22:16," *JSNT* 37 (1989):103-116.

[3] Z. C. Hodges, "The First Horseman of the Apocalypse," *BibSac* 119 (1962):332.

Come, Lord. Amen.

COMMENTARY

The Spirit and the bride. The Spirit probably is a name for God. The bride is the church or the community. Jointly, the two subjects constitute the two parties to the contract. The invitation to **come** was issued both by God and by the chosen people who would inhabit the city of Zion.

Let him who is thirsty come. Palestine in the summer is a **thirsty** land, but Zion was distinguished as the city with this wonderful spring of Siloam, which provided clear water to quench the **thirst** of **thirsty** people.

The water of life. **The water of** life was a name given for **the** water that flowed freely from the Spring of Siloam underneath the threshold of the temple. It was available free of **charge** for the inhabitants of the city. It was the unique factor of Zion. In a land where most **water** sources dry up during the summer, this spring flowed generously all year around. The city of Zion was established originally 5,000 years ago because of this **water** source. This was one of the main reasons David wanted to control Zion in the first place. **Life** was a legal term given to those who were members of the contract made between God and his people. Palestine was called the Land of **Life**. **Water of life** was used for purification from ritual defilement. This can either be flowing **water** or **water** of at least a certain quantity. Water of **life** was that **water** which provided **life** by removing defilement. For the gentile this was proselyte baptism; for the defiled party to the contract it was the bath of sanctification. In both cases it was **the water** for the ritual necessary to admit the entrant into the community where **life** was possible. In one case for the first time; in the other case to readmit one who was temporarily removed because of defilement.

The water of life that flowed from the Spring of Siloam at Zion was so closely related to early Jewish and Christian theology that those who had entered the new contract and had become apostate were said to have "turned away from the well of the water of life" (CD 19:B34).

I, John, bear witness. This is the way John ended his addition and supporting endorsement to **the prophecy**. His few additions were introductory and supportive. He concluded with a scriptural invitation to those who had been as well impressed with **the prophecy** he had included between his introduction and conclusion as he had been. If the book had not already been Christianized, then he made the necessary additions to give it Christian authority. The final statement was a curse called down upon anyone who might make any further additions to the document.

Who hears the words of the prophecy of this book. **The words of the prophecy of this book** were **the words** of **the prophecy** reported in Rev 4:1-22:5. John expected the officers in charge of each of the churches to read this **prophecy** aloud to the members of the churches. There was to be a blessing on the one **who reads and those who hear the word of this prophecy** (Rev 1:3). The one **who reads** was the officer of the church and **those who hear** were the members of the churches.

JOHN'S COPYRIGHT

TEXT

Revelation	First Testament
	^{Deut 29:18-19}It will happen when he hears the words of this curse and he will bless himself to himself, saying, "The peace of the Lord be mine! For I will walk in the stubbornness of my mind" so as to add drunkenness to thirst. Yehowah will not be willing to forgive him, because then the nostrils of Yehowah and his jealousy will smoke against that man, and every curse
If anyone **adds to** them God will **add to** him the plagues **that are written in this scroll**, ¹⁹and	**that is written in this scroll** will lie in wait for him, and Yehowah will blot out his name from under heaven.
	^{Deut 13:1}Every word which I command you shall guard to do. You shall not **add on to** it; you shall not **take from** it.
	^{Deut 4:2}You shall not **add to** the word which I am commanding you, and you shall not **take away from** it [but you shall] keep the commandment of Yehowah your God which I am commanding you.
if anyone **takes away from** the words of the **book** of **this prophecy**, God will take away his share from	
	^{Gen 2:9}Yehowah God produced from the ground every tree that was pleasant to see and good for food,
the tree of life and from the holy city of those things written in this book. ²⁰The one who bears witness to these things says, "Yes, I am coming	**the tree of life** in the midst of the court yard, and **the tree of** the knowledge of good and evil.

quickly. Amen! Come Lord Jesus!"
²¹The grace of the Lord Jesus be with the saints.

COMMENTARY

God will take away his share from the tree of life. **The tree of life** grew in the Garden of Eden before the fall. That was when the inhabitants (Adam and Eve) were celibate. Monks were reliving those days in hopes that the Garden of Eden with its **tree of life** would be restored to Zion. The term was not mentioned in the prophecy, but it is here repeated from Rev 2:7 where **the tree of life which is in the paradise of God** was promised to those who conquer—i.e., the monks. It was part of John's vocabulary. Taking away one's **share from the Tree of life** meant exclusion from the new Jerusalem.

I am coming quickly. Amen! Come Lord Jesus! The original hearers were expected to know how Jesus was to **come,** but that is not clear today. Was he to **come** with the clouds of heaven, as the son of Man in Dan 7 or was he promising to be legally present where two or three are gathered in his name? **The one who bears witness to these things** was evidently some Christian who acted as Jesus' legal agent, and as such, could speak in Jesus' name, in his behalf, and at his responsibility.

With the saints. There are several variants of this reading. Some texts have, **with all the saints** (*pm*sy); still others read, **with all of you** (vg^{el}); and another, **with all your saints** (*et* 2329). NA accepted the reading **with everyone**. Sinaiticus may have intentionally used the word **saints** here to cohere with Rev 1:1 to form an inclusion. There he opens John's introduction with the revelation God gave Jesus **to show his saints**, and here he closes John's conclusion with the petition that grace of the Lord Jesus be **with the saints.** The *inclusio* relationship is further strengthened by John's initial and concluding appeal for grace (Rev 1:4; 22:21).

The poem. The unit in Rev 2:18-19 is a poem, ABAB:[1]
    A. If anyone . . .
    B. God will . . .
    A. If anyone . . .
    B. God will . . .

If anyone adds to them. Consistent with the methodology used both by John and by the prophet who wrote the basic message, John concluded his message by paraphrasing the warning given in Deuteronomy to anyone who heard the words of the contract and either **added** anything to them or failed to keep them. Deuteronomy promised that he would then receive the curses that were listed in the oaths of the

---

[1] This is not a chiasm, ABBA, as Boring, *Continuing Voice*, p. 162, claimed.

contract taken. John classified this prophecy in the same category as Deuteronomy. It was the word of God to be treated with the utmost respect.

The plagues that are written in this scroll. The curses in Deuteronomy associated with the contract threatened that if the Israelites broke the contract and were unfaithful, then God would also break the contract and divorce the Israelites. Instead of the curses listed in Deuteronomy or Leviticus, John threatened with **the plagues** that were promised in the prophecy when the seven angels emptied their bowls. John further threatened with excommunication. This meant the one rejected would have no portion in the Garden of Eden where the tree of life flourished. This was the new Jerusalem.

There were no copyright laws in those days, so the only protection an author had was to place the readers and scribes under the threat of curses. This was a common practice. In the Letter of Aristeas 311 supposedly reporting the magical way in which the OG was composed, the author said that after the work was completed they pronounced a curse over it to prevent anyone from changing it.[1] The same kind of curse was supposedly placed over Second Enoch (2Enoch 48:7-8). At the end of Irenaeus' treatise, *On the Ogdoad*, he wrote, "

> I place you under oath, you who copy this book, by our Lord, Jesus Christ, and by his glorious parousia, when he comes to judge the living and the dead, that you copy and correct it carefully with this text you are copying, and you shall likewise copy this oath and place it in the copy (*HE* 5:20.2).

An ancient cuneiform tablet ends with the following curse: "Whoever destroys this tablet, may the gods annihilate his name!"[2] See also Deut 4:2; 12:32; 1Enoch 1.4:10; Letter of Aristeas 310-11).

Those who have read the manuscript this far have learned all that the Book of Revelation teaches, both the prophecy and the introduction and conclusion of John are included here. That which is left is in the final chapter. What does all of this mean to the twenty first century Christian or Jew. That chapter will summarize the insights of the first 22 chapters.

---

[1] Noticed by Charles, *Revelation* I, p. 223.
[2] J. Nougayrol, *Le Palais Royal d'Ugarit III* (Paris, 1955), quoted in F. I. Andersen, "The Socio-Juridical Background of the Naboth Incident," *JBL* 85 (1966):50.

CONCLUSIONS

THE BASIC MESSAGE

The Book of Revelation is divided into two general parts:

1) The introduction and conclusion, and
2) The prophecy, which is a collection of many smaller sources developed as an anthology.

The basic message of the prophecy (Rev 4:1-22:5) is the same as the basic message of John's introduction and conclusion (Rev 1:1-3:22 and 22:6-21). It is that Rome was about to be completely destroyed and the Promised Land would be restored to the chosen people with the capital at Jerusalem. Throughout the document, Palestine, the Messiah (Lamb), the chosen people (the new saints of the Most High), the heavenly angels, and the Lord God almighty were shown in very favorable terms. All of these are joined in battle against the Romans, the Roman leaders and agents, the city of Rome, and Satan. The crowns of the Messiah (Rev 19:12) and the woman clothed in the sun (Rev 12:1) are contrasted to the crowns of the dragon (Rev 12:3). The conflict involved is not just a psychological conflict that takes place in the lives of individuals as they work out their emotional problems, reading the Book of Revelation as the required ink blot for the Rorschach test.[1] The conflict is military and national. The times of the writings and all of the future times anticipated happened nearly two centuries ago. None of these authors dreamed of the twenty-first century or anticipated anything that might happen then.

This conflict between Israel and its enemies is pictured as an antitype of earlier conflicts between Jews and the city of Tyre, the city of Babylon, or the conflict between North Israel and Nineveh. Jeremiah had predicted that Babylon would destroy Jerusalem and would itself later be destroyed. Tyre had gloated over the fall of Jerusalem (Ezek 26:2), so Ezekiel foresaw the future destruction of Tyre when Jews would have their turn to gloat. First century Jews and Christians thought of Rome as the new Babylon or the new Tyre, and they gloated when Rome began to burn (Rev 19:1-9). They used the terms, Babylon and Tyre, as code words when they were speaking disparagingly about Rome. Babylon and Tyre were both destroyed just as Jeremiah and Ezekiel prophesied. The author of these anti-Roman passages in the Book of Revelation hated Rome as much as Ezekiel and Jeremiah hated Babylon and Tyre. They also believed that God had destroyed Tyre and Babylon and was at that moment in the process of destroying Rome, requiring vengeance for the evil Rome had done to the Jews and/or Christians.

Contrasts between these two powers were presented in several ways. Rome was caricatured as a wicked woman who was a harlot, luring people into her evil

---

[1] A. Y. Collins, *Crisis and Catharsis* (Philadelphia: Westminster Press, c1984).

business. On the other hand, Israel was shown as a pious woman, wrapped in a cloud. She was pregnant with the Messiah and was always living in a crisis, but in the midst of her suffering she and the Messiah could expect to be delivered by miracles sent from God. On the other hand Israel was also displayed as a virgin destined to be the righteous bride of the Messiah, who was called the Lamb. The two would be joined in marriage by the new contract that Jeremiah promised. The Messiah was the legal agent of God, pictured as the groom. The wedding anticipated was that of the Messiah, who was to be married to the chosen people. The people were organized as a legal corporation and played the role of the bride. Since the Messiah was God's legal agent, acting in his behalf, the wedding constituted the new marriage contract between God with his people. Rome was the wicked woman who was both drunk and lustful. Rome was also described insultingly as a dragon with beasts for agents. In various ways like this Rome was cartooned in despicable ways.

During the time of Moses God had entered into a marriage contract with the chosen people through the agency of Moses. As God's legal agent, Moses had the authority to speak in God's name, in his interests, and at his responsibility. The people whom he represented before God were guilty of the crime of unfaithfulness. They had broken the contract they had made with God, so they were made to receive the curses associated with the contract. The Lord issued a divorce document and drove the Jews and North Israelites out of Yehowah's houses, his temples, and off the land. Israel could not be restored to her former position of favoritism until she retraced her steps taken in earlier years, reliving the experiences of Egypt, Babylon, the wilderness, and the conquest. The Lord was in charge of all of these events, so he punished Israel, on the one hand, and Rome, on the other. Israel was punished as the unfaithful wife and Rome was punished as the enemy. Israel had to receive the curses of the contract, and Rome had to receive the antitype of the plagues of Egypt.

The term "antitype" was used when some later event, institution, or person was compared by identification with some earlier well known event, institution, or person. The earlier event, institution, or person was known as the "type," and the later one was known as the "antitype." There was always something about the earlier type which called attention to the same character in the later antitype. In these instances the earlier type was a country that Jews hated, and Rome was a later antitype that Jews also hated in the same way and for the same reason.

The authors of the various units in this document, like their readers, were firmly convinced that they had to retrace the earlier steps of the nation, reliving the sufferings of the wilderness before they could reenter the Promised Land. Because they thought suffering was a necessary part of the past that had to be repeated, they rejoiced in their sufferings. They thought each injury would pay off some of the obligations charged against Israel. The souls of the martyrs would be stored in the heavenly membership books that were kept under the altar in the heavenly temple. The good news of their afflictions was that these punishments were the last ones they would receive. The end was in sight. It was expected within the lifetimes of the authors. This was evident from comparing the current events to earlier events in Israel's history.

An important theme throughout the document was the renewal of God's marriage contract with his people. Without a contract with Yehowah, Israel had no legal claim to anything and could expect no promises to be fulfilled and no provisions to be granted. Before the time of John of Patmos there were evidently several small essays narrating the importance of renewing the contract. The editor who collected these units evidently chose the ones that he thought were the best and fit in best with his anthology. These still exist in the Book of Revelation. These narratives were told in terms of a people holding a contract that was preserved in a scroll that was sealed, because they had no one with the authority to open the seals. Then, finally, when the Messiah appeared, the scroll would be opened. This emphasized the longing for the Messiah that was evident during that period. The period when the seals were being broken was the period when the authors lived. They were called the "birth pangs of the Messiah."

Another reference was to a scroll given by a divine figure, coming down from heaven, wrapped in a cloud and accompanied with the kinds of sounds that appeared to Moses when he received the marriage contract the first time. The heavenly character provided a scroll for the author giving him instructions to consume it, probably meaning that he should study it until it was memorized or **written on [his] mind** (Jer 31:33). This was the contract proposed to be offered to Israel for a reestablishment of a favorable relationship with the Lord. Since the contract was a marriage contract, and the Messiah was the Lord's legal agent, one narrative told of a wedding between the righteous bride of Israel and the Messiah. There were other narratives that just alluded to the contract by including items like thunder, lightning, and other noises like those that accompanied the provision of the contract at Sinai. Central to the hopes of the author and readers was the renewal of the marriage contract with the Lord.

STRUCTURE AND LITERARY IDENTIFICATION

The outline. Many scholars basically agree on the general organization of the Book of Revelation. There is disagreement in details, and there is even some basic disagreement. Among the variant opinions is that of Bauckham, who said that Revelation is not just a literary unity, but "one of the most unified works of the New Testament."[1] Revelation is a unity only in the way that an anthology is a unity. It has similar points of view, similar emphases, and a similar style, written by different people. Years ago, Charles held that there was a basic unity of authorship. Because the style was similar throughout, he said the same author wrote the entire document. He believed that Rev 1:1-20:3 was preserved basically undisturbed. The final chapters, however, had been misorganized by some unlearned editor who misplaced some of the materials (Rev 20:4-22:21).[2].

---

[1] R. Bauckham, *The Climax of Prophecy: Studies in the Book of Revelation* (Edinburgh: T. & T. Clark, 1993), p. 1, fn. 1.
[2] R. H. Charles, *A Critical and Exegetical Commentary on the Revelation of St. John the Divine*

Boismard held that there are two basic sources behind the Book of Revelation,[1] but, like Charles, he proposed the same author as the one responsible for both sources, for the same reasons that Charles gave—uniformity of style. These sources were both apocalypses written at different times and later put together to form one unit. Charles thought the uniform style excluded the possibility that there were several sources

Neither of these scholars considered the role of a translator in providing a uniform style. Translators use their own vocabularies and styles when they render the works of someone else into their own language. The vocabulary and style of Revelation probably reflects the uniform style and language of John of Patmos, the translator of Rev 4:1-22:5. There are different theories that explain this fact, but that fact is that there are many units in Revelation which reflect a uniform language.

Lohmeyer said the document is unified, except for the introduction and conclusion, which means that he found unity in the prophecy, but not in the work of John of Patmos. His solution to this problem is to propose that the same author wrote the introduction and conclusion as a separate document and later joined it to the other chapters.[2]

Like Charles and Boismard, Kraft thought the entire document was the composition of one author, but he thought it was written in three different stages, each indicated by a new conclusion.[3]

Collins held that although there is no plot to the Book of Revelation that it is organized into two large cycles of visions: Rev 1:9-11:19 and Rev 12:1-22:5. Each cycle consists of three series of seven.[4] Rousseau divided the document into five layers with an epilogue to each of the layers.[5] Beale presented a four part outline: 1) Introduction (Rev 1:1-18); 2) Rev 1:19-3:22; 3) Rev 4:1-22:5; 4) conclusion (Rev 22:6-21). He did not label parts 2 and 3, but it is clear that he thought there was a definite break between Rev 3:22 and Rev 22:6, which constituted the main part of the book.

He noted the verbal relationship between Daniel and Rev 1:1-3:22 and Rev 22:6-21, which he did not notice in the rest of the book.[6] Düsterdieck divided the book into three parts: 1) introduction (Rev 1:1-3:22), 2) the chief theme (Rev 4:1-22:5), and 3) the epilogue (Rev 22:6-21). He argued, however, for the unity of the document.[7] Other scholars have followed his lead, even though they have divided

---

(Edinburgh: T. & T. Clark, 1920).
[1] M. E. Boismard, "'L'Apocalypse', ou 'Les Apocalypses' de Saint Jean," *RB* 56 (1949):507-41.
[2] E. Lohmeyer, "Die Offenbarung des Johannes 1920-1934," *TRu* 6 (1934):301.
[3] H. Kraft, *Die Offenbarung des Johannes* (Tübingen: J. C. B. Mohr—Siebeck, 1974).
[4] A. Y. Collins, *The Apocalypse* (Wilmington: Glazier, 1979), pp. ix, 31-32.
[5] F. Rousseau, *L'Apocalypse et le milieau prophétique du Nouveau Testament: Structure et préhistoire du texte* (Tournai: Desclée, 1971).
[6] G. K. Beale, "The Influence of Daniel upon the Structure and Theology of John's Apocalypse," *JETS* 27 (1984):413-23.
[7] F. Düsterdieck, *Critical and Exegetical Handbook to the Revelation of John*, tr. H. E. Jacobs (Winona Lake: Alpha Publications, 1884), pp. ix, 22.

the chief theme into more units than one. He did not suggest that John wrote only the introduction and the conclusion--an observation which seems obvious.

Schüssler-Fiorenza argued that there was no linear temporal sequence in the Book of Revelation. Many of the units took place or were expected to take place at the same time, even though they are organized one after the other. This is not surprising for an anthology that contains units that were composed at different times and were organized on some principle other than chronology. She correctly claimed that units are organized thematically rather than temporally. Schüssler-Fiorenza also considered the central section to be Rev 4:1-22:5, although she did not distinguish this section from the introduction and conclusion as having been composed by different authors.[1]

It is not difficult to divide the Book of Revelation into a few major units, and many scholars have done that. The most logical first division is to separate the prophecy (Rev 4:1-22:5) from the introduction (Rev 1-3) and the conclusion (Rev 22:6-21). Many scholars have made these divisions. For example, from the standpoint of the use made of the word for "martyr" and "martyrdom" alone, Marshall argued that the meanings given in Rev 1-3 and 22:6-21 are different from the rest of the book. This further separates the introduction, letters, and conclusion from the prophecy (Rev 4:1-22:5).[2]

Whealon correctly believed that the Book of Revelation had as its basis a Jewish apocalypse (Rev 4:1-22:7) to which a Christian introduction, conclusion, and a few interpolations had been added. In addition to the literary evidence that points in this direction, Whealon was convinced that Christians would not approve of the war-like character of the Lamb, which was not at all like Jesus, in his judgment.[3] He did not explain why the Christian, John of Patmos, was so favorably impressed with such a war-like messiah that he could identify him with Jesus. Vanni and Aune divided the Book of Revelation into two parts: 1) Rev 1:4-3:22 and 4:1-22:21. The second part is the main part. Aune called the main part the first edition and the other section the second edition. Both took Rev 1:1-3 as a prologue and Rev 22:6-21 as an epilogue.[4]

Feuillet argued that the letters could not have been composed at the same time as the rest of the document.[5] He believed that Revelation 4-11 belonged to one unit and Rev 12-22 to another. All of these were composed during the time of Domitian, but Rev 4-11 was composed as if it belonged to the period before the fall of Jerusalem. This unit was a message to Judaism, and Rev 12-22 was directed to the

---

[1] E. Schüssler-Fiorenza, "Eschatology and the Composition of the Apocalypse," *CBQ* 30 (1968):553, 567-68.
[2] I. H. Marshall, "Martyrdom and the Parousia in the Revelation of John," *SE* 4 (1968):333-39.
[3] J. F. Whealon, "New Patches on an Old Garment: The Book of Revelation," *BTB* 11 (1981):54-59.
[4] U. Vanni, "L'Apocalypse Johannique," J. Lambrecht (ed.), *L'Apocalypse johannique et L'Apocalyptique dans le Noveau Testament* (Gembloux: Duculot, c1980), p. 26, fn. 16; D. E. Aune, *Revelation 1-5* (Dallas: Word Books, c1997), p. c, cxxi.
[5] A. Feuillet, *L'Apocalypse: état de la Question* (Paris: Desclée de Brouwer, c1962), pp. 20-21, 29, 63.

world.¹ Giet set different boundaries for the central unit. He considered Rev 4:1-19:8 to be a major unit and Rev 1-3 and Rev 19:9-22 to be another.²

With all of the differences among scholars there is much agreement in the position that the basic division of materials is between Rev 1-3 and 4-22. Several even went further and divided the final recommendation from the rest of the message, calling it an epilogue. This is the basic distinction claimed in this commentary. There is, first of all, the Jewish prophecy that has been slightly Christianized, and later a testimony by someone named John who introduced others to the prophecy and finally recommended it enthusiastically

The prophecy (Rev 4:1-22:5) contains some large units that are easy to identify. For example Rev 4-5 is either one unit or two based on a scene in heaven with the Lord sitting on the throne of judgment, surrounded by angels, the Messiah, appropriate furniture, and some heavenly beasts. Rev 12 presents an exciting narrative about a "dragon" chasing a pregnant woman. Rev 13 contains two narratives about two different "beasts." In similar ways the entire book is divided into units and subunits. Some units are based on Daniel and others on Ezekiel, Isaiah, Jeremiah, or some Psalm or Torah passage. Although they are related to the same subject material and sometimes move logically from one chapter to another, several of these units would make sense, each one, all by itself, separated from the rest of the book.

Although these facts are apparent to all, nearly every scholar who examines the Book of Revelation proposes a different outline. Some are those proposed by Lambrecht,³ Schüssler-Fiorenza, and Giblin.⁴ One of the thought-provoking outlines was proposed by Strand. In broad strokes he offered an eight unit division to the Book of Revelation:⁵

	1:1-10a Prologue
I	1:10b-3:22 Church Militant
II	4:1-8:1 God's Ongoing Work of Salvation
III	8:2-11:18 Trumpet Warnings
IV	11:19-14:20 Evil Powers
V	15:1-16:17 Bowl Plagues
VI	16:18-18:24 Evil Powers Judged by God
VII	19:1-21:4 God's Judgment Finale
VIII	21:5-22:5 Church Triumphant
	Epilogue

---

[1] A. Feuillet, "Essai d'Interpretation du Capitre XI de l'Apocalypse,"*NTS* 4 (1957/58):183-200.
[2] S. Giet, *L'Apocalypse et L'Histoire* (Paris: Presses Universitaires de France, 1957), pp. 146, 177.
[3] J. Lambrecht, "A Structuration of Revelation 4, 1-22, 5," J. Lambrecht (ed.), *L'Apocalypse*, pp. 78-104. His outline is on pages 85-86.
[4] C. H. Giblin, *The Book of Revelation* (Collegeville: The Liturgical Press, c1991), pp. 12-18.
[5] K. A. Strand, "The Eight Basic Visions in the Book of Revelation," *AUSS* 25 (1987):107-21.

This is a good outline of the prophetic section. The only problem arises in deciding whether Rev 1-3 should be considered two categories, or just one. If there is to be a division it should probably be made between the letters and the prologues. Nothing matches the letters anywhere else in the book. That which seems to be true here is the division of the prophecy (Rev 4:1-22:5) into seven units, with John's work as a separate introduction and conclusion (Rev 1:1-3:22 and Rev 22:6-22). Within the prophecy there are seven victorious introductions, one for each vision.[1]

It is much easier to find a broad outline for the book than a more detailed one, so there is more disagreement in the details. Although there are some large units within the book, the book is an anthology, composed of many separate units, some of which are overlapping in content with others. They were composed by different authors at different times and later assembled by some editor, because they were all related to the same subject. Recognizing the format of the Book of Revelation comes from reading many other collections of literature of the same kind that have been recorded by the medieval Jewish scholars. It has been closely identified with historical events between the fall of Jerusalem to the end of the Crusades.[2]

The Midrash. Rabbis called the various commentaries on Scripture "midrash." Some midrashim are continuous comments on verses of Scripture, one verse after the other. Other midrashim are sermons or arguments centered around one or two texts. Still others are narrative midrashim that narrate a story by alluding to Scripture passages throughout. The Book of Revelation is flooded with references to the First Testament (FT). These passages are called midrashim. As early as 1909, Swete correctly said,

> No book in the New Testament is so thoroughly steeped in the thought and imagery of the Old Testament.[3]

Trudinger lists about 600 verses in the Book of Revelation that allude to passages in the FT.[4] Notably scholars like Beale argue that Daniel is the basic biblical source behind the Book of Revelation. Ruiz and Vogelgesang hold, instead, that the controlling text was Ezekiel.[5] There are also differences of opinion about the references. References which one scholar claims to be controlling, others say are not central. Individual texts are debatable, but the same methodology of composition is

---

[1] There is no uniformity in this effort to outline the Book of Revelation. E. Schüssler-Fiorenza, "Composition and Structure of the Revelation of John," *CBQ* 39 (1977), for example, p. 364, also organized the book into seven units, but she included the entire document, dividing the prophecy (Rev 4:1-22:5) into only four parts.
[2] For a collection of these, see Buchanan, *Jewish Messianic Movements from AD 70 to AD 1300* (Eugene, Oregon: Wipf and Stock Publishers, 2003).
[3] H. B. Swete, *The Apocalypse of St. John* (London: Macmillan, 1909), p. liii.
[4] L. P. Trudinger, *The Text of the Old Testament in the Book of Revelation* (unpublished Th.D. dissertation, Boston University School of Theology, 1963).
[5] Scholars like Baird, Ruiz, Shea, Strand, and Vogelgesang, who have concentrated their efforts in discovering how the authors and editors in Revelation used FT sources, are all on the right track. That is one of the best ways to learn the meaning of the Book of Revelation.

basically consistent throughout the document. Those who composed the different units based their arguments on Scripture, and they used the Scripture that seemed best suited to their needs for their various arguments. These midrashic authors were rhetoricians, just as lawyers are rhetoricians. They used the scripture when arguing cases, just as lawyers use earlier legal materials. Lawyers argue cases based on the constitution and later precedents. Midrashic authors do the same, basing their cases on the Pentateuch and on various prophets, psalmists, and other later wisdom writers. Anyone accustomed to reading cases in law journals should be comfortable reading biblical documents—especially one like the Book of Revelation which is well documented by the authors' use of earlier precedents in scripture.

Each author was trying to prove on the basis of Scripture that God was soon going to restore the Promised Land to his chosen people at the time that he wrote. In so doing the authors involved used texts from Ezekiel, Daniel, Zechariah, First and Second Isaiah, and Jeremiah, according to their needs. They frequently wove texts from two or three different biblical books into one narrative. Texts were not always quoted *verbatim*, and frequently authors alluded to passages of FT with only a word or two. The logic behind all of this was that this Scripture constituted God's word by which he had entered into a contract with his people. Therefore, he could be trusted to fulfill the promises he made in that contract.

In a court of law two witnesses were required to prove a case. The same legal principle was applied to Scripture. If Isaiah and Daniel or Ezekiel agreed in their witness of promising the same event, the author could be certain that it would be fulfilled. It was not difficult to find agreement among these scriptural books, because later authors in FT also based their arguments on earlier books, just the way current legal journals collect arguments that have used earlier precedents. For example most of the times that Jeremiah made a prophecy claiming it to be the word of the Lord, he quoted verbatim from Deuteronomy, Exodus, Numbers, or Leviticus. He also used Hosea.[1] The first chapters of Zechariah are crowded with quotations and allusions to earlier Scripture. This methodology and doctrine did not stop with NT times.

Literature that closely resembles the Book of Revelation in style, content, and purpose continued to be written through the period of the Crusades. The Israeli scholar, Ibn Shemuel called this literature "Redemption Midrash" (*Mee-dreh-sháy Geh-oo-láh*, מדרשי גאולה), because, on the one hand, it was saturated with scriptural references so as to qualify as midrashic. On the other hand, its subject matter was concentrated on the near future redemption of Israel. Redemption is a financial metaphor which, biblically, refers to the deliverance of Israel from foreign powers and its restoration to the promised rule under the leadership of its own king. Just as notes for money that has been borrowed can by redeemed by paying the loan, so Jews and Christians believed fines for crimes committed could be redeemed by performing virtues in payment. The person who paid, either for the borrowed money

---

[1] See further Buchanan, *Biblical and Theological Insights from Ancient and Modern Civil Law* (Lewiston: The Edwin Mellen Press, c1992), pp. 113-139.

or the committed crimes, was called a redeemer. There were three major redemptions in Israel's history:

1) redemption from Egypt;
2) redemption from Babylon; and
3) redemption from Syrian Greeks.

Medieval Jews anticipated a future redemption from Moslems, Christians, or both. Redemption was never merely a philosophical concept for Jews. It always involved politics and real estate. The means by which it could be obtained involved war and international manipulation.

Early deliverances provided patterns by which medieval Jews could compare their current historical situation. Since they believed that God functioned according to repetitious patterns, authors of Redemption Literature made prophecies by comparing current events, typologically, to earlier redemption events, assuming that since God had fulfilled earlier promises in this way they might expect him to do it again through the same steps. Sources for their prophecies were scriptural passages related to historical redemption events.

1) For the redemption from Egypt they searched for passages from the Torah and some Psalms;
2) for the deliverance from Babylon, they read Jeremiah, Ezekiel, Ezra, Nehemiah, Haggai, Zechariah, Song of Solomon, and some Psalms;
3) for the redemption from the Greeks they had Daniel and some Psalms.

Some of this literature consisted of major sermons for feast days, like those in "Pesikta de Rav Kahana" and "Pesikta Rabbati." There were also small sermonettes like "Heavenly Jerusalem," based on the text, **This is none other than the house of God** (Gen 28:17),[1] and "Redemption and War," based on the Scripture, **Open for me, my sister, my beloved** (Cant 5:2).[2] There are scores of small prayers, poems, and hymns that express Jews' longing for redemption. For example, there is the long poem of Judah Halevy, "Longing for Zion." This poem has more than one Scripture reference for every two lines.[3] One poetic prophecy, obviously written after the event, "foresaw" the Battle of Acre that was fought between the Moslems and Christians. Christians were badly defeated. The author interpreted the event as the one preceding the arrival of the Messiah.[4] Some of the narratives and characters in this literature seem to reflect a familiarity with the Book of Revelation.

There are also anthologies in which many of these units are joined together, rather loosely, to form a greater unit. For many of these units there are two, three, or

---

[1] Buchanan, *Jewish Messianic Movements*, pp. 526-31.
[2] Buchanan, *Jewish Messianic Movements*, pp. 448-50.
[3] Buchanan, *Jewish Messianic Movements* , pp. 254-57.
[4] "That Day," tr. by Buchanan, *Jewish Messianic Movements* , pp. 291-92. The Battle of Acre was fought in IA 1291.

four versions that vary slightly. Two of the best known of these are "The Book of Zerubbabel"[1] and "The Prayer, Secrets, and Mysteries of Rabbi Shimon Ben Yohai."[2] Sometimes the units are obvious. They begin and end with the same words, forming an inclusion, or one subject comes to a complete end just before another subject begins in a different writing style. Some units have the same basic message and Scripture quotations, but are told differently. The same author would not have written both and included them in the same anthology. For example in the Book of Zerubbabel there are two introductions, both of which begin with Zerubbabel at the gate of heaven. Apparently some later editor put together two collections of redemption units that had been previously collected and attributed to Zerubbabel.

There are four variant texts of the Book of Zerubbabel. Some of the units included here are also included in other collections. For instance, the story of Armilos, the Jewish equivalent of the Antichrist, occurs in the Bodleian Library version twice. This story may have its origin in Rev 11 and Ecclesiastical History of Eusebius. It developed over hundreds of years and was modified to suit the historical situation of the person who used it. It appears at least 15 times in extant literature. One of the versions in the Book of Zerubbabel reflects the events of 629 IA and another characterizes Armilos (the Christian church) as having two heads, indicating a time after the schism of 1020 IA. Some units prophesy the deliverance of Israel in 1060 IA, with a variant text of 960 IA. Although there is an overall unity to the book, it is clear that some parts of the book were written at one time and place and some at another. That which unifies the document is the theme of deliverance or redemption of Jews from the political dominance of the Moslems and/or Christians.

The end anticipated is the end of these powers and the reestablishment of Israel as a free nation, centered around the capital city of Jerusalem, ruling the world. The redemption anthology attributed to Rabbi Shimon ben Yohai is also composed of several units, some of which, such as the story of Armilos, are also included in the Book of Zerubbabel. This collection, however, is more closely related to the events belonging to the Moslems than is the Book of Zerubbabel. It includes a long "prophecy" of events that had occurred when the Moslems were in power, including the report of the Battle of Acre in 1291 IA.

Anyone who reads this medieval redemption literature will be reminded of other literature that is already familiar. Anthologies like the Book of Zerubbabel and the Prayer, Secrets, and Mysteries of Rabbi Shimon ben Yohai are very similar to other anthologies like Daniel, Enoch, Isaiah, Zechariah, and Fourth Ezra. These biblical and other Jewish books also include midrashic developments of earlier texts, and they are also principally centered around the topic of redemption. Redemption literature is not confined to one particular form or style. It can be in the form of prophecy, poetry, letters (called *responsa* by medieval Jews), or sermons, or prayers. It can also be composed of several units that have been collected into some sort of unity. Like the Prayer, Secrets, and Mysteries of Rabbi Shimon ben Yohai, the Book

---

[1] Buchanan, *Jewish Messianic Movements*, pp. 338-82.
[2] Buchanan, *Jewish Messianic Movements*, pp. 387-418.

of Zerubbabel, the Book of Enoch, or the Book of Daniel, redemption literature can be pseudepigraphical, but that is not a requirement. There exists redemption literature, like Zechariah, the Book of Revelation, or the *responsa* of Maimonides which is not pseudepigraphical. In other words redemption literature is a very broad general term that includes many kinds of midrashic literary expression. The Book of Revelation easily fits into this category.

Revelation and Redemption Midrash. Scholars have argued about the proper name to describe the kind of literature illustrated by the Book of Revelation. On the one hand, it is the only book of this classification which contains the word, "apocalypse." The apocalypse, however, is not the entire Book of Revelation. In fact it probably was not used by John to describe a literary form at all. The apocalypse was the insight John received from God when he read the prophecy brought to him by the messenger. The prophecy which he received from the messenger probably still exists and consists of the material between Rev 4:1 and 22:5. Therefore, if any literature is to be called apocalyptic it should be the prophetic section of the Book of Revelation--not because it was an apocalypse, but because it inspired an apocalypse in John's mind. On the other hand, this prophecy lacks some of the qualifications that are typical of pseudepigraphal documents which have been called "apocalyptic,"[1] even though the word never occurs in any of the Greek documents used for defining the term. Vogelgesang calls Revelation anti-apocalyptic, because he considers apocalyptic literature to be confined to *Hecalot* and *Mercavah* literature,[2] which also never mention the word "apocalypse." If anyone starts with the same presupposition that Vogelgesang did, he or she is likely to agree with his conclusion. This is the advantage and disadvantage of rhetoric.

The Book of Revelation is not as esoteric as this other literature Vogelgesang called "apocalyptic," and it does not fit neatly into this category. The differences he noted between Revelation and apocalyptic literature are two:

1) Inside the document Revelation is called a prophecy;
2) Revelation is not pseudonymous.[3]

Although he has observed that John may not have written the entire document,[4] Vogelgesang treats the entire document as if John wrote it all and wrote with a conscious intent of refuting other so-called apocalyptic literature. It is much easier to show factual differences than it is to prove conscious refutation. This is especially true of a document, like Revelation, which contains many sources from different

---

[1] In fact some scholars, like J. M. Vogelgesang, *The Interpretation of Ezekiel in the Book of Revelation* (Ann Arbor: University Microfilms, 1986), pp. 281-86, who follow Georgi, argue that Revelation is "anti-apocalyptic." G. E. Ladd, "The Revelation and Jewish Apocalyptic," *EvQ* 29 (1957):94, correctly argued that Revelation really was not apocalyptic. It was a prophecy alongside *First Testament* prophetic books.
[2] Vogelgesang, *Interpretation*, pp. 168-308.
[3] Vogelgesang, *Interpretation*, pp. 286-87.
[4] Vogelgesang, *Interpretation*, p. 286, fn. 192.

authors and different periods. Who was the consciously intending refuter? the individual authors of sources? the editor of the prophecy? John of Patmos? Without any conscious effort at refuting authors of *Hecalot* or *Mercavah* literature these various authors may have simply emphasized different points, or the editor of the prophecy may have chosen sources that emphasized different points. Vogelgesang has driven one more coffin nail to the faulty assumption that apocalyptic literature is a well defined genre, and that the Book of Revelation fits into its category.[1]

John of Patmos called the central portion of this book a prophecy, and he also referred to it as the source of revelation which God sent to him. The letter which John attached to this prophecy is also redemption midrash. It is like other NT epistles or medieval *responsa*, as a literary form. Like most medieval redemption letters it is not pseudepigraphical. Scholars who have limited their scope to pseudepigraphical literature as the bases for their definition have had difficulty in defining the genre of the Book of Revelation. Even though John of Patmos related only the prophecy to the apocalypse, some scholars claim that the entire book is a prophecy and not an apocalypse.

This whole literary genre called "apocalyptic" is rather confusing. We might take a clue from Ibn Shemuel and compare the Book of Revelation with other literature, called "redemption literature," or "redemption midrash." Ruiz mistakenly criticized Beale for calling Revelation's use of Daniel "midrashic."[2] This is a nitpicking attempt of Ruiz to confine the term "midrash" to a narrower meaning than the rabbis ever intended. Rabbis used the Scripture in many ways, always claiming authority from it. Anyone who reads hundreds of pages of rabbinic midrash will recognize when reading Revelation its use, not only of Daniel, Ezekiel, Zechariah, and Jeremiah, but of other Scripture. He or she will also recognize it as the same kind of material as other Jewish commentaries. This kind of literature is called "midrash." Most scholars insist that there is a basic unity to the document, but they differ on the question of the divisions. For example, Beasley-Murray said,

> One controlling hand, one master mind has been at work to produce a vision of the end wherein many originally diverse elements have been worked into a panorama of wonderful symmetry.[3]

Goulder followed a pattern from beginning to end that constituted a liturgy for an entire year of weekly readings.[4] Hartman compared Revelation to *Gulliver's*

---

[1] Others who challenge the identification of Revelation with apocalyptic literature are F. D. Mazzaferri, *The Genre of the Book of Revelation from a Source-critical Perspective* (New York: DeGruyter, 1989), p. 3, and J. Kallas, "The Apocalypse--An Apocalyptic Book?," *JBL* 76 (1967):69-80.
[2] J. -P. Ruiz, *Ezekiel in the Apocalypse: the Transformation of Prophetic Language in Revelation 16,17 - 19,10* (New York: Peter Lang, c1989), p. 121.
[3] G. R. Beasley-Murray, *The Book of Revelation* (London, 1961), p. 18.
[4] M. D. Goulder, "The Apocalypse as an Annual Cycle of Prophecies," *NTS* 27 (1981):342-67.

Travels, because neither fits neatly into a precise genre.[1] It is the "precise" genre where Revelation does not fit, but it does fit into a more general genre, like redemption midrash. It has within it units of various kinds. It contains an epistle, poetry, drama, hermeneutics, prophecy, and other variant kinds of literature, but they are all put together, anthologically, into one unit that defies precise definition. It belongs to the same group as the Book of Zerubbabel, First Enoch, Fourth Ezra, Zechariah, and other similar literature developed around the restoration of the Promised Land to the chosen people.

The reason scholars disagree about the divisions is that the book is composite. Different authors wrote different parts at different times; later some of these were modified and updated an unknown number of times. Still later some unknown editor organized these units in a way that is more or less unified[2] and seems to fit into some of the plans of organization suggested. This organized unit is the document John called a prophecy that became his revelation. Like the Book of Zerubbabel, however, the Book of Revelation has more than one account of the same basic story. For example, the sea of glass (Rev 4; 15); four beasts and 24 elders (Rev 4; 19); the 144,000 (Rev 7; 14); the seven angels who bring curses to the world (Rev 8; 9; and 11:14-18); the bottomless pit (Rev 9; 20); Satan thrown from heaven (Rev 12; 20); the seven headed beast with ten horns (Rev 13; 17) who comes up from the abyss (Rev 13:1, 11; 17:8); Babylon's fall (Rev 14; 15); seven angels and seven last plagues (Rev 15; 16; 17; 21); the narratives about the book (Rev 5:1-14 and 10:9-11); and the measurement of Jerusalem (Rev 11; 21).[3] Furthermore there are some conflicting commands in the book which reflect different authorship. In Rev 10:4, for instance, the author was ordered to seal up the scroll and stop writing. In Rev 22:10-11, an obviously different author was commanded not to seal up the words of the scroll.[4]

Midrash as Prophecy. Schüssler-Fiorenza makes a false distinction between midrash and prophecy:

> While the homily is the interpretation of the divine word in Scripture, prophecy claims to be the revelation and authority of the Kyrios.[5]

She evidently did not know that FT prophets also got their authority from earlier Scripture. This can be recognized by studying the works of such prophets as Jeremiah, Ezekiel, Isaiah, Second Isaiah, Zechariah, Habakkuk, and various Psalms

---

[1] L. Hartman, "Survey of the Problem of Apocalyptic Genre," *Apocalypticism in the Mediterranean World and the Near East*, ed. D. Hellholm (Tübingen: J. C. B. Mohr, 1983), p. 301.
[2] J. Weiss, *Die Offenbarung des Johannes* (Göttingen: Vandenhoeck & Ruprecht, 1908), p. 601, early in the twentieth century, held that the book was finalized by an editor or compiler.
[3] K. A. Strand, *Interpreting the Book of Revelation* (Naples, Fla.: Ann Arbor Publishers, c1979), p. 44, noticed this.
[4] Vogelgesang, *Interpretation*, p. 315, also noticed this, but he gave this a different explanation.
[5] E. Schüssler-Fiorenza, "Apokalypsis and Propheteia: the Book of Revelation in the Context of Early Christian Prophecy," J. Lambrecht (ed), *L'Apocalypse johannique*, p. 109.

and Wisdom documents.[1] In her attempt to show that John did not belong to a Jewish apocalyptic community but a Christian prophetic community in Asia Minor Schüssler-Fiorenza tried to show similarities between Revelation and the writings of Paul, such as the salutation at the beginning of the document. These, of course, were probably standard formulae for addressing letters in that day. Since Paul was also a Jew it is not surprising to find doctrines to which both agree.

This does not mean that they were both Pauline or that they came from the same geographical territory. Schüssler-Fiorenza thought there were great similarities between Paul's salutations and that of Revelation, but Hartman pointed out the differences. The normal form should give the title of the book, mention something about its content and the author. Instead, the title in Revelation told how the message was received and it introduced John in the third person. This is more like the beginning of Enoch than any of Paul's letters.[2] We do not have enough extant letters of that period from Jewish Christians to show how similar and how different they would be from Paul's, but Revelation begins more as a book than as a letter. The fact that Paul was in conflict with the Judaizers in Asia Minor shows that there were more than Paulinists in Asia Minor. The assumption that Revelation was composed entirely in Asia Minor has not been demonstrated.

John of Patmos called the central section of the Book of Revelation a prophecy by means of which he received a revelation from God. There is very little reason to think he was incorrect in calling it a prophecy as a literary form. Since it provided him with new insights, he also said he received a revelation in close relationship to the prophecy he received, but the word "revelation" described the prophecy's function in relationship to John--not its literary form.

The Introduction and Conclusion. The last units of the Book of Revelation to be written were the introduction, the letters to the churches, and the conclusion. These parts were composed by John of Patmos. Both the introduction and the conclusion were written by the same person, who intentionally structured them in such a way as to form a unit of the entire Book of Revelation as it now exists. He unified the document with four *inclusios*:

1) quoting the same Scripture both at the beginning and at the end--Rev 1:1; 22:6: **the things that must happen** (Dan 2:28, 45);
2) references to an angel sent to **John** at both ends (Rev 1:1; 22:6);
3) the term, **I, John** (Rev 1:9; 22:8), in both places; and
4) the mention of **the words of the prophecy** (Rev 1:3), at the introduction and **the words of this book** (Rev 22:9), at the end.

---

[1] See, for example, Buchanan, "Midrashim Pre-Tannaïtes," *RB* 72 (1965):227-39; "The Function of Agency in the Formation of Canon," *Explorations* 8 (1990):63-79; and *Insights*, pp. 123-25.
[2] See L. Hartman, "Form and Message: A Preliminary Discussion of 'Partial Texts' in Rev 1-3 and 22, 6 ff.," *L'Apocalypse johannique*, p. 132.

The words added by John tell of the way John received the prophecy included in Rev 4:1-22:5, together with the midrashic, redemption letters addressed to seven churches in Asia Minor (modern Turkey). In the conclusion John recommended that the prophecy be read and observed. The message included between the introduction and the conclusion is the prophecy about which John wrote. The prophecy begins with a vision of heaven (Rev 4). This is followed by a narrative constructed around seven seals that are systematically opened (Rev 5-7). Next are the seven trumpets (Rev 8-14) and the seven curses (Rev 15-16). The distinction between the Johannine additions and the prophecy are so obvious that many scholars, who assume that John of Patmos wrote the entire document, nevertheless, consider Rev 1-3 and 22:6-21 to be separate divisions, which they call the "prologue" and the "epilogue."[1]

DATES AND PLACES OF COMPOSITION

The Book of Revelation was not composed at one time by one author, but many scholars believe that it was. Most of these follow Irenaeus and date the composition of the book about 90-95 IA, during the reign of Domitian.[2] There were some, like Boring, who held that the book had to have been written after 70 IA, because it identified Rome with Babylon.[3] These scholars argue that since Babylon burned Jerusalem in 586 BIA Rome could not have been considered an antitype of Babylon until it had also burned Jerusalem. Typology, however, does not require that both items fit at every point. Since Babylon, like Egypt, once ruled the Israelites or Jews either one would be a good antitype for Rome. Jerusalem is nowhere described in the Book of Revelation as having burned, although the burning of Rome is vividly described. Fourth Ezra, on the other hand, describes the burning both of Jerusalem (4Ezra 10:21; 12:44-50) and Rome (12:1-3). Parts of the Book of Revelation may have been composed after the fall of Jerusalem, but the use of Babylon as a type is no clue that Jerusalem had been burned.

Others, who also thought Revelation was completed during the time of Domitian, believed that there were many sources of the book that were composed earlier.[4] Boismard, however, thought the book was composed of two units, both of which were written during the seventh decade,[5] and Bell, Lipinski, and Newman all date the book during the war between the Jews and the Romans (IA 66-70).[6]

There is no single date or place that will satisfy the data provided by the Book of Revelation. The introduction and conclusion related John of Patmos to the

---

[1] For example, see Vanni, "L'Apocalypse," p. 26, fn. 16.
[2] For example Vanni, "L'Apocalypse,", p. 28, and Weiss, *Offenbarung*, p. 599.
[3] M. E. Boring, *Revelation* (Louisville: John Knox Press, c1989), p. 10.
[4] Such as A. S. Peake, *The Revelation of John* (London: Holborn, n.d.), pp. 5-10, and A. Loisy, *L'Apocalypse de Jean* (Paris: Emile Nourry, 1963), pp. 37-42.
[5] M. E. Boismard, "'L'Apocalypse', ou 'les Apocalypses'" pp. 507-41; "Notes sur l'Apocalypse," *RB* 59 (1952): 172-81; *L'Apocalypse* (Paris: Les Editions du Cerf, 1959), pp. 520-21; 538-41.
[6] Albert A. Bell, Jr., "The Date of John's Apocalypse. The Evidence of Some Roman Historians Reconsidered," *NTS* 25 (1978):93-102; E. Lipinski, "L'Apocalypse et le Martyre de Jean à Jérusalem," *NovT* 11 (1969):225-32; and B. Newman, "The Fallacy of the Domitian Hypothesis," *NTS* 10 (1963/64):133-39.

area around Asia Minor. Some messenger (*áhn-geh-laws*) brought him the prophecy at Patmos, but there is no certainty that he translated the document and wrote his introduction and conclusion at Patmos. He was later reported to have lived at Ephesus (HE 3:3, 6). He described the events related to his reception of the prophecy in the past tense. The event would have occurred before the writing whether he wrote at Patmos or some other location.

The only references to the Asia Minor area are those written by John, and the date given by Irenaeus relates only to the time John made his additions and circulated the document. That was the part Irenaeus said was done during the time of Domitian. The geographical locations given in the prophecy (Rev 4:1-22:5) are places like Mount Megiddo, Jerusalem, the Kidron Valley, the Mount of Olives, mountains, caves, and other situations descriptive of places in Palestine. It also mentions adjoining places, like Euphrates, the East, and symbolic places like Egypt and Babylon. None of these is related to Asia Minor. This shows that the prophecy was not composed at the same date and place as the introduction and conclusion.

We who live in the twenty-first century have to deduce most of the dates for the literature in the Book of Revelation. Some parts of the prophecy may have been written as early as 37 BIA, describing Herod the Great as a beast and King Antigonus as the Lamb. Other parts may have been written more than a hundred years later--as late as 69-70 IA, when Jerusalem was involved in a civil war, and Rome was burning. Other parts, like the description of the second beast may have been composed during the reigns of Emperor Gaius and King Agrippa (ca. 37-44 IA).

Sometime after 70 IA the prophecy was organized by some editor into the prophecy that now is preserved as Rev 4:1-22:5. The editor who did the organization may have also added the few Christianizing statements, making the prophecy more or less Christian. Some time after 70 IA the prophecy was brought to John at Patmos. Most scholars accept the dating given by Irenaeus who said it was written by John during the reign of Domitian (ca. 81-96 IA). This is the only written testimony preserved that offers a possible date for John's authorship. Although Irenaeus may have had false information, he was made bishop in 177 IA, which is much closer in time than the twentieth century. Therefore it cannot be justly ignored. The possible extremes of estimation, then, are 70 IA when parts of the prophecy were composed, and approximately 177 IA when Irenaeus was made bishop. This space can be further reduced by the occurrence of the Bar Cochba War (132-35 IA), after which all hope of immediate restoration of the Promised Land to the chosen people had vanished. Charles Hill argued that Irenaeus used the entire Book of Revelation, indicating that the complete book was well known in its present form before the end of the second century.[1]

If it were not for Irenaeus's testimony (HE 3:18, 3; 5:8, 6) Domitian's reign would not have been the time most reasonably chosen to conjecture. A more likely time for John to have functioned would have been closer to Bar Cochba's

---

[1] Charles E. Hill, *The Johannine Corpus in the Early Church* (Oxford: The University Press, c2004), p. 96.

movement. Eschatological excitement, such as that which John exhibited when he received the prophecy, usually requires more than a time of persecution, such as that possibly administered by Domitian. It also demands some hope of redemption. For example, Second Isaiah was written after the author knew that Jews had made a treaty with Cyrus of Persia to work together to overthrow Babylon and allow Jews to return to Palestine. Zechariah was written after Babylon had been taken by Persia.

There was a great deal of eschatological excitement between IA 66 and IA 70, not just because Jews were suffering hardship, but because they had defeated Cestius at the Battle of Beth-horon (66 IA), and especially after Vespasian left Jerusalem to settle a civil war in Rome, and Rome was burned in the process (69 IA). That was a time when prophets thought Rome was going to be destroyed and Jews were about to receive possession of the Promised Land again. There was no such movement during the time of Domitian.

Neither had a Jubilee of years elapsed between 70 IA and 95 IA. That Jubilee would have occurred about 120 IA. A Jewish rebellion broke out in Egypt in 115 IA (HE 4:2, 1-5), but this seemed to be local. Hadrian became emperor in 117 IA and began to develop good relationships with the Jews. He planned to rebuild Jerusalem, and Jews thought he was going to rebuild the Jewish temple for Jews. When Jews learned the temple was going to be dedicated to Jupiter, resistance began, which finally developed into an all-out war that lasted from 132 to 135 IA. Any time during the Hadrianic period, someone like John might have read the prophecy included in the Book of Revelation and concluded that the events prophesied were **the things that had to happen *quickly*** (Dan 2:28, 45; Rev 1:1). This deduction does not rule out the testimony of Irenaeus. There may have been resistance movements that occurred during Domitian's reign which have not been reported. This discussion offers more data to be considered in reconstructing history.

Among the possible conjectures some that are most likely are that the prophecy (Rev 4:1-22:5) was written before the introduction and conclusion (Rev 1:1-3:22 and 22:6-21). The prophecy was composed at many different times and finally organized after 70 IA. The prophecy was probably composed in Palestine, partly in Jerusalem. The introduction and conclusion were composed in western Asia Minor, possibly at Patmos Island or Ephesus, between 70 IA and 135 IA.

THE AUTHORS AND THE COMMUNITIES OF THE DOCUMENT

Author or Authors. It would be easy, but naive, to presume that the Book of Revelation is a unified document, composed entirely by one author, whose name was John. The document, however, has a complex origin whose parts have come from different periods and have been updated an unknown number of times before they were all put together into one prophecy. It is true that John is the only person mentioned as an author in the Book of Revelation, and the only biographical materials given in the book are related to him, and they occur only in the introduction and conclusion of the document. Therefore John will be given most of the attention devoted to authorship in the Book of Revelation.

We know the name of one author, **John,** because it is given in the text. The author did not give any detail about his qualifications—no genealogy, no attempt to distinguish himself from all of the other **Johns** of the NT. He did not claim to be an apostle or an elder, although Justin (*Dial.* 81:4) claimed in 155 IA that he was an apostle, and Eusebius reported that Papias listed him among the elders (HE 7:25, 12-16). Even though both of these facts have been widely circulated and accepted, it is not certain that John held either of these qualifications.

John simply wrote affirmatively, boldly and voluntarily, **I, John,** just as if he were testifying before a court and had sworn to tell the truth, the whole truth, and nothing but the truth. He did not tell more about himself, except to identify himself with the Christian brothers, apparently a courageous thing to do during the turbulent time about which he wrote.

He identified himself with the message he sent--not as if he were the author—but as if he valued it highly, recommended it, and put his signature to his recommendation. As Bovon correctly said, he was not discreet about it. He made no attempt to be anonymous, but he used his own personal pronoun and his own name. This would draw him closer to his readers or listeners.[1] He used his name only twice in the entire document, once here in the introduction, and again at the end (Rev 22:8), he put his signature to his recommendation.

A Christian Leader. John was presented in relationship to the *ahn-geh-laws* (angel, messenger) in a way that seems rather normal in historical concepts. He was not "taken up" and moved through the heavens nor did he go from one geographical location or section of the universe to another, the way Ezekiel and Enoch did (Ezek 3:12-15; 8:3, 7, 16; 11:1, 24; 40:1-3, 17, 24, 35, 48; 41:1, 15; 43:1, 5; 44:1, 4; 46:19, 21; 47:1-2; Enoch 14:8; 17:4-5; 23:1; 28:1; 29.1; 30:1; 32:2-3; 33:1; 35:1; 36:1-2). John was no ancient, like Noah, Moses, Enoch, Daniel, and other heroes in whose names some redemption literature has been falsely written. Neither was this composition attributed to any ancient leader like David, Solomon, or Moses.

In fact if John merely transcribed a book the *áhn-geh-laws* brought him, the book he was brought is not attributed to anyone. John apparently was a real human being who lived at the very time he professed to have received the prophecy. John referred to himself as the Lord's servant (Rev 1:1); the *áhn-geh-laws* was a fellow servant (Rev 22:9), and the recipients of the message were also called God's servants (Rev 22:6). Other believers for whom the message was intended were called "brothers" and "prophets" (Rev 22:9). John, too, was called a "brother" (Rev 1:9) and was probably a member of a brotherhood known as prophets (Rev 22:9). John and his readers were all Christians who interpreted Jesus' death as expiatory (Rev 1:5-6). The fact that John punctuated Exod 19:9 to read, **And he made you a**

---

[1] F. Bovon, "John's Self-presentation in Revelation 1:9-10," *CBQ* 62 (2000):693-700.

kingdom, priests to God (Rev 1:6), may mean that this brotherhood was composed of priests, but it may instead have been a general allusion, as in 1Pet 2:9.

Possible Problems. Bauckham gathered important instances in extra-canonical literature that might indicate that it was normal for angels to object to human worship.[1] His first example is of the angel who escorted Isaiah in a vision through six heavens to the seventh. When they reached the second heaven where angels were worshiping the one who sat on the throne, Isaiah also began to worship--not his escorting angel, but the being on the throne. He was forbidden, however, by the angel, to worship any being or at any time until directed to do so by his escorting angel (AsIsa 7:21-22). This would take place in the seventh heaven. When they reached the sixth heaven, Isaiah referred to his escort as "Lord." The angel objected, saying that he was not Isaiah's lord but his companion (AsIsa 8:5). When he finally reached the seventh heaven he was instructed to worship the angel of the Holy Spirit, which he did (AsIsa 9:36-10:6). Then the Father of Jesus told Isaiah that he was no longer of human likeness, but rather like all of the angels of heaven. This made him superior to the angels of the world (AsIsa 10:7-11), but a companion of the angels from the seventh heaven who escorted him from earth.

This is not really comparable to the angel who refused to allow John to worship him. One situation took place in heaven where Isaiah was taken only in a vision and was transformed into a being like heavenly angels. The other was not in a vision but in a historical account of a situation that took place on earth with an angel who was not distinguished as a heavenly angel. In one instance Isaiah attempted to worship someone sitting on a throne, on the other, John attempted to worship the angel to whom he was speaking.

In another example Tobit was told by the angel Raphael to worship God, but he did not say he could not also worship the angel Raphael as well (Tob 12:16-22). In still a third vision Zephaniah imagined that he was being visited by the Lord Almighty, and fell down to worship him. The being turned out to be, instead, the angel Eremiel, who warned him not to worship him, but to worship only the Lord Almighty (ApocZeph 6:4-15). This place was not on earth, but in Hades.

Visions in heaven cannot be ruled out of consideration automatically, because they provide clues to the beliefs of the people who composed the visions, but even here the beliefs shown in the visions are not those of earthly people in their earthly form confronting angels on earth. Some of the visions indicated that the people involved in the visions were transformed in heaven so that they had a status that was different from people on earth. They were of a status equal to that of the angels they accompanied and might have attempted to worship. These do not rule out the consideration of an *áhn-geh-laws* being a human being, functioning precisely the way a human *áhn-geh-laws* should--bringing messages to other human beings. The context of the *ángelos* with John, while John told of his personal experience in receiving a certain prophecy in a certain geographical location, while not having a vision, has convinced me that John was a historical human being and not a heavenly

---

[1] R. Bauckham, "The Worship of Jesus in Apocalyptic Christianity," *NTS* 27 (1981):322-41.

angel, but others may reach different conclusions. These are every reader's prerogatives. Now to continue the situation with John of Patmos.

The Cost of Convictions. John said he was reporting a revelation he had received from God after he had been given a prophecy on a scroll from an *áhn-geh-laws*. When he opened the scroll so that he could read it, he called this unrolling a revelation. The insight he gained from this was **a revelation of Jesus Christ** (Rev 1:1). John was not the only one of the group to suffer for his faith. He shared with his readers in tribulation, a kingdom, and the endurance of Jesus (Rev 1:9). When he received this prophecy he was on Patmos Island, not only because of the word of God, but also for the testimony of Jesus (Rev 1:9). The kind of testimony most likely to have prompted Rome to punish Jews and Christians was that understood by Romans to constitute a political threat. Like the zealots who fought in the wars concluding with the fall of Jerusalem and the defeat of Bar Cochba, Christians and Jewish martyrs hoped to expel Rome from Palestine. John may have sympathized with them. John's religious and ethical points of view are evident from the types of behavior he commended and those he disapproved.

Approved Behavior. John praised the leading officer of the church at Ephesus because of his work, labor, and endurance (Rev 2:2). He had no tolerance for evil people (*kah-koós,* κακούς). He also did not take people at their word, but put them to the test, and in so doing they found that some who called themselves apostles were false (Rev 2:2). John did not want any doctrinally unapproved leaders among his flock. He was pleased that the Ephesian officer was able to endure and that he had borne patiently because of God's or Jesus' name and had not grown weary (Rev 2:3). Furthermore, like Jesus and/or God, he hated the works of the Nicolaitans (Rev 2:6). John encouraged the officer of the church at Smyrna because he had already suffered tribulation and poverty (Rev 2:8-9), and he would soon face still more suffering and imprisonment (Rev 2:10). John considered this kind of steadfastness to the faith highly commendable. In Pergamum, John praised the example of Antipas, who died for the faith (Rev 2:13). He also approved the way the officer at Thyatira worked harder as time passed.

The officer at Sardis had been lax. He was responsible for the character of the Christians at Sardis. There were still a few in Sardis, however, who were worthy, who had not defiled their garments (Rev 3:4), and had walked with John in white. The officer at Philadelphia had pleased John by the way he upheld John's work, not denying his name (Rev 3:8, 10). He distinguished himself from the superficial Jews who belonged to the synagogue of Satan (Rev 3:9). John also scolded the officer at the church of Laodicia for being superficial. John could not tolerate moderation

From his short composition, John's views come loud and clear. He was a very strict law-observing Christian, who was willing to die for his faith, and he believed all other Christians should be similarly prepared. He demanded rigorous observance of religious laws. He had no tolerance for liberal Christians. The same views are evident from his definition of unapproved behavior.

Unacceptable Behavior. John did not approve of any type of laxness. Those in Ephesus who had left their first love (Rev 2:4), the officer in Sardis who had a name of being alive but was really dead from a religious point of view (Rev 3:1), and the leader in Laodicia who was lukewarm (Rev 3:15) were all given strong warnings. Some of these backsliders accepted the teaching of "Balaam" who taught Balak to put a stumbling block before the children of Israel, causing them to eat food offered to idols and to commit adultery (Rev 2:14). These same people also accepted the teaching of the Nicolaitans (Rev 2:15). The background of these insults was Num 24 and 25. The story of Balaam who tried to place a curse on Israel and the condition of the Israelites before Phineas interfered and put a stop to the mingling with foreign peoples, like the Midianites, was the basis for his allusions. There was evidently someone in John's time who advocated liberal teaching, permitting mingling with gentiles (called committing adultery) and eating food that was not *kasher*.[1]

These followers of Balaam seemed also to be Nicolaitans, who also were lax in their practices. In fact the Nicolaitans may have been the same liberal Jewish Christians whom John called the followers of Balaam. Another heretical teacher against whom Christians were warned was called **Jezebel,** to remind scriptural students of the pagan queen who persecuted Elijah (1Kings 16:31). This **Jezebel** called herself a prophetess, but she was not. She led John's flock astray by teaching liberal teachings concerning mingling with gentiles and eating food offered to idols (Rev 2:20). John called her associates those who **committed adultery** with her (Rev 2:22). Those who accepted her teachings knew the depth of Satan (Rev 2:24). The church at Philadelphia was warned against those who called themselves Jews but were not; instead they belonged to the synagogue of Satan (Rev 3:9).

There were not only false Jews and false prophetesses, but also false apostles against whom John's flock needed warning (Rev 2:3). These people whom John considered false were evidently Christians who were not very strict in their Jewish law observance. Like Paul and his followers, they were willing to mingle with gentiles and eat food that had not been purchased at a kasher meat market.

Goats and Sheep. John's approvals and disapprovals all indicate that John not only did not mingle with gentiles, but he looked forward to a new Jerusalem (Rev 3:12), which he believed would come soon (Rev 3:3, 10).

John the Zealot. The fact that John was imprisoned by the Romans for his faith at a time when Jewish and Christian insurrection was a serious annoyance to Rome together with his anticipation of a restored Jerusalem implies that he was himself considered by Romans to be a saboteur or active insurrectionist. His admonitions to the churches suggest that Rome was right in its judgment. The type of revelation which would have attracted him would have been one that understood the events of that time as a fulfillment of prophecy prior to the end of the Roman rule and the reestablishment of the Promised Land.

---

[1] Buchanan, *The Consequences of the Covenant* (Leiden: E. J. Brill, 1970), pp. 184-89.

The fact that John was imprisoned at Patmos Island, and not some island near Palestine, suggests that he was one of the faithful Jewish nationalists of the diaspora who became a Christian at a time when Christianity was still a part of Judaism. The choice of churches near the Island of Patmos suggests that he originally was at home some place in modern Turkey. There were many Jews in NT times in old Asia Minor (modern Turkey). Jewish wars were never confined to Palestine. There were thousands of Jews in the diaspora, and they were involved in every war. Many of these were as terroristic as native Palestinian Jews. John belonged to some group who was active away from Palestine.

John's familiarity with Scripture. **John** was a very apt student of Scripture, especially of those passages related to various events in Israel's history just prior to the end of foreign domination and the beginning of Israel's reign. In one six-verse passage (Rev 1:12-17), he alluded to seven quotations from the FT (Zech 4:2, 10; Dan 7:9, 13; 10:5-6; Ezek 1:24; Isa 49:2; Judges 5:31; Dan 10:9-12). If these were not understood as scriptural passages, the entire unit would sound ridiculous, but the nature of these references was so selected that **John's** feeling about his new insights is clear. In Rev 1-3 and Rev 22:6-20, **John** used passages from the Pentateuch, earlier and latter prophets, Psalms, and wisdom literature. John, however, did not write the entire Book of Revelation. There were several other earlier authors involved. Their identity and character can only be deduced from the contents of their messages. The same is true of the communities to whom they wrote. The fact, however, that the prophecy the messenger brought to John was such a favorable revelation to him indicates that the authorship and the communities involved were religiously similar to that related to John.

The primary communities to which the various units of the prophecy are addressed are not the seven churches in Rev 2-3. Each of the many units within the book had its origin in its own community. Rev 13, for example, apparently contains two documents that may have been composed during the period of the two Herods-- Herod the Great (d. 4 BIA, Rev 13:1-10) and Herod Agrippa (d. 44 IA, Rev 13:11-18) before it was updated to fit the needs of later communities. If this deduction is correct then the first narrative in Rev 13 would have been addressed to a Palestinian community that was pro-Hasmonean and, like **John** of Patmos, anti-Roman. The second document most likely would also have been omposed in Palestine. It was not necessarily pro-Hasmonean, but it certainly reflects and anti-Roman and anti-Herodian attitude.

Rev 16:12, 16-19 reflects a very precise period, between July 69 and August, 70 IA. This was after Vespasian had withdrawn his troops from Jerusalem to settle a civil war in Rome. The Palestinian Jewish author believed that, in a matter of a few months, God would settle the civil war among the three factions who were battling in Jerusalem. He was a Palestinian nationalist who anticipated the redemption of Israel, and he may have been one of the residents inside Jerusalem at that time. It is even possible that he was one of the prophets Josephus described as false.

Rev 11-14 reflect the same period and situation. All of these documents (i.e., Rev 11, 12, 13, and 14) were written by and for zealots inside Jerusalem. Rev 19 reflects a situation during 69 or 70 IA when Rome's civil war resulted in a terrible fire in Rome that burned the Capitol and its temples. Like the units of Rev 11-14, Rev 19 was written by and for Jewish terrorists, who were religiously convinced that God intended Jews to have control of the land of Palestine and who believed the Hasmonean victory was being reenacted.

The first two identified the Herods with the beasts of Daniel, and they believed that they would both be destroyed before God raised up a messiah to lead his people to victory. The final editor collected the materials some time after 70 IA when all of the earlier sources had been composed. He edited the sources to result in the prophecy that was brought to John of Patmos, sometime between the time of the editor's work and 150 IA when church fathers wrote of the document. Prior to that time some Christian editor made a few additions to identify the Lamb with Jesus and thereby adapt the document for Christian use.

Although the Book of Revelation is not as esoteric as *Hecalot* literature, much of it, nevertheless, was written in code so that only those who were well versed in Scripture and Jewish tradition would be able to understand it. This means it was written by and for legalists, monks, and others with special training. Vogelgesang overstated the case when he said,

> In Revelation, the Christian community as a whole is on an equal basis with John, and *anyone* [emphasis his] may read and understand the book.[1]

Mealy was also wrong in assuming that the book was written for a wide range of levels of familiarity with the FT.[2] It was written only for those who knew as much Scripture as the authors. All the authors who have contributed to the Book of Revelation wanted the common era to come to an end and the holy era to begin. The common era was that ruled by idolaters; the holy era was to be ruled by God's chosen people (Christians and/or Jews) from the central base of Jerusalem.

INSIGHTS FROM REVELATION

After nearly half a century of research I have come to the following conclusions that I did not know when I first taught the class on Revelation back in 1956:

1. The Book of Revelation is neither the ranting and ravings of a crazy person nor an almanac that promises the future for Christians in the twenty-first century.
2. John of Patmos wrote only the introduction (Rev 1), the letters to the leaders of seven churches in western Turkey (Rev 2-3), and the recommendation for readers (Rev 22:6-22).

---

[1] Vogelgesang, *Interpretation*, p. 294.
[2] J. W. Mealy, *After the Thousand Years* (Sheffield: JSOT Press, c1992), p. 63.

3. The prophecy (Rev 4:1-22:5) consists of an anthology of literary units, every one of which told about the expected redemption of Israel. All of these units expected their predictions to be fulfilled before the end of the first century IA. None of them was designed as prophecies for the twentieth or twenty-first centuries.

4. At the time when John of Patmos sent the prophecy out to his churches Christianity was only one branch of Judaism. There were only two basic differences between Christians and other Jews: Christians believed that Jesus was the promised Messiah, whereas other Jews anticipated another Messiah.

Christians believed that Jer 31:31 and Isa 55:3 were correct in holding God had divorced his people and a new contract had to be made before God would be the Lord's people again. Jesus acted as God's legal agent to establish that contract. Other Jews agreed with Isa 50:1 that there had never been a divorce. Therefore a new contract was not necessary. The contract involved was a legal liturgy. Both groups accepted the FT as valid and interpreted it in similar ways.

5. The Book of Revelation is one of the most comprehensive and well written anthologies of redemption literature in either Jewish or Christian extant writings. It is one of the clearest expressions of aggressive Jewish and Christian conquest theology of NT times. Conquest theology was not unique to Revelation. It was basic to the conquest of Canaan by Joshua, the expansion of David and Solomon, the reconquest of Ezra and Nehemiah, the rebellion of the Maccabees, and the rebellion of Bar Kochba. The conquest theology of Revelation was not satisfied during the time expected, but the zeal for conquest continued on many fronts until its military fulfillment was finally achieved during the reign of Constantine.

6. The authors of Revelation were rhetoricians. A rhetorician is one who is trained to argue cases in court on the bases of earlier constitutions and legal precedents. Rhetoricians are not objective research scholars whose goal is to learn and expose truth. They are trained to defend conclusions they have accepted at the outset.

7. The rules by which these rhetoricians functioned were all included in the Scripture. That which was not in the Scripture was not in the world, so far as their arguments were concerned. Rules designed by Romans, Greeks, or any other people that had not been also included in Scripture could not be used for argument. No one was allowed to question the ethics or logic of Scripture.

8. It was assumed that God was the great judge who approved all of the rules, predictions, and practices of Scripture. Therefore God was required to judge on the bases of Scripture and to act according to rhetorical arguments prescribing the way they should be interpreted. Jewish and Christian prophets, like authors of parts of the Book of Revelation, deduced from Scripture arguments needed to persuade both other believers and also God that God was obligated to act as they prescribed.

9. Revelation was written for a group of insiders, all of whom understood all of the allusions and thought-forms involved and accepted its beliefs and goals. These have long been forgotten by many Jews and Christians. Many of those who still understand these thought-forms do not agree with them. Therefore, there has been a strong

motivation to reinvent the document and produce fictions that the original authors would never have recognized. This commentary has not depended upon the inventions of modern interpreters of Revelation. Instead it has worked carefully to learn what the message really meant two thousand years ago and express these insights in ways most Christians can understand.

Revelation is part of Christian and Jewish tradition. It belongs in our canon of religious literature. It should be learned, studied, and understood—not as a prescription for the future, but as a basis for understanding our past. It helps to explain how we became the people we are and why we act the way we still do, today. It provides important information and questions for extensive discussion.

GENERAL INDEX
WORDS

abyss 75, 242-244, 248-249, 284-286, 291, 372, 493-494, 561-563, 570, 582, 591, 608, 611, 672, 685, 709

adultery 106, 111, 114, 131, 395, 407, 452, 521, 717

agent 14, 19, 20, 25, 26, 36, 40, 47, 48, 52, 70, 85, 86, 89-91, 101, 102, 108, 112, 119, 123, 124, 131, 137-140, 144, 147, 150, 152, 153, 161, 168, 169, 171, 172, 177, 200, 201, 217, 221, 224, 265, 270, 283-285, 288, 289, 301, 302, 305, 306, 324, 328, 343-345, 347, 348, 350, 352, 361, 362, 364, 367, 368, 386, 387, 394, 409, 422, 450, 472, 473, 478, 490, 496, 500, 503, 505, 525, 529, 530, 542, 544, 551, 592, 599, 609, 619, 620, 623, 625-627, 635, 652, 654, 670, 676, 677, 685, 697-699, 720

alcohol..514

Alexandrian..........….....................347, 394

almanac...............................…10, 39, 719

altar 24, 52, 64, 69, 72, 78, 130, 134, 156, 171, 190-192, 230-232, 236, 249, 250, 261, 269, 271, 272, 274-276, 307, 355, 386, 400-402, 414, 415, 420, 422, 427, 435, 436, 444, 445, 461, 513, 578, 605, 606, 614, 624, 625, 630, 639, 640, 651-654, 657, 658, 665, 670, 677, 679, 698

angel 14, 18, 22, 39, 40, 49, 53, 68, 70, 74, 75, 77-82, 85-89, 97, 98, 114, 118, 119, 122-124, 130, 132-134, 137, 145, 146, 149, 153, 160, 163, 164, 174, 175, 177, 178, 189, 190, 192, 203-207, 209, 216-218, 221, 226, 227, 229-234, 236-238, 240-245, 248-252, 255-263, 266-268, 270, 271, 279, 283, 295, 297, 300, 301, 314, 317, 320, 323-326, 355, 372, 383, 384, 396, 401, 403, 406, 408, 410, 413-417, 420-424, 427, 429, 430, 434-446, 448, 451-454, 461, 464, 466, 467, 470-472, 474, 475, 481-483, 489, 491, 507, 508, 510, 512, 513, 527, 530, 536, 547, 551, 556, 557, 562, 564, 570, 595, 596, 606, 609, 611, 615-618, 632-634, 636, 638, 639, 644, 645, 655, 666, 681, 684, 685, 687, 697, 702, 709, 710, 714, 715

antichrist 92, 210, 300, 342-344, 346-348, 369, 371, 372, 669, 706

antiquities 14, 290, 363, 535

antitype 2, 9, 12, 15-19, 21, 34, 37, 38, 58, 70, 112, 107, 114, 115, 131, 132, 190, 204-206, 209, 210, 216, 219, 239, 244, 251, 255, 258, 262, 265, 276-278, 280, 281, 284, 285, 289, 290, 292, 294, 295, 316, 318, 347, 348, 352, 355, 357, 360, 366, 376, 382, 392, 394 398, 399, 409, 412, 430, 432, 436, 438, 442, 460, 464, 470, 472, 474, 479, 487, 490, 493, 494, 506, 512, 521, 523, 536, 538, 546, 547, 567, 571, 577-579, 582, 669, 697, 698, 711

apartheid....................................... 8, 426

apocalypse 1, 2, 8, 20, 24, 33, 34-36, 41-43, 45, 47, 48, 53, 57, 60, 70, 79, 80, 91, 106, 110, 113, 125, 143, 153, 156, 162, 178, 183, 192, 194 , 200, 206, 213, 217, 236, 241, 244-247, 250, 259, 262, 268, 271, 272, 280, 287, 294, 295, 302, 309, 315, 328, 336, 342, 346-348, 350, 357, 359, 381, 383, 386, 389, 390, 398, 403 , 414, 416, 442, 460, 462, 463, 465, 467, 471, 477-479, 484, 486, 487, 492, 493, 521, 523, 525, 546, 551, 556, 558, 580, 583, 584, 619, 634, 666, 679-681, 685, 687, 688, 692, 699-703, 707-709

apostate 524, 534, 583, 584, 603, 630, 632, 693

apostle 19, 20, 40, 58, 85, 86, 89, 90-92,

96, 113, 140, 144, 282, 315, 345, 373, 388, 389, 391, 396, 397, 422, 466, 496, 510, 527, 529, 530, 542, 546, 581, 626, 628, 634, 636-638, 675, 685, 714, 716, 717

Arab 191, 250, 290, 320, 349, 372, 446, 449, 608, 614, 641

Arabian.............................. 290, 449, 641

Arabic...................... 250, 446, 608, 614

Aramaic 30, 31, 47, 142, 344, 359, 373, 386, 414, 436, 437, 555, 600, 619

archetype 15, 113, 412, 614

Assyrian 8, 20, 37, 181, 207, 215, 400, 413-415, 418, 422, 423, 426, 458, 462, 554, 557, 558, 607, 664, 608

atone 9, 16, 26, 51, 52, 94, 95, 168, 192, 201, 212, 214, 215, 229, 231, 232, 272, 273, 290, 375, 401, 419, 420, 436, 533, 689

atonement 9, 16, 26, 51, 52, 94, 95, 168, 192, 201, 212, 214, 215, 229, 232, 272, 273, 290, 375, 419, 420, 436, 635, 639, 652, 676, 689

avenge 129, 130, 189, 191, 193, 194, 260, 261, 353, 412, 517, 529, 532, 533, 536, 538, 557, 559, 568

Babylonian 17, 18, 21, 37, 38, 53, 57, 73, 84, 101, 125, 126, 129, 130, 207, 244, 282, 302, 306, 318, 360, 365, 377, 394, 400, 406, 407, 412, 452, 453, 464, 487-489, 503, 535, 584, 610, 613, 614, 620, 634

baptism 97, 110, 191, 217, 224, 282, 524, 544, 583, 694

Baptist...2, 16, 58, 77, 282, 294, 346, 498

beast 13, 15, 64, 69, 70, 126, 131, 133, 145, 149, 151, 152, 155-157, 164-166, 170, 174-178, 180, 182, 185-189, 214, 216, 217, 226, 229, 245, 246, 274, 275, 284-286, 289, 291, 296, 299, 309, 312, 317, 320, 322-325, 330, 333, 337-340, 342-356, 358-362, 364-366, 368, 369, 371-373, 378, 380, 387, 394, 398, 401, 403, 406, 408-412, 427, 431, 433, 434, 436, 441, 442, 446, 447, 451, 462, 470, 471, 473, 478, 482, 483, 488, 490-499, 501-503, 505, 508, 511, 516, 539, 540, 546, 556-560, 562, 563, 574, 575, 578, 588, 592, 595, 611, 651, 698, 702, 709, 712, 719

bedouin 145, 146, 198, 199, 333, 609

Bible 6, 16, 31, 79, 92, 128, 129, 169, 195, 201, 322, 335, 347, 373, 378, 393, 399, 463, 476, 560, 609, 614, 643

blaspheme 149, 355, 445, 446, 471, 476

blessing 39, 41, 65, 66, 80, 84, 98, 104, 109, 110, 134, 181, 191, 210, 216, 308, 361, 384, 396, 403, 404, 479, 546, 571, 608, 623, 640, 653, 655, 684, 694

blood 24, 25, 45, 52, 58, 63, 140, 170, 173, 174, 191-193, 195, 198, 203, 209, 218-220, 225, 226, 234, 237, 238, 273, 278, 284, 285, 296, 298, 326, 329, 349, 358, 366, 384, 407, 421, 423-426, 432, 441-445, 447-449, 470, 477, 478, 491, 510, 527, 531, 533, 536, 539, 545, 548-551, 553, 554, 556-559, 578, 588, 611, 630, 660, 665, 688

Bodleian...................................341, 706

boil 239, 410, 441, 442, 451, 470, 478, 558, 631, 679

bowl 28, 66, 77, 85, 133, 151, 206, 226, 236, 279, 301, 309, 429, 434, 436-442, 445-447, 451, 454, 461, 464, 466, 467, 470-475, 477, 478, 481, 482, 544, 564, 632-634, 696, 702

bribe ..167, 233, 288-290, 499, 576, 577

bride 65, 94, 132, 139, 140, 342, 391, 482, 483, 485, 428, 431, 510, 528, 531, 541-546, 604, 619, 620, 627, 632, 634, 679, 692, 693, 699, 700

bridegroom 139, 140, 510, 528, 531, 541, 543, 604, 619, 634

calculate 8, 265, 277, 375, 567, 568, 588, 641

Canaanite 96, 128-130, 195, 245, 356, 464

Capitol 469, 484, 503, 504, 522, 527, 538, 594, 595, 718

captive 8, 9, 20, 21, 167, 21, 229, 246, 278, 286, 289, 301, 349, 358, 374-376,

410, 555, 571, 589,
captivity 8, 10, 16, 20, 21, 53, 56, 73, 84, 109, 129, 207, 222, 264, 318, 325, 357, 358, 374, 375, 377, 394, 400, 410, 418, 452, 462, 490, 491, 535, 564, 570, 589, 611, 612, 620
carbuncle....................……........641, 645-647
caricature 18, 178, 338, 341-343, 345, 348, 409, 698
Catholic.............5, 38, 371, 524, 563, 575
Caucasian......................................590, 591
cavalry 182, 226, 247, 249, 251, 252, 323
cave 59, 132, 189, 196, 198, 308, 321, 333, 352, 377, 448, 450, 557, 559, 600, 640, 655, 712
celibate 12, 52, 53, 98, 217, 251, 380, 385, 388-393, 396, 398-401, 545, 546, 578, 652, 671, 675, 676, 695
chariot 73, 180, 183, 204, 248, 460, 588, 663
cherubim..........72, 151, 153, 156, 166, 178, 231, 234, 379, 436, 539, 541, 651, 652
Chinese..315, 317
chosen 9, 16, 22, 30, 42, 52, 70, 102, 124, 131, 147, 153, 163, 164, 167-169, 173, 181, 183, 195, 198, 200, 217, 219, 224, 232, 239, 263-265, 295, 305, 306, 313, 324, 328, 344, 348, 358 374, 376, 382, 389, 394, 410, 438, 444, 453, 462, 467, 477, 486, 490, 542, 564, 577, 581, 599, 625, 630, 631, 635, 656, 674, 690, 693, 697, 698, 704, 708, 709, 712, 719
Christ 1, 33-35, 50, 53, 59, 74, 79, 80, 86, 92, 140, 167, 168, 190, 209, 210, 217, 226, 315, 319, 329, 336, 343, 373, 384, 390, 397, 415, 462, 536, 550, 565, 628, 631, 682, 716
clerk...144
cloud 9, 13, 14, 22, 28, 53, 54, 66, 68-70, 141, 142, 144, 145, 150, 151, 231, 234, 235, 244, 255-257, 283, 293, 299, 307, 323, 413-417, 421, 422, 434-436, 475, 591, 608, 621, 624, 632, 633, 636, 641, 648, 695, 699

comfort 8, 112, 223, 224, 229, 318, 319, 464, 594, 625, 672, 704
Commagene...456
commerce 461, 487, 490, 519, 521, 531, 654
common 8, 16, 33, 83, 88, 116, 124, 149, 193, 212, 230, 270, 272, 373-377, 411, 547, 561, 571, 572, 614, 635, 650, 656, 667, 671, 680, 681, 685, 687, 696, 719
conclusion 2, 3, 15, 22, 31, 32, 42, 43, 55, 63, 66, 71, 79, 83, 86, 101, 102, 108, 133, 142, 161, 168, 196, 208, 231, 244, 256, 258, 301, 309, 329, 336, 340, 345, 371, 373, 378, 383, 390, 435, 462, 474, 477, 523 542, 545, 547, 567, 605, 628, 628, 665, 667, 678, 680-682, 684, 687, 693, 695-697. 700-703, 707, 710-713, 715, 719, 720
confess 41, 92, 118, 122, 125, 178, 246, 328, 398, 429, 444, 536, 551
conquest 10, 23, 60, 73, 130, 200, 225, 229, 230, 314, 376, 424, 426, 454, 484, 485, 524, 535, 564, 570, 588, 610, 698, 700, 720
continence.. 392
contract 7, 16, 21, 37, 43-45, 50, 60, 65, 66, 84, 89, 93-98, 102, 104, 105, 108, 109, 114-117, 120, 121, 137, 140, 142, 144, 147, 150, 154, 156, 159, 162-164, 169, 171, 172, 174, 181-183, 188-190, 192, 193, 199, 200-202, 209, 211, 223, 227-230, 233, 236, 240, 258, 259, 262, 267, 268, 284, 294, 295, 306-308, 313, 319, 320, 325, 336, 342, 355, 391, 394, 401-404, 412, 429, 430, 432, 435, 436, 438, 439, 444, 449, 451, 467, 468, 470, 474, 476-479, 489, 495, 503, 508, 536, 542-546, 568, 605, 610, 619, 620, 622-627, 629, 630, 632, 634, 635, 650, 652, 653, 688-690, 693, 696, 698, 699, 704, 720
convert 98, 245, 256, 397, 416, 417, 654, 673
Coptic.. 76, 80
Corinthians.......................... 26, 109, 396
cosmic 4, 133, 195, 201, 259, 314, 530,

608, 609, 612, 627, 655
cosmos 5, 10, 128, 195, 197, 201, 261, 574, 607, 610-613
council 145, 146, 153, 154, 168, 171, 174, 325, 355, 502, 539, 564, 575, 576, 578, 585, 652, 669
covenant 1, 20, 65, 66, 75, 80, 84, 95, 132, 221, 250, 262, 270, 376, 390, 452, 614, 615, 655, 680, 691, 717
crisis 2, 215, 216, 266, 278, 295, 346, 378, 392, 491, 498, 523, 532, 534, 655, 697, 698
Crusade 11, 146, 288, 296, 407, 459, 501 524, 567, 568, 588, 590, 702, 704
curse 21, 24, 44, 45, 49, 50, 55, 66, 71, 95, 106, 108, 114-116, 133, 136, 181, 182, 186, 188-190, 192, 199, 209, 211, 225, 226, 236, 238, 239, 243, 244, 246, 249, 255, 261, 283, 301, 308, 313, 333, 334, 403, 422, 429, 438, 447, 451, 467, 468, 474, 477, 508, 530, 536, 560, 599, 612, 624, 630, 631, 671, 675, 676, 693, 694, 696, 698, 709, 711, 717
cycle 2, 4, 9, 10, 12, 13, 15, 23, 24, 39, 49, 59, 70, 73, 76, 83, 148, 216, 314, 325, 344, 426, 529, 568, 570, 642, 653, 700, 708
cyclical 10, 23, 39, 49, 69, 302, 570, 571, 581, 589
Davidic 10, 12, 22, 25, 46, 117, 133, 140, 148, 258, 283, 409, 495, 536, 542, 580, 610, 632
debt 7, 9, 12, 52, 95, 125, 172, 357, 363, 374, 389, 445, 518, 545, 599
debtor 6-10, 20, 21, 129, 374, 375, 389, 518
defend   4, 198, 362, 542, 549, 720
defendant 13, 50, 51, 69, 142, 202, 221, 233, 256, 328, 331, 444, 483, 494, 517, 518, 536, 560, 564, 576, 596, 601, 623, 677
defense 32, 38, 51, 144, 169, 192, 205, 207, 221, 231, 333, 347, 362, 366, 460, 461, 530, 564, 601, 641, 660, 662-664
demon 14, 43, 52, 66, 87, 96, 122, 209, 251, 252, 265, 342, 352, 359, 360, 398,
402, 436-438, 447, 462, 470, 479, 508, 511, 514, 550, 564, 573, 574, 592,
depend 24, 34, 35, 76, 86, 92, 126, 137, 142-144, 148, 159, 192, 212, 215, 228, 236, 257, 258, 265, 274, 318, 342, 350, 367, 368, 378, 409, 410, 414, 415, 421, 452, 455, 487, 495, 500, 507, 513, 518, 521-523, 525, 531, 534, 543, 551, 554, 574, 576, 590, 602
Deuteronomy 20, 26, 60, 193, 208, 360, 365, 398, 423, 695, 696
devil 100, 103, 318, 324, 325, 327, 328, 343, 437, 490, 562, 563, 570, 587, 593-596
diaspora 9, 17, 18, 20, 21, 84, 120, 132, 173, 211-215, 218, 223, 317, 335-337, 417, 458, 591, 592, 654, 718
dignity 149, 288, 347, 492, 513, 575, 577, 685
dirge..................................513, 522, 531
disk 14, 67, 68, 73, 240, 257, 310, 314, 315
divorce 37, 104, 181, 183, 267, 308, 394, 489, 514, 545, 546, 619, 624-626, 635, 696, 720
dog..689, 690
dragon 13, 246, 309, 311-313, 315-319, 323-327, 330-335, 337, 338, 340, 343, 345-348, 350-352, 355, 359, 362, 364, 369, 372, 378, 394, 398, 409, 463, 471, 473, 483, 489, 490, 493, 494 562-564, 570, 583, 585, 592, 697, 698, 702
drama 13, 69, 70, 98, 99, 112, 148, 228, 259, 308, 314, 315, 318, 323, 325-327, 331, 332, 334, 337, 345, 355, 359, 392, 436, 464, 483, 504, 543, 546, 558, 564, 566, 594, 600, 607, 609, 631, 635, 709
drink 96, 221, 384, 398, 406-409, 443, 453, 475, 482, 487, 488, 491, 506, 512, 514, 630
dying 39, 49, 57, 114, 117, 146, 168, 287, 314, 412, 521, 551, 570
dynasty 44, 50, 138, 316, 346-348, 375, 492-494, 499
Edomite 296, 299, 320, 360, 412, 425, 503, 619

Egyptian 18, 21, 22, 57, 132, 153, 195, 210, 225, 236-238, 244, 245, 302, 305, 308, 431, 432, 439, 441, 442, 444, 451, 456, 460, 461, 463, 473, 477, 551, 610

elder 40, 88, 96, 145, 150, 152, 153, 157, 158, 160, 165, 166, 170-172, 174-178, 216-218, 223, 303, 305, 307, 355, 380, 401, 410, 526, 537, 539, 546, 574-578, 585, 628, 648, 709, 714

end 1-4, 6-10, 12, 23, 32, 35, 38, 46, 56, 58, 69, 75, 76, 78, 84, 103, 108, 109, 112, 114, 116, 128, 133, 138, 140, 143, 148, 156, 159, 180, 187, 191, 192, 195, 197, 201, 203, 205, 211, 219, 222, 228, 230, 233, 234, 244, 247, 252, 259-265, 270, 277, 278, 282, 296, 301, 318, 321-323, 329, 333, 343, 359, 360, 373, 375-378, 381, 406, 410, 416-418, 424, 429, 435, 439, 442, 448, 457-460, 478, 481, 483, 484, 487, 493, 497, 501, 512, 519, 522, 525, 530, 531, 534, 541, 549, 555, 560, 565-568, 571, 572, 574, 583, 585, 591, 592, 594, 616, 618, 630, 631, 640, 641-644, 649, 655, 660, 662, 663, 669, 672, 675, 679, 681, 682, 684, 685, 689, 696, 698, 703, 706, 708, 712, 714, 719

enemy 11, 14, 45, 68, 70, 73, 133, 178, 183, 191, 204, 215, 230, 240, 241, 257, 274, 281, 284-286, 288, 295, 314, 315, 327, 328, 332, 340, 343, 353, 357, 378, 411, 412, 415-418, 420, 423, 424, 433, 435, 436, 442, 444, 458, 461, 462, 467, 473, 476, 485, 490, 502, 550, 552, 554, 558, 568, 572, 573, 590, 593-595, 608, 664, 698

Ephesian................................ 91-94, 716
epilogue.................... 681, 700-702, 711
epistle...............78, 142, 217, 238, 572
eschatology 4, 6-8, 12, 13, 76, 83, 195, 205, 262, 347, 375, 410, 545, 581, 701
Essene......... 92, 391, 392, 394, 395, 399
Ethiopian..........................110, 398, 584
ethrog...673
exile 20, 37, 59 60, 92, 181, 230, 294, 299, 306, 332, 363, 374, 394, 569, 572, 583, 683

exodus 20-22, 27, 28, 31, 42, 56, 57, 129, 130, 173, 198, 200, 205, 210, 225, 236, 257, 325, 332, 397, 429-431, 435, 437, 442, 445, 454, 461, 470, 474, 478, 504, 535, 570, 590, 608, 610, 642, 647, 704

famine 21, 22, 182, 185-190, 209, 215, 225, 229, 237, 312, 357, 368, 508, 516, 519, 559

feast 10, 38, 99, 102, 132, 139, 146, 156, 174, 206, 212-215, 218, 222, 238, 275, 286, 330, 356, 360, 386, 400, 429, 434, 436, 453, 457, 517, 542, 546, 558, 565, 581, 589, 615, 624, 655, 670, 705

fertility...690
first fruits 380, 390, 397, 398, 400, 401, 410, 424, 545
foreclose................................. 5, 516, 518
forehead 56, 135, 202, 204, 207-210, 215, 229, 243, 245, 246, 249-251, 263, 341, 343, 368, 369, 379, 387, 394, 398, 400, 407, 409, 411, 412, 488, 490, 574, 578, 673, 676, 677

forgive 5, 37, 51, 94, 118, 232, 630, 631, 694
forgiven 52, 95, 342, 419, 420, 599, 630, 631
forgiveness.................. 5, 51, 94, 95, 631
fortress 87, 101, 119, 147, 156, 197, 198, 204, 211, 254, 271, 274-276, 319, 337, 371, 382, 386, 390, 401, 459-462, 468, 484, 536, 550, 565, 605, 615, 637, 639, 653, 659-661, 668, 690

foundation 74, 314, 320, 326, 354, 356, 357, 362, 381, 390, 437, 494, 501, 504, 633, 636, 637, 645, 646, 679

freedom 20-22, 59, 125, 215, 236, 285, 375, 452, 563, 656
frog...........225, 470, 472, 473, 478, 479
future 1, 2, 5, 6, 14, 20, 34-36, 38, 39, 42, 49, 56, 74, 76, 77, 88, 90, 116, 122, 125, 135, 138, 146, 148, 152, 160, 174, 191, 192, 200, 218, 254, 257, 258, 263, 264, 271, 272, 274, 277, 292, 314, 344, 358, 361, 363, 368, 411, 414, 493, 494, 496, 498, 520, 531, 534, 536, 549, 556, 557, 559, 563 565, 579, 581, 584, 588, 589,

593, 601, 603, 608-610, 616, 618, 619, 631, 640, 643, 664, 666, 667, 670, 672, 679, 682, 685, 687, 697, 704, 705 719, 721
Galatian..109
gematria............................370, 371, 399
Galilean...........................247, 355 576
Gitite.. 307, 403
gnostic...........................45, 97, 109, 172
gospel 22, 58, 97, 99, 127, 131, 140, 183, 211, 323, 336, 340, 380, 391, 396, 399, 401, 403, 404, 406, 422, 423, 495, 560, 600, 635, 652, 665, 685
guerrilla 10, 12, 38, 58, 168, 198, 315, 321, 332, 333, 352, 438, 455, 456
guilt 19, 41, 51, 87, 100, 104, 109, 189, 193, 220, 221, 232, 233, 375, 390, 400, 515, 531, 536, 576, 578, 584, 585, 601, 654, 698
Hades 73-75, 80, 185, 188, 189, 592, 596, 598, 602, 603, 685, 715
Hanukkah 58, 68, 70, 201, 212, 214, 219, 276, 288, 378, 420, 426, 492, 567, 682, 687
harlot 107, 113, 131, 133, 174, 183, 193, 343, 439, 452, 459, 462, 469, 481-489, 492-494, 501-505, 507, 508, 511, 512, 514, 521, 533, 536, 546, 548, 563, 564, 570, 592, 634, 689, 690, 697
harvest 7, 132, 190, 215, 233, 400, 413, 414, 416-421, 423, 424, 672
heretic...97, 109, 113, 115, 343, 657, 717
Hittite...65, 129
holy 11, 21, 28, 45, 52, 53, 60, 66, 72, 98, 99, 122-124, 132, 145, 147, 149, 152, 156, 157, 171, 173, 182, 183, 192, 197, 204, 205, 208, 209, 221, 224, 227, 229, 232, 234, 251, 256, 269, 271-276, 278, 281, 282, 296-299, 301-303, 309, 315, 323, 353-355, 359, 373, 374, 376, 377, 380, 381, 386, 389, 394, 395, 400, 403, 408, 410, 419, 422, 424, 426, 428, 434, 436, 443, 448-452, 495, 501, 524, 530, 568, 571, 576, 580, 582, 583, 586, 589, 593, 595, 596, 598, 604-606, 612-614, 616-625, 631, 632, 635, 639, 640, 642, 643, 646, 647, 650-652, 654, 656, 657, 659, 663, 666, 667, 672, 676-678, 688, 690-692, 694, 715, 719
hostility...............306, 367, 506, 538, 563
idolater..................26, 626, 629, 689, 719
inclusio 78, 159, 180, 322, 505, 605, 618, 674, 681, 695, 706, 710
inequities......................................5, 667
inherit 11,111, 117, 128, 129, 163, 181, 309, 313, 335, 399, 552, 571, 580, 587, 603, 613, 618, 629, 631, 632, 655, 678
introduction 1, 3, 4, 15, 42, 43, 58, 62, 63, 66, 74, 82, 83, 89, 91, 99, 119, 140, 143, 160, 172, 183, 210, 214, 243, 261, 295, 314, 325, 336, 340, 344, 383, 384, 386, 414, 435, 440, 460, 462, 483, 506, 507, 529, 541, 547, 548, 583, 605, 606, 627, 681-683, 687, 693, 695, 697, 700, 701, 703, 706, 710-714, 719
Jebusites 274, 386, 608, 612, 624, 637, 646, 662
Jubilee 4, 6-10, 13, 20, 21, 172, 227, 299, 230, 232, 235, 236, 263, 299, 314, 325, 374-376, 416, 497, 555, 567, 569, 608, 609, 624, 666, 713
justice 4, 6, 7, 9-11, 19, 21, 25, 26, 57, 89, 99, 101, 108, 129, 172, 173, 193, 271, 375, 382, 428, 444, 445, 483, 550, 574, 601, 628
king 6, 11, 12, 14, 15, 17, 22, 25, 33, 40, 50, 51, 55, 65, 68, 75, 89, 95, 100, 112, 113, 117, 120, 133, 137, 141, 144, 149, 150, 152, 158, 160, 165-168, 173, 177, 179, 183, 188, 216, 221, 224, 247, 249, 251, 257, 262, 263, 274, 282, 285, 288-291, 294, 296, 298, 301-303, 305-307, 311, 312, 314, 316, 320, 325, 328, 331-333, 341, 342, 349-351, 353, 357, 360, 362-265, 367, 371-376, 386-388, 409, 416, 420, 423, 425, 428, 429, 433, 449, 455, 457, 459-461, 466, 478, 494, 496-501, 523, 540, 542-545, 549, 550, 553-555, 559, 562, 564, 572, 573, 578, 586, 591, 593, 594, 597, 600, 601, 605, 609-611, 613, 622, 624, 625, 627, 629, 648, 649, 652-654, 670, 676, 684, 685, 688,

712

kingdom 4, 6, 9-14, 20, 22, 26, 27, 45, 46, 51-53, 57-59, 70, 75-77, 88, 89, 97, 104, 109, 117, 125, 142, 149, 158, 161, 167, 170-175, 177, 186, 201, 224, 226, 232, 233, 251, 258, 262, 267, 271, 275, 278, 280-282, 300-303, 326-328, 340, 345-347, 356, 359, 362, 364, 365, 367, 388, 391, 392, 396, 409, 410, 415-417, 419, 420, 429, 433, 437, 438, 440, 446, 454, 456, 470, 481, 483, 494, 497, 498, 500-502, 505, 512, 513, 519, 535, 540, 542, 559, 571, 573-575, 578-581, 583, 584, 603, 610, 611, 620, 629 632, 633, 635, 653, 669, 674, 676-679, 687, 690, 714, 716

lamentation 23, 137, 162, 261, 321, 329, 508, 516, 520, 538, 586, 622, 628, 632

lamp 15-18, 28, 66, 68-70, 75, 77, 82, 85, 89, 90, 93, 95, 119, 139, 151, 152, 154, 156, 169, 238, 279, 282, 432, 510, 528, 531, 544, 648, 651, 653, 654, 674

land 6-11, 13, 16, 18, 20, 21, 35, 37, 52, 54, 60, 69, 70, 72, 73, 77, 89, 94, 99, 102, 126-134, 137, 142, 144, 154, 164, 167, 169, 171, 173, 174, 182, 184, 187, 192-196, 198, 200, 203, 205-207, 209, 219, 222, 223, 229, 232-237, 240-247, 250-252, 258, 259, 262-264, 266-268, 271, 277, 282-285, 291-294, 298, 299, 301, 305-307, 319, 325, 329, 331-333, 340, 343, 344, 350, 354, 356, 359, 360, 362-364, 368, 374-377, 381, 383, 388-390, 397, 400, 403, 405, 408-410, 414, 417, 418, 420, 421, 423, 424, 427, 429, 431, 437, 442, 444, 446, 448, 449, 452, 457, 460, 461, 463, 468, 474, 476, 479, 487, 488, 494, 495, 506, 508-510, 513, 515, 519, 521-523, 526, 529, 533-537, 539, 541-543, 548, 551, 555-557, 560, 566-568, 572, 578, 580-582, 584-586, 588-593, 595, 597, 600, 601, 604, 606-613, 616, 617, 619, 620, 622, 623-625, 627, 629, 632, 634, 635, 639, 641, 642, 649-651, 655, 666, 667, 671, 676, 679, 683, 690, 693, 697, 704, 709, 712, 713,

716-719

language 3, 24, 31, 32, 42, 47, 65, 67, 72, 81, 85, 93, 112, 128, 131, 136, 170, 173, 174, 176, 193, 212-214, 252, 267, 268, 285, 287, 292, 354, 356, 358, 364, 371, 381-383, 393, 402, 404, 405, 467, 487, 501, 503, 531, 611, 700-708

lapus lazli 149, 150

lawless 117, 567

legal 6, 9, 13, 19, 20, 24-26, 40, 47, 50-53, 55, 58-60, 66, 70, 78, 84-86, 89-92, 94, 95, 97, 98, 101, 104, 105, 108, 109, 112, 114-116, 119-121, 123, 124, 135, 137, 138, 140, 144, 145, 147, 150, 152, 153, 158, 161, 163, 164, 168, 169, 171, 172, 177, 181, 191, 200, 201, 217, 219-221, 224, 231, 265, 270, 280, 288, 294, 302, 305, 306, 313, 314, 318, 328, 345, 349, 352, 361, 367-369, 383, 386-388, 394, 396, 399, 400, 409, 412, 415, 422, 444, 445, 472, 473, 478, 480, 490, 501, 524, 530, 534, 542-545, 551, 553, 576-578, 583, 584, 599, 603, 606, 609, 612, 615, 619, 620, 623, 625-627, 630, 631, 635, 643, 652, 654, 670, 671, 676, 677, 679, 684-686, 691-693, 695, 698, 699, 704, 719-720

Levite 16, 24, 25, 52, 133, 145, 174, 401, 584, 676

Levitical 12, 16, 19, 102, 373, 385, 480, 627, 654, 656

lilith 436, 437

lion 132, 160, 161, 163, 164, 168, 169, 172, 256, 259, 360, 387

Maccabean 9, 18, 23, 37, 70, 148, 167, 219, 260, 262, 277, 278, 323, 325, 344, 345, 375, 453, 456, 458, 464, 490, 501, 554, 578

Maccabee 10, 13, 14, 18, 23, 37-39, 52, 54, 68-70, 142, 148, 167, 172, 174-176, 183, 206, 214, 216, 219, 220, 277, 278, 281, 308, 318, 320, 321, 333, 357, 377, 394, 415, 417, 420, 456, 489, 490, 566, 571, 572, 575, 579, 585, 591, 669, 691, 720

magical 56, 57, 96, 198, 200, 229, 331-

333, 564, 636, 665, 696
manna............…107, 109, 110, 325, 551
marriage 37, 93, 94, 319, 349, 357, 391, 393, 396, 489, 542-545, 612, 619, 620, 623-625, 627, 634, 635, 671, 676, 690, 698, 699
martyr................ 40, 168, 192, 219, 550
Mazdean....................................... 14, 573
menorah.. 69, 89
merchant 84, 133, 448, 507-510, 512, 514, 515, 521-529, 531, 532, 591, 592, 595, 602
merit 5, 6, 10, 90, 95, 101, 112, 121, 139, 172, 192, 202, 206, 329, 356, 396, 411, 413, 418, 445, 451, 545, 547, 569, 571, 573, 629
messenger 14,16, 20, 28, 33, 39, 40-43, 53, 56, 61-66, 69, 74, 75, 77, 78, 80, 85-88, 109, 119, 135, 137, 142, 144, 149, 184, 204-206, 210, 258, 259, 324, 384, 385, 418, 449, 477, 544, 546, 574, 607, 678, 680, 682-687, 691, 707, 711, 714, 718
messianic 8, 36, 61, 69, 99, 131-133, 135, 147, 152, 155, 167, 188, 194, 202, 286, 288, 289, 299, 309, 320, 321, 341-342, 356, 375, 386, 407, 415, 416, 422, 425, 447, 459, 491, 501, 542, 556, 564, 567-569, 571-573, 580, 582, 583, 590, 596, 602, 607, 613-615, 618, 631, 641-643, 654, 655, 660, 666, 669-673, 677-680, 703, 705, 706
Midianite.............27, 108, 113, 459, 717
midrash 4, 18, 19, 23, 24, 27, 28, 36, 37, 56, 61, 63, 93, 99, 121, 125, 163, 170, 262, 263, 273, 278, 287, 320, 337, 365, 366, 373, 382, 399, 401, 403, 404, 416, 417, 421-423, 479, 506, 510, 544, 545, 560, 590, 600, 613, 653, 665, 672, 703, 704, 706-710
military 5, 3, 19, 22, 60, 88, 117, 132, 145, 166-169, 176, 182, 183, 206, 214, 245, 251, 257, 278, 288, 290, 305, 315, 320, 323, 324, 347, 349, 350, 353, 362, 366, 368, 414, 415, 422, 426 452-454, 457-461, 463, 484, 506, 521, 523, 535,
542, 549, 551, 554, 557, 566, 567, 590, 592, 594, 650, 662, 664, 679, 690, 691, 697, 720
millennium 132, 149, 262, 322, 555, 565-571, 573, 574, 580, 583, 584, 588, 589
millenialist................................ 372, 572
miracle 16, 21, 23, 28, 132, 148, 247, 296, 308, 332, 351, 364-366, 377, 433, 453, 454, 461, 602, 635, 698
Mishnah.............................114, 377, 635
Moabite................................27, 106, 113
monk 52, 58, 99, 101, 104, 145, 157, 211, 387, 390, 392, 394-396, 399-401, 546, 578, 612, 644, 675, 676, 695, 719
Moslem 343, 425, 449, 463, 547, 572, 615, 705, 706
mourn 54, 162, 243, 256, 267, 320, 368, 379, 399, 504, 507-511, 519-522, 525-527, 540, 567, 595, 625
Mysteries 33, 75, 77, 97, 202, 260, 262-264, 425, 568, 618, 677, 705, 706
mystical 12, 217, 247, 454, 460, 461, 464, 554
Nicolaitan 90, 95-97, 102, 106-109, 359, 628, 716, 717
oil 68, 185, 187, 188, 279, 282, 653, 665
omnipotent..542
ontological....................................80, 626
orthodox 91-98, 101,102, 108, 110, 113, 116, 122, 125, 140, 158, 164, 212, 398, 480, 488, 514, 523, 529, 584, 605, 651, 657
pagan 16, 18, 20, 26, 41, 93, 99, 106, 108, 113, 130, 135, 230, 276, 353, 356, 361, 398, 399, 418, 600, 605, 614, 626, 651, 656, 657, 682, 717
Palestinian 126, 129, 130, 132, 133, 173, 192, 212, 287, 326, 333, 335, 352, 355, 360, 368, 385, 402, 409, 424, 430, 452, 454, 460-462, 467, 474, 493, 494, 497, 506, 532, 559, 579, 595, 638, 679, 718
palm...........................132, 212-215, 656
paradise ..90, 98, 99, 104, 560, 611, 612, 643, 666, 672, 679, 695
pardon.......................................5, 94, 232
Partheon 132, 167, 183, 206, 207, 220,

251, 288, 289, 349, 350, 352, 355, 357, 360, 453, 456-459, 461-464, 468, 474, 524, 555, 593
Passover 6, 56, 139, 140, 205, 206, 210, 212, 315, 394, 543, 551, 675, 689
Paulinist........................ 34, 97, 106, 711
Pentacontad 205, 206, 214, 215, 262, 263, 375, 376, 416, 418, 419, 424, 624, 689
Pentacost...205
Persian........................278, 314, 323, 453
Pesikta de Rav Kahana...............614, 705
Pesikta Rabbati.................. 426, 477, 705
pestilence 21, 111, 114, 182, 185, 186, 188, 189, 209, 225, 229, 234, 237, 298, 312, 357, 358, 508, 516, 519, 548, 559, 587, 630
Pharaoh 17, 51, 207, 236, 237, 312, 431, 440, 444, 451, 460, 461, 479, 504, 566
Pharisee......................... 20, 355, 396, 418
Philippians.......................................1, 109
Philistine.......73, 284, 402, 403, 608, 646
Phoenician.. 538
plague 18, 66, 78, 106, 130, 132, 188, 196, 198, 200, 203, 225, 226, 232, 236, 238, 245, 246, 248, 250, 252, 284, 308, 427, 429, 430, 432, 434-439, 442-444, 446-448, 451, 464, 467, 470-474, 476, 477, 479, 508, 519, 536, 632, 634, 683, 694, 696, 698, 702, 709
plaintiff 13, 50, 205, 231, 233, 256, 331, 444, 478, 517, 518, 623
poetry 8, 11, 31, 176, 177, 508, 707, 710
political 3, 5, 8, 11, 12, 14, 33, 50, 58, 60, 64, 88, 104, 124, 149, 163, 172, 192, 198, 294, 301, 315, 347-349, 363, 368, 369, 382, 410, 460, 461, 467, 485, 492, 494, 497, 503, 507, 534, 543, 568, 569, 576, 577, 580, 581, 589, 609, 612, 624, 626, 680, 706, 708
politics..462, 706
pope...371, 372
prayer 11, 51, 57, 86, 144, 149, 150, 170-172, 178, 202, 228, 230-233, 259, 304, 373, 425, 444, 544, 568, 571, 577, 586, 615, 618, 677, 705, 706

predestine 12, 23, 38, 70, 76, 88, 148, 200, 201, 252, 258, 260, 262, 277, 302, 314, 318, 320, 327, 356-358, 410, 461, 536, 570, 571, 589
pregnant 310, 311, 314, 318, 326, 613, 664, 671, 676, 698, 702
priest 11, 16, 18, 19, 22, 24-26, 39, 40, 45, 52, 53, 55, 69, 77, 89, 102, 113, 122, 129, 130, 133, 135, 144, 145, 153, 156, 158, 171-174, 220, 221, 223, 227, 229, 230, 232, 256, 264, 265, 272, 273, 275, 276, 281-283, 289-291, 305, 309, 324-326, 361, 365-367, 373, 376, 389, 390, 394, 395, 400, 418, 434-436, 439, 482, 484, 504, 535, 539, 544, 562, 574, 582, 584, 585, 605, 616, 625, 632, 633, 637, 639, 646, 652, 657, 660, 669, 676, 714
prison 5, 20, 21, 51, 59, 100, 103, 363, 464, 497, 508, 511, 534, 571, 585, 588, 591
prologue 65, 66, 75, 84, 90, 95, 101, 105, 112, 403, 701, 702, 711
promiscuity................107, 407, 487, 490
prophecy 17, 21, 24, 27, 33, 34-37, 39, 41-43, 45, 48, 49, 52, 56, 60, 62-64, 66, 68, 70, 71, 74-77, 79-81, 83, 87, 93, 98, 99, 109, 110, 113, 116, 117, 124, 132, 135, 140, 142, 143, 161, 178, 179, 181, 184, 196, 201, 207, 215, 216, 223, 225, 236, 239, 258, 259, 268, 271, 280, 281, 284, 286, 301, 307, 308, 314, 319, 335, 349, 358, 366, 371, 374, 381, 383-385, 398, 399, 401, 403, 407, 411, 412, 417, 418, 429, 431, 432, 434, 435, 444, 467, 477, 483, 487, 491, 496, 503, 520, 521, 529-531, 538, 542, 545-549, 554, 559, 574, 585, 595, 606, 612, 618, 627, 628, 634, 638, 642, 659, 667-669, 671, 674, 678, 681, 683-687, 692-697, 700-720
prophet 16, 20, 23, 24, 26, 27, 36-43, 61, 62, 77, 79-83, 88, 89, 92, 108, 113, 126, 128, 143, 145, 147, 148, 181, 184, 193, 198, 201, 205, 208, 211, 216, 247, 254, 258, 259, 263-268, 277, 280-282, 285, 287, 291, 298, 299, 303, 304, 306, 321, 322, 336, 344, 346, 347, 349, 364-366,

385, 391, 406, 418, 419, 430, 432, 443-445, 452, 470-474, 478, 479, 487, 488, 490, 510, 512-514, 527-531, 533, 536, 544, 547, 554, 557-560, 565, 588, 591, 596, 598, 602, 611, 624, 626, 628, 630, 635, 636, 643-644, 669, 674, 680-681, 682-686, 692, 695, 702, 704, 707-709, 711, 714, 715, 717, 718, 720
prosecute.................................... 331, 564
proselyte...............53, 174, 584, 656, 693
prostitute 484, 485, 488, 490, 513, 519, 690
Protestant.........................5, 192, 371, 399
prototype...... 15, 23, 132, 133, 147, 614
Psalm 27, 28, 50, 52, 137, 172, 283, 306, 401, 402, 433, 518, 539, 580, 600, 613, 627, 630, 637, 646, 667, 668, 674, 689, 702, 704, 709, 718
Pseudo-Jonathan.................. 47, 375, 647
punish 60, 114, 126, 133, 188, 236, 238, 260, 358, 401, 427, 435, 438, 467, 477, 478, 506, 516-518, 520, 532, 595, 602, 609, 624, 687, 688, 699, 717
rabbi 18, 94, 152, 184, 194, 202, 209, 233, 263, 284, 287, 288, 376, 425, 477, 478, 482, 514, 551, 568, 576, 577, 609, 613, 615, 616, 618, 619, 625, 630, 641-644, 656, 660, 663, 666, 668-671, 677, 678, 686, 698, 716
ransom 5, 124, 125, 328, 380, 386, 388-390
recessional..........................513, 521
reconcile............... 37, 52, 232, 361, 689
redeem 4, 5, 7, 37, 45, 47, 51, 52, 54, 55, 68, 75, 100, 125, 129, 139, 168, 173, 219, 278, 318, 343, 380, 388-390, 392, 397, 400, 401, 447, 451, 519, 573, 626, 630, 644, 657, 669, 676, 688, 704
redemption 5, 7, 9-11, 20, 21, 23, 35-37, 44, 51, 52, 64, 68, 81, 82, 84, 95, 97, 99, 101, 104, 109, 117, 139, 146, 164, 172, 173, 178, 192, 206, 219, 227, 233, 246, 258, 259, 266, 269, 277, 278, 283, 297, 298, 309, 322, 336, 338, 343-345, 372, 382, 390, 397, 400, 401, 410, 417, 421, 423, 432, 447, 531, 555, 561, 563, 568, 569, 572, 574, 579, 595, 596, 618, 631, 644, 652, 670, 671, 676, 704-710, 712, 714, 718-720
rejoice 27, 28, 126, 131, 183, 213, 216, 222, 285, 287, 318, 320, 326, 327, 329, 410, 426, 445, 510, 527-529, 541, 569, 572, 573, 604, 612, 616, 617, 620, 622, 634, 655, 666, 699
release 5, 7, 8, 16, 20, 21, 45, 47, 51, 52, 108, 116, 122, 132, 143, 189, 191, 199, 206, 210, 226, 236, 249, 262, 314, 325, 363, 367, 374, 375, 411, 429, 434, 437 438, 458, 461, 472, 477, 562, 570, 585, 588, 589, 592, 593
repent 52, 84, 90, 93-95, 107, 108, 111, 114, 118, 121, 136, 139, 140, 226, 245, 252, 253, 419, 429, 445-447, 451, 604, 631, 687, 689, 693
responsa...............................84, 707-709
rest 23, 27, 30, 46, 62, 81, 83, 88, 90, 96, 103, 111, 115, 130, 132, 144, 152, 157, 161, 205, 210, 222, 226, 240, 243, 252, 253, 262, 276, 286, 293, 295, 298, 299, 334, 335, 337, 339, 364, 374, 376, 377, 388, 394, 398, 400, 401, 403, 408, 412, 433, 449, 461, 473, 488, 507, 519, 544, 557, 558, 568, 574, 582, 585, 588, 596, 602, 604, 608, 612, 631, 641, 643, 656, 609, 664, 666, 678, 680, 690, 701-703
reveal 33-36, 75, 146, 184, 263, 264, 298, 303, 309, 326, 460, 477, 490, 572, 606, 613-615, 618, 647, 680, 687
reward 6, 98, 116, 190, 223, 228, 616, 625, 688, 689
rhetorical 16, 32, 68, 138, 194, 202, 352, 382, 383, 385, 392, 425, 426, 504, 567, 667, 721
ridge 156, 273, 386, 612, 637, 646, 655, 660-662, 664, 671, 680
river 23, 59, 88, 99, 100, 120, 132, 151, 206, 207, 249-251, 266, 287, 299, 319, 331-333, 363, 451-455, 457, 458, 462, 464, 470, 472, 474-476, 497, 602, 611, 624, 642, 658, 659, 665, 666, 670-672
robe 29, 66, 67, 69, 123, 125, 136, 153, 191, 192, 213, 218, 219, 310, 323, 371,

372, 472, 498, 526, 541, 544, 545, 553, 604, 616, 636, 655, 688, 689
sabbath 4, 6-10, 13, 21, 61, 62, 88, 89, 159, 172, 216, 229, 262, 373, 374, 376, 416, 420, 569, 580, 583, 656, 607
sabotage............... 60, 113, 333, 486, 504
saboteur..717
saint 109, 347, 373, 381, 390, 462, 465, 604, 612, 654, 666, 671, 674, 676, 678, 695, 697, 699
Samaritan 6, 24, 115, 163, 211, 283, 373-375, 445, 456, 588, 592, 637
Satan 101-103, 105, 106, 126, 132, 221, 318, 325, 326, 328, 331, 342, 437, 562-565, 570, 571, 583, 585, 588-590, 592, 593, 595, 611, 627, 628, 697, 709, 716, 717
scales..........................190, 233, 473, 656
scavenger...559
Scripture 2, 5, 7, 16, 24, 26, 32, 35, 37, 41-43, 48, 49, 53, 55, 56, 61-63, 68, 70, 81, 83, 95, 99, 104, 112, 113, 122, 146-148, 154, 157, 162, 176, 193, 197, 202, 211, 246, 247, 264-266, 270, 281, 284, 296, 314, 323, 327, 333, 336, 340, 349, 360, 367, 388, 392, 398, 410, 411, 414, 422, 423, 430, 434, 445, 448, 467, 482, 483, 486, 491, 501, 516, 544, 551, 554, 556, 558, 559, 563, 564, 566, 568, 576, 588, 600, 602, 614, 617, 620, 629, 632, 637, 639, 642-644, 664, 665, 668, 672, 678, 684, 686, 687, 703-705, 708-710, 718-720
scroll 31, 34, 35, 39, 41, 43, 52, 61, 62, 64, 66, 69, 75, 78-80, 83, 112, 132, 140, 153, 154, 160-164, 169, 170, 174, 182, 186, 199, 200, 256-259, 262, 263, 266-268, 344, 349, 357, 377, 385, 438, 527, 560, 609, 619, 640, 652, 655, 660-662, 665, 676, 679, 683, 684, 686, 687, 689, 694, 696, 699, 709, 716
sea 7, 8, 11, 12, 14, 22, 35, 37, 52, 53, 70, 77, 78, 131, 133, 134, 138, 139, 155, 156, 166, 170, 174, 177, 184, 199, 205-209, 214, 223, 226, 233, 236-238, 241, 256, 257, 259-261, 265, 266, 270, 282,
308, 315, 320, 327, 333, 334, 337-339, 344, 360, 372, 375, 393, 402, 216, 426, 427, 430-433, 436, 438, 441-443, 447, 450, 453, 455, 461, 464, 470, 482, 486, 489, 494, 504, 507, 509, 520, 523, 525, 526, 530, 535, 550, 554, 557, 591-593, 597, 598, 600, 602, 604, 605, 607, 608, 611, 614, 619, 629, 640, 641, 649, 651, 652, 655, 658, 659, 665, 670, 671, 673, 676, 679, 689, 709
seal 15, 34, 130, 163, 181, 183, 189, 192, 198, 199, 201, 203, 204, 206, 207, 209, 217, 227-229, 233, 236, 243, 246, 249, 256, 259, 262, 263, 301, 398, 436, 437, 472, 478, 598, 677, 686, 687, 699, 709, 711
secrets 12, 34, 35, 77, 96, 97, 140, 303, 315, 368, 392, 404, 495, 551, 572
Seleucid 46, 278, 316, 347, 348, 455, 499
Semitic 31, 47, 52, 53, 93, 115, 134, 165, 173, 176, 187, 218, 256, 268, 286, 302, 332, 350, 383, 492, 493, 507, 613, 692
Septuagint.. 127
Seraphim...................................... 156, 230
serpent 105, 210, 250, 312, 315, 317, 324, 325, 328, 330, 332, 333, 335, 562, 563, 570
sexual 97, 99, 105-107, 113, 253, 390, 393, 395, 406, 407, 482, 485, 487, 488, 508-510, 512, 514, 519, 521, 629
Shebuoth..624
Shekinah........................…..616, 645, 678
Sibyl 207, 323, 456, 473, 516, 532, 611, 614, 615, 641, 656
sickle 215, 403, 413, 414, 418, 420-424, 554
sign 135, 142, 150, 204, 207-209, 215, 230, 331 245-247, 310, 313, 314, 331 364, 369, 392, 400, 409, 411, 412, 422, 427, 429, 435, 454, 484, 490, 578, 592, 628, 630, 676
smoke 145, 231, 232, 242, 244, 274, 279, 283, 386, 408, 410, 430, 434, 436, 449, 508-510, 513, 520, 521, 526, 527, 537, 539, 594, 595, 606, 624, 625, 636, 651, 653, 676, 678, 694

Son of God 11, 51, 110, 112, 224, 350, 422
Son of man 13, 15, 20, 28, 51 54, 66, 69, 70, 103, 117, 142, 165, 167, 172, 174-176, 200, 206, 218, 256, 266, 267, 302, 317, 387, 403, 409, 413, 415-417, 422, 424, 467, 489, 494, 546, 575, 578, 579, 584, 585, 594, 638, 676, 687, 695
soul 191, 329, 396, 426, 427, 441, 442, 509, 524, 533, 541, 572, 587, 604, 616-618, 631, 686, 698
Spanish.................................. 31, 524, 592
Sphinx................155, 156, 178, 436, 539
spirit 17, 49, 59, 61, 65, 80, 84, 87, 90, 92, 98, 100, 107, 111, 113, 114, 118, 119, 124, 137, 143, 147, 154, 155, 165, 169, 282, 286, 293, 309, 366, 368, 384, 408, 489, 546, 547, 557, 568, 574, 617, 618, 632-635, 692, 693
spring 39, 72, 99, 132, 156, 198, 212, 224, 247, 254, 259, 274, 275, 314, 386, 388, 398, 414, 415, 468, 554, 606, 608, 611, 623, 624, 629, 630, 652, 653, 658-665, 668-670, 672, 676, 679, 691, 693
stagger.............................408, 488, 511
strip......................320, 501, 502, 516, 619
suffer 26, 209, 222, 451, 505, 624, 625, 677, 698, 703, 716
sword 18, 21, 29, 67, 68, 72, 105, 107, 108, 123, 144, 169, 180, 185, 186, 188, 189, 209, 229, 230, 235, 237, 312, 324, 357, 358, 364, 368, 419, 425, 427, 452, 469, 477, 478, 484, 487, 508, 511, 512, 535, 548, 550-554, 558-560, 577-579
symbol 69, 73, 93, 95, 164, 184, 257, 314, 336, 369, 371, 415, 416, 420, 442, 476, 484, 492, 530, 609, 619, 628, 634, 635, 641, 712
synagogue 78, 86, 100-102, 120, 122, 123 125, 126, 134, 156, 233, 272, 361, 384, 583, 627, 628, 647, 716, 717
Syrian 9, 10, 14, 38, 88, 130, 190, 216, 219, 277, 278, 316-318, 321, 376, 394, 409, 415, 438, 453, 456, 492, 567, 577, 601, 705
taboo...6, 161
talmud...347, 377
talmudist.................................... 426, 580
targum................….......31, 47, 56, 334, 603
targumist......425, 592, 602, 630, 653, 678
temple 10, 13-17, 19, 23, 38, 52, 53, 61, 69, 70, 72, 73, 77, 78, 88, 94, 95, 99, 109, 110, 124, 132-135, 144, 146-148, 150, 152-156, 159, 161, 171, 184, 188, 190, 191, 201, 202, 204, 206, 211, 215, 216, 219, 222, 228, 231, 246, 247, 253, 259, 263, 265, 267, 269, 271-279, 281, 282, 292, 298, 299, 307-309, 318, 320, 321, 325, 329, 341, 342, 345, 353, 355, 361, 366-368, 375, 376, 385-388, 390, 392, 394, 395, 398, 400, 401, 412, 414-416, 418, 420, 422-424, 426, 430, 431, 434-436 438-441, 451, 456, 464, 466, 468, 470-473, 475, 478, 480, 491, 512, 523, 537-539, 543, 545, 549, 554, 560, 566, 568, 570, 571, 588, 589, 594-596, 599, 602, 605-615, 617, 618, 622-628, 630, 636-643, 647, 648, 651-654, 656-663, 665-674, 678, 679, 690, 693, 698, 713, 718
tent 14, 77, 146, 223-225, 282, 307, 355, 402, 434-436, 605, 607, 609, 610, 615, 621-628, 629, 632, 639, 651, 653, 662, 665, 670, 673, 697
Therapeutae..394
Tishbite..283
Torah 8, 24, 26, 43, 52, 53, 93, 97, 137, 153, 174, 264, 267, 282, 296, 308, 309, 334, 349, 408, 411, 412, 450, 577, 618, 640, 647, 702-705
torture 1, 59, 122, 126, 131, 183, 219, 223, 236, 243-249, 265, 286, 287, 325, 355, 408, 410, 446, 503, 508, 516, 518, 520, 523, 588, 595, 596
Tosephta.......................................377, 635
treasury 5, 10, 12, 101, 109, 112, 121, 139, 172, 192, 275, 276, 400, 413, 545, 549, 628
treaty 10, 65, 75, 89, 94, 97, 98, 101, 108, 251, 375, 457-459, 713
tribulation 9, 10, 38, 57-59, 68, 100, 101, 103, 111, 183, 190, 192, 213, 218, 219,

223, 224, 229, 233, 247, 262, 277, 278, 281, 308, 311, 329, 335, 569, 655, 716
triumph 16, 208, 385, 563, 573, 583
typology 2, 4, 15, 16, 18, 20-23, 69, 76, 131, 216, 244, 285, 314, 316, 319, 323, 325, 348, 375, 463 , 473, 487, 612, 711
unclean 367, 373, 380, 398, 470, 472, 473, 479, 480, 489, 508, 511, 513, 605, 650, 652, 654, 656
utopian..652
vengeance 96, 188, 191-194, 201, 223, 269, 278, 299, 407, 408, 411, 421, 423, 515-517, 533, 536, 539, 698
verbatim.........................……....634, 704
verdict 13, 15, 25, 109, 142, 143, 175, 186, 202, 206, 246, 256, 259, 416, 419, 420, 422, 424, 444, 484, 490, 494, 536, 554, 576, 578, 595, 598, 601, 677
version 30, 72, 210, 295, 296, 317, 421, 453, 472, 563, 599, 600, 614, 705, 706, virgin 202, 342, 389, 391, 398, 511, 513, 514, 697, 698
vizier................................ 153, 305
wadi............223, 332, 424, 624, 658, 659
wage... 515

wand 198, 200, 234, 236, 237, 284, 441, 447, 473, 476, 479
wedding 139, 140, 313, 319, 320, 541-546, 619, 620, 627, 698, 699
widow.. 485
wine 131, 187, 188, 252, 253, 269, 405, 408-410, 419, 421, 423-425, 464, 471, 475, 478, 479, 482, 487, 490, 506, 508, 511, 514, 552-554, 629, 688
witchcraft   481, 488, 510, 528, 529, 531
witness 33, 41, 44, 50, 55, 56, 58, 62, 63, 76, 79, 104, 109, 117, 122, 130, 136-138, 193, 280, 281, 289, 290, 294, 296, 394, 416, 444, 518, 547, 576, 579, 604, 660, 692, 693, 695, 704
worship 13, 53, 79, 80, 102, 107, 120, 131, 159, 172, 178, 252, 267, 269, 272, 273, 276, 295, 298, 351, 359, 362, 363, 365, 366, 385, 402, 408-410, 431, 432, 438, 442, 538, 545-547, 605, 607, 649, 655, 676, 679, 684, 685, 715
worthy 19, 120, 158, 160, 163, 164, 170, 174, 184, 298, 632, 684, 716
Zadokite...52
zealous......12, 18, 19, 139, 194, 352, 506
zodiac............ 69, 156, 244, 315, 646, 647

GEOGRAPHICAL LOCATIONS

Achor ....…......604, 659
Acre..............................572, 706, 707
Adiabene...............................173, 458
Aegean...88
Africa....................... 451, 454, 455, 591
Ain 222, 274, 388, 402, 443, 659, 665, 675, 676
Alexandria 97, 132, 347, 394, 496, 584, 641
Alps..455, 590
Ammon.......................................27, 45
Anthedon...130
Antioch..........................210, 216, 550
Antonia 156, 204, 274, 276, 468, 605, 615, 637, 647, 653, 663, 665, 690

Arad.......…........................274-276, 639
Armageddon 226, 372, 381, 453, 459, 460, 461, 536
Armenia..................... 456, 457, 463, 469
Ascalon..130, 425
Ashdod... 425, 514
Asia 29, 76, 78, 84, 126, 187, 392, 397, 472, 550
Asia Minor 46, 86, 88, 100, 106, 109, 115, 120, 247, 259, 294, 332, 337, 360, 372, 382, 383, 385, 400, 424, 454, 455, 462, 464, 472, 532, 590, 591, 711-714, 719
Assyria... 20, 21, 298-325, 331-333, 374, 375, 488
Baghdad... 449

Beitar..424
Beth Alpha................................. 156, 647
Beth-horon 10, 13, 14, 76, 190, 201, 219, 234, 250, 263, 277, 278, 281, 288, 321, 333, 375, 376, 417, 420, 426, 438, 492, 571, 678, 682, 687, 714
Beth Shan...647
Bethel.......................................145, 653
Bethlehem.................. 309, 320, 333, 353
Byzantium... 469
Caesarea....130, 184, 367, 522, 592, 656
Camelot...611
Canaan 11, 14, 27, 73, 128, 167, 229, 305, 314, 535, 610, 721
Capernaum...............................134, 492
Carmel 133, 365, 366, 433, 457, 459, 460, 467, 494, 608, 641, 642
Carrhae..456
Carthage....................................455, 524
Caucasian..................................590, 591
Caystar...88
Chalcis..............................316, 496, 498
China...121, 332, 372, 463, 526, 554, 590
Colossie...137
Constantinople............296, 341, 465, 496
Corinth.......26, 87, 88, 97, 102, 109, 396
Cush... 591
Cyprus..611
Damascus..............................53, 641, 642
Dead Sea 7, 8, 11, 12, 35, 37, 52, 53, 70, 77, 174, 206, 209, 214, 223, 265, 270, 282, 375, 393, 438, 442, 482, 504, 507, 550, 593, 611, 614, 619, 640, 651, 652, 655, 659, 665, 668-671, 675-679, 689,
Decision......................................297, 460, 472
Eden 22, 93, 98, 202, 334, 399, 589, 604, 612, 613, 642, 643, 644, 666, 667, 669-672, 675-679, 690, 695,
Edom 24, 27, 278, 341, 362, 407, 412, 425, 478, 539, 554, 555, 589
Elam..203
Ephesus 46, 59, 61, 85, 87-89, 91, 92, 94, 95, 99, 100, 104, 110, 119, 132, 137, 712, 713, 716
Ephraim...............136, 138, 286, 295, 296
Esdraelon.............................21, 459, 460
Ethiopia 110, 124, 398, 484, 591, 617, 643, 666, 671
Euphrates 21, 132, 206, 207, 226, 249-251, 388, 406, 438, 447, 451-454, 456, 457, 459, 461-463, 468, 470, 472, 474-476, 483, 500, 503, 527, 530, 643, 667, 671, 712
Europe 31, 46, 197, 372, 454, 455, 523, 524, 581, 591, 663,
Fertile Crescent.................. 460, 461, 591
Gadara.. 130
Galilee 20, 134, 208, 247, 349, 443, 523, 593, 611, 651
Gaza......................... 130, 425, 514, 587
Gehenna............................395, 612
Gehinnom...568, 596, 603, 632, 677, 678
Gerasa..130
Gezer......................................460, 661, 664
Gibraltar... 461
Gihon 222, 274, 275, 388, 402, 414, 560, 623, 653, 661, 665, 667, 675, 676
Giliad..283
Gishon.. 671
Gog..556
Gomorrah 226, 242, 244, 285, 408, 410, 411, 413, 629
Gozen..299
Great River 249, 250, 319, 332, 451, 452, 470, 475, 476
Greece 64, 69, 70, 74, 174, 287, 345, 454-456, 492, 522, 642
Hades............75, 185, 188, 598, 602, 603, 686
Halak..299
Hamath............................. 156, 617, 647
Har Mageden.....................................447
Havilah..671
Hazor.. 460, 661
Hellespont... 455
Hermon......................................445, 642
Hierapolis...137
Himalya...592
Hippos... 130
Idumea...............................247, 291, 349, 593
India........5, 448, 454, 463, 524, 591, 620
Izmir... 64, 100
Jabneh... 338

Jericho.................. 23, 229, 230, 247, 469
Jezreal....................... 460, 501, 505, 588
Joppa...641
Jordan 21, 23, 333, 400, 453, 454, 464, 588, 592, 595, 597, 600, 614, 673
Judaea............…..168, 320, 364, 366, 377
Judah 20, 37, 69, 89, 132, 169, 172, 176, 181, 184, 190, 204, 286, 295, 297, 298,314, 315, 331-333, 358, 362, 374, 386, 387, 403, 408, 411, 412, 417, 425, 456, 513, 531, 542, 560, 603, 608, 615, 633, 644, 655, 658, 688, 705
Kadesh... 428, 461
Kerioth..587
Kidron 98, 99, 132, 156, 215, 223, 386, 414-417, 420, 422-424, 426, 460, 463, 473, 480, 554, 557, 560, 566, 568, 572, 592, 595, 602, 607, 608, 612, 637, 653, 659, 660, 663, 664, 668, 670-672, 677, 712
Kishon......................................460, 608
Lachish........................…..........274-276, 639
Lagash... 614
Laodicea.........................136, 138-140
Lebanon......250, 270, 275, 449, 452, 642
Libya..454
Macedonia..........….396, 454-456, 500, 524
Magnesia............................... 62, 120, 458
Magog 294, 426, 451, 459, 480, 556, 572, 573, 585-587, 589-593, 643, 666
Masada..............................290, 349, 661
Meander River..................... 59, 455, 458
Media.................. 38, 64, 254, 406, 670, 686, 715
Mediterranean 34, 46, 187, 205, 259, 320, 337, 430-433, 442, 443, 446, 455, 456, 459, 461, 523, 564, 593, 602, 611, 641, 649, 651, 658, 708
Megiddo 73, 133, 271, 275, 438, 452, 457, 459-561, 463, 468, 470, 472, 474-476, 480, 594, 661, 712
Memphis..370
Moab…....…..27, 45, 106, 110, 113, 587, 691
Moriah..642
Mount of Olives 250, 415, 467, 554, 592, 607, 634, 672, 712
Mount Sinai 14, 42, 54, 60, 147, 150, 152, 230, 232, 233, 242, 244, 268, 295, 308, 319, 464, 468, 476, 477, 608, 614, 619, 626, 636, 641, 644, 646, 647, 666, 670, 672, 675, 695, 700,
Murraba'at.. 377
Nile.................................….237, 238, 441
Nineveh 3, 270, 375, 407, 442, 485, 487,491, 507, 512-514, 613, 641, 698
Palestine 15, 20-22, 35, 38, 69, 99, 126-134, 167, 168, 173, 187, 189, 198, 200, 210, 229, 232, 239-241, 245-247, 249, 251, 252, 254, 259, 260, 277, 278, 282, 287, 292, 305, 306, 315-317, 319, 321, 328, 332-335, 337, 341, 344, 347, 349, 352, 353, 356, 360, 363, 365-367, 375, 382, 383, 385, 390, 397, 400, 404, 405, 409, 415, 418, 424, 431, 437, 439, 449, 453-455, 457-459, 461, 462, 464, 470, 473, 476, 484, 487, 489, 490, 497, 500, 505, 517, 523, 524, 532, 538, 539, 564, 85, 589, 590, 592-595, 599, 603, 605, 609, 612, 624, 672, 683, 693, 697, 712, 713, 716-719
Paradise 90, 98, 99, 104, 560, 611, 612, 643, 666, 672, 679, 695
Parthia 132, 167, 183, 206, 207, 220, 251, 288, 289, 316, 347-350, 352, 353, 355, 357, 360, 456-459, 461-464, 468, 474, 500, 523, 524, 555, 593, 666
Pella.................................. 130, 315, 316
Perea..93
Pergamum 46, 61, 64, 88, 96, 105-108, 112, 717
Persia 15, 33, 64, 69, 70, 74, 120, 206, 207, 278, 314, 323, 341, 345, 452-454, 456, 458, 461, 500, 517, 555, 591, 713
Petra.. 647
Philadelphia 2, 46, 61, 64, 87, 104, 109, 110, 123-126, 134, 135, 137, 140, 149, 150, 210, 271, 295, 346, 347, 372, 381, 382, 390, 392, 393, 430, 437, 460, 491, 496, 523, 529, 536, 607, 697, 716, 717
Philistia................….......................... 45
Pishon...........................…...............671
Qumran 8, 38, 99, 223, 390, 413, 549, 619, 640, 655, 659, 660, 668, 671, 676, 680

Rhodes.. 257, 290
River Cebar.......................................151
Samaria 130, 138, 182, 185, 186, 211, 286, 295, 364, 367, 454
Sardis..46, 64, 118-122, 124, 137, 716
Scythopolis.......................................130
Seba.. 124, 649
Sebaste..130
Sebonitis...130
Sepphoris..641
Sheba..591, 649
Shiloh..372,
Shinar..617
Shittim......................105, 602, 658, 669
Sicily..370
Sidon..45
Sinai 14, 43, 54, 60, 84, 230, 232, 242, 295, 308, 435, 467, 476-478, 619, 641, 647, 666
Sippar...613
Smyrna 46, 61, 64, 100-104, 106, 110, 124, 137, 717
Sodom 22, 133, 226, 242, 244, 272, 285-287, 289, 408, 410, 411, 513, 629
Spain 155, 372, 455, 496, 526, 592, 609, 649, 672
Syria........................182, 215, 455-457, 492
Tabor.......................445, 459, 641, 642
Tarshish..................... 520, 591, 649, 650
Taurus..455, 458
Tekoa..333
Thebes... 641
Thrace....................... 370, 454, 455, 523
Thyatira............ 46, 61, 64, 110-117, 716
Tiber 156, 287, 316, 348, 363, 452, 483, 484, 486, 487, 496, 497, 502, 503
Tigris............21, 476, 503, 643, 667, 671
Tograma.....................................590, 591
Tubal................................522, 586, 590, 591
Tunisia..449
Turkey 46, 59, 64, 84, 88, 100, 137, 523, 591, 712, 719, 720
Tyre 45, 80, 412, 424, 481, 485-487, 490, 506, 507, 512, 513, 519, 521, 522, 525, 526, 528-531, 538, 606, 611, 645, 652, 698
Ugarit...454, 697
Uphaz........................29, 67, 540, 548
Verdict 13, 15, 25, 109, 142, 143, 175, 186, 202, 206, 246, 256, 259, 416, 419, 422, 424, 444, 484, 490, 494, 536, 554, 556, 576, 578, 595, 598, 601, 677
Vesuvius.. 238
Wadi el Arish...................................424
Yemen...449, 572
Zion ...90, 132, 150, 152, 156, 191, 205, 215, 219, 222, 271, 273, 282, 314, 318-320, 326, 354, 379, 386-390, 397, 398, 401, 414-416, 419, 424, 430, 435, 476, 490, 514, 531, 554, 557, 569, 571, 576, 587, 604, 608, 609, 612, 614, 615, 618, 619, 621, 623-625, 627, 630, 632, 635-637, 642-644, 646, 648, 650, 651, 653, 655, 659, 661, 662, 666, 668, 669, 671, 672, 675, 676, 678, 679, 690, 693, 695, 705

ANCIENT PERSONALITIES

Aaron 19, 53, 198, 200, 209, 231, 236, 237, 244, 280, 284, 285, 436, 473, 479, 616, 652
Abedneggo.............................365, 558
Abraham 17, 22, 47, 128, 129, 154, 156, 181, 242, 250, 294, 305, 400, 451, 574, 610, 671
Abram...............................293, 294, 474
Adam 22, 98, 399, 419, 570, 612, 613, 643, 644, 669-671, 675, 676, 695
Adonijah.. 274
Adso... 343
Aesop... 15
Ahab 110, 113, 115, 253, 283, 312, 315, 505, 533,
Ahaz....................... 314, 459, 460, 595
Ahaziah........................... 459, 460, 595
Akiba... 263, 287
Alcimus..394
Alexander 11, 51, 120, 245, 289, 390, 394, 445, 453-455, 463, 492, 500, 524, 551, 591

Amiel..............................147, 341
Amos 25, 27, 55, 56, 195, 199, 202, 208, 225, 230, 231, 235-240, 259, 263-265, 282, 303, 444, 445, 506, 511, 513, 528, 540, 587, 595
Ananaus..........................291, 535
Anthony............247, 289, 376, 457, 503
Antigonus 167, 168, 176, 179, 220, 247, 288-291, 328, 349, 350, 352, 357, 457, 578, 593
Antiochus 10, 13, 15, 38, 46, 69, 120, 131, 137, 142, 164, 183, 219, 263, 265, 273, 276, 277, 281, 316, 318, 325, 337, 345, 348, 459, 352, 353, 355, 363, 366, 375-377, 415, 436, 438, 454-456, 458, 489, 492, 494, 498, 499, 523, 559, 566, 571, 575, 579, 601, 669
Antipas 105, 106, 316, 348, 363, 496, 497
Antipater.................289, 316, 496, 497
Apollo...............................249, 294
Archelaus 28, 130, 168, 176, 335, 348, 458
Aristeas............... 660-662, 665, 696
Aristobulus.............................289
Aristophanes..........................72
Armilos 286, 295-300, 340-343, 348, 371, 378, 450, 669, 706
Artabanus...........................456, 457
Artemis................................88, 120
Asher.................................204, 633
Athrongaeus......................... 357
Attalus............................... 88, 106
Augustus 294, 316, 348, 361, 370, 404, 496, 503
Azazel............................562-564, 570
Azekah...................................234
Baal 25, 107, 110, 113, 115, 116, 239, 265-267, 275,
Balaam 96, 105-108, 115, 448, 628, 717
Balak...............................105, 106, 717
Bar Cochba.........102, 103, 318, 713, 716
Barak..................68, 105, 133, 257, 450
Barnabas................................80, 566
Baruch 35, 191, 192, 194, 204, 206, 263, 514, 566, 570, 571, 578, 585, 589, 610, 672
Beliar..................................574
Beliel................................. 296, 341
Balshazzar..........................252, 253
Ben Kisma............................ 577
Benedictus........................... 371
Benjamin 89, 107, 204, 212, 535, 567, 569, 634, 647
Berenice............................. 363
Caesar 130, 184, 294, 319, 337, 347-349, 352, 356, 360, 364, 367, 370, 373, 377, 458, 463, 484, 490, 492, 496, 497, 499, 503, 504, 522, 554, 592, 656
Caligula 316, 346, 347, 366-368, 371, 431, 496, 498
Calvin................................371
Caracella...........................456
Cestius........250, 334, 337, 347, 367, 713
Charlemagne.........................371
Claudius 40, 187, 316, 348, 361-364, 367, 496, 498, 503, 505, 636, 647
Cleopatra............................290
Constantine 302, 342, 459, 486, 500, 588, 620
Corbulo..............................457
Crassus..............................251
Cybele............................... 120
Cyril................................246, 398, 584
Cyrus 21, 33, 120, 206, 207, 452, 458, 517, 584, 630, 713
Daniel 4, 13, 14, 17, 18, 24, 30, 33-38, 54, 57, 58, 60, 64, 68-72, 74-77, 80, 81, 100, 102, 103, 112, 131, 142, 148, 155, 157, 175-178, 189, 205, 219, 253, 257, 260-265, 267, 273, 276-278, 281, 285, 291, 297, 315, 323, 330, 333, 339, 340, 344-347, 351, 355, 359, 365-368, 371, 374, 376, 387, 409, 411, 416, 419-421, 423, 446, 483, 490, 492, 494, 497, 499, 500, 506, 513, 526, 539, 541, 549, 559, 564, 567, 570, 575-578, 585, 588, 600, 614, 618, 682, 684-687, 700, 702-708, 714, 719
Dante..................................583
David 11, 17, 40, 50, 89, 95, 123, 125,

132, 137, 138, 161, 166, 168, 171, 175, 215, 217, 270, 273-275, 282, 283, 295, 296, 298, 299, 301, 307, 308, 341, 355, 386, 387, 402, 403, 435, 450, 455, 457, 469, 535, 549, 592, 605, 606, 608, 610, 616, 617, 623-625, 630, 632, 637, 642, 643, 646, 651-654, 657, 660-662, 664, 665, 668, 670, 671, 676-679, 691-693, 714, 720

Deborah   39, 68, 73, 133, 257, 314, 460
Dio..288, 294
Dio Cassius.. 81
Diocletian...316
Diogenes   434, 591, 641
Diotrephes..92
Dolabella..88
Dominic...280
Domitian 40, 187, 347 371-373, 474, 487, 496, 498, 704, 711-713
Eleazar......... 25, 133, 320, 328, 468, 482
Elharizi.. 568, 618
Eli...26, 484, 403
Eliakim....................................... 123-125
Eliezer........................ 168, 176, 220, 642
Elijah 2, 16, 17, 19, 22, 31, 113, 130, 140, 279-281, 283-285, 293, 295, 298, 299, 320, 321, 341, 362, 365, 366, 450, 543, 544, 587, 594 , 595, 598, 602, 611, 613, 618, 669, 717
Elisha 19, 113, 115, 130, 182, 185, 186, 280, 281, 283, 285, 536, 544
Epanetus.. 397
Ephraim......136, 138, 286, 288, 295, 296
Epiphanius...................................40, 389
Esau 160, 296, 299, 361, 412, 450, 492, 493, 535, 548
Esther................................. 292, 367, 567
Eusebius......97, 342, 343, 620, 706, 714
Eve 98, 315, 317, 399, 612, 613, 670, 676
Ezekias................................. 349, 357
Ezekiel 17, 22, 24, 26, 36, 42, 43, 45, 61, 68, 72-74, 79, 81, 99, 120, 132, 135, 143, 147, 150, 155, 156, 162, 169, 170, 178, 189, 198, 205, 207-210, 212, 215, 218, 236, 246, 247, 258, 267, 268, 270-274 293, 294, 297, 306, 373, 386, 388, 392, 394, 398, 399, 400, 422, 423, 426, 451, 463, 467, 472, 477, 478, 488, 506, 512, 513, 521-523, 526, 529, 532, 541, 547, 549, 555-558, 560, 590-595, 613, 620, 624, 627, 630, 634-637, 639-642, 644, 659, 663-672, 679, 686, 697, 702-705, 707-709, 714
Felix..505
Festus..19, 505
Florus.. 245-247
Francis.....................62, 280, 421, 557
Gabriel................................. 74, 209, 229
Gad..212
Gaius 40, 348, 362-364, 366-368, 370, 377, 409, 412, 431, 433, 459, 497, 498, 503, 713
Galba.. 316, 497
Gerundi...573
Gideon..459
Gog 236, 294, 411, 426, 451, 480, 556, 557, 572, 573, 586, 589, 590-593, 643, 666
Habakkuk 35, 241, 264, 265, 407, 411-413, 482, 483, 593, 595, 709
Hadrian..713
Haggai.. 39, 77, 705
Hanina.................................209, 477
Hanna..166, 206 607, 616, 617, 643, 653, 672, 690, 691, 700
Hannibal...................120, 454, 455, 463
Hasmonean 10, 12, 18, 19, 22, 58-60, 68, 69, 73, 76, 102, 166-168, 174, 176, 179, 184, 201, 220, 265, 276-278, 288, 290, 291, 303, 311, 316, 318, 321, 325, 344, 345, 349, 350, 355, 357, 360, 375, 387, 394, 409, 415, 438, 453, 457, 492, 494, 495, 535, 543, 577, 578, 581, 582, 589, 642, 662, 682, 691, 718, 719
Hecate.. 75
Heliodorus..................................... 549
Hermas......................................92, 619
Herod 16, 130, 132, 167, 168, 176, 179, 206, 220, 247, 273, 278, 280, 281, 286-292, 294, 316, 318, 319, 346, 348-350,

352, 355-357, 359-364, 367, 369, 377, 378, 409, 412, 447, 456-458, 488, 490, 493, 494, 496-498, 503, 505, 521, 559, 576, 593, 595, 640, 647, 668, 712, 718
Herodotus................... 207, 453, 454, 458
Hezekiah 215, 271, 311, 414, 415, 423, 659, 662-664, 665, 675
Hofni..284
Hunia..514
Hyrcanus................................ 289, 349
Ignatius..61-63, 109
Innocence.........................1, 256, 262, 271
Irenaeus 40, 96, 348, 373, 377, 497, 696, 711-713
Isaac......47, 156, 361, 535, 573, 574, 671
Isaiah 8, 11, 21, 22, 24, 27, 38, 52, 53, 57, 68, 74, 101, 110, 124, 125, 128, 135, 147, 167, 173, 176, 198, 199, 206, 215, 222, 224, 232, 239, 243, 253, 254, 271, 278, 299, 314, 318, 327, 329, 332, 333, 357, 374, 375, 400, 406, 412, 414, 415, 421-423, 436, 452, 453, 458, 463, 464, 487, 490, 506, 513, 514, 529-532, 534, 538, 558-560, 570, 581, 584, 599, 603, 606, 607, 610, 612, 614, 620, 623, 625, 627, 628, 630, 634, 635, 652, 654, 656, 664, 679, 684, 686, 702, 704, 706, 709, 713, 715
Ishmael.184, 194, 288, 425, 643, 671, 678
Issachar 204, 633
Ithamar 25
Jacob 47, 145, 146, 163, 210, 222, 299, 361, 492, 527, 529, 535, 548, 574, 603, 607, 616, 617, 643, 653, 572, 690, 691, 700
Jannaeus.. 289
Japeth..585
Jehoshaphat 132, 202, 413, 419, 420, 423-425, 560, 568, 596, 608, 631, 677
Jehu.................. 113-115, 253, 505, 536,
Jeremiel..190
Jesse......................................50, 161, 691
Jesus 2, 11, 12, 14, 16, 19, 20, 33-36, 40, 43, 45, 47, 49-52, 54, 59, 60, 62, 63, 74, 79, 80, 83, 91, 92, 98, 99, 101, 119,
122, 137, 140, 168, 171-173, 184, 195, 206, 214, 215, 219, 233, 277, 278, 282, 283, 291, 302, 316, 319, 321, 326, 328, 331, 335, 336, 342, 357, 366, 373, 377, 378, 384, 388-393, 395-399, 411, 413, 416, 422, 460, 462, 494, 497, 498, 509, 530, 543, 545-547, 550, 551, 564, 574, 579, 580, 605, 614, 620, 627, 636, 638, 652, 671, 675, 679, 681, 682, 691, 695, 696, 701, 714-716, 719, 719, 720
Jezebel 97, 107, 111, 113, 115, 253, 505, 536, 628, 718
Joash................................ 27, 180, 182
Johanan............................ 275, 609, 613
Jonah.......................270, 407, 491, 617
Jonathan 31, 34, 47, 204, 284, 375, 459, 647
Jose.....................576, 577, 641, 656
Joseph 17, 167, 207, 247, 295, 299, 315, 341, 363, 393, 450, 539
Josephus 23, 156, 173, 188, 211, 216, 246, 265, 273, 280-291, 348, 360, 362, 363, 366, 367, 388, 417, 458, 468, 531, 535, 559, 591, 596, 636, 641, 646, 647, 661, 663, 665, 668, 718
Josiah.............................. 459, 460, 551
Judah... 26, 160, 163, 168, 219, 286, 295
Judas 9, 10, 13, 14, 15, 21, 37-39, 52, 54, 68-70, 76, 142, 148, 167, 172, 174-176, 183, 190, 209, 210, 216, 219, 229, 265, 277, 278, 281, 288, 308, 317, 318, 321, 325, 328, 329, 333, 355, 357, 375-377, 394, 409, 415, 417, 420, 426, 438, 456, 489, 490, 492, 494, 500, 566, 571, 572, 575, 579, 585, 599, 601, 669, 678, 691
Jupiter..69, 713
Justin Martyr..40, 619
Korah....................332, 333, 617, 669
Leto..11, 317
Levi.....16, 477, 478, 574, 599, 643, 666
Livy......... 81, 82, 337, 454, 457, 459, 717
Lysias..216

Lysymachus 454
Macrobius 361
Manassah 210
Marcion 103
Mariamme 349, 357
Mary 316
Mattathias 18, 19
Maxentius 459
Melchizedek 16, 22, 375
Menahem 147, 320, 341
Meshach 365, 432
Micah 233, 311, 318, 319, 418, 502, 567, 635
Micaiah 166
Michael 24, 78, 98, 229, 257, 278, 297, 299, 313, 317, 323, 324, 352, 392, 450, 465
Mithradates 455
Naphtali 633
Nebuchadnezzar 17, 33, 75, 77, 79, 147, 253, 263, 294, 312, 351, 365, 432, 464, 478, 500, 531, 675, 684
Nero 130, 133, 346-348, 359, 370, 371, 377, 378, 457, 463, 496, 522
Nicanor 288
Nicalaus 96
Nidaba 613
Noah 22, 150, 535, 603, 714
Origen 392
Otho 316, 497
Paetus 251, 457
Pappus 290, 291, 578
Paul 19, 26, 34, 46, 58, 80, 91, 92, 102, 103, 108, 109, 134, 183, 280, 282, 292, 395, 396, 517, 532, 536, 544, 579, 614-616, 619, 628, 638, 652, 685, 710, 717
Pegasus 156
Peter 19, 24, 38, 42, 75, 244, 280, 373, 467, 532, 566, 638, 647, 656
Petronius 366-368, 412, 431, 432, 466, 467
Phillip 87, 316, 363, 495, 496
Philo 3, 67, 69, 614, 615, 626, 646, 682, 705
Phineas 18, 19, 27, 108, 233, 284, 310,
Pilate 353

Pliny 59, 88, 104, 106, 124, 171, 238, 383, 385
Plutarch 81
Polybius 398, 454-456, 459
Polycarp 100
Pompey 260, 276, 353, 370, 371, 377, 411, 455, 456, 531
Popilius 337, 456, 459
Ptolemy 454, 550
Raguel 229
Rahab 312, 315
Remiel 229
Reuben 107, 204, 598, 631, 633
Romulus 286, 341, 371, 484
Salome 361
Samuel 166, 571
Satan 100-103, 105, 106, 111, 115, 123, 125, 126, 132, 134, 209, 221, 248, 252, 272, 296, 318, 324-326, 328, 329, 331, 341, 342, 346, 437, 450, 490, 493, 562-565, 570, 571, 583, 585, 588-590, 592, 593, 595, 611, 627, 628, 697, 709, 716, 717
Saul 34, 115, 166, 282, 454, 535, 538
Scipio 120, 455, 458
Sejanus 287, 363
Seleucus 454
Sennacherib 215
Seraiah 530
Seutonius 187, 503, 554
Shadrach 365, 432, 558
Silas 685
Simon 215, 468, 479, 535, 633, 661, 662, 665
Sirach 188
Sisera 68, 73, 133, 257, 333, 426, 433, 459-461, 588, 608
Solomon 10-12, 14, 17, 51, 77, 89, 134, 155, 162, 177, 223, 274, 275, 301, 305, 307, 308, 369, 409, 435, 436, 573, 605, 609, 612, 615, 625, 629, 632, 637, 639, 640, 642, 646-648, 651, 652, 665, 667, 705, 714, 720
Sossius 167, 288, 289
St. Peter 647
Stephanas 397

Suidas..72
Tacitus 81, 100, 251, 454, 458, 469, 504, 507, 522, 538, 594, 666
Talitha...19
Tertullian......................................40, 619
Theodocian...................................34, 72
Theudas... 23
Thucydides......................................664
Thutmose..461
Tiamat... 315
Tiberius....................................156, 363
Titus 22, 184, 211, 238, 247, 254, 265, 273, 276, 316, 371, 396, 468, 469, 474, 496, 531, 594, 637
Uriel..229
Uzzah..403
Vespasian 22, 211, 238, 251, 254, 316, 334, 335, 337, 346-348, 371, 424, 457-459, 464, 465, 468, 474, 484, 487, 496, 497, 504, 507, 527, 529, 593, 594, 713, 718
Victoria........................... 485, 513, 520
Victorinus...................96, 109, 300, 369
Vitellius 251, 316, 335, 457, 459, 468, 484, 497, 504, 593, 594
Vologenses....................................251
Xerxes.. 454
Yahozabad....................................227
275, 280, 282, 285, 289, 291, 292, 341, 407, 564, 582, 602, 705, 706, 709
Zabad..27
Zadok................................20, 52, 355
Zebedee... 45
Zerubbabel 39, 69, 70, 76, 89, 99, 146, 275, 280, 282, 285, 289, 291,292, 341, 407, 564, 582, 602, 705, 706, 709
Zeus... 80
Zimri..............................18, 27, 108

MODERN SCHOLARS

Abegg..7
Aland.................30, 35, 42, 56, 143, 149
Alexander.................. 390, 463, 551, 591
Allen.. 418
Allison.. 134, 445
Allo......................... 218, 383, 462, 465
Altink.............................. 402, 403, 404
Anderson...591
Ariel... 668
Aune 57, 61, 74, 77, 87, 93, 108, 121, 122, 123, 126, 143, 166, 182, 194, 205, 208, 217-219, 225, 257, 276, 288, 304, 306, 349, 350, 388, 389, 394, 404, 417, 431, 432 , 457, 467, 468, 484, 490, 529, 530, 543, 551, 605, 636, 692, 701
Bachmann...................................... 183
Baillet......................................619, 640
Baines.. 371
Barclay...529
Barr..41
Bauckham.............. 478, 477, 699, 716
Bauer..97
567-569, 571-573. 576-578, 582, 583,
Baur...97, 109
Beagley 106, 125, 126, 192, 199, 213, 241, 245, 348, 389, 405, 463, 466, 486, 504, 521, 523
Beale......................4, 500, 700, 703, 708
Beasley-Murray 108, 213, 371, 381, 390, 392, 398, 460, 462, 465, 604, 709
Beatty............................ 288, 294, 327
Beauvery................................484, 487
Beckwith........................460, 462, 463
Bell..................................711, 713, 720
Bengel.................218, 321, 322, 329, 641
Benoit...377
Bergman...19
Bergmeier..........255, 258, 370, 483, 492
Betz...36, 57, 445
Bird...22
Bleek..218
Bloom..2, 631
Bodinger...347
Bogaert.................................. 194, 206
Boismard...........287, 492, 699, 701, 711
Boring......35, 38, 43 101, 162, 187, 195,

277, 278, 321, 329, 359, 426, 447, 460, 471, 491, 497, 538, 550, 553, 573, 682, 685, 686, 695, 711.
Bornkamm.................................. 182, 447
Bousset...59, 97, 218, 272, 371, 383, 462
Boutflower... 8
Bovon.. 58, 714
Bowman............................378, 392, 608
Böcher.................................... 43, 549
Brady................................. 371, 372
Braude.................................... 262
Braumann................................109
Briggs..................................27, 373
Brown.................................. 127
Brownlee.....................................53
Buchanan...............1, 4, 6, 8, 11, 13, 15, 19, 20, 23, 31, 36, 37, 49, 50, 51, 54, 61, 76, 92, 93, 95, 98, 99, 106, 132, 133, 135, 140, 147, 155, 167, 171, 192, 194, 202, 207, 211, 215, 221, 250, 259, 262, 270, 273, 286, 288, 294, 299, 309, 320, 321, 341, 349, 376, 383, 384, 390, 392, 396, 399, 405, 407, 415, 416, 422, 423, 425, 447, 452, 459, 491, 544, 554, 564, 590, 596, 602, 607, 608, 613-615, 618, 619, 620, 631, 640-643, 646, 665, 666, 668-673, 677-678, 686, 690, 703, 706, 709. 717
Burrows.................................... 613
Butts..................................... 391
Cadbury..............................81, 82
Caird 2, 3, 46, 79, 97, 101, 117, 142, 164, 169, 190, 194, 198, 208, 217, 228, 265, 306, 332, 335, 381, 382, 287, 390, 391-393, 398, 404, 426, 431, 446, 447, 460, 462, 465, 473, 476, 478, 525, 554, 565, 581
Carrington...466
Cary.......................................591
Charles 13, 63, 71, 78, 127, 128, 143, 176, 187, 209, 213, 280, 324, 340, 346, 383, 384, 390, 392, 465, 507, 508, 547, 574, 636, 679, 685, 690, 696, 699, 700, 712
Charlesworth...............................685
Cohen..................................361, 418
Cole.. 88
Collins 192, 258, 295, 317, 322, 346, 378, 381, 383, 391, 392, 407, 491, 498, 523, 532, 697, 700
Comblin.....................................217, 670
Considine......................................271, 283
Conzelmann................................. 526
Corsini......................................392, 465
Court... 338
Cowley........................110, 398, 584
Cox......................................372
Cross................................. 163, 182
Crowfoot..................................640
Cumont......................................14
Danielou................................. 376
Daremberg.................................514
Davis.....................42, 53, 145, 154
Deere...581
Daube.....................................129
De Jonge......................302, 328, 580
Derrett......................................26
Deutsch............ 607, 619, 626-628, 635
DeVaux..619
Divine..398
Dodd...13
DosSantos.....................................127
Downey..73
Draper..218
Duling..555
Düsterdieck 40, 61, 71, 79, 87, 127, 143, 146, 147, 153, 156, 161, 163, 177, 181, 184, 186, 187, 192, 201, 213, 228, 247, 250, 258, 275, 292, 315, 316, 319, 328, 344, 345, 359, 381, 389, 390, 392, 393, 404, 418, 419, 424, 460, 461, 463, 465, 493, 496, 555, 580, 590, 607, 690, 700
Dyer.. 483
Eiselen..373
Eliade...................5, 93, 574, 613
Evans..............................99, 423, 665
Ewald......................................79, 377
Farmer.. 666
Farrar..418
Farrer.....................................68, 462
Faust...661
Fekkes.................................... 620

Feuillet............... 183, 217, 272, 398, 701
Fishbane......................24, 270, 370
Flusser..............................613, 614
Ford 71, 127, 199, 220, 258, 292, 347, 348, 392, 405, 424, 436-438, 462, 521, 523
Frey.....................................418
Fritsch..................................613
Giblin 187, 193, 194, 211, 261, 292, 346, 378, 387, 404, 417, 534, 568, 583, 702
Giet 245-247, 250, 254, 263, 280, 287, 701
Glasson.......................393, 565, 566
Goodenough....................69, 89, 156
Goppelt..................................22
Goulder.......................24, 200, 708
Gunther.................................40
Guy..................................62, 463
Gry....................................600
Hailey 91, 101, 107, 183, 210, 243, 261, 272, 306, 386, 389, 393, 399, 460, 465, 476, 529, 583, 589, 599, 602, 681, 683
Hall....................................155
Halver................463, 613, 614, 621
Hannah................................166
Hanson............373, 381, 390, 393, 465
Hartman..................681, 708, 711
Heber.................................157
Hedrick...............................317
Helmhold..........................45, 76
Hemer 29, 75-77, 84, 87, 94, 126, 138, 187
Henderson............................418
Hendrickson.........................247
Higger...............................447
Hilgenfeld........................97, 109
Hill, Charles..............36, 371, 713
Hill, David..........................280
Hillers..............................377
Hodges..........................183, 692
Holmes..........................193, 194
Holtzmann.......................218, 465
Holz..................................336
Holy Bible Confraternity..........373
Horgan................................38
Hoskier..............................294

Huffman..............................669
Hughes...................565, 577, 583
Hummel..............................613
Ibn Shemuel.............36, 704, 708
Isbell...............................436
Jacobs 40, 87, 127, 143, 161, 181, 213, 228, 247, 275, 315, 344, 359, 381, 393, 404, 461, 493, 555, 580, 608, 690, 700
Jacobson............................361
Jastrow.............................377
Jellinek 287, 341, 399, 447, 611, 618, 631
Johnson.........................262, 416
Kallas...............................708
Karrer..............................382
Kaufmann.............................8
Kern............................662, 664
Kesser..............................218
Kim................................485
Kio................................442
Klausner...........................375
Koester............................109
Köhler........................280, 576
Kraft 35, 365, 389, 390, 393, 394, 399, 462, 466, 473, 700
Kramer.......................149, 150
Kraus..............................418
Ladd...........79, 199, 389, 390, 465, 483
Lagrange............................8
Lambert.............................5
Lambrecht 48, 194, 206, 302, 309, 328, 336, 403, 556, 619, 679, 701, 702, 709
Lampe............................15-18
Landman...........................418
Laperrousaz.......................647
LaRondelle........................476
Lattimore.........................600
Laughlin..........................383
Lauha.............................591
Lewis, B..........................591
Lewis, C. T.................321, 642
Lewis R. B........................62
Lewy.....................6, 416, 624
Lilje.................347, 393, 399
Lindsey........................13, 372
Lipinski..........................711

Loasby...476
Lohmeyer..........1, 77, 101, 389, 461, 462, 473, 700
Loisy 43, 59, 60, 70, 87, 113, 143, 156, 162, 178, 244, 259, 280, 348, 357, 359, 386, 398, 414, 462, 479, 525, 546, 551, 558, 583, 590, 680
Longnecker.......................................547
Lundquist..669
Lupieri....................................... 263, 496
Lust..556
Makrakis........................390, 463, 465
Marcus................................... 290, 456
Margolis... 448
Marmorstein.................................. 447
Marshall...701
Marti...419
Martin.............................274, 663, 668
Martin-Achard...............................614
Martinez... 641
Marx... 448
May..1, 2
Mazar...647
Mazzafarri 36, 41, 43, 162, 227, 257, 258, 291, 322, 388, 709
McCullough......................................27
McGinn....................281, 343, 371, 372
McIlraith................................. 543, 545
McKelvey....................................... 218
McNicol.. 272
Mealy 104, 461, 471, 472, 560, 564, 567, 576, 577, 588, 589, 592, 595, 600, 604, 719
Mernold...6
Mendenhall................................65, 669
Milik..............................377, 619, 640
Miller, K. E..................................... 545
Miller, P. D..14
Milliere..437
Minear 50, 198, 199, 241, 334, 565, 568
Moberly... 597
Moffatt........................258, 292, 393, 394
Montgomery....................................437
Morgenstern.........................6, 416, 624
Morris...42, 47, 147, 186, 187, 217; 229, 243, 247, 261, 287, 352, 389, 390, 393,

397, 398, 405, 415, 418, 424, 456, 460, 465, 486, 496, 565, 568, 603, 641, 654, 690
Mounce 50, 71, 199, 213, 258, 291, 292, 347, 389, 393, 465
Mulholland.....................62, 76, 421, 557
Munck..280
Mussies.........................47, 48, 383, 666
Nestle...............30, 35, 42, 56, 143, 149
Neusner.........................211, 655, 680
Newman............109, 372, 373, 474, 711
Newport 52, 120, 122, 173, 268, 332, 350, 383, 434, 692
Nodet..214
North...6
Nougayrol.. 696
O'Rourke.......................... 176, 177, 217
Oppenheim................................ 207, 458
Osbourn..551
Pagán... 8
Paulien...336
Peake 59, 86, 87, 189, 276, 301, 322, 338, 346, 373, 377, 477, 640, 711
Perrin..391
Petrement...315
Peuch....................................... 11, 37
Pieters... 323
Pinches.. 6
Porter...373
Preston..............373, 381, 390, 393, 465
Preuss..371
Prigent............................679, 681, 685
Pritchard...149, 153, 207, 305, 316, 458, 461
Provon......................................506, 507
Pusey..419
Reader.....................................276, 287
Renan.......................................109, 371
Rissi 125, 138, 200, 261, 280, 325, 391, 397, 433, 534, 536, 549, 557, 559, 563,
Rist...70, 393
Robinson, G. L................................ 419
Robinson, J. A. T.............................. 295
Rousseau..701
Ross... 591
Rowland..................2, 167, 175, 176, 220

Rowley...36
Royce...294
Ruiz 24, 42, 43, 268, 466, 467, 478, 704, 709
Saglio..14
Sanders..436
Sarna.. 27
Scheftelowitz...........................348, 492
Schnutenhaus................................. 14
Shrenk... 218
Schüssler-Fiorenza 43, 87, 89, 97, 99, 101, 102, 108, 172, 197, 198, 211, 227, 254, 271, 272, 319, 337, 371, 382, 383, 388-392, 399, 401, 404, 416, 424, 462, 484, 565, 594, 682, 701, 703, 710
Scott C. A...79
Scott R. B. Y..................................383
Segoreia... 390
Shanks..........164, 347, 361, 661,663, 668
Shea...................65, 84, 322, 453, 507
Shiloh, S..372
Shiloh, Y..668
Shimon ben Yohai 202, 308, 425, 568, 618, 619, 677, 706, 707
Singer......................188, 220, 373
Sinor... 591
Skehan.................................. 373, 555
Slater...500
Smith, J. B...................... 388, 390, 460
Smith, M..............................34, 97
Soggin...11
Sowers..614
Spina...670
Spitta..346
Stadelmann........................563, 583
Staples... 445
Stegner.......................... 99, 423, 666
Steindorf..80
Steiner.. 663
Steinmann......................................471
Stevenson................... 153, 158
Stott.. 63
Strand 65, 66, 104, 143, 272, 280, 282, 435, 483, 507, 607, 703, 704, 710
Strobel.. 498
Sudilovsky..................................668

Sun....................................128
Sweeney.........................201, 560
Sweet 2, 61, 71, 194, 199, 210, 268, 346, 359, 381, 387, 389, 397-399, 430, 433, 460, 461, 465, 496, 608
Swete......29, 79, 381, 465, 473, 690, 704
Tabor.. 668, 677
Talmon... 656, 680
Taylor... 27
Terry.......................393, 462, 463, 465
Thackeray.. 535
Thomas...43
Thompson, S........47, 187, 350, 383, 493
Thompson, H................................ 405
Topham.. 359
Torrance..................................... 200
Torrey................................... 383
Trask.. 5, 574, 613
Trench..78
Trites.............................. 41, 280, 576
Trudinger..................................... 704
Ulfgard...... 174, 218, 565, 580, 581, 589
Van Houten.......................... 8, 374, 376
Van Shaik.................................... 403
VanderKam...............................14, 610
Vanhoye...24
Vanni...702, 711
Vasiliadis..............................41, 547
Vincent................................ 321, 642
Visher........................ 346, 373, 381
Vogelgesang 24, 178, 258, 704, 708, 710, 719, 720
Volkmar..................................... 109
Von Orieli................................ 419
Von Rad................................ 376
Vriezen...613
Wacholder..7
Walvoord...................373, 390, 462, 473
Warren................... 661, 662-664, 668
Weiss, B. 241, 252, 268, 280, 292, 306, 315, 346, 360, 362, 371, 462, 466, 496, 581, 629
Weiss, J. 77, 114, 169, 183, 211, 220, 228, 255, 276, 284, 295, 349, 360, 369, 371, 496, 532, 546, 555, 560, 593, 599, 611, 636, 679, 682, 709

Wellhausen................138, 340, 346
Wenham................................. 376
Wertheimer........................ 341, 618, 671
Wetstein................71, 465, 466
Whealon 43, 292, 335, 356, 411, 479, 491, 524, 529, 546, 551, 579, 584, 638, 684, 702
White...........................13, 372
Widengren............................670
Wilcox....................620, 635, 656, 682
Wilson......................153, 305, 461
Windisch............................11, 12
Winkle................................. 210
Wise..........................669, 677
Woolcombe..................... 15-18
Yadin.................614, 641, 660, 661
Zahn 34-36, 38, 59, 61, 78-80, 96, 106, 147, 153, 194 , 201, 210-212, 218, 228, 238, 251, 315, 316, 346-349, 370, 391, 393, 404, 406, 415, 432, 531, 537, 538
Zalcman............................. 514
Zwingli................................. 2

www.ingramcontent.com/pod-product-compliance
Lightning Source LLC
Chambersburg PA
CBHW080526300426
44111CB00017B/2629